The English Novel 1770–1829: A Bibliographical Survey
of Prose Fiction Published in the British Isles

Volume II: 1800–1829

General Editors: Peter Garside, James Raven, and
Rainer Schöwerling

# The English Novel 1770–1829:
# A Bibliographical Survey of Prose Fiction
# Published in the British Isles

## Volume II: 1800–1829

PETER GARSIDE

and

RAINER SCHÖWERLING

with the assistance of
CHRISTOPHER SKELTON-FOORD
and KARIN WÜNSCHE

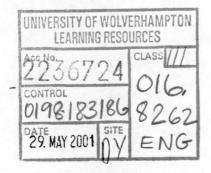
**OXFORD**
UNIVERSITY PRESS

# OXFORD
### UNIVERSITY PRESS

Great Clarendon Street, Oxford ox2 6DP
Oxford University Press is a department of the University of Oxford.
It furthers the University's objective of excellence in research, scholarship,
and education by publishing worldwide in

Oxford New York

Athens Auckland Bangkok Bogotá Buenos Aires Calcutta
Cape Town Chennai Dar es Salaam Delhi Florence Hong Kong Istanbul
Karachi Kuala Lumpur Madrid Melbourne Mexico City Mumbai
Nairobi Paris São Paulo Singapore Taipei Tokyo Toronto Warsaw

and associated companies in Berlin Ibadan

Oxford is a registered trade mark of Oxford University Press
in the UK and certain other countries

Published in the United States
by Oxford University Press Inc., New York

British Library Cataloguing in Publication Data

Data available

Library of Congress Cataloging in Publication Data

Data available

ISBN 0–19–818318–6

1 3 5 7 9 10 8 6 4 2

Typeset in Minion by
Jayvee, Trivandrum, India
Printed in Great Britain
on acid-free paper by
Biddles Ltd.,
Guildford and King's Lynn

# Acknowledgments

The Anglo-German co-operation which underlies this volume has greatly benefited from generous support given to the two main research centres at Cardiff
University and the Universität-Gesamthochschule Paderborn. Grants have also
facilitated travel between these two centres and to library collections in both Europe
and North America. Projekt Corvey at Paderborn is especially indebted to the
owner of the Fürstliche Bibliothek Corvey, Franz Albrecht von Metternich-Sándor,
Herzog von Ratibor und Fürst von Corvey, who opened his library for international
scholarship, and to the general administration at Schloss Corvey, in particular to
Dr C.-D. Seidel. The Ministerium für Schule und Weiterbildung, Wissenschaft und
Forschung des Landes Nordrhein-Westfalen, generously provided financial
support for Projekt Corvey's cataloguing and microfiching of the Corvey Library,
which in turn led to participation in the present bibliography. The Deutscher
Akademischer Austauschdienst [DAAD], in co-operation with the British Council,
provided finance for a number of exchange visits to Cardiff University and to
research libraries in Britain and Ireland; while grants from the Deutsche
Forschungsgemeinschaft [DFG] funded visits to libraries in the USA as well as
research assistance. The Universität-Gesamthochschule Paderborn also supplied
funding for a research assistant and provided general administrative help. Research
at Cardiff University has benefited from general support given by the University,
through its School of English, Communication and Philosophy [ENCAP], in the
form of research leave, travel funding, equipment, research assistance, and major
library purchases. More particularly, funding was provided by ENCAP for the
provision of a Corvey Senior Studentship in Bibliography, held by Christopher
Skelton-Foord from October 1992 to September 1995. Two major awards were
made by the British Council, in association with the DAAD, to support a series of
visits from Cardiff to Paderborn. The award of a Houghton Mifflin Visiting Fellow-
ship in Publishing History at Harvard University, held in Summer 1994, enabled
Christopher Skelton-Foord to carry out essential work in the Houghton and
Widener Libraries at Harvard, while also paying visits to other key research libraries
such as the Beinecke Library at Yale University.

Many libraries have been visited during the compilation of this volume, and it is
regrettably not possible to mention all those curators and staff of rare book and
research libraries who have offered help and advice. The editors would nevertheless
like to offer special thanks to the following for facilitating their researches at vital
stages: Myrtle Anderson-Smith (Aberdeen University Library); Michael Bott
(University of Reading Library); William S. Brockman (University of Illinois
Library, Urbana-Champaign); Charlotte B. Brown (University of California
Library, Los Angeles); Graham Jefcoate (British Library); William Kelly (National

Library of Scotland); Nick Lee (University of Bristol Library); Lionel Madden (National Library of Wales); George Riser (Alderman Library at the University of Virginia, Charlottesville); and Richard Wendorf (Houghton Library, Harvard). Thanks are also due to the university library at Paderborn; and to the Arts and Social Studies Library at Cardiff University, where the staff, in particular Tom Dawkes, have provided invaluable day-to-day assistance. The editors are grateful too to the trustees of the National Library of Scotland for permission to cite and quote from manuscripts in their care; and to Longmans for permission to publish materials from the Longman archives held at Reading University.

Many dozens of scholars have assisted in the compilation of this volume, either through providing help in retrieving information and checking the entries, or through answering queries and sending in suggestions. Activities at Paderborn have been greatly enhanced through assistance provided by Verena Ebbes, Werner Huber, and Angelika Schlimmer; and at Cardiff by Claire Connolly, Andrew Davies, Mike Franklin, and Gillian Garside. Anthony Mandal, as part of the Centre for Editorial and Intertextual Research at Cardiff, worked tirelessly in constructing a database and drawing up tables and graphs, as well as overseeing other aspects of the preparation of the entries in their final form. Thanks are also due to the Corvey Institut für Buch- und Bibliotheksgeschichte and to Günter Tiggesbäumker for help and advice. Gwen Averley and Frank Robinson, of the *Nineteenth-Century Short-Title Catalogue* project, in addition to allowing permission to cite materials, generously sent electronic copy of the fiction categories from the indexes of the second series (1816–1870) before the latter's completion in published form. Amongst other scholars who have contributed with their knowledge and expertise, the editors would particularly like to thank J. H. Alexander, Margareta Björkman, David Bryant, Peter Buse, Pamela Clemit, Emma Clery, Ian Duncan, Paula R. Feldman, Antonia Forster, David Hewitt, Malcolm Kelsall, Stephen Knight, Angela Koch, Alison Lumsden, Joan Percy, Julie Shaffer, and David Skilton.

Without the assistance of these and numerous other scholars and book custodians, and their maintenance of the principle of allowing free access to library materials regardless of particular affiliations, many of the novels in this volume could not have been located and studied. The general editors of this bibliography are hugely indebted to this world-wide community of librarians and scholars.

# Contents

# Tables, Figures, and Illustrations

# Abbreviations

| | |
|---|---|
| * | No copy of first edition located |
| ? | doubtful |
| ABu | Aberdeen University Library |
| adv. | advertisement/advertised |
| Allibone | S. Austin Allibone, *A Critical Dictionary of English Literature, and British and American Authors.* 3 vols. (London and Philadelphia, 1859–71) |
| Alston | R. C. Alston, *A Checklist of Women Writers 1801–1900* (London, 1990) |
| App | Appendix |
| AWn | National Library of Wales, Aberystwyth |
| BDLA | *Biographical Dictionary of the Living Authors of Great Britain and Ireland* (London, 1816) |
| Bent03 | William Bent, *The Modern Catalogue of Books [. . .] since the year 1792* (London, 1803) |
| Bent22 | William Bent, *London Catalogue of Books [. . .] since the year 1800 to October 1822* (London, 1822) |
| Bentley | G. E. Bentley, Jun., 'Copyright Documents in the George Robinson Archive: William Godwin and Others 1713–1820', *Studies in Bibliography* 35 (1982), 67–110 |
| BI | Britain and Ireland |
| BL | British Library |
| Blakey | Dorothy Blakey, *The Minerva Press 1790–1820* (London: The Bibliographical Society, 1939 [for 1935]) |
| Blanck | Jacob Blanck, *A Bibliography of American Literature.* 9 vols. (New Haven, 1955–91) |
| BLC | British Library Catalogue |
| Block | Andrew Block, *The English Novel 1740–1850: A Catalogue including Prose Romances, Short Stories, and Translations of Foreign Fiction* (London, 1939; revised 1961; reprinted 1968) |
| BN | Catalogue of the Bibliothèque Nationale, Paris |
| BRu ENC | Bristol University Library, Early Novels Collection |
| c. | circa |
| C | Cambridge University Library |
| CaAEU | University of Alberta |
| CaOHM | Mills Memorial Library, McMaster University |
| CFu | Cardiff University Library |
| CG | The card index of Chester Noyes Greenough, Houghton Library, Harvard |

| | |
|---|---|
| CLU-S/C | Special Collections, University of California, Los Angeles |
| CME | Corvey Microfiche Edition |
| Corson | James C. Corson, *Notes and Index to Sir Herbert Grierson's Edition of the Letters of Sir Walter Scott* (Oxford, 1979) |
| Corvey | Corvey, Fürstliche Bibliothek zu Corvey |
| CR | *The Critical Review.* 1st ser., 70 vols. (London, 1756–90), 2nd ser., 39 vols. (London, 1791–1803), 3rd ser., 24 vols. (1804–11) |
| CSmH | Henry E. Huntington Library, San Marino, California |
| CtY | Sterling Library, Yale University |
| CtY-BR | Beinecke Library, Yale University |
| D | National Library of Ireland, Dublin |
| d. | died |
| DBI | Deutsches Bibliotheksinstitut/German Library Institute, Berlin: database-service (DBI-LINK), Union Catalogue (DBIopac VK97) |
| DGW | George Washington University |
| DLC | Library of Congress, Washington DC |
| DNB | Dictionary of National Biography |
| Dt | Trinity College Library, Dublin |
| E | National Library of Scotland, Edinburgh |
| EA | Continental Europe, Australasia, Asia, and Africa |
| ECB | *English Catalogue of Books 1801–1836*, ed. Robert Alexander Peddie and Quintin Waddington (London, 1914; Kraus Reprint, New York, 1963) |
| ed. | edited |
| edn. | edition |
| EM | Eighteenth-Century Microfilm Series, Primary Source Media (formerly RPI or Research Publications International) |
| ER | *Edinburgh Review.* 250 vols. (1802–1929) |
| ESTC | *English Short-Title Catalogue* (formerly *Eighteenth-Century Short-Title Catalogue*) on-line via BLAISE and RLIN; CD-ROM 1992; CD-ROM 1997 |
| Facs: BWN | Facsimile (London: Routledge/ Thoemmes, 1992) *British Women Novelists, 1750–1850* |
| Facs: EC | Facsimile (Stuttgart: Belser Verlag, 1988) *Edition Corvey* |
| Facs: GNI | Facsimile (New York: Arno, 1972) *Gothic Novels I* |
| Facs: GNII | Facsimile (New York: Arno, 1974) *Gothic Novels II* |
| Facs: GNIII | Facsimile (New York: Arno, 1977) *Gothic Novels III* |
| Facs: IAN | Facsimile (New York: Garland, 1979) *Irish and Anglo-Irish Novelists* |
| Facs: N | Facsimile (New York: Garland, 1979) *The Novel: 1720–1805* |
| Facs: RR | Facsimile (Oxford: Woodstock Books, 1989–) *Revolution and Romanticism, 1789–1834* |
| Facs: RWN | Facsimile (London: Routledge/ Thoemmes, 1995) *The Romantics: Women Novelists* |

| | |
|---|---|
| FC | Virginia Blain, Isobel Grundy, and Patricia Clements (eds.), *The Feminist Companion to Literature in English* (London, 1990) |
| Frank | Frederick S. Frank, *The First Gothics: A Critical Guide to the English Gothic Novel* (New York, 1987) |
| Gecker | Sidney Gecker, *English Fiction to 1820 in the University of Pennsylvania Library* (Philadelphia, 1954) |
| Gilson | David Gilson, *A Bibliography of Jane Austen* (Oxford, 1982) |
| GOT | Niedersächsische Staats- und Universitätsbibliothek, Göttingen |
| H&L | Samuel Halkett and John Laing, *Dictionary of Anonymous and Pseudonymous Literature*, new and enlarged edn., 7 vols. (Edinburgh, 1926–34) |
| Hardy | J. C. Hardy, *A Catalogue of English Prose Fiction mainly of the Eighteenth Century from a Private Library* (Frenich, Foss, 1982) |
| Henderson | The Gothic Novel in Wales (1790–1820), *National Library of Wales Journal*, 11 (1959–60), 244–54 |
| IaU | University of Iowa |
| ICN | Newberry Library, Chicago |
| ICU | Regenstein Library, University of Chicago |
| ill. | illustrated |
| InU-Li | Lilly Library, Indiana University |
| IU | University of Illinois, Urbana-Champaign |
| IinFI | Stephen J. Brown, *Ireland in Fiction: A Guide to Irish Novels and Tales, Romances and Folklore* (1919; reprinted New York, 1970) |
| IinFII | Stephen J. Brown and Desmond Clarke, *Ireland in Fiction: A Guide to Irish Novels and Tales, Romances and Folklore*, vol. 2 (Cork, 1985) |
| Jackson | J.R. de J. Jackson, *Romantic Poetry by Women: A Bibliography, 1770–1835* (Oxford, 1993) |
| Jarndyce | Jarndyce Antiquarian Booksellers, Catalogues of |
| KIK | The Baikie Collection, Tankerners House, Kirkwall, Orkney |
| Lics | University of London Institute of Commonwealth Studies |
| Mayo | Robert D. Mayo, *The English Novel in the Magazines 1740–1815* (Evanston, Illinois, 1963) |
| MB | Boston Public Library |
| MdBJ | Johns Hopkins University |
| MGD | M. G. Devonshire, *The English Novel in France 1830–1870* (London, 1929) |
| MH | Harvard University |
| MH-H | Houghton Library, Harvard University |
| MiU | University of Michigan, Ann Arbor |
| ML | Maurice Lévy, 'Bibliographie chronologique', in his *Le Roman 'gothique' anglais 1764–1824* (Toulouse, 1968) |
| MLC | Maurice Lévy, 'English Gothic and the French Imagination: A Calendar of Translations 1767–1828', in *The Gothic Imagination: Essays in Dark Romanticism*, ed. G. R. Thompson (Pullman, Wash., 1974) |

| | |
|---|---|
| MnU | Meredith Wilson and James Ford Bell Libraries, University of Minnesota |
| MR | *The Monthly Review*, 1st ser., 81 vols. (London, 1749–1789), n.s., 108 vols. (London, 1790–1825) |
| MRu | John Rylands Library, Manchester |
| MS | manuscript |
| NA | North America |
| NCBEL | *The New Cambridge Bibliography of English Literature*, ed. George Watson, vol. 3 (1969) |
| NcD | William R. Perkins Library, Duke University |
| NcU | Wilson Library, University of North Carolina, Chapel Hill |
| NCu | Newcastle upon Tyne University Library |
| n.d. | no date |
| NIC | Cornell University |
| NjP | Princeton University |
| NN | New York Public Library |
| NNS | New York Society Library |
| n.p. | no place of publication |
| n.s. | new series |
| NSTC | *Nineteenth-Century Short-Title Catalogue*: Series I, 1801–1815. 6 vols. (1984–6); Series II, 1816–1870, 56 vols. (1986–95); CD-ROM, 1996 |
| NUC | *National Union Catalog* |
| O | Bodleian Library, Oxford |
| OAkU | University of Akron |
| OBgU | Bowling Green State University, Ohio |
| opp. | opposite |
| p.c. | private copy |
| Pigoreau | Alexandre Pigoreau, *Petite Biographico-Romancière, ou Dictionnaire des Romanciers* (1821; Slatkine Reprints, 1968) |
| PPL | Library Company of Philadelphia |
| pseud. | pseudonym |
| PU | University of Pennsylvania |
| QR | *Quarterly Review*. 305 vols. (1809–1967) |
| rev. | review |
| RLF | The Royal Literary Fund 1790–1918: Archives (London: World Microfilms, 1984). References are to the reel and entry number. |
| RS | Rainer Schöwerling and Verena Ebbes, 'Die Rezeption englischer Romane in Deutschland 1790–1834. Eine Bibliographie' (project in progress at the University of Paderborn) |
| Sadleir | Michael Sadleir, *XIX Century Fiction: A Bibliographical Record based on his own Collection*. 2 vols. (Cambridge, 1951) |
| ScU | University of South Carolina |

| | |
|---|---|
| SEK | Selkirk, Borders Regional Library |
| ser. | series |
| s.l. | spine label |
| SU | Barr Smith Library, University of Adelaide |
| Summers | Montague Summers, *A Gothic Bibliography* (London, [1940]; reprinted 1969) |
| t.p. | title-page |
| trans. | translation |
| *trans.* | translator |
| TxU | Humanities Research Centre, University of Texas at Austin |
| unn. | unnumbered; no page numbers marked |
| ViU | University of Virginia |
| vol. | volume |
| WSW I | William S. Ward, *Literary Reviews in British Periodicals 1798–1820*. 2 vols. (New York, 1972) |
| WSW II | William S. Ward, *Literary Reviews in British Periodicals 1821–1826* (New York, 1977) |
| Wolff | Robert Lee Wolff, *Nineteenth-Century Fiction: A Bibliographical Catalogue*. 5 vols. (New York, 1981–6) |
| xESTC | not entered in the *English Short-Title Catalogue* (at February 1998) |
| xNSTC | not entered in the *Nineteenth-Century Short-Title Catalogue* |
| ZAP | Auckland Public Library |

# GENERAL INTRODUCTION

*Peter Garside, James Raven, and Rainer Schöwerling*

What was a novel in the late eighteenth and early nineteenth centuries? Did popular novels address a broad range of topics and plots and characterizations or were they generally confined to domestic, sedentary themes? Were there as many historical as contemporary settings, as many novels in letters as in continuous narrative? How many were based on real events? Who wrote them? Who published and sold them? How expensive were they? What was their appeal and popularity? How were they reviewed? These and other questions are the starting point for this bibliography.

The period is the first great age of the popular English novel. Post-Richardson and pre-Dickens, these are the years of Burney, Austen, Edgeworth, and Scott, of Beckford, Godwin, Hogg, Inchbald, M. G. Lewis, and Mary Shelley. It is also the age of hundreds of other writers of novels. But what does the full cast of British novelists of the late eighteenth century and Romantic period look like? Who were the most popular writers in their own day? We know that the young Jane Austen cantered through scores of novels, that Leigh Hunt devoured them like crumpets before the fire, that critics complained of a plague of the things. We also know that Austen was far from the most popular writer of her generation, and that the literary fame of most of her rivals was transitory. The authors of one-hit wonders have been forgotten—however influential or notorious they were in their own day. Some writers, indeed, guarded their identity at the time. Many novelists, including Ann Radcliffe and William Godwin, published their first work anonymously; many others were unable or unwilling to acknowledge their authorship throughout their lives. Burney, Austen, and Scott were not named in the original title-pages to any of their novels.

The questions are not trivial: they are essential for anyone examining the literary history of the period and the background to the success—or failure—of particular authors, the representativeness of particular literary genres, the allusions made to other writers and fiction of the day, the exact timing of publication and reprinting, the potential audience, and the contemporary critical reception of the early novel. The absence of such study is apparent in recent republications. Prefaces to dozens of reissued 'lost' novels of the period have lamented current ignorance about the fuller publishing profile of those years and the occurrence of particular literary tropes and styles.

This historical bibliography of fiction therefore addresses the void faced by generations of literary scholars and historians concerned with the development of the English novel. It attempts, for the first time, to provide a basis for an assessment of the work of all novelists of the period. It seeks to list all novels of the period whether or not surviving in extant copies, their publication and pricing details, and contemporary review information. In the case of surviving novels it supplies full references to allow their consultation either on microform or in modern library and research collections all over the world. A copy of every identified surviving novel has been examined for the bibliography. By providing a transcription of the title and title-page, which often includes a contemporary proposal of genre, and further bibliographical and historical information (sometimes including evidence of imitation and plagiarism), the bibliography allows users to make their own comparisons between novels.

Despite the long-acknowledged need for such a bibliography, until now it has been impossible to identify the full range of fiction published in Britain in the late eighteenth century or during the Romantic period. The standard existing guide is Andrew Block's *The English Novel, 1740–1850*, first published in 1939, but it is often unreliable, while offering very little detail on author and title (and none on other issues).[1] Check-lists of specific genres such as those for the gothic novel and the epistolary novel vary greatly in range and detail. Without considering the broader context of all fiction production, these check-lists can give an inflated sense of the importance in the period of the genre under survey.[2] Dorothy Blakey's cataloguing of the publications of William Lane has been a model for other check-lists of leading publishers of fiction of the period, but her survey is incomplete and, in respect of research in recent years, dated.[3] Listings in the *Cambridge Bibliography of English Literature* are very selective, and although a new edition is now underway, it does not intend to include details of all popular fiction of the period. Check-lists based on particular collections are naturally bounded by the range of the particular holdings used, and some do not extend their otherwise very important coverage beyond a certain date or theme.[4] In recent years, women writers have been better served than their male counterparts, but even the fullest existing guides remain limited in their coverage of publication and reception details and, by their nature, do not offer information about the location of consultable copies of novels.[5]

---

[1] An attempt to replace Block (new and revised edn. 1961; reprinted 1963, 1967, 1968), Leonard Orr, *Catalogue Checklist of English Prose Fiction, 1750–1800* (Troy, NY, 1979) falls far short of doing so.

[2] Frederick S. Frank, *The First Gothics: A Critical Guide to the English Gothic Novel* (New York, 1987); Maurice Lévy, 'Bibliographie chronologique du roman "gothique" 1764–1824,' in his *Le Roman 'gothique' anglais 1764–1824* (Toulouse, 1968); Dan J. McNutt, *The Eighteenth-Century Gothic Novel: An Annotated Bibliography of Criticism and Selected Texts* (London, 1975); R. D. Spector, *The English Gothic: A Bibliographic Guide to Writers from Horace Walpole to Mary Shelley* (Westport, CT, and London, 1984); Montague Summers, *A Gothic Bibliography* (London, [1940]; reprinted 1969); Frank Gees Black, *The Epistolary Novel in the Late Eighteenth Century* (Eugene, OR, 1940).

[3] Dorothy Blakey, *The Minerva Press 1790–1820* (London, 1939). Cf. James Raven, 'The Noble Brothers and Popular Publishing', *The Library*, 6th ser., 12 (1990): 293–345; Peter Garside, 'J. F. Hughes and the Publication of Popular Fiction, 1803–1810', *The Library*, 6th ser., 9 (1987): 240–58; and Deborah McLeod, 'The Minerva Press', unpublished PhD dissertation University of Alberta, 1997.

[4] For example, William H. McBurney's *English Prose Fiction 1700–1800 in the University of Illinois Library* (Urbana, 1965) excludes the rich nineteenth-century fiction holdings.

[5] Janet Todd, ed., *A Dictionary of British and American Women Writers 1660–1800* (Totowa, NJ, 1985); J. R. de J. Jackson, *Romantic Poetry by Women: A Bibliography 1770–1835* (Oxford, 1993); Virginia

The continuing *English Short-Title Catalogue* (now subsuming the *Eighteenth-Century Short-Title Catalogue*) has transformed our understanding of the range of eighteenth-century publications and of the libraries that currently hold them. ESTC allows on-line computer and CD-ROM searches for specific words in the title and short form of publication line (amongst other information in each entry), but it has no genre field. The best alternative, a title-word search on 'novel',[6] produces listings of under ten per cent of those works clearly identifiable as novels. Bibliographical assistance for early nineteenth-century English literature is even more problematic for those attempting to identify novels. The *Nineteenth-Century Short-Title Catalogue* now offers a rich resource for locating nineteenth-century literature, but its restricted library coverage and its retention of the Dewey Decimal classification frequently leads to limited or inappropriate subject guidance for the early nineteenth-century novel.

This bibliography will complement existing check-lists for the period before 1770, and together they will provide a full research guide to prose fiction from 1700 to 1830. A series of fiction check-lists spanning the period 1700–1770 has been compiled over many years, starting with W. H. McBurney's *Check List of English Prose Fiction 1700–1739* (1960), followed by J. C. Beasley's *Check List of English Prose Fiction 1740–1749* (1972), and James Raven's *British Fiction, 1750–1770* (1987). The following work continues this series, but is also much more extensive than its predecessors in the bibliographical, literary, and holding-library information that it offers.

It has to be restated that no bibliography of this kind can escape difficult editorial decisions over inclusion and exclusion. 'Novel' was by no means an agreed term in the eighteenth century, and books which do not now appear to us to be novels were then reviewed under that category. But the instability of the term also points to the new opportunities provided by this survey in chronicling contemporary notions of fiction and in understanding the broader cultural and historical significance of the 'rise of the novel'. The bibliography aims to add to our understanding of the character of fiction in this period, while seeking to avoid rigid categories of sub-genres. From the evidence of reprinting and patronage to that of the mediating response of critical reviewers, the bibliography aims to identify authorship, communities of writing, the themes embraced and repeated by writers, the circumstances of novel production, and the nature of literary circulation and reception. Existing literary canons might be challenged, refined, or better understood by revisiting this history of the novel, by the contextualizing of the fuller output of imaginative prose of the period, by the recovery of rare books now scattered across the world, and by the very basic reconstruction of books now lost.

---

Blain et al. eds., *The Feminist Companion to Literature in English* (London, 1990); Dale Spender, *Mothers of the Novel: 100 Good Women Writers before Jane Austen* (London and New York, 1986).

[6] It is also possible to search for the term 'novel' using the ESTC '500 note field', but that field has been applied patchily and cannot be used in all cases.

*Scope*

The bibliography records the first editions of all known novels in English published in the British Isles between 1770 and 1829 inclusive, and gives details of subsequent editions to 1850. Also included are the first English translations in this period of novels originally published elsewhere in Europe.[7] Novels in English first published in North America in this period and subsequently published in the British Isles before 1830 are described in an entry for the first British edition. The bibliography does not include subsequent editions of novels first published before 1770. It also includes brief references to subsequent editions up to 1850, including the first American editions and German and French first translations.

The listings adopt a more rigorous definition of the 'novel' than in earlier volumes by McBurney, Beasley, and Raven. This is partly because of the huge upturn in the number of publications over this period (especially from the 1790s), but also because the forms of the prose novel became more readily identifiable. The bibliography includes what contemporaries thought of as novels, incorporating works categorized as 'novels' in contemporary periodical reviews and under 'novels' headings in circulating library catalogues, but excludes religious tracts, chapbooks, literature written only for children and juveniles, and very short separately issued tales. Collections of tales (including some mixed genre compilations) are included; separate verse novels are not.

The bibliography gives a full description (together with catalogue number) of the copy of the novel examined (more complete details are given below of the arrangement within each entry). To assist detailed recovery of the publication history of each novel, detailed imprint information and a variety of contemporary source references are also given. The imprint line is exactly reproduced (save for the exceptions detailed below under 'Components of each entry'). Other printing or publishing information is also given in a further notes section within each entry. The full publishing information is given in detail unavailable in other bibliographies.

Each entry also provides information concerning other copies of the novels held at libraries and research institutions world-wide. These holding details are taken from current short-title catalogues and other on-line resources, but the compilers of this bibliography have also undertaken extensive further research in individual libraries and special collections.

---

[7] Sources used to verify translations into English include Alexandre Cioranescu, *Bibliographie de la littérature Française du dix-huitième siècle*, 3 vols. (Paris, 1969); Angus Martin, Vivienne G. Mylne, and Richard Frautschi, eds., *Bibliographie du genre romanesque français 1751–1800* (London and Paris, 1977). Sources used to identify translations from English into German include Mary Bell Price and Lawrence Marsden Price, *The Publication of English Literature in Germany in the Eighteenth Century* (Berkeley, Ca, 1934); Norbert Otto Eke and Dagmar Olasz-Eke, *Bibliographie: Der deutsche Roman, 1815–1830* (Munich, 1994); Rainer Schöwerling and Verena Ebbes, *Rezeption englischer Romane in Deutschland 1790–1834, eine Bibliographie* (forthcoming); and the 'English authors in Germany, 1680–1810' project, University of Münster (forthcoming).

A further significant feature within the entries are the references to reviews and listings in *The Monthly Review*, *The Critical Review*, *The Quarterly Review*, *The Edinburgh Review*, and other contemporary reviews and notices.[8] The periodicals provide evidence that the title was considered to be fiction by contemporaries, and also supply corroborative information about pricing, format, and general date of issue. Appropriate extracts from review notices are also given in the pre-1800 entries, with the name of the reviewer where identified.[9] *The Monthly Review* and *The Critical Review* are listed in volume I wherever they supply a review either in the main or the subsidiary section of the periodical. References to periodicals other than the *Monthly* and *Critical* are cited when these offer the only review of the novel before 1800, together with other review references in existing bibliographies. In many cases newspaper advertisement references are listed to pin-point publication dates. In addition, booksellers' advertisements found within novels examined are cited where they supply useful further evidence for the dating and verification of other novels. For the post-1800 period, when contemporary reviewing policy was changing, the references given correspond mainly to simple lists of new publications given in *The Edinburgh* and *The Quarterly*, although full reviews of novels in these two journals are also noted.

## Procedure

The guiding principle has been to work from a range of eighteenth- and nineteenth-century bibliographical records and to examine actual copies of all known surviving novels entered in the bibliography. In identifying the existence of rare copies and their location, ESTC and NSTC have been complemented by other catalogues and extended by use of on-line resources such as the *OCLC WorldCat* database. Copies of novels identified from contemporary sources, OCLC, the STCs, the *National Union Catalog* (NUC), and other catalogues were all examined afresh and further searches undertaken in libraries and collections. Library stack-work has ensured in particular that the bibliography corrects and amplifies existing bibliographical aids to novels of the period. The importance of this hands-on work is underlined by the number of titles located during the course of research but not listed by the eighteenth- and nineteenth-century short-title catalogues. The bibliography is not, therefore, merely a derivative or synthesis of catalogues and bibliographical databases. It includes rare editions not identified by the STCs, as well as titles which have not survived in extant copies and whose existence and further details have been ascertained by printing and publishing records[10] or contemporary

---

[8] See also below under Contemporary Review References, pp. 10–11.

[9] Using the copy of the MR marked up by its editor, Ralph Griffiths, and held in the Bodleian Library, Oxford; also, Benjamin Christie Nangle, *The Monthly Review First Series 1749–1789: Indexes of Contributors and Articles* (Oxford: Clarendon Press, 1934) and Benjamin Christie Nangle, *The Monthly Review Second Series 1790–1815: Indexes of Contributors and Articles* (Oxford: Clarendon Press, 1955).

[10] These include the archives of John Murray, Albermarle St., London; the archives of Longmans

reviews, or by a combination of corroborative sources such as advertisements and circulating library catalogues.[11] These last two sources must usually be taken together, as some advertising puffs are not by themselves proof of certain publication (some seem to have been wishful thinking or attempts at relaunches) and at least some of the entries in early library catalogues are loose descriptions that can mislead.

Similarly, review references have been identified from contemporary periodical reviews and magazines, and not merely from existing published guides to the reviews. As a result, the bibliography both locates reliable references for novels no longer surviving in extant copies and excludes the many ghost entries which litter earlier attempts at such a bibliography.[12] For the 1790s in particular, a trawl of newspaper advertisements has revealed much new detail about publication dates and confirmation of authorship, pricing, and (for lost works) title. Where later editions of non-surviving first editions do exist, further details of these are included in the entry.

Where, as in the great majority of entries, copies of novels do survive, recording practice for the examined copy is uniform, with reproduction of title-page information and a basic formula for the description of each volume (full details are given below in the explanation of the constituent parts to each entry). Measurements of title-pages (as often included in the NUC for example) are not included. Novels were often cut back drastically when bound or otherwise presented, and dimensions vary considerably between different copies. Instead each entry provides basic format information by collation of leaves. In the past, many catalogues and check-lists have included erroneous multiplication of editions as a consequence of one library listing a book as 8$^{vo}$ and another listing it as 12$^{mo}$. One of the benefits of the hands-on research for these volumes is the elimination of such ghost entries. Format information is also followed by the price of the novel, according to its condition cited in given contemporary sources. The usual distinction was between sewed (that is, sewed with paper covers), bound, or in boards.

As will be clear from the entries, a very large number of libraries have been visited world-wide. Often relatively small collections preserve unique copies of novels, but

held at Reading University; the records of the Bowyers (Keith Maslen and John Lancaster, *The Bowyer Ledgers: The Printing Accounts of William Bowyer, father and son . . .* (London and New York, 1991); and copyright documents belonging to George Robinson held at Manchester Central Library.

[11] In entries before 1800 many newspapers—such as the *St James's Chronicle* and the *Public Advertiser*—were consulted where appropriate. The introduction to volume 1 provides a full list and discussion. In the same volume, various booksellers' catalogues and advertisements are cited, including for example, those of the Noble brothers (but all usually only as corroboration to other sources, given the often unreliable titles and details provided). In volume II *The English Catalogue of Books 1801–1836* and catalogues by William Bent are used. Full details are given in the volume introduction.

[12] Ghosts are plentiful in Block, *The English Novel*; and even more so in the repository of file cards collected from libraries and scholars worldwide by Chester Noyes Greenough and on deposit at the Houghton Library, Harvard University. The Greenough file (with its broad, miscellaneous coverage) was nevertheless a valuable early guide, particularly for volume II, and its suggestions were followed up. The editors are grateful to the Trustees of the Houghton Library.

most of the major libraries have also contributed significantly to the following work. This does not mean, however, that all their novels were listed in their own catalogues. Recent moves at the British Library, for example, uncovered many eighteenth-century editions not surviving elsewhere but also believed to have been lost by the Library. Our research at the Bodleian Library similarly included copies of numerous novels listed in the library's pre-1920 catalogue but not listed in ESTC. Amongst many other examples, full checks were made of the novels in the closed stacks at Aberdeen University, the Early Novels Collection at Bristol University Library, the post-1800 titles in the stacks at the University of Illinois, Urbana-Champaign, card index files for the Sadleir-Black collection at the University of Virginia, Charlottesville, and card index files recording fiction at Trinity College, Dublin. One recently rediscovered library has also been a major contributor to the project. For the years between 1795 and 1830, the collection of novels at Schloss Corvey, near Höxter, Germany, assembled by two Romantic *belles-lettres* enthusiasts, has been a vital resource. It is listed in its own right in the library location-line of each entry.[13]

## Arrangement

Entries are arranged chronologically by year of imprint. Within each year, anonymous works are ordered alphabetically by title and precede entries for novels by known authors and/or translators, ordered alphabetically by author's name or by the given pseudonymous name where no real author's name has been found. Evidence of authorship has been scrutinized afresh. Where some doubt remains about an attribution a question mark is placed before the author's name; where major doubt exists the novel is entered as anonymous (with further possible attribution details in the notes to the entry). *All's Right at Last* (1774), for example, remains an anonymous work given that the *Critical Review*'s allusion to the style of Frances Brooke is ambiguous. All author references (as here to Mrs Brooke) are entered in the author index. Pseudonyms of identified authors do not appear in the author line but are given appropriate cross-references within each year and index entries. Remaining pseudonyms treated as authors' names for the sake of the alphabetical listing include the false appropriation of real names. Examples include the use, again in 1774, of 'Mr Helvetius' when the novel (*The Child of Nature*) is clearly not by Claude-Adrien Helvétius. Entries for authors with several works in one year are ordered alphabetically by title. Where necessary, further details of the precise chronology are given in the final notes to each entry.

[13] A provisional account of the fiction holdings is given in Peter Garside, 'Collections of English Fiction in the Romantic Period: The Significance of Corvey', in Rainer Schöwerling and Hartmut Steinecke, eds., *Die Fürstliche Bibliothek Corvey* (Munich, 1992), pp. 70–81. A further description is also given in Rainer Schöwerling, Hartmut Steinecke, and Günter Tiggesbäumker, eds., *Literatur und Erfahrungswandel 1789–1830* (Munich, 1995).

Novels are entered under the year of their title-page imprint date, irrespective of evidence of earlier and (very rarely) later issue. Post-dating on imprints—to make a fashionable work seem more up to date—was common. Evidence for an earlier publication is often apparent from periodical reviews, newspaper advertisements, or, later in the period, from the dates of publication given in *The English Catalogue of Books, 1801–1836* (ECB).

Occasionally, it is highly problematic—or even impossible—to determine which of two editions (or translations) of a novel was issued first in a particular year. In such cases separate 'a' and 'b' entries are given. Only one entry is given for editions published in the same year but where the order of publication is clear and uncontroversial. In all cases, the final notes section provides further information on the alternative edition.

Novels with volumes published in different years are not normally separately entered under the respective years of publication, unless, for example, a significant break occurred in their publication. The bibliography attempts a distinction between those volumes of a novel issued in successive seasons as a single entity, and those volumes of a novel often published with the same title and as a deliberate continuation, but conceived as a separate publication (and often separated from the earlier volumes by several years). This point is of particular importance for the pre-1800 volume where the separate listing of successively issued volumes would misleadingly inflate the number of entries. A publishing season (from September to May) also, of course, crossed two calendar years, and certain novels have volumes bearing different imprint dates but were actually issued in the same season. The notes section to novels whose constituent parts are entered separately provide full cross-referencing to the subsequent or previous volumes. Where titles are entered according to the imprint date of the first volume, cross-references back to this entry are given from the years in which the subsequent volume(s) were published.

Cross-referencing is provided by the indexes, and, where necessary, within the main body of entries. This is especially important for women writers changing to married names during the period covered by each volume, but also to locate novels which a reader might associate with one of the many mistaken former attributions. Cross-references are also given to works whose authorship and (very occasionally) publication date is in doubt. Many attributions are made for the first time in this bibliography and in the case of well-known works the cross-reference is intended as an additional aid. Volume indexes are provided to authors (including pseudonyms) and translators; to titles; and to booksellers, publishers, printers, and place of publication.

Where no copy of a novel survives, and its title and publication details are reconstituted from outside evidence, the reconstituted entry is marked with an asterisk * before the title and the absence of any located copy is noted in the line reserved for shelf-marks and catalogues. Where not already explicit, sources are given for the various elements of the reconstitution.

*Components of each entry*

A standard entry consists of the following:

Entry number (within each year)
Author's name
Full title
Place of publication and imprint publication details
Pagination, format, and price
Contemporary review references
Location and shelf-mark of copy examined and references to other copies and catalogues
Notes

ENTRY NUMBER
Numbering starts afresh each year. Cross-references and indexes cite the number prefixed by the year—e.g. 1770: 26, 1829: 43.

AUTHOR'S NAME
Each entry opens with the name of the author(s) and translator(s) where known (or where attribution can be made with some certainty, as further described in the entry). Unless bracketed, names are given as they appear on the title-page. Square brackets are used around names supplied wholly by outside evidence. Additions which complete names, and which are, again, derived from outside sources rather than the novel itself, are also given in square brackets—as, for example, JONES, A[nne]. Occasionally, although no author's name appears on the title-page or it appears in shortened or altered form, the novel itself supplies valuable additional details, for instance at the end of a preface or dedication. Where the author's name is derived from this internal evidence, either wholly or substantially, it is enclosed by curly brackets. 'Mr', 'Mrs', and 'Miss' are omitted unless these are the only qualification to the surname or the only indication of gender. Where no author has been identified 'ANON.' is given. Entries for anonymous works, listed in alphabetical order by title, precede entries with known authors or remaining pseudonymous names. Doubtful attribution is indicated by a question mark. Where a novel is listed as anonymous evidence about possible attributions may also be given in the notes section.

Translators are treated similarly to authors, but with the addition of '(*trans.*)' immediately after the name. Square brackets indicate the attribution of a translator. Further information about the translation may also be given in the notes to each entry.

FULL TITLE
The title is taken in full from the title-page. Because it has been impossible to replicate exactly the original—and sometimes eccentric—mixture of uppercase, lowercase, small capitals, italic, black letter and other fonts, titles are reproduced in

simple uppercase throughout, but with original punctuation retained. This offers a much fuller reproduction than the short titles of ESTC and NSTC. Mottoes are excluded. Other points of interest may be recorded in the notes section. Use of '[*sic*]' to indicate the given spelling or typography is sparing but included where necessary. Where there is significant variation in the titles of the different volumes of a novel, each title is reproduced in full, or in the case of minor variation, the differences are recorded in the notes section.

PLACE OF PUBLICATION AND IMPRINT PUBLICATION DETAILS

The first-named town of publication is given first, followed (after a colon) by the full details of booksellers and publishers as they appear on the title-page up to the imprint date. A comma separates this information from the date, which is always given in arabic numerals even when in roman in the original. Where a town of publication is not named but inferred from other imprint details this is given in square brackets. Where no date is given on the title-page this is recorded as 'n.d.' followed by an attributed date in square brackets, with source reference where necessary. Where title-page publication details vary between volumes of the novel, this is fully indicated. Where such details are identical in each volume except for the dates, these are combined—e.g. '1770/71'. Where further significant publication or printing details are given in the novels (usually in the colophon or prefatory material), these are recorded under the notes section.

PAGINATION, FORMAT, AND PRICE

The last roman and arabic page number of each volume is given. These are preceded, in the case of multi-volume novels, by the volume number in upper-case roman. Where volumes were published in different years this is indicated in parentheses after the volume numbers. Where pagination information is unavailable because no copy has survived, the number of volumes only is indicated.

The format of each volume—usually 8$^{vo}$ or 12$^{mo}$—has been individually checked by collation of leaves (existing secondary references have not been trusted).

Price is given in shillings (s) and pence (d) as on the title-page and/or in review and newspaper notices, with given form ('sewed', 'boards', &c). The source for the price is also given, including title-page (t.p.), spine label (s.l.), CR, MR, ER, and QR. Where reviews are absent or insufficient to provide publication date and pri-cing information, use is made of other contemporary sources. Conflicts between sources are frequent; all variants are provided. For the post-1800 period, *The English Catalogue of Books 1801–1836* (ECB) is used extensively for information relating to retail price and date of publication.

CONTEMPORARY REVIEW REFERENCES

References are given to the appearance of the novel in the major eighteenth-century periodical reviews, *The Monthly Review* and *The Critical Review,* and in *The Edinburgh Review* and *The Quarterly Review* in the early nineteenth century.

The abbreviations (CR, MR, for example) are followed by volume, page, and date references. *The Monthly* is cited consistently to 1803 when *The Edinburgh* (founded 1802) began extensive listings. Similarly, *The Critical* is cited up to 1809 when *The Quarterly* was founded. References are also given to any further reviews of the novel, as already indexed to 1800 by Antonia Forster, and to 1826 by William S. Ward.[14] The absence of a reference to a review in any of the leading periodicals (or to Forster and Ward) is therefore significant. For novels listed in volume I (1770–1799) and *not* reviewed by *The Monthly* and *The Critical*, a direct reference (to short-cut Forster) is given to a review found in another periodical (*The Analytical Review*, *The British Critic*, *The European Magazine*, and *The Gentleman's Magazine*, for example).

LOCATION AND SHELF-MARK OF COPY EXAMINED AND REFERENCES TO OTHER COPIES AND CATALOGUES

This line always begins with an abbreviation for the location of the copy of the novel examined (or statement of apparent non-survival), followed by the holding library's own shelf-mark. In the case of novels held at the Corvey Library, where no current catalogue numbers exist, the ISBN of the Corvey Microfiche (CME) is given as the most useful and accessible identifying call number.

The examined copy's shelf-mark or Corvey ISBN is followed (as applicable) by the ECB page number, the novel's reference number in the Primary Source Media Eighteenth-Century Microfilm series (EM), and the verified ESTC record control number or the NSTC entry number. EM numbers, identifying novels available in microfilm (although often not the copies examined for this bibliography) are given for the filming completed and published by December 1997. Where the novel has been microfilmed by the Primary Source Media project but is not yet published, this is indicated by the abbreviation 'EMf' [Eighteenth-Century Microfilms forthcoming].

In volume I (1770–1799), up to nine further holding libraries are cited in addition to that of the copy examined (although in practice many novels are extremely rare and survive at very few locations). All ESTC numbers are followed in parenthesis by an indication of the verified location in other libraries (given in standard abbreviation) of copies of this edition of the novel. Unverified locations, including those listed in ESTC but marked as unverified, are excluded. In a surprisingly large number of cases, holding libraries (including the location of the examined copy) are not amongst the major libraries of the world. Where a novel is held by many libraries, priority is given to the five main holding libraries in the British Isles (including Ireland, denoted as 'BI'), to eleven main libraries in North America (denoted as 'NA'), and up to three libraries elsewhere (Continental Europe,

---

[14] Antonia Forster, *Index to Book Reviews in England 1749–1774* (Carbondale, IL, 1990), and *Index to Book Reviews in England 1775–1800* (London, 1997); and William S. Ward, *Literary Reviews in British Periodicals 1798–1820*, 2 vols. (New York, 1972); William S. Ward, *Literary Reviews in British Periodicals 1821–1826* (New York, 1977).

Australasia, and other, denoted as 'EA'), in addition to the location of the copy examined.[15] In all cases, however, where further locations are listed in ESTC (used by the pre-1800 volume as the basis for further holding-library references) an indication ('&c') is given. It is important to note, however, that the volume offers corrections to previously published editions of ESTC. Details of some new findings were supplied to the ESTC on-line project team.

The libraries given priority listing for novels published before 1801 are as follows:

BI

British Library, London; University Library, Cambridge; National Library of Ireland, Dublin; National Library of Scotland, Edinburgh; Bodleian Library, Oxford.

NA

Henry E. Huntington Library, California; Sterling Library and Beinecke Rare Books Library, Yale University; Library of Congress, Washington; Newberry Library, Chicago; Library of the University of Illinois, Urbana-Champaign; Houghton Library, Harvard University; Princeton University Library; New York Public Library; Library of the University of Pennsylvania; Harry Ransom Humanities Research Center, University of Texas at Austin; Library of the University of Virginia.

Very occasional examples have been found of a library listed by ESTC in which the apparently verified copy cannot be found. In these cases references to the libraries are omitted. Similarly, research for these volumes has often identified further copies, not listed in ESTC, but these are included in the main holding library lists.

In the case of the second volume, 1800–1829, NSTC has served as the main source for libraries holding copies of the titles listed. NSTC has been compiled from a more limited library consultation than ESTC, but its citations are presented in a manner similar to that of volume I, with the NSTC reference number given first, followed by holding libraries in parenthesis. In cases where NSTC includes more than one number for the same title (under both author and title, for example), the number cited is normally the one based on author, or (in the case of works without identified authors) the most substantial. In each instance, cited holding libraries are taken from all the NSTC entries for this title. Because NSTC begins with the year 1801, and contains relatively few original works actually published in 1800, the first year in volume II of this bibliography is supplemented by material from ESTC entered under the same guide-lines as used in volume I. Because entries in NSTC are based on printed catalogues of the libraries rather than fresh examination of their holdings, it naturally carries over mistakes from earlier cataloguers, and a number of errors concerning matters such as title description and author attribution have been corrected and recorded. NSTC Series 1 (1801–1815) records holdings at six major libraries:

---

[15] This policy is adopted to provide references to leading research libraries holding copies of the novel, avoiding, in the case of widely held novels, a short-list restricted to abbreviations from the start of the alphabet (and usually, therefore, exclusively Canadian libraries).

British Library; University Library, Cambridge; Trinity College, Dublin; National Library of Scotland, Edinburgh; University of Newcastle Library; Bodleian Library, Oxford.

NSTC Series 2 (1816–1870) supplements these libraries by two others:

Library of Congress, Washington; Harvard University.

When one of the libraries listed in ESTC or NSTC provides the actual copy consulted for the entry (and given therefore with shelf-mark at the beginning of the line), the library is omitted from the holding libraries abbreviated later in parenthesis. In cases where the specific edition of the novel forming the entry is absent from ESTC (pre-1801) or NSTC (post-1800), this is indicated by xESTC and xNSTC.

NOTES

These notes are not intended to be comprehensive but to record additional information thought to be of particular interest to readers, including, for example, dedications, subscription lists, and advertisements within the novels. In the case of translations from another language, basic details are provided of the original title and date and place of publication. These are followed by any additional information about authors and translators, as well as past mis-attributions of authorship. Further notes are given in much the same order as the other parts of the full entry. In the first (eighteenth-century) volume, epistolary novels are noted because this form was then both distinctive and significant. For the years to 1777, information from Keith Maslen's *Bowyer Ledgers* is also included to give an indication of the size of the edition.

Also listed are further editions of the novel published up to and including 1850. In the case of reissues first published before 1801, ESTC and the *OCLC WorldCat* online database have provided rich sources of information. NSTC is used as a source of reference for further editions in both volumes: in the case of the first volume it is supplemented by *OCLC* and in the case of the second volume by other catalogues, notably NUC, and by reliable sources such as the published records of the nineteenth-century fiction collections of Michael Sadleir and Robert Lee Wolff.[16] In volume I up to five further editions are listed in chronological order with place and date of publication and ESTC entry number. If more than five editions were published before 1850, the number of these is also given in the form of the number of further entries in ESTC (an important distinction because separate ESTC entries sometimes record variant rather than separate editions). Such references also allow readers to pursue further detail in ESTC entries. Where the further editions include the first Irish edition, booksellers and basic format details of this edition are given. In such a case we include all the information on booksellers of these subsequent

[16] Michael Sadleir, *XIX Fiction: A Bibliographical Record based on his own Collection*, 2 vols. (Cambridge, 1951); Robert Lee Wolff, *Nineteenth-Century Fiction: A Bibliographical Catalogue*, 5 vols. (New York, 1981–6).

Irish editions given by ESTC, but it should be noted that ESTC practice is variable in this instance, sometimes listing all the names of booksellers in what were often large publishing associations, but sometimes listing only a few, followed by the number of others omitted.[17]

In the second volume slightly different editorial procedures are followed with regard to subsequent editions. Up to five further editions published in Britain and Ireland are listed, with supporting references given in parenthesis. Places of publication for these further editions are recorded when they differ from that of the main entry. Where more than five further editions have been identified, the number of additional editions, as evident from NSTC when viewed in conjunction with other catalogues, is given in square brackets (e.g. as 'at least 8 more edns. to 1850'). Because the practice of producing pirate or parallel Dublin editions virtually disappears after the Act of Union of 1800 (when English copyright laws were extended to Ireland), Irish editions are placed in the same chronological sequence as British editions, without additional details being supplied. The sequence of British and Irish editions is then followed by citation of the first known North American edition before 1850, except in cases where the American edition preceded the British (in which case the latter supplies the full entry). In cases where editions were published in different places in North America during the first known year of publication there, the first of these alphabetically by place of publication is given, followed by the others in square brackets.

Both volumes also list the first known translations into German and French.

In the first volume (with fewer entries overall), space has allowed the inclusion of extracts from the reviews. These are reproduced with original spelling and punctuation except in cases of ambiguity (round brackets replace square brackets, for example).

---

[17] This means that while the imprint index, including booksellers, printers and others listed in the imprint line, can be used to identify Irish booksellers involved in the publication of all novels *first* published in this period, the index is no guide to determine *all* the Irish booksellers involved in the novel reprint trade.

# THE ENGLISH NOVEL IN THE ROMANTIC ERA: CONSOLIDATION AND DISPERSAL

*Peter Garside*

The years from 1800 to 1829 are indisputably of pivotal importance in the history of the novel. Traditionally the Romantic period in terms of fiction is viewed as the age of Walter Scott and Jane Austen, whose input into the larger tradition of the novel has been commented on at length, and whose published works have enjoyed intense bibliographical scrutiny. In recent years other novelists, such as Maria Edgeworth and Mary Shelley, have benefited from the bibliographical attention that goes with scholarly editing, and a broader interest in certain generic fields, notably the Gothic and women's fiction, has led to both facsimile series and specialist check-lists. Commencing in the immediate wake of an efflorescence of female novel-writing, yet also characterized by some commentators as involving in its later stages the hijacking of prose fiction by male writers for male readers, the period evidently stands at an important crossroads in terms of the gender distribution of authorship. During this period the understanding of what constitutes a novel tightened, production and marketing became increasingly professional, output of fiction almost certainly overtook that of poetry, and the genre eventually gained new respectability. Concurrently, the three-volume form developed into the norm (though in turn encouraging fresh variants), more prestigious octavos challenged the smaller duodecimo format, and famously a guinea-and-a-half (31s 6d) became the optimum price for a three-volume novel—a price that was to endure virtually until the end of the century.

Yet fiction of the Romantic period has long been overshadowed in academic study by poetry, and as a whole remains one of the least well-researched fields in English literature—certainly one of the most unevenly researched. It has not been known with any degree of certainty how many original novels were produced over these years, or whether the bulk of these were recoverable or not. Relatively little was known about the larger body of uncelebrated authors whose works once filled the shelves of contemporary circulating libraries, and less still about whether they originally wrote anonymously, pseudonymously, or as named authors. Nor has it been clear how many publishers were involved, and what might have been their market share. In view of such imponderables, a whole series of questions, some now especially enticing, have remained virtually unanswerable. Did the number of original titles increase in this period? How did the output of women writers relate to that of their male counterparts? To what extent was production dominated by specialist publishing concerns such as the Minerva Press? Was the Gothic mode dominant in the earlier years of the century, and how true is the notion that it was 'replaced' by historical fiction? To what degree might one validly discriminate between different levels of fiction, say, between 'quality' retail titles and a more common type of 'circulating library' novel? Is it possible to gauge the popularity of authors and titles, did they appeal to different audiences, and what might have been the length of a best-seller's success? These questions demand fresh and continuing research; the present volume provides a number of tools which make an initial survey of the full field now possible.

## (1) Resources

To a degree the above-mentioned uncertainties stem directly from the imperfect (if tantalizing) picture left behind by contemporary records of output. In some respects, the age might be said to fall between the later eighteenth-century endeav-our to evaluate all literary output and the Victorians' almost obsessive cataloguing of their increasingly mechanized production. Not unnaturally bibliographers of eighteenth-century fiction have turned to periodicals as a useful foundation: notably to the monthly *Critical* and *Monthly* reviews, which characteristically pro-vided either full appraisals of novels in their main sections, or, failing that, shorter notices in the 'Novels' section of their end monthly catalogues. A sudden surge in novel production in the later 1780s, followed by fresh peaks in the 1790s, neverthe-less stretched this system to breaking point, so that by the beginning of the new cen-tury the policy of all-inclusion had become well nigh untenable. About half the novels belonging to 1800 and 1801 were reviewed, albeit for the most part briefly, by the *Critical Review*; but by the mid-decade this proportion had dipped to about one quarter, with less than twenty novels with 1806 imprints receiving any notice at all.[1] The *Monthly Review*'s coverage was even more sparse, with only 21 of the 81 novels listed under 1800 in this bibliography receiving any attention, a figure which diminishes to only 18 and 11 in relation to 1801 and 1802 titles respectively. Several gaps of three or four months without any fiction component are evident in the *Monthly* between 1800 and 1803, and there is also a noticeable tardiness in the take-up of some of those titles that do appear. Anne Plumptre's *Something New* (1801: 58) must surely have lost some of its shine when finally noticed there in May 1803.[2]

A more draconian outlook comes into view with the advent of the new-style quarterlies, whose concentration on longer articles broke the mould of reviewing practice early in the nineteenth century. From its inception in 1802 to the end of the 1820s the Whig *Edinburgh Review* gave reviews to fiction on just over thirty

---

[1] Figures relating to numbers of novels produced in the period, and statistics founded on these, relate to the entries in the main annual listings in this volume unless otherwise stated.

[2] MR, n.s. 41 (May 1803), 103.

occasions. This figure is only slightly exceeded by the Tory *Quarterly*, which included barely forty reviews involving fiction between 1809 and 1829, though noticeably allowing greater leeway in the 1820s (partly through the use of composite reviews). A broad distaste for the common 'female' novel is apparent in both journals,[3] and even authors of celebrity were not free from being pushed in the direction of the general pit. Frances Burney's *The Wanderer* (1814: 17), according to one disappointed *Quarterly* reviewer, could hardly 'claim any very decided superiority over the thousand-and-one volumes with which the Minerva Press inundates the shelves of circulating libraries, and increases, instead of diverting, the ennui of the loungers at watering places'.[4] A valuable record of those teeming volumes is nevertheless to be found in 'Novels and Romances' sections of the 'New Publications' listings regularly appended to both journals. Between 1810 and 1829, when the two were operating side by side, the *Edinburgh* and *Quarterly* listed no less than 1,190 and 942 items respectively in this way.[5] These listings match earlier Monthly Catalogues by usually giving details of price, and also (when used guardedly) can offer a rough idea of what part of the year a novel might have been first issued. Unlike their predecessors, however, they provide no indication of publisher, and, in lacking commentary, offer no absolute safeguard that a novel actually existed.

The number of titles so included in these two journals ebbs and flows in interesting ways. The years 1807 and 1808 are especially rich in the *Edinburgh Review*, and the lists of both journals swell noticeably in 1825 (88 items in the *Edinburgh*, 105 in the *Quarterly*), that is, immediately before the 'crash' in the book trade of 1826. As an indicator of total output, however, they have a limited usefulness. Both journals failed to include a high proportion of novels published outside London and Edinburgh. Thinly represented too are novels published 'for the author' or by the subscription method, both of which were unlikely to be pushed by the book trade. Works managed by some publishers gained fuller inclusion than those of others. While only 45 per cent of new titles published by A. K. Newman from the Minerva Press featured in the *Quarterly*'s lists between 1820 and 1829, the percentages for the respectable wholesale house of Longmans and the pushing novel-specialist Henry Colburn are 53 and 63 per cent respectively. Not surprisingly in view of his proprietorship of the review, the relatively small number of novels managed by Archibald Constable did unusually well in the *Edinburgh* (23 out of 25 works). So too did those of John Murray in the *Quarterly*, where a disproportionate number of Murray imprints, including Austen's *Emma* and the first series of Scott's *Tales of My Landlord*, received full reviews (both of those mentioned by Scott himself!). While

---

[3] For a powerful analysis of the derogative female-gendered terms used to describe the 'common' novel in reviews such as the *Edinburgh* and *Quarterly*, see Ina Ferris, *The Achievement of Literary Authority: Gender, History, and the Waverley Novels* (Ithaca and London, 1991), esp. Chs. 1 and 2.

[4] QR, 11 (Apr. 1814), 124.

[5] This count includes a few repeated items and occasional items of misplaced non-fiction. For an annual breakdown, see Peter Garside, 'Collections of English Fiction in the Romantic Period: The Significance of Corvey', in Rainer Schöwerling and Hartmut Steinecke (eds.), *Die Fürstliche Bibliothek Corvey* (Munich, 1992), pp. 70–81 (Table 2, p. 80).

the lists offer a fair starting point for a more complete survey, anyone attempting to construct even the most basic listing of titles on these grounds alone would soon fall into error. The *Quarterly* (especially) includes a number of poems, misled sometimes it would seem by the sub-title 'A Tale'; and the lists of both journals occasionally include miscellaneous works, such as the non-fictional Scott spin-offs which proliferated in the 1820s. Variations in numbers recorded—for example, the radical dip in titles provided by the *Edinburgh* in 1826, when Constable fell bankrupt—might reflect factors other than output itself.

An even fuller array of novel titles can be found in surviving catalogues of circulating libraries. Undoubtedly the bulk of novels read at this time were borrowed rather than individually purchased, especially in the pre-Scott years, and some of the larger libraries (rather like video emporiums today) evidently made an attempt to include all available titles for their clientele. A. K. Newman's 1814[–1819] *Catalogue* of the Minerva Library in Leadenhall Street, London, contains as a whole some 3,500 items under its unusually elongated heading 'Novels, Romances, Imaginary Histories, Lives and Adventures', representing in the region of 40 per cent of the library's total holdings.[6] Analysis moreover of the annual supplements (Parts II–VII) which help make up the surviving catalogue reveals that accessions of fiction averaged about 100 titles a year (a sum which includes reprints and a few retrospective purchases). The Minerva Library is the institution of its kind most commonly associated with novel-reading, but examination of comparable catalogues shows that it was far from exceptional by this time. *A Catalogue of Horne's Public Library, Queen Street, Cheapside* 1824[–1827] incorporates in all 11,607 items, of which nearly 35 per cent are fiction (its 1827 Appendix pointing to an intake of about sixty 'Novels, Romances, &c.' annually).[7] Alexander Mackay's *Catalogue of the Edinburgh Circulating Library* [1810–1816] lists in all 7,094 items, of which nearly 30 per cent are fiction, while the library of Robert Kinnear, more fashionably positioned in the Edinburgh New Town, had acquired by 1825 some 7,646 volumes, consisting of about 70 per cent fiction.[8] An indication of the kind of holdings offered by the larger libraries in spa towns and resorts can be found in

---

[6] *Catalogue of A. K. Newman & Co.'s Circulating Library, Minerva Office, 32 & 33 Leadenhall-Street, London; Consisting of a General Selection of Books in Every Department of Literature, and Particularly Embracing the Whole of Modern Publications*, 7 parts (London: printed at the Minerva Press, February 1814[–1819]). The catalogue (now held in the Bodleian Library) lists 7,967 items in its main section, increasing to 10,692 through the supplements.

[7] Horne's *Catalogue*, now in the Bodleian Library, incorporates as 'Part 1' the [1807] catalogue of *Richards's Library*, of 9, Cornhill, which Horne had presumably absorbed.

[8] Mackay's library stood in the Edinburgh High Street, and claimed its origin from Allan Ramsay's circulating library founded in 1725, reputedly the earliest of this kind in Britain. Kinnear's was at 29 Frederick Street, and its core *Catalogue of Robert Kinnear's Circulating Library, Containing Several Thousand Volumes* [1808] is supplemented by an Appendix [1814] and two addenda [1819, 1823], the latter with MS additions to 1825. Interestingly, whereas Mackay's single Supplement [1816] indicates an intake of fiction on a similar level to that indicated by the core catalogue, Kinnear's appendices point to an increasingly heavy proportion of novels acquired in later years. Both catalogues are in the Edinburgh Public Library.

catalogues such as that of Godwin [1819–1823] in Bath, with 25 per cent fiction from 4,206 items and an intake of 40–50 novels annually. Even smaller provincial libraries, some little more than market stalls, could carry surprisingly large collections of recent novels, through a policy of concentrating almost exclusively on fiction. J. Brown's library in Wigan, 'opposite the Royal Hotel, Standishgate', according to its 1821 catalogue contained 275 'Novels and Romances' from among 375 items. In Salisbury, libraries conducted at the end of the 1810s by C. Fellows (70 per cent fiction from 1,854 items) and Gilmour (90 per cent from 664 items) competed on nearly level terms, though with Gilmour offering slightly more attractive lending terms (20s annually rather than 21s), perhaps in compensation for a smaller stock.[9] Considering that the price for an up-market three-volume novel had by then exceeded a guinea it is not surprising that, as Jane Austen observed in 1814, consumers should be 'more ready to borrow & praise, than to buy'—lamentable as the fact might appear to Austen as an author hoping for sales rather than as a reader.[10]

Compilation of the present volume has involved examination of catalogues belonging to more than thirty commercial circulating libraries of the period. Attention has also been given to the holdings of ten proprietary Library Societies,[11] whose largely professional and male members were share-holders rather than casual fee-payers, and which, having generally eschewed fiction in earlier years, were themselves starting to build up fairly extensive fiction holdings. Such records offer a unique view of reading patterns, pointing to the popularity of certain modes and authors, the existence of possible regional variations, and the wider appeal of fiction in the 1820s. The presence of a title under the 'Novels and Romances' headings commonly found in larger catalogues also helps isolate the output of fiction, while providing a valuable indication of what were considered as novels at the time. Occasionally catalogues include privileged information: local knowledge presumably enabled Mackay to identify 'Mrs Richardson' as the author of the anonymous *Adonia, A Desultory Story* (1801: 59), and the Newman Catalogue of 1814 is a useful source for Minerva authors. In a number of instances, circulating library catalogues

---

[9] Fuller details of the libraries mentioned above, and their holdings of fiction, will be found in Christopher Skelton-Foord, 'Circulating Fiction 1780–1830: The Novel in British Circulating Libraries of the Romantic Era', Ph.D. thesis (Cardiff, 1997).

[10] Letter to Fanny Knight, 30 Nov. 1814, in Deirdre Le Faye (ed.), *Jane Austen's Letters*, 3rd edn. (Oxford, 1995), p. 287. See also Lee Erickson, 'The Economy of Novel Reading: Jane Austen and the Circulating Library', in his *The Economy of Literary Form: English Literature and the Industrialization of Publishing, 1800–1850* (Baltimore and London, 1996), pp. 125–41; and Christopher Skelton-Foord, 'To buy or to borrow? Circulating libraries and novel reading in Britain, 1778–1828', *Library Review*, 47: 7 (1998), 348–54.

[11] Library societies whose in-period Catalogues (years in parentheses) have been examined are: Bristol (1814, Appendix 1824), Birmingham (1821), Sheffield ([1816], 1821, 1831), Liverpool (1814, Appendix 1820), Manchester Subscription (1818, 1831), Tavistock (1822), Macclesfield (1823), Subscription Library for Promoting General Knowledge, Manchester (1828), Edinburgh (1833), and Morpeth (1834). While particular circumstances naturally differ, the general impression gained is that the novels holdings of these institutions doubled between 1815 and 1830, with some libraries (e.g. the Macclesfield Subscription Library) holding as much as 15 per cent fiction.

have helped disclose titles which might otherwise have been overlooked. Sarah Wilkinson's *The Child of Mystery, A Novel* (1808: 110), published by the somewhat unscrupulous James Fletcher Hughes, is found in a number of catalogues, including those of Newman, Mackay, Kinnear, and Brown. It appears not to have received any reviews, however, and is absent in modern bibliographies of fiction, perhaps as a result of being obscured by Hannah Maria Jones's similarly titled *Child of Mystery* (1837). Extreme care nevertheless needs to be taken when handling materials found in this way. Circulating libraries were notoriously disorganized affairs,[12] catalogues often garbled or truncated titles to the point of non-recognizability, and proprietors engaged in a variety of deceptions such as turning to a secondary title in an effort to give a work fresh currency. Accordingly no title in the present bibliography has been accepted on this kind of evidence alone, though it should be added that virtually all the suggestions brought up in this way have led to actual works of fiction, the vast majority in the shape of surviving copies.

The final contemporary source field originates from the book trade's own record of its output. At its most basic, this is found in the form of notices of novels and romances 'Just Published' or 'In the Press', which are frequently found in individual works of fiction of the period. Some of these lists, such as those by Lane and Newman, B. Crosby and Co., J. F. Hughes, and Henry Colburn, are especially long and detailed, and offer a clear signal of the publisher's commitment to fiction, or even desire to corner the market in the genre. As a record of production, however, advertisements of this kind need to be approached with caution, and quite a few works vaunted as being 'In the Press' apparently never materialized. A more comprehensive record is provided by the various updates of William Bent's *London Catalogue of Books*, a compilation (based on trade lists) which first appeared in 1773, and which usually provide basic details of title, publisher, format, price, and (much less frequently) authorship. Unfortunately, whereas earlier issues of Bent had sometimes granted 'Novels and Romances' a section on their own, the issues after 1800 generally fail to make this distinction, at best listing fiction in a broader 'Miscellaneous' category. Bent's compilation was also a record of the London trade and often omits provincial publications or alternatively obliterates a primary publisher by superimposing the London agent. A similar focus and arrangement is evident in *The English Catalogue of Books, 1801–1836*, a retrospective compilation, published in 1914, under the editorship of R. A. Peddie and Quintin Waddington.[13] This incorporates periodical trade catalogues that preceded *The Publishers' Circular* as well as information from the various editions of Bent's *London Catalogue*, checked in cases of doubt against the then current Catalogue of the British Museum. Entries are listed alphabetically in a single continuous list by author or

---

[12] According to Thomas Wilson, in *The Use of Circulating Libraries Considered* ([London], 1797), 'I have seen many catalogues, some of them so confused, that the librarian himself has hardly known where to look for any particular work' (p. 30).

[13] Fuller details of the catalogues and bibliographies mentioned in this Introduction, when not provided with a footnote, will be found in the abbreviation list to this volume.

title (with cross-references from title to author, where identified), with full entries usually providing details of price, format, publisher, and date (the latter often by month as well as year). Cross-checking against other sources, such as reviews, indicates that the details provided (e.g. of price) almost invariably refer to the initial publication of a title, though in a few cases a reprint is offered instead of (or as an adjunct to) the original edition.

At a rough estimate, the *English Catalogue of Books* (ECB) contains some 27,000 entries for the years 1801–1829, of which approximately 2,400 titles are broadly describable as fiction. In a more specific survey, John Sutherland isolated 3,740 entries belonging to the four years between 1824 and 1827, of which 393 were fiction, representing 10.5 per cent of output.[14] This fiction tally though is likely to be swollen by the inclusion of a number of titles for the purposes of this bibliography not counted as novels (an issue discussed more fully below). At the same time, the ECB is far from complete, areas of absence including provincial publications, works privately published, and those issued by smaller presses. It also evidently carries over some mistakes from contributing sources, rendering for example the author Edward Moore as 'Mawe (Edw.)', the publisher Fearman as 'Fearson', and *The Dwarf of Westerbourg* (1827: 66) as 'Dwarf of Westerbony'. Occasionally entries silently overwrite an earlier edition, most noticeably in the case of non-London issues, and sometimes one publisher is given where several were concerned, or alternatively the subsequent purchaser of the copyright features rather than the original bookseller. And while the specific dates provided serve as a useful adjunct to those suggested by the reviews, and like them occasionally point to publication prior to the actual imprint date, due care needs to be taken for possible cases of over-optimistic anticipation.[15] As a basic secondary source of information, ECB stands on at least an equal footing with review listings. Accordingly regular references are provided by the present volume in all instances—more than 1,750 cases in all—where a title is found there (normally within the main entry when apparently identical, and in the 'Notes' field if a later edition). Additionally, ECB is used as an authority for price details throughout, as well as for time of publication where no review dating is evident and/or where publication prior to the imprint date is indicated. Pricing information for the year 1800, which is not covered there, is entered in lieu from Bent's *Modern Catalogue of Books, with their Sizes and Prices . . . since the Year 1792* (1803).

The two standard modern catalogues of fiction most likely to be consulted prior to the present bibliography both date back to the 1930s, and each in its sprawling nature and vulnerability to error might be said to mirror aspects of the contemporary

[14] John Sutherland, 'The British Book Trade and the Crash of 1826', *The Library*, 6th ser., 9: 2 (June 1987), 148–61.

[15] An instance is provided by the 'Dec. 1814' dating of Scott's *Guy Mannering* (1815: 46), which in actuality was first issued in Edinburgh on 24 Feb. 1815, several days in advance of the London sale. Here the ECB dating no doubt reflects the earliest newspaper announcements, and, beyond that, the expectations of the managing London house of Longmans, as originally fuelled by Scott's literary agent, John Ballantyne.

documents so far described. Andrew Block's *The English Novel 1740–1850: A Catalogue including Prose Romances, Short Stories, and Translations of Foreign Fiction* (1939; revised 1961), an alphabetical listing by author or title, contains in excess of 3,000 entries for the period 1800–1829.[16] This number, however, is inflated by the inclusion of chapbooks, 'shilling shockers', didactic tracts, memoirs, and quasi-fictional materials not definable in normative terms as novels. Block also occasionally provides entries for works that are non-fictional, amongst them Scott's *Tales of a Grandfather*, a children's history; and even some poems are entered, usually on the authority of review listings. A number of other titles prove on examination to be 'ghosts', that never actually existed, the product of Block's over-trusting acceptance of uncorroborated contemporary sources (or earlier reference works, such as Allibone, when based on such materials). Double entries abound, and not always through a mistaken inclusion under both author and title. *All Sorts of Lovers* (1811: 76) is attributed to Henry Somerset and Henry Summersett alike; while *The Vaults of Lepanto* (1814: 57), with variations in the title, features under both T. R. Tucker and (more correctly) T. R. Tuckett. Block is particularly vulnerable where works have been reissued under changed titles: a device not infrequently used by the book trade as a means of giving old/unsold material fresh currency. To give just one instance from several such: *The Royal Sufferer* (1810) and *Secret Memoirs of an Illustrious Princess* (1813), both listed under John Agg, are one and the same work (see 1810: 21). Another weakness is found in a tendency to date uncertain items in round numbers, so that (say) 1810 and 1820 are considerably inflated in any annual count. As a whole, the foundation of entries can vary between rare copies actually seen in antiquarian bookshops (including Block's own) to jottings made from other secondary works and palpably unreliable records such as publishers' adverts.

Similar uncertainties underlie Montague Summers's *A Gothic Bibliography* [1940], which unlike Block usually offers no indication of source. Some detailed entries give the impression that a copy was actually in hand, while others might well have been culled from the lists of other works 'by the author' commonly found on title-pages. Summers's use of 'Gothic' in his own title is something of a misnomer, since the elastic policy declared at the onset is stretched to the point that effectively nearly all 'popular' non-canonical fiction is potentially open for inclusion. Like Block, Summers shows a penchant for the Gothic chapbooks which proliferated in the 1800s and early 1810s; and a prioritizing of the output of the Minerva Press undoubtedly helps give an exaggerated sense of the dominance of that concern over the years. A descriptive 'Index of Authors' accompanies the alphabetical listing of titles, though there are noticeable disparities between the two, and some titles given

---

[16] An annual breakdown of 4,195 entries in Block relating to 1780–1830 is given in Peter Garside, 'The English Novel in the 1820s: Consolidation and Dispersal', in Rainer Schöwerling, Hartmut Steinecke, and Günter Tiggesbäumker (eds.), *Literatur und Erfahrungswandel 1789–1830* (Munich, 1996), pp. 179–93 (p. 192, Table 1). For the period under view the count is 877 (1800s), 920 (1810s), and 1,268 (1820s). The 1968 edn. of Block used for this analysis, and referred to elsewhere in this volume, is a reprint of the 'New and Revised edition' published in 1961.

under author lists are not repeated in the main listing. The imprint information given for individual entries is also frequently found to be wanting, when compared against actual copies. Anne Ker's *Edric, the Forester* can hardly have been issued by J. F. Hughes in 1817, several years after his disappearance from the bookselling scene through bankruptcy: and the true publisher then, as the present entry (1817: 36) reveals, was actually T. Hughes. Yet even here there is the enticing possibility of an earlier attempted issue, with which the other Hughes might feasibly have been associated (see 1804: 30). Summers's work still has the capacity to offer unexpected leads and insights, but as a source of bibliographical information it should be handled with great caution.

Later bibliographical studies have generally cast the net less widely. Gothic fiction in particular has been well served, though practitioners in the field often risk giving an exaggerated idea of the prevalence of the mode in relation to output of novels generally. The check-list of titles 1764–1824 appended to Maurice Lévy's *Le Roman 'gothique' anglais* (1968) includes some 340 titles overall, with 215 items occurring between 1800 and 1826.[17] While library sources are cited on a number of occasions, there remains an element of uncertainty sometimes about whether an actual copy has been consulted or not, and in a handful of cases no form of authentication is supplied. Frederick S. Frank's *The First Gothics* (1987) carries the Gothic torch further, offering brief bibliographical descriptions as well as plot synopses of 500 Gothic fictions, of which 324 fall into the years covered by the present volume. A closer breakdown shows 193 in the 1800s, 95 in the 1810s, and a much diminished 36 in the 1820s. Most of these are full-length novels, though Frank does include chapbooks and 'shilling shockers', as well as Gothic parodies, carefully distinguishing these when they appear. While the Sadleir-Black collection at the University of Virginia evidently served as the main archival base for this study, no specific information is given about copies consulted, and in some instances one doubts whether a copy has been seen at all. In the case of one tantalizing title, *Durston Castle; or, the Ghost of Eleonora, A Gothic Story* (1804), which Summers and Lévy both list, defeat is openly acknowledged: 'until a copy is exhumed and examined, *Durston Castle* must remain an unverified Gothic and a bibliographical mystery'.[18]

A more recent growth area, the study of fiction by women, has so far been more successful in announcing the extensiveness of output than in offering clear-cut results. Dale Spender's listing of 568 novels by '106 women authors before Jane Austen' undoubtedly had a useful propagandist effect when it appeared in her

---

[17] Maurice Lévy, 'Bibliographie chronologique du roman "gothique" 1764–1824', in his *Le Roman 'gothique' anglais 1764–1824* (Toulouse, 1968), pp. 684–708. A breakdown post-1800 shows 142 titles in the 1800s, followed by 59 in the 1810s, and only 14 between 1820 and 1826. This count omits the French translations of English Gothic titles which Lévy incorporates in his annual lists. The latter element was later expanded by Lévy's 'English Gothic and the French Imagination: A Calendar of Translations 1767–1828', in *The Gothic Imagination: Essays in Dark Romanticism*, ed. G. R. Thompson (Pullman, Wash., 1974), pp. 150–70.

[18] Frederick S. Frank, *The First Gothics: A Critical Guide to the English Gothic Novel* (New York, 1987), Item 117, p. 99. Further details concerning *Durston Castle* are given later in this Introduction.

*Mothers of the Novel* (1986).[19] Yet it is relatively thin in content after 1800, and has hardly any direct bibliographical value, having been somewhat sketchily assembled from chiefly secondary sources. R. C. Alston's *A Checklist of Women Writers 1801–1900* (British Library, 1990) valuably shifts the spotlight to the nineteenth century, where an abundance of imaginative writing by women is again in evidence. However, this compilation offers no full generic indicators to distinguish prose fiction from poetry and drama, and its entries, largely determined by a sweep of shelf-mark ranges in the British Library, do not include unidentified anonymous works. A fertile source of information is also to be found in a publication of the same year, *The Feminist Companion to Literature in English,* a biographical guide which contains a variety of entries on authors in the Romantic period.[20] All are accurately researched, some containing fresh information through reference to the archives of the Royal Literary Fund. Titles are not indexed, however, and can only be traced through reading entries, which themselves are understandably selective in mentioning works by prolific authors.

As a thoroughgoing investigation, no published study has yet really surpassed Dorothy Blakey's *The Minerva Press 1790–1820* (1939). Blakey's main 'Chronological List of Publications'—offered as an Appendix, but in effect a full bibliography—contains from 1800 to 1820 inclusive some 435 original fiction titles published by William Lane and his successor A. K. Newman, of which slightly more than 60 per cent have been examined at first hand.[21] Generally speaking, it still holds up well during these years as a record of the Minerva output. Yet there is still a noticeable disparity between, on the one hand, the particularly fine entries provided where actual copies have been seen and, on the other, the much briefer and less reliable descriptions constructed from secondary sources, notably reviews. One side effect of this is found in the fairly frequent placing of unseen items under the wrong year. As a whole, mistakes are most apparent in the 1800s, where the recovery rate is at its lowest, with only 115 copies seen out of a total of 232 fiction entries for that decade. Granted that Blakey had pursued copies on both sides of the Atlantic, as well as having access to private collections such as that of Michael Sadleir, the prospects for completing a copy-based bibliography incorporating all novels produced in the period might seem remote in the extreme.

One immediate problem facing the present-day researcher is how to locate and isolate those novels that have survived in major libraries. The British Library undeniably contains a uniquely rich and diverse collection of novels belonging to the early

---

[19] Dale Spender, *Mothers of the Novel: 100 Good Women Writers before Jane Austen* (London and New York, 1986), pp. 119–37.

[20] Virginia Blain, Isobel Grundy, and Patricia Clements (eds.), *The Feminist Companion to Literature in English: Women Writers from the Middle Ages to the Present* (London, 1990). While contributions originate from a number of hands, one senses especially the presence of Isobel Grundy in the entries relating to the Romantic period.

[21] These figures exclude acknowledged later editions, miscellanies, periodicals, and other nonfiction items included by Blakey, though prose tales for children and remainder issues of novels found in the main listings are counted.

nineteenth century, gathered not only as a copyright library, but also through the intake of other collections and an inspired purchasing policy. Extensive fiction holdings are grouped together under a number of set shelf-marks (most obviously, the 'N' prefix), but there is no certainty that a title so catalogued will prove to be a novel on examination. Conversely, as entries in the present volume will show, there are significant numbers of novels that are not directly traceable through shelf-mark at all, including several recent accessions. Even the privilege of direct access to the holdings, as Alston acknowledges, would entail searching amongst miles of shelving. A not dissimilar situation is faced at the Bodleian Library, Oxford, which probably houses the second strongest holdings of Romantic fiction in Britain, and in particular a number of rare Gothic and scandal fictions. Here a good spread of fiction is found with the prefix '249.s', a grouping searched extensively in the production of this bibliography, but other novels are likely to be found under a myriad of other headings, some relating to extremely small collections. The Compact Disc (CD-ROM) versions of the British Library General Catalogue to 1975 and the Bodleian Pre-1920 Catalogue of Printed Books have vastly facilitated title searching, making it possible for example to isolate titles within combinations of years and shelf-marks. Neither database, however, includes a searchable fiction or novel genre field.

The Nineteenth-Century Short-Title Catalogue (NSTC), incorporating catalogued holdings of all the main British copyright libraries, only partially helps obviate the above difficulties through its adoption of the Dewey Decimal Classification system (823 English Fiction, 833 German Fiction, 843 French Fiction etc.). The fiction category is applied there to a wide range of texts, including chapbooks, miscellanies, collections, tracts, and some children's books. The granting of separate entries for reprints and translations, as well as the presence often of multiple entries for the same work, will also inevitably swell any annual count. A Boolean search for English fiction (823) titles by decade on the CD-ROM version (1996) of Series I and II results in the magnified totals of 1,246 (1800s), 1,883 (1810s), and 3,027 (1820s). Closer scrutiny uncovers a number of other deficiencies, including ambiguities or mistakes concerning date and place of publication, and the occasional egregious error in classification. Mary Sabilla Novello's A Day in Stowe Gardens (1825: 62), clearly a novel, is given a Dewey classification of 635, namely 'Agriculture—Garden Crops, Vegetables'. As well as being limited by its catalogue origins, NSTC is based on the holdings of a relatively small number of libraries, some likely to be unsympathetic to seemingly ephemeral literature when originally making accessions. Compilation of this volume has revealed a surprisingly high number of novels either entirely absent there or not recorded in their original edition.[22]

---

[22] More than 20 per cent of the original editions which provide the entries in the main listings in this volume (affecting 460 entries in all) are absent in NSTC, though on some 50 occasions the title is found there in the form of a subsequent edition or editions (in which case the NSTC number of the earliest edition is given under 'Further Editions(s)' in the entry). In the 1800s the absences are especially striking, with more than 40 per cent of titles belonging to 1801–1809 (288 from 692 entries) not being present in NSTC in the original edition given.

Comparable impediments can be met in searching North American libraries, where exceptional holdings are found at a number of institutions, including Harvard and Yale universities, the University of Illinois at Urbana-Champaign, and the University of California, Los Angeles. One difficulty stems from an apparent uncertainty about the status of books belonging to the early nineteenth century. At Urbana a renowned collection of eighteenth-century fiction, as recorded in a published check-list by William H. McBurney in 1965,[23] is housed in the Rare Book room, but equally rich holdings in the early nineteenth century are mostly dispersed on the open stacks amongst other later fiction. In two libraries visited, apparently unique copies have been found available for general loan, while in others texts are guarded with zealous care and can only be called up singly. The *National Union Catalog* (NUC) offers invaluable help in establishing locations of surviving copies, but provides little guidance about genre apart from what is apparent from titles, while the quality of entries varies considerably according to the lead contributing library. The *OCLC WorldCat* database has also served usefully in searching extremely rare novels, but again includes no suitable genre-specific mechanism.

One way of easing the problem of making wide-sweeping library searches is to concentrate on special collections of fiction. Here, however, the early nineteenth century has suffered unduly in falling between two established areas of book collection, the eighteenth century and the Victorian period. Sidney Gecker's *English Fiction to 1820 in the University of Pennsylvania Library* (1954) contains in all 1,112 items (including reprints), of which only 163 titles were first published between 1800 and 1820 (84 in the 1810s, and 79 in the 1820s). Even then, the high proportion of Irish, American, and later British editions, makes it of limited use for a survey of original titles. A similar sense of the Romantic period serving as a kind of overspill area is found in J. C. Hardy's *A Catalogue of English Prose Fiction mainly of the Eighteenth Century* (1982). This record of a private library lists 826 items, nearly all of them original editions, of which just 104 titles belong to the period from 1800. Looking from the opposite direction, the post-Scott era is unquestionably the main focus of interest in two catalogues of privately built collections of nineteenth-century fiction, assembled by Michael Sadleir and Robert Lee Wolff, though the few pre-1830 entries found in Sadleir are impeccably constructed and Wolff's in-period commentaries can be extremely useful.[24]

Three established library collections, two in Britain and one in North America, have none the less proved invaluable in the construction of the present volume. The Early Novels Collection in the University of Bristol Library presently contains in the region of 2,000 volumes, with a heavy concentration in the Romantic period.

---

[23] *English Prose Fiction 1700–1800 in the University of Illinois Library,* compiled by William H. McBurney with the assistance of Charlene M. Taylor (Urbana, 1965). This includes just 19 titles relating to the year 1800.

[24] Michael Sadleir, *XIX Century Fiction: A Bibliographical Record based on his own Collection,* 2 vols. (Cambridge, 1951); Robert Lee Wolff, *Nineteenth-Century Fiction: A Bibliographical Catalogue,* 5 vols. (New York, 1981–6).

The collection was originally created and built up by W. L. Cooper, Librarian of the University (1923–1946), and, until the production of a pamphlet catalogue in 1994,[25] was only recorded in the form of a manuscript handlist. Omitting repeated titles and collected works, some 250 original novels belong to the period 1800–1829, several of which are now extremely rare (see, for examples, 1811: 34, 1814: 49, and 1818: 62 in this volume). Overall, the collection is strong in works by popular 'named' authors of the period, for instance those of Anna Maria Porter and Amelia Opie, and relatively weak in novels such as Gothic pot-boilers, whose survival rate has been poorer. An even less well-known resource exists at Aberdeen University, which, as one of the ancient Scottish universities, enjoyed the privileges of a copyright library up till 1836. In about 1814, at the beginning of the Scott era, the Librarian must have decided to take up his right to claim novels registered at Stationers' Hall. The University Library contains on its closed shelves a sequence of some 870 items of fiction belonging to the period 1810–1837, nearly all in their original boards and with spine labels often in place. An annual breakdown of 605 titles between 1814 and 1829 shows ten 1814 titles, followed thereafter by an intake of between 30 to 50 annually: the years 1821 to 1825 forming a steady plateau, no single year dipping below 40, and with a bumper crop in 1829 (54 titles).[26] Works having a Scottish provenance or interest are understandably in evidence, and children's literature and evangelical tract fiction are also strongly represented (though not dominant).

Unlike these two relatively unknown British resources, the Sadleir–Black Collection at the University of Virginia Library, Charlottesville, is more strongly weighted in favour of the earlier years under survey. No printed catalogue is available, but an index by call number lists some 325 original novels belonging to the period 1800–1829, a figure which excludes a large number of chapbooks also in the collection and other items such as drama and German language titles. Any specialist library collection, however, is bound to some degree to be an artificial construction, determined by factors quite distinct from those that affected earliest readers. The Bristol collection no doubt reflects the availability and affordability of titles in West Country antiquarian bookshops, as well as the retrospective judgments of those making accessions. The Aberdeen holdings likewise must not only mirror registrations at Stationers' Hall, but also probably those titles which the librarian felt fit to take up and/or keep on his shelves. Most obviously, the Sadleir–Black Collection is a monument to the purchasing priorities of its bibliophile founders, whose main focus of interest was the male Gothic 'horror' tradition represented by M. G. ('Monk') Lewis and Charles Robert Maturin. In spite of individual differences, all the above collections seem noticeably light in those more 'commonplace' titles that can be viewed at large in contemporary documents such as circulating library catalogues.

[25] *Early Novels Collection*, compiled by Nick Lee (University of Bristol Library, March 1994).
[26] A full annual breakdown of the holdings at Aberdeen, and at Bristol, is given in Garside, 'Collections of English Fiction', p. 80 (Tables 1 and 2).

Illustration 1. 'Die Fürstliche Bibliothek' (Princely Library) at Schloss Corvey

One recently rediscovered collection has the capacity to transform our understanding of the fiction of the Romantic era. 'Die Fürstliche Bibliothek' (Princely Library) at Schloss Corvey, near Höxter, is a German aristocratic family library, including some 25,000 titles in 73,000 volumes, mainly in German, French, and English, with a distinct tailing off after 1834. Its most important collectors were Victor Amadeus (1779–1834), Landgrave of Hesse-Rotenburg, and his second wife Elise (1790–1830), who both had connections with the English royal family.[27] One striking feature as it now stands is the large component of English fiction, comprising over 2,450 titles between 1790 and 1834. It is probable that many of these books entered into the collection through a German bookseller from Göttingen specializing in English works, called Dr Möller. Whatever the case, the overall result is much the same as if all the promptings of the reviews, as well as the trade catalogues of publishers specializing in fiction, had been taken up virtually *in toto*. Apart from the house-style decorated leather bindings, and elegant glass-fronted

---

[27] In 1821 Victor Amadeus acquired Schloss Corvey, through a territorial exchange; though it is useful to bear in mind that the collection and extension of the library initially took place at Rotenburg (some 45 miles to the south of Schloss Corvey), the books only being moved to their present home between 1825 and 1833. In the eighteenth century Rotenburg housed a fairly unexceptional German court library of its kind, the intake of English books only becoming really significant after the French Revolution. For a recent account of the Corvey library and its fiction holdings, see Christopher Skelton-Foord, ' "Universalbibliothek der Trivialliteratur", 1800–1830: Castle Corvey and the Distribution of Circulating-Library Fiction in English', *Library History*, 14 (Nov. 1998), 117–32.

cases which now keep out tourists in summer and mice in winter, it is almost as if the fiction stocks of one of the leading contemporary circulating libraries, with yearly accessions intact, had been transported mysteriously to Germany.

In August 1985, a contract was signed between the state of North Rhine-Westphalia and the Duke of Ratibor and Corvey, which gave the University of Paderborn exclusive rights for the extensive cataloguing of the collection at Corvey. Cataloguing began with *belles lettres*, in German, French, and English, and books were brought over in consignments to the Projekt Corvey rooms in the nearby University Library at Paderborn to be processed in three ways: (i) all title-pages were xeroxed; (ii) basic bibliographical details of each item were sent to the North Rhine-Westphalian library computing system at Cologne; and (iii) microfiches were made of the full text of individual books. The English language series of the Corvey Microfiche edition (CME), published by Belser Wissenschaftlicher Dienst of Stuttgart from 1989, comprising in all 3,290 titles, includes most (but not all) of the English fiction held in Schloss Corvey.[28] As a concentrated collection of English novels belonging to the Romantic period Corvey is exceptional, while numerically its holdings almost certainly exceed those found in this area in any other library, including the British Library.

## (2) Recovery and Exclusions

Historically the present volume originates from the coming together of two separate bibliographical enterprises, as first reported on at the International Corvey Symposium held in October 1990. The first project consisted of a card index file of novels between 1780 and 1830, compiled by the present writer in an eclectic way from various sources, such as circulating library catalogues, Bent's London Catalogues, review listings, and so on. When finally settling down in the late 1980s, the file incorporated 2,897 titles, representing it then seemed at least 95 per cent of novels originally published in the period. This allowed a number of observations to be made—about the market share of publishers, gender distribution of authorship, and such like—but always with the proviso that in many cases only secondary sources (albeit in combination) had been employed. As a result of contact established with Projekt Corvey in May 1990, it became possible to check the card index file against the entries made for the Cologne library system, which by then included all fiction titles held at Corvey. In addition to confirming the extensiveness of Corvey, the exercise threw light on the kinds of novel that are *absent* from the library. Prominent here were translations into English of works previously published in French or

---

[28]  An early check-list of the English fiction holdings at Corvey will be found in John Graham, *Novels in English: The Eighteenth- and Nineteenth-Century Holdings at Schloss Corvey, Höxter, Germany* (New York, 1983). This, however, only offers short bibliographical descriptions, and there are numerous errors, the product it would seem of hasty transcriptions and an over-reliance on Block and similar sources when assembling the final author/title list. There are also some omissions, notwithstanding 2,107 entries. In view of the immensity of the project, it is perhaps not surprising that the Belser catalogue lists provided with the Microfiche edition also contain a number of misattributions and other errors.

German, many of which exist in the library in the original versions. Other areas where omissions were found included: subscription novels and works published 'for the author'; titles issued by publishers who were not fully established (e.g. Henry Colburn in his early days); scandal fictions; and titles which might be taken to indicate a bawdy content. While the large proportion of holdings are in first editions, in some cases where a book was popular, or unexpectedly broke onto the scene, it is found in a subsequent edition, indicating something of a time-lag in purchasing. Also thrown up by this process were some 50–60 titles that had not become known through the sources used in the card index file. Furthermore, comparison against catalogues such as NSTC and NUC indicated that a significant number of the novels at Corvey were probably unique copies.[29]

Procedurally the general rule in the present volume has been to use Corvey as the foundation in cases where a first edition is held there. As a result, more than 1,600 entries are based on a copy held at Corvey, freshly examined and checked to provide the main entry. In a handful of instances, where the Corvey copy is incomplete or otherwise imperfect (e.g. lacks a subscription list), alternative copies have been sought to provide the entry, the presence of a copy in Corvey in these cases being signalled by the inclusion of the CME ISBN number after the shelf-mark of the actual contributing library. More broadly, on some 125 occasions where the copy at Corvey is a later edition, or a reissue, this copy again has not been used for the main entry, though its presence is indicated under 'Further Editions' at the end of the Notes field of the entry. One secondary result of the above procedure is that the present volume offers a record of over 1,750 English novels held at Corvey in a first or early subsequent edition, with CME numbers provided in all cases where microfiches are available. During the preparation of this stage of the bibliography the holdings of the Corvey library were again thoroughly surveyed, and a number of previously overlooked or disregarded titles have been progressively added as entries.

The search for original editions not held at Corvey has involved visits to numerous libraries on both sides of the Atlantic. Generally speaking, the British Isles copyright libraries have provided the main alternative resource. In all, some 380 entries

---

[29] Checks against a wide variety of catalogues and on-line databases, in addition to ESTC and NSTC, indicate that more than 100 of the copies recorded in this volume are possibly unique to the Corvey collection. The following original editions, by entry number, have not as yet been discovered in another source, and may possibly represent the only surviving copy of the work: 1800: 4; 1800: 9; 1801: 1; 1801: 10; 1801: 12; 1802: 6; 1802: 19; 1803: 4; 1803: 12; 1803: 13; 1803: 47; 1803: 69; 1803: 70; 1803: 72; 1804: 6; 1804: 7; 1804: 15; 1804: 30; 1804: 44; 1804: 66; 1804: 68; 1805: 12; 1805: 18; 1805: 34; 1805: 52; 1805: 56; 1805: 65; 1805: 70; 1805: 73; 1806: 2; 1806: 3; 1806: 11; 1806: 13; 1806: 16; 1806: 19; 1806: 41; 1806: 45; 1806: 46; 1806: 61; 1806: 69; 1807: 2; 1807: 22; 1807: 51; 1807: 61; 1807: 65; 1808: 1; 1808: 26; 1808: 27; 1808: 28; 1808: 30; 1808: 50; 1808: 53; 1808: 58; 1808: 84; 1808: 86; 1808: 87; 1808: 99; 1808: 104; 1808: 107; 1809: 3; 1809: 19; 1809: 23; 1809: 47; 1809: 52; 1809: 59; 1809: 79; 1810: 15; 1810: 79; 1810: 82; 1811: 10; 1811: 12; 1811: 52; 1811: 71; 1812: 11; 1812: 32; 1812: 38; 1812: 39; 1812: 53; 1812: 55; 1812: 61; 1813: 13; 1813: 32; 1813: 36; 1813: 40; 1814: 1; 1814: 35; 1814: 51; 1814: 57; 1814: 58; 1815: 3; 1815: 21; 1818: 36; 1818: 42; 1819: 5; 1819: 15; 1820: 11; 1821: 53; 1822: 5; 1822: 31; 1822: 42. Additionally, the following first editions in Corvey have not been located in another source, though the work apparently survives elsewhere in a later edition: 1805: 1; 1805: 22; 1805: 74; 1806: 55; 1808: 20; 1813: 26; 1816: 9; 1817: 36; 1822: 14, 1829: 8. In two cases a later edition in Corvey may possibly represent the only surviving copy of the work (see 1802: 8 and 1816: 27).

in this volume are based on copies located in the British Library, over 30 were found at the Bodleian, and altogether some 40 more originate from the National Library of Scotland, Edinburgh, Cambridge University Library, and Trinity College Library, Dublin. Direct access to the Bristol Early Novels Collection and to the closed stacks at Aberdeen (19 and 10 entries respectively) allowed direct comparison to be made between copies there and entries already compiled from Corvey and other sources. On some occasions this disclosed variants between supposedly similar editions, and, in a few instances, the survey led to the addition of titles previously not considered for entry. In particular, the spine labels at Aberdeen proved a useful additional source of information on price, and information gained in this way is provided in the entries when no other accurate data is available.

Libraries in North America have been chiefly (though not exclusively) used in cases where copies were not available in Corvey or Britain and Ireland, with holding locations generally being ascertained through the use of the *National Union Catalog* and the OCLC database. Regular visits have been paid to leading centres, including: the Houghton and Widener libraries at Harvard; the Beinecke and Sterling libraries at Yale University; the Alderman Library, University of Virginia; the library of the University of Illinois, Urbana-Champaign; the New York Public Library; and the library of the University of California at Los Angeles. In total, these between them have provided over 100 title entries. In addition to the Sadleir–Black collection at Virginia, two resources allowed wider surveys to be carried out. Systematic stack checks at Urbana helped corroborate the existence there of a number of earlier states of editions, and also led to a few previously unexpected novels (see, for example, entries 1824: 14 and 1824: 93). An extensive check was also made against the card index catalogue compiled by Chester Noyes Greenough, housed in the Houghton Library at Harvard. Not unlike Block's *English Novel* in its diversity, this threw up a plethora of 'overlooked' titles, all of which were checked against other bibliographical sources, and where necessary against actual copies, the large majority proving unsuitable for entry. The density of Greenough's record also made it a useful ancillary source for later editions, especially American ones; and occasional clues relating to author attribution were also thrown up. In addition to large resource centres like Harvard, numerous other libraries have been visited, sometimes in pursuit of apparently unique single copies (see entries 1811: 35 and 1814: 30 for examples). A final sweep of North American libraries also took in the Newberry and Regenstein libraries in Chicago, the Library of Congress, and Princeton University Library.[30]

[30]  While location and examination of copies was taking place, further searches were conducted in secondary sources. With the completion of Series II of NSTC in 1995, a comprehensive survey was made of all titles with classifications (823 etc.) relating to fiction, in sorted form; this in turn being followed by a further comparison by year using the CD-ROM version. A similar trawl has also been made through items categorized as Fiction (F) in William S. Ward's two relevant bibliographies of reviews of literary works, *Literary Reviews in British Periodicals 1798–1820: A Bibliography*, 2 vols. (New York, 1972) and *Literary Reviews in British Periodicals 1821–1826: A Bibliography* (New York, 1977). Further details relating to reviews in the year 1800 will be found in Antonia Forster's *Index to Book Reviews in England 1775–1800* (British Library, 1997), which, as affecting one year only, is not used as a reference source in this volume.

The notion that fiction of this period represents an unfathomable lake has proved in the event not to be justified. Nor is it true that a significant number of known titles are now unrecoverable. Only in some 40 cases, where there is compelling evidence that a novel did actually exist, has it proved not possible to locate and examine a copy. The reconstituted entries supplied for these 'missing' novels, signified by an asterisk before the title, break down by decade as follows: 20 in the 1800s, 19 in the 1810s, and a mere two in the 1820s. The high survival of novels from the 1820s is no doubt symptomatic of the enhanced status of fiction, making it a more collectable item, and the larger number of copies being sold to individuals. In the 1810s, some of the 'reconstituted' entries are based on subsequent editions, and it is not impossible that in one or two cases no 'first' edition ever existed, the publisher using a misleading title-page to simulate a runaway popularity. In the 1800s, moreover, it is noticeable that half the titles in this category are translations of foreign works, all between 1800 and 1806, none of these being of a particularly high-profile nature, and all naturally lacking the kind of local associations which might lead to copies being specially preserved.

In addition to the reconstituted titles included in this volume, there are a further twenty or so that have not been included in the main listings, usually on the grounds that the existence of an original publication is not established conclusively by secondary sources. *Fitzherbert. A Novel*, which Summers lists as a work by Mrs Pilkington in 1808, may possibly have had a brief life and then been banned as having a scandalous content. Alternatively, it could have fallen foul of the bankruptcy of J. F. Hughes, who advertised such a title as 'In the Press' in both 1808 and 1810, first as by Mrs Pilkington, and then as by Sarah Isdell. Or a novel of this name might have been remaindered at a later date, which could explain the presence of such a work by Isdell in Horne's 1824 circulating library catalogue. Unusually elusive later in the period is the not inappropriately-named *The Phantom; or Mysteries of the Castle* (1825), listed by both Block and Summers as by Mrs Mathews, but which, granting its existence, may possibly have been a shorter tale and/or a work recycled from an earlier publication. Fuller details of the last two titles mentioned, as well as other comparable cases, will be found in the last section (F: 1–F: 5) of the Appendix near the end of this volume.

Preparation of this volume has also led to the discovery of a number of more tangible 'ghosts'. Some titles catalogued as fiction prove on examination not to be novels at all: Alfred Thornton's *Adventures of a Post Captain* (1817), though included in Block and classified as fiction in NSTC, is actually a narrative in verse. Other works, while clearly prose fiction, never existed as independent novels. Miss C. D. Haynes's 'Castle [of] Le Blanc', listed as 'by the author' in her *The Foundling of Devonshire* (1818: 35), was actually serialized in *The Lady's Magazine* and appears never to have been published separately. George Moore's *The Married Man*, listed in Block and catalogued by the British Library, is in fact part of the same author's *Tales of the Passions* (1808: 80), and was apparently never issued on its own.

Also excluded are some 25 titles which are not original works but rather reissues of an earlier one in a different guise. Most involve manipulation of the original title, such as transposition of the original two parts, the adoption of the secondary as the solitary title, the addition of fresh words and/or excision of others, and so on, although very occasionally a completely fresh title is used. A few announced themselves as new editions, but the greater part are silent reissues, with cancel title-pages the only true difference, the rest of the novel consisting of the original printed sheets. A fairly characteristic instance is provided by *The Benevolent Recluse; A Novel* (1810: 40), which was published by E. Kerby and is now extremely rare, and *Suspicion; or, the Benevolent Recluse, A Novel*, issued by A. K. Newman at the Minerva Press, in 1814, also as 'by Lady—'. Both Block and Summers list the second title as if an original novel, and it is likewise catalogued as such by the British Library. First-hand examination of copies of each title, however, makes it clear that the second is a remainder reissue, with the original sheets having probably been sold by the first publisher to Newman.

Normally in such circumstances only the original issue is used for a full entry, with details of the reissue being given under 'Further editions', and with later cross-reference from the year where the re-titled version appeared. In a handful of cases, however, as when there are significant textual or bibliographical differences, both versions are granted separate entries. The bibliography thus provides separate entries for both *Woman; or, Minor Maxims* (1818: 24) and *Helena Egerton; or, Traits of Female Character* (1824: 19), in spite of these being essentially the same work by Maria Elizabeth Budden, on the grounds that the second version is a full reprint claiming significant authorial revisions. Examples of reissues and reprints that have not been granted entries in the main listings (together with sample translations rejected as not representing the first) will be found in the Appendix (E: 1–E: 8).

Further exclusions have occurred through implementation of the general policy of omitting 'religious tracts, chapbooks, literature written only for children and juveniles, and very short separately issued tales' (see General Introduction, p. 4). Owing to special factors relating to the production of fiction in this period, this ruling has probably led to a higher proportion of non-qualifying titles being omitted compared with the first volume of this Bibliography. Not recorded generally are the large number of short chapbooks (usually 36 pages) and blue-backed 'shilling shockers' which proliferated in the 1800s and early 1810s, many of which were themselves distillations of popular novels, notably Gothic titles.[31] An exception has been made, however, in the case of *The Ghost of Harcourt* (1803: 8), which is 72 pages long and contains two chapbook-like tales, but which in other respects is better viewed as a fairly routine product of the Minerva Press, artificially replicating the chapbook form.

Likewise excluded are propagandist materials such as Legh Richmond's pious tale *The Dairyman's Daughter* [1809], issued by the Religious Tract Society, and

---

[31] For a general account, though now badly dated, see William W. Watt, *Shilling Shockers of the Gothic School: A Study of Chapbook Gothic Romances* (Cambridge, Mass., 1932; repr. New York, 1967). Valuable additional information can be found in Angela Koch, 'Bluebooks: Unterhaltungsliteratur im England des frühen 19. Jahrhunderts und ihre Beziehungen zum gotischen Roman', Diss. phil. (Paderborn, 1997).

short anti-radical tracts such as *Jem Gudgeon, or Radical Conduct* (1821). Occasionally a writer is found operating both as a tract-writer and as a conventional novelist. The Revd Henry Duncan's *William Douglas; or, the Scottish Exiles* (1826: 31), an historical novel after the manner of Scott, is thus included, but the same writer's polemical *The Young South Country Weaver [. . .] A Tale for the Radicals* (1821) is not. There have also been a number of exclusions of short, sometimes amateurishly produced, single tales, of a kind usually not found in circulating library catalogues of the time. This volume includes, at the edge of its page limitation, Lord John Russell's *The Nun of Arrouca* (1822: 64) and Polidori's seminal Gothic tale, *The Vampyre* (1819: 55), both of which enjoyed considerable public attention (the latter not least through its Byron connection). But it excludes, for example, an anonymous *The Avalanche; or, the Old Man of the Alps, A Tale, Translated from the French* (Clapham, 1829), in which the main story runs from pp. 5–69, followed by an 'Account of the Avalanche of Bergemoletto, in 1755' (pp. 71–8).

Another category that has been viewed cautiously is the miscellaneous collection, especially when the fictional component provides only a loose framework, or when there is no real linkage between largely idiosyncratic ingredients. The volume includes J. W. Cunningham's *Sancho, or the Proverbialist* (1816: 24), which has a clear narrative dynamic, but excludes his popular *The Velvet Cushion* (1814), where narrative linkage is for the most part lost amongst a mixture of whimsy and Anglican polemic. In the 1820s, the titles of collections sometimes almost seem to celebrate a random organization (e.g. *Odd Moments; or Time Beguiled* (1825, Appendix B: 3), followed by *More Odd Moments* (1826)). And while such items are commonly catalogued as fiction, generically they often have a greater affinity with the keepsakes and annuals whose numbers were then burgeoning, as well as too with periodical literature generally.[32]

Two other main areas developing with great rapidity during this period are: (i) the short religious tale; and (ii) children's fiction, especially that projected at 'young people'. The shorter moral tale, generally retailing at 5s–6s a volume, and often including a frontispiece illustration, is a fairly common feature of the 1820s, when a number of specialist publishers operated in this field. On some occasions, polemical concerns almost completely overwhelm the fictional component, and such cases are usually excluded in the listings. Sometimes a weighting of this kind is reflected in the title itself, as in the case of *The West Indian: or the Happy Effects of Diligence and Self-Control; exemplified in the History of Philip Montague* (1827), which has not been included. Occasionally an author can be found operating at various points along the

---

[32] Also omitted are a number of quasi-fictional titles of the period which are sometimes catalogued as fiction. These include: Anne Grant's *Letters from the Mountains* (1806), consisting of actual correspondence; William Hazlitt's *Liber Amoris, or the New Pygmalion* (1823), with its strong autobiographical element; and Anna Brownell Jameson's *A Lady's Diary* (1826: and reissued that year as *Diary of an Ennuyée*), a fictional travel autobiography. Amongst historical memoirs considered to have a more significant biographical as opposed to fictional element are: William Collins's *Memoirs of a Picture* (1805), based on the life of the artist George Morland; and Elizabeth Hamilton's *Memoirs of the Life of Agrippina* (1804; Appendix D: 2), an historical life with dialogue in a fictional style.

scale from the purely doctrinal to conventional-seeming novel writing. Grace Kennedy's *Dunallan; or, Know What You Judge* (1825: 48) has a clear evangelical focus, but in other respects follows the usual pattern of a three-volume novel. It is also found in several commercial circulating library catalogues, entered into the Corvey library in its second edition, and was listed by the *Edinburgh Review* as a new novel. *Father Clement; A Roman Catholic Story* (1823: 51), though more directly polemical, none the less evidently enjoyed a wide sale, and is found included as a work of fiction in a high proportion of libraries, of both the commercial and proprietary kind. A similar ubiquitousness is not evident in the case of Kennedy's shorter (92-page) moral tale, *Jessy Allan, the Lame Girl; A Story Founded on Facts* (1823), which has a title-page motto from the New Testament, and whose frontispiece caption reads 'They worked together and the Bible open by them'. This more tract-like publication, with its not uncharacteristic evangelical emphasis on 'Facts', is excluded, along with the same author's *Anna Ross. A Story for Children* (1824).

As the last title cited indicates, literature targeted at children and 'young people' not infrequently overlaps at this period with the kind of moral writing outlined above. While fiction for juveniles has generally been excluded, in a very few instances, where a work evidently enjoyed a wider currency, an exception has been made. Three novels adjudged to have effectively entered the mainstream, notwithstanding more pointed titular statements of intent, are Maria Edgeworth's *Moral Tales for Young People* (1801: 25), Rachel Hunter's *The Schoolmistress; A Moral Tale for Young Ladies* (1811: 46), and Jane Taylor's *Display. A Tale for Young People* (1815: 50). Omitted on the other hand are the full range of works by a number of authors who appear to have worked exclusively during this period in the juvenile market, including Mary Elliott, Maria Hack, and Mary Sherwood. Some authors appear to have followed two paths. Mary Pilkington's *The Asiatic Princess* (2 vols., 1800), while bearing the outer marks of a novel, is omitted as having closer affinities with her specialist fiction aimed at children; five adult novels by her, beginning with *Crimes and Characters* (1805: 60), are however included, the last three coming from the Minerva Press. Likewise omitted are Barbara Hofland's *Son of a Genius: A Tale for the Use of Youth* (1812), one of her most successful works, and a parallel *Daughter of a Genius* (1823), both of which are addressed to a juvenile respondent (her son in the first instance). The bibliography on the other hand includes *The History of a Clergyman's Widow* (1812: 36), one of several such tales by the author in which the narrative focus rests on a woman seeking independence and respect, as well as more conventional novels by Hofland, beginning with *Says She to her Neighbour, What?* (1812: 37) and *Iwanowna; or, the Maid of Moscow* (1813: 27).

In the 1820s, when literature for youth developed increasingly as a specialist publishing activity, more than one author can be seen operating simultaneously in different markets. Isabella Stoddart's *Annals of the Family of M'Roy* (1823: 79) was advertised by its publisher (W. Wetton) as an adult book in a distinctly different way from her tales for youth, such as *The Scottish Orphans* (1822, Appendix A: 6), which were also written under the pseudonym of Mrs Blackford and published by

Wetton. A similarly firm line of demarcation can be sensed in Amelia Opie's willingness to publish a children's book, *Tales of the Pemberton Family* (1825), after forsaking adult fiction and in the same year as joining the Quakers. Similarly, Christian Isobel Johnstone's *Diversions of Hollycot; or, the Mother's Art of Thinking* (1828), aimed at 'the younger reader', is generically distinct from her multi-volume novels, *Clan-Albin* (1815: 32) and *Elizabeth de Bruce* (1827: 44). By the later 1820s the didactic tale for youth, frequently merging with the kind of evangelical tract fiction described earlier, clearly represented one of the largest growth areas in publishing, its attractions magnified for the trade by the new opportunities for direct retail sales. This still largely uncharted phenomenon, however, requires a separate bibliography of its own, and any attempt to include output at large would seriously unbalance the present volume's record of the English novel at this period.

While this volume does not attempt to track every manifestation of prose fiction in the early nineteenth century, it undoubtedly offers a fuller and more cohesive record of the English novel of the Romantic era than is provided in any previously published bibliography. Advances can be claimed on three fronts. (i) The present volume provides full details, based on examined copies, of works previously listed as fiction but considered unrecoverable as actual texts. One striking example is provided by the recovery of *Durston Castle* (1804: 68), no longer a bibliographical mystery, and whose author can now be identified as Mary Tuck, the proprietor of a circulating library, 'near the Adam and Eve, Peckham'. (ii) Through the policy of returning to earliest editions, a significant number of cases have come to light where the imprint information previously recorded in bibliographies has proved to be based on a reissue. More broadly, the same policy has had the effect of helping remove accretions that have built up on novels since their first publication, making it possible to perceive more clearly how works were originally presented to their earliest readers. (iii) Lastly, the present volume contains a significant number of novels that have fallen altogether from the record, through (say) a similar title overwriting its predecessor. In the case of *First Love. A Novel* (1801: 6) and *First Love; A Tale of My Mother's Times* (1824: 6), both unidentified anonymous works, Block and Summers give only the first title whereas the *English Catalogue of Books* records only the second. Two entirely distinct works with *The Castle of Villeroy* (1801: 52, 1827: 12) as the lead title are both absent in Block, while only the second is present in Summers, somewhat overshadowed there by better-known and more fully recorded 'Castle' titles.

## (3) Number of Titles

The present volume provides entries for 2,256 fiction titles first published in Britain in the thirty years between 1800 and 1829. In nine cases, when the precedence between two versions of the same title is unclear (as when rival translations appeared in the same year), double entries are given, so that in all 2,265 books are described in the main listings.

# DURSTON CASTLE;

OR,

## THE GHOST

OF

## *ELEONORA.*

𝔄 𝔊𝔬𝔱𝔥𝔦𝔠 𝔖𝔱𝔬𝔯𝔶.

*LONDON:*

PRINTED, BY C. AND W. GALABIN,
· Ingram-Court, Fenchurch-Street,

FOR M. TUCK, CIRCULATING LIBRARY,
NEAR THE ADAM AND EVE, PECKHAM.

1804.

Illustration 2. Title-page of Mary Tuck, *Durston Castle* (1804: 68)

Output at this period needs to be seen against the backdrop of an upsurge of new titles in the later 1780s, followed by the new peaks achieved during the 1790s. As Figure 1 suggests, the high level of output reached in the late 1790s was largely sustained during the 1800s. A slight dip nevertheless is apparent in the years 1801 to 1802, and a distinct peak occurs in 1808 (the only single year for the whole period to exceed 100 titles). Output in the 1810s, however, is nearly 15 per cent lower than in the 1800s (662 titles as opposed to 770), with a clear trough apparent in the middle years of the decade. In the 1820s (824 titles in all) output of new titles again began to rise. From a base of 70 in 1820, production rose by more than 25 per cent in four years, leading to a figure of 99 original titles in 1824. The economic difficulties of the book trade in 1826 help explain the slightly deflated figure of 77 in that year, but the novel's power of recovery is evident in the rise of output again to more than 80 titles in both 1828 and 1829. Of ten years with 80 titles or more in evidence, all but four occur in the 1820s, while only three years (1815, 1816, 1817) fall beneath 60 titles. The remaining years show a fairly regular output of between 60 and 80 new titles, a level of production which roughly correlates with the kind of annual intake indicated by surviving catalogues of some of the larger circulating libraries of the period.

Overall, the period does not reveal the kind of uninterrupted upward path that has been implicitly claimed by some commentators.[33] Impression numbers for first editions certainly increased in specific areas, with Scott's novels in the early 1820s reaching

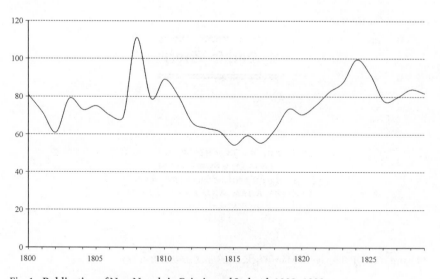

Fig. 1. **Publication of New Novels in Britain and Ireland, 1800–1829**

[33] An instance is found in Chart I in Frank Gees Black's *The Epistolary Novel in the Late Eighteenth Century* (Eugene, OR, 1940), p. 174, where the line showing 'Production of fiction in English' has an upward arrow at 1800 breaking through the 90 titles upper limit.

a high mark of 12,000 copies, and a larger proportion of established authors meriting a first impression in the 1,500–2,000 band. On the other hand, a one-off run of 500–750 copies remained the norm for all but exceptional works, and publishing records such as the Longman Letter Books reveal how difficult it could be to dispose even of these, once the first sale had passed.[34] A rapidly expanding population, and increasing urbanization, offered a potentially new audience for fiction, but there are nevertheless strong indications that novel reading remained for the most part an upper- and middle-class vogue. Two of the main factors underlying its expansion in the Romantic era, the influx of women readers and the marketing of fiction as commodity by entrepreneurs like William Lane, were already in place by the beginning of the new century.[35] The high price of books, exacerbated by wartime conditions, ensured that novels continued to be borrowed rather than bought; and it is arguable that the organization of circulating libraries, whose catalogues often displayed the price of the books listed, militated against any large expansion in titles or undercutting of retail prices. Publishers too were wary about extending their lists or taking on untried authors in an uncertain economic climate. As Scott wrote to his friend Mrs Pascoe, apropos her *Coquetry* (1818: 47): 'The public they imagine has a certain limited degree of appetite for novels and will not devour more than its usual allowance at a time.'[36]

Charles Knight was later to claim, from the vantage point of an expansionist era, that the great publishers of the 1820s actively contributed to the negative forces at play by fostering a cult of exclusivity: 'They paid most liberally for copyright, and they looked only to an exclusive sale for their remuneration.'[37] Whatever the underlying causes, technological innovations in the early nineteenth century, such as the steam-driven rotary press (employed to print *The Times* in 1814) and the development of stereotype plates, were slow to affect the book trade at large, and appear not to have significantly altered the production of novels until the later 1820s. Most novels were set by compositors using moveable type and produced on hand presses, an especially laborious business in the case of multi-volume novels.[38] Only the full exploitation of James Ballantyne's twenty or so presses, with compositors and pressmen working round the clock, made it possible to produce the first editions of

[34] For example, on 22 November 1821, Sir Samuel Egerton Brydges was informed that 300 out of the 500 copies printed of his *Hall of Hellingsley* (1821: 23) had been cleared (Longman Letter Books, I, 101, no. 191). A letter to Alicia Lefanu on 14 April 1821 told her that 'we have sold altogether 279 copies of "Leolin Abbey"'(see 1819: 44), with only £5 0s 5d remaining due to the author (I, 101, no. 122). The Longman Papers, as cited here and elsewhere in this Introduction, are housed in the University of Reading Library.

[35] See Terry Lovell, *Consuming Fiction* (London, 1987), esp. Ch. 3 ('The Novel as Commodity: 1770–1820'); and, for the turning of women to fiction as both readers and authors, Lawrence Stone, *The Family, Sex and Marriage in England, 1500–1800* (Harmondsworth, 1979), p. 190.

[36] National Library of Scotland (henceforth in this Introduction NLS), MS 5317, f. 19 [1818].

[37] Charles Knight, *The Old Printer and the Modern Press* (London, 1854), p. 239.

[38] Accepting Charles Knight's calculation that a 10,000 edition of a schoolbook would engage two men operating a single press for almost three-quarters of a year, a three-volume novel in an impression of 1,000 produced in the same way might take up to two months to complete. Knight's estimate is based on a schoolbook consisting of 20 sheets; the calculation for a novel follows this through for a 3-volume duodecimo consisting of 40 sheets (i.e. 960 pages). See *Old Printer and the Modern Press*, p. 253.

the Waverley novels in months rather than years. As a whole the period is best viewed as one of consolidation rather than outright expansion, with developments taking place in particular channels, though by the 1820s there are clear signs of the forces which would lead to a further explosion in the fiction market in the early Victorian era.

Closer examination of the figures by decades also helps reveal some of the more particular factors which could affect the output of new titles at a given time. The slight dip evident in 1801 to 1802 might reflect a delayed reaction to the battering which the novel had received at the hands of the reactionary anti-Jacobin movement in the late 1790s, with journals such as the *Anti-Jacobin Review* continuing in the new century to carry out a policy of surveillance, excoriating any suggestion of Godwinian sympathies or apparent laxness in depicting gender relations. Certainly an air of unusual caution can be sensed in some of the prefatory statements found in novels at this time, for instance in the reluctance of both Maria Edgeworth and Amelia Opie to acknowledge 'a Novel' (see 1801: 24, 54), and clearly the genre was struggling to regain respectability as it sought fresh channels of expression. The slight resurgence apparent in 1803 is largely explainable in terms of an increased intake of new translated works by foreign writers, the majority of these (some 20 out of up to 27 translations in all) originating from French source titles. This sudden invasion was no doubt facilitated by the brief 14-month interlude in the war with France brought about by the Peace of Amiens, 27 March 1802, the slight delay before the actual appearance of these works matching the time needed for translation and printing. (It should be borne in mind in any calculation that the amount of time taken in producing a novel, and the occasional practice of post-dating,[39] means that many titles are likely to have been embarked on in the year preceding the imprint date.) In the case of Madame de Staël's *Delphine*, which was to cause a sensation, at least two rival translations were set in motion (see 1803, 67[a], 67[b]). As a whole the 1800s are the richest in terms of translated titles, with as many as 116 original titles having a foreign source, representing 15 per cent of output. This contrasts with the much diminished intake in the 1810s, and even compares favourably with the 1820s, when translations from the German began to match their French equivalents (for an overall view, see Table 1).[40]

---

[39] Publishing archives of this period frequently indicate that November was considered the most auspicious time for releasing a novel. Constable & Co thus recommended to Maturin, for his *Women* (1818: 41), 'that publication took place as soon as possible, say about November (the beginning of the publishing season) ... [or] as soon after that as practicable' (NLS, MS 789, p. 823; 29 July 1817). In cases of works published at that point, the temptation to employ the following year for the imprint date was naturally strong. More flagrant post-dating appears to be relatively uncommon in this period.

[40] Works are generally counted as translations when a foreign author is identified and/or the original source title is known. Additionally the following 'questionable' titles, which claim to be translated or partly translated, are incorporated as translations in Table 1: 1800: 21; 1800: 81; 1801: 39; 1803: 4; 1803: 16; 1803: 22; 1804: 59; 1806: 3; 1809: 79; 1810: 75; 1819: 32; 1819: 58; 1820: 52; 1828: 41. Two compilations (1810: 83, 1826: 37) are also included. Obvious deceits are excluded, and allegations about a foreign origin found in sources such as reviews (see, e.g., 1800: 12) are not considered adequate evidence on their own.

Table 1. First Editions of English Translations of Foreign Novels, 1800–1829

| Imprint Year | French | German | Other | Non-Translated | Total New Novels |
|---|---|---|---|---|---|
| 1800 | 4 | 3 | 2 | 72 | 81 |
| 1801 | 1 | 1 | 1 | 69 | 72 |
| 1802 | 4 | 3 | — | 54 | 61 |
| 1803 | 20 | 4 | 3 | 52 | 79 |
| 1804 | 11 | 9 | — | 53 | 73 |
| 1805 | 6 | 4 | — | 65 | 75 |
| 1806 | 4 | 6 | 1 | 59 | 70 |
| 1807 | 7 | 4 | — | 58 | 69 |
| 1808 | 9 | 1 | — | 101 | 111 |
| 1809 | 5 | 3 | — | 71 | 79 |
| *1800s* | *71* | *38* | *7* | *654* | *770* |
| % | *9.2* | *4.9* | *0.9* | *85.0* | |
| 1810 | 3 | — | 1 | 85 | 89 |
| 1811 | 4 | 2 | — | 74 | 80 |
| 1812 | 1 | 1 | — | 64 | 66 |
| 1813 | 2 | 2 | — | 59 | 63 |
| 1814 | — | — | 1 | 60 | 61 |
| 1815 | 2 | — | — | 52 | 54 |
| 1816 | 2 | 2 | — | 55 | 59 |
| 1817 | 3 | 0 | 1 | 51 | 55 |
| 1818 | 2 | 1 | 1 | 58 | 62 |
| 1819 | 2 | 1 | — | 70 | 73 |
| *1810s* | *21* | *9* | *4* | *628* | *662* |
| % | *3.2* | *1.3* | *0.6* | *94.9* | |
| 1820 | 2 | 1 | 2 | 65 | 70 |
| 1821 | 3 | 1 | — | 71 | 75 |
| 1822 | 2 | — | — | 80 | 82 |
| 1823 | 2 | 2 | 1 | 82 | 87 |
| 1824 | 1 | 3 | — | 95 | 99 |
| 1825 | 4 | 3 | — | 84 | 91 |
| 1826 | 3 | 7 | — | 67 | 77 |
| 1827 | 1 | 2 | — | 76 | 79 |
| 1828 | 1 | 1 | 1 | 80 | 83 |
| 1829 | 2 | — | — | 79 | 81 |
| *1820s* | *21* | *20* | *4* | *779* | *824* |
| % | *2.5* | *2.5* | *0.5* | *94.5* | |
| **Total** | *113* | *67* | *15* | *2,061* | *2,256* |
| % | *5.0* | *3.0* | *0.7* | *91.3* | |

The increasing number of new titles evident in the later 1800s, and in particular the sudden peak found in 1808, are less easily explained in terms of imports. Of 111 titles with 1808 imprint dates more than one hundred were apparently the product of indigenous writers, between them producing virtually twice as many non-translated works as are found for 1803. Here it is possible to point to a particular domestic reason for increased output. Though it was a general adage in the book trade that moments of political upheaval had a negative effect on sales, the furore caused by the ascendancy of Lord Grenville's 'Ministry of all the Talents', between February 1806 and March 1807, appears to have acted as a positive impetus, inspiring both a pamphlet war and a flood of scurrilous satires in various forms. An additional stimulus was provided by the scandal caused by the separation of the Prince of Wales and Princess of Wales, which reached new intensity with the 'delicate investigation' of the Princess by leading members of the Whig cabinet. One result of this was a flood of 'royal' titles, in some ways reminiscent of revelations concerning a later Princess of Wales, many of which adopted a fictitious manner in purporting to uncover some of the more indelicate truths behind the investigation. Those keen to hear more about the Prince's part in the affair had a choice between *The Royal Eclipse; or, Delicate Facts Exhibiting the Secret Memoirs of Squire George and his Wife* (1807: 19), *The Royal Legend. A Tale* (1808: 15); *The R—l Stranger. A Tale* (1808: 16), J. P. Hurstone's *Royal Intrigues: or, Secret Memoirs of Four Princesses* (1808: 64), or Sarah Green's *The Private History of the Court of England* (1808: 49)—the latter a fairly easily decoded *roman-à-clef* set at the time of the Wars of the Roses.

More broadly, 1807–1808 represents the highpoint for a special kind of acerbic scandal fiction, often intersecting with the specific royal issues mentioned above, but also claiming to lay bare infidelities rife amongst the *haut ton* at large. Many of these are identifiable through direct allusion in their titles to the fashionable 'seasons', a pattern set by Thomas Skinner Surr's highly successful *A Winter in London; or, Sketches of Fashion* (1806: 64), and followed by eye-catching variants such as Mary Julia Young's *A Summer at Brighton. A Modern Novel* (1807: 69), J. P. Hurstone's *An Autumn at Cheltenham; or, Mysteries in High Life* (1808: 60), and Young's *A Summer at Weymouth; or, the Star of Fashion* (1808: 111). Both the Young titles were published by the then rapidly expanding J. F. Hughes, fashionably positioned just off Cavendish Square in the London West End. The latter's keenness to exploit this trend is apparent in his opportunistic re-titling of a novel by Mrs Bayfield as *A Winter at Bath* (1807: 9) to run against an anonymous *Winter in Bath* (see 1807: 7), published by his former associates B. Crosby and Co. Hughes's main author in this field was Charles Sedley, whose rake-like persona introduces no less than three 'fashionable' fictions with 1808 imprints: *A Winter in Dublin* (1808: 98), *The Faro Table; or, the Gambling Mothers* (1808: 97), and *Asmodeus; or, the Devil in London* (1808: 96). The scurrilous content of this series, which at one point led to the beating-up of Hughes in his shop by an offended victim (see 1808: 97), noticeably intensifies and darkens, to the point that a circulating library can be presented in *Asmodeus* as a front for a brothel.[41] Whether this kind of scandal fiction actually attracted a genuinely fashionable audience seems unlikely. Rather it appears to have been pitched to satisfy the prurient curiosities of an urban middle-class audience, capable of finding vicarious pleasure in glowing accounts of the lifestyle and accoutrements of the *beau monde*, yet at the same time hostile towards the kind of amorality and injustice depicted. A breakdown of the 111 titles belonging to 1808 suggests that as many as a third had a primarily scandalous content, at least matching the number of Gothic/Historical novels then produced, and outweighing more conventional Domestic/Sentimental fictions.

This phase of 'fashionable' fiction was to prove relatively short-lived, though fascination with Princess Caroline, eminently serviceable as an icon for Whig opposition, continued to help generate successes such as Thomas Ashe's *The Spirit of "The Book"* (1811: 15). One fairly immediate cause for its demise came from within the genre, in the form of influential corrective works such as Hannah More's evangelical *Cœlebs in Search of a Wife* (1808: 81) and the first series of Maria Edgeworth's pointedly titled *Tales of Fashionable Life* (1809: 22), the first attempting the moral rearmament of the upper ranks, the latter an enlargement of their rational capabilities. Even more run-of-the-mill novelists show signs of wanting to distance themselves from the general decline in standards. In this spirit, Mary Ann Hanway used the preliminaries of her *Falconbridge Abbey* (1809: 30), a fairly unexceptional Minerva publication, to castigate at length 'an era, like the present, when every rank of the community devour, with avidity, all the crude and indigestible trash, that load the shelves of circulating libraries'.[42] A similar sense of a teeming, uncontrolled, socially deleterious outpouring of titles is found in Walter Scott's anonymous review of Charles Robert Maturin's Gothic novel, *Fatal Revenge; or, the Family of Montorio* (1807: 42), in the *Quarterly Review* for May 1810. Claiming to have 'sent to our Publisher for an assortment of the newest and most fashionable novels', Scott skims the resultant hamper of its surface of 'a few thin volumes of simple and insipid sentiment', before hitting on a deeper vein of new scurrility: 'We have our Winters in London, Bath, and Brighton, of which it is the dirty object to drag forth the secret history of the day, and to give to Scandal a court of written record.'[43] Delving deeper, he confronts various Gothic novels in the style of both Ann Radcliffe and M. G. Lewis, amid which Maturin's *Fatal Revenge* stands out as the product of an unusually gifted, if misdirected, author.[44]

---

[41] For further details about the almost certainly pseudonymous Charles Sedley, and the incidents described, see Peter Garside, 'J. F. Hughes and the Publication of Popular Fiction', *The Library*, 6th ser., 9: 3 (Sept. 1987), 241–58 (pp. 250–1).

[42] Hanway's diatribe goes on to complain how 'under the seductive title of fashionable novels, are produced licentious and profligate publications, fraught with the most vivid descriptions of love, and its effects on our conduct, exemplified by baneful examples, pourtrayed in language warm, flowing, and dangerous as the lava of Vesuvius, that, in its destructive course, sweeps away alike the humble cottage and the stately palace' (Preface, vol. 1, p. xii).

[43] QR, 3 (May 1810), 341.

[44] In Scott's mind, one suspects, the ultimate treasure to be brought to light that year was to be his own *Waverley; or, 'Tis Sixty Years Since* (1814: 52), which could well have been begun either in 1808 or early in 1810, in spite of authorial intimations of an 1805 inception. *Waverley* was advertised as part of

A conservative backlash against 'low' fiction offers one immediate reason for the decline that begins early in the 1810s. The length of the trough that follows, with an average production of only sixty new titles between 1812 and 1818, is however more fully explained by difficult economic conditions in the late years of the Napoleonic war. In particular restrictions in importing the raw materials for making paper (linen rags) from the Continent helped force up the cost of the demy sheets used in the production of novels, offsetting any advantage gained by the introduction in the later 1800s of Fourdrinier paper-making machines.[45] Paper represented by far the largest cost in the production of books, accounting for two-thirds of the bill even in the case of a novel such as Scott's *Guy Mannering* (1815: 46), notwithstanding James Ballantyne's high printing costs and the unusual (for a novel) supply of proofs to the author.[46] As Lee Erickson convincingly argues, the proportionately higher cost of materials had the effect of encouraging shorter literary forms, notably poetry, at the expense of expansive prose fiction.[47] A symptom of this is the fashionable narrative poem, especially early in the decade, as produced by Scott and Byron. Such conditions also help explain the cult of the 'exceptional' writer, whose latest fashionable works were capable of commanding a premium price, above the level of 'common' literature and even more so above that of cheap reprint series, which at this time were largely limited to reproducing classics from the later Augustan era. The economic depression in the immediate post-war years also discouraged growth in the publishing trade, leading even such sanguine operators as Archibald Constable to shorten their lists and concentrate on the most reliable and/or immediately saleable items. These are the conditions Constable described to his partner Robert Cadell while on his annual visit to the London trade sales in 1816, news of which Cadell then relayed to Scott:

Mr Constable writes me that Trade in the South is generally speaking very dull—and of course the Book Trade is affected by the stagnation. Books of first-rate merit however, sell better now, than at any former period—those of a middle walk in Literature do not sell at all—& almost all periodical Works of talent increase in circulation.[48]

Scott's strategy from the commencement of the Waverley novels was to create a 'superior' kind of fiction, calculated through shared discourses to appeal to the

John Ballantyne's list of 'New Works and Publications for 1809–10', and an unspecified portion of the novel was sent by Scott to James Ballantyne for evaluation in mid-September 1810. See 'A History of the Text of *Waverley*', in *Waverley; or, 'Tis Sixty Years Since*, ed. Claire Lamont (Oxford, 1981), pp. xxiv–xxv; and for further evidence, relating especially to the manuscript, P. D. Garside, 'Dating *Waverley*'s Early Chapters', *The Bibliotheck*, 13: 3 (1986), 61–81.

[45] Fourdrinier machines were being manufactured in Britain by 1807, but it was not until the 1820s that the production of machine-made paper exceeded that of paper made by hand (see Philip Gaskell, *A New Introduction to Bibliography* (Oxford, 1974), pp. 214, 216).

[46] Ballantyne's bill for the first edn. of 2,000, as entered under Feb. 20 [1815], in the Longman ledgers, lists £309 as the cost of paper (206 reams of demy at 30s) out of total printing costs of £467 19s 8d, this latter sum including an 18 guinea fee for transcribing Scott's manuscript (Longman Impression Book 5, f. 178).

[47] Lee Erickson, 'The Poets' Corner: The Impact of Technological Changes in Printing on English Poetry, 1800–1850', in *The Economy of Literary Form*, pp. 19–48. An earlier version of this essay appeared in *English Literary History*, 52: 4 (Winter 1985), 893–911.

[48] NLS, MS 789, p. 615 (9 Aug. 1816).

*Edinburgh* and *Quarterly* reviews, whose own sales by this point had exceeded 10,000.[49] Shortly before printing *Waverley; or, 'Tis Sixty Years Since* (1814: 52), James Ballantyne had enquired of Constable whether paper should be ordered for an impression of 750 or 1,000, Constable bravely opting for the larger number. Before this first edition was sold out, early in August 1814, a second of 2,000 had been ordered, followed by two of a thousand each in the Autumn, and three more (totalling 4,500) in the subsequent three years. Caution on the part of Longmans, the managing publisher, largely explains the limitation of the first edition of its successor, *Guy Mannering* (1815: 46), to 2,000 copies; but in the case of *The Antiquary* (1816: 52), managed directly from Edinburgh by Constable, no less than 6,000 were produced and (more amazingly still) disposed of within weeks. For *Rob Roy* (1818: 55), Scott's fifth novel, a first edition of 10,000 was ordered, effectively launching 'the author of *Waverley*' as the first regular best-seller in the history of the novel.[50]

While Scott's success clearly served as a main motor for this essentially new phenomenon of the up-market best-selling novel, there are also signs of broader divisions taking place within the fiction industry throughout the decade. Scott himself, in returning to complete *Waverley*, had no doubt been impressed by the sums paid out for Maria Edgeworth's most recent fiction: £1,050 for the second series (1812) of *Tales of Fashionable Life*, followed by £2,100 for her less popular *Patronage* (1814: 20).[51] Before venturing to take a share of *Waverley*, Longmans had already decided to mark Frances Burney's return as a novelist with an impression of 6,000 of her *The Wanderer* (1814: 17), planning to divide the second 3,000 into several subsequent editions, not all of which were marketed owing to unexpectedly poor sales.[52] Jane Austen's *Emma* (1816: 16), bearing the imprint of John Murray, the publisher of Byron, and with its dedication to the Prince Regent, was clearly at a guinea for the three volumes a different article from contemporary Minerva publications (then generally retailing at about 5s a volume). As if to hammer the point home, Scott in his *Quarterly* review of *Emma* lauded the author's previous work for having 'attracted, with justice, an attention from the public far superior to what is granted to the ephemeral productions which supply the regular demand of watering-places and circulating libraries'.[53] William Blackwood, in Edinburgh, whose main venture

[49] Sales figures for periodicals of the period are given in Richard D. Altick, *The English Common Reader: A Social History of the Mass Reading Public 1800–1900* (Chicago, 1957), p. 392.

[50] For an overview of the publishing history of the earlier Waverley novels, see Peter Garside, 'Rob's Last Raid: Scott and the Publication of the Waverley Novels', in *Author/Publisher Relations in the Eighteenth and Nineteenth Centuries*, ed. Robin Myers and Michael Harris (Oxford, 1983), pp. 88–118.

[51] Figures as listed by Edgeworth and recorded in Marilyn Butler, *Maria Edgeworth: A Literary Biography* (Oxford, 1972), Appendix B, pp. 490–3. Butler herself notes the contrast with the £300 given for *Belinda* (1801: 24).

[52] 'The second 3000 copies were divided into three editions of 1000 each—the fourth & half of the third editions were wasted with the concurrence of Dr Burney' (to Mme. D'Arblay [1817], Longman Letter Books, I, 100, no. 133).

[53] QR, 14 (Oct. 1815), 189. Austen is listed along with Burney and Edgeworth as an example of the kind of author promoted by 'carriage-trade publishers', in Edward Copeland, *Women Writing About Money: Women's Fiction in England, 1790–1820* (Cambridge, 1995), p. 161.

in fiction hitherto had involved taking a share with Murray of the first series of Scott's *Tales of My Landlord* (1816: 53), felt confident enough near the end of the decade to chance a first edition of 1,500 with both Susan Ferrier's *Marriage* (1818: 29), a first novel, and James Hogg's *The Brownie of Bodsbeck* (1818: 37), the latter representing its author's first attempt at making a success in what by then must have seemed a more lucrative field than poetry.[54] Stronger financial inducements no doubt encouraged a number of other authors to turn to fiction at this time. Of the 73 titles with 1819 imprints, at least 70 appear to be the product of indigenous authors, a figure only exceeded in five of the preceding 18 years under survey.

As in several other spheres, it is difficult not to associate Scott, himself the author of three novels bearing 1820 imprint dates, with the expansion in the number of new titles found during the early 1820s. In its opening article for January 1820, the *Edinburgh Review* celebrated 'the author of *Waverley*' as a 'prodigy of fertility', redirecting earlier metaphorical suggestions of female excess into a picture of masculine potency.[55] Clearly, however, other factors were at work. With freer access to raw materials, the benefits of mechanical manufacture of paper became more fully apparent, making longer works of literature more viable. 'Paper is falling every day', Constable and Co. insisted to a London supplier on 16 January 1821, and the implications for an expansionist concern such as theirs were plain.[56] Less easy to chart is a shift in readership, but there is strong evidence that Scott's influence helped encourage a fairly widespread return of male readers to the fold as acknowledged novel-readers.[57] Impression numbers for best-selling titles, and the higher rate of survival of bound copies from the 1820s, both indicate a marked shift towards individual purchases. Scott's pulling power had diminished by mid-decade, the first clear sign of this being the decision to reduce the impression of *Peveril of the Peak* (1822: 67) from 12,000 to 10,500.[58] Nevertheless 1823 to 1825 was a time of optimum production, almost matching, though in a less erratic way, the three-year high found in 1808–1810 (277 as opposed to 279 titles).

Another significant feature, itself indicative of the decade's capacity to absorb fresh materials, is the growing number of British reprints of works originally

---

[54]  For an account of the virtually contemporaneous publication of these two works, and the differing fortunes of each, see Peter Garside, 'Three Perils in Publishing: Hogg and the Popular Novel', *Studies in Hogg and his World*, 2 (1991), 45–63 (pp. 52–3).

[55]  ER, 33 (1820), 1. The reviewer was Francis Jeffrey.

[56]  NLS, MS 791, pp. 228 (to Longman & Dickinson). According to Erickson, the cost of demy dropped from 32s a ream in 1810 to 20s a ream in 1835 ('The Poets' Corner', in *The Economy of Literary Form*, p. 27). In addition to reducing manufacturing costs, the mechanical method created a superior quality product, thus reducing losses through wastage in printing.

[57]  Such a change is implicitly forecast by J. B. S. Morritt (a landowner and MP), in describing to Scott his responses having read *Guy Mannering*: 'I hope the said author will proceed & give us a new tone in prose narrative that shall restore it to the dignity from which it gradually slipped before it dwindled into a manufacture for the circulating library' (16 Mar. 1815; NLS, MS 3886, f. 100).

[58]  NLS, MS 791, p. 589 (Robert Cadell to James Ballantyne, 22 July 1822). Cadell mentioned the difficulty in disposing of the 3rd edn. of *The Fortunes of Nigel* (1822: 66) as the main reason behind the decision. Scott produced three novels with 1822 imprints, matching his 1820 performance, and it is not unlikely that the market was being over-stretched.

published in America. Whereas in the 1800s there had been only six such 'imported' titles (four of them by Charles Brockden Brown), and in the 1810s just one (Brown's *Wieland* (1811)), as many as 25 'new' titles in the 1820s had appeared in earlier American editions, the British imprint sometimes directly displaying its provenance in this respect. James Fenimore Cooper's novels are most apparent here, but this grouping also contains lesser-known items such as the anonymous *Zelica, the Creole* (1820: 12), which was offered by its publisher as part of 'a Series of Novels that have been transmitted [...] from America'. Other American 'imports' include works by Catharine Maria Sedgwick, John Neal, James MacHenry, and the German-born Karl Magnus Postl (see 1829: 66). The 1820s also saw a moderate revival in the output of first translations of French and German titles (some 20 apiece), with a new enthusiasm for German literature evident particularly in 1824–1826.

As previously stated, the economic difficulties of the book trade in 1825–1826, precipitated by the crash of Constable's London associates, Hurst, Robinson and Co., probably best explain the break in an ascending line at this point. While traditional accounts of mass bankruptcies amongst publishers are undoubtedly exaggerated, there is clear evidence of some houses actively backing off from producing novels in the later years of the decade. One publisher, Henry Colburn, none the less refused to draw his horns in, actually quadrupling his output of new novels at this time, and marketing them with an efficiency which brought cries of protest from potential rivals. Robert Cadell, in writing to J. G. Lockhart in May 1828 apropos Scott's *The Fair Maid of Perth* (see 1828: 72), notes with barely concealed resentment 'how different his [Scott's] works are from the trash with which the public are now flooded from the Colburn press—the puffs of the rubbish are absolutely nauseous'.[59] It is possible that Colburn's artificially high prices and his projection of material primarily still at a circulating library clientele (to whom the same prices would help stress the good value of subscriptions) had a partly negative effect in so far as output of fiction as a whole is concerned. Less specialist publishers still operating in the field at the end of the decade, such as William Blackwood, complained that a preoccupation with public events—the debate concerning Catholic emancipation and agitation for Reform—was making the sale of new works of literature well-nigh impossible.[60] In actuality, the novel at this time stood on the verge of a new phase of development, with a potential for tapping a vastly expanded readership, though the first signs of any full realization of this market came in the form of reprint series such as the Magnum Opus edition of Scott's Waverley Novels.[61]

Any overall estimate of output of novels relative to the total production of new books is bound to be limited by the elusive, sometimes contrary, figures available for the period as a whole. Charles Knight calculated on the basis of Bent's *London Catalogue* that 15,888 new books were published between 1800 and 1827, averaging

[59] NLS, MS 794, f. 291.

[60] For an account of negative factors affecting the trade at this stage, see Royal A. Gettmann, *A Victorian Publisher: A Study of the Bentley Papers* (Cambridge, 1960), pp. 9–11.

[61] See Jane Millgate, *Scott's Last Edition: A Study in Publishing History* (Edinburgh, 1987), *passim*.

588 titles annually, though this analysis necessarily reflects Bent's limited scope and offers no account of movement between years.[62] Ian Jack's figures taken from copies of the lists of books entered at Stationers' Hall sent to the Librarian at Cambridge University, between 1815 and 1825, supplemented by his breakdown for later years from Bent's *Monthly Literary Advertiser*, probably between them offer a truer picture. The Stationers' Hall figures indicate a fairly gentle rise from 1,121 titles in 1815 to 1,346 in 1825, with a few single years (e.g. 1818 and 1821) slipping back slightly during this progression, and the 1,390 titles of 1822 representing a bumper crop. If allowance is made for the slightly lower returns listed by the *Monthly Literary Advertiser*, then the upward curve continues later in the decade, leading to a rise in 1829 which is then sustained into the 1830s.[63] A more comprehensive view of general output over the full period, as well as of movements between years, has been provided by Simon Eliot, whose calculations are based on a variety of sources, including records of paper production. At their most tentative for the early nineteenth century, these suggest a single peak in 1803 (perhaps swollen by political pamphlets), a rising trend from 1805–1809, a pattern of fluctuation in the second decade, and an overall rising pattern in the 1820s.[64] As a whole, output of new novels as indicated by the present volume would seem generally to reflect overall movements within the book trade, with fiction titles representing in the region of 8 per cent of new output. However, the sudden upsurge of novels near the end of the 1800s has no clear parallel in the wider projections, and the trough in the 1810s is apparently not matched by an equivalent decline in general production. The steep ascent in the output of new fiction titles in the early 1820s, furthermore, would appear to outmatch the general trend then, particularly if the size of novels (normally by that stage in three volumes) is also taken into account, and even more so if subsidiary forms such as children's fiction and evangelical tract literature are brought into calculations.

By the end of the 1820s there is every indication that fiction had become the dominant imaginative literary genre. Certainly there are clear signs of poetry losing some of the shine that had made it so attractive as a fashionable article earlier in the period. In the early 1820s ambitious younger authors clearly saw the novel, with its increasingly large impressions, as representing the main area of opportunity. The decline of poetry sales, 'even for a Wordsworth', was noted in pointed terms by

---

[62] Knight, *Old Printer and the Modern Press*, p. 238. These figures had originally appeared in Knight's paper, *The Printing Machine*, in 1834, and are adopted for 1800–1827 in M. Henry Meidinger's 'A Statistical Account of the Book Trade of various Countries. Part II' in *Journal of the Statistical Society of London*, 3 (Jan. 1841), 376–86 (p. 384). Meidinger also provides the figures of 842 and 1,064 for the years 1828 and 1829, as calculated from Bent's *Monthly Literary Advertiser*.

[63] Ian Jack, *English Literature, 1815–1832* (Oxford, 1963), p. 38 n. Erickson adjusts the less full figures from Bent to suggest an increase of 23 per cent between 1815 and 1828 (1,121 titles as compared to 1,377) and of 30 per cent between 1828 and 1832 (1,377 titles compared to an estimated 1,789). See 'The Poets' Corner', in *The Economy of Literary Form*, p. 26. Even these perhaps somewhat sanguine projections are exceeded by the rise of the number of new novels from 54 in 1815 to 83 in 1828, representing an increase of more than 50 per cent.

[64] Simon Eliot, *Some Patterns and Trends in British Publishing 1800–1919* (London, 1994), esp. pp. 19, 24, 109–10.

J. G. Lockhart in his review for *Blackwood's Magazine* of John Wilson's *Lights and Shadows of Scottish Life* (1822: 82): 'we suppose his publishers never think of venturing beyond a 500 or 750 edition, which, as editions go now, is just nothing.'[65] Even in the face of continuing disappointment, James Hogg persisted in the belief that fiction would bring fortune and fame, while his poetry was forced into finding an outlet in periodicals and the new literary annuals. The production of individual volumes of new poetry had definitely slackened off by the end of the 1820s,[66] as a new and more extensive generation of readers, whose first expectation in imaginative literature was prose fiction, increasingly made its presence felt.

## (4) Kinds of Title

In a period when large numbers of new novels were published anonymously,[67] titles naturally played a crucial part in signalling the specific generic character of individual works. Even where authors were named on the title-page, or otherwise known, the general tendency in circulating library catalogues was to list by title, with only a few celebrated authors such as Maria Edgeworth being granted the privilege of having works entered under their surname. Choosing a certain lead word for a title could have the effect of placing a work in flattering company, as well as opening up the possibility of enticing readers looking for novels similar to well-known favourites. A title beginning 'Mystery/ies' or 'Mysterious'—as is the case with nearly thirty novels in the present volume—would thus in all likelihood share the same area of space in a Catalogue as Ann Radcliffe's *The Mysteries of Udolpho* (1794), arguably the most successful of all Gothic novels. On the other hand, proximity of this kind could lead a novel with literary ambitions into unwanted obscurity amongst a crowd of similar titles. Elizabeth Anne Le Noir, apparently for such reasons, altered her *Clara de Montfier, A Moral Tale* (1808: 71) to *The Maid of La Vendee* for its second edition, alleging that the original title had led to confusion owing to a number of other 'Clara' titles, notably Sophie Cottin's *Claire d'Albe*, which in its translated version appeared as *Clara; A Novel* (1808: 39). The addition of a subsidiary ('or') title offered a further opportunity to broadcast the generic characteristics and/or arresting qualities of a work, as well as leaving open the possibility of a later transposition of the two titles. Approximately 45 per cent of the novels in the present volume have dual titles of this nature, the practice of double titling being sustained throughout the bulk of the period under view, with a tailing-off only really apparent in the later 1820s.

---

[65] *Blackwood's Magazine*, 11 (June 1822), 669.

[66] See 'The Poets' Corner', in *The Economy of Literary Form*, esp. pp. 28–9, 33–5. A breakdown of entries in J. R. de J. Jackson's *Annals of English Verse, 1770–1835* (New York, 1985) shows a clear tailing off of new poetry titles in the later 1820s (see Table 1, in Garside, 'The English Novel in the 1820s', p. 192). A slightly different picture is given in J. R. de J. Jackson's *Romantic Poetry by Women: A Bibliography 1770–1835* (Oxford, 1993), which indicates a fairly steady output of around 30–35 first editions between 1821 and 1829, after a highpoint of 42 in 1820 (see Jackson's 'Note on the Annual Rate of Publication', pp. 392–4).

[67] An issue discussed more fully in the following section on 'Authors'.

There is strong evidence in surviving records that publishers could exert considerable pressure on authors, or even override them completely, when titles were finalized. C. R. Maturin used the Preface of his *Women; or, Pour et Contre* (1818: 41) to complain how his *Family of Montorio* had been 'misnomed by the bookseller "The Fatal Revenge", a very book-selling appellation'—though, without this alleged intrusion, the Gothic character of the work would have been less immediately apparent. In the naming of *Women* itself, Maturin had been warned off his first-choice lead title of 'De Courcy' by his present publisher, Archibald Constable, on the grounds that this had been used 'oftner than once'.[68] In fact, this name had appeared as a constituent part in no less than four titles of novels between 1800 and 1813 (1802: 54, 1806: 3, 1808: 2, and 1813: 21).[69] Longmans in writing to John Phillips on 12 March 1818, in relation to *Lionel; or, the Last of the Pevenseys* (1818: 50), asked for a choice of alternatives to replace the (unnamed) title first submitted. Similarly, Elizabeth Lester was informed on 20 November 1818: 'We do not find the Title a happy one—if you could give us several we could point out the one we thought best.'[70] Other concerns were no doubt less circumspect in their dealings. Title-pages were usually set and printed in the last stages of producing a novel, and tell-tale signs of a last-minute change of plan by the publisher are perhaps to be discovered in some of those cases where disparities exist between the main titles and the title given within the book, as in the drop-head title placed immediately above the text proper of a novel. For example, in the case of Ann Mary Hamilton's *The Maiden Wife; or, the Heiress of De Courcey. A Most Interesting Tale* (1813: 21), where the drop-head title reads 'The Heiress of De Courcy [*sic*]', and where there is no evidence of a prior issue, it is by no means impossible that the arresting lead title was arrived at late in the day and from a bookselling rather than authorial vantage point. As a jobbing authoress, without any special clout, Hamilton would have been especially vulnerable to such arbitrary treatment (see also below).

Table 2. **Keywords in Titles, 1800–1829**

| Imprint Years | 'Novel' | Novel % | 'Romance' | Romance % | 'Tale/s' | Tale/s % |
|---|---|---|---|---|---|---|
| 1800s | 277 | 36.0 | 141 | 18.3 | 129 | 16.8 |
| 1810s | 235 | 35.5 | 86 | 13.0 | 138 | 20.8 |
| 1820s | 118 | 14.3 | 74 | 9.0 | 283 | 34.3 |
| Total | *630* | *27.9* | *301* | *13.3* | *550* | *24.4* |

Even the three most common basic descriptive labels, 'Novel', 'Romance', and 'Tale(s)', could carry special significance in conveying differences of content. As

---

[68] NLS, MS 789, p. 829 (Constable to Maturin, 8 Aug. 1817).

[69] In addition to the post-1800 titles listed here, it is possible to add *Sidney Castle; or the Sorrows of De Courci* (1792), *Edward de Courcy* (1794), and *Adeline de Courcy* (1797), all anonymous novels.

[70] Longman Letter Books, I, 100, nos. 234, 248.

Table 2 illustrates, 'Novel' was the most frequently used over the period as a whole, followed by 'Tale(s)', and then 'Romance'. While sometimes these terms can seem virtually interchangeable, generally the term 'Novel' is found in titles which contain contemporary domestic matter, whereas 'Romance' more usually describes fiction with an historical, fantastical, or exotic orientation. 'Tale' is naturally used for shorter works, and in the plural for compilations, though its relative freedom from negative connotations also gave it an attraction as an alternative for 'Novel'. Elizabeth Appleton, in the preliminaries of her *Edgar: A National Tale* (1816: 14), thus explains how 'tale' rather than 'novel' had been used in the title, as more appropriate for 'moral fiction';[71] just as eleven years later, Henry Constantine Phipps, in somewhat aloof terms, warned readers of his *Matilda; A Tale of the Day* (1825: 66) not to 'expect "a novel", in the circulating library sense of the word' (Preface, p. [iii]).

Not unwilling to declare her family 'great Novel-readers',[72] Jane Austen evidently had no such qualms, pinning her colours firmly to the mast through the titling of all four of the works published in her lifetime as 'A Novel'. Walter Scott, more wary of contamination, avoided the term in all the original editions of his fictional works, notwithstanding the gradual adoption of the generic label 'Waverley novels' and his subsequent reputation as the founder of the 'Historical Novel'. The choice of 'Novels and Tales' as the title for the collected editions of his first ('Scottish') sequence of novels, with largely post-1660 settings, and that of 'Historical Romances' to contain the largely non-Scottish and more fustian titles stemming from the medieval *Ivanhoe* (1820: 63), eventually offered a kind of quasi-official reinforcement of the main lines of demarcation. More particularly, Scott's previous use of the mantle title *Tales of My Landlord*, originally with the intention of combining several tales,[73] but in the event involving the incorporation of no more than two stories (and in the case of the second series only one: see 1818: 56), provides the clearest single explanation for an increase of works of fiction titled 'Tale(s)' later in the period. This is first apparent in a sudden surge in 1818–1819, and leads on to a situation where the term is included in more than a third of titles (34.3 per cent) belonging to the 1820s, compared with significantly lower proportions for the same span in the case of both 'Novel' and 'Romance' (14.3 per cent and 9 per cent respectively).

As a whole, a title could contain as many as three components—title, sub-title, and basic generic label—all capable on their own of sending out a signal about the kind of novel on offer. Even the basic labels of Novel etc. were expandable to give a more specific generic indication, an additional epithet sometimes overriding in importance the root term (as in Fashionable Novel/Fable/Tale). Seen in unison

---

[71] 'To the Public', vol. 1, pp. vii–viii. Appleton's statement concludes: 'It remains for the public alone to determine, whether these volumes are worthy of a higher rank in literature than that of a *Novel*' (p. viii).

[72] Le Faye (ed.), *Jane Austen's Letters*, p. 26 (to Cassandra Austen, 19 Dec. 1798).

[73] The original intention with the first series (1816) of *Tales of My Landlord* was for each of the four volumes to contain a separate tale, illustrative of a different region of Scotland; but this was overtaken by the expansion of the second tale, *Old Mortality*, to fill the final three volumes.

various elements of a title might point more closely to distinctions within a broad mode, such as Gothic. A combination of 'Romance' with any one of a number of keywords, including (in addition to 'Mysteries') 'Castle', 'Monastery', 'Abbey', 'Cavern', almost invariably points towards a Gothic novel in the essentially female tradition of Ann Radcliffe. 'Romance' and 'Castle', for example, feature together in some forty titles belonging to the 1800s, nearly all of the works concerned being Radcliffian in nature. 'Monk', on the other hand, especially when combined with some less decorous words, is more likely to intimate a novel in the more 'male' horror tradition of M. G. Lewis's *The Monk* (1796). At the same time, titles taken at face value can sometimes have a deceptive effect. *Atrocities of a Convent* (1808: 92) might at second hand appear to indicate a pot-boiler in the coarser Lewisian tradition; but examination of the possibly unique copy in the library of the University of California, Los Angeles, not only revealed a satire of ideas, but also identified the author as the radical writer Thomas 'Clio' Rickman. In some cases, no doubt, booksellers forced a sensational title on generically inappropriate materials. Scott told a story of how a novel by Henry Siddons, the actor–manager, had been re-christened by William Lane of the Minerva Press as 'The Mysterious Bridal'. '"Saar," as poor Harry used to say, "there was neither mystery nor bridal in my poor book. So . . . the consequence was I took my own book out of a circulating library for some new reading for Mrs. Siddons, and never found it out till I was far in the first volume"'.[74]

A few titles of the period move in the opposite direction of (usually mock) non-signification, as in Mary Meeke's *Something Odd! A Novel* (1804: 49), one of four novels by the author that year, followed by her *Something Strange. A Novel* (1806: 46). Alternatively, the reader might be offered a blank space to fill in, as with Alethea Lewis's *A Tale Without a Title: Give it What You Please* (1804: 42) or Mrs Llewellyn's *Read, and Give it a Name. A Novel* (1813: 40). In these circumstances, however, the use of an established pseudonym (e.g. Eugenia de Acton in the case of Lewis), or a listing of previous works 'by the author', could have a significant compensatory effect. Any full study of generic movements within fiction at this time would necessitate close analysis of all the novels in this volume, and even then researchers would soon encounter problems such as those arising from the generic instability of a number of the works under view. The following observations concerning trends are therefore necessarily tentative and provisional. While title-page information offers a useful initial indicator of mode, first-hand knowledge of texts is utilized wherever possible, and guidance is also sought from a number of previous studies of specific genres.[75]

One feature of the earlier years under survey is the paucity of titles indicating a picaresque content in the older eighteenth-century manner. Those titles that do indicate such qualities, usually through the use of 'Life' and 'Adventures' as lead words, appear to have come from the periphery of novel production, and rarely

---

[74] *The Letters of Sir Walter Scott*, ed. H. J. C. Grierson, 12 vols. (London, 1932–7), VI, 145.

[75] In addition to the studies of specific modes mentioned below, a valuable contribution to the taxonomy of Romantic fiction will also be found in Gary Kelly, *English Fiction of the Romantic Period 1789–1830* (London, 1989), *passim*.

seem to have enjoyed a wide circulation. William Linley's *The Adventures of Ralph Reybridge* (1809: 43) actually announces in its preliminaries that the work was written in Madras in 1801, shortly after the author's arrival at the Presidency but without his yet having secured a suitable position. Daniel George's *The Adventures of Dick Distich* (1812: 30), again apparently written some years before publication, was listed by the *Edinburgh Review*, in an unusual indication there of style, as 'Written after the manner of Fielding, Smollett, and Cervantes'. The anonymous *Brambleton Hall, a Novel, Being a Sequel to the Celebrated Humphrey [sic] Clinker, by Tobias Smollet [sic], M.D.* (1818: 3), in addition to leading the constructor of the title-page into two spelling errors, carried an instructional Preface addressed to readers who had not 'perused the preceding volumes of the Expedition of Humphry Clinker'. In the case of the provincially published *The History and Adventures of Godfrey Ranger* (1813: 45), by David William Paynter, a Preface ostensibly by its publisher deprecated the work in an apparent effort to forestall criticism. (The switch of the title to *Godfrey Ranger. A Novel* for the Newman remainder issue of 1816 is perhaps indicative of the unserviceability by that time of titles with the prefix 'History and Adventures'.) It is noticeable that very few novels of this nature entered into the Corvey Library, in line with its apparent accessions policy of avoiding masculinist titles with a potentially bawdy content.

Two distinct phases of re-appropriation of the picaresque form are nevertheless worth noting. The first is evident in an upturn in the number of 'spy'-like titles, in the manner of Le Sage, during the period 1808–1812, at the height of the contemporary craze for 'scandal' fictions. Representative cases will be found in a number of publications by J. F. Hughes, among them John Canton's *The English Gil Blas; or, the Adventures of Gabriel Tangent* (1807: 13) and Charles Sedley's *Asmodeus; or, the Devil in London* (1808: 96). Other examples include *Rhydisel. The Devil in Oxford* (1811: 47), possibly by Anthony Gregory Johnstone, Ann Mary Hamilton's *The Adventures of a Seven-Shilling Piece* (1811: 37), and the evocatively titled but anonymous *Adventures of an Ostrich Feather of Quality* (1812: 1). The second phase occurs on a much broader front in the 1820s, and is indicative of a large-scale return of male readers to prose fiction. This phenomenon involves a number of independent strands: perambulatory 'travel' fictions, such as the *Hermit* titles by Felix Macdonogh (1819: 46 etc.) and Thomas Colley Grattan's three series of *High-Ways and By-Ways* (1823: 39 etc.); exotic tales in the style of James Justinian Morier's *The Adventures of Hajji Baba, of Ispahan* (1824: 70); and the Tom and Jerry 'man about town' adventures of Pierce Egan's *Life in London* (1821: 31), which set the pattern for other originally serialized works by Egan or in the Egan manner.

There is little sign, on the other hand, of any recovery by the epistolary novel, a form which had dominated production from about 1776–1784, but which was already well in decline by the later 1790s. Only seven titles in the listings contain the once potent phrase 'In a Series of Letters', which had introduced more than one hundred new novels between 1770 and 1790. Prefatory materials likewise rarely announce, still less celebrate, an epistolary content. Elizabeth Lefanu, writing in her mid-forties, adopts a slightly apologetic air in *The India Voyage* (1804: 39), when justifying 'the epistolary, or, rather, the journal style', on the grounds that it 'appeared to her more favourable to the development of character than the narrative'. Another (younger) Irish writer, then just about to break on to a wider literary stage, provides a striking exception here. Sydney Owenson's first work of fiction, *St. Clair; or, the Heiress of Desmond* (1803: 55), published originally in Dublin, offers a daring reinterpretation of the illicit triangular relationships of Rousseau's *Julie, ou la Nouvelle Héloïse* (1761) and (the more immediate model) Goethe's *Die Leiden des jungen Werthers* (1774). The letter form was employed again by Owenson in *The Wild Irish Girl; A National Tale* (1806: 54), one of the most striking successes of the 1800s, though in this case the uninterrupted epistolary sequence provided by its main male protagonist gives the impression of a first-person narrative. Nicola J. Watson argues that the emphasis on individual subjectivity in epistolary fiction, as well as the subversive reputation acquired by the letter at the time of the French Revolution, had the effect of giving the mode a duplicitous if not dangerous appearance.[76] More tangibly, one suspects that the mechanics of the epistolary form had become an impediment to a readership eager for the thrills and escapades available in newer direct narrative modes, notably the Gothic novel. In these circumstances, publishers are likely to have discouraged unmediated epistolary structures. One appears to have taken direct action. In the 'Advertisement' to her *The Irishwoman in London, A Modern Novel* (1810: 49), Ann Mary Hamilton complained how her publisher (J. F. Hughes) had altered the text 'from Letters to Chapters' in her absence, 'conceiving it not so saleable' in its original form.

Frank Gees Black lists 169 English epistolary fictions belonging to the 1780s, 155 in the 1790s, followed by 62 in the 1800s, 38 in the 1810s, and a mere 26 in the 1820s.[77] While a handful of overlooked titles have been discovered during the preparation of this volume, particularly in the early 1800s, little has been found to contradict the general picture of a disappearing mode. In fact, for the later period, where it is highly unusual to find a complete epistolary novel, Black's figures are probably over-sanguine. J. G. Lockhart's *The History of Matthew Wald* (1824: 60), for instance, which is included in Black's list, is effectively a first-person narrative, albeit concluded by a brief letter 'enclosing the foregoing Memoirs'. When letters *are* incorporated within a narrative during this later period, as through the inclusion of a sentimental correspondence in Scott's *Guy Mannering* (1815: 46), they are usually employed self-consciously or to provide a special period ambience. Such instabilities, combined with the difficulties of defining 'epistolary' content in diverse narratives like James Hogg's *The Private Memoirs and Confessions of a Justified Sinner* (1824: 50), underlie the decision not to denote epistolary novels in the individual entries of this volume.

---

[76] Nicola J. Watson, *Revolution and the Form of the British Novel 1790–1825: Intercepted Letters, Interrupted Seductions* (Oxford, 1994), p. 69. Watson goes on to consider various strategies, evident in the post-Revolutionary period, for redirecting the letter in a fictional framework.

[77] Black, 'Chronological List of Epistolary Fiction', in his *Epistolary Novel*, pp. 160–8.

Apart from exceptions such as Owenson's *St. Clair*, there are scant signs of a revival in fiction of the cult of 'sentiment' and 'sensibility', which had stood at its height in Britain from the 1770s to the mid-1790s. An unusual instance of the once familiar combination of sensibility with the epistolary form is evident in the first entry in the present listings, *Alphonso di Borgo; or, a Sentimental Correspondence of the Sixteenth Century* (1800: 1). References thereafter to the sentimental, when they do appear, are likely to be in a pejorative or facetious rather than in a laudatory vein, as in *The Tears of Camphor; or, Love and Nature Triumphant* (1804: 19), written under the raffish-sounding pseudonym of Henrico Fernandez Glysticus. At the same time, it is possible to point to a recycling and re-assimilation of older 'retreatist' forms of feeling into a new ideology of social community and domestic cohesion. A transmutation of this kind helps explain the extraordinary appetite earlier in the period for the pictures of familial attachment offered by the German writer, August Lafontaine. In fact, the sentimental component in his writing appears sometimes to be actively reinforced by the English versions, as through the sub-titling of Eliza Parson's translation *Love and Gratitude; or, Traits of the Human Heart* (1804: 35), itself one of six translations of Lafontaine to appear with 1804 imprints. A different model was provided by Amelia Opie's much reprinted *The Father and Daughter* (1801: 54), whose transgressive heroine painfully seeks rehabilitation in an at first unforgiving community. Titles signalling a comparable pathetic focus include: Sarah Wilkinson's *The Thatched Cottage; or, Sorrows of Eugenia* (1806: 69), a domestic melodrama, with aristocratic protagonists; Robert Bayles's *The Sorrows of Eliza; or a Tale of Misfortune* (1810: 23), comprising 'authentic Memoirs of a young Lady in the Vicinity of London'; and the perennial 'orphan' favourite, *Fatherless Fanny; or, the Memoirs of a Little Mendicant, and her Benefactors* (1811: 31). The most frequently reprinted translated work of this period, Sophie Cottin's *Elizabeth; or, the Exiles of Siberia* (1807: 15), which depicts its young heroine's journey to plead with the Czar for her parents' release, apparently owed much of its success to its usefulness as a manual in filial obedience and perseverance.

A movement from a subjective sentimentalism to one based on social consensus is also apparent in the fairly large number of works (more than thirty in all) which describe themselves as 'A Domestic Tale/Story' etc. These are apparent throughout the whole period: from William Mudford's picture of innocence destroyed in *Augustus and Mary; or, the Maid of Buttermere. A Domestic Tale* (1803: 51), through didactic fictions such as Barbara Hofland's *The Sisters; A Domestic Tale* (1813: 29), to Catherine G. Ward's originally serialized *The Forest Girl; or, the Mountain Hut: An Original and Interesting Domestic Tale* (1826: 74). More broadly still, the basic narrative trajectory of the earlier English domestic sentimental novel, culminating usually in the marriage of a previously bereft or socially vulnerable heroine, continued to help shape the plots of innumerable novels in this period.

The one form that was undeniably buoyant at the beginning of the new century is the Gothic novel. Noticeably, both the two main specialist listings of Gothic fiction available, by Lévy and by Frank, include a larger number of entries for the

1800s than for the 1790s (142 as opposed to 112, and 193 compared with 115).[78] Annual counts in each suggest that the optimum years for the mode were between 1796 and 1806. This tallies with Robert B. Mayo's broad claim in 1950 that 'During the years from 1796 to 1806 at least one-third of all novels published in Great Britain were Gothic in character.'[79] Table 3 shows the number of Gothic titles entered in the present listings: it incorporates all the novels listed by Lévy and Frank, with the exception of parodies and some works better classified as historical fiction, as well as including a significant number of Gothic novels not known to, or overlooked by, these previous bibliographers. As a whole, the new figures confirm the ubiquitousness of Gothic romance in the 1800s (199 titles in all), compared with the 1810s (89 titles), and even more so the 1820s (42 titles). Mayo's claim that the genre was responsible for more than a third of total production, however, proves to be somewhat exaggerated, with only two years (1800 and 1802) matching this criterion. Within the 1800s it is also interesting to note a drop in output in 1803 and (more especially) 1804, though a revival is perceptible in the years 1805–1807 and (to a lesser extent) in 1810. Production then falls away, with the largest drop occurring in 1813–1814, during which two years only nine Gothic titles are found. A slight resurgence however is apparent in 1819–1820, in the immediate wake of the publication of Mary Shelley's *Frankenstein; or, the Modern Prometheus* (1818: 57). After that Gothic novels are found in small numbers, and it has not been possible to find any clear instance in the final year surveyed.

Table 3. **Publication of Gothic Novels, 1800–1829**

| Imprint Year | No. Titles | % of Total | Imprint Year | No. Titles | % of Total | Imprint Year | No. Titles | % of Total |
|---|---|---|---|---|---|---|---|---|
| 1800 | 27 | 33.3 | 1810 | 22 | 24.7 | 1820 | 10 | 14.3 |
| 1801 | 20 | 27.8 | 1811 | 13 | 16.3 | 1821 | 4 | 5.3 |
| 1802 | 22 | 36.1 | 1812 | 9 | 13.6 | 1822 | 4 | 4.9 |
| 1803 | 19 | 24.1 | 1813 | 5 | 7.9 | 1823 | 5 | 5.7 |
| 1804 | 10 | 13.7 | 1814 | 4 | 6.6 | 1824 | 5 | 5.1 |
| 1805 | 22 | 29.3 | 1815 | 8 | 14.8 | 1825 | 1 | 1.1 |
| 1806 | 22 | 31.4 | 1816 | 6 | 10.2 | 1826 | 4 | 5.2 |
| 1807 | 21 | 30.4 | 1817 | 6 | 10.9 | 1827 | 6 | 7.6 |
| 1808 | 21 | 18.9 | 1818 | 5 | 8.1 | 1828 | 3 | 3.6 |
| 1809 | 15 | 19.0 | 1819 | 11 | 15.1 | 1829 | — | — |
| *1800s* | *199* | *25.8* | *1810s* | *89* | *13.4* | *1820s* | *42* | *5.1* |
| | | | | | | Total | 330 | 14.6 |

[78] Maurice Lévy, 'Bibliographie chronologique', in his *Le Roman 'gothique' anglais 1764–1824*, pp. 684–708; Frederick S. Frank, 'Annual Chronology', Appendix 3 in his *The First Gothics*, pp. 457–68.

[79] Robert D. Mayo, 'Gothic Romance in the Magazines', *Publications of the Modern Language Association*, 65 (1950), 762–89 (p. 766). Mayo's claim about the predominance of Gothic novels, since

It is worth bearing in mind that the above observations about trends involve only Gothic novels, and do not take into account the often more graphic Gothic chapbooks and stage melodramas of the period. The bulk of the fictions under view are relatively decorous in nature, with novels in the Radcliffian manner far outweighing their Lewisian counterparts. Spectres and spirits are both more commonplace than ghosts, just as 'banditti' prevail over 'robber/s' and convents outnumber nunneries. 'Monk'-like fictions only fully come into view with an outcrop of sensational titles, characterized by their sadism and voyeurism, published by J. F. Hughes in the later 1800s. Notable here are *The Demon of Sicily* (1807: 44) and *The Legends of a Nunnery* (1807: 45), both by Edward Montague; and *The Friar Hildargo* (1807: 46) and *Montoni; or, the Confessions of the Monk of Saint Benedict* (1808: 82), by an interchangeable-sounding Edward Mortimer. Sometimes the effort to display Gothic credentials leads to a mixture of Radcliffian and Lewisian elements, as in T. J. Horsley Curties's *The Monk of Udolpho* (1807: 16), or in the case of *Manfroné; or, the One-handed Monk* (1809: 61), where the ascription to 'Mary Anne Radcliffe' may or may not lead to the true author. Arguably the most heavily signalled Gothic novel of all—though there are several strong contenders—is *The Mysterious Baron, or the Castle in the Forest, A Gothic Story* (1808: 91), by Eliza Ratcliffe. Rather remarkably, this is one of only five novels actually incorporating the word 'Gothic' in the title, a salutary reminder that this term has a much wider currency in modern criticism of the mode than in the kind of fiction it chiefly describes.

The listings also contain a number of clear counter-versions to the Gothic, most noticeably in the period from 1800 to 1814. Two novels early in the 1800s clearly signal their *lack* of Gothic credentials. Rachel Hunter's *Letitia; or, the Castle without a Spectre* (1801: 35) does so by its title, whereas Mary Goldsmith's *Casualties. A Novel* (1804: 20), itself a moral domestic fiction, renounces what are clearly regarded as formulaic ingredients in an unusual title-page declaration of intent: 'No Subterranean Caverns—Haunted Castles—Enchanted Forests—Fearful Visions—Mysterious Voices—Supernatural Agents—Bloody Daggers—Dead Men's Skulls—Mangled Bodies—*Nor* Marvellous Lights, from any Part of the present Work; but will be found, on Perusal, to arise out of Natural Incidents.' It was between these two publications, probably early in 1803, that Jane Austen's burlesque 'Susan' (later published posthumously as *Northanger Abbey* (1818: 19)) was sold to B. Crosby and Co. for £10, though Crosby, in spite of advertising the work, failed to have it printed and published.[80] The conjecture that Crosby held back as a result of his commitment to genuine Gothic fictions is probably misjudged. From

frequently echoed, originates from selected lists of 'New Publications' in the *Monthly Magazine*. A fuller account of shifting taste, based on fiction contributed to the *Lady's Magazine*, is given in Mayo's 'How Long was Gothic Fiction in Vogue?', *Modern Language Notes*, 58 (1943), 58–64. This earlier article traces a rising curve from the 1790s, leading to a high water mark in 1805, followed by a drop in 1807–9, spiralling down to a total absence of Gothic content in 1813–1814.

[80] See Jan Fergus, *Jane Austen. A Literary Life* (London, 1991), pp. 111–13. Fergus considers the novel submitted at this stage, and reclaimed by Austen in 1809, to be substantially the same as the published *Northanger Abbey*.

twelve novels with 1803 or 1804 imprints, bearing Crosby's name, at least four show Gothic characteristics; yet it is also worth considering that the years 1803–1804 saw a decline in the output of Gothic novels generally, and in this latter respect Austen could be seen as swimming with rather than against the tide. Probably Austen's lack of success is better attributed to the choice of a publisher dealing in fairly nondescript fiction and whose output of novels, for whatever reason, noticeably dips in the mid-1800s.

The highest concentration of burlesques, perhaps not surprisingly, is found in the years when production of Gothic novels was starting to fall significantly. Notable titles at this turning-point include Sarah Green's *Romance Readers and Romance Writers* (1810: 46), *Love and Horror, A Modern Romance* (1812: 41), by 'Ircastrensis', and Eaton Stannard Barrett's *The Heroine, or Adventures of a Fair Romance Reader* (1813: 9), the popularity of the last work effectively marking the end of the pure Radcliffian mode, at least as a fashionable form of reading. Thomas Love Peacock's *Nightmare Abbey* (1818: 48), though published in the same year as Austen's *Northanger Abbey*, was targeted at an essentially different kind of dark 'Byronic' Gothicism, characterized for Peacock by its post-Revolutionary morbidity. In the 1820s a fairly clear division occurs between a relatively small number of conscious 'intellectual' developments of the Gothic, of which Maturin's *Melmoth the Wanderer* (1820: 51) is a striking example, and more 'populist' offshoots of terror writing such as Sarah Wilkinson's self-professedly commercial *The Spectre of Lanmere Abbey* (1820: 70), the serialized 'Mystery' titles of Catherine G. Ward, and the Gothic fictions still being produced for A. K. Newman, notably by Miss C. D. Haynes (1821: 45, 1827: 31).

In some instances the lionizing of a particular writer or the prominence gained by a single work could lead to a succession of imitations and mock sequences. The outstanding success of Maria Edgeworth's *Tales of Fashionable Life* (1809, 1812) encouraged a number of such offshoots, amongst them the anonymous *Tales of Real Life. Forming a Sequel to Miss Edgeworth's Tales of Fashionable Life* (1810: 18), an early opportunist publication by Henry Colburn. In exasperation, Joseph Johnson, the publisher of the original work, mounted a public campaign to assert the integrity of the Edgeworthian canon.[81] Probably the most influential single work in this period, however, was Hannah More's *Cœlebs in Search of a Wife* (1808: 81), which had reached its fourteenth edition by 1813. A deliberate appropriation of the novel form by its famous evangelical author, this took as its brief the reformation of 'nominal Christians' from among the upper ranks, though ultimately one suspects its large sales were generated by supporters rather than potential converts. Offshoots vary between the adulatory and purely imitative, those offering alternative agendas, and the nakedly facetious. Amongst the more self-evident can be counted *Cœlebs Suited* (1809: 62), by a pseudonymous Sir George Rover, *Cœlebs in*

---

[81] Johnson, e.g., took space in the *Morning Post* for 8 Feb. 1810 to list Edgeworth's genuine works, in an effort to counter the spurious *Tales of Real Life*.

*Search of a Mistress* (1810: 7), which offers a free thinker's counter-version, and the epistolary *Sequel to Cœlebs* (1812: 14). Those preferring to track the basic marriage plot from a feminine viewpoint could choose between Robert Torrens's rationalist *Coelibia Choosing a Husband* (1809: 72), Jane Best's *Celia Suited, or the Rival Heiresses* (1810: 27), and William Mudford's *Nubilia in Search of a Husband* (1809: 53), which its author acknowledges having written in less than a month.

More generally, More's intervention encouraged a number of novels in the following years which can be broadly categorized as 'moral-evangelical' in character. Some hardly manage to develop further than their original programmatic intent: Henry Kett's *Emily, A Moral Tale* (1809: 37), for example, incorporates letters from a father to his daughter, guiding her proper religious development amid the perils of London society. In other hands, the mode presented fresh possibilities for psychological analysis and moral discrimination. Mary Brunton's *Self-Control: A Novel* (1811: 25) focuses on the inner struggles of its heroine in resisting an advantageous-seeming match, in spite of its being condoned by her dying father, on the grounds that her aristocratic suitor is and remains 'unprincipled'. Unusual in being managed by an Edinburgh concern, Manners and Miller, the success of this work in the south at first surprised the London publishers, Longmans, though shortages were soon to lead to a succession of new editions.[82] The pattern set by Brunton— whose second title, *Discipline: A Novel* (1814: 14), if anything casts a sterner air— led to a chain of similar morally charged domestic fictions, often discernible through their deliberately unadorned titles, these sometimes consisting only of single words reflecting moral qualities. Characteristic examples include: Amelia Opie's *Temper, or Domestic Scenes* (1812: 52), more obtrusively religious than any of her earlier works; Margaret Roberts's *Duty, A Novel* (1814: 47), which contains an obituary of the author by Opie, outlining her impeccable moral history as the daughter of a clergyman and clergyman's wife; and Anne Raikes Harding's *Correction. A Novel* (1818: 33), which was shortly followed by her *Decision. A Tale* (1819: 37), both publications being issued by Longmans. One noticeable feature of such works is the apparent willingness to employ the term 'Novel', even in conjunction with the most severe-sounding titles, which indicates a measure of rehabilitation for the form itself at this time; another is the relative scarcity of 'or' sub-titles, these perhaps being regarded as redundant by a newly 'serious' female readership, in addition to having associations with a more 'common' circulating-library fiction.

Jane Austen's later novels, especially *Mansfield Park* (1814: 11), share a number of interesting characteristics with this broad phenomenon, though Austen's

---

[82] See Longman Letter Books, I, 97, nos. 50, 86, 96, 150, 290, for a sequence of communications to Manners and Miller between 30 Mar. 1811 and 11 Feb. 1812. These describe accelerating sales in London, shortages of copies, and the pressing need for new editions. 750 is suggested as the 'proper number' on 30 Mar. 1811, 'a third edition of 1250' is demanded on 24 May 1811 (no. 86), and a new edition of '1250 as before' is called for on 22 Oct. 1811 (no. 150). The last letter in the sequence states: 'We have not had a copy to sell for some time.'

conservative Anglicanism (allied no doubt with other reservations) militated against any unequivocal avowal of the evangelical cause. On the other side of the spectrum, more severe evangelicals, such as those of the 'Clapham Sect', continued to hold deep suspicions about imaginative fiction of any kind, even when drawn by the thought of its potential usefulness as a means of promulgating ideas. As Zachary Macaulay observed, in a review of Edgeworth's *Tales of Fashionable Life* for the *Christian Observer*: 'every novel by an author of reputation is an object of solicitude to the guardians of the public morals. It is a work likely to pass through the hands of nine-tenths of the reading part of the community.'[83] The young Thomas Babington Macaulay, in his 'Observations on Novel Reading', which appeared in the December 1816 number of the same journal, showed greater leniency than his father when approving of both moral novels ('which may be read with considerable benefit') and religious novels ('which ought to be read'). Compared with these, he was careful to stress, 'bad novels' should be thrown in the fire, and 'the harmless and entertaining ... read but occasionally'. Even so, Macaulay's sixteen-year old enthusiasm for the latter category, especially those novels which offer 'spirited and striking descriptions of national manners and customs' (Scott's *Waverley* is the cited example), is still palpable and offers a useful indication of changing attitudes to fiction with a new generation.[84]

    This bibliography provides a fuller and firmer base against which to judge Scott's credentials as the 'father' of the modern historical novel. One noticeable feature is the large number of novels before the publication of *Waverley* in 1814 claiming through their titles to be historical fictions. In all the listings contain some fifty novels describing themselves as Historic/al Romances or (less commonly) Historical Novels in their title, of which half appeared before Scott's public appearance as a novelist. Rainer Schöwerling, in a fuller survey of the field, lists no less than 211 'pseudo-historical' novels before *Waverley*, of which 142 fall into the years 1800–1814, with noticeable bulges during the time of the second and third coalition war against France (1799–1802 and 1804–1808), and at the time of the wars in Spain and Portugal from 1808–1814.[85] Many of the earlier of these novels on examination prove to be little more than sentimental fictions in period costume, or are closer generically by modern standards to Gothic rather than standard Historical fiction. Some evidently use an historical setting as a thin disguise for retailing current scandalous matter. A number of others, however, quite clearly involve more genuine attempts to recreate the 'manners' of an earlier period, even when driven by a larger moralistic or patriotic purpose.

    A patriotic impulse is especially apparent in the panoramic fictions of the Porter

[83]  *Christian Observer*, 8 (Dec. 1809), 781.

[84]  *Christian Observer*, 15 (Dec. 1816), 784–5. Macaulay's essay was in response to an earlier, disapproving letter to the editor, Aug. 1815, under the same page-top heading, and signed 'A. A.'.

[85]  Rainer Schöwerling, 'Sir Walter Scott and the Tradition of the Historical Novel before 1814—With a Checklist', in Uwe Böker, *et al.* (eds.), *The Living Middle Ages: Studies in Medieval English Literature and its Tradition* (Stuttgart, 1989), pp. 227–62.

sisters, with their focus on national identities threatened by Napoleonic pan-Europeanism, as in Anna Maria Porter's *Don Sebastian; or, the House of Braganza. An Historical Romance* (1809: 60). Jane Porter's seminal *The Scottish Chiefs* (1810: 68), celebrating national resistance to tyranny and written at a time of notable successes by Highland troops in the Peninsular War, can also be seen as part of the same phenomenon. More deliberate attempts to recreate the public conflicts and domestic life of past eras are found in works such as Jane West's two late historical fictions, *The Loyalists: An Historical Novel* (1812: 64) and *Alicia de Lacy; An Historical Romance* (1814: 60), while a concern for distinctive 'manners' is manifest in Elizabeth Strutt's *The Borderers. An Historical Romance, illustrative of the Manners of the Fourteenth Century* (1812: 58), which as an addition provides informational end notes. In some instances, one senses the influence of Scott's poetical romances in this predominantly female-authored body of work. An opportunistic anonymous publication, *The Lady of the Lake: A Romance . . . Founded on the Poem so called by Walter Scott, Esq.* (1810: 12), actively highlighted such a connection. Issued by Thomas Tegg, a specialist in remainder sales, this might possibly have caught Scott's eyes when advertised in the Edinburgh papers in August 1810.[86] If so, it could well have helped galvanize him into turning to exploit the genre actively himself.

The large number of 'national' tales evident in the years 1808–1814 further complicates the issue of priority. In his own carefully constructed genealogy of the Waverley novels, Scott singled out the 'well-merited fame' of Maria Edgeworth as a leading encouragement for his resumption of *Waverley* in 1813.[87] Edgeworth's reputation as a novelist of Irish 'manners' stemmed primarily from the Irish stories in her *Tales of Fashionable Life*, notably 'Ennui' (1809) and 'The Absentee' (1812), and less obviously from *Castle Rackrent, An Hibernian Tale* (1800: 30), with its particular focus on issues relating to the Union of 1800. No mention is made by Scott of Sydney Owenson (by then Lady Morgan) whose reputation for Whig 'radicalism' had led to her severe treatment in the *Quarterly Review*.[88] Yet it was Owenson's *Wild Irish Girl* (1806: 54) which first employed the generic label 'A National Tale'; and it is this work that most obviously stands at the head of a sequence of 'Irish' titles found concentrated between 1808 and 1810. Examples include Maturin's *Wild Irish Boy* (1808: 75), a fairly evident spin-off, Henrietta Rouviere Mosse's *The Old Irish Baronet; or, Manners of My Country* (1808: 83), Theodore Melville's *The Irish Chieftain, and His Family* (1809: 49), John Agg's *Mac Dermot; or, the Irish Chieftain* (1810: 20), and Ann Mary Hamilton's *The Irishwoman in London* (1810: 49). Some

---

[86] This work was advertised as 'Arrived this morning' in the *Edinburgh Evening Courant*, 16 Aug. 1810; another advert appeared on 20 Sept. 1810.

[87] 'General Preface', *Waverley Novels*, 48 vols. (Edinburgh 1829–33), I, xii–xiii. See also Peter Garside, 'Popular Fiction and National Tale: Hidden Origins of Scott's *Waverley*', *Nineteenth-Century Literature*, 46 (1991), 30–53.

[88] In a review of *Woman: or, Ida of Athens* (1809: 55), QR, 1 (Feb. 1809), 50–2. The reviewer was Scott's friend, John Wilson Croker.

of these tales clearly pandered to a taste for comic Irishness, as no doubt did Charles Henry Wilson's *The Irish Valet; or, Whimsical Adventures of Paddy O'Haloran* (1811: 80); but others seriously addressed issues of Anglo-Irish relationships, while sometimes in the process offering appealing images of social cohesion and far-flung loyalty. The same years saw a number of 'English' tales, a new concern for regional manners being evident in titles such as Mary Linwood's *Leicestershire Tales* (1808: 73), Mary Ann Hanway's *Falconbridge Abbey. A Devonshire Story* (1809: 30), John Brewster's *Yorkshire Characters* (1810: 28), and John Hamilton Roche's *A Suffolk Tale* (1810: 69).

Less fully recognized than some of their Irish counterparts are a number of Scottish titles clustered in the years immediately before *Waverley*, almost exclusively by female authors. A debt to Elizabeth Hamilton's essentially didactic *The Cottagers of Glenburnie* (1808: 52) was acknowledged in the last-chapter 'Postscript' to *Waverley*, and there are reports of Scott having later admitted to George IV that Porter's *Scottish Chiefs* was 'the parent in his mind of the Waverley novels'.[89] No room has been found in literary history, however, for such works as *Caledonia; or, the Stranger in Scotland: A National Tale* (1810: 24), probably by Catherine Bayley, Sarah Wigley's *Glencarron: A Scottish Tale* (1811: 79), and a sequence of titles by Honoria Scott,[90] including *The Vale of Clyde: A Tale* (1810: 73) and *Strathmay: or Scenes in the North, illustrative of Scottish Manners* (1813: 54). Even after *Waverley*'s publication, two female writers implicitly questioned its claims to absolute precedence in the preliminaries to their apparently pre-empted novels. In the 'Advertisement' to *Clan-Albin: A National Tale* (1815: 32), Christian Isobel Johnstone asserted that 'the first half of this Tale was not only written but *printed*' long before Scott's 'animated' account had appeared and 'rendered a second journey all but hopeless'. Likewise, in the Preface to her *The Lairds of Glenfern* (1816: 37), Mary Johnston claimed that 'The whole of the first, and great part of the second volume, have been written nearly four years.' Notwithstanding such uncertainties, acknowledgments of indebtedness were rapidly to become the order of the day, Johnstone's dedication of the second edition of *Clan-Albin* 'To Walter Scott, Esq.' probably representing the first in a chain of such apparent acts of homage.

The extensiveness of Scott's influence is apparent in the high proportion of historical novels found in the 1820s, matching in some respects the dominance of the Gothic mode in the 1800s. One of the most prolific writers of historical romance in the earlier 1820s was Louisa Sidney Stanhope, whose previous output had included several standard Gothic fictions. Historical fictions by Stanhope include: *The Crusaders. An Historical Romance, of the Twelfth Century* (1820: 66), *The Festival of Mora. An Historical Romance* (1821: 68), *The Siege of Kenilworth. An Historical*

---

[89] Obituary notices of Porter containing this story are cited in Ann H. Jones, *Ideas and Innovations: Best Sellers of Jane Austen's Day* (New York, 1986), pp. 132–3, 302. See also A. D. Hook, 'Jane Porter, Sir Walter Scott, and the Historical Novel', *Clio*, 5 (1976), 181–92.

[90] For Honoria Scott's possible true identity as Susan Fraser, see 1810: 74 in the listings.

*Romance* (1824: 90), and *Runnemede. An Ancient Legend* (1825: 76). Later years however see the construction of a tighter-seeming, more 'professional' kind of historical novel, spearheaded by male writers, amongst whom can be counted Horatio Smith and (at the very edge of the period under view) G. P. R. James. Other generic regroupings in this period were acknowledged in the *Edinburgh* and *Quarterly* reviews, under composite headings such as 'Secondary Scottish Novels' (John Galt, J. G. Lockhart, and John Wilson) and 'Irish Novels' (the Banim brothers, Eyre Evans Crowe, and William Hamilton Maxwell), the chosen exponents almost invariably being male authors. An important shift occurs with the appearance in 1825 of three new-style fashionable novels, all hugely puffed by Henry Colburn: *Tremaine, or the Man of Refinement* (1825: 85), by Robert Plumer Ward; *Matilda; A Tale of the Day* (1825: 66), by Constantine Henry Phipps, later Marquis of Normanby; and (albeit with a post-dated imprint) Thomas Henry Lister's *Granby. A Novel* (1826: 51). These works triggered the craze for 'silver fork' fiction, which was soon to involve also a number of female authors, such as Lady Charlotte Bury and Marianne Spencer Hudson (née Stanhope), as well as the inevitable imitations from Leadenhall Street.

The male invasion of mainstream fiction is even more pronounced with a wave of nautical–military titles, first fully apparent in 1826. By 1829 these had become virtually the most dominant single mode, with titles that year including George Robert Gleig's *The Chelsea Pensioners* (1829: 35), William Hamilton Maxwell's *Stories of Waterloo* (1829: 60), Joseph Moyle Sherer's *Tales of the Wars of our Times* (1829: 77), and Frederick Marryat's *The Naval Officer* (1829: 59). The transitions evident at this point are striking, and reflect more profound changes in the authorship, production, and readership of fiction.

## (5) Authors

This volume lists novels under some 870 different author names. Of these 40 are actual or probable pseudonyms, several of which effectively operated as recognized author names (for example, Rosalia St Clair and Anthony Frederick Holstein). Also included in the listings are some 60 translators, of whom almost a third were also original authors. As a whole then the bibliography records the output of over 900 distinguishable authors and translators involved in the production of fiction from 1800 to 1829, a figure which would no doubt expand beyond 1,000 if the writers of a hard residue of unidentified titles were also known.

The authors identified range from some of the most prolific in the history of fiction to others whose single title in the bibliography probably represents their only published work. More than 500 authors have only one entry in this volume; nearly 90 published five or more titles within the time span covered; and 18 stand out by having produced 10 or more original titles. Table 4 lists the amount of original novels produced by these 18 most productive authors in the period, with the total number of volumes per author in the following column.

Table 4. **Most Productive Authors of Novels, 1800–1829**

| Authors | Novels | Volumes |
|---|---|---|
| Scott, Sir Walter | 22 | 71 |
| Hofland, Barbara | 21 | 46 |
| Meeke, Mary [a] | 19 | 70 |
| Lafontaine, August | 18 | 49 |
| Lathom, Francis | 17 | 50 |
| Genlis, Stéphanie | 17 | 40[b] |
| Ward, Catherine George | 17 | 24[c] |
| Galt, John | 16 | 28 |
| Green, Sarah[d] | 15 | 43 |
| Stanhope, Louisa | 14 | 52 |
| Hatton, Anne | 13 | 60 |
| Holstein, Anthony | 12 | 41 |
| Harvey, Jane | 12 | 37 |
| Mosse, Henrietta R. | 11[e] | 40 |
| Roche, Regina Maria | 11[f] | 39 |
| Opie, Amelia | 11[g] | 31 |
| Thomas, Elizabeth | 10 | 33 |
| Porter, Anna Maria | 10[h] | 32 |

(a)  count excludes 4 translations (13 vols.).
(b)  includes 2-vol. version of *Petrarch and Laura* (1820: 28[b]), instead of
      1-vol. version.
(c)  includes 11 large 1-vol. serialised works.
(d)  count excludes 1 translation (2 vols.).
(e)  includes 1 questionable work (4 vols.).
(f)  includes 1 questionable work (2 vols.).
(g)  includes 2 newly attributed works (4 vols.).
(h)  excludes 2 works co-authored with Jane Porter (5 vols.).

Not surprisingly, Scott—whose output was considered phenomenal by contemporaries—stands at the head with 22 novels in 71 volumes. All these works, furthermore, were published within the last 16 years covered by this volume (his last original work of fiction, the 4th series of *Tales of My Landlord*, appeared in 1831). Yet Scott is not without his challengers, and the table noticeably includes a number of highly prolific female authors. Operating at the other end of the market, writing exclusively for the Minerva Press, Mary Meeke is almost as productive with 19 works in 70 volumes, all published between 1800 and 1823. Moreover, if four translated works by Meeke (in 13 volumes) are added, then her overall output exceeds Scott, the margin becoming wider still if seven novels of hers written before 1800 also enter into calculations. The list of Barbara Hofland's in-period fiction would likewise expand beyond the 21 entries in this volume to overtake Scott, at least in terms of number of titles produced, if her children's books were included. Other productive Minerva authors, in addition to Meeke, include Anne Hatton ('Anne of Swansea'), the pseudonymous Holstein, Henrietta Rouviere Mosse, Regina Maria Roche, Louisa Sidney Stanhope, and Elizabeth Thomas, with Francis Lathom representing the only clear known male in this grouping. Madame de Genlis and August Lafontaine stand out as by far the most productive and popular of translated authors, the publication of Lafontaine's 18 titles (10 by Minerva) between 1802 to 1813 representing an especially concentrated output.

Among prolific authors operating outside the Minerva circle can be counted Amelia Opie and Anna Maria Porter, both essentially Longman authors. Sarah Green and Jane Harvey moved between publishers, though never quite left Minerva. John Galt, matching Scott's output in the early 1820s (to the point of producing like him three titles bearing 1822 imprints), began with Henry Colburn, became a regular of the house of Blackwood, but then for a while moved to the rival Edinburgh firm of Oliver and Boyd. Catherine George Ward's output shifted in direction most dramatically of all, from the production of regular novels, mainly with Minerva, to the writing of serialized fiction in weekly parts, which were then sold separately usually in large single volumes. Ward under the name Mason continued as a prolific writer in this new mode, with some 20 novels and six works of poetry to 1833. Newly emergent writers whose output began late in the 1820s, and whose representation is therefore limited in the present volume, include W. H. Ainsworth, Edward Bulwer Lytton, Catherine Gore, and Frederick Marryat. Nearer the beginning of the listings will likewise be found the last works of some of the more productive novelists of the later eighteenth century, among them Eliza Parsons and Charlotte Smith.

One of the advantages of the documentation provided by this bibliography, in particular its full transcription of title-page details, is that it allows a better view than has been previously available of the ways in which authors were projected at their readership when their novels were originally published. Mary Meeke can be seen to have chiefly alternated between acknowledging herself as 'Mrs Meeke' and the use of the pseudonym 'Gabrielli' (though two works attributed to her are anonymous). This effectively created two chains of writing, partly motivated perhaps by a desire to avoid the appearance of over-production. In contrast, all Francis Lathom's novels carried his own name, the main differences between title-pages lying in the amount of works given as 'by the author': a generally accumulative process, reaching its highest point with *Puzzled and Pleased* (1822: 53), which lists fourteen such titles on its title-page. Barbara Hofland's first work of fiction was published anonymously, and all but one of her next seven fictions followed the 'by the author of . . .' pattern (the exception is the use of the pseudonym 'An Old-Fashioned Englishman' for 1812: 37). With *A Visit to London* (1814: 34), however, the authorship of 'Mrs. Hofland' was acknowledged fully on the title-page, a procedure usually followed thereafter, and carried over to the long sequence of her works published by Longmans in the 1820s.

Walter Scott—whose part ownership of the press where his novels were printed gave him an unusual degree of control—effectively constructed several distinct strands within his own *œuvre*. Thus the *Tales of My Landlord* series, by an obviously pseudonymous 'Jedidiah Cleishbotham', could run parallel with works by 'the author of *Waverley*', albeit with enough clues left in place for an overall kinship to be recognizable. In the case of less powerful authors, however, it was frequently the publisher who called the tune. For Maturin's *Women; or, Pour et Contre* (1818: 41) Archibald Constable strongly recommended 'by the author of "Bertram"', preferring to highlight a celebrated drama instead of the author's name (which had not appeared on any previous novels by Maturin).[91] Longmans, on the other hand, were insistent that James Hogg's name should appear on the title-page of *The Three Perils of Man* (1822: 44),[92] in spite of the appeals of a Scott-like anonymity to its author. It is also noticeable that all four of Hogg's acknowledged novels (though three different publishers were involved) prominently display the poem *The Queen's Wake*, his one unquestionable literary success, as a work by the author.

Nevertheless, the general tendency during the period as a whole was towards anonymity. Of the 2,256 titles in this volume, almost a half were anonymous when first published, with only some 970 carrying the author's name on the title-page (or a description full enough to point to the identity of the true author), and a further 190 titles being issued pseudonymously. Of the 1,100 or so anonymous titles, less than 350 offer some measure of identification by listing a previous work or works by the author, with the remainder providing no sign of a previous track record, though very infrequently they might offer descriptive indications of gender and/or social status ('By a Lady', etc.). There are fairly apparent reasons why authors themselves should wish to remain anonymous. Some women writers clearly felt a threat to their respectability in openly acknowledging authorship, especially at a time when the status of fiction was low. According to Elizabeth Sarah Villa-Real Gooch, in the Preface to her *Sherwood Forest* (1804: 21): 'An acknowledged Novel-writer is, perhaps, one of the most difficult names to support with credit and reputation.' Prefatory materials in novels by women writers also abound in anxious references to anticipated unfavourable criticism, and anonymity at least offered some measure of protection from public humiliation at the hands of the predominantly male reviewers. Even Amelia Opie, operating virtually as a semi-professional writer, evidently felt unease in appearing 'as an avowed Author at the bar of public opinion' with her first acknowledged work of fiction (see 1801: 54). And Sarah Wilkinson, notwithstanding many a novel and chapbook behind her, still gives the impression of consciously breaking ranks when acknowledging 'profit' as a main motive, in the Preface to *The Spectre of Lanmere Abbey* (1820: 70): 'Knowing

---

[91] NLS, MS 789, p. 830 (Constable to Maturin, 8 Aug. 1817).
[92] 'we would wish to have your name in the Title' (to Hogg, 18 Oct. 1821, Longman Letter Books, I, 101, no. 174C).

how eager the fair sex are for something *new* and *romantic*, I determined on an attempt to *please* my fair sisterhood, hoping to *profit* myself thereby.'

Male authors too evidently had their own reasons for remaining anonymous. In the earlier period, fear of association with a predominantly female mode might possibly have played a part. Certainly Anna Maria Mackenzie appears to acknowledge the existence of such a disincentive in the Preface to her *The Irish Guardian* (1809: 45): 'The Author perceives she cannot conclude without paying a feeble tribute of praise to those male writers, who have thought it no degradation of their dignity . . . to . . . improve and amuse in the form of a novel.' Other male writers might have wished to avoid compromising their professional life. This is one of several possible reasons for anonymity given in the Preface of the third edition (1814) of Scott's *Waverley*, others there including the unwillingness of a new author to risk an avowal, the fear of a 'hackneyed author' of making too frequent appearances, and the snobbish fears of a man of fashion—none of the above approaching too closely Scott's own true situation! Undoubtedly Scott's own example did much to help create a cult of anonymity in the 1820s, with the somewhat contradictory result that as the novel's reputation improved acknowledged authors became less in evidence.

Again, publishers appear to have had a major hand in determining trends. An interesting case history is provided by two historical romances written by Anna Eliza Bray, both with 1828 imprints. *The White Hoods* (1828: 22), the first to appear, and published by Longmans, has a full author description on the title-page, further elaborated by reference to Bray's previous identity as Mrs Charles Stothard. *The Protestant* (1828: 21), on the other hand, for which Henry Colburn outbid Longmans, bears no description other than authorship of her two earlier novels. During the 1820s Longmans produced 43 novels by female writers, of which 30 name the author on the title-page. Colburn in contrast published 17 novels by women in the same period, though only in three exceptional cases—a translation of Genlis's *Petrarch and Laura* (1820: 28 [b]), Lady Morgan's *The O'Briens and the O'Flahertys* (1827: 54), and Ann Radcliffe's posthumously published *Gaston de Blondeville* (1826: 66)—was a direct author description given. Whereas Longmans were still promoting regular female writers, and in the case of the *White Hoods* also probably had in mind a number of cousin 'Stothard' titles, Colburn, himself by now far more heavily committed to male writers, was more interested in creating a kind of mystique by not naming his authors. As these instances suggest, a number of factors could affect procedure in any individual case. As a whole, however, an increasing tendency towards anonymity is apparent in the 1820s. In 1829, no less than 66 out of a total 81 novels were published without any direct author name on the title-page. This contrasts with 35 cases where the author's name is given out of an equal number of new novels produced in 1800, at which time it might have seemed that the general tendency was towards acknowledged novels.

On the other hand, any count of anonymity based on first edition title-pages is bound to underestimate the degree to which authors were known during the period. Word of mouth obviously played a part in revealing the authorship of a number of talked-about successes. Mary Brunton's identity, for example, was evidently well known before her official public 'outing' by her husband, through the 'Memoir of Her Life' prefixed to the posthumously published *Emmeline* (1819: 28). As Walter Scott had written to Lady Abercorn on 18 September 1811: 'The authoress of Selfcontroul is the wife of a Revd Mr. Brunton a clergyman in Edinburgh; at least that seems the admitted report.'[93] Scott himself was widely mentioned as the author of the Waverley novels long before the financial disasters of 1825–1826 necessitated his claiming the works.[94] Occasionally, full author names are found within a novel—as in a signed Preface, or through the inclusion of an engraved portrait or additional title-page—when the main title-page offers no direct authorial description. Augusta Ann Hirst's *Helen; or Domestic Occurrences* (1807: 28), for example, carries only the bare title on its title-page, though the full author's name appears immediately afterwards in a Dedication to the Countess Fitzwilliam, and the author's name later featured directly on the title-page in the Minerva reissue of 1808. Of some twenty such cases discovered, the majority involve female authors, several of whom no doubt contrived by this process to place their mark in their novel while avoiding a more open public acknowledgment.[95]

Additionally, the fairly common procedure of an author's name appearing after several earlier works had been written anonymously could have the effect of identifying the earlier titles (which, if reprinted, would then be likely to bear the author's name). Later editions of a single work too sometimes reveal an author's name, no doubt as the result of confidence having been gained through the initial success. An example will be found in the case of W. Clayton's *The Invisible Hand* (1815: 19), which closely identified the author in its second edition through a combination of title-page ascription and a dedication to the author's mother. The third edition of *Anastasius* (1819: 42) has a signed Dedication by Thomas Hope, the true author, effectively countering widespread reports that the novel had been written by Lord Byron (which in the interim must have hugely benefited sales). Reviews could also disclose a novel's authorship, the *Monthly Review* for example identifying 'Miss Cullen, a native of the northern part of our island' as 'the fair writer' of *Home.*

---

[93] *Letters of Scott*, ed. Grierson, III, 2.

[94] As by Jane Austen, in response to *Waverley*, 28 Sept. 1814: 'Walter Scott has no business to write novels, especially good ones' (Le Faye (ed.), *Jane Austen's Letters*, p. 277). Even after Scott's avowal of authorship in 1827, the Waverley novels continued to be published without his name, the only exception being the signed Introduction to *Chronicles of the Canongate* (see 1827: 63).

[95] For further examples where names appear in prefaces etc., but are absent on the title-page, see: 1801: 72, 1804: 68, 1809: 79, 1813: 19, 1814: 17, 1815: 21, 1816: 23, 1816: 44, 1818: 25, 1821: 53, 1821: 69, 1824: 71, 1825: 27, 1826: 52. Such cases are not counted as instances of 'named' authorship for the purposes of analysis in this Introduction, but clearly represent an interesting middle ground between anonymity and acknowledged authorship.

*A Novel* (1802: 21).[96] In the case of John Moore's *Mordaunt* (1800: 56), 'by the author Zeluco & Edward', the *Monthly*'s review has the page-top heading 'Moore's *Mordaunt*' and refers throughout to 'Dr. Moore' as the author; just as the *Edinburgh Review* was later to describe *The Wanderer* (1814: 17) in its header as 'by Madame D'Arblay', though strictly speaking its title-page mentions only 'the author of Evelina, Cecilia, and Camilla'. Advertisements, as well as circulating library catalogues, could likewise disclose the authorship of ostensibly anonymous titles. *Strathmay: or Scenes in the North* (1813: 54), 'by the author of A Winter in Edinburgh [etc.]' includes opposite its title-page a list of five novels just brought out by its publishers, including 'A Winter in Edinburgh . . . by Honoria Scott', thus effectively naming the author of the present title (or at least her pseudonym). Moreover, at least one case has been discovered where a surviving contemporary spine label provides an author's name not found on the title-page (see Appendix A: 3).

The present volume identifies the authorship of almost twice as many novels as were directly acknowledged on first publication. In all some 1,780 novels are attributed to an author; while a further 75 appear in the listings under a pseudonym—or probable pseudonym—in lieu of an identified true author. At the same time, a remaining hard core of 400 or so titles resist satisfactory identification, and are hence listed under 'Anon[ymous]'. Attributions have necessarily been inherited from a variety of secondary sources, to the extent that in some cases it is difficult to trace the precise origin of an identification. Great care nevertheless has been taken to verify authorship, especially in circumstances where contrary information is given, and in a significant number of cases accepted attributions have been rejected. In some instances wrong ascriptions can be traced back to the original publishers. Four novels published by the Minerva Press under the name of Pigault-Lebrun, and widely catalogued as translations of his work, are in fact based on original French novels by Charles Augustin de Bassompierre Sewrin (see 1804: 60, 61, 62, 63). In view of the greater marketability of Pigault-Lebrun's name, it is difficult here not to suspect an element of deliberate deception. On other occasions, genuine errors seem to have taken place in the general disorder and rush to complete. A notable instance is the Minerva Press's title-page attribution of Amelia Beauclerc's *Eva of Cambria; or, the Fugitive Daughter* (1811: 19) to Emma de Lisle [the pseudonym of Emma Parker]: a mistake which might well have gone unrecorded, and led to further misattributions, had not Emma Parker described the circumstances in the Preface of her *Fitz-Edward; or, the Cambrians* (see 1811: 65).

On other occasions, the desire to boost a novel's credentials apparently involved both authors and publishers in extending the list of titles 'by the author' beyond the bounds of veracity. This kind of licence probably helps explain a complicated chain of some twenty novels, stretching between *The Aunt and the Niece* (1804: 3) and

---

[96] MR, n.s. 41 (May 1803), 102.

*The Revealer of Secrets* (1817: 8)—the latter 'by the author of Eversfield Abbey, Banks of the Wye, Aunt and Niece, Substance and Shadow &c. &c.'—components of which have since been variously and implausibly attributed to Mrs E. M. Foster, J. H. James, or Mrs E. G. Bayfield. If the shadowy Mrs E. M. Foster is a linking factor, then it would involve an authorship stretching from 1795 to 1817, with a number of unexplained breaks in the sequence of connection. The involvement of the last two authors evidently results from more localized mistakes. A confusion between *A Winter in Bath* (1807: 7), 'by the author of two popular novels' and one of the titles involved in the chain, and Mrs E. G. Bayfield's *A Winter at Bath* (1807: 9), opportunistically re-titled by its publisher from *Love As It May Be*, almost certainly represents the sole reason why Mrs Bayfield's 'chaste pen' ever became associated with this sequence. Likewise 'J. H. James' probably enters into the equation only as a result of a similarity in title between *The Banks of the Wye* (1808: 1), another key link in the chain, and *The Banks of the Wye; and Other Poems* (1856), by the mid-Victorian barrister-poet James Henry James. In the absence of any alternative author, even for parts of the chain, all these novels are entered as anonymous in the present listings.

The disentangling of other confusions caused by similarly titled works has led to a number of titles being rescued from false author attributions. Modern cataloguers have struggled bravely, though not always successfully, to distinguish three works of fiction titled *Decision* which came out within fifteen years of each other: *The Decision; A Novel* (1811: 6), 'by the author of Caroline Ormsby'; *Decision. A Tale* (1819: 37), by Anne Raikes Harding; and Barbara Hofland's *Decision. A Tale* (1824: 48). Yet it is the presence of another *The Decision* (1821), a first work by Grace Kennedy written in the form of a play, which has created the greatest difficulty in this area. The title-page description of *Willoughby; or Reformation* (1823: 17) as 'by the author of "The Decision", "Caroline Ormsby" [etc.]' has led to this novel and three associated titles (see 1810: 1, 1810: 6, and 1811: 6) being wrongly attributed to Kennedy in a number of catalogues. A similar instance will be found in the case of titles wrongly attributed to Ann Yosy, through an apparent confusion between her non-fictional *Switzerland* (1815) and *Tales from Switzerland* (1822: 12), the latter the first of a sequence of probably male-authored evangelical fictions (see 1823: 1, 1824: 13).

Arguably the most considerable authorial unravelling that has been achieved concerns the figure of Mrs Ross, whose output if previous attributions were to be accepted would place her as one of the most productive authors in the period. According to the entry in the *Feminist Companion to Literature in English* (1990), this 'obscure but remarkable author' produced 'at least 13 novels and groups of stories, 1811–25'.[97] Viewed together, however, this body of work reveals two quite separate sequences, the first seven titles with imprints from 1811 to 1817 all being published by the Minerva Press, and the second sequence consisting of titles

---

[97]  Blain *et al.*, *Feminist Companion*, p. 922.

published by Longmans between 1817 and 1825. The dividing point occurs with two novels which viewed casually might give the impression of being companion works: *The Balance of Comfort; or the Old Maid and Married Woman* (1817: 50), bearing Mrs Ross's name and post-dated from 1816, and *The Bachelor and the Married Man, or the Equilibrium of the "Balance of Comfort"* (1817: 37), published anonymously and whose title provides the main link with the succeeding five titles. Closer examination of these two novels not only reveals a number of stylistic and presentational dissimilarities, but also points to basic ideological differences (a much stronger religious bent is evident in the latter). Nor is there much in *The Bachelor and the Married Man* to indicate that it was written as a counter-title, apart from a final passing reference, and it is not unlikely that Longmans suggested the title at a late stage, encouraged by the way in which Mrs Ross's title had caught the public imagination. In this case the Longman Letter Books have helped resolve the issue (see 1817: 37), the true author of the novels in the second sequence almost certainly being Elizabeth B. Lester, whose only directly acknowledged novel was the Opie-esque *The Quakers; A Tale* (1817: 38).

In addition to cancelling false ascriptions, the listings contain a significant number of other new attributions. Several discoveries have been made through evidence found within novels themselves, often in rare or unique copies. The discovery of Mary Tuck's authorship of *Durston Castle* through its signed Address to Mrs Crespigny has already been mentioned. A comparable case is found with *The Castles of Marsange & Nuger* (1809: 79), where another signed Dedication points to the involvement of a previously unknown Henrietta Maria Young, though an element of uncertainty remains over the degree to which Young operated as a translator or original author. Comparison between the possibly unique Corvey copy of *Maids As They are Not* (1803: 70), 'by Mrs. Martha Homely', and the rare Yale copy of *The Three Old Maids of the House of Penruddock* (1806: 66), which includes an Introduction signed 'Martha Homely', indicates that the first title almost certainly constitutes the earliest novel written by Elizabeth Thomas—whose more usual pseudonym was Mrs Bridget Bluemantle. Reissues can also lead to a previously unrecognized authorship. The second and third volumes of the Bodleian copy of *A Set-Down at Court* (1812: 20), both reissues with an 1816 imprint, describe the author as 'Mrs Bayley' rather than (as in the first volume) 'Kate Mont Albion', this suggesting the possibility of an authorship by Catharine Bayley, and potentially unlocking in turn two previous novels written under the Montalbion pseudonym.

Archival materials have also encouraged a number of fresh attributions. The Longman Letter Books, as well as disclosing Elizabeth Lester's contribution, also point strongly to John Phillips's authorship of *Lionel: or, the Last of the Pevenseys* (1818: 50). One of the titles claimed by Louisa Theresa Bellenden Ker in her various appeals to the Royal Literary Fund was *Manfroné; or, the One-Handed Monk* (1809: 61), this opening up the possibility that 'Mary Anne Radcliffe' as found here is a manufactured name, and also in turn leading to Ker's possible authorship of the virtually unknown *Ida of Austria; or the Knights of the Holy Cross* (1812: 53), 'by the author of "Manfrone"'.[98] The archives of the Royal Literary Fund also reveal Mary Julia Young to be the translator, rather than original author, of *The Mother and Daughter, A Pathetic Tale* (see 1804: 12), though the title itself is an obvious spin-off from Amelia Opie's *The Father and Daughter*. On the basis of surviving correspondence, Opie's own *œuvre* is extended by two titles which might possibly be hers: *The Only Child; or, Portia Bellenden. A Tale* (1821: 61) and *Much to Blame, A Tale* (1824: 73), the latter ('by a Celebrated Author') appearing two years after her last acknowledged novel, *Madeline, A Tale* (1822: 60).

In spite of remaining elements of uncertainty, such as the possibility that some 'real' author names are in fact pseudonyms, the present bibliography offers the fullest base yet available against which to judge the gender distribution of authorship during this period. Table 5 gives a numerical breakdown employing three divisions within gender: (i) 'named', which applies to cases where the author appeared on the title-page; (ii) 'identified', referring to cases where a work appeared anonymously or pseudonymously, but where the author has since been identified; and (iii) 'implied', which relates to unidentified pseudonyms and gender-implicit tags such as 'By a Lady' or 'By a Bengal Officer'.[99] In all, novels by named/identified/ implied female authors outnumber those by their male counterparts by 979 (43.4 per cent) to 899 (39.8 per cent), with a residue of 378 (16. 8 per cent) titles resisting adequate gender identification.

---

[98]   See 1809: 61. For the existence of a real Mary Ann(e) Radcliffe (*c*.1746-*post* 1810?), feminist writer and the possible author of novels in the 1790s, see Joanne Shattock, *The Oxford Guide to British Women Writers* (Oxford, 1993), pp. 352–3. However, later residence in Edinburgh and the publication in 1809 of *Manfroné* by J. F. Hughes sit uneasily together. Hughes himself was not averse to using authorial names likely to be confused with well-known novelists—witness the case of 'Caroline Burney', an apparently invented name which led to protests by Henry Colburn (see 1809: 14, 1812: 24). On the other hand, it should be observed that some of Ker's other claims to authorship of novels appear to be somewhat stretched (see 1803: 29, 1804: 52).

[99]   In the last category, some allowance perhaps should be made for the possibility that pseudonyms and gender-implicit tags might disguise the true gender of the author. As a whole, however, little evidence of gender switching of this kind has been discovered during the period. Mary Meeke's pseudonym of Gabrielli appears to have been intended to indicate an Italianate Gothic flavour rather than simply maleness as such. Barbara Hofland's use of 'an Old-Fashioned Englishman' for her *Says She to her Neighbour, What?* (1812: 37) should be seen in connection with the success enjoyed by Edward Nares's *Think's-I-To-Myself* (1811: 59), which encouraged a number of spin-offs (e.g. 1812: 6). 'Geoffry Jarvis' and 'Peregrine Rover', found in the preliminaries of (respectively) Elizabeth Hamilton's *Memoirs of Modern Philosophers* (1800: 39) and Eliza Logan's *St Johnstoun* (1823: 58), are both fairly evident pseudonyms, the first being quickly exploded and the latter manifestly in the spirit of Scott's comic personas. Claims in the reviews that Sarah Green must be a male author, since no woman could have experienced such a variety of scenes, reflect more on the male reviewers' lack of vision than on the Green's own credentials (see 1810: 45). Nevertheless the possibility (though faint) that a 'Bengal Officer' is a lady and 'A Lady' is a Bengal officer necessarily remains, a factor which provides one reason for keeping pseudonyms and gender-implicit tags in a special 'implied' category.

Table 5. **Authorship of New Novels by Gender, 1800–1829**

| Imprint Year | Female | | | Male | | | Unknown | Total New Titles |
|---|---|---|---|---|---|---|---|---|
| | Named | Identified | Implied | Named | Identified | Implied | | |
| 1800 | 17 | 18 | 4 | 18 | 10 | — | 14 | 81 |
| 1801 | 27 | 14 | 2 | 13 | 4 | 1 | 11 | 72 |
| 1802 | 17 | 10 | 1 | 12 | 6 | 2 | 13 | 61 |
| 1803 | 18 | 14 | 1 | 27 | 8 | — | 11 | 79 |
| 1804 | 22 | 6 | 2 | 21 | 11 | 3 | 8 | 73 |
| 1805 | 22 | 9 | 3 | 23 | 6 | — | 12 | 75 |
| 1806 | 24 | 11 | 2 | 15 | 4 | 2 | 12 | 70 |
| 1807 | 24 | 7 | — | 18 | 7 | 6 | 7 | 69 |
| 1808 | 34 | 15 | 1 | 28 | 6 | 7 | 20 | 111 |
| 1809 | 22 | 13 | 2 | 20 | 6 | 5 | 11 | 79 |
| *1800s* | *227* | *117* | *18* | *195* | *68* | *26* | *119* | *770* |
| % | *29.5* | *15.2* | *2.3* | *25.3* | *8.8* | *3.4* | *15.5* | |
| 1810 | 27 | 16 | 6 | 13 | 6 | 3 | 18 | 89 |
| 1811 | 21 | 13 | 3 | 21 | 9 | 2 | 11 | 80 |
| 1812 | 12 | 21 | — | 6 | 5 | 5 | 17 | 66 |
| 1813 | 25 | 12 | 1 | 10 | 6 | 3 | 6 | 63 |
| 1814 | 22 | 17 | 1 | 7 | 6 | 3 | 5 | 61 |
| 1815 | 18 | 6 | — | 7 | 6 | 4 | 13 | 54 |
| 1816 | 20 | 11 | — | 5 | 9 | 1 | 13 | 59 |
| 1817 | 22 | 8 | — | 4 | 9 | 3 | 9 | 55 |
| 1818 | 16 | 11 | 3 | 5 | 10 | 4 | 13 | 62 |
| 1819 | 22 | 8 | 2 | 7 | 11 | 1 | 22 | 73 |
| *1810s* | *205* | *123* | *16* | *85* | *77* | *29* | *127* | *662* |
| % | *31.0* | *18.6* | *2.4* | *12.8* | *11.6* | *4.4* | *19.2* | |
| 1820 | 16 | 6 | 4 | 16 | 17 | — | 11 | 70 |
| 1821 | 17 | 8 | 1 | 16 | 14 | 3 | 16 | 75 |
| 1822 | 17 | 9 | 2 | 12 | 25 | 2 | 15 | 82 |
| 1823 | 17 | 10 | — | 11 | 29 | 2 | 18 | 87 |
| 1824 | 23 | 15 | 2 | 13 | 32 | 2 | 12 | 99 |
| 1825 | 10 | 13 | — | 19 | 33 | 2 | 14 | 91 |
| 1826 | 13 | 13 | 1 | 8 | 35 | — | 7 | 77 |
| 1827 | 11 | 14 | 3 | 7 | 31 | 1 | 12 | 79 |
| 1828 | 10 | 15 | 1 | 7 | 32 | 3 | 15 | 83 |
| 1829 | 6 | 15 | 1 | 9 | 38 | — | 12 | 81 |
| *1820s* | *140* | *118* | *15* | *118* | *286* | *15* | *132* | *824* |
| % | *17.0* | *14.3* | *1.8* | *14.3* | *34.7* | *1.8* | *16.1* | |
| Total | *572* | *358* | *49* | *398* | *431* | *70* | *378* | *2,256* |
| % | *25.3* | *15.9* | *2.2* | *17.6* | *19.1* | *3.1* | *16.8* | |

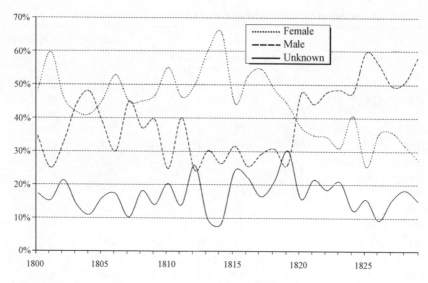

Fig. 2. **Authorship of New Novels, 1800–1829: Gender Breakdown**

Figure 2 provides a supplementary view of this broad gender breakdown in percentage rather than numerical terms. As this illustrates, from a high level inherited from the 1790s, the female line of authorship rises to a brief peak in 1801 (reflecting 43 female- as opposed to 18 male-authored titles), but then descends to become entangled with the male line in 1803–1804 (when male titles outnumber female by 70 to 63). It ascends again in 1805–1806 (71 female works as opposed to 50 male titles), briefly touches the male line again in 1807 (31 titles by males and female authors alike), but then rises again in 1808–1809 (87 female titles, 72 by males). As a whole in the 1800s, 362 female-authored works outnumber 289 novels by males, with 119 gender unknown titles. Female titles that originally carried the name of the author, at the same time, roughly match as a proportion the total named male titles (29.5 per cent female named, 25.3 per cent male named). The overall numerical balance noticeably moves more strongly in favour of female writers if foreign translated works are excluded from the calculation, in which case 320 female-authored titles clearly outweigh some 220 native male equivalents.

The 1810s show an even clearer pattern of female dominance, with women novelists out-producing their male counterparts in every year, and accounting for over 50 per cent of titles in six of the eight years between 1810 and 1817. Male-authored works in contrast hover awkwardly around the 30 per cent mark between 1812 and 1819, with the lowest year in percentage terms (24.2 per cent) occurring in 1812. In numerical terms female-authored works outnumber those by male authors by two-to-one or more in years 1810 (49 female titles, 22 male), 1812 (33, 16), 1813 (38, 19), 1814 (40, 16), and 1816 (31, 15). Another surprising feature of the 1810s is the high proportion of novels by named female authors, representing 31 per cent of total output, this increased proportion noticeably overshadowing male named novels, themselves reduced to less than 13 per cent. As these figures indicate, the *publication* of Jane Austen's novels was achieved not against the grain but during a period of female ascendancy. It is noticeable too that Scott's earliest historical novels were launched when male authorship of fiction was at a lower than usual ebb. The full tally for this decade as a whole is 344 female—as opposed to 191 male-authored works, with 127 gender unknown titles.

The tendency in the 1820s generally reverses what is evident in the 1810s. Novels by male authors now outnumber their female counterparts by 419 to 273, with 132 gender unknown cases, the male category thus claiming more than half (50.8 per cent) the total number of titles. A resurgence is immediately apparent in 1820, with male titles out-numbering female ones by 33 to 26, this year being the first to show a clear male pre-dominance since 1804. This new level is sustained for the following three years, with 114 male-authored works outnumbering 81 by women writers, though in 1824 a measure of equivalence returns, with 40 female titles almost balancing 47 by males. However, for 1825 imprints the balance again shifts dramatically, with twice as many novels by men compared with women (54 to 23). And in 1829, perhaps an unusual year, 47 male-authored works outweigh 22 female ones (with 12 gender unknown). One salient feature in this decade is the high proportion (nearly 35 per cent of total output) of novels by 'identified' male writers, whose works were originally published anonymously, with the number of novels by named female authors shrinking at the same time to scarcely 17 per cent. Another significant factor is the disproportionate 'maleness' of novels written and produced in Scotland at this time, with only 14 of 95 titles managed by Edinburgh publishers in the 1820s originating from identifiable women writers.

Clues to the gender of authors of unidentified anonymous works are occasionally found in prefatory materials, as when the author refers to 'her pen'. This information has been added in the notes of entries, when discovered, but is not considered firm or consistent enough evidence to determine gender for the purposes of the breakdown given above. From a fairly small number of such instances found, indirect female indications of authorship outnumber male equivalents by about two to one, with the proportion increasing in their favour if 'by the author of' title connections are followed through. Clearly there are female writers waiting to be discovered. A tantalizing glimpse, for example, is found in Maria Edgeworth's reference to widowed Mrs Blair, who had fallen on hard times after the financial ruin of her husband: 'She now writes novels if not for bread for butter.'[100] In the first twenty years under view there appears to be a greater likelihood that novels whose gender origin is indeterminate were written by women rather than men, though in the 1820s the cult of male anonymity must also be taken into consideration.

A clearer snapshot, though of a more specialist nature, is provided by novels

---

[100] Maria Edgeworth, *Letters from England, 1813–44*, ed. Christina Colvin (Oxford, 1971), p. 173 (4 Mar. 1819).

containing subscription lists, where authors are nearly always declared. As a whole this volume includes and describes 69 novels with such lists, a figure which exceeds the number of titles listed in existing published records of subscription literature.[101] Of the 34 titles which fall in the 1800s, 27 can be attributed to female authors, and six to male authors, with one uncertain case. In the 1810s, from 24 instances, 18 clear female titles again outmatch five male subscription novels.[102] But in the 1820s the balance shifts, with six titles by male writers outnumbering five female subscription novels. Granted that female writers are likely to have attracted more sympathy as objects of charity, and bearing in mind the special attractions of this method for women, who were likely to have experienced greater difficulty in approaching publishers without support, the balancing out to a more even situation in the 1820s (though the sample is small) is perhaps telling.

## (6) Publishers, Booksellers, and Printers

A large number of the novels in this volume originated from London publishing concerns. Of 2,265 books entered in the listings (a figure which incorporates both items in the case of double entries), 2,030 have London as the first (or only) place of publication in their imprint. For both the 1800s and 1810s, the proportion of London publications exceeds 90 per cent of total output, though in the 1820s this proportion dips to slightly less than 85 per cent (see Table 6, for fuller details). The reduction here is almost exclusively due to the sudden burgeoning of Edinburgh as an alternative centre of production, a phenomenon that will be described more fully at the end of this section.

Table 6. Place of Publication of New Novels, 1800–1829

| Imprint Years | London | Scotland | Ireland | English Provincial | Other | Total* |
|---|---|---|---|---|---|---|
| 1800s | 716 | 4 | 9 | 44 | — | 773 |
| % | 92.6 | 0.5 | 1.2 | 5.7 | — | — |
| 1810s | 611 | 29 | 4 | 17 | 1 | 662 |
| % | 92.3 | 4.4 | 0.6 | 2.6 | 0.1 | — |
| 1820s | 703 | 100 | 14 | 10 | 3 | 830 |
| % | 84.7 | 12.0 | 1.7 | 1.2 | 0.4 | — |
| Total | 2,030 | 133 | 27 | 71 | 4 | 2,265 |
| % | 89.6 | 5.9 | 1.2 | 3.1 | 0.2 | — |

* Numbers and percentages relate to both items in the case of dual (a/b) entries.

[101] F. J. G. Robinson and P. J. Wallis, *Book Subscription Lists: A Revised Guide* (Newcastle-upon-Tyne, 1975); *Book Subscription Lists: Extended Supplement to the Revised Guide by P. J. Wallis*, completed and edited by Ruth Wallis (Newcastle-upon-Tyne, 1996). These together give only 19 of the 69 lists noted in this volume.

[102] For the purposes of the gender breakdown in this case—but not for the general statistical analyses given for output as a whole—translators override foreign original authors. Counts of the subscription lists will be found in the individual entries in the listings.

There is little evidence of any revival in Ireland, since the demise in the 1790s of new novels produced in Dublin. In fact, it would seem that the disappearance of the reprint industry, as a result of the extension of British copyright law to Ireland in 1800, had a generally depressive effect on the trade, without providing any stimulus for the production of new titles. An early instance of a Dublin imprint none the less will be found in the case of Sydney Owenson's *St. Clair* (1803: 55). Unlike Maria Edgeworth, whose *Castle Rackrent* was published first in London through her father's link with the bookseller, Joseph Johnson, the relatively unconnected Owenson faced the more difficult task of finding a publisher at home. In her autobiography she describes having entered into a Dublin bookseller's shop almost at random, only to be told by the proprietor that he was 'not a publisher of novels at all', before being directed more propitiously elsewhere. Even then, it was not long before Owenson was negotiating for a London edition: 'I have got a price far beyond my most sanguine wishes for *St. Clair*. Mr. Harding, of Pall Mall, says, it will be done in a very superior style, and will be certainly at Archer's [the Dublin subsidiary] in three weeks.'[103] After this, all Owenson's novels would be published from London, Joseph Johnson and Richard Phillips vying with each other for the copyright of *The Wild Irish Girl* (1806: 54), and Henry Colburn securing the now Lady Morgan as his leading name through the purchase of *O'Donnel* (1814: 41) at £550 and *Florence Macarthy* (1818: 44) for £1,200.[104]

In all nearly thirty Irish original novels are included, 21 with Dublin imprints, the remainder originating from Cork, Belfast, and Limerick. Three distinct groupings here are worth noting. The first is a sequence of four titles—including two by Anna Millikin, and one by Catharine Selden—printed in Cork by John Connor, whose imprints indicate also proprietorship of the 'Circulating Library, Grand-Parade'. The extended imprint of the fourth of these titles, the anonymous *Soldier of Pennaflor* (1810: 16), points to an established link with A. K. Newman in London, with the Minerva Press effectively importing and redistributing Irish materials from Connor. A moment of unusual confidence is evident in the issuing of three titles in 1820 by John Cumming (more usually apparent as an Irish subsidiary), under his own imprint, one in connection with Minerva and two with Longmans (see 1820: 7, 11, 50). The absence of any later imprints of this kind, however, is perhaps explainable in terms of a poor take-up on the domestic front (or a lack of interest in Irish-managed works among the British trade). Also worthy of note are a number of evangelical fictions published in the late 1820s, mainly by William Curry, whose imprints at first include other publishers specializing in the tract trade, such as William Oliphant in Edinburgh, and Hatchard in London. Extended imprints of this kind, where Curry is sometimes found as the Irish subsidiary, reveal a

---

[103] *Lady Morgan's Memoirs: Autobiography, Diaries and Correspondence*, ed. W. Hepworth Dixon and G. Jewsbury, 2 vols. (London, 1862), I, 187, 237.

[104] Letters between Johnson and Phillips are given in *Lady Morgan's Memoirs*, I, 269–77. Phillips finally won the auction, offering £300 for the three-volume work and £50 for each subsequent edition (see I, 271, 275). Prices for the two later works are given in Jones, *Ideas and Innovations*, p. 188.

widespread system of interconnection in the marketing of such publications throughout Britain and Ireland.

Novels first published in England outside London are more in evidence in the earlier years under view, with the number of titles in the 1800s (44) outmatching similar publications in the following decades (27 in total only). Apart from the exceptional case of Philip Norbury's publication of 16 novels at Brentford, in close proximity to the main London book trade, only two provincial centres managed to produce five or more original novels over the period as a whole. The majority of the eight titles produced in Bath indicate a situation where the author was resident. The Bath producer (e.g. Cruttwell or Hazard) too is normally given as the printer, and the London 'seller' of the book is usually to all intents and purposes its main promoter. Five Norwich imprints equally indicate a strong linkage with London publishers, though in these cases the Norwich producer is usually styled as the seller of the book rather than just its printer. From the 42 other provincial imprints included, a larger proportion (30 titles or more) originate from the south of England, especially the Home Counties and East Anglia. Imprints relating to the north of England are comparatively rare, and, where found, generally do not indicate the same level of co-operation with the London trade. Titles which appear to have involved only a local bookseller include: William Fardely's translation, *Francis and Josepha* (1807: 29), whose Leeds imprint reads 'Printed by Edward Baines'; and David Paynter's *History and Adventures of Godfrey Ranger* (1813: 45), where the original Manchester imprint reads 'Printed & sold by R. & W. Dean, Market-Street'. In both these cases, the author might conceivably have been the main instigator, so that an element of vanity publishing was possibly involved. A novel published locally without a clear London link would almost certainly generate only small sales, at least without the backing of a substantial prior subscription, and this is manifest in the remaindering of Paynter's work as a Minerva publication in 1816.[105]

In view of the emergence of Edinburgh later in the period as a rival to London, it is surprising to find so few Scottish imprints before the publication of Scott's *Waverley* in 1814. Robert Couper's *The Tourifications of Malachi Meldrum* (1803: 25), printed in Aberdeen, and including on its imprint A[lexander] Brown, proprietor of the Aberdeen Circulating Library, is apparently something of a one-off; and even here, the presence of William Creech of Edinburgh and Joseph Johnson of London points to a broader arrangement, not too unlike the more familiar pattern at this time of a Scottish bookseller appearing as the agent of a London publisher.

---

[105] In addition to the non-London imprints discussed above, this volume includes two titles originating from Wales: an unusual Cardiff imprint, *Leave of Absence* (1824: 14), published in association with Longmans; and the Aberystwyth-printed *Adventures and Vagaries of Twm shon Catti* (1828: 65), sometimes claimed to represent the first indigenous Welsh novel. The volume also overrides the general policy of excluding imprints outside Britain and Ireland by incorporating two 'foreign' productions: the Jamaica-printed *Montgomery* (1812: 9), which entered into the Corvey collection, as well as being reviewed in Britain; and the first translation of Manzoni's influential historical novel, *The Betrothed Lovers* (1828: 57), which, notwithstanding its Pisa imprint, appears to have been generally distributed in Britain.

The first two Edinburgh imprints in the listings are: Joseph Strutt's *Queenhoo-Hall* (1808: 101), printed by James Ballantyne, largely as a result of Walter Scott's influence, but essentially a publication of John Murray in London; and Elizabeth Hamilton's *The Cottagers of Glenburnie* (1808: 52), again printed by Ballantyne, but this time for the Edinburgh firm of Manners and Miller, in association with two leading London booksellers. Manners and Miller were also the Edinburgh publishers of Mary Brunton's *Self-Control* (1811: 25), one of the few unqualified successes to come from Scotland before *Waverley*. John Ballantyne's *The Widow's Lodgings* (1813: 8), published nominally by Ballantyne's own firm, in association with Longmans, might possibly represent some kind of testing of the waters before Scott's own appearance as a novelist. The presence of several Edinburgh printers in novels before Scott—George Ramsay, and G. R. Clarke, in addition to James Ballantyne— also points to the potential of Edinburgh as a manufacturing centre. Yet even in the period from 1814 to 1819, if Scott's own seven novels are excluded from the count, only 14 titles have primary Edinburgh imprints. This makes the explosion which took place in the 1820s seem even more dramatic.

In all, some 450 booksellers and publishers are in evidence in the listings. The enterprises recorded vary over a wide range: from provincial printers with a single press, who might also possibly keep a market stall for selling books, to the largest of London wholesale houses. Of this total, some 280 booksellers/publishers can be designated 'primary publishers', on the basis that their name features on the title-page alone or as the initiator and/or manager of the publication. Even in London, where the vast majority of primary publishers were located, considerable variations are to be found. In his *Reminiscences of Literary London*, Thomas Rees distinguishes between three types of London bookseller: (i) specialist concerns dealing in reprint series, number publication etc.; (ii) 'the greater wholesale booksellers and publishers'; and (iii) 'booksellers who chiefly dealt in retail; whose traffic was mostly with their brother tradesmen'.[106] Generally, original novels were produced at this period by those in the latter two categories. Smaller bookselling concerns are more likely to be found operating in association with fellow tradesmen, who might share some of the capital risk, or undertake to purchase at a discount a certain number of copies. At the same time, there is increasing evidence of larger concerns operating primarily as the wholesale distributor of a work, a far greater emphasis being placed on marketing and distribution than on individual retail sales. Another noticeable feature, especially evident in the later stages of the period under view, is the development of a number of associations between Edinburgh and London houses. Notable combinations in the 1820s, where the Edinburgh firm was dominant, include William Blackwood's association with Thomas Cadell in London, and the ill-fated arrangement between Archibald Constable and Hurst, Robinson, and Co.

---

[106] Dr Thomas Rees, *Reminiscences of Literary London from 1779 to 1853*, with additions by John Britton (London, 1896), pp. 31, 61. Rees was the younger brother of Owen Rees, the first partner to join Thomas Norton Longman.

An associated element is the increasing use of 'publisher' and 'published by' to describe the activities of (especially) the larger houses in marketing their novels. This contrasts with the situation found in the eighteenth century, and evident too at the beginning of the period under view, where the term 'bookseller' had a broad application, covering most aspects of the publication and retailing of books. The word is thus employed, apparently without any underlying innuendo, in Elizabeth Hamilton's address to 'Mr. Robinson, Bookseller, Pater-Noster-Row', at the beginning of her *Memoirs of Modern Philosophers* (1800: 39). According to Thomas Rees, George Robinson's concern at this time 'carried on the largest business of any house in London, as general publishers, and also as wholesale and retail booksellers'.[107] As Royal Gettmann suggests, however, an element of disparagement tends to enter into the use of the word later in the period, at least in certain mouths and situations.[108] The imprints in this volume certainly point to its diminishing use as a means of self-description by those issuing books. By contrast there are only six clear cases of 'published' in the 1800s, whereas more than fifty instances are discoverable in the 1820s, most frequently in the form of standard imprints, such as 'Published by Sherwood, Neely, and Jones', 'Published by George Virtue', and 'Published by Oliver & Boyd'.

The period also reveals a number of interesting developments in the relationship between publishers and authors. Four types of financial arrangement, as detailed below, are evident from surviving publishing records and other sources.

(i) *Publication by subscription.* In these cases, the author effectively guaranteed the sale of the work, or at least a portion, through procuring advance promises to pay for copies from subscribers. This might give a publisher the confidence to proceed, though, on the other hand, his profit was likely to be limited to a commission, the bulk of the subscription going to the author once costs were covered. In the latter respect, publishers had little incentive to promote a novel once subscribed copies had been distributed, and a number of instances will be found of remaindered copies being reissued by concerns such as the Minerva Press (see, e.g., 1802: 31, 1803: 37, 1806: 51, 1813: 38, 1822: 11). As previously noted, the listings contain nearly 70 subscription novels, though there is a distinct tailing-off with only 11 examples in the 1820s (representing 1.3 per cent of total output compared with 5.5 per cent for the years 1800–4).

(ii) *Publication by the author.* In such circumstances the cost of production and advertising was borne by the author, the publisher taking a commission on copies sold retail and to other booksellers at trade or 'sale' price (usually two-thirds of the retail price), with the author profiting from any remaining receipts. It was on this basis that Jane Austen's *Sense and Sensibility* (1811: 16) was first published, with Austen, according to her brother, so unsure about the sale 'that she actually made a

---

[107] Dr Thomas Rees, *Reminiscences of Literary London from 1779 to 1853*, p. 37.
[108] See Gettmann, *A Victorian Publisher*, pp. 1–2.

reserve from her very moderate income to meet the expected loss'.[109] As in the case of subscription fiction, sale on a commission basis was likely to prove less of a spur to publishers than the larger slice of profits available in the case of novels where they had purchased the copyright. In all 86 novels in the period are described on their imprint as being printed or published 'for the author',[110] of which some 20 were also subscription novels. As in the case of subscription fiction, as a means of publication 'by the author' is much less evident later in the period, with only 17 examples in the 1820s (as opposed to 35 in the 1800s, and 34 in the 1810s).

(iii) *'Half profits'*. The system of dividing profits is described in a letter to George Wilkins from Longmans on 21 February 1825: 'on the publication of the edition, we will make up a statement of account, and after deducting the amount of paper, printing, & advertising from the amount of the whole impression at the trade sale price, we will, without your having to wait the event of the sale pay you in cash half the balance of probable profits'.[111] Longmans in this instance were keen to retain Wilkins, who was threatening to leave for Messrs Rivington, and the terms of payment in cash before the sale were better than most were offered on this front. Some authors had to wait through regular intervals (normally six months) to receive payment, with the final settlement only being made after a protracted period. Normally Longmans' practice was to offer 'half profits' to untried authors or to those whose sales were declining. Thus Anna Eliza Bray on 25 September 1827 was informed that the sale of her *De Foix* (1826: 19) had 'not been such as to warrant our purchasing the copyright of your new work; but we would with pleasure undertake it on the plan of dividing the profits'.[112] A striking exception here is Walter Scott, who insisted on contracting all his novels on a half profits basis, this allowing him to keep a tighter grip on the supply of paper and print (in which, as co-owner of Ballantyne's press, he had strong interests) and also opening up the prospect of enhanced profits on the less costly subsequent editions, with which Scott could turn to other publishers if need be.[113] Few (if any) authors were able to exercise such control. Charlotte Pascoe and her sister, notwithstanding Scott's backing, had to wait three years before receiving from Constable half profits of £79 16s 8d on the 1,000 impression of *Coquetry* (1818: 47), the last 241 having been disposed of at a trade sale for 1s 8d a copy.[114] Others received next to nothing. On 14 April 1821, Alicia

---

[109] Henry Austen, 'Biographical Notice', in *Northanger Abbey* (1818: 19), vol. 1, p. xiii.

[110] In these cases, for the purposes of the statistical breakdowns in this Introduction, the bookseller/publisher given on the imprint is counted as the 'secondary publisher'.

[111] Longman Letter Books, I, 101, no. 494B.     [112] Longman Letter Books, I, 102, no. 52B.

[113] Subsequent editions were cheaper in not requiring a transcript of Scott's manuscript (made to preserve anonymity) and also in involving less heavy proofing and corrections. For the first edn. (2,000 copies) of *Guy Mannering* (1815), after production costs and advertising had been deducted, a profit of £849 9s 1d was shared between the author and the publishers. In the case of the 4th edn. of *Guy* (1817), also an impression of 2,000, the profit divided was £1,015, with £507 10s 0d going to the author. This increase in profits was aided by a reduction in the cost of the paper used (23s a ream rather than 30s). Details are taken from Longman Impression Book, 5, f. 178; 6, f. 123.

[114] NLS, MS 791, pp. 428–30 (Constable to Scott, 29 Nov. 1821).

Lefanu was told by Longmans that only 279 of her *Leolin Abbey* (1819: 44) had been sold, producing half-profits totalling £15 2s 7d for the author.[115] In the case of the 1,000 impression of James Hogg's *Confessions of a Justified Sinner* (1824: 50), the firm's Divide Ledger indicates no profits were made available until the final closing of the account in June 1828, with £16 1s 2d being sent to William Blackwood (the 'Author' having been crossed out).[116]

(iv) *Purchase of copyright.* As a whole, this probably represents the most common procedure. Longmans usually paid their leading regular women novelists a one-off payment for copyright, sometimes allowing generous advances before delivery. Jane West on 23 January 1812 was offered 200 guineas for *The Loyalists* (1812: 64), the same sum as she had received for *The Refusal* (1810: 87); while Jane Porter on 11 September 1823 was granted a further advance of £100 on her *Duke Christian of Luneburg* (1824: 77), which 'on the publication of your new Romance if agreeable to you we shall make up [to] the amount of Six Hundred Guineas'. Two years later, at the beginning of the military-nautical craze, Captain Joseph Moyle Sherer was offered £500 for the copyright for *The Story of a Life* (1825: 74), an extremely large sum for a first work of fiction.[117] Other novelists and translators evidently settled for much less. Sophia Elizabeth Shedden apparently had to wait until the whole edition of her translation of Bellin de la Liborlière's *La Nuit anglaise* (see 1817: 14) was cleared before being able to claim £25 from its publisher. If Thomas Rees is to be believed, Minerva authors worked at a minuscule rate compared with their more favoured sisters under the wing of the house of Longman: 'From ten to twenty pounds were the sums usually paid to authors for those novels of three volumes.'[118]

Printers generally played a less obtrusive part, at least publicly, in the production of fiction at this time. In some 75 cases the printer is also nominated in the imprint as the bookseller, a large proportion (60 per cent) of these cases occurring in provincial imprints. The remaining such cases apply much more sporadically to London, no clear instances having been found of printers describing themselves also as the seller of the book in either Dublin or Edinburgh imprints. In general, the entries in this volume only record printer information where it appears on the title-page, though in certain cases information found elsewhere (as in end-of-volume colophons) is included on an optional basis in the notes field. One interesting procedure revealed is the practice of placing different volumes of a novel in the hands of different printers. This occurs most noticeably in the case of translated works of

---

[115] Longman Letter Books, I, 101, no. 122. Another letter to Lefanu, 28 Aug. 1821, states that 'In consequence of the little success we have had with your former work, we beg leave to decline engaging in the one you have now the goodness to propose to us' (I, 101, no. 167A). A. K. Newman of the Minerva Press published Lefanu's subsequent three novels.

[116] Longman Divide Ledger 2D, p. 239. It is possible Hogg had signed over his share to Blackwood.

[117] Longman Letter Books, I, 97, no. 283; I, 101, no. 421A; I, 101, no. 509C (to Sherer, 25 May 1825).

[118] Rees, *Reminiscences,* p. 87. See also Dorothy Blakey, *The Minerva Press 1790–1820* (London, 1939), pp. 73–4, for further indications relating to payment, none of which essentially contradict Rees's statement.

note, where there was a rush to reach the market first. The pattern is also found in the case of some original works of a high profile nature (see, e.g., the three printers involved in producing Edgeworth's *Belinda* (1801: 24)), and with unusually long novels (see, e.g., 1804: 38 and 1806: 24).

An overview of changing patterns in the publication of novels is provided by Tables 7: 1, 2, 3, which show the output of different concerns as primary publishers within ten-year periods. Noticeably absent, as main producers in the 1800s, are some of the booksellers who had been most conspicuous in the 1790s, including Thomas Hookham, John Bell, and Vernor and Hood. A symbiotic relationship between circulating libraries and the production of fiction is still evident, however, with six of the top producers (Lane at the Minerva, Dutton, Earle, Colburn, Chapple, and Norbury) also being library proprietors. This connection is less evident in the 1810s, though Henry Colburn continued to operate his library, and the sons of Thomas Hookham, who kept the celebrated reading rooms at 15, Old Bond Street, revived a once common imprint as publishers of novels. During this middle period Robinson and Co., producers of some of the most significant titles of earlier years, effectively disappear from view. In the 1820s, Colburn challenges the dominance of A. K. Newman at Minerva as the most prolific producer of titles. This period is also marked by the full emergence of two Scottish houses, Blackwoods and Constable and Co. The appearance of George Virtue, a specialist in serialized fiction, is also significant in indicating the development of new channels for fiction.

Table 7.1.  **Primary Publishers, 1800–1809**

| Publisher/Concern | Count | % | Imprints Include |
|---|---|---|---|
| Minerva | 214 | 27.7 | William Lane; Lane & Newman; Lane, Newman & Co.; A. K. Newman & Co. |
| Hughes, James Fletcher | 77 | 9.9 | J. F. Hughes; J. F. & G. Hughes |
| Longmans | 53 | 6.9 | T. N. Longman & O. Rees; Longman, Hurst, Rees & Orme |
| Crosby & Co. | 43 | 5.6 | B. Crosby & Co.; Crosby & Letterman |
| Robinson & Co. | 23 | 3.0 | G., G. & J. Robinson; G. & J. Robinson; George Robinson |
| Dutton, Robert | 22 | 2.8 | R. Dutton |
| Earle, William | 17 | 2.2 | W. Earle; Earle & Hemet |
| Colburn & Co. | 16 | 2.1 | Henry Colburn |
| Chapple, Clement | 13 | 1.7 | C. Chapple |
| Johnson, Joseph | 12 | 1.5 | J. Johnson |
| Norbury, Philip | 12 | 1.5 | P. Norbury |
| Other | 271 | 35.1 | |
| Total | 773 | | |

Table 7.2. **Primary Publishers, 1810–1819**

| Publisher/Concern | Count | % | Imprints Include |
|---|---|---|---|
| Minerva | 163 | 24.6 | A. K. Newman & Co. |
| Longmans | 60 | 9.0 | Longman, Hurst, Rees & Orme; Longman, Hurst, Rees, Orme & Brown |
| Colburn & Co. | 43 | 6.5 | Henry Colburn |
| Sherwood & Co. | 37 | 5.6 | Sherwood, Neely & Jones |
| Baldwin & Co. | 16 | 2.4 | R. Baldwin; Baldwin, Cradock & Joy |
| Hughes, James Fletcher | 16 | 2.4 | J. F. Hughes |
| Crosby & Co. | 13 | 2.0 | B. Crosby & Co.; B. & R. Crosby & Co. |
| Simpkin & Marshall | 13 | 2.0 | W. Simpkin & R. Marshall |
| Chapple, Clement | 12 | 1.8 | C. Chapple |
| Hookham & Co. | 11 | 1.7 | T. Hookham jun. & E. T. Hookham jun.; T. Hookham jun. & Co.; Thomas Hookham |
| Other | 278 | 42.0 | |
| Total | 662 | | |

Table 7.3. **Primary Publishers, 1820–1829**

| Publisher/Concern | Count | % | Imprints Include |
|---|---|---|---|
| Minerva | 145 | 17.5 | A. K. Newman & Co. |
| Colburn & Co. | 104 | 12.6 | Henry Colburn; Henry Colburn & Co.; Henry Colburn & Richard Bentley |
| Longmans | 84 | 10.1 | Longman, Hurst, Rees, Orme & Brown; L., H., R., O., B. & Green; L., R., O., B. & G. |
| Whittaker & Co. | 58 | 7.0 | G. & W. B. Whittaker; Geo. B. Whittaker; Whittaker, Treacher & Arnot; Whittaker, Treacher & Co. |
| Blackwood | 35 | 4.2 | William Blackwood |
| Constable & Co. | 17 | 2.0 | Archibald Constable & Co. |
| Saunders & Otley | 17 | 2.0 | Saunders & Otley |
| Baldwin & Co. | 16 | 1.9 | Baldwin, Cradock & Joy; Baldwin & Cradock |
| Virtue | 14 | 1.7 | George Virtue |
| Sherwood & Co. | 14 | 1.7 | Sherwood, Neely & Jones; Sherwood, Jones & Co.; Sherwood, Gilbert & Piper |
| Other | 326 | 39.3 | |
| Total | 830 | | |

In spite of the plethora of booksellers involved across the field, four leading concerns were responsible, as primary publishers, for no less than 975 of the novels entered in this volume. Two of these, Minerva and Longmans, regularly produced new fiction titles during the period. Henry Colburn began publishing novels in

1807, but only really comes into view as a major producer in the later 1820s. The presence of J. F. Hughes—a specialist in fiction—in this grouping is primarily due to a sudden burst of production in 1807–1808, though his imprints stretch from 1803–1811.

The success of William Lane, the founder of the Minerva establishment, was based on three interrelating enterprises: the Minerva Library, the Minerva Press, and Lane's activities as a commissioning publisher, chiefly of novels. Nearly all the new titles issued from Leadenhall Street were published under the current regular Minerva imprint, the only exceptions being eight cases where a novel is published 'for the author', and seven cases where Lane's successor, A. K. Newman, appears as the secondary publisher on the imprint. Excluding these instances, the listings include 522 original novels published by William Lane and/or A. K. Newman, representing 23 per cent of total output. This confirms the established view concerning the dominance of Minerva novels in the Romantic period, but fails to corroborate more exaggerated pictures of a total saturation of the market. For the years 1800–1820, the sum total of 390 is slightly less than the number of fiction titles listed by Dorothy Blakey, whose check-list overlaps for these years.[119] This is partly owing to a number of cases where a supposedly original Minerva title has proved to be a reissue of a novel previously published by another concern. Unlike Blakey, too, the present volume excludes a number of titles aimed at the juvenile market.

Output of new novels by Minerva was at its strongest in the earlier years under view. Between 1800 and 1806 the Press produced on average 24 new titles annually, market share in this respect never falling below 27 per cent, and in 1802 actually rising as high as 43.5 per cent. In 1802 the Minerva imprint changes from 'William Lane' to 'Lane and Newman', as a result of Lane's taking Newman, a former apprentice, into partnership. It then changes again in 1803 to 'Lane, Newman and Co.', indicating the inclusion of other partners (amongst whom was the printer supervisor of the Minerva press, John Darling). Having amassed a large personal fortune, Lane retired from business altogether in 1808, the description 'A. K. Newman and Co.' first appearing on 1809 imprints. The disruption caused by this transitional period perhaps best explains a drop in output around 1807–1808, with only 29 new novels appearing with imprint dates belonging to those years, and the Minerva's share of new output dropping as low as 16 per cent. In the middle 1810s production again picked up, with a regular output of between 15 and 17 new novels, representing between 25 to 30 per cent of output generally in those relatively fallow years. However, there are distinct signs by now that the Minerva's list, which in the early 1800s had mirrored current trends, was beginning to acquire a rather tired and predictable look. It is at this time too that Newman shifts most noticeably to juvenile titles, as if in search of an alternative outlet.

The Minerva Press as such apparently came to an end in 1820, the familiar

---

[119] See above, p. 24, and note.

prefix 'Printed at the Minerva Press' last appearing in two novels with 1821 imprints, both of which were actually published in November 1820 (see 1821: 43, 45).[120] In the early 1820s, a roughly similar output of between 17 and 19 new novels is found annually, though against a rapidly expanding total production, so that in 1824–1825 the number of new Minerva titles falls below 17 per cent of output. In the following three years, with only 36 titles, the decline becomes more apparent, and in 1829 Newman brought out only nine new novels. During this period, too, the material issued becomes increasingly formulaic and imitative (for example, of the fashionable novel), or, like Haynes's Gothic titles, gives the impression of being almost deliberately retrogressive. Newman also stuck with a predominantly female authorship, at a time when male novelists were attracting most attention.

Little is known about James Fletcher Hughes's origins, though it is conceivable that he was related to Thomas Hughes, of Ludgate Street, a dealer in 'shilling shockers' early in the century. Hughes's own premises at Wigmore Street, off Cavendish Square, placed him close to the 'fashionable' residents of the West End squares, and some of his earliest imprints indicate a connection (perhaps not entirely invited) with the Whig aristocratical circles surrounding the Prince of Wales. Some early imprints show an association with Crosby and Co., usually with Hughes as the secondary publisher, though there is also a possibility that on occasions variant title-pages were employed, giving Hughes as the publisher for his share of the impression (see 1803: 68). By 1804 his familiar Wigmore Street imprint, often involving D. N. Shury as printer, was well in place. Hughes showed no qualms from the start about dramatically magnifying the attractions of nondescript authors and works. *Hell Upon Earth*, by Joseph Gruber—one of several translations issued by Hughes—was evidently promoted as by the more eye-catching August Kotzebue (see 1804: 23). Likewise, a number of Hughes's authors have names suspiciously similar to better-known novelists. 'Miss West', the author of *The Two Marillos* (1804: 69), bore no relation to Mrs Jane West, then celebrated for her moral fictions, yet in the catalogue of Mackay's Edinburgh Circulating Library her novel is listed as 'West's two Marillos'. Nevertheless, Hughes did manage to attract one genuinely high-profile author, M. G. Lewis, publishing Lewis's genuinely successful *Bravo of Venice* (1805: 75), itself based on an original title by J. H. Zschokke, as well as his less digestible *Feudal Tyrants* (1806: 50), again 'taken from the German' [of Christiane Naubert]. This laid the path for a number of lurid 'Monk'-like titles in 1807–1808, by hack authors, such as perhaps Hughes had wished Lewis had provided himself. These were accompanied by numerous 'scandal' titles, in the manner of T. S. Surr's *Winter in London*, which were to prove the largest contributing factor in Hughes's brief success. Hughes's 1808 output included 27 new fiction titles, representing nearly 25 per cent of total production in a bumper year.

---

[120] Though the Minerva Press disappears from imprints, John Darling continued to print works at Leadenhall Street for A. K. Newman (see, e.g., 1824: 63, 1827: 36).

Yet in 1809 output of new fiction by J. F. Hughes ground almost to a halt, with only seven titles bearing that year's imprint, and Wigmore Street giving way to an alternative address in Berners Street. The best explanation lies in Hughes's bankruptcy, which was listed in the *London Gazette* in November 1808. The whole enterprise had mushroomed without the network of provincial connections that Crosby and Co. had built up, the extent of which is made pointedly apparent in the imprint of the latter's *A Winter in Bath* (see 1807: 7). Moreover, unlike other main publishers of novels, Hughes lacked the support of his own circulating library and connections with other libraries. An attempted comeback is evident in 1810, with 15 new titles belonging to that year, supported by widespread advertising in papers such as the *Morning Post*, but at this point Hughes effectively disappears from view. Some late imprints of his feature the 15, Paternoster Row address of the printer-bookseller Michael Allen, who might have provided a refuge, and who (under the imprint of Allen and Co.) possibly managed to salvage some of the titles that Hughes had commissioned in his last burst of activity.[121]

Hughes's frenetic career contrasts sharply with the steady output of generally middle-market fiction produced by the house of Longman throughout the period. In all Longmans published nearly 200 novels directly under their own imprint, as well as serving in a 'secondary' capacity as the London distributor in some 50 other cases, many of these latter being provincial publications where Longmans in effect operated as the main outlet. The firm had begun issuing novels on a regular basis from the later 1790s, shortly after Thomas Norton Longman had been joined by Owen Rees in 1794, and the intake of fresh partners, evident in the expanding imprints of the new century, is indicative of the scale of operation of this broadly based publishing concern. Early in the 1800s, Longmans had striking successes with Amelia Opie's *Father and Daughter* (1801: 54) and Jane Porter's *Thaddeus of Warsaw* (1803: 59), both of which were followed by a chain of new editions. Opie and Porter stayed on to form part of a group of regular (mainly female) authors, with literary credentials noticeably higher than their Minerva counterparts, and to whom Longmans remained creditably loyal—at least as far as commercial considerations allowed. Between 1800 and 1818 output of new novels never exceeded eight titles in any one year, with an average annual rate of just over five titles. In 1814 the firm became associated with Scott's fiction, through Archibald Constable offering them a 700 share of the 1,000 first edition of *Waverley*; and in the case of *Guy Mannering* (1815: 46) they were handed the management, mainly as a result of Scott's relish for their firm bills of payment. Scott however soon became concerned that Longmans were not 'pushing' enough as sellers of books,[122] and from

---

[121] For a fuller account, see Garside, 'J. F. Hughes and the Publication of Popular Fiction', *passim*.

[122] See Scott's letter to Joanna Baillie, 17 Mar. 1817: 'our friends Longman & co have a sort of mercantile mode of treating all their books alike and according to what they call the rules of trade which is unfavourable to rapid sale.... There is a *selling time* for every popular work which may last perhaps from four to six months or a year at most. A pushing bookseller keeps the market full during that period and contents himself with smaller profits on each copy that he may be reimbursed by the quantity disposed of' (*Letters*, ed. Grierson, IV, 411).

*The Antiquary* (1816: 52) onwards the management usually went to Constable, with Longmans also eventually losing their position as main London agents for the Waverley novels.

In 1818 Longmans' output of new novels reached double figures (11 titles) for the first time, and generally remained at that level until 1827, with a noticeable dropping off in 1828 and 1829 (6 and 2 titles only). In the early 1820s the firm still cultivated their regular female authors, while developing new areas such as the evangelical short story. Later in the decade, there are signs of a shift in yet another direction. In negotiating terms for Anna Maria and Jane Porter's *Coming Out; and the Field of the Forty Footsteps* (1828: 64), Longmans on 29 November 1827 offered 'the same for this work as for "Honor O'Hara" [1826: 63] viz £420, though the sale of neither that work nor the Tales [*Tales Round a Winter Hearth*: 1826: 64] fully warrant it'. A month earlier (30 October) Captain Sherer had been encouraged to proceed full steam ahead: 'You should by all means devote yourself to the "Tales of the Wars of our Times" [1829: 77] which we shall be most happy to engage in. You cannot employ yourself on any thing better.'[123]

Henry Colburn apparently began his career in the book trade as an assistant to William Earle, a bookseller in Albemarle Street, and it was possibly through Earle that he acquired the English and Foreign Circulating Library, at 48 Conduit Street, New Bond Street, in the heart of the West End. This proprietorship is widely displayed in the two earliest novels published by Colburn (see 1807: 21, 32). Of sixteen novels produced by Colburn between 1807 and 1809, nine were translations from foreign languages, predominantly French, one of these vying directly with another translation commissioned by J. F. Hughes (see 1808: 44). In the 1810s his output dips, and between 1818 and 1824 Colburn was responsible for two or three titles annually. These carefully selected up-market items, however, helped keep Colburn and his library in the public eye, and occasionally reaped the rewards of daring.[124]

Colburn's capacity for marketing his wares was enhanced by his founding of the *New Monthly Magazine* in 1814 and the setting-up in 1817 of the *Literary Gazettte*, an innovatory weekly review. Nevertheless, it is only in the years 1826–1829, after the disposal of his library in 1824, that Colburn becomes prominent as a large-scale producer of fiction titles. In 1826, when most publishers were in retreat, Colburn doubled his output with 13 new novels, this in turn being followed by 17 new titles with 1827 imprints, and 24 with 1828 imprints. The 34 new fiction titles issued by Colburn for 1829—some displaying his new partnership with the printer, Richard Bentley—represent 42 per cent of total production for that year. This occurs exactly at the moment when Minerva's output slips dramatically and Longmans appear to falter in their commitment to fiction (see Figure 3). Colburn's titles also

---

[123] Longman Letter Books, I, 102, nos. 60C, 56B.
[124] For a fuller account of Colburn's marketing activities, see John Sutherland, 'Henry Colburn Publisher', *Publishing History*, 19 (1986), 59–83.

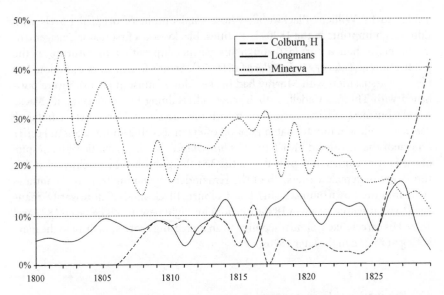

Fig. 3. Leading Publishers, 1800–1829, by Publication of New Novels

contributed heavily to the masculinization of fiction at this time. Of the 93 new novels managed by his firm between 1825 and 1829, only 14 were female-authored (as opposed to 72 male titles, and seven unknown).

Another striking feature of the 1820s is the sudden burgeoning of novel production in Edinburgh. The 95 novels with Edinburgh imprints in this decade outnumber their equivalents in the previous twenty years by three to one, and the number would swell to nearly 130 if cases where Edinburgh appears as the secondary place of publication were added. Undoubtedly the runaway success of the Waverley novels—known as the 'Scotch' novels as much for their provenance as content—served as a strong impetus. But more general factors also undoubtedly played a part. The development of the Edinburgh New Town opened a new market for polite literature. Beyond that, Edinburgh was in a strong position to supply the rapidly developing industrial areas in the North of England. Records of Edinburgh publishing houses at this time show them directly supplying not only Scotland, but also much of the industrial North, as well as Ireland. Edinburgh was also developing fast as a major force in the print industry. James Bertram, who worked as an apprentice in the trade in the 1830s, recalled with some relish that by 1837 there were more booksellers (128) than barbers in Edinburgh and 'over eighty letter-press printers . . . great and small'.[125]

The optimum period for the production of original novels in Scotland occurs between 1822 and 1825, when 51 titles bear Edinburgh imprints, 21 of which were

---

[125] James Bertram, *Some Memories of Books, Authors, and Events* (Westminster, 1893), pp. 85–6.

published by William Blackwood, whose total output of original novels with Edinburgh imprints in the 1820s is 35 titles. Blackwood's first major engagement in the genre had occurred through his partnership with John Murray in the publication of *Tales of My Landlord* (1816: 53), Scott's fourth work of fiction; but after his association with Murray had broken down, most of his titles were published with Thomas Cadell, with Blackwood retaining the management. Blackwood's business efficiency, combined with the success of *Blackwood's Edinburgh Magazine*, allowed him to match London offers in securing authors, Susan Ferrier reportedly being offered £1,000 for *The Inheritance* (1824: 33). Noticeably, in spite of the Ferrier connection, only five of the 35 titles published by Blackwood at this time were by female writers, 26 of the remainder originating from male authors (with four unknown or uncertain). Like Colburn, Blackwood (if more warily) managed to weather the storm of 1825/6, producing eight new novels between 1827 and 1829. His career, like Colburn's, points to an increasing professionalism in the marketing of fiction in the later 1820s.

## (7) Production, Marketing, and Dissemination

Although large-scale technological developments only began to affect the manufacture of fiction substantially in the 1830s, a number of significant changes in the production of the novel are still traceable through the period under view. On one level, it is possible to point to a greater degree of standardization, as an increasingly professional publishing industry advanced and consolidated the gains made by the genre since the beginning of the century. At the same time, the 1820s in particular saw the development of a number of alternatives for the marketing of fiction, as well as a much broader dissemination of the English novel in the form of American editions, translations, and a new species of standard reprint.

One significant transformation in production is found in the move towards the three-decker (3-volume) novel as the standard for mainstream fiction. As Table 8 indicates, during the 1800s novels in two volumes are almost as prevalent as those in three volumes, and works of four or more volumes are not uncommon either. Novels in two volumes with imprint years 1800, 1803, 1805, and 1806, in fact, outnumber three-volume novels for those years. Moreover four-volume titles are the most common of any type in 1801 (26 cases), and in 1809 manage to match their otherwise ascendant three-volume equivalents (25 titles apiece). At this period the bulk of copies produced almost certainly still went to circulating libraries, where extensiveness was not necessarily a difficulty. Library proprietors buying novels in batches would have been able to accommodate longer sets in their budget, and with the added advantage of being able to display goods out of the reach of most of their subscribers as retail items. Multi-volume sets could also be lent out by the volume, allowing a greater number of clients access to new and popular novels.

Table 8. Volume Structure of New Novels, 1800–1829

| Imprint Year | I | II | III | IV | V+ | Total* |
|---|---|---|---|---|---|---|
| 1800s | 87 | 237 | 244 | 177 | 28 | 773 |
| % | 11.2 | 30.7 | 31.6 | 22.9 | 3.6 | |
| 1810s | 91 | 154 | 256 | 132 | 29 | 662 |
| % | 13.7 | 23.3 | 38.7 | 19.9 | 4.4 | |
| 1820s | 228 | 146 | 365 | 78 | 13 | 830 |
| % | 27.5 | 17.6 | 44.0 | 9.4 | 1.5 | |
| Total | 406 | 537 | 865 | 387 | 70 | 2265 |
| % | 17.9 | 23.7 | 38.2 | 17.1 | 3.1 | |

\* Numbers and percentages relate to both items in the case of dual (a/b) entries.

A clearer shift to the three-volume form is evident in the 1810s, this occurring mainly at the expense of the two-volume novel. The changeover is most apparent in the case of 1814 imprints, with 25 three-volume works outmatching only eight novels in two volumes (though this year also includes 22 titles in four volumes or more). The first year when three-volume novels outmatch all other alternatives is 1819, when 38 three-deckers are found amongst a total production of 73 titles. During the 1820s the three-volume novel is the most common form in all years except for 1824, when 42 single-volume titles momentarily outnumber 37 three-volume novels. A complete dominance over all other types, as in 1819, is found again in 1828 and 1829, where 44 and 48 three-volume novels are found respectively.

A number of causes undoubtedly contributed to the ascendancy of the three-decker novel, which was to survive as a norm virtually to the end of the century,[126] but in these transitional years commercial considerations appear to have been a major factor. In the later years under view, and especially in the wake of Scott's earliest successes, individual purchases almost certainly began to account for a much larger proportion of sales. Much of the pressure for three volumes accordingly came from publishers convinced that this was the maximum size the market could bear. The Longman archives provide several instances of would-be expansive authors being advised to cut back: 'A novel in three volumes we always consider more salable than one in four', James Hogg was told on 5 May 1823 with regard to his forthcoming *Three Perils of Woman* (1823: 43).[127] For the veteran writer, Henry Mackenzie, whose greatest success had been the single-volume tale, *The Man of Feeling* (1771), the rule had an opposite effect in encouraging unnecessary amplification: 'The mystical Number 3 seems in modern times to be worshipped, as in some Eastern Countries,

---

[126] The novel 'in three volumes' eventually expired in the mid-1890s and was succeeded by the single volume at 6s as the main form for new novels. The term 'three-decker' itself does not appear to have come into use until the 1830s.

[127] Longman Letter Books I, 101, no. 357. On being informed on 21 Mar. 1821 that only 377 of the 750 impression of his *Sir Francis Darrell* (1820: 21) were sold, R. C. Dallas was offered a similar analysis: 'We are of opinion that a Novel of *three* is of more ready sale than one of *four* Volumes' (I, 101, no. 101A).

by Authors or their Booksellers, that being the common standard for the Number of Vols in which most of the favorite [*sic*] Fictions of the day are set forth.'[128]

Another main change at this time relates to the format in which fiction was produced. Generally novels in the earlier period were in duodecimo (12mo) format, one of the smallest sizes for books then, which involved creating gatherings of 24 pages (12 leaves) from the sheets on which text was printed. This allowed ease of handling, suitable it might seem for a leisurely style of reading by a predominantly female readership. At the same time, however, it physically embodied the low status of fiction in comparison to other literary modes (it is not uncommon to find novels gathered under the heading 'Duodecimos' in contemporary library catalogues). The larger octavo (8vo) format, where gatherings include sixteen pages, and which was commonly used for works such as histories and travel books, is only found in the case of 5.8 per cent of novels in the 1800s, and 4.4 per cent in the 1810s. Novels appearing in this larger format in the early 1800s are usually of the kind that featured under author names in catalogues and received full literary reviews. Instances include Elizabeth Hamilton's *Memoirs of Modern Philosophers* (1800: 39), a corrective anti-Jacobin fiction, Dr John Moore's *Mordaunt* (1800: 56), whose sub-title suggests a standing equivalent to non-fiction, and the continuations of Harriet and Sophia Lee's up-market *Canterbury Tales* (see 1801: 42, 1805: 49). Hannah More's *Cœlebs in Search of a Wife* (1808: 81) also declared that it was no ordinary novel through its larger format. This in turn set a precedent for a number of other moral-evangelical fictions, brought out in octavo, including Brunton's three novels (1811: 25, 1814: 14, 1819: 28), Henry Kett's *Emily, A Moral Tale* (1809: 37), and Laetitia-Matilda Hawkins's *The Countess and Gertrude; or, Modes of Discipline* (1811: 40). Yet no larger shift in this direction is apparent at this juncture. On the contrary, between 1813 and 1818 only 10 genuine octavos (as ascertained by collation of leaves) are to be found in the listings, with every other item there being a duodecimo.

A distinct shift is apparent in 1819, when six novels with that year's imprint are in octavo, including Thomas Hope's *Anastasius; or, Memoirs of a Greek* (1819: 42), Polidori's *The Vampyre; A Tale* (1819: 55), and Andrew Reed's *No Fiction* (1819: 56). Nevertheless the largest single contributing factor was undoubtedly *Ivanhoe* (1820: 63), Scott's first novel to focus on English history, which was actually published in December 1819. From the beginning, it was planned that this work was to be produced as an octavo, on good quality paper, and in a smaller more distinct type.[129] All Scott's subsequent historical romances were produced in the same octavo style. Implicitly the novel now claimed a status comparable to other works produced in octavo. No less than 60 of the novels produced with 1824 and 1825 imprints are genuine octavos, this representing almost a third of total output, the overall proportion for the 1820s being 20.8 per cent.

---

[128] In an unpublished review of J. G. Lockhart's *Valerius; A Roman Story* (1821: 56), NLS, MS 4846, f. 30.

[129] For a full account, see Jane Millgate, 'Making It New: Scott, Constable, Ballantyne, and the Publication of *Ivanhoe*', *Studies in English Literature*, 34 (1994), 795–811.

The cost of new fiction soared in this period, with the most frequently charged retail price for a three-volume novel tripling from 10s 6d in 1800 to 31s 6d in the later 1820s. Earlier in the period a distinction is sometimes made between the cost 'sewed' or 'in boards', referring to books comprising gathered sheets stitched together with paper wrappers and those covered with two sheets of stiff card, the differential between the two (when apparent) being 6d a volume. None of the sources used for prices in this volume, however, give a 'sewed' price for post-1807 titles, and it seems reasonable to assume that most novels were marketed from that point in boards, usually with the printed labels on the spines.[130] Through the period as a whole the most frequent price for a novel in three volumes rises to 12s (1802–1805), 13s 6d (1806–1807), 15s (1808–1812), 18s (1813–1817), 21s (1818–1825), finally reaching 31s 6d (a guinea-and-a-half) in 1826. Between 1800 and 1814 the rising prices generally match the inflationary situation in the war years, with costs for raw materials being exacerbated in the case of books by the high prices charged for paper. But even after the war prices for new novels continued to be pushed upwards in a generally deflationary situation. There can be little doubt that Scott's apparently unstoppable appeal in the market served as the main spearhead for this process. With *The Antiquary* (1816: 52), his third novel, Constable decided at the last moment to increase the retail price from 21s to 24s, telling Longmans that 'the additional profit would be considerable, and we do not think one dozen less of the Book would be sold'.[131] Constable's confidence was justified, the first edition of 6,000 selling out within three weeks, generating half profits of £1,682 to the author and considerable sums to the two publishers.[132] Additional hikes in the price charged for the Waverley novels occurred with the four-volumed second series of *Tales of My Landlord* (1818: 56), which retailed at 32s compared with the 28s charged for the first series, and then again with *Ivanhoe*, whose superior appearance encouraged Constable and his associates to charge 30s, though at one point 31s 6d had been contemplated.[133] The final leap was made with the three-volume *Kenilworth* (1821: 64), which was sold at 31s 6d in boards, all Scott's subsequent novels managing to sustain the set price of 10s 6d a volume.

While *Kenilworth* is often represented as setting the mould for subsequent three-decker novels, both in terms of format and price, it was not the first octavo novel to charge a guinea-and-a-half. On 5 December 1819, just as *Ivanhoe* was about to go on sale, Robert Cadell wrote to Constable that 'Murray yesterday subscribed a Book in three Vols crown 8vo at £1 11s 6d!!! . . . it is a Novel—and why may we not do the

---

[130] Labels were supplied by the printer on a spare leaf, and are sometimes found unused within novels that have been specially bound (see, e.g., 1816: 58, and Appendix A: 3). Another development in the binding of books for retail sale, found only late in the period, is the use of cloth-covered boards. A copy of *Elizabeth de Bruce* (1827: 44), in the present writer's possession, is in boards covered in brown silk-like cloth, and has the original spine labels, stating the price to be £1 11s 6d.

[131] NLS, MS 789, p. 538.

[132] For a detailed analysis of costs and profits, see David Hewitt (ed.), Walter Scott, *The Antiquary*, Edinburgh Edition of the Waverley Novels (Edinburgh, 1995), 'Essay on the Text', pp. 363–4.

[133] Millgate, 'Making It New', 808.

same thing?'[134] The novel in question was Thomas Hope's *Anastasius* (1819: 42), an unusually large work of fiction, issued from John Murray's decidedly up-market headquarters at Albemarle Street, and carrying in its early days the additional allurement of a rumoured authorship by Byron. It was *Kenilworth* nevertheless that created the clearest precedent for a standard novel at 31s 6d, and by 1826 virtually a third of new novels in three volumes were set at the same high price. The sense of a stereotype forming, however, only becomes fully apparent with Henry Colburn's lists of 'new novels' late in the decade. Out of 45 three-decker novels published by Colburn with 1828 or 1829 imprints, no less than 31 were priced at 31s 6d. On the other hand, the movement to octavo format in his case, at least in technical terms, was something of an illusion. All of Colburn's 1829 three-deckers turn out on examination to be duodecimos, though widely puffed as 'post octavo'.[135] Colburn's pricing at the same time helped open up a broader division in the market than is evident at the beginning of the century. Whereas the Minerva Press's output under William Lane had generally matched other novels as a whole in appearance and market value,[136] the rather tired-looking three-decker duodecimos produced by A. K. Newman at the end of the 1820s were priced at between 16s 6d and 18s, well below Colburn's market-leaders. Still more glaring differences opened up between premium new titles and cheap reprint fiction. In 1826 two volumes of *Limbird's Edition of British Novelists*, containing all Anne Radcliffe's main fiction, were advertised at 10s in the same newspaper in which Colburn announced the posthumous publication of the same author's *Gaston de Blondeville* (1826: 66), retailing at 38s, '4 vols, post 8vo'.[137]

   In some respects the consolidation found in the 1820s has more the air of an enforced conformism, and in a number of areas there are signs of fresh outlets being explored and developed. One form of resistance to the formula of the three-decker is found in several attempts to promote single volumes containing full-length texts at a cheaper price. Sir Richard Phillips in 1820, under the title 'The Periodical

[134]   NLS, MS 323, f. 107.

[135]   As ascertained by counting leaves between signatures, the method used to establish format in this bibliography. Examination of some copies of Colburn's novels with uncut leaves, and in the original boards, indicates that these were not necessarily dissimilar in dimension to novels in octavo such as the post-*Kenilworth* Waverley novels. The size of leaves of course varied with the dimensions of the sheets used in printing. Some duodecimos in the entries were printed on half sheets, and collate in sixes.

[136]   One noticeable feature of Minerva novels early in the 1800s is the use of engraved frontispiece illustrations, which are found in 24 titles between 1800 and 1803, illustrating both Gothic and sentimental fictions. In the 1820s none of the novels issued by A. K. Newman appear to have been illustrated.

[137]   John Limbird's advertisement appeared on 12 June 1826 in the *Morning Chronicle*, where Colburn had been promoting Radcliffe's 'new' work for several months. Limbird, a retail stationer in the Strand, also offered certain shorter fictions for as little as 6d, but met fierce resistance from the established trade (see Altick, *English Common Reader*, pp. 266–7). Other reprint series sold during the period include: Cooke's *Pocket Library* (titles varying from 6d to 9s 6d according to length); Tegg's *Miniature Novelists* (distillations at 6d); and Henshall's *Pocket Library*. Collections include: Anna Barbauld's *British Novelists*, 50 vols. (1810), consisting mainly of eighteenth-century classics, but also including an authorially revised version of Edgeworth's *Belinda*; W. Mudford's *British Novelists* (1810–1817), issued in shilling parts; and *Ballantyne's Novelist's Library*, 10 vols. (1821–1824), including fiction from Fielding to Radcliffe, with introductions by Walter Scott.

Novelist, or Circulating Library' offered a full John Galt novel, *Glenfell; or, Macdonalds and Campbells* (1820: 26), at '6s half-bound and lettered, or 5s 3d in quires [i.e. ungathered sheets]', the first price apparently aimed at retail purchasers, and the latter at circulating library proprietors wishing to provide their own house bindings. With its second item, the series set a one-volume translation of Madame de Genlis's *Petrarch and Laura* (1820: 28[a]), at the same prices, against a rival two-volume Colburn translation retailing at 10s 6d. Nevertheless it is the Colburn version which is most common in surviving circulating library catalogues, and the series evidently folded after its third issue, a somewhat unappealing-looking translation from the Italian and Spanish with the lead title *Andrew of Padua* (1820: 24). The 'Advertisement to the Series' prefixed to *Glenfell* recommends the compactness of its books for both 'Private and Family Libraries' and 'all the Circulating Libraries and Book Societies', and one difficulty seems to have stemmed from the series appealing to contradictory markets. Phillips too was no longer at the centre of the fiction market, compared with the days when he had courted and won Lady Morgan, and distribution could have been another problem, notwithstanding the link with William Sams's Pall-Mall circulating library evident in the imprints.

In spite of this failure, a new popularity for the single volume tale or novel form is more broadly manifest in the output of the 1820s, with 27.5 per cent of titles falling into this category. A number of titles published by William Blackwood in the mid-1820s, such as J. G. Lockhart's *The History of Matthew Wald* (1824: 60), exploited the smaller sharper print style now in fashion to offer nearly full-scale works of fiction at 10s 6d. The tally of one-volume works is also considerably boosted at this time by the popularity of the shorter moral evangelical tale, produced not only by specialist concerns such as Francis Westley, but also increasingly favoured by more general producers such as Longmans. In introducing her *The Lettre de Cachet; A Tale* (1827: 32), Catherine Gore also argued eloquently in favour of the single-volume form, in terms which anticipate more modern predilections for reading matter within the same covers.[138]

Another area of development, this time outside the aegis of the main trade, is found in the form of number publication (i.e. serialized fiction). Two of the leading authors here were Catherine George Ward and Hannah Maria Jones [later Lowndes], Ward having previously worked as a Minerva author. The main publisher specializing in this field was George Virtue, whose imprints show a number of London addresses, as well as branches in Bristol and Liverpool, from which travelling salesmen moved out selling instalments on a door-to-door basis. Twelve titles by Ward originally serialized in this way, and seven by Jones, are included in the bibliography, where a handful of similar such publications (see, e.g., 1825: 27, 37; 1827: 57) are also found, the criterion for entry being a later sale as a single

---

[138] 'I am told there is a general prejudice against a *single volume*. If so, it must exist in the bookselling, not in the book-reading world' (Preface, p. [iii]). Gore goes on to specify a number of classic shorter works, such as *The Vicar of Wakefield*, a list which interestingly ends with J. G. Lockhart's *Adam Blair* (1822: 54).

entity. Usually weekly numbers consisting of 24 pages were sold at the price of 6d each, though double numbers were sometimes issued at the same price, and there was also the option of buying monthly parts at 2s. Engraved illustrations, usually eight plus an engraved title-page, were presumably supplied as part of the general package. A valuable illustration of the pattern of publication is provided by the copy in the British Library of the first number (24 pp.) of Ward's *The Widow's Choice* (1823: 84), issued by John Saunders, whose Ivy Lane, Paternoster Row address places him immediately next to Virtue's main London headquarters. The original paper wrapper announces: 'This truly interesting Work will be printed from Stereotype Plates on a superfine paper, embellished with beautiful Copperplate Engravings, and completed in about 25 numbers, price 6d each, or in Parts, at 2s each.' The majority of titles of this kind entered in the listings have been discovered in the form of large single volumes, consisting of between 600 and 800 large octavo-size pages, made up from the assembled numbers. The presence usually in these of an additional title-page indicates a separate sale once the serialization had been completed, probably at the price of the sum total of the numbers.

Another interesting feature of serial publication, evident in a number of joint entries in the listings, is the issuing of at least some works independently in multi-volume forms. Three of Hannah Maria Jones's titles were apparently reprinted and published jointly with the serialized versions as conventional three- or four-volume novels. The price given for these latter in sources such as the *English Catalogue of Books* (ECB) noticeably exceeds the sum total charged for the serialized version by a considerable extent. For example, the three-volume version of Jones's *Rosaline Woodbridge* (1827: 46[a]) is listed as costing 25s in ECB and as 25s in boards by the *Edinburgh Review*, whereas the 712 pages found in the serialized version (see 1827: 46[b])), representing probably 30 numbers, are likely to have cost no more than 15s. This indicates strongly that the multi-volume versions were directed primarily at circulating libraries rather than at individual purchasers. In fact, this is made explicit in the preliminaries to the 1824 four-volume reprint of Ward's *The Mysterious Marriage* (1820: 68):

If unprecedented demand and extensive circulation be a just criterion of the merits of a literary work, the Mysterious Marriage may claim a rank amongst the standard novels of our country. And the Publisher, in offering the present edition, is actuated by a wish to introduce it to the notice of the numerous supporters of Public Libraries . . .[139]

According to Mihai H. Handrea, the *Mysterious Marriage* was initially sold in 27 numbers at 6d each, totalling 13s 6d,[140] whereas the price given in ECB for the four-volume version is 21s. The existence of parallel publications of this kind is itself indicative of an increasing diversification in the fiction market.

---

[139] 'Advertisement', dated London, July 1824. The presence of this edition at Corvey, rather than the one-volume version, is also significant.

[140] 'Books in Parts and the Number Trade', in Richard G. Landon (ed.), *Book Selling and Book Buying: Aspects of the Nineteenth-Century British and North American Book Trade* (Chicago, 1978), pp. 34–51 (p. 41).

Of the 2,256 titles in this volume, less than a quarter went into a subsequent edition in Britain or Ireland. (Irish reprints themselves, it should be noted, are extremely rare after 1800/1.) The existence of further editions, of course, offers a less than perfect guide in gauging the popularity of particular works. Novels which had a wide and long-lasting currency in the circulating libraries, for example, are likely to have generated fewer editions, since copies were shared, than novels of the moment, such as T. S. Surr's *Winter in London* (1806: 64), where a succession of editions probably reflects a high proportion of retail sales. Generally the practice in this period was to describe editions in successive numerical terms (as 2nd, 3rd, 4th etc.), and these descriptions are followed in the entries under 'Further edition(s)'.[141] In all, slightly more than twenty novels appear to have generated six or more later editions in non-collected forms up to 1850. It is noticeable that the bulk of these titles belong to the first half of the period covered by this volume, with Scott's *Waverley* (1814: 52) representing the last of the main grouping, and Thomas Moore's *The Epicurean* (1827: 53) representing a rare late example. Obviously works earlier in the period had a greater opportunity to accrue later editions to 1850; but, even allowing for this, the preponderance of early titles is striking. One explanation no doubt lies in the smaller impressions generally produced for first editions at that time. While many of the titles in this category clearly enjoyed a wide circulation, reference even to seven pre-1815 cases where ten or more subsequent editions are found reveals different patterns of popularity.

Sophie Cottin's *Elizabeth; or, the Exiles of Siberia* (1807: 15), at the head of the group with at least twenty further editions, clearly benefited both from its relative cheapness as a non-copyright reprint and (as suggested earlier) its appeal as a homiletic instrument. *Fatherless Fanny* (1811: 31), originally attributed to Mrs Edgeworth, acquired a new popularity as a number publication and was frequently reprinted under both London and provincial imprints. Hannah More's *Cœlebs in Search of a Wife* (1808: 81) had the full weight of the polite evangelical movement behind it, the number of surviving copies still found in antiquarian bookshops indicating a predominantly retail sale. Jane Porter's *Thaddeus of Warsaw* (1803: 59), on the other hand, with a steady flow of new editions by Longmans, evidently enjoyed success both as a circulating library novel and as an individual purchase. Among Maria Edgeworth's fiction, both *Castle Rackrent* (1800: 30) and *Tales of Fashionable Life* (1809: 22) generated at least 10 further editions. The earlier tale's tally, however, is aided by a number of parallel Dublin reprints, reflecting an immediate topical significance, whereas a more extensive success appears to have been

---

[141] Care naturally needs to be taken in counting editions. It was not uncommon procedure for publishers to divide the same impression into different editions as a marketing ploy. Another practice was to add cancel title-pages, claiming a new edition, as a means of giving unsold stock a new look. In some cases where gaps between surviving editions are found, it is unclear whether intervening editions are lost or not. Yet, even allowing for such uncertainties, a number of subsequent editions seems a fair token of a work having enjoyed a wider or longer circulation than was usual. The obverse certainly seemed to be the case to Maturin, when writing the Preface to his *Women* (1818: 41): 'None of my former prose works have been popular. The strongest proof of which is, none of them arrived at a second edition.'

achieved by the two series of the larger (and much costlier) second publication. Elizabeth Hamilton's *Cottagers of Glenburnie* (1808: 52), with both compactness and evangelical correctness on its side, was probably further buoyed up by a newly emergent vogue for 'national' tales and rustic 'manners'. Reference to other elements available in the entries, such as the number of surviving copies in copyright libraries, the reviews received by a work, and existence of translated versions, will also help build up the profile of individual works in terms of their early reception.

In addition to British and Irish subsequent editions, the entries give the first American edition as discovered in the secondary sources used in preparing this volume. Naturally this procedure does not apply in those cases where the entry itself describes the first British edition of a work originally published in America.[142] Table 9 lists the number of British titles, by year of original publication, which have been found in American editions up to 1850, and also records the number of such titles which were reprinted in America either in the same year as, or the year immediately following, the original date of publication. If the 30 or so titles in the listings originally published in America are excluded from the calculations, then the 73 American reprints based on British titles belonging to the 1800s represent 9.5 per cent of novels for that decade, with the 118 relating to the 1810s representing 17.9 per cent, and the 183 stemming from the 1820s reaching as high as 23 per cent of output. Just as revealing is the increasing proportion in later years of novels published within a year of the original British edition, with 83 per cent of reprints matching this criterion in the 1820s, as

Table 9. **American Editions of New British Titles, 1800–1829 (to 1850)**

| Imprint Year | Total US edns. | US edns. within 1 yr | Imprint Year | Total US edns. | US edns. within 1 yr | Imprint Year | Total US edns. | US edns. within 1 yr |
|---|---|---|---|---|---|---|---|---|
| 1800 | 14 | 9 | 1810 | 6 | 5 | 1820 | 14 | 13 |
| 1801 | 7 | 1 | 1811 | 11 | 7 | 1821 | 15 | 12 |
| 1802 | 4 | 2 | 1812 | 14 | 12 | 1822 | 18 | 15 |
| 1803 | 5 | 1 | 1813 | 9 | 2 | 1823 | 14 | 11 |
| 1804 | 2 | 1 | 1814 | 11 | 6 | 1824 | 18 | 16 |
| 1805 | 6 | 2 | 1815 | 10 | 9 | 1825 | 12 | 9 |
| 1806 | 7 | 4 | 1816 | 11 | 11 | 1826 | 18 | 15 |
| 1807 | 7 | 5 | 1817 | 16 | 15 | 1827 | 20 | 16 |
| 1808 | 10 | 5 | 1818 | 18 | 13 | 1828 | 26 | 23 |
| 1809 | 11 | 6 | 1819 | 12 | 11 | 1829 | 28 | 22 |
| *1800s* | *73* | *36* | *1810s* | *118* | *91* | *1820s* | *183* | *152* |
| | | | | | | Total | 374 | 279 |

[142] Some 30 British reprints of titles originally published in America are included in the listings, six in the 1810s, one only in the 1810s, and the remainder in the 1820s. For further details, see above, p. 47.

opposed to less than 50 per cent in the 1800s. Individual factors, such as the Anglo-American war of 1813–1814, obviously underlie some more particular fluctuations.

By the 1820s, with unimpeded and improved communications, a number of relationships had clearly developed between British publishers and their counterparts in centres such as Boston, New York, and Philadelphia. While copyright restrictions did not apply in either direction, there was a clear incentive for American publishers to make an arrangement so as to be first on the market with a high-profile title. Prepublication sheets of Scott's novels, beginning with *Rob Roy* in 1818, were regularly sent over the Atlantic, and in 1822 the Philadelphia firm of Carey and Lea established in writing its right to be sole recipients of such materials.[143] This factor helps explain the speed with which some American imprints, including syndicated publications in different towns, appeared after the original British publication. As Maria Edgeworth noted on 4 February 1822: 'every English book of celebrity is reprinted in America with wonderful celerity. For instance on the twenty ninth day after one of Walter Scott's novels was published in London it was republished in Philadelphia and sold at a third less than the London price—a guinea instead of a guinea and a half.'[144]

The degree to which arrangements of this kind affected other authors is uncertain, but clearly similar engagements took place. A letter of Longmans to an American correspondent in September 1813 refers to his offer of £500 'for a duplicate M.S. copy' of Frances Burney's *The Wanderer* (1814: 17), a work which indeed appeared with some alacrity in its New York edition.[145] The direct display of the original publisher in several London reprints by A. K. Newman would seem to indicate a prior arrangement rather than outright piracy, and it is not unlikely that other publishers specializing in American materials had running agreements with overseas counterparts. Any full appraisal of the kinds of title imported into America would require further research and analysis, though a preference for popular mainstream titles is fairly evident, with the main centres often apparently producing independent editions in the same year.

This volume also points to an increasing outflow from the English fiction market to those in France and Germany.[146] As Table 10 indicates, as a whole the listings record the translation of 341 English novels into French and/or German: 250 into French, 204 into German, with 113 of these titles receiving translations into both

[143] See David Kaser, 'Waverley in America', *Papers of the Bibliographical Society of America*, 51 (1957), 163–7; also his *Messrs. Carey & Lea of Philadelphia: A Study in the History of the Booktrade* (Philadelphia, 1957). A detailed example of the relationship between different American editions is given in J. H. Alexander, 'The First American editions of Scott's *Kenilworth*', *The Bibliotheck*, 18 (1992–3), 11–21.

[144] Edgeworth, *Letters from England, 1813–1844*, ed. Colvin, p. 341. Edgeworth's informant was Gerald Ralston, a citizen of Philadelphia, and both were guests of David Ricardo.

[145] Longman Letter Books I, 98, no. 63: 6 Sept. 1813 (to Mr Breevort).

[146] Recovery of translations has greatly benefited from the ongoing research at Paderborn University, by Rainer Schöwerling and Verena Ebbes, in preparation of their *Die Rezeption englischer Romane in Deutschland 1790–1834. Eine Bibliographie* (forthcoming). In the present volume the actual titles of French and German translations are only given (with an authority) when significantly differing from, or adding to, the English source title.

languages. If works translated into English from foreign languages are excluded from calculations,[147] then French translations up to 1850 are found in the case of about 12 per cent of total British output 1800–1829 and German translations in the case of slightly less than 10 per cent. In the course of this period, Britain evidently becomes the dominant partner in the interchange with both countries. Whereas the 71 works translated from French into English in the 1800s slightly exceed the 68 titles belonging to that decade translated into French, for the 1820s the 21 titles translated from French into English are far exceeded by 111 English novels translated into French. In the case of Germany, the degree of saturation attained by English origin titles is even more remarkable. For the 1800s, 38 titles translated from German into English almost exactly balance 37 titles belonging to that decade translated into German; but in the case of 1820s output, 20 works translated from the German are far outweighed by no less than 134 novels translated from English into German. In fact, the number of novels from the 1820s that received translations in Germany noticeably exceeds the number of equivalent translations into French (134 as opposed to 111).

Generally speaking, translations in French were more likely to appear before those in German, though in the later 1820s German translators in a number of instances responded at least as quickly as their French counterparts in picking out and processing key novels. Of 113 titles translated into both French and German, 63 appeared in France first, 18 in Germany first, and 32 were issued in the same year. France's position as the leading partner in the reception and translation of English fiction is at its most evident in the case of novels originating from the 1810s, with 17 of the titles translated into both languages appearing first in French and only one title having a prior German translation. In the case of 1820s titles, however, from 71 titles translated into both languages, 12 appeared in German first and 26 in the same year in the two countries.

Of the 204 German first translations recorded in this bibliography, almost 70 per cent (142) were published in the 1820s, compared with 19 in the 1800s and 20 in the 1810s (the remainder being post-1829). In France the spread by ten-year periods is less uneven, with 38 translations being published in the 1800s, 73 in the 1810s, and 118 in the 1820s (all but one of the remaining 21 being issued in the 1830s). Seen in yearly terms, the French intake of English novels shows a fairly regular progression, though there is a distinct surge in the immediate post-war years (22 works translated in 1816–1817, as opposed to nine in 1814–1815): a level sustained in the 1820s, in which 1824 represents the optimum year (19 translations). In the case of Germany, translations are virtually non-existent in the years 1804–1809 (four novels translated only) and 1811–1814 (four again only). Thereafter there is a noticeable increase between 1816 and 1820 (15 translations), followed by a rapid acceleration during the 1820s, with 1827 (26 translations) representing the maximum year.

---

[147] See Table 1 above, p. 41, for information concerning the numbers of translated titles so excluded.

Table 10. New Novels in English, 1800–1829, Translated into French and German (to 1850)

| Imprint Year | French & German | French Only | German Only | Total Translated |
|---|---|---|---|---|
| 1800 | 2 | 7 | 7 | 16 |
| 1801 | 6 | 9 | 2 | 17 |
| 1802 | — | 4 | 1 | 5 |
| 1803 | 3 | 2 | 1 | 6 |
| 1804 | 1 | 3 | — | 4 |
| 1805 | 1 | 5 | 1 | 7 |
| 1806 | 3 | 6 | 3 | 12 |
| 1807 | 1 | 6 | — | 7 |
| 1808 | 1 | 4 | 1 | 6 |
| 1809 | 3 | 1 | — | 4 |
| *1800s* | *21* | *47* | *16* | *84* |
| 1810 | — | 4 | — | 4 |
| 1811 | 2 | 6 | 1 | 9 |
| 1812 | — | 3 | 1 | 4 |
| 1813 | 3 | 3 | 2 | 8 |
| 1814 | 4 | 6 | 1 | 11 |
| 1815 | 1 | 2 | 3 | 6 |
| 1816 | 3 | 7 | — | 10 |
| 1817 | 1 | 7 | 1 | 9 |
| 1818 | 4 | 8 | 1 | 13 |
| 1819 | 3 | 4 | 2 | 9 |
| *1810s* | *21* | *50* | *12* | *83* |
| 1820 | 8 | 5 | 1 | 14 |
| 1821 | 4 | 7 | 3 | 14 |
| 1822 | 8 | 8 | 5 | 21 |
| 1823 | 6 | 3 | 10 | 19 |
| 1824 | 8 | 5 | 6 | 19 |
| 1825 | 8 | 3 | 6 | 17 |
| 1826 | 6 | 3 | 9 | 18 |
| 1827 | 8 | — | 9 | 17 |
| 1828 | 8 | 4 | 6 | 18 |
| 1829 | 7 | 2 | 8 | 17 |
| *1820s* | *71* | *40* | *63* | *174* |
| Total | *113* | *137* | *91* | *341* |

As in the case of American editions, further research is required before a full pic-ture can emerge of the kinds of English fiction absorbed by both countries. Some salient trends are nevertheless fairly apparent. As a whole the French translated more English novels by female writers than male (126 to 115, with 9 gender unknown), though in the case of 1820s titles the balance shifts to male-authored works (79 to 27 female, 5 unknown). In Germany a much larger proportion of male-authored works were translated (122 male, 75 female, and 7 gender unknown), the disparity com-pared with the French gender balance being partly explainable by the heavier intake of English source titles from the 1820s. French readers appear to have been more responsive to sentimental/Gothic titles and works by known women writers in the earlier period, whereas the much fewer German translations covering those years tend to pick out key popular titles, Maria Edgeworth's *Belinda* (1801: 24) and William Godwin's *Fleetwood* (1805: 33) alike. German translations of the earlier Waverley novels are likely to lag several years behind the first French version, but from the beginning of the 1820s French and German translations usually appeared contemporaneously, often in the same year as the original British publication. The craze for Scott in France did not obliterate other interests: the American novels of James Fenimore Cooper were quickly translated, and an appetite for the Irish novels of the Banim brothers is also apparent. In Germany the enthusiasm for the Waverley novels seems at points to have been almost all-consuming, leading to the rapid trans-lation of historical fictions by Horatio Smith and others working in the Scott vein, as well as the fabrication of at least one Scott title and the cultivation of a number of non-existent Scott associations.[148]

The year 1829 marks a watershed in the production of fiction in Britain, with the first clear realization of an extended middle-class market. Writing to Scott on 21 March 1828, Robert Cadell relayed the report of an associate about the extensive sale of the Waverley series in Germany:

So great is the run for the novels throughout that Country that one bookseller assured him he had sold 10,000 sets at one shilling a Novel—or 3d a Volume—and that they print 40,000 and 50,000 at a time!!![149]

Cadell was on the point of launching the Magnum Opus edition of the Waverley Novels, which offered single volumes in cloth-covered boards at 5s published monthly, starting in June 1829. Sales, which had been projected at 12,000, rose as high as 30,000; the printing process also involved stereotype plates, and steam printing, which so far had been under-exploited in the production of regular fiction.[150] The Magnum was the model for Colburn and Bentley's Standard Novels

---

[148] The best-known illustration of 'Scottomanie' (a contemporary term) in Germany is *Walladmor* (see 1825: 38), allegedly a novel by Scott translated by Georg Wilhelm Heinrich Häring (the true author), and 're-translated' back into English by De Quincey. Amongst several works wrongly ascribed to Scott in their German translation is Christian Isobel Johnstone's *Clan-Albin* (1815: 32).

[149] NLS, MS 796, f. 249. The associate was Mr Bowring.

[150] See Millgate, *Scott's Last Edition*, passim.

series, which began in February 1831 with Fenimore Cooper's *The Pilot*, in one volume, priced at 6s.[151] In some respects, this marks the beginning of the end of the distinct cultural phase which is recorded in this bibliography. At the same time, it would be mistaken to allow the apparent cohesion of the bulk of the works listed to obscure radical changes which took place in the production of fiction in the Romantic era, not least the contrary forces of consolidation and dispersal increasingly evident in the 1820s.

[151] For further details of the series, which eventually ran to 127 volumes, the last of which appeared in 1854, see Gettmann, *Victorian Publisher*, pp. 28–54, and Michael Sadleir, 'Bentley's Standard Novel Series: Its History and Achievement', *Colophon*, 10 (1932), [45]–[60]. In including recent work by living writers, by agreement, the series broke from the copyright restraints that had governed earlier reprint series, themselves further hampered by the extension of copyright in 1814 to 28 years or the life of the author. While not breaking the established pattern of three volumes at 31s 6d for new works, the series did herald the Victorian practice of following expensive first editions with cheaper reprints.

# An Historical Bibliography of
# Prose Novels in English
# First Published in the British Isles
# 1800–1829

PETER GARSIDE

and

RAINER SCHÖWERLING

with the assistance of Christopher Skelton-Foord
and Karin Wünsche

# 1800

1800: 1    ANON.

ALPHONSO DI BORGO; OR, A SENTIMENTAL CORRESPONDENCE OF THE SIXTEENTH CENTURY.

London: Printed for J. and T. Carpenter, Old Bond Street, 1800.
iv, 147p. 8vo. 3s 6d (Bent03); 4s boards (CR).
CR 2nd ser. 32: 470 (Aug 1801); WSW I: 10.
BL 012612.df.31; EM 334: 6; ESTC t068057 (NA TxU).

*Notes.* Dedication to Lady Harry Parker signed 'The Author, London, June 1800'.


1800: 2    ANON.

ALUREDUS, KNIGHT OF MALTA. IN THREE VOLUMES.

London: Printed by J. D. Dewick, Aldersgate Street, for R. Dutton, 10, Birchin Lane, Cornhill, 1800.
I 276p; II 288p; III 312p. 12mo. 13s 6d (Bent03).
Corvey; CME 3-628-47050-1; ESTC n031338 (NA CaAEU, CtY).


1800: 3    ANON.

THE BARONET: A NOVEL. FOUNDED ON FACTS. IN THREE VOLUMES.

London: Printed by J. D. Dewick, 20, Aldersgate Street; for R. Dutton, 10, Birchin Lane, Cornhill, 1800.
I 226p; II 220p; III 177p. 12mo. 10s 6d (Bent03).
Corvey; CME 3-628-47107-9; ESTC n032364 (NA PU).


1800: 4    ANON.

THE CHILD OF HOPE; OR, INFIDELITY PUNISHED. A NOVEL. BY A LADY. IN THREE VOLUMES.

London: Printed for Vernor and Hood, No. 31, Poultry, by J. Cundee, Ivy-Lane, 1800.
I 226p; II 239p; III 239p. 12mo. 10s 6d (Bent03); 10s 6d sewed (CR).
CR 2nd ser. 31: 115–16 (Jan 1801); WSW I: 23–4.
Corvey; CME 3-628-47263-6; ESTC t212844.


1800: 5    ANON.

HORATIO, OF HOLSTEIN. IN THREE VOLUMES.

London: Printed for R. Dutton, Birchin-Lane, Cornhill, 1800.
I 264p; II 240p; III 248p. 12mo. 12s (Bent03); 12s sewed (CR).
CR 2nd ser. 31: 116–17 (Jan 1801); WSW I: 55.
Corvey; CME 3-628-47683-6; EM 998: 4; ESTC n001748 (NA ICU, MH-H).

1800: 6   ANON.

## IDALIA. A NOVEL. FOUNDED ON FACTS. IN TWO VOLUMES.

> London: Printed for the Author, at the Minerva-Press, by William Lane, Leadenhall-Street, 1800.
> I 251p; II 269p. 12mo. 7s (Bent03).
> Corvey; CME 3-628-47869-3; ESTC t129873 (BI BL; NA CaAEU, MH-H).

*Notes.* List of subscribers (8 pp. unn.) at beginning of vol. 1, including *c.*145 names.

1800: 7   ANON.

## JULIA COLVILLE. IN THREE VOLUMES.

> Chester: Printed and sold by W. Minshull, at the Eastgate. Sold also by Crosby and Letterman, No. 4, Stationers-Court, near Paternoster-Row, London, 1800.
> I iv, 222p; II iv, 189p; III iv, 191p. 12mo. 9s (Bent03).
> CaAEU PR.3991.A1.J94.1800; ESTC n055261.

## THE LIBERTINES; OR, MONKISH MYSTERIES! A ROMANCE.

See Vol. 1, 1798: 11; also present Vol., Appendix E: 1

1800: 8   ANON.

## THE LORD OF HARDIVYLE, AN HISTORICAL LEGEND OF THE FOURTEENTH CENTURY.

> London: Printed for W. Treppass, No. 31, St. Martin's-Le-Grand. J. Rider, Printer, Little-Britain, 1800.
> 174p. 12mo. 2s 6d (Bent03); 3s 6d boards (CR).
> CR 2nd ser. 28: 478 (Apr 1800); WSW I: 68.
> Corvey; CME 3-628-48113-9; xESTC.

1800: 9   ANON.

## MIDSUMMER EVE, OR THE COUNTRY WAKE. A TALE OF THE SIXTEENTH CENTURY. IN TWO VOLUMES.

> Newcastle upon Tyne: Printed for the Author by Edward Walker, Pilgrim-Street; and sold by Joseph Mawman, Poultry, London, 1800.
> I 157p; II 179p. 12mo. 6s sewed (CR, MR); 6s (ECB).
> CR 2nd ser. 32: 107–8 (May 1801); MR n.s. 35: 333 (July 1801); WSW I: 76.
> Corvey; CME 3-628-48129-5; ECB 383; xESTC.

*Notes.* ECB dates Jan 1801, with Mawman as publisher.
Further edn: French trans., 1801 [as *La Soirée d'été*, spuriously attributed to M. G. Lewis (MLC)].

1800: 10   ANON.

## THE MYSTERIOUS PENITENT; OR, THE NORMAN CHATEAU. A ROMANCE.

> Winchester: Printed and sold by Ja. Robbins; sold also by Crosby and Letterman, Stationer's-Court, Ludgate Hill, London, 1800.

I 227p; II 165p. 12mo. 6s sewed (CR); 6s (ECB).
CR 2nd ser. 32: 469–70 (Aug 1801); WSW I: 81.
Corvey; CME 3-628-48180-5; ECB 403; EM 1289: 5; ESTC n010244 (NA MH-H).

*Notes.* ECB dates Mar 1801, and gives Crosby as publisher.
Further edns: Dublin 1801 (NUC); New York (from 3rd London edn.) 1834 (NUC).

## 1800: 11 ANON.
### THE NEIGHBOURHOOD, A TALE. IN TWO VOLUMES.

London: Printed for A. and J. Black, and H. Parry, Leadenhall-Street, 1800.
I iv, 234p; II iv, 263p. 12mo. 8s (Bent03); 7s sewed (CR, MR).
CR 2nd ser. 30: 230–1 (Oct 1800); MR n.s. 33: 207 (Oct 1800); WSW I: 82.
BL C.175.n.19; ESTC t131306 (NA CSmH, MB, MH-H &c.).

## 1800: 12 ANON.
### THE PICTURE OF THE AGE. A NOVEL. IN TWO VOLUMES.

London: Printed for H. D. Symonds, Paternoster-Row, 1800.
I xiii, 205p; II 181p. 8vo. 7s (Bent03); 7s boards (CR); 6s sewed (MR).
CR 2nd ser. 29: 471 (Aug 1800); MR n.s. 35: 429–30 (Aug 1801); WSW I: 92.
Corvey; CME 3-628-48439-1; ESTC n061593 (NA NcD, PU).

*Notes.* CR states: 'Though this work is brought forward as an orginal, we have no doubt, from a great number of passages, that it is a translation from the French'. No French original, however, has been discovered. Printer's mark (in square brackets) after imprint date reads: 'T. Davison, Lombard-Street, Fleet-Street'.

## 1800: 13 ANON.
### THE SAILOR BOY. A NOVEL. IN TWO VOLUMES.

London: Printed at the Minerva-Press, for William Lane, Leadenhall-Street, 1800.
I 239p; II 242p. 12mo. 8s (Bent03).
Corvey; CME 3-628-48591-6; EM 168: 3; ESTC t066390 (BI BL; NA CaAEU, IU, MH-H).

*Notes.* Further edn: Boston 1801 (NUC).

## 1800: 14 ANON.
### SELINA, A NOVEL, FOUNDED ON FACTS. BY A LADY. IN THREE VOLUMES.

London: Printed for C. Law, Avemaria-Lane, by Bye and Law, St. John's-Square, Clerkenwell, 1800.
I viii, 239p; II 268p; III 254p. 12mo. 10s 6d (Bent03); 10s 6d sewed (CR, MR).
CR 2nd ser. 30: 230 (Oct 1800); MR n.s. 32: 93 (May 1800); WSW I: 109.
Corvey; CME 3-628-48643-2; EM 131: 3; ESTC t066392 (BI BL; NA IU).

## 1800: 15 ANON.
### A SHORT STORY: INTERSPERSED WITH POETRY. BY A YOUNG LADY. IN TWO VOLUMES.

London: Printed and published by Geo. Cawthorn, British Library, No. 132, Strand, Bookseller to Her Royal Highness the Princess of Wales; sold also by Messrs. Richardson,

Royal-Exchange; H. D. Symonds, J. Wallis, West and Hughes, Paternoster-Row; and J. Wright, Piccadilly, 1800.

I vii, 201p; II 204p. 12mo. 7s (Bent03); 7s sewed (CR).

CR 2nd ser. 31: 116 (Jan 1801); WSW I: 111.

Corvey; CME 3-628-48689-0; EM 170: 4; ESTC t066394 (BI BL; NA CaAEU, NNS).

1800: 16   ANON.
THE SPIRIT OF TURRETVILLE: OR, THE MYSTERIOUS RESEMBLANCE. A ROMANCE OF THE TWELFTH CENTURY: IN TWO VOLUMES.

London: Printed by J. D. Dewick, 20, Aldersgate Street; for R. Dutton, 10, Birchin Lane, Cornhill, 1800.

I iv, 200p; II 223p. 12mo. 7s (Bent03); 7s sewed (CR).

CR 2nd ser. 31: 114–15 (Jan 1801).

Corvey; CME 3-628-48800-1; EM 131: 4; ESTC t066395 (BI BL).

*Notes.* 'Advertisement', regarding subject of novel, states: 'The Proprietor of an extensive circulating library informed him [the author], that he could not keep a ghost or a spirit at home' (p. [iii]).

Further edn: German trans., 1834?

1800: 17   ANON.
TALES OF TRUTH. BY A LADY. UNDER THE PATRONAGE OF THE DUCHESS OF YORK. IN FOUR VOLUMES.

London: Printed by T. Plummer, Seething-Lane; for R. Dutton, No. 10, Birchin-Lane, Cornhill, 1800.

I 153p; II 179p; III 170p; IV 168p. 8vo. 14s (Bent03); 14s sewed (CR).

CR 2nd ser. 31: 475 (Apr 1801); WSW I: 118.

Corvey; CME 3-628-48874-5; EM 1279: 10; ESTC n013589 (NA MH-H, NjP).

*Notes.* Dedication to the Duchess of York signed 'E. H.'. Main text preceded by 2 poems, 'Sonnet to Gratitude' and 'Lines Addressed to her R.H. the Duchess of York'.

BENNETT, Anna Maria, DE VALCOURT
See LAKE, Eliza

1800: 18   BISSET, Robert.
DOUGLAS; OR, THE HIGHLANDER. A NOVEL. IN FOUR VOLUMES. BY ROBERT BISSET, L.L.D. AUTHOR OF THE LIFE OF BURKE, &C.

London: Printed at the Anti-Jacobin Press, by T. Crowder, Temple Lane, Whitefriars; and sold by C. Chapple, Pall Mall; T. Hurst, Paternoster Row; and J. and E. Kerby, Bond Street, 1800.

I vi, xxviii, 323p; II v, 300p; III viii, 315p; IV xii, 382p. 12mo. 18s (Bent03).

CR 2nd ser. 30: 116 (Sept 1800); WSW I: 158.

Corvey; EM 240: 1; ESTC t068561 (BI BL, E; NA CaAEU, MH-H).

*Notes.* Dedication to 'the most noble George, Marquis of Huntley', dated Sloane Terrace, 1 Feb 1800.

Further edn: Dublin 1800 (NUC).

1800: 19   [BROWN, Charles Brockden].
ORMOND; OR THE SECRET WITNESS. BY THE AUTHOR OF
WIELAND, ARTHUR MERVYN, &C. &C.

London: Printed at the Minerva-Press, for William Lane, Leadenhall-Street, 1800.
iv, 338p. 12mo. 4s 6d (Bent03).
WSW I: 174.
Corvey; CME 3-628-47138-9; ESTC t131855 (BI BL; NA CtY).

*Notes.* Dedication to I. E. Rosenberg. Collates in sixes. ECB 78 lists Colburn edn., Nov 1810,
15s. Originally published New York 1799 (Blanck).
Further edns: 1811 (NSTC); 1822 (NUC); 1839 (NSTC); German trans., 1802 (ascribed to
William Godwin).

1800: 20   [BURKE, Mrs].
ELLIOTT: OR, VICISSITUDES OF EARLY LIFE. IN TWO VOLUMES. BY
A LADY.

London: Printed and published by Geo. Cawthorn, British Library, No. 132, Strand,
Bookseller to Her Royal Highness the Princess of Wales; sold also by Messrs.
Richardson, Royal-Exchange; H. D. Symonds, J. Wallis West and Hughes, Paternos-
ter-Row; and J. Wright, Piccadilly, 1800.
I viii, 338p; II 295p. 12mo. 8s (Bent03); 7s sewed (CR); 8s sewed (MR).
CR 2nd ser. 31: 353–4 (Mar 1801); MR n.s. 35: 332 (July 1801).
Corvey; CME 3-628-47524-4; ESTC t210673 (BI BL; NA IU, PU).

*Notes.* 'A List of Subscribers' Names', vol. 1, pp. [i]–viii, headed by 'His Royal Highness the
Duke of Gloucester, 3 sets', and with *c.*215 other names (many titled).

1800: 21   BUTLER, Weeden (*trans.?*).
ZIMAO, THE AFRICAN. TRANSLATED BY THE REV. WEEDEN
BUTLER, M.A. OF SIDNEY SUSSEX COLLEGE, CAMBRIDGE.

London: Printed for Vernor and Hood, in the Poultry; by S. Rousseau, Wood Street,
Spa Fields, 1800.
xi, 105p. 8vo.
BL 837.b.35(1); ESTC t075674 (BI O).

*Notes.* ESTC states this appears not to be a translation. Small engraving on t.p. Preface
addressed to 'Courteous Reader' and signed W. B., Cheynè Walk, Chelsea. Dedication 'to A
Lady eminent for her private qualities and her public station', pp. [v]–x; six-line verse quo-
tation from Darwin, p. xi. Text ends on p. 71 and the rest is an appendix concerning slavery.
Further edns: Dublin, 1800 (Printed by Brett Smith, for Gilbert and Hodges, Burnett, Porter,
Halpin, Rice [and 5 others]), ESTC t075675; 2nd edn. 1807 (NSTC).

1800: 22   [CARVER, Mrs].
THE OLD WOMAN. A NOVEL. IN TWO VOLUMES. BY THE AUTHOR
OF THE HORRORS OF OAKENDALE ABBEY.

London: Printed for the Author, at the Minerva-Press, by William Lane, Leadenhall-
Street, 1800.

I 218p; II 255p. 12mo. 7s (Bent03).

Corvey; CME 3-628-48255-0; ESTC t223030 (BI BL).

*Notes.* Blakey notes attributed to Mrs Carver in Minerva Library Catalogue of 1814.

1800: 23   CLARK, Emily.

ERMINA MONTROSE; OR, THE COTTAGE OF THE VALE. IN THREE VOLUMES. WITH CHARACTERS FROM LIFE. BY EMILY CLARK, GRAND-DAUGHTER OF THE LATE COLONEL FREDERICK, AND AUTHOR OF "IANTHE; OR, THE FLOWER OF CAERNARVON."

London: Printed for the Author, and sold by James Wallis, Paternoster-Row, 1800.

I viii, 239p; II 272p; III 244p. 12mo. 12s (Bent03); 12s boards (CR).

CR 2nd ser. 31: 355–6 (Mar 1801).

Corvey; CME 3-628-47290-3; EM 131: 5; ESTC t070069 (BI BL; NA CaAEU, MH-H).

*Notes.* Dedication 'to the Right Honorable Countess of Shaftesbury', signed Emily Clark, No 4, Cockspur-street, Haymarket. 'List of Subscribers' (*c.*110 names), vol. 1, pp. [iii]–viii, includes Maria Edgeworth ('twenty copies').

1800: 24   ?COBBE, Sarah.

JULIA ST. HELEN; OR, THE HEIRESS OF ELLISBOROUGH. A NOVEL. IN TWO VOLUMES. PUBLISHED BY SARAH COBBE, RELICT OF THE REV. RICHARD CHALONER COBBE, RECTOR OF BRADENHAM IN BUCKINGHAMSHIRE, AND CHAPLAIN TO THE RIGHT HONOURABLE THE EARL OF MOIRA.

London: Printed by J. Nichols, Earl's Court, Leicester-Square; sold by Earle and Hemet, No. 47, Albemarle-Street, Piccadilly, 1800.

I xvii, 228p; II 240p. 12mo. 8s (Bent03).

BL 12654.f.10; ESTC t107266.

*Notes.* Dedication to 'the Right Honourable the Earl of Moira, Baron Rawdon, &c. &c. &c. &c.', dated 15 June 1800. Preface states 'that Julia St. Helen *is not mine*, but has been kindly obtained for me from the deceased author's relatives, through the interference of a friend, and upon the condition that I should publish it by subscription' (p. [vii]). 'List of Subscribers' (*c.*410 names), vol. 1, pp. [ix]–xvii, followed by 1 p. (unn.) adv. for 'Original French and English Circulating Library, W. Earle'.

1800: 25   [CRAIK, Helen].

ADELAIDE DE NARBONNE, WITH MEMOIRS OF CHARLOTTE DE CORDET. A TALE. IN FOUR VOLUMES. BY THE AUTHOR OF HENRY OF NORTHUMBERLAND.

London: Printed at the Minerva-Press, for William Lane, Leadenhall-Street, 1800.

I 286p; II 267p; III 283p; IV 304p. 12mo. 16s (Bent03).

WSW I: 7.

BL 12612.dd.2; EM 273: 1; ESTC t066881 (BI MRu; NA CaAEU).

*Notes.* Blakey notes attributed to Craik by Minerva Library Catalogue of 1814.

1800: 26   [CRAIK, Helen].
## HENRY OF NORTHUMBERLAND, OR THE HERMIT'S CELL. A TALE OF THE FIFTEENTH CENTURY. IN THREE VOLUMES.

London: Printed at the Minerva-Press, for William Lane, Leadenhall-Street, 1800.
I xii, 233p, ill.; II 247p; III 249p. 12mo. 12s (Bent03); 10s 6d sewed (CR).
CR 2nd ser. 29: 115–16 (May 1800); WSW I: 52.
Corvey; CME 3-628-47777-8; ESTC t200843 (NA CaAEU, CLU-S/C).

*Notes.* Further edn: Dublin 1800 (Printed by William Folds, for P. Wogan, W. Porter, B. Dornin, J. Rice, and G. Folingsby, 2 vols., 12mo), ESTC n032935.


1800: 27   CROFFTS, Mrs.
## ANKERWICK CASTLE. A NOVEL. IN FOUR VOLUMES. BY MRS. CROFFTS.

London: Printed at the Minerva-Press, for William Lane, Leadenhall-Street, 1800.
I 286p; II 251p; III 259p; IV 249p. 12mo. 14s (Bent03); 14s sewed (CR).
CR 2nd ser. 31: 235–6 (Feb 1801); WSW I: 227.
Corvey; CME 3-628-47352-7; ESTC n042635 (NA IU).

*Notes.* Further edn: German trans., 1801 [as *Schloß Ankerwick. Ein Sittengemälde nach der Natur* (RS)].


1800: 28   [DUBOIS, Edward].
## ST. GODWIN: A TALE OF THE SIXTEENTH, SEVENTEENTH, AND EIGHTEENTH CENTURY. BY COUNT REGINALD DE ST. LEON.

London: Printed for J. Wright, Piccadilly, 1800.
xxiii, 235p. 12mo. 3s 6d (Bent03, MR).
MR n.s. 33: 224 (Oct 1800); WSW I: 251.
BL 12613.d.8; EM 276: 4; ESTC t070070 (BI MRu; NA CtY-BR, CSmH, IU, MH-H, NN, TxU &c.).

*Notes.* Dedication to Mrs Sheridan. Preface dated 26 Dec 1799. A satire of William Godwin's *St. Leon* (1799).
Further edns: 2nd edn. (corrected) 1800 (BRu ENC); Dublin, 1800 (Printed for P. Wogan, W. Porter, B. Dornin, H. Fitpatrick, J. Rice, G. Folingsby, and E. Mercier, 1 vol., 12mo), ESTC t160333.


1800: 29   [EARLE, William (jun.)].
## OBI; OR, THE HISTORY OF THREE-FINGERED JACK. IN A SERIES OF LETTERS FROM A RESIDENT IN JAMAICA TO HIS FRIEND IN ENGLAND.

London: Printed for Earle and Hemet, No. 47, Albemarle-Street, Piccadilly, 1800.
vi, 232p. 12mo. 4s (Bent03).
ViU PR.3431.E171800; ESTC t176735 (BI BL, Lics; NA NjP, PU).

*Notes.* 'Advertisement' signed 'W. E. J.'.
Further edns: Worcester, Mass., 1804 (NUC). Also numerous chapbook versions of this story (and songs from the pantomime version) with similar titles. For example, BL 1076.l.24(15), with the same lead title (Newcastle: Printed by M. Angus & Son [1800?]), is 24 pp.

1800: 30   [EDGEWORTH, Maria].

CASTLE RACKRENT, AN HIBERNIAN TALE. TAKEN FROM FACTS, AND FROM THE MANNERS OF THE IRISH SQUIRES, BEFORE THE YEAR 1782.

> [London]: Printed for J. Johnson, St. Paul's Church-Yard, 1800.
> xliv, 182p. 8vo. 4s (ECB).
> WSW I: 255.
> BL 12611.f.4; ECB 178 (3rd edn.); EM 58: 1; ESTC t057317 (BI C, D, Dt; NA CaOHM, PU, TxU &c.).

*Notes.* Printer information, 'By J. Crowder, Warwick-Square', after imprint date. 'Advertisement to the English Reader', followed by 'Glossary', pp. [xv]–xliv.
Further edns: 1800, EM 4582: 3, ESTC t143397; Dublin, 1800 (Printed for P. Wogan, H. Colbert, P. Byrne, W. Porter, J. Halpen, [and 5 others in Dublin]), ESTC t111009; 2nd edn. Dublin 1801 (NSTC); 3rd edn. 1801 (Corvey), CME 3-628-47575-9; 3rd edn. Dublin 1802 (NSTC); 4th edn. 1804 (NSTC); 5th edn. 1810 (NSTC); 5th edn. Dublin 1810 (NSTC); [at least 3 more edns. to 1850]; Boston 1814 (NUC); German trans., 1802.
Facs: IAN (1979).

1800: 31   [ELSON, Jane].

ROMANCE OF THE CASTLE. IN TWO VOLUMES.

> London: Printed at the Minerva-Press, for William Lane, Leadenhall-Street, 1800.
> I ii, 236p, ill.; II 238p. 12mo. 7s (Bent03).
> WSW I: 105.
> Corvey; CME 3-628-48470-7; ESTC t200842 (NA CaAEU, CtY, IaU).

*Notes.* Price given as '7s sewed' in adv. on verso of last page of *The Faux Pas* (1800: 47).

1800: 32   {F}[OSTER, Mrs] {E. M.}.

EMILY OF LUCERNE. A NOVEL. IN TWO VOLUMES. BY THE AUTHOR OF THE DUKE OF CLARENCE.

> London: Printed at the Minerva-Press, for William Lane, Leadenhall-Street, 1800.
> I 240p; II 304p. 12mo. 7s (Bent03).
> Corvey; CME 3-628-47563-5; ESTC n030766 (NA PU).

*Notes.* Dedication in the 2nd vol. after t.p. 'to Her Royal Highness the Princess of Wales' signed 'E. M. F.'.

1800: 33   {F}[OSTER, Mrs] {E. M.}.

FREDERIC & CAROLINE, OR THE FITZMORRIS FAMILY. A NOVEL. IN TWO VOLUMES. BY THE AUTHOR OF REBECCA, JUDITH, MIRIAM, &C.

> London: Printed at the Minerva-Press, for William Lane, Leadenhall-Street, 1800.
> I 256p; II 296p. 12mo. 7s (Bent03).
> BL 12613.aaa.11; CME 3-628-47838-3; EM 199: 2; ESTC t068576 (NA CaAEU).

*Notes.* Dedication 'to Her Royal Highness, the Princess of Wales', signed 'E. M. F'. The Dedication is not found in the Corvey copy of this title. Drop-head title and running-titles read 'Fitzmorris'.

1800: 49   LATHOM, Francis.

MYSTERY, A NOVEL: IN TWO VOLUMES. BY FRANCIS LATHOM, AUTHOR OF MEN AND MANNERS, OF WHICH A NEW EDITION IS JUST PUBLISHED; THE MIDNIGHT BELL; THE CASTLE OF OLLADA, &C.

London: Printed for H. D. Symonds, Paternoster-Row, by T. Davison, Lombard-Street, White-Friars, 1800.
I viii, 292p; II 268p. 12mo. 8s (Bent03); 7s sewed (MR).
CR 2nd ser. 30: 116 (Sept 1800); MR n.s. 33: 207 (Oct 1800); WSW I: 362.
Corvey; CME 3-628-47961-4; London edn. xESTC.

*Notes.* Further edn: Dublin, 1800 (Printed for P. Wogan, W. Porter, B. Dornin, J. Rice, P. Moore, G. Folingsby, and J. Stockdale. By Thomas Burnside, 1 vol., 12mo), EM 7472: 10, ESTC t121180.

1800: 50   [LECLERCQ, Michel-Théodore].

THE INVISIBLE MAN, OR DUNCAM CASTLE. IN TWO VOLUMES. FROM THE FRENCH.

London: Printed at the Minerva-Press, for William Lane, Leadenhall-Street, 1800.
I 227p; II 215p. 12mo. 7s (Bent03).
BL C.192.a.173; ESTC t226755.

*Notes.* Trans. of *Le Château de Duncam, ou l'homme invisible* [Paris, n.d.]. Summers wrongly attributes to Pigault-Lebrun, and Blakey questions his authorship.

1800: 51   LINLEY, William.

FORBIDDEN APARTMENTS. A TALE. IN TWO VOLUMES. BY WILLIAM LINLEY.

London: Printed at the Minerva-Press, for William Lane, Leadenhall-Street, 1800.
I x, 280p; II 328p. 12mo. 8s (Bent03); 8s boards (CR).
CR 2nd ser. 32: 231 (June 1801).
MH-H *EC8.L6487.800f; EM 1007: 26; ESTC n002288 (NA CaAEU, CtY, NjP; EA GOT).

*Notes.* Preface argues the case for compactness in fiction, compared with stories by some female authors 'made to drag through six volumes' (p. vii).
Further edn: French trans., 1801 [as *Le Jeune Héritier, ou les appartements défendus* (MLC)].

1800: 52   LITTLEJOHN, P.

THE MISTAKE: OR, SOMETHING BEYOND A JOKE. IN THREE VOL-UMES. BY P. LITTLEJOHN, AUTHOR OF HENRY AND THE CIPHER.

London: Printed for the Author, by J. Bonsor, Salisbury Square. And sold by T. Hurst, Paternoster-Row, Kerbys', Bond Street, and Dutton, Birchin Lane, 1800.
I xi, 238p; II 240p; III 266p. 12mo. 12s (Bent03); 12s boards (CR, MR).
CR 2nd ser. 31: 355 (Mar 1801); MR n.s. 35: 331–2 (July 1801); WSW I: 375.
Corvey; CME 3-628-48033-7; EM 7474: 3; ESTC t110147 (BI BL; NA CaAEU, MH-H).

1800: 53   MACKENZIE, Anna Maria.
FEUDAL EVENTS, OR, DAYS OF YORE. AN ANCIENT STORY. IN TWO
VOLUMES. BY ANNA MARIA MACKENZIE, AUTHOR OF NEAPOLI-
TAN, DUSSELDORF, &C. &C.

> London: Printed at the Minerva-Press, for William Lane, Leadenhall-Street, 1800.
> I xi, 242p, ill.; II 276p. 12mo. 7s (Bent03).
> Corvey; CME 3-628-48095-7; EM 1282: 5; ESTC n006527 (NA MH-H).

*Notes.* Dedication 'to Mrs. Tennant, of Bromley, Middlesex, (With Permission.)'. 'Postcript'
[*sic*], facing first page of novel text, justifies 'the modernised diction of this ancient tract'.


1800: 54   [MARTIN, Mrs].
JEANNETTE. A NOVEL. IN FOUR VOLUMES. BY THE AUTHOR OF
MELBOURNE, REGINALD, DELORAINE, &C.

> London: Printed at the Minerva-Press, for William Lane, Leadenhall-Street, 1800.
> I 279p; II 263p; III 254p; IV 216p. 12mo. 14s (Bent03); 14s boards (CR).
> CR 2nd ser. 31: 356 (Mar 1801).
> Corvey; CME 3-628-48012-4; ESTC n067472 (NA CtY).

*Notes.* Blakey notes attributed by Minerva Library Catalogue of 1814 to Mrs Martin.


1800: 55   [MEEKE, Mary].
ANECDOTES OF THE ALTAMONT FAMILY. A NOVEL. IN FOUR VOL-
UMES. BY THE AUTHOR OF THE SICILIAN, &C.

> London: Printed at the Minerva-Press, for William Lane, Leadenhall-Street, 1800.
> I 250p; II 266p; III 306p; IV 365p. 12mo. 16s (Bent03).
> Corvey; CME 3-628-47059-5; EM 221: 1; ESTC t089386 (BI BL; NA NjP).


MINIFIE, Susannah
See GUNNING, Susannah


1800: 56   [MOORE, John].
MORDAUNT. SKETCHES OF LIFE, CHARACTERS, AND MANNERS,
IN VARIOUS COUNTRIES; INCLUDING THE MEMOIRS OF A
FRENCH LADY OF QUALITY. BY THE AUTHOR OF ZELUCO &
EDWARD.

> London: Printed for G. G. and J. Robinson, Paternoster-Row; S. Hamilton, Falcon-
> Court, Fleet-Street, 1800.
> I ii, 403p; II ii, 408p; III ii, 460p. 8vo. 21s (Bent03); 21s boards (CR, MR).
> CR 2nd ser. 28: 264–76 (Mar 1800) full review; MR n.s. 32: 149–52 (June 1800) full
> review; WSW I: 404.
> BL 12611.h.16; CME 3-628-48297-6; EM 197: 1; ESTC t057357 (BI C, E &c; NA CaAEU,
> CLU-S/C, PU &c.; EA SU).

*Notes.* Corvey copy has misbound pages at end of vol. 1. MR indexes as 'Moore's *Mordaunt*',
and refers to 'Dr. Moore' passim in its review.

Further edns: Dublin, 1800 (Printed for W. Watson and Son—G. Burnet—P. Wogan—P. Byrne—H. Colbert [and 12 others in Dublin], 3 vols., 12mo), ESTC t077681; Chiswick 1830 (NSTC); New York 1801 (NUC).

1800: 57    MOSER, Joseph.
**TALES AND ROMANCES, OF ANCIENT AND MODERN TIMES. IN FIVE VOLUMES. BY JOSEPH MOSER, ESQ. AUTHOR OF TURKISH TALES, HERMIT OF CAUCASUS, TIMOTHY TWIG, MORAL TALES, &C. &C. &C.**

> London: Printed by Sampson Low, Berwick Street, Soho; for T. Hurst, Paternoster Row, 1800.
> I 271p; II 244p; III 229p; IV 292p; V 244p. 12mo. 20s (Bent03).
> WSW I: 412.
> Corvey; CME 3-628-48337-9; ESTC n046778 (BI MRu; NA NjP).

*Notes.* I Cara Rustines, a Turkish Tale; II The History of Achmet Beg and Sadi. A Turkish Tale; III The Pictures; The Turban, a Turkish Tale; IV Adelfrid, a Christmas Tale; The Cadi of Adrianople; The Adventures of Frank Fidget; V The Greek Alphabet; or, Black and White. The last page of vol. 3 is mistakenly numbered 129.

1800: 58    PARSONS, [Eliza].
**THE MISER AND HIS FAMILY. A NOVEL. IN FOUR VOLUMES. BY MRS. PARSONS, AUTHOR OF THE VALLEY OF ST. GOTHARD, MYS-TERIOUS WARNINGS, &C.**

> Brentford: Printed by and for P. Norbury; and sold by J. Wallis, No. 46, Pater-Noster-Row, London, 1800.
> I 238p; II 263p; III 288p; IV 326p. 12mo. 16s (Bent03); 16s boards (CR).
> CR 2nd ser. 32: 105–6 (May 1801); WSW I: 430.
> Corvey; CME 3-628-48397-2; ESTC t173325 (BI BL, C; NA CtY, IU, NjP).

*Notes.* Further edn: Dublin 1801 (NUC).

1800: 59    [PESTALOZZI, Johann Heinrich; LEDGARD, Sir J. (*trans.*)].
**LEONARD & GERTRUDE. A POPULAR STORY, WRITTEN ORIGIN-ALLY IN GERMAN; TRANSLATED INTO FRENCH, AND NOW ATTEMPTED IN ENGLISH; WITH THE HOPE OF ITS BEING USEFUL TO THE LOWER ORDERS OF SOCIETY.**

> Bath: Printed and sold by S. Hazard: sold also by Cadell and Davies, Strand, London; Todd, York; Pennington, Kendal; Bulgin, Bristol; and all other Booksellers, 1800.
> 367p. 12mo. 3s (Bent03); 3s sewed (CR, MR).
> CR 2nd ser. 33: 354 (Oct 1801); MR n.s. 33: 446 (Dec 1800); WSW I: 65.
> BL C.171.bb.2; EM 2555: 13; ESTC t117390.

*Notes.* Trans. of *Lienhard und Gertrud* (1st pt. Berlin, 1781; 2nd, 3rd pt. Frankfurt 1783–5). French translation: *Léonard et Gertrude* (1st, 2nd pt. Lausanne, 1784). Dedication to William Wilberforce, Esq., signed 'The Translator'. ECB 443 lists 2 vols. Mawman 1825 edn., 10s 6d. Further edns: 1824 (another trans.) (NSTC); 1825 (NSTC); Philadelphia 1801 (NUC).

1800: 60    [?PIGAULT-LEBRUN, Charles-Antoine].
THE MONK OF THE GROTTO, OR EUGENIO & VIRGINIA. A TALE. IN
TWO VOLUMES. FROM THE FRENCH.

> London: Printed at the Minerva-Press, for William Lane, Leadenhall-Street, 1800.
> I xxx, 238p; II 249p. 12mo. 7s (ECB).
> Corvey; CME 3-628-48265-8; ECB 391; xESTC.

*Notes.* French original not discovered. Summers states original by Pigault-Lebrun, but both
Gecker and Blakey question his authorship. ECB treats as anon. and dates Jan 1801. Continu-
ous roman and arabic pagination in vol. 1, with novel proper beginning at p. [31].
Further edn: Boston 1846 (NUC).


1800: 61    PROBY, William Charles.
THE SPIRIT OF THE CASTLE, A ROMANCE. IN TWO VOLUMES. BY
WILLIAM CHARLES PROBY, AUTHOR OF THE MYSTERIOUS SEAL, &C.

> London: Printed by J. W. Myers, No 2, Paternoster-Row, for Crosby and Letterman,
>      Stationer's Court, Paternoster-Row, 1800.
> I 264p; II 221p. 12mo. 7s (Bent03).
> WSW I: 452.
> Corvey; CME 3-628-48400-6; ESTC n037353 (NA CaAEU).

*Notes.* Further edn: Baltimore 1801 (NUC).


1800: 62    [REGNAULT-WARIN, Jean Baptiste Joseph].
*THE CAVERN OF STROZZI. A VENETIAN TALE.

> William Lane, 1800.
> 1 vol. 12 mo. 3s 6d (Bent03); 3s 6d sewed (CR).
> CR 2nd ser. 31: 355 (Mar 1801).
> No copy of 1st edn. located.

*Notes.* Trans. of *La Caverne de Strozzi* (Paris, 1798). Details mainly from Blakey (copy not seen).
Further edns: New York 1801 (NUC); 1812 [n.p.] (NUC).


1800: 63    ROCHE, Regina Maria.
NOCTURNAL VISIT. A TALE. IN FOUR VOLUMES. BY MARIA
REGINA [*sic*] ROCHE, AUTHOR OF THE CHILDREN OF THE ABBEY,
MAID OF THE HAMLET, VICAR OF LANSDOWNE, AND CLERMONT.

> London: Printed at the Minerva-Press, for William Lane, Leadenhall-Street, 1800.
> I 309p; II 290p; III 260p; IV 395p. 12mo. 21s (Bent03).
> Corvey; CME 3-628-48463-4; ESTC t127131 (BI BL; NA CaAEU, IU).

*Notes.* Further edns: Philadelphia 1801 (NUC); French trans., 1801; German trans., 1802.
Facs: GNIII (1977).


1800: 64    SCHILLER, [Johann Christoph] F[riedrich]; RENDER, W[ilhelm] (*trans.*).
THE ARMENIAN; OR, THE GHOST-SEER. A HISTORY FOUNDED ON
FACT. TRANSLATED FROM THE GERMAN OF F. SCHILLER, AUTHOR
OF THE ROBBERS, DON CARLOS &C. BY THE REV. W. RENDER.

London: Printed by C. Whittingham, Dean Street, Fetter Lane, for H[.] D. Symonds,
Paternoster Row, 1800.

I vi, 223p; II 243p; III 255p; IV 256p. 12mo. 14s (Bent03).

BL 1154.i.8; EM 2903: 2; ESTC t100181 (BI O; NA CaOHM, CSmH, CLU-S/C &c.).

*Notes.* Trans. of *Der Geisterseher. Eine Geschichte aus den Papieren des Grafen von O\*\**
(Leipzig, 1789); 2nd and 3rd part continued by X. Y. Z. (i.e. Emanuel Friedrich Wilhelm
Ernst Follenius) (Leipzig, 1796–7). This follows an earlier translation by D. Boileau of
Schiller's original first part only, under the title *The Ghost-Seer; or Apparitionist* (London,
1795). Imprint in vols. 2 and 3 changes to: 'Printed by J. Cundee, Ivy Lane, [etc.]'.

Further edn: Dublin, 1800 (Printed by William Folds, for P. Wogan, H. Colbert, J. Rice, B.
Dornin, G. Folingsby, and P. Moore, 2 vols., 12mo), EM 4850: 5, ESTC t084060; Philadelphia
1801 (NUC).

1800: 65    [SELDEN, Catharine].
## THE SAILORS. A NOVEL. IN TWO VOLUMES. BY THE AUTHORESS OF COUNT DE SANTERRE, THE ENGLISH NUN, AND LINDAR.

Reading: Printed by R. Snare and Co. and sold by Crosby and Letterman, Stationer's-
Court, Paternoster-Row, London, 1800.

I 236p; II 180p. 12mo. 7s (Bent03); 7s sewed (CR).

CR 2nd ser. 31: 235 (Feb 1801).

O Vet.A5.ef.2351, 2352; ESTC t178629 (NA NcU).

*Notes.* Collates in sixes.

1800: 66    SELDEN, Catharine.
## SERENA. A NOVEL. IN THREE VOLUMES. BY CATHARINE SELDEN, AUTHOR OF THE ENGLISH NUN, &C.

London: Printed at the Minerva-Press, for William Lane, Leadenhall-Street, 1800.

I 234p; II 216p; III 221p. 12mo.

Corvey; CME 3-628-48637-8; EM 126: 3; ESTC t070705 (BI BL).

1800: 67    [SHERIFFE, Sarah].
## HUMBERT CASTLE, OR THE ROMANCE OF THE RHONE. A NOVEL. IN FOUR VOLUMES.

London: Printed at the Minerva-Press, for William Lane, Leadenhall-Street, 1800.

I ii, 312p, ill.; II 318p; III 293p; IV 336p. 12mo. 16s (Bent03); 18s boards (CR).

CR 2nd ser. 32: 231 (June 1801); WSW I: 56.

Corvey; CME 3-628-47752-2; ESTC n033323 (BI E; NA CaAEU).

*Notes.* Dedication to 'Mrs. F——R'. Allibone gives attribution to Mrs Sarah Sheriffe, who is
there stated to have died in 1849 in her 77th year, writing 3 novels when she was still Miss
Bennet (the title above, plus *Correlia* (1802: 57), and *The Forest of Hohenelbe* (1803: 64) ).

1800: 68    SICKELMORE, Richard.
## MARY-JANE. A NOVEL. IN TWO VOLUMES. BY RICHARD SICKEL-MORE, AUTHOR OF EDGAR, OR THE PHANTOM OF THE CASTLE, AGNES AND LEONORA; &C. &C.

London: Printed for the Author, at the Minerva-Press, by William Lane, Leadenhall Street, 1800.

I 229p, ill.; II 235p. 12mo. 7s (Bent03); 7s sewed (CR).

CR 2nd ser. 31: 236 (Feb 1801).

Corvey; CME 3-628-48691-2; EM 7474: 1; ESTC t127132 (BI BL; NA CaAEU, CtY-BR, MH-H).

*Notes.* Dedication to Sir Godfrey Webster, Bart. signed by Richard Sickelmore.

1800: 69    SMITH, Charlotte.
### THE LETTERS OF A SOLITARY WANDERER: CONTAINING NARRATIVES OF VARIOUS DESCRIPTION. BY CHARLOTTE SMITH.

London: Printed by and for Sampson Low, Berwick Street, Soho, 1800/02.

I (1800) vii, 307p; II (1800) 317p; III (1801) 381p; IV (1802) viii, 276p; V (1802) 306p. 12mo. 13s 6d sewed (CR, MR) for first 3 vols; 10s boards (CR, MR) for vols. 4 and 5; 25s for 5 vols. (Bent03); 10s (ECB) for vols. 4 and 5.

CR 2nd ser. 32: 35–42 (May 1801) full review for first 3 vols; CR 2nd ser. 37: 54–8 (Jan 1803) full review for vols. 4 and 5; MR n.s. 35: 332 (July 1801) for first 3 vols., 39: 428 (Dec 1802) for vols. 4 and 5; WSW I: 503.

Corvey; CME 3-628-48660-2; ECB 544; EM 989: 14; ESTC n003685 (BI E, O, MRu; NA CtY, MH-H, PU, NjP &c.); NSTC S2380 (BI E, O).

*Notes.* Preface in vol. 1 dated 20 Oct 1800. Preface to the 4th and 5th vols. dated 1 Feb 1802. Imprint in vols. 4 and 5 changes to 'Printed for T. N. Longman and O. Rees, Paternoster-Row'.

Further edns: Dublin 1801 (NSTC); German trans., 1802; French trans., 1806 [of 'The Story of Corsiande' as *Corsiande de Beauvilliers* (BLC)] and 1819 [of 'The Story of Henrietta' as *Les Cavernes des Montagnes-Bleues, ou Orgueil et haine* (BLC)].

Facs: RR (of vols. 1–3; 1995).

1800: 70    SMITH, [Horatio].
### A FAMILY STORY, IN THREE VOLUMES. BY MR. SMITH.

London: Printed by C. Boult, for Crosby and Letterman, Stationers-Court, near Paternoster-Row, 1800.

I 268p; II 244p; III 262p. 12mo. 10s 6d (Bent03).

CR 2nd ser. 28: 477 (Apr 1800); WSW I: 502.

Corvey; CME 3-628-48655-6; ESTC n067809 (NA CaAEU).

*Notes.* 'This day published', 12 Dec 1799, *General Evening Post.* Summers dates 1797, but apparently in error.

1800: 71    SMITH, [Horatio].
### THE RUNAWAY; OR, THE SEAT OF BENEVOLENCE. A NOVEL. IN FOUR VOLUMES. BY MR. SMITH.

London: Printed for Crosby and Letterman, Stationers'-Court, Ludgate-Street, 1800.

I 255p; II 247p; III 267p; IV 261p. 12mo. 16s (Bent03); 14s sewed (CR, MR).

CR 2nd ser. 31: 474 (Apr 1801); MR n.s. 34: 204 (Feb 1801); WSW I: 502–3.

Corvey; CME 3-628-48657-2; ESTC t196606 (BI BL, O).

1800: 72 [?SUMMERSETT, Henry].
**JAQUELINE OF OLZEBURG: OR, FINAL RETRIBUTION. A ROMANCE.**

London: Printed by T. Plummer, Seething-Lane; and sold by Chapple, Pall-Mall; and R. Dutton, Birchin-Lane, Cornhill, 1800.
191p. 12mo. 3s 6d (Bent03); 3s 6d sewed (CR).
CR 2nd ser. 31: 115 (Jan 1801); WSW I: 60.
Corvey; CME 3-628-47992-4; EM 1010: 16; ESTC n001023 (NA MH-H).

*Notes.* Attributed to Summersett on the t.p. of his *Martyn of Fenrose* (1801: 63).

1800: 73 SUMMERSETT, Henry.
**LEOPOLD WARNDORF. A NOVEL. IN TWO VOLUMES. BY HENRY SUMMERSETT, AUTHOR OF THE MAD MAN OF THE MOUNTAIN, &C. &C. &C.**

London: Printed at the Minerva-Press, for William Lane, Leadenhall-Street, 1800.
I viii, 294p; II 311p. 12mo. 7s (Bent03).
BL 12613.aa.20; EM 240: 3; ESTC t068569 (NA CaAEU).

1800: 74 THICKNESSE, {A}[nn].
**THE SCHOOL FOR FASHION, IN TWO VOLUMES. BY MRS. THICK-NESSE.**

London: Printed by H. Reynell, No. 21, Piccadilly, for Debrett and Fores, Piccadilly; Hookham, Old Bond Street; and Robinsons, Paternoster-Row, 1800.
I xviii, 234p, ill.; II 286p, ill. 8vo. 12s (ECB); 12s boards (MR).
CR 2nd ser. 31: 479–80 (Apr 1801); MR n.s. 35: 430–1 (Aug 1801); WSW I: 535.
CtY-BR 1975.801; ECB 584; ESTC n036333 (BI C; NA PPL).

*Notes.* List of 'Subscribers' (44 names) , vol. 1, pp. [iii]–iv; 'Dedication. To Fashion', signed 'A. T.', vol. 1, pp. [v]–xvii. Frontispiece portrait of 'Mrs. Thickness', opp. t.p. in vol. 1; similar portrait of 'Phil^p. Thickness E^sq' opp. t.p. in vol. 2. Collates in fours. ECB dates June 1802.

1800: 75 VULPIUS, [Christian August]; HINCKLEY, [John] (*trans.*).
**THE HISTORY OF RINALDO RINALDINI, CAPTAIN OF BANDITTI. TRANSLATED FROM THE GERMAN OF VULPIUS. BY I. HINCKLEY, ESQ. IN THREE VOLUMES.**

London: Printed by A. Strahan, Printers-Street, for Longman and Rees, Paternoster-Row; and C. Geisweiler, Parliament-Street, 1800.
I viii, 269p; II 247p; III 200p. 12mo. 10s 6d (Bent03); 10s 6d boards (MR).
MR n.s. 33: 207 (Oct 1800).
ViU PZ2.V84H.1800; ESTC t219039 (EA ZAP).

*Notes.* Trans. of *Rinaldo Rinaldini, der Räuberhauptmann* (Leipzig, 1799). Half-titles, drop-head and running-titles all read: 'Rinaldo Rinaldini'. Preface, vol. 1, pp. [iii]–viii, incorporating 'The Author's Preface [. . .] written on St. Rosalia's day 1798'. 8 pp. (unn.) list of 'Books Printed for T. N. Longman and O. Rees' at end of vol. 3. ECB 494 lists Newman edn., 1831, 13s 6d.

Further edns: Dublin 1801 (NSTC); 1801 (NSTC); 1831 as *Rinaldo Rinaldini, Captain of Banditti* (NSTC); '4th edn.' 1841 (NSTC, NUC); Charleston, SC, 1814 (NUC).

1800: 76   WALKER, George.
THE THREE SPANIARDS, A ROMANCE. BY GEORGE WALKER, AUTHOR OF THE VAGABOND, &C. IN THREE VOLUMES.

>    London: Printed by Sampson Low, for G. Walker, No. 106, Great Portland Street; and
>    Hurst, No. 32, Paternoster-Row, 1800.
>    I 295p; II 262p; III 250p. 12mo. 12s (Bent03).
>    WSW I: 551.
>    Corvey; CME 3-628-48815-X; ECB 619; ESTC t181013 (BI O).

*Notes.* Further edns: Dublin 1800 (Printed by Brett Smith, for P. Wogan, J. Rice, G. Folingsby, and B. Dornin, 2 vols., 12mo), ESTC n027345; Dublin 1802 (NUC); 1821 (NSTC); New York 1801 (NUC); French trans., 1805.

1800: 77   WELLS, Helena.
CONSTANTIA NEVILLE; OR, THE WEST INDIAN. A NOVEL. IN THREE VOLUMES. BY HELENA WELLS, AUTHOR OF "THE STEP-MOTHER," &C.

>    London: Printed by C. Whittingham, Dean-Street, Fetter-Lane, for T. Cadell, jun. and
>    W. Davies, Strand; and W. Creech, Edinburgh, 1800.
>    I xxviii, 340p; II vii, 432p; III viii, 380p. 12mo. 15s (Bent03); 15s sewed (CR, MR).
>    CR 2nd ser. 29: 472 (Aug 1800); MR n.s. 33: 206 (Oct 1800); WSW I: 27, 555–6.
>    BL 12613.d.3; EM 291: 7 and 292: 1; ESTC t070084 (BI KIK; NA InU-Li).

*Notes.* Preface dated Little Park-Street, Westminster, 15 Apr 1800. 'List of Subscribers' (*c.*375 names), followed by 'Subscribers on the Continent' (13 'Berlin' names, 28 more 'At Hamburgh'), and 'Subscribers in Charleston, South Carolina' (55 listed), vol. 1, pp. [ix]–xxiv. 4 pp. adv. at end of vol. 3 for 2nd edn. of same author's *The Step-Mother*, and for her *Letters on Subjects of Importance to the Happiness of Young Females*, both with extracts from reviews.
Further edns: 2nd edn. 1800 (Corvey), CME 3-628-48886-9; French trans., 1801 [as *Constantia Neville, ou la jeune Américaine* (Pigoreau)].

1800: 78   WILLIAMS, William Frederick.
FITZMAURICE: A NOVEL. BY WILLIAM FREDERICK WILLIAMS, AUTHOR OF SKETCHES OF MODERN LIFE; OR, MAN AS HE OUGHT NOT TO BE. IN TWO VOLUMES.

>    London: Printed by S. Gosnell. Little Queen Street, for J. Murray and S. Highley, No. 32,
>    Fleet Street; and J. Harding, St. James's Street, 1800.
>    I vi, 210p; II 190p. 12mo. 6s (Bent03); 5s sewed (CR); 6s sewed (MR).
>    CR 2nd ser. 30: 351–2 (Nov 1800); MR n.s. 33: 103 (Sept 1800); WSW I: 564.
>    Corvey; CME 3-628-48965-2; EM 1290: 31; ESTC 006003 (BI BL; NA CaAEU, MH-H).

*Notes.* Vol. 2 imprint differs: 'London: Printed by Luke Hansard, Great Turnstile, Lincoln's-Inn Fields, [etc.]'.

1800: 79 [?WYNDHAM, Revd].

TOURVILLE: OR, THE MYSTERIOUS LOVER: A SENTIMENTAL NOVEL, IN TWO VOLUMES.

> London: Printed for Crosby and Letterman, Stationers Court, Paternoster-Row, 1800.
> I iv, 184p; II 184p. 12mo. 7s (Bent03); 7s sewed (CR).
> CR 2nd ser. 31: 357 (Mar 1801); WSW I: 122.
> Corvey; CME 3-628-48764-1; EM 1493: 21; ESTC n013717 (NA MH-H).

*Notes.* 'R. Noble, Printer, Old Bailey' below imprint date. Treated as anonymous in ESTC and NUC: the title however apparently links with *Men and Women* (see 1805: 72), which is attributed to the Revd Mr Wyndham by Summers.

1800: 80 YEATES, Mrs.

ELIZA, A NOVEL: IN TWO VOLUMES. BY MRS. YEATES, DAUGHTER OF THE LATE HOLLAND COOKSEY, ESQ. OF BRACES LEIGH, IN THE COUNTY OF WORCESTER.

> Lambeth: Printed and published by S. Tibson, No. 7, Westminster-Bridge-Road; and
> sold by C. Chapple, Pall-Mall; J. and E. Kerby, Old Bond-Street; J. Lee, No. 77, Fleet-
> Street; and West and Hughes, Paternoster-Row, 1800.
> I xii, 168p; II 180p. 12mo. 7s (Bent03); 7s sewed (CR, t.p.).
> CR 2nd ser. 31: 356–7 (Mar 1801); WSW I: 576.
> Corvey; CME 3-628-48984-9; ESTC t144767 (BI BL).

*Notes.* Dedication 'to the amiable and humane Mrs. Bland, of Ham-Court in the County of Worcester'. Preface presents author as 'tremblingly alive to all the fears which the first attempt naturally excites' (p. [v]). 'Names of Subscribers' (*c.*125 listed), vol. 1, pp. [vii]–xii. 'Elegy on the Death of Sir William Jones [. . .], written by R. Cooksey, Esq.', vol. 2, pp. [177]–180; novel proper ends on p. 176. CR states: 'This is avowed to be Mrs. Yeates's first production' (p. 357).

1800: 81 [YORKE, Mrs. R. P. M. (*trans.?*)].

VALLEY OF COLLARES, OR THE CAVERN OF HORRORS. A ROMANCE. IN THREE VOLUMES. TRANSLATED FROM THE POR-TUGUESE.

> London: Printed for the Author, at the Minerva-Press, by William Lane, Leadenhall-
> Street, 1800.
> I 247p; II 273p; III 264p. 12mo. 10s 6d (Bent03).
> Corvey; CME 3-628-48853-2; xESTC.

*Notes.* No Portuguese original discovered. Blakey notes 'Dedication to Sir Charles Gould Morgan, Bart.', but not found in Corvey copy.

# 1801

1801: 1   ANON.

**ADAMINA, A NOVEL, BY A LADY. IN TWO VOLUMES.**

London: Printed by J. D. Dewick, Aldersgate-Street, for Vernor and Hood, 31, Poultry, 1801.

I 187p; II 187p. 12mo. 7s sewed (CR, MR), 7s (ECB).

CR 2nd ser. 33: 461 (Dec 1801); MR n.s. 38: 312 (July 1802); WSW I: 7.

Corvey; CME 3-628-47013-7; ECB 4; xNSTC.

**ADONIA**

See RICHARDSON, Caroline E.

1801: 2   ANON.

**AGNES. A NOVEL. IN THREE VOLUMES. BY THE AUTHOR OF FRED-ERICA RISBERG.**

London: Printed at the Minerva-Press, for William Lane, Leadenhall-Street, 1801.

I 324p; II 369p; III 380p. 12mo. 15s (CR); 13s 6d (ECB).

CR 2nd ser. 33: 114 (Sept 1801).

Corvey; CME 3-628-47026-9; ECB 8; xNSTC.

1801: 3   ANON.

**CLARA, A TALE. IN TWO VOLUMES.**

London: Printed for G. Kearsley, Fleet-Street, 1801.

I 262p; II 203p. 12mo. 8s sewed (CR); 8s (ECB).

CR 2nd ser. 32: 470 (Aug 1801); WSW I: 25.

Corvey; CME 3-628-47286-5; ECB 117; NSTC C2048 (BI BL, O).

*Notes.* 'T. Davison, Lombard-Street, White-Friars' in square brackets after imprint date.

1801: 4   ANON.

**DOROTHEA, OR A RAY OF THE NEW LIGHT. IN THREE VOLUMES.**

London: Printed for G. G. and J. Robinson, Paternoster-Row; by R. Noble, in the Old Bailey, 1801.

I 204p; II 183p; III 161p. 12mo. 10s 6d sewed (CR, MR); 10s 6d (ECB).

CR 2nd ser. 34: 238 (Feb 1802); MR n.s. 37: 425 (Apr 1802).

Corvey; ECB 169; NSTC D1596 (BI O).

*Notes.* Further edn: Dublin 1801 (BL C.193.a.43).

1801: 5   ANON.

**FARTHER EXCURSIONS OF THE OBSERVANT PEDESTRIAN, EXEM-PLIFIED IN A TOUR TO MARGATE. IN FOUR VOLUMES. BY THE**

## AUTHOR OF THE "OBSERVANT PEDESTRIAN," IN TWO VOLUMES, "MYSTIC COTTAGER," "MONTROSE," &C.

London: Printed for R. Dutton, No. 10, Birchin-Lane, Cornhill. By J. D. Dewick, Aldersgate-Street, 1801.
I xii, 239p; II 237p; III 240p; IV 235p. 12mo.
WSW I: 42.
Corvey; CME 3-628-47635-6; NSTC M1127 (BI BL, O).

*Notes.* Introductory 'To The Reviewers In General' strongly asserts female authorship, in relation to the preceding *Observant Pedestrian* (1795): 'how will they be surprised to learn, that the subject is the sole effusions of a *female* pen, although the deep penetration of a *certain* critical class, coud neither discern or imagine such ideas were composed by a *woman*' (pp. vi–vii).

## 1801: 6 ANON.
### FIRST LOVE. A NOVEL. IN THREE VOLUMES.

London: Printed at the Minerva-Press, for William Lane, Leadenhall-Street, 1801.
I 284p; II 345p; III 365p. 12mo. 18s boards (CR).
CR 2nd ser. 32: 352 (July 1801).
Corvey; CME 3-628-47554-6; xNSTC.

*Notes.* Lacks sub-title of 'or, The history of Lady Frances Sullivan' given in Blakey (copy not seen). Distinct from *First Love* (1824: 6); and again from *First Love: A Novel* (1830), by Margracia Loudon.

## 1801: 7 ANON.
### THE KNIGHT AND MASON; OR, HE WHO RUNS MAY READ. A NOVEL. IN FOUR VOLUMES.

London: Printed for Crosby and Letterman, Stationer's-Court; by Rowland Hurst, Wakefield, 1801.
I 216p; II 214p; III 219p; IV 192p. 12mo. 18s boards (CR); 16s (ECB).
CR 2nd ser. 33: 237 (Oct 1801); WSW I: 62.
Corvey; CME 3-628-47923-1; ECB 323; NSTC K758 (BI O).

*Notes.* Drop-head and running-titles (unlike t.ps.) read 'The Knight and the Mason'. Colophons read: 'R. Hurst, Printer, Wakefield'.

## 1801: 8 ANON.
### LUSIGNAN, OR THE ABBAYE OF LA TRAPPE. A NOVEL. IN FOUR VOLUMES.

London: Printed at the Minerva-Press, for William Lane, Leadenhall-Street, 1801.
I 200p, ill.; II 205p; III 217p; IV 239p. 12mo. 14s (ECB).
Corvey; CME 3-628-48126-0; ECB 356; xNSTC.

*Notes.* 'Founded on Baculard D'Arnaud's first play *Les Amans Malheureux, ou le comte de Comminge* (1765), itself a dramatization of Madame de Tencin's story *Les Mémoires du comte de Comminge*' (Summers, p. 394). ECB dates May 1801.

1801:9   ANON.
THE MONASTERY OF GONDOLFO. A ROMANCE. BY A YOUNG
LADY.

> Limerick: Printed by John and Thomas M'Auliff, at the Circulating Library, near the
>    Exchange, 1801.
> 142p. 12mo.
> Dt OLS.188.r.80; NSTC M2821.

*Notes.* Collates in sixes.


1801:10   ANON.
MYSTERIOUS FRIENDSHIP: A TALE. IN TWO VOLUMES.

> London: Printed by Knight & Compton, Middle Street, Cloth Fair, for Earle and Hemet,
>    47, Albemarle Street, Piccadilly, 1801.
> I 236p; II 267p. 12mo. 8s sewed (CR); 8s (ECB).
> CR 2nd ser. 34: 117 (Jan 1802).
> Corvey; CME 3-628-48179-1; ECB 403; xNSTC.


1801:11   ANON.
ST. MARY'S ABBEY. A NOVEL. IN TWO VOLUMES. BY AN OFFICER
IN THE BRITISH MILITIA.

> Chelmsford: Printed for the Author, by R. C. Stanes, and Co., 1801.
> I xii, 134p; II 187p. 12mo.
> Corvey; CME 3-628-48491-X; xNSTC.

*Notes.* 'List of Subscribers' (100 names, about half of these militia officers), vol. 1,
pp. [vii]–xii. Collates in sixes. ECB 512 lists Badcock edn., Feb 1802, 7s; but not discovered in
this form.


1801:12   ANON.
THE SCOURGE OF CONSCIENCE. A ROMANCE. IN FOUR VOLUMES.

> London: Printed for R. Dutton, Birchin-Lane, Cornhill, 1801.
> I 204p; II 204p; III 284p; IV 279p. 12mo. 16s (ECB).
> Corvey; CME 3-628-48600-9; ECB 522; xNSTC.

*Notes.* ECB dates Nov 1801.


1801:13   ANON.
THE SOLDIER BOY. A NOVEL. IN THREE VOLUMES. BY THE
AUTHOR OF THE SAILOR BOY.

> London: Printed at the Minerva-Press, for William Lane, Leadenhall-Street, 1801.
> I 238p; II 238p; III 216p. 12mo. 12s sewed (CR).
> CR 2nd ser. 31: 475 (Apr 1801).
> Corvey; CME 3-628-48718-8; NSTC S2795 (BI BL).

*Notes.* Evidently by the same author as that of *Nobility Run Mad* (1802: 9) and *Diurnal Events*
(1816: 2). ECB only lists *Soldier Boy* (1831) and *Sailor Boy* (1830), by Rosalia St. Clair.

1801: 14    ANON.

THE WISE MEN OF GOSMANTHORPE. A TALE.

London: Printed by Burney and Gold, Shoe-Lane. For T. Reynolds, Oxford-Street, 1801.
xx, 206p. 12mo. 4s 6d (CR); 3s 6d (ECB).
CR 2nd ser. 33: 114 (Sept 1801).
O 249.s.514; ECB 644; NSTC G1522 (BI BL).

*Notes.* Includes several long digressions on non-fictional subjects.

1801: 15    BELLAMY, Thomas.

THE BEGGAR BOY: A NOVEL, IN THREE VOLUMES. BY THE LATE MR. THOMAS BELLAMY. TO WHICH ARE PREFIXED, BIOGRAPHI-CAL PARTICULARS OF THE AUTHOR, BY MRS. VILLA-REAL GOOCH.

London: Printed for Earle and Hemet, No. 47, Albemarle-Street, Piccadilly, by Hare
and Co. King-Street, Covent-Garden, 1801.
I xlvi, 182p, ill.; II 225p; III 230p. 12mo. 12s (ECB).
WSW I: 152.
Corvey; CME 3-628-47189-3; ECB 49; NSTC B1418 (BI BL).

*Notes.* Frontispiece portrait of 'Mr. Thomas Bellamy', carrying the legend 'Published as the
Act directs, December 20th 1800, by Earle & Hemet Albemarle Street'. Preface signed by
Elizabeth Sarah Villa-Real Gooch, Nov 1800. ECB dates Feb 1801.
Further edn: Alexandria, VA, 1802 (NSTC).

1801: 16    CHARLTON, Mary.

THE PIRATE OF NAPLES. A NOVEL. IN THREE VOLUMES. BY MARY CHARLTON, AUTHOR OF ROSELLA, ANDRONICA, PHEDORA, &C.

London: Printed at the Minerva-Press, for William Lane, Leadenhall-Street, 1801.
I 303p, ill.; II 308p; III 300p. 12mo. 13s 6d boards (CR); 13s 6d (ECB).
CR 2nd ser. 34: 476 (Apr 1802); WSW I: 203.
Corvey; CME 3-628-47256-3; ECB 107; xNSTC.

*Notes.* Further edns: French trans., 1801; German trans., 1803 [as *Der Seeräuber von Neapel
[. . .] Eine abentheuerliche Geschichte* (RS)].

1801: 17    [COLPOYS, Mrs].

THE IRISH EXCURSION, OR I FEAR TO TELL YOU. A NOVEL. IN FOUR VOLUMES.

London: Printed at the Minerva-Press, for William Lane, Leadenhall-Street, 1801.
I 310p; II 300p; III 298p; IV 297p. 12mo. 18s boards (CR); 18s (ECB).
CR 2nd ser. 32: 107 (May 1801); WSW I: 216.
Corvey; CME 3-628-47462-0; ECB 300; NSTC C3182 (BI BL, Dt).

*Notes.* Vignette, consisting of two hands, clasping a rose, thistle, and shamrock, on t.p.
Further edn: Dublin 1801 (NUC).

1801: 18    CROFFTS, Mrs.

SALVADOR, OR BARON DE MONTBELLIARD. IN TWO VOLUMES. BY MRS. CROFFTS, AUTHOR OF ANKERWICK CASTLE, &C.

London: Printed at the Minerva-Press, for William Lane, Leadenhall-Street, 1801.
I 256p; II 270p. 12mo. 8s (ECB).
Corvey; CME 3-628-47344-6; ECB 144; NSTC C4234 (BI O).

*Notes.* ECB dates May 1801.
Further edn: French trans., 1801.

1801: 19   CURTIES, T. J. Horsley.
ANCIENT RECORDS, OR, THE ABBEY OF SAINT OSWYTHE. A
ROMANCE. IN FOUR VOLUMES. BY T. J. HORSLEY CURTIES,
AUTHOR OF ETHELWINA, OR THE HOUSE OF FITZ-AUBURNE.

London: Printed at the Minerva-Press, for William Lane, Leadenhall-Street, 1801.
I viii, 408p, ill.; II 396p; III 350p; IV 319p. 12mo. 18s boards (CR); 18s (ECB).
CR 2nd ser. 32: 232 (June 1801).
BL 1578/3545; CME 3-628-47383-7; ECB 148; NSTC C4586.

*Notes.* Dedication 'to Mrs. Watson, Poets' Corner, Westminster', and signed 'No. 1
Bury Street, Bloomsbury Square, Jan. 10, 1801'. Preface, vol. 1, pp. [v]–viii, states of the
author: 'He sent his *Ethelwina* into the world as an orphan, whose father feared to acknowledge it, and under his *Christian* appellation of HORSLEY. The public have fostered it;
and now, with some degree of pride, he can claim it as his own by his *surname* of
CURTIES' (p. v).
Further edn: French trans., 1813 [as *L'Abbaye de Saint-Oswithe* (BN)].

1801: 20   DALLAS, R[obert] C[harles].
PERCIVAL, OR NATURE VINDICATED. A NOVEL. BY R. C. DALLAS,
ESQ. IN FOUR VOLUMES.

London: Printed by A. Strahan, Printers-Street, for T. N. Longman and O. Rees, Pater-
noster-Row, 1801.
I xxiv, 315p; II xi, 263p; III xii, 250p; IV viii, 250p; 12mo. 16s (ECB); 18s boards
(MR).
MR n.s. 37: 425 (Apr 1802); WSW I: 234.
BL 12612.dd.4; CME 3-628-47395-0; ECB 150; NSTC D102.

*Notes.* Dedication to 'Her [. . .] whose maternal virtues have raised around me a family of
young friends', signed R. C. Dallas.
Further edn: 2nd edn. 1802 (NSTC).

1801: 21   [DAMER, Anne Seymour].
BELMOUR: A NOVEL. IN THREE VOLUMES.

London: Printed for J. Johnson, in St. Paul's Church Yard, 1801.
I 256p; II 300p; III 332p. 12mo. 10s 6d (ECB); 10s 6d boards (MR).
MR n.s. 38: 314 (July 1802).
Corvey; CME 3-628-47234-2; ECB 49; xNSTC.

*Notes.* 'Luke Hansard, Printer, Lincoln's-Inn Fields' after imprint date.
Further edns: Dublin 1801 (NSTC D180); New edn. 1827 (Corvey); French trans., 1804 [as
*Belmont* (BN)].

1801: 22   [DUBOIS, Edward].

## OLD NICK: A SATIRICAL STORY. IN THREE VOLUMES. BY THE AUTHOR OF A PIECE OF FAMILY BIOGRAPHY, &C.

London: Printed for Murray and Highley, No. 32, Fleet-Street, 1801.

I xxxii, 198p; II xii, 266p; III xiii, 273p. 12mo. 10s 6d sewed (CR, MR); 10s 6d (ECB).

CR 2nd ser. 34: 449–53 (Apr 1802) full review; MR n.s. 36: 53–67 (Sept 1801) full review; WSW I: 251.

Corvey; CME 3-628-48252-6; ECB 172; NSTC D2013 (BI BL, C).

*Notes.* Dedication 'to Thomas Hill, Esq.', dated 10 Oct 1800.

Further edns: Dublin 1801 (NSTC); 2nd edn. 1803 (NSTC).

1801: 23   EARLE, William (jun.).

## THE WELSHMAN, A ROMANCE, IN FOUR VOLUMES. BY WILLIAM EARLE, JUN. AUTHOR OF NATURAL FAULTS, A COMEDY; OBI, OR THREE-FINGER'D JACK, &C.

London: Printed by J. D. Dewick, Aldersgate Street, for Earle and Hemet, 47, Albemarle Street, Piccadilly, 1801.

I xiv, 271p; II 238p; III 262p; IV 245p. 12mo. 16s sewed (CR); 16s (ECB).

CR 2nd ser. 34: 116–17 (Jan 1802).

Corvey; CME 3-628-47508-2; ECB 176; NSTC E40 (BI BL).

*Notes.* Dedication 'to him, to whom I am indebted for life [. . .] To her, whose arms have cradled me'.

1801: 24   EDGEWORTH, Maria.

## BELINDA. BY MARIA EDGEWORTH. IN THREE VOLUMES.

London: Printed for J. Johnson, St. Paul's Churchyard, 1801.

I 8, 370p; II 387p; III 359p. 12mo. 13s 6d boards (CR); 16s 6d (ECB); 16s 6d boards (MR).

CR 2nd ser. 34: 235–7 (Feb 1802); MR n.s. 37: 368–74 (Apr 1802) full review; WSW I: 255.

BL 012611.e.31; ECB 178; NSTC E229 (BI C, O).

*Notes.* Printer information, found at foot of half-titles, differs between vols. Vol. 1 reads 'Printed by J. Crowder, Warwick Square'; vol. 2 reads 'Printed by S. Hamilton, Falcon Court, Fleet Street'; vol. 3 reads 'Printed by G. Woodfall, Paternoster Row'. 'Advertisement', dated 20 Apr 1801, offers the work as 'a Moral Tale—the author not wishing to acknowledge a Novel'.

Further edns: Dublin 1801 (NSTC); 2nd edn. 1802 (Corvey), CME 3-628-47557-0; Dublin 1802 (NSTC); 1810 (NSTC); 3rd edn. 1811 (NSTC); 4th edn. 1821 (NSTC); [at least 2 more edns. to 1850]; Boston 1814 (NUC); French trans., 1802; German trans., 1803.

1801: 25   EDGEWORTH, Maria.

## MORAL TALES FOR YOUNG PEOPLE. BY MARIA EDGEWORTH, AUTHOR OF PRACTICAL EDUCATION, &C.

London: Printed for J. Johnson, in St. Paul's Churchyard, by G. Woodfall, Paternoster-Row, 1801.

I xi, 238p, ill.; II 197p, ill.; III 192p, ill.; IV 190p; V 190p. 12mo. 3s each (ECB, vols. 3, 4, 5); 15s 6d boards (MR).

MR n.s., 39: 334–5 (Nov 1802) full review; WSW I: 255.
BL Ch.800/132; ECB 178; NSTC E239 (BI O).

*Notes*. I Forester; II Angelina, and the Knapsack; III The Prussian Vase, and Mademoiselle Panache; IV The Good Aunt; V The Good French Governess. Preface signed by R. L. Edgeworth. MR comments: 'These tales for young people may be perused with benefit by people of all ages' (p. 334). ECB lists only vols. 3–5; also 3rd edn., May 1806, 10s 6d.
Further edns: 1802 (NSTC: 3 vols.); 2nd edn. 1806 (NSTC); 5th edn. 1809 (NSTC); 6th edn. 1813 (NSTC); 7th edn. 1816 (NSTC); [at least 2 more edns. to 1850]; Philadelphia 1810 (NUC); French trans., 1804; German trans., 1828.

1801: 26    EVANS, Robert.
**THE DREAM, OR NOBLE CAMBRIANS. A NOVEL. IN TWO VOLUMES. BY ROBERT EVANS, A.M. AUTHOR OF THE STRANGER.**

London: Printed at the Minerva-Press, for William Lane, Leadenhall-Street, 1801.
I 304p; II 258p. 12mo. 8s (ECB).
CtY-BR In.Ev158.801D; ECB 193; xNSTC.

*Notes*. ECB dates July 1801.

FORTNUM, Sophia
See KING, Sophia

1801: 27    [FOSTER, Mrs E. M.].
**CONCEALMENT, OR THE CASCADE OF LLANTWARRYHN. A TALE. IN TWO VOLUMES. BY THE AUTHOR OF MIRIAM, JUDITH, FEDARETTA, &C.**

London: Printed at the Minerva-Press, for William Lane, Leadenhall-Street, 1801.
I 222p; II 322p. 12mo. 8s (ECB).
Corvey; CME 3-628-47307-1; ECB 129; xNSTC.

*Notes*. 'To The Reader' (unn.) refers to 'The authoress of the ensuing work'. This novel is different from *Concealment* (1821: 4). ECB dates July 1801.

1801: 28    FRERE, B[enjamin].
**THE MAN OF FORTITUDE; OR, SCHEDONI IN ENGLAND. IN THREE VOLUMES. BY B. FRERE.**

London: Printed for James Wallis, No. 46, Pater-Noster-Row, 1801.
I 211p; II 236p; III 213p. 12mo. 10s 6d boards (CR); 10s 6d (ECB, MR).
CR 2nd ser. 32: 231 (June 1801); MR n.s. 37: 27–30 (Jan 1802) full review; WSW I: 274.
Corvey; CME 3-628-47839-1; ECB 219; NSTC F1764 (BI O).

*Notes*. Printer's mark after imprint date reads: 'T. Davison, Lombard-Street, White-Friars'.

1801: 29    GOOCH, Eliz{abeth} Sarah Villa-Real.
**TRUTH AND FICTION: A NOVEL, IN FOUR VOLUMES. BY ELIZ. SARAH VILLA-REAL GOOCH. AUTHOR OF THE CONTRAST, WANDERINGS OF IMAGINATION, FANCIED EVENTS, &C. &C.**

London: Printed at the Apollo Press, by G. Cawthorn, No. 132, Strand, Bookseller and
  Printer to Her Royal Highness the Princess of Wales, 1801.
I xvi, 271p, music; II 252p; III 244p; IV 233p. 12mo. 18s boards (CR); 18s (ECB).
CR 2nd ser. 36: 117–18 (Sept 1802).
Corvey; CME 3-628-48916-4; ECB 236; xNSTC.

*Notes.* Preface, vol. 1, pp. i–xvi, signed Elizabeth Sarah Villa-Real, and dated 'Michael's Place,
Brompton, 1801'. Drop-head title to vol. 1 reads 'Truth & Fiction'; those to vols. 2 and 3 read,
more extensively, 'Truth & Fiction. The History of Antonio, Count Genzano; or The Dominion
of the Passions. Addressed to Father St. Pietro, his Confessor at Naples'. ECB dates June 1802.

1801: 30   GUION, Miss.
THE ITALIAN ROMANCE, IN TWO VOLUMES. BY MISS GUION,
AUTHOR OF IMMELINA, A GERMAN STORY, IN THREE VOLUMES.

  Brentford: Printed by and for P. Norbury; and sold by J. Wallis, No. 46, Pater-Noster-Row, 1801.
  I vii, 195p; II 194p. 12mo.
  Corvey; CME 3-628-47915-0; ECB 249; NSTC G2366 (BI O).
*Notes.* ECB dates Jan 1801, and lists under Gutton, Miss.

1801: 31   HATFIELD, Miss {S.}.
SHE LIVES IN HOPES; OR, CAROLINE. A NARRATION FOUNDED
UPON FACTS. BY MISS HATFIELD, OF MANCHESTER. (BY PERMIS-
SION) DEDICATED TO HER ROYAL HIGHNESS THE PRINCESS OF
ORANGE AND NASSAU. IN TWO VOLUMES.

  London: Published for the Authoress, and sold by Parsons and Son, Ludgate-Hill; Ver-
    nor and Hood, Poultry; Carpenter and Co. Old Bond-Street; Clarks, Bancks, and
    Thomson, Manchester; and Merritts and Wright, Liverpool, 1801.
  I vii, 311p; II 297p. 12mo. 9s sewed (CR, MR); 9s (ECB).
  CR 2nd ser. 32: 470 (Aug 1801); MR n.s. 38: 313 (July 1802); WSW I: 301–2.
  BL 12611.bbb.17; ECB 258; NSTC H870.
*Notes.* Dedication signed S. Hatfield, London, 16 Apr 1801.

1801: 32   HELME, Elizabeth.
ST. MARGARET'S CAVE: OR, THE NUN'S STORY. AN ANCIENT LEG-
END. IN FOUR VOLUMES. BY ELIZABETH HELME, AUTHOR OF
ALBERT, FARMER OF INGLEWOOD FOREST, LOUISA, &C. &C.

  London: Printed for Earle and Hemet, Albemarle Street, 1801.
  I xxviii, 260p; II 294p; III 296p; IV 320p. 12mo. 21s boards (CR); 21s (ECB).
  CR 2nd ser. 34: 237–8 (Feb 1802).
  Corvey; CME 3-628-47789-1; ECB 263; NSTC H1231 (BI BL, E, O).
*Notes.* Further edns: 2nd edn. 1819 (NSTC); French trans., 1803; German trans., 1803.
Facs: GNIII (1977).

1801: 33   HOLFORD, M[argaret] [née WRENCH].
FIRST IMPRESSIONS; OR, THE PORTRAIT. A NOVEL. IN FOUR VOLUMES.
BY M. HOLFORD, AUTHOR OF SELIMA, GRESFORD VALE, POEMS, &C.

London: Printed at the Minerva-Press, for William Lane, Leadenhall-Street, 1801.
I iv, 271p, ill.; II 354p; III 344p; IV 349p. 12mo. 18s boards (CR).
CR 2nd ser. 32: 232–3 (June 1801); WSW I: 321.
Corvey; CME 3-628-47727-1; xNSTC.

*Notes.* Dedication to Miss Seward. Blakey lists under 1800, but copy not seen.
Further edn: French trans., 1813 [as *Maria Doriville, ou le séducteur vertueux* (BN)].

1801: 34   HOLSTEN, Esther.
ERNESTINA; A NOVEL. DEDICATED, BY PERMISSION, TO HER
ROYAL HIGHNESS THE DUCHESS OF YORK. BY ESTHER HOLSTEN.
IN TWO VOLUMES.

London: Printed by J. Cundee, Ivy-Lane, for Crosby and Letterman, Stationers'-Court,
    Ludgate-Hill, 1801.
I x, 277p; II 213p. 12mo. 7s sewed (CR); 7s (ECB).
CR 2nd ser. 33: 113 (Sept 1801); WSW I: 325.
Corvey; CME 3-628-47741-7; ECB 278; xNSTC.

*Notes.* Dedication 'to Her Royal Highness, the Duchess of York'. Introduction dated
Feb 1801.

1801: 35   HUNTER, [Rachel].
LETITIA: OR, THE CASTLE WITHOUT A SPECTRE. BY MRS. HUNTER,
OF NORWICH. IN FOUR VOLUMES.

Norwich: Printed for W. Robberds; and sold by Longman and Rees, Paternoster-Row,
    London. Wilks and Taylor, Printers, Chancery-Lane, 1801.
I xvi, 384p; II 345p; III 342p; IV 360p. 12mo. 21s boards (CR, MR); 21s (ECB).
CR 2nd ser. 34: 355–6 (Mar 1802); MR n.s. 39: 427 (Dec 1802); WSW I: 65, 335.
Corvey; CME 3-628-47786-7; ECB 289; NSTC H3176 (BI BL, C).

1801: 36   [ISAACS, Mrs].
ARIEL, OR THE INVISIBLE MONITOR. IN FOUR VOLUMES.

London: Printed at the Minerva-Press, for William Lane, Leadenhall-Street, 1801.
I 359p, ill.; II 269p; III 297p; IV 344p. 12mo. 18s sewed (CR).
CR 2nd ser. 34: 356 (Mar 1802).
Corvey; CME 3-628-47070-6; xNSTC.

*Notes.* Further edn: German trans., 1804.

1801: 37   KELLY, Isabella.
RUTHINGLENNE, OR THE CRITICAL MOMENT. A NOVEL. IN
THREE VOLUMES. DEDICATED, BY PERMISSION, TO LADY
DALLING. BY ISABELLA KELLY, AUTHOR OF MADELINE, ABBEY OF
ST. ASAPH, AVONDALE PRIORY, EVA, &C. &C.

London: Printed at the Minerva-Press, for William Lane, Leadenhall-Street, 1801.
I xii, 298p; II 284p; III 260p. 12mo. 13s 6d (ECB).
Corvey; CME 3-628-47929-0; ECB 317; NSTC K138 (BI BL, O).

*Notes.* Dedication to Lady Dalling, vol. 1, pp. [ii]–vi, signed Isabella Kelly. 'List of Subscribers' (63 names), vol. 1, pp. [viii]–xii. ECB dates June 1801.
Further edn: French trans., 1818 [as *Le Prieuré de Ruthinglenne* (Pigoreau)].

1801: 38   KER, Anne.
EMMELINE; OR, THE HAPPY DISCOVERY; A NOVEL, IN TWO VOLUMES. BY ANNE KER, AUTHOR OF THE HEIRESS DI MONTALDE, ADELINE ST. JULIAN, &C.

> London: Printed by J. Bonsor, Salisbury Square. For J. and E. Kerby, Bond Street; and
> T. Hurst, Paternoster Row, 1801.
> I viii, 271p; II 280p. 12mo. 8s (ECB).
> Corvey; CME 3-628-48003-5; ECB 186; NSTC K380 (BI BL, O).

*Notes.* Dedication to Lady Jerningham, dated 24 Feb 1801. ECB dates Apr 1801.

1801: 39   ?KIDDERSLAW, Johanson; [MACKENZIE, Anna Maria (*trans.?*)].
SWEDISH MYSTERIES, OR HERO OF THE MINES. A TALE. IN THREE VOLUMES. TRANSLATED FROM A SWEDISH MANUSCRIPT, BY JOHANSON KIDDERSLAW, FORMERLY MASTER OF THE ENGLISH GRAMMAR SCHOOL AT UPSAL.

> London: Printed at the Minerva-Press, for William Lane, Leadenhall-Street, 1801.
> I 288p, ill.; II 303p; III 320p. 12mo. 13s 6d boards (CR); 13s 6d (ECB).
> CR 2nd ser. 34: 476 (Apr 1802).
> Corvey; CME 3-628-48793-5; ECB 321; xNSTC.

*Notes.* Frank (Item 258) calls this a 'sham translation'. CR states: 'We have not leisure to examine whether this novel be really a translation from the Swedish, or whether it be the original production of him who calls himself the translator'. Kidderslaw has not been located in Swedish bibliographies and may be a spurious name. Several catalogues attribute directly to Mackenzie. Blakey (copy not seen) gives title as continuing '[…] of Dalecarlia', but Corvey copy does not include this.

1801: 40   KING, Sophia [afterwards FORTNUM].
THE FATAL SECRET, OR, UNKNOWN WARRIOR; A ROMANCE OF THE TWELFTH CENTURY, WITH LEGENDARY POEMS. BY SOPHIA KING, AUTHOR OF WALDORF, OR THE DANGERS OF PHILOSOPHY; CORDELIA, A ROMANCE OF REAL LIFE; AND THE VICTIM OF FRIENDSHIP, A GERMAN ROMANCE.

> London: Printed for the Author, by J. G. Barnard, George's Court, Clerkenwell; and
> sold by J. Fiske, Wigmore Street, Cavendish Square, and all other Booksellers, 1801.
> vii, 211p. 8vo. 4s (ECB).
> BL N.2048(3); ECB 321; NSTC K593.

*Notes.* 'Preface', pp. [i]–vii, indicates this work is the author's 'fourth attempt' (p. iv). ECB dates Dec 1801.

1801: 41   KING, Sophia [afterwards FORTNUM].
*THE VICTIM OF FRIENDSHIP; A GERMAN ROMANCE. BY SOPHIA KING, AUTHOR OF TRIFLES FROM HELICON, &C.

London: R. Dutton, 1801.

2 vols. 12mo. 7s boards (CR).

CR 2nd ser. 32: 232 (June 1801); WSW I: 355.

No copy located.

*Notes.* Sophia King was a sister of Charlotte Dacre, with whom she published *Trifles of Helicon* (1798), a collection of verse (see Jackson, p. 95).

1801: 42   LEE, Harriet.

## CANTERBURY TALES. VOLUME THE FOURTH. BY HARRIET LEE.

London: Printed for G. and J. Robinson, Paternoster-Row, 1801.

490p. 8vo. 8s boards (CR).

CR 2nd ser. 35: 207–15 (Oct 1801) full review; WSW I: 367.

Corvey; CME 3-628-48017-5; ECB 336; NSTC L978 (BI BL).

*Notes.* 'The poet's address' (1 p. unn.). Contains 'The German's Tale: Kruitzner' and 'The Scotsman's Tale: Claudina'.

Further edns: 2nd edn. 1803 (NUC); (as part of collected edns.): 1832 (NSTC); 1837 (NSTC); 1842 (NSTC); Philadelphia 1833 (NSTC); German trans., 1810. *Kruitzner* (separately) 5th edn. 1823 (NSTC); New York & Philadelphia 1823 (NSTC).

1801: 43   [LESLIE, Mrs].

## A PLAIN STORY. IN FOUR VOLUMES.

London: Printed at the Minerva-Press, for William Lane, Leadenhall-Street, 1801.

I 384p, ill.; II 322p; III 324p; IV 366p. 12mo.

Corvey; CME 3-628-48474-X; xNSTC.

*Notes.* Blakey notes attributed to Mrs Leslie in Minerva Library Catalogue of 1814.

1801: 44   [LEWIS, Alethea].

## THE MICROCOSM. BY THE AUTHOR OF VICISSITUDES IN GENTEEL LIFE. IN FIVE VOLUMES.

London: Printed for J. Mawman, in the Poultry, 1801.

I xxviii, 248p; II vii, 255p; III vii, 264p; IV vii, 243p; V iv, 204p. 12mo. 20s sewed (CR, MR); 20s (ECB).

CR 2nd ser. 33: 460 (Dec 1801); MR n.s. 35: 428–9 (Aug 1801); WSW I: 75.

Corvey; CME 3-628-48128-7; ECB 383; NSTC L1464 (BI BL, O).

*Notes.* Printer's mark after imprint date reads: 'By T. Gillet, Salisbury-Square'. Dedication to 'Sir Edward Littleton, Bart, one of the Representatives of the County of Stafford'. 'Prefatory Letter. Addressed to the Rev. William Johnstone'.

1801: 45   LUCAS, Charles.

## THE INFERNAL QUIXOTE. A TALE OF THE DAY. IN FOUR VOLUMES. BY CHARLES LUCAS, A.M. AUTHOR OF THE CASTLE OF ST. DONATS, &C.

London: Printed at the Minerva-Press, for William Lane, Leadenhall-Street, 1801.

I viii, 291p, ill.; II 411p; III 348p; IV 375p. 12mo. 20s boards (CR); 18s (ECB).

CR 2nd ser. 33: 113 (Sept 1801); WSW I: 378.

Corvey; CME 3-628-48119-8; ECB 355; NSTC L2560 (BI BL, O).

*Notes.* Further edn: French trans., 1802.

1801: 46   [LYTTLETON, Mr].
**THE FOLLIES OF FASHION: A DRAMATIC NOVEL. IN THREE VOLUMES.**

> London: Printed by A. Strahan, Printers-Street; for T. N. Longman and O. Rees, Pater-
> noster-Row, 1801.
> I 270p; II 302p; III 324p. 12mo. 13s 6d boards (CR, MR); 13s 6d (ECB).
> CR 2nd ser. 34: 475 (Apr 1802); MR n.s. 41: 105 (May 1803).
> Corvey; CME 3-628-47798-0; ECB 210; NSTC F995 (BI BL).

*Notes.* ECB dates Jan 1802.

MACKENZIE, Anna Maria
See KIDDERSLAW, Johanson

1801: 47   [MARTIN, Mrs].
**THE ENCHANTRESS, OR WHERE SHALL I FIND HER? A TALE. BY
THE AUTHOR OF MELBOURNE, DELORAINE, REGINALD, &C.**

> London: Printed at the Minerva-Press, for William Lane, Leadenhall-Street, 1801.
> 335p. 12mo. 4s 6d (ECB).
> WSW I: 38.
> Corvey; CME 3-628-47565-1; ECB 186; NSTC E865 (BI BL).

*Notes.* Blakey notes attributed to Mrs Martin in Minerva Library Catalogue of 1814. ECB
treats as anon., and dates Apr 1801.

1801: 48   [?MATHEWS, Eliza Kirkham].
**WHAT HAS BEEN. A NOVEL. IN TWO VOLUMES.**

> London: Printed at the Minerva-Press, for William Lane, Leadenhall-Street, 1801.
> I 288p; II 268p. 12mo. 8s boards (CR).
> CR 2nd ser. 32: 351–2 (July 1801); WSW I: 129.
> Corvey; CME 3-628-48898-2; xNSTC.

*Notes.* Attributed to 'Mrs Mathews' on t.p. of the American edn., Alexandria 1803, as seen at
PU. Blakey and Summers treat this work as anonymous, the latter adding 'The first literary
attempt of a lady'. FC nevertheless includes this as a late work of Eliza Kirkham Mathews
(1772–1802) in its entry on that author.
Further edn: Alexandria, VA, 1803 (NUC).

1801: 49   MATTHEW, Charlotte.
**INTROSPECTION; OR A PEEP AT REAL CHARACTERS. A NOVEL.—
IN FOUR VOLS. BY CHARLOTTE MATTHEW.**

> Bath: Printed by R. Cruttwell; and sold by Messrs. Carpenter (Booksellers to his R.H.
> The Duke of York) Old Bond-Street, London, 1801.
> I vi, 207p; II 258p; III 304p; IV 312p. 12mo. 18s (ECB).
> MH-H EC8.M4312.801; ECB 373; xNSTC.

*Notes.* This title is listed by Summers under Mrs Charlotte Mathews along with others usually attributed to Eliza Kirkham (Mrs Charles) Mathews.
Further edn: 1802 (Corvey—a reissue by the Minerva Press with a cancel t.p.), CME 3-628-
48197-X.

1801: 50   [MEEKE, Mary].

**MYSTERIOUS HUSBAND. A NOVEL. IN FOUR VOLUMES. BY GABRIELLI, AUTHOR OF THE MYSTERIOUS WIFE, &C. &C.**

London: Printed at the Minerva-Press, for William Lane, Leadenhall-Street, 1801.
I 286p; II 273p; III 297p; IV 298p. 12mo. 18s (CR).
CR 2nd ser. 33: 353 (Nov 1801).
Corvey; CME 3-628-47882-0; xNSTC.

*Notes.* Further edn: French trans., 1804.

1801: 51   MEEKE, [Mary].

**WHICH IS THE MAN? A NOVEL. IN FOUR VOLUMES. BY MRS. MEEKE, AUTHOR OF ANECDOTES OF THE ALTAMONT FAMILY, ELLESMERE, &C.**

London: Printed at the Minerva-Press, for William Lane, Leadenhall-Street, 1801.
I 275p, ill.; II 271p; III 288p; IV 256p. 12mo. 18s boards (CR).
CR 2nd ser. 32: 469 (Aug 1801).
Corvey; CME 3-628-48052-3; ECB 378; NSTC M1958 (BI BL).

1801: 52   MILLS, Frances Mary.

**THE CASTLE OF VILLEROY, A ROMANCE. BY FRANCES MARY MILLS.**

London: Printed by D. N. Shury, Berwick-Street; and sold by T. Hurst, Paternoster-
   Row, 1801.
xiii, 226p. 12mo.
Corvey; CME 3-628-48165-1; xNSTC.

*Notes.* 'Dedication to the Subscribers', pp. [iii]–vi, signed 'Frances Mary Mills. 14, Blenham's Buildings, Camberwell'. 'List of Subscribers' (*c.* 270 names), pp. [vii]–xiii. A different novel from *The Castle of Villeroy*, written under the pseudonym of Ann of Kent (see 1827: 12). BL has a variant copy (C.192.a.219) bearing the imprint of J. Skirven, but with the same Shury colophon as above and identical pagination (plus subscription list). Imprint of this cancel t.p. reads as follows: 'London: Printed by J. Skirven, Ratcliff-Highway; for William Harris, No. 96, High-Street, Shadwell'.

1801: 53   MUSGRAVE, Agnes.

**THE CONFESSION: A NOVEL, IN FIVE VOLUMES. BY AGNES MUS-GRAVE, AUTHOR OF CICELY OF RABY, THE SOLEMN INJUNCTION, &C.**

London: Printed at the Apollo Press, by G. Cawthorn, British Library, Strand; Book-
   seller and Printer to Her Royal Highness the Princess of Wales, 1801.
I 266p; II 256p; III 247p; IV 260p; V 231p. 12mo. 20s boards (CR); 20s (ECB).
CR 2nd ser. 33: 237 (Oct 1801).
Corvey; CME 3-628-48171-6; ECB 402; NSTC M3773 (BI O).

*Notes.* Last page of vol. 1 mistakenly numbered 262.

1801: 54   OPIE, {Amelia} [Alderson].

**THE FATHER AND DAUGHTER, A TALE, IN PROSE: WITH AN EPIS-TLE FROM THE MAID OF CORINTH TO HER LOVER; AND OTHER POETICAL PIECES. BY MRS. OPIE.**

London: Printed by Davis, Wilks, and Taylor, Chancery-Lane; and sold by Longman
and Rees, Paternoster-Row, 1801.

vii, 244p. 12mo. 4s 6d (CR 2nd edn., ECB); 4s 6d boards (MR).

CR 2nd ser. 35: 114–16 (May 1802); MR n.s. 35: 163–6 (June 1801) full review; WSW
I: 43, 421.

C S.727.d.80.29; ECB 423; NSTC O385 (BI O).

*Notes.* Dedication to 'Dr. Alderson, of Norwich', signed 'Amelia Opie, Berners Street, 1800'.
'To the Reader' expresses apprehension felt 'as an avowed Author at the bar of public opinion', and offers not 'a Novel' but 'a simple, moral Tale' (pp. [vi]–vii). Tale ends at p. 206,
followed by poems.

Further edns: 2nd edn. 1801 (NSTC); 3rd edn. 1802 (Corvey), CME 3-628-48261-5; 4th edn.
1804 (NSTC); 5th edn. 1806 (NSTC); 7th edn. 1813 (NSTC); Dublin 1814 (NSTC); [at least
3 more edns. to 1850]; Richmond 1806 (NUC); French trans., 1802; German trans., 1803 [as
*Vater und Tochter. Ein Familiengemälde* (RS)].

Facs: RWN (1995).


1801: 55   PARSONS, [Eliza].

THE PEASANT OF ARDENNE FOREST: A NOVEL. IN FOUR VOL-
UMES. BY MRS. PARSONS, AUTHOR OF ANECDOTES OF TWO
WELL-KNOWN FAMILIES THE MISER, THE VALLEY OF ST.
GOTHARD, AN OLD FRIEND WITH A NEW FACE, WOMAN AS SHE
SHOULD BE, MYSTERIOUS WARNING, &C.

Brentford: Printed by and for P. Norbury; and sold by T. Hurst, No. 32, Paternoster
Row; J. Hatchard, Piccadilly; Carpenter and Co. Old-Bond-Street; and Didier and
Tibbett, St. James's-Street, London, 1801.

I 276p; II 287p; III 296p; IV 328p. 12mo. 20s (ECB).

WSW I: 430.

Corvey; CME 3-628-48401-4; ECB 435; NSTC P566 (BI O).

*Notes.* ECB dates Dec 1801.

Further edn: French trans., 1803.


1801: 56   PIGAULT-LEBRUN, [Charles-Antoine].

MY UNCLE THOMAS. A ROMANCE. IN FOUR VOLUMES. FROM THE
FRENCH OF PIGAULT LEBRUN.

London: Printed at the Minerva-Press, for William Lane, Leadenhall-Street, 1801.

I 264p; II 240p; III 255p; IV 257p. 12mo. 16s boards (CR); 16s (ECB).

CR 3rd ser. 3: 237 (Oct 1804).

CtY-BR Hfd29.615M; ECB 335; xNSTC.

*Notes.* Trans. of *Mon oncle Thomas* (Paris, 1795). Some pages wanting in vol. 2.

Further edn: New York 1810 (NUC).


1801: 57   [PLUMPTRE, Annabella].

THE WESTERN MAIL: BEING A SELECTION OF LETTERS MADE
FROM THE BAG TAKEN FROM THE WESTERN MAIL, WHEN IT WAS
ROBBED BY GEORGE——, IN 17—. NOW FIRST PUBLISHED.

London: Printed by Davis, Wilks, and Taylor, Chancery-Lane, for J. Mawman, Successor to Mr. Dilly, in the Poultry, 1801.
iv, 282p. 12mo. 3s (CR); 4s (ECB).
CR 2nd ser. 32: 352 (July 1801).
Corvey; CME 3-628-48897-4; ECB 631; NSTC P2155 (BI BL, C, O).

1801: 58    PLUMPTRE, Anne.
SOMETHING NEW: OR, ADVENTURES AT CAMPBELL-HOUSE. IN THREE VOLUMES. BY ANNE PLUMPTRE.

London: Printed by A. Strahan, Printers-Street; for T. N. Longman and O. Rees, Paternoster-Row, 1801.
I iv, 348p; II 334p; III 355p. 12mo. 15s boards (CR, MR); 15s (ECB).
CR 2nd ser. 34: 475–6 (Apr 1802); MR n.s. 41: 103 (May 1803); WSW I: 441.
Corvey; CME 3-628-48477-4; ECB 455; NSTC P2162 (BI BL, C).

*Notes.* 'Prologue' in verse, vol. 1, pp. [iii]–iv.

1801: 59    [RICHARDSON, Caroline E.].
ADONIA, A DESULTORY STORY, IN FOUR VOLUMES. INSCRIBED, BY PERMISSION, TO HER GRACE THE DUCHESS OF BUCCLEUGH.

London: Printed for A. & J. Black & H. Parry, Leadenhall-Street; and Bell & Bradfute, Edinburgh, 1801.
I 3, 300p; II 295p; III 343p; IV 372p. 12mo. 18s boards (CR); 18s (ECB); 18s sewed (MR).
CR 2nd ser. 31: 474 (Apr 1801); MR n.s. 35: 427–8 (Aug 1801); WSW I: 7.
BL 12614.cc.15; ECB 6; NSTC A479 (BI E, O).

*Notes.* Dedication by 'the Authoress' dated London, 19 Jan 1801. *Catalogue* [1810–16] of Mackay's Circulating Library (Edinburgh) lists as 'by Mrs. Richardson' Also identified in Jackson as Richardson, Caroline E., Mrs George G. (1777–1853), the wife of George Richardson, a servant of the East India Company, and herself eventually proprietor of the *Berwick Advertiser*. This is a different author from Charlotte Caroline Richardson, author of *The Soldier's Child* (1821: 63).

1801: 60    SICKELMORE, Richard.
RAYMOND, A NOVEL. IN TWO VOLUMES. INSCRIBED, BY PERMISSION, TO GEORGE PORTER, ESQ. M.P. BY RICHARD SICKELMORE, AUTHOR OF MARY-JANE, &C.

London: Printed by W. and C. Spilsbury, Snowhill, for Didier and Tebbett, St. James's Street; and sold by Crosby and Letterman, Stationers Court, Ludgate-Hill, 1801.
I vii, 267p; II 270p. 12mo.
Corvey; CME 3-628-48694-7; NSTC S1916 (BI C).

*Notes.* Dedication to 'George Porter, Esq. M.P.'.

1801: 61    SMITH, [Horatio].
TREVANION; OR, MATRIMONIAL ERRORS. A NOVEL. BY MR. SMITH, AUTHOR OF . . . "FAMILY STORY"—"THE RUNAWAY," &C. IN FOUR VOLUMES.

London: Printed for Earle and Hemet, No. 47, Albemarle Street, Piccadilly, 1801.
I 211p; II 209p; III 211p; IV 214p. 12mo. 14s (ECB).
Corvey; CME 3-628-48658-0; ECB 545; NSTC S2434 (BI BL).

*Notes.* Further edn: Dublin 1801 (NSTC).

1801: 62   SMITH, Maria Lavinia.
THE FUGITIVE OF THE FOREST. A ROMANCE. IN TWO VOLUMES.
BY MARIA LAVINIA SMITH.

London: Printed at the Minerva-Press, for William Lane, Leadenhall-Street, 1801.
I 232p; II 240p. 12mo.
Corvey; CME 3-628-48662-9; NSTC S2542 (BI O).

*Notes.* Vignettes after each chapter.
Further edn: French trans., 1803.

1801: 63   SUMMERSETT, Henry.
MARTYN OF FENROSE; OR, THE WIZARD AND THE SWORD. A
ROMANCE. BY HENRY SUMMERSETT, AUTHOR OF LEOPOLD
WARNDORF, JAQUELINE OF OLZEBURG, &C. &C.

London: Printed for R. Dutton, No. 10, Birchin-Lane, Cornhill; and sold by Cobbett
and Morgan, Crown and Mitre, Pall-Mall; Miller, Bond-Street; and Hurst, Pater-
Noster-Row, 1801.
I iv, 239p; II 252p; III 226p. 12mo. 13s boards (CR); 13s 6d (ECB); 9s sewed (MR).
CR 2nd ser. 33: 112 (Sept 1801); MR n.s. 40: 207 (Feb 1803); WSW I: 526.
Corvey; CME 3-628-48734-X; ECB 569; NSTC S4367 (BI C).

*Notes.* Preface dated London, 1800.

1801: 64   SURR, T[homas] S[kinner].
SPLENDID MISERY. A NOVEL, IN THREE VOLUMES. BY T. S. SURR,
AUTHOR OF GEORGE BARNWELL, CONSEQUENCES, &C.

London: Printed for T. Hurst, Paternoster-Row, 1801/02.
I (1801) 254p; II (1801) 249p; III (1802) iii, 274p. 12mo. 15s boards (CR); 13s 6d (ECB).
CR 2nd ser. 35: 112 (May 1802); WSW I: 115, 527.
BL 12612.dd.1; ECB 570; NSTC S4393 (BI C, O).

*Notes.* Dedication in vol. 3 to Richard Brinsley Sheridan; also Preface in same vol., dated
London, Feb 1802.
Further edns: 2nd edn. 1802 (Corvey), CME 3-628-48738-2; Dublin 1802 (NUC); 3rd edn.
1803 (NSTC); 4th edn. 1807 (NSTC); 5th edn. 1814 (NSTC); German trans., 1802 [as *Graf
Latimore, oder die Märtyrer des Glaubens* (RS)]; French trans., 1807 [as *Splendeur et souf-
france* (BN)].

1801: 65   [THELWALL], John.
THE DAUGHTER OF ADOPTION; A TALE OF MODERN TIMES. IN
FOUR VOLUMES. BY JOHN BEAUFORT, LL.D.

London: Printed for R. Phillips, St. Paul's Church-Yard; sold by T. Hurst, J. Wallis, and
West and Hughes, Paternoster-Row, 1801.

I iv, 335p; II 324p; III 319p; IV 309p. 12mo. 16s sewed (CR); 16s boards (MR).
CR 2nd ser. 31: 234–5 (Feb 1801); MR n.s. 35: 356–61 (Aug 1801) full review; WSW I: 149.
Corvey; CME 3-628-47132-X; NSTC T559 (BI BL, O).

*Notes.* Printer's mark after imprint date reads: 'T. Davison, White-Friars' (in square brackets).
This differs in the 3rd and 4th vols: 'Printed by Davis, Wilks, and Taylor, Chancery-Lane'.
Further edn: Dublin 1801 (BRu ENC).

1801: 66 VENTUM, Harriet.
**JUSTINA; OR, THE HISTORY OF A YOUNG LADY. IN FOUR VOL-
UMES. BY HARRIET VENTUM, AUTHOR OF SELINA, &C. &C.**

London: Printed for J. Badcock, Paternoster-Row, by J. D. Dewick, Aldersgate-Street, 1801.
I iv, 264p; II 256p; III 215p; IV 215p. 12mo. 18s sewed (CR, MR); 18s (ECB).
CR 2nd ser. 33: 460–1 (Dec 1801); MR n.s. 38: 313 (July 1802); WSW I: 548.
CtY-BR In.V567.801J; ECB 612; xNSTC.

*Notes.* Dedication to the Marchioness of Abercorn, dated London, Dec 1801. Drop-head title
'Justina Trecothick. In a Series of Letters'; running-title 'Justina Trecothick'. Vol. 4 colophon
'Printed by W. Calvert, Great Shire Lane, Temple Bar'; vols. 1 and 2 colophons 'Printed by
J. D. Dewick, Aldersgate-Street'. Vol. 4, despite its colophon, still has identical imprint to
vols. 1–3, with Dewick's name.
Further edn: 1802 (Corvey), CME 3-628-48909-1.

1801: 67 [WHITFIELD, Henry].
**GERALDWOOD. BY THE AUTHOR OF VILLEROY, AND SIGISMAR.**

London: Printed for R. Dutton, No. 10, Birchin-Lane, Cornhill. By J. D. Dewick, Alders-
gate-Street, 1801.
I vi, 232p; II 217p; III 218p; IV 234p. 12mo. 18s (ECB).
WSW I: 48.
Corvey; CME 3-628-47823-5; ECB 228; NSTC G678 (BI BL).

*Notes.* ECB dates Nov 1801.

1801: 68 WINGROVE, Ann.
**THE SPINSTER'S TALE; IN WHICH IS INTRODUCED, LANGBRIDGE
FORT, A ROMANCE. BY ANN WINGROVE, AUTHOR OF LETTERS
MORAL AND ENTERTAINING. IN THREE VOLUMES.**

London: Printed by T. Plummer, Seething-Lane; for R. Dutton, Birchin-Lane, Cornhill,
1801.
I 192p; II 202p; III 180p. 12mo. 10s 6d (ECB).
Corvey; CME 3-628-48936-9; ECB 643; NSTC W2440 (BI BL).

*Notes.* Dedication 'to Her Royal Highness the Duchess of York', dated Bath, 1 Oct 1801.
ECB dates Oct 1801.

1801: 69 [WOLZOGEN, Caroline von]; [SHOWES, Mrs (*trans.*)].
**AGNES DE LILIEN. A NOVEL. FROM THE GERMAN. IN THREE VOL-
UMES. BY THE AUTHOR OF STATIRA, AND THE RESTLESS MATRON.**

London: Printed at the Minerva-Press, for William Lane, Leadenhall-Street, 1801.

I 263p; II 264p; III 332p. 12mo. 12s (ECB).
BL 12551.bb.23; ECB 8; NSTC L1620.

*Notes.* Trans. of *Agnes von Lilien* (Berlin, 1798). ECB dates Sept 1801.

1801: 70 [WRIGHT, Elizabeth].
A MARVELLOUS PLEASANT LOVE-STORY. IN TWO VOLUMES.

London: Printed at the Minerva-Press, for W. Lane, Leadenhall-Street, 1801.
I v, 358p; II 348p. 8vo. 12s (ECB).
WSW I: 72.
Corvey; CME 3-628-48118-X; ECB 371; NSTC W3023 (BI BL, O).

*Notes.* Dedication 'to His Royal Highness Edward Duke of Kent'. ECB dates May 1801.

1801: 71 YORKE, Mrs [R. P. M.].
THE HAUNTED PALACE, OR THE HORRORS OF VENTOLIENE; A ROMANCE, BY MRS. YORKE, AUTHOR OF VALLEY OF COLLARES, ROMANCE OF SMYRNA, &C. &C. &C. IN THREE VOLUMES.

London: Printed by C. Stower, King Street Covent Garden, for Earle and Hemet, Albemarle-Street, Piccadilly, 1801.
I 276p; II 268p; III 293p. 12mo. 13s 6d (ECB).
Corvey; CME 3-628-48987-3; ECB 652; NSTC Y116 (BI O).

*Notes.* Dedication 'to the Right Honorable Joshua Allen, Viscount Allen, in the county of Kildare, and Baron Allen, of Stillorgan, in the county of Dublin', dated 31 May 1801. ECB dates June 1801.

1801: 72 {YORKE}, [Mrs] {R. P. M.}.
THE ROMANCE OF SMYRNA; OR, THE PREDICTION FULFILLED!!! IN FOUR VOLUMES.

London: Printed for Earle and Hemet, No. 47, Albemarle Street, Piccadilly, 1801.
I 198p; II 231p; III 227p; IV 258p. 12mo. 14s (ECB).
WSW I: 105.
Corvey; CME 3-628-48988-1; ECB 652; xNSTC.

*Notes.* Dedication 'to Sir William Sidney Smith' signed 'R. P. M. Yorke'. ECB dates Feb 1801.

# 1802

1802: 1 ANON.
THE AUTHOR AND THE TWO COMEDIANS; OR THE ADOPTED CHILD; A NOVEL.

London: Printed for M. Allen, 15, Paternoster-Row; and sold by all Booksellers in the United Kingdom, 1802.
iv, 228p. 12mo. 3s 6d sewed (MR).

MR n.s. 40: 208 (Feb 1803); WSW I: 13.
ICN Y.155.A961; xNSTC.

*Notes.* Imprint on t.p. after imprint date reads: 'The Profits of this Edition will be appropri-
ated to the Benefit of the Charity-Schools of Castle-Baynard Ward and Pentonville'.

1802: 2    ANON.
THE CASTLE OF PROBATION, OR, PRECEPTIVE ROMANCES; CHIEFLY
TAKEN FROM LIFE. BY A CLERGYMAN. IN TWO VOLUMES.

> London: Printed for H. D. Symonds, Paternoster-Row; by Bye and Law, St. John's-
> Square, Clerkenwell, 1802.
> I 240p; II 240p. 12mo.
> Corvey; CME 3-628-47219-9; NSTC C2432 (BI BL).

1802: 3    ANON.
DELAVAL. A NOVEL. IN TWO VOLUMES.

> London: Printed at the Minerva-Press, for William Lane, Leadenhall-Street, 1802.
> I 266p, ill.; II 216p. 12mo. 8s boards (CR); 8s (ECB).
> CR 2nd ser. 34: 476 (Apr 1802); WSW I: 32.
> Corvey; CME 3-628-47405-1; ECB 158; xNSTC.

*Notes.* Further edn: Newbern, NC, 1804 (NUC).

1802: 4    ANON.
HATRED, OR THE VINDICTIVE FATHER. A TALE OF SORROW. IN
THREE VOLUMES.

> London: Printed at the Minerva-Press, for Lane and Newman, Leadenhall-Street, 1802.
> I 228p; II 272p; III 269p. 12mo. 12s (ECB).
> WSW I: 51.
> Corvey; CME 3-628-47851-0; ECB 258; xNSTC.

*Notes.* ECB dates July 1802.

1802: 5    ANON.
THE HISTORY OF NETTERVILLE, A CHANCE PEDESTRIAN. A NOVEL.
IN TWO VOLUMES.

> London: Printed by J. Cundee, Ivy-Lane, for Crosby and Co. Stationer's-Court, 1802.
> I 300p; II 300p. 12mo. 8s boards (CR); 6s sewed (MR).
> CR 2nd ser. 34: 356 (Mar 1802); MR n.s. 40: 207–8 (Feb 1803); WSW I: 54.
> Corvey; CME 3-628-47672-0; ECB 273; NSTC N578 (BI O).

*Notes.* Dedication, signed 'The Authoress', describes this as a 'second attempt in the region of
fiction'.

1802: 6    ANON.
JEALOUSY, OR THE DREADFUL MISTAKE. A NOVEL. IN TWO VOL-
UMES. BY A CLERGYMAN'S DAUGHTER.

> London: Printed at the Minerva-Press, for William Lane, Leadenhall-Street, 1802.

I 306p; II 266p. 12mo. 8s (ECB).

WSW I: 60.

Corvey; CME 3-628-47931-2; ECB 306; xNSTC.

*Notes.* See the same author's *Castle of Santa Fe* (1805: 3), for a possible authorship by Miss Cleeve. ECB dates Dec 1801.


1802: 7   ANON.

## MASSOUF, OR THE PHILOSOPHY OF THE DAY. AN EASTERN TALE.

London: Printed at the Minerva-Press, for Lane and Newman, Leadenhall-Street, 1802. 210p. 12mo. 3s 6d sewed (CR); 3s 6d (ECB).

CR 2nd ser. 36: 117 (Sept 1802); WSW I: 72–3.

BL 12611.c.24; ECB 372; NSTC M1633 (BI O).


1802: 8   ANON.

## *THE MYSTERIES OF ABRUZZO, BY THE AUTHOR OF THE CHILD OF DOUBT, &C. IN TWO VOLUMES.

London: Printed by and for R. Cantwell, 33, Bell Yard, Temple Bar; and sold by Hughes, No. 5, Wigmore Street, Cavendish Square, 1802.

I iv, 190p; II 172p. 12mo. 7s (ECB).

No copy of 1st edn. located; ECB 403.

*Notes.* Details above replicate Corvey 2nd edn., where 'Advertisement' indicates female authorship. *Eliza Beaumont and Harriet Osborne; or, The Child of Doubt* (1789) is by Indiana Brooks, but apart from the similarity of the subtitle no evidence has been discovered about the authorship of this title. ECB (no edn. specified) dates June 1802. Collates in sixes. Further edn: 2nd edn. 1802 (Corvey), CME 3-628-48177-5.


1802: 9   ANON.

## NOBILITY RUN MAD, OR RAYMOND AND HIS THREE WIVES. A NOVEL. IN FOUR VOLUMES. BY THE AUTHOR OF THE SAILOR BOY AND SOLDIER BOY.

London: Printed at the Minerva-Press, for Lane and Newman, Leadenhall-Street, 1802. I 280p; II 272p; III 275p; IV 294p. 12mo. 6s (ECB).

WSW I: 84.

Corvey; CME 3-628-48230-5; ECB 415; NSTC N1115 (BI BL).

*Notes.* ECB dates Apr 1802.


1802: 10   ANON.

## THE NOBLE WANDERERS. A NOVEL. IN TWO VOLUMES.

London: Printed at the Minerva-Press, for Lane and Newman, Leadenhall-Street, 1802. I 284p; II 304p. 12mo.

WSW I: 84.

Corvey; CME 3-628-48232-1; ECB 415; xNSTC.

*Notes.* ECB dates Aug 1802.

1802: 11  ANON.
### THE ORPHANS OF LLANGLOED. A MODERN TALE. IN THREE VOLUMES. BY THE AUTHOR OF LUSIGNAN.

> London: Printed at the Minerva-Press, for Lane and Newman, Leadenhall-Street, 1802.
> I 256p; II 298p; III 235p. 12mo. 10s 6d boards (CR).
> CR 2nd ser. 37: 237–8 (Feb 1803); WSW I: 88.
> Corvey; CME 3-628-48316-6; xNSTC.

1802: 12  ANON.
### SCENES IN WALES; OR, THE MAID OF LLANGOLF. BY A CLERGYMAN.

> London: Printed by J. Wright, Denmark Court, for R. H. Westley, 159 Strand, and E.
>   Hennah, St. Austell, Cornwall, 1802.
> viii, 219p. 12mo. 4s (ECB).
> WSW I: 108.
> Corvey; CME 3-628-48532-0; ECB 516; xNSTC.

*Notes.* ECB dates Mar 1802. Collates in sixes.

1802: 13  ANON.
### THE STROLLING PLAYER; OR, LIFE AND ADVENTURES OF WILLIAM TEMPLETON. IN THREE VOLUMES.

> London: Printed by B. M'Millan, Bow-Street, Covent-Garden; sold by H. D. Symonds,
>   Paternoster-Row, 1802.
> I 293p; II 262p; III 294p. 12mo. 12s (ECB); 12s boards (MR).
> MR n.s. 40: 208 (Feb 1803); WSW I: 116.
> Corvey; CME 3-628-48680-7; ECB 566; NSTC T476 (BI BL).

*Notes.* BLC and NUC both list under Templeton, William, but text indicates that this name is part of the fiction.

1802: 14  ANON.
### WELSH LEGENDS: A COLLECTION OF POPULAR ORAL TALES.

> London: Printed by J. D. Dewick, Aldersgate-Street, for J. Badcock, Paternoster-Row, 1802.
> vi, 280p, ill. 12mo.
> MR n.s. 40: 109 (Jan 1803); WSW I: 129.
> Corvey; CME 3-628-51169-0; ECB 176; NSTC W1193 (BI BL).

*Notes.* Frontispiece carries the legend: 'Publish'd as the Act directs Nov. 1 1801 by Earle and Hemet, Albemarle Street Piccadilly.' 5 legends included, the 2nd of which is in verse. ECB dates 1801, and gives Earle as publisher. It also attributes the authorship to William Earle (jun.), who himself apparently claims authorship in letters of 6 May 1829 and 23 Aug 1830 to the Royal Literary Fund (RLF 20: 654). Block also attributes to Earle, though BLC and NUC treat as anon. Collates in sixes. MR also gives 10s 6d for 8vo, but not discovered in this form.

1802: 15  [ARNOLD, Ignaz Ferdinand]; GEISWEILER, Maria (*trans.*).
### THE BRIDE'S EMBRACE ON THE GRAVE: OR, THE MIDNIGHT WEDDING IN THE CHURCH OF MARIENGARTEN. IN TWO VOLUMES. TAKEN FROM THE GERMAN, BY MARIA GEISWEILER.

London: Printed by G. Sidney, Black-Horse-Court, Fleet Street; for Constantine Geisweiler, No. 42, Parliament Street, Westminster; and sold by all Booksellers in Town and Country, 1802.

I xii, 180p; II 242p. 12mo. 8s (ECB).

BL C.192.a.201; ECB 224; xNSTC.

*Notes.* Trans. of *Der Brautkuß auf dem Grabe, oder die Trauung um Mitternacht in der Kirche zu Mariengarten* (Rudolstadt/Arnstadt, 1801). Notice, dated 20 Mar 1802, in which the author/translator apologizes 'for the inaccuracies which may be found in the first volume of this work; also for the delay in publication; owing to some very unpleasant occurrences at the printing-office where it was first began, and from which it was necessary to remove it to another for its completion'. List of Subscribers (*c.*160) vol. 1, pp. [v]–xii. Variant imprint on t.p. of vol. 2 reads: 'London: Printed by Evans & Ruffy, 27, Leadenhall Street; [etc.]'.

1802: 16   [BRYDGES, Sir Samuel Egerton].
LE FORESTER, A NOVEL. BY THE AUTHOR OF ARTHUR FITZ-ALBINI. IN THREE VOLUMES.

London: Printed for J. White, Fleet Street, by T. Bensley, Bolt Court, 1802.

I vii, 294p; II 250p; III 226p. 12mo. 10s 6d sewed (CR); 10s 6d (ECB).

CR 2nd ser. 36: 357 (Nov 1802); WSW I: 178.

Corvey; CME 3-628-47799-9; ECB 336; NSTC L1048 (BI BL).

*Notes.* 'The Author To His Book' (in verse), dated 6 Sept 1802.

1802: 17   CHARLTON, Mary.
THE WIFE AND THE MISTRESS. A NOVEL. IN FOUR VOLUMES. BY MARY CHARLTON, AUTHOR OF THE PIRATE OF NAPLES, ROSELLA, ANDRONICA, &C. &C.

London: Printed at the Minerva-Press, for Lane and Newman, Leadenhall-Street, 1802.

I 344p; II 353p; III 328p; IV 327p. 12mo. 14s (ECB).

BL N.2506; ECB 107; NSTC C1530 (BI C).

*Notes.* ECB dates July 1802.

Further edn: 2nd edn. 1803 (Corvey), CME 3-628-47261-X.

1802: 18(a)   CHATEAUBRIAND, [François René, Vicomte] de.
ATALA. FROM THE FRENCH OF MR DE CHATEAUBRIANT [*sic*]. WITH EXPLANATORY NOTES.

London: Printed for G. & J. Robinson, Paternoster Row, by W. Meyler, Bath, 1st August, 1802.

ix, 147p, ill. 8vo. 5s boards (CR).

CR 2nd ser. 37: 117 (Jan 1803).

BL 12511.c.29; NSTC C1560.

*Notes.* Trans. of *Atala, ou les amours de deux sauvages dans le désert* (Paris, 1801). Engraved t.p. only. 'Preface of the Translator', dated Bath, July 1802. ECB 107 lists Ridgway edn., July 1801, 3s 6d; but no such edn. has been located.

Further edns: Numerous later American and British translations. NSTC states that London 1817 edn. contains the same trans. as the entry above; the translator of the Boston edn. of 1802 was Caleb Bingham.

1802: 18(b)   [CHATEAUBRIAND, François René, Vicomte de].

ATALA: OR THE AMOURS OF TWO INDIANS, IN THE WILDS OF AMERICA. DESCRIPTIVE OF THE GREAT DANGERS THEY ENCOUNTERED WHEN MAKING THEIR ESCAPE FROM THE WOOD OF BLOOD. THEIR ABODE WITH A VENERABLE RECLUSE, WHO LIVED THIRTY YEARS ON A HIGH MOUNTAIN. THE TRAGICAL CATASTROPHE OF ATALA, AND PIOUS REMONSTRANCES OF THE HOLY HERMIT, TO CHAETAS HER LOVER.

> London: Printed for J. Lee, No. 12, King-Street, Covent-Garden, 1802.
> 129p, ill. 12mo. 'Price One Shilling' (t.p.).
> BL RB.23.a.12436; xNSTC.

*Notes.* Trans. of *Atala, ou les amours de deux sauvages dans le désert* (Paris, 1801). Frontispiece with the legend: 'Pub. Sept$^r$. 17. 1801 by I. Gouyn'. Colophon reads: 'Printed by W. and C. Spilsbury, Snow-hill'.
Further edns: see under 1802: 18(a).

1802: 19   CORRY, John.

MEMOIRS OF ALFRED BERKLEY; OR, THE DANGER OF DISSIPATION. BY JOHN CORRY, AUTHOR OF "A SATIRICAL VIEW OF LONDON," "THE DETECTOR OF QUACKERY," &C.

> London: Printed for R. Dutton, 45, Gracechurch-Street; Crosby and Co. Stationers'-Court; J. F. Hughes, Wigmore-Street; J. Henderson, Tavistock-Street; and C. Chapple, Pall-Mall, 1802.
> x, 228p. 12mo.
> WSW I: 220.
> Corvey; CME 3-628-47367-5; ECB 137; xNSTC.

*Notes.* Dedication to 'The Ladies of The United Kingdom'.

1802: 20   [CRAIK, Helen].

STELLA OF THE NORTH, OR THE FOUNDLING OF THE SHIP. A NOVEL. IN FOUR VOLUMES. BY THE AUTHOR OF ADELAIDE DE NARBONNE, &C.

> London: Printed at the Minerva-Press, for Lane and Newman, Leadenhall-Street, 1802.
> I 295p, ill.; II 309p; III 323p; IV 341p. 12mo.
> Corvey; CME 3-628-48786-2; xNSTC.

1802: 21   [CULLEN, Margaret].

HOME. A NOVEL. IN FIVE VOLUMES. EXPECT NOT A STORY DECK'D IN THE GARB OF FANCY,—BUT LOOK AT HOME.

> London: Printed for J. Mawman, Poultry; and by and for T. Wilson, and R. Spence, High-Ousegate, York, 1802.
> I 334p; II 312p; III 288p; IV 319p; V 364p. 12mo. 20s sewed (CR, MR).
> CR 2nd ser. 36: 356 (Nov 1802); MR n.s. 41: 102–3 (May 1803); WSW I: 229.
> Corvey; CME 3-628-47807-3; ECB 146; NSTC C4436 (BI BL).

*Notes.* Inscription at the end of vol. 5 to the memory of the author's father. MR identifies the author as 'Miss Cullen, a native of the northern part of our island' (p. 102). ECB 278, the fuller entry, lists Mawman edn., 1822, 21s.

Further edns: 2nd edn. 1803 (NSTC); 1822 (ECB, Summers); 4th edn. 1835 (NSTC, NUC); Philadelphia 1813 (NUC).

1802: 22    CURTIES, T. J. Horsley.
THE SCOTTISH LEGEND, OR THE ISLE OF SAINT CLOTHAIR. A ROMANCE. IN FOUR VOLUMES. BY T. J. HORSLEY CURTIES, AUTHOR OF ETHELWINA AND ANCIENT RECORDS.

 London: Printed at the Minerva-Press, for William Lane, Leadenhall-Street, 1802.
 I iii, 344p, ill.; II 331p; III 331p; IV 324p. 12mo. 18s sewed (CR); 18s (ECB).
 CR 2nd ser. 36: 117 (Sept 1802); WSW I: 232.
 Corvey; CME 3-628-47464-7; ECB 148; NSTC C4590 (BI BL).

*Notes.* Dedication 'to Mrs. Morton, Twickenham', signed No. 28, Hart-Street, Bloomsbury-Square. ECB dates Nov 1801.

1802: 23    DUCRAY-DUM[I]NIL, [François-Guillaume].
*VICTOR; OR, THE CHILD OF THE FOREST. IN FOUR VOLUMES. FROM THE FRENCH OF M. DUCRAY-DUMENIL.

 London: Printed at the Minerva-Press, for Lane and Newman, Leadenhall-Street, 1802.
 4 vols. 12mo. 16s boards (CR).
 CR 2nd ser. 38: 115–16 (May 1803).
 No copy located.

*Notes.* Trans. of *Victor, ou l'enfant de la forêt* (Paris, 1797). Title and imprint details from Blakey, whose entry is based on Stonehill (Booksellers) copy.

1802: 24    ELSON, Jane.
THE VILLAGE ROMANCE. IN TWO VOLUMES. BY JANE ELSON, AUTHOR OF THE ROMANCE OF THE CASTLE, &C.

 London: Printed at the Minerva-Press, for Lane and Newman, Leadenhall-Street, 1802.
 I 316p, ill.; II 311p. 12mo. 7s boards (CR).
 CR 2nd ser. 36: 478 (Dec 1802); WSW I: 260.
 Corvey; CME 3-628-47558-9; ECB 185; xNSTC.

1802: 25    FIÉVÉE, [Joseph].
*FREDERIC; TRANSLATED FROM THE FRENCH OF M. FIÉVÉE, AUTHOR OF SUZETTE'S DOWRY, &C.

 London: Wynne and Scholey, 1802.
 3 vols. 12s boards (CR).
 CR 2nd ser. 36: 357 (Nov 1802).
 No copy located.

*Notes.* Trans. of *Frédéric* (Paris, 1799). Bent03 gives Wallis as publisher, and prices at 10s 6d. MR n.s. 34: 531–2 (App [Apr/May 1801]) gives full review of an edn. published in London by De Bouffe, apparently in French (though an extract quoted is in English).

GEISWEILER, Maria
See ARNOLD, Ignaz Ferdinand

1802: 26   GUNNING, [Elizabeth] [afterwards PLUNKETT].
THE FARMER'S BOY; A NOVEL: IN FOUR VOLUMES. BY MISS GUN-
NING, AUTHOR OF "LOVE AT FIRST SIGHT"—"GIPSY COUNTESS,"
&C. &C. &C.

> London: Printed by J. Cundee, Ivy-Lane; for B. Crosby & Co. Stationers'-Court; T.
>      Hurst, No. 32, and M. Jones, No. 1, Paternoster-Row, 1802.
> I 226p, ill.; II 230p; III 226p; IV 262p. 12mo. 16s (ECB).
> WSW I: 291.
> Corvey; CME 3-628-47582-1; ECB 248; xNSTC.

*Notes.* Frontispiece portrait of 'Miss Gunning'. Of the two titles mentioned as by the author,
only the second is by Elizabeth Gunning, *Love at First Sight* supposedly being by her mother
Susannah. ECB dates June 1802.

1802: 27   GUNNING, [Susannah] [née MINIFIE] and GUNNING,
[Elizabeth] [afterwards PLUNKETT].
THE HEIR APPARENT: A NOVEL. BY THE LATE MRS. GUNNING,
AUTHOR OF THE DELBOROUGH FAMILY, MEMOIRS OF MARY, &C.
REVISED AND AUGMENTED BY HER DAUGHTER, MISS GUNNING.
IN THREE VOLUMES.

> London: Printed for James Ridgway, York Street, St. James's Square; and H. D.
>      Symonds, No. 20, Paternoster Row, 1802.
> I viii, 251p; II 296p; III 298p. 12mo. 12 boards (CR); 12s (ECB); 12s sewed (MR).
> CR 2nd ser. 35: 477 (Aug 1802); MR n.s. 40: 208 (Feb 1803); WSW I: 291.
> Corvey; CME 3-628-47584-8; ECB 248; NSTC G2393 (BI O).

*Notes.* Preface, 'written by a friend', explains how Miss [Elizabeth] Gunning had completed
the greater part of her deceased mother's project.

1802: 28   HARVEY, Jane.
*MINERVA CASTLE: A TALE. BY JANE HARVEY.

> London: William Lane, 1802.
> 3 vols. 12mo. 13s 6d (ECB).
> No copy located; ECB 257.

*Notes.* Listed by Blakey, but not seen; Frank (Item 163) gives a minimal synopsis. ECB dates
Jan 1802; listed in Bent03 as Lane, 13s 6d. Not found in contemporary circulating library catalogues. Possibly a 'ghost' title, or a variant of the same author's *Warkfield Castle* (1802: 29).

1802: 29   HARVEY, Jane.
WARKFIELD CASTLE. A TALE. IN THREE VOLUMES. BY JANE
HARVEY.

> London: Printed at the Minerva-Press, for Lane and Newman, Leadenhall-Street, 1802.
> I 317p; II 322p; III 292p. 12mo. 13s 6d (ECB).

WSW I: 300.

Corvey; CME 3-628-47855-3; ECB 257; xNSTC.

*Notes.* ECB dates Feb 1802.

1802: 30   HASW[ORTH], H. H.

THE LADY OF THE CAVE, OR MYSTERIES OF THE FOURTEENTH CENTURY. AN HISTORICAL ROMANCE. IN THREE VOLUMES. BY H. H. HASWDH [*sic*].

> London: Printed at the Minerva-Press, for Lane and Newman, Leadenhall-Street, 1802.
> I 230p; II 287p; III 272p. 12mo. 12s (ECB).
> Corvey; CME 3-628-47856-1; ECB 258; xNSTC.

*Notes.* ECB dates June 1802. ECB, Allibone, and Blakey all give author's name as Hasworth.

1802: 31   HOOK, Sarah Ann.

CELINA; OR, THE WIDOWED BRIDE. A NOVEL. FOUNDED ON FACTS. BY SARAH ANN HOOK. IN THREE VOLUMES.

> London: Printed for the Author, and sold No. 14, Warwick Court, Holborn. A. Paris, Printer, Rolls' Buildings, 1802.
> I xxii, 226p; II 237p; III 214p. 12mo.
> IU 823.H764c; xNSTC.

*Notes.* 'A List of Subscribers Names' (*c.*190 names, many from NW England), vol. 1, pp. [xv]–xxii. Imprint on t.p. of vols. 2 and 3 reads: 'London: Printed for the Author, by A. Paris, Rolls' Building, Fetter Lane, and sold No. 14, Warwick Court, Holborn. Also by all the Bookseller's [*sic*], 1802'. Collates in sixes.

Further edn: 1803 as *The Widowed Bride, or Celina* (Corvey—a reissue by Lane and Newman with similar pagination and the same colophon of 'A. Paris, Printer, Rolls' Buildings, Fetter Lane' in all vols.), CME 3-628-47696-8.

1802: 32   HUNTER, [Rachel].

THE HISTORY OF THE GRUBTHORPE FAMILY, OR THE OLD BACH- ELOR AND HIS SISTER PENELOPE. BY MRS. HUNTER, OF NOR- WICH; AUTHOR OF LETITIA. IN THREE VOLUMES.

> Norwich: Printed for W. Robberds; and sold by Longman and Rees, Paternoster-Row, London. Wilks and Taylor, Printers, Chancery-Lane, 1802.
> I viii, 270p; II 310p; III 310p. 12mo. 13s 6d (ECB).
> Corvey; CME 3-628-47654-2; ECB 289; NSTC H3173 (BI C, O).

*Notes.* ECB dates Oct 1802.

1802: 33   KELLY, Isabella.

THE BARON'S DAUGHTER: A GOTHIC ROMANCE. BY ISABELLA KELLY, AUTHOR OF MADELINE, ABBEY ST. ASAPH, AVONDALE PRIORY, EVA, RUTHINGLENNE, ETC. IN FOUR VOLUMES.

> London: Printed for J. Bell, No. 148, Oxford-Street, by Wilks and Taylor, Chancery- Lane, 1802.

I iv, 244p; II 212p; III 176p; IV 182p. 12mo. 16s boards (CR); 14s (ECB).
CR 2nd ser. 36: 117 (Sept 1802); WSW I: 350.
BL 12611.bb.13; ECB 317; NSTC K134.

*Notes.* Further edn: 2nd edn. 1805 (Corvey), CME 3-628-47924-X.

## KNIGGE, Adolf Franz Friedrich Ludwig von, FAMILY MISFORTUNES; OR THE HISTORY OF FREDERICK GUTMAN

See THE HISTORY OF THE AMTSRATH GUTMAN, Vol. 1, 1799: 57; also present Vol., Appendix E: 2

### 1802: 34   LAFONTAINE, August [Heinrich Julius]; [HEMET, John (*trans.*)]. ODD ENOUGH, TO BE SURE! OR, EMILIUS IN THE WORLD. A NOVEL. IN TWO VOLUMES. FROM THE GERMAN OF AUGUSTUS LA FONTAINE.

London: Printed at the Minerva-Press, for Lane and Newman, Leadenhall-Street, 1802.
I x, 295p; II 268p. 12mo. 9s (ECB).
Corvey; CME 3-628-47470-1; ECB 326; NSTC L161 (BI BL).

*Notes.* Trans. of *Der Sonderling; ein Gemälde des menschlichen Herzens* (Vienna and Prague, 1799). ECB dates Jan 1802.

### 1802: 35   LAFONTAINE, August [Heinrich Julius]; [CHARLTON, Mary (*trans.*)]. THE REPROBATE. A NOVEL. IN TWO VOLUMES. TRANSLATED BY THE AUTHOR OF THE WIFE AND THE MISTRESS, &C. THE ORIGINAL BY AUGUSTUS LA FONTAINE.

London: Printed at the Minerva-Press, for Lane and Newman, Leadenhall-Street, 1802.
I 334p; II 300p. 12mo. 8s boards (CR); 8s (ECB); 8s sewed (ER).
CR 2nd ser. 37: 238 (Feb 1803); ER 4: 498 (July 1804); WSW I: 203.
BL 1152.h.6; ECB 326; NSTC L159.

*Notes.* Trans. of *Tableaux de famille, ou journal de Charles Engelmann* (Paris, 1801); original German title, *Carl Engelmanns Tagebuch* (Berlin, 1800).

### 1802: 36   LATHOM, Francis. ASTONISHMENT!!! A ROMANCE OF A CENTURY AGO, IN TWO VOLUMES, BY FRANCIS LATHOM, AUTHOR OF "MEN AND MANNERS— MYSTERY—MIDNIGHT BELL—CASTLE OF OLLADA—DASH OF THE DAY—ORLANDO AND SERAPHINA, OR THE FUNERAL PILE—HOLIDAY TIME, OR THE SCHOOL-BOY'S FROLIC—CURIOSITY", &C. &C.

London: Printed for T. N. Longman and O. Rees, Paternoster-Row, 1802.
I iv, 318p; II 309p. 12mo. 9s boards (CR); 9s (ECB).
CR 2nd ser. 37: 116–17 (Jan 1803); WSW I: 363.
Corvey; CME 3-628-47953-3; ECB 330; NSTC L539 (BI BL).

*Notes.* Note (unn.) stating that 'For the Poetry interspersed in these Volumes, the Author is indebted to a Female Friend'; followed by 'A Few Words to Begin With' (vol. 1, pp. [iii]–iv). Vignette design of 'Payne, Printer, Norwich' at end of both vols.
Further edn: Newman edn. 1821 (NUC).

1802: 37   [LYTTLETON, Mr].

ISABEL, OR THE ORPHAN OF VALDARNO. A FLORENTINE ROMANCE. FOUNDED DURING THE CIVIL WARS IN ITALY. IN THREE VOLUMES. BY A STUDENT OF TRINITY COLLEGE, CAMBRIDGE.

London: Printed at the Minerva-Press, for Lane and Newman, Leadenhall-Street, 1802.
I 286p, ill.; II 325p; III 392p. 12mo.
WSW I: 59.
Corvey; CME 3-628-47870-7; xNSTC.

1802: 38   LYTTLETON, Mr.

THE LOTTERY OF LIFE, OR THE ROMANCE OF A SUMMER. IN THREE VOLUMES. BY MR. LYTTLETON, THE AUTHOR OF ISABEL.

London: Printed at the Minerva-Press, for Lane and Newman, Leadenhall-Street, 1802.
I 270p; II 276p; III 243p. 12mo. 12s boards (CR); 12s (ECB).
CR 2nd ser. 38: 115 (May 1803); WSW I: 379.
Corvey; CME 3-628-48074-4; ECB 357; xNSTC.

1802: 39   MACKENZIE, Anna Maria.

MARTIN & MANSFELDT, OR THE ROMANCE OF FRANCONIA. IN THREE VOLUMES. BY ANNA MARIA MACKENZIE, AUTHOR OF MYSTERIES ELUCIDATED, FEUDAL EVENTS, &C.

London: Printed at the Minerva-Press, for Lane and Newman, Leadenhall-Street, 1802.
I xxiii, 232p; II 325p; III 352p. 12mo. 12s (ECB).
WSW I: 381.
Corvey; CME 3-628-48096-5; ECB 360; NSTC M345 (BI BL).

*Notes.* 'Introduction by the Editor', signed Anna Maria Mackenzie, stating that the present work is translated from an old German manuscript; but no German original discovered.

1802: 40   [MALARME, Charlotte de Bournon].

*MIRALBA, THE CHIEF OF THE BANDITTI. TRANSLATED FROM THE FRENCH.

London: Hurst, 1802.
2 vols. 12mo. 8s (ECB).
No copy located; ECB 388.

*Notes.* Trans. of *Miralba, chef de brigands* (Paris, 1800). Publisher taken from Summers. ECB dates June 1802.

1802: 41   [MARTIN, H.].

HELEN OF GLENROSS; A NOVEL. BY THE AUTHOR OF HISTORIC TALES. IN FOUR VOLUMES.

Printed for G. and J. Robinson. Paternoster-Row. By J. Cundee, Ivy-Lane, 1802.
I iv, 264p; II 264p; III 331p; IV 269p. 12mo. 16s boards (CR, MR); 16s (ECB).
CR 2nd ser. 34: 356 (Mar 1802); MR n.s. 41: 103 (May 1803).
Corvey; CME 3-628-47724-7; ECB 263; xNSTC.

*Notes.* Dedication 'To **** *****', and signed '******* ******', dated Nov 1801. Preface (1 p. unn.) at beginning of vol. 2, dated Jan 1802, apologises for typographical errors in the first two vols. 'occasioned by the Author's absence from the press, and by the Editor's not having this part of the Work submitted to him until it was printed'. Author listed as Harriet Martin, d. 1846, in some catalogues.

Further edns: Boston 1802 (NUC); French trans., 1812.

1802: 42   [MEEKE, Mary].

INDEPENDENCE. A NOVEL. IN FOUR VOLUMES. BY GABRIELLI, AUTHOR OF THE MYSTERIOUS HUSBAND, &C.

> London: Printed at the Minerva-Press, for Lane and Newman, Leadenhall-Street, 1802.
> I 280p; II 237p; III 272p; IV 264p. 12mo. 16s boards (CR); 16s (ECB).
> CR 2nd ser. 37: 237 (Feb 1803); WSW I: 394.
> Corvey; CME 3-628-47846-4; ECB 293; xNSTC.

1802: 43   MEEKE, [Mary].

MIDNIGHT WEDDINGS. A NOVEL. IN THREE VOLUMES. BY MRS. MEEKE, AUTHOR OF ANECDOTES OF THE ALTAMONT FAMILY, ELLESMERE, &C. &C.

> London: Printed at the Minerva-Press, for William Lane, Leadenhall-Street, 1802.
> I 297p; II 298p; III 319p. 12mo. 12s (ECB).
> Corvey; CME 3-628-48209-7; ECB 378; NSTC M1955 (BI BL).

*Notes.* ECB dates Nov 1801.

Further edn: French trans., 1820 [as *Les Mariages nocturnes, ou Octave et la famille Browning* (BN)].

1802: 44   MELVILLE, Theodore.

THE WHITE KNIGHT, OR THE MONASTERY OF MORNE. A ROMANCE. IN THREE VOLUMES. BY THEODORE MELVILLE, ESQ.

> London: Printed, at the Oriental Press, by Wilson & Co. for Crosby and Letterman, Stationers Court, Ludgate-Street, 1802.
> I iv, 223p; II 182p; III 262p. 12mo. 10s 6d sewed (CR); 12s (ECB).
> CR 2nd ser. 35: 476–7 (Aug 1802); MR n.s. 39: 427 (Dec 1802); WSW I: 394.
> Corvey; CME 3-628-48057-4; ECB 379; xNSTC.

1802: 45   MILLIKIN, Anna.

PLANTAGENET: OR, SECRETS OF THE HOUSE OF ANJOU. A TALE OF THE TWELFTH CENTURY. WRITTEN BY ANNA MILLIKIN, AUTHOR OF "CORFE CASTLE,"—"EVA,"—"THE CASKET," &C. &C. IN TWO VOLUMES.

> Cork: Printed by J. Connor, Circulating-Library, Grand-Parade, 1802.
> I 224p; II 258p. 8vo. 7s boards (CR).
> CR 2nd ser. 37: 117 (Jan 1803); WSW I: 396.
> Corvey; CME 3-628-48132-5; ECB 454; NSTC M2411 (BI Dt).

*Notes.* ECB dates Aug 1802.

MINIFIE, Susannah
See GUNNING, Susannah

1802: 46    MOORE, George.
**THEODOSIUS DE ZULVIN, THE MONK OF MADRID: A SPANISH TALE,
DELINEATING VARIOUS TRAITS OF THE HUMAN MIND. BY GEORGE
MOORE, AUTHOR OF GRASVILLE ABBEY. IN FOUR VOLUMES.**

> London: Printed for G. and J. Robinson, Paternoster-Row; by S. Hamilton, Falcon-
> Court, Fleet-Street, 1802.
> I xii, 288p; II 279p; III 268p; IV 276p. 12mo. 14s (ECB).
> WSW I: 404.
> Corvey; CME 3-628-48279-8; ECB 394; xNSTC.

*Notes.* Dedication 'to the Inhabitants of the Isle of Wight', dated Tottenham Court Road,
4 June 1802. Preface contains information about the author having lived on the Isle of Wight
from 1798 to Autumn 1799 and then returning to London. ECB dates Nov 1802. For records
of an impression of 1000, and payments to the author, see Bentley, pp. 93 and 106.

1802: 47    MOORE, Marian.
**LASCELLES. INTERSPERSED WITH CHARACTERSTIC SKETCHES
FROM NATURE. IN THREE VOLUMES. BY MARIAN MOORE.**

> London: Printed at the Minerva-Press, for Lane and Newman, Leadenhall-Street, 1802.
> I 288p; II 295p; III 270p. 12mo. 12s (ECB).
> Corvey; CME 3-628-48284-4; ECB 394; xNSTC.

*Notes.* Dedication to 'T—s L—e, Esq.'. 'Advertisement' (unn.), signed M. M., and stating the
Authoress to be 'very young and inexperienced'. ECB dates Apr 1802.

1802: 48    OAKES, Susanna.
**THE RULES OF THE FOREST. IN THREE VOLUMES. BY SUSANNA OAKES.**

> Derby: Printed by J. Drewry, and sold by all Booksellers in the three Kingdoms, n.d. [1802].
> I 278p, ill.; II 296p; III (1802) 464p. 12mo. 12s (ECB); 10s 6d/13s 6d (end 'Advertise-
> ment').
> Corvey; CME 3-628-48242-9; ECB 419; NSTC O15 (BI O).

*Notes.* Frontispiece, depicting the authoress as 'keeper of the circulating library at Ashborne
in the County of Derby'. 'Advertisement' (unn.) at the end vol. 1 offers an apology for 'the
repeated delays during the process of the foregoing pages', and promises that the remaining
vols. will be 'brought forward as expeditiously as possible'. List of 'Subscribers Names' (4 pp.
unn.) at the beginning of vol. 3; this includes 92 names, with subscriptions alongside (most
commonly 10s 6d). Vol. 3 t.p. is dated 1802. Novel proper ends on p. 462, followed by 'Errata'
(p. 463) and a final 'Advertisement' (p. 464) stating that the length of the last vol., and
expense of paper, has necessitated raising the price: 'First Subscriptions, 10s. 6d.—with additions, 13s. 6d.' ECB dates Nov 1802. Collates in sixes.

1802: 49    [ORMSBY, Anne].
**MEMOIRS OF A FAMILY IN SWISSERLAND; FOUNDED ON FACTS.
IN FOUR VOLUMES.**

London: Printed by A. Strahan, Printers-Street, for T. N. Longman, and O. Rees, Pater-
noster-Row, 1802.
I 220p; II 224p; III v, 240p; IV vii, 230p. 12mo. 14s boards (CR).
CR 2nd ser. 36: 236 (Oct 1802); WSW I: 423.
Corvey; CME 3-628-48060-4; NSTC O481 (BI BL, E, O).

1802: 50   P., F. H.
THE CASTLE OF CAITHNESS. A ROMANCE OF THE THIRTEENTH
CENTURY. IN TWO VOLUMES. BY F. H. P.

London: Printed at the Minerva-Press, for Lane and Newman, Leadenhall-Street, 1802.
I 225p; II 256p. 12mo. 8s boards (CR).
CR 2nd ser. 36: 478 (Dec 1802); WSW I: 22, 426.
Corvey; CME 3-628-47225-3; xNSTC.

1802: 51   PARKER, Mary Elizabeth.
ALFRED; OR THE ADVENTURES OF THE KNIGHT OF THE CASTLE. A
NOVEL. IN THREE VOLUMES. BY MARY ELIZABETH PARKER.

London: Printed at the Apollo Press, by G. Cawthorn, British Library, Strand Bookseller
and Printer to Her Royal Highness The Princess of Wales, 1802.
I 343p; II 224p; III 194p. 12mo. 13s 6d (ECB).
Corvey; CME 3-628-48383-2; ECB 433; xNSTC.

*Notes.* ECB dates June 1802.

1802: 52   [PARNELL, William].
JULIETTA, OR THE TRIUMPH OF MENTAL ACQUIREMENTS OVER
PERSONAL DEFECTS.

London: Printed for J. Johnson, St. Paul's Church-Yard, 1802.
206p. 8vo. 3s 6d (ECB); 3s 6d boards (MR).
MR n.s. 40: 205–7 (Feb 1803); WSW I: 61.
Corvey; CME 3-628-48014-0; ECB 315; NSTC J1212 (BI BL, O).

1802: 53   PARSONS, [Eliza].
THE MYSTERIOUS VISIT: A NOVEL, FOUNDED ON FACTS. IN FOUR
VOLUMES. BY MRS. PARSONS, AUTHOR OF THE PEASANT OF
ARDENNE FOREST, THE VALLEY OF ST. GOTHARD, THE MISER
AND HIS FAMILY, &C. &C. &C.

Brentford: Printed by and for P. Norbury; and sold by T. Hurst, No. 32, Paternoster
Row; J. Hatchard, Piccadilly; Carpenter and Co. Old-Bond-Street; and Didier and
Tibbett, St. James's-Street, London, 1802.
I 271p; II 259p; III 264p; IV 272p. 12mo. 20s (ECB).
WSW I: 430.
Corvey; CME 3-628-48399-9; ECB 435; NSTC P565 (BI O).

*Notes.* ECB dates Jan 1803.

1802: 54   [PILKINGTON, Miss].
THE ACCUSING SPIRIT, OR DE COURCY AND EGLANTINE. A
ROMANCE. IN FOUR VOLUMES. BY THE AUTHOR OF DELIA,
ROSINA, AND THE SUBTERRANEAN CAVERN.

London: Printed at the Minerva-Press, for Lane and Newman, Leadenhall-Street, 1802.
I 295p, ill.; II 276p; III 292p; IV 304p. 12mo. 18s (ECB).
Corvey; CME 3-628-47004-8; ECB 3; NSTC B4627 (BI O).

*Notes*. Blakey notes attributed by Minerva Library Catalogue of 1814 to Miss Pilkington. This
is apparently a different author from Mary Pilkington (1766–1839), who is listed separately
in FC—see her *Crimes and Characters* (1805: 60). NSTC (following Bodleian) lists under
Brooke, Frances (1724–1789). ECB dates Jan 1802.


PLUNKETT, Elizabeth
See GUNNING, Elizabeth


1802: 55   [PURBECK, Jane].
NEVILLE CASTLE; OR, THE GENEROUS CAMBRIANS. A NOVEL, IN
FOUR VOLUMES. BY THE AUTHOR OF RAYNSFORD PARK.

London: Printed by T. Plummer, Seething-Lane; for R. Dutton, 45, Gracechurch-
    Street; and J. Cawthorn, Catherine-Street, Strand, 1802.
I iv, 256p; II 288p; III 299p; IV 312p. 12mo. 14s boards (CR); 14s (ECB).
CR 2nd ser. 38: 358 (July 1803); WSW I: 83.
Corvey; CME 3-628-48189-9; ECB 410; xNSTC.

*Notes*. 'Preface' states that 'the following pages were written several years since' (p. [i]); and
the first-person writer praises Madame de Genlis, and the authors of *Camilla*, and of *The
Mysteries of Udolpha* [*sic*] and *The Italian*. Several catalogues attribute to the Misses Purbeck
(i.e. Elizabeth and Jane). 'Literary Intelligence' (unn.) at the end of the 3rd vol. announces
the removal of R. Dutton's Circulating Library from Birchin-Lane to No. 45, Gracechurch-
Street, dated 2 June 1802.
Further edn: French trans., 1803.


1802: 56   [SANDS, James].
MONCKTON; OR, THE FATE OF ELEANOR. A NOVEL. IN THREE
VOLUMES. TO WHICH IS PREFIXED, A GENERAL DEFENCE OF
MODERN NOVELS. BY THE AUTHOR OF COUNT DI NOVINI.

London: Printed for G. and J. Robinson, Pater-Noster-Row. By J. Crowder and E. Hem-
    sted, Warwick-Square, 1802.
I xxi, 263p; II 240p; III 246p. 12mo. 10s 6d boards (CR).
CR 2nd ser. 37: 356 (Mar 1803); WSW I: 78.
Corvey; CME 3-628-48221-6; NSTC S417 (BI BL, C).

*Notes*. Dedication (in verse) to Sir M. W. Ridley, Bart. M.P. 'A General Defence of Modern
Novels', vol. 1, pp. [i]–xxi. Continuous roman and arabic pagination, with novel beginning
at p. [23].

1802: 57   [SHERIFFE, Sarah].
**CORRELIA, OR THE MYSTIC TOMB. A ROMANCE. IN FOUR VOL-
UMES. BY THE AUTHOR OF HUMBERT CASTLE.**

>  London: Printed at the Minerva-Press, for Lane and Newman, Leadenhall-Street, 1802.
>  I xii, 324p; II 335p; III 350p; IV 363p. 12mo.
>  Corvey; CME 3-628-47366-7; xNSTC.

*Notes.* Further edn: German trans., 1803 [as *Corelia, oder die Geheimnisse des Grabes* (RS)].


1802: 58   SLEATH, Eleanor.
**WHO'S THE MURDERER? OR THE MYSTERY OF THE FOREST. A
NOVEL. IN FOUR VOLUMES. BY ELEANOR SLEATH, AUTHOR OF
THE ORPHAN OF THE RHINE, &C.**

>  London: Printed at the Minerva-Press, for Lane and Newman, Leadenhall-Street, 1802.
>  I 362p, ill.; II 387p; III 370p; IV 398p. 12mo.
>  WSW I: 501.
>  Corvey; CME 3-628-48757-9; ECB 542; xNSTC.

*Notes.* ECB dates July 1802.
Further edn: French trans., 1819 [as *Les Mystères de la forêt, ou quel est le meurtrier?* (MLC)].


**SMITH, Charlotte, THE LETTERS OF A SOLITARY WANDERER**
See 1800: 69


**SURR, Thomas Skinner, SPLENDID MISERY**
See 1801: 64


1802: 59   [TYLER, Royall].
**THE ALGERINE CAPTIVE; OR, THE LIFE AND ADVENTURES OF
DOCTOR UPDIKE UNDERHILL, SIX YEARS A PRISONER AMONG
THE ALGERINES.**

>  London: Printed for G. and J. Robinson, Paternoster-Row, by S. Hamilton, Falcon-
>  Court, Fleet-Street, 1802.
>  I xxiv, 190p; II xi, 228p. 12mo. 6s (CR, ECB); 6s boards (MR).
>  CR 2nd ser. 35: 113–14 (May 1802); MR n.s. 42: 86–97 (Sept 1803) full review; WSW I:
>  547.
>  Corvey; CME 3-628-47038-2; ECB 12; xNSTC.

*Notes.* Dedication to 'His Excellency David Humphreys, Esq. Minister of the United States at
the Court of Lisbon, &c.', signed Updike Underhill, 20 June 1797. Originally published Walpole, NH, 1797 (NUC).


1802: 60   [WEST, Jane].
**THE INFIDEL FATHER; BY THE AUTHOR OF "A TALE OF THE
TIMES," "A GOSSIP'S STORY," &C. IN THREE VOLUMES.**

>  London: Printed by A. Strahan, Printers-Street, for T. N. Longman and O. Rees, Pater-
>  noster-Row, 1802.

I iv, iii, 306p; II vii, 345p; III iv, 346p. 12mo.
WSW I: 556.
Corvey; CME 3-628-48892-3; NSTC W1345 (BI BL, C, O).

1802: 61    [WILSON, Ann].
**LADY GERALDINE BEAUFORT. A NOVEL IN THREE VOLUMES. BY A
DAUGHTER OF THE LATE SERJEANT WILSON.**

> London: Printed for G. and J. Robinson, Paternoster-Row, by S. Hamilton, Falcon-
> Court, Fleet-Street, 1802.
> I 278p; II 240p; III 291p. 12mo. 12s boards (CR); 12s (ECB); 10s 6d boards (MR).
> CR 2nd ser. 35: 477 (Aug 1802); MR n.s. 41: 103–4 (May 1803); WSW I: 565.
> Corvey; CME 3-628-47890-1; ECB 641; xNSTC.

*Notes.* ECB attributes to Miss Ann Wilson: see also *Scotch Lawsuits* (1812: 66) for further evidence supporting attribution to this author. Drop-head title reads: 'The History of Lady
Geraldine Beaufort'.


# 1803


1803: 1    ANON.
**ALGERNON PERCY: OR THE VICTIM OF ENVY. A ROMANCE.
INTERSPERSED WITH BALLADS; IN IMITATION OF THE ANTIENTS.
IN TWO VOLUMES.**

> London: Printed for J. Bell, No. 148, Oxford-Street, by Wilks and Taylor, Chancery
> Lane, 1803.
> I 187p; II 189p. 12mo. 6s (ECB).
> MH-H EC8.A100.803a; ECB 12; NSTC A896.5 (BI BL).

*Notes.* ECB dates Apr 1803.


1803: 2    ANON.
**BARBARA MARKHAM; OR, THE PROFLIGATE REQUITED. A NOVEL.**

> London: Printed by the Philanthropic Society, St. George's-Fields, for W. J. and J.
> Richardson, Royal Exchange; and Vernor and Hood, Poultry, 1803.
> I x, 184p; II 184p. 12mo. 7s boards (CR); 7s (ECB).
> CR 3rd ser. 2: 113–14 (May 1804); ER 3: 260 (Oct 1803); WSW I: 14.
> Corvey; CME 3-628-47100-1; ECB 39; xNSTC.

*Notes.* Dedication 'to Her Grace The Duchess of Bedford'. Collates in sixes.


1803: 3    ANON.
**THE CHANCES; OR, NOTHING OF THE NEW SCHOOL: A NOVEL. IN
THREE VOLUMES. BY A DISCIPLE OF THE OLD SCHOOL.**

London: Printed for Cuthell and Martin, Middle-Row, Holborn; by W. Blackader, 10,
Took's Court, Chancery Lane, 1803.
I vi, 295p; II 312p; III 318p. 12mo. 10s 6d (ECB).
WSW I: 23.
Corvey; CME 3-628-47248-2; ECB 105; NSTC C1336.5 (BI BL).

*Notes.* 'To The Reader', dated Duck-Lane, 1 Jan 1803. ECB dates May 1803.

1803: 4   ANON.
THE CONVENT OF ST. MICHAEL, A TALE: TAKEN FROM A GERMAN
MANUSCRIPT OF THE SEVENTEENTH CENTURY. IN TWO VOLUMES.

London: Printed by J. Cundee, Ivy-Lane, for T. Hurst, Paternoster-Row; and C. Chap-
ple, Pall-Mall, 1803.
I viii, 210p; II 208p. 12mo. 7s boards (CR); 7s (ECB).
CR 2nd ser. 38: 237 (June 1803); WSW I: 27.
Corvey; CME 3-628-47327-6; ECB 132; xNSTC.

*Notes.* Preface signed 'The Editor' and dated London, 1803. Introduction states the story is
based on an Italian [*sic*] manuscript, which was procured by 'Madam Soranza' and then
passed to 'Lady M—', widow of the ambassador to Venice.

1803: 5   ANON.
DON SANCHO; OR, THE MONK OF HENNARES. A SPANISH ROMANCE.
IN TWO VOLUMES.

London: Printed by D. N. Shury, Berwick Street, Soho; for J. F. Hughes, Wigmore
Street, 1803.
I 275p; II 231p. 12mo. 7s (ECB).
Corvey; CME 3-628-47447-7; ECB 168; xNSTC.

*Notes.* ECB dates Dec 1803.

1803: 6   ANON.
ECCENTRIC PHILANTHROPY. A NOVEL, IN THREE VOLUMES.

London: Printed for J. Booth, 14, Duke-Street, Portland Place; and sold by E. Kirby,
Stafford Street, Bond Street, C. Chapple, Pall Mall, and T. Hurst, 1803.
I 288p; II 288p; III 264p. 12mo. 10s 6d boards (CR); 10s 6d (ECB).
CR 2nd ser. 37: 478 (Apr 1803); WSW I: 35.
Corvey; CME 3-628-47579-1; ECB 177; xNSTC.

*Notes.* CR states: 'A scion from the German stock [. . .] The work is decidedly a translation,
and far from a correct one'. But no German original discovered.

1803: 7   ANON.
FALSE APPEARANCES; OR, MEMOIRS OF HENRY AUBERVILLE
INTERSPERSED WITH LEGENDARY ROMANCES.

Dublin: Printed for William Porter, Grafton-Street, 1803.
179p. 12mo.
IU X823.f.1982; xNSTC.

*Notes.* Dedication (p. [3]) 'to Sir Fenton Aylmer, Bart.'. Preface (pp. [5]–6) dated Dublin, May 1803. Summers (p. 314) comments 'There is, I believe, an English edition of the same year but some months earlier'. No such edn. has been located.

1803: 8  ANON.
## THE GHOST OF HARCOURT. A ROMANCE. TO WHICH IS ADDED THE FAIR MAID OF PORTUGAL.

> London: Printed at the Minerva-Press, for Lane, Newman, and Co. Leadenhall-Street, 1803.
> 72p. 12mo.
> BL 12619.e.39(2); NSTC H478.

*Notes.* 'The Ghost of Harcourt', pp. [1]–30; 'The Fair Maid of Portugal', pp. [31]–72. Closely printed pages; presentationally bearing a similarity to contemporary chapbooks containing Gothic material, but unusual in being packaged as a Minerva publication.

1803: 9  ANON.
## HUMAN FRAILTIES. A NOVEL, IN THREE VOLUMES. INTER-SPERSED WITH POETRY. BY THE AUTHOR OF THE "OBSERVANT PEDESTRIAN"—"MONTROSE"—"MYSTIC COTTAGER," &C. &C.

> London: Printed by John Abraham, Clement's Lane; for R. Dutton, 45, Gracechurch Street; T. Hurst, Paternoster Row; J. Cawthorn, Catherine Street; and Chapple, Pall-Mall, 1803.
> I 227p; II 240p; III 238p. 12mo. 12s boards (CR); 10s 6d (ECB).
> CR 3rd ser. 1: 237–8 (Feb 1804); ER 3: 506 (Jan 1804); WSW I: 55.
> Corvey; CME 3-628-47680-1; ECB 288; NSTC F1342 (BI BL).

1803: 10  ANON.
## LETTERS OF MISS RIVERSDALE. A NOVEL. IN THREE VOLUMES.

> London: Printed for J. Johnson, St. Paul's Church-Yard, 1803.
> I viii, 372p; II 367p; III 425p. 12mo. 13s 6d (ECB).
> WSW I: 65.
> Corvey; CME 3-628-48039-6; ECB 342; NSTC R1112 (BI BL, O).

*Notes.* Dedication to 'Mrs. Blandford'. ECB dates Apr 1803.

1803: 11  ANON.
## NOTHING NEW, A NOVEL; IN WHICH IS DRAWN CHARACTERIS-TIC SKETCHES FROM MODERN AND FASHIONABLE LIFE. IN THREE VOLUMES.

> London: Printed for J. Booth, Duke-Street, Portland-Place; and T. Hurst, Paternoster-Row, 1803.
> I 262p; II 316p; III 306p. 12mo. 10s 6d boards (CR); 10s 6d (ECB).
> CR 2nd ser. 37: 478 (Apr 1803); WSW I: 84.
> Corvey; CME 3-628-48239-9; ECB 417; xNSTC.

*Notes.* Printer's mark verso of t.p. reads: 'Printed by J. Barfield, Wardour-Street, Printer to His Royal Highness the Prince of Wales'. ECB lists Hurst only as publisher. NUC enters an apparently variant issue: 'Nothing new! or, Louisa, the orphan of Lennox Abbey; a novel. London, J. Barfield. 1803'. The Corvey copy is an epistolary novel, featuring Lenox [*sic*] Abbey and in which Louisa is a central character. See also 1807: 1, below.

1803: 12    ANON.
THE VALE OF CONWAY. A NOVEL. BY A LADY. IN FOUR VOLUMES.

> London: Printed for Vernor and Hood, 31, Poultry. By T. Appleby, North Shields, 1803.
> I vi, 269p; II 269p; III 303p; IV 323p. 12mo. 12s boards (CR); 14s (ECB).
> CR 2nd ser. 38: 478 (Aug 1803); WSW I: 125.
> Corvey; CME 3-628-48851-6; ECB 609; xNSTC.

*Notes.* Collates in sixes.

1803: 13    [AUMONT, Mme. de] Pienne, Duchesse [d'].
ITALIAN JEALOUSY: OR, THE HISTORY OF LADY GEORGINA CECIL. BY THE DUCHESS OF PIENNE. IN THREE VOLUMES.

> London: Printed for Thomas Hurst, No. 32, Pater-Noster-Row, by Wilks and Taylor,
>    Chancery-Lane, 1803.
> I 296p; II 285p; III 345p. 12mo. 13s 6d (ECB).
> Corvey; CME 3-628-48440-5; ECB 450; xNSTC.

*Notes.* French original not discovered. ECB dates Feb 1803.

1803: 14    B[ACULARD] D'ARNAUD, [François-Thomas-Marie de].
LORIMON, OR MAN IN EVERY STAGE OF LIFE. A NOVEL. IN TWO VOLUMES. BY B. D'ARNAUD. TRANSLATED FROM THE FRENCH.

> London: Printed at the Minerva-Press, for Lane and Newman, Leadenhall-Street, 1803.
> I xii, 206p; II 228p. 12mo. 7s boards (CR); 7s (ECB).
> CR 2nd ser. 38: 477–8 (Aug 1803).
> Corvey; CME 3-628-47422-1; ECB 353; xNSTC.

*Notes.* Trans. of *Lorimon, ou l'homme tel qu'il est* (Paris, n.d.). Preface by the Translator.

1803: 15    BARTON, James.
THE REMORSELESS ASSASSIN; OR THE DANGERS OF ENTHUSIASM. BY JAMES BARTON, L.M. TRANSLATOR OF MARGARET OF STRAF-FORD, THE DEPRAVED HUSBAND AND PHILOSOPHIC WIFE, &C. &C. IN TWO VOLUMES.

> London: Printed by R. Exton, Great Portland-Street; for J. F. Hughes, Wigmore-Street,
>    Cavendish-Square, 1803.
> I 202p; II 224p. 12mo.
> Corvey; CME 3-628-47110-9; ECB 43; NSTC B840 (BI BL).

*Notes.* Collates in sixes.

1803: 16    BROMLEY, Eliza Nugent (*trans.?*).
THE CAVE OF COSENZA: A ROMANCE OF THE EIGHTEENTH CENTURY. ALTERED FROM THE ITALIAN. BY ELIZA NUGENT

BROMLEY; AUTHOR OF LAURA AND AUGUSTUS. DEDICATED, BY PERMISSION, TO HIS ROYAL HIGHNESS THE DUKE OF YORK. IN TWO VOLUMES.

> London: Printed by W. Calvert, Great Shire-Lane, Temple-Bar; for G. and J. Robinson, Paternoster-Row; and Hookham and Ebers, Old Bond-Street, 1803.
> I 330p; II 349p. 12mo. 12s boards (CR); 12s (ECB).
> CR 3rd ser. 1: 119 (Jan 1804); ER 3: 506 (Jan 1804).
> Corvey; CME 3-628-47162-1; ECB 77; xNSTC.

*Notes.* No Italian original discovered. CR states: 'The work is said to be altered from the Italian; and there is seemingly an incongruous mixture of the English and the Italian stories'. Dedication dated London, Dec 1803. 'List of Subscribers' (7 pp. unn.), at the beginning of vol. 1: this is headed by the Duke and Duchess of York, and the Dukes of Clarence and Kent, followed by 104 other subscribers. For records of payments in the George Robinson archive, see Bentley pp. 86, 100 (notes 12, 13).

1803: 17   BROOKE, [Charlotte].
EMMA; OR THE FOUNDLING OF THE WOOD. A NOVEL. BY MISS BROOKE, DAUGHTER OF THE LATE HENRY BROOKE, AUTHOR OF THE FOOL OF QUALITY, ETC.

> London: Printed for J. F. Hughes, 5, Wigmore-Street, Cavindish[*sic*]-Square; by J. Swan, Angel Street, Newgate Street. And sold by B. Crosby and Co. Stationers'-Court, Ludgate-Street, 1803.
> vii, 180p. 12mo. 3s 6d (ECB).
> WSW I: 173.
> Corvey; CME 3-628-47163-X; ECB 77; xNSTC.

*Notes.* ECB dates Mar 1803.

1803: 18   BROWN, C[harles] B[rockden].
ARTHUR MERVYN. A TALE. IN THREE VOLUMES. BY C. B. BROWN, AUTHOR OF EDGAR HUNTLY, WIELAND, ORMOND, &C.

> London: Printed at the Minerva-Press, for Lane and Newman, Leadenhall-Street, 1803.
> I iv, 318p; II 299p; III 311p. 12mo. 12s boards (CR); 12s (ECB).
> CR 2nd ser. 39: 119 (Sept 1803); WSW I: 174.
> Corvey; CME 3-628-47134-6; ECB 78; xNSTC.

*Notes.* 'Preface' signed 'C. B. B.'. ECB dates Nov 1802. Originally published Philadelphia 1799, followed by 'Second Part' New York 1800 (Blanck). Further edn: 1821 (NUC).

1803: 19   BROWN, C[harles] B[rockden].
EDGAR HUNTLY, OR MEMOIRS OF A SLEEP-WALKER. A NOVEL. IN THREE VOLUMES. BY C. B. BROWN, AUTHOR OF ARTHUR MERVYN, WIELAND, ORMOND, &C.

> London: Printed at the Minerva-Press, for Lane and Newman, Leadenhall-Street, 1803.
> I 259p; II 255p; III 288p. 12mo. 12s boards (CR); 10s 6d (ECB).

CR 3rd ser. 3: 360 (Nov 1804); WSW I: 174.
Corvey; CME 3-628-47136-2; ECB 78; xNSTC.

*Notes.* ECB dates Nov 1802. Originally published Philadelphia 1799 (Blanck).
Further edns: 1831 (NSTC 2B51809); 1842 (NSTC).

1803: 20    BRUNO, Louis de.
LIONCEL; OR, THE EMIGRANT: AN HISTORICAL NOVEL. TRANS-
LATED FROM THE FRENCH OF LOUIS DE BRUNO, A NATIVE OF
THE BANKS OF THE GANGES. IN TWO VOLUMES. EMBELLISHED
WITH FRONTISPIECES.
London: Printed for John Stockdale, Piccadilly, 1803.
I viii, 188p; II 155p? 12mo. 7s (ECB).
CR 2nd ser. 38: 478 (Aug 1803).
NN NKV (Bruno); ECB 81; xNSTC.

*Notes.* Trans. of *Lioncel, ou l'émigré, nouvelle historique* (Paris, 1800). Vol. 1 only found;
vol. 2 pagination from BL copy of 2nd edn., 1803 (12451.ccc.2), which has the same pagination in vol. 1. No illustrations discovered in NN copy. Dedication to Mrs Samuel Johnson, of
Devonshire Street, Portland Place, signed 'the Translator', London, 28 Feb 1803. 'Advertisement' indicates male translator.
Further edn: 2nd edn. 1803 (NSTC B5006).

1803: 21    BYERLEY, J[ohn Scott].
NATURE; OR, A PICTURE OF THE PASSIONS. TO WHICH IS PRE-
FIXED, AN ESSAY ON NOVEL WRITING. BY J. BYERLEY. IN FOUR
VOLUMES.
London: Printed for S. Highley, (Successor to the late Mr. John Murray) No. 24, Fleet-
Street; E. Williams, No. 11, Strand; and James Asperne, Cornhill, 1803/04.
I (1804) xvi, 32, 142p; II (1803) 225p; III (1804) 204p; IV (1804) 228p. 12mo. 14s boards (CR).
CR 3rd ser. 1: 358 (Mar 1804); ER 3: 506 (Jan 1804); WSW I: 184.
BL 1578/5116; NSTC B6020.5.

*Notes.* Dedication to George Brewer, Esq., dated London, 1 July 1803. 'An Essay on Novel
Writing' occupies vol. 1, pp. [3]–32 (first sequence), and is dated 16 Oct 1803. Printer's mark
verso of t.p. in vol. 1 'T. Burton, Printer, Little Queen-Street'; in vols. 2, 3, and 4 'Printed by
W. Glendinning, No. 25, Hatton-Garden'. Nevertheless colophon in vol. 2 reads 'Printed by
B. M'Millan Bow-Street, Covent-Garden'; colophons in vols. 3 and 4 are those of W.
Glendinning.
Further edn: 1804 (Corvey), CME 3-628-47152-4.

1803: 22    [CHARLTON, Mary (*trans.?*)].
THE PHILOSOPHIC KIDNAPPER. A NOVEL. IN THREE VOLUMES.
ALTERED FROM THE FRENCH BY THE AUTHOR OF THE WIFE AND
THE MISTRESS.
London: Printed at the Minerva-Press, for Lane and Newman, Leadenhall-Street, 1803.
I iv, 277p; II 280p; III 286p. 12mo. 12s (ECB).
Corvey; CME 3-628-47255-5; ECB 447; xNSTC.

*Notes.* No French original discovered. Preface by the Translator. ECB dates Mar 1803.

1803: 23   C[OTTIN, Sophie Ristaud].
**AMELIA MANSFIELD. TRANSLATED FROM THE FRENCH OF MADAME C\*\*\*. AUTHOR OF MALVINA & CLAIRE D'ALBE.**

> London: Printed by Cox, Son, and Baylis, Great Queen-Street, for Gameau and Co. No. 51, Albemarle-Street. And sold by Boosey, Broad-Street, Royal Exchange, and Booth, Corner of Duke-Street, Portland Place, 1803.
> I vi, 272p; II 239p; III 299p; IV 360p. 12mo. 14s (CR).
> CR 3rd ser. 2: 114–15 (May 1804).
> BL 12611.a.21; NSTC C3811.

*Notes.* Trans. of *Amélie Mansfield* (Paris, 1802). Vol. 2 lacks t.p. ECB 138 lists Colburn edn., Dec 1809, 16s 6d. QR 1: 304–15 (May 1809) gives full review of French language version, published by Colburn (London 1809).
Further edn: 1809 (NSTC).

1803: 24   C[OTTIN, Sophie Ristaud]; GUNNING, [Elizabeth] [afterwards PLUNKETT] (*trans.*).
**MALVINA, BY MADAME C\*\*\*\*, AUTHORESS OF CLARE D'ALBE, AND AMELIA MANSFIELD. TRANSLATED FROM THE FRENCH, BY MISS GUNNING, IN FOUR VOLUMES.**

> London: Printed for T. Hurst, Paternoster-Row; C. Chapple, Pall-Mall, and Southampton-Row, Russell-Square; and R. Dutton, Gracechurch-Street. H. Reynell, Printer, 21, Piccadilly, 1803.
> I 237p; II 246p; III 236p; IV 261p. 12mo. 16s (ECB).
> ER 3: 506 (Jan 1804).
> O 249.s.513; ECB 365; NSTC P2191.

*Notes.* Trans. of *Malvina* (Paris, 1800). 1 p. (unn.) adv. for C. Chapple's Circulating Library at end of vol. 4. ECB dates Dec 1803.
Further edns: 1804 (Corvey—with identical t.p. details, apart from date, and similar pagination), CME 3-628-47645-3; 2nd edn. 1810 (NSTC).

1803: 25   COUPER, Robert.
**THE TOURIFICATIONS OF MALACHI MELDRUM ESQ. OF MELDRUM-HALL. BY DR. ROBERT COUPER.**

> Aberdeen: Printed by J. Chalmers and Co. for J. Johnson, London; W. Creech, Edinburgh; and A. Brown, Aberdeen, 1803.
> I 226p; II 256p. 12mo. 10s 6d boards (MR).
> ER 3: 505 (Jan 1804); MR n.s. 42: 131–42 (Oct 1803) full review; WSW I: 222.
> Corvey; CME 3-628-47342-X; ECB 139; NSTC C3858 (BI C).

*Notes.* Dedication to 'the most noble Marquis of Huntly &c &c &c.', signed Fochabers, Dec 1802. Introductory poems in each vol: 'To the Highland Society' (vol. 1), and 'Inchstevranna' (vol. 2), plus further poems throughout the text. 'Glossary' of Scots at end of vol. 2, pp. [221]–256. NSTC lists also a London 1803 imprint at BL, E, O, but BL 12350.aaa.33 has same Aberdeen imprint as above, and a separate London edn. seems doubtful. Copy in BRu ENC has price as 10s 6d on t.p.

1803: 26   CURTIES, T. J. Horsley.
**THE WATCH TOWER; OR, THE SONS OF ULTHONA. AN HISTORIC ROMANCE. IN FIVE VOLUMES. BY T. J. HORSLEY CURTIES, AUTHOR OF ETHELWINA, ANCIENT RECORDS, AND THE SCOTTISH LEGEND.**

> Brentford: Printed by and for P. Norbury; and sold by T. Hurst, No. 32, Paternoster Row; Carpenter and Co. Old-Bond-Street; J. Hatchard, Piccadilly; and Didier and Tibbett, St. James's-Street, London; also by W. Ansell, Richmond, Surrey, 1803/04.
> I (1804) viii, 360p; II (1804) 336p; III (1803) 307p; IV (1804) 312p; V (1804) 351p. 12mo. 25s (ECB).
> ER 3: 506 (Jan 1804); WSW I: 328.
> Corvey; CME 3-628-47465-5; ECB 148; xNSTC.

*Notes.* Dedication to E. H. Elcock Brown, Esq., North-Walsham, Norfolk, signed Hart-Street, Bloomsbury-Square, Dec 1803.

1803: 27   [CUTHBERTSON, Catherine].
**ROMANCE OF THE PYRENEES. IN FOUR VOLUMES.**

> London: Printed for G. and J. Robinson, Paternoster-Row; by S. Hamilton, Falcon-Court, Fleet-Street, 1803.
> I 337p; II 324p; III 336p; IV 346p. 12mo. 18s boards (CR); 18s (ECB); 20s boards (ER).
> CR 2nd ser. 37: 477–8 (Apr 1803); ER 10: 492 (July 1807); WSW I: 232–3.
> ViU PZ2.C874R.1803; ECB 501; xNSTC.

*Notes.* Further edns: 3rd edn. 1807 (NSTC C4644); 4th edn. 1812 (Corvey), CME 3-628-48508-8; 5th edn. 1822 (NSTC); 1840 (NSTC); 1844 (NSTC); Amherst, NH, 1809 (NUC); French trans. 1809 [as *Les Visions du château des Pyrénées*, spuriously attributed to Ann Radcliffe (BN)].

1803: 28   DUCRAY-DUMINIL, [François-Guillaume]; MEEKE, [Mary] (*trans.*).
**A TALE OF MYSTERY, OR CELINA. A NOVEL. IN FOUR VOLUMES. ALTERED FROM THE FRENCH OF DUCRAY-DUMINIL, BY MRS. MEEKE, AUTHOR OF WHICH IS THE MAN, THE SICILIAN, &C. &C.**

> London: Printed at the Minerva-Press, for Lane and Newman, Leadenhall-Street, 1803.
> I 278p; II 323p; III 312p; IV 327p. 12mo. 16s boards (CR).
> CR 2nd ser. 37: 478 (Apr 1803); WSW I: 252.
> BL 1607/2020; CME 3-628-48249-6; NSTC D2046.

*Notes.* Trans. of *Cœlina, ou l'enfant du mystère* (Paris, 1798). 'Advertisement' (1 p. unn.) states: 'it has been deemed necessary to make material alterations from the French Author [...] The two last volumes, indeed, may be considered as mere imitations of the original.' CR gives title as 'Celina, or Tale of Mystery', and comments: 'The first two volumes of this work are professedly translated from the French novel which furnished Mr. Holcroft with his celebrated melo-drama, The Tale of Mystery. The last two are imitations only, and somewhat faint'.

1803: 29   [DUPERCHE, J.-J.-M.]; DUFOUR, Camilla (*trans.*).
**AURORA, OR THE MYSTERIOUS BEAUTY. ALTERED FROM THE FRENCH. BY CAMILLA DUFOUR. IN TWO VOLUMES.**

> London: Printed by R. Exton, Great Portland-Street; for B. Crosby and Co. Stationers' Court; and J. F. Hughes, Wigmore-Street, Cavendish-Square, 1803.
> I 190p; II 172p. 12mo. 7s (ECB).
> Corvey; CME 3-628-47490-6; ECB 173; xNSTC.

*Notes.* Trans. of *Aurora, ou l'amante mystérieuse* (Paris, 1802), itself based on Friedrich Julius Heinrich von Soden's *Aurora, oder das Kind der Hölle* (Chemnitz, 1795), a play. Dedication to Lady Sarah Bailey by 'The Editor', dated 'Wigmore-Street, May 30, 1803'. ECB dates Dec 1803. The title was listed by Louisa Theresa Bellenden Ker as one of her own publications, when appealing for support from the Royal Literary Fund (RLF 11: 400, Item 6 [1822?]). According to Summers, Camilla Dufour (the translator as stated on t.p.) was a favourite singer at Drury Lane and married to J. H. Sarrett (himself the acknowledged translator of a chapbook version of *Koenigsmark*, from the German of Raspe, another title listed by Ker). For other novels likewise claimed by Louisa Theresa Bellenden Ker, see 1804: 52 and 1809: 61.

1803: 30   [FOSTER, Mrs. E. M.].
**LIGHT AND SHADE: A NOVEL. BY THE AUTHOR OF FEDERETTA; REBECCA; MIRIAM; AND CONCEALMENT, OR THE CASCADE OF LANTWARRYBN.**

> Bath: Printed by R. Cruttwell; and sold by G. and J. Robinson, Pater-Noster-Row, London, 1803.
> I 219p; II 247p; III 181p; IV 181p. 12mo. 14s boards (CR); 14s (ECB).
> CR 3rd ser. 1: 238–9 (Feb 1804); ER 3: 506 (Jan 1804); WSW I: 146.
> Corvey; CME 3-628-48099-X; ECB 346; NSTC F1158 (BI BL).

1803: 31   GENLIS, [Stéphanie-Félicité, Comtesse de]; [?BARTON, James (*trans.*)].
**THE DEPRAVED HUSBAND AND THE PHILOSOPHIC WIFE. IN TWO VOLUMES. BY MADAME GENLIS.**

> London: Printed by W. S. Betham, Furnival's-Inn-Court, Holborn; for B. Crosby and Co. Stationer's Court, Ludgate-Hill; and J. F. Hughes, Wigmore-Street, Cavendish-Square, 1803.
> I 186p; II 139p. 12mo. 6s (ECB).
> WSW I: 239.
> CtY-BR Hfd29.370; ECB 225; xNSTC.

*Notes.* Trans. of *Le Mari corrupteur suivie de la femme philosophe* (Paris, 1803), itself based on Charles Lloyd's *Edmund Oliver* (Bristol, 1798). End of text in both vols. signed 'Ducrest Genlis'. James Barton is described as the translator in the title of the *The Remorseless Assassin* (see 1803: 15). Vol. 1, pp. [1]–30: 'Dialogue, between two literary Characters'; pp. 31–186: 'The Philosopher taken at his Word; or, the Depraved Husband' (drop-head title on p. 31). Vol. 2: 'The Philosophic Wife' (drop-head title on p. [1]). ECB dates May 1803.

1803: 32   [GUÉNARD, Elisabeth]; SARRETT, H. J. (*trans.*).
THE THREE MONKS!!! FROM THE FRENCH. BY H. J. SARRETT. IN
TWO VOLUMES.

> London: Printed by W. S. Betham, Furnival's-Inn-Court, Holborn, for B. Crosby and
> Co. Stationer's Court, and J. F. Hughes, Wigmore Street, n.d. [1803].
> I 191p; II 204p. 12mo. 7s sewed (CR); 7s 6d (ECB).
> CR 2nd ser. 39: 235 (Oct 1803).
> Corvey; CME 3-628-48526-6; ECB 590; NSTC G2326 (BI BL).

*Notes.* Trans. of *Les Capucins, ou le secret du cabinet noir, histoire véritable, publiée par M. de
Faverolles* (Paris, 1801); or *Les Trois Moines, par M. de Faverolles* (Paris, 1802?, 1815).
Faverolles was the maiden name, or a pseudonym, of Elisabeth Guénard, Baronne de Méré.
Dedication to 'M. G. Lewis, Esq. M.P.', dated Wigmore Street, 28 Mar 1803. Collates in sixes.


1803: 33   GUNNING, {Elizabeth} [afterwards PLUNKETT].
THE WAR-OFFICE: A NOVEL. BY MISS GUNNING, AUTHOR OF "THE
PACKET," "FARMER'S BOY," &C. &C. IN THREE VOLUMES.

> London: Printed by J. Cundee, Ivy-Lane; published for the Author, by M. Jones, No. 1,
> Paternoster-Row, 1803.
> I viii, 239p; II 218p; III 220p. 12mo.
> WSW I: 291.
> Corvey; CME 3-628-47588-0; xNSTC.

*Notes.* Dedication 'to His Royal Highness the Duke of York', signed Elizabeth Gunning and
dated 1 Dec 1802.


GUNNING, Susannah
See MINIFIE, Susannah


1803: 34   HELME, Elizabeth.
ST. CLAIR OF THE ISLES: OR, THE OUTLAWS OF BARRA, A SCOT-
TISH TRADITION. BY ELIZABETH HELME. IN FOUR VOLUMES.

> London: Printed by A. Strahan, Printers-Street, for T. N. Longman and O. Rees, Pater-
> noster-Row, 1803.
> I iv, 264p; II 216p; III 240p; IV 251p. 12mo. 14s (ECB).
> ER 3: 505 (Jan 1804); WSW I: 309.
> Corvey; CME 3-628-47757-3; ECB 278; NSTC H1230 (BI E, O).

*Notes.* Dedication 'to the Most Noble The Marchioness of Abercorn'. Text in vol. 2 ends at
p. 214, followed by 2 numbered pages of advs.
Further edns: 2nd edn. 1817 (NUC); 3rd edn. 1824 (NUC); 1825 (NSTC); Manchester 1825
(NSTC); 1833 (NSTC); [at least 4 more edns. to 1850]; French trans., 1808; German trans., 1810.


1803: 35   HIGGINS, William.
THE AMERICAN. A NOVEL. IN TWO VOLUMES. BY WILLIAM
HIGGINS.

> London: Printed for J. Ridgway, York Street, St. James's Square, 1803.

I 292p; II 248p. 12mo. 8s boards (CR); 8s (ECB).

CR 2nd ser. 38: 237–8 (June 1803), 3rd ser. 3: 239 (Oct 1804); WSW I: 312.

Corvey; CME 3-628-47686-0; ECB 268; xNSTC.

*Notes.* Dedication 'to Isaac Swainson, Esq.'.


HOMELY, Martha

See THOMAS, Elizabeth


1803: 36    HOLSTEN, Esther.

**MIRANDA; OR, THE MYSTERIOUS STRANGER. A NOVEL: IN TWO VOL-UMES. DEDICATED, BY PERMISSION, TO THE RT. HON. VISCOUNTESS BULKELEY. BY ESTHER HOLSTEN, AUTHOR OF "ERNESTINA."**

London: Printed by J. Cundee, Ivy Lane, for M. Jones, Paternoster-Row, 1803.

I 189p; II 225p. 12mo. 7s (ECB).

Corvey; CME 3-628-47743-3; ECB 278; xNSTC.

*Notes.* Dedication dated Jan 1803. 'List of Subscribers' (8 pp. unn.), with *c.*125 names, at beginning of vol. 1. ECB dates Jan 1803. Collates in sixes.


HOOK, Sarah Ann, THE WIDOWED BRIDE, OR CELINA

See 1802: 31


1803: 37    [JULLIEN, Jean-Auguste]; BARNBY, Mrs. (*trans.*).

**KERWALD CASTLE, OR, MEMOIRS OF THE MARQUIS DE SOLANGES. IN TWO VOLUMES: TRANSLATED FROM THE FRENCH, BY MRS. BARNBY, AUTHOR OF THE ROCK; OR, ALFRED AND ANNA: A SCOTTISH TALE.**

Maidstone: Printed for the Author by D. Chalmers, and sold by Wilkie, Symonds, and Hurst, Paternoster Row, London, n.d. [1803].

I x, 192p; II 190p. 12mo.

CR 2nd ser. 38: 478 (Aug 1803); ER 3: 260 (Oct 1803).

BL N.1899; NSTC J1215 (BI O).

*Notes.* Trans. of *Mémoires du marquis de Solanges* (Amsterdam, 1766). List of Subscribers (*c.*185 names), vol. 1, pp. [iii]–x. ER spells as 'Thorwald Castle'.

Further edn: 1804 (Corvey—a Minerva reissue, but lacking the subscription list), CME 3-628-47985-1.


1803: 38    KARAM[Z]IN, Ni[k]olai [Mikhailovich]; ELRINGTON, John Battersby (*trans.*).

**RUSSIAN TALES. BY NICOLAI KARAMSIN. TRANSLATED INTO ENG-LISH BY JOHN BATTERSBY ELRINGTON.**

London: Printed by G. Sidney, Northumberland-Street, 1803.

262p, ill. 8vo.

ER 3: 506 (Jan 1804).

BL 12591.h.21; NSTC K39.

*Notes.* Engraved frontispiece portrait of Karamzin. BL copy is presentation copy to Dr William Tenant. Prefatory address 'To my friends' signed J. B. E., dated Borough, 10 Oct 1803, and 'To the World' signed 'The Translator'. Contains 'Lisa', 'Flor Silin', 'Natalia', and 'Julia'. BLC states that the translation is also attributed to A[ndreas] A[ndersen] Feldborg. ER lists *Tales from the Russian.*
Further edn: 1804, reissued (without translator's name) as *Tales from the Russian of Nicolai Karamsin* (BL 12590.f.9; NSTC K40).

1803: 39   KELLY, Isabella.
**A MODERN INCIDENT IN DOMESTIC LIFE. IN TWO VOLUMES. BY ISABELLA KELLY, AUTHOR OF MADELINE, ABBEY ST. ASAPH, AVONDALE PRIORY, EVA, RUTHINGLENNE, BARON'S DAUGH-TERS, &C. &C. &C.**
> Brentford: Printed by and for P. Norbury; and sold by T. Hurst, No. 32, Paternoster Row; J. Hatchard, Piccadilly; Carpenter and Co. Old-Bond-Street; and Didier and Tibbett, St. James-Street, London, 1803.
> I viii, 240p; II 225p. 12mo. 9s (ECB).
> Corvey; CME 3-628-47981-9; ECB 317; NSTC K136 (BI BL).

*Notes.* Dedication 'to the Right Honorable Lady Anne Culling Smith', dated 31 Jan 1803. ECB dates Mar 1803.

1803: 40   KER, Anne.
**THE MYSTERIOUS COUNT; OR, MONTVILLE CASTLE. A ROMANCE, IN TWO VOLUMES. BY ANNE KER.**
> London: Printed by D. N. Shury, Berwick-Street, Soho, for the Author, and sold by Crosby and Co. Stationers' Court, Ludgate Street, 1803.
> I iv, 232p; II 240p. 12mo. 7s (ECB).
> ER 3: 260 (Oct 1803).
> Corvey; CME 3-628-47997-5; ECB 403; xNSTC.

*Notes.* 'List of Subscribers' (28 names), vol. 1, pp. [iii]–iv.

1803: 41   LAFONTAINE, August [Heinrich Julius].
**THE VILLAGE PASTOR AND HIS CHILDREN. A NOVEL. IN FOUR VOLUMES. FROM THE GERMAN OF AUGUSTUS LA FONTAINE.**
> London: Printed at the Minerva-Press, for Lane and Newman, Leadenhall-Street, 1803.
> I 256p; II 264p; III 238p; IV 271p. 12mo. 16s boards (CR).
> CR 2nd ser. 39: 236–7 (Oct 1803).
> CtY-BR HKc14.306M; NSTC L152 (BI BL).

*Notes.* Trans. of *Leben eines armen Landpredigers* (Berlin, 1802).
Further edns: 1849 as *Family Pictures; or, the Life of a Poor Village Pastor and His Children* (NSTC 2L1634); New York 1810 (NUC).

1803: 42   LANTIER, É[tienne] F[rançois] [de]; [SHOBERL, Frederick (*trans.*)].
**ADOLPHE AND BLANCHE; OR, TRAVELLERS IN SWITZERLAND. BY E. F. LANTIER. TRANSLATED FROM THE FRENCH.**

London: Printed by M. Allen, Paternoster-Row, for John Badcock, Paternoster-Row,
   1803/04.
I (1803) iv, 234p; II (1803) 257p; III (1803) 235p; IV (1804) 198p; V (1804) 207p; VI
   (1804) 184p. 12mo. 24s boards (CR); 12s (ECB, for 3 vols.).
CR 3rd ser. 2: 235–6 (June 1804); ER 3: 506 (Jan 1804); WSW I: 362.
Corvey; CME 3-628-47900-2; ECB 6; NSTC L463 (BI BL).

*Notes*. Trans. of *Les Voyageurs en Suisse* (Paris, 1803). Printers change between vols: vols. 1
and 6 printed by M. Allen, Paternoster-Row; vols. 2–5 printed by J. D. Dewick, Aldersgate-
Street. The last page of vol. 1 is mistakenly numbered 238. Copy at National Library of Scot-
land (GB/A.1168) has t.p. reading 'Travellers in Switzerland, By E. F. Lantier [. . .] Translated
from the French by Frederic Shoberl. In Six Volumes. London: Printed by J. D. Dewick,
Aldergate Street, for John Badcock, Pater-Noster Row; and S. Highley, Fleet-Street, 1804'.
Pagination suggests a reissue with cancel t.p.
Further edn: 1804 as *Travellers in Switzerland* (NSTC—see above).


1803: 43   LATHOM, Francis.
VERY STRANGE, BUT VERY TRUE! OR, THE HISTORY OF AN OLD
MAN'S YOUNG WIFE. A NOVEL. BY FRANCIS LATHOM, AUTHOR
OF—"MEN AND MANNERS"—"MYSTERY" "ASTONISHMENT! OR, A
ROMANCE OF A CENTURY AGO"—"MIDNIGHT BELL"—"CASTLE
OF OLLADA" &C. &C. &C. IN FOUR VOLUMES.

   London: Printed by A. Strahan, Printers-Street, for T. N. Longman and O. Rees, Pater-
      noster-Row, 1803.
   I 244p; II 236p; III 235p; IV 216p. 12mo. 14s (ECB).
   WSW I: 363.
   Corvey; CME 3-628-47965-7; ECB 612; NSTC L547 (BI BL).

*Notes*. Text proper in vol. 2 ends on p. 234; pp. [235]–236: 'Works by the same Author'. Text
proper in vol. 4 ends on p. 211, followed by advs. pp. [212]–216. ECB dates June 1803.


LATHOM, Francis
See RICCOBONI, Marie-Jeanne; and also ROUSSEL, Pierre Joseph Alexis


1803: 44   LYTTLETON, Mr.
THE GERMAN SORCERESS. A ROMANCE. IN THREE VOLUMES. BY
MR. LYTTLETON.

   London: Printed at the Minerva-Press, for Lane and Newman, Leadenhall-Street, 1803.
   I 240p; II 260p; III 256p. 12mo. 10s 6d (ECB).
   ER 3: 260 (Oct 1803).
   Corvey; CME 3-628-48073-6; ECB 357; xNSTC.


1803: 45   LYTTLETON, Mr.
LA BELLE SAUVAGE, OR A PROGRESS THROUGH THE BEAU-
MONDE. A NOVEL. IN TWO VOLUMES. BY MR. LYTTLETON,
AUTHOR OF THE FOLLIES OF FASHION, LOTTERY OF LIFE, &C.

London: Printed at the Minerva-Press, for Lane and Newman, Leadenhall-Street, 1803.
I xvi, 260p; II 246p. 12mo.
WSW I: 16.
Corvey; CME 3-628-48169-4; NSTC L2754 (BI BL).

1803: 46   [LYTTLETON, Mr].
PEREGRINE, OR THE FOOL OF FORTUNE. A NOVEL. IN THREE VOL-
UMES. BY THE AUTHOR OF THE FOLLIES OF FASHION, LOTTERY
OF LIFE, LA BELLE SAUVAGE, &C.

London: Printed at the Minerva-Press, for Lane and Newman, Leadenhall-Street, 1803.
I 267p; II 278p; III 291p. 12mo. 12s boards (CR); 12s (ECB).
CR 2nd ser. 39: 236 (Oct 1803); WSW I: 91.
Corvey; CME 3-628-48431-6; ECB 442; NSTC P1183 (BI BL).

1803: 47   ?MINIFIE, [Susannah] [afterwards GUNNING] or ?MINIFIE,
[Margaret].
THE UNION: A NOVEL, IN THREE VOLUMES. BY MISS MINIFIE,
AUTHOR OF THE COUNT DE POLAND.

London: Printed by J. D. Dewick, Aldersgate-Street, for R. Dutton, Gracechurch-Street;
    sold also by T. Hurst, Paternoster-Row; J. Cawthorn, Catharine-Street, Strand; and
    C. Chapple, Pall-Mall, 1803.
I 247p; II 262p; III 249p. 12mo. 9s sewed (CR).
CR 3rd ser. 1: 238 (Feb 1804); WSW I: 398.
Corvey; CME 3-628-48167-8; xNSTC.

1803: 48   MONTJO[I]E, F[élix] L[ouis] C[hristophe].
D'AVEYRO; OR, THE HEAD IN THE GLASS CAGE: A NOVEL. BY F. L. C.
MONTJOYE, AUTHOR OF THE "HISTOIRE DES QUATRE ESPAGNOLS."
TRANSLATED FROM THE FRENCH.

London: Printed by J. Cundee, Ivy-Lane, for M. Jones, Paternoster-Row, 1803.
I ix, 242p; II 268p; III 215p; IV 223p. 12mo. 16s boards (CR); 16s (ECB).
CR 2nd ser. 39: 480 (Dec 1803).
ViU PZ2.M65D.1803; ECB 153; xNSTC.

Notes. Trans. of *Histoire de la conjuration de Maximilien Robespierre* (Paris, 1794)? Drop-
head title reads 'D'Aveyro; or, the Italian Manuscript'. The last two pages of vol. 4 are both
numbered 222; on verso of the second of these begin advs. (3 pp. unn.) of 'Books published
by T. Ostell, Ave-Maria Lane'. ECB gives subtitle as 'or, the Man in the glass cage', and publisher as Ostell, Mar 1803.

1803: 49   MONTJO[I]E, F[élix] L[ouis] C[hristophe].
*MOUNT PAUSILLYPPO; OR, A MANUSCRIPT FOUND AT THE
TOMB OF VIRGIL. TRANSLATED FROM THE FRENCH OF F. L. C.
MONTJOYE.

London: Symonds, 1803.
5 vols. 12mo. 20s (ECB).

ER 3: 506 (Jan 1804).

No copy located; ECB 393.

*Notes.* Trans. of *Manuscrit trouvé au mont Pausilype* (Paris, 1802). ECB dates Oct 1803. ECB spells as Pausillyppo, ER as Pausilyppo, and Bent03 as Pausilippo.


1803: 50   MOORE, Marian.

**ARIANA AND MAUD. A NOVEL. IN THREE VOLUMES. BY MARIAN MOORE, AUTHOR OF LASCELLES.**

London: Printed at the Minerva-Press, for Lane and Newman, Leadenhall-Street, 1803.
I iv, 287p; II 261p; III 240p. 12mo. 10s 6d boards (CR); 10s 6d (ECB).
CR 2nd ser. 37: 356 (Mar 1803); WSW I: 405.
Corvey; CME 3-628-48283-6; ECB 394; xNSTC.

*Notes.* Dedication to Sir Sidney Smith.


MORGAN, Lady Sydney
See OWENSON, Sydney


1803: 51   MUDFORD, William.

**AUGUSTUS AND MARY; OR, THE MAID OF BUTTERMERE. A DOMESTIC TALE. BY WILLIAM MUDFORD.**

London: Printed for M. Jones, No. 1, Paternoster-Row, by B. M'Millan, Bow-Street, Covent-Garden, 1803.
xiv, 187p, ill. 8vo. 4s boards (CR); 5s (ECB).
CR 2nd ser. 38: 358 (July 1803); WSW I: 412–13.
Corvey; CME 3-628-48391-3; ECB 32; NSTC M3536 (BI BL).

*Notes.* Frontispiece carries the legend: 'Pub. May 14 1803, by M. Jones, Paternoster row'. Dedication to 'Truth, Innocence, and Simplicity'.


1803: 52   [NAUBERT, Christiane Benedicte Eugenie]; YOUNG, Mary Julia (*trans.*).

**LINDORF AND CAROLINE; OR, THE DANGER OF CREDULITY. IN THREE VOLS. TRANSLATED FROM THE GERMAN OF PROFESSOR KRAMER, BY MARY JULIA YOUNG, AUTHOR OF ROSE MOUNT CASTLE; THE EAST INDIAN; THE KINSMEN OF NAPLES; POEMS, &C.**

London: Printed for B. Crosby and Co. Stationers'-Court, Ludgate-Street, by W. S. Betham, Furnival's-Inn-Court, Holborn, 1803.
I vi, 221p; II 228p; III 247p. 12mo. 10s 6d (ECB).
ViU PZ2.N38Li.1803; ECB 325; xNSTC.

*Notes.* Trans. of 'Lindorf und Caroline', according to NUC, but no such German original discovered. BN lists French trans. *Lindorf et Caroline; ou les dangers de la crédulité, traduit de l'auteur d'Hermann d'Unna* (Paris, 1802). Dedication to Viscountess Wentworth, by 'the Translator'. 1 leaf [2 pp.] advs. following Dedication, before start of novel (8 titles). ECB dates Mar 1803.

1803: 53    [NAUBERT, Christiane Benedicte Eugenie].
WALTER DE MONBARY, GRAND MASTER OF THE KNIGHTS TEM-
PLARS. AN HISTORICAL ROMANCE. IN FOUR VOLUMES. FROM THE
GERMAN OF PROFESSOR KRAMER, AUTHOR OF HERMAN OF UNNA.

> London: Printed at the Minerva-Press, for Lane and Newman, Leadenhall-Street, 1803.
> I 288p, ill.; II 272p; III 248p; IV 245p. 12mo.
> Corvey; CME 3-628-48818-4; NSTC N349 (BI BL).

*Notes.* Trans. of *Walter von Montbarry, Großmeister des Tempelherrnordens* (Leipzig, 1786).
ECB 325 lists Newman 2nd edn., Jan 1816, 20s; but not discovered in this form. Bent03 list-
ing at 10s perhaps more accurately reflects original price.
Further edn: 1808 (NUC).

1803: 54    [NOTT, John].
SAPPHO. AFTER A GREEK ROMANCE.

> London: Printed for Cuthell and Martin, Middle-Row, Holborn, by Wilks and Taylor,
>     Chancery-Lane, 1803.
> viii, 310p. 12mo. 3s 6d (ECB).
> WSW I: 408.
> Corvey; CME 3-628-52603-5; ECB 514; NSTC N1309 (BI BL).

*Notes.* 'Advertisement' signed 'The Author'. ECB dates May 1803.
Further edn: German trans., 1806 [as *Sappho und Phaon, oder der Sturz von Leukate* (RS)].

1803: 55    O[WENSON], S[ydney] [afterwards MORGAN, Lady Sydney].
ST. CLAIR; OR, THE HEIRESS OF DESMOND. BY S. O.

> Dublin: Printed by Brett Smith, for Messrs. Wogan, Brown, Halpin, Colbert, Jon
>     Dornin, Jackson, and Medcalf, 1803.
> iv, 240p. 12mo. 4s (ECB).
> ER 3: 506 (Jan 1804); WSW I: 424–5.
> Dt 192.r.141; ECB 396; xNSTC.

*Notes.* Preface dated 7 Nov 1802. ECB dates 1804, and probably refers to the London 1803
edn. (which was preceded by the Dublin edn.).
Further edns: London 1803 (Corvey; NSTC O736), CME 3-628-47460-4; 3rd edn. London
1812 (NSTC); Philadelphia 1807 (NSTC); French trans., 1813; German trans., 1827.
Facs: RWN (of 3rd edn. 1812; 1995).

1803: 56    PALMER, John.
THE WORLD AS IT GOES; OR, PORTRAITS FROM NATURE. A
NOVEL. BY JOHN PALMER, AUTHOR OF THE HAUNTED CAVERN.
IN TWO VOLUMES.

> London: Printed by W. Flint, Old Bailey, for Moore and Beauclerc, No. 332, Oxford-
>     Street, 1803.
> I 218p; II 227p. 12mo.
> Corvey; CME 3-628-48379-4; xNSTC.

*Notes.* Dedication to Sir Francis Burdett, dated Oct 1802.

1803: 57   PICKERSGILL, Joshua (jun.).
THE THREE BROTHERS: A ROMANCE. BY JOSHUA PICKERSGILL,
JUN. ESQ. IN FOUR VOLUMES.

> London: Printed for John Stockdale, Piccadilly, 1803.
> I 230p; II 300p; III 468p; IV 462p. 12mo. 20s (ECB).
> WSW I: 438.
> Corvey; CME 3-628-48438-3; ECB 449; NSTC P1643 (BI O).

*Notes.* Colophons differ: vols. 1 and 2 printed by T. Gillet; vol. 3 by Davison and Gillet; and vol. 4 by T. Burton. ECB dates June 1803.

1803: 58   PIGAULT-LEBRUN, [Charles-Antoine].
*MONSIEUR BOTTE. A ROMANCE. IN THREE VOLUMES. BY
PIGAULT LEBRUN. AUTHOR OF MY UNCLE THOMAS, THE BARONS
OF FELSHEIM, &C. &C.

> London: Printed at the Minerva Press, for Lane and Newman, Leadenhall-Street, 1803.
> 3 vols. 12mo. 12s boards (CR).
> CR 3rd ser. 3: 237–8 (Oct 1804); WSW I: 366.
> No copy located; ECB 335.

*Notes.* Trans. of *Monsieur Botte* (Paris, 1802). Title and imprint details from Blakey, whose entry is based on Stonehill (Booksellers) copy. ECB dates Sept 1803. The 4 vol. 1803 edn. listed by NSTC (P1729) is in French.

PLUNKETT, Elizabeth
See GUNNING, Elizabeth

1803: 59   PORTER, [Jane].
THADDEUS OF WARSAW. IN FOUR VOLUMES. BY MISS PORTER.

> London: Printed by A. Strahan, Printers-Street, for T. N. Longman and O. Rees, Paternoster-Row, 1803.
> I xi, 247p; II 224p; III 236p; IV 238p. 12mo. 14s boards (CR, ER); 14s (ECB).
> CR 2nd ser. 39: 120 (Sept 1803); ER 4: 499 (July 1804) 2nd edn; ER 7: 257 (Oct 1805) 3rd edn; WSW I: 448.
> Corvey; CME 3-628-48362-X; ECB 464; xNSTC.

*Notes.* Inscription to Sir Sidney Smith. ER 7: 257 (Oct 1805) gives 3rd edn. price as 14s boards, and states: 'This edition has undergone an attentive Revisal by the Authoress; who has occasionally amplified and retrenched the Subjects, according to the Suggestions of her maturer Judgment'. Further edns: 2nd edn. 1804 (NSTC P2615); 3rd edn. 1805 (Dt); 4th edn. 1806 (NSTC); 5th edn. 1809 (NSTC); 6th edn. 1812 (NSTC); [at least 8 more edns. to 1850]; Boston 1809 (NUC) [also New York 1809 (NUC)]; French trans., 1809 [as *Le Polonais* (Pigoreau)]; German trans., 1825 [as *Thaddäus Constantin, Graf von Sobieski*, also as *Graf Sobieski; historischer Roman* (RS)].

1803: 60   [RICCOBONI, Marie-Jeanne Laboras de Mézières]; LATHOM,
Francis (*trans.*).
ERESTINA, A TALE, TAKEN FROM THE FRENCH, WITH ALTERATIONS
AND ADDITIONS OF THE TRANSLATOR, BY FRANCIS LATHOM.

Norwich: Printed and sold by J. Payne, Bookseller, Market-Place: sold also by Messrs. Longman and Rees, Paternoster-Row, London, and by all other Booksellers, n.d. [1803?].
162p. 12mo.
Corvey; CME 3-628-47894-4; xNSTC.

*Notes.* NUC lists as a free translation of Riccoboni's *Histoire d'Ernestine.* The tale was published variously within Riccoboni's works, the earliest edn. found being her *Recueil de pièces détachées, par Madame Riccoboni,* Paris 1765. CR 2nd ser. 39: 119–20 (Sept 1803) has 2 vols., 12mo, 6s boards, Payne, and comments: 'How much of Erestina is taken from the French, and how much is Mr. Lathom's own, we cannot inform our readers'. ER 11: 238 (Oct 1807) has 'Erestina. A Tale from the French. By Francis Lathom Edar [*sic*], 3s'. No version in 2 vols. has been located; the evidently single vol. edn. listed by ER may or may not relate directly to the present entry.

1803: 61   [RICE, Mrs].
THE DESERTED WIFE. A TALE OF MUCH TRUTH. IN TWO VOLUMES.

London: Printed at the Minerva-Press, for Lane, Newman, and Co. Leadenhall-Street, 1803.
I 212p; II 245p. 12mo. 7s boards (CR).
CR 2nd ser. 39: 353 (Nov 1803).
Corvey; CME 3-628-47446-9; xNSTC.

1803: 62   [ROUSSEL, Pierre Joseph Alexis]; LATHOM, Francis (*trans.*).
THE CASTLE OF THE TUILERIES: OR, A NARRATIVE OF ALL THE EVENTS WHICH HAVE TAKEN PLACE IN THE INTERIOR OF THAT PALACE, FROM THE TIME OF ITS CONSTRUCTION TO THE EIGHT-EENTH BRUMAIRE OF THE YEAR VIII. TRANSLATED FROM THE FRENCH, BY FRANCIS LATHOM. IN TWO VOLUMES.

London: Printed for T. N. Longman and O. Rees, Paternoster-Row, 1803.
I xii, 367p; II vi, 392p. 8vo. 14s (ECB).
BL 1560/336; ECB 100; NSTC R1773 (BI C, O).

*Notes.* Trans. of *Le château des Tuileries* (Paris, 1802). ECB dates June 1803. MR has review of original French title, 2 vols. Paris, 'Imported by De Boffe London, Price 12 shillings sewed', in 39: 474–6 (App [Dec 1801/Jan 1802]).

1803: 63   ST. AUBIGNÉ, Chevalier de; BYERLEY, J[ohn Scott] (*trans.*).
THE CATASTROPHE; A TALE FOUNDED ON FACTS. FROM THE FRENCH OF THE CHEVALIER DE ST. AUBIGNÉ. BY J. BYERLEY.

London: Printed for S. Highley (Successor of the late Mr. J. Murray) No. 24, Fleet-Street; William Miller, Old Bond-Street; James Carpenter, Old Bond-Street; E. Lawrence, No. 378, Strand; E. Williams, No. 11, Strand; E. Harding, No. 100, Pall-Mall; and J. Asperne, No. 32, Cornhill, 1803.
viii, 231p, ill. 8vo.
ER 3: 506 (Jan 1804).
Corvey; CME 3-628-49010-3; NSTC S195 (BI BL).

*Notes.* French original not discovered.

1803: 64   [SHERIFFE, Sarah].
THE FOREST OF HOHENELBE. A TALE. IN THREE VOLUMES. BY
THE AUTHOR OF HUMBERT CASTLE AND CORRELIA.

London: Printed at the Minerva-Press, for Lane and Newman, Leadenhall-Street, 1803.
I 367p; II 347p; III 362p. 12mo. 13s 6d boards (CR); 13s 6d (ECB).
CR 3rd ser. 1: 239 (Feb 1804); WSW I: 46.
Corvey; CME 3-628-47800-6; ECB 211; xNSTC.

*Notes.* Further edn: French trans., 1807 [as *La Forêt de Hohenelbe, ou Albert de Veltzlar*
(MLC)].


1803: 65   [SIDDONS, Henry].
REGINAL [*sic*] DI TORBY, OR THE TWELVE ROBBERS. A ROMANCE.
IN TWO VOLUMES.

London: Printed at the Minerva-Press, for Lane and Newman, Leadenhall-Street, 1803.
I xiv, 294p; II 274p. 12mo.
ER 3: 260 (Oct 1803); WSW I: 102.
Corvey; CME 3-628-48616-5; NSTC R486 (BI BL).

*Notes.* Dedication 'To oblivion, who has always been so kind as to take care of the works of
the numerous tribe of my brother authors'.


1803: 66   [SINGER, Mr].
EDWIN, OR THE HEIR OF ÆLLA. AN HISTORICAL ROMANCE. IN
THREE VOLUMES. BY THE AUTHOR OF THE WANDERER OF THE
ALPS, AND THE MYSTIC CASTLE.

London: Printed at the Minerva-Press, for Lane, Newman, and Co. Leadenhall-Street,
   1803.
I 272p, ill.; II 278p; III 352p. 12mo.
ER 3: 505 (Jan 1804); WSW I: 35.
Corvey; CME 3-628-47520-1; xNSTC.


1803: 67(a)   STAËL-HOLSTEIN, [Anne Louise Germaine] de.
DELPHINE: A NOVEL. BY MADAME DE STAEL-HOLSTEIN. TRANS-
LATED FROM THE FRENCH. IN THREE VOLUMES.

London: Printed for G. and J. Robinson, Paternoster-Row, by Wilks and Taylor,
   Chancery-Lane, 1803.
I xxiv, 461p; II 357p; III 301p. 12mo. 15s boards (CR); 15s (ECB).
CR 2nd ser. 38: 48–58 (May 1803) full review; WSW I: 242.
BL 12510.bb.21; ECB 557; NSTC S3440 (BI C).

*Notes.* Trans. of *Delphine* (Geneva, 1802). 'Advertisement', dated 14 Feb 1803, reads: 'The
following translation of Madame de Stael's novel was ready for publication twelve days ago,
when a fire breaking out in the printing-house of Mr. Hamilton, in Falcon-court, Fleet-
street, the whole impression of the first volume was unfortunately destroyed. It has been
reprinted, and in part re-translated, with great expedition; and if any inaccuracies should
have arisen from the circumstance, the reader, it is hoped, will have the indulgence to pardon

them.' Colophon reads 'Wilks and Taylor, Printers, Chancery-Lane' in vols. 1 and 3; 'Taylor and Wilks, Printers, Chancery-lane' in vol. 2. Each vol. is divided into two 'Parts', noted on t.ps., making six in all.

1803: 67(b)    STAËL-HOLSTEIN, [Anne Louise Germaine] de.
**DELPHINE. BY MADAME DE STAEL-HOLSTEIN. IN SIX VOLUMES.**

> London: Printed for J. Mawman, in the Poultry, 1803.
> I 344p; II 382p; III 327p; IV 286p; V 252p; VI 203p. 12mo. 21s (ECB).
> ER 2: 172–7 (Apr 1803) full review; WSW I: 242.
> CtY-BR Hfd29.490D; ECB 557; xNSTC.

*Notes.* Trans. of *Delphine* (Geneva, 1802). Printers after date on t.p. imprints differ: vols. 1 and 5 'By T. Gillet, Salisbury-Square'; vols. 2 and 4 'W. and C. Spilsbury, Printers, Snow-hill'; vol. 3 'W. Flint, Printer, Old Bailey'. Gecker (Item 1009) and NUC (PU) list yet another edn., Lackington, Allen, & Co., London, 4 vols., 12mo, 1805.

1803: 68    ?STAËL[-HOLSTEIN, Anne Louise Germaine] de; [BARTON, James (*trans.*)].
**MARGARET OF STRAFFORD, AN HISTORICAL ROMANCE: INTER-SPERSED WITH SEVERAL ANECDOTES OF THE REIGN OF CHARLES II. AND OTHER MEMORIALS RELATIVE TO THE REVOLUTION. IN FIVE VOLS. BY MADAME DE STAEL, AUTHOR OF DELPHINE, &C. &C.**

> London: Printed by R. Exton, Great Portland-Street; for J. F. Hughes, Wigmore-Street, Cavendish-Square, 1803.
> I 211p; II 205p; III 247p; IV 217p; V 191p. 12mo. 15s (CR); 17s (ECB).
> CR 3rd ser. 2: 115 (May 1804); ER 3: 260 (Oct 1803).
> Corvey; CME 3-628-47500-7; ECB 557; xNSTC.

*Notes.* Trans. of *Marguerite de Strafford, roman historique* (Paris, 1803). NSTC describes the French original as 'By Madame de ***'. This title is not normally associated with de Staël, and the attribution to her may well be spurious. Publishers change between vols: vols. 1, 4–5, see above; vols. 2 and 3 'Printed by R. Exton, Great-Portland-Street; for B. Crosby and Co. Stationers'-Court; and J. F. Hughes, Wigmore-Street, Cavendish-Square, 1803'. This matches the imprints in BL copy (C.190.aa.21). MR n.s. 41: 510–12 (App [Aug/Sept 1803]) has review of *Marguerite de Strafford*, Paris, 1803, 'Imported by De Boffe, Price 15 shillings sewed', but this probably relates to a French language edn.

1803: 69    [TAYLOR, Miss].
**THE NOBLEMAN AND HIS STEWARD, OR MEMOIRS OF THE ALBANY FAMILY. A NOVEL. IN THREE VOLUMES.**

> London: Printed at the Minerva-Press, for Lane and Newman, Leadenhall-Street, 1803.
> I 263p, ill.; II 271p; III 304p. 12mo. 12s (ECB).
> Corvey; CME 3-628-48231-3; ECB 415; xNSTC.

*Notes.* Blakey (under 1802; copy not seen) notes attributed by Minerva Library Catalogue of 1814 to Miss Taylor, and indexes this author separately from Eliza Taylor, the author of *Education* (see 1817: 53). BLC and Summers also list separately; FC, however, appears to consider that the same Eliza Taylor 'published several Minerva novels, 1799–1817' (p. 1057). ECB dates Jan 1803.

1803: 70   [THOMAS, Elizabeth].

**MAIDS AS THEY ARE NOT, AND WIVES AS THEY ARE. A NOVEL. IN FOUR VOLUMES. BY MRS. MARTHA HOMELY.**

> London: Printed by J. D. Dewick, Aldersgate-Street, for W. Earle, jun. 43, Wigmore-Street, 1803.
> I iv, 190p; II iv, 297p; III 4, 224p; IV iv, 189p. 12mo. 16s (ER); 14s boards (ER).
> ER 4: 249 (Apr 1804), 4: 499 (July 1804).
> Corvey; CME 3-628-47681-X; xNSTC.

*Notes.* 'Martha Homely' appears again as the signature to the Introduction of *The Three Old Maids of the House of Penruddock* (see 1806: 66), 'By Bridget Bluemantle' (the pseudonym of Elizabeth Thomas). Summers (p. 13) identifies Martha Homely as one of Thomas's pseudonyms. Adv. for Earle's 'French, English, & Italian Library, No. 43, Wigmore-Street, Cavendish-Square', at the end of vol. 2. 'Preface to Volume the Third' thanking 'unknown' corrector of the press.

1803: 71   THOMSON, J[ames].

**WINNIFRED, A TALE OF WONDER. IN TWO VOLUMES. BY THE REV. J. THOMSON, AUTHOR OF MAJOR PIPER, THE DENIAL, &C.**

> London: Printed at the Minerva-Press, for Lane and Newman, Leadenhall-Street, 1803.
> I 157p; II 179p. 12mo.
> BL 12613.aaa.25; NSTC T857.

*Notes.* Colophon at end of each vol: 'Newcastle upon Tyne; Printed by Edw. Walker, Pilgrim-Street'.

1803: 72   VANZEE, Maria.

**FATE; OR, SPONG CASTLE. BY MARIA VANZEE.**

> London: Printed for Parsons and Son, Circulating Library, Ludgate-Hill, 1803.
> vi, 231p. 12mo. 3s boards (CR); 4s (ECB).
> CR 3rd ser. 2: 236 (June 1804); ER 3: 506 (Jan 1804); WSW I: 548.
> Corvey; CME 3-628-48857-5; ECB 612; xNSTC.

*Notes.* Preface, claiming the original is a German manuscript dug up in Yorkshire! 'Terms of Subscriptions at Parsons & Son's London Circulating Library, Ludgate-Hill', followed by adv. for 'A Peep at the World [. . .] by Henry Somerset', at end of vol. ECB lists under Venzee, Maria and dates Dec 1803.

1803: 73   WALKER, George.

**DON RAPHAEL, A ROMANCE. BY GEORGE WALKER, AUTHOR OF THE THREE SPANIARDS, VAGABOND, POEMS, &C. IN THREE VOLUMES.**

> London: Printed for G. Walker, Bookseller, 106, Great Portland-Street; and T. Hurst, 32, Pater-Noster-Row; by Exton, Great Portland-Street, 1803.
> I 338p; II 291p; III 273p. 12mo. 13s 6d boards (CR); 13s 6d (ECB).

CR 2nd ser. 39: 235–6 (Oct 1803); WSW I: 551.

Corvey; CME 3-628-48813-3; ECB 619; NSTC W213 (BI C, O).

*Notes.* ECB dates Jan 1801, but evidently in error.

Further edn: New York 1803 (NUC).

1803: 74    WHITE, T[homas] H[enry].

**BELLGROVE CASTLE; OR, THE HORRID SPECTRE! A ROMANCE. IN FOUR VOLUMES. BY T. H. WHITE.**

> London: Printed by J. Norris, No. 2, Old Round-Court, Strand, for T. H. White, Duke's-Court, St. Martin's-Lane, and W. Jee, No. 447, Strand, 1803.
> I vi, 223p; II 209p; III 234p; IV 279p. 12mo. 14s (ECB).
> WSW I: 560.
> Corvey; CME 3-628-48904-0; ECB 635; NSTC W1686 (BI BL, O).

*Notes.* Dedication 'to the Ladies of Great Britain', signed Duke's Court, St. Martin's Lane. Vol. 2 imprint differs by reading: 'London: Printed at the Minerva-Press, for Lane and Newman, Leadenhall-Street, 1803'. Vignette shield device at end of vols. (including vol. 2) with the name and address of printer, and the date 1803. ECB dates Feb 1803, and gives publisher as Jee only.

1803: 75    [WHITFIELD, Henry].

**LEOPOLD; OR, THE BASTARD. IN TWO VOLUMES.**

> London: Printed for S. Highley, (Successor to the late Mr. John Murray) No. 24, Fleet Street; E. Harding, No. 100, Pall-Mall; E. Williams, No. 11, Strand; and J. Asperne, Cornhill, 1803.
> I viii, 308p; II 351p. 12mo. 8s sewed (CR); 8s (ECB).
> CR 2nd ser. 38: 441–4 (Aug 1803) full review; ER 3: 260 (Oct 1803); WSW I: 561.
> Corvey; CME 3-628-48029-9; ECB 338; NSTC W1747 (BI BL).

1803: 76    WILLIAMS, W[illiam] F[rederick].

**TALES OF AN EXILE. IN TWO VOLUMES. BY W. F. WILLIAMS, AUTHOR OF SKETCHES OF MODERN LIFE, FITZMAURICE, &C.**

> London: Printed at the Minerva-Press, for Lane, Newman, and Co. Leadenhall-Street, 1803.
> I ix, 242p; II 259p. 12mo. 6s boards (CR).
> CR 2nd ser. 39: 353 (Nov 1803); WSW I: 564.
> Corvey; CME 3-628-48966-0; xNSTC.

1803: 77    WOODFALL, Sophia.

**FREDERICK MONTRAVERS; OR, THE ADOPTED SON. A NOVEL. IN TWO VOLUMES. BY SOPHIA WOODFALL.**

> London: Printed for B. Crosby and Co. Stationers' Court, Paternoster Row, by Barnard & Sultzer, Water Lane, Fleet Street, 1803.
> I x, 190p; II 231p. 12mo. 6s boards (CR).
> CR 2nd ser. 39: 353 (Nov 1803); WSW I: 570.
> Corvey; CME 3-628-48981-4; ECB 647; NSTC W2737 (BI BL).

*Notes.* ECB dates 1802.

1803: 78　YOUNG, Mary Julia.
MOSS CLIFF ABBEY; OR, THE SEPULCHRAL HARMONIST. A MYSTE-
RIOUS TALE. IN FOUR VOLS. BY MARY-JULIA YOUNG, AUTHOR OF
ROSE MOUNT CASTLE; THE EAST INDIAN; THE KINSMEN OF
NAPLES; POEMS, &C.

> London: Printed by W. S. Betham, Furnival's-Inn-Court, Holborn, for B. Crosby and
> 　Co. Stationer's Court, Ludgate-Hill; and J. F. Hughes, Wigmore Street, 1803.
> I 198p; II 215p; III 196p; IV 216p. 12mo. 12s boards (CR).
> CR 3rd ser. 1: 119 (Jan 1804); ER 3: 260 (Oct 1803); WSW I: 577.
> Corvey; CME 3-628-48993-8; ECB 654; xNSTC.

*Notes.* Imprint in vol. 2: 'London: Printed by W. S. Betham, Furnival's-Inn-Court, Holborn,
for B. Crosby and Co. Stationer's Court, Ludgate-Hill; J. F. Hughes, Wigmore Street; and C.
Fourdrinier, Charing Cross, 1803'. Imprint in vol. 3: 'London: Printed by D. N. Shury,
Berwick-Street, Soho, for B. Crosby and Co. Stationer's Court, Ludgate Hill; and J. F.
Hughes, Wigmore Street, 1803'. Imprint in vol. 4: 'London: Printed by D. N. Shury, Berwick-
Street, Soho; for B. Crosby and Co. Stationer's Court, Ludgate Hill; and J. F. Hughes,
Wigmore-Street, 1803'.

1803: 79　YOUNG, Mary Julia.
RIGHT AND WRONG; OR, THE KINSMEN OF NAPLES. A ROMANTIC
STORY, IN FOUR VOLUMES. BY MARY JULIA YOUNG, AUTHOR OF
ROSE MOUNT CASTLE, THE EAST INDIAN, MOSS CLIFF ABBEY,
POEMS, &C. &C.

> London: Printed by D. N. Shury, Berwick Street; for Crosby and Co. Stationers' Court;
> 　and Hughes, Wigmore Street, 1803.
> I 232p; II 228p; III 201p; IV 242p. 12mo. 12s boards (CR); 14s (ECB).
> CR 3rd ser. 3: 471 (Dec 1804); ER 3: 260 (Oct 1803); WSW I: 577.
> Corvey; CME 3-628-48995-4; ECB 654; NSTC Y236 (BI BL, E).

*Notes.* Dedication to G. E. A. Wright, Esq. Young features as 'author of The Kinsmen of
Naples' in both *Lindorf and Caroline* (1803: 52) and *Moss Cliff Abbey* (1803: 78), though a
copy with this section of the title appearing first has not been discovered. Summers (p. 380)
states Hughes adv. 'The Kinsmen of Naples', 2nd edn. 1808, but again no such edn. has been
located.

1804: 1 ANON.

## ADELAIDE DE GRAMMONT; A ROMANCE OF THE FIFTEENTH CEN-
TURY.

> [London]: Albion Press: Printed by J. Cundee, Ivy-Lane, for T. Hurst, Paternoster-Row, 1804.
> 240p. 12mo. 4s 6d (ECB, ER).
> ER 4: 498 (July 1804).
> BL 12604.df.30; ECB 6; xNSTC.

*Notes.* Collates in sixes.

1804: 2 ANON.

## AMASINA, OR THE AMERICAN FOUNDLING. IN TWO VOLUMES. DEDICATED BY PERMISSION TO LADY COTTER.

> London: Printed at the Minerva-Press, for Lane, Newman, and Co. Leadenhall-Street, 1804.
> I 261p; II 324p. 12mo. 8s (ECB); 8s sewed (ER).
> ER 4: 249 (Apr 1804); WSW I: 10.
> Corvey; CME 3-628-47052-8; ECB 14; NSTC A1082 (BI O).

*Notes.* Dedication signed 'the Authoress'. T.p. attribution later indicates by the same author as *The Soldier of Pennaflor* (see 1810: 16).

1804: 3 ANON.

## THE AUNT AND THE NIECE. A NOVEL. IN TWO VOLUMES.

> London: Printed at the Minerva-Press, for Lane, Newman, and Co. Leadenhall-Street, 1804.
> I 248p; II 247p. 12mo. 6s (CR); 8s sewed (ER).
> CR 3rd ser. 3: 471–2 (Dec 1804); ER 5: 252 (Oct 1804); WSW I: 146.
> Corvey; CME 3-628-47079-X; NSTC A2010.5 (BI BL).

*Notes.* This title appears (as by the author) several times again in a sequence of works which have been attributed variously to Mrs E. G. Bayfield, James Henry James, and Mrs E. M. Foster (see 1806: 7, 1808: 19, 1812: 16, and 1817: 8). For the unlikelihood of Bayfield and James being the author of this sequence, see *A Winter in Bath* (1807: 7), itself a key title in the chain. If Mrs E. M. Foster is the author, it would involve an authorship stretching from 1795 to 1817. In the present case, granting the possibility of Mrs Foster's involvement, it seems odd that no previous works are cited in the title (an invariable procedure in earlier instances). Blakey treats this work as anonymous. See also *The Corinna of England* (1809: 4).

1804: 4 ANON.

## THE CASTLE OF ST. CARANZA. A ROMANCE. IN TWO VOLUMES.

London: Printed at the Minerva-Press, for Lane, Newman, and Co. Leadenhall-Street, 1804.

I 260p, ill.; II 248p. 12mo. 7s (ECB).

WSW I: 22.

Corvey; CME 3-628-47222-9; ECB 100; NSTC C961 (BI BL).

*Notes.* ECB dates Dec 1803.

1804: 5   ANON.

## THE CITIZEN'S DAUGHTER; OR WHAT MIGHT BE.

London: Printed by N. Biggs, Crane-Court, Fleet-Street, for Vernor and Hood, 31, Poultry, 1804.

284p. 12mo. 4s (ECB); 8s sewed (ER).

ER 4: 249 (Apr 1804); WSW I: 25.

Corvey; CME 3-628-47283-0; ECB 117; NSTC C1992 (BI BL, O).

*Notes.* For another work, apparently by the same author, see 1805: 7.

1804: 6   ANON.

## COMMON LIFE, AN ARTLESS TALE; INTENDED TO ILLUSTRATE THE EFFECTS OF EDUCATION.

London: Printed for J. Ginger, Bookseller to His Royal Highness the Prince of Wales, No. 169, Piccadilly, and T. Hurst, Paternoster Row, 1804.

I 217p; II 196p. 12mo. 7s (ECB); 7s sewed (ER).

ER 4: 498 (July 1804).

Corvey; CME 3-628-47277-6; ECB 128; xNSTC.

1804: 7   ANON.

## THE MAD DOG; A ROMANCE. IN THREE VOLUMES.

London: Printed by Nichols and Son, Red Lion Passage, Fleet Street, for W. Earle, at the original French and English Circulating Library, No. 47, Albemarle Street, Piccadilly, 1804.

I iv, 236p; II 228p; III 220p. 12mo. 12s (ER).

ER 5: 500 (Jan 1805); WSW I: 70.

Corvey; CME 3-628-48143-0; xNSTC.

1804: 8   ANON.

## THE REFORMED REPROBATE. A NOVEL. IN THREE VOLUMES.

London: Printed by D. N. Shury, No. 7, Berwick Street, Soho; for J. F. and G. Hughes, Wigmore Street, Cavendish Square, 1804.

I 278p; II 223p; III 227p. 12mo. 12s boards (CR, ER); 12s (ECB).

CR 3rd ser. 3: 116 (Sept 1804); ER 5: 252 (Oct 1804).

BL 12611.bbb.21; ECB 484; NSTC R688.

*Notes.* CR states: 'it is only from a foreign journal, that we learn its author was Augustus la Fontaine'. Modern catalogues however, treat as anonymous. But see also *The Reprobate* (1802: 35) for a possible connection.

1804: 9    ANON.

THE TALISMAN: OR, SINGULAR ADVENTURES OF AN OLD OFFI-
CER; WITH ITS CONSEQUENCES. WRITTEN BY HIMSELF.

> London: Printed for R. Dutton, No. 45, Gracechurch Street; J. Cawthorn, Catherine
> Street; Chapple, Pall-Mall; and T. Hurst, Paternoster Row; by John Abraham,
> Clement's Lane, 1804.
> I 240p; II 240p. 12mo. 8s (ECB).
> WSW I: 119.
> Corvey; CME 3-628-48940-7; ECB 576; xNSTC.

*Notes.* ECB dates Apr 1804.

1804: 10    BARTON, James.

HONORINA, OR THE INFATUATED CHILD. A NOVEL. IN TWO VOL-
UMES. BY JAMES BARTON, L.M.

> London: Printed at the Minerva-Press, for Lane, Newman, and Co. Leadenhall-Street,
> 1804.
> I 263p, ill.; II 268p. 12mo. 7s boards (CR).
> CR 3rd ser. 3: 360 (Nov 1804); WSW I: 145.
> Corvey; CME 3-628-47111-7; NSTC B839 (BI BL).

1804: 11    BARTON, J[ames].

TRAVELS OF YOUNG CANDID AND DOCTOR PANGLOSS TO THE
COUNTRY OF EL-DORADO, TOWARDS THE END OF THE EIGHT-
EENTH CENTURY; BEING A CONTINUATION OF VOLTAIRE'S
CANDID. BY J. BARTON, L.M. AUTHOR OF THE INFATUATED
CHILD, REMORSELESS ASSASSIN, MONK OF HENNARES, &C. &C. IN
THREE VOLUMES.

> London: Printed by D. N. Shury, Berwick Street, Soho, for J. F. Hughes, Wigmore
> Street, 1804.
> I 212p; II 182p; III 184p. 12mo. 12s (ECB); 12s boards (ER).
> ER 4: 249 (Apr 1804).
> BL 1508/1687; ECB 42; NSTC B841.

1804: 12    [BERTHIER, J. B. C.]; YOUNG, Mary Julia (*trans.*).

THE MOTHER AND DAUGHTER, A PATHETIC TALE, BY MARY
JULIA YOUNG, AUTHOR OF MOSS CLIFFE ABBEY, KINSMEN OF
NAPLES, ROSE MOUNT CASTLE, EAST INDIAN, &C. &C. IN THREE
VOLUMES.

> London: Printed by R. Exton, Great Portland-Street; for J. F. Hughes, Wigmore-Street,
> Cavendish-Square, 1804.
> I 261p; II 226p; III 218p. 12mo.
> ER 3: 506 (Jan 1804).
> Corvey; CME 3-62-48994-6; NSTC Y234 (BI BL, C).

*Notes.* Trans. of *Felix et Éléonore, ou les colons malheureux* (Paris, 1801). Mary Julia Young
states that *Mother and Daughter* is a translation from Berthier in a letter to the Royal Literary

Fund committee (20 Mar 1808, RLF 6: 216). While such an origin is not mentioned on the t.p. and there are no preliminaries, Young's narrative describes a journey to the Americas from France in 1789 and has Felix and Eleonora as key characters. The source title above is listed in BN, and is the only work given there by the author.

1804: 13   BISSET, Robert.
**MODERN LITERATURE: A NOVEL, IN THREE VOLUMES. BY ROBERT BISSET, L.L.D.**

> London: Printed for T. N. Longman and O. Rees, Paternoster-Row, 1804.
> I xxviii, 313p; II xii, 332p; III xii, 280p. 12mo. 10s boards (CR); 15s (ECB); 15s boards (ER).
> CR 3rd ser. 3: 238 (Oct 1804); ER 4: 498 (July 1804); WSW I: 158.
> Corvey; CME 3-628-47199-0; ECB 59; NSTC B3058 (BI BL).

*Notes.* Preface dated Sloane-Terrace, 8 May 1804. The author's degree is represented more normally as 'LL.D' on t.ps. of vols. 2 and 3.

1804: 14   BROWN, C[harles] B[rockden].
**JANE TALBOT. A NOVEL. IN TWO VOLUMES. BY C. B. BROWNE [*sic*], AUTHOR OF ARTHUR MERVYN, EDGAR HUNTLEY, &C.**

> London: Printed at the Minerva-Press, for Lane, Newman, and Co. Leadenhall-Street, 1804.
> I 263p; II 336p. 12mo. 8s (ECB).
> WSW I: 174.
> Corvey; CME 3-628-47137-0; ECB 78; xNSTC.

*Notes.* ECB dates Apr 1804. Originally published Philadelphia 1801 (Blanck).

**BYERLEY, John Scott, NATURE; OR A PICTURE OF THE PASSIONS**
See 1803: 21

1804: 15   CANTON, John.
**ALVAR AND SERAPHINA; OR, THE TROUBLES OF MURCIA. AN HIS-TORIC ROMANCE. IN TWO VOLUMES. BY JOHN CANTON.**

> London: Printed for Lane, Newman, and Co. Minerva Press, Leadenhall-Street, 1804.
> I 238p, ill.; II 222p. 12mo. 6s (CR).
> CR 3rd ser. 3: 470 (Dec 1804); ER 3: 505 (Jan 1804); WSW I: 201.
> Corvey; CME 3-628-47210-5; xNSTC.

**CURTIES, T. J. Horsley, THE WATCH TOWER**
See 1803: 26

1804: 16   DALLAS, R[obert] C[harles].
**AUBREY: A NOVEL. BY R. C. DALLAS ESQ. AUTHOR OF PERCIVAL.**

> London: Printed for T. N. Longman and O. Rees, Paternoster-Row, 1804.
> I xxvii, 212p; II iv, 268p; III vii, 299p; IV viii, 390p. 12mo. 18s (ECB); 18s boards (ER).

ER 4: 498 (July 1804); WSW I: 234–5.

Corvey; CME 3-628-47390-X; ECB 150; NSTC D95 (BI BL).

*Notes.* Dedication 'to M. Bertrand De Moleville, one of the confidental ministers of Louis XVI', dated Camberwell Grove, 23 Mar 1804. Text proper in vol. 1 ends on p. 210, followed by 2 pp. of advs.

### 1804: 17 EDGEWORTH, Maria.
## POPULAR TALES. BY MARIA EDGEWORTH, AUTHOR OF PRACTICAL EDUCATION, BELINDA, CASTLE RACKRENT, IRISH BULLS, &C. &C.

[London]: Printed for J. Johnson, St. Paul's Church-Yard, by C. Mercier and Co. Northumberland-Court, Strand, 1804.

I iv, 384p; II 367p; III 394p. 12mo. 15s (ECB).

ER 4: 329–37 (July 1804) full review; WSW I: 255.

Corvey; CME 3-628-47576-7; ECB 178; NSTC E242 (BI BL, O).

*Notes.* Preface, signed 'Richard Lovell Edgeworth. Edgeworth's Town, Feb. 1804'. This comments: 'Burke supposes that there are eighty thousand readers in Great Britain, nearly one hundredth part of its inhabitants! Out of these we may calculate that ten thousand are nobility, clergy, or gentlemen of the learned professions. Of seventy thousand readers which remain, there are many who might be amused and instructed by books, which were not professedly adapted to the classes that have been enumerated. With this view the following volumes have been composed' (vol. 1, pp. ii–iii).

Further edns: 2nd edn. 1805 (NSTC); 3rd edn. 1807 (NSTC); 4th edn. 1811 (NSTC); 5th edn. 1814 (NSTC); 6th edn. 1817 (NSTC); [at least 4 more edns. to 1850]; Philadelphia 1804 (NUC); German trans., 1807 [as *Einfache Erzählungen* (RS)]; French trans., 1823.

### FLORIAN, Jean Pierre Claris de, GALATEA: A PASTORAL ROMANCE
See Vol. 1, 1791: 35; also present Vol., Appendix E: 3

### 1804: 18 GENLIS, [Stéphanie-Félicité, Comtesse] de; [?LENNOX, Charles (*trans.*)].
## THE DUCHESS OF LA VALLIERE. AN HISTORICAL ROMANCE. BY MADAME DE GENLIS. TRANSLATED FROM THE FRENCH. IN TWO VOLUMES.

London: Printed for John Murray, No. 32, Fleet-Street, 1804.

I xxxv, 264p; II 319p. 12mo. 8s boards (CR); 10s 6d (ECB); 10s 6d sewed (ER); 9s boards (ER).

CR 3rd ser. 3: 239 (Oct 1804); ER 4: 498 (July 1804), 5: 252 (Oct 1804); WSW I: 239–40.

CtY-BR Hfd29.351.V; ECB 225; xNSTC.

*Notes.* Trans. of *La Duchesse de la Vallière* (Paris, 1804). ECB and ER both state translated by Charles Lennox. Translator is also identified by Summers as Charles Lennox, but no indication of identity is apparently given in the long Preface. NUC entry does not mention Lennox.

### 1804: 19 GLYSTICUS, Henrico Fernandez [pseud.].
## THE TEARS OF CAMPHOR; OR, LOVE AND NATURE TRIUMPHANT. A SATIRICAL TALE OF THE NINETEENTH CENTURY. INTERSPERSED WITH ORIGINAL POETRY. BY HENRICO FERNANDEZ

GLYSTICUS, LL.D. F.R.S. F.S.A. &C. &C. AND SITTING MEMBER OF THE UNIVERSITY OF GALLIPOT-OMUS. IN THREE VOLUMES.

> London: Printed for J. Ginger, Piccadilly; C. Chappel [*sic*], and J. Budd, Pall-Mall, 1804.
> I xv, xi, 284p, ill.; II xiv, 294p; III xiv, 264p. 12mo. 15s boards (CR, ER); 15s (ECB).
> CR 3rd ser. 3: 116 (Sept 1804); ER 4: 498 (July 1804); WSW I: 281.
> Corvey; CME 3-628-48946-6; ECB 233; NSTC G1225 (BI BL).

*Notes.* Dedication to 'His Supreme Highness The Devil', signed 'Henrico Fernandez Glysticus', dated England, 24 June 1804. Preface, dated the same and signed H. F. G., anticipates unfavourable reviews: with the *Critical Review*, for example, noticing 'A vapid, senseless, stupid, and indecent novel, which every careful parent ought to forbid' (p. xi).

1804: 20    GOLDSMITH, Mary.
CASUALTIES. A NOVEL. IN TWO VOLUMES. BY MARY GOLDSMITH, AUTHOR OF THE COMEDY ENTITLED SHE LIVES! OR, THE GENEROUS BROTHER.

> London: Printed by Roden and Lewis, Paternoster-Row; for T. Hughes, Stationers-Court,
>     Ludgate-Street; and sold by Jordan Hookham, New Bond-Street; Harding, Pall-Mall;
>     Lloyd, Harley-Street, Cavendish-Square; and J. Ridgeway, York-Street, St. James's, 1804.
> I xvi, 182p; II 166p. 12mo. 6s (ECB); 6s boards (ER).
> ER 4: 498 (July 1804); WSW I: 282.
> BL 12612.ccc.14; CME 3-628-47820-0; ECB 235; NSTC G1323.

*Notes.* Dedication 'to the Honorable Mrs. A. M. Egerton', signed 'Mary Goldsmith'. 'Subscribers' (27 names), vol. 2, pp. 165–6. T.p. carries the following statement: 'No Subterranean Caverns—Haunted Castles—Enchanted Forests—Fearful Visions—Mysterious Voices—Supernatural Agents—Bloody Daggers—Dead Men's Skulls—Mangled Bodies—*Nor* Marvellous Lights, from any Part of the present Work; but will be found, on Perusal, to arise out of Natural Incidents'. Corvey copy lacks list of subscribers.

1804: 21    GOOCH, {Elizabeth Sarah} Villa-Real.
SHERWOOD FOREST; OR NORTHERN ADVENTURES. A NOVEL. IN THREE VOLUMES. BY MRS. VILLA-REAL GOOCH.

> London: Printed for S. Highley, (Successor of the late Mr. John Murray,) No. 24, Fleet-
>     Street, 1804.
> I xii, 228p; II 192p; III 234p. 12mo. 12s (ECB); 12s boards (ER).
> CR 3rd ser. 3: 115–16 (Sept 1804); ER 4: 498 (July 1804); WSW I: 283.
> Corvey; CME 3-628-47837-5; ECB 236; xNSTC.

*Notes.* Dedication 'to James Wardell, Esq. Wine merchant, Pall Mall', signed Elizabeth Sarah Villa-Real Gooch, King Street, Hammersmith, 12 Apr 1804. Preface, vol. 1, pp. [ix]–xii, begins with the statement: 'An acknowledged Novel-writer is, perhaps, one of the most difficult names to support with credit and reputation'. CR gives Lane as publisher, and Blakey (copy not seen) includes as a title of the Minerva Press.

1804: 22    GRAGLIA, G[uiseppe] A.
THE LABYRINTH OF CORCIRA: OR, THE MOST EXTRAORDINARY AND SURPRISING HISTORY OF THE INCOMPARABLE DON

FERNANDO D'AVALO, HEREDITARY PRINCE OF SALERNO, AND
THE BEAUTIFUL AND VIRTUOUS ISIDORA, DUCHESS OF CATANIA.
TOGETHER WITH THE SURPRISING EVENTS OF THE COUNTESS OF
LIPARY HIS SISTER. BY G. A. GRAGLIA. IN TWO VOLUMES.

> London: Printed by Cox, Son, and Baylis, No. 75, Great Queen-Street, Lincoln's-Inn-
> Fields, for the Author, No. 22, Castle-Street, Leicester-Fields, 1804.
> I viii, 203p; II 218p. 12mo.
> Corvey; CME 3-628-47793-X; NSTC G1609 (BI BL).

1804: 23　[GRUBER, Johann Gottfried].
HELL UPON EARTH. IN TWO VOLUMES. TRANSLATED FROM THE
GERMAN.

> London: Printed by D. N. Shury, Berwick Street, Soho, for J. F. Hughes, Wigmore
> Street, 1804.
> I 278p; II 223p. 12mo. 4s boards (CR); 7s (ECB).
> CR 3rd ser. 1: 358 (Mar 1804); ER 3: 506 (Jan 1804).
> Corvey; CME 3-628-47725-5; ECB 263; NSTC H1214 (BI BL).

*Notes.* Trans. of *Die Hölle auf Erden: ein Roman* (Leipzig, 1800). ER lists as 'by the author of
Pizarro, &c.', giving (misleading) impression that author is Kotzebue. ECB dates Dec 1803.

1804: 24　[GUÉNARD, Elisabeth].
THE CAPTIVE OF VALENCE; OR THE LAST MOMENTS OF PIUS VI.
IN TWO VOLUMES.

> London: Printed for G. and J. Robinson, Pater-Noster-Row, by W. Meyler, Grove, Bath, 1804.
> I 253p, ill.; II 268p, ill. 8vo.
> ER 5: 252 (Oct 1804); WSW I: 21.
> BL 12512.aaa.26; NSTC P2020 (BI O).

*Notes.* Trans. of *Le Captif du Valence ou les derniers moments de Pie VI* (Paris, 1802). 'To the
Reader' states: 'The Author from whom the following sheets are translated, asserts the various incidents contained in the succeeding narrative to be founded in fact, though clad in the
guise of a novel'. BN and NUC both give Guénard as the author of the French original.

HELME, Elizabeth, THE PENITENT OF GODSTOW
See 1812: 35

1804: 25　HOOK, Sarah Ann.
SECRET MACHINATIONS. A NOVEL, IN FOUR VOLUMES. BY SARAH
ANN HOOK, AUTHOR OF THE WIDOWED BRIDE, OR, CELINA.

> London: Printed for R. Dutton, Gracechurch-Street; and C. Chapple, Pall-Mall; by J. D.
> Dewick, Aldersgate-Street, 1804.
> I viii, 276p; II 270p; III 206p; IV 254p. 12mo. 16s sewed (ER).
> ER 5: 500 (Jan 1805); WSW I: 326.
> Corvey; CME 3-628-47691-7; NSTC H2395 (BI O).

*Notes.* 'Terms of Subscription to R. Dutton's Circulating Library' (2 pp. unn.) at the end of
vol. 2.

1804: 26  HUNTER, [Rachel].
THE UNEXPECTED LEGACY, A NOVEL. BY MRS. HUNTER, OF NOR-
WICH; AUTHOR OF LETITIA; THE HISTORY OF THE GRUBTHORPE
FAMILY; AND MRS. PALMERSTONE'S LETTERS TO HER DAUGH-
TER. IN TWO VOLUMES.

> London: Printed for T. N. Longman and O. Rees, Paternoster-Row; and W. T. Rob-
> berds, Norwich; by R. Taylor, Black-Horse-Court, Fleet Street, 1804.
> I xvii, 243p; II 363p. 12mo. 9s (ECB).
> ER 4: 249 (Apr 1804); WSW I: 336.
> Corvey; CME 3-628-47787-5; ECB 289; NSTC H3178 (BI BL, O).

1804: 27  [IRELAND, Samuel William Henry].
*BRUNO; OR, THE SEPULCHRAL SUMMONS.

> London: Earle and Hemet, 1804.
> 4 vols. 12mo.
> No copy located.

*Notes.* Listed in Summers, who indicates published under the initials 'W. H. I.'. Frank (Item
200) gives short synopsis.

1804: 28  [IRELAND, Samuel William Henry].
THE WOMAN OF FEELING. IN FOUR VOLUMES.

> London: Printed by D. N. Shury, No. 7, Berwick Street, Soho, for William Miller, Old
> Bond Street, and Didier and Tebbett, 75, St. James's Street, 1804.
> I xii, 216p; II viii, 234p; III vii, 215p; IV vii, 254p. 12mo. 16s (ECB); 16s sewed (ER).
> ER 4: 498 (July 1804); WSW I: 339.
> Corvey; CME 3-628-48974-1; ECB 645; NSTC P1261 (BI BL).

*Notes.* Dedication to 'Miss Sarah Colepeper', signed 'The Baronet's Nephew' [fictive]. The last
chapter in vol. 4, 'A Penny for my Reader's Thoughts' (pp. 249–54) is signed 'Paul Persius'.

1804: 29  [JONES, John Gale].
GALERIO AND NERISSA, INCLUDING ORIGINAL CORRESPON-
DENCE, THE HISTORY OF AN ENGLISH NOBLEMAN AND LADY;
SEVERAL POETICAL EFFUSIONS, AND A FEW DOMESTIC ANEC-
DOTES.

> London: Printed for the Author, and sold by Messrs. Jordan and Maxwell, No. 180,
> Fleet Street, 1804.
> xvi, 131p. 8vo. 'Four Shillings in Boards' (t.p.).
> WSW I: 347.
> BL 12612.f.19; NSTC J972 (BI O).

*Notes.* 'Subscribers Names' (162 listed), pp. (v)–xii; 'Introductory Narrative', dated Aug
1804; 'Poetical Effusions' pp. 103–31 [a separate section]. Collates in fours.

KARAMZIN, Nikolai Mikhailovich, TALES FROM THE RUSSIAN
See 1803: 38

1804: 30   KER, {Anne}.

**MODERN FAULTS, A NOVEL, FOUNDED ON FACTS. BY MRS. KER, AUTHOR OF "THE HEIRESS DI MONTALDE." &C. &C. &C. IN TWO VOLUMES.**

> London: Printed by J. M'Gowen, Church Street, Blackfriars Road. For J. Ker, 34, Great Surry Street, Black Friars Road; sold also by John Badcock, Paternoster Row, 1804.
> I 228p, ill.; II 234p. 12mo. 6s boards (CR); 7s (ECB); 7s sewed (ER).
> CR 3rd ser. 3: 116 (Sept 1804); ER 4: 498 (July 1804); WSW I: 354.
> Corvey; CME 3-628-48016-7; ECB 320; xNSTC.

*Notes.* Frontispiece portrait of 'M^rs. Anne Ker'. Adv. for Mrs Ker's *Edric the Forester*, in 3 vols. forthcoming in Dec at 10s 6d, below text in vol. 2, p. 234 (followed by colophon of 'M'Gowen, Printer, Church Street, Blackfriars Road'). The earliest edn. of this title discovered, however, was published more than a decade later (see 1817: 36).

1804: 31   LAFONTAINE, August [Heinrich Julius].

**\*BARON DE FLEMING; OR, THE RAGE OF NOBILITY. FROM THE GERMAN OF AUGUSTUS LA FONTAINE.**

> London: Lane, Newman, and Co. 1804.
> 3 vols. 12mo. 12s (ECB); 12s sewed (ER).
> ER 4: 498 (July 1804); WSW I: 357.
> No copy located; ECB 326.

*Notes.* Trans. of *Leben und Thaten des Freiherrn Quinctius Heymeran von Flaming* (Berlin, 1795–6). *Literary Journal, A Review*, 3 (16 June 1804), p. 682, lists this and the following title as separate works, with Lafontaine's name positioned immediately beneath *Baron de Fleming, the Son* while apparently relating to each. ECB dates both titles May 1804.

1804: 32   LAFONTAINE, August [Heinrich Julius].

**BARON DE FLEMING, THE SON; OR THE RAGE OF SYSTEMS. A NOVEL. IN THREE VOLUMES. FROM THE GERMAN OF AUGUSTUS LA FONTAINE.**

> London: Printed at the Minerva-Press, for Lane, Newman, and Co. Leadenhall-Street, 1804.
> I 246p; II 260p; III 243p. 12mo. 12s (ECB); 12s sewed (ER).
> ER 4: 498 (July 1804).
> BL 12548.f.23; ECB 326; NSTC L154.

*Notes.* Trans. of *Leben und Thaten des Freiherrn Quinctius Heymeran von Flaming* (Berlin, 1795–6). ECB and ER both describe this title as 'a continuation' of 'Baron de Fleming'.

1804: 33   LAFONTAINE, August [Heinrich Julius].

**HENRIETTA BELLMANN: OR, THE NEW FAMILY PICTURE. A NOVEL. BY AUGUSTUS LA FONTAINE. IN TWO VOLUMES.**

> London: Printed for Vernor and Hood in the Poultry, 1804.
> I 271p; II 304p. 12mo. 8s (ECB); 8s sewed (ER).

CR 3rd ser. 6: 215–16 (Oct 1805); ER 4: 249 (Apr 1804); WSW I: 357.
BL 12547.ccc.14; ECB 326; NSTC L151.

*Notes.* Trans. of *Henriette Bellmann* (Berlin, 1802). 'By T. Gillet, Crown-Court, Fleet-Street' after imprint date.

1804: 34   LAFONTAINE, August [Heinrich Julius]; MEEKE, [Mary] (*trans.*).
**LOBENSTEIN VILLAGE. A NOVEL. IN FOUR VOLUMES. TRANS-LATED BY MRS. MEEKE, FROM THE FRENCH OF AUGUSTUS LA FONTAINE.**

London: Printed at the Minerva-Press, for Lane, Newman, and Co. Leadenhall-Street, 1804.
I 270p, ill.; II 292p; III 276p; IV 266p. 12mo. 16s boards (CR).
CR 3rd ser. 2: 114 (May 1804).
BL 1607/1867; NSTC L162.

*Notes.* Trans. of *Le Village de Lobenstein, ou le nouvel enfant trouvé* (Genève et Paris, 1802), itself a trans. of the original German title, *Theodor, oder Kultur und Humanität* (Berlin, 1802).

1804: 35   LAFONTAINE, August [Heinrich Julius]; PARSONS, [Eliza] (*trans.*).
**LOVE AND GRATITUDE; OR, TRAITS OF THE HUMAN HEART. SIX NOVELS, TRANSLATED FROM AUGUSTUS LA FONTAINE. IN THREE VOLUMES. PREPARED FOR THE PRESS BY MRS. PARSONS, AUTHOR OF MYSTERIOUS WARNING, GIRL OF THE MOUNTAIN, MURRAY HOUSE, THE MISER AND HIS FAMILY, THE PEASANT OF ARDENNE FOREST, THE VALLEY OF ST. GOTHARD, MYSTERIOUS VISIT, &C. &C.**

Brentford: Printed by and for P. Norbury; and sold by Longman, Hurst, Rees, and Orme, Pater-Noster Row; Carpenter and Co. Old-Bond-Street; Earle, Albemarle-Street; Hatchard, Piccadilly; and Didier and Tibett, St. James's Street, London; also by W. Ansell, Richmond, Surrey, 1804.
I 264p; II 234p; III 268p. 12mo. 12s (CR); 13s 6d (ECB); 12s sewed (ER).
CR 3rd ser. 5: 330 (July 1805); ER 5: 500 (Jan 1805).
Corvey; CME 3-628-48396-4; ECB 326; NSTC L145 (BI BL, O).

*Notes.* Trans. of *Liebe und Dankbarkeit* (Berlin/Leipzig, 1799). The other five novels are trans. from *Die Gewalt der Liebe* (Berlin, 1791–4).

1804: 36   LAFONTAINE, August [Heinrich Julius]; [CHARLTON, Mary (*trans.*)].
**THE RAKE AND THE MISANTHROPE. A NOVEL. IN TWO VOLUMES. FROM THE GERMAN OF AUGUSTUS LA FONTAINE.**

London: Printed at the Minerva-Press, for Lane, Newman, and Co. Leadenhall-Street, 1804.
I 243p; II 232p. 12mo. 7s 6d (ECB); 7s sewed (ER).
ER 4: 249 (Apr 1804).
CtY-BR HKc14.310R; ECB 326; xNSTC.

*Notes.* German original not discovered.

1804: 37   LA MARTELIÈRE, [Jean Henri Ferdinand].
THE THREE GIL BLAS, OR FOLLIES OF YOUTH. A NOVEL. IN FOUR
VOLUMES. FROM THE FRENCH OF LA MARTELIERE.

>  London: Printed at the Minerva-Press, for Lane, Newman, and Co. Leadenhall-Street,
>     1804.
>  I iv, 255p; II 272p; III 266p; IV 290p. 12mo. 16s (ECB); 16s sewed (ER).
>  ER 5: 252 (Oct 1804).
>  Corvey; CME 3-628-48958-X; ECB 327; NSTC L240 (BI BL).

*Notes.* Trans. of *Trois Gil Blas, ou cinq ans de folie* (Paris, 1802).

LANTIER, Étienne François de, TRAVELLERS IN SWITZERLAND
See 1803: 42

1804: 38   LEE, Sophia.
THE LIFE OF A LOVER. IN A SERIES OF LETTERS. BY SOPHIA LEE. IN
SIX VOLUMES.

>  London: Printed for G. & J. Robinson, Paternoster-Row, 1804.
>  I xi, 320p; II 336p; III 314p; IV 363p; V 298p; VI 376p. 8vo. 36s (CR); 36s 6d boards (ER).
>  CR 3rd ser. 2: 324–30 (July 1804) full review; ER 4: 498 (July 1804); WSW I: 367–8.
>  Corvey; CME 3-628-47973-8; ECB 336; NSTC L1009 (BI BL, C).

*Notes.* Colophons differ: vols. 1–4 'S. Hamilton, Printer, Shoe Lane, Fleet-Street'; vols. 5–6
'T. Davison, White-Friars'.
Further edn: French trans., 1808 [as *Savinia Rivers, ou le danger d'aimer* (BN)].

1804: 39   LEFANU, [Elizabeth].
THE INDIA VOYAGE; BY MRS. H. LEFANU, DAUGHTER OF THE
LATE THOMAS SHERIDAN, M.A. IN TWO VOLUMES.

>  London: Printed for G. and J. Robinson, Paternoster-Row, 1804.
>  I 267p; II 298p. 12mo. 8s (ECB).
>  ER 5: 252 (Oct 1804); WSW I: 368.
>  Corvey; CME 3-628-48047-7; ECB 295; NSTC L1045 (BI BL).

*Notes.* Untitled notice misbound at end of vol. 2 begins: 'The author of the following sheets,
has adopted the epistolary, or, rather, the journal style; as it appeared to her more favourable
to the development of character than the narrative'. Block and Summers both attribute to
Alicia Lefanu, but t.p. description of the authoress as 'Mrs. H. Lefanu' indicates Elizabeth
Lefanu, mother of Alicia and wife of Henry Lefanu. See also *Strathallan* (1816: 43).

1804: 40   LE NOIR, [Elizabeth Anne].
VILLAGE ANECDOTES; OR, THE JOURNAL OF A YEAR, FROM
SOPHIA TO EDWARD. WITH ORIGINAL POEMS. BY MRS. LE NOIR.
IN THREE VOLUMES.

>  London: Printed for Vernor and Hood, 31, Poultry, by A. Wilson, Wild Court, Lin-
>     coln's Inn Fields, 1804.
>  I iv, 262p; II 306p; III 303p. 12mo. 12s (ECB).

ER 3: 506 (Jan 1804); WSW I: 369–70.

Corvey; CME 3-628-48170-8; ECB 338; NSTC L1168 (BI BL).

*Notes.* Further edn: 2nd edn. Reading [1807] (NSTC).

1804: 41   LENOX, Miss [pseud.].

MEMOIRS OF HENRY LENOX, INTERSPERSED WITH LEGENDARY ROMANCES. BY THE HON. MISS LENOX.

> London: Printed by D. N. Shury, No. 7, Berwick Street, Soho, for J. F. and G. Hughes, Wigmore Street, Cavendish Square, 1804.
> 211p. 12mo.
> ER 5: 252 (Oct 1804).
> BL 1153.l.8; ECB 338; NSTC L1179 (BI O).

1804: 42   [LEWIS, Alethea].

A TALE WITHOUT A TITLE: GIVE IT WHAT YOU PLEASE. IN THREE VOLUMES. BY EUGENIA DE ACTON, AUTHOR OF ESSAYS ON THE ART OF BEING HAPPY, THE MICROCOSM, &C.

> London: Printed at the Minerva-Press, for Lane, Newman, and Co. Leadenhall-Street, 1804.
> I 280p, ill.; II 286p; III 266p. 12mo. 12s boards (CR).
> CR 3rd ser. 3: 360 (Nov 1804); WSW I: 238.
> Corvey; CME 3-628-47008-0; ECB 575; xNSTC.

1804: 43   LEWIS, Isabella.

TERRIFIC TALES. BY ISABELLA LEWIS.

> London: Printed by R. Cantwell, 33, Bell-Yard, Temple-Bar, for J. F. Hughes, No. 5, Wigmore-Street, Cavendish-Square, 1804.
> 229p. 12mo.
> Corvey; CME 3-628-51086-4; xNSTC.

*Notes.* Collates in sixes.

1804: 44   MALARME, Charlotte de Bournon; GOOCH, [Elizabeth Sarah] Villa-Real (*trans.*).

CAN WE DOUBT IT? OR, THE GENUINE HISTORY OF TWO FAMILIES OF NORWICH. BY CHARLOTTE BOURNON-MALARME, MEMBER OF THE ACADEMY OF ARCADES OF ROME. TRANSLATED FROM THE FRENCH, BY MRS. VILLA-REAL GOOCH. IN THREE VOLUMES.

> London: Printed by J. Swan, No. 76, Fleet-Street, for B. Crosby and Co. Stationers' Court, Paternoster-Row, 1804.
> I 215p; II 213p; III 179p. 12mo. 10s 6d (CR, ECB, ER).
> CR 3rd ser. 4: 446–7 (Apr 1805); ER 5: 501 (Jan 1805).
> Corvey; ECB 236; xNSTC.

*Notes.* Trans. of *Qui ne s'y serait trompé?* (Paris, 1810). No earlier edn. of French original discovered. Preface 'By the translator'. Postscript at the end of vol. 3 claims a true story about two families, with changed names.

### 1804: 45    MALDEN, Miriam.
JESSICA MANDAVILLE, OR THE WOMAN OF FORTITUDE, IN FIVE VOLUMES, BY MIRIAM MALDEN.

> Richmond: Printed by and for G. A. Wall; and sold by Longman, Hurst, Rees, and Orme, London, 1804.
> I vii, 298p; II 258p; III 284p; IV 282p; V 275p. 12mo. 17s 6d (ECB); 17s 6d boards (ER).
> ER 5: 252 (Oct 1804); WSW I: 384.
> Corvey; CME 3-628-48145-7; ECB 364; NSTC M806 (BI BL).

*Notes.* Dedication to 'H— C—, Esq.'.

### 1804: 46    MEEKE, [Mary].
AMAZEMENT. A NOVEL. IN THREE VOLUMES. BY MRS. MEEKE, AUTHOR OF ELLESMERE, MIDNIGHT WEDDINGS, &C.

> London: Printed at the Minerva-Press, for Lane, Newman, and Co. Leadenhall-Street, 1804.
> I 276p; II 279p; III 274p. 12mo. 12s sewed (ER).
> ER 4: 499 (July 1804); WSW I: 394.
> Corvey; CME 3-628-48206-2; NSTC M1952 (BI BL, O).

### 1804: 47    MEEKE, [Mary].
THE NINE DAYS' WONDER. A NOVEL. IN THREE VOLUMES. BY MRS. MEEKE, AUTHOR OF THE OLD WIFE AND YOUNG HUSBAND, AMAZEMENT, &C. &C.

> London: Printed at the Minerva-Press, for Lane, Newman, and Co. Leadenhall-Street, 1804.
> I 284p; II 269p; III 251p. 12mo. 12s sewed (ER).
> ER 5: 253 (Oct 1804); WSW I: 394.
> Corvey; CME 3-628-48210-0; ECB 415; xNSTC.

### 1804: 48    MEEKE, [Mary].
THE OLD WIFE AND YOUNG HUSBAND. A NOVEL. IN THREE VOL-UMES. BY MRS. MEEKE, AUTHOR OF ELLESMERE, PALMIRA AND ERMANCE, &C.

> London: Printed at the Minerva-Press, for Lane, Newman, and Co. Leadenhall-Street, 1804.
> I 264p; II 280p; III 277p. 12mo.
> ER 4: 498 (July 1804); WSW I: 394.
> Corvey; CME 3-628-48211-9; xNSTC.

### 1804: 49    [MEEKE, Mary].
SOMETHING ODD! A NOVEL. IN THREE VOLUMES.

London: Printed at the Minerva-Press, for Lane, Newman, and Co. Leadenhall-Street, 1804.

I vii, 286p; II 273p; III 278p. 12mo. 12s boards (CR); 12s (ECB).

CR 3rd ser. 3: 238 (Oct 1804); WSW I: 394.

Corvey; CME 3-628-48654-8; ECB 549; xNSTC.

*Notes.* 'A Dialogue between the Author and his Pen', vol. 1, pp. [i]–vii.


1804: 50    MILLIKIN, Anna.

THE RIVAL CHIEFS; OR, BATTLE OF MERE. A TALE OF ANCIENT TIMES. BY ANNA MILLIKIN, AUTHOR OF "CORFE CASTLE," "PLAN-TAGENET," &C.

Cork: Printed by J. Connor, 1804.

215p. 12mo. 3s 6d (ECB).

WSW I: 396.

BL 12651.b.25; ECB 495; NSTC M2412.

*Notes.* 'Entered at Stationer's Hall' after imprint date. ECB entry dates Mar 1805, and probably relates to the Minerva edn. (see below).

Further edn: 1805 (Corvey—a reissue by Lane, Newman, and Co., with 'Connor, Printer, Cork' on verso of t.p.), CME 3-628-48164-3.


1804: 51    [MOSSE], Henrietta Rouviere.

LUSSINGTON ABBEY. A NOVEL. IN TWO VOLUMES. BY HENRIETTA ROUVIERE.

London: Printed at the Minerva-Press, for Lane, Newman, and Co. Leadenhall-Street, 1804.

I iv, 347p; II 308p. 12mo. 9s sewed (ER).

ER 5: 253 (Oct 1804); WSW I: 474.

Corvey; CME 3-628-48348-4; xNSTC.

*Notes.* 'To the Reviewers', signed Henrietta Rouviere.

Further edn: French trans., 1807.


1804: 52    [MURRAY, Hugh].

THE SWISS EMIGRANTS: A TALE.

London: Printed for T. N. Longman and O. Rees, Paternoster Row, 1804.

126p. 12mo. 4s boards (CR); 4s (ECB).

CR 3rd ser. 1: 357–8 (Mar 1804); ER 3: 506 (Jan 1804); WSW I: 414.

Corvey; CME 3-628-48796-X; ECB 572; NSTC M3703 (BI BL, E).

*Notes.* Preface (19 pp. unn.) outlining background of Swiss Revolution in 1798. Advs. (15 pp. unn.) at the end incorporating a long critique, from the *Monthly Review*, of Henry Zschokke's *History of the Invasion of Switzerland. The Swiss Emigrants* is one of several works subsequently claimed by Louisa Theresa Bellenden Ker (see RLF 11: 400, Item 6 [1822?]), though this title has hitherto been widely attributed to Hugh Murray. See also *Corasmin* (1814: 42).

Further edn: 2nd edn. 1806 (NSTC).

1804: 53   [NERI, Mary Anne].
THE EVE OF SAN-PIETRO. A TALE. IN THREE VOLUMES.

> London: Printed for T. Cadell and W. Davies, Strand; by I. Gold, Shoe-Lane, Fleet-
> Street, 1804.
> I 290p; II 278p; III 250p. 12mo. 10s 6d sewed (ER).
> ER 4: 498 (July 1804); WSW I: 40.
> Corvey; CME 3-628-47638-0; NSTC N563 (BI BL, C, O).

*Notes.* Further edn: French trans., 1823 [as *La Veille de Saint Pierre, ou la vengeance* (MLC)].

1804: 54   PARSONS, [Eliza].
MURRAY HOUSE. "A PLAIN UNVARNISHED TALE." IN THREE VOL-
UMES. BY MRS. PARSONS, AUTHOR OF ERRORS OF EDUCATION,
WOMAN AS SHE SHOULD BE, MYSTERIOUS WARNING, GIRL OF
THE MOUNTAIN, THE PEASANT OF ARDENNE FOREST, THE VAL-
LEY OF ST. GOTHARD, THE MISER AND HIS FAMILY, MYSTERIOUS
VISIT, &C. &C.

> Brentford: Printed by and for P. Norbury; and sold by Hurst, No. 32, Paternoster Row;
> Carpenter and Co. Old-Bond-Street; Earle, Albemarle-Street; Hatchard, Piccadilly;
> and Didier and Tibbett, St. James's-Street, London; also by W. Ansell, Richmond,
> Surrey, 1804.
> I 296p; II 264p; III 331p. 12mo. 15s (ECB, ER).
> ER 4: 498 (July 1804); WSW I: 430–1.
> Corvey; CME 3-628-48398-0; ECB 378; NSTC P564 (BI BL).

*Notes.* Attributed to Mary Meeke, not Parsons, in ER, BDLA, ECB, and NCBEL. The title (as
above) however clearly attributes this work to Eliza Parsons; the Brentford/Norbury imprint
also matches other works by Parsons, but not those by Mary Meeke (a Minerva Press author).

1804: 55   PI[CQ]UENARD, J[ean] B[aptiste].
ZOFLORA, OR, THE GENEROUS NEGRO GIRL. A COLONIAL STORY.
FROM THE FRENCH OF J. B. PIGUENARD. IN TWO VOLUMES.

> London: Printed for Lackington, Allen, and Co. Temple of the Muses, Finsbury Square,
> 1804.
> I iv, 201p; II 235p. 12mo. 7s (ECB); 7s boards (ER).
> ER 4: 249 (Apr 1804); WSW I: 132.
> Corvey; CME 3-628-49004-9; ECB 450; NSTC P1648 (BI BL, O).

*Notes.* Trans. of *Zoflora, ou la bonne négresse, aventure coloniale* (Paris, 1799). Printer's mark
after imprint date reads: '(By T. Appleby, North Shields)'. Collates in sixes.

1804: 56   PIGAULT-LEBRUN, [Charles-Antoine].
THE BARONS OF FELSHEIM. A ROMANCE. IN THREE VOLUMES.
FROM THE FRENCH OF PIGAULT LEBRUN, AUTHOR OF MY UNCLE
THOMAS, MONSIEUR BOTTE, &C.

> London: Printed at the Minerva-Press, for Lane, Newman, and Co. Leadenhall-Street,
> 1804.

I 248p; II 271p; III 287p. 12mo. 12s boards (CR); 12s (ECB).
CR 3rd ser. 2: 236 (June 1804).
ViU PZ2.P534B.1804; ECB 335; xNSTC.

*Notes.* Trans. of *Les Barons de Felsheim* (Paris, 1798). ECB dates Dec 1803.

PIGAULT-LEBRUN, [Charles-Antoine]
See also SEWRIN, Charles Augustin de Bassompierre (1804: 60, 61, 62, 63)

1804: 57   PORTER, Anna Maria.
THE LAKE OF KILLARNEY: A NOVEL, IN THREE VOLUMES. BY
ANNA MARIA PORTER, AUTHOR OF OCTAVIA, WALSH COLVILLE,
&C. &C.

London: Printed for T. N. Longman and O. Rees, Paternoster-Row, 1804.
I viii, 279p; II 307p; III 354p. 12mo.
ER 5: 252 (Oct 1804); WSW I: 446.
Corvey; CME 3-628-48345-X; NSTC P2591 (BI O).

*Notes.* Dedication 'to the Reverend Percival Stockdale, Rector of Lesbury In Northumberland'. Preface dated Thames Ditton, 1804. ECB 464 lists Newman edn. 1833, 16s 6d.
Further edns: 1833 (ECB, Summers); 1838 (NSTC); New edn. 1839 (NUC); Philadelphia
1810 (NUC).

1804: 58   [ROBERTSON, Eliza Frances].
DESTINY: OR, FAMILY OCCURRENCES: AN INTERESTING NARRA-
TIVE. IN TWO VOLUMES.

London: Printed by William Burton, 82, Fetter Lane. Sold by Mr. Ryan, near Pantheon,
    Oxford Street; and may also be had of the principal Booksellers in the United King-
    doms; and at all the Circulating Libraries, n.d. [1804?].
I 176p; II 174p. 12mo. 'Common Edition, Price 6s. Fine 8s. in Boards' (t.p.).
ER 3: 260 (Oct 1803).
BL N.1898; NSTC D947.

*Notes.* Recto following t.p. reads: 'CARD. The Author presents most respectful Thanks to
those Ladies and Gentlemen who did her the Honor of subscribing for this Work; but being
few in number, and some, from a Wish to conceal their Benevolence, having forbid their
Names to appear, a List of Subscribers is omitted.' Eliza Robertson was imprisoned for debt,
and died in the Fleet Prison (Jackson). Collates in sixes. ECB 496 lists 2nd edn. 1804. ER listing points to possible 1803 (or earlier) publication of 1st edn; BLC dates as [*c.* 1810].
Further edn: 2nd edn. 1804 as *Destiny: or, family occurrences of the House of Derwentwater; an
interesting narrative, including the life of the author* (Corvey—with 'Miss Robertson, Late of
Blackheath' and date as '1804' on t.p., and a Preface (in verse) dated and signed 'Fleet, Jan. 1,
1804. E. R.'), CME 3-628-48652-1.

1804: 59   SELDEN, Catherine (*trans.?*).
GERMAN LETTERS, TRANSLATED INTO ENGLISH, BY CATHERINE
SELDEN, AUTHOR OF—"THE ENGLISH NUN,"—"COUNT DE SAN-
TERRE,"—"SERENA,"—&C. &C. ENTERED AT STATIONER'S HALL.

Cork: Printed by J. Connor, Circulating Library, Grand-Parade, 1804.
iv, 153p. 12mo. 3s (ECB).
Corvey; CME 3-628-48636-X; ECB 525; NSTC S1076 (BI BL, C).

*Notes.* Preface asserts that the translated letters are probably the work of 'the same hand', and also acknowledges having condensed some of the material and added direct narrative at points (pp. iii–iv). According to FC 'poses as a translation of a work like *Werther*, which CS had earlier disapproved' (p. 963). ECB dates June 1805, and gives Lane as publisher. Blakey lists as a publication of the Minerva Press (copy not seen) under 1805; no copy of such an edn., however, has been located.

1804: 60   [SEWRIN, Charles Augustin de Bassompierre].
BRICK BOLDING; OR, WHAT IS LIFE? AN ENGLISH, FRENCH, AND ITALIAN ROMANCE. IN TWO VOLUMES. FROM THE FRENCH OF PIGAULT-LEBRUN.

London: Printed at the Minerva-Press, for Lane, Newman, and Co. Leadenhall-Street, 1804.
I vii, 259p; II 226p. 12mo. 6s boards (CR).
CR 3rd ser. 3: 115 (Sept 1804); ER 5: 252 (Oct 1804).
BL 12520.cc.19; ECB 335; NSTC P1721.

*Notes.* Trans. of *Brick Bolding, ou Qu'est-ce que la vie? Roman anglo-franco-italien* (Paris, 1799). BLC enters under Pigault-Lebrun, but suggests a suppositious work. For three other titles attributed by the Minerva Press to Pigault-Lebrun, but actually by Sewrin, see 1804: 61, 62, 63 below. A German trans., *Brick Bolding, oder Was ist das Leben*, apparently from the French, was published in Leipzig, 1800 (RS).

1804: 61   [SEWRIN, Charles Augustin de Bassompierre].
THE FIRST NIGHT OF MY WEDDING. TRANSLATED FROM THE FRENCH OF PIGAULT LEBRUN, AUTHOR OF THE BARONS OF FELSHEIM, MONSIEUR BOTTE, MY UNCLE THOMAS, &C. &C.

London: Printed at the Minerva-Press, for Lane, Newman, and Co. Leadenhall-Street, 1804.
I xii, 240p; II 204p. 12mo. 8s (ECB); 8s sewed (ER).
ER 4: 498 (July 1804).
BL 1608/1629; ECB 335; NSTC P1722.

*Notes.* Trans. of *La Première nuit de mes noces, traduit du champenois par l'auteur de Brick Bolding* (Paris, 1802).

1804: 62   [SEWRIN, Charles Augustin de Bassompierre].
THE HISTORY OF A DOG. WRITTEN BY HIMSELF, AND PUBLISHED BY A GENTLEMAN OF HIS ACQUAINTANCE. TRANSLATED FROM THE FRENCH OF PIGAULT LEBRUN, AUTHOR OF THE BARONS OF FELSHEIM, MONSIEUR BOTTE, MY UNCLE THOMAS, &C. &C.

London: Printed at the Minerva-Press, for Lane, Newman, and Co. Leadenhall-Street, 1804.
viii, 208p. 12mo. 4s boards (CR).

CR 3rd ser. 3: 238 (Oct 1804); ER 5: 252 (Oct 1804); WSW I: 366.
BL 12835.b.33; ECB 335; NSTC P1722.

*Notes.* Trans. of *Histoire d'un chien, écrit par lui-même et publiée par un homme de ses amis* (Paris, 1802).

1804: 63    [SEWRIN, Charles Augustin de Bassompierre].
PAPA BRICK; OR, WHAT IS DEATH? AN ENGLISH, FRENCH, AND ITALIAN ROMANCE. BEING THE SUITE OF BRICK BOLDING. FROM THE FRENCH OF PIGAULT LEBRUN.

London: Printed at the Minerva-Press, for Lane, Newman, and Co. Leadenhall-Street, 1804. 202p. 12mo. 3s 6d boards (CR).
CR 3rd ser. 3: 115 (Sept 1804); ER 5: 252 (Oct 1804); WSW I: 89.
CtY Hfd29.617H; ECB 335; xNSTC.

*Notes.* Trans. of *Papa Brick, ou Qu'est-ce que la mort?* (Paris, 1801). 'The Author and the Bookseller; or a Dialogue by way of a Preface', pp. [1]–8; 'Brick Bolding to his Readers', pp. 9–11. Throughout the first of these the 'Author' speaks of Pigault-Lebrun, whom he greatly admires, as a third party. Novel proper begins p. [13].

1804: 64    SIDDONS, Henry.
VIRTUOUS POVERTY, A TALE. IN THREE VOLUMES. BY HENRY SIDDONS.

London: Printed for Richard Phillips, No. 71, St. Paul's, 1804.
I xii, 267p; II viii, 275p; III vii, 255p. 12mo. 13s 6d (ECB); 13s 6d boards (ER).
ER 4: 498 (July 1804); WSW I: 499.
Corvey; CME 3-628-48697-1; ECB 537; NSTC S1923.5 (BI BL).

*Notes.* Printer's mark after imprint date reads: 'By T. Gillet, Crown-court'. Dedication to the author's mother, dated Hampstead, Monday, 30 Apr 1804.

1804: 65    SINCLAIR, Harvey [pseud.?].
A PEEP AT THE WORLD; OR, THE CHILDREN OF PROVIDENCE. A NOVEL. IN THREE VOLUMES. BY HARVEY SINCLAIR.

London: Printed for Parsons and Son, at their new London Library, No. 46, Ludgate Hill, by J. Adlard, Duke-Street, Smithfield, 1804.
I viii, 236p; II 224p; III 228p. 12mo. 12s boards (CR); 12s (ECB).
CR 3rd ser. 2: 235 (June 1804); ER 3: 506 (Jan 1804); WSW I: 500.
Corvey; CME 3-628-48704-8; ECB 440; NSTC S2070.5 (BI BL).

*Notes.* Dedication 'to Benj. Cooke Griffinhoose, Esq.'. Adv. at end of *Fate; or, Spong Castle* (1803: 72) attributes this title (complete with subtitle) to 'Henry Somerset', and states 'just published'. This opens up the possibility that Henry Sinclair is a pseudonym, and that the true author is Henry Summerset. Allibone gives Harvey Sinclair R.A. as author of this work and of *Remarks on the Army* (1791), though ESTC attributes the latter to Lieut. Henry Sinclair. ECB dates Dec 1803.

1804: 66    SUMMERSETT, Henry.
THE WORST OF STAINS. A NOVEL. BY HENRY SUMMERSETT. IN TWO VOLUMES.

London: Printed for R. Dutton, Gracechurch Street, 1804.
I iv, 200p; II 206p. 12mo. 8s (ECB).
WSW I: 526.
Corvey; CME 3-628-48735-8; ECB 569; xNSTC.

SUMMERSETT, Henry
See SINCLAIR, Henry, A PEEP AT THE WORLD

1804: 67   THOMSON, [Anna? or Harriet?].
THE PRIDE OF ANCESTRY: OR, WHO IS SHE? A NOVEL. IN FOUR
VOLUMES. BY MRS. THOMSON, AUTHOR OF EXCESSIVE SENSIBIL-
ITY—FATAL FOLLIES—THE LABYRINTHS OF LIFE—GERALDINE—
AND ROBERT AND ADELA, &C.
    London: Printed for Parsons & Son, Circulating Library, Ludgate Hill, 1804.
    I 256p; II 227p; III 225p; IV 184p. 12mo. 16s boards (CR); 16s (ECB).
    CR 3rd ser. 2: 235 (June 1804); ER 3: 506 (Jan 1804); WSW I: 537.
    Corvey; CME 3-628-48955-5; ECB 469; NSTC T792 (BI BL).

*Notes.* For the alternative attribution of this title to Anna rather than Harriet Thomson, see
note to *The Labyrinths of Life*, in Vol. 1, 1791: 70. Harriet Thomson (née Pigott) is given as the
author in NUC.

1804: 68   {TUCK, Mary}.
DURSTON CASTLE; OR, THE GHOST OF ELEONORA. A GOTHIC
STORY.
    London: Printed, by C. and W. Galabin, Ingram-Court, Fenchurch-Street, for M. Tuck,
        Circulating Library, near the Adam and Eve, Peckham, 1804.
    vii, 169p. 12mo. 3s (ER).
    ER 5: 253 (Oct 1804).
    Corvey; CME 3-628-47493-0; xNSTC.

*Notes.* 'Address' to Mrs Crespigny, signed 'Mary Tuck', 'Circulating-Library, near the Adam
and Eve, Peckham'. In this, Tuck writes of 'employing my pen to preserve a young family
from immediate distress' (p. vi). Frank (Item 117) states 'until a copy is exhumed and examined, *Durston Castle* must remain an unverified Gothic and a bibliographical mystery'. This
bibliographical mystery is now resolved!

1804: 69   WEST, Miss [pseud.?].
THE TWO MARILLOS; OR, THE MYSTERIOUS RESEMBLANCE. A
ROMANCE, IN THREE VOLUMES. BY MISS WEST.
    London: Printed by Brimmer and Jennings, No. 32, Upper Mary-le-Bone Street; for J.
        F. Hughes, Wigmore-Street, Cavendish-Square, 1804.
    I 207p; II 201p; III 160p. 12mo. 9s boards (CR); 10s 6d (ECB).
    CR 3rd ser. 1: 357 (Mar 1804); ER 3: 506 (Jan 1804).
    Corvey; CME 3-628-48894-X; ECB 630; xNSTC.

*Notes.* 'Notes' at the end of the last vol. (pp. 143–60). The author bears no relation to Mrs
(Jane) West, author of *A Gossip's Story* (1796), and other conservative moral fictions, though

the two are sometimes confused in contemporary circulating library catalogues (a confusion perhaps not counter to the publisher's intentions). ECB dates Dec 1803.

1804: 70   WHITFIELD, Henry.
A PICTURE FROM LIFE: OR, THE HISTORY OF EMMA TANKERVILLE AND SIR HENRY MORETON. BY HENRY WHITFIELD, M.A. IN TWO VOLUMES.

> London: Printed for S. Highley, (Successor to the late Mr. John Murray) No 24, Fleet Street, 1804.
>
> I xxii, 228p; II viii, 232p. 12mo. 8s boards (CR, ER); 8s (ECB).
>
> CR 3rd ser. 2: 348 (July 1804); ER 4: 499 (July 1804); WSW I: 561.
>
> Corvey; CME 3-628-48906-7; ECB 635; NSTC W1750 (BI BL, O).

*Notes.* Further edn: 2nd edn. 1808 (NUC).

1804: 71   WIELAND, C[hristoph] M[artin]; ELRINGTON, John Battersby (*trans.*).
CONFESSIONS IN ELYSIUM, OR THE ADVENTURES OF A PLATONIC PHILOSOPHER; TAKEN FROM THE GERMAN OF C. M. WIELAND; BY JOHN BATTERSBY ELRINGTON, ESQ.

> London: Printed for J. Bell, No. 148, Oxford-Street; by G. Sidney, Northumberland-Street, Strand, 1804.
>
> I xvi, 200p; II 223p; III 228p. 12mo. 12s boards (CR); 12s (ECB); 10s 6d sewed (ER).
>
> CR 3rd ser. 3: 359–60 (Nov 1804); ER 5: 252 (Oct 1804).
>
> MiU 838.W64ge.tE5; ECB 130; xNSTC.

*Notes.* Trans. of *Geheime Geschichte des Philosophen Peregrinus Proteus* (Leipzig, 1790–1). Dedication 'To His Royal Highness Prince William Frederick of Glocester [*sic*]', signed I. B. Elrington, London, 1 Mar 1804. 'To Subscribers', signed 'The Translator' (1 p. unn.): no proper subscription list found. 'To The World', signed 'I. B. E.', dated London, 1 Mar 1804. 24 pp. 'Modern Publications [. . .] printed for Longman, Hurst, Rees, and Orme, Paternoster-Row', dated 1 Aug 1807, bound in at end of vol. 2.
Further edn: 1804 (NSTC W1820). BL 12548.bb.42 has the imprint of the Minerva Press, and identical pagination, indicating a same-year reissue.

1804: 72   WILLIAMS, William Frederick.
THE WORLD WE LIVE IN. A NOVEL. IN THREE VOLUMES. BY WILLIAM FREDERICK WILLIAMS, AUTHOR OF SKETCHES OF MODERN LIFE, FITZMAURICE, TALES OF AN EXILE, &C. &C.

> London: Printed at the Minerva-Press, for Lane, Newman, and Co. Leadenhall-Street, 1804.
>
> I 264p; II 231p; III 243p. 12mo. 10s 6d sewed (ER).
>
> ER 5: 253 (Oct 1804); WSW I: 564.
>
> Corvey; CME 3-628-48928-8; ECB 640; xNSTC.

*Notes.* Dedication 'to Madame Catharine Marie de Vattier'. Mispagination in vol. 2, with sequences from [1]–216 and 145–159.

[?WYNDHAM. Revd], MEN AND WOMEN. A NOVEL

See 1805: 72

1804: 73    [?WYNDHAM, Revd].

**WHAT YOU PLEASE OR, MEMOIRS OF MODERN CHARACTERS; A NOVEL, IN FOUR VOLUMES. BY THE AUTHOR OF 'TOURVILLE.'**

> Bristol: Printed for J. Lansdown, St. John-Street; J. Mills, St. Augustine's Back—Long-man and Rees, T. Hurst, T. Ostell, and Crosby and Co. London, 1804.
>
> I xi, 211p; II 191p; III 220p; IV 241p. 12mo. 1s [*sic*] (ECB); 16s boards (ER).
>
> ER 4: 498 (July 1804); WSW I: 130.
>
> Corvey; CME 3-628-48899-0; ECB 632; NSTC W1495 (BI BL).

*Notes.* Printer's mark after imprint date reads: 'Printed by J. Mills, Bristol' in vols. 1 and 2, and 'J. Mills, Printer' in vols. 3 and 4. For attribution see title of *Men and Women* (1805: 72).

YOUNG, Mary Julia
See BERTHIER, J. B. C.

# 1805

1805: 1    ANON.

**THE ABBEY OF WEYHILL. A ROMANCE. IN TWO VOLUMES. INTER-SPERSED WITH POETRY.**

> London: Printed for the Author, and sold by Lane, Newman, and Co. Leadenhall-Street, 1805.
>
> I 187p; II 189p. 12mo. 6s (ECB, ER).
>
> ER 5: 501 (Jan 1805).
>
> Corvey; CME 3-628-47005-6; ECB 1; xNSTC.

*Notes.* ECB dates Dec 1804.
Further edn: New York 1814 (Early American imprints. Second series; no. 30606 (micro-film)).

1805: 2    ANON.

**BELVILLE-HOUSE, A NOVEL: IN TWO VOLUMES.**

> London: Printed for Chapple, Pall-Mall; and H. D. Symonds, Paternoster-Row; Con-stable, Edinburgh; and Archer, Dublin, 1805.
>
> I 296p; II 312p. 12mo. 8s (ECB, ER).
>
> CR 3rd ser. 7: 106–7 (Jan 1806); ER 6: 493 (July 1805); WSW I: 16.
>
> Corvey; CME 3-628-47235-0; ECB 50; NSTC B1511 (BI BL, O).

1805: 3   ANON.

THE CASTLE OF SANTA FE. A NOVEL. IN FOUR VOLUMES. BY A CLER-
GYMAN'S DAUGHTER, AUTHOR OF JEALOUSY, OR THE DREAD-
FUL MISTAKE.

> London: Printed at the Minerva-Press, for Lane, Newman, and Co. Leadenhall-Street,
> 1805.
> I 260p, ill.; II 267p; III 358p; IV 324p. 12mo. 18s (ECB).
> CR 3rd ser. 5: 218 (June 1805); WSW I: 22.
> Corvey; CME 3-628-47223-7; ECB 100; NSTC C2390 (BI BL, O).

*Notes.* Dedication to the Honourable Mrs Ariana Egerton, with a footnote stating 'This Dedication was designed for the Press, by the truly amiable and lamented Author of this Work, a
short time before she—DIED!'. BL and Bodleian catalogues list under Cleeve, Miss; though
Blakey treats both this title and *Jealousy* (1802: 6) as anonymous. No further information
about Miss Cleeve has been discovered.


1805: 4   ANON.

EDMOND IRONSIDE, OR, THE CAVE OF OSMER; A LEGEND OF THE
NINTH CENTURY. IN THREE VOLUMES.

> London: Printed by D. N. Shury, Berwick-Street, Soho; for J. F. Hughes, Wigmore
> Street, Cavendish Square, 1805.
> I 216p; II 240p; III 260p. 12mo. 12s (ER).
> ER 5: 501 (Jan 1805).
> Corvey; CME 3-628-47578-3; xNSTC.


1805: 5   ANON.

THE FISHERMAN'S HUT; OR ALZENDORF. A NOVEL. IN THREE
VOLUMES.

> London: Printed at the Minerva-Press, for Lane, Newman, and Co. Leadenhall-Street,
> 1805.
> I 263p, ill.; II 291p; III 236p. 12mo. 12s (ECB); 12s sewed (ER).
> ER 5: 501 (Jan 1805); WSW I: 45.
> Corvey; CME 3-628-47601-1; ECB 207; xNSTC.

*Notes.* ECB dates Nov 1804.


1805: 6   ANON.

HYPPOLITUS; OR, THE WILD BOY. A NOVEL. IN FOUR VOLUMES.
TRANSLATED FROM THE FRENCH.

> London: Printed at the Minerva-Press, for Lane, Newman, and Co. Leadenhall-Street,
> 1805.
> I viii, 212p; II 230p; III 212p; IV 224p. 12mo. 16s (ECB); 12s (ER).
> ER 7: 508 (Jan 1806).
> Corvey; CME 3-628-47667-4; ECB 292; NSTC H3572 (BI BL).

*Notes.* Trans. of *Hyppolite, ou l'enfant sauvage* (n.p., 1801).

1805: 7   ANON.

### THE IDIOT HEIRESS. A NOVEL. IN TWO VOLUMES.

London: Printed at the Minerva-Press, for Lane, Newman, and Co. Leadenhall-Street, 1805.
I 242p; II 255p. 12mo. 7s (ECB, ER).
ER 7: 256 (Oct 1805); WSW I: 56.
Corvey; CME 3-628-47878-2; ECB 292; xNSTC.

*Notes.* A later tale 'for youth', *My Bird and My Dog* (1816), attributes on its t.p. this novel and
*The Citizen's Daughter* (1804: 5) to the same author (see Blakey, pp. 216, 255).

1805: 8   ANON.

### MEMOIRS OF M. DE BRINBOC: CONTAINING SOME VIEWS OF ENGLISH AND FOREIGN SOCIETY. IN THREE VOLUMES.

London: Printed for T. Cadell and W. Davies, in the Strand, 1805.
I 290p; II 272p; III 264p. 12mo. 12s (ECB, ER).
CR 3rd ser. 5: 443 (Aug 1805); ER 6: 493 (July 1805); WSW I: 74.
BL N.2333–35; ECB 380; NSTC B4325.

1805: 9   ANON.

### THE MYSTERIOUS FATHER; OR, TRIALS OF THE HEART. A NOVEL. IN FOUR VOLUMES. WRITTEN BY A LADY.

[London]: Albion Press printed, published by J. Cundee, Ivy-Lane; and sold by Chapple, Pall-Mall; and Booth, Duke-Street, Portland-Chapel, 1805.
I iv, 244p; II 249p; III 241p; IV 272p. 12mo. 16s (ECB); 16s boards (ER).
ER 6: 251 (Apr 1805); WSW I: 81.
Corvey; CME 3-628-48178-3; ECB 403; xNSTC.

1805: 10   ANON.

### THE MYSTERIOUS PROTECTOR: A NOVEL. DEDICATED TO LADY CRESPIGNY. IN TWO VOLUMES.

London: Printed for George Robinson, 25, Paternoster-Row, 1805.
I 232p; II 203p. 12mo. 7s (ECB); 7s boards (ER).
ER 7: 257 (Oct 1805), 7: 508 (Jan 1806); WSW I: 467.
Corvey; CME 3-628-48181-3; ECB 403; NSTC P3227 (BI BL).

*Notes.* Dedication signed 'M. C.'. Novel proper ends vol. 2, p. 198, followed by 'Fugitive
Verses' (pp. [199]–203).

1805: 11   ANON.

### ROSETTA, A NOVEL. IN FOUR VOLUMES. BY A LADY, WELL KNOWN IN THE FASHIONABLE WORLD.

Richmond: Printed by and for G. A. Wall, and sold by Longman, Hurst, Rees, and
Orme, Paternoster-Row, London, 1805.
I 244p; II 260p; III 201p; IV 250p. 12mo. 14s (ECB, ER).
CR 3rd ser. 6: 216–17 (Oct 1805); ER 6: 493 (July 1805); WSW I: 106.
Corvey; CME 3-628-48550-9; ECB 503; xNSTC.

*Notes.* Summers lists two novels with the same lead title: *Rosetta: A Novel,* Minerva Press, 1805; and one matching the present full title, but published by Longman, 1807; he also states that the first *Rosetta* has been ascribed by Stephen Jones to Mrs Parsons. It seems not unlikely that in actuality the two *Rosettas* are the same novel, as above.

1805: 12   ANON.
## TIMES PAST; OR SKETCHES OF THE MANNERS OF MANKIND IN THE LAST CENTURY. A ROMANTIC MELANGE. IN THREE VOLUMES.

> London: Printed at the Minerva-Press, for Lane, Newman, and Co. Leadenhall-Street, 1805.
> I xx, 188p; II 279p; III 264p. 12mo. 12s (ECB).
> WSW I: 121.
> Corvey; CME 3-628-48961-X; ECB 591; xNSTC.

*Notes.* Dedication 'to the Nobility and Gentry of the British Empire'. ECB dates Feb 1805.

1805: 13   ANON.
## THE TWO PILGRIMS. A ROMANCE. IN TWO VOLUMES.

> London: Printed at the Minerva-Press, for Lane, Newman, and Co. Leadenhall-Street, 1805.
> I 208p; II 212p. 12mo. 7s (ECB, ER).
> ER 6: 494 (July 1805); WSW I: 124.
> Corvey; CME 3-628-48848-6; ECB 605; xNSTC.

1805: 14   ANON.
## VALOMBROSA; OR THE VENETIAN NUN. A NOVEL. IN TWO VOLUMES.

> London: Printed at the Minerva-Press, for Lane, Newman, and Co. Leadenhall-Street, 1805.
> I 264p; II 306p. 12mo. 12s (CR); 8s (ECB); 12s sewed (ER).
> CR 3rd ser. 4: 329–30 (Mar 1805); ER 5: 253 (Oct 1804); WSW I: 125.
> Corvey; CME 3-628-48855-9; ECB 609; xNSTC.

*Notes.* Evidently by the same author as that of *Forresti* and *Vesuvia* (see 1806: 9 and 1807: 6). CR states: 'We cannot congratulate this gentleman (for a male performance it must certainly be) on the slightest ambition to imitate that delicacy which is one of the many beauties so profusely scattered over the writings of Mrs. Radcliffe' (p. 329). CR lists this title as 3 vols., Lane and Co., 1804, and ER likewise states 3 vols. Blakey also lists as 3 vols., under 1804, but copy not seen. ECB dates Nov 1804, but in 2 vols. No 1804 edn. in 3 vols. has been located.

1805: 15   [ANDERSON, Andreas].
## *MENTAL RECREATIONS. FOUR DANISH AND GERMAN TALES. BY THE AUTHOR OF TOUR IN ZEALAND.

> London: Baldwin, 1805.
> 158p. 8vo. 2s 6d (ECB).

CR 3rd ser. 6: 326 (Nov 1805); WSW I: 74.

No copy located; ECB 381.

*Notes.* ECB, unlike CR, lists publisher as Dutton, and gives format as 12mo. CR recommends as a 'fire-screen'.

1805: 16    BERKENHOUT, Helena.

**THE HISTORY OF VICTORIA MORTIMER. BY MRS. HELENA BERKEN-HOUT. IN FOUR VOLUMES.**

London: Printed by I. Gold, Shoe-Lane, for the Author; and sold by James Wallis, 19, Paternoster-Row, 1805.

I 279p; II 296p; III 312p; IV 286p. 12mo. 18s (ER).

ER 7: 256 (Oct 1805).

Corvey; CME 3-628-47117-6; xNSTC.

*Notes.* Dedication 'to the Right Honourable Lord Auckland'.

1805: 17    BURKE, Mrs.

**THE SECRET OF THE CAVERN. A NOVEL. IN TWO VOLUMES. BY MRS. BURKE, AUTHOR OF THE SORROWS OF EDITH, ELLIOTT, &C.**

London: Printed at the Minerva-Press, for Lane, Newman, and Co. Leadenhall-Street, 1805.

I 221p; II 244p. 12mo. 8s (ECB, ER).

ER 6: 493 (July 1805); WSW I: 180.

Corvey; CME 3-628-47172-9; ECB 85; NSTC B5594 (BI O).

1805: 18    CECIL, Henry Montague.

**THE MYSTERIOUS VISITOR; OR MARY, THE ROSE OF CUMBER-LAND. A NOVEL BY HENRY MONTAGUE CECIL. IN TWO VOLUMES.**

London: Printed for Longman, Hurst, Rees, and Orme, Paternoster-Row; A. Constable and Co. Edinburgh; and by and for F. Jollie, Carlisle, 1805.

I 329p; II 379p. 12mo. 9s (ECB, ER).

ER 6: 493 (July 1805); WSW I: 201.

Corvey; CME 3-628-47243-1; ECB 403; xNSTC.

*Notes.* Colophon of 'F. Jollie, Printer, Carlisle' in both vols. Collates in sixes.

*Further edn:* 1808 as *The Rose of Cumberland* (Corvey—a reissue by the Minerva Press, with a cancel t.p. and the same colophon of F. Jollie), CME 3-628-47244-X.

1805: 19    CHARLTON, Mary.

**THE HOMICIDE. A NOVEL. TAKEN FROM THE COMEDIE DI GOLDONI, BY MARY CHARLTON, AUTHOR OF "THE WIFE AND MISTRESS" &C. IN TWO VOLUMES.**

London: Printed at the Minerva-Press, for Lane, Newman, and Co. Leadenhall-Street, 1805.

I 300p; II 208p. 12mo. 9s (ECB); 5s (ER).

ER 6: 494 (July 1805).

Corvey; CME 3-628-47249-0; ECB 235; xNSTC.

*Notes.* Based on *Commedie scelte di Carlo Goldoni.* Price given as '9s, sewed' on verso of last page of *The Three Old Maids of the House of Penruddock* (1806: 66).

Further edns: 2nd edn. 1813 as *Rosaura di Viralva; or, The Homicide* (NUC); French trans., 1817 [as *Rosaura di Viralva, ou l'homicide* (BN)].

1805: 20   CLARK, Emily.
THE BANKS OF THE DOURO; OR, THE MAID OF PORTUGAL. A TALE. IN THREE VOLUMES. BY EMILY CLARK, GRAND-DAUGHTER OF THE LATE COLONEL FREDERICK, AND AUTHOR OF TANTHE [*sic*] AND ERMINA MONTROSE.

> London: Printed at the Minerva-Press, for Lane, Newman, and Co. Leadenhall-Street, 1805.
> I 294p; II 300p; III 336p. 12mo. 13s 6d (ECB).
> ER 6: 493 (July 1805); WSW I: 206.
> Corvey; CME 3-628-47289-X; ECB 118; NSTC C2080 (BI BL).

*Notes.* Dedication 'to the Right Honorable the Countess of Euston'. 'Ianthe' is spelled correctly on t.ps. of vols. 2 and 3.

1805: 21   CONOLLY, L[uke] A[ylmer].
THE FRIAR'S TALE; OR, MEMOIRS OF THE CHEVALIER ORSINO. WITH OTHER NARRATIVES, BY L. A. CONOLLY, A.B. IN TWO VOLUMES.

> London: Printed for T. Cadell and W. Davies, Strand, 1805.
> I viii, 240p; II 221p. 12mo. 7s (ECB, ER).
> ER 6: 494 (July 1805); WSW I: 218.
> Corvey; CME 3-628-47318-7; ECB 130; NSTC C3384 (BI BL).

*Notes.* Dedication 'To Him'. Preface dated Trinity College, Dublin, Mar 1805.

1805: 22   COTTIN, [Sophie Ristaud].
THE SARACEN, OR MATILDA AND MELEK ADHEL, A CRUSADE-ROMANCE, FROM THE FRENCH OF MADAME COTTIN, WITH AN HISTORICAL INTRODUCTION BY J. MICHAUD, THE FRENCH EDITOR. IN FOUR VOLUMES.

> London: Printed for R. Dutton, 45, Gracechurch-Street, 1805.
> I lxxiii, 279p; II 296p; III 263p; IV 264p. 12mo.
> Corvey; CME 3-628-47580-5; xNSTC.

*Notes.* Trans. of *Mathilde, ou mémoires tirés de l'histoire des croisades* (Paris, 1805). Introduction, vol. 1, pp. [iii]–lxxiii, signed 'J. Michaud, Editor'. Continuous roman and arabic pagination, with novel proper beginning at p. [75]. ECB 138 lists 1809 edn., 20s.

Further edns: 1809 as *Matilda and Malek Adhel, the Saracen [. . .] to which is prefixed a Memoir of the Life of the Authoress by Mr. D. Boileau* (BL 1508/151; NSTC C3821); 3rd edn. 1816 (also as *Matilda and Malek Adhel*) (NSTC); 1833 (NSTC); New York 1810 (NSTC).

1805: 23    [?CRAIK, Helen].
THE NUN AND HER DAUGHTER; OR, MEMOIRS OF THE COUR-
VILLE FAMILY. A NOVEL. IN FOUR VOLUMES.

> London: Printed at the Minerva-Press, for Lane, Newman, and Co. Leadenhall-Street,
>    1805.
> I 315p; II 311p; III 316p; IV 348p. 12mo. 18s (ECB, ER).
> ER 6: 493 (July 1805); WSW I: 84.
> Corvey; CME 3-628-48241-0; ECB 418; NSTC C3896 (BI BL).

*Notes.* Blakey notes attributed to Miss Helen Craik in Minerva Library Catalogue of 1814;
ECB lists under title only.


1805: 24    [DACRE, Charlotte].
CONFESSIONS OF THE NUN OF ST. OMER. A TALE, IN THREE VOL-
UMES. BY ROSA MATILDA.

> London: Printed by D. N. Shury, No. 7, Berwick Street, Soho; for J. F. Hughes, Wigmore
>    Street, Cavendish Square, 1805.
> I 234p; II 192p; III 192p. 12mo. 13s 6d sewed (ER).
> ER 6: 251 (Apr 1805); WSW I: 26, 233.
> Corvey; CME 3-628-47385-3; NSTC D45 (BI BL).

*Notes.* Dedication to 'M. G. Lewis, Esq.'.
Facs: GNI (1972).


1805: 25    DALLAS, R[obert] C[harles].
THE MORLANDS. TALES ILLUSTRATIVE OF THE SIMPLE AND SUR-
PRISING. BY R. C. DALLAS, ESQ. IN FOUR VOLUMES.

> London: Printed for Longman, Hurst, Rees, and Orme, Paternoster-Row, 1805.
> I viii, 233p; II 270p; III 468p; IV 385p. 12mo. 21s (ECB, ER).
> CR 3rd ser. 8: 24–33 (May 1806) full review; ER 7: 508 (Jan 1806); WSW I: 235.
> Corvey; CME 3-628-47393-4; ECB 150; NSTC D99 (BI BL, C, E).

*Notes.* Introduction contains dialogue between author and friend.


1805: 26    [DAVIS, John].
WALTER KENNEDY: AN AMERICAN TALE.

> London: Printed for Longman, Hurst, Rees, and Orme, Paternoster-Row, 1805.
> vii, 192p. 12mo. 4s 6d (ECB, ER).
> ER 6: 494 (July 1805); WSW I: 128.
> Corvey; CME 3-628-48817-6; ECB 621; NSTC D513 (BI BL).

*Notes.* Further edn: 1808 as *Walter Kennedy: An Interesting American Tale* (NUC).


1805: 27    DESFORGES, [Pierre Jean Baptiste] C[houdard].
EUGENE & EUGENIA; OR, ONE NIGHT'S ERROR. A NOVEL. IN THREE
VOLUMES. ALTERED FROM THE FRENCH OF C. DESFORGES.

London: Printed at the Minerva-Press, for Lane, Newman, and Co. Leadenhall-Street, 1805.

I 243p; II 255p; III 251p. 12mo. 12s (ECB, ER).

ER 7: 256 (Oct 1805).

Corvey; CME 3-628-47612-7; ECB 192; xNSTC.

*Notes.* Trans. of *Eugène et Eugénie* (Paris, [1799]).

1805: 28   [D'ISRAELI, Isaac].
FLIM-FLAMS! OR, THE LIFE AND ERRORS OF MY UNCLE, AND THE AMOURS OF MY AUNT! WITH ILLUSTRATIONS AND OBSCURITIES, BY MESSIEURS TAG, RAG, AND BOBTAIL. WITH AN ILLUMINATING INDEX! IN THREE VOLUMES, WITH NINE PLATES.

London: Printed for John Murray, 32, Fleet Street, 1805.

I xvi, 220p, ill.; II 236p, ill.; III 279p, ill. 8vo. 18s boards (CR, ER); 8s (ECB).

CR 3rd ser. 4: 155–7 (Feb 1805) full review; ER 6: 251 (Apr 1805); WSW I: 247.

Corvey; CME 3-628-47756-5; ECB 209; NSTC D1360 (BI BL, C, O).

*Notes.* 'Advertisement. The Reviewers Anticipated!!!', at the beginning of vol. 1, followed by a variety of Shandean preliminaries. 'An Illuminating Index' (22 pp. unn.) at the end of vol. 3. Further edn: 1806 (NSTC).

1805: 29   EDGEWORTH, [Maria].
THE MODERN GRISELDA. A TALE. BY MISS EDGEWORTH, AUTHOR OF PRACTICAL EDUCATION, BELINDA, CASTLE RACKRENT, HISTORY OF IRISH BULLS, LETTERS FOR LITERARY LADIES, POPULAR TALES, &C.

London: Printed for J. Johnson, No. 72, St. Paul's Churchyard; by Bye and Law, St. John's Square, 1805.

170p. 8vo. 5s (CR); 3s (ECB, ER).

CR 3rd ser. 4: 218–19 (Feb 1805); ER 5: 501 (Jan 1805); WSW I: 77, 255–6.

BL 1078.e.34; ECB 178; NSTC E238 (BI C, Dt, O).

*Notes.* ECB dates Dec 1804.

Further edns: 2nd edn. 1805 (Corvey), CME 3-628-47573-2; 3rd edn. 1813 (NSTC); 4th edn. 1819 (NSTC); [1820] (NSTC); 1833 (NSTC); Georgetown 1810 (NUC); French trans., 1813 [as *Les Deux Griseldis* (BN)].

1805: 30   FORTNUM, Sophia [née KING].
THE ADVENTURES OF VICTOR ALLEN. BY MRS. FORTNUM, (LATE SOPHIA KING,), AUTHOR OF WALDORF, OR THE DANGERS OF PHILOSOPHY; CORDELIA, A ROMANCE OF REAL LIFE; THE VICTIM OF FRIENDSHIP, A GERMAN ROMANCE; THE FATAL SECRET, OR UNKNOWN WARRIOR; &C. IN TWO VOLUMES.

London: Printed by D. N. Shury, Berwick-Street, Soho; for W. Hodgson, No. 20, Strand, 1805.

I 182p; II 167p. 12mo. 7s (ER).

ER 7: 256 (Oct 1805); WSW I: 272.

Corvey; CME 3-628-48015-9; NSTC K592 (BI BL).

## 1805: 31   [FRANK, . . . ].
## CECILY FITZ-OWEN; OR, A SKETCH OF MODERN MANNERS. IN TWO VOLUMES.

London: Printed for Vernor and Hood, Poultry; By W. Blackader, 10, Took's Court, Chancery Lane, 1805.

I 283p; II 271p. 12mo. 7s (ER).

ER 5: 501 (Jan 1805); WSW I: 273.

Corvey; CME 3-628-47245-8; NSTC F797 (BI BL).

*Notes.* Attribution is found in H&L and WSW.

## 1805: 32   [GÉRARD, L'Abbé Louis Philippe].
## THE COUNT DE VALMONT; OR, THE ERRORS OF REASON. TRANS-LATED FROM THE FRENCH. IN THREE VOLUMES.

London: Printed for J. Hatchard, Bookseller to Her Majesty, No. 190, opposite Albany House, Piccadilly, 1805.

I vii, 312p; II 310p; III 239p. 12mo. 13s 6d (ECB, ER).

CR 3rd ser. 6: 325–6 (Nov 1805); ER 7: 257 (Oct 1805).

C S735.d.80.18; ECB 139; NSTC G686 (BI O).

*Notes.* Trans. of *Le Comte de Valmont, ou les égarements de la raison* (Paris, 1801). Translator's Preface (vol. 1, pp. [v]–vii) states that only the first of two parts in the original French work in six volumes has been translated; the translator also acknowledges having omitted 'whole pages which I thought uninteresting, or unadapted to an English and a Protestant reader' (p. vi).

## 1805: 33   GODWIN, William.
## FLEETWOOD: OR, THE NEW MAN OF FEELING. BY WILLIAM GOD-WIN. IN THREE VOLUMES.

London: Printed for Richard Phillips, No. 6, Bridge-Street, Blackfriars, 1805.

I xii, 300p; II 295p; III 342p. 12mo. 15s (CR, ECB).

CR 3rd ser. 4: 383–91 (Apr 1805) full review; ER 6: 182–93 (Apr 1805) full review, 6: 251 (Apr 1805); WSW I: 281–2.

Corvey; CME 3-628-47850-2; ECB 234; NSTC G1251 (BI BL, C, O).

*Notes.* Preface dated 14 Feb 1805. BRu ENC copy has 'Georgina Craven Feb. 22 1805' written on front of each vol., matching ECB dating of Feb 1805.
Further edns: 1832 (NSTC); New York 1805 (NSTC); French trans., 1805; German trans., 1806.
Facs: N (1979).

GOLDONI, Carlo
See CHARLTON, Mary

1805: 34   HARRAL, T[homas].
**SCENES OF LIFE. A NOVEL. IN THREE VOLUMES. BY T. HARRAL, ESQ.**

> London: Printed by J. Swan, 76, Fleet Street. For B. Crosby and Co. Stationers'-Court, Paternoster-Row, 1805.
> I viii, 208p; II 199p; III 214p. 12mo. 10s 6d (CR, ER).
> CR 3rd ser. 5: 421–3 (Aug 1805) full review; ER 6: 494 (July 1805); WSW I: 299.
> Corvey; CME 3-628-47628-3; xNSTC.

*Notes.* Dedication 'to John Gifford, Esq.', dated 28 May 1805.


1805: 35   HELME, Elizabeth.
**THE PILGRIM OF THE CROSS; OR, THE CHRONICLES OF CHRISTA-BELLE DE MOWBRAY. AN ANCIENT LEGEND. IN FOUR VOLUMES. BY ELIZABETH HELME, AUTHOR OF ST. MARGARET'S CAVE, OR THE NUN'S STORY; LOUISA, OR THE COTTAGE ON THE MOOR; ST. CLAIR OF THE ISLES, &C. &C.**

> Brentford: Printed by and for P. Norbury; and sold by T. Ostell, Ave-Maria-Lane; Long-man, Hurst, Rees, and Orme, Pater-noster Row; Hatchard, Piccadilly; Carpenter and Co. Old-Bond-Street; and Earle, Albemarle-Street, London; also by W. Ansell, Rich-mond, Surrey, 1805.
> I xii, 263p; II 254p; III 266p; IV 264p. 12mo. 18s (ECB, ER).
> CR 3rd ser. 7: 215 (Feb 1806); ER 7: 508 (Jan 1806); WSW I: 309.
> Corvey; CME 3-628-47788-3; ECB 263; NSTC H1229 (BI BL, C, O).

*Notes.* Dedication 'to the Princess Sophia Matilda of Gloucester'.
Further edn: French trans., 1807.


1805: 36   HERNON, G. D.
**LOUISA; OR THE BLACK TOWER. A NOVEL, IN TWO VOLUMES. BY G. D. HERNON, ESQ.**

> London: Printed for H. D. Symonds, Paternoster-Row, 1805.
> I 207p; II 190p. 12mo. 9s (ECB, ER).
> ER 7: 256 (Oct 1805).
> Corvey; CME 3-628-47782-4; ECB 354; xNSTC.

*Notes.* Imprint in vol. 2 differs by reading: 'Printed for W. Gordon, Circulating Libary, 357, Oxford Street, near the Pantheon'. Collates in sixes.


1805: 37   HOLCROFT, Thomas.
**MEMOIRS OF BRYAN PERDUE: A NOVEL. BY THOMAS HOLCROFT. IN THREE VOLUMES.**

> London: Printed for Longman, Hurst, Rees, and Orme, Paternoster-Row, 1805.
> I viii, 290p; II 268p; III 268p. 12mo. 15s (ECB, ER).
> CR 3rd ser. 7: 14–24 (Jan 1806) full review; ER 7: 256 (Oct 1805); WSW I: 320.
> Corvey; CME 3-628-47729-8; ECB 276; NSTC H2131 (BI BL, C).

*Notes.* Preface dated Berner-Street, London, 5 Sept 1805.
Facs: N (1979).


1805: 38    IRELAND, [Samuel] W[illiam] H[enry].
GONDEZ, THE MONK. A ROMANCE, OF THE THIRTEENTH CEN-
TURY. IN FOUR VOLUMES. BY W. H. IRELAND, AUTHOR OF THE
ABBESS, &C. &C. &C.

> London: Printed for W. Earle, Albemarle-Street, and J. W. Hucklebridge. And sold by
>     Longman, Hurst, Rees, and Orme, Paternoster-Row. And all other Booksellers, 1805.
> I xii, 204p; II iv, 228p; III v, 228p; IV iv, 228p. 12mo. 16s (ECB, ER).
> ER 5: 500 (Jan 1805); WSW I: 340.
> Corvey; CME 3-628-47945-2; ECB 300; NSTC I433 (BI BL, O).

*Notes.* 'Entered at Stationers' Hall' on verso of t.ps. Dedication (in verse) to 'Lumley St.
George Skeffington, Esq. of Skeffington Lodge, Leicestershire'. ECB dates Dec 1804.


1805: 39    [ISAACS, Mrs].
GLENMORE ABBEY; OR, THE LADY OF THE ROCK. A NOVEL. IN
THREE VOLUMES. BY THE AUTHOR OF "ARIEL."

> London: Printed at the Minerva-Press, for Lane, Newman, and Co. Leadenhall-Street,
>     1805.
> I 259p; II 254p; III 250p. 12mo. 12s (ER).
> ER 7: 256 (Oct 1805); WSW I: 343.
> Corvey; CME 3-628-47819-7; xNSTC.


1805: 40    [ISDELL, Sarah].
THE VALE OF LOUISIANA, AN AMERICAN TALE; IN TWO VOLUMES.

> Dublin: Printed by B. Smith, 38, Mary-Street, 1805.
> I 224p; II 243p. 12mo.
> MH-H *EC8.Is247.805v; xNSTC.

*Notes.* Dedication to 'Mrs. O. H.'. This work is given as by the author on the t.p. of Isdell's
*The Irish Recluse* (1809: 34).


1805: 41    KELLY, Isabella.
THE SECRET. A NOVEL. IN FOUR VOLUMES. BY ISABELLA KELLY,
AUTHOR OF MADELINE, ABBEY ST. ASAPH, AVONDALE PRIORY,
EVA, RUTHINGLENNE, BARON'S DAUGHTER, A MODERN INCI-
DENT IN DOMESTIC LIFE, &C. &C.

> Brentford: Printed by and for P. Norbury; and sold by Longman, Hurst, Rees, and
>     Orme, Pater-noster Row; Hatchard, Piccadilly; Carpenter and Co. Old-Bond-Street;
>     Earle, Albemarle-Street; and Didier and Tibett, St. James's Street, London; also by W.
>     Ansell, Richmond, Surrey, 1805.
> I 264p; II 272p; III 254p; IV 263p. 12mo. 18s (ER).
> CR 3rd ser. 6: 437 (Dec 1805); ER 7: 256 (Oct 1805); WSW I: 350.
> Corvey; CME 3-628-47925-8; NSTC K139 (BI BL).

KING, Sophia
See FORTNUM, Sophia

1805: 42   LAFONTAINE, August [Heinrich Julius].
**DOLGORUCKI AND MENZIKOF. A RUSSIAN TALE. IN TWO VOLUMES. FROM THE GERMAN OF AUGUSTUS LA FONTAINE.**

> London: Printed at the Minerva-Press, for Lane, Newman, and Co. Leadenhall-Street, 1805.
> I 314p; II 305p. 12mo. 8s (ECB); 8s sewed (ER).
> ER 5: 501 (Jan 1805).
> BL 12554.aa.38; ECB 326; NSTC L148.

*Notes.* Trans. of *Fedor und Marie, oder Treue bis zum Tode* (Berlin, 1802). ECB dates Nov 1804.

1805: 43   LAFONTAINE, August [Heinrich Julius].
***HERMAN AND EMILIA. FROM THE GERMAN OF AUGUSTUS LA FONTAINE.**

> London: Lane, Newman, and Co., 1805.
> 4 vols.
> No copy located.

*Notes.* Trans. of *Herrmann et Emilie, traduit de l'allemande* (Paris, 1802), original German title *Herrmann Lange* (Berlin, 1799). *Literary Journal*, Sept 1805, p. 1002, gives price as 18s and comments: 'This is said to be a translation from the German of Augustus La Fontaine, who, if everything be his that is laid to his charge, must be allowed to be a most indefatigable novel writer.'

1805: 44   LAFONTAINE, [August Heinrich Julius].
**RODOLPHUS OF WERDENBERG. TRANSLATED FROM THE GERMAN OF LA FONTAINE. IN TWO VOLUMES.**

> London: Printed by D. N. Shury, No. 7, Berwick Street, Soho; for J. F. Hughes, Wigmore Street, Cavendish Square, 1805.
> I 154p; II 160p. 12mo. 7s (ECB, ER).
> ER 6: 494 (July 1805).
> BL 12611.aaa.18; ECB 326; NSTC L160.

*Notes.* Trans. of *Rudolph von Werdenberg* (Berlin, 1793). For an alternative, professedly far more complete version of the German source title, see 1807: 34.

1805: 45   LAMBERT, C. D. L.
**THE ADVENTURES OF COOROO, A NATIVE OF THE PELLEW ISLANDS. BY C. D. L. LAMBERT.**

> Norwich: Printed and sold by Stevenson and Matchett; sold also by Scatcherd and Letterman, Ave-Maria-Lane, London, and all other Booksellers. Entered at Stationers' Hall, n.d. [1805].
> viii, 275p. 8vo. 5s (CR).

CR 3rd ser. 5: 330–1 (July 1805); WSW I: 361.

BL 12612.ff.14; CME 3-628-48026-4; NSTC L286 (BI C, Dt, O).

*Notes.* Dedication to Lady Harriet Berney. 'List of Subscribers' (85 names), pp. [iii]–iv. 'The Author's Apology to the Reader', pp. [vii]–viii, dated Norwich, Feb 1805.


1805: 46   LATHOM, Francis.
THE IMPENETRABLE SECRET, FIND IT OUT! A NOVEL. IN TWO VOLUMES. BY FRANCIS LATHOM, AUTHOR OF MEN AND MANNERS; THE MYSTERY, &C. &C.

London: Printed at the Minerva-Press, for Lane, Newman, and Co. Leadenhall-Street, 1805.
I xi, 277p, ill.; II 259p. 12mo. 9s (ECB, ER).
CR 3rd ser. 6: 438 (Dec 1805); ER 7: 508 (Jan 1806); WSW I: 363.
Corvey; CME 3-628-47955-X; ECB 330; NSTC L544 (BI BL).

*Notes.* Further edn: 2nd edn. 1831 (NSTC).


1805: 47   LATHY, T[homas] P[ike].
THE PARACLETE. A NOVEL. IN FIVE VOLUMES. BY T. P. LATHY, AUTHOR OF USURPATION, &C.

London: Printed at the Minerva-Press, for Lane, Newman, and Co. Leadenhall-Street, 1805.
I 278p; II 258p; III 260p; IV 240p; V 216p. 12mo. 20s (ECB, ER).
ER 7: 256 (Oct 1805); WSW I: 364.
Corvey; CME 3-628-47969-X; ECB 331; NSTC L593 (BI BL).


1805: 48   LATHY, T[homas] P[ike].
USURPATION; OR, THE INFLEXIBLE UNCLE. A NOVEL. IN THREE VOLUMES. BY T. P. LATHY.

London: Printed at the Minerva-Press, for Lane, Newman, and Co. Leadenhall-Street, 1805.
I 246p; II 235p; III 261p. 12mo. 12s (ECB).
WSW I: 364.
Corvey; CME 3-628-47970-3; ECB 331; xNSTC.

*Notes.* ECB dates Mar 1805.


1805: 49   LEE, Harriet.
CANTERBURY TALES. VOLUME THE FIFTH. BY HARRIET LEE.

London: Printed for Geo. Wilkie and John Robinson, No. 57; and Geo. Robinson, No. 25, Paternoster-Row, 1805.
528p. 8vo. 16s (ECB, vols. 4 and 5).
WSW I: 367.
Corvey; CME 3-628-48017-5; ECB 336; NSTC L978 (BI BL).

*Notes.* Containing 'The Landlady's Tale', 'The Friend's Tale', 'The Wife's Tale'.

Further edns: 2nd edn. 1805 (NUC); (as part of collected edns.): 1832 (NSTC); 1837 (NSTC); 1842 (NSTC); Philadelphia 1833 (NSTC); German trans., 1810.

1805: 50   [LEWIS, Alethea].
THE NUNS OF THE DESERT; OR, THE WOODLAND WITCHES. IN
TWO VOLUMES. BY EUGENIA DE ACTON. AUTHOR OF ESSAYS ON
THE ART OF BEING HAPPY; A TALE WITHOUT TITLE, &C.

> London: Printed at the Minerva-Press, for Lane, Newman, and Co. Leadenhall-Street,
> 1805.
> I xii, 319p; II 296p. 12mo. 9s (ECB); 10s (ER).
> ER 6: 493 (July 1805); WSW I: 84, 238.
> Corvey; CME 3-628-47007-2; ECB 3; xNSTC.

LEWIS, Matthew Gregory, THE BRAVO OF VENICE
See ZSCHOKKE, Johann Heinrich

1805: 51   LUCAS, William.
THE DUELLISTS; OR, MEN OF HONOUR: A STORY; CALCULATED TO
SHEW THE FOLLY, EXTRAVAGANCE, AND SIN OF DUELLING. BY
WILLIAM LUCAS.

> [London]: Albion Press printed: Published by J. Cundee, Ivy-Lane, Paternoster-Row;
> Williams and Smith, No. 12, and W. Suttaby, No. 2, Stationers'-Court; and C. Chap-
> ple, Pall-Mall, 1805.
> xvii, 183p, ill. 12mo. 3s 6d (ECB).
> CR 3rd ser. 6: 218 (Oct 1805); WSW I: 378–9.
> BL 1608/4076; ECB 355; NSTC L2568 (BI C, O).

*Notes.* Frontispiece bears the legend 'Pub. July 1 1805 by Williams & Smith, Stationers
Court'.

1805: 52   LYTTLETON, Mr.
FIESCO, COUNT OF LAVAGNE. AN HISTORICAL NOVEL. IN FOUR
VOLUMES. BY MR. LYTTLETON, AUTHOR OF THE FOLLIES OF
FASHION, PEREGRINE, &C.

> London: Printed at the Minerva-Press, for Lane, Newman, and Co. Leadenhall-Street,
> 1805.
> I 250p, ill.; II 231p; III 204p; IV 204p. 12mo. 14s (ECB).
> WSW I: 379.
> Corvey; CME 3-628-48075-2; ECB 357; xNSTC.

1805: 53   [MEEKE, Mary].
THE WONDER OF THE VILLAGE. A NOVEL. IN THREE VOLUMES.

> London: Printed at the Minerva-Press, for Lane, Newman, and Co. Leadenhall-Street,
> 1805.
> I 263p; II 222p; III 230p. 12mo. 12s (ECB).

WSW I: 131.
Corvey; CME 3-628-48978-4; ECB 378; xNSTC.

*Notes.* Introductory note (unn.) states: 'It is with gratitude we express our thanks to an unknown Correspondent for the outlines and plan on which this Novel has been formed. It was accompanied by a Note, signifying that they were found among the papers of a Lady deceased, whose Executors presented them gratuitously to the Proprietors of the Minerva Office'. ECB dates June 1805.

1805: 54  MONTOLIEU, [Jeanne-Isabelle-Pauline Polier de Bottens, Baronne] de.
TALES, BY MADAME DE MONTOLIEU, AUTHOR OF CAROLINE OF LICHTFIELD. IN THREE VOLUMES.

> London: Printed for C. Chapple, 66, Pall-Mall; and sold by all other Booksellers. Henry Reynell, Printer, 21, Piccadilly, 1805.
> I xi, 155p; II 200p; III 152p. 12mo. 10s 6d (ECB); 12s sewed (ER).
> ER 7: 257 (Oct 1805).
> BL 1153.l.15; ECB 393; NSTC P2364 (BI O).

*Notes.* Trans. of *Recueil de contes* (Geneva, 1803). Preface [translator's], vol. 1, pp. [vii]–xi.

1805: 55  MORLEY, G. T.
DEEDS OF DARKNESS; OR, THE UNNATURAL UNCLE: A TALE OF THE SIXTEENTH CENTURY; INCLUDING INTERESTING MEMOIRS, FOUNDED ON FACTS. BY G. T. MORLEY. IN TWO VOLUMES.

> London: Printed by J. D. Dewick, Aldersgate-Street, for Tipper and Richards, Leadenhall-Street, 1805.
> I x, 251p; II 252p. 12mo. 8s (ECB, ER).
> CR 3rd ser. 7: 107–8 (Jan 1806); ER 6: 494 (July 1805); WSW I: 409.
> Corvey; CME 3-628-48333-6; ECB 397; xNSTC.

*Notes.* Dedication to 'Mrs. Wackerbarth (Seymour-House, Mary-La-Bonne)', dated Cold Bath Square, 1 Apr 1805.

1805: 56  NORRIS, Mrs.
SECOND LOVE; OR, THE WAY TO BE HAPPY. A NOVEL. IN TWO VOLUMES. BY MRS. NORRIS.

> London: Printed for B. Crosby & Co. Stationers Court, Paternoster-Row. By Lewis and Roden, Paternoster-Row, 1805.
> I 286p; II 276p. 12mo. 8s (ECB); 7s (ER).
> ER 6: 494 (July 1805); WSW I: 418.
> Corvey; CME 3-628-48237-2; ECB 416; xNSTC.

1805: 57  OPIE, [Amelia Alderson].
ADELINE MOWBRAY, OR THE MOTHER AND DAUGHTER: A TALE, IN THREE VOLUMES. BY MRS. OPIE.

> London: Printed for Longman, Hurst, Rees, & Orme, Paternoster Row; and A. Constable and Co. Edinburgh, 1805.

I 237p; II 237p; III 296p. 8vo. 3s 6d [*sic*] (CR); 13s 6d (ECB); 12s boards (ER); 13s 6d boards (ER).

CR 3rd ser. 4: 219–21 (Feb 1805); ER 5: 500 (Jan 1805), 6: 251 (Apr 1805); WSW I: 7, 421–2.

Corvey; CME 3-628-48260-7; ECB 423; NSTC O382 (BI BL, E, O).

*Notes.* Further edns: 2nd edn. 1805 (NSTC); 3rd edn. 1810 (NUC); 1844 (NSTC); George-town 1808 (NUC); French trans., 1806.

Facs: RR (1995).

1805: 58   PICKAR, Mary.
THE CASTLE OF ROVIEGO; OR, RETRIBUTION. A ROMANCE, IN FOUR VOLUMES. BY MARY PICKAR.

London: Printed by J. Barfield, Wardour Street, for J. Booth, Duke Street, Portland Place, 1805.
I 321p; II 311p; III 270p; IV 295p. 12mo. 21s (ER).
ER 7: 256 (Oct 1805), 10: 492 (July 1807); WSW I: 438.
Corvey; CME 3-628-48414-6; xNSTC.

*Notes.* Block gives the author's name as Pickard, Frank as Picard, and Summers as Pickhard! The present spelling is found, however, in the George Robinson archive, where Mary Pickar appears as the translator of Soulavie's *Mémoires* (see Bentley, pp. 94, 108).

1805: 59   PIGAULT-LEBRUN, [Charles-Antoine].
THE POLANDERS, THE LYING FAMILY, AND THE LIFE OF MY UNCLE, WITH HIS PORTFOLIO. IN TWO VOLUMES. TRANSLATED FROM THE FRENCH OF PIGAULT LEBRUN, AUTHOR OF THE BARONS OF FELSHEIM, MONSIEUR BOTTE, MY UNCLE THOMAS, &C. &C.

London: Printed at the Minerva-Press, for Lane, Newman, and Co. Leadenhall-Street, 1805.
I 260p; II 276p. 12mo. 8s (ECB, ER).
ER 6: 493 (July 1805).
BL 12511.aaa.20; ECB 335; NSTC P1723.

*Notes.* The first title is a trans. of *Métusko, ou les Polonais*, in *Les Cent-vingt jours, ou les quatre nouvelles* (Paris, 1800). 'The Lying Family' begins at vol. 1, p. [149], and is prefaced by a 'Dialogue Between the Author and the Bookseller by way of a Preface'.

1805: 60   PILKINGTON, [Mary].
CRIMES AND CHARACTERS; OR, THE NEW FOUNDLING. IN THREE VOLUMES. BY MRS. PILKINGTON, AUTHOR OF PARENTAL DUPLI-CITY, &C. &C.

London: Printed for W. Earle, and J. W. Hucklebridge; and sold by W. Earle, 47, Albe-marle Street; G. Robinson, Paternoster-Row; Crosby and Co. Stationers' Court; and all other Booksellers, 1805.
I 240p; II 256p; III 248p. 12mo. 12s (ECB); 13s 6d boards (ER).

ER 6: 494 (July 1805); WSW I: 440.

Corvey; CME 3-628-48442-1; ECB 450; NSTC P1762 (BI BL).

*Notes.* 'Entered at Stationers' Hall' on verso of t.ps. Evidently the first fully adult work of fiction by Mary (Hopkins) Pilkington (1766–1839). The Miss or Mrs Pilkington who wrote *The Accusing Spirit* (see 1802: 54), the last of a sequence of novels for the Minerva Press, is apparently another author.

1805: 61   [PORTER, Anna Maria].

A SAILOR'S FRIENDSHIP, AND A SOLDIER'S LOVE. IN TWO VOL-UMES.

London: Printed for Longman, Hurst, Rees, and Orme, Paternoster-Row, 1805.

I viii, 318p; II 184p. 12mo. 8s (ECB, ER).

ER 7: 257 (Oct 1805); WSW I: 106.

Corvey; CME 3-628-48592-4; ECB 511; NSTC P2593 (BI BL).

*Notes.* Dedication to 'the late Lord Duncan'. 'Preface by the Editor', stating that the stories originated from an 'old maiden lady, with whom I became acquainted at Bath' and a 'younger friend of hers' (p. [v]).

1805: 62   RICE, Mrs.

MONTEITH, A NOVEL, FOUNDED ON SCOTTISH HISTORY. BY MRS. RICE, AUTHOR OF "THE DESERTED WIFE." IN TWO VOLUMES.

Gainsborough: Printed by and for H. Mozley: and sold by Longman, Hurst, Rees, and Orme, London, 1805.

I 178p; II 186p. 12mo. 8s (ECB, ER).

ER 7: 507 (Jan 1806); WSW I: 463.

Corvey; CME 3-628-48571-1; ECB 492; NSTC R820 (BI E).

*Notes.* Collates in sixes.

1805: 63   SELDEN, Catherine.

VILLA NOVA; OR, THE RUINED CASTLE. A ROMANCE. IN TWO VOLUMES. BY CATHERINE SELDEN, AUTHOR OF COUNT DE SAN-TERRE, THE SAILORS, ENGLISH NUN, &C.

London: Printed for Lane, Newman, and Co., 1805.

I 240p; II 194p. 12mo. 7s (ECB).

WSW I: 491.

Corvey; CME 3-628-48638-6; ECB 525; NSTC S1077 (BI BL).

*Notes.* Printer's mark reads: 'Connor, Printer, Cork'. ECB dates Apr 1805.

1805: 64   SERRES, {Olivia} [Wilmot].

ST. JULIAN: IN A SERIES OF LETTERS. BY MRS. J. T. SERRES.

London: Printed by D. N. Shury, Berwick-Street, Soho; for J. Ridgway, 170, Piccadilly, 1805.

167p, ill. 8vo.

CR 3rd ser. 6: 326–7 (Nov 1805); WSW I: 492.

MH-H EC8.Se685.805s; xNSTC.

*Notes.* Frontispiece portrait of 'Olivia Serres'.

1805: 65    SICKELMORE, Richard.

RASHLEIGH ABBEY; OR, THE RUIN ON THE ROCK. A ROMANCE. IN THREE VOLUMES. BY RICHARD SICKELMORE, AUTHOR OF RAY-MOND; MARY-JANE; AGNES AND LEONORA; EDGAR, OR THE PHAN-TOM OF THE CASTLE, &C. &C.

London: Printed at the Minerva-Press, for Lane, Newman, and Co. Leadenhall-Street, 1805.

I vii, 244p; II 260p; III 239p. 12mo. 12s (ECB, ER).

ER 7: 508 (Jan 1806); WSW I: 499.

Corvey; CME 3-628-48693-9; ECB 537; xNSTC.

*Notes.* Dedication 'to the Right Honourable Lady Charlotte Lennox'.

1805: 66    SPENCE, Elizabeth Isabella.

THE NOBILITY OF THE HEART: A NOVEL. BY ELIZABETH ISABELLA SPENCE, AUTHOR OF HELEN SINCLAIR. IN THREE VOLUMES.

London: Printed for Longman, Hurst, Rees, and Orme, Paternoster-Row, 1805.

I 299p; II 281p; III 251p. 12mo. 13s 6d (ECB); 13s 6d boards (ER).

CR 3rd ser. 5: 218 (June 1805); ER 5: 500 (Jan 1805); WSW I: 517–18.

Corvey; CME 3-628-48722-6; ECB 554; xNSTC.

SUMMERSETT, Henry, ALL SORTS OF LOVERS

See 1811: 76

1805: 67    [TAYLOR, Miss].

THE HEIRESS OF AVONMORE. A NOVEL. IN THREE VOLUMES. BY THE AUTHOR OF THE NOBLEMAN AND HIS STEWARD.

London: Printed at the Minerva-Press, for Lane, Newman and Co. Leadenhall-Street, 1805.

I 247p, ill.; II 343p; III 328p. 12mo. 12s (ECB); 12s sewed (ER).

ER 5: 501 (Jan 1805).

Corvey; CME 3-628-47723-9; ECB 263; xNSTC.

*Notes.* For author attribution, see *The Nobleman and his Steward* (1803: 69). ECB dates Nov 1804.

1805: 68    TEMPLE, Mrs. {F.}.

FERDINAND FITZORMOND; OR, THE FOOL OF NATURE. BY MRS. TEMPLE. IN FIVE VOLUMES.

London: Printed for Richard Phillips, No. 6, Bridge-Street, Blackfriars; by B. M'Millan, Bow-Street, Covent-Garden, 1805.

I vii, 303p; II 368p; III 347p; IV 298p; V 341p. 12mo. 21s (ER).

ER 7: 257 (Oct 1805); WSW I: 533.

Corvey; CME 3-628-48948-2; ECB 582; NSTC T460 (BI BL).

*Notes.* 'Advertisement', signed 'F. Temple', dated London, May, 1805.

1805: 69   WILLIAMS, William Frederick.
THE WITCHERIES OF CRAIG ISAF. IN TWO VOLUMES. BY WILLIAM
FREDERICK WILLIAMS, AUTHOR OF TALES OF AN EXILE, THE
WORLD WE LIVE IN, &C. &C.

London: Printed at the Minerva-Press, for Lane, Newman, and Co. Leadenhall-Street,
1805.
I 272p; II 260p. 12mo. 6s (CR); 8s sewed (ER).
CR 3rd ser. 3: 470 (Dec 1804); ER 5: 253 (Oct 1804), 5: 501 (Jan 1805); WSW I: 564.
Corvey; CME 3-628-48967-9; ECB 640; xNSTC.

*Notes.* Blakey places under 1804, but copy not seen.

1805: 70   WILLIAMS, W[illiam] F[rederick].
THE YOUNG FATHER. A NOVEL. IN THREE VOLUMES. BY W. F. WIL-
LIAMS, AUTHOR OF TALES OF AN EXILE; THE WITCHERIES OF
CRAIG ISAF; THE WORLD WE LIVE IN, &C. &C.

London: Printed at the Minerva-Press, for Lane, Newman, and Co. Leadenhall-Street,
1805.
I 265p; II 280p; III 252p. 12mo. 12s (ECB, ER).
ER 7: 508 (Jan 1806); WSW I: 564.
Corvey; CME 3-628-48929-6; ECB 640; xNSTC.

*Notes.* ER lists as 'The Young Husband'.

1805: 71   WOODFALL, Sophia.
ROSA; OR, THE CHILD OF THE ABBEY. A NOVEL. IN FOUR VOL-
UMES. BY SOPHIA WOODFALL, AUTHOR OF MONTRAVERS.

London: Printed by D. N. Shury, No. 7, Berwick Street, Soho, for J. F. Hughes, Wigmore
Street, Cavendish-Square, 1805.
I 216p; II 246p; III 244p; IV 232p. 12mo. 16s (ECB); 16s boards (ER).
ER 5: 501 (Jan 1805).
Corvey; CME 3-628-48982-2; ECB 647; xNSTC.

*Notes.* ECB dates Oct 1804.

1805: 72   [?WYNDHAM, Revd].
MEN AND WOMEN, A NOVEL, IN THREE VOLUMES. DEDICATED
TO SIR JAMES MACKINTOSH, BY THE AUTHOR OF 'WHAT YOU
PLEASE,' 'TOURVILLE,' &C.

Bristol: Printed for J. Lansdown, St. John-Street; J. Mills, St. Augustine's Back—Longman
and Co. T. Ostell, Crosby and Co. Lane and Newman, London.—Mozley, Gainsborough, and Wilson and Spence, York. J. Mills, Printer, St. Augustine's Back, Bristol, 1805.

I iv, 210p; II 206p; III ii, 238p. 12mo. 13s 6d (ECB); 12s boards (ER); 13s 6d boards (ER).
ER 5: 501 (Jan 1805), 6: 251 (Apr 1805); WSW I: 74.
Corvey; CME 3-628-47482-5; ECB 381; NSTC W3133.5 (BI BL).

*Notes.* Dedication to Sir James Mackintosh, Recorder of Bombay. Attributed to the Revd Mr Wyndham by Summers (p. 412). BL 1568/8750 is an incomplete set (wanting vols. 1 and 2), with imprint reading 'Bristol: Printed for J. Lansdown, St. John-Street; J. Mills, St. Augustine's Back—Longman and Rees, T. Hurst, T. Ostell, and Crosby and Co. London. J. Mills, Printer, 1804'. No other evidence has been discovered, however, in support of publication in 1804. ECB dates Jan 1805.

1805: 73   [YORKE, Mrs. R. P. M.].
MY MASTER'S SECRET; OR, THE TROUBLESOME STRANGER. IN TWO VOLUMES.

> London. Printed at the Minerva-Press, for Lane, Newman, and Co. Leadenhall-Street, 1805.
> I 268p; II 312p. 12mo. 7s (ECB, ER).
> ER 5: 501 (Jan 1805); WSW I: 81.
> Corvey; CME 3-628-48173-2; ECB 652; xNSTC.

*Notes.* Dedication 'to Her Grace The Duchess Of Bedford', signed 'The Editor'. ECB dates Dec 1804.

1805: 74   YOUNG, Mary Julia.
DONALDA; OR, THE WITCHES OF GLENSHIEL. A CALEDONIAN LEGEND, IN TWO VOLUMES. BY MARY JULIA YOUNG, AUTHOR OF MOSS CLIFF ABBEY; RIGHT AND WRONG; THE EAST INDIAN; ROSE MOUNT CASTLE, &C.

> London: Printed by D. N. Shury, No. 7, Berwick Street, Soho; for J. F. Hughes, Wigmore Street, Cavendish Square, 1805.
> I 288p; II 315p. 12mo. 13s (ECB); 10s (ER).
> ER 6: 251 (Apr 1805); WSW I: 577.
> Corvey; CME 3-628-48991-1; ECB 653; xNSTC.

*Notes.* Further edn: [1843] (NSTC 2Y2017).

1805: 75   [ZSCHOKKE, Johann Heinrich]; LEWIS, M[atthew] G[regory] (*trans.*).
THE BRAVO OF VENICE, A ROMANCE: TRANSLATED FROM THE GERMAN BY M. G. LEWIS.

> London: Printed by D. N. Shury, No. 7, Berwick Street, Soho, for J. F. Hughes, Wigmore Street, Cavendish Square, 1805.
> viii, 340p. 8vo. 6s (CR, ECB); 6s boards (ER).
> CR 3rd ser. 5: 252–6 (July 1805) full review; ER 5: 501 (Jan 1805); WSW I: 371.
> BL 12547.g.29; ECB 343; NSTC Z92 (BI C, E, O).

*Notes.* Trans. of *Abällino, der große Bandit* (Leipzig, 1803). Dedication to the Earl of Moira, signed M. G. Lewis, Inveraray Castle, 27 Oct 1804. Summers states actually published in Dec

1804, and that some few copies carry this date on t.p.; no copy with this imprint date, however, has been located. ECB dates Dec 1804.

Further edns: 2nd edn. 1805 (Corvey), CME 3-628-48040-X; 5th edn. 1807 (NSTC); 6th edn. 1809 (NSTC); 7th edn. 1818 (NSTC); 8th edn. 1826 (NUC); [at least 4 more edns. to 1850]; New York [1804] (NUC); French trans. 1806.

Facs: GNI (1972).


# 1806


1806: 1   ANON.

THE BRAVO OF BOHEMIA; OR, THE BLACK FOREST. A ROMANCE. IN FOUR VOLUMES. BY A LADY.

> London: Printed at the Minerva Press, for Lane, Newman, and Co. Leadenhall-Street, 1806.
> I ii, 279p; II 222p; III 303p; IV 292p. 12mo. 18s (ECB).
> WSW I: 18.
> ViU PZ2.B7371806; ECB 72; xNSTC.

*Notes.* Dedication to Lady Emily M'Leod, dated 30 Apr 1806. ECB dates Oct 1806. Title in 2nd edn. of 1819, also issued by the Minerva Press, lists the author's other publications as 'Jessy, or the Rose of Donald's Cottage; Yamboo, or the North American Slave, &c. &c'. This helps link a chain of three novels by this female author—see 1812: 18 and 1818: 10.
Further edns: 2nd edn. 1819 (Corvey; NSTC 2B39354), CME 3-628-47274-1; 3rd edn. 1832 (NSTC).


1806: 2   ANON.

THE CHILDREN OF ERROR. A NOVEL. IN TWO VOLUMES. BY AN OFFICER OF DRAGOONS.

> Brentford: Printed by and for P. Norbury; and sold by T. Ostell, Ave Maria Lane, London, 1806.
> I 216p; II 238p. 12mo. 7s (ECB, ER).
> ER 9: 500 (Jan 1807); WSW I: 24.
> Corvey; CME 3-628-47281-4; ECB 110; xNSTC.


1806: 3   ANON.

CONSTANTIA DE COURCY, A NOVEL, IN TWO VOLUMES. IMITATED FROM THE FRENCH.

> London: Printed for the Author, by J. Whiting, Finsbury Place; and published by J. Richardson, Royal Exchange, 1806.
> I 202p; II 192p. 12mo. 6s (ER).

ER 9: 248 (Oct 1806); WSW I: 27.
Corvey; CME 3-628-47322-5; xNSTC.

*Notes.* No French original discovered.

1806: 4 ANON.
THE COTTAGER'S DAUGHTER. A TALE OF THE NINETEENTH CEN-
TURY. IN TWO VOLUMES.

> London: Printed for B. Crosby and Co. Stationers' Court, Paternoster-Row, 1806.
> I ii, 220p; II 234p. 12mo. 8s (ECB, ER).
> ER 8: 229 (Apr 1806); WSW I: 28.
> BL C.171.a.15; ECB 138; NSTC C3799.

*Notes.* Preface dated London, 1 Oct 1805.

1806: 5 ANON.
DELLINGBOROUGH CASTLE; OR, THE MYSTERIOUS RECLUSE. A
NOVEL. IN TWO VOLUMES.

> London: Printed at the Minerva-Press, for Lane, Newman, and Co. Leadenhall-Street,
> 1806.
> I 238p; II 200p. 12mo. 7s (ECB, ER).
> ER 9: 248 (Oct 1806); WSW I: 32.
> Corvey; CME 3-628-47407-8; ECB 158; NSTC D807 (BI BL).

1806: 6 ANON.
DONALD. A NOVEL. IN THREE VOLUMES.

> London: Printed by I. Gold, Shoe-Lane, for Longman, Hurst, Rees, and Orme, Pater-
> noster-Row, 1806.
> I 335p; II 324p; III 213p. 12mo. 13s 6d (ECB); 13s 6d boards (ER).
> ER 9: 500 (Jan 1807); WSW I: 34.
> Corvey; CME 3-628-47448-5; ECB 168; NSTC D1544 (BI BL, C).

1806: 7 ANON.
EVERSFIELD ABBEY: A NOVEL. BY THE AUTHORESS OF THE AUNT
AND THE NIECE.

> London: Printed for B. Crosby and Co. Stationers'-Court, 1806.
> I 244p; II 269p; III 273p. 12mo. 12s (ECB, ER).
> CR 3rd ser. 7: 329 (Mar 1806); ER 7: 508 (Jan 1806); WSW I: 146.
> Corvey; CME 3-628-47594-5; ECB 194; NSTC E1542 (BI BL).

*Notes.* See *The Aunt and the Niece* (1804: 3) for a possible link with Mrs E. M. Foster and other
authors.

1806: 8 ANON.
FERDINAND AND AMELIA. A NOVEL. IN THREE VOLUMES.

> London: Printed by Dewick and Clarke, Aldersgate-Street, for B. Crosby and Co.
> Stationers'-Court, Paternoster-Row, 1806.

I 211p; II 243p; III 224p. 12mo. 10s 6d (ECB, ER).
CR 3rd ser. 7: 328–9 (Mar 1806); ER 7: 508 (Jan 1806); WSW I: 43.
Corvey; CME 3-628-47504-X; ECB 203; xNSTC.

1806: 9    ANON.
**FORRESTI; OR, THE ITALIAN COUSINS. A NOVEL. IN THREE VOL-
UMES. BY THE AUTHOR OF VALAMBROSA [*sic*].**

London: Printed at the Minerva-Press, for Lane, Newman, and Co. Leadenhall-Street,
1806.
I 290p; II 280p; III 299p. 12mo. 13s 6d (CR, ECB).
CR 3rd ser. 11: 96–7 (May 1807).
Corvey; CME 3-628-47824-3; ECB 211; xNSTC.

*Notes.* 'P.S.' at the end of vol. 3 concerning over-severe 'criticism upon his last publication'
(see 1805: 14) in the *Critical Review*: male authorship implied.

1806: 10    ANON.
**GLENCORE TOWER; OR, THE FEUDS OF SCOTLAND. A LEGEND OF
THE THIRTEENTH CENTURY. IN TWO VOLUMES.**

London: Printed at the Minerva-Press, for Lane, Newman, and Co. Leadenhall-Street,
1806.
I 242p; II 264p. 12mo. 8s (ECB).
Corvey; CME 3-628-47857-X; ECB 233; NSTC G1180 (BI E).

*Notes.* ECB dates July 1806.

1806: 11    ANON.
**HIDE AND SEEK; OR, THE OLD WOMAN'S STORY. A NOVEL. IN
THREE VOLUMES.**

London: Printed at the Minerva-Press, for Lane, Newman, and Co. Leadenhall-Street,
1806.
I vii, 226p; II vii, 214p; III vii, 220p. 12mo. 10s 6d (ECB, ER).
ER 7: 508 (Jan 1806); WSW I: 53.
Corvey; CME 3-628-47684-4; ECB 267; xNSTC.

1806: 12    ANON.
**THE LAST MAN, OR OMEGARUS AND SYDERIA, A ROMANCE IN
FUTURITY. IN TWO VOLUMES.**

London: Printed for R. Dutton, 15, Gracechurch-Street, 1806.
I 220p; II 204p. 12mo. 7s (ER).
CR 3rd ser. 8: 443 (Aug 1806); ER 8: 479 (July 1806); WSW I: 64.
Corvey; CME 3-628-47899-5; NSTC L528 (BI BL, O).

1806: 13    ANON.
**THE MYSTERIOUS SISTERS, A SPANISH ROMANCE. IN TWO VOLUMES.**

London: Printed for J. F. Hughes, 5, Wigmore Street, Cavendish-Square, by R. Wilks,
80, Chancery Lane, 1806.

I 6, 251p; II 190p. 12mo. 7s (ER).

ER 7: 508 (Jan 1806); WSW I: 81.

Corvey; CME 3-628-48182-1; xNSTC.

*Notes.* 'Preface by the Translator' identifies the source story as *Avalos, or The Three Sisters of the Castle de Fuente* by Don Francisco Sancho Assensio; but no Spanish original discovered. Drop-head title in vol. 2 reads: 'It is, and it is not; or, The Three Sisters of the Castle De Fuente'.

1806: 14   ANON.

A SIMPLE NARRATIVE; OR, A VISIT TO THE NEWTON FAMILY. IN TWO VOLUMES.

London: Printed at the Minerva Press, for Lane, Newman, and Co. Leadenhall-Street, 1806.

I 249p; II 245p. 12mo. 7s (ECB); 7s sewed (ER).

ER 9: 500 (Jan 1807).

Corvey; CME 3-628-48700-5; ECB 538; NSTC N865 (BI BL).

1806: 15   ANON.

THE STRANGER; OR, THE NEW MAN OF FEELING.

[London] Albion Press: Printed by and for James Cundee, Ivy-Lane; and M. Jones, Paternoster-Row, 1806.

138p, ill. 8vo. 4s (ECB, ER).

ER 9: 248 (Oct 1806); WSW I: 115.

Corvey; CME 3-628-54710-5; ECB 565; NSTC S4142 (BI BL).

*Notes.* Dedication to William Dacre and George Elliott, dated London, July 1806; followed by a letter to 'William Dacre, Esq. Kirklinton Hall, Cumberland' signed 'J. C*********', headed Pentonville, 8 July 1806.

1806: 16   ANON.

TWO GIRLS OF EIGHTEEN. IN TWO VOLUMES. BY AN OLD MAN.

London: Printed by J. Barfield, Wardour-Street, Soho. Published and sold by G. Walker, 106, Great Portland-Street. Sold also by T. Ostell, Ave-Maria-Lane, 1806.

I 265p; II 289p. 12mo. 8s (ER).

ER 8: 479 (July 1806).

Corvey; CME 3-628-48845-1; ECB 619; xNSTC.

*Notes.* ECB and NCBEL attribute to George Walker, though this is not substantiated by other catalogues.

1806: 17   ARMSTRONG, Leslie.

THE ANGLO-SAXONS; OR, THE COURT OF ETHELWULPH. A ROMANCE. IN FOUR VOLUMES. BY LESLIE ARMSTRONG, ESQ.

London: Printed at the Minerva-Press, for Lane, Newman, and Co. Leadenhall-Street, 1806.

I xxiv, 282p; II 282p; III 286p; IV 300p. 12mo. 18s (ECB, ER).

ER 9: 248 (Oct 1806); WSW I: 134.
Corvey; ECB 26; NSTC A1659 (BI BL).

1806: 18   BENNETT, [Anna Maria].
VICISSITUDES ABROAD; OR, THE GHOST OF MY FATHER. A
NOVEL. IN SIX VOLUMES. BY MRS. BENNETT, AUTHOR OF ANNA;
JUVENILE INDISCRETIONS; AGNES DE COURCI; ELLEN; BEGGAR
GIRL, &C.
> London: Printed at the Minerva-Press, for Lane, Newman, and Co. Leadenhall-Street,
> 1806.
> I vi, 308p; II 340p; III 323p; IV 355p; V 316p; VI 384p. 12mo. 36s (ECB, ER).
> ER 8: 229 (Apr 1806).
> Corvey; CME 3-628-47253-9; ECB 50; NSTC B1579 (BI BL).

*Notes.* Further edn: French trans., 1808 [as *La Malédiction paternelle, ou l'ombre de mon père*
(DBI)].

1806: 19   BRISTED, John.
EDWARD AND ANNA; OR, A PICTURE OF HUMAN LIFE. A NOVEL.
BY JOHN BRISTED, OF THE HONOURABLE SOCIETY OF THE INNER
TEMPLE, AUTHOR OF THE SYSTEM OF THE QUAKERS EXAMINED.
IN TWO VOLUMES.
> London: Printed by Dewick and Clarke, Aldersgate-Street, for B. Crosby and Co.
> Stationers'-Court, 1806.
> I xvi, 233p; II 210p. 12mo. 7s (ER).
> ER 8: 479 (July 1806); WSW I: 172.
> Corvey; CME 3-628-47159-1; xNSTC.

*Notes.* Dedication 'to the Rev. Nathaniel Bristed, Vicar of Sherborne, in Dorsetshire' (the
author's father), dated Inner Temple, 16 Jan 1806.

1806: 20   BUTLER, Harriet.
VENSENSHON; OR, LOVE'S MAZES. A NOVEL. IN THREE VOLUMES.
BY MRS. HARRIET BUTLER.
> London: Printed for the Author, by Brimmer and Jennings, No. 32, Upper Mary-Le-
> Bone Street, 1806.
> I 231p; II 230p; III 244p. 12mo. 15s (ER).
> ER 8: 229 (Apr 1806); WSW I: 183.
> Corvey; CME 3-628-47151-6; ECB 89; xNSTC.

*Notes.* 'Advertisement', signed 'H. B——.', dated Mar 1806.

1806: 21   BYRON, [Elizabeth] [afterwards STRUTT].
ANTI-DELPHINE: A NOVEL, FOUNDED ON FACTS. BY MRS. BYRON.
IN TWO VOLUMES.
> London: Printed for J. Mawman, 22, Poultry, by W. Flint, Old Bailey, 1806.
> I x, 305p; II 290p. 12mo. 8s (CR, ECB, ER).

CR 3rd ser. 11: 99 (May 1807); ER 8: 229 (Apr 1806); WSW I: 185.
Corvey; CME 3-628-47154-0; ECB 90; NSTC S4206 (BI BL).

*Notes.* Dedication to the author's mother, dated Hull, Feb 1806.
Further edn: 1818 (NUC).


1806: 22   CAREY, D[avid].
SECRETS OF THE CASTLE; OR, THE ADVENTURES OF CHARLES
D'ALMAINE. IN TWO VOLUMES. BY D. CAREY, AUTHOR OF THE
PLEASURES OF NATURE, REIGN OF FANCY, &C.

> London: Printed by J. Swan, 76, Fleet Street, for B. Crosby and Co. Stationers' Court,
> Paternoster Row, 1806.
> I 215p; II 212p. 12mo. 7s (ER).
> ER 8: 479 (July 1806); WSW I: 197.
> Corvey; CME 3-628-47213-X; xNSTC.

*Notes.* Dedication 'to the Right Honourable W. Windham, M.P.'.


1806: 23   CURTIES, T. J. Horsley.
ST. BOTOLPH'S PRIORY; OR, THE SABLE MASK. AN HISTORIC
ROMANCE. BY T. J. HORSLEY CURTIES, ESQ. AUTHOR OF ETHEL-
WINA, ANTIENT RECORDS, SCOTISH LEGENDS, AND THE WATCH
TOWER. IN FIVE VOLUMES.

> London: Printed by D. N. Shury, Berwick Street, Soho; for J. F. Hughes, Wigmore
> Street, Cavendish Square, 1806.
> I 312p; II 256p; III 327p; IV 324p; V 363p. 12mo. 25s (ER).
> ER 7: 508 (Jan 1806); WSW I: 232.
> Corvey; CME 3-628-47747-6; ECB 148; NSTC C4589 (BI BL).

*Notes.* Dedication 'to the Right Honourable the Earl of Macclesfield', dated Oct 1805, Vale
Place, Hammersmith Road.


1806: 24   [CUTHBERTSON, Catherine].
SANTO SEBASTIANO: OR, THE YOUNG PROTECTOR. A NOVEL. IN
FIVE VOLUMES. BY THE AUTHOR OF "THE ROMANCE OF THE
PYRENÉES."

> London: Printed for George Robinson, 25, Paternoster-Row, 1806.
> I 418p; II 405p; III 416p; IV 422p; V 455p. 12mo. 30s (ECB, ER).
> ER 9: 500 (Jan 1807); WSW I: 233.
> BL 12650.aaa.166; ECB 514; NSTC C4645 (BI E).

*Notes.* Colophon in vol. 1 reads: 'T. Davison, Printer, Whitefriars'; vols. 2, 3, and 4 read:
'Printed by William Ballintine, Duke-Street, York-buildings, Strand'; vol. 5 reads: 'Printed
by S. Hollingsworth, Crane-Court, Fleet-street'. ECB dates Oct 1806.
Further edns: 2nd edn. 1809 (NSTC); 3rd edn. 1814 (Corvey), CME 3-628-48619-X; 4th edn.
1820 (NUC); 1847 (NSTC); Philadelphia 1813 (NUC). Published in penny numbers as *The
Heiress of Montalvan; or, First and Second Love*, W. Caffyn, Oxford Street, London, 1845–6
(Summers).

1806: 25    DACRE, Charlotte.
ZOFLOYA; OR, THE MOOR: A ROMANCE OF THE FIFTEENTH CEN-
TURY. IN THREE VOLUMES. BY CHARLOTTE DACRE, BETTER
KNOWN AS ROSA MATILDA, AUTHOR OF THE NUN OF ST. OMERS,
HOURS OF SOLITUDE, &C.

> London: Printed for Longman, Hurst, Rees, and Orme, Paternoster-Row, 1806.
> I 283p; II 283p; III 236p. 12mo. 13s 6d (ECB); 12s (ER).
> ER 8: 479 (July 1806); WSW I: 233–4.
> Corvey; CME 3-628-47388-8; ECB 149; NSTC B6026 (BI O).

*Notes.* Further edn: French trans., 1812.
Facs: GNII (1974).

1806: 26    [DAVIS, John].
THE POST-CAPTAIN; OR, THE WOODEN WALLS WELL MANNED;
COMPREHENDING A VIEW OF NAVAL SOCIETY AND MANNERS.

> London: Printed for Thomas Tegg, 111, Cheapside, by G. Hazard, 49, Beech-Street, 1806.
> 300p. 8vo. 7s (CR).
> CR 3rd ser. 10: 325–6 (Mar 1807); WSW I: 404.
> Corvey; CME 3-628-48364-6; xNSTC.

*Notes.* Vignette t.p., with illustration of a man-of-a-war. Sadleir (Item 678) states that 3rd
edn. (and perhaps also the 2nd edn.), carried on its t.p. an ascription of the work 'to the
author of Zeluco' [i.e. Dr John Moore]. R. H. Case in his edn. of 1928 identifies the true
author as John Davis (1775–1854). ECB 465 lists new edn., Vernor, 1810, 7s.
Further edns: 3rd edn. 1808 (NSTC P2699); 4th edn. 1810 (NUC); 5th edn. 1811 (NSTC);
1813 (NSTC); 1815 (NSTC); [at least 4 more edns. to 1850]; New York 1813 (NUC).

1806: 27    [DENNIS, Thomasine].
SOPHIA ST. CLARE. A NOVEL. IN TWO VOLUMES.

> London: Printed for J. Johnson, St. Paul's Churchyard, 1806.
> I 200p; II 204p. 12mo. 6s (CR, ECB, ER).
> CR 3rd ser. 10: 402–3 (Apr 1807) full review; ER 8: 479 (July 1806); WSW I: 241.
> Corvey; CME 3-628-48714-5; ECB 550; NSTC S199 (BI BL).

1806: 28    EDGEWORTH, Mrs.
ADELAIDE; OR, THE CHATEAU DE ST. PIERRE. IN FOUR VOLUMES.
A TALE OF THE SIXTEENTH CENTURY. BY MRS. EDGEWORTH.

> London: Printed by D. N. Shury, Berwick Street, Soho, for J. F. Hughes, No. 5, Wig-
> more-Street, Cavendish-Square, 1806.
> I 218p; II 227p; III 247p; IV 228p. 12mo. 18s (ECB, ER).
> ER 9: 248 (Oct 1806); WSW I: 255.
> BL 12611.bbb.9; ECB 178; NSTC E222.

1806: 29    EDGEWORTH, [Maria].
LEONORA. BY MISS EDGEWORTH. IN TWO VOLUMES.

London: Printed for J. Johnson, No. 72, St. Paul's Churchyard, 1806.

I 291p; II 291p. 8vo. 10s (ECB); 10s 6d (ER).

CR 3rd ser. 7: 215–16 (Feb 1806); ER 8: 206–13 (Apr 1806) full review, 8: 229 (Apr 1806); WSW I: 256.

Corvey; CME 3-628-47571-6; ECB 178; NSTC E235 (BI BL, C, Dt, E, O).

*Notes.* ECB (mistakenly?) gives Baldwin as publisher.

Further edns: 1815 (NSTC); New York 1806 (NSTC); French trans., 1807; German trans., 1807?


1806: 30    [FRANCES, Sophia].
**VIVONIO; OR, THE HOUR OF RETRIBUTION. A ROMANCE. IN FOUR VOLUMES. BY A YOUNG LADY.**

London: Printed at the Minerva-Press, for Lane, Newman, and Co. Leadenhall-Street, 1806.

I 286p; II 272p; III 298p; IV 348p. 12mo. 8s (ECB); 18s (ER).

ER 8: 229 (Apr 1806); WSW I: 127.

Corvey; CME 3-628-47834-0; ECB 616; NSTC V497.5 (BI BL).

*Notes.* Further edn: French trans., 1820.


1806: 31    GENLIS, [Stéphanie-Félicité, Comtesse de].
**ALPHONSINE: OR, MATERNAL AFFECTION. A NOVEL. BY MADAME GENLIS. IN FOUR VOLUMES.**

London: Printed for J. F. Hughes, 5, Wigmore-Street, Cavendish-Square; by R. Wilks, 89, Chancery-Lane, 1806.

I 372p; II 309p; III 424p; IV 355p. 12mo. 22s (ER).

ER 9: 248 (Oct 1806); WSW I: 240.

CtY-BR Hfd29.298c; ECB 225; xNSTC.

*Notes.* Trans. of *Alphonsine, ou la tendresse maternelle* (Paris, 1806). ECB dates 1807.
Further edn: 2nd edn. 1807 (NSTC 2B4975).


1806: 32    GENLIS, [Stéphanie-Félicité, Comtesse de].
**\*THE IMPERTINENT WIFE: A MORAL TALE, FROM THE FRENCH OF MADAME GENLIS.**

London: Lane, Newman, and Co., 1806.

1 vol. 12mo. 3s 6d (ECB, ER).

ER 8: 479 (July 1806).

No copy located; ECB 225.

*Notes.* Trans. of *L'Épouse impertinente* (Paris, 1804). In Blakey, but copy not seen. Fuller title (given above) follows ER.


1806: 33    GENLIS, [Stéphanie-Félicité, Comtesse] de.
**MADAME DE MAINTENON, TRANSLATED FROM THE FRENCH OF MADAME DE GENLIS.**

London: Printed for Longman, Hurst, Rees and Orme, Pater-Noster Row, 1806.
I xxiv, 263p; II 263p. 12mo. 8s (ECB, ER).
ER 8: 479 (July 1806).
MH-H *FC7.G2875.Eg806mc; ECB 225; xNSTC.

*Notes.* Trans. of *Madame de Maintenon* (Paris, 1806). 'Dedicatory Epistle to Mrs. Chinnery'. CR 3rd ser. 9: 476–9 (Supplement [Dec 1806/Jan 1807]) offers full review of '*Madam* [*sic*] *de Maintenon, intended as a Sequel to the History of the Duchess de la Vallière.* By Madame de Genlis. 2 vols. small 8vo. Paris. Imported by Deconchy. 1806'; though it is unclear whether this refers to an edn. in French or English.

1806: 34   HAMILTON, [Ann] M[ary].
THE FOREST OF ST. BERNARDO. A NOVEL, IN FOUR VOLUMES. BY
MISS M. HAMILTON.

London: Printed by D. N. Shury, Berwick-Street, Soho. For J. F. Hughes, No. 5,
Wigmore-Street, Cavendish-Square, 1806.
I 176p; II 236p; III 216p; IV 236p. 12mo. 18s (ER).
ER 8: 229 (Apr 1806); WSW I: 296.
O 249.s.67–70; NSTC H299.

*Notes.* Further edn: 2nd edn. 1806 (Corvey), CME 3-628-47548-1.

1806: 35   HARVEY, Jane.
THE CASTLE OF TYNEMOUTH. A TALE. BY JANE HARVEY, AUTHOR
OF WARKFIELD CASTLE, &C. &C. IN TWO VOLUMES.

London: Printed for Longman, Hurst, Rees, & Orme, Paternoster-Row; and Vernor,
Hood, and Sharpe, Poultry, 1806.
I viii, 208p; II 194p. 12mo. 7s 6d (ECB, ER).
ER 8: 229 (Apr 1806); WSW I: 300–1.
Corvey; CME 3-628-47643-7; ECB 257; NSTC H763 (BI O).

*Notes.* Preface dated Newcastle, 12 Feb 1806. Imprint on vol. 2 reads: 'Printed for Vernor, Hood, and Sharpe, Poultry; and Longman, Hurst, Rees, and Orme, Paternoster-Row'. Colophon in both vols. reads: 'North Shields: Printed by T. Appleby'.
Further edn: 2nd edn. Newcastle-upon-Tyne 1830 (NSTC).

1806: 36   HUNTER, [Rachel].
LADY MACLAIRN, THE VICTIM OF VILLANY [*sic*]. A NOVEL. IN
FOUR VOLUMES. BY MRS. HUNTER, OF NORWICH, AUTHOR OF
LETITIA; THE UNEXPECTED LEGACY; THE HISTORY OF THE
GRUBTHORPE FAMILY; PALMERSTONE'S LETTERS, &C. &C.

London: Printed for W. Earle and J. W. Hucklebridge; and sold by W. Earle, No. 47,
Albemarle Street; George Robinson, Paternoster Row; B. Crosby and Co. Stationer's
Court; Tho. Ostell, Ave Maria Lane; and all other Booksellers, 1806.
I iv, 316p; II 368p; III 340p; IV 311p. 12mo. 21s (ER).
ER 8: 479 (July 1806).
Corvey; CME 3-628-47802-2; NSTC H3174 (BI BL, O).

1806: 37   [ISAACS, Mrs].
THE WOOD NYMPH, A NOVEL; IN THREE VOLUMES. BY THE
AUTHOR OF "ARIEL," AND "GLENMORE ABBEY."

London: Printed for C. Chapple, Pall Mall; and Southampton-Row, Russell-Square. By
C. Stower, Pater-noster Row, 1806.
I 224p; II 224p; III 208p. 12mo. 12s (ER).
ER 9: 248 (Oct 1806); WSW I: 343.
BL C.171.aa.4; NSTC I524.

Notes. Variant printer information on t.p. of vol. 3: 'By J. G. Barnard, 57, Snow-Hill'.
Further edn: 1806 (Corvey—a reissue by the Minerva Press, with identical pagination and
the same colophon of 'C. Stower, Printer, Paternoster-row' in vols. 1 and 2), CME 3-628-
48980-6.

1806: 38   KENDAL, Mrs. [A.].
MORELAND MANOR; OR, WHO IS THE HEIR? A NOVEL, IN THREE
VOLUMES. BY MRS. KENDAL, AUTHOR OF DERWENT PRIORY, CAS-
TLE ON THE ROCK, &C. &C.

London: Printed for Longman, Hurst, Rees, and Orme, Paternoster-Row, 1806.
I viii, 246p; II 296p; III 254p. 12mo. 12s (ECB, ER).
ER 9: 248 (Oct 1806); WSW I: 351.
Corvey; CME 3-628-47916-9; ECB 318; NSTC K241 (BI BL).

1806: 39   KENLEY, Marianne.
THE COTTAGE OF THE APPENINES, OR, THE CASTLE OF NOVINA.
A ROMANCE. IN FOUR VOLUMES. DEDICATED, BY PERMISSION,
TO THE MOST NOBLE THE MARCHIONESS OF DONEGALL. BY
MARRIANNE [sic] KENLEY.

Belfast: Printed at the Public Printing-Office, 1806.
I 251p; II 226p; III 210p; IV 208p. 12mo.
BL 12603.aa.11; NSTC K272.

Notes. Dedication and 'An Address to the Reader and Critic', both dated May 1802. Collates
in sixes.

1806: 40   LAFONTAINE, August [Heinrich Julius]; POWELL, J[ames] (trans.).
THE VILLAGE OF FRIEDEWALDE: OR, THE ENTHUSIAST. A NOVEL.
TRANSLATED FROM THE ORIGINAL GERMAN OF AUGUSTUS
LAFONTAINE, BY J. POWELL. IN THREE VOLUMES.

London: Printed for J. F. Hughes, 5, Wigmore Street, Cavendish-Square, by R. Wilks,
89, Chancery-Lane, 1806.
I 230p; II 189p; III 174p. 12mo. 13s 6d (ER).
ER 8: 229 (Apr 1806).
BL 12547.bb.25; NSTC L155.

Notes. BLC lists as a trans. of Das Nadelöhr, oder die Schwärmerei; but no further information
concerning an original source title has been discovered.

1806: 41   LAKE, Eliza.
THE WHEEL OF FORTUNE. A NOVEL. IN THREE VOLUMES. BY
ELIZA LAKE, AUTHOR OF DE VALCOURT.

> London: Printed by D. N. Shury, No. 7, Berwick Street, Soho, for J. F. Hughes, Wigmore
> Street, Cavendish Square, 1806.
> I iv, 256p; II 251p; III 261p. 12mo. 13s 6d (ECB).
> Corvey; CME 3-628-47895-2; ECB 632; xNSTC.

*Notes.* Preface signed 'E. Lake', 38, Upper John Street, Fitzroy Square, 1805. ECB dates Sept
1805.

1806: 42   LATHOM, Francis.
THE MYSTERIOUS FREEBOOTER: OR, THE DAYS OF QUEEN BESS. A
ROMANCE. IN FOUR VOLUMES. BY FRANCIS LATHOM, AUTHOR
OF MEN AND MANNERS; MYSTERY; ASTONISHMENT; THE IMPEN-
ETRABLE SECRET, &C. &C.

> London: Printed at the Minerva-Press, for Lane, Newman, and Co. Leadenhall-Street,
> 1806.
> I xii, 339p; II 316p; III 336p; IV 391p. 12mo. 21s (ECB); 20s (ER).
> CR 3rd ser. 8: 327 (July 1806); ER 8: 229 (Apr 1806); WSW I: 363.
> Corvey; CME 3-628-48229-1; ECB 330; NSTC L545 (BI O).

*Notes.* Further edns: 3rd edn. 1829 (NSTC); 1844 (NSTC).

1806: 43   LATHY, T[homas] P[ike].
THE INVISIBLE ENEMY; OR, THE MINES OF WIELITSKA. A POLISH
LEGENDARY ROMANCE. IN FOUR VOLUMES. BY T. P. LATHY,
AUTHOR OF USURPATION, THE PARACLETE, &C. &C.

> London: Printed at the Minerva-Press, for Lane, Newman, and Co. Leadenhall-Street,
> 1806.
> I xii, 308p; II 264p; III 283p; IV 345p. 12mo. 20s (ECB, ER).
> CR 3rd ser. 8: 328 (Nov 1806); ER 9: 248 (Oct 1806); WSW I: 364.
> Corvey; CME 3-628-47968-1; ECB 331; NSTC L592 (BI BL, O).

1806: 44   [LESLIE, Mrs].
FIRESIDE STORIES; OR, THE PLAIN TALES OF AUNT DEBORAH AND
HER FRIENDS. IN THREE VOLUMES. BY THE AUTHOR OF A PLAIN
STORY, GLEANINGS OF A WANDERER, &C.

> London: Printed at the Minerva-Press, for Lane, Newman, and Co. Leadenhall-Street,
> 1806.
> I 178p; II 232p; III 235p. 12mo. 8s (ECB); 9s (ER).
> ER 9: 248 (Oct 1806); WSW I: 44.
> Corvey; CME 3-628-47552-X; ECB 206; xNSTC.

*Notes.* Blakey notes attributed to Mrs Leslie in Minerva Library Catalogue of 1814.

LEWIS, Matthew Gregory, FEUDAL TYRANTS
See NAUBERT, Christiane Benedicte Eugenie

1806: 45    MANNERS, [Catherine].
CASTLE NUOVIER; OR, HENRII AND ADELINA. A ROMANCE. IN
TWO VOLUMES. BY MRS. MANNERS.

> London: Printed for B. Crosby and Co. Stationers' Court, Paternoster Row; by Swan
> and Son, 76, Fleet Street, 1806.
> I 316p; II 323p. 12mo. 8s (ECB, ER).
> ER 8: 479 (July 1806); WSW I: 386.
> Corvey; CME 3-628-48085-X; ECB 366; xNSTC.

1806: 46    [MEEKE, Mary].
SOMETHING STRANGE. A NOVEL. IN FOUR VOLUMES. BY
GABRIELLI, AUTHOR OF THE MYSTERIOUS HUSBAND, INDEPEND-
ENCE, &C. &C.

> London: Printed at the Minerva-Press, for Lane, Newman, and Co. Leadenhall-Street,
> 1806.
> I 280p; II 324p; III 332p; IV 353p. 12mo. 18s (ECB, ER).
> ER 8: 479 (July 1806); WSW I: 394.
> Corvey; CME 3-628-47884-7; ECB 549; xNSTC.

1806: 47    MILLER, J[ohann] M[artin]; HAWKINS, Lætitia-Matilda (*trans.*).
SIEGWART: A MONASTIC TALE. TRANSLATED FROM THE GERMAN
OF J. M. MILLER BY LÆTITIA-MATILDA HAWKINS. IN THREE
VOLUMES.

> London: Printed for J. Carpenter, Old Bond Street, 1806.
> I xix, 331p; II 351p; III 405p. 12mo. 15s (ER).
> ER 8: 229 (Apr 1806).
> BL 12547.f.10; NSTC M2382.

*Notes.* Trans. of *Siegwart: Eine Klostergeschichte* (Leipzig, 1776). Introduction (vol. 1, pp.
[v]–xvi) claims a fuller and more accurate translation than *Sigevart, A Tale* (1799): 'Two very
small volumes, containing the outline of the story, and that very much mutilated, were printed
at Chelsea in 1799, for G. Polidore [*sic*], with no other designation than the initials H. L.' (p. xiv).

1806: 48    MONTAGUE, Edward.
THE CASTLE OF BERRY POMEROY. A NOVEL. IN TWO VOLUMES.
BY EDWARD MONTAGUE, AUTHOR OF MONTONI, OR THE CON-
FESSIONS OF THE MONK OF ST. BENEDICT, &C.

> London: Printed at the Minerva-Press, for Lane, Newman, and Co. Leadenhall-Street,
> 1806.
> I 296p; II 320p. 12mo. 9s (ECB, ER).
> ER 9: 248 (Oct 1806); WSW I: 401.
> Corvey; CME 3-628-48268-2; ECB 392; NSTC M2911.5 (BI BL).

MORGAN, Lady Sydney
See OWENSON, Sydney

1806: 49    [MOSSE], Henrietta Rouviere.
**THE HEIRS OF VILLEROY. A ROMANCE. IN THREE VOLUMES. BY HENRIETTA ROUVIERE, AUTHOR OF LUSSINGTON ABBEY, &C.**

> London: Printed at the Minerva-Press, for Lane, Newman, and Co. Leadenhall-Street, 1806.
> I xi, 236p, ill.; II 274p; III 380p. 12mo. 12s (ECB); 13s 6d (ER).
> ER 7: 508 (Jan 1806); WSW I: 474.
> Corvey; CME 3-628-48347-6; ECB 399; NSTC R1780 (BI O).

*Notes.* ECB dates Nov 1805.

1806: 50    [NAUBERT, Christiane Benedicte Eugenie]; LEWIS, M[atthew] G[regory] (*trans.*).
**FEUDAL TYRANTS; OR, THE COUNTS OF CARLSHEIM AND SARGANS. A ROMANCE. TAKEN FROM THE GERMAN. IN FOUR VOLUMES. BY M. G. LEWIS, AUTHOR OF THE BRAVO OF VENICE, ADELGITHA, RUGANTINO, &C.**

> London: Printed by D. N. Shury, Berwick-Street, Soho, for J. F. Hughes, Wigmore Street, Cavendish Square, 1806.
> I 310p; II 352p; III 410p; IV 338p. 12mo. 28s (ECB, ER).
> CR 3rd ser. 11: 273–8 (July 1807) full review; ER 9: 500 (Jan 1807); WSW I: 372.
> BL 1156.3.22; ECB 343; NSTC L1499 (BI C).

*Notes.* A free trans. of *Elisabeth Erbin von Toggenburg, oder Geschichte der Frauen von Sargans in der Schweiz* (Leipzig, 1789).
Further edns: 2nd edn. 1807 (Corvey), CME 3-628-48043-4; 3rd edn. 1807 (NSTC); French trans., 1810 [as *Les Orphelines de Werdenberg* (MLC)].

1806: 51    NORRIS, Mrs.
**THE STRANGERS; A NOVEL. IN THREE VOLUMES. BY MRS. NORRIS, AUTHOR OF SECOND LOVE, &C.**

> London: Printed by W. Glendinning, 25, Hatton Garden; and published for the Author, by Vernor, Hood, and Sharpe, Poultry, London, 1806.
> I xxiii, 306p; II 376p; III 364p. 12mo. 15s (ER).
> CR 3rd ser. 8: 443 (Aug 1806); ER 8: 479 (July 1806).
> IU 823.N79s; NSTC N1196 (BI Dt).

*Notes.* 'To The Reader', dated London, Apr 1806. 'List of Subscribers' (*c.*240 names), vol. 1, pp. [ix]–xxiii.
Further edn: 1807 as *Olivia and Marcella; or, the Strangers* (Corvey), CME 3-628-48236-4. This 'second edition' was issued by B. Crosby and Co., and, apart from lacking the subscription list, has identical pagination.

1806: 52    OPIE, [Amelia Alderson].
**SIMPLE TALES: BY MRS. OPIE. IN FOUR VOLUMES.**

> London: Printed for Longman, Hurst, Rees, and Orme, Paternoster Row, 1806.

I 352p; II 301p; III 321p; IV 282p. 12mo. 21s (ECB, ER).

CR 3rd ser. 8: 443–6 (Aug 1806); ER 8: 229 (Apr 1806), 8: 465–71 (July 1806) full review, 8: 479 (July 1806); WSW I: 422.

BRu ENC; ECB 423; xNSTC.

*Notes.* Further edns: 2nd edn. 1806 (NSTC O387); 3rd edn. 1809 (Corvey), CME 3-628-51111-9; 4th edn. 1815 (NSTC); Georgetown 1807 (NUC); German trans., 1819 [as *Kleine Romane und Erzählungen* (RS)].

1806: 53    OWENSON, [Sydney] [afterwards MORGAN, Lady Sydney].
**THE NOVICE OF SAINT DOMINICK. BY MISS OWENSON, AUTHOR OF ST. CLAIR. IN FOUR VOLUMES.**

London: Printed for Richard Phillips, No. 6, Bridge-Street, Blackfriars, by T. Gillet, Salisbury-Square, 1806.
I 364p; II 379p; III 393p; IV 395p. 12mo. 'Price Eighteen Shillings, in boards' (t.p.); 20s (ECB, ER).
ER 7: 256 (Oct 1805); WSW I: 425.
Corvey; CME 3-628-48325-5; ECB 396; NSTC O732 (BI BL, C, O).

*Notes.* ECB dates Sept 1805.
Further edns: 2nd edn. 1806 (NSTC); 3rd edn. 1808 (NSTC); 4th edn. 1823 (BRu ENC); Philadelphia 1807 (NUC); French trans., 1817.

1806: 54    OWENSON, [Sydney] [afterwards MORGAN, Lady Sydney].
**THE WILD IRISH GIRL; A NATIONAL TALE. BY MISS OWENSON, AUTHOR OF ST. CLAIR, THE NOVICE OF ST. DOMINICK, &C. &C. &C. IN THREE VOLUMES.**

London: Printed for Richard Phillips, 6, Bridge Street, Blackfriars, 1806.
I xxxiii, 261p; II 265p; III 264p. 12mo. 15s (ECB); 13s 6d (ER).
CR 3rd ser. 9: 327–8 (Nov 1806); ER 9: 248 (Oct 1806); WSW I: 425.
Corvey; CME 3-628-48373-5; ECB 396; NSTC O737 (BI BL).

*Notes.* 'Introductory Letter', vol. 1, pp. [i]–xxxiii. Continuous roman and arabic pagination, with 'Letter 1' beginning at p. [35].
Further edns: 3rd edn. 1807 (NSTC); 4th edn. 1808 (NUC); 5th edn. 1813 (NSTC); 1846 (NSTC); 1850 (NSTC); New York 1807 (NUC) [also Philadelphia 1807 (NSTC, NUC)]; German trans., 1807 [as *Glorwina, das Naturmädchen in Irland* (RS)]; French trans., 1813 [as *Glorvina, ou la Jeune Irlandaise* (BN)].
Facs: IAN (1979); RR (1995).

1806: 55    PALMER, John.
**THE MYSTIC SEPULCHRE; OR, SUCH THINGS HAVE BEEN. A SPANISH ROMANCE. IN TWO VOLUMES. BY JOHN PALMER, AUTHOR OF THE "HAUNTED CAVERN"—"MYSTERY OF THE BLACK TOWER"—'WORLD AS IT GOES," &C.**

London: Printed by J. Nichols, Earl's-Court, Leicester-Square, for W. Earle, Albemarle-Street, Piccadilly, 1806.

I 192p; II 192p. 12mo. 8s (ECB); 8s boards (ER).
ER 11: 238 (Oct 1807).
Corvey; CME 3-628-48378-6; ECB 431; xNSTC.

*Notes.* Dedication to 'George Ambrose Baker, Esq. of Salisbury', dated London, 20 May 1806. ECB dates July 1807.
Further edns: 1807 (NSTC P177); French trans., 1810 [as *Le Tombeau mystérieux, ou les familles de Hénarez et d'Almanza* (BN)].

1806: 56    RAYNER, W. H.
**VIRTUE AND VICE. A NOVEL. IN TWO VOLUMES. BY W. H. RAYNER.**

London: Printed for the Author, and sold by W. Thiselton, Circulating Library, 37 Goodge Street, 1806.
I iv, 224p; II 223p. 12mo. 9s (ECB, ER).
ER 7: 508 (Jan 1806); WSW I: 458.
Corvey; CME 3-628-48454-5; ECB 480; NSTC R291 (BI O).

*Notes.* Preface signed 'W. H. Rayner'. Colophons read: 'W. Matthew Thiselton, Printer, Goodge Street, London'. ECB dates Dec 1805 and gives the publisher as Ostell. A catalogue of the Minerva Library of 1814 lists the author as Mr Rayner.

1806: 57    ROBERTS, Mrs. {D.}.
**DELMORE, OR MODERN FRIENDSHIP. A NOVEL. IN THREE VOLUMES. BY MRS. ROBERTS.**

London: Printed for the Author, and sold by R. Faulder, New Bond-Street, 1806.
I xii, 228p; II 236p; III 234p. 12mo.
Corvey; CME 3-628-48653-X; xNSTC.

*Notes.* Dedication 'to Her Royal Highness the Princess of Wales' signed D. Roberts, Clarence Place. 'List of Subscribers' (*c.*110 names), vol. 1, pp. [viii]–xiii. 'Additional Subscribers' (7 more names) at end of vol. 3. NUC lists as by Margaret Roberts (née Wade), d. 1813, but this title is apparently by a different author: see also note to 1814: 47. ECB 496 lists Crosby edn., Oct 1809, 12s.
Further edn: 1809 (NSTC R1164).

1806: 58    RYMER, M.
**THE SPANIARD; OR, THE PRIDE OF BIRTH. A TALE, BY M. RYMER.**

London: Printed for G. Robinson, 25, Paternoster-Row, 1806.
224p. 12mo. 3s 6d (ECB, ER).
ER 9: 500 (Jan 1807); WSW I: 476.
Corvey; CME 3-628-48590-8; ECB 509; NSTC R2209 (BI O).

*Notes.* NUC attributes to James Malcolm Rymer, who however only appears to have published after 1839; another Rymer, James (fl. 1775–1822) was a surgeon writer. Allibone, NSTC, and Summers all attribute this title to M. Rymer, without expansion.
Further edns: 1815 (NSTC); German trans., 1826 [as *Pedrosa's Abentheuer* (RS)].

1806: 59    [SANDS, James].
**THE EVENTFUL MARRIAGE, A TALE. IN FOUR VOLUMES. BY THE AUTHOR OF "COUNT DI NOVINY" AND "MONCKTON".**

London: Printed by C. Stower, Pater-noster Row. For B. Crosby and Co. Stationers'-Court, 1806.
I 325p; II 307p; III 325p; IV 332p. 12mo. 18s (ECB, ER).
CR 3rd ser. 7: 329 (Mar 1806); ER 7: 508 (Jan 1806); WSW I: 40–1.
Corvey; CME 3-628-47639-9; ECB 194; xNSTC.

*Notes.* Introductory poem (1 p. unn.), described as 'a parody on "Blest as the immortal gods is he, &c." Mr. Philip's admirable translation from the Greek of Sappho'. Last page in vol. 3 mistakenly numbered 337. ECB dates Dec 1805.

1806: 60   SEMPLE, Robert.
**CHARLES ELLIS: OR, THE FRIENDS; A NOVEL. COMPRISING THE INCIDENTS AND OBSERVATIONS OCCURRING ON A VOYAGE TO THE BRAZILS AND WEST INDIES, ACTUALLY PERFORMED BY THE WRITER, ROBERT SEMPLE: AUTHOR OF "WALKS AND SKETCHES AT THE CAPE OF GOOD HOPE." IN TWO VOLUMES.**
London: Printed by and for C. and R. Baldwin, New Bridge-Street, 1806.
I iv, 258p; II 241p. 12mo. 9s (CR); 12s (ECB); 7s (ER).
CR 3rd ser. 10: 102 (Jan 1807); ER 9: 500 (Jan 1807); WSW I: 491.
Corvey; CME 3-628-48645-9; ECB 527; xNSTC.

*Notes.* Preface dated London, 1 July 1805.

1806: 61   [SHOWES, Mrs. (*trans.*)].
**DOMESTIC SCENES. FROM THE GERMAN. IN THREE VOLUMES. BY THE AUTHOR OF AGNES DE LILIEN, STATIRA, RESTLESS MATRON, &C. &C.**
London: Printed at the Minerva Press, for Lane, Newman, and Co. Leadenhall-Street, 1806.
I 352p; II 329p; III 323p. 12mo. 13s 6d (ECB, ER).
ER 7: 508 (Jan 1806).
Corvey; CME 3-628-47478-7; ECB 168; xNSTC.

*Notes.* German original not discovered. Distinct from *Domestic Scenes*, by 'Lady Humdrum' (1820: 38).

1806: 62   SIDDONS, Henry.
**THE MAID, WIFE, AND WIDOW, A TALE. IN THREE VOLUMES. BY HENRY SIDDONS, AUTHOR OF VIRTUOUS POVERTY.**
London: Printed for R. Phillips, Bridge-Street, Black-Friars, 1806.
I xxxiii, 256p; II 263p; III 277p. 12mo. 13s 6d (ER).
ER 8: 479 (July 1806); WSW I: 499.
Corvey; CME 3-628-48695-5; ECB 537; NSTC S1920 (BI BL, E, O).

*Notes.* Dedication to 'the Rev. John Middleton, A.M.', dated Brewer-Street, Bloomsbury, Mar 1806.

1806: 63   [STANHOPE, Louisa Sidney].
**MONTBRASIL ABBEY; OR, MATERNAL TRIALS. A TALE. IN TWO VOLUMES.**
London: Printed at the Minerva-Press, for Lane, Newman, and Co. Leadenhall-Street, 1806.

I iv, 266p; II 205p. 12mo. 8s (ECB, ER).
ER 9: 248 (Oct 1806); WSW I: 79.
Corvey; CME 3-628-48272-0; ECB 392; xNSTC.

STRUTT, Elizabeth
See BYRON, Elizabeth

1806: 64    SURR, T[homas] S[kinner].
A WINTER IN LONDON; OR, SKETCHES OF FASHION: A NOVEL, IN
THREE VOLUMES, BY T. S. SURR.

London: Printed for Richard Phillips, Bridge-Street, Blackfriars, 1806.
I vii, 282p; II 272p; III 267p. 12mo. 13s 6d (ECB, ER).
CR 3rd ser. 8: 318–20 (July 1806) full review; ER 8: 229 (Apr 1806); WSW I: 527.
BL 012638.r.13; ECB 570; NSTC S4394 (BI C, O).

*Notes.* Dedication to the Countess of Moira. Preface dated London, Jan 1806.
Further edns: 2nd edn. 1806 (NSTC); 3rd edn. 1806 (NUC); 4th edn. 1806 (Corvey), CME
3-628-48739-0; 5th edn. 1806 (NSTC); 8th edn. 1806 (NSTC); 9th edn. 1807 (NSTC); [at
least 2 more edns. to 1850, including '13th edn.' 1824 (NSTC)]; Baltimore 1808 (NUC);
French trans., 1810; German trans., 1815.

1806: 65    [TAYLOR, Miss].
THE FATHER AND SON; OR, DE CLAREMONT. A DESULTORY TALE.
IN THREE VOLUMES.

London: Printed at the Minerva-Press, for Lane, Newman, and Co. Leadenhall-Street,
     1806.
I 232p; II 240p; III 282p. 12mo. 12s (ECB, ER).
ER 8: 479 (July 1806).
Corvey; CME 3-628-47502-3; ECB 201; NSTC T270 (BI BL).

*Notes.* Attributed to Miss Taylor in a Minerva Library Catalogue of 1814 (Blakey). Blakey,
BLC, and Summers treat this author as distinct from Eliza Taylor, author of *Education* (1817:
53); see also 1803: 69.

1806: 66    [THOMAS, Elizabeth].
THE THREE OLD MAIDS OF THE HOUSE OF PENRUDDOCK.
A NOVEL. IN THREE VOLUMES. BY MRS. BRIDGET BLUEMANTLE.

London: Printed at the Minerva-Press, for Lane, Newman, and Co. Leadenhall-Street,
     1806.
I 249p; II 276p; III 264p. 12mo. 12s (ECB, ER).
ER 8: 479 (July 1806); WSW I: 121.
CtY-BR In.T362.806; ECB 590; xNSTC.

*Notes.* Introduction (vol. 1, pp. 1–2) signed 'Martha Homely'.

1806: 67    [WÄCHTER, Georg Philipp Ludwig Leonhard]; POWELL, J[ames] (*trans.*).
WOLF; OR, THE TRIBUNAL OF BLOOD: A ROMANCE, FROM THE
ORIGINAL GERMAN OF VEIT WEBER, AUTHOR OF THE SORCERER,

BLACK VALLEY, &C. BY J. POWELL, TRANSLATOR OF "THE VILLAGE OF FRIEDEWALDE," &C. &C. IN TWO VOLUMES.

> London: Printed for J. F. Hughes, 5, Wigmore-Street, Cavendish-Square, by R. Wilks, 89, Chancery-Lane, 1806.
> I 193p; II 173p. 12mo. 8s (ER).
> ER 8: 229 (Apr 1806).
> BL 12548.bb. 41; NSTC W1007.

*Notes.* Trans. of *Wolf* in: *Sagen der Vorzeit*, vol. 2 (Berlin, 1788). Verso of vol. 2, p. 173 [Notice] stating: 'The whole of the Works of Weber, that have not yet appeared in English, are now translating from the original German, by J. Powell, and will shortly be published.' Veit Weber is a pseudonym for G. P. L. L. Wächter.


1806: 68   WARREN, Caroline Matilda.
CONRADE; OR, THE GAMESTERS. A NOVEL, FOUNDED ON FACTS. IN TWO VOLUMES. BY CAROLINE MATILDA WARREN.

> London: Printed at the Minerva-Press, for Lane, Newman, and Co. Leadenhall-Street, 1806.
> I xi, 216p; II 214p. 12mo. 7s (ECB); 5s (ER).
> ER 8: 229 (Apr 1806); WSW I: 553.
> Corvey; CME 3-628-48877-X; ECB 624; NSTC W670 (BI BL).

*Notes.* Preface dated Sutton, Feb 1806.


1806: 69   WILKINSON, Sarah [Scudgell].
THE THATCHED COTTAGE; OR, SORROWS OF EUGENIA. A NOVEL. IN TWO VOLUMES. BY SARAH WILKINSON.

> London: Printed for T. Hughes, 1, Stationer's-Court, by Dewick & Clarke, Aldersgate-Street, 1806.
> I vii, 272p; II 265p. 12mo.
> WSW I: 563.
> Corvey; CME 3-628-48926-1; ECB 638; xNSTC.

*Notes.* Dedication 'to Mrs. Fielding', signed 10, William-Street, Pimlico. 'List of Subscribers' (*c.*155 names), vol. 1, pp. [v]–vii. ECB dates 1805.


1806: 70   [?ZSCHOKKE, Johann Heinrich].
THE POLISH CHIEFTAIN: A ROMANCE. TRANSLATED FROM THE GERMAN OF THE AUTHOR OF "ABALLINO."

> London: Printed for J. F. Hughes, 5, Wigmore-Street, Cavendish-Square, by R. Wilks, 89, Chancery Lane, 1806.
> 172p. 12mo. 4s 6d (ER).
> ER 8: 479 (July 1806).
> Corvey; CME 3-628-48479-0; xNSTC.

*Notes.* German original not discovered.

# 1807

1807: 1   ANON.
*LOUISA; OR, THE ORPHAN OF LENOX ABBEY.

> London: J. Booth?, 1807.
> 3 vols? 12mo. 10s 6d (ECB).
> No copy located; ECB 354.

*Notes. Mandeville Castle; or, the Two Elinors* (see 1807: 2) lists this title as a work by its author. Title also adv. in *Susan* (1809: 9). ECB apparently mis-spells as '*Senex* Abbey', dating Apr 1807. For a possible earlier issue of the same work, see *Nothing New* (1803: 11).

1807: 2   ANON.
MANDEVILLE CASTLE; OR, THE TWO ELINORS. IN TWO VOLUMES. BY THE AUTHOR OF LOUISA, THE ORPHAN OF LENOX ABBEY.

> London: Printed for J. Booth, Duke Street, Portland Place; and T. Ostell, Ave-Maria Lane, Ludgate Street; by J. Barfield, Wardour Street, 1807.
> I 200p; II 186p. 12mo. 7s (CR, ECB); 7s boards (ER).
> CR 3rd ser. 11: 91–3 (May 1807) full review; ER 10: 492 (July 1807); WSW I: 71.
> Corvey; CME 3-628-48088-4; ECB 365; xNSTC.

1807: 3   ANON.
*MARGARETTA; OR THE INTRICACIES OF THE HEART.

> London: Longman, 1807.
> 1 vol? 12mo. 6s (ECB); 12s boards (ER).
> ER 11: 238 (Oct 1807).
> No copy located; ECB 368.

*Notes.* Neither ER nor ECB state number of vols., though the prices given might indicate one and two vols. respectively. NUC gives 1807 edns. with both Charleston and Philadelphia imprints, indicating a title originally published in America.

1807: 4   ANON.
RETRIBUTION; OR, THE SISTERS OF ULSTIEN. IN TWO VOLUMES.

> London: Printed and sold, for the Author, by R. Causton & Son, 21, Finch-Lane, Corn-hill, 1807.
> I 218p; II 224p. 12mo.
> BL RB.23.a.12459; xNSTC.

1807: 5   ANON.
THEODORE; OR, THE ENTHUSIAST. IN FOUR VOLUMES.

> London: Printed for Longman, Hurst, Rees, and Orme, Paternoster-Row, 1807.
> I 346p; II 332p; III 332p; IV 360p. 12mo. 21s (ECB); 21s boards (ER).

ER 10: 492 (July 1807); WSW I: 120.

Corvey; CME 3-628-48950-4; ECB 584; NSTC T581 (BI BL).

*Notes.* Dedication 'to Her Serene Highness the Reigning Duchess of Saxe-Weimar'.

1807: 6    ANON.

VESUVIA; OR, ANGLESEA MANOR. A NOVEL. IN THREE VOLUMES. BY THE AUTHOR OF VALAMBROSA [*sic*], AND FORRESTI.

> London: Printed at the Minerva-Press, for Lane, Newman, and Co. Leadenhall-Street, 1807.
> I 282p; II 275p; III 243p. 12mo. 13s 6d (ECB); 13s 6d sewed (ER).
> ER 10: 492 (July 1807).
> Corvey; CME 3-628-48920-2; ECB 612; xNSTC.

*Notes.* For probable male authorship, see 1805: 14 and 1806: 9.

1807: 7    ANON.

A WINTER IN BATH. IN FOUR VOLUMES. BY THE AUTHOR OF TWO POPULAR NOVELS.

> London: Printed by J. G. Barnard, Snow-Hill, for B. Crosby and Co. Stationer's Court, Paternoster Row: sold by all the Booksellers in Bath; Richardson, Bristol; Donaldson, Brighton; Harvey, Weymouth; Skelton, and Mrs. Street, Southampton; Garner, Margate; Barry, Hastings; Nash, Tunbridge-Wells; Leek, Cromer; Ruff, Cheltenham; and Burgess, Ramsgate, n.d. [1807].
> I 295p; II 244p; III 269p; IV 227p. 12mo.
> CR 3rd ser. 11: 290–3 (July 1807) full review; WSW I: 146.
> BL 12654.ee.58; NSTC B1035.

*Notes.* Wrongly attributed to Mrs E. G. Bayfield in pencil on inside cover of vol. 1 in BL copy. 'Second Edition' (BL 1208.d.32) is again undated, but on the verso of t.p. of vol. 1 there is a statement 'To the Booksellers and the Public at large', headed 'Literary Fraud', complaining that J. F. Hughes has 'altered the Title of a Novel several months previously announced for Publication under the Title of "Love as it may Be", only, to "*A Winter at Bath*", and by misrepresentation and deceit introduced it into the hands of the Trade, as the novel solely announced by B. Crosby and Co. for Publication upwards of six months before, under the Title of "*A Winter in Bath*"; and which was done at the moment intended for the Publication of B. Crosby and Co.'s work, with a view to profit by the popularity of their Novel . . . '. The same statement adds: 'The candid avowal which Crosby and Co. have received from Mrs. Bayfield, the authoress of "Love as it may Be", of the Title having been altered by the publishers without her knowledge or consent, also deserves our particular acknowledgements.' It concludes by noting that legal proceedings are pending. This statement makes clear that Mrs Bayfield is author of *A Winter at Bath* (see 1807: 9), and not the above title, in spite of its attribution to her in several catalogues. The alternative attribution to J. H. James (Block, NSTC) also appears unlikely: see *The Banks of the Wye* (1808: 1), for further information. The present title also features in a string of attributions within titles, which themselves have been linked with Mrs E. M. Foster: see *The Corinna of England* (1809: 4). CR assumes a male author: 'His insipid tale might safely be consigned to the flames' (p. 292). Further edn: 2nd edn. [1807] (NSTC).

1807: 8   [BARRETT, Eaton Stannard].
**THE RISING SUN, A SERIO-COMIC SATIRIC ROMANCE. BY CER-
VANTES HOGG, F.S.M.**

> London: Printed for Appleyards, Wimpole-Street, 1807.
> I 197p, ill.; II 171p, ill. 12mo. 21s (CR 3rd edn., ECB).
> CR 3rd ser. 11: 427–8 (Aug 1807) full review (3rd edn.); ER 10: 241 (Apr 1807); WSW
>    I: 142.
> BL N.1662; ECB 494; NSTC B675 (BI O).

*Notes.* Collates in sixes.
Further edns: 2nd edn. 1807 (NSTC); 3rd edn. 1807 (NSTC); 4th edn. 1807 (NSTC); 5th edn.
1809 (NSTC).

1807: 9   BAYFIELD, Mrs. [E. G.].
**\*A WINTER AT BATH; OR, LOVE AS IT MAY BE, AND FRIENDSHIP AS
IT OUGHT TO BE; A NOVEL IN 4 VOLS. FROM THE CHASTE AND
CLASSICAL PEN OF MRS. BAYFIELD.**

> London: J. F. Hughes, 1807.
> 4 vols. 12mo. 18s (ECB); 18s boards (ER).
> ER 10: 492 (July 1807).
> No copy located; ECB 44.

*Notes.* Title details from Summers, where a further extended version is given. Mrs Bayfield,
who also wrote *Fugitive Poems* (1805), is sometimes wrongly identified as the author of
*A Winter in Bath*, a rival publication, and so apparently with a string of publications stemming
for that other work. For further details, see *A Winter in Bath* (1807: 7).

1807: 10   BROWN, C[harles] B[rockden].
**PHILIP STANLEY; OR, THE ENTHUSIASM OF LOVE. A NOVEL. IN
TWO VOLUMES. BY C. B. BROWN, AUTHOR OF ARTHUR MERVYN,
EDGAR HUNTLY, JANE TALBOT, &C.**

> London: Printed at the Minerva-Press, for Lane, Newman, and Co. Leadenhall-Street,
>    1807.
> I viii, 221p; II 200p. 12mo. 7s (ECB); 7s sewed (ER).
> ER 11: 238 (Oct 1807), 11: 504 (Jan 1808).
> Corvey; CME 3-628-47139-7; ECB 78; NSTC B4731 (BI BL).

*Notes.* A re-titled version of Brown's *Clara Howard* (Philadelphia, 1801).

1807: 11   BUTLER, {H}[arriet].
**COUNT EUGENIO; OR, FATAL ERRORS: A TALE, FOUNDED ON
FACT. BY MRS. BUTLER. IN TWO VOLUMES.**

> London: Printed for J. F. Hughes, 5, Wigmore Street, 1807.
> I viii, 258p; II 270p. 12mo. 10s (ER).
> ER 10: 492 (July 1807).
> Corvey; CME 3-628-47149-4; ECB 89; xNSTC.

*Notes.* Dedication 'to a Member of the British Senate', dated May 1807 and signed 'H. B.'.

BYERLEY, John Scott
See LE MAIRES, Henri

1807: 12   BYRON, [Elizabeth] [afterwards STRUTT].
DRELINCOURT AND RODALVI; OR, MEMOIRS OF TWO NOBLE
FAMILIES. A NOVEL, IN THREE VOLUMES. BY MRS. BYRON,
AUTHOR OF ANTI-DELPHINE.
> London: Printed for J. Mawman, in the Poultry, by G. Hazard, Beech-Street, 1807.
> I iii, 241p; II 260p; III 293p. 12mo. 12s (ECB); 12s boards (ER).
> CR 3rd ser. 11: 212–13 (June 1807); ER 10: 492 (July 1807); WSW I: 185.
> Corvey; CME 3-628-47176-1; ECB 90; NSTC B6043 (BI O).

*Notes.* Further edn: 2nd edn. 1819 (NSTC).

1807: 13   CANTON, John.
THE ENGLISH GIL BLAS; OR, THE ADVENTURES OF GABRIEL TAN-
GENT. A NOVEL. BY JOHN CANTON, AUTHOR OF ALVAR AND
SERAPHINA; OR, THE TROUBLES OF MURICA. IN THREE VOL-
UMES.
> London: Printed by R. Wilks, Chancery-Lane, for J. F. Hughes, Wigmore Street,
>     Cavendish Square, 1807.
> I 233p; II 232p; III 221p. 12mo. 13s 6d (ECB, ER).
> CR 3rd ser. 13: 106 (Jan 1808); ER 10: 492 (July 1807).
> BL 12612.aa.11; ECB 187; NSTC C532.

1807: 14   [CORP, Harriet].
AN ANTIDOTE TO THE MISERIES OF HUMAN LIFE, IN THE HIS-
TORY OF WIDOW PLACID, AND HER DAUGHTER RACHEL.
> London: Printed by James Cundee, Ivy Lane, for Williams and Smith, Stationers' Court,
>     Paternoster Row, 1807.
> vi, 137p. 12mo.
> WSW I: 219.
> BL 4413.ff.46(1); NSTC C3714.

*Notes.* A response in part to James Beresford's *The Miseries of Human Life* (1806), which
itself is not in the form of a fictional narrative. Collates in sixes.
Further edns: 2nd edn. 1808 (NSTC); 3rd edn. 1808 (NSTC); 4th edn. 1808 (NSTC); 5th edn.
1808 (NSTC); 6th edn. 1810 (NUC); [at least 4 more edns. to 1850]; New York 1808 (NUC).

1807: 15   COTTIN, [Sophie Ristaud]; MEEKE, [Mary] (*trans.*).
ELIZABETH; OR, THE EXILES OF SIBERIA. A TALE, FOUNDED ON
FACTS. ALTERED FROM THE FRENCH OF MADAME DE COTTIN, BY
MRS. MEEKE.
> London: Printed at the Minerva-Press, for Lane, Newman, and Co. Leadenhall-Street,
>     1807.
> vi, 237p. 12mo. 4s 6d (ER).

ER 10: 241 (Apr 1807), 10: 493 (July 1807).
CtY Hfd29.602m; xNSTC.

*Notes.* Trans. of *Élisabeth, ou les exilés de Sibérie* (Paris, 1806). This story also appeared with Meeke's translation of Ducray-Duminil's *Julien; or, My Father's House*, published by the Minerva Press with the same year imprint—see 1807: 22. French language version of this tale received a full review in ER, 11: 448–62 (Jan 1808). ECB 138 lists 3rd edn. 1809, Tegg, 3s. Further edns: 1808 (NSTC C3815); 3rd edn. 1809 (NSTC); 1810 (NSTC); Dublin 1811 (NSTC); 1814 (NSTC); [at least 15 more edns. to 1850]; Philadelphia 1808 (NUC).

1807: 16    CURTIES, T. J. Horsley.
THE MONK OF UDOLPHO; A ROMANCE. IN FOUR VOLUMES. BY T. J. HORSLEY CURTIES, ESQ. AUTHOR OF THE SABLE MASK, THE WATCH TOWER, SCOTTISH LEGENDS, ANCIENT RECORDS, AND ETHELWINA.

> London: Printed by D. N. Shury, 7, Berwick Street, Soho, for J. F. Hughes, Wigmore Street, Cavendish Square, 1807.
> I viii, 232p; II 244p; III 265p; IV 232p. 12mo. 22s (ECB).
> WSW I: 232.
> O 249.s.244; ECB 391; NSTC C4588.

*Notes.* Preface dated Chelsea Park, Little Chelsea, 20 Oct 1806. ECB dates Nov 1806.
Further edn: 1807 (BL C.192.a.226)
Facs: GNIII (1977).

1807: 17    DACRE, Charlotte.
THE LIBERTINE; BY CHARLOTTE DACRE, BETTER KNOWN AS ROSA MATILDA, AUTHOR OF HOURS OF SOLITUDE, NUN OF ST. OMER'S, ZOFLOYA, &C. IN FOUR VOLUMES.

> London: Printed for T. Cadell and W. Davies, Strand, 1807.
> I 268p; II 260p; III 245p; IV 224p. 12mo. 18s (ECB); 18s boards (ER).
> ER 10: 492 (July 1807); WSW I: 233.
> IU 823.D119l; ECB 149; xNSTC.

*Notes.* Further edns: 2nd edn. 1807 (NSTC D47); 3rd edn. 1807 (Corvey), CME 3-628-47386-1; French trans., 1816 [as *Angelo, comte d'Albini, ou les dangers du vice* (BN)]; German trans., 1829 [as *Der Wüstling* (RS)].
Facs: GNII (1974).

1807: 18    DIBDIN, [Charles].
HENRY HOOKA. A NOVEL. BY MR. DIBDIN, AUTHOR OF HANNAH HEWETT—YOUNGER BROTHER—MUSICAL TOUR—PROFESSIONAL LIFE—HARMONIC PRECEPTOR—HISTORY OF THE STAGE, &C. &C. IN THREE VOLUMES.

> London: Printed for C. Chapple, Pall-Mall, 1807.
> I 216p; II 220p; III 304p. 12mo. 12s (ECB); 12s sewed (ER).

ER 10: 492 (July 1807); WSW I: 243.

Corvey; CME 3-628-47454-X; ECB 162; NSTC D1038 (BI BL, C).

*Notes.* Printer's mark after imprint date reads: '[J. G. Barnard, Printer, Snow-hill]'. ECB also lists new edn., 3 vols. 1827; but not discovered in this form.

1807: 19    DIOGENES [pseud.].
**THE ROYAL ECLIPSE; OR, DELICATE FACTS EXHIBITING THE SECRET MEMOIRS OF SQUIRE GEORGE AND HIS WIFE. WITH NOTES. BY DIOGENES.**

> London: Printed by D. N. Shury, Berwick Street, Soho, for J. F. Hughes, Wigmore Street, Cavendish Square, 1807.
> xi, 172p. 12mo. 7s (ECB); 7s boards (ER).
> CR 3rd ser. 11: 428–9 (Aug 1807) full review; ER 10: 493 (July 1807); WSW I: 246.
> BL 1608/3327; ECB 505; NSTC D1298 (BI E).

*Notes.* Further edn: 2nd edn. 1807 (NSTC).

1807: 20    D{OHERTY}, H{ugh}.
**THE DISCOVERY; OR, THE MYSTERIOUS SEPARATION OF HUGH DOHERTY, ESQ. AND ANN HIS WIFE. BY H. D. ESQ.**

> London: Printed by G. Sidney, Northumberland-Street, Strand. To be had only at No. 12, Temple Place, Blackfriars Road, 1807.
> xcv, 223p. 12mo.
> WSW I: 248.
> ViU CT848.D6A3.1807; ECB 164; xNSTC.

*Notes.* 'To the Reader', pp. [v]–xcv, signed 'Hugh Doherty, Half-pay, late 23d Lt. Dragoons. 12, Temple Place, Blackfriars-road, London'. Drop-head title on p. [1] reads: 'The Discovery; a Domestic Tale'. Quasi-fictional romance, with epistolary exchanges, relating to the author's elopement with his wife and her subsequent desertion of him. See also Ann Doherty's *Ronaldsha* (1808: 41).
Further edns: 3rd edn. 1807 (NSTC D16); 4th edn. 1807 (NSTC); 5th edn. 1807 (NSTC).

1807: 21    [?DUCRAY-DUMINIL, François-Guillaume].
**THE CONVENT OF NOTRE DAME: OR, JEANNETTE. IN TWO VOLUMES. BY THE AUTHOR OF A TALE OF MYSTERY, OR CELINA.**

> London: Printed for Henry Colburn, (English and Foreign Circulating Library,) No. 48, Conduit Street, New Bond-Street; by S. Rousseau, Wood Street, Spa Fields, 1807.
> I xv, 251p; II viii, 271p. 12mo. 9s (ECB); 9s sewed (ER); 10s (ER).
> ER 9: 500 (Jan 1807), 10: 492 (July 1807).
> Corvey; CME 3-628-47326-8; ECB 132; xNSTC.

*Notes.* Ducray-Duminil was the author of the French source title for *A Tale of Mystery, or Celina*, as translated by Mary Meeke—see 1803: 28. No French original for this present title, however, has been discovered. Dedication (of 'the novel of Jeannette') 'To the Right Honourable Lady Elizabeth Monck', signed 'By her Ladyship's Most obedient and humble Servant, The Translator and Publisher'. Notice at beginning of vols. 1 and 2 announcing the circulating library of H. Colburn ('from Earle's'), at 48, Conduit Street, New Bond Street.

1807: 22   DUCRAY-DUMINIL, [François-Guillaume]; MEEKE, [Mary] (*trans.*).
JULIEN; OR, MY FATHER'S HOUSE. A NOVEL, ALTERED FROM THE
FRENCH OF DUCRAY-DUMINIL, BY MRS. MEEKE. IN FOUR VOL-
UMES. TO WHICH IS ADDED, ELIZABETH, OR THE EXILES OF
SIBERIA, A TALE, FOUNDED ON FACTS, FROM THE FRENCH OF
MADAME DE COTTIN.

> London: Printed at the Minerva-Press, for Lane, Newman, and Co. Leadenhall-Street,
> 1807.
> I 254p; II 287p; III 324p; IV 309p. 12mo. 18s (ECB); 18s sewed (ER); 20s sewed (ER).
> ER 10: 493 (July 1807), 11: 238 (Oct 1807).
> Corvey; CME 3-628-48208-9; ECB 173; xNSTC.

*Notes.* Trans. of *Jules, ou le toit paternel* (Paris, 1806) and Cottin, Sophie Ristaud: *Élisabeth,
ou les exilés de Sibérie* (Paris, 1806). *Julien* ends vol. 4, p. 71, followed by the tale *Elizabeth* with
separate t.p., and 'Author's Preface' (pp. [iii]–vi); the tale proper starts at p. [79]. See also
1807: 15 for the separate publication of *Elizabeth*.


1807: 23   FRANCES, Sophia.
CONSTANCE DE LINDENSDORF; OR, THE FORCE OF BIGOTRY. A
TALE. IN FOUR VOLUMES. BY SOPHIA FRANCES, AUTHOR OF
VIVONIO, &C.

> London: Printed at the Minerva-Press, for Lane, Newman, and Co. Leadenhall-Street,
> 1807.
> I 286p, ill.; II 266p; III 244p; IV 260p. 12mo. 18s (ECB, ER).
> ER 10: 241 (Apr 1807).
> Corvey; CME 3-628-47831-6; ECB 215; NSTC F1451 (BI C).

*Notes.* Further edn: French trans., 1808 [as *Constance de Lindensdorf, ou la tour de Wolfenstad*
(BN under Lathom, Francis)].


1807: 24   FRANCES, Sophia.
THE NUN OF MISERECORDIA; OR, THE EVE OF ALL SAINTS. A
ROMANCE. IN FOUR VOLUMES. BY SOPHIA FRANCES, AUTHOR OF
VIVONIO, CONSTANCE DE LINDENSDORF, &C.

> London: Printed at the Minerva-Press, for Lane, Newman, and Co. Leadenhall-Street,
> 1807.
> I 263p; II 253p; III 263p; IV 271p. 12mo. 18s (ECB); 18s sewed (ER).
> ER 11: 504 (Jan 1808).
> O 249.s.462–465; ECB 215; NSTC F1452.

*Notes.* Further edn: French trans., 1809.


1807: 25   [?GUÉNARD, Elisabeth].
BARON DE FALKENHEIM. A GERMAN TALE OF THE SIXTEENTH
CENTURY. IN TWO VOLUMES.

> London: Printed at the Minerva-Press, for Lane, Newman, and Co. Leadenhall-Street,
> 1807.

I 304p; II 303p. 12mo. 9s (ECB); 9s sewed (ER).
ER 9: 500 (Jan 1807).
Corvey; CME 3-628-47106-0; ECB 41; xNSTC.

*Notes.* French original not discovered. The present title, however, is connected through t.p.
attribution with *Mystery upon Mystery* and *The Black Banner* (see 1808: 51, 1811: 36), both of
which have strong associations with Elisabeth Guénard.

1807: 26   [?GUION, Miss].
THE THREE GERMANS. MYSTERIES EXEMPLIFIED IN THE LIFE OF
HOLSTEIN OF LUTZTEIN. A GERMAN ROMANCE. IN THREE VOL-
UMES.

> London: Printed for J. F. Hughes, Wigmore-Street, Cavendish-Square, 1807.
> I 179p; II 151p; III 188p. 12mo. 20s bound (ER).
> ER 11: 238 (Oct 1807).
> Corvey; CME 3-628-48956-3; NSTC H2272 (BI BL).

*Notes.* No German original discovered. List of works 'Just Published' (1 p. unn.) at end of
vol. 3 of *St. Botolph's Priory* (1806: 23) includes this title 'by Miss Guion'.

1807: 27   HERBERT, William.
THE SPANISH OUTLAW, A TALE. BY WILLIAM HERBERT, ESQ. IN
FOUR VOLUMES.

> London: Printed for J. F. Hughes, Wigmore-Street, Cavendish-Square, 1807.
> I 295p; II 341p; III 379p; IV 388p. 12mo. 22s (ECB); 21s (ER).
> ER 10: 493 (July 1807).
> Corvey; CME 3-628-47780-8; ECB 265; NSTC H1374 (BI BL).

1807: 28   {HIRST, Augusta Ann}.
HELEN; OR DOMESTIC OCCURRENCES. A TALE. IN TWO VOLUMES.

> London: Printed for the Author: sold by W. Bent, Paternoster-Row, 1807.
> I xxx, 266p; II 263p. 12mo. 10s 6d (CR, ECB); 10s 6d boards (ER).
> CR 3rd ser. 11: 438 (Aug 1807); ER 10: 492 (July 1807).
> MH-H *EC8.H6181.807h; ECB 271; NSTC H1826 (BI O).

*Notes.* Dedication 'to the Right Honorable Countess Fitzwilliam', signed Augusta Ann Hirst,
London, 6 Apr 1807. 'Names of Subscribers' (568 listed), vol. 1, pp. [xi]–xxx.
Further edn: 1808 (Corvey—a reissue by the Minerva Press with the author's name on t.p.,
but minus the preliminaries), CME 3-628-47712-3.

1807: 29   HUBER, [Therese]; FARDELY, William (*trans.*).
FRANCIS AND JOSEPHA. A TALE. FROM THE GERMAN OF HUBER.
BY WILLIAM FARDELY.

> Leeds: Printed by Edward Baines, 1807.
> viii, 101p. 8vo. 3s (ECB).
> CR 3rd ser. 11: 213–14 (June 1807).
> BL 1509/297; ECB 286; NSTC H2897.

*Notes.* Trans. of *Franz und Josephe. Eine Erzählung,* from *Taschenbuch für Damen auf das Jahr 1802* (Tübingen, 1801). Collates in fours. Preface signed 'The Translator'. ECB dates Dec 1808, and gives Lane as publisher; but not discovered in this form.

1807: 30   HUNTER, [Rachel].
FAMILY ANNALS; OR, WORLDLY WISDOM. A NOVEL. IN FIVE VOLUMES. BY MRS. HUNTER, OF NORWICH; AUTHOR OF LÆTITIA;—GRUBTHORPE FAMILY;—UNEXPECTED   LEGACY;—LADY   PALMERSTON'S   LETTERS; &C. &C.

> London: Printed for J. F. Hughes, Wigmore-Street, Cavendish-Square, 1807.
> I xvi, 243p; II 227p; III 226p; IV 234p; V 209p. 12mo. 25s (ECB); 25s boards (ER).
> ER 10: 493 (July 1807), 11: 238 (Oct 1807).
> Corvey; CME 3-628-47805-7; ECB 289; xNSTC.

*Notes.* Further edn: 2nd edn. 1808 (NSTC H3172).

1807: 31   IRELAND, [Samuel] W[illiam] H[enry].
THE CATHOLIC, AN HISTORICAL ROMANCE. BY W. H. IRELAND, AUTHOR OF THE ABBESS, 4 VOL. GONDEZ, OR THE MONK, 4 VOL. &C. &C. &C.

> London: Printed for W. Earle, Albemarle-Street, 1807.
> I 223p; II 234p; III 304p. 12mo. 15s (ECB); 15s boards (ER).
> ER 11: 238 (Oct 1807).
> Corvey; CME 3-628-47944-4; ECB 300; xNSTC.

*Notes.* 'To the Reader' (in verse) at beginning of vol. 3, followed by 1 p. (unn.) advs. of 'Books lately published, by W. Earle'.

1807: 32   KOTZEBUE, August [Friedrich Ferdinand] von.
THE PASTOR'S DAUGHTER, WITH OTHER ROMANCES. FROM THE GERMAN OF AUGUSTUS VON KOTZEBUE, AUTHOR OF THE STRANGER, LOVER'S VOWS, PIZARRO, &C. IN FOUR VOLUMES.

> London: Printed for Henry Colburn, (English and Foreign Library,) No. 48, Conduit
>    Street, New Bond Street, 1807.
> I 296p; II 239p; III viii, 215p; IV ii, 251p. 12mo. 21s (ECB); 18s boards (ER).
> CR 3rd ser. 10: 167–79 (Feb 1807) full review; ER 9: 500 (Jan 1807).
> C 8746.d.82–85; ECB 325; NSTC K904.

*Notes.* Trans. of *Des Pfarrers Tochter,* from *Kleine Romane, Erzählungen, Anecdoten und Miscellen* (Leipzig, 1805–10). Dedication to the Countess of Jersey by 'Henry Colburn'. Pagination at the end of vols. 2 and 4 incorporates advs. for both Colburn's Circulating Library and 'Works just published'; the text of the novel in these cases ends at pp. 237 and 249 respectively. Further edn: 2nd edn. 1807 (NUC).

1807: 33   LAFONTAINE, A[ugust Heinrich Julius].
EDWARD AND ANNETTE. A MORAL TALE, FROM THE GERMAN, OF A. LAFONTAINE. WITH A FRONTISPIECE.

London: Printed for J. F. Weise, 31, King Street, Soho, 1807.
239p, ill. 12mo.
BL 12612.bb.13; NSTC L147.

*Notes.* German original not discovered. Collates in sixes.

1807: 34   LAFONTAINE, August [Heinrich Julius]; POWELL, J[ames] (*trans.*).
THE MONK OF DISSENTIS: A ROMANCE. FOUNDED ON THE REVO-
LUTIONS OF SWITZERLAND, IN THE 13TH AND 14TH CENTURIES.
TRANSLATED FROM THE ORIGINAL GERMAN OF AUGUSTUS
LAFONTAINE. BY J. POWELL. IN THREE VOLUMES.

London: Printed by J. G. Barnard, 57, Snow-Hill, for B. Crosby and Co. Stationers'
Court, Paternoster-Row, 1807.
I iv, 265p; II 241p; III 340p. 12mo. 12s (ECB, ER).
ER 10: 241 (Apr 1807).
BL C.193.a.1; ECB 326; xNSTC.

*Notes.* Trans. of *Rudolph von Werdenberg* (Berlin, 1793). 'Advertisement', vol. 1, pp. [iii]–iv,
identifies the source title, and adds: 'The reason for changing the title in this its English dress
was, that since the present translation has been finished, a Romance entitled *Rudolph of Werdenberg* has appeared in which little resemblance to the original is to be found, it containing
not one third of the matter, and even that mutilated and altered, so as not to be recognized as
the work of *Lafontaine*'. ECB dates Dec 1806. For the mutilated rival, see 1805: 44.

1807: 35   LATHOM, Francis.
THE FATAL VOW; OR, ST. MICHAEL'S MONASTERY, A ROMANCE,
IN TWO VOLUMES. BY FRANCIS LATHOM. AUTHOR OF THE MYS-
TERIOUS FREEBOOTER—MEN AND MANNERS—HUMAN BEINGS—
MYSTERY—THE INPENETRABLE SECRET—THE MIDNIGHT BELL,
&C. &C.

London: Printed for B. Crosby and Co. Stationers' Court. By C. Stower, Paternoster
Row, 1807.
I 323p; II 268p. 12mo. 9s (ECB); 9s bound (ER).
CR 3rd ser. 13: 105 (Jan 1808); ER 11: 504 (Jan 1808), 12: 267 (Apr 1808); WSW I: 364.
BL 12611.d.4; CME 3-628-47956-8; ECB 330; NSTC L542.

1807: 36   LATHOM, Francis.
HUMAN BEINGS, A NOVEL. IN THREE VOLUMES. BY FRANCIS
LATHOM, AUTHOR OF MEN AND MANNERS—THE MYSTERIOUS
FREEBOOTER—MYSTERY—THE IMPENETRABLE SECRET—ASTO-
NISHMENT—THE MIDNIGHT BELL—ERESTINA, &C. &C.

London: Printed for B. Crosby and Co. Stationers-Court. By J. and E. Hodson, Cross
Street, Hatton Garden, 1807.
I viii, 295p; II 303p; III 309p. 12mo. 13s 6d (ECB).
CR 3rd ser. 10: 101–2 (Jan 1807); WSW I: 363–4.
Corvey; CME 3-628-47958-4; ECB 330; NSTC L543 (BI BL).

*Notes.* ECB dates Nov 1806.

1807: 37   LATHY, T[homas] P[ike].
**GABRIEL FORRESTER; OR, THE DESERTED SON. A NOVEL. IN FOUR VOLUMES. BY T. P. LATHY, AUTHOR OF USURPATION; THE PARACLETE; THE INVISIBLE ENEMY, OR MINES OF WIELITSKA, &C. &C.**

> London: Printed for Oddy and Co. 27, Oxford-Street; W. Oddy, 108, Newgate-Street; J. Goodwin, Brook-Street, Holborn; and Appleyards, Wimpole-Street, n.d. [1807].
> I 354p; II 328p; III 348p; IV 343p. 12mo. 21s (ER).
> CR 3rd ser. 12: 331–4 (Nov 1807); ER 10: 493 (July 1807), 13: 506 (Jan 1809); WSW I: 364.
> Corvey; CME 3-628-47967-3; ECB 221; NSTC L591.5 (BI BL).

*Notes.* Printer's marks after imprint date in vols. 1–3 read: 'Lewis and Hamblin, Printers, Paternoster-row'; printer's mark after imprint date in vol. 4 reads: 'T. Gillet, Printer, Wild-Court'. ECB dates June 1807.

1807: 38   {LE MAIRES}, [Henri]; BYERLEY, J[ohn] S[cott] (*trans.*).
**THE CONSCRIPT, A SERIO-COMIC ROMANCE. IN TWO VOLUMES. BY J. S. BYERLEY, ESQ.**

> London: Printed for C. Chapple, 66, Pall Mall, 1807.
> I 168p; II 164p. 12mo. 7s (ECB); 7s boards (ER).
> ER 10: 492 (July 1807); WSW I: 184.
> Corvey; CME 3-628-47152-4; ECB 90; NSTC B6019 (BI BL).

*Notes.* Trans. of *Le Conscrit ou les billets de Logement* (Paris, 1800). 'Advertisement', dated Hammersmith, 20 May 1807, acknowledging 'The following volumes are founded on M. Le Maires's exquisite little tale of "Le Conscrit ou les billets de Logement"', but with the proviso that this represents not a translation but a recasting.

1807: 39   LONEY, T. C.
**THE MAN IN ARMOUR, OR THE INVISIBLE SWORD, A ROMANCE. BY T. C. LONEY.**

> Macclesfield: Printed by J. Wilson, 1807.
> ii, 186p. 12mo.
> Corvey; CME 3-628-48112-0; NSTC L2274 (BI BL).

*Notes.* 'To the Reader', dated July 1807. Collates in sixes.
Further edn: 1811 reissued by Henry Colburn as *Sebastian and Isabel; or, the Invisible Sword* (ViU PZ2.L65S.1811; NUC). For further details, see Appendix E: 5.

1807: 40   [MANGIN, Edward].
**GEORGE THE THIRD. A NOVEL. IN THREE VOLUMES.**

> London: Printed for James Carpenter, Old Bond Street, 1807.
> I vii, 226p; II 228p; III 225p. 12mo. 13s 6d (ECB); 12s boards (ER).
> ER 10: 492 (July 1807); WSW I: 385.
> Corvey; CME 3-628-47728-X; ECB 228; NSTC M977 (BI BL, Dt, O).

1807: 41   MATHEWS, [Eliza Kirkham?].
**GRIFFITH ABBEY, OR, MEMOIRS OF EUGENIA. BY MRS. C. MATHEWS. IN TWO VOLUMES.**

London: Printed by W. Burton, Fetter Lane, for Oddy and Co. 27, Oxford Street, and J.
  Goodwin, Brook Street, Holborn, 1807.
I 251p; II 244p. 12mo. 9s (ECB); 9s boards (ER).
ER 10: 493 (July 1807).
BL 12613.bb.20; ECB 246; NSTC M1664.

*Notes.* BLC and NUC both attribute to Eliza Kirkham Mathews [née Strong], who married
Charles Mathews (the actor) in 1797, but who died in 1802 (see F. C., Jackson). Frank (Item
264) and Summers attribute to a somewhat opaque Charlotte Matthews (see also 1801: 49).
Collates in sixes.
Further edn: New York 1808 (NUC).

1807: 42   [MATURIN, Charles Robert].
**FATAL REVENGE; OR, THE FAMILY OF MONTORIO. A ROMANCE.
BY DENNIS JASPER MURPHY. IN THREE VOLUMES.**

London: Printed for Longman, Hurst, Rees, and Orme, Paternoster Row, 1807.
I xiii, 400p; II 518p; III 493p. 12mo. 21s (ECB); 21s boards (ER).
ER 11: 238 (Oct 1807); QR 3: 339–47 (May 1810) full review; WSW I: 414.
Corvey; CME 3-628-48395-6; ECB 201; NSTC M1726 (BI BL, Dt).

*Notes.* Preface signed 'Dennis Jasper Murphy', dated Dublin, 15 Dec 1806.
Further edns: 2nd edn. 1824 (NSTC); 4th edn. 1840 (NSTC); 1841 (NSTC); New York 1808
(NUC); French trans., 1822 [as *La Famille de Montorio, ou la fatale vengeance* (BN)].
Facs: GNII (1974).

1807: 43   MELVILLE, Theodore.
**THE BENEVOLENT MONK; OR, THE CASTLE OF OLALLA. A
ROMANCE. IN THREE VOLUMES. BY THEODORE MELVILLE, ESQ.
AUTHOR OF THE WHITE KNIGHT, OR THE MONASTERY OF
MOURNE.**

London: Printed for B. Crosby & Co. Stationers'-Court, Paternoster Row, 1807.
I 288p; II 295p; III 344p. 12mo. 13s 6d (ECB); 13s 6d boards (ER).
CR 3rd ser. 12: 104 (Sept 1807); ER 10: 241 (Apr 1807), 10: 492 (July 1807); WSW I:
  394–5.
Corvey; CME 3-628-48055-8; ECB 379; NSTC M2019 (BI BL).

1807: 44   MONTAGUE, Edward.
**THE DEMON OF SICILY. A ROMANCE, IN FOUR VOLUMES, BY
EDWARD MONTAGUE ESQ. AUTHOR OF LEGENDS OF A NUNNERY,
THE CASTLE OF BERRY POMEROY, &C. &C. &C.**

London: Printed for J. F. Hughes, Wigmore Street, Cavendish Square, 1807.
I 260p; II 216p; III 256p; IV 264p. 12mo. 20s (ECB); 20s boards (ER).
ER 10: 493 (July 1807).
O 249.s.404–407; ECB 392; NSTC M2913.

*Notes.* Vol. 4 t.p. mistakenly reads 'Volume the First', which is corrected in hand in the
Bodleian copy.
Further edn: 1830? (NSTC).

1807: 45 MONTAGUE, Edward.
**THE LEGENDS OF A NUNNERY. A ROMANCE. IN FOUR VOLUMES. BY EDWARD MONTAGUE, ESQ. AUTHOR OF "THE CASTLE OF BERRY POMEROY."**

> London: Printed by J. Dennet, Leather Lane, for J. F. Hughes, Wigmore Street, Cavendish Square, 1807.
> I 238p; II 234p; III 218p; IV 257p. 12mo. 20s (ECB); 20s sewed (ER).
> ER 10: 492 (July 1807).
> BL 1154.i.11; ECB 392; NSTC M2914 (BI C).

1807: 46 MORTIMER, Edward [pseud.?].
**THE FRIAR HILDARGO. A LEGENDARY TALE. IN FIVE VOLUMES. BY EDWARD MORTIMER, ESQ.**

> London: Printed by J. Dennett, Leather Lane, for J. F. Hughes, Wigmore Street, Cavendish Square, 1807.
> I 234p; II 278p; III 296p; IV 213p; V 209p. 12mo. 21s (ER).
> ER 10: 493 (July 1807).
> Corvey; CME 3-628-48334-4; ECB 219; xNSTC.

*Notes.* Drop-head title reads: 'Friar Hildargo. A Tale of the Thirteenth Century'. ER, Allibone, and Block give author as E. Martin, though apparently in error.

1807: 47 [MOSSE], Henrietta Rouviere.
**A PEEP AT OUR ANCESTORS. AN HISTORICAL ROMANCE. IN FOUR VOLUMES. BY HENRIETTA ROUVIERE, AUTHOR OF LUSSINGTON ABBEY, HEIRS OF VILLEROY, &C.**

> London: Printed at the Minerva-Press, for Lane, Newman, and Co. Leadenhall-Street, 1807.
> I xv, 190p, ill.; II 219p; III 253p; IV 284p. 12mo. 20s (ECB); 18s (ER); 20s sewed (ER).
> ER 11: 238 (Oct 1807), 11: 504 (Jan 1808).
> Corvey; CME 3-628-48350-6; ECB 399; NSTC R1781 (BI BL).

*Notes.* Frontispiece portrait of the author. Dedication to 'His Grace the late Duke of Leinster', dated London, 1 Oct 1807. List of 'Subscribers' (46 names, predominantly with Irish addresses), vol. 1, pp. [viii]–x.

**NORRIS, Mrs, OLIVIA AND MARCELLA; OR, THE STRANGERS**
See 1806: 51

1807: 48 ORLANDO [pseud.].
**A SUMMER BY THE SEA. A NOVEL. IN TWO VOLUMES. BY ORLANDO.**

> London: Printed at the Minerva-Press for Lane, Newman, and Co. Leadenhall-Street, 1807.
> I 339p; II 368p. 12mo. 10s (ECB); 10s sewed (ER); 6s (ER).
> ER 9: 500 (Jan 1807), 10: 241 (Apr 1807).
> Corvey; CME 3-628-48314-X; ECB 569; NSTC O455 (BI BL).

1807: 49   ORMSBY, Anne.

THE SOLDIER'S FAMILY; OR, GUARDIAN GENII. A ROMANCE. IN FOUR VOLUMES. BY ANNE ORMSBY, AUTHOR OF MEMOIRS OF A FAMILY IN SWISSERLAND.

> London: Printed by J. G. Barnard, Snow-Hill, for B. Crosby and Co. Stationer's-Court, Paternoster-Row, 1807.
>
> I 411p; II 396p; III 488p; IV 472p. 12mo. 26s (ECB); 26s boards (ER).
>
> CR 3rd ser. 12: 104 (Sept 1807); ER 10: 493 (July 1807); WSW I: 423–4.
>
> Corvey; CME 3-628-48315-8; ECB 425; NSTC O482 (BI BL).

1807: 50   PARSONS, [Eliza].

THE CONVICT, OR NAVY LIEUTENANT. A NOVEL. BY MRS. PARSONS, AUTHOR OF THE MISER AND HIS FAMILY; MURRAY HOUSE; THE MYSTERIOUS VISIT, &C. &C. &C. FOUR VOLUMES.

> Brentford: Printed by and for P. Norbury; and sold by T. Ostell, Ave-Maria-Lane; Carpenter and Co. Old-Bond-Street; Earle, Albemarle-Street; and Hatchard, Piccadilly, London, 1807.
>
> I 259p; II 272p; III 264p; IV 350p. 12mo. 12s (ECB).
>
> WSW I: 431.
>
> Corvey; CME 3-628-48425-1; ECB 435; NSTC P563 (BI BL, O).

*Notes.* ECB dates Nov 1806.

1807: 51   PILKINGTON, [Mary].

ELLEN; HEIRESS OF THE CASTLE. IN THREE VOLUMES. BY MRS. PILKINGTON.

> London: Printed by E. Thomas, Golden-Lane, Barbican; for B. Crosby, and Co. Stationers'-Court, Ludgate-Street, 1807.
>
> I xi, 326p; II 348p; III 323p. 12mo. 13s (CR); 12s (ECB); 12s boards (ER).
>
> CR 3rd ser. 12: 102–4 (Sept 1807); ER 10: 493 (July 1807); WSW I: 440.
>
> Corvey; CME 3-628-48443-X; ECB 450; xNSTC.

*Notes.* Preface dated Hammersmith, 25 June 1807.

1807: 52   PORTER, Anna Maria.

THE HUNGARIAN BROTHERS. BY MISS ANNA MARIA PORTER. IN THREE VOLS.

> London: Printed by C. Stower, 32, Paternoster Row, for Longman, Hurst, Rees, and Orme, Pater-Noster Row, 1807.
>
> I vii, 234p; II 274p; III 278p. 12mo. 13s 6d (CR, ECB, ER).
>
> CR 3rd ser. 13: 442–3 (Apr 1808); ER 10: 492 (July 1807); WSW I: 446–7.
>
> BL N.2499; ECB 463; NSTC P2590 (BI C, O).

*Notes.* Preface, dated Mar 1807.

Further edns: 2nd edn. 1808 (Corvey), CME 3-628-48300-X; 3rd edn. 1814 (NSTC); 4th edn. 1819 (NSTC); 1832 (NSTC); 1839 (NSTC); Philadelphia & New York 1809 (NUC); French trans., 1818.

1807: 53   REEVE, Sophia.
THE MYSTERIOUS WANDERER. A NOVEL: IN THREE VOLUMES.
DEDICATED, BY PERMISSION, TO THE RIGHT HON. LADY ELIZA-
BETH SPENCER. BY SOPHIA REEVE.

> London: Printed for the Author, by C. Spilsbury, Angel-Court, Snow-Hill; and sold by
> Richardson and Son, Royal-Exchange; J. Highley, Fleet-Street; and Didier and Teb-
> bett, St. James's-Street, 1807.
> I ix, 252p; II 248p; III 246p. 12mo. 12s (ECB, ER).
> CR 3rd ser. 11: 326 (July 1807); ER 10: 241 (Apr 1807); WSW I: 458–9.
> MH-H *EC8.R2592.807m; ECB 483; xNSTC.

*Notes.* 'Advertisement', dated 1 Feb 1807. Dedication to Lady Elizabeth Spencer. 'Subscribers
Names' (204 listed), vol. 1, pp. [xi]–[xiv].

1807: 54   [?ROCHE, Regina Maria].
ALVONDOWN VICARAGE. A NOVEL. IN TWO VOLUMES.

> London: Printed at the Minerva-Press, for Lane, Newman, and Co. Leadenhall-Street,
> 1807.
> I 279p; II 290p. 12mo. 9s (ECB); 9s sewed (ER).
> ER 10: 493 (July 1807).
> Corvey; CME 3-628-47051-X; ECB 14; NSTC R1414 (BI O).

*Notes.* Widely catalogued as by Roche, though listed under title only in ECB; the absence of
the author's name on t.p. is also perhaps significant, and the presentation is noticeably sparse
compared with 1807: 55.

1807: 55   ROCHE, Regina Maria.
THE DISCARDED SON; OR, HAUNT OF THE BANDITTI. A TALE. IN FIVE
VOLUMES. BY REGINA MARIA ROCHE, AUTHOR OF THE CHILDREN
OF THE ABBEY, &C.

> London: Printed at the Minerva-Press, for Lane, Newman, and Co. Leadenhall-Street,
> 1807.
> I 315p; II 317p; III 320p; IV 264p; V 350p. 12mo. 27s 6d (ECB); 27s 6d sewed (ER).
> ER 10: 492 (July 1807); WSW I: 470.
> Corvey; CME 3-628-48458-8; ECB 498; NSTC R1415 (BI BL, C).

*Notes.* Further edns: 1825 (NUC); New York 1807 (NUC); French trans., 1808 [as *Le Fils
banni, ou la retraite des brigands* (DBI)].

1807: 56   ST. VENANT, [Catherine-Françoise-Adélaide] de; BYERLEY,
J[ohn] S[cott] (*trans.*).
LEOPOLD DE CIRCE; OR, THE EFFECTS OF ATHEISM. BY M. DE ST.
VENANT, MEMBER OF THE NATIONAL INSTITUTE. TRANSLATED
BY J. S. BYERLEY, ESQ.

> London: Printed for C. Chapple, Pall Mall, 1807.
> I 171p; II 163p. 12mo. 8s (ECB); 8s bound (ER).
> ER 11: 504 (Jan 1808).
> BL 12510.b.27; ECB 90; NSTC S231 (BI O).

*Notes.* Trans. of *Léopold de Circé, ou les effets de l'athéisme.* (Paris, 1803). Pp. 37–38 are missing in BL copy.

1807: 57    SEDLEY, Charles [pseud.?].
THE BAROUCHE DRIVER AND HIS WIFE: A TALE FOR HAUT TON. CONTAINING A CURIOUS BIOGRAPHY OF LIVING CHARACTERS, WITH NOTES EXPLANATORY. IN TWO VOLUMES. BY CHARLES SEDLEY, ESQ. AUTHOR OF "THE INFIDEL MOTHER," "THE MASK OF FASHION," &C. &C. &C.

> London: Printed by D. N. Shury, Berwick Street, Soho, for J. F. Hughes, Wigmore Street, Cavendish Square, 1807.
> I xv, 176p; II 189p. 12mo. 'Price Fourteen Shillings' (half-title); 14s (ECB).
> WSW I: 491.
> BL 12613.g.14; ECB 525; NSTC S1060 (BI C).

*Notes.* 'From the Author' written in hand (ink) on half-title to vol. 1. Dedication to the Earl and Countess of Jersey, dated Brighton Cliffs, 19 July 1807. 'Postscript' at end of vol. 2 (verso of p. 189), dated Brighton Cliffs, 22 July 1807.
Further edns: 2nd edn. 1807 (NSTC); 4th edn. 1808 (Corvey), CME 3-628-48633-5.

1807: 58    SEDLEY, Charles [pseud.?].
THE INFIDEL MOTHER: OR, THREE WINTERS IN LONDON. BY CHARLES SEDLEY, ESQ. AUTHOR OF 'THE MASK OF FASHION,' &C. &C. IN THREE VOLUMES.

> London: Printed by D. N. Shury, Berwick Street, Soho, for J. F. Hughes, Wigmore-Street, Cavendish-Square, 1807.
> I 275p; II 283p; III 236p. 12mo. 18s (ECB); 18s sewed (ER).
> ER 10: 492 (July 1807); WSW I: 491.
> IU 823.Se3i; ECB 525; xNSTC.

*Notes.* Preface signed 'The Author', dated London, Mar 1807. Vol. 2 t.p. imprint differs by reading: 'Printed by R. Zotti, Broad Street, Golden Squ.'
Further edn: 2nd edn. 1807 (Corvey; NSTC S1062), CME 3-628-48634-3.

1807: 59    [?SEDLEY, Charles] [pseud.?].
THE MASK OF FASHION; A PLAIN TALE; WITH, ANECDOTES FOREIGN AND DOMESTIC. IN TWO VOLUMES.

> London: Printed for I. [*sic*] F. Hughes, No. 5, Wigmore Street, Cavendish Square, 1807.
> I xxi, 252p; II vii, 230p. 12mo. 9s (ECB, ER).
> ER 9: 500 (Jan 1807); WSW I: 527.
> O 249.s.259; ECB 372; NSTC S4391.

*Notes.* Dedication to the Duchess of St Albans, dated London, Nov 1806. 'T. S. Surr' written in pencil on first t.p. of the Bodleian copy, an attribution also found in Block. This title is given as by Charles Sedley, however, on the t.p. of both *The Infidel Mother* and *Winter in Dublin* (see 1807: 58, 1808: 98). Imprint on t.p. of vol. 2 has publisher, more normally, as J. F. Hughes. ECB dates Nov 1806.

1807: 60   SMITH, {Catherin}[e].

THE MISANTHROPE FATHER; OR, THE GUARDED SECRET: A NOVEL,
IN THREE VOLUMES. BY MISS SMITH.

> London: Printed for Appleyards, Wimpole-Street; and sold by Appleyard and Co., 108,
> Newgate-Street, 1807.
> I iii, 246p; II 255p; III 258p. 12mo. 15s (ECB); 15s boards (ER).
> ER 11: 238 (Oct 1807); WSW I: 76.
> BL 12614.aa.25; ECB 544; NSTC S2363.

*Notes.* Introductory Address (in verse), dated London, 29 Nov 1806, and signed 'Catharina'.


1807: 61   SMITH, [Horatio].

HORATIO: OR, SKETCHES OF THE DAVENPORT FAMILY. A NOVEL,
IN FOUR VOLUMES. BY MR. SMITH, AUTHOR OF THE FAMILY
STORY; THE RUNAWAY; AND TREVANION.

> Richmond: Printed by and for G. A. Wall, Hill-Street, 1807.
> I 268p; II 255p; III 261p; IV 264p. 12mo. 20s (ECB, ER).
> ER 11: 504 (Jan 1808).
> Corvey; CME 3-628-48656-4; ECB 544; xNSTC.

*Notes.* ECB gives Longman as publisher, and dates Sept 1807; but not discovered in this
form.


1807: 62   SPENCE, Elizabeth Isabella.

THE WEDDING DAY, A NOVEL, BY ELIZABETH ISABELLA SPENCE,
AUTHOR OF "THE NOBILITY OF THE HEART," &C. &C.

> London: Printed by C. Stower, 32, Paternoster Row, for Longman, Hurst, Rees, and
> Orme, Paternoster Row, 1807.
> I 194p; II 168p; III 215p. 12mo. 12s (CR, ECB, ER).
> CR 3rd ser. 11: 437–8 (Aug 1807); ER 10: 492 (July 1807); WSW I: 518.
> Corvey; CME 3-628-48724-2; ECB 554; xNSTC.

*Notes.* CR states: 'The morality of the piece is what might be expected from the niece of
Dr. Fordyce: for such we understand Miss Spence to be' (p. 438).


1807: 63(a)   STAËL-HOLSTEIN, [Anne Louise Germaine] de.

CORINNA, OR ITALY. BY MAD. DE STAËL HOLSTEIN. IN THREE
VOLUMES.

> London: Printed for Samuel Tipper, Leadenhall-Street, 1807.
> I 398p; II 420p; III 440p. 12mo. 20s (ECB, ER); 15s (ER).
> CR 3rd ser. 12: 281–4 (Nov 1807) full review; ER 10: 493 (July 1807), 11: 238 (Oct 1807);
> WSW I: 242.
> BL 1206.g.2-4; ECB 557; NSTC S3432 (BI O).

*Notes.* Trans. of *Corinne, ou l'Italie* (Paris, 1807). A different translation from b) below.
French language version of this novel received a full review in ER, 11: 183–95 (Oct 1807). ER
prices 15s (July 1807), 20s (Oct 1807), both in relation to 3 vols.

1807: 63(b)    STAËL-HOLSTEIN, [Anne Louise Germaine] de; LAWLER, D[ennis] (*trans.*).
**CORINNA; OR, ITALY. BY MAD. DE STAËL HOLSTEIN. IN FIVE VOL-UMES. TRANSLATED FROM THE FRENCH, BY D. LAWLER.**

> London: Printed for Corri, No. 15, Little Newport Street, Leicester Square; and sold by Colburn, No. 48, Conduit Street, New Bond Street, and Mackenzie, No. 24, Old Bailey, 1807.
> I iv, 251p; II 263p; III 264p; IV 253p; V 278p. 12mo.
> WSW I: 242.
> BL 1456.b.16; ECB 557; NSTC S3431 (BI C, Dt).

*Notes.* Trans. of *Corinne, ou l'Italie* (Paris, 1807). Translator's Preface signed D. L., 20 July 1807. This acknowledges the existence of a 'rival translation' (see above), and justifies the choice of five rather than three volumes: 'as I have affixed to it the same price as that in three, while I trust it will bear competition with it as to the paper, &c. the public will, I hope, believe, that in thus varying the number of volumes I could have had no other object in view than the convenience of my purchasers' (vol. 1, p. iii). ECB also lists: Corinne. Transl. by Isabel Hill. With metrical versions of the 'Chants' by Miss Landon. (Standard Novels, no. 24.) 12mo, 6s, Bentley, Feb. 1833.

1807: 64    [STANHOPE, Louisa Sidney].
**THE BANDIT'S BRIDE; OR, THE MAID OF SAXONY. A ROMANCE. IN FOUR VOLUMES. BY THE AUTHOR OF MONTBRASIL ABBEY, &C.**

> London: Printed at the Minerva-Press, for Lane, Newman, and Co. Leadenhall-Street, 1807.
> I 264p; II 254p; III 243p; IV 239p. 12mo. 18s (ECB); 18s sewed (ER).
> ER 10: 493 (July 1807).
> CtY-BR In.St24.807; ECB 558; xNSTC.

*Notes.* Further edns: 2nd edn. 1818 (Corvey), CME 3-628-48771-4; 3rd edn. 1827 (NUC); Philadelphia 1820 (NSTC 2S36106); French trans., 1809.

STRUTT, Elizabeth
See BYRON, Elizabeth

**SURR, Thomas Skinner, THE MASK OF FASHION**
See SEDLEY, Charles

1807: 65    THARMOTT, Maria.
**SANS SOUCI PARK; OR, THE MELANGE. A NOVEL, IN THREE VOL-UMES. BY MARIA THARMOTT.**

> London: Printed for B. Crosby, and Co. Stationers' Court. By C. Stower, Paternoster-Row, 1807.
> I 316p; II 263p; III 229p. 8vo. 13s 6d (ECB, ER).
> ER 10: 241 (Apr 1807); WSW I: 535.
> Corvey; CME 3-628-48949-0; ECB 583; xNSTC.

1807: 66   THOMSON, [Anna? or Harriet?].

**LAURETTE; OR, THE CAPRICES OF FORTUNE. A NOVEL. IN THREE VOLUMES. BY MRS. THOMSON.**

> London: Printed at the Minerva-Press, for Lane, Newman, and Co. Leadenhall-Street, 1807.
> I 254p; II 228p; III 247p. 12mo. 13s 6d (ECB); 13s 6d boards (ER); 13s 6d sewed (ER).
> ER 10: 241 (Apr 1807), 10: 492 (July 1807).
> Corvey; CME 3-628-48954-7; ECB 586; xNSTC.

*Notes.* For the alternative attribution of this title to Anna rather than Harriet Thomson, see note to *The Labyrinths of Life*, in Vol. 1, 1791: 70. Harriet Thomson (née Pigott) is given as the author in FC.

1807: 67   [WHITFIELD, Henry].

**BUT WHICH? OR, DOMESTIC GRIEVANCES OF THE WOLMORE FAMILY. BY THE AUTHOR OF "LEOPOLD."**

> London: Printed for Edward Bentley, Paternoster Row, 1807.
> I viii, 303p; II 312p. 12mo. 10s (ECB, ER).
> CR 3rd ser. 11: 325–6 (July 1807); ER 11: 238 (Oct 1807); WSW I: 561–2.
> Corvey; CME 3-628-47148-6; ECB 88; NSTC W1748 (BI BL).

*Notes.* Dedication 'to the Right Honourable William Windham'. ECB lists Lane as publisher, but not discovered in this form.

1807: 68   WILKINSON, Sarah [Scudgell].

**THE FUGITIVE COUNTESS; OR, CONVENT OF ST. URSULA. A ROMANCE. IN FOUR VOLUMES. BY SARAH WILKINSON.**

> London: Printed for J. F. Hughes, Wigmore-Street, Cavendish-Square, 1807.
> I ii, 213p; II 212p; III 233p; IV 184p. 12mo. 18s (ER).
> ER 10: 493 (July 1807), 11: 238 (Oct 1807).
> Corvey; CME 3-628-48924-5; ECB 638; NSTC W1943 (BI BL).

*Notes.* Dedication 'to Lady de Crespigny', signed 'No. 2, Smith-Street, Westminster'.

1807: 69   [YOUNG, Mary Julia].

**A SUMMER AT BRIGHTON. A MODERN NOVEL, IN THREE VOLUMES.**

> London: Printed by D. N. Shury, Berwick Street, Soho, for J. F. Hughes, Wigmore Street, Cavendish Square, 1807.
> I 256p; II 257p; III 246p. 12mo. 13s 6d (ECB).
> WSW I: 577.
> BL 12611.bbb.6; ECB 569; NSTC Y231 (BI O).

*Notes.* T.p. to vol. 3 only carries the words 'Second Edition'.
Further edns: 2nd edn. 1807 (Corvey), CME 3-628-48731-5; 3rd edn. 1807, with additional 4th vol. containing *The Story of the Modern Lais* (NUC); 4th edn. 1807 (NSTC); 5th edn. 1808 (NSTC). ECB dates Dec 1806.

**ATROCITIES OF A CONVENT**
See RICKMAN, Thomas 'Clio'

1808: 1   ANON.
THE BANKS OF THE WYE: OR, TWO SUMMERS AT CLIFTON. IN
FOUR VOLUMES. BY THE AUTHOR OF A WINTER IN BATH, &C. &C.

> London: Printed by C. and R. Baldwin, New Bridge-Street; for B. Crosby and Co. Sta-
> tioners' Court, Paternoster-Row: sold also by all the Booksellers in Bath and Bristol;
> Donaldson, Brighton; Harvey, Weymouth; Mrs. Street, Southampton; Bettison,
> Margate; Barry, Hastings; Mannder and Co. Tunbridge-Wells; Leek, Cromer; and
> Burgess, Ramsgate, n.d. [1808].
> I 271p; II 247p; III 268p; IV 259p. 12mo. 18s (ECB, ER).
> ER 12: 267 (Apr 1808); WSW I: 146.
> Corvey; CME 3-628-47098-6; ECB 38; xNSTC.

*Notes.* Verso of t.p. of vol. 1 carries a statement 'To the Booksellers and the Public at large',
concerning 'Literary Fraud' by J. F. Hughes, similar in wording to that found in *A Winter in
Bath*—see 1807: 7. Block and Summers attribute to J. H. James, but no other evidence about
such an author writing in the period has been discovered. James Henry James (fl. 1856–62)
was the author of *The Banks of the Wye: and Other Poems* (1856) which possibly explains the
attribution of this title (and sequence of novels connected with it) to J. H. James.

1808: 2   ANON.
THE BARON DE COURCY; OR, READING ABBEY: A LEGENDARY
TALE. IN TWO VOLUMES.

> London: Printed by B. Clarke, Well-Street, Cripplegate, for J. F. Hughes, Wigmore-
> Street, Cavendish-Square, 1808.
> I 199p; II 210p. 12mo. 9s (ECB).
> Corvey; CME 3-628-47105-2; ECB 41; NSTC C3861 (BI BL).

*Notes.* Drop-head title reads: 'Reading Abbey'. ECB dates Nov 1807.

1808: 3   ANON.
CITY NOBILITY; OR, A SUMMER AT MARGATE: A NOVEL, IN THREE
VOLUMES. BY THE AUTHOR OF TWO POPULAR NOVELS.

> London: Printed for J. F. Hughes, No. 15, Paternoster-Row, & 5, Wigmore-Street,
> Cavendish Square, 1808.
> I 223p; II 260p; III 196p. 12mo. 15s (ER).
> ER 13: 225 (Oct 1808).
> BL 12611.bb.14; NSTC M1126.

*Notes.* 'By the author of two popular novels' corresponds with *Winter in Bath* (1807: 7),
though the connection is probably arbitrary.

1808: 4   ANON.

**THE HERMIT OF THE WOOD; OR, THE INTRIGUES OF ARMANDA. IN THREE VOLUMES.**

> London: Printed by D. N. Shury, Berwick Street, Soho, for J. F. Hughes, Wigmore Street, Cavendish Square, and 15, Paternoster Row, 1808.
> I 227p; II 256p; III 272p. 12mo.
> CLU-S/C PR.3991.A1H428; xNSTC.

*Notes.* Summers (p. 426) lists *The Monk and His Daughter; or, the Intrigues of Amanda*, 3 vols., Hughes, 1808, which may represent a differently-tilted version of the same work. 'The Monk and His Daughter' is adv. as 'Just Published' at the end of another Hughes publication, *Wolf* (1806: 67), as 'by Drusilla Davies, of Covent Garden Theatre'.

1808: 5   ANON.

**THE IMAGINARY ADULTRESS. IN TWO VOLUMES.**

> London: Printed by E. Thomas, Golden-Lane, Barbican; for Corri, and Co. No. 15, Little Newport-Street, Leicester-Square; and Colburn, Conduit-Street, New Bond-Street, 1808.
> I 169p; II 183p. 12mo. 8s (ECB, ER).
> ER 11: 504 (Jan 1808).
> Corvey; CME 3-628-47881-2; ECB 292; NSTC A481 (BI BL).

*Notes.* ECB gives Symonds as publisher, but not discovered in this form.

1808: 6   ANON.

**LIFE AS IT IS; OR, A PEEP INTO FASHIONABLE PARTIES. A NOVEL. IN THREE VOLUMES.**

> London: Printed at the Minerva-Press, for Lane, Newman, and Co. Leadenhall-Street, 1808.
> I 239p; II 289p; III 251p. 12mo. 15s (ECB).
> WSW I: 66.
> Corvey; CME 3-628-48044-2; ECB 345; xNSTC.

*Notes.* ECB dates Dec 1807.

1808: 7   ANON.

**MARIANNA; OR, MODERN MANNERS. A NOVEL. IN TWO VOLUMES.**

> London: Printed by Luke Hansard & Sons, for T. Cadell and W. Davies, in the Strand, 1808.
> I vii, 209p; II 304p. 12mo. 8s (ER).
> CR 3rd ser. 14: 439–40 (Aug 1808); ER 12: 525 (July 1808); WSW I: 72.
> Corvey; CME 3-628-48157-0; NSTC M1136 (BI BL, C).

*Notes.* Preface dated London, 1 June 1808; this implies male authorship.

1808: 8   ANON.

**THE MASTER PASSION; OR, THE HISTORY OF FREDERICK BEAU-MONT. IN FOUR VOLUMES.**

London: Printed for William Miller, Albemarle Street, 1808.

I vi, 314p, music; II 288p; III 296p; IV 230p. 12mo. 16s (ER).

CR 3rd ser. 14: 220–2 (June 1808); ER 12: 267 (Apr 1808); WSW I: 73.

Corvey; CME 3-628-48136-8; NSTC M1639.5 (BI BL).

*Notes.* 'To My Reader' (vol. 1, pp. v–vi). CR refers to 'The fair lady, who is the author of the Master Passion' (p. 220).

1808: 9    ANON.

MEMOIRS OF FEMALE PHILOSOPHERS, IN TWO VOLUMES. BY A MODERN PHILOSOPHER OF THE OTHER SEX.

London: Printed for Henry Colburn, English, French, and Italian Subscription Library, No. 50, Conduit Street, 1808.

I xi, 204p; II 213p. 12mo. 10s (ECB, ER).

ER 11: 503 (Jan 1808).

BL 12611.c.25; ECB 379; NSTC M2035.

*Notes.* Dedication to Lady Haggerston by 'the Editor and Publisher'. ECB dates Nov 1807. Adv. for four other novels 'Just Published' by Henry Colburn follows immediately after the text on vol. 1, p. 204, and further advs. are similarly found at vol. 2, pp. 213–[14].

1808: 10    ANON.

THE MONKS AND THE ROBBERS; A TALE OF THE FIFTEENTH CENTURY. IN TWO VOLUMES.

London: Printed for George Robinson, 25, Paternoster-Row, 1808.

I 284p; II 244p. 12mo. 8s (ER).

ER 12: 525 (July 1808); WSW I: 78.

Corvey; CME 3-628-48266-6; xNSTC.

*Notes.* Originally published in 53 parts in the *Lady's Magazine*, over an unprecedented period of nearly eleven years (Aug 1794–Nov 1794, Apr 1798–May 1805). The story, written by a reader, was abandoned after three parts, and resumed by a volunteer, 'A. Percy', in 1798 (see Mayo, Item 913).

1808: 11    ANON.

NEWMINSTER ABBEY, OR THE DAUGHTER OF O'MORE. A NOVEL, FOUNDED ON FACTS. AND INTERSPERSED WITH ORIGINAL POETRY AND PICTURESQUE AND FAITHFUL SKETCHES OF VARIOUS COUNTRIES. IN TWO VOLUMES.

London: Printed by B. Clarke, Well-Street, Cripplegate, for J. F. Hughes, Wigmore-Street, Cavendish-Square, 1808.

I iv, 223p; II 272p. 12mo.

Corvey; CME 3-628-48194-5; NSTC O334 (BI BL).

*Notes.* Preface, pp. [iii]–iv, implies male authorship.

THE NOBLE CORNUTOS

See HURSTONE, J. P.

1808: 12   ANON.
**THE RED TYGER; OR, THE TRUTH WILL OUT. IN TWO VOLUMES.**

> London: Printed for B. Crosby and Co. Stationers' Court, by C. Stower, Paternoster Row, 1808.
> I 257p; II 352p. 12mo. 9s (ECB, ER).
> ER 12: 267 (Apr 1808).
> MH-H *EC8.A100.808r; ECB 482; NSTC T1127 (BI BL).

1808: 13   ANON.
**THE RING AND THE WELL; OR, THE GRECIAN PRINCESS. A ROMANCE. IN FOUR VOLUMES.**

> London: Printed for Longman, Hurst, Rees, and Orme, Paternoster-Row, 1808.
> I 271p; II 220p; III 249p; IV 300p. 12mo. 18s (ECB, ER).
> ER 12: 524 (July 1808), 13: 507 (Jan 1809); WSW I: 104.
> Corvey; CME 3-628-48607-6; ECB 494; NSTC G1895 (BI E).

1808: 14   ANON.
**THE ROMANCE OF THE APPENNINES. IN TWO VOLUMES.**

> London: Printed for Henry Colburn, English, French, and Italian Subscription Library, No. 50, Conduit Street, 1808.
> I 199p; II 199p. 12mo. 9s (ECB, ER).
> ER 11: 504 (Jan 1808).
> BL 12611.b.2; ECB 501; NSTC A1470.

*Notes.* Dedication to Sir Francis Hartwell, Bart., signed 'The Author'. ECB dates Nov 1807.

1808: 15   ANON.
**THE ROYAL LEGEND. A TALE.**

> London: Printed by Ballantine and Law, Duke-Street, Adelphi, Strand; for Effingham Wilson, Paternoster-Row, 1808.
> ii, 195p. 12mo. 5s (ECB); 5s bound (ER).
> ER 11: 504 (Jan 1808), 12: 267 (Apr 1808); WSW I: 106.
> Corvey; CME 3-628-48558-4; ECB 505; xNSTC.

*Notes.* 'Motto' (pp. [i]–ii) from Shakespeare's *Henry IV.* Preface (pp. [1]–5). Introduction (pp. [7]–17). Novel proper starts at p. [19]. ER 12: 267 (Apr 1808) also gives, as if subtitle: 'in which are detailed the Characters of Bardolph, Lupo, Waldon, and other dangerous Companions for a Prince'. ECB dates Nov 1807.

1808: 16   ANON.
**THE R—L STRANGER. A TALE. IN ONE VOLUME.**

> London: Printed for J. F. Hughes, 15, Paternoster-Row, and 5, Wigmore-St. Cavendish-Square, 1808.
> 158p. 12mo. 'Five Shillings' (t.p.).
> DLC PR.3991.A1R62; xNSTC.

1808: 17   ANON.

SAINT HILARY, THE CRUSADER. A ROMANTIC LEGEND. IN THREE
VOLUMES.

> London: Printed for J. F. Hughes, Wigmore-Street, Cavendish-Square, 1808.
> I iii, 214p; II 228p; III 224p. 12mo. 13s 6d (ER).
> ER 11: 504 (Jan 1808).
> Corvey; CME 3-628-48487-1; xNSTC.

1808: 18   ANON.

SKETCHES OF CHARACTER, OR SPECIMENS OF REAL LIFE. A NOVEL,
IN THREE VOLUMES.

> London: Printed for Longman, Hurst, Rees, and Orme, Paternoster-Row; B. Crosby,
> Stationer's-Court: and J. Lansdown, Bristol, by Mills & Co. St. Augustine's-Back,
> Bristol, 1808.
> I x, 282p; II 308p; III 392p. 12mo. 15s (ECB).
> CR 3rd ser. 15: 88–92 (Sept 1808) full review; WSW I: 112.
> PU PR.3991.A1.S54.1808; ECB 541; NSTC S2186 (BI BL).

*Notes.* MS note on fly-leaf in ViU copy (PZ2.S556.1808) reads, in contemporary hand, 'By
Richard Brinsley Sheridan, author of Critic'; this copy has the Preface mistakenly bound near
end of last vol. NUC entry states 'also attributed to Amelia Opie'. It is worth noting too, per-
haps, the similarity of the imprint to those found in a sequence of novels attributable to the
Revd Mr Wyndham (see e.g. 1805: 72).
*Further edns:* 2nd edn. 1813 (Corvey), CME 3-628-48753-6; 3rd edn. 1815 (NSTC).

1808: 19   ANON.

THE WOMAN OF COLOUR, A TALE. BY THE AUTHOR OF "LIGHT
AND SHADE," "THE AUNT AND THE NIECE," "EBERSFIELD [*sic*]
ABBEY", &C. IN TWO VOLUMES.

> London: Printed for Black, Parry, and Kingsbury, Booksellers to the Honourable East
> India Company, Leadenhall-Street, 1808.
> I 264p; II 220p. 12mo. 10s (ECB, ER).
> ER 13: 507 (Jan 1809); WSW I: 146.
> BL 12614.k.3; ECB 645; xNSTC.

*Notes.* The three titles listed as by the author suggest a possible connection with Mrs E. M.
Foster, though her authorship is not generally granted. Colophon reads 'Printed by S. Hamilton, Weybridge, Surry'. ECB dates Oct 1808.

1808: 20   ANON.

THE YOUNG MOTHER; OR, ALBINIA. A NOVEL. IN THREE VOLUMES.

> London: Printed at the Minerva-Press, for Lane, Newman, and Co. Leadenhall-Street,
> 1808.
> I 209p; II 215p; III 226p. 12mo. 15s (ECB).
> Corvey; CME 3-628-48990-3; ECB 653; xNSTC.

*Notes.* Half-title, drop-head title, and running-title all read: 'Albinia'. ECB dates Oct 1808.
*Further edn:* Baltimore 1833 as *Albinia; or, the Young Mother* (NUC).

1808: 21   AMPHLETT, J[ames].
## NED BENTLEY, A NOVEL, IN THREE VOLUMES. BY J. AMPHLETT.

Stafford: Printed by J. Drewry; and published by Longman, Hurst, Rees and Orme, London, 1808.
I xxi, 227p; II 252p; III 252p. 12mo. 15s (ER).
CR 3rd ser. 16: 89–93 (Jan 1809) full review; ER 13: 507 (Jan 1809); WSW I: 5.
Corvey; CME 3-628-47056-0; xNSTC.

*Notes.* Dedication 'to the Right Hon. R. B. Sheridan'. Preface dated Stafford, 2 Oct 1808. 'Subscribers' Names' (*c.*230 listed), vol. 1, pp. [xiii]–xxi. Collates in sixes.


1808: 22   [ARNOLD, Lieut.].
## THE BRITISH ADMIRAL. A NOVEL. IN THREE VOLUMES. BY A NAVAL OFFICER.

London: Printed at the Minerva-Press, for Lane, Newman, and Co. Leadenhall-Street, 1808.
I xv, 314p; II 354p; III 364p. 12mo. 16s 6d (ECB, ER).
ER 13: 225 (Oct 1808).
Corvey; CME 3-628-47160-5; ECB 75; xNSTC.

*Notes.* Dedication 'to Sir Home Popham, Knight, Commander of His Majesty's Squadron at the Glorious Capture of Buenos Ayres, on the 27th of June, 1806', dated 1 May 1808. This is followed by a list headed by Her Royal Highness the Princess of Wales, followed by more than twenty other names ranging from other members of the royal family to contemporary actresses, and including 'Mr. Chapple, 66, Pall Mall, (who is so good as to receive subscriptions)'. The author describes how he has received donations from the above while imprisoned for more than ten months for 'a debt of thirty pounds only'. Blakey notes attributed to Lieut. Arnold in Minerva Library Catalogue of 1814.


1808: 23   BARNBY, Mrs.
## *THE AMERICAN SAVAGE; OR, ORAB AND PHOEBE. BY MRS BARNBY.

London: Robinson, 1808.
2 vols. 12mo. 9s (ECB, ER).
ER 15: 529 (Jan 1810); WSW I: 141.
No copy located; ECB 40.

*Notes.* Details mainly from ECB, which dates Sept 1808. Summers gives Maidstone as place of publication.


1808: 24   BARRELL, Miss [P.].
## RICHES AND POVERTY: A TALE. BY MISS BARRELL.

London: Printed for Samuel Tipper, 37, Leadenhall Street; and Joseph Robins, 57, Tooley Street, 1808.
212p, ill. 12mo. 5s (ECB, ER).
CR 3rd ser. 14: 108–9 (May 1808); ER 12: 524 (July 1808); WSW I: 141.
BL 12611.bbb; ECB 41; NSTC B651.

1808: 25   [BARRETT, Eaton Stannard].
THE MISS-LED GENERAL; A SERIO-COMIC, SATIRIC, MOCK-HEROIC
ROMANCE. BY THE AUTHOR OF THE RISING SUN.

> London: Printed for H. Oddy, Oxford-Street, 1808.
> 197p, ill. 12mo. 7s (ECB).
> WSW I: 142–3.
> Corvey; CME 3-628-48215-1; ECB 389; NSTC B672 (BI BL, C, O).

*Notes.* A satire on Frederick, Duke of York. Collates in sixes. ECB dates Nov 1807.
Further edn: 2nd edn. 1808 (NSTC).

1808: 26   BOUNDEN, Joseph.
THE MURDERER; OR, THE FALL OF LECAS. A TALE. IN TWO VOL-
UMES. BY JOSEPH BOUNDEN.

> London: Printed at the Minerva-Press, for Lane, Newman, and Co. Leadenhall-Street,
> 1808.
> I 194p; II 187p. 12mo. 8s (ECB, ER).
> ER 13: 225 (Oct 1808).
> Corvey; CME 3-628-47012-9; ECB 68; xNSTC.

1808: 27   BOUVERIE, Sophia.
LORD HUBERT OF ARUNDEL: A ROMANCE, IN TWO VOLUMES. BY
SOPHIA BOUVERIE, AUTHOR OF ST. JUSTINS [*sic*]; OR THE HOUR
OF TRIAL.

> London: Printed for J. F. Hughes, Paternoster-Row; and No. 5, Wigmore-Street,
> Cavendish-Square, 1808.
> I 192p; II 231p. 12mo.
> Corvey; CME 3-628-47269-5; xNSTC.

1808: 28   BOUVERIE, Sophia.
ST. JUSTIN; OR, THE HOUR OF TRIAL. A ROMANCE, IN THREE VOL-
UMES. BY SOPHIA BOUVERIE, AUTHOR OF "LORD HUBERT OF
ARUNDELL [*sic*]."

> London: Printed for J. F. Hughes, 5, Wigmore-Street, Cavendish-Square, and 15, Pater-
> Noster-Row, 1808.
> I vii, 232p; II 243p; III 200p. 12mo. 15s (ER).
> ER 13: 225 (Oct 1808).
> Corvey; CME 3-628-47270-9; xNSTC.

*Notes.* Colophon in vol. 1 (only): 'Printed by J. F. Hughes, Wigmore Street'. Colophon in
vol. 2 reads: 'Printed by R. Juigné, 17, Margaret-street, Cavendish-square.' Novel proper
ends at vol. 3, p. 189; pp. 190–200 consists of a list of 'Popular Novels, Romances &c. &c. &c.'
published by Hughes, listing 66 items in all.

1808: 29   BREWER, George.
THE WITCH OF RAVENSWORTH; A ROMANCE, IN TWO VOLUMES.
BY GEORGE BREWER, AUTHOR OF "HOURS OF LEISURE."

London: Printed for J. F. Hughes, 15, Pater-noster-Row, and 5, Wigmore-Street,
    Cavendish-Square, 1808.
I 228p; II 212p. 12mo. 10s (ER).
ER 13: 506 (Jan 1809); WSW I: 131.
Corvey; CME 3-628-47196-6; ECB 73; NSTC B4246 (BI BL).

*Notes.* Further edn: Durham 1842 (NSTC).

1808: 30   BREWER, J[ames] N[orris].
MOUNTVILLE CASTLE, A VILLAGE STORY: IN THREE VOLUMES. BY
J. N. BREWER, AUTHOR OF "A WINTER'S TALE," IN 4 VOLS.

London: Printed by M. Allen, 15, Paternoster-Row, for Corri & Co. No. 15, Little New-
    port-Street, Leicester-Square; and Colburn, Conduit-Street, New Bond-Street, 1808.
I ii, 226p; II 242p; III 252p. 12mo. 15s (ECB); 15s boards (ER).
ER 11: 504 (Jan 1808); WSW I: 171.
Corvey; CME 3-628-47097-8; ECB 73; xNSTC.

*Notes.* ECB dates Oct 1807.

1808: 31   BREWER, James Norris.
SECRETS MADE PUBLIC. A NOVEL. IN FOUR VOLUMES. BY JAMES
NORRIS BREWER, AUTHOR OF A WINTER'S TALE, THOUGHTS ON
THE PRESENT STATE OF THE ENGLISH PEASANTRY, &C.

London: Printed at the Minerva-Press, for Lane, Newman, and Co. Leadenhall-Street,
    1808.
I xxxi, 244p; II 293p; III 279p; IV 276p. 12mo. 20s (ECB, ER).
ER 12: 524 (July 1808).
Corvey; CME 3-628-47671-2; ECB 73; xNSTC.

*Notes.* 'Advertisement' incorporating the following statement: 'The Author begs leave to
submit, that a Book (professing to be a Novel) lately published under the title of "Mountville
Castle, by the Author of A Winter's Tale," was written in *very early life, previously* to *The Winter's Tale*. Had the bookseller (in whose hands it lay nine years) apprised the writer of his
intention, so childish a composition should have been suppressed.' This is followed by 'Hints
toward a Just Taste in Novel Reading' (pp. [i]–xxxi). Continuous roman and arabic pagination, with novel proper beginning at p. [33].

1808: 32   [BURNEY, Sarah Harriet].
GERALDINE FAUCONBERG. IN THREE VOLUMES. BY THE AUTHOR
OF CLARENTINE.

London: Printed for G. Wilkie and J. Robinson, 57, Paternoster-Row, 1808.
I viii, 288p; II 300p; III 392p. 12mo. 18s (ECB, ER); 12s (ER).
CR 3rd ser. 16: 104–5 (Jan 1809); ER 13: 225 (Oct 1808), 13: 507 (Jan 1809); WSW
    I: 181.
BL N.2346-48; ECB 228; NSTC B5717 (BI O).

*Notes.* ER price 12s Oct 1808, 18s Jan 1809.
Further edns: 2nd edn. 1812 (Corvey), CME 3-628-47175-3; Boston 1817 (NUC); French
trans., 1825 [as *Miss Fauconberg, traduit de l'anglois de Miss Burney* (BN)].

1808: 33   BYRON, ['Medora Gordon'].
THE ENGLISH-WOMAN. A NOVEL. IN FIVE VOLUMES. BY MISS
BYRON.

> London: Printed at the Minerva-Press, for Lane, Newman, and Co. Leadenhall-Street,
> 1808.
> I 286p; II 298p; III 348p; IV 331p; V 302p. 12mo. 25s (ECB, ER).
> ER 13: 225 (Oct 1808); WSW I: 185.
> MH-H *EC8.B9965.808e; ECB 91; NSTC B6041 (BI BL).

*Notes.* The first novel by 'Miss Byron', who should be distinguished from Mrs Byron (afterwards Elizabeth Strutt). It seems likely Miss Byron and 'A Modern Antique' (see 1809: 15,
1814: 15, 1816: 21) are the same author. The forenames Medora Gordon, misleadingly suggesting a connection with Lord Byron, appeared in the Minerva Catalogue 1816 (see FC) and
were commonly associated with this author.
Further edn: 2nd edn. 1812 (Corvey), CME 3-628-47179-6.


1808: 34   CAMBRIENSIS [pseud.].
EDMUND FITZAUBREY. A NOVEL. BY CAMBRIENSIS. IN THREE
VOLUMES.

> London: Printed for Richard Phillips, Bridge-Street, Blackfriars, 1808.
> I 271p; II 223p; III 257p. 12mo. 15s (ER).
> ER 12: 524 (July 1808); WSW I: 194.
> Corvey; CME 3-628-47516-3; NSTC C328 (BI BL).

*Notes.* Printer's mark after imprint date reads: 'T. Gillet, Crown-Court'.


1808: 35   CAMPBELL, Dr.
THE FEMALE MINOR. A NOVEL. IN TWO VOLUMES. BY DOCTOR
CAMPBELL.

> London: Printed for George Richards, Cornhill, 1808.
> I vii, 206p; II 199p. 12mo.
> BL 12612.aa.10; NSTC C361.

*Notes.* 'Prefatory Epistle', vol. 1, pp. [v]–vii.


1808: 36   [CAVENDISH-BRADSHAW, Mary Ann].
MEMOIRS OF MARIA, COUNTESS OF D'ALVA: BEING NEITHER
NOVEL NOR ROMANCE, BUT APPERTAINING TO BOTH. INTER-
SPERSED WITH HISTORIC FACTS & COMIC INCIDENTS; IN THE
COURSE OF WHICH ARE INTRODUCED, FRAGMENTS & CIRCUM-
STANCES, NOT ALTOGETHER INAPPLICABLE TO THE EVENTS OF
THIS DISTRACTED AGE, AND TO THE MEASURES OF THE FORE-
SIGHTED DEFENDERS OF OUR HOLY FAITH. IN TWO VOLUMES. BY
PRISCILLA PARLANTE.

> London: Printed by J. Barfield, Wardour-Street, for William Miller, Albemarle-Street,
> 1808.
> I xvi, 384p, ill.; II 494p, ill. 8vo. 21s (ER).

CR 3rd ser. 15: 104–5 (Sept 1808); ER 12: 524 (July 1808).
BL 12613.gg.15; CME 3-628-48618-1; NSTC P461.

*Notes.* Preface 'to the Man in the Moon'. CR begins: 'If this production be neither novel nor romance, it becomes an exceedingly difficult task to determine how it is to be entitled'. It concludes: 'In short, we can find nothing to distinguish this from any other of the numerous productions of the day' (p. 105).

**CECIL, Henry Montague, THE ROSE OF CUMBERLAND**
See 1805: 18

1808: 37　CORDOVA, Cordelia.
**THE ILLUSIONS OF YOUTH: OR, ROMANCE IN WALES, AND COMMON SENSE IN LONDON. A NOVEL, IN FOUR VOLUMES, BY CORDELIA CORDOVA.**

> Hampstead: Printed by and for T. Wallis, and sold by Longman, Hurst, Rees, and Orme, Paternoster Row, 1808.
> I xxvii, 196p; II 223p; III 213p; IV 210p. 12mo. 18s (ER).
> ER 13: 225 (Oct 1808).
> BL 838.b.29-30; NSTC C3658.

*Notes.* Dedication to 'Captain Macnamara', dated Hampstead, 22 Aug 1808. Preface (vol. 1, pp. [vii]–xxviii) also dated Hampstead, 22 Aug 1808, and signed Cordelia Cordova. ViU copy (PZ2.C76.I.1809) is a presentation copy with the author's MS corrections.
Further edn: 1809 (Corvey), CME 3-628-47280-6.

1808: 38　CORRY, John.
**THE MYSTERIOUS GENTLEMAN FARMER; OR, THE DISGUISES OF LOVE: A NOVEL. IN THREE VOLUMES. BY JOHN CORRY, AUTHOR OF "A SATYRICAL VIEW OF LONDON," &C. &C.**

> London: Printed for B. Crosby & Co. Stationer's Court, Paternoster-Row; By J. & E. Hodson, 15, Cross Street, Hatton Garden, 1808.
> I 233p; II 241p; III 209p. 12mo. 13s 6d (ECB, ER).
> ER 12: 267 (Apr 1808); WSW I: 220.
> Corvey; CME 3-628-47368-3; ECB 137; NSTC C3752 (BI O).

1808: 39　COTTIN, [Sophie Ristaud].
**CLARA; A NOVEL, IN TWO VOLUMES. BY MADME. COTTIN, AUTHOR OF ELIZABETH, OR THE EXILES OF SIBERIA; THE SARACEN, &C. &C.**

> London: Published by Henry Colburn, Conduit-Street, New Bond-Street, 1808.
> I vii, 194p; II 188p. 12mo. 10s (CR); 9s (ER).
> CR 3rd ser. 15: 278–87 (Nov 1808) full review; ER 12: 524 (July 1808); WSW I: 220.
> BL 12511.e.27; ECB 138; NSTC C3813.

*Notes.* Trans. of *Claire d'Albe* (Paris, 1799).

1808: 40   DALLAS, R[obert] C[harles].

THE KNIGHTS: TALES ILLUSTRATIVE OF THE MARVELLOUS. BY
R. C. DALLAS, ESQ. IN THREE VOLUMES.

> London: Printed for Longman, Hurst, Rees, and Orme, Paternoster-Row, 1808.
> I xiii, 279p; II 272p; III 274p. 12mo. 15s (ECB).
> CR 3rd ser. 14: 95–6 (May 1808) full review; WSW I: 235.
> Corvey; CME 3-628-47392-6; ECB 150; NSTC D98 (BI BL, E).

*Notes.* Dedication to 'Mr. Pratt', dated Chelsea, 20 Feb 1808.


1808: 41   DOHERTY, {Ann}.

RONALDSHA; A ROMANCE, IN TWO VOLUMES. BY MRS. DOHERTY,
WIFE OF HUGH DOHERTY, ESQ. AUTHOR OF THE "DISCOVERY;
OR, MYSTERIOUS SEPARATION."

> London: Published by H. D. Symonds, Paternoster-Row; and may be had of all the
>     Booksellers in the United Kingdom, 1808.
> I xlv, 173p; II 262p. 12mo. 10s 6d (ER).
> CR 3rd ser. 14: 331–2 (July 1808); ER 12: 524 (July 1808); WSW I: 248.
> Corvey; CME 3-628-47442-6; ECB 167; xNSTC.

*Notes.* Inscription to 'Thomas Hunter, Esq. and Hannah, his Wife', signed 'Hugh Doherty'.
'Dedication', vol. 1, pp. [vii]–xvii, again signed 'Hugh Doherty', and dated '4, Melina Place,
Westminster Road', London, 25 Apr 1808. Preface, vol. 1, pp. [xxi]–xlv, also signed 'Hugh
Doherty', describing how the novel was written by his wife when they lived together in Hert-
fordshire, before her desertion of him and their child. 'Apology', at the end of vol. 2,
pp. 259–62, signed and dated like the Dedication. This is followed by an adv. for a new edn.,
'just published', of 'The Discovery; or, the Mysterious Separation of Hugh Doherty, Esq. and
Ann, his Wife'.
Further edn: Boston (from 2nd London edn.) 1809 (NUC).


1808: 42   DUNCOMBE, Mrs. {A}.

THE VILLAGE GENTLEMAN, AND THE ATTORNEY AT LAW; A NAR-
RATIVE. BY MRS. DUNCOMBE. IN TWO VOLUMES.

> London: Printed for J. Hatchard, Bookseller to Her Majesty, No. 190, Piccadilly, 1808.
> I v, 355p; II 280p. 12mo. 10s 6d (ECB).
> CR 3rd ser. 14: 218 (June 1808).
> BL 838.b.27; ECB 174; NSTC D2184 (BI E, O).

*Notes.* Dedication to the Countess of Albemarle, signed A. Duncombe. 'Subscribers' Names'
(56 listed), vol. 1, pp. [iii]–v. According to FC, this novel is falsely ascribed to Susanna Duncombe (née Highmore), whose husband's Christian name was John.


1808: 43   EDGEWORTH, Mrs.

THE MATCH GIRL. A NOVEL, IN THREE VOLUMES. BY MRS. EDGE-
WORTH.

> London: Printed by J. Dennett, Leather Lane, Holborne; for J. F. Hughes, 15, Paternos-
>     ter Row, and 5, Wigmore Street, Cavendish Square, 1808.

I 241p; II 215p; III 188p. 12mo. 15s (ER).
ER 13: 225 (Oct 1808).
BL 1509/4148; NSTC E223.5.

1808: 44    GENLIS, [Stéphanie-Félicité, Comtesse] de.
**BELISARIUS; TRANSLATED FROM THE FRENCH OF MADAME DE
GENLIS. IN TWO VOLUMES.**
London: Published by Henry Colburn, Conduit-Street, and Bond-Street, 1808.
I xviii, 170p; II missing. 12mo.
BL 12512.aaa.22; NSTC B4976 (BI E).

*Notes.* Trans. of *Bélisaire* (Paris, 1808). The second vol. of the BL copy belongs to another
translation, published by J. F. Hughes, with the t.p. date of 1809. The copy at E cited by NSTC
is in fact a microfilm of the BL copy. MH-H 40588.21.100 is the full Hughes edn., titled *Belisarius; An Historical Romance*, both vols. (I xxxiii, 142p; II 173p) with 1809 imprint. ECB 225
gives publisher as Dulau, 1808, 7s.
Further edn: Baltimore 1810, as *Belisarius: A Historical Romance* (NUC).

1808: 45    GENLIS, [Stéphanie-Félicité, Comtesse] de.
**THE DUKE OF LAUZUN; AN HISTORICAL ROMANCE; INTERSPERSED
WITH NUMEROUS ANECDOTES OF THE COURT OF LOUIS XIV. AND
FORMING A COMPANION TO THE DUCHESS OF LA VALLIERE.
BY MADAME DE GENLIS. IN TWO VOLUMES.**
London: Printed for Henry Colburn, English, French, and Italian Library, No. 50, Con-
     duit Street, 1808.
I 208p; II 256p. 12mo. 10s (ECB).
ER 11: 504 (Jan 1808).
MH-H 40588.21.80; ECB 173; xNSTC.

*Notes.* No French original discovered. ECB lists under title not Genlis, and dates Nov 1807.
CR 3rd ser. 13: 449–57 (Jan 1808) gives full review, but apparently of an edn. in French published in London by Dulau.

1808: 46    GENLIS, [Stéphanie-Félicité, Comtesse] de.
**THE EARL OF CORK; OR, SEDUCTION WITHOUT ARTIFICE. A
ROMANCE. TO WHICH ARE ADDED, SIX INTERESTING TALES. IN
THREE VOLUMES. BY MADAME DE GENLIS, AUTHOR OF ALPHON-
SINE, TALES OF THE CASTLE, SIEGE OF ROCHELLE, &C. &C.**
London: Printed for J. F. Hughes, 5 Wigmore Street, Cavendish Square; and 15, Pater-
     noster-Row, 1808.
I xiii, 218p; II 216p; III ii, 167p. 12mo.
ICU PQ.1985.G.5A641808; xNSTC.

*Notes.* Trans. of *Le Comte de Corke surnommé le Grand, ou la séduction sans artifice, suivi de six
nouvelles* (Paris, 1805). Preface gives biographical details about Earl of Cork (d. 1613). Vol. 2
contains three additional titles 'The young Penitent' (to p. 90), 'Zumelinde; or, the young old
Lady' (pp. 91–135), 'The Lovers without Love' (pp. 137–216); vol. 3 contains 'Introduction',
'The Tulip Tree; an Oriental Tale' (pp. 3–61), 'The Savinias; or the Twins' (pp. 63–167).

1808: 47    GENLIS, [Stéphanie-Félicité, Comtesse] de.
SAINCLAIR, OR THE VICTIM OF THE ARTS AND SCIENCES. TRANS-
LATED FROM THE FRENCH OF MADAME DE GENLIS.

> London: Printed by Cox, Son, and Baylis, Great Queen Street, for B. Dulau and Co.
>   Soho Square, 1808.
> v, 141p. 12mo. 3s (ECB).
> WSW I: 240.
> BL 12512.aaa.20; ECB 225; NSTC B4992 (BI O).

*Notes.* Trans. of *Sainclair; ou la victime des sciences et des arts* (Paris, 1808). ECB dates May
1808. 'Preface by the Translator', pp. [i]–v, followed by advs. with following statement: 'M.
Dulau and Co. beg leave to inform the Public, that all the works of that celebrated writer
Mme. de Genlis, may be had of them, either separate or together. And it is their intention to
present the public with the earliest editions of her future works, both in French and English,
having made arrangements to publish them in English sooner than anybody else'.
Further edn: Georgetown 1813 (NUC).

1808: 48    GENLIS, [Stéphanie-Félicité, Comtesse] de; DALLAS, R[obert]
C[harles] (*trans.*).
THE SIEGE OF ROCHELLE; OR, THE CHRISTIAN HEROINE. BY
MADAME DE GENLIS. TRANSLATED BY R. C. DALLAS, ESQ.

> London: Printed by Cox, Son, and Baylis, 75, Gt. Queen Street, for B. Dulau and Co.
>   Soho Square; and J. Hughes, Wigmore Street, Cavendish Square, 1808.
> I xxiii, 214p; II 252p; III 216p. 12mo. 13s 6d (ECB); 12s (ER).
> ER 12: 525 (July 1808).
> BRu ENC; ECB 225; NSTC B4993 (BI BL, C).

*Notes.* Trans. of *Le Siège de la Rochelle, ou le malheur et la conscience* (Paris, 1808). Vol. 2 t.p.
imprint reads 'Printed by P. Da Ponte, 15, Poland Street, Oxford Street . . . [etc.]'; vol. 3 t.p.
reads 'Printed by R. Juigné, 17 Margaret-Street, Cavendish Square . . . [etc.]'. CR 3rd ser. 13:
525–8 (App [Apr/May 1808]) has full review of *The Siege of La Rochelle &c. By Madame de
Genlis*, Dulau, 1808: this probably relates to a French language edn.

1808: 49    [GREEN, Sarah].
THE PRIVATE HISTORY OF THE COURT OF ENGLAND. IN TWO VOLUMES.

> London: Printed for the Author, and sold by B. Crosby & Co. Stationers' Court,
>   Ludgate-Street, 1808.
> I xxiv, 287p; II xi, 252p. 12mo. 12s (CR, ECB).
> CR 3rd ser. 14: 217–18 (June 1808); WSW I: 288.
> BL 808.c.19; ECB 471; NSTC G1946 (BI C, O).

*Notes.* Further edn: 2nd edn. 1808 (NSTC).

1808: 50    [GREEN, Sarah].
TANKERVILLE FAMILY, IN THREE VOLUMES. BY A LADY.

> London: Printed for R. Dutton, Gracechurch-Street, and C. Chapple, Pall-Mall, 1808.
> I 239p; II 239p; III 248p. 12mo. 13s 6d (ECB).
> Corvey; CME 3-628-48941-5; ECB 577; xNSTC.

*Notes. The Festival of St. Jago* (1810: 44), more commonly attributed to Green, is described on its t.p. as 'by the Author of Tankerville Family'. Summers attributes to Green and lists as *History of the Tankerville Family*, Minerva Press, 1806; but not discovered in this form. ECB dates May 1809.

1808: 51    [?GUÉNARD, Elisabeth].
MYSTERY UPON MYSTERY. A TALE OF EARLIER TIMES. IN FOUR
VOLUMES. BY THE AUTHOR OF THE BARON DE FALKENHEIM.

> London: Printed at the Minerva-Press, for Lane, Newman, and Co. Leadenhall-Street,
> 1808.
> I 271p, ill.; II 268p; III 280p; IV 259p. 12mo. 20s (ECB).
> Corvey; CME 3-628-48185-6; ECB 403; NSTC M3825 (BI BL).

*Notes.* Trans. of *Mystères sur mystères, ou les onze chevaliers* (Paris, 1807)? ECB dates Dec 1807, and lists under title only.

GUNNING, Elizabeth
See PLUNKETT, Elizabeth

1808: 52    HAMILTON, Elizabeth.
THE COTTAGERS OF GLENBURNIE; A TALE FOR THE FARMER'S
INGLE-NOOK. BY ELIZABETH HAMILTON, AUTHOR OF THE ELEM-
ENTARY PRINCIPLES OF EDUCATION, MEMOIRS OF MODERN
PHILOSOPHERS, &C. &C. &C.

> Edinburgh: Printed by James Ballantyne and Co. for Manners and Miller, and S.
> Cheyne; T. Cadell and W. Davies, Strand, and William Miller, Albemarle-Street,
> London, 1808.
> xv, 402p. 8vo. 7s 6d (ECB, ER).
> CR 3rd ser. 15: 421–30 (Dec 1808) full review; ER 12: 401–10 (July 1808) full review, 13:
> 225 (Oct 1808); WSW I: 295–6.
> BL 012643.pp.83; ECB 252; NSTC H314 (BI E).

*Notes.* Dedication to Hector Macneill Esq., dated George-Street, 3 May 1808.
Further edns: 2nd edn. 1808 (NSTC); 3rd edn. 1808 (NSTC); 4th edn. 1810 (NSTC); 5th edn.
1810 (NSTC); 6th edn. 1815 (NSTC); [at least 5 more edns. to 1850]; New York 1808 (NUC);
German trans., 1827 [as *Die Hütten-Bewohner von Glenburnie* (RS)].

1808: 53    HARVEY, Jane.
THE GOVERNOR OF BELLEVILLE. A TALE. BY JANE HARVEY. IN
FOUR VOLUMES.

> London: Printed for Vernor, Hood, and Sharpe, Poultry. (By T. Appleby, North
> Shields.), 1808.
> I 273p; II 282p; III 219p; IV 174p. 12mo. 14s (ECB); 14s bound (ER).
> ER 11: 504 (Jan 1808).
> Corvey; CME 3-628-47646-1; ECB 257; xNSTC.

*Notes.* ECB dates Nov 1807.

1808: 54 HERBERT, W[illiam].
**ELLA ROSENBERG, A ROMANCE. BY W. HERBERT, ESQ. AUTHOR OF THE "SPANISH OUTLAW." IN TWO VOLUMES.**

> London: Printed by and for J. F. Hughes, 15, Pater-Noster Row, and 5, Wigmore Street, Cavendish Square, 1808.
> I 206p; II 188p. 12mo.
> Corvey; CME 3-628-47666-6; NSTC H1373 (BI BL).

*Notes.* Colophons read: 'Printed by J. F. Hughes, Wigmore Street'.

1808: 55 [HOLBROOK, Ann Catherine].
**REBECCA, OR THE VICTIM OF DUPLICITY; A NOVEL, IN THREE VOLUMES.**

> Uttoxeter: Printed by R. Richards; sold by Lackington, Allen, & Co. London, 1808.
> I 203p; II 202p; III 223p. 12mo. 12s (ECB).
> CR 3rd ser. 15: 331–2 (Nov 1808); WSW I: 319.
> ICN Case Y 155.H695; ECB 481; xNSTC.

*Notes.* Colophons read: 'R. Richards, Printer, Uttoxeter'. ECB lists Crosby as publisher, and dates Feb 1808.

1808: 56 HOLSTEIN, Anthony Frederick [pseud.].
**SIR OWEN GLENDOWR, AND OTHER TALES. IN THREE VOLUMES. BY ANTHONY FREDERICK HOLSTEIN.**

> London: Printed at the Minerva-Press, for Lane, Newman, and Co. Leadenhall-Street, 1808.
> I 224p; II 224p; III 191p. 12mo. 13s 6d (ECB).
> CR 3rd ser. 18: 218–19 (Oct 1809); WSW I: 324.
> Corvey; CME 3-628-51048-1; ECB 278; xNSTC.

1808: 57 [HOOK, Theodore Edward].
**THE MAN OF SORROW. A NOVEL. IN THREE VOLUMES. BY ALFRED ALLENDALE, ESQ.**

> London: Printed for Samuel Tipper, Leadenhall-Street, 1808.
> I iii, 263p; II 274p; III 236p. 12mo. 13s (ECB); 15s (ER).
> CR 3rd ser. 14: 330–1 (June 1808); ER 12: 524 (July 1808); WSW I: 327.
> IU x823.H76man; ECB 14; xNSTC.

*Notes.* Dedication to 'the prettiest girl in England', signed 'Alfred Allendale'. Further edn: 1842 (NSTC 2H28939).

1808: 58 HOWARD, Charles.
**THE CONVENT OF ST. MARC; A ROMANCE, IN FOUR VOLUMES. BY CHARLES HOWARD.**

> London: Printed for J. F. Hughes, No. 5, Wigmore Street, Cavendish Square; and No. 15, Paternoster-Row, 1808.
> I 226p; II 234p; III 237p; IV 206p. 12mo.

ER 13: 506 (Jan 1809).
Corvey; CME 3-628-47751; xNSTC.

1808: 59   HURRY, [Margaret].
**ARTLESS TALES: BY MRS. IVES HURRY. IN THREE VOLUMES.**

> London: Printed for Longman, Hurst, Rees, and Orme, Paternoster-Row, 1808.
> I xvi, 230p; II 200p; III 196p. 12mo. 15s (ECB, ER).
> ER 12: 524 (July 1808); WSW I: 337.
> Corvey; CME 3-628-51053-8; ECB 290; NSTC H3354 (BI BL).

*Notes.* 'List of Subscribers' (*c.*320 names), vol. 1, pp. [v]–xvi.

1808: 60   HURSTONE, J. P.
**AN AUTUMN AT CHELTENHAM; OR, MYSTERIES IN HIGH LIFE. A FASHIONABLE NOVEL. IN THREE VOLUMES. BY J. P. HURSTONE, ESQ. AUTHOR OF "THE PICCADILLY AMBULATOR."**

> London: Printed by J. Dean, 57. Wardour Street, Soho. For G. Hughes, 212, Tottenham
> Court-Road, and H. D. Symonds, Paternoster-Row, 1808.
> I 216p; II 192p; III 207p. 12mo. 15s (ER).
> ER 13: 507 (Jan 1809).
> BL 12612.bb.11; NSTC H3358.

*Notes.* Dedication to Sir Francis Burdett, M.P., dated May 1808.

1808: 61   HURSTONE, J. P.
**DORINDA GRAFTON, A DOMESTIC TALE. BY J. P. HURSTONE. IN THREE VOLUMES.**

> London: Printed by B. Clarke, Well-Street, Cripplegate, for J. F. Hughes, Wigmore-
> Street, Cavendish-Square, 1808.
> I iv, 283p; II 232p; III 267p. 12mo. 15s (ER).
> ER 11: 504 (Jan 1808).
> Corvey; CME 3-628-47754-9; NSTC H3359 (BI BL).

1808: 62   [?HURSTONE, J. P.].
**THE NOBLE CORNUTOS: BEING A SERIES OF TALES, FOR THE AMUSEMENT OF THE FASHIONABLE WORLD. IN TWO VOLUMES.**

> London: Printed by and for J. F. Hughes, 15, Pater-Noster Row, and 5, Wigmore-St.
> Cavendish-Square, 1808.
> I 211p; II 190p. 12mo. 10s (ER).
> ER 13: 225 (Oct 1808).
> BL 12611.b.8; NSTC C3703.

*Notes.* This title is listed as a work by the author on the t.p. of J. P. Hurstone's *Royal Intrigues* (1808: 64).

1808: 63   HURSTONE, J. P.
**THE PICCADILLY AMBULATOR; OR, OLD Q: CONTAINING MEM-OIRS OF THE PRIVATE LIFE OF THAT EVER-GREEN VOTARY OF**

VENUS! THROUGHOUT WHICH ARE INTERSPERSED ANECDOTES OF THE MOST NOTED FASHIONABLES, HIS CONTEMPORARIES. IN TWO VOLUMES. BY J. P. HURSTONE, ESQ.

> Printed by J. Dean, 57, Wardour Street, Soho. For G. Hughes, 212, Tottenham-Court-Road; and H. D. Symonds, 20, Paternoster-Row, 1808.
>
> I xii, 143p, ill.; II 115p. 12mo. 10s (ER).
>
> ER 12: 525 (July 1808); WSW I: 337.
>
> BL 12611.b.11; NSTC H3360 (BI C, O).

*Notes.* Folding coloured illustration: 'A View taken from the Grand Park'. Preface dated London, Feb 1808. Dedication 'to the Rising Generation of British Nobility'.


1808:64   HURSTONE, J. P.
ROYAL INTRIGUES: OR, SECRET MEMOIRS OF FOUR PRINCESSES: INVOLVING NUMEROUS INTERESTING AND CURIOUS ANEC-DOTES CONNECTED WITH THE PRINCIPAL COURTS OF EUROPE. IN TWO VOLUMES. BY J. P. HURSTONE, ESQ. AUTHOR OF "THE NOBLE CORNUTOES," &C. &C. &C.

> London: Printed by M. Allen, Paternoster-Row, for J. F. Hughes, 15, Paternoster-Row; and 5, Wigmore-Street, Cavendish-Square, n.d. [1808].
>
> I xxxv, 148p; II 192p. 12mo.
>
> MH-H *EC8.H9465.808r; xNSTC.

*Notes.* Introductory letter 'to the editors of the publication, entitled The Satirist, or Monthly Meteor', signed J. P. Hurstone, 10 July 1808. Four semi-fictional reworkings of historical tales.


1808:65   JONES, Jenkin.
UNFORTUNATE AMOURS: WITH BIOGRAPHIC SKETCHES OF NOTED AND ECCENTRIC CHARACTERS. INCLUDING MEMOIRS OF THE SARCASTIC ALEXANDER MUCKLE. IN FOUR VOLUMES. BY JENKIN JONES, AUTHOR OF PROS AND CONS FOR CUPID AND HYMEN—HOBBY HORSES—THE PHILANTHROPIST, &C.

> London: Printed and published by M. Allen, No. 15, Paternoster-Row, 1808.
>
> I xvi, 247p; II 244p; III 248p; IV 146p, [1]–97p. 12mo. 20s (ER).
>
> ER 12: 525 (July 1808).
>
> E NF.555.d.4; NSTC J940.

*Notes.* 'Advertisement' states: 'A Brief account of Julius, and his correspondence with Eliza, having been receiv'd so favorably, the Publisher is now induced to offer a more complete Edition of those sarcastic and eccentric compositions, containing many novel pieces, revis'd and rang'd in proper order by Eliza; whose melancholy history is now prefix'd, accompanied by biographic sketches of her associates, lovers, friends, and literary colleagues'. Novel proper ends vol. 4, p. 146; pp. [1]–97 (fresh sequence) in vol. 4 comprises an 'Appendix, containing the Poetical Pieces Incident to the Foregoing Memoirs'.
Further edn: 1811 (NSTC).

1808: 66   [KRÜDENER, Barbara Juliane von].
THE SORROWS OF GUSTAVUS, OR THE HISTORY OF A YOUNG
SWEDE. IN TWO VOLUMES.

> London: Printed for Henry Colburn, No. 50, Conduit-Street, 1808.
> I viii, 232p; II 210p. 12mo. 10s (ECB, ER).
> ER 11: 504 (Jan 1808).
> BL 1152.d.3; ECB 146; NSTC G2449.

*Notes.* Trans. of *Valérie ou lettres de Gustave de Linar à Ernest de G* . . . (Paris, 1804). Translated by Dorothea Schlegel from French into German as *Valerie, oder Briefe Gustav's von Linar an Ernst von G\*\*e* (Leipzig, 1804). English text probably translated from the German trans., as names of characters and German places are correct. Running-title reads: Gustavus de Linar. ECB dates Nov 1807. NSTC K913 indicates 1802 imprint at Bodleian, but this is incorrect.

1808: 67   LATHOM, Francis.
THE UNKNOWN; OR, THE NORTHERN GALLERY. A ROMANCE. IN
THREE VOLUMES. BY FRANCIS LATHOM, AUTHOR OF THE MYS-
TERIOUS FREEBOOTER, THE IMPENETRABLE SECRET, MYSTERY,
&C. &C.

> London: Printed at the Minerva-Press, for Lane, Newman, and Co. Leadenhall-Street,
> 1808.
> I xi, 336p, ill.; II 376p; III 362p. 12mo. 18s (ECB, ER).
> ER 12: 267 (Apr 1808), 12: 524 (July 1808); WSW I: 364.
> Corvey; CME 3-628-47964-9; ECB 331; NSTC L546.5 (BI BL).

*Notes.* Further edns: 1826 (NSTC); French trans., 1810.

1808: 68   LAWLER, Dennis.
THE SOLDIER'S COTTAGE; A TALE. IN ONE VOLUME. BY DENNIS
LAWLER, TRANSLATOR OF CORINNA.

> London: Printed for the Editor, by E. Thomas, Golden-Lane, Barbican; and sold by
>       Chapple, Pall-Mall; Colburn, Conduit-Street, New Bond-Street; and Richards,
>       Cornhill, 1808.
> 197p. 12mo. 4s (ECB).
> BL N.2487; ECB 333; NSTC L759.

*Notes.* ECB dates May 1808, and gives publisher as Symonds (but not discovered in this form).

1808: 69   LAWLER, Dennis.
VICISSITUDES IN EARLY LIFE; OR, THE HISTORY OF FRANK
NEVILLE, A SERIO-COMIC, SENTIMENTAL, AND SATIRICAL TALE:
INTERSPERSED WITH COMIC SKETCHES, ANECDOTES OF LIVING
CHARACTERS, AND ORIGINAL POETRY; ELEGIAC, AMATORY,
HUMOUROUS, LYRICAL, AND DESCRIPTIVE. WITH A CARICATURE
FRONTISPIECE. IN TWO VOLUMES. BY DENNIS LAWLER.

London: Printed by Deans & Dunne, Hart-Street, Covent Garden; sold by C. Chapple,
  Pall Mall; and may be had of every Bookseller in the United Kingdom, n.d. [1808?].
I vii, 207p; II 203p. 12mo.
BL 12613.aaa.21; NSTC L762.

*Notes.* Dedication to 'Dr. Willan, of Bloomsbury-Square', dated 31 Dec 1807. T.p. of vol. 2
similar to that of vol. 1, with the addition of the date 1808 at bottom. Though there is a
reference in the title to a frontispiece, none exists in the BL copy. Pagination in vol. 2 skips
from 199 to 203, though without any apparent loss of text. BLC dates [1807].

1808: 70    [?LAYTON, Jemima or ?STARCK, Henry Savile de].
**BERTRAND; OR, MEMOIRS OF A NORTHUMBRIAN NOBLEMAN IN
THE SEVENTEENTH CENTURY; WRITTEN BY HIMSELF. IN THREE
VOLUMES.**

London: Printed at the Minerva-Press, for Lane, Newman, and Co. Leadenhall-Street,
  1808.
I xv, 259p; II 249p; III 251p. 12mo. 15s (ECB).
WSW I: 17.
Corvey; CME 3-628-47119-2; ECB 53; NSTC L866 (BI C, NCu, O).

*Notes.* Blakey, of the Bodleian copy, Notes. 'This copy has a manuscript note on the fly-leaf of
vol. 1 which is accepted in the Bodleian catalogue as evidence of authorship: "Presented to me
by the author Henry Savile de Starck. W. B. [= William Beckford?]". The authorship is attributed by *Notes & Queries*, clxiii, 80, to Mrs. F. Layton.' NSTC, reflecting this, ascribes both to
Jemima Layton (L866) and to de Starck (D946). ECB lists under title only, and dates Mar 1808.

1808: 71    LE NOIR, Elizabeth Anne.
**CLARA DE MONTFIER, A MORAL TALE. WITH ORIGINAL POEMS. IN
THREE VOLUMES. RESPECTFULLY INSCRIBED TO THE RIGHT HON.
LADY CHARLOTTE GREVILLE. BY ELIZABETH ANNE LE NOIR,
AUTHOR OF VILLAGE ANECDOTES.**

Reading: Printed for the Author, by A. M. Smart and Co. and sold by Messrs. Riving-
  ton's [*sic*], St. Paul's Church Yard, London, 1808.
I iv, 308p; II 403p; III 413p. 12mo. 20s (ECB, ER).
ER 15: 242 (Oct 1809); WSW I: 370.
Corvey; CME 3-628-48100-7; ECB 338; NSTC L1167 (BI BL).

*Notes.* Dedication 'to the Right Honorable Lady Charlotte Greville', dated 8 Nov 1808. ECB
dates July 1809. Collates in sixes.
Further edn: 2nd edn. 1819 as *The Maid of La Vendee* (BL 12612.e.13; NSTC). Preface to this
2nd edn. explains the change of title as owing to confusion caused by number of other similar 'Clara' titles, and in particular Mme. Cottin's *Claire d'Albe* (see 1808: 39).

1808: 72    LEWIS, M[atthew] G[regory].
**ROMANTIC TALES, BY M. G. LEWIS, AUTHOR OF THE MONK, ADEL-
GITHA, &C. IN FOUR VOLUMES.**

London: Printed by D. N. Shury, 7, Berwick Street, for Longman, Hurst, Rees, and
  Orme, Paternoster-Row, 1808.

I xxiii, 307p; II 335p; III 276p; IV 326p. 12mo. 24s (ECB).

CR 3rd ser. 15: 355–66 (Dec 1808) full review; ER 13: 225 (Oct 1808); WSW I: 372.

Corvey; CME 3-628-51092-9; ECB 343; NSTC L1509 (BI BL, C, O).

*Notes.* Dedication to Lady Charlotte Maria Campbell, dated London, 21 June 1808. I Mistrust; or, Blanche and Osbright; The Admiral Guarino; King Rodrigo's Fall; Bertrand and Mary-Belle; The Lord of Falkenstein; Sir Guy, the Seeker; II The Anaconda; The Dying Bride; The Four Facardins, Part I; III The Four Facardins, Part II; Oberon's Henchman, or the Legend of the Three Sisters; IV My Uncle's Garret-Window; Bill Jones; Amorassan, or the Spirit of the Frozen Ocean.

Further edns: 1838 (NSTC: selection); 1848 (NSTC: selection); New York 1809 (NUC); French trans., of 'My Uncle's Garret-Window', 1821.

1808: 73   LINWOOD, Mary.
**LEICESTERSHIRE TALES. BY MISS MARY LINWOOD. IN FOUR VOLUMES.**

London: Printed for the Author, and sold by Richard Phillips, Bridge Street, Blackfriars. Rider & Weed, Printers, Little Britain, 1808.

I 251p; II 239p; III 238p; IV 247p. 12mo. 21s (ER).

ER 13: 225 (Oct 1808); WSW I: 374.

Corvey; CME 3-628-51093-7; NSTC L1756 (BI BL).

*Notes.* Dedication 'to the Right Honourable the Countess Dowager of Moira, Huntington, Hastings, &c. &c. &c.'. 'Advertisement' dated Leicester, 1 Jan 1808.

1808: 74   LUCAS, Charles.
**THE ABISSINIAN REFORMER, OR THE BIBLE AND SABRE. A NOVEL. IN THREE VOLUMES. BY CHARLES LUCAS, M.A. AUTHOR OF THE INFERNAL QUIXOTE, &C. &C.**

London: Printed for George Richards, Cornhill, 1808.

I xii, 240p; II 227p; III 200p. 12mo. 15s (ECB).

CR 3rd ser. 14: 186–90 (June 1808) full review; WSW I: 378.

BL 12613.bbb.22; ECB 355; NSTC L2558.

*Notes.* Tear on vol. 1 t.p. obscures 'M.A.', though the letters are present in following vols.

1808: 75   [MATURIN, Charles Robert].
**THE WILD IRISH BOY. IN THREE VOLUMES. BY THE AUTHOR OF MONTORIO.**

London: Printed for Longman, Hurst, Rees, and Orme, Paternoster-Row, by J. D. Dewick, Aldersgate-Street, 1808.

I xi, 276p; II 342p; III 406p. 12mo. 21s (ECB); 12s (ER).

ER 12: 267 (Apr 1808); WSW I: 390.

Corvey; CME 3-628-48922-9; ECB 637; NSTC M1728 (BI BL, Dt, O).

*Notes.* Dedication 'to the Right Honorable the Earl of Moira', signed 'The Author of Montorio'. Preface stating that 'My first work was said to be too defective in female characters and female interest' (p. [ix]).

Further edns: 2nd edn. 1824 (NUC); New York 1808 (NUC); French trans., 1828 [as *Le Jeune Irlandais* (BN)].
Facs: GNIII (1977); IAN (1979).


1808: 76    MAXWELL, Caroline.
ALFRED OF NORMANDY: OR, THE RUBY CROSS. AN HISTORICAL ROMANCE, IN TWO VOLUMES. BY CAROLINE MAXWELL.

> London: Printed and sold by A. Seale, 160, Tottenham Court Road, and may be had of all Booksellers in Town and Country, 1808.
> I 179p; II 165p. 12mo.
> Corvey; CME 3-628-48202-X; NSTC M1816 (BI BL).

*Notes.* Collates in sixes.


1808: 77    MEEKE, [Mary].
"THERE IS A SECRET, FIND IT OUT!" A NOVEL. IN FOUR VOLUMES. BY MRS. MEEKE, AUTHOR OF AMAZEMENT, OLD WIFE AND YOUNG HUSBAND, WONDER OF THE VILLAGE, &C. &C.

> London: Printed at the Minerva-Press, for Lane, Newman, and Co. Leadenhall-Street, 1808.
> I 330p; II 372p; III 384p; IV 379p. 12mo. 24s (ECB).
> Corvey; CME 3-628-48018-3; ECB 378; NSTC M1957 (BI BL).

*Notes.* ECB dates Mar 1808.


1808: 78    MONTAGUE, Edward.
MODERN CHARACTERS. A NOVEL. IN THREE VOLUMES. BY EDWARD MONTAGUE, ESQ.

> London: Printed for G. Hughes, 212, Tottenham-Court Road, opposite Goodge-Street, 1808.
> I vi, 255p; II 230p; III 215p. 12mo. 18s (ECB, ER).
> ER 11: 504 (Jan 1808).
> CLU-S/C PR.5029.M782m; CME 3-628-48269-0; ECB 392; NSTC M2915 (BI BL, C).

*Notes.* ECB dates Nov 1807. Vols. 2 and 3 t.ps. in the Corvey set state 'Second Edition': a similar pattern is found in BL 12612.bbb.19.
Further edn: 1808 (see note above).


1808: 79    [MONTOLIEU, Jeanne-Isabelle-Pauline Polier de Bottens, Baronne de].
CHRISTINA; OR, MEMOIRS OF A GERMAN PRINCESS. BY THE AUTHOR OF CAROLINE OF LICHTFIELD. IN TWO VOLUMES.

> London: Printed for Henry Colburn, Conduit-Street, New Bond-Street, 1808.
> I 208p; II 272p. 12mo. 10s (ECB); 9s (ER).
> CR 3rd ser. 13: 443 (Jan 1808); ER 11: 504 (Jan 1808).
> Corvey; CME 3-628-47282-2; ECB 114; NSTC M2956 (BI BL).

*Notes.* Trans. of *La Princesse de Wolfenbuttel* (Paris, 1807), itself based on Johann Heinrich Daniel Zschokke's *Die Prinzessin von Wolfenbüttel* (Zurich, 1804). ECB dates Nov 1807. Further edn: 2nd edn. 1809 (NSTC).

1808: 80   MOORE, George.
TALES OF THE PASSIONS; IN WHICH IS ATTEMPTED AN ILLUSTRA-TION OF THEIR EFFECTS ON THE HUMAN MIND: EACH TALE COM-PRISED IN ONE VOLUME, AND FORMING THE SUBJECT OF A SINGLE PASSION. BY GEORGE MOORE.

> London: Printed for G. Wilkie and J. Robinson, Paternoster Row, 1808/11.
> I (1808) xvi, 415p; II (1811) xi, 455p. 8vo. 19s 6d (ECB); 10s 6d (ER, QR, for vol. 2).
> ER 18: 266 (May 1811); QR 5: 537 (May 1811); WSW I: 404.
> Dt OLS.L-1-689-690; ECB 394; NSTC M3038 (BI BL, C).

*Notes.* General Preface to vol. 1 states: 'In each volume, it is my intention to comprise a single tale, in which a delineation of one of the principal passions shall form the general basis'. Secondary t.p. to vol. 1 reads: 'The Courtezan, an English Tale: in which is attempted an illustration of the passion of revenge, in its effects on the human mind'. Dedication to J. P. Kemble, Esq. for this tale. Secondary t.p. to vol. 2 reads: 'The Married Man; an English Tale: in which is attempted an illustration of the passion of jealousy, in its effects on the human mind'. Dedication in vol. 2 'to a beloved and respected Mother', dated Mar 1811. BL N.2017 comprises a copy of the *The Married Man*, with this undated t.p. introducing the vol., but is evidently not a separate publication. ECB dates 1st vol. Dec 1807, 2nd vol. Mar 1811. Colophon of 'S. Hamilton, Weybridge' at end of both vols.
Further edn: 2nd edn. 1814 (Corvey—a reissue by A. K. Newman), CME 3-628-48281-X).

1808: 81   [MORE, Hannah].
CŒLEBS IN SEARCH OF A WIFE. COMPREHENDING OBSERVA-TIONS ON DOMESTIC HABITS AND MANNERS, RELIGION AND MORALS. IN TWO VOLUMES.

> London: Printed for T. Cadell and W. Davies, in the Strand, 1808.
> I xi, 351p; II 469p. 8vo. 12s (ECB, QR).
> CR 3rd ser. 16: 252–64 (Mar 1809) full review; ER 14: 145–51 (Apr 1809) full review; QR
>    1: 236 (Feb 1809); WSW I: 408.
> BL 1608/2725; ECB 124; NSTC M3150 (BI O).

*Notes.* Preface signed 'Cœlebs'. ECB dates Jan 1809.
Further edns: 2nd edn. 1809 (NSTC); 3rd edn. 1809 (NSTC); 4th edn. 1809 (NSTC); 5th edn. 1809 (NSTC); 6th edn. 1809 (NSTC); [at least 9 more edns. to 1850]; New York 1809 (NSTC); German trans., 1816 [as *Cölebs, oder der junge Wanderer, der eine Gattin sucht* (RS)]; French trans., 1817 [as *Cœlebs, ou le choix d'une épouse* (BN)]. Corvey copy is 14th edn. 1813, CME 3-628-47303-9.

1808: 82   MORTIMER, Edward [pseud.?].
MONTONI; OR, THE CONFESSIONS OF THE MONK OF SAINT BENE-DICT. A ROMANCE. IN FOUR VOLUMES. BY EDWARD MORTIMER, ESQ. AUTHOR OF FRIAR HILDARGO.

London: Printed by B. Clarke, Well-Street, Cripplegate, for J. F. Hughes, Wigmore-Street, Cavendish-Square, 1808.

I 219p; II 188p; III 204p; IV 210p. 12mo. 18s (ER).

ER 11: 504 (Jan 1808); WSW I: 410.

Corvey; CME 3-628-48335-2; NSTC M3407 (BI BL).

1808: 83    [MOSSE], Henrietta Rouviere.
THE OLD IRISH BARONET; OR, MANNERS OF MY COUNTRY. A NOVEL. IN THREE VOLUMES. BY HENRIETTA ROUVIERE, AUTHOR OF LUSSINGTON ABBEY, HEIRS OF VILLEROY, A PEEP AT OUR ANCESTORS, &C. &C.

London: Printed at the Minerva-Press, for Lane, Newman, and Co. Leadenhall-Street, 1808.

I 236p; II 216p; III 260p. 12mo. 15s (ECB, ER).

ER 13: 225 (Oct 1808).

Corvey; CME 3-628-48349-2; ECB 399; xNSTC.

1808: 84    MUSGRAVE, Agnes.
WILLIAM DE MONTFORT; OR, THE SICILIAN HEIRESSES. BY AGNES MUSGRAVE, AUTHOR OF CICELY OF RABY, SOLEMN INJUNCTIONS, &C. IN THREE VOLUMES.

London: Printed by W. Nicholson, Warner Street, for George Richards, 9, Cornhill, 1808.

I vii, 292p; II 294p; III 280p. 12mo. 15s (ECB, ER).

CR 3rd ser. 14: 218–20 (June 1808); ER 12: 267 (Apr 1808); WSW I: 415.

Corvey; CME 3-628-48172-4; ECB 402; xNSTC.

1808: 85    NERI, Mary Anne.
THE HOUR OF TRIAL: A TALE. BY MARY ANNE NERI; AUTHOR OF "THE EVE OF SAN PIETRO." IN THREE VOLUMES.

London: Printed for Longman, Hurst, Rees & Orme, Paternoster-Row, 1808.

I vii, 240p; II 232p; III 334p. 12mo. 15s (ECB, ER).

ER 13: 225 (Oct 1808); WSW I: 416.

BL 12614.eee.23; ECB 409; NSTC N564.

1808: 86    NORRIS, Mrs.
JULIA OF ENGLAND. A NOVEL. IN FOUR VOLUMES. BY MRS. NORRIS, AUTHOR OF THE STRANGERS, SECOND LOVE, &C.

London: Printed for Samuel Tipper, Leadenhall-Street, 1808.

I 214p; II 222p; III 255p; IV 238p. 12mo. 20s (ECB); 18s (ER).

ER 12: 524 (July 1808).

Corvey; CME 3-628-48235-6; ECB 416; xNSTC.

1808: 87    [PECK, Frances].
THE MAID OF AVON. A NOVEL FOR THE HAUT TON. IN THREE VOLUMES. BY AN IRISHWOMAN.

London: Printed at the Minerva-Press, for Lane, Newman, and Co. Leadenhall-Street, 1808.

I 219p; II 202p; III 228p. 12mo. 15s (ECB); 13s 6d (ER).

ER 11: 504 (Jan 1808); WSW I: 418.

Corvey; CME 3-628-48147-3; ECB 363; xNSTC.

*Notes.* ECB dates Dec 1807.


1808: 88   [PECK, Frances].
THE WELCH PEASANT BOY. A NOVEL. IN THREE VOLUMES. BY THE AUTHOR OF THE MAID OF AVON.

London: Printed at the Minerva-Press, for Lane, Newman, and Co. Leadenhall-Street, 1808.

I 210p; II 170p; III 173p. 12mo. 12s (ECB, ER).

ER 13: 225 (Oct 1808).

Corvey; CME 3-628-48882-6; ECB 629; NSTC P915 (BI BL).


PERCY, A.

See ANON., THE MONKS AND THE ROBBERS


1808: 89   PIGAULT-LEBRUN, [Charles-Antoine]; W., E. (*trans.*).
THEODORE; OR, THE PERUVIANS. FROM THE FRENCH OF PIGAULT LE BRUN. BY E. W.

London: Printed for B. Crosby and Co. No. 4, Stationers-Court, Ludgate-Street, 1808.

160p. 8vo. 4s 6d (ECB).

BL 12654.i.25; ECB 335; NSTC P1727 (BI O).

*Notes.* Trans. of *Théodore, ou les Péruviens* (Paris, 1800). ECB dates Aug 1808.


1808: 90   PLUNKETT, [Elizabeth] [née GUNNING].
THE EXILE OF ERIN, A NOVEL, IN THREE VOLUMES. BY MRS. PLUN-KETT, LATE MISS GUNNING.

London: Printed by T. Plummer, Seething-Lane, for B. Crosby and Co. Stationers'-Court, Ludgate Hill, 1808.

I viii, 290p; II 239p; III 268p. 12mo. 13s 6d (ECB, ER).

ER 12: 267 (Apr 1808).

BL 12611.aaa.8; ECB 248; NSTC P2193 (BI Dt, O).

*Notes.* Further edn: Alexandria, VA, 1809 (NUC).


1808: 91   RATCLIFFE, Eliza.
THE MYSTERIOUS BARON, OR THE CASTLE IN THE FOREST, A GOTHIC STORY. BY ELIZA RATCLIFFE.

London: Printed by J. B. G. Vogel, 13, Poland St. Oxford Street. Sold by C. Chapple, Pall Mall, and may be had by every Bookseller in the United Kingdom, 1808.

184p. 12mo. 3s 6d (ECB).

Corvey; CME 3-628-48453-7; ECB 480; xNSTC.

*Notes.* Dedication 'to Miss Mary Ann Davies of Fleet-Street', signed 'The Editor'. ECB dates June 1808. 'Errata' at end states: 'By an oversight of the Transcriber, not an error of the Printer, Sir Oswald's Secretary is at the commencement of the Romance called Owen instead of Jones.'

1808: 92 {RICKMAN, Thomas Clio}.
ATROCITIES OF A CONVENT, OR THE NECESSITY OF THINKING FOR OURSELVES, EXEMPLIFIED IN THE HISTORY OF A NUN. BY A CITIZEN OF THE WORLD.

> London: Printed by and for Clio Rickman, Upper Mary-le-Bone-Street; and to be had of all Booksellers, 1808.
> I 223p; II 220p; III 178p. 12mo. 13s 6d (ER).
> ER 12: 525 (July 1808); WSW I: 13.
> CLU-S/C PZ2.1.A882; xNSTC.

*Notes.* Vol. 3 contains at end 4 pp. (unn.) advs. headed 'Also written and published by Thomas Clio Rickman'. This list contains works which are known to have been authored by Thomas 'Clio' Rickman (1761–1834), who was also featured in a contemporary portrait by Robert Dighton as 'A Citizen of the World' (see DNB). The attribution of this rare novel to him has apparently not been previously made.

1808: 93 RYLEY, S[amuel] W[illiam].
THE ITINERANT, OR MEMOIRS OF AN ACTOR. IN THREE VOLUMES. BY S. W. RYLEY.

> London: Printed for Taylor and Hessey, 93, Fleet Street, 1808/27.
> I (1808) 326p; II (1809) 332p; III (1809) 398p; IV (1816) 155p, 162p; V (1817) 371p; VI (1817) 446p, ill.; VII (1827) 336p; VIII (1827) 322p; IX (1827) 322p. 12mo. 63s (ECB).
> WSW I: 476.
> BL 12613.e.15; ECB 509; NSTC R2207 (BI NCu, O; NA MH).

*Notes.* T.p. of vol. 2 differs as follows: London: Printed for Sherwood, Neely, and Jones, (Successors to Mr. H. D. Symonds) Paternoster Row; t.p. of vol. 4 has same publisher but without text in brackets; new t. p. of vol. 7 reads: *The Itinerant, in Scotland. By S. W. Ryley.* London: Printed for Sherwood and Co. Paternoster-Row; Constable, Edinburgh; and Griffin, Glasgow, 1827. Dedication to Sir William Roscoe, Esq. in vols. 1 and 4. Vol. 4 includes a 'Preface or no Preface', running to p. 155, and dated Chapel Cottage, Parkgate, 3 Feb 1813. Dedication in vol. 7 to the Earl of Sefton, dated Liverpool, 17 Apr.
Further edns: 2nd edn. 1816/17 (NSTC); 1817/27 (NSTC); New York 1810 (NUC) [also Philadelphia 1810 (NSTC, NUC)].

1808: 94 ST. JOHN, A[ndrew].
TALES OF FORMER TIMES. EMBELLISHED WITH TWO ELEGANT ENGRAVINGS. BY A. ST. JOHN. IN TWO VOLS.

> London: Printed for B. Crosby and Co. Stationers Court, Paternoster Row, 1808.
> I vi, 293p, ill.; II iv, 305p, ill. 12mo. 9s (ECB, ER).
> ER 12: 267 (Apr 1808); WSW I: 477.
> BL 1459.e.4; ECB 511; NSTC S205.

*Notes.* Preface ([iv]–vi) states the contents are adapted from 'the Old English Metrical Romances'. ECB dates Dec 1807.

1808: 95   ST. VICTOR, Helen [pseud.?].
THE RUINS OF RIGONDA; OR, THE HOMICIDIAL [*sic*] FATHER. A ROMANCE, IN THREE VOLUMES. BY HELEN ST. VICTOR.
>London: Printed for C. Chapple, 66, Pall Mall, 1808.
>I 198p; II 189p; III 170p. 12mo. 13s 6d (ECB, ER).
>ER 13: 507 (Jan 1809).
>Corvey; CME 3-628-48504-5; ECB 506; NSTC S232 (BI BL).

*Notes.* Collates in sixes.

1808: 96   [SEDLEY, Charles] [pseud.?].
ASMODEUS; OR, THE DEVIL IN LONDON: A SKETCH. IN THREE VOLUMES. BY THE AUTHOR OF "THE FARO TABLE," "A WINTER IN DUBLIN," &C. &C. &C.
>London: Printed by J. Dean, 57, Wardour Street, Soho. For J. F. Hughes, 15, Paternoster-Row, & 5, Wigmore Street, Cavendish Square, 1808.
>I xiii, 192p; II 206p; III 213p. 12mo. 'Price One Guinea' (t.p.).
>ER 13: 225 (Oct 1808); WSW I: 491.
>Corvey; CME 3-628-47076-5; NSTC S1059 (BI BL).

*Notes.* Preface, signed 'the Author', and dated London, Apr 1808.

1808: 97   {SEDLEY, Charles} [pseud.?].
THE FARO TABLE; OR, THE GAMBLING MOTHERS. A FASHIONABLE FABLE. IN TWO VOLUMES. BY THE AUTHOR OF "THE BAROUCHE DRIVER AND HIS WIFE," &C. &C. &C.
>London: Printed by J. Dean, 57, Wardour Street, Soho. For J. F. Hughes, Wigmore-Street, Cavendish-Square, 1808.
>I xxiv, 158p; II 190p. 12mo.
>WSW I: 42.
>BL 12611.aaa.25; ECB 525; NSTC S1061 (BI O).

*Notes.* Preface signed Charles Sedley, London, 21 Dec 1807. 'Postcript [*sic*] by the Publisher' (vol. 2, pp. 181–90), describing an attack on his person by Hon. Richard Augustus Butler Danvers, and which also mentions that 'Charles Sedley was a fictitious person' (p. 182), signed J. F. Hughes, 5, Wigmore Street.
Further edns: 2nd edn. 1808 (NUC); 3rd edn. 1808. A facsimile of the 3rd edn., with an Introduction by Beverley Nichols, was published by Nash and Grayson (London, 1931).

1808: 98   SEDLEY, Charles [pseud.?].
A WINTER IN DUBLIN: A DESCRIPTIVE TALE. BY CHARLES SEDLEY, ESQ. AUTHOR OF THE BAROUCHE DRIVER, INFIDEL MOTHER, MASK OF FASHION, &C. &C. &C. IN THREE VOLUMES.

London: Printed by D. N. Shury, Berwick Street, Soho, for J. F. Hughes, Wigmore Street, Cavendish Square, 1808.

I xiv, 234p; II 252p; III 227p. 12mo. 21s bound (ER).

ER 11: 504 (Jan 1808); WSW I: 131, 491.

BL 12613.b.18; ECB 525; NSTC S1063 (BI C, Dt, O).

*Notes.* Dedication to Mr Sheriff Phillips, signed 'the Publisher', 5 Wigmore Street, 24 Oct 1807. Preface, signed Charles Sedley, Ramsgate, 17 Oct 1807.

Further edn: 3rd edn. 1808 (Corvey), CME 3-628-48635-1.


1808: 99 SOUTHWOOD, T.

**DELWORTH; OR, ELEVATED GENEROSITY. IN THREE VOLUMES. BY T. SOUTHWOOD.**

London: Printed for B. Crosby and Co. Stationer's Court. By C. Stower, 32 Paternoster Row, 1808.

I xxiv, 325p; II 359p; III 270p. 12mo. 15s (CR, ECB).

CR 3rd ser. 15: 221 (Oct 1808); WSW I: 517.

Corvey; CME 3-628-48715-3; ECB 552; xNSTC.

*Notes.* Dedication 'To a Friend of my Youth'; 'Introductory Dialogue between the Author and a Friend' (implies male authorship). CR refers to author as Mr Southwood.


1808: 100 STANHOPE, Louisa Sidney.

**STRIKING LIKENESSES; OR, THE VOTARIES OF FASHION. A NOVEL. IN FOUR VOLUMES. BY LOUISA SIDNEY STANHOPE, AUTHOR OF 'MONTBRASIL ABBEY,' AND 'THE BANDIT'S BRIDE.'**

London: Printed by B. Clarke, Well-Street, Cripplegate, for J. F. Hughes, Wigmore-Street, Cavendish-Square, 1808.

I 244p; II 256p; III 259p; IV 230p. 12mo.

WSW I: 116.

Corvey; CME 3-628-48782-X; ECB 558; NSTC S3498 (BI BL, O).


STARCK, Henry Savile de

See LAYTON, Jemima


1808: 101 STRUTT, Joseph.

**QUEENHOO-HALL, A ROMANCE: AND ANCIENT TIMES, A DRAMA. BY THE LATE JOSEPH STRUTT, AUTHOR OF "RURAL SPORTS AND PASTIMES OF THE PEOPLE OF ENGLAND," &C. IN FOUR VOLUMES.**

Edinburgh: Printed by James Ballantyne & Co. for John Murray, Fleet-Street, London, and Archibald Constable & Co. Edinburgh, 1808.

I vii, vi, 253p; II ii, 247p; III ii, 242p; IV 211p. 8vo. 18s (ECB); 13s boards (ER).

CR 3rd ser. 14: 406–9 (Aug 1808) full review; ER 13: 225 (Oct 1808); WSW I: 525.

Corvey; CME 3-628-48681-5; ECB 566; NSTC S4214 (BI BL, C, E, NCu).

*Notes.* 'Advertisement', explaining that the present text is founded on papers acquired after

the author's death, is dated London, 1 Apr 1808. Strutt's antiquarian romance was completed by Sir Walter Scott. *Ancient Times* begins at vol. 4, p. [97].
Further edn: 2nd edn. London 1812 (NUC).

1808: 102    STUART, A[u]gusta Amelia.
LUDOVICO'S TALE, OR, THE BLACK BANNER OF CASTLE DOUGLAS.
A NOVEL, IN FOUR VOLUMES. BY AGUSTA [*sic*] AMELIA STUART.
> London: Printed for J. F. Hughes, Wigmore Street, Cavendish Square, 1808.
> I viii, 224p; II 246p; III 229p; IV 224p. 12mo. 20s (ER).
> ER 11: 504 (Jan 1808).
> Corvey; CME 3-628-48685-8; NSTC S4230 (BI BL).

*Notes.* ECB 567 lists as 'Ludovicus: a tale', 1801, and under title (355) 'Ludovicus: tale', 1810; both apparently in error. Allibone lists 'Ludovicus; a Tale, 1810', which also appears in Block.

1808: 103    [SYKES, Henrietta].
MARGIANA; OR, WIDDRINGTON TOWER. A TALE OF THE FIFTEENTH
CENTURY. IN FIVE VOLUMES.
> London: Printed at the Minerva-Press, for Lane, Newman, and Co. Leadenhall-Street,
> 1808.
> I 275p; II 254p; III 258p; IV 292p; V 286p. 12mo. 21s (ECB).
> Corvey; CME 3-628-48079-5; ECB 368; NSTC S4581 (BI C, O).

*Notes.* ECB dates Oct 1808.

1808: 104    [THOMAS, Elizabeth].
THE HUSBAND AND WIFE; OR, THE MATRIMONIAL MARTYR. A
NOVEL. IN THREE VOLUMES. BY MRS. BRIDGET BLUEMANTLE,
AUTHOR OF THE THREE OLD MAIDS, &C.
> London: Printed at the Minerva-Press, for Lane, Newman, and Co. Leadenhall-Street,
> 1808.
> I 271p; II 316p; III 351p. 12mo. 15s (ECB).
> Corvey; CME 3-628-47125-7; ECB 63; xNSTC.

*Notes.* ECB dates Dec 1807.

1808: 105    THOMPSON, Benjamin.
THE FLORENTINES, OR SECRET MEMOIRS OF THE NOBLE FAMILY
DE C**. BY BENJAMIN THOMPSON, TRANSLATOR OF THE STRAN-
GER, GERMAN THEATRE, &C. &C.
> London: Printed by B. Clarke, Well-Street, for J. F. Hughes, Wigmore-Street,
> Cavendish-Square, 1808.
> 275p. 12mo.
> ER 11: 238 (Oct 1807).
> BL 012611.e.4; NSTC T751 (BI O).

*Notes.* 'No Chapter, or the one preceding Chapter the first', pp. [1]–26; t.p. falls on p. [27]; Chapter 1 begins p. 29.

1808: 106   TRELAWNEY, Anne.
CHARACTERS AT BRIGHTON. A NOVEL, IN FOUR VOLUMES. BY
ANNE TRELAWNEY, AUTHOR OF THE OFFSPRING OF MORTIMER,
&C. &C.

> London: Printed by J. Dennett, Leather Lane, Holborn; for J. F. Hughes, 15, Paternoster Row, and 5, Wigmore Street, Cavendish Square, 1808.
> I 241p; II 242p; III 274p; IV 330p. 12mo. 24s (CR).
> CR 3rd ser. 14: 440–1 (Aug 1808); WSW I: 23.
> BL 12611.bb.21; ECB 598; xNSTC.

*Notes.* Dedication to His Royal Highness the Prince of Wales, signed 'The Editor'.
Further edns: 2nd edn. 1808 (NUC); 3rd edn. 1808 (Corvey), CME 3-628-487688-4.

1808: 107   TRELAWNEY, Anne.
OFFSPRING OF MORTIMER; OR MEMOIRS OF THE STRATFORD
FAMILY. A DOMESTIC NOVEL. IN FOUR VOLUMES. BY ANNE
TRELAWNEY.

> London: Printed by J. Dennett, Leather Lane; for J. F. Hughes, Wigmore Street, Cavendish Square, 1808.
> I 262p; II 244p; III 236p; IV 192p. 12mo.
> Corvey; CME 3-628-48769-2; xNSTC.

1808: 108   WARNER, [Ellen Rebecca].
HERBERT-LODGE; A NEW-FOREST STORY. IN THREE VOLUMES. BY
MISS WARNER, OF BATH.

> Bath: Printed by Richard Cruttwell, St. James's-Street; and sold by Longman, Hurst, Rees, and Orme, Paternoster-Row, London, 1808.
> I xx, 205p; II 213p; III 218p. 12mo.
> CtY-BR W242.808; ECB 624; xNSTC.

*Notes.* 'Subscribers' Names', vol. 1, pp. [ix]–xx; followed by 'Names sent too late for insertion in the List' [xxi]: *c.*730 in all listed. Imprint of BRu ENC copy differs by reading: '[. . .] and sold by Wilkie and Robinson, Paternoster-Row, London, 1808'. ECB dates 1810.

1808: 109   [WEIMAR, Miss].
ALZYLIA, A NOVEL, IN FOUR VOLUMES.

> London: Printed for the Author, by T. Collins, Harvey's Buildings, Strand, and published by C. Chapple, Pall-Mall, 1808.
> I 194p; II 210p; III 219p; IV 258p. 12mo. 21s (ECB).
> BL N.1895,96; ECB 628; NSTC W1057.

*Notes.* 'Entered at Stationers' Hall', in square brackets after imprint date. 'List of the Subscribers' (*c.*100 names), vol. 1, pp. [1]–4. ECB dates Nov 1808.

1808: 110   WILKINSON, Sarah [Scudgell].
THE CHILD OF MYSTERY, A NOVEL, IN THREE VOLUMES, FOUNDED
ON RECENT EVENTS. BY SARAH WILKINSON.

London: Printed for J. F. Hughes, 15, Pater-Noster-Row, and 5, Wigmore-Street,
   Cavendish-Square, 1808.
I 228p; II 229p; III 217p. 12mo.
BL 1486.de.37; NSTC W1941.

*Notes.* Advs. at the end of vol. 2 (3 pp. unn.) and vol. 3 (5 pp. unn.), consecutively listing
'Popular Novels, Romances, &c. &c. &c.' from 1 to 58.

1808: 111   [YOUNG, Mary Julia].
**A SUMMER AT WEYMOUTH; OR, THE STAR OF FASHION. A NOVEL,
IN THREE VOLUMES. BY THE AUTHOR OF A SUMMER AT
BRIGHTON, &C. &C.**

London: Printed for J. F. Hughes, Wigmore Street, Cavendish Square, 1808.
I 264p; II 252p; III 250p. 12mo. 15s (ECB, ER).
ER 11: 504 (Jan 1808).
Corvey; CME 3-628-48732-3; ECB 569; xNSTC.

*Notes.* ECB dates Nov 1807.

# 1809

1809: 1   ANON.
**ARNOLD; OR, A TRAIT, AND IT'S CONSEQUENCES, OF CIVIL WAR.
A NOVEL. IN TWO VOLUMES.**

London: Printed for G. Robinson, 25, Paternoster-Row, 1809.
I x, 206p; II 280p. 12mo.
BL 12612.aa.9; ECB 26; NSTC A1699.

1809: 2   ANON.
**THE BANKS OF THE CARRON; OR, THE TOWERS OF LOTHIAN: A
SCOTTISH LEGEND. BY THE AUTHOR OF THE "TWO PILGRIMS."**

London: Printed for J. F. Hughes, 5, Wigmore-Street, Cavendish-Square; and 15, Pater-
   noster-Row, 1809.
I 226p; II 256p; III 266p; IV 222p. 12mo.
Corvey; CME 3-628-47096-X; NSTC C827 (BI BL).

*Notes.* See also 1809: 11, which is apparently identical apart from t.ps.

1809: 3   ANON.
**THE BEAU MONDE: OR, SCENES IN FASHIONABLE LIFE. IN THREE
VOLUMES.**

London: Printed at the Minerva-Press, for A. K. Newman and Co. (Successors to Lane,
   Newman, & Co.) Leadenhall-Street, 1809.

I 236p; II 235p; III 236p. 12mo. 15s (ECB, ER, QR).

ER 15: 529 (Jan 1810); QR 3: 268 (Feb 1810).

Corvey; CME 3-628-47130-3; ECB 45; xNSTC.

*Notes.* ECB dates May 1810.

1809: 4    ANON.

THE CORINNA OF ENGLAND, AND A HEROINE IN THE SHADE;
A MODERN ROMANCE, BY THE AUTHOR OF "THE WINTER IN
BATH," "THE BANKS OF THE WYE," "THE WOMAN OF COLOUR,"
"LIGHT AND SHADE," &C. &C.

London: Printed for B. Crosby and Co., Stationers' Court, Paternoster-Row, 1809.

I 232p; II 245p. 12mo. 8s (ECB); 9s (ER).

ER 13: 507 (Jan 1809); WSW I: 146, 147.

Corvey; CME 3-628-47338-1; ECB 136; NSTC C3663 (BI BL).

*Notes.* Attributed variously to Mrs E. G. Bayfield (BLC, Hardy, H&L, WSW), J. H. James
(Block), and to Mrs E. M. Foster (FC). For the probable cause of the attribution to Bayfield
and to James, see *A Winter in Bath* (1807: 7) and *The Banks of the Wye* (1808: 1). The attribution to Foster apparently hinges on a chain of ascriptions within titles, stretching to 1817, and
must without further evidence be considered unlikely: see *The Aunt and the Niece* (1804: 3).

1809: 5    ANON.

THE ENGLISH BROTHERS; OR, ANECDOTES OF THE HOWARD
FAMILY. IN FOUR VOLUMES.

London: Printed for William Miller, Albemarle Street, 1809.

I 323p; II 340p; III 323p; IV 379p. 12mo. 21s (ECB, ER, QR).

ER 14: 519 (July 1809); QR 1: 462 (May 1809); WSW I: 38.

Corvey; CME 3-628-47567-8; ECB 187; xNSTC.

*Notes.* Dedication 'to the most exemplary of Women, and the best of Parents' signed 'The
Author'.

1809: 6    ANON.

GOTHIC LEGENDS. A ROMANCE, IN TWO VOLUMES.

London: Printed for J. F. Hughes, 38, Berners Street, Oxford Street, 1809.

I 221p; II 225p. 12mo.

BL 012612.de.4; xNSTC.

1809: 7    ANON.

THE MONK AND THE VINE-DRESSER: OR, THE EMIGRANTS OF
BELLESME. A MORAL TALE. BY A LADY.

Edinburgh: Printed for Manners & Miller, A. Constable & Co. and Brown & Crombie;
    and Constable, Hunter, Park, & Hunter, London, 1809.

ii, 183p. 12mo. 3s (ER).

ER 15: 528 (Jan 1810); WSW I: 78.

E Hall.278.e; NSTC L103.

*Notes.* 'Address to the Public', dated Oct 1809. Collates in sixes.

1809: 8   ANON.

ROSA IN LONDON, AND OTHER TALES; BY THE AUTHOR OF THE YOUNG MOTHER, OR ALBINIA. IN FOUR VOLUMES.

> London: Printed for Henry Colburn, English and Foreign Library, Conduit-Street, Bond-Street, 1809.
> I 264p; II 247p; III 220p; IV 261p. 12mo. 22s (ECB, ER, QR).
> ER 15: 528 (Jan 1810); QR 3: 267 (Feb 1810).
> Corvey; CME 3-628-48513-4; ECB 502; NSTC R1622 (BI BL).

*Notes.* Further edn: Philadelphia 1813 (NUC).


1809: 9   ANON.

SUSAN. A NOVEL. IN TWO VOLUMES.

> London: Printed by J. Barfield, 91, Wardour-Street, for J. Booth, Duke-Street, Portland-Place, Mary-le-bone, 1809.
> I 220p; II 200p. 12mo. 8s (ECB, QR).
> QR 1: 462 (May 1809); WSW I: 117.
> IU 823.Su81; ECB 570; xNSTC.

*Notes.* Final two lines of novel (vol. 2, p. 200) followed by 'Books of esteemed Characters, lately published by J. Booth', comprising 5 titles (3 novels).


1809: 10   ANON.

TALES OF OTHER REALMS. COLLECTED DURING A LATE TOUR THROUGH EUROPE. BY A TRAVELLER. IN TWO VOLUMES.

> London: Printed for Longman, Hurst, Rees, and Orme, Paternoster-Row, 1809.
> I viii, 199p; II 208p. 12mo. 8s (ECB, ER, QR).
> ER 15: 242 (Oct 1809); QR 2: 466 (Nov 1809); WSW I: 118.
> Corvey; CME 3-628-51155-0; ECB 575; NSTC T131 (BI O).

*Notes.* Preface dated London, May 1809.


1809: 11   ANON.

THE TOWERS OF LOTHIAN; OR, THE BANKS OF CARRON: A SCOTTISH LEGEND. IN FOUR VOLUMES. BY THE AUTHOR OF THE "TWO PILGRIMS."

> London; Printed by M. Allen, Paternoster-Row, for Holmes and Whitterton, No. 15, Paternoster-Row, 1809.
> I 226p; II 256p; III 266p; IV 222p. 12mo. 20s (CR, ECB); 20s boards (ER).
> CR 3rd ser. 16: 111 (Jan 1809), 3rd ser. 16: 331–2 (Mar 1809); ER 14: 272 (Apr 1809); WSW I: 122.
> BL N.2741; ECB 595; NSTC L2355 (BI E).

*Notes.* Apparently identical to *The Banks of the Carron* (1809: 2), apart from different t.p.


1809: 12   ANON.

TRUTH IN THE GARB OF FICTION; OR, SKETCHES FROM REAL LIFE. A NOVEL. IN FOUR VOLUMES. BY A DISCIPLE OF THE OLD SCHOOL.

London: Printed by C. Stower, Paternoster-Row, for C. Chapple, Pall Mall, 1809.
I 325p; II 346p; III 352p; IV 324p. 12mo. 24s (QR).
QR 3: 268 (Feb 1810).
Corvey; CME 3-628-48839-7; xNSTC.

1809: 13   [ARNOLD, Lieut.].
LUCKY ESCAPES; OR, SYSTEMATIC VILLANY. A NOVEL. IN THREE
VOLUMES. BY THE AUTHOR OF THE BRITISH ADMIRAL, &C.

London: Printed at the Minerva-Press, for Lane, Newman, and Co. Leadenhall-Street,
1809.
I vii, 244p; II 272p; III 257p. 12mo. 15s (ECB).
Corvey; CME 3-628-48124-4; ECB 355; NSTC A1700 (BI O).

*Notes.* Dedication 'to Mrs. Billington'.

1809: 14   BURNEY, Caroline [pseud.?].
SERAPHINA; OR, A WINTER IN TOWN. A MODERN NOVEL, IN
THREE VOLUMES. BY CAROLINE BURNEY.

London: Printed for J. F. Hughes, 38, Berners Street, Oxford Street, 1809.
I 215p; II 194p; III 285p. 12mo.
WSW I: 181.
Corvey; CME 3-628-47174-5; xNSTC.

*Notes.* 'Advertisement' to Sarah Harriet Burney's *Traits of Nature* (1812: 24) states: 'The publisher [i.e. Henry Colburn] of this Work thinks it proper to state that Miss Burney is *not* the
Author of a Novel called "Seraphina," published in the year 1809, under the assumed name
of Caroline Burney.'

1809: 15   [BYRON, 'Medora Gordon'].
CELIA IN SEARCH OF A HUSBAND. BY A MODERN ANTIQUE. IN
TWO VOLUMES.

London: Printed at the Minerva-Press, for A. K. Newman and Co. (Successors to Lane,
Newman, and Co.) Leadenhall-Street, 1809.
I iv, 322p; II 306p. 8vo. 12s (ECB).
CR 3rd ser. 18: 219–20 (Oct 1809); WSW I: 193.
BL 1152.f.8; ECB 103; NSTC B6077 (BI E).

*Notes.* It seems likely that the chain of three novels published as by 'A Modern Antique', and
those under the name of Miss Byron, are by the same author (see 1808: 33).
Further edns: 2nd edn. 1809 (NSTC); 3rd edn. 1809 (NSTC).

1809: 16   BYRON, ['Medora Gordon'].
HOURS OF AFFLUENCE, AND DAYS OF INDIGENCE. A NOVEL. IN
FOUR VOLUMES. BY MISS BYRON, AUTHOR OF THE ENGLISH-
WOMAN, &C.

London: Printed at the Minerva-Press, for Lane, Newman, and Co. Leadenhall-Street,
1809.
I 225p; II 244p; III 258p; IV 268p. 12mo. 20s (ECB, QR).

QR 2: 240 (Aug 1809); WSW I: 185.
Corvey; CME 3-628-47181-8; ECB 91; NSTC B6042 (BI BL, O).

1809: 17    [CORP, Harriet].
A SEQUEL TO THE ANTIDOTE TO THE MISERIES OF HUMAN LIFE.
CONTAINING A FURTHER ACCOUNT OF MRS. PLACID AND HER
DAUGHTER RACHEL. BY THE AUTHOR OF THE ANTIDOTE.
>London: Printed for Williams and Smith, Stationers'-Court, 1809.
>viii, 175p. 12mo.
>BL 4413.ff.46(2); NSTC C3715 (BI O).

*Notes.* Collates in sixes.
Further edns: 2nd edn. 1809 (NSTC); 3rd edn. 1811 (NUC); 4th edn. 1814 (NSTC); 5th edn.
1820 (Corvey, NSTC); New York 1810 (NUC).

1809: 18    COSTELLO, Mrs.
THE SOLDIER'S ORPHAN: A TALE. BY MRS. COSTELLO. IN THREE
VOLUMES.
>London: Printed for Longman, Hurst, Rees, and Orme, Paternoster-Row, 1809.
>I 226p; II 211p; III 195p. 12mo. 13s 6d (ECB, ER, QR).
>ER 14: 272 (Apr 1809); QR 1: 462 (May 1809); WSW I: 220.
>Corvey; CME 3-628-47370-5; ECB 100; NSTC C3780 (BI O).

*Notes.* The author is evidently different from Louisa Stuart Costello (1799–1870), author of
several novels in the 1840s.
Further edn: New York 1812 (NSTC).

COTTIN, Sophie Ristaud, MATILDA AND MALEK ADHEL
See 1805: 22

1809: 19    [COURTENAY, Charles].
EUSTON. A NOVEL, IN TWO VOLUMES.
>London: Printed for C. Chapple, 66, Pall-Mall, 1809.
>I 188p; II 260p. 12mo. 9s (ER).
>CR 3rd ser. 18: 109–10 (Sept 1809); ER 15: 242 (Oct 1809); WSW I: 40.
>Corvey; CME 3-628-47636-4; ECB 140; xNSTC.

*Notes.* Allibone and Block give author as above for the title *Ereston, a Novel* (1809), itself
almost certainly a misspelled form of the present entry.

1809: 20    CUMBERLAND, Richard.
JOHN DE LANCASTER. A NOVEL. BY RICHARD CUMBERLAND, ESQ.
IN THREE VOLUMES.
>London: Printed for Lackington, Allen, and Co. Temple of the Muses, Finsbury Square,
>    1809.
>I 300p; II 292p; III 292p. 8vo. 21s (ECB, ER, QR).

ER 14: 272 (Apr 1809); QR 1: 337–48 (May 1809) full review, 1: 462 (May 1809); WSW I: 230.
BRu ENC; ECB 147; NSTC C4483 (BI BL, C, NCu, O).

*Notes.* Further edns: 2nd edn. 1809 (Corvey), CME 3-628-47361-6; New York 1809 (NUC).

1809: 21   DUDLEY, Frederick.
**AMOROSO; A NOVEL, IN TWO VOLUMES, FOUNDED ON FACT. BY FREDERICK DUDLEY.**

London: Printed and published by T. Collins, Harvey's Buildings, Strand, 1809/10.
I (1809) vi, 164p; II (1810) 165p. 12mo. 10s (QR).
QR 3: 268 (Feb 1810).
CLU-S/C PR.4629.D86a; ECB 173; xNSTC.

*Notes.* T.p. of vol. 2 reads: 'London: Printed by and for T. Collins and Son, Harvey's Buildings, Strand, and sold by Cradock and Joy, Paternoster Row, 1810'. ECB lists publisher as Cradock, and dates 1810.

1809: 22   EDGEWORTH, [Maria].
**TALES OF FASHIONABLE LIFE, BY MISS EDGEWORTH, AUTHOR OF PRACTICAL EDUCATION, BELINDA, CASTLE RACKRENT, ESSAY ON IRISH BULLS, &C. IN THREE VOLUMES.**

London: Printed for J. Johnson St. Paul's Churchyard, 1809/12.
I (1809) vii, 400p; II (1809) 338p; III (1809) 369p. IV (1812) iv, 460p; V (1812) 392p; VI
   (1812) 466p. 12mo. 39s (ECB, for 6 vols.).
ER 14: 375–88 (July 1809) full review, 20: 100–26 (July 1812) full review; QR 2: 146–54
   (Aug 1809) full review, 7: 329–42 (June 1812) full review; WSW I: 256.
BRu ENC; ECB 178; NSTC E246 (BI BL, Dt, O).

*Notes.* I Ennui; II Almeria, Madame de Fleury, and the Dun; III Manoeuvring; IV Vivian; V Emilie de Coulanges and the Beginning of The Absentee; VI The Conclusion of The Absentee. Preface in vol. 1, signed 'Richard Lovell Edgeworth. Edgeworth's Town, March 1809'. With vols. 4 to 6 t.ps. read: 'In Six Volumes' and imprint changes to: 'Printed for J. Johnson and Co., St. Paul's Church-Yard, 1812'. Preface to vol. 4, is signed 'R. L. Edgeworth, May 1812', followed by 'A List of all the Works written by Mr. and Miss Edgeworth / Published only by J. Johnson and Co. St. Paul's Church-Yard'.
Further edns: 2nd edn. 1809 (NSTC); 3rd edn. 1809 (NSTC); 4th edn. 1813 (Corvey), CME 3-628-47534-1; 1815 (NSTC); 1818/24 (NSTC); [at least 5 more edn. to 1850]; Georgetown 1809 (NUC); French trans. of vols. 4–6, 1813–14 [as *Scènes de la vie du grand monde* (BN)], also of 'Ennui', 1812; German trans. of 'Manoeuvring', 1814 [as *Schleichkünste* (RS)], and 'Ennui', 1814 [as *Denkwürdigkeiten des Grafen von Glenthorn* (RS)], and 'Vivian', 1814 [as *Vivian, oder der Mann ohne Charakter* (RS)], and 'Emilie de Coulanges', 1815 [as *Emilie, oder der Frauenzwist* (RS)]. Facs: IAN (of *Ennui* and of *The Absentee*, 1979).

1809: 23   EGESTAS [pseud.].
**OLD TIMES REVIVED, A ROMANTIC STORY OF THE NINTH AGE; WITH PARALLELS OF CHARACTERS AND EVENTS OF THE EIGHTEENTH AND NINETEENTH CENTURIES. BY EGESTAS, AUTHOR OF WAYS AND MEANS, POLITICAL VERSATILITY, &C. &C.**

London: Printed by D. Deans, Hart-Street, Covent Garden; for J. Cawthorn, (Bookseller to Her Royal Highness the Princess of Wales,) No. 5, Catherine-Street, Strand, 1809.
I viii, 237p; II 203p; III 229p; IV 262p. 12mo. 20s (ER).
ER 15: 528 (Jan 1810).
Corvey; CME 3-628-48254-2; xNSTC.

1809: 24    [?ENGLISH, John].
MODERN TIMES; OR, ANECDOTES OF THE ENGLISH FAMILY. IN THREE VOLUMES.

London: Printed for J. Budd, Bookseller to his Royal Highness the Prince of Wales, at the Crown and Mitre, Pall-Mall; and Sharpe and Hailes, No. 186, Piccadilly, 1809.
I xxiv, 264p; II 230p; III 261p. 12mo. 15s (ECB, ER).
ER 15: 529 (Jan 1810); WSW I: 78.
Corvey; CME 3-628-48219-4; ECB 390; NSTC M2772 (BI O).

*Notes.* Preface dated Buen-Retiro, Sept 1809. For attribution to John English, see his *Castlethorpe Lodge* (1816: 27).
Further edn: 1810 (NUC).

1809: 25    FLORIAN, [Jean Pierre Claris] de; HEWETSON, William B. (*trans.*).
WILLIAM TELL; OR, SWISSERLAND DELIVERED. BY THE CHEVALIER DE FLORIAN, MEMBER OF THE ROYAL ACADEMIES OF PARIS, MADRID, FLORENCE, &C. &C. A POSTHUMOUS WORK. TO WHICH IS PREFIXED, THE LIFE OF THE AUTHOR, BY JAUFFRET. TRANSLATED FROM THE FRENCH, BY WILLIAM B. HEWETSON, AUTHOR OF "THE BLIND BOY," "THE FALLEN MINISTER," &C. &C.

London: Printed for Sherwood, Neely, and Jones, (Successors to Mr. H. D. Symonds) Paternoster Row, 1809.
xxxvi, 115p, ill. 12mo. 5s (CR, ECB).
CR 3rd ser. 17: 440 (Aug 1809).
BL 1607/3574; ECB 209; NSTC H1494.

*Notes.* Trans. of *Guillaume Tell, ou la Suisse libre* (Paris, 1801). Colour frontispiece bears the legend: 'Pub. by Sherwood, Neely, & Jones, May 27 1809'. 'Life of Florian' on pp. [vii]–xxxvi. This appears to be the first full English translation of a work which, according to Michaud (*Biographie Universelle*, 1854), was written in 1793 but not published before the death of the author in 1794. Later rival translations include *William Tell, or the Patriot of Switzerland* (London, 1823).
Further edns: 1836 (NSTC); [1844] (NSTC); Concord 1843 (NSTC).

1809: 26    FRANCES, Sophia.
ANGELO GUICCIARDINI; OR, THE BANDIT OF THE ALPS. A ROMANCE. IN FOUR VOLUMES. BY SOPHIA FRANCES, AUTHOR OF VIVONIO, CONSTANCE DE LINDENSDORF, AND THE NUN OF MISERICORDIA.

London: Printed for Henry Colburn, English and Foreign Library, Conduit-Street,
Bond-Street, 1809.
I 272p; II 284p; III 258p; IV 376p. 12mo. 24s (ECB, QR).
QR 3: 267 (Feb 1810).
Corvey; CME 3-628-47810-3; ECB 215; NSTC S2967 (BI BL).

*Notes.* Further edn: French trans., 1817.

1809: 27 GENLIS, [Stéphanie-Félicité, Comtesse] de.
**ALPHONSO; OR, THE NATURAL SON. BY MADME. DE GENLIS,
AUTHOR OF SAINCLAIR, THE SIEGE OF ROCHELLE, THE RECOL-
LECTIONS OF FELICIA, THE EARL OF CORK, &C. &C. TRANSLATED
FROM THE FRENCH. IN THREE VOLUMES.**

London: Printed for Henry Colburn, English and Foreign Library, Conduit-Street,
Bond-Street, 1809.
I iv, 174p; II 183p; III 190p. 12mo. 13s 6d (ECB, ER, QR).
ER 15: 242 (Oct 1809); QR 3: 267 (Feb 1810).
BL 12511.c.20; ECB 225; NSTC B4973.

*Notes.* Trans. of *Alphonse, ou le fils naturel* (Paris, 1809).

1809: 28 [GREEN, Sarah].
**TALES OF THE MANOR. BY THE AUTHOR OF THE PRIVATE HIS-
TORY OF THE COURT OF ENGLAND, &C. &C. IN TWO VOLUMES.**

London: Printed for B. Crosby and Co. Stationers'-Court, Paternoster-Row, 1809.
I 270p; II 219p. 12mo. 10s (ECB, ER).
ER 13: 507 (Jan 1809), 14: 272 (Apr 1809); WSW I: 288.
Corvey; CME 3-628-48873-7; ECB 576; NSTC G1950 (BI O).

*Notes.* Vol. 1 printed by J. & E. Hodson, Cross-Street, Hatton-Garden; vol. 2 by R. Wilks,
Chancery Lane. Collates in sixes.

1809: 29 HALL, W. H.
**FEMALE CONFESSIONS; OR, SCENES IN LIFE. AN INTERESTING
DOMESTIC STORY. IN TWO VOLUMES. BY W. H. HALL, ESQ. AUTHOR
OF THE SCHOOL OF VIRTUE, &C.**

London: Printed for W. Turmaine, No. 10, Gate-Street, Lincoln's-Inn-Fields. And sold
by T. Mason, Cambridge-Street, Golden-Square, 1809.
I xii, 171p; II 187p. 12mo. 'Price Nine Shillings' (t.p.).
WSW I: 294.
BL 1568/8463; NSTC H242.5.

*Notes.* Half-title reads: 'The Museum; or, Female Confessions. A Domestic Story.' Preface
characterizes the author as 'a man of fashion'. This suggests a different person from William
Henry Hall (d. 1807), author of *The New Royal Encyclopaedia* (1791), and other works.

1809: 30 HANWAY, {Mary Ann}.
**FALCONBRIDGE ABBEY. A DEVONSHIRE STORY. IN FIVE VOLUMES.
BY MRS. HANWAY, AUTHOR OF ELLINOR, AND ANDREW STUART.**

London: Printed at the Minerva-Press, for Lane, Newman, and Co. Leadenhall-Street,
    1809.
I xxiv, 299p; II 280p; III 286p; IV 312p; V 376p. 12mo. 27s 6d (CR, ECB); 25s (ER).
CR 3rd ser. 16: 110 (Jan 1809); ER 13: 507 (Jan 1809); WSW I: 297.
Corvey; CME 3-628-47621-6; ECB 254; NSTC H477 (BI BL).

*Notes.* Dedication 'to James Buller, Esq. Member of Parliament for Exeter' signed 'Mary Ann
Hanway', and dated Blackheath, 15 Dec 1808. ECB dates Dec 1808. Preface, vol. 1, pp. v–xxiv,
complains about 'all the crude indigestible trash, that load the shelves of circulating libraries'
(p. xii).

1809: 31   HILL, Mary.
THE FOREST OF COMALVA, A NOVEL; CONTAINING SKETCHES OF
PORTUGAL, SPAIN, AND PART OF FRANCE. IN THREE VOLUMES.
BY MARY HILL.

London: Printed for Richard Phillips, New Bridge-Street, Blackfriars, 1809.
I v, 231p; II 210p; III 261p. 12mo. 15s (ECB, ER).
ER 14: 272 (Apr 1809); WSW I: 313.
Corvey; CME 3-628-47688-7; ECB 269; NSTC H1688 (BI BL).

*Notes.* Preface in vol. 1, pp. [iii]–v, in which the authoress refers to 'this first production of
her pen', is dated Jan 1809.

1809: 32   [HOFLAND, Barbara].
THE HISTORY OF AN OFFICER'S WIDOW, AND HER YOUNG FAMILY.

London: Printed for J. Harris, (Successor to E. Newberry) Corner of St. Paul's Church
    Yard, 1809.
vii, 182p. 12mo.
WSW I: 327.
BL 12611.c.21; NSTC H2420.

*Notes.* Further edns: 3rd edn. 1814 (NSTC); 5th edn. 1822 (NUC); 1834 (NSTC); New York
1830 (NUC).

1809: 33   ISAACS, Mrs.
ELLA ST. LAURENCE; OR, THE VILLAGE OF SELWOOD AND ITS
INHABITANTS: A NOVEL, IN FOUR VOLUMES. BY MRS. ISAACS,
AUTHOR OF ARIEL, GLENMORE ABBEY, AND THE WOOD-NYMPH.

London: Printed for C. Chapple, 66, Pall Mall, 1809.
I 291p; II 267p; III 275p; IV 282p. 12mo. 22s (ECB, ER).
ER 15: 242 (Oct 1809); WSW I: 343.
Corvey; ECB 301; NSTC I522 (BI BL).

*Notes.* Collates in sixes.

1809: 34   ISDELL, Sarah.
THE IRISH RECLUSE; OR, A BREAKFAST AT THE ROTUNDA. IN
THREE VOLUMES. BY SARAH ISDELL, AUTHOR OF THE VALE OF
LOUISIANA.

London: Printed for J. Booth, Duke-Street, Portland-Place, 1809.
I iv, 260p, ill.; II 226p, ill.; III 249p, ill. 12mo. 13s 6d (ECB, ER, QR).
ER 15: 242 (Oct 1809); QR 2: 466 (Nov 1809); WSW I: 343.
MH-H *EC8.Is247.809i; ECB 300; NSTC I527 (BI Dt).

*Notes.* Dedication to Sir Edward Denny, Bart., Tralee Castle. Vol. 3, p. 249, where text ends, concludes with adv. for a non-fictional work, 'Spain and Portugal', the following p. [250] containing advs. for 'New Novels, &c.'.

1809: 35   JONES, Evan.
**THE BARD; OR, THE TOWERS OF MORVEN. A LEGENDARY TALE. BY EVAN JONES, ROYAL NAVY.**

London: Printed for the Author, and sold by R. Dutton, 45, Gracechurch-Street, 1809.
vi, 160p. 12mo.
CFu WG16.9.J; xNSTC.

*Notes.* Introduction, pp. [v]–vi, giving origin in North Wales tradition, and in which author apologises for 'the numerous errors with which this first production of his pen abounds' (p. vi). Colophon reads: 'Printed by W. Darton, and J. and J. Harvey, Gracechurch-Street.' Further edn: 1810 (Corvey—a reissue by A. K. Newman), CME 3-628-51083-X. The Corvey copy has the same printer's mark and colophon as the 1809 Dutton edn.

1809: 36   JONES, Harri{e}t.
**THE FAMILY OF SANTRAILE; OR, THE HEIR OF MONTAULT. A ROMANCE IN FOUR VOLUMES. BY HARRIOT [*sic*] JONES, AUTHORESS OF BELMONT LODGE, A NOVEL.**

London: Printed for J. Cawthorn, 5, Catherine-Street, Strand, 1809.
I xii, 333p, ill.; II 299p; III 286p; IV 300p. 12mo.
WSW I: 347.
ViU PZ2.J66F.1809; xNSTC.

*Notes.* 'Address to the Public', signed Harriet Jones, Maidstone Nunnery, 1808. On t.ps. to vols. 2–4, the author's name is spelt 'Harriet'.
Further edn: 2nd edn. 1818 (Corvey), CME 3-628-48001-9.

KER, Louisa Theresa Bellenden
See RADCLIFFE, Mary Anne

1809: 37   KETT, Henry.
**EMILY, A MORAL TALE, INCLUDING LETTERS FROM A FATHER TO HIS DAUGHTER, UPON THE MOST IMPORTANT SUBJECTS. BY THE REV. HENRY KETT, FELLOW OF TRINITY COLLEGE, OXFORD, AND AUTHOR OF THE ELEMENTS OF GENERAL KNOWLEDGE, &C. IN TWO VOLUMES.**

London: Printed for Messrs. Rivingtons, No. 62, St. Paul's Church-Yard; Payne, Pall-Mall; Lunn, Soho Square; Egerton, Charing-Cross; and Hatchard, Piccadilly, 1809/11.

I (1809) vii, 327p; II (1809) 328p; III (1811) 328p. 8vo. 21s 6d (ECB).
QR 2: 314–19 (Nov 1809) full review; WSW I: 354–5.
BRu ENC; ECB 320; NSTC K473 (BI BL, O).

*Notes.* Dedication to 'their Royal Highnesses the Princesses Augusta, Elizabeth, Mary, Sophia, and Amelia'. 'Advertisement to the Third Volume of Emily' begins: 'As the two Volumes which originally composed this work have been very favourably received, the author is encouraged to introduce a THIRD to the notice of the public'. Vol. 3 title is similar to those of vols. 1 and 2 apart from reading: 'In Three Volumes'. Imprint to vol. 3 differs as follows: London: Printed for Messrs. Rivingtons, No. 62, St. Paul's Church-Yard; Payne, Pall-Mall; Egerton, Charing-Cross; and Hatchard, Piccadilly; by Law and Gilbert, St. John's Square, 1811. ECB dates May 1809, Feb 1812.
Further edn: 2nd edn. 1809 (NSTC).

1809: 38   KOTZEBUE, August [Friedrich Ferdinand] von.
LEONTINA: A NOVEL. IN THREE VOLUMES. BY AUGUSTUS VON KOTZEBUE. TRANSLATED FROM THE GERMAN.

> London: Printed for Henry Colburn, Conduit-Street, New Bond-Street, 1809.
> I 212p; II 234p; III 216p. 12mo. 15s (ER).
> ER 14: 272 (Apr 1809).
> C Rom.3.53; NSTC 902.

*Notes.* Trans. of *Leontine* (Riga, 1808).

KOTZEBUE, Amalie Johanna Karoline
See LUDECUS, Amalie Johanna Karoline

KOTZEBUE, August Friedrich Ferdinand, von, LEVITY AND SORROW
See LUDECUS, Amalie Johanna Karoline

1809: 39   LATHOM, Francis.
LONDON; OR, TRUTH WITHOUT TREASON. A NOVEL. IN FOUR VOLUMES. BY FRANCIS LATHOM, AUTHOR OF THE MYSTERIOUS FREEBOOTER, THE UNKNOWN, MYSTERY, ERESTINA, &C. &C.

> London: Printed at the Minerva-Press, for Lane, Newman, and Co. Leadenhall-Street, 1809.
> I viii, 296p; II 312p; III 295p; IV 322p. 12mo. 22s (ECB, ER, QR).
> ER 14: 272 (Apr 1809); QR 1: 462 (May 1809); WSW I: 364.
> Corvey; CME 3-628-47959-2; ECB 330; xNSTC.

*Notes.* ECB dates Dec 1808.

1809: 40   LATHOM, Francis.
THE ROMANCE OF THE HEBRIDES; OR, WONDERS NEVER CEASE! IN THREE VOLUMES. BY FRANCIS LATHOM, AUTHOR OF LONDON; THE UNKNOWN; MYSTERIOUS FREEBOOTER; MYSTERY; &C.

> London: Printed at the Minerva-Press, for A. K. Newman and Co. (Successors to Lane, Newman, & Co.) Leadenhall-Street, 1809.

I viii, 282p; II 288p; III 256p. 12mo.

Corvey; CME 3-628-47963-0; NSTC L546 (BI BL, E).

*Notes.* Preface (vol. 1, pp. [v]–viii) states: 'The period at which the following tale is supposed to have taken place, is about the middle of the thirteenth century, and the theatre of action principally the Scottish Isles'.

1809: 41   LATHY, T[homas] P[ike].
*LOVE, HATRED, AND REVENGE; A SWISS ROMANCE. BY T. P. LATHY.

> London: A. K. Newman, 1809.
> 3 vols. 12mo. 15s (ER).
> ER 15: 529 (Jan 1810).
> No copy located.

*Notes.* Newman is given as publisher by Bent22.

1809: 42   [LEWIS, Alethea].
THE DISCARDED DAUGHTER. A NOVEL, IN FOUR VOLUMES. BY EUGENIA DE ACTON, AUTHOR OF "ESSAYS ON THE ART OF BEING HAPPY," AND MANY OTHER POPULAR WORKS.

> London: Printed for J. F. Hughes, 38, Berners-Street, Oxford-Street, 1809/10.
> I (1810) 239p; II (1810) 215p; III (1809) 269p; IV (1809) 247p. 12mo. 22s (QR).
> QR 3: 268 (Feb 1810); WSW I: 238.
> Corvey; CME 3-628-47006-4; xNSTC.

*Notes.* No author appears on the t.p. of vols. 3 and 4. Blakey (copy not seen) lists under 1810 as a Minerva publication, but not discovered in this form. ECB 3 lists Lane edn., 1810, 21s.

1809: 43   LINLEY, William.
THE ADVENTURES OF RALPH REYBRIDGE: CONTAINING SKET-CHES OF MODERN CHARACTERS, MANNERS, AND EDUCATION. BY WILLIAM LINLEY, ESQ. IN FOUR VOLUMES.

> London: Printed for Richard Phillips, Bridge-Street, Blackfriars, 1809.
> I xii, 307p; II viii, 303p; III vii, 268p; IV xii, 268p. 12mo.
> Corvey; CME 3-628-48102-3; NSTC L1727 (BI BL, C).

*Notes.* 'Prefatory Address to the Reader' (vol. 1, pp. [iii]–viii) begins: 'The following pages were written at Madras in the year 1801, soon after the Author's arrival at that Presidency, and before he was appointed to fill any office of responsibility in the service.' 'Introductory Chapter to the Fourth Volume', vol. 4, pp. [vii]–xii.

1809: 44   [LUDECUS, Amalie Johanna Karoline]; BIANCHI, Michael Angelo (*trans.*).
LEVITY AND SORROW; A GERMAN STORY, IN TWO VOLUMES: WITH A PREFACE BY A. VON KOTZEBUE. TRANSLATED BY MICHAEL ANGELO BIANCHI.

> London: Printed at the Minerva-Press, for A. K. Newman, and Co. (Successors to Lane, Newman, & Co.) Leadenhall-Street, 1809.

I xii, 256p; II 266p. 12mo. 10s (ECB, ER, QR).
ER 14: 519 (July 1809); QR 1: 462 (May 1809).
BL 12547.dd.9; ECB 343; NSTC B1986.

*Notes.* Trans. of *Louise, oder die unseligen Folgen des Leichtsinns. Mit einer Vorrede von Kotze-bue* (Leipzig, 1800). The German original title was written by August Kotzebue's daughter Amalie, who published under her married name of Ludecus. 'Preface of the Translator' (vol. 1, pp. [iii]–vii) states: 'I should have willingly made the version from the original in German; but the interdiction of the means of procuring a copy, has induced me to attempt it from a Danish translation, casually fallen into my hands' (p. v). This is followed by 'Preface of Mr. A. von Kotzebue' (pp. [viii]–xii), which of the authorship states: 'Thus much I can assure you, upon my honor [*sic*], that she [the author] is neither my mother, wife, or sister; but happy he that is in any degree connected with her' (p. xii).
Further edn: 1819 (NSTC).

1809: 45   MACKENZIE, {Anna Maria}.
**THE IRISH GUARDIAN, OR, ERRORS OF ECCENTRICITY. IN THREE VOLUMES. BY MRS. MACKENZIE.**

London: Printed for Longman, Hurst, Rees, and Orme, 39, Paternoster-Row, 1809.
I iv, 296p; II 292p; III 279p. 12mo. 15s (ECB, QR).
QR 1: 462 (May 1809).
BL 1153.i.17; ECB 360; NSTC M344.

*Notes.* Preface, vol. 1, pp. [i]–iv, signed Anna Maria Mackenzie, reads: 'The Author perceives she cannot conclude without paying a feeble tribute of praise to those male writers, who have thought it no degradation of their dignity [. . .] to [. . .] improve and amuse in the form of a novel' (p. iv). Colophon in all vols. of 'J. Rackham, Printer, Bury St. Edmund's'.
Further edn: 1811 as *Almeria D'Aveiro; or, the Irish Guardian* (Corvey—a reissue by A. K. Newman, with same colophon), CME 3-628-48094-9.

1809: 46   MANNERS, C[atherine].
**THE LORDS OF ERITH, A ROMANCE, IN THREE VOLUMES. BY C. MANNERS.**

London: Printed by J. Dean, 57, Wardour Street, Soho. For R. Ryan, 353, Oxford-Street, and G. Shade, 62, Poland-Street, Oxford-Street. Sold by Sherwood, Neeley, and Jones, Paternoster-Row, 1809.
I 214p; II 248p; III 259p. 12mo. 15s (ECB).
ER 15: 242 (Oct 1809).
Corvey; CME 3-628-48080-9; ECB 366; NSTC M1001 (BI BL).

1809: 47   MAXWELL, C[aroline].
**LIONEL; OR, THE IMPENETRABLE COMMAND. AN HISTORICAL ROMANCE. IN TWO VOLUMES. BY MRS. C. MAXWELL, AUTHOR OF ALFRED OF NORMANDY, &C.**

London: Printed at the Minerva-Press, for Lane, Newman, and Co. Leadenhall-Street, 1809.
I 220p; II 212p. 12mo. 8s (ECB, ER).

ER 13: 507 (Jan 1809).
Corvey; CME 3-628-48205-4; ECB 375; xNSTC.

*Notes.* ECB dates Dec 1808.

1809: 48 [MEEKE, Mary].
**LANGHTON PRIORY. A NOVEL. IN FOUR VOLUMES. BY GABRIELLI, AUTHOR OF MYSTERIOUS WIFE, MYSTERIOUS HUSBAND, &C. &C.**

London: Printed at the Minerva-Press, for Lane, Newman, and Co. Leadenhall-Street, 1809.
I 299p; II 316p; III 330p; IV 340p. 12mo. 20s (QR).
QR 1: 462 (May 1809), 2: 240 (Aug 1809).
Corvey; CME 3-628-47845-6; NSTC M1954 (BI O).

*Notes.* Blakey, Block, Summers etc. all spell as 'Laughton Priory', presumably in error.

1809: 49 MELVILLE, Theodore.
**THE IRISH CHIEFTAIN, AND HIS FAMILY. A ROMANCE. IN FOUR VOLUMES. BY THEODORE MELVILLE, ESQ. AUTHOR OF THE WHITE KNIGHT, THE BENEVOLENT MONK, &C.**

London: Printed at the Minerva-Press, for Lane, Newman, and Co. Leadenhall-Street, 1809.
I 208p; II 226p; III 236p; IV 240p. 12mo. 20s (ECB, ER, QR).
ER 14: 272 (Apr 1809); QR 1: 462 (May 1809), 2: 240 (Aug 1809).
Corvey; CME 3-628-48056-6; ECB 379; NSTC M2020 (BI BL).

*Notes.* Colophon in each vol. reads: 'J. Dennett, Printer, Leather-Lane, Holborn'.

1809: 50 MOORE, Thomas George.
**THE BACHELOR: A NOVEL, IN THREE VOLUMES. BY THOMAS GEORGE MOORE, ESQ.**

London: Printed for Henry Colburn, Conduit-Street, New Bond-Street, 1809.
I 184p; II 220p; III 228p. 12mo. 15s (CR, ER).
CR 3rd ser. 16: 111 (Jan 1809), 3rd ser. 16: 430–1 (Apr 1809); ER 14: 272 (Apr 1809); WSW I: 408.
Corvey; CME 3-628-48288-7; xNSTC.

MORGAN, Lady Sydney
See OWENSON, Sydney

1809: 51 MORRINGTON, J.
*****THE COTTAGE OF MERLIN VALE. A NOVEL BY J. MORRINGTON.**

London, 1809.
2 vols. 12mo. 10s (ER, QR).
ER 14: 519 (July 1809); QR 1: 461 (May 1809).
No copy located.

*Notes.* Listed by Henderson as being in National Library of Wales, but not found there. Allibone, Summers, and Henderson give author as above; Block lists as by 'Isabella Morrington'.

ER gives sub-title as 'A History Founded on Facts'; QR as 'A Rational, Moral, Sentimental, Literary, and Entertaining History, founded on Facts'.

1809: 52 [MOUHY, Charles de Fieux, Chevalier de]; HUNT, John Proteus (*trans.*).
**THE IRON MASK; OR, THE ADVENTURES OF A FATHER & A SON, A ROMANCE, TRANSLATED FROM A SPANISH MANUSCRIPT, BY THE REVEREND JOHN PROTEUS HUNT. IN THREE VOLUMES.**

> London: Printed by J. Dean, 57, Wardour Street, Soho. For George Hughes, 212, Tottenham-Court-Road, and sold by Sherwood, Neely, and Jones, 20, Paternoster-Row, 1809.
> I xlv, 208p; II 208p; III 193p. 12mo. 15s (CR).
> CR 3rd ser. 16: 110 (Jan 1809).
> Corvey; CME 3-628-47669-0; xNSTC.

*Notes.* Trans. of *Le Masque de fer, ou les aventures admirables du père et du fils* (La Haye, 1747). 'The English Translator's Preface' (vol. 1, pp. [v]–ix), signed 'J. P. H.', begins: 'The History of the *Iron Mask* was originally written in Spanish, and was published by the French Translator, who favours us with the annexed ingenious and interesting preface, in the original language, and in French, at the Hague, about the year 1726–7'. Dedication 'to Her Ladyship the Countess of Tremes', signed 'L. C. D***'. Preface, pp. [xiii]–xlv. Continuous roman and arabic pagination, with novel proper beginning on p. [47]. Frank (Item 193) treats Hunt's work as an original title, and gives A. K. Newman as publisher.

1809: 53 [MUDFORD, William].
**NUBILIA IN SEARCH OF A HUSBAND; INCLUDING SKETCHES OF MODERN SOCIETY, AND INTERSPERSED WITH MORAL AND LITERARY DISQUISITIONS.**

> London: Printed for J. Ridgeway, Piccadilly; and Sherwood, Neely, and Jones, Paternoster-Row, 1809.
> 456p. 8vo. 9s (ECB).
> CR 3rd ser. 17: 439 (Aug 1809); WSW I: 413.
> BL 12614.d.23; ECB 418; NSTC N1351 (BI E, O).

*Notes.* Preface (3 pp. unn.) ends: 'It is not to deprecate criticism that it is told, the following work was commenced on the 10th of May, 1809, and finished on the 3d of June following'. Further edns: 2nd edn. (with two additional chapters) 1809 (NSTC); 4th edn. 1809 (NSTC); Philadelphia 1809 (NUC).

1809: 54 ORLANDO [pseud.].
**THE CHAMBER OF DEATH; OR, THE FATE OF ROSARIO. AN HISTORICAL ROMANCE OF THE SIXTEENTH CENTURY. IN TWO VOLUMES. BY ORLANDO, AUTHOR OF "A SUMMER BY THE SEA."**

> London: Printed at the Minerva-Press, for A. K. Newman and Co. (Successors to Lane, Newman, & Co.) Leadenhall-Street, 1809.
> I 211p; II 183p. 12mo. 9s (ECB).
> Corvey; CME 3-628-47247-4; ECB 104; xNSTC.

1809: 55   OWENSON, {Sydney} [afterwards MORGAN, Lady Sydney].
WOMAN: OR, IDA OF ATHENS. BY MISS OWENSON, AUTHOR OF
THE "WILD IRISH GIRL," THE "NOVICE OF ST. DOMINICK," &C. IN
FOUR VOLUMES.

> London: Printed for Longman, Hurst, Rees, and Orme, Paternoster-Row, 1809.
> I xxviii, 223p; II 272p; III 192p; IV 290p. 12mo. 21s (ECB, ER, QR).
> ER 14: 272 (Apr 1809); QR 1: 50–2 (Feb 1809) full review, 1: 236 (Feb 1809); WSW I: 425.
> Corvey; CME 3-628-48374-3; ECB 396; NSTC O738 (BI BL, C, E, O).

*Notes.* 'To the Public', vol. 1, pp. [iii]–vii, signed 'Sydney Owenson' and dated Dublin, 18 Nov 1808. This carries a footnote which states: 'The "Wild Irish Girl" was written in six weeks; the "Sketches" in one; and "Woman," though I had long revolved its plan and tendency in my mind, and frequently mentioned it in society, was not begun until the 20th of last July. It was written at intervals, in England, Wales, and Ireland, and almost always in the midst of what is called the world. It was finished on the 18th of October, and is now printed from the first copy' (p. vn). Notes (2 pp. unn.) at the end of vol. 4; notes at end of other vols. within the main sequence of pagination.
Further edns: Philadelphia & New York & Baltimore 1809 (NUC); French trans., 1812; German trans., 1820 [as *Ida von Athen* (RS)].

1809: 56   [PALMER, Alicia Tyndal].
THE HUSBAND AND THE LOVER. AN HISTORICAL AND MORAL
ROMANCE. IN THREE VOLUMES.

> London: Printed for Lackington, Allen, and Co. Temple of the Muses, Finsbury Square,
>     1809.
> I xi, 302p; II 315p; III 374p. 12mo. 18s (ECB, ER, QR).
> ER 15: 242 (Oct 1809), 16: 259 (Apr 1810); QR 2: 466 (Nov 1809); WSW I: 427.
> Corvey; CME 3-628-47679-8; ECB 290; xNSTC.

*Notes.* 'Introductory Letters from Father Theodore, to the Youthful Guardian of Sabina de Montresor', vol. 1, pp. [v]–xi, which form a fictive introduction belonging to the novel proper. Adv. at the end of vol. 1 for 'A Circulating Library, to be sold for an hundred pounds, (*Which is exceedingly cheap.*)', consisting of a thousand volumes (750 of them novels and romances), and to be had from Lackington, Allen, and Co. Novel proper ends, vol. 3, p. 371. Author's note in vol. 3, pp. 373–4 states: 'The Author has endeavoured, in this work, carefully to avoid violating any important historic fact. She has founded her little tale on the circumstance of John Sobieski, after ascending the throne of Poland, having so far acknowledged a son of the Marchioness de Briscacier to be his, as to exert his influence with Louis XIV. to confer on *that son* the title of Duke'. Her note also calls the novel 'this first essay of her pen'.

1809: 57   PECK, {Frances}.
THE YOUNG ROSINIERE; OR, SKETCHES OF THE WORLD. A NOVEL,
IN THREE VOLUMES; BY MRS. PECK, AUTHOR OF THE MAID OF
AVON, WELCH PEASANT BOY, &C.

> London: Printed for Henry Colburn, English and Foreign Subscription Library, Con-
>     duit-Street, Bond-Street, 1809.
> I 255p; II 172p; III 197p. 12mo. 15s (ECB, QR).

QR 3: 267 (Feb 1810); WSW I: 435.

Dt 200.r.122–124; ECB 477; NSTC P916.

*Notes.* Dedication 'to the Right Hon. the Countess of Londonderry', signed Frances Peck. 2nd vol. is mistakenly described as 'vol. III' on t.p., and in signatures; 3rd vol. lacks a t.p., but is mistakenly described in signatures as 'vol. IV'. This error presumably arose through a misunderstanding by the printers: vol. 1 colophon reads: 'Printed by E. Hemsted, New-Street, Fetter-Lane'; colophons in vols. 2 and 3 read: 'B. Clarke, Well Street, Cripplegate'. QR gives as 'By Mr. Rach, of Dublin', ECB lists under 'Rach'.

1809: 58    PEREGRINE, Peter [pseud.].
**MATILDA MONTFORT; A ROMANTIC NOVEL. IN FOUR VOLUMES. BY PETER PEREGRINE, ESQ.**

London: Printed by W. M'Dowall, Pemberton Row, Gough Square, for R. Spencer, No. 22, Great-Ormond-Street, 1809.

I 231p; II 239p; III 251p; IV 220p. 12mo. 21s (ER, QR).

ER 14: 272 (Apr 1809), 15: 242 (Oct 1809); QR 1: 462 (May 1809), 2: 466 (Nov 1809); WSW I: 436.

Corvey; CME 3-628-48432-4; xNSTC.

1809: 59    PILKINGTON, [Mary].
**SINCLAIR; OR, THE MYSTERIOUS ORPHAN. A NOVEL. IN FOUR VOLUMES. BY MRS. PILKINGTON, AUTHOR OF CRIMES AND CHARACTERS, PARENTAL DUPLICITY, &C.**

London: Printed at the Minerva-Press, for A. K. Newman and Co. (Successors to Lane, Newman, and Co.) Leadenhall-Street, 1809.

I 274p; II 233p; III 254p; IV 261p. 12mo. 20s (ECB).

Corvey; CME 3-628-48471-5; ECB 450; xNSTC.

1809: 60    PORTER, Anna Maria.
**DON SEBASTIAN; OR, THE HOUSE OF BRAGANZA. AN HISTORICAL ROMANCE. IN FOUR VOLUMES. BY MISS ANNA MARIA PORTER. AUTHOR OF THE HUNGARIAN BROTHERS.**

London: Printed for Longman, Hurst, Rees, and Orme, Paternoster Row, 1809.

I xvi, 278p; II 314p; III 303p; IV 320p. 12mo. 21s (ECB, ER, QR).

ER 15: 242 (Oct 1809); QR 2: 466 (Nov 1809); WSW I: 447.

Corvey; CME 3-628-48516-9; ECB 463; NSTC P2589 (BI BL, C, Dt, E, O).

*Notes.* Preface, dated Aug 1809, states: 'I am told that there has been a novel written in French on the same story, which forms the ground work of mine, but I have not seen it'.
Further edns: 1838 (NSTC); [1850?] (NSTC); Philadelphia 1810 (NUC); French trans., 1820 [as *Don Sebastian, roi de Portugal* (BN)]; German trans., 1821 [as *Der Kreuzritter, oder Don Sebastian, König von Portugal. Ein historischer Ritterroman* (RS)].

1809: 61    ?RADCLIFFE, Mary Anne or [?KER, Louisa Theresa Bellenden].
**MANFRONÉ; OR, THE ONE-HANDED MONK. A ROMANCE, IN FOUR VOLUMES. BY MARY ANNE RADCLIFFE.**

London: Printed for J. F. Hughes, 38, Berners Street, Oxford Street, 1809.
I 224p; II 228p; III 230p; IV 222p. 12mo.
WSW I: 457.
ViU PZ2.R335M.1809; xNSTC.

*Notes.* This title was later claimed by Louisa Theresa Bellenden Ker, as part of several appeals to the Royal Literary Fund (RLF 11: 400, Items 6, 11, 16); for Ker herself, see the entry under her name in FC.
Further edns: 2nd edn. 1819 (Corvey), CME 3-628-48446-4; 3rd edn. 1828 (NUC); 1839 (NUC).
Facs: GNI (of 1828 edn; 1972).

1809: 62    ROVER, Sir George [pseud.].
**CŒLEBS SUITED, OR THE OPINIONS AND PART OF THE LIFE OF CALEB CŒLEBS, ESQ. A DISTANT RELATION OF THE LATE CHARLES CŒLEBS, ESQ. DECEASED. BY SIR GEORGE ROVER, BART.**

London: Printed for Edmund Lloyd, Harley Street, Cavendish Square, 1809.
vi, 322p. 8vo.
WSW I: 474.
Corvey; CME 3-628-48557-6; NSTC R1784 (BI BL, C).

1809: 63    SICKELMORE, Richard.
**OSRICK; OR, MODERN HORRORS. A ROMANCE. INTERSPERSED WITH A FEW ANECDOTES, &C. THAT HAVE THEIR FOUNDATION IN TRUTH, AND WHICH ARE OCCASIONALLY POINTED OUT TO THE READER. IN THREE VOLUMES. BY RICHARD SICKELMORE, AUTHOR OF MARY-JANE; RAYMOND; AGNES AND LEONORA; EDGAR; RASHLEIGH ABBEY; &C. &C.**

London: Printed at the Minerva-Press, for Lane, Newman, and Co. Leadenhall-Street, 1809.
I viii, 219p; II 210p; III 246p. 12mo. 15s (ECB, ER, QR).
ER 15: 242 (Oct 1809); QR 2: 241 (Aug 1809), 2: 466 (Nov 1809).
Corvey; CME 3-628-48692-0; ECB 537; NSTC S1915 (BI O).

*Notes.* Dedication 'to the Right Honourable the Countess Craven'.

1809: 64    SIDDONS, Henry.
**THE SON OF THE STORM, A TALE. BY HENRY SIDDONS. IN FOUR VOLUMES.**

Richmond: Printed by G. A. Wall, for Longman, Hurst, Rees, and Orme, Paternoster Row, London, 1809.
I 261p; II 255p; III 226p; IV 224p. 12mo. 18s (ECB, ER).
ER 15: 528 (Jan 1810).
Corvey; CME 3-628-48696-3; ECB 537; NSTC S1921 (BI BL).

*Notes.* Dedication 'to B. C. Griffinhoofe, Esq.', a former school-fellow of the author.

1809: 65    SINCLAIR, Caroline.
THE MYSTERIOUS FLORENTINE. A ROMANCE, IN FOUR VOLUMES.
BY CAROLINE SINCLAIR.

> London: Printed for J. F. Hughes, 38, Berners Street, Oxford Street, 1809.
> I 221p; II 201p; III 182p; IV 183p. 12mo. 18s (ER, QR).
> ER 15: 242 (Oct 1809); QR 2: 466 (Nov 1809).
> Corvey; CME 3-628-48703-X; NSTC S2066 (BI O).

1809: 66    SLEATH, Eleanor.
THE BRISTOL HEIRESS; OR, THE ERRORS OF EDUCATION. A TALE.
IN FIVE VOLUMES. BY ELEANOR SLEATH, AUTHOR OF WHO'S THE
MURDERER? THE ORPHAN OF THE RHINE, &C.

> London: Printed at the Minerva-Press, for Lane, Newman, and Co. Leadenhall-Street,
> 1809.
> I 295p; II 332p; III 339p; IV 336p; V 339p. 12mo. 25s (ECB, ER).
> ER 13: 507 (Jan 1809); WSW I: 307, 501.
> Corvey; CME 3-628-48754-4; ECB 542; xNSTC.

*Notes.* ER lists as 'The British Heiress'.

1809: 67    SMITH, [Catherine].
THE CASTLE OF ARRAGON; OR THE BANDITTI OF THE FOREST. A
ROMANCE, IN FOUR VOLUMES. BY MISS SMITH.

> London: Printed for Henry Colburn, English and Foreign Library, Conduit-Street,
> Bond-Street, 1809/10.
> I (1809) 236p; II (1810) 264p; III (1810) 195p; IV (1810) 167p. 12mo. 22s (ER); 20s
> (QR).
> ER 15: 528 (Jan 1810); QR 3: 267 (Feb 1810).
> Corvey; CME 3-628-48760-9; xNSTC.

1809: 68    SPIESS, [Christian Heinrich]; HEWETSON, William B. (*trans.*).
THE FALLEN MINISTER, AND OTHER TALES. IN TWO VOLUMES.
FROM THE GERMAN OF SPIESS, BY WILLIAM B. HEWETSON, AUTHOR
OF THE DRAMA OF "THE BLIND BOY."

> London: Printed at the Minerva-Press, for A. K. Newman and Co. (Successors to Lane,
> Newman, & Co.) Leadenhall-Street, 1809.
> I vi, 213p; II 223p. 12mo. 10s (ECB, ER).
> ER 15: 242 (Oct 1809).
> BL 12548.f.23; ECB 555; NSTC S3325.

*Notes.* No German original discovered. Contains 7 tales.

1809: 69    STANHOPE, Louisa Sidney.
THE AGE WE LIVE IN. A NOVEL. IN THREE VOLUMES. BY LOUISA
SIDNEY STANHOPE, AUTHOR OF MONTBRASIL ABBEY, THE BAN-
DIT'S BRIDE, STRIKING LIKENESSES, &C. &C.

London: Printed at the Minerva-Press, for A. K. Newman and Co. (Successors to Lane, Newman, & Co.) Leadenhall-Street, 1809.
I 222p; II 245p; III 238p. 12mo. 15s (ECB, ER).
ER 15: 242 (Oct 1809).
Corvey; CME 3-628-48770-6; ECB 558; NSTC S3494 (BI BL, O).

1809: 70    [SYMMONS, Caroline].
THE COTTAGE OF THE VAR, A TALE. IN THREE VOLUMES.
London: Printed for Samuel Tipper, 37, Leadenhall Street, 1809.
I 262p; II 228p; III 227p. 12mo. 15s (ECB).
CR 3rd ser. 17: 330–1 (July 1809); WSW I: 528–9.
BL N.2482; ECB 138; NSTC S4598.

1809: 71    [THOMAS, Elizabeth].
MONTE VIDEO; OR, THE OFFICER'S WIFE AND HER SISTER. A NOVEL. IN FOUR VOLUMES. BY MRS. BRIDGET BLUEMANTLE, AUTHOR OF THE HUSBAND AND WIFE, THREE OLD MAIDS, &C. &C.
London: Printed at the Minerva-Press, for A. K. Newman, and Co. (Successors to Lane, Newman, & Co.) Leadenhall-Street, 1809.
I 208p; II 205p; III 228p; IV 231p. 12mo. 18s (ECB).
Corvey; CME 3-628-47126-5; ECB 63; xNSTC.
*Notes.* Novel proper ends vol. 4, p. 230, followed by an apology for the novel by 'The Author of the foregoing pages' (p. 231).
Further edn: Philadelphia 1816 (NUC).

1809: 72    TORRENS, R[obert].
COELIBIA CHOOSING A HUSBAND; A MODERN NOVEL, IN TWO VOLUMES. BY R. TORRENS, ESQ.
London: Printed by D. N. Shury, Berwick-Street, Soho, for J. F. Hughes, 28, Berners-Street, 1809.
I 202p; II 198p. 12mo. 10s (ECB, ER).
ER 15: 242 (Oct 1809); WSW I: 542.
BL 12611.aa.19; ECB 594; NSTC T1332.

1809: 73    TROTTER, J[ohn] B[ernard].
STORIES FOR CALUMNIATORS: INTERSPERSED WITH REMARKS ON THE DISADVANTAGES, MISFORTUNES, AND HABITS OF THE IRISH. IN TWO VOLUMES. BY J. B. TROTTER, ESQ.
Dublin: Printed by H. Fitzpatrick, No. 4, Capel-Street, 1809.
I xiii, 265p; II 323p. 12mo. 11s (ECB).
WSW I: 544.
BL 12614.e.3; ECB 600; NSTC T1701.
*Notes.* Dedication 'to the Right Honourable Lord Holland', dated Richmond, Dec 1809. ECB dates 1810, and gives publisher as Ridgway; but not discovered in this form.

1809: 74    VERE, Horace [pseud.].
## GUISCARD; OR, THE MYSTERIOUS ACCUSATION. A ROMANCE. IN TWO VOLUMES. BY HORACE VERE.

> London: Printed at the Minerva-Press, for A. K. Newman and Co. (Successors to Lane, Newman, and Co.) Leadenhall-Street, 1809.
> I 250p; II 294p. 12mo. 10s (ECB, ER).
> ER 15: 242 (Oct 1809); WSW I: 548–9.
> Corvey; CME 3-628-48910-5; ECB 612; NSTC V218 (BI BL).

1809: 75    [WERTHES, Friedrich August Clemens].
## EDWARD AND LAURA: A NOVEL. TRANSLATED FROM THE FRENCH. IN TWO VOLUMES. BY A BENGAL OFFICER.

> London: Printed by J. Dean, 57, Wardour Street, for R. Ryan, No. 353, Oxford Street, to be had of all Booksellers, 1809.
> I xii, 177p; II 188p. 12mo.
> ER 15: 243 (Oct 1809); QR 2: 466 (Nov 1809).
> CLU-S/C PT.2557.W52E2; xNSTC.

*Notes.* Trans. of *Les Aventures d'Edouard Bomston* (Lausanne, 1789), itself a trans. of *Begebenheiten Eduard Bomstons in Italien* (Altenburg, 1782). 'The French Translator's Dedication', vol. 1, pp. [v]–viii, addressed to 'To my Friend. My dear C*****', and signed 'De S*******', Lausanne, 1 July 1789. 'The English Translator's Address' (pp.[ix]–xii), dated Camp near Saoronj, 20 May 1807. Text proper ends vol. 2, p. 168; pp. [169]–188, contains 'List of Subscribers' (330 names).

1809: 76    WILLIAMSON, T{homas}.
## THE DOMINICAN; A ROMANCE: OF WHICH THE PRINCIPAL TRAITS ARE TAKEN FROM EVENTS RELATING TO A FAMILY OF DISTINCTION, WHICH EMIGRATED FROM FRANCE DURING THE REVOLUTION. BY CAPTAIN T. WILLIAMSON, AUTHOR OF THE WILD SPORTS OF THE EAST. IN THREE VOLUMES.

> London: Printed for Longman, Hurst, Rees, and Orme, Paternoster Row, 1809.
> I ix, 248p; II 305p; III 281p. 12mo. 15s (ECB, ER, QR).
> ER 14: 272 (Apr 1809); QR 1: 462 (May 1809); WSW I: 564.
> Corvey; CME 3-628-48930-X; ECB 640; NSTC W2178 (BI BL).

*Notes.* Dedication 'to His Most Christian Majesty, Louis XVIII. King of France and Navarre' signed 'Thomas Williamson', dated London, 5 Feb 1809. 'Explanation of the Plate, which shews the Route across Switzerland', preceding text proper; but no map located in Corvey or BL copy.
Further edns: 1812 (NSTC); New York 1810 (NUC).

1809: 77    WILMOT, R. H.
## SCENES IN FEUDAL TIMES. A ROMANCE. IN FOUR VOLUMES. BY R. H. WILMOT.

> London: Printed for George Robinson, 25, Paternoster-Row, 1809.

I 271p; II 270p; III 203p; IV 188p. 12mo. 16s (ECB, QR).

QR 3: 268 (Feb 1810); WSW I: 565.

Corvey; CME 3-628-48935-0; ECB 641; NSTC W2233 (BI BL).

1809: 78   WOODTHORPE, Augusta Maria.
THE HOUR OF TWO: A NOVEL. IN THREE VOLUMES. BY AUGUSTA
MARIA WOODTHORPE.

> London: Printed for W. Turmaine, No. 10, Gate-Street, Lincoln's-Inn-Fields; and sold
> by T. Mason, 5, Cambridge-Street, Soho, 1809.
> I 207p; II 194p; III 185p. 12mo. 13s 6d (t.p.).
> BL 12611.b.18; ECB 647; NSTC W2796.

1809: 79   {YOUNG, Henrietta Maria (*trans.?*)}.
THE CASTLES OF MARSANGE & NUGER; OR, THE NOVITIATE DE
ROUSILLON. A TALE, ALTERED FROM THE FRENCH BY A LADY. IN
WHICH IS INTRODUCED THE HISTORY OF PAULINA & ISABELLA.
BY THE TRANSLATOR. IN THREE VOLUMES.

> Faversham: Printed and sold by Warren; sold in London by J. Richardson, Royal
> Exchange; B. Crosby and Co. Stationer's Court; and the other Booksellers, 1809.
> I x, 228p; II 204p; III 231p. 12mo. 12s (ECB, ER).
> ER 15: 529 (Jan 1810).
> Corvey; CME 3-628-47220-2; ECB 101; xNSTC.

*Notes.* No French original discovered. Dedication 'to the Right Hon. Lady Sondes' signed
'Henrietta Maria Young', Faversham, Sept 1809. Preface signed 'The Translator'. Collates in
sixes.

# 1810

1810: 1   ANON.
THE ACCEPTANCE. BY THE AUTHOR OF CAROLINE ORMSBY, &C.
IN THREE VOLUMES.

> London: Printed for John Booth, Duke Street, Portland Place, 1810.
> I iv, 225p; II iv, 263p; III iv, 282p. 12mo. 15s (ECB, ER).
> ER 16: 509 (Aug 1810); WSW I: 6.
> Corvey; CME 3-628-47002-1; ECB 2; NSTC A147 (BI BL).

*Notes.* Mistakenly attributed in some catalogues to Grace Kennedy—see note to *The Decision*
(1811: 6). Final numbered page of last vol. includes advs. for New Novels.

1810: 2   ANON.

THE ADULTERESS; OR, ANECDOTES OF TWO NOBLE FAMILIES. A
TALE. IN FOUR VOLUMES. BY AN ENGLISH-WOMAN.

> London: Printed for the Authoress; and sold by Sherwood, Neely, and Jones, 20, Pater-
> noster Row, 1810.
> I vii, 293p; II 329p; III 298p; IV 347p. 12mo. 21s (ER).
> ER 16: 259 (Apr 1810), 16: 510 (Aug 1810); WSW I: 7.
> NN NCV (Ford Collection); xNSTC.

*Notes.* Prefatory Address to Mrs West, signed 'An English-Woman', 23 Dec 1809.


1810: 3   ANON.

ANNE OF BRITTANNY: AN HISTORICAL ROMANCE. IN THREE VOL-
UMES.

> London: Printed for C. Cradock and W. Joy, (Successors to the late T. Ostell) No. 32,
> Paternoster Row, 1810.
> I viii, 180p; II 202p; III 180p. 12mo. 13s 6d (ECB, ER, QR).
> ER 16: 510 (Aug 1810); QR 4: 277 (Aug 1810); WSW I: 11.
> Corvey; CME 3-628-47064-1; ECB 20; xNSTC.

*Notes.* Further edns: New York 1811 (Gecker); French trans., 1814.


1810: 4   ANON.

THE AVENGER; OR, THE SICILIAN VESPERS: A ROMANCE OF THE
THIRTEENTH CENTURY, NOT INAPPLICABLE TO THE NINETEENTH.
IN THREE VOLUMES.

> London: Printed for J. J. Stockdale, No. 41, Pall-Mall, 1810.
> I iii, 296p; II 372p; III 340p. 12mo.
> ER 15: 242 (Oct 1809); QR 2: 466 (Nov 1809); WSW I: 14.
> Corvey; CME 3-628-47083-8; NSTC S1912 (BI E).

*Notes.* 'Dedicatory Epistle. To Lady Mill, Mottisfont House, Hampshire', signed 'The Publisher'. This presents the romance as 'in my judgment, very far above mediocrity' (p. [1]).
Jarndyce CXXV, Item 6, notes that the novel might be by the publisher, John Joseph Stockdale, or by his sister Mary Stockdale, who wrote mostly poetry; though both suggestions are
speculative. ER and QR list as 'Retribution, or the Sicilian Vespers'.


1810: 5   ANON.

BLACK ROCK HOUSE; OR, DEAR BOUGHT EXPERIENCE. A NOVEL.
BY THE AUTHOR OF "A WINTER IN BATH," "EVERSFIELD ABBEY,"
"THE CORINNA OF ENGLAND," "BANKS OF THE WYE," "THE
WOMAN OF COLOUR," &C. &C. &C. IN THREE VOLUMES.

> London: Printed for B. Crosby and Co., Stationers' Court, Paternoster-Row; Meyler
> and Son, Bath; and J. Richardson, Bristol, 1810.
> I 261p; II 281p; III 245p. 12mo. 15s (ECB, ER).
> ER 15: 529 (Jan 1810); WSW I: 146–7.
> Corvey; CME 3-628-47204-0; ECB 59; xNSTC.

*Notes.* Mrs E. G. Bayfield, to whom this title is sometimes attributed, was not the author of Crosby's *Winter in Bath*—see 1807: 7. This and 3 other titles listed are attributed to J. H. James by Block, but no clear evidence of an author with this name writing in this period has been discovered: see *The Banks of the Wye* (1808: 1) for a possible explanation of the confusion. ECB dates Nov 1809.

1810: 6  ANON.
CAROLINE ORMSBY; OR THE REAL LUCILLA: A TALE FOR THE FEMALE SEX. INTERSPERSED WITH SKETCHES MORAL AND RELIGIOUS.

> London: Printed for Henry Colburn, English and Foreign Library, Conduit Street, Bond Street, 1810.
> vi, 221p. 12mo. 5s (ECB, ER, QR).
> ER 15: 528 (Jan 1810); QR 3: 267 (Feb 1810); WSW I: 22.
> CLU-S/C PR.3991.A1C22; ECB 98; xNSTC.

*Notes.* Apparently by the same author as *The Acceptance* (1810: 1), and not by Grace Kennedy: see also note to *The Decision* (1811: 6). ECB dates Dec 1809.
Further edn: 2nd edn. 1812 (NUC).

1810: 7  ANON.
CŒLEBS IN SEARCH OF A MISTRESS. A NOVEL, IN TWO VOLUMES.

> London: Published by Thomas Tegg, 111, Cheapside; and Wm. Allason, 31, New Bond-Street. Printed by G. Mazard Beech-Street, 1810.
> I 192p; II 197p. 12mo. 10s (ER).
> ER 15: 528 (Jan 1810).
> Corvey; CME 3-628-47302-0; xNSTC.

*Notes.* Preface (2 pp. unn.), implying authorship by a 'Man of Honor', dated 111 Cheapside, Jan 1810. At end of Preface, adv. for (as 'In the Press') 'A History of the Rise, Progress, and Temptation of the O.P. WAR, in a series of humorous Epistles'; 'Subscriptions received by the Author, 111, Cheapside'.

1810: 8  ANON.
THE DAUGHTER. IN TWO VOLUMES.

> London: Printed for J. Hatchard, Bookseller to Her Majesty, 190, Piccadilly, 1810.
> I vii, 233p; II 189p. 12mo. 9s (ECB).
> BL 12613.d.15; ECB 153; NSTC D379.

*Notes.* ECB dates July 1810.

1810: 9  ANON.
EGBERT, OR THE MONK OF PENMON. A ROMANCE. BY THE AUTHOR OF TWO POPULAR NOVELS. IN TWO VOLUMES.

> London: Printed for the Author, by R. Cantwell, 29, Bell Yard, Lincoln's Inn; and sold by Sherwood, Neely, and Jones, (Successors to Mr. H. D. Symonds,) No. 20, Paternoster Row, 1810.

I 225p; II 200p. 12mo.
ER 18: 265 (May 1811); WSW I: 36.
Corvey; CME 3-628-47530-9; xNSTC.

1810: 10   ANON.
FAULCONSTEIN FOREST. A ROMANTIC TALE.

London: Printed for T. Hookham, junior, and E. T. Hookham, 15, Old Bond Street,
1810.
176p. 8vo. 6s 6d (ER).
ER 15: 529 (Jan 1810); WSW I: 43.
BL N.1999; NSTC F301 (BI O).

*Notes.* Dedication to 'Rev. W****** B******', by 'his sincere friend, **** ********'.

HENRY FREEMANTLE
See 1816: 7

1810: 11   ANON.
THE HOUSE OF LANCASTER; OR, THE STORY OF AP THOMAS. AN
HISTORICAL NOVEL. IN TWO VOLUMES.

London: Printed for J. F. Hughes, 15, Paternoster-Row, 1810.
I 220p; II 204p. 12mo.
BL 12611.a.19; CME 3-628-47668-2; NSTC A1518.

*Notes.* The Corvey copy contains a subscription list and dedication to the Prince of Wales,
vol. 2, preceding page [1], identical to those found in *Julia de Vienne* (see 1811: 8); presumably as a result of a binding error. No such list is found in the BL copy.

1810: 12   ANON.
THE LADY OF THE LAKE: A ROMANCE, IN TWO VOLUMES.
FOUNDED ON THE POEM SO CALLED BY WALTER SCOTT, ESQ.

London: Printed for Thomas Tegg, No. 111, Cheapside. And sold by Wm. Allason,
No. 31, New Bond Street, 1810.
I 186p; II 178p. 12mo.
WSW I: 63.
BL 12612.aaa.40; NSTC S872 (BI E).

*Notes.* Adv. in *Fatal Ambition* (1811: 33) gives price as 10s.

1810: 13   ANON.
MADNESS THE RAGE; OR, MEMOIRS OF A MAN WITHOUT A NAME.
IN TWO VOLUMES.

London: Printed for Sherwood, Neely, and Jones, Paternoster-Row; and T. Gillet,
Crown-Court, Fleet-Street, 1810.
xxiii, 211p; II 255p. 12mo. 9s (ER).
ER 16: 259 (Apr 1810).
O 249.s.266; NSTC M671.

*Notes.* Printer's mark after imprint date reads: 'T. Gillet, Printer, Crown-court, Fleet-street'.

1810: 14   ANON.

## THE MAN OF SENSIBILITY; OR THE HISTORY OF EDWARD AND MATILDA. IN TWO VOLUMES.

London: Printed for Vernor, Hood, and Sharpe, 31, Poultry, 1810.
I 214p; II 215p. 12mo. 8s (ECB, ER).
ER 16: 259 (Apr 1810).
BL 12612.aa.32; ECB 365; NSTC M918.

1810: 15   ANON.

## PRESENT TIMES AND MODERN MANNERS; OR, TALE OF A REC-TOR'S FAMILY. IN FOUR VOLUMES.

London: Printed by J. D. Dewick, 46, Barbican, for Appleyards, Wimpole-Street, 1810.
I 267p; II 309p; III 291p; IV 311p. 12mo.
Corvey; CME 3-628-48371-9; xNSTC.

1810: 16   ANON.

## THE SOLDIER OF PENNAFLOR: OR, A SEASON IN IRELAND. A TALE OF THE EIGHTEENTH CENTURY. IN FIVE VOLUMES.

Cork: Printed by John Connor, and sold by A. K. Newman and Co. Leadenhall-Street, London, 1810.
I 308p; II 404p; III 316p; IV 356p; V 383p. 12mo.
BL 1489.g.9; NSTC P1027.

*Notes.* Collates in sixes. Colophon in each vol: 'Printed by John Connor Grand-Parade, Cork'. 1 p. prefatory address 'To The Reader' (unn.) precedes p. 1 in vol. 4.
Further edn: London 1811 (Corvey), CME 3-628-48719-6. This Corvey copy has the imprint: 'Printed for A. K. Newman & Co. (Successors to Lane, Newman, & Co.) Leadenhall-Street, 1811'. Colophon reads: 'Printed by John Connor, Cork'. It also states 'By the author of *Amasina, or the American Foundling*' on t.p.: see 1804: 2 for this title and its implied female authorship.

1810: 17   ANON.

## SPLENDID FOLLIES. A NOVEL, IN THREE VOLUMES. FOUNDED ON FACTS. BY THE AUTHOR OF THE "OBSERVANT PEDESTRIAN," "MONTROSE," "MYSTIC COTTAGER." &C. &C.

London: Printed for J. F. Hughes, 15, Paternoster-Row, 1810.
I 202p; II 207p; III 197p. 12mo. 15s (s.l., ER).
ER 16: 259 (Apr 1810).
BL 12612.bb.9; NSTC F996.

*Notes.* Price cited as s.l. above is from extra (unn.) leaf at end of vol. 3 containing titles for use on spine of each volume.

1810: 18   ANON.

## TALES OF REAL LIFE. FORMING A SEQUEL TO MISS EDGEWORTH'S TALES OF FASHIONABLE LIFE. IN THREE VOLUMES.

London: Printed for Henry Colburn, English and Foreign Public Library, Conduit-Street, New Bond-Street, 1810.

I 200p; II 208p; III 208p. 8vo. 18s (ER, QR).

ER 15: 529 (Jan 1810); QR 3: 268 (Feb 1810); WSW I: 118.

O 249.s.255; NSTC T133.

*Notes.* Drop-head title in all vols. reads: 'Tales Moral, Historical, and Sentimental'. 25 tales in all.

1810: 19   ANON.

WHO CAN HE BE, OR, WHO IS HIS FATHER? A NOVEL, IN TWO VOL-UMES. BY THE AUTHOR OF TWO POPULAR WORKS, LATELY PUB-LISHED.

London: Published by J. Dick, 24, Hollywell-Street, Strand, (late Chiswell-Street); and sold by all the Booksellers, 1810.

I 228p; II 235p. 12mo. 9s (ECB, ER).

ER 17: 248 (Nov 1810).

Corvey; CME 3-628-48907-5; ECB 636; NSTC F295 (BI BL).

1810: 20   AGG, John.

MAC DERMOT; OR, THE IRISH CHIEFTAIN. A ROMANCE, INTEN-DED AS A COMPANION TO THE SCOTTISH CHIEFS. BY JOHN AGG. IN THREE VOLUMES.

London: Printed by J. Dean, 57, Wardour Street, Soho. For George Shade, 26, Princes Street, Cavendish Square. Sold by Sherwood, Neely, and Jones, Paternoster-Row, 1810.

I 228p; II 230p; III 227p. 12mo.

Corvey; CME 3-628-47024-2; xNSTC.

*Notes.* The last pages of vol. 2 are mistakenly numbered 128–130. Adv. facing t.p. of vol. 1 for (as 'In the Press') 'Craniology; or, a Dissertation upon Skulls', by Patrick Pericranium, Esq.

1810: 21   AGG, John.

THE ROYAL SUFFERER; OR, INTRIGUES AT THE CLOSE OF THE EIGHTEENTH CENTURY. A FASHIONABLE NOVEL. INTERSPERSED WITH ANECDOTES, CONNECTED WITH THE BRITISH COURT. BY JOHN AGG. IN THREE VOLUMES.

London: Printed by E. Thomas, Golden-Lane: for George Hughes, No. 221, Totten-ham-Court Road; Bookseller to Her Royal Highness the Princess of Wales, 1810.

I 221p; II 199p; III 204p. 12mo. 15s 6d (ER, QR); 13s 6d (ER, QR).

ER 16: 510 (Aug 1810), 17: 500 (Feb 1811); QR 4: 276 (Aug 1810), 4: 542 (Nov 1810), 5: 267 (Feb 1811).

BL N.2336-8; ECB 8; NSTC A595.

*Notes.* QR lists as 13s 6d in Aug 1810, and 15s 6d in Nov 1810 and Feb 1811; ER also gives 13s 6d in Aug 1810, and 15s 6d in Feb 1811.

Further edn: reissued 1813 as *The Secret Memoirs of an Illustrious Princess; or, the Royal Sufferer* (NjP 3602.098.384; Wolff, Item 26).

1810: 22   [ARNOLD, Lieut.].

THE IRISHMEN; A MILITARY-POLITICAL NOVEL, WHEREIN THE IDIOM OF EACH CHARACTER IS CAREFULLY PRESERVED, AND THE UTMOST PRECAUTION CONSTANTLY TAKEN TO RENDER THE EBULLITIONARY PHRASES, PECULIAR TO THE SONS OF ERIN, INOFFENSIVE AS WELL AS ENTERTAINING. IN TWO VOLUMES. BY A NATIVE OFFICER.

> London: Printed at the Minerva-Press, for A. K. Newman and Co. (Successors to Lane, Newman and Co.) Leadenhall-Street, 1810.
> I xiii, 254p; II 243p. 12mo. 9s (ER).
> ER 17: 248 (Nov 1810).
> BL 12612.aaa.35; NSTC I485.

*Notes.* Dedication to Mrs Edwin. Blakey cites attribution to Lieut. Arnold in a Minerva Library Catalogue of 1814.


1810: 23   {BAYLES, Robert} [B.].

THE SORROWS OF ELIZA; OR A TALE OF MISFORTUNE.

> London: Printed by G. Davidson, Old Boswell Court, St. Clement's, 1810.
> xi, 131p. 12mo. 7s 6d (ECB, ER, QR).
> ER 17: 500 (Feb 1811); QR 5: 267 (Feb 1811); WSW I: 147.
> BL 12613.dd.3; ECB 44; NSTC B1040 (BI C).

*Notes.* The author's name appears on vignette t.p. which immediately precedes the normal t.p. The vignette t.p. reads: 'The Sorrows of Eliza; or, A Tale of Misfortune: being the authentic Memoirs of a young Lady in the Vicinity of London. By R. Bayles, Esq$^r$. London: Published by Longman, Rees, Orme & Brown, Paternoster Row, 1810'. Introductory address to the Right Honourable Henry Richard (Vassal) Lord Holland, signed Robert Bayles. ECB lists as Longman, 1810.


1810: 24   [?BAYLEY, Catharine].

CALEDONIA; OR, THE STRANGER IN SCOTLAND: A NATIONAL TALE, IN FOUR VOLUMES. ILLUSTRATIVE OF THE STATE OF CIVIL SOCIETY AND DOMESTIC MANNERS IN SCOTLAND, AT THE PRESENT PERIOD. BY KATE MONTALBION. AUTHOR OF "LOVER'S LABOURS," "SPANISH LADY," "NORMAN KNIGHT," &C.

> London: Printed for J. F. Hughes, 15, Paternoster Row, 1810.
> I 223p; II 193p; III 181p; IV 201p. 12mo. 20s (ER, QR).
> ER 16: 509 (Aug 1810); QR 4: 277 (Aug 1810).
> Corvey; CME 3-628-48270-4; NSTC M2919 (BI O).

*Notes.* For the issue of author attribution, see *A Set-Down at Court* (1812: 20).


1810: 25   [?BAYLEY, Catharine].

THE SPANISH LADY, AND THE NORMAN KNIGHT. A ROMANCE OF THE ELEVENTH CENTURY. IN TWO VOLUMES, BY KATE MONTALBION.

London: Printed for J. F. Hughes, 15, Paternoster-Row, 1810.
I xvi, 173p; II 207p. 12mo. 10s (ER).
ER 16: 259 (Apr 1810).
Corvey; CME 3-628-48271-2; NSTC M2920 (BI BL, O).

*Notes.* Dedication to 'Her Royal Highness The Princess Elizabeth'. For the issue of author attribution, see 1812: 20. BLC and Bodleian catalogue both suggest 1816, not 1810, as the actual publication date, which seems unlikely in the light of advs. facing t.p. in both vols. (e.g. for *Lindamira* (1810: 29) in vol. 1), and the ER listing above.

1810: 26   BENSON, Maria.
THE WIFE. A NOVEL. IN THREE VOLUMES. BY MARIA BENSON, AUTHOR OF "THOUGHTS ON EDUCATION".

London: Printed for Longman, Hurst, Rees, and Orme, Paternoster-Row, 1810.
I xii, 290p; II 290p; III 218p. 12mo. 16s 6d (ECB, ER).
ER 16: 259 (Apr 1810).
Corvey; CME 3-628-47115-X; ECB 51; NSTC B1621 (BI BL, E).

*Notes.* Preface to Mr Benson, Ackworth, Yorkshire, dated London, 20 Feb 1810.

1810: 27   [BEST, Jane].
CELIA SUITED, OR THE RIVAL HEIRESSES; COMPRISING NEW SKETCHES OF MODERN FEMALE HABITS AND MANNERS, RELI-GION AND MORALS. IN TWO VOLUMES.

London: Printed by T. Harper, jun. Crane Court, Fleet Street, for H. Colburn, English and Foreign Library, Conduit Street, New Bond Street, 1810.
I v, 204p; II 218p. 12mo. 12s (ECB, ER, QR).
ER 15: 528 (Jan 1810); QR 2: 466 (Nov 1809), 3: 267 (Feb 1810).
Corvey; CME 3-628-47246-6; ECB 103; NSTC B1863 (BI BL, O).

*Notes.* Preface dated 9 Nov 1809. ECB dates Dec 1809.

1810: 28   BREWSTER, John.
YORKSHIRE CHARACTERS: A NOVEL. IN TWO VOLUMES. BY JOHN BREWSTERR [*sic*].

London: Printed for J. F. Hughes, 15, Paternoster-Row, 1810.
I 220p; II 238p. 12mo.
Corvey; CME 3-628-47121-4; NSTC B4275 (BI BL).

*Notes.* Author at end signs himself 'John Brewster'.

1810: 29   BURNEY, Caroline [pseud.?].
LINDAMIRA; OR, AN OLD MAID IN SEARCH OF A HUSBAND. A SATIRICAL NOVEL, IN THREE VOLUMES. BY CAROLINE BURNEY, AUTHOR OF "SERAPHINA," &C. &C.

London: Printed for J. F. Hughes, 15, Paternoster Row, 1810.
I 199p; II 215p; III 181p. 12mo. 15s (ER).

ER 16: 259 (Apr 1810).

Corvey; CME 3-628-47173-7; xNSTC.

*Notes.* Vol. 2, pp. [213–215] mistakenly numbered as 193–195. For evidence about the pseudonymous nature of the authorship, see *Seraphina* (1809: 14). *Lindamira* ends on p. 99 of vol. 3; this is followed by 'Theodore and Martha. A Tale, by Another Author', which fills pp. [103]–181. Adv. facing t.p. of vol. 1 for (as 'will be published in a few days') 'The Paradise of Love, A Utopian Romance, in 4 vols, 12mo', an 'extraordinary Novel' which 'has been translated in every language on the Continent'. No novel with this title has been discovered; but for a possible alternative version, see 1811: 49.

1810: 30   BYRON, ['Medora Gordon'].

THE ALDERMAN AND THE PEER; OR, THE ANCIENT CASTLE & MODERN VILLA. IN THREE VOLUMES. BY MISS BYRON, AUTHOR OF THE ENGLISHWOMAN, HOURS OF AFFLUENCE AND DAYS OF INDIGENCE, &C.

> London: Printed at the Minerva-Press, for A. K. Newman and Co. (Successors to Lane, Newman, & Co.) Leadenhall-Street, 1810.
> I 215p; II 190p; III 216p. 12mo.
> Corvey; CME 3-628-47177-X; ECB 91; xNSTC.

*Notes.* Appears in Blakey (copy not seen) as 'The Modern Villa and Ancient Castle; or, the Peer and the Alderman', but no copy with this title arrangement has been located; also listed in ECB as 'The modern villa and the ancient castle'. 2 pp. (unn.) adv. at end of vol. 2 for *Celia in Search of a Husband* (1809: 15), 'With the Reviewers' Opinion'.

1810: 31   [CAVENDISH-BRADSHAW, Mary Ann].

FERDINAND AND ORDELLA, A RUSSIAN STORY; WITH AUTHENTIC ANECDOTES OF THE RUSSIAN COURT AFTER THE DEMISE OF PETER THE GREAT. TO WHICH IS ADDED, A PREFATORY ADDRESS TO THE SATIRIST, UPON PATRONS AND DEDICATIONS, REFORMERS AND REFORMATIONS. BY PRISCILLA PARLANTE. IN TWO VOLUMES.

> London: Printed for Samuel Tipper, Leadenhall-Street, by W. Flint, Old Bailey, 1810.
> I lxii, 274p; II 380p. 12mo. 12s (ER).
> ER 16: 259 (Apr 1810).
> Corvey; CME 3-628-47539-2; NSTC P460 (BI BL, E).

*Notes.* 'Dissertation respecting Patrons and Dedications', vol. 1, pp. [i]–lxii.

CAZOTTE, Jacques, BIONDETTA, OR THE ENAMOURED SPIRIT

See ALVAREZ; OR, IRRESISTIBLE SEDUCTION, Vol. 1, 1791: 32; also present Vol., Appendix E: 4

1810: 32   CLIFFORD, Frances.

THE RUINS OF TIVOLI; A ROMANCE. IN FOUR VOLUMES. BY FRANCES CLIFFORD.

> London: Printed for J. F. Hughes, 38, Berners Street, Oxford Street, 1810.

I 240p; II 219p; III 245p; IV 237p. 12mo. 20s (QR).
QR 3: 268 (Feb 1810).
Corvey; CME 3-628-47295-4; ECB 121; NSTC C2468 (BI BL).

*Notes.* Block and Summers both state 1804, but BLC and NUC copies are 1810. Adv. as 'Just published' in *The House of Lancaster* (1810: 11). Drop-head title reads: 'Eudora; or, The Ruins of Tivoli'.

1810: 33   COTTIN, [Sophie Ristaud].
CHEVALIER DE VERSENAI, A NOVEL, IN TWO VOLUMES, TRANS-
LATED FROM THE FRENCH OF MAD. COTTIN, AUTHOR OF "ELIZA-
BETH, OR, THE EXILES OF SIBERIA," &C. &C.

London: Printed for J. F. Hughes, 15, Paternoster-Row, by J. D. Dewick, 46. Barbican,
   1810.
I xx, 272p; II 293p. 12mo. 10s (ER).
ER 16: 259 (Apr 1810).
NjP Ex.3243.22.325.5; xNSTC.

*Notes.* French original not discovered.

1810: 34   [?COWLEY, Hannah].
THE ITALIAN MARAUDERS[.] A ROMANCE, IN FOUR VOLUMES. BY
ANNA MATILDA.

London: Printed by J. Dean, 57, Wardour Street, Soho. For George Hughes, 221,
   Tottenham-Court-Road, near Store-Street; sold by Sherwood, Neeley, and Jones,
   Paternoster-Row, 1810.
I 227p; II 216p; III 216p; IV 240p. 12mo. 20s (ER, QR).
ER 15: 242 (Oct 1809); QR 2: 466 (Nov 1809).
ViU PZ2.C691.1810; NSTC A1343 (BI O).

*Notes.* ViU catalogues as by Hannah Cowley, who used the pseudonym Anna Matilda for her *Poetry* (1788); however, Hannah Cowley died in 1809.

1810: 35   CUMBERLAND, George.
ORIGINAL TALES, BY GEORGE CUMBERLAND. IN TWO VOLUMES.

London: Printed and published by Miller and Pople, 72, Chancery-Lane, 1810.
I 257p; II 227p. 12mo. 10s (ECB).
WSW I: 229.
Corvey; CME 3-628-51009-0; ECB 147; NSTC C4461 (BI BL, O).

*Notes.* Tales end vol. 2, p. 179, followed by 'Poems', pp. [183]–227. Mistakenly attributed to Richard Cumberland in Block.

1810: 36   [CUTHBERTSON, Catherine].
FOREST OF MONTALBANO: A NOVEL. IN FOUR VOLUMES. BY THE
AUTHOR OF "SANTO SEBASTIANO," AND "THE ROMANCE OF THE
PYRENEES."

London: Printed for George Robinson, 25, Paternoster-Row, 1810.

I 453p; II 446p; III 398p; IV 392p. 12mo. 28s (ECB, ER, QR).

ER 17: 248 (Nov 1810); QR 4: 542 (Nov 1810).

Corvey; CME 3-628-47538-4; ECB 211; NSTC M2918 (BI BL, E).

*Notes.* Further edns: Philadelphia 1812 (NUC); French trans., 1813.

1810: 37   DARLING, Peter Middleton.
**THE ROMANCE OF THE HIGHLANDS. BY PETER MIDDLETON DAR-LING. IN TWO VOLUMES.**

Edinburgh: Printed by George Ramsay and Co. for the Author; and sold by Peter Hill and J. Sutherland, Edinburgh; and Longman, Hurst, Rees, and Orme, London, 1810.
I x, 200p; II 244p. 12mo. 12s (ECB, ER).
ER 16: 509 (Aug 1810).
Corvey; CME 3-628-47421-3; ECB 152; NSTC D306 (BI E, O).

*Notes.* List of 'Subscribers' (137 names), vol. 1, pp. [iii]–x. Collates in sixes.

1810: 38   DUCRAY-DUMINIL, [François-Guillaume].
**THE LITTLE CHIMER; A TALE. ALTERED FROM THE FRENCH OF DUCRAY DUMINIL, AUTHOR OF "CŒLINA," &C. &C. IN FOUR VOLUMES.**

London: Printed for Henry Colburn, English and Foreign Public Library, Conduit-Street, New Bond-Street, 1810.
I 252p; II 260p; III 244p; IV 259p. 12mo. 22s (ECB, ER, QR).
ER 16: 510 (Aug 1810); QR 4: 277 (Aug 1810).
C Syn.7.81.208-211; ECB 173; NSTC D2045.

*Notes.* Trans. of *Le Petit Carillonneur* (Paris, 1809). ECB gives title as 'The little chimer: a romantic novel'.

1810: 39   [DUCRAY-DUMINIL, François-Guillaume].
**THE NOVICE OF SAINT URSULA. BY THE AUTHOR OF "A TALE OF MYSTERY," "JEANNETTE," &C. IN FOUR VOLUMES.**

London: Printed for Henry Colburn, English and Foreign Public Library, Conduit-Street, New Bond-Street, 1810.
I 224p; II 232p; III 264p; IV 205p. 12mo. 21s (ECB, ER, QR).
ER 16: 259 (Apr 1810), 16: 510 (Aug 1810); QR 4: 277 (Aug 1810).
IU 845.D856.OnE; ECB 173; xNSTC.

*Notes.* French original not discovered. Drop-head title reads: 'Elvina, or the Novice of Saint Ursula' [misspelt Ursulu in vol. 1]. QR lists as 'The Novice of St. Ursula, or Elvina'.

**DUDLEY, Frederick, AMOROSO**
See 1809: 21

1810: 40   [?DUNN], Lady.
**THE BENEVOLENT RECLUSE; A NOVEL, IN TWO VOLUMES. BY LADY ——.**

London: Printed for E. Kerby, Bookseller, Stafford-Street, Bond-Street, by A. Macpherson, Russell-Court, Covent-Garden, 1810.

I vi, 252p; II 320p. 12mo. 11s (ER).
ER 16: 259 (Apr 1810).
CtY-BR In.B435.810; xNSTC.

*Notes.* The last page of vol. 1 is mistakenly numbered 226. Block lists as by Lady Dunn, and Summers also attributes the reissue of 1814 (see below) to this author. NUC and (for the re-issue) NSTC treat as unidentified. Allibone has Lady Dunn as author of *Recluse, a Novel*, 2 vols, but mentions no other work by her.

Further edn: reissued 1814 by A. K. Newman as *Suspicion; or, the Benevolent Recluse* (BL Cup.408.m.21; NSTC S4409.5).

1810: 41   EDGEWORTH, Mrs.
THE WIFE; OR, A MODEL FOR WOMEN. A TALE, IN THREE VOL-UMES. BY MRS. EDGEWORTH.

London: Printed for J. F. Hughes, 38, Berners Street, Oxford Street, 1810.
I 201p; II 239p; III 223p. 12mo. 15s (ER).
ER 16: 259 (Apr 1810).
Corvey; CME 3-628-47556-2; xNSTC.

*Notes.* Further edn: French trans., 1813 [as *Le Modèle des femmes* (BN under Edgeworth, Maria)].

1810: 42   ENGLISH, John.
THE GREY FRIAR, AND THE BLACK SPIRIT OF THE WYE: A ROMANCE. IN TWO VOLUMES. BY JOHN ENGLISH, ESQ. OF BLACKWOOD HALL.

London: Printed at the Minerva-Press, for A. K. Newman and Co. (Successors to Lane, Newman, and Co.) Leadenhall-Street, 1810.
I 276p; II 299p. 12mo. 10s (ECB, QR).
QR 3: 268 (Feb 1810).
Corvey; CME 3-628-47568-6; ECB 188; NSTC E1008 (BI O).

1810: 43   FARROW, Witham.
THE BRAVO'S SON; OR, THE CHIEF OF ST. MALDO, A ROMANCE. INTERSPERSED WITH POETRY. IN TWO VOLUMES. BY WITHAM FARROW, AUTHOR OF SEVERAL FUGITIVE PIECES.

London: Printed by J. Dean, 57. Wardour Street, Soho. For George Hughes, 221, Tottenham-Court-Road, near Store-Street; sold by Sherwood, Neeley, and Jones, Paternoster-Row, 1810.
I 24, 195p; II 156p. 12mo. 7s (ER).
ER 15: 528 (Jan 1810).
BL 12612.bb.7; NSTC F283 (BI Dt).

1810: 44   [GREEN, Sarah].
THE FESTIVAL OF ST. JAGO. A SPANISH ROMANCE. IN TWO VOL-UMES. BY THE AUTHOR OF THE TANKERVILLE FAMILY, PRIVATE HISTORY OF THE COURT OF ENGLAND, &C.

London: Printed at the Minerva-Press, for A. K. Newman and Co. (Successors to Lane, Newman, and Co.) Leadenhall-Street, 1810.
I vii, 205p; II 203p. 12mo.
WSW I: 43.
Corvey; CME 3-628-47497-3; NSTC G1944 (BI BL).

1810: 45   {G}[REEN], {S}[arah].
THE REFORMIST!!! A SERIO-COMIC POLITICAL NOVEL. IN TWO VOLUMES.

London: Printed at the Minerva Press, for A. K. Newman and Co. (Successors to Lane, Newman and Co.), Leadenhall-Street, 1810.
I xii, 254p; II 199p. 12mo. 10s 6d (ECB, ER); 10s (ER).
ER 16: 510 (Aug 1810), 17: 248 (Nov 1810); WSW I: 288–9.
BL 12612.aa.19; ECB 484; NSTC G22.

*Notes.* Preface signed S. G****, Westminster. Reviewer in MR n.s. 64: 216–17 (Feb 1811) casts doubt on the gender of the author: 'While, however, we own that we have been diverted by the broad humour which runs through this work, we cannot be such dupes of the preface as to believe that the experience of a lady could have furnished all the scenes which are here delineated; and much less would we attribute to a female pen the great illiberality which occasionally displays itself' (p. 217). ER 2nd citation (Nov 1810) gives price as 10s.
Further edn: 2nd edn. 1816 as *Percival Ellingford: or the Reformist* (Corvey), CME 3-628-47854-5.

1810: 46   {G}[REEN], {S}[arah].
ROMANCE READERS AND ROMANCE WRITERS: A SATIRICAL NOVEL. IN THREE VOLUMES. BY THE AUTHOR OF 'A PRIVATE HISTORY OF THE COURT OF ENGLAND, &C.'

London: Printed for T. Hookham, junior, and E. T. Hookham, 15, Old Bond Street, 1810.
I xxxvi, 209p; II 204p; III 233p. 12mo. 15s (ER).
ER 15: 529 (Jan 1810); WSW I: 289.
ViU PR.4728.G28R6.1810; NSTC G1948 (BI BL).

*Notes.* 'Literary Retrospection', vol. 1, pp. [v]–xxxvi, signed 'S. G****, the Author, Westminster'. Drop-head title in all 3 vols. reads: 'The Effects of Romance Reading'.

1810: 47   GREEN, [Sarah].
*THE ROYAL EXILE; OR, VICTIMS OF HUMAN PASSIONS: AN HISTORICAL ROMANCE OF THE SIXTEENTH CENTURY. BY MRS. GREEN, AUTHOR OF ROMANCE READERS AND ROMANCE WRITERS, &C. IN FOUR VOLUMES.

London: Printed for John Joseph Stockdale, No. 41, Pall Mall, 1810.
I 218p; II 218p; III 215p; IV 250p. 12mo. 20s (ER, QR).
ER 17: 500 (Feb 1811); QR 4: 542 (Nov 1810), 5: 267 (Feb 1811); WSW I: 289.
No copy of 1st edn. located.

*Notes.* Details follow 2nd edn. of 1811 (BL 12613.d.14; NSTC G1949), which is likely to have been very similar to its close predecessor.

Further edn: 2nd edn. 1811 (see note above).

GUNNING, Elizabeth
See PLUNKETT, Elizabeth

1810: 48    H——, Miss.
THE PROFLIGATE MOTHER; OR, THE FATAL CABINET. BY MISS H——.

> London: Printed by W. Lewis, Paternoster-Row; for Appleyards, Wimpole-Street, 1810.
> I 204p; II 180p. 12mo.
> O 249.s.245; NSTC H5.

*Notes.* Further edn: Boston 1810, as *The Fatal Cabinet; or, the Profligate Mother* (NUC).

1810: 49    HAMILTON, Ann [Mary].
THE IRISHWOMAN IN LONDON, A MODERN NOVEL, IN THREE VOLUMES. BY ANN HAMILTON.

> London: Printed for J. F. Hughes. 15, Paternoster Row, 1810.
> I 218p; II 216p; III 236p. 12mo.
> WSW I: 295.
> BL 12613.aa.14; CME 3-628-47589-9; NSTC H300.

*Notes.* 'Advertisement' (2 pp. unn.) stating that the novel had originally been epistolary: 'Immediately after disposing of it, the Author left town, and the Publisher conceiving it not so saleable, altered it from Letters to Chapters; the Author was ignorant of such an alteration having been made till the First Volume was nearly printed.'

1810: 50    HARVEY, Jane.
*ETHELIA: A NOVEL. BY JANE HARVEY.

> London: Longman, 1810.
> 3 vols. 12mo. 12s (ECB, ER).
> ER 16: 239 (Apr 1810).
> No copy of 1st edn. located; ECB 257.

*Notes.* Publisher from ECB.

Further edn: 2nd edn. 1814 (Corvey), CME 3-628-47644-5. This reissue by A. K. Newman (sub-titled 'A Tale') has a colophon reading 'H. Mozley, Printer, Gainsborough' in all vols., and may represent a remaindered copy of the original edn. Collates in sixes.

1810: 51    [HATTON, Anne Julia Kemble].
CAMBRIAN PICTURES; OR, EVERY ONE HAS ERRORS. BY ANN OF SWANSEA. IN THREE VOLUMES.

> London: Printed for E. Kerby, Stafford-Street, Bond-Street, 1810.
> I xxviii, 276p; II 364p; III 448p. 12mo.
> WSW I: 302.
> IU 823.H289c; xNSTC.

*Notes.* Dedication to 'A. Cherry, Esq. Late of the Theatre Royal, Drury Lane, Author of the Soldier's Daughter, Travellers, &c. &c. &c. present Manager of the Swansea Theatre, &c. &c. &c.', signed Ann of Swansea. Colophon of 'B Clarke, Printer, Well-Street, London' in all vols., and in the 1813 Corvey copy (see below). BL 12612.dd.16 has same t.p. as Corvey, but with imprint date blocked out. NSTC A1350, based on this copy, follows the erroneous dating for that edn. of [1810?]. ECB 20 lists Newman edn., 1813, 16s 6d.

Further edn: 1813 (Corvey—a reissue by A. K. Newman), CME 3-628-48741-2.

1810: 52 HOLSTEIN, Anthony Frederick [pseud.].
THE ASSASSIN OF ST. GLENROY; OR, THE AXIS OF LIFE. A NOVEL. IN FOUR VOLUMES. BY ANTHONY FREDERICK HOLSTEIN, AUTHOR OF SIR OWEN GLENDOWR, &C.

> London: Printed at the Minerva-Press, for A. K. Newman and Co. (Successors to Lane, Newman, & Co.) Leadenhall-Street, 1810.
> I xv, 218p; II 227p; III 241p; IV 300p. 12mo.
> ER 15: 529 (Jan 1810); WSW I: 324.
> Corvey; CME 3-628-47783-2; NSTC H2273 (BI BL).

1810: 53 HOLSTEIN, Anthony Frederick [pseud.].
LOVE, MYSTERY, AND MISERY! A NOVEL. IN TWO VOLUMES. BY ANTHONY FREDERICK HOLSTEIN, AUTHOR OF SIR OWEN GLEN-DOWR, THE ASSASSIN OF ST. GLENROY, &C.

> London: Printed at the Minerva-Press, for A. K. Newman and Co. (Successors to Lane, Newman, and Co.) Leadenhall-Street, 1810.
> I v, 247p; II 250p. 12mo. 10s (ECB, ER).
> ER 16: 509 (Aug 1810); WSW I: 324.
> Corvey; CME 3-628-47739-5; ECB 278; NSTC H2277 (BI BL).

*Notes.* 'Prefatory Apology', dated Jan 1810.

1810: 54 HOLSTEIN, Anthony Frederick [pseud.].
THE MISERIES OF AN HEIRESS. A NOVEL. IN FOUR VOLUMES. BY ANTHONY FREDERICK HOLSTEIN, AUTHOR OF SIR OWEN GLEN-DOWR; THE ASSASSIN OF ST. GLENROY; LOVE, MYSTERY, AND MISERY, &C.

> London: Printed at the Minerva-Press, for A. K. Newman and Co. (Successors to Lane, Newman, and Co.) Leadenhall-Street, 1810.
> I xviii, 288p; II 307p; III 271p; IV 302p. 12mo.
> ER 17: 248 (Nov 1810); QR 4: 542 (Nov 1810); WSW I: 324.
> Corvey; CME 3-628-47733-6; xNSTC.

1810: 55 HORWOOD, Caroline.
THE CASTLE OF VIVALDI, OR THE MYSTERIOUS INJUNCTION, A NOVEL, IN FOUR VOLUMES. BY CAROLINE HORWOOD.

> London: Printed by D. N. Shury, Berwick Street, Soho, for J. F. Hughes, 15, Pater-Noster Row, 1810.

I 240p; II 229p; III 212p; IV 211p. 12mo. 18s (ECB); 20s (ER).

ER 16: 259 (Apr 1810).

Corvey; CME 3-628-47748-4; ECB 257; xNSTC.

*Notes.* Further edn: 1840 as *The Castle of Vivaldi; or, the Mysterious Casket* (NSTC 2H3167).


1810: 56   HOUGHTON, Mary.
*THE MYSTERIES OF THE FOREST: A NOVEL. BY MISS MARY HOUGHTON.

> London: A. K. Newman?, 1810.
> 3 vols. 12mo. 18s (ER, QR).
> ER 16: 509 (Aug 1810); QR 4: 277 (Aug 1810); WSW I: 329.
> No copy of 1st edn. located; ECB 284.

*Notes.* Publisher from Summers, though evidence of 2nd edn. (see below) throws some doubt on this. Fuller title detail from ECB.
Further edn: 2nd edn. 1822 (Corvey; NSTC 2H32140), CME 3-628-47750-6. This edn. by A. K. Newman and Co. (sub-titled 'A Romance') has printer's marks and colophons in each vol. of J. Gillet, Crown-Court, Fleet-Street, London, perhaps indicating a remainder issue.


HUISH, Robert
See LAMBE, George


1810: 57   JANSON, Charles William.
EDWARD FITZ-YORKE: A NOVEL. IN FOUR VOLUMES. BY CHARLES WILLIAM JANSON, ESQ. AUTHOR OF "THE STRANGER IN AMERICA," &C. &C.

> London: Printed by E. Thomas, Golden Lane, for Sherwood, Neely, and Jones, Paternoster-Row; and J. Colbourn, Conduit-Street, Bond-Street, n.d. [1810? (BLC)].
> I 213p; II 215p; III 215p; IV 224p. 12mo.
> BL 12611.bbb.14; NSTC J255.


1810: 58   ?LAMBE, G[eorge].
THE MYSTERIES OF FERNEY CASTLE; A ROMANCE OF THE SEVENTEENTH CENTURY. IN FOUR VOLUMES. BY G. LAMBE, ESQ.

> London: Printed for Henry Colburn, English and Foreign Library, Conduit-Street, Bond-Street, 1810.
> I 214p; II 264p; III 250p; IV 268p. 12mo. 22s (ECB, ER, QR).
> ER 15: 528 (Jan 1810); QR 2: 466 (Nov 1809), 3: 267 (Feb 1810).
> Corvey; CME 3-628-47896-0; ECB 327; xNSTC.

*Notes.* Robert Huish later apparently claimed this title as his own: see *The Brothers* (1820: 36). ECB dates Dec 1809.


1810: 59   ?LEE, Sophia.
ORMOND; OR, THE DEBAUCHEE. COMPREHENDING SKETCHES OF REAL CHARACTERS, AND ILLUSTRATIVE OF THE MANNERS

AND CUSTOMS OF FASHIONABLE LIFE, AT THE CLOSE OF THE YEAR 1809. IN THREE VOLUMES. BY SOPHIA LEE.

> London: Printed by J. Dean, 57, Wardour Street, Soho. For George Hughes, 221, Tottenham-Court Road, near Store-Street; sold by Sherwood, Neeley, and Jones, Paternoster-Row, 1810.
>
> I 200p; II 212p; III 210p. 12mo. 15s (ER, QR).
>
> ER 16: 510 (Aug 1810); QR 4: 277 (Aug 1810).
>
> ViU PZ2.L44Or.1810; xNSTC.

*Notes.* The association of Sophia Lee with such an imprint is unusual, and perhaps the authorship should be viewed with some suspicion. Vol. 2 t.p. imprint differs by beginning 'London: Printed by W. M. Thiselton, Goodge Street'.


LEWIS, Alethea, THE DISCARDED DAUGHTER

See 1809: 42


1810: 60    [LLOYD, Charles].

ISABEL. A TALE. IN TWO VOLUMES.

> London: Sold by Longman, Hurst, Rees, and Orme; and Sherwood, Neely, and Jones. Ulverston: Printed and sold by J. Soulby, 1810.
>
> I xliv, 203p; II 270p. 12mo.
>
> MH-H 18494.38*; xNSTC.

*Notes.* Preface, dated 1 Nov 1809, states: 'The following Tale was, in the main, written more than ten years ago: it has since undergone some alterations'. ECB 350 lists Baldwin edn., 1820, 10s. WSW I: 375 lists only 1820 reviews.

Further edn: 1820 (NSTC 2L18659, Corvey), CME 3-628-48036-1. BL C.39.g.26 (Charles and Henry Baldwin, London, 1820) includes an 'Advertisement' stating that the work was first printed in 1810 'in a remote country place, in the North of England, at which the author resided', and then laid aside until a change of location encouraged publication in 1820. The Bodleian copy (256.e.14895) and Corvey copy have no 'Advertisement', and a different imprint, reading: 'London: C. & J. Ollier, Vere Street, Bond Street, 1820'. Both 1820 issues seen acknowledge Lloyd's authorship on the t.p.


1810: 61    MANNERS, William.

THE BOON, BEING AN ANTIDOTE TO "THE REFUSAL;" AND CONTAINING INCIDENTS IN THE UNMARRIED LIFE OF A WELL-KNOWN LADY OF FASHION AND QUALITY. IN THREE VOLUMES. BY WILLIAM MANNERS, ESQ.

> London: Printed by J. Dean, 57, Wardour Street, Soho, for G. Hughes, Tottenham Court-Road; Bookseller to Her R.H. the Princess of Wales: sold by Sherwood, Neely, and Jones, Paternoster-Row, 1810.
>
> I 195p; II 199p; III 211p. 12mo. 13s 6d (QR).
>
> QR 4: 277 (Aug 1810).
>
> O 249.s.466-468; NSTC M1009.

*Notes.* An antidote, that is, to Jane West's *The Refusal* (1810: 87). QR has 'By Captain Manners'.

1810: 62 MAXWELL, [Caroline].
THE EARL OF DESMOND; OR, O'BRIEN'S COTTAGE. AN IRISH STORY, IN THREE VOLUMES. BY MRS. MAXWELL, AUTHOR OF "LIONEL, OR THE IMPENETRABLE SECRET," &C. &C.

> London: Printed for J. F. Hughes, 38, Berners-Street, Oxford-Street, 1810.
> I 180p; II 159p; III 197p. 12mo.
> Corvey; CME 3-628-48203-8; NSTC M1817 (BI BL).

*Notes.* Adv. *Morning Post*, 25 Dec 1809, as 'an interesting Irish story'.

MONTALBION, Kate
See BAYLEY, Catharine

1810: 63 [MURRAY, Mrs].
HENRY COUNT DE KOLINSKI, A POLISH TALE.

> London: Printed for James Cawthorn, Bookseller to her Royal Highness the Princess of Wales, No. 24, Cockspur Street, 1810.
> 153p. 12mo.
> WSW I: 414.
> O 249.s.237; NSTC M3685 (BI E).

*Notes.* Princess of Wales feathers on t.p. Collates in sixes.

1810: 64 NORRIS, Mrs.
EUPHRONIA, OR THE CAPTIVE; A ROMANCE, BY MRS. NORRIS, AUTHOR OF "JULIA OF ENGLAND, &C." IN THREE VOLUMES.

> London: Printed for Henry Colburn, English and Foreign Library, Conduit Street, Bond Street, 1810.
> I 211p; II 216p; III 225p. 12mo. 15s (ECB, ER, QR).
> ER 15: 528 (Jan 1810); QR 3: 267 (Feb 1810); WSW I: 418.
> Corvey; CME 3-628-48234-8; ECB 416; xNSTC.

*Notes.* ECB dates Dec 1809.

1810: 65 PALMER, Alicia Tyndal.
THE DAUGHTERS OF ISENBERG: A BAVARIAN ROMANCE. IN FOUR VOLUMES. BY ALICIA TYNDAL PALMER; AUTHOR OF "THE HUS-BAND AND THE LOVER."

> London: Printed for Lackington, Allen, and Co. Temple of the Muses, Finsbury Square, 1810.
> I xvi, 298p; II 324p; III 342p; IV 426p. 12mo. 24s (ECB, ER, QR).
> ER 16: 510 (Aug 1810), 17: 500 (Feb 1811); QR 4: 61–7 (Aug 1810) full review, 4: 277 (Aug 1810), 4: 542 (Nov 1810), 5: 267 (Feb 1811); WSW I: 427.
> Corvey; CME 3-628-48376-X; ECB 430; NSTC P168 (BI BL).

*Notes.* Dedication 'to John Burrows, Esq. of Hadley, in the County of Middlesex'.

1810: 66   [PARKER], Emma.
A SOLDIER'S OFFSPRING; OR, THE SISTERS. A TALE. IN TWO VOL-
UMES. BY EMMA DE LISLE.

> London: Printed at the Minerva-Press, for A. K. Newman and Co. (Successors to Lane,
> Newman, and Co.) Leadenhall-Street, 1810.
> I iv, 348p; II 278p. 12mo. 10s (ECB).
> Corvey; CME 3-628-48107-4; ECB 158; NSTC D801 (BI BL, O).

*Notes.* 'Dedicatory Lines' to 'my Mother'. ECB dates 1809.


1810: 67   PLUNKETT, [Elizabeth] [née GUNNING].
DANGERS THROUGH LIFE: OR, THE VICTIM OF SEDUCTION. A
NOVEL. IN THREE VOLUMES. BY MRS. PLUNKETT, (LATE MISS
GUNNING,) AUTHOR OF THE PACKET, ORPHANS OF SNOWDON,
&C. &C.

> London: Printed for J. Ebers, 23, Old Bond-Street, 1810.
> I xxiv, 232p; II 231p; III 304p. 12mo. 15s (ER).
> ER 15: 529 (Jan 1810); WSW I: 291.
> Corvey; CME 3-628-48478-2; NSTC G2392 (BI E).

*Notes.* A different novel from the same author's *The Victims of Seduction* (1815: 28).
Further edn: 1812 (Blakey).


1810: 68   PORTER, Jane.
THE SCOTTISH CHIEFS. A ROMANCE. IN FIVE VOLUMES. BY MISS
JANE PORTER, AUTHOR OF THADDEUS OF WARSAW, AND
REMARKS ON SIDNEY'S APHORISMS.

> London: Printed for Longman, Hurst, Rees, and Orme, Paternoster-Row, 1810.
> I xi, 357p, iv; II 367p; III 411p; IV 386p; V 396p. 12mo. 35s (ECB); 25s (ER).
> ER 16: 259 (Apr 1810); WSW I: 448.
> BRu ENC; ECB 464; NSTC P2613 (BI BL, E, NCu, O).

*Notes.* Preface dated Long Ditton, Dec 1809.
Further edns: 2nd edn. 1811 (Corvey), CME 3-628-48361-1; 3rd edn. 1816 (NSTC); 4th edn.
1820 (CG, Summers); 5th edn. 1825 (NSTC); 1831 (NSTC); [at least 4 more edns. to 1850];
New York 1810 (NUC) [also Philadelphia 1810 (NUC)]; French trans., 1814.


1810: 69   ROCHE, [John] Hamilton.
A SUFFOLK TALE; OR, THE PERFIDIOUS GUARDIAN. IN TWO VOL-
UMES. BY HAMILTON ROCHE, ESQ.

> London: Printed for the Author; and sold by T. Hookham, jun. and E. T. Hookham, 15,
> Old Bond Street, 1810.
> I xii, 207p; II 179p. 12mo. 9s (ECB).
> Corvey; CME 3-628-48426-X; ECB 498; NSTC R1409 (BI BL).

*Notes.* 'Entered at Stationers' Hall' printed on page facing t.p. Dedication to Lady Hippisley,
dated Sudbury, 1809.

1810: 70   ROCHE, Regina Maria.
## THE HOUSES OF OSMA AND ALMERIA; OR, CONVENT OF ST. ILDE-FONSO. A TALE. IN THREE VOLUMES. BY REGINA MARIA ROCHE, AUTHOR OF THE CHILDREN OF THE ABBEY, DISCARDED SON, &C.

> London: Printed at the Minerva-Press, for A. K. Newman and Co. (Successors to Lane, Newman, & Co.) Leadenhall-Street, 1810.
> I 208p; II 257p; III 270p. 12mo. 18s (ECB, QR).
> QR 3: 268 (Feb 1810).
> Corvey; CME 3-628-48462-6; ECB 498; NSTC D147 (BI BL).

*Notes.* Advs. of new works, 'With the Reviewers' Opinion', at end of vols. 2 and 3.
Further edn: Philadelphia 1810 (NUC).


1810: 71   ST. HILAIRE, Bridget.
## THE PRIORY OF SAINT MARY. A ROMANCE FOUNDED ON DAYS OF OLD. IN FOUR VOLUMES. BY BRIDGET ST. HILAIRE.

> London: Printed by J. Dean, 57, Wardour Street, for R. Ryan, 353, Oxford Street, and G. Shade, 26, Princes Street, Cavendish Square. Sold by Sherwood, Neely, and Jones, Paternoster-Row, 1810.
> I 275p; II 264p; III 264p; IV 249p. 12mo. 20s (ER).
> ER 15: 528 (Jan 1810).
> IU 823.Sa232; xNSTC.

*Notes.* The last page of vol. 2 is mistakenly numbered 210, and pp. 245–249 in vol. 4 are mistakenly numbered 235–239.
Further edn: 2nd edn. 1810 (Corvey), CME 3-628-47157-5. This 'edition', involving the same publishers, has identical pagination.


1810: 72   SCOTT, Honoria [pseud.?].
## AMATORY TALES OF SPAIN, FRANCE, SWITZERLAND, AND THE MEDITERRANEAN: CONTAINING THE FAIR ANDALUSIAN; ROSO-LIA OF PALERMO; AND THE MALTESE PORTRAIT: INTERSPERSED WITH PIECES OF ORIGINAL POETRY. IN FOUR VOLUMES. BY HONORIA SCOTT, AUTHOR OF THE WINTER IN EDINBURGH, &C.

> London: Published for J. Dick, 55, Chiswell Street; and sold by all the Booksellers, 1810.
> I 235p; II 238p; III 226p; IV 256p. 12mo. 16s (ECB); 20s (ER, QR).
> ER 16: 509 (Aug 1810); QR 4: 277 (Aug 1810).
> Corvey; CME 3-628-48538-X; ECB 520; NSTC S759 (BI BL).

*Notes.* 'To the Reader' (1 p. unn.), dated 'Chiswell Street, May, 1810'. This states: 'Owing to the Absence of the Author from Town during the Time this Work was in the Press, several Errors have unavoidably crept in, particularly with respect to the Names of Places in Malta &c. [...]. Should a Second Edition be called for, the whole shall be carefully revised and corrected.' Adv. opp. t.p. in vols. 2, 3, 4 for the same writer's 'The Authoress' (as 'In the Press', but evidently never published), promising 'a characteristic Work of Humour and Anecdote, containing the Author's Literary Adventures, with a Sketch of her Life'. For the possible identity of this author, see *A Winter in Edinburgh* (1810: 74). ECB dates Jan 1811.

1810: 73   SCOTT, Honoria [pseud.?].

THE VALE OF CLYDE: A TALE, BY HONORIA SCOTT, AUTHOR OF "A WINTER IN EDINBURGH," &C. IN TWO VOLUMES.

> London: Published by J. Dick, 24, Hollywell-Street, Strand, (late Chiswell-Street); and sold by all the Booksellers, 1810.
> I 229p; II 206p. 12mo. 9s (ECB).
> Corvey; CME 3-628-48543-6; ECB 520; NSTC S762 (BI BL, E).

*Notes.* For the possible identity of the author, see 1810: 74. ECB dates Jan 1811.

1810: 74   SCOTT, Honoria [pseud.?].

A WINTER IN EDINBURGH; OR, THE RUSSIAN BROTHERS; A NOVEL. IN THREE VOLUMES. BY HONORIA SCOTT.

> London: Published by J. Dick, 55, Chiswell Street, 1810.
> I 268p; II 244p; III 210p. 12mo. 15s (ECB, ER, QR).
> ER 15: 529 (Jan 1810); QR 3: 268 (Feb 1810); WSW I: 480.
> Corvey; CME 3-628-48544-4; ECB 520; NSTC S763 (BI BL, E, O).

*Notes.* H&L attributes this work to 'Mrs. Frazer' citing a newspaper cutting of July 1824. This may or may not refer to Mrs Susan Fraser, author of *Camilla de Florian, and other poems* (1809) and *Poems* (1811). If the attribution is correct, then Fraser is likely to be the author of all four novels written under the pseudonym of Honoria Scott (see also 1810: 72, 73 and 1813: 54). 'Advertisement', dated No. 55, Chiswell Street, 22 Nov 1809, in which Dick, the publisher, replies to T. F. [*sic*] Hughes's accusation that the title 'A Winter in Edinburgh' has been copied from a prospective Hughes publication: no such title seems in fact to have been published by J. F. Hughes. ECB dates Jan 1811.
Further edn: 2nd edn. 1822 (NSTC).

1810: 75   SENATE, E.

FAMILY PRIDE AND HUMBLE MERIT. A NOVEL, FOUNDED ON FACTS, AND PARTLY TAKEN FROM THE FRENCH. BY E. SENATE, M.D. IN THREE VOLUMES.

> London: Printed for Sherwood, Neely, and Jones, (Successors to Mr. H. D. Symonds) No. 20, Paternoster Row, 1810.
> I viii, 311p; II 288p; III 306p. 12mo. 18s (ECB, ER).
> ER 16: 259 (Apr 1810).
> BL N.2027; ECB 527; NSTC S1141.

*Notes.* Preface by the author, dated Jan 1810.

1810: 76   S[HELLEY], P[ercy] B[ysshe].
ZASTROZZI, A ROMANCE. BY P. B. S.

> London: Printed for G. Wilkie and J. Robinson, 57, Paternoster Row, 1810.
> 252p. 12mo. 5s (ECB, ER).
> ER 16: 259 (Apr 1810); WSW I: 497.
> Corvey; CME 3-628-48997-0; ECB 654; NSTC S1642 (BI BL, O).

*Notes.* Facs: GNIII (1977).

1810: 77   SLEATH, [Eleanor].
THE NOCTURNAL MINSTREL; OR, THE SPIRIT OF THE WOOD. A
ROMANCE. IN TWO VOLUMES. BY MRS. SLEATH, AUTHOR OF THE
ORPHAN OF THE RHINE, WHO'S THE MURDERER? BRISTOL
HEIRESS, &C. &C.

> London: Printed at the Minerva-Press, for A. K. Newman and Co. (Successors to Lane,
> Newman, and Co.) Leadenhall-Street, 1810.
> I 208p; II 191p. 12mo. 10s (ECB, QR).
> QR 3: 268 (Feb 1810).
> Corvey; CME 3-628-48755-2; ECB 542; NSTC S2265 (BI BL, O).

*Notes.* Facs: GNI (1972).


SMITH, Catherine, THE CASTLE OF ARRAGON
See 1809: 67


1810: 78   [SMITH, Julia].
THE PRISON OF MONTAUBAN; OR, TIMES OF TERROR. A REFLEC-
TIVE TALE. BY THE EDITOR OF LETTERS OF THE SWEDISH COURT.

> London: Printed for C. Cradock and W. Joy, (Successors to Mr. Ostell,) 32, Paternoster
> Row, 1810.
> xi, 254p. 12mo. 6s (ECB, ER).
> ER 16: 259 (Apr 1810); WSW I: 506–7.
> O 256.f.3043; CME 3-628-48482-0; ECB 471; NSTC S2536.


1810: 79   SQUIRE, Miss [C.].
INCIDENT AND INTEREST; OR, COPIES FROM NATURE. BY MISS
SQUIRE.

> London: Printed for Longman, Hurst, Rees, Orme, and Brown, Paternoster-Row, by J.
> M'Creery, Black-Horse-Court, 1810.
> I iv, 275p; II 171p. 12mo. 9s (ECB, ER, QR).
> ER 17: 500 (Feb 1811); QR 5: 267 (Feb 1811).
> Corvey; CME 3-628-54711-3; ECB 557; xNSTC.

*Notes.* 'Advertisement' dated London, Nov 1810. 'Wives as They Should Be! A Comedy in
Three Acts' (drama) fills vol. 2, pp. [77]–171.


1810: 80   ?STAËL-HOLSTEIN, [Anne Louis Germaine] de.
THE LIBERTINE HUSBAND. A NOVEL, IN TWO VOLUMES. TRANS-
LATED FROM THE FRENCH OF MADAME DE STAEL HOLSTEIN,
AUTHOR OF "DELPHINE," "CORINNA," &C.

> London: Printed for J. F. Hughes, 38, Berners Street, Oxford Street, 1810.
> I 162p; II 171p. 12mo.
> BL 12510.bb.20; NSTC S3445.

*Notes.* The publisher's attribution to de Staël is doubtful. No French original discovered.

1810: 81   STANHOPE, Louisa Sidney.
DI MONTRANZO; OR, THE NOVICE OF CORPUS DOMINI. A
ROMANCE. IN FOUR VOLUMES. BY LOUISA SIDNEY STANHOPE,
AUTHOR OF MONTBRASIL ABBEY; THE BANDIT'S BRIDE; STRIK-
ING LIKENESSES; THE AGE WE LIVE IN, &C. &C.

> London: Printed at the Minerva-Press, for A. K. Newman and Co. (Successors to Lane,
>   Newman, and Co.) Leadenhall-Street, 1810.
> I 254p; II 228p; III 250p; IV 270p. 12mo. 21s (ECB).
> O 256.e.17071; CME 3-628-48775-7; ECB 558; NSTC S3496 (BI BL).

*Notes.* ECB dates June 1810.


1810: 82   STUART, Augusta Amelia.
THE EXILE OF PORTUGAL: A TALE OF THE PRESENT TIME, IN TWO
VOLUMES, BY AUGUSTA AMELIA STUART, AUTHOR OF LUDO-
VICO'S TALE &C.

> London: Printed for J. F. Hughes, 38, Berners Street, 1810.
> I v, 198p; II 191p. 12mo. 9s (ER, QR).
> ER 15: 242 (Oct 1809); QR 2: 466 (Nov 1809).
> Corvey; CME 3-628-48684-X; ECB 567; xNSTC.

*Notes.* ECB dates 1806, but no copy belonging to this year located.


1810: 83   [TAYLOR, William (*trans.*)].
TALES OF YORE. IN THREE VOLUMES.

> London: Printed for J. Mawman, 22, Poultry, 1810.
> I iv, 336p; II iv, 340p; III iv, 345p. 12mo. 15s (ECB, ER).
> ER 15: 528 (Jan 1810); WSW I: 119.
> Corvey; CME 3-628-52308-7; ECB 576; NSTC T414 (BI BL).

*Notes.* 20 tales in all, from different foreign languages. ECB dates Dec 1809.


1810: 84   TURNER, {Margaret}.
INFATUATION; OR SKETCHES FROM NATURE. BY MRS. TURNER,
AUTHOR OF "ORIGINAL POEMS." IN TWO VOLUMES.

> London: Printed for Richard Phillips, Bridge-Street, Blackfriars, 1810.
> I xii, 262p; II 249p. 12mo. 10s 6d (ECB, ER).
> ER 16: 509 (Aug 1810).
> Corvey; CME 3-628-48843-5; ECB 603; NSTC T1885 (BI BL).

*Notes.* Dedication to Henry Lidgbird, Esq., signed Margaret Turner. Printer's mark after
imprint date reads: 'Gillet and Son, Printers, Crown-court, Fleet-Street'.


1810: 85   [WALSH, Miss].
THE OFFICER'S DAUGHTER; OR, A VISIT TO IRELAND IN 1790. BY
THE DAUGHTER OF A CAPTAIN IN THE NAVY, DECEASED. IN
FOUR VOLUMES.

London: Printed by Joyce Gold, Shoe Lane, 1810.
I xiv, 221p; II 252p; III 210p; IV 251p. 12mo. 21s (QR).
QR 4: 277 (Aug 1810); WSW I: 552.
IU 823.Of 25; xNSTC.

*Notes.* Dedication to the Hon. Mrs Fane. 'List of Subscribers' (224 names), vol. 1, pp. [v]–xiv. Printer's colophon 'G. Sidney, Printer, Northumberland-Street, Strand' in vol. 1; 'Printed by Joyce Gold, Shoe Lane, London', vols. 2 and 3; 'T. Bensley Printer, Bolt Court, Fleet Street, London', vol. 4. Summers attributes to Miss Walsh, Gecker to Mrs Walsh.

1810: 86   WARD, Catherine G[eorge].
THE DAUGHTER OF ST. OMAR. A NOVEL. IN TWO VOLUMES. BY CATHARINE G. WARD.

London: Printed at the Minerva-Press, for A. K. Newman and Co. (Successors to Lane, Newman, & Co.) Leadenhall-Street, 1810.
I 263p; II 214p. 12mo.
Corvey; CME 3-628-48822-2; ECB 623; NSTC W505 (BI BL).

1810: 87   [WEST, Jane].
THE REFUSAL. BY THE AUTHOR OF THE "TALE OF THE TIMES," "INFIDEL FATHER," &C.

London: Printed for Longman, Hurst, Rees, and Orme, Paternoster Row, 1810.
I 318p; II vii, 385p; III vii, 422p. 12mo. 21s (ECB).
ER 15: 529 (Jan 1810); WSW I: 557.
Corvey; CME 3-628-48895-8; ECB 631; NSTC W1351 (BI BL, C, E, O).

*Notes.* Further edn: Philadelphia 1810 (NUC).

1810: 88   WILKINSON, [Sarah Scudgell].
CONVENT OF GREY PENITENTS; OR, THE APOSTATE NUN. A ROMANCE, IN TWO VOLUMES. BY MISS WILKINSON.

London: Printed for J. F. Hughes, 38, Berners Street, Oxford Street, 1810.
I 198p; II 191p. 12mo. 9s (ECB, ER); 10s (QR).
ER 15: 529 (Jan 1810); QR 3: 268 (Feb 1810).
Corvey; CME 3-628-48923-7; ECB 638; NSTC W1942 (BI BL)

1810: 89   YOUNG, Mary Julia.
THE HEIR OF DRUMCONDRA; OR, FAMILY PRIDE. IN THREE VOL-UMES. BY MARY JULIA YOUNG, AUTHOR OF THE SUMMER AT WEYMOUTH, THE SUMMER AT BRIGHTON, DONALDA, ROSE-MOUNT CASTLE, EAST INDIAN, &C. &C.

London: Printed at the Minerva-Press, for A. K. Newman and Co. (Successors to Lane, Newman, & Co.) Leadenhall-Street, 1810.
I 224p; II 217p; III 255p. 12mo. 15s (ECB).
Corvey; CME 3-628-48992-X; ECB 653; NSTC Y237 (BI E).

*Notes.* Last page of vol. 2 is mistakenly numbered 241. ECB dates May 1810.

# 1811

1811: 1    ANON.

ALIDIA AND CLORIDAN; OR, THE OFFSPRING OF BERTHA. A
ROMANCE OF FORMER TIMES. IN TWO VOLUMES.

> London: Printed for, and published by, N. L. Pannier, Bookseller to his Royal Highness
> the Duke of Kent; and sold by J. M. Richardson, 23, Cornhill, and all other Book-
> sellers, 1811.
> I 266p; II 255p. 12mo. 10s (ER, QR).
> ER 17: 500 (Feb 1811); QR 4: 542 (Nov 1810), 5: 267 (Feb 1811).
> Corvey; CME 3-628-47041-2; NSTC A903 (BI BL).

*Notes*. ER and QR both mistakenly give first name in title as 'Alicia'.

1811: 2    ANON.

AMONAIDA; OR, THE DREADFUL CONSEQUENCES OF PARENTAL
PREDILECTION. A ROMANCE, IN FOUR VOLUMES. BY THE AUTHOR
OF ALIDIA AND CLORIDAN.

> London: Printed for, and published by, N. L. Pannier, at the English and Foreign
> Library, No. 15, Leicester-Place, Leicester-Square; and sold by J. M. Richardson, 23,
> Cornhill, and all other Booksellers, 1811.
> I 223p; II 208p; III 201p; IV 204p. 12mo.
> Corvey; CME 3-628-47054-4; NSTC A1162 (BI BL).

1811: 3    ANON.

BATH AND LONDON; OR, SCENES IN EACH. A NOVEL. IN FOUR
VOLUMES.

> London: Printed at the Minerva-Press, for A. K. Newman and Co. (Successors to Lane,
> Newman, and Co.) Leadenhall-Street, 1811.
> I 227p; II 219p; III 246p; IV 296p. 12mo. 21s (ECB).
> Corvey; CME 3-628-47128-1; ECB 43; NSTC B942 (BI BL).

*Notes*. ECB dates May 1811.

1811: 4    ANON.

*THE BRITISH SOLDIER AND SAILOR, THEIR FAMILIES, AND FRIENDS.

> 2 vols. 12s (ER); 12s 6d (QR).
> ER 18: 517 (Aug 1811); QR 5: 537 (May 1811); WSW I: 18.
> No copy located.

1811: 5    ANON.

THE DEAD LETTER OFFICE; AND A TALE FOR THE ENGLISH
FARMER'S FIRE-SIDE. BY THE AUTHOR OF CORINNA OF ENGLAND,

WINTER IN BATH, EVERSFIELD ABBEY, WOMAN OF COLOUR, BANKS OF THE WYE, &C. &C.

> London: Printed for B. Crosby and Co. Stationers'-Court, Paternoster-Row, n.d. [1811].
>
> I 262p; II 251p. 12mo. 10s (ECB).
>
> Corvey; CME 3-628-47380-2; ECB 156; xNSTC.

*Notes.* Introduction, vol. 1, pp. 1–16, suggests female authorship. 'Observations by the Author' at end (vol. 2, pp. 250–1) indicates indebtedness to Miss Hamilton's 'Tale for the Ingle Nook' [i.e. *The Cottagers of Glenburnie* (1808: 52)]. Sometimes attributed to Mrs E. G. Bayfield or to J. H. James, but see notes to *A Winter in Bath* (1807: 7) and *The Banks of the Wye* (1808: 1). ECB dates July 1811.

1811: 6  ANON.
THE DECISION; A NOVEL. BY THE AUTHOR OF CAROLINE ORMSBY, OR THE REAL LUCILLA; THE ACCEPTANCE, &C. &C. IN THREE VOLUMES.

> London: Printed for Henry Colburn, English and Foreign Public Library, Conduit-Street, Hanover-Square, 1811.
>
> I 207p; II 192p; III 167p. 12mo. 15s (ECB).
>
> QR 6: 563 (Dec 1811); WSW I: 31.
>
> Corvey; CME 3-628-47381-0; ECB 156; xNSTC.

*Notes.* This title has misled some catalogues into attributing works by this unidentified author to Grace Kennedy, though the latter's *The Decision* (1821, and her first work) is in the form of a play (BL 4410.f.14). Block attributes this 1811 *Decision* to Barbara Hofland, almost certainly mistaking it for Hofland's 1 vol. *Decision: A Tale* (see 1824: 48). This work is also distinct from Anne Raikes Harding's 3 vol. *Decision: A Tale* (see 1819: 37).

1811: 7  ANON.
FREDERICK; OR, MEMOIRS OF MY YOUTH. INTERSPERSED WITH OCCASIONAL VERSE. IN TWO VOLUMES.

> London: Printed for William Miller, Albemarle-Street; and J. Parker, Oxford, 1811.
>
> I 284p; II 271p. 12mo. 12s (ECB, ER, QR).
>
> ER 18: 266 (May 1811); QR 5: 537 (May 1811); WSW I: 46.
>
> E NF.1325.b.5; ECB 216; NSTC F1583.

1811: 8  ANON.
JULIA DE VIENNE. A NOVEL. IN FOUR VOLUMES. IMITATED FROM THE FRENCH, BY A LADY.

> London: Printed for Henry Colburn, English and Foreign Public Library, Conduit-Street, New Bond-Street, 1811.
>
> I 214p; II 227p; III 256p; IV 256p. 12mo. 21s (ECB, ER, QR).
>
> ER 17: 500 (Feb 1811); QR 5: 267 (Feb 1811).
>
> Corvey; CME 3-628-48005-1; ECB 314; xNSTC.

*Notes.* French original not discovered. Dedication to the Prince of Wales, introducing 'this my first attempt', followed by 'List of Subscribers' (2 pp. unn.) containing 43 names. The same dedication and list are found in the Corvey copy of *The House of Lancaster* (see 1810: 11).

1811:9    ANON.

THE MOUNTAIN CHIEF; OR, THE DESCENDANT OF WILLIAM TELL, THE DELIVERER OF SWITZERLAND. A ROMANCE, IN FOUR VOLUMES.

> London: Printed by John Dean, 57, Wardour Street, Soho. For George Hughes, 221, Tottenham-Court Road. Bookseller to her R.H. the Princess of Wales, 1811.
> I 240p; II 216p; III 190p; IV 220p. 12mo. 20s (ER, QR).
> ER 17: 500 (Feb 1811); QR 4: 542 (Nov 1810), 5: 267 (Feb 1811).
> Corvey; CME 3-628-48353-0; xNSTC.

1811:10    ANON.

ST. BRIDE'S MANOR. A NOVEL, IN TWO VOLUMES.

> London: Printed for J. F. Hughes, 15, Paternoster Row, 1811.
> I 217p; II 193p. 12mo. 8s (ECB).
> Corvey; CME 3-628-48594-0; xNSTC.

*Notes.* ECB 511 lists Crosby edn. July 1811; but no copy located.

1811:11    ANON.

THE SPECTRE OF THE MOUNTAIN OF GRENADA; A ROMANCE. IN THREE VOLUMES.

> London: Printed by John Dean, 57, Wardour Street, Soho. For George Hughes, 221, Tottenham-Court Road. Bookseller to her R.H. the Princess of Wales, 1811.
> I 268p; II 224p; III 255p. 12mo. 15s (ER, QR).
> ER 17: 500 (Feb 1811); QR 4: 542 (Nov 1810), 5: 267 (Feb 1811).
> Corvey; CME 3-628-48668-8; xNSTC.

*Notes.* Listed by Blakey (copy not seen) as a Minerva publication; but not located in this form. Pigoreau lists a French title *Le Spectre de la Montagne de Grenade* (1809), by 'Désirée Castellerat' [Castéra?], which may possibly represent the source title. MLC however lists a French trans., 1811, as if the English title represented the original. NUC and BN both contain several novels by Désirée de Castéra, published in French between *c.*1800–20, but not the present title. Since some other titles attributed by Pigoreau to 'Castellerat' are among these, it is likely that Pigoreau misrepresents the surname.
Further edn: see note above.

1811:12    ANON.

THE TIMES, A NOVEL. IN TWO VOLUMES.

> London: Printed for Henry Colburn, English and Foreign Public Library, Conduit Street, Bond Street, 1811.
> I viii, 186p; II 172p. 12mo. 10s (ECB, ER, QR).
> ER 18: 266 (May 1811); QR 5: 537 (May 1811).
> Corvey; CME 3-628-48957-1; ECB 591; xNSTC.

*Notes.* Dedication to Mrs Hamilton.

1811: 13   ANON.

A WINTER IN PARIS; OR MEMOIRS OF MADAME DE C****: WRIT-
TEN BY HERSELF. IN THREE VOLUMES.

> London: Printed for Henry Colburn, English and Foreign Public Library, Conduit-
> Street, New Bond-Street, 1811.
> I 224p; II 231p; III 190p. 12mo. 15s (ECB); 18s (ER, QR).
> ER 18: 266 (May 1811); QR 5: 537 (May 1811).
> BL 12623.e.6; ECB 644; NSTC C6 (BI E).

1811: 14   AGG, John.

EDWY AND ELGIVA, AN HISTORICAL ROMANCE OF THE TENTH
CENTURY. IN FOUR VOLUMES. BY JOHN AGG, AUTHOR OF "MAC
DERMOT," &C. &C.

> London: Printed for C. Chapple, 66, Pall-Mall, 1811.
> I 221p; II 216p; III 208p; IV 199p. 12mo. 21s (ECB, ER, QR).
> ER 20: 502 (Nov 1812); QR 7: 471 (June 1812); WSW I: 2.
> Corvey; CME 3-628-47025-0; ECB 181; NSTC A587 (BI BL).

1811: 15   ASHE, Thomas.

THE SPIRIT OF "THE BOOK;" OR, MEMOIRS OF CAROLINE,
PRINCESS OF HASBURGH, A POLITICAL AND AMATORY ROM-
ANCE. IN THREE VOLUMES. EDITED BY THOMAS ASHE, ESQ.

> London: Printed and published by Allen & Co. No. 15, Paternoster-Row, 1811.
> I x, 230p; II 250p; III 272p. 12mo. 15s (ER, QR); 25s (ER).
> ER 18: 517 (Aug 1811), 19: 252 (Nov 1811); QR 6: 309 (Oct 1811); WSW I: 135.
> BL G.5114-16; ECB 28; NSTC C717 (BI C, E).

*Notes.* ER 18: 517 (Aug 1811) gives subtitle as 'or Memoirs of a Great Personage' and price
as 15s.
Further edns: 2nd edn. 1811 (NSTC); 3rd edn. 1811 (NSTC); 4th edn. 1812 (NSTC);
abridgement 1812 (NSTC); Philadelphia (from 3rd London edn.) 1812 (NUC); French
trans., 1813; German trans., 1813.

1811: 16   [AUSTEN, Jane].

SENSE AND SENSIBILITY: A NOVEL. IN THREE VOLUMES. BY A
LADY.

> London: Printed for the Author, by C. Roworth, Bell-Yard, Temple-Bar, and published
> by T. Egerton, Whitehall, 1811.
> I 317p; II 278p; III 301p. 12mo. 15s (ECB, ER, QR).
> ER 19: 252 (Nov 1811), 20: 501 (Nov 1812); QR 6: 563 (Dec 1811); WSW I: 136.
> BL C.71.bb.14; ECB 527; NSTC A2018 (BI O).

*Notes.* Further edns: 2nd edn. 1813 (NSTC); 1833 (NSTC); 1837 (NSTC); 1844 (NSTC);
1849 (NSTC); Philadelphia 1833 (NSTC); French trans., 1815 [as *Raison et Sensibilité, ou les
deux manières d'aimer* (BN)].

1811: 17 [BARTHES DE MARMORIÈRES, Antoine].
*ELNATHAN; OR, THE AGES OF MAN. AN HISTORICAL ROMANCE.
BY A PHILOSOPHER.

London: A. K. Newman, 1811.
3 vols. 12mo. 15s (ECB); 13s (ER, QR).
ER 19: 252 (Nov 1811); QR 6: 309 (Oct 1811).
No copy located; ECB 185.

*Notes.* Trans. of *Elnathan; ou les âges de l'homme, traduit du chaldéen* (Paris, 1802). Listed in Blakey, but copy not seen.


1811: 18 [BARRETT, Eaton Stannard].
THE METROPOLIS; OR, A CURE FOR GAMING. INTERSPERSED
WITH ANECDOTES OF LIVING CHARACTERS IN HIGH LIFE. IN
THREE VOLUMES. BY CERVANTES HOGG, ESQ. AUTHOR OF THE
RISING SUN, THE SETTING SUN, &C. &C.

London: Printed at the Minerva-Press, for A. K. Newman and Co. (Successors to Lane,
Newman, and Co.) Leadenhall-Street, 1811.
I 218p; II 248p; III 259p. 12mo. 15s (ER).
ER 18: 265 (May 1811).
Corvey; CME 3-628-47700-X; NSTC B671 (BI O).

*Notes.* A different work from *The Metropolis: A Novel* (1819: 13). ECB 383 lists Newman edn.
June 1822, 16s 6d; but not discovered in this form.


1811: 19 [BEAUCLERC, Amelia].
EVA OF CAMBRIA; OR, THE FUGITIVE DAUGHTER. A NOVEL. IN
THREE VOLUMES. BY EMMA DE LISLE, AUTHOR OF THE SOLDIER'S
OFFSPRING, &C. &C.

London: Printed at the Minerva-Press, for A. K. Newman and Co. (Successors to Lane,
Newman, & Co.) Leadenhall-Street, 1811.
I 264p; II 269p; III 279p. 12mo.
Corvey; CME 3-628-48106-6; xNSTC.

*Notes.* Blakey (p. 232) states that this title is not by Emma de Lisle [the pseudonym of Emma
Parker], but the production of another author, sent to the press by mistake for hers; and that
her manuscript was later published as *Fitz-Edward* (see 1811: 65). *Ora and Juliet* (1811: 20),
almost certainly by Beauclerc, states on its t.p. that it is 'by the author of Eva of Cambria'.


1811: 20 [BEAUCLERC, Amelia].
ORA AND JULIET; OR, INFLUENCE OF FIRST PRINCIPLES. A NOVEL.
IN FOUR VOLUMES. BY THE AUTHOR OF EVA OF CAMBRIA, &C.

London: Printed at the Minerva-Press, for A. K. Newman and Co. (Successors to Lane,
Newman, & Co.) Leadenhall-Street, 1811.
I 238p; II 228p; III 233p; IV 231p. 12mo. 20s (ER, QR).
ER 19: 252 (Nov 1811); QR 6: 563 (Dec 1811).
Corvey; CME 3-628-48310-7; xNSTC.

1811: 21    BIGLAND, John.

THE PHILOSOPHICAL WANDERERS; OR, THE HISTORY OF THE
ROMAN TRIBUNE, AND THE PRIESTESS OF MINERVA: EXHIBITING
THE VICISSITUDES THAT DIVERSIFY THE FORTUNES OF NATIONS
AND INDIVIDUALS. BY JOHN BIGLAND, AUTHOR OF "THE HIS-
TORICAL AND GEOGRAPHICAL VIEW OF THE WORLD;" "LETTERS
ON ANCIENT AND MODERN HISTORY," &C. &C.

> London: Printed for Longman, Hurst, Rees, Orme and Brown, Paternoster-Row; Ver-
> nor, Hood and Sharpe, Poultry; and James Cundee, Ivy-Lane, 1811.
>
> xii, 286p. 12mo. 6s (ECB, ER).
>
> ER 18: 265 (May 1811).
>
> BL 12614.d.5; ECB 56; NSTC B2895.

1811: 22    BOSWELL, H.

THE IDIOT; OR, PICTURES OF LIFE. IN THREE VOLUMES. BY H.
BOSWELL.

> London: Printed by G. E. Miles, 127, Oxford Street; for G. Shade, 26, Princes Street,
> Cavendish Square, 1811.
>
> I 213p; II 214p; III 213p. 12mo.
>
> ViU PZ2.B672I.1811; xNSTC.

*Notes.* Summers (p. 571) attributes to G. H. Boswell; Allibone and Block give author as Miss
H. Boswell. Colophon in vol. 3 reads: 'Printed by J. Dean, 57, Wardour St. Soho'; colophons
in other vols. match t.p.

1811: 23    BREWER, James Norris.

AN OLD FAMILY LEGEND; OR, ONE HUSBAND AND TWO MARRIAGES.
A ROMANCE. IN FOUR VOLUMES. BY JAMES NORRIS BREWER,
AUTHOR OF A WINTER'S TALE, SECRETS MADE PUBLIC, A DESCRIP-
TIVE AND HISTORICAL ACCOUNT OF SPLENDID PALACES, &C.

> London: Printed at the Minerva-Press, for A. K. Newman and Co. (Successors to Lane,
> Newman, & Co.) Leadenhall-Street, 1811.
>
> I iv, 200p; II 234p; III 232p; IV 244p. 12mo. 20s (ECB); 21s boards (ER); 21s (QR).
>
> ER 18: 517 (Aug 1811); QR 5: 537 (May 1811).
>
> Corvey; CME 3-628-47197-4; ECB 73; NSTC B4249 (BI BL).

*Notes.* Dedication to Richard Cumberland, Esq., signed J. Norris Brewer, Hurst, Berks.

1811: 24    BROWN, C[harles] B[rockden].

WIELAND, OR THE TRANSFORMATION, AN AMERICAN TALE. BY
B. C. [*sic*] BROWN, AUTHOR OF ORMOND, OR THE SECRET
WITNESS, &C. &C. IN THREE VOLUMES.

> New York printed, London: Re-printed for H. Colburn, English and Foreign Public
> Library, Conduit-Street, New Bond-Street, 1811.
>
> I viii, 218p; II 200p; III 175p. 12mo. 15s (ECB, ER, QR).

ER 17: 248 (Nov 1810); QR 4: 452 (Nov 1810); WSW I: 174.
BL 12703.f.5; ECB 78; NSTC B4734 (BI O).

*Notes.* Dedication to Richard Brinsley Sheridan, signed Henry Colburn; 'Advertisement' signed 'B. C. B.' and dated Sept 1798. ECB gives title as 'Wieland; or, the Transformation: a romance', and dates Nov 1810. Originally published New York 1798 (Blanck, ESTC). Further edns: New edn. 1822, as *Wieland, an American tale* (NUC); French trans., 1841 [as *Wieland, ou la voix mystérieuse . . . (traduction faite sur la dernière édition de Londres)* (BN)].

1811: 25 [BRUNTON, Mary].
SELF-CONTROL: A NOVEL.

Edinburgh: Printed by George Ramsay & Co. for Manners and Miller; and Longman, Hurst, Rees, Orme, and Brown, London, 1811.
I x, 388p; II 468p. 8vo. 21s (ECB); 24s (ER, 3rd edn., QR, 2nd edn.).
ER 18: 517 (Aug 1811) [for 3rd edn.]; QR 5: 537 (May 1811) [for 2nd edn.]; WSW I: 177.
BL 1608/742; ECB 526; NSTC B5017 (BI C, E, O).

*Notes.* Dedication to Miss Joanna Baillie, dated Jan 1811.
Further edns: 2nd edn. 1811 (NSTC); 3rd edn. 1811 (NSTC); 4th edn. 1812 (Corvey), CME 3-628-48640-8; London 1832 (NSTC); 1844 (NSTC); [at least 2 more edns. to 1850]; New York 1811 (NUC); French trans., 1829 [as *Laure Montreville, ou l'empire sur soi-même* (BN)].

1811: 26 CAMPBELL, Dr.
THE HEROINE OF ALMEIDA, A NOVEL: FOUNDED ON FACTS, RELATING TO THE CAMPAIGNS IN SPAIN AND PORTUGAL, UNDER LORD WELLINGTON, AND GENERAL BERESFORD. BY DR. CAMP-BELL, AUTHOR OF "THE FEMALE MINOR", &C. &C.

Dublin: Printed by J. Charles, No. 49, Mary-Street, 1811.
v, 145p. 12mo.
Dt OLS.186.o.34; xNSTC.

*Notes.* 'A Prefatory Address to the Reader', pp. [iii]–v, clearly presents this as a novel.

1811: 27 CARD, Henry.
BEAUFORD: OR, A PICTURE OF HIGH LIFE. BY HENRY CARD, M.A. OF PEMBROKE COLLEGE, OXFORD. IN TWO VOLUMES.

London: Printed for F. C. and J. Rivington, No. 62, St. Paul's Church-Yard; by Law and Gilbert, St. John's-Square, Clerkenwell, 1811.
I vii, 325p; II 312p. 8vo. 15s (ECB, QR).
QR 6: 563 (Dec 1811); WSW I: 197.
Corvey; CME 3-628-47212-1; ECB 97; NSTC C587 (BI BL, Dt).

*Notes.* Dedication 'to Henry David Erskine, Esq.', dated Chapel Hill, near Margate, Oct 1811.

1811: 28 CRANDOLPH, Augustus Jacob.
THE MYSTERIOUS HAND; OR, SUBTERRANEAN HORROURS! A ROMANCE. IN THREE VOLUMES. BY AUGUSTUS JACOB CRANDOLPH.

London: Printed at the Minerva-Press, for A. K. Newman and Co. (Successors to Lane, Newman, & Co.) Leadenhall-Street, 1811.

I ii, 218p; II 217p; III 254p. 12mo. 15s (ER, QR).

ER 17: 500 (Feb 1811); QR 5: 267 (Feb 1811).

Corvey; CME 3-628-47350-0; ECB 479; NSTC C4094 (BI BL).

*Notes.* Dedication 'to Her Royal Highness, The Princess Mary', dated Nov 1810. Novel dated Jan 1811 at end of vol. 3. ECB lists under Randolph (A. J.).

Further edn: French trans., 1819.


1811: 29   [DACRE, Charlotte].

**THE PASSIONS. IN FOUR VOLUMES. BY ROSA MATILDA, AUTHOR OF HOURS OF SOLITUDE; THE NUN; ZOFLOYA; LIBERTINE, &C.**

London: Printed for T. Cadell, and W. Davies, Strand, 1811.

I 287p; II 292p; III 252p; IV 340p. 12mo. 21s (ECB, ER, QR).

ER 18: 517 (Aug 1811); QR 5: 537 (May 1811); WSW I: 234.

Corvey; CME 3-628-47387-X; ECB 149; NSTC D48 (BI BL, O).

*Notes.* Facs: GNII (1974).


1811: 30   [D'ISRAELI, Isaac].

**DESPOTISM: OR THE FALL OF THE JESUITS. A POLITICAL ROMANCE, ILLUSTRATED BY HISTORICAL ANECDOTES.**

London: Printed for John Murray, Fleet-Street; and W. Blackwood, Edinburgh, 1811.

I xvi, 230p; II [231]–478p. 8vo. 12s (ECB, ER, QR).

ER 18: 517 (Aug 1811); QR 5: 537 (May 1811); WSW I: 247–8.

BL 12613.d.19; ECB 160; NSTC D936 (BI C, O).

*Notes.* 'Preface', vol. 1, pp. [iii]–xi, provides 'An historical introduction to a fictitious Narrative'. Novel proper ends vol. 2, p. 312, followed by notes, pp. 313–474, and an 'Index to the Notes which particularly relate to the Jesuits', pp. [475]–478.


1811: 31   EDGEWORTH, Mrs.

**FATHERLESS FANNY; OR, THE MEMOIRS OF A LITTLE MENDI-CANT, AND HER BENEFACTORS. A MODERN NOVEL, IN FOUR VOL-UMES. BY MRS. EDGEWORTH. AUTHORESS OF "THE WIFE; OR, A MODEL FOR WOMEN," &C. &C.**

London: Printed by J. Dean, 57. Wardour Street, Soho. For James Taylor, and Co. 25, Dean Street; and Sherwood, Neeley, and Jones, Paternoster Row, 1811.

I 212p; II 187p; III 212p; IV 212p. 12mo. 20s (ER, QR).

ER 18: 517 (Aug 1811); QR 6: 309 (Oct 1811).

Corvey; CME 3-628-47529-5; NSTC E234 (BI O).

*Notes.* This work was much reprinted, and has been attributed to Clara Reeve (d. 1807) and to Thomas Peckett Prest (born *c.*1810). ER 18: 517 (Aug 1811) lists misleadingly as 'by Miss Edgeworth'. The edn. published by Fisher, Son & Co, London 1833 (p.c.), is titled '*Fatherless Fanny; or a Young Lady's First Entrance into Life*, By the late Miss Taylor. Edited and enlarged by Mrs. Sarah Green': the ending of this also differs from earlier versions. The 1811 edn. described in this entry represents the first known printing (and attribution) of the work. Further edns: 1818 (NSTC); 1819 (BL N.2006, NSTC); 1820 (NUC); 1821 (NUC); Manchester 1822 (MH, NSTC); [also frequently reprinted, under London and provincial imprints, to 1850]; New York 1836 (NSTC); French trans., 1812 [as *Fanny, ou mémoires d'une jeune orpheline et de ses bienfaiteurs* (BN under Edgeworth, Maria)].

1811:32 EDGEWORTH, Theodore.
THE SHIPWRECK; OR, MEMOIRS OF AN IRISH OFFICER AND HIS FAMILY. IN THREE VOLUMES. BY THEODORE EDGEWORTH, ESQ.

> London: Printed for Thomas Tegg, No. 111, Cheapside, and sold by all other Booksellers, 1811.
> I 216p; II 216p; III 192p. 12mo. 15s (ECB, ER).
> ER 18: 265 (May 1811); WSW I: 257.
> Corvey; CME 3-628-47518-X; ECB 178; NSTC E264 (BI BL, Dt).

1811:33 FORSTER, A. V.
FATAL AMBITION, OR, THE MYSTERIES OF THE CAVERNS. A ROMANCE OF THE THIRTEENTH CENTURY. IN THREE VOLUMES. BY A. V. FORSTER, ESQ. ROYAL WEST MIDDLESEX MILITIA.

> London: Printed for Thomas Tegg. No. 111, Cheapside, and sold by all other Booksellers, 1811.
> I 214p; II 192p; III 176p. 12mo. 15s (ECB, ER, QR).
> ER 18: 265 (May 1811); QR 5: 537 (May 1811).
> MH-H 18485.20; ECB 211; xNSTC.

*Notes.* Opp. t.p. of all 3 vols. advs. for 'New Popular Novels just Published, by Thomas Tegg', viz. 'The Shipwreck', 'The Lady of the Lake', and ('in the press') 'The Hottentot Venus; or, Love in Africa, A Romance'—no copy of such a work as the last has been discovered.

1811:34 [GOULBURN, Edward].
FREDERICK DE MONTFORD. A NOVEL. IN THREE VOLUMES. BY THE AUTHOR OF THE PURSUITS OF FASHION.

> London: Printed for John Ebers, 23, Old Bond-Street, 1811.
> I vi, 254p; II 252p; III 250p. 12mo. 21s (ER).
> ER 19: 252 (Nov 1811); WSW I: 284.
> BRu ENC; xNSTC.

1811:35 GREEN, {S}[arah].
GOOD MEN OF MODERN DATE. A SATIRICAL TALE. IN THREE VOLUMES. BY MRS. GREEN, AUTHOR OF ROMANCE READERS AND ROMANCE WRITERS, REFORMIST, ROYAL EXILE, &C.

> London: Printed for Thomas Tegg, No. 111, Cheapside, 1811.
> I xii, 184p; II missing; III 179p. 12mo. 15s (ECB, QR).
> QR 7: 231 (Mar 1812); WSW I: 289.
> DGW PR.4728.G26G661811; ECB 244; xNSTC.

*Notes.* 'To the Reviewers, in particular to the British and Critical Reviewers' signed 'Westminster. S. Green'. Vol. 2 missing in DGW. ECB also dates Mar 1812.
Further edn: Philadelphia 1813 (NUC).

1811: 36   [?GUÉNARD, Elisabeth].
THE BLACK BANNER; OR, THE SIEGE OF CLAGENFURTH. A
ROMANTIC TALE. IN FOUR VOLUMES. BY THE AUTHOR OF THE
BARON DE FALKENHEIM, MYSTERY UPON MYSTERY, &C. &C.

> London: Printed at the Minerva-Press, for A. K. Newman and Co. (Successors to Lane,
> Newman, & Co.) Leadenhall-Street, 1811.
> I 272p; II 290p; III 288p; IV 322p. 12mo.
> Corvey; CME 3-628-47198-2; NSTC G2325 (BI BL).

*Notes.* Apparently a trans. of *La Bannière noire; ou le siège de Clagenforth*, though the earliest
copy of this title in French discovered in catalogues is dated 1820. BN attributes to Guénard,
though MLC treats as a French *translation* of this title.

1811: 37   HAMILTON, A[nn] [Mary].
THE ADVENTURES OF A SEVEN-SHILLING PIECE. IN TWO VOL-
UMES. BY A. HAMILTON, AUTHOR OF MONTALVA, &C. &C. &C.

> London: Printed by R. Juigné, 17, Margaret-St. Cavendish-Sq. for N. L. Pannier, at the
> English, Foreign and Classical Library, 15, Leicester-Place, Leicester-Square, and
> sold by J. M. Richardson, 23, Cornhill, and all other Booksellers, 1811.
> I xvi, 207p; II 240p. 12mo.
> BL 12612.ff.12; NSTC H298 (BI O).

1811: 38   HAMILTON, A[nn] [Mary].
MONTALVA; OR ANNALS OF GUILT. A TALE. BY A. HAMILTON,
AUTHOR OF THE IRISHMAN IN LONDON.

> London: Printed for, and published by, N. L. Pannier, at the English and Foreign
> Library, No. 15, Leicester-Place, Leicester-Square; and sold by J. M. Richardson, 23,
> Cornhill, and all other Booksellers, 1811.
> I 272p; II 293p. 12mo. 10s 6d (ER).
> ER 18: 517 (Aug 1811).
> Corvey; CME 3-628-47585-6; NSTC H302 (BI O).

1811: 39   HAMILTON, A[nn] [Mary].
A WINTER AT ST. JAMES'S; OR, MODERN MANNERS. A NOVEL, IN
FOUR VOLUMES. BY A. HAMILTON, AUTHOR OF "THE IRISH-
WOMAN IN LONDON," &C.

> London: Printed and published by Allen & Co. No. 15, Paternoster-Row, 1811.
> I 246p; II 244p; III 231p; IV 234p. 12mo. 20s (ECB, ER).
> ER 18: 265 (May 1811).
> Corvey; CME 3-628-47599-6; ECB 252; xNSTC.

*Notes.* ECB and BDLA give author as Emma Hamilton.

1811:40   HAWKINS, Lætitia-Matilda.

**THE COUNTESS AND GERTRUDE; OR, MODES OF DISCIPLINE. BY LÆTITIA-MATILDA HAWKINS. IN FOUR VOLUMES.**

> London: Printed for F. C. and J. Rivington, 62, St. Paul's Church-Yard; by Law and Gilbert, St. John's Square, Clerkenwell, 1811.
>
> I xxxi, 383p; II 415p; III 408p; IV 425p. 8vo. 36s (ECB, QR).
>
> QR 6: 563 (Dec 1811); WSW I: 303.
>
> BL 12643.ppp.32; ECB 259; NSTC H990 (BI Dt, E, O).

*Notes.* Dedication to Mrs H. M. Bowdler, signed Twickenham, Nov. 1811.
Further edn: 2nd edn. 1812 (Corvey), CME 3-628-47540-6.


1811:41   [HEYNE, Christian Leberecht]; [ROBINSON, Henry Crabb (*trans.*)].

**AMATONDA. A TALE, FROM THE GERMAN OF ANTON WALL.**

> London: Printed for Longman, Hurst, Rees, Orme, and Brown, Paternoster-Row, 1811.
>
> xxiii, 288p. 12mo. 6s (ECB, ER, QR).
>
> ER 18: 266 (May 1811); QR 5: 537 (May 1811).
>
> Corvey; CME 3-628-51023-6; ECB 620; NSTC A1463 (BI BL).

*Notes.* Trans. of *Persische Märchen: Amathonte* (Altenburg, 1799). Anton Wall was the pseudonym for Christian Leberecht Heyne. Drop-head sub-title reads: 'A Persian Tale'. Text proper ends on p. 274, followed by 'Note referred to in Page 260', pp. 275–88.


1811:42   HOLSTEIN, Anthony Frederick [pseud.].

**THE INHABITANTS OF EARTH; OR, THE FOLLIES OF WOMAN. A NOVEL. IN THREE VOLUMES. BY ANTHONY FREDERICK HOLSTEIN, AUTHOR OF SIR OWEN GLENDOWR; LOVE, MYSTERY, & MISERY; THE ASSASSIN OF ST. GLENROY; THE MISERIES OF AN HEIRESS, &C.**

> London: Printed at the Minerva-Press, for A. K. Newman and Co. (Successors to Lane, Newman, and Co.) Leadenhall Street, 1811.
>
> I iv, 233p; II 235p; III 303p. 12mo. 16s 6d (ECB, ER, QR).
>
> ER 19: 252 (Nov 1811); QR 6: 309 (Oct 1811).
>
> Corvey; CME 3-628-47735-2; ECB 278; NSTC H2275 (BI BL).

*Notes.* Preface dated London, Mar 1811.


1811:43   [HOLSTEIN, Anthony Frederick] [pseud.].

**ISADORA OF MILAN. IN FIVE VOLUMES.**

> London: Printed for Henry Colburn, English and Foreign Public Library, Conduit Street, New Bond Street, 1811.
>
> I 202p; II 204p; III 211p; IV 202p; V 212p. 12mo. 25s (ECB, ER, QR).
>
> ER 17: 500 (Feb 1811); QR 5: 267 (Feb 1811); WSW I: 59.
>
> Corvey; CME 3-628-47873-1; ECB 301; NSTC H2276 (BI BL, O).

*Notes.* A (fictional) 'Addenda, by the Editor', vol. 5, pp. 210–12, signed 'Willoughby Clive', states that 'The foregoing Narrative was written by Walter, Lord St. Aubin'. ECB lists under title only; this work is however attributed to Holstein in the title of *L'Intriguante* (see 1813: 33).

1811:44   [HORWOOD, Caroline].
ST. OSTBERG, OR THE CARMELITE MONK. A ROMANCE. IN FOUR
VOLUMES.

> London: Printed by J. Dean, 7. Wardour Street, Soho. Published and sold by M. Taylor
> and Co. 25, Dean Street, Soho, and by all Booksellers, 1811.
> I 212p; II 212p; III 212p; IV 224p. 12mo. 21s (ER, QR).
> ER 19: 252 (Nov 1811); QR 6: 563 (Dec 1811).
> Corvey; CME 3-628-47215-6; xNSTC.

1811:45   HOWARD, Miss.
MARRIED LIFE; OR, FAULTS ON ALL SIDES. A NOVEL. IN FIVE VOL-
UMES. BY MISS HOWARD.

> London: Printed at the Minerva-Press, for A. K. Newman and Co. (Successors to Lane,
> Newman, and Co.) Leadenhall-Street, 1811.
> I 286p; II 243p; III 230p; IV 242p; V 235p. 12mo. 25s (ECB); 15s (ER, QR).
> ER 17: 500 (Feb 1811); QR 5: 267 (Feb 1811).
> Corvey; CME 3-628-47746-8; ECB 285; xNSTC.

*Notes.* Further edn: Philadelphia 1812 (NUC).

1811:46   HUNTER, [Rachel].
THE SCHOOLMISTRESS; A MORAL TALE FOR YOUNG LADIES. IN
TWO VOLUMES. BY MRS. HUNTER, OF NORWICH, AUTHOR OF LETI-
TIA, LADY MACLAIRN, UNEXPECTED LEGACY, HISTORY OF THE
GRUBTHORPE FAMILY, MRS. PALMERSTONE'S LETTERS, &C. &C.

> London: Printed at the Minerva-Press, for A. K. Newman and Co. (Successors to Lane,
> Newman, and Co.) Leadenhall-Street, 1811.
> I 208p; II 192p. 12mo. 9s (ECB).
> Corvey; CME 3-628-47803-0; ECB 289; NSTC H3177 (BI BL).

*Notes.* ECB dates May 1811. Presence in the 'Novels and Romances' section of a number of
circulating library catalogues indicates a general audience; the tone is also adult.

1811:47   [?JOHNSTONE, Anthony Gregory].
RHYDISEL. THE DEVIL IN OXFORD. IN TWO VOLUMES.

> London: Printed for the Author; and sold by Sherwood, Neely, and Jones, Paternoster-
> Row, 1811.
> I xii, 256p; II iv, 318. 12mo. 10s 6d (ECB, ER).
> ER 18: 517 (Aug 1811); WSW I: 104.
> O G.A.Oxon.8° 88,89; ECB 491; NSTC J844 (BI E).

*Notes.* ECB dates *c.*1830, probably in error. Author attribution from the Bodleian catalogue,
which is repeated in NSTC; Wolff (Item 7556) lists as anonymous.

KETT, Henry, EMILY, A MORAL TALE
See 1809: 37

1811:48   LAFONTAINE, August [Heinrich Julius].
FAMILY QUARRELS. A NOVEL. IN THREE VOLUMES. BY AUGUSTUS
LAFONTAINE, AUTHOR OF "LOBENSTEIN VILLAGE,"—"THE RAKE
AND THE MISANTHROPE."—"BARON DE FLEMING,"—"HERMANN
AND EMILIA,"—"RODOLPHUS OF WERDENBURGH," "SAINT JULIEN,"
&C. &C.

> London: Printed and published by John Dean No. 7, Wardour Street, Soho: sold by all
> Booksellers, 1811.
> I 211p; II 216p; III 196p. 12mo. 15s (QR).
> QR 6: 563 (Dec 1811).
> BL 1152.b.1; NSTC L150.

*Notes.* Trans. of *Das Haus Barburg, oder der Familienzwist* (Berlin, 1805). 'The Translator's Preface', vol. 1, pp. [5]–13, points to the greater challenge presented by translation from the German
rather than French: 'The German novels are usually more difficult to translate, and contain
many more intricate passages than those of the French school' (p. [5]). The present title,
however, more closely matches *Les querelles de famille* (Paris, 1809), itself from the German.


1811:49   LAWRENCE, James [Henry].
THE EMPIRE OF THE NAIRS; OR, THE RIGHTS OF WOMEN. AN
UTOPIAN ROMANCE, IN TWELVE BOOKS. BY JAMES LAWRENCE,
AUTHOR OF "THE BOSOM FRIEND," "LOVE, AN ALLEGORY," ETC.
IN FOUR VOLUMES.

> London: Printed for T. Hookham, jun. and E. T. Hookham, No. 15, Old Bond Street,
> 1811.
> I viii, xliii, 216p; II 242p; III 254p; IV 262p, v. 12mo. 22s (ER, QR).
> ER 18: 517 (Aug 1811), 20: 502 (Nov 1812); QR 6: 309 (Oct 1811); WSW I: 365.
> BL 1459.b.5-6; NSTC L772.

*Notes.* Vol. 1 includes 'An Essay on the Nair System of Gallantry and Inheritance'. 'Advertisement', vol. 1, pp. [v]–viii, states that this Essay had been previously published, with the
encouragement of Wieland, in the *German Mercury* in 1793, and that the novel was similarly
published, with the encouragement of Schiller, in the *Journal der Romane* for 1801, 'under
the title of "*Das Paradies der Liebe*"', subsequently appearing again under the title *Das Reich
der Nairen*. The same Advertisement also describes a French translation by the present
author, published under the title of *L'Empire des Nairs* in 1803. It continues by explaining
that this English translation has been issued in an attempt to forestall another by 'a man of
letters' who 'has already delivered his manuscript to a bookseller'. See 1810: 29 for a possible
adv. for this putative rival version.
Further edns: 2nd edn. 1811 (NUC); 1813 (NUC); 1824 (NUC); French trans., 1814.


1811:50   LEADBEATER, Mary.
COTTAGE DIALOGUES AMONG THE IRISH PEASANTRY. BY MARY
LEADBEATER. WITH NOTES AND A PREFACE BY MARIA EDGE-
WORTH, AUTHOR OF CASTLE RACKRENT, &C.

> London: Printed for J. Johnson and Co. St. Paul's Churchyard, 1811.

v, 343p. 12mo. 12s (ECB, for 2 parts).
WSW I: 366.
BL 8275.aa.18; ECB 335; NSTC L877 (BI C, E, O).

*Notes.* Advertisement to the Reader, signed Maria Edgeworth, Edgeworth Town, 1 July 1810. 'Glossary and Notes for the Use of the English Reader' occupies pp. 269–343. ECB dates Apr 1811. This work was also published in a Dublin edn., 'Printed by J. and J. Carrick, Bachelor's-Walk, 1811', 167p, with a 'List of Subscribers', pp. iii–xi. It was followed by the same author's *Cottage Dialogues [. . .] Part Two* (Dublin, 1813), 140p, and *The Landlord's Friend, intended as a sequel to Cottage Dialogues* (Dublin, 1813), 113p. These short works, strongly polemical in character, are not itemised separately in this Bibliography.
Further edns: Dublin 1811 (NSTC); 4th edn. Dublin 1813 (NSTC); Philadelphia 1811 (NUC).

## LONEY, T. C., SEBASTIAN AND ISABEL; OR, THE INVISIBLE SWORD
See 1807: 39

## MACKENZIE, Anna Maria, ALMERIA D'AVEIRO; OR, THE IRISH GUARDIAN
See 1809: 45

### 1811: 51    MARCHANT, M. A.
*RUDOLPH AND ADELAIDE; OR, THE FORT OF ST. FERNANDOS. BY M. A. MARCHANT.

> London: Sherwood, 1811.
> 3 vols. 8vo.
> QR 6: 563 (Dec 1811).
> No copy located.

*Notes.* Publisher from Block and Summers; format from Summers.

### 1811: 52    MAXWELL, Caroline.
LAURA; OR THE INVISIBLE LOVER. A NOVEL, IN FOUR VOLUMES. DEDICATED BY PERMISSION, TO HER GRACE, THE DUTCHESS [*sic*] OF DEVONSHIRE, BY MRS. CAROLINE MAXWELL, AUTHOR OF "ALFRED OF NORMANDY;" "LIONEL;" AND THE "EARL OF DESMOND."

> London: Printed for the Author, and sold by E. Jones, 5, Newgate Street, and may be had of every Bookseller in the Kingdom, 1811.
> I xii, 211p; II 188p; III 131p; IV 153p. 12mo. 20s (adv. end of vol. 4).
> Corvey; CME 3-628-48204-6; xNSTC.

*Notes.* Dedication to the Duchess of Devonshire, signed 'Georgiana Caroline Maxwell. Upper Mary le-bone Street', 31 Jan 1811.

### 1811: 53    [MEEKE, Mary].
STRATAGEMS DEFEATED. A NOVEL. IN FOUR VOLUMES. BY GABRIELLI, AUTHOR OF LANGHTON PRIORY; MYSTERIOUS WIFE; MYSTERIOUS HUSBAND; HARCOURT, &C.

London: Printed at the Minerva-Press, for A. K. Newman and Co. (Successors to Lane, Newman, & Co.) Leadenhall Street, 1811.

I 348p; II 379p; III 379p; IV 370p. 12mo. 24s (ECB).

Corvey; CME 3-628-47858-8; ECB 565; xNSTC.

*Notes.* ECB dates May 1811.

1811:54 MONTOLIEU, [Jeanne-Isabelle-Pauline Polier de Bottens, Baronne] de; PLUNKETT, [Elizabeth] (*trans.*).

SENTIMENTAL ANECDOTES, BY MADAME DE MONTOLIEU, AUTHOR OF "TALES", "CAROLINE OF LICHFIELD [*sic*]," &C. &C. &C. IN TWO VOLUMES. TRANSLATED FROM THE FRENCH BY MRS. PLUNKETT, FORMERLY MISS GUNNING.

London: Printed for C. Chapple, Pall-Mall, opposite St. James's Palace, 1811.

I 154p; II 146p. 12mo. 7s (ECB).

O 249.s.272; ECB 393; NSTC P2363.

*Notes.* I Containing Eliza and Albert; II Containing Marcel; or, the Cobbler of the Cottage. Sophia; or, the Blind Girl. Eleonore; or, the Beautiful Eyes. Drop-head/running title vol. 1: 'Eliza and Albert: a Swiss Anecdote'; vol. 2: 'Marcel; or, the Cobbler of the Cottage' [3]–45; 'Sophia; or, the Blind Girl' [49]–94; 'Eleonore; or, the Beautiful Eyes' [97]–146. In vol. 2 each story has its own half-title; drop-head of 'Sophia' also includes 'The Recital of Henry P. at Twenty-five' and that of 'Eleonore' is headed 'Conclusion of the Blind Girl' and has 'The Recital of Henry P. at Thirty-five'. ECB dates Aug 1811.

Further edn: Philadelphia 1812 (NSTC).

MORGAN, Lady Sydney

See OWENSON, Sydney

1811:55 MOORE, Edward.

SIR RALPH DE BIGOD. A ROMANCE OF THE NINETEENTH CEN-TURY, INTERSPERSED WITH ANECDOTES OF REAL LIFE. IN FOUR VOLUMES. BY EDWARD MOORE, ESQ.

London: Printed at the Minerva-Press, for A. K. Newman and Co. (Successors to Lane, Newman, and Co.) Leadenhall-Street, 1811.

I 303p; II 300p; III 304p; IV 302p. 12mo. 21s (ECB, ER, QR).

ER 18: 517 (Aug 1811); QR 6: 309 (Oct 1811).

Corvey; CME 3-628-48278-X; ECB 375; xNSTC.

*Notes.* ECB gives author as 'Edwd. Mawe'.

MOORE, George, THE MARRIED MAN and TALES OF THE PASSIONS

See 1808: 80

1811:56 MORIARTY, H[enrietta] M[aria].

BRIGHTON IN AN UPROAR; COMPRISING ANECDOTES OF SIR TIM-OTHY FLIGHT, MR. ABRAHAMS, SOLOMONS, ALIAS MODISH AND

FAMILY, &C. &C. &C. A NOVEL, FOUNDED ON FACTS, BY H. M.
MORIARTY . . . IN TWO VOLUMES.

> London: Printed for, and sold by the Author, 29, Villier's-Street, Strand; and by all the
> Booksellers, 1811.
> I 240p; II 200p. 12mo. 12s (QR).
> QR 6: 563 (Dec 1811).
> BL 12654.t.24; ECB 396; NSTC M3282.

*Notes.* Further edn: 2nd edn. 1811 (NSTC).


1811: 57   MOWER, Arthur.
THE WELCH MOUNTAINEER. BY ARTHUR MOWER. IN TWO VOL-
UMES.

> London: Printed for B. Crosby and Co. Stationers' Court, Paternoster Row, by F. Vig-
> urs, 5, Princes Street, Leicester Square, 1811.
> I xix, 147p; II 128p. 12mo. 8s (ECB, ER); 7s (ER, QR).
> ER 18: 517 (Aug 1811), 19: 252 (Nov 1811); QR 6: 309 (Oct 1811); WSW I: 412.
> Corvey; CME 3-628-48389-1; ECB 399; NSTC M3508 (BI BL).

*Notes.* Dedication 'The Author, to Himself', dated London, May 1811. Preface complaining
of the superfluity and similarity of novels, dated London, June 1811. ER Aug 1811 prices at 8s.


1811: 58   [MUDFORD, William].
THE LIFE AND ADVENTURES OF PAUL PLAINTIVE, ESQ. AN
AUTHOR. COMPILED FROM ORIGINAL DOCUMENTS, AND INTER-
SPERSED WITH SPECIMENS OF HIS GENIUS, IN PROSE AND
POETRY. BY MARTIN GRIBALDUS SWAMMERDAM, (HIS NEPHEW
AND EXECUTOR.)

> London: Printed by W. Flint, Old Bailey; for Sherwood, Neely, and Jones, Paternoster-
> Row, 1811.
> I xxii, 237p; II 264p. 12mo. 10s 6d (ER, QR).
> ER 19: 252 (Nov 1811); QR 6: 563 (Dec 1811); WSW I: 413.
> BL 1152.b.7; NSTC M3541 (BI O).

*Notes.* 'Dedication to William Mudford', signed M. G. Swammerdam, 20 Aug 1811. This is
followed by a separate Preface dated 17 Aug 1811, signed M. G. S.


1811: 59   [NARES, Edward].
THINK'S-I-TO-MYSELF. A SERIO-LUDICRO, TRAGICO-COMICO
TALE, WRITTEN BY THINK'S-I-TO-MYSELF WHO? IN TWO VOL-
UMES.

> London: Printed by Law and Gilbert, St. John's Square, Clerkenwell: and sold by Sher-
> wood, Neely, and Jones, 20, Paternoster Row; Hatchard, Piccadilly; and Asperne,
> Cornhill, 1811.
> I 226p; II 206p. 12mo. 10s 6d (ER, QR); 10s 6d boards (ER).
> ER 18: 265 (May 1811), 18: 517 (Aug 1811); QR 5: 537 (May 1811); WSW I: 415.
> BL 12612.d.18; NSTC N290.

*Notes.* Further edns: 2nd edn. 1811 (NSTC); 3rd edn. 1811 (NSTC); 5th edn. 1811 (NSTC); 6th edn. 1812 (NSTC); 7th edn. 1812 (NUC); [at least 4 more edns. to 1850]; Boston 1812 (NUC) [also New York 1812 (NUC)]; German trans., 1827.

1811:60   O'KEEFFE, {Adelaide}.
PATRIARCHAL TIMES; OR, THE LAND OF CANAAN: A FIGURATIVE HISTORY, IN SEVEN BOOKS. COMPRISING INTERESTING EVENTS, INCIDENTS, & CHARACTERS, FOUNDED ON THE HOLY SCRIP-TURES. BY MISS O'KEEFFE. IN TWO VOLUMES.

> London: Printed by J. Dennett, Leather Lane, Holborn; for Gale and Curtis, Paternos-ter Row; J. Hatchard, Piccadilly; and T. Williams, Stationers' Court, 1811.
> I ii, ii, 286p; II 360p. 12mo. 10s 6d (ECB).
> WSW I: 420.
> BL 4414.ee.6; ECB 421; NSTC O247 (BI C, O).

*Notes.* Prefatory statement that 'the subject of this Work begins at the Eighth Verse of the Twenty-first Chapter of Genesis, and ends at the Twenty-ninth verse of the Forty-sixth Chapter', signed Adelaide O'Keeffe, Greenford, Middlesex, Apr 1811. ECB dates Apr 1811. Further edns: 3rd edn. 1820 (Corvey), CME 3-628-48247-X; 4th edn. 1826 (NSTC); New York 1822 (NUC).

1811:61   OWENSON, [Sydney] [afterwards MORGAN, Lady Sydney].
THE MISSIONARY: AN INDIAN TALE. BY MISS OWENSON. WITH A PORTRAIT OF THE AUTHOR. IN THREE VOLUMES.

> London: Printed for J. J. Stockdale, No. 41, Pall Mall, 1811.
> I 228p, ill.; II 255p; III 222p. 12mo. 21s (ER, QR).
> ER 18: 265 (May 1811); QR 5: 537 (May 1811); WSW I: 425–6.
> Dt OLS.188.o.102-104; NSTC O731.

*Notes.* Frontispiece portrait of Miss Owenson based on a drawing by Sir Thomas Lawrence, who is not however named. Dedication to the Marchioness of Abercorn. 'Notice' by the Pub-lisher at end of vol. 3, drawing attention to another of his publications, 'The History of the Inquisitions'; verso of this unn. leaf carries adv. for 'Calcutta, a Poem', 'this day published'. Further edns: 2nd edn. 1811 (NSTC); 3rd edn. 1811 (Corvey), CME 3-628-48324-7; 4th edn. 1811 (NUC); New York 1811 (NUC); French trans., 1812; German trans., 1825 [as *Die Prophetin von Caschimir, oder Glaubenskraft und Liebesglück* (RS)].

1811:62   PALMER, Alicia Tyndal.
THE SONS OF ALTRINGHAM, A NOVEL. IN THREE VOLUMES. BY ALICIA TYNDAL PALMER, AUTHOR OF "THE HUSBAND AND THE LOVER," AND "THE DAUGHTERS OF ISENBERG."

> London: Printed for Lackington, Allen, and Co. Temple of the Muses, Finsbury Square, 1811.
> I 399p; II 390p; III 328p. 12mo. 18s (ECB, QR).
> QR 7: 231 (Mar 1812); WSW I: 427.
> Corvey; CME 3-628-48377-8; ECB 430; NSTC P169 (BI BL).

*Notes.* Drop-head sub-title vol. 1: 'Cecil, or the Vengeance of the redeemed Captive'; vol. 2: 'Mortimer, or, the Election and the Four-in-Hand Club'; vol. 3: 'Orlando; or, the matrimonial Contest for Snap-Dragon Lodge'.

1811: 63    PALMER, John.
LIKE MASTER LIKE MAN: A NOVEL. IN TWO VOLUMES. BY THE LATE JOHN PALMER, (OF THE THEATRE ROYAL, IN THE HAYMARKET:) SON TO THE DECEASED AND CELEBRATED JOHN PALMER, OF THE THEATRE ROYAL DRURY-LANE, AND OF THE ABOVE MENTION'D THEATRE. WITH A PREFACE, BY GEORGE COLMAN, THE YOUNGER.

> London: Printed *for the Relief of the Author's Widow*, and sold by W. Earle, at his Original English and Foreign Library, Albemarle Street, Piccadilly, 1811.
> I xxxii, 261p; II 213p. 12mo. 12s (ECB).
> BL 12613.bbb.30; ECB 430; NSTC P175 (BI O).

*Notes.* Preface, signed 'George Colman, The Younger' and dated 10 Apr 1811, followed by 'List of Subscribers' (*c.*85 names), pp.[xxix]–xxxii. ECB dates July 1811.

1811: 64    PARKER, Emma.
ELFRIDA, HEIRESS OF BELGROVE. A NOVEL, IN FOUR VOLUMES. BY EMMA PARKER.

> London: Printed for B. Crosby and Co., Stationer's Court, Paternoster Row; J. Painter, Wrexham, and Wright and Cruikshanks, Liverpool, 1811.
> I 262p; II 320p; III 416p; IV 318p. 12mo. 20s (ECB, ER, QR).
> ER 17: 500 (Feb 1811); QR 5: 267 (Feb 1811); WSW I: 428–9.
> Corvey; CME 3-628-48385-9; ECB 433; NSTC P394 (BI BL, C).

*Notes.* ECB dates Dec 1810.

1811: 65    [PARKER, Emma].
FITZ-EDWARD; OR, THE CAMBRIANS. A NOVEL. INTERSPERSED WITH PIECES OF POETRY. IN THREE VOLUMES. BY EMMA DE LISLE, AUTHOR OF A SOLDIER'S OFFSPRING, ELFRIDA, OR THE HEIRESS OF BELLEGROVE, &C. &C.

> London: Printed at the Minerva-Press, for A. K. Newman and Co. (Successors to Lane, Newman, & Co.) Leadenhall-Street, 1811.
> I iii, 235p; II 204p; III 210p. 12mo. 15s (ECB, ER); 15s boards (QR).
> ER 18: 517 (Aug 1811); QR 5: 537 (May 1811).
> Corvey; CME 3-628-48105-8; ECB 158; NSTC D800 (BI E).

*Notes.* Preface reads: 'It is necessary here to observe, that this Work would have appeared many months since; but, owing to a mistake, another manuscript, the production of *another* author, was sent to the press instead of *mine*, and, through inadvertency, printed under a similar supposition. *This* has already been explained as far as it was possible; and I have only here to add, that the following Work is *that* which *was* announced some months ago, as being *about* to be published under the title of "Eva of Cambria;" but as another person's Novel has, through an error, been published under that name, it was necessary to give a new title to the present Work.' Amelia Beauclerc was probably the true author of the published *Eva of Cambria* (see 1811: 19).

1811: 66   PARKER, Emma.
VIRGINIA; OR THE PEACE OF AMIENS. A NOVEL. IN FOUR VOL-
UMES. BY MISS EMMA PARKER, AUTHOR OF ELFRIDA, HEIRESS OF
BELGROVE.

> London: Printed for B. Crosby and Co. Stationers'-Court, Ludgate-Hill, 1811.
> I xii, 376p; II xi, 348p; III xi, 336p; IV xii, 344p. 12mo. 24s (ECB, ER, QR).
> ER 19: 252 (Nov 1811); QR 6: 309 (Oct 1811); WSW I: 429.
> Corvey; CME 3-628-48423-5; ECB 433; xNSTC.

*Notes.* All four vols. prefaced by a 'Prelude'.

1811: 67   PHILLIPS, Charles.
*THE LOVES OF CELESTINE AND ST. AUBERT: A ROMANTIC TALE.
BY CHARLES PHILLIPS, A.B., AND STUDENT OF THE MIDDLE
TEMPLE. WITH A PORTRAIT OF AUTHOR. IN TWO VOLUMES.

> London: Printed for J. J. Stockdale, No. 41, Pall Mall, 1811.
> I viii, 130p, ill.; II 127p. 12mo. 10s 6d (ER).
> ER 18: 265 (May 1811); WSW I: 437.
> No copy of 1st edn. located.

*Notes.* Details follow 2nd edn. of 1811 (O 249.r.13,14; NSTC P1503). The Bodleian copy has a Dedication 'to Madame la Comtesse de St. Marguerite', dated 31 Jan 1811, 1, Duke Street, Adelphi; but wants the portrait.

1811: 68   [RHODES, Henrietta].
ROSALIE; OR, THE CASTLE OF MONTALABRETTI. IN FOUR VOL-
UMES.

> Richmond: Printed for Longman, Hurst, Rees, Orme, and Brown, Paternoster Row,
> London, 1811.
> I vi, 215p; II 200p; III 221p; IV 313p. 12mo. 20s (ECB, QR).
> QR 6: 563 (Dec 1811); WSW I: 462.
> Corvey; CME 3-628-48514-2; ECB 502; xNSTC.

*Notes.* Preface states: 'The story of *Bianca Capello*, has already appeared in Print; but it is so well deserving of being better known, that the Author hopes to be pardoned, for having introduced it'.

1811: 69   ROSE, Edward [H.].
THE SEA-DEVIL, OR, SON OF A BELLOWS-MENDER. A TRAGI-
COMIC ROMANCE OF THE PRESENT DAY. IN TWO VOLUMES. BY
EDWARD ROSE, SEAMAN.

> Plymouth-Dock: Printed and published by J. Roach; and may be had of the principal
> Booksellers in Town and Country, 1811.

I xi, 188p; II 188p. 12mo. 9s (QR).

QR 7: 231 (Mar 1812); WSW I: 473.

BL 12613.f.17; ECB 502; NSTC R1657.

*Notes.* Summers notes (p. 497): 'Vol. 1 was written by Edward H. Rose who died before the work was completed. Vol. 2 was written by Mr. Wild'.

Further edn: 2nd edn. 1818 (Corvey), CME 3-628-48549-5.

1811: 70     [ROSS, Mrs].

**THE COUSINS; OR, A WOMAN'S PROMISE AND A LOVER'S VOW. A NOVEL. IN THREE VOLUMES.**

> London: Printed at the Minerva-Press, for A. K. Newman and Co. (Successors to Lane, Newman, & Co.) Leadenhall-Street, 1811.
>
> I 214p; II 204p; III 223p. 12mo. 15s (ECB, ER, QR).
>
> ER 19: 252 (Nov 1811); QR 6: 309 (Oct 1811).
>
> Corvey; CME 3-628-47346-2; ECB 503; xNSTC.

1811: 71     S——, Mrs.

**GOTHA: OR, MEMOIRS OF THE WURTZBURG FAMILY. FOUNDED ON FACTS. IN TWO VOLUMES. BY MRS. S——.**

> London: Printed for C. Chapple, Pall Mall, opposite St. James's Palace, 1811.
>
> I 309p; II 279p. 12mo. 18s (ER, QR); 13s (ECB, ER, QR).
>
> ER 18: 517 (Aug 1811), 20: 502 (Nov 1812); QR 5: 537 (May 1811), 6: 309 (Oct 1811), 7: 471 (June 1812); WSW I: 476.
>
> Corvey; CME 3-628-47795-6; ECB 237; xNSTC.

*Notes.* ECB dates Mar 1812. ER 2nd citation (Nov 1812) and QR 3rd citation (June 1812) give price as 13s.

1811: 72     [SHELLEY, Percy Bysshe].

**ST. IRVYNE; OR, THE ROSICRUCIAN: A ROMANCE. BY A GENTLE-MAN OF THE UNIVERSITY OF OXFORD.**

> London: Printed for J. J. Stockdale, 41, Pall Mall, 1811.
>
> 236p. 12mo. 4s (ECB); 6s (ER, QR).
>
> ER 17: 500 (Feb 1811); QR 5: 267 (Feb 1811); WSW I: 497.
>
> Corvey; CME 3-628-48489-8; ECB 511; NSTC S1640 (BI BL, O).

*Notes.* Further edn: 1822 (NSTC).

Facs: GNIII (1977).

1811: 73     SLEATH, Eleanor.

**PYRENEAN BANDITTI. A ROMANCE. IN THREE VOLUMES. BY ELEANOR SLEATH, AUTHOR OF THE NOCTURNAL MINSTREL, BRISTOL HEIRESS, WHO'S THE MURDERER, &C. &C.**

> London: Printed at the Minerva-Press, for A. K. Newman and Co. (Successors to Lane, Newman, and Co.) Leadenhall-Street, 1811.

I 243p; II 243p; III 225p. 12mo. 15s (ECB).
Corvey; CME 3-628-48756-0; ECB 476; xNSTC.

*Notes.* ECB dates *c.*1810.

1811: 74   SMITH, [Catherine].
THE CALEDONIAN BANDIT; OR, THE HEIR OF DUNCAETHAL. A
ROMANCE OF THE THIRTEENTH CENTURY. IN TWO VOLUMES. BY
MRS. SMITH, OF THE THEATRE-ROYAL, HAYMARKET.

London: Printed at the Minerva-Press, for A. K. Newman and Co. (Successors to Lane,
Newman, and Co.) Leadenhall-Street, 1811.
I ii, 242p; II 233p. 12mo. 10s (ECB, ER, QR).
ER 19: 252 (Nov 1811); QR 6: 309 (Oct 1811).
Corvey; CME 3-628-48759-5; ECB 544; xNSTC.

*Notes.* ER and QR both have 'Banditti' rather than 'Bandit' in title.

1811: 75   [SOUZA-BOTELHO, Adélaide-Marie-Émilie Filleul, Marquise de
Flahaut].
A PEEP INTO THE THUILLERIES; OR, PARISIAN MANNERS: INCLUD-
ING THE AMOURS OF EUGENE DE ROTHELIN. A NOVEL, IN TWO
VOLUMES. BY THE AUTHOR OF 'ADELA DE SENANGE'.

London: Printed and published by Allen & Co. No.15, Paternoster-Row, 1811.
I 228p; II 185p. 12mo.
BL 12611.c.32; NSTC T1807.

*Notes.* Trans. of *Eugène de Rothelin* (Paris, 1808). Drop-head title in vol. 1 reads: 'Eugene de
Rothlin' [*sic*]; in vol. 2 'Eugene de Rothelin'.

1811: 76   SUMMERSETT, Henry.
ALL SORTS OF LOVERS; OR, INDISCRETION, TRUTH, AND PER-
FIDY. A NOVEL. IN THREE VOLUMES. BY HENRY SUMMERSETT,
AUTHOR OF THE FATE OF SEDLEY, LEOPOLD WARNDORFF, &C.

London: Printed at the Minerva-Press, for A. K. Newman and Co. (Successors to Lane,
Newman, & Co.) Leadenhall-Street, 1811.
I 234p; II 236p; III 278p. 12mo.
Corvey; CME 3-628-48733-1; ECB 569; xNSTC.

*Notes.* Blakey (copy not seen) and ECB date 1805, but no further evidence for an earlier edn.
discovered.

1811: 77   [THOMAS, Elizabeth].
MORTIMER HALL; OR, THE LABOURER'S HIRE. A NOVEL. IN FOUR
VOLUMES. BY MRS. BRIDGET BLUEMANTLE, AUTHOR OF HUS-
BAND AND WIFE, THREE OLD MAIDS OF THE HOUSE OF PENRUD-
DOCK, MONTE VIDEO, &C. &C.

London: Printed at the Minerva-Press, for A. K. Newman and Co. (Successors to Lane,
Newman, & Co.) Leadenhall-Street, 1811.

I 245p; II 216p; III 227p; IV 236p. 12mo. 21s (ECB, ER, QR).
ER 18: 517 (Aug 1811); QR 5: 537 (May 1811).
Corvey; CME 3-628-47127-3; ECB 63; xNSTC.

1811: 78   TICKEN, William.
SANTOS DE MONTENOS; OR, ANNALS OF A PATRIOT FAMILY.
FOUNDED ON RECENT FACTS. IN THREE VOLS. BY WILLIAM
TICKEN, ESQ.

> London: Printed for N. L. Pannier, Bookseller to His R.H. The Duke of Kent, at the Eng-
> lish, Foreign and Classical Library, 15, Leicester-Place, Leicester-Square, and sold by
> J. M. Richardson, 23, Corn-Hill, and all Booksellers, 1811.
> I vii, 222p; II 205p; III 186p. 8vo. 18s (ECB, ER).
> ER 19: 252 (Nov 1811).
> Corvey; CME 3-628-48960-1; ECB 590; NSTC T1112 (BI BL).

*Notes.* Dedication to the recently-deceased Duke of Alburquerque[*sic*], 'by the Publisher',
dated 17 May 1811.

1811: 79   WIGLEY, {Sarah}.
GLENCARRON: A SCOTTISH TALE. IN THREE VOLUMES. BY MISS
WIGLEY.

> London: Printed for Henry Colburn, English and Foreign Public Library, Conduit-
> Street, New Bond-Street, 1811.
> I 231p; II 222p; III 240p. 12mo. 15s (ECB).
> Corvey; CME 3-628-48921-0; ECB 637; xNSTC.

*Notes.* Dedication to the Marquis of Huntly, signed Sarah Wigley, High Street, Mary-le-
bone, 15 May 1811, at beginning of vol. 3; followed by 'Subscribers' (4 pp. unn.), including
87 names. ECB dates Aug 1811.

1811: 80   WILSON, C[harles] H[enry].
THE IRISH VALET; OR, WHIMSICAL ADVENTURES OF PADDY
O'HALORAN: WHO, AFTER BEING SERVANT TO SEVERAL MASTERS,
BECAME MASTER OF MANY SERVANTS. BY THE LATE C. H. WILSON,
ESQ. OF THE MIDDLE TEMPLE. AUTHOR OF POLYANTHEA,
BROOKIANA, BEAUTIES OF BURKE, WANDERING ISLANDER, &C.
&C. TO WHICH IS PREFIXED, THE LIFE OF THE AUTHOR.

> London: Printed and published by M. Allen, No. 15, Paternoster-Row, 1811.
> xxiv, 192p. 12mo. 5s (ER).
> ER 18: 265 (May 1811); WSW I: 565.
> D Ir.8237.g.W1; NSTC W2254 (BI O).

*Notes.* Dedication 'to the Right Honorable Earl Moira', signed 'the Editor'.

1812: 1 ANON.

## THE ADVENTURES OF AN OSTRICH FEATHER OF QUALITY.

London: Printed for Sherwood, Neely, and Jones, Paternoster-Row, 1812.
155p. 8vo. 4s (ECB).
WSW I: 7–8.
MH-H 19463.001.10*; ECB 6; NSTC A489 (BI BL).

*Notes.* ECB lists Allman as publisher.
Further edn: 2nd edn. 1819 (Corvey), CME 3-628-47020-X. Corvey 2nd edn. t.p. reads: 'By the author of "The Intriguing Beauty, and the Beauty without Intrigue"'; and imprint is 'London: Printed for T. and J. Allman, Princes Street, Hanover Square; and Baldwin, Cradock, and Joy, Paternoster-Row, 1819'.

1812: 2 ANON.

## ALEXIS, THE TYRANT OF THE EAST. A PERSIAN TALE.

London: Printed for Henry Colburn, Public Library, Conduit-Street, Hanover-Square, 1812.
iv, 194p. 12mo. 5s (ECB, ER, QR).
ER 19: 511 (Feb 1812); QR 7: 231 (Mar 1812).
BL 1489.t.83; ECB 11; NSTC A876.

*Notes.* ECB dates Dec 1811.

1812: 3 ANON.

## THE BOOK!! OR, PROCRASTINATED MEMOIRS. AN HISTORICAL ROMANCE.

London: Printed for Sherwood, Neely, and Jones, Paternoster-Row, 1812.
x, 174p. 12mo.
BL 012633.m.34; NSTC B3601.

*Notes.* See Olivia Wilmot Serres's *Memoirs of a Princess* (1812: 54) for possible clue to authorship. Collates in sixes.

## THE CAPRICIOUS MOTHER

See 1816: 27

1812: 4 ANON.

## ELTON; OR, THE HEROINE OF SORROW. A NOVEL.

London: Printed for E. Wilson, No. 88, Cornhill: by E. Thomas, Golden-Lane, 1812.
vi, 207p. 12mo. 7s (ECB).
BL 12614.aaa.13; ECB 185; NSTC E757.

1812: 5   ANON.
*FRIENDS AND LOVERS.
> London: Chapple, 1812.
> 3 vols. 15s (ER, QR).
> ER 19: 511 (Feb 1812); QR 7: 231 (Mar 1812).
> No copy located.

*Notes.* Publisher from Bent22.

1812: 6   ANON.
I'LL CONSIDER OF IT! A TALE, IN THREE VOLUMES, IN WHICH "THINKS I TO MYSELF" IS PARTIALLY CONSIDERED.
> London: Printed for Thomas Tegg, No. 111, Cheapside, 1812.
> I 225p; II 215p; III 219p. 12mo. 21s (ER, QR).
> ER 20: 501 (Nov 1812); QR 7: 471 (June 1812); WSW I: 56.
> Corvey; CME 3-628-47880-4; NSTC I1 (BI BL, O).

*Notes.* NSTC (N280) attributes to Edward Nares.

1812: 7   ANON.
LAURA BLUNDEL AND HER FATHER. A NOVEL. IN THREE VOL-UMES.
> London: Printed at the Minerva-Press, for A. K. Newman and Co. Leadenhall-Street, 1812.
> I iv, 223p; II 203p; III 206p. 12mo. 15s (ECB, ER, QR).
> ER 20: 252 (July 1812); QR 7: 471 (June 1812).
> Corvey; CME 3-628-47971-1; ECB 332; NSTC B3423 (BI BL).

*Notes.* Preface dated Jan 1812.

1812: 8   ANON.
THE LENNOX FAMILY; OR, WHAT D'YE THINK OF THE WORLD? A NOVEL, IN THREE VOLUMES.
> London: Printed for J. Rodwell (Successor to Mr. Faulder), New Bond-Street, 1812.
> I iv, 249p; II 246p; III 258p. 12mo. 18s (ECB, QR).
> QR 7: 471 (June 1812); WSW I: 65.
> Corvey; CME 3-628-48101-5; ECB 338; NSTC L1161 (BI E).

1812: 9   ANON.
MONTGOMERY; OR, THE WEST-INDIAN ADVENTURER. A NOVEL, IN THREE VOLUMES. BY A GENTLEMAN RESIDENT IN THE WEST-INDIES.
> Jamaica: Printed at the Office of the Kingston Chronicle, 1812.
> I xiii, 368p; II vii, 461p; III viii, 523p. 8vo.
> WSW I: 79.
> Corvey; CME 3-628-48273-9; NSTC M2934 (BI BL, E).

*Notes.* 'To the Reader' dated Jamaica, 1811. Presence in Corvey and in WSW both indicate a circulation in Britain.

1812: 10   ANON.

MY OWN TIMES, A NOVEL. CONTAINING INFORMATION ON THE LATEST FASHIONS, THE IMPROVED MORALS, THE VIRTUOUS EDUCATION, AND THE IMPORTANT AVOCATIONS OF HIGH LIFE. TAKEN FROM "THE BEST AUTHORITIES," AND DEDICATED, WITHOUT PERMISSION, TO "THOSE WHO WILL UNDERSTAND IT."

> London: Printed for Longman, Hurst, Rees, Orme, & Brown, Paternoster-Row, 1812.
> I 237p; II 216p. 12mo. 9s (ECB).
> WSW I: 81.
> Corvey; CME 3-628-48175-9; ECB 403; xNSTC.

*Notes.* ECB dates Oct 1812.

1812: 11   ANON.

OLD TIMES AND NEW; OR, SIR LIONEL AND HIS PROTEGÉE. A NOVEL. IN FOUR VOLUMES.

> London: Printed at the Minerva-Press, for A. K. Newman and Co. Leadenhall-Street, 1812.
> I viii, 238p; II 268p; III 272p; IV 268p. 12mo. 22s (ECB, ER).
> ER 20: 502 (Nov 1812); WSW I: 86.
> Corvey; CME 3-628-48573-8; ECB 422; xNSTC.

*Notes.* 'Introduction' indicates female authorship.

1812: 12   ANON.

A PEEP AT THE THEATRES! AND BIRD'S-EYE VIEWS OF MEN IN THE JUBILEE YEAR! A NOVEL, SATIRICAL, CRITICAL, AND MORAL, IN THREE VOLUMES; BY AN OLD NAVAL OFFICER.

> London: Printed for C. Chapple, Pall-Mall, 1812.
> I xii, 231p; II 254p, III 276p. 12mo. 18s (ECB, QR).
> QR 7: 231 (Mar 1812).
> MH-H 19463.43.A*; ECB 440; xNSTC.

*Notes.* 'List of Subscribers' (30 listed), vol. 1, pp. [v]–vi. Prefatory address 'To the Subscribers', dated Pall-Mall, Feb 1812. Dedications to the Prince Regent, vol. 1, to the Duke of York, vol. 2, and to the Duke of Kent, vol. 3.

1812: 13   ANON.

THE PROFLIGATE PRINCE; OR COURT OF ETHELRED. A NOVEL.

> London: Printed by W. Oxberry, 11, Clarendon Square, Somers Town. Published by Sherwood, Neely, and Jones, Paternoster-Row, 1812.
> 223p. 12mo. 5s (ECB).
> BL 12604.df.29; ECB 472; NSTC P3107.

1812: 14   ANON.

A SEQUEL TO CŒLEBS; OR, THE STANLEY LETTERS: CONTAINING OBSERVATIONS ON RELIGION AND MORALS; WITH ANECDOTES FOUNDED ON FACT.

London: Published by M. Jones, No. 5, Newgate-Street and sold by Setchell and Son, 23, King-Street, Covent Garden; Booth, Duke-Street, Portland-Place; Mercer, 230, Piccadilly, 1812.

iv, 372p. 12mo. 8s (ECB, ER).

ER 20: 502 (Nov 1812); WSW I: 110.

BL 4371.aaa.20; ECB 527; NSTC B563.

*Notes.* Dedication to Mrs M., signed F. Barlow, jun. and dated New College, 15 Jan 1812. Consists of letters between Dr Barlow, a character in the original Hannah More novel (see 1808: 81), and members of his family.

1812: 15    ANON.
### SILVANELLA, OR THE GYPSEY; A NOVEL. IN FOUR VOLUMES.

Gloucester: Printed by Joseph Wood, for Longman, Hurst, Rees, Orme, and Browne [*sic*], Pater-Noster-Row, [London;] Brisley, Stroud; and Washbourn, Gloucester, 1812.

I xii, 251p; II 279p; III 267p; IV 224p. 12mo. 21s (ER).

ER 20: 502 (Nov 1812); WSW I: 111.

BL 12611.dd.9; ECB 537; NSTC S1967.

*Notes.* In the case of the t.ps. for vols. 2–4, the line reading 'for Longman [...] London' is covered by a piece of paper stuck over this part of the imprint; in vol. 1 it has been removed, though 'London' is still obscured. Prefatory poem 'To a Fair Friend' (1 p. unn.), with footnote: 'These lines are contributed by a literary friend of the Authoress's'. 'List of Subscribers, to Silvanella, or The Gypsey', vol. 1, pp. [v]–xii, beginning with 'His Royal Highness the Duke of Clarence' and 'His Royal Highness the Duke of Cumberland' (in all *c*.185, a large number from Gloucestershire; plus two additional names in hand on BL copy).
Futher edn: 1812 (Corvey), CME 3-628-48699-8. Imprint details on Corvey copy read: 'London: Printed at the Minerva-Press, for A. K. Newman and Co. Leadenhall-Street, 1812'; and title is spelt 'Gipsey'. This Minerva edn. also includes the subscription list.

1812: 16    ANON.
### SUBSTANCE AND SHADOW; OR, THE FISHERMAN'S DAUGHTERS OF BRIGHTON. A PATCHWORK STORY. IN FOUR VOLUMES. BY THE AUTHOR OF LIGHT AND SHADE; EVERSFIELD ABBEY; BANKS OF THE WYE; AUNT AND NIECE, &C. &C.

London: Printed at the Minerva-Press, for A. K. Newman and Co. Leadenhall-Street, 1812.

I 221p; II 264p; III 265p; IV 288p. 12mo. 22s (ER).

ER 20: 502 (Nov 1812).

Corvey; CME 3-628-48687-4; NSTC B4322 (BI BL).

*Notes.* Attributed in some catalogues to Mrs E. G. Bayfield, and also connected with a chain of novels associated with J. H. James, though authorship by either of these seems unlikely: see 1807: 7 and 1808: 1.

1812: 17    ANON.
### *WILLIAM AND AZUBAH; OR, THE ALPINE RECESS, A NOVEL.

London: Crosby, 1812.
2 vols. 12mo. 8s (ECB).
No copy located; ECB 638.

*Notes.* Extended title from Block, who gives *New Monthly Magazine* as source.

1812: 18   ANON.
YAMBOO; OR, THE NORTH AMERICAN SLAVE. A TALE. IN THREE
VOLUMES. BY THE AUTHOR OF THE BRAVO OF BOHEMIA.

London: Printed at the Minerva-Press, for A. K. Newman and Co. Leadenhall-Street,
1812.
I 243p; II 270p; III 216p. 12mo. 15s (ECB, QR).
QR 6: 563 (Dec 1811).
Corvey; CME 3-628-47474-4; ECB 651; xNSTC.

*Notes.* Dedication to 'Major-General Hunter, President of his Majesty's Hon. Privy Council,
and Commander in Chief of the Province of New Brunswick', dated Frederictown, New
Brunswick, British North America, 5 Feb 1811. ECB dates Nov 1811.

1812: 19   ASHE, Thomas.
THE LIBERAL CRITIC; OR, MEMOIRS OF HENRY PERCY. CONVEY-
ING A CORRECT ESTIMATE OF THE MANNERS AND PRINCIPLES OF
THE PRESENT TIMES. BY THOMAS ASHE, ESQ. AUTHOR OF THE
SPIRIT OF THE BOOK; TRAVELS IN AMERICA, &C. &C.

London: Printed for B. and R. Crosby and Co. Stationers' Court, Paternoster Row,
1812.
I 360p; II 364p; III 332p. 12mo. 21s (ECB); 21s boards (ER, QR).
ER 20: 252 (July 1812); QR 7: 231 (Mar 1812), 7: 471 (June 1812); WSW I: 135.
Corvey; CME 3-628-47074-9; ECB 28; NSTC A1806 (BI BL, O).

BARLOW, F. jun., A SEQUEL TO CŒLEBS
See 1812: 14

1812: 20   [?BAYLEY, Catharine].
A SET-DOWN AT COURT; INCLUDING A SERIES OF ANECDOTES IN
HIGH LIFE, AND THE HISTORY OF MONTHEMAR. A NOVEL,
FOUNDED ON FACT. IN FOUR VOLUMES. BY KATE MONT ALBION,
AUTHOR OF "CALEDONIA,"— "LOVER'S LABOURS,"— "SPANISH
LADY AND NORMAN KNIGHT," &C. &C.

London: Printed and published by Allen & Co. No. 15, Paternoster-Row, 1812/16.
I (1812) iv, 220p; II (1816) 212p; III (1816) 223p; IV (1812) 202p. 12mo. 21s (ER, QR).
ER 20: 502 (Nov 1812); QR 7: 471 (June 1812).
O 256.e.16177; NSTC B1041.

*Notes.* Vols. 2 and 3 have a different t.p., with 'The Haut-Ton' as the main title, and 'Mrs. Bayley' given as author. This indicates a reissuing of the work by Allen & Co. in 1816. Catharine

Bayley was the acknowledged author of *Vacation Evenings*, and the translator of Voltaire's *Zadig and Astarte*.

1812: 21 [BEAUCLERC, Amelia].
ALINDA, OR THE CHILD OF MYSTERY. A NOVEL. IN FOUR VOL-
UMES. BY THE AUTHOR OF "ORA AND JULIET, CASTLE OF TAR-
IFFA, &C."

London: Printed for B. and R. Crosby and Co. Stationers' Court, Ludgate Street, 1812.
I 288p; II 312p; III 336p; IV 356p. 12mo. 20s (ECB, ER).
ER 21: 258 (Feb 1813); WSW I: 240.
Corvey; CME 3-628-47042-0; ECB 12; NSTC B1129 (BI BL).

1812: 22 [BEAUCLERC, Amelia].
THE CASTLE OF TARIFFA; OR, THE SELF-BANISHED MAN. A
NOVEL. IN FOUR VOLUMES. BY THE AUTHOR OF THE FUGITIVE
DAUGHTER, OR EVA OF CAMBRIA, ORA AND JULIET, OR INFLU-
ENCE OF FIRST PRINCIPLES.

London: Printed for B. Crosby and Co. Stationers' Court, Paternoster Row, 1812.
I 288p; II 332p; III 248p; IV 292p. 12mo. 20s (ECB, QR).
QR 7: 231 (Mar 1812).
Corvey; CME 3-628-47250-4; ECB 100; NSTC T190 (BI BL).

1812: 23 [?BENGER, Elizabeth Ogilvy or ?PILE, Barbara].
MARIAN, A NOVEL. IN THREE VOLUMES.

Edinburgh: Printed for Manners and Miller; and Longman, Hurst, Rees, Orme, and
Brown, London, 1812.
I 288p; II 271p; III 250p. 12mo. 15s (ECB, ER, QR).
ER 19: 511 (Feb 1812); QR 7: 471 (June 1812).
Corvey; CME 3-628-48156-2; ECB 368; NSTC M1135 (BI BL, E, O).

*Notes.* Benger is given as the author in FC and NUC; Mme.[?] Barbara Pile is listed as apparently the author in Bentley (p. 94) (also spelt Pilon (p. 72)).
Further edn: Philadelphia 1812 (NUC).

BYRON, Elizabeth
See STRUTT, Elizabeth

1812: 24 BURNEY, [Sarah Harriet].
TRAITS OF NATURE, BY MISS BURNEY, AUTHOR OF CLARENTINE,
&C. IN FIVE VOLUMES.

London: Printed for Henry Colburn, English and Foreign Public Library, Conduit
Street, Hanover Square, 1812.
I 293p; II 277p; III 307p; IV 247p; V 251p. 12mo. 30s (ECB, ER, QR).
ER 20: 501 (Nov 1812); QR 7: 471 (June 1812); WSW I: 181.
BL 012618.df.20; ECB 87; NSTC B5718 (BI O).

*Notes.* 'Advertisement', verso of vol. 1, p. 293, states: 'The publisher [i.e. Henry Colburn] of this Work thinks it proper to state that Miss Burney is *not* the Author of a Novel called "Seraphina," published in the year 1809, under the assumed name of Caroline Burney.' For this allegedly misleading publication see 1809: 14. Summers (p. 536) says the first edn. of *Traits of Nature* sold out within 3 months.

Further edns: 2nd edn. 1812 (NUC); 3rd edn. 1813 (Corvey), CME 3-628-47146-X; Philadelphia 1812 (NUC); French trans., 1819 [as *Le Jeune Cleveland, ou traits de nature* (BN)].

1812: 25   [BURY, Lady Charlotte Susan Maria].
**SELF-INDULGENCE; A TALE OF THE NINETEENTH CENTURY. IN TWO VOLUMES.**

> Edinburgh: Printed by Thomas Allan & Company, for G. R. Clarke, South St. Andrew's Street, and Longman, Hurst, Rees, Orme, & Brown, London, 1812.
> I 240p; II 251p. 12mo. 12s (ECB, ER).
> ER 20: 501 (Nov 1812); WSW I: 182.

Corvey; CME 3-628-48642-4; ECB 526; NSTC B5879 (BI BL, C, E, O).
*Notes.* Further edns: Boston 1812 (NUC) [also Philadelphia 1812 (NUC)].

1812: 26   BYRON, ['Medora Gordon'].
**THE ENGLISHMAN. A NOVEL. IN SIX VOLUMES. BY MISS BYRON, AUTHOR OF THE ENGLISHWOMAN; HOURS OF AFFLUENCE AND DAYS OF INDIGENCE; MODERN VILLA AND ANCIENT CASTLE, &C. &C.**

> London: Printed at the Minerva-Press, for A. K. Newman and Co. Leadenhall-Street, 1812.
> I 231p; II 227p; III 220p; IV 223p; V 271p; VI 273p. 12mo. 30s (ECB, QR).
> QR 6: 563 (Dec 1811).

Corvey; CME 3-628-47180-X; ECB 91; NSTC B6040 (BI BL).
*Notes.* ECB dates Nov 1811.

1812: 27   CASTIGATOR [pseud.].
**NOTORIETY, OR FASHIONABLES UNVEILED, A TALE FOR THE HAUT-TON. INTERSPERSED WITH ELEGANT AND ORIGINAL ANECDOTES, AND FORMS A GALLERY OF DISTINGUISHED AND INTERESTING PORTRAITS. BY CASTIGATOR. IN THREE VOLUMES.**

> London: Printed by J. Dean and G. Schulze, 13, Poland Street. Published by Sherwood, Neeley and Jones, Paternoster Row, and Earle and Taylor, 25, Dean Street, Soho, sold by all Booksellers, 1812.
> I 240p; II 240p; III 203p. 12mo. 18s (ER, QR).
> ER 20: 501 (Nov 1812); QR 7: 471 (June 1812).

O Vet.A6e.488; NSTC C954 (BI BL).
*Notes.* Castigator was a pseudonym used by Charles Dibdin (1745–1814), but no connection with this author has been established in the present case.
Further edn: 2nd edn. 1812 (Corvey), CME 3-628-48240-2.

1812: 28   CHATEAUBRIAND, F[rançois René, Vicomte de]; WALTER, W. Joseph (*trans.*).
THE MARTYRS; OR, THE TRIUMPH OF THE CHRISTIAN RELIGION. BY F. A. DE CHATEAUBRIAND, AUTHOR OF THE GENIE DE CHRISTIANISME, ATALA, ETC. TRANSLATED FROM THE FRENCH, BY W. JOSEPH WALTER, LATE OF ST. EDMUND'S COLLEGE. TO WHICH IS ADDED, AN APPENDIX, CONSISTING OF EXTRACTS FROM HIS "ITINERAIRE." IN TWO VOLUMES.

> London: Printed and sold for the Author, by J. Ebers, 23, Old Bond-Street; and by J. Booker, 61, New Bond-Street, 1812.
> I xxviii, 372p; II 372p. 8vo.
> p.c.; xNSTC.

*Notes.* Trans. of *Les Martyrs, ou le triomphe de la religion Chrétienne* (Paris, 1809). 'The Translator's Preface' followed by 'The Author's Preface'.
Further edns: 2nd edn. 1819 as *The Two Martyrs* (NSTC 2C16973); New York 1812 (NUC).


1812: 29   [CORP, Harriet].
COTTAGE SKETCHES; OR, ACTIVE RETIREMENT. BY THE AUTHOR OF AN ANTIDOTE TO THE MISERIES OF HUMAN LIFE, TALENTS IMPROVED, &C.

> London: Printed by E. Blackader, Took's Court, Chancery Lane. For Gale, Curtis, and Fenner, Paternoster-Row, 1812.
> I 249p; II 273p. 12mo. 9s (ECB, ER).
> ER 20: 501 (Nov 1812); WSW I: 219.
> BRu ENC; ECB 138; xNSTC.

*Notes.* Further edns: 2nd edn. 1813 (NSTC C3716); Boston 1813 (NUC).


1812: 30   [DANIEL, George].
THE ADVENTURES OF DICK DISTICH. IN THREE VOLUMES.

> London: Published by Effingham Wilson, 88, Cornhill, 1812.
> I v, v, 205p; II iv, 201p; III v, 270p. 12mo. 18s (ECB, ER).
> ER 20: 502 (Nov 1812); WSW I: 8.
> BL 12614.bb.10; ECB 6; NSTC D246 (BI C).

*Notes.* On a blank leaf at the beginning of the BL copy is written in hand: 'The Adventures of Dick Distich (the three volumes bound in one) written by George Daniel in the years 1807 and 1808. Now entirely out of print and scarce 1820'. Wolff (Item 1718) notes that the holograph MS came on the market in 1866 with a note saying that the work had been begun 'about September' 1808 and finished 31 Jan 1809. ER states 'Written after the manner of Fielding, Smollett, and Cervantes'.


1812: 31   [DOHERTY], Ann.
THE CASTLES OF WOLFNORTH AND MONT EAGLE. BY ST. ANN. EMBELLISHED WITH ORIGINAL DESIGNS. IN FOUR VOLUMES.

> London: Printed for T. Hookham, junr. and E. T. Hookham, Old Bond Street, 1812.

I 381p, ill.; II 355p, ill.; III 343p, ill.; IV 328p, ill. 12mo. 26s (ECB); 21s 'or on fine paper' 34s (ER); 24s or 34s 'on fine paper' (QR).
ER 20: 502 (Nov 1812); QR 7: 471 (June 1812); WSW I: 476.
Corvey; CME 3-628-47239-3; ECB 167; NSTC D1516 (BI O).

*Notes.* Postscript signed 'Devonshire Street'.

## EDGEWORTH, Maria, TALES OF FASHIONABLE LIFE
See 1809: 22

1812: 32    HAMILTON, [Ann Mary].
**THE MONK'S DAUGHTER; OR, HYPOCRISY PUNISHED. A NOVEL, IN THREE VOLUMES. BY MRS. HAMILTON, AUTHOR OF "A WINTER AT ST. JAMES'S,"—"FRENCH EMIGRANTS, OR SUPPOSITIOUS HEIRESS," &C. &C.**

London: Printed and published by Allen & Co. No. 15, Paternoster-Row, 1812.
I 243p; II 239p; III 230p. 12mo. 15s (ER, QR).
ER 20: 252 (July 1812); QR 7: 231 (Mar 1812).
Corvey; CME 3-628-47586-4; xNSTC.

1812: 33    HARVEY, Jane.
**MEMOIRS OF AN AUTHOR. BY JANE HARVEY, AUTHOR OF ETHELIA, TYNEMOUTH CASTLE, GOVERNOR OF BELLEVILLE, WARKFIELD CASTLE, &C. &C. IN THREE VOLUMES.**

Gainsborough: Printed by and for Henry Mozley: and sold by Longman, Hurst, Rees, Orme and Brown, London, 1812.
I 301p; II 294p; III 279p. 12mo. 13s 6d (ECB); 15s 6d (QR).
QR 7: 231 (Mar 1812); WSW I: 301.
O 249.s.247; ECB 257; NSTC H764.

*Notes.* Collates in sixes.
Further edn: 1814 as *Auberry Stanhope; or, Memoirs of an Author* (Corvey—a reissue by A. K. Newman), CME 3-628-47642-9. Apart from replacement t.ps., the Corvey copy and the above entry are apparently identical.

1812: 34    [HATTON, Anne Julia Kemble].
**SICILIAN MYSTERIES, OR THE FORTRESS DEL VECHII. A ROMANCE. IN FIVE VOLUMES.**

London: Printed for Henry Colburn, English and Foreign Public Library, Conduit-Street, Hanover-Square, 1812.
I 312p; II 244p; III 256p; IV 239p; V 263p. 12mo. 27s 6d (ECB, QR).
QR 7: 231 (Mar 1812).
Corvey; CME 3-628-48690-4; ECB 536; NSTC S1911 (BI BL).

*Notes.* Dedication to the Countess of Derby, dated Swansea, 14 Nov 1811. ECB dates Dec 1811.

1812: 35   HELME, Elizabeth.

MAGDALEN; OR, THE PENITENT OF GODSTOW. AN HISTORICAL NOVEL. IN THREE VOLUMES. BY ELIZABETH HELME, AUTHOR OF ST. MARGARET'S CAVE, OR THE NUN'S STORY, THE PILGRIM OF THE CROSS, &C. &C.

> Brentford: Printed by and for P. Norbury; and sold by C. Cradock and W. Joy, No. 32, Pater-Noster-Row, London, 1812.
> I 264p; II 264p; III 260p. 12mo. 16s 6d (ECB, ER, QR).
> ER 20: 502 (Nov 1812); QR 7: 471 (June 1812).
> Corvey; CME 3-628-47479-5; ECB 263; xNSTC.

*Notes.* Summers also lists as 'The Penitent of Godstow; or, the Magdalen', 3 vols., Craddock [*sic*], 1804, but no evidence found for such an earlier edn.
Further edn: Boston 1813 (NUC).


1812: 36   [HOFLAND, Barbara].

THE HISTORY OF A CLERGYMAN'S WIDOW AND HER YOUNG FAMILY. BY THE AUTHOR OF AN OFFICER'S WIDOW AND HER YOUNG FAMILY.

> London: Printed at the Minerva-Press, for A. K. Newman and Co. Leadenhall-Street, 1812.
> 240p, ill. 12mo. 4s (ECB, QR).
> QR 6: 563 (Dec 1811).
> BL 12613.f.1; ECB 121; NSTC H1855 (BI C, E).

*Notes.* ECB dates Nov 1811 and gives title as 'Clergyman's widow and her young family'.
Further edns: 2nd edn. 1814 (Corvey), CME 3-628-47713-1; 5th edn. 1822 (NSTC); 6th edn. 1823 (NSTC); 7th edn. 1825 (NSTC); [1845?] (NSTC); Boston [182–] (NSTC).


1812: 37   [HOFLAND, Barbara].

SAYS SHE TO HER NEIGHBOUR, WHAT? IN FOUR VOLUMES. BY AN OLD-FASHIONED ENGLISHMAN.

> London: Printed at the Minerva-Press, for A. K. Newman and Co. Leadenhall-Street, 1812.
> I 285p; II 291p; III 336p; IV 336p. 12mo. 28s (ECB).
> WSW I: 108.
> Corvey; CME 3-628-48530-4; ECB 516; NSTC H2426 (BI BL).

*Notes.* ECB dates Aug 1812.
Further edn: New York 1815 (NUC).


1812: 38   HOLSTEIN, Anthony Frederic[k] [pseud.].

BOUVERIE, THE PUPIL OF THE WORLD. A NOVEL. IN FIVE VOLUMES. BY ANTHONY FREDERIC HOLSTEIN, AUTHOR OF THE ASSASSIN OF ST. GLENROY; THE MISERIES OF AN HEIRESS; THE INHABITANTS OF EARTH, &C. &C.

> London: Printed at the Minerva-Press, for A. K. Newman and Co. Leadenhall-Street, 1812.

I x, 239p; II 252p; III 298p; IV 280p; V 242p. 12mo. 27s 6d (ECB, ER, QR).

ER 20: 501 (Nov 1812); QR 7: 471 (June 1812); WSW I: 324.

Corvey; CME 3-628-47742-5; ECB 278; xNSTC.

*Notes.* WSW I dates 1814, and lists reviews of 1814 and 1815. Blakey (copy not seen) also cites the same reviews, but places under 1812.

1812: 39   HOLSTEIN, Anthony Frederick [pseud.].

**THE MODERN KATE; OR, A HUSBAND PERPLEXED. A NOVEL. IN TWO VOLUMES. BY ANTHONY FREDERICK HOLSTEIN, AUTHOR OF SIR OWEN GLENDOWR; THE ASSASSIN OF ST. GLENROY; LOVE, MYSTERY, AND MISERY; THE MISERIES OF AN HEIRESS, &C. &C.**

London: Printed at the Minerva-Press, for A. K. Newman and Co. Leadenhall-Street, 1812.

I xv, 237p; II 218p. 12mo. 16s 6d (ECB); 10s (QR).

QR 6: 563 (Dec 1811).

Corvey; CME 3-628-47740-9; ECB 278; xNSTC.

*Notes.* Dedication 'to the Right Hon. Lady **** *******', dated Sept 1811.

1812: 40   HUTCHINSON, [Miss] A. A.

**FRIENDS UNMASKED; OR, SCENES IN REAL LIFE. A NOVEL FOUNDED IN FACTS. BY A. A. HUTCHINSON, AUTHOR OF THE EXHIBITIONS OF THE HEART, &C. &C. IN THREE VOLUMES.**

London: Printed for Longman, Hurst, Rees, Orme, and Brown, Paternoster-Row, 1812.

I vii, 254p; II 257p; III 249p. 12mo. 20s (ECB, ER).

ER 20: 501 (Nov 1812); WSW I: 47, 337.

Corvey; CME 3-628-47863-4; ECB 290; NSTC H3399 (BI BL).

1812: 41   IRCASTRENSIS [pseud.].

**LOVE AND HORROR, A MODERN ROMANCE. BY IRCASTRENSIS. AN IMITATION OF THE PRESENT, AND A MODEL FOR ALL FUTURE ROMANCES.**

London: Printed by T. Bensley, Bolt-Court, Fleet-Street, 1812.

vii, 219p. 12mo. 5s (ER, QR, 1815).

ER 25: 560 (Oct 1815); QR 13: 531 (July 1815); WSW I: 339.

BL 1208.f.6; NSTC I410.

*Notes.* Dedication reads: 'I should have wished to dedicate this little Book to a Noble Family, with which I have been connected for some time [...]. But the thing is not worthy of them'. ER 25: 560 (Oct 1815) lists as 'Love and Honour [*sic*], A Romance'; both this and the other reviews cited evidently relate to 1815 edn.

Further edns: 1815 (NUC); 1825 (MH-H 19463.31.20*). Both these edns. were published by J. J. Stockdale. T.p. of Harvard 1825 copy has as 'By Ircastrensis, Author of A Short Excursion in France, and Annals of Orlingbury, a Novel'.

1812: 42 [JACSON, Frances].
THINGS BY THEIR RIGHT NAMES; A NOVEL, IN TWO VOLUMES. BY
A PERSON WITHOUT A NAME.

London: Printed for George Robinson, 25, Paternoster-Row, 1812.
I v, 279p; II 274p. 12mo.
ER 20: 501 (Nov 1812); WSW I: 120.
BL 12612.e.16; ECB 585; NSTC L1465 (BI C, NCu, O).

*Notes*. For the attribution of this (and other) titles to Jacson, rather than to Alethea Lewis, see
Joan Percy, 'An unrecognized novelist: Frances Jacson (1754–1842)', *British Library Journal*,
23: 1 (Spring 1997), 81–97.
Further edns: 2nd edn. 1814 (Corvey), CME 3-628-48952-0; Boston 1812 (NUC).


KER, Louisa Theresa Bellenden
See RADCLIFFE, Mary Anne


1812: 43 LAFONTAINE, August [Heinrich Julius]; GREEN, [Sarah]
(*trans.*).
RAPHAEL; OR PEACEFUL LIFE. IN TWO VOLUMES. TRANSLATED
FROM THE GERMAN OF AUGUSTUS LAFONTAINE. BY MRS. GREEN.
AUTHOR OF THE ROYAL EXILE; ROMANCE READERS AND
ROMANCE WRITERS; REFORMIST; PRIVATE HISTORY OF THE
COURT OF ENGLAND &C. &C.

London: Printed by T. Wallis, Hampstead, for James Taylor, and Co. 25, Dean Street,
Soho; and sold by all Booksellers, 1812.
I 200p; II 222p. 12mo. 10s (ER).
ER 20: 501 (Nov 1812).
BL 1153.l.6; NSTC L157.

*Notes*. Trans. of *Raphael, oder das stille Leben* (Halle and Leipzig, 1809).


1812: 44 L[EVERLAND], G[ervase] C.
THE VIRTUOUS WIFE, A SENTIMENTAL TALE. BY G. C. L. AUTHOR
OF THE HONEST CRIMINAL, LOUISA, THE HUMOURIST, &C. &C.

Sudbury: Printed for the Author, by J. Burkitt, 1812.
xxv, 142p, ill. 8vo.
BL 12614.cc.5; NSTC L1438 (BI O).

*Notes*. Collates in fours.


1812: 45 MACNEILL, Hector.
THE SCOTTISH ADVENTURERS, OR, THE WAY TO RISE; AN HIS-
TORICAL TALE. BY HECTOR MACNEILL, ESQ. IN TWO VOLUMES.

Edinburgh: Printed for William Blackwood; and J. Murray, Fleet Street, and R. Baldwin,
Paternoster-Row, London, 1812.
I vii, 287p; II 257p. 12mo. 12s (ECB, QR); 12s boards (ER).

ER 19: 511 (Feb 1812); QR 7: 231 (Mar 1812); WSW I: 383.
ABu SB.82379.McNe; ECB 361; NSTC M547 (BI C, E).

*Notes.* Dedication 'to John Campbell, Esq. Tertius', dated Edinburgh, 4 Feb 1812.
Further edns: 2nd edn. 1812 'with alterations' (Corvey), CME 3-628-48091-2; New York 1812 (NSTC) [also Philadelphia 1812 (NUC)].


1812: 46   [MATURIN, Charles Robert].
## THE MILESIAN CHIEF. A ROMANCE. BY THE AUTHOR OF MONTO-RIO, AND THE WILD IRISH BOY. IN FOUR VOLUMES.

London: Printed for Henry Colburn, Public Library, Conduit-Street, Hanover-Square, 1812.
I vi, 228p; II 218p; III 239p; IV 204p. 12mo. 21s (ECB, ER, QR).
ER 19: 511 (Feb 1812); QR 7: 231 (Mar 1812); WSW I: 390.
Corvey; CME 3-628-48130-9; ECB 384; NSTC M1727 (BI BL, C, Dt, O).

*Notes.* Dedication to the Quarterly Reviewers, dated Dublin, 12 Dec 1811. Drop-head titles and running-titles read: 'The Milesian'. ECB dates Dec 1811.
Further edns: Philadelphia 1812 (NUC); French trans., 1828 [as *Connal, ou les Milésiens* (BN)].
Facs: IAN (1979).


1812: 47   [?MAXWELL, Caroline].
## MALCOLM DOUGLAS; OR, THE SIBYLLINE PROPHECY. A ROM-ANCE. IN THREE VOLS.

London: Printed for T. Hookham, jun. & E. T. Hookham, Old Bond Street, n.d. [1812?].
I 224p; II 194p; III 210p. 12mo.
O 249.s.248; CME 3-628-48152-X; NSTC 2D17641 (BI BL).

*Notes. Malcolm Douglas* is attributed to Caroline Maxwell on the t.p. of her *The Actress* (1823: 62). This author also published a collection of poetical *Feudal Tales* [1810?] with the same publishers as above (see Jackson, p. 217). Bodleian catalogue gives date of present entry as [1824?], but 2 pp. advs. of 'new works' published by Hookham at end of vol. 2 point to earlier date: novels there include *Faulconstein Forest* (1810), *Romance Readers and Romance Writers* (1810), and *The Empire of the Nairs* (1811).


1812: 48   MEEKE, [Mary].
## MATRIMONY, THE HEIGHT OF BLISS, OR THE EXTREME OF MIS-ERY. A NOVEL. IN FOUR VOLUMES. BY MRS. MEEKE, AUTHOR OF "THERE IS A SECRET," FIND IT OUT! OLD WIFE AND YOUNG HUS-BAND, &C.

London: Printed at the Minerva-Press, for A. K. Newman and Co. Leadenhall-Street, 1812.
I 240p; II 244p; III 240p; IV 264p. 12mo. 21s (ECB, QR).
QR 6: 563 (Dec 1811).
Corvey; CME 3-628-48264-X; ECB 378; xNSTC.

MONTALBION, Kate
See BAYLEY, Catharine

1812: 49   MORIARTY, H[enrietta] M[aria].
**CRIM. CON. A NOVEL, FOUNDED ON FACTS. BY H. M. MORIARTY, AUTHORESS OF "BRIGHTON IN AN UPROAR," &C. &C. &C. IN TWO VOLUMES.**

> London: Printed for and sold by the Authoress, at Messrs. Seaton and Smith's, Stationers, 40, Oxford Street (Corner of Newman Street); and may be had of all Booksellers, 1812.
> I viii, 220p; II 216p. 12mo. 15s (ER).
> ER 20: 502 (Nov 1812); WSW I: 409.
> BL 12614.g.27; ECB 396; NSTC M3283 (BI C).

*Notes.* Preface 'To the Public', dated Apr 1812.
Further edn: 2nd edn. 1812 (Corvey), CME 3-628-48330-1.


1812: 50   MOSSE, Henrietta Rouviere.
**ARRIVALS FROM INDIA; OR, TIME'S A GREAT MASTER. A NOVEL. IN FOUR VOLUMES. BY HENRIETTA ROUVIERE MOSSE, AUTHOR OF LUSSINGTON ABBEY; HEIRS OF VILLEROY; PEEP AT OUR ANCESTORS; OLD IRISH BARONET, &C. &C.**

> London: Printed at the Minerva-Press, for A. K. Newman and Co. Leadenhall-Street, 1812.
> I 280p; II 258p; III 255p; IV 255p. 12mo.
> WSW I: 412.
> Corvey; CME 3-628-48339-5; xNSTC.


1812: 51   [NARES, Edward].
**I SAYS, SAYS I; A NOVEL. BY THINKS-I-TO-MYSELF. IN TWO VOLUMES.**

> London: Printed for J. Johnston, 98, Cheapside, and sold by all Booksellers, 1812.
> I xi, 186p; II 200p. 12mo. 10s (ECB); 10s 6d (ER, QR).
> ER 20: 501 (Nov 1812); QR 7: 471 (June 1812); WSW I: 415.
> BL 1154.g.8; ECB 292; NSTC N279.

*Notes.* Further edns: 2nd edn. 1812 (Corvey), CME 3-628-47874-X; Boston 1812 (NUC); German trans., 1827.


1812: 52   OPIE, [Amelia Alderson].
**TEMPER, OR DOMESTIC SCENES: A TALE, IN THREE VOLUMES, BY MRS. OPIE.**

> London: Printed for Longman, Hurst, Rees, Orme, and Brown, Paternoster-Row, 1812.
> I 323p; II 431p; III 369p. 12mo. 21s (ECB, ER, QR).
> ER 20: 502 (Nov 1812); QR 7: 471 (June 1812); WSW I: 422.
> BL 1152.a.2; ECB 423; NSTC O389 (BI C, Dt, NCu, O).

*Notes.* Further edns: 2nd edn. 1812 (NSTC); 3rd edn. 1813 (Corvey), CME 3-628-48308-5; Boston 1812 (NUC) [also New York 1812 (NUC)]; French trans., 1813 [as *Emma de Saint-Aubin, ou caractères et scènes de la vie privée* (BN)].

PILE, Barbara
See BENGER, Elizabeth Ogilvy


1812: 53   [?RADCLIFFE, Mary Anne or ?KER, Louisa Theresa Bellenden].
IDA OF AUSTRIA; OR THE KNIGHTS OF THE HOLY CROSS. A
ROMANCE, IN THREE VOLUMES, BY THE AUTHOR OF "MANFRONE."
>  London: Printed by T. Wallis, Hampstead. For Earle, Taylor, and Co., 25, Dean Street,
>      Soho; and sold by all Booksellers, 1812.
>  I 204p; II 205p; III 212p. 12mo. 15s (QR).
>  QR 6: 563 (Dec 1811).
>  Corvey; CME 3-628-47867-7; xNSTC.

*Notes. Manfroné; or, the One-Handed Monk* is attributed on its t.p. to Mary Anne Radcliffe
(see 1809: 61), though this title was later claimed by Louisa Theresa Bellenden Ker (see FC).
Drop-head title in vol. 1 reads: 'Ida of Altenburgh; or the Knights of the Holy Cross'.


1812: 54   S[ERRES], Olivia W[ilmot].
MEMOIRS OF A PRINCESS; OR, FIRST LOVE. AN HISTORICAL
ROMANCE. IN TWO VOLUMES. BY OLIVIA W. S——. AUTHOR OF
"THE BOOK."
>  London: Published by John Maynard, 9, Panton-Street, Haymarket, 1812.
>  I x, 194p; II 165p. 12mo.
>  BL 12614.c.22; NSTC S50.

*Notes.* Dedication to 'the unmarried fair of Great Britain'. An anonymous romance, titled
*The Book!!,* appearing in the same year (see 1812: 3), may or may not also have been written
by Serres.


1812: 55   [SOANE, George].
THE EVE OF SAN MARCO. A ROMANCE. IN THREE VOLUMES.
>  London: Hildyard, Printer, Poppin's-Court. Published by W. Oxberry, Clarendon
>      Square, Somers-Town. Sold by Sherwood, Neely, and Jones, Paternoster-Row, 1812.
>  I xvi, 243p; II 368p; III 396p. 12mo. 20s (QR).
>  QR 7: 471 (June 1812).
>  Corvey; CME 3-628-47650-X; ECB 548; xNSTC.

*Notes.* Dedication 'to the most noble the Marchioness of Hertford'. Verse Address 'To the
Ladies', vol. 1, pp. [xiii]–xvi.


1812: 56   SOANE, George.
*KNIGHT DAEMON AND ROBBER CHIEF. BY GEORGE SOANE.
>  London: Sherwood, Neely, and Jones, 1812.
>  1 vol. 12mo. 6s (ECB).
>  No copy located; ECB 548.

*Notes.* Frank (Item 428) gives a synopsis, stating the work to be a derivative of German
Gothicism.

1812: 57    STANHOPE, Louisa Sidney.
THE CONFESSIONAL OF VALOMBRE. A ROMANCE. IN FOUR VOL-
UMES. BY LOUISA SIDNEY STANHOPE, AUTHOR OF MONTEBRASIL
ABBEY; THE BANDIT'S BRIDE; STRIKING LIKENESSES, &C. &C.

> London: Printed at the Minerva-Press, for A. K. Newman and Co. Leadenhall-Street,
> 1812.
> I 273p; II 269p; III 274p; IV 268p. 12mo. 22s (ECB, ER, QR).
> ER 20: 252 (July 1812), 20: 502 (Nov 1812); QR 7: 471 (June 1812).
> Corvey; CME 3-628-48772-2; ECB 558; NSTC S3495 (BI BL, O).

1812: 58    [STRUTT, Elizabeth; formerly BYRON].
THE BORDERERS. AN HISTORICAL ROMANCE, ILLUSTRATIVE OF
THE MANNERS OF THE FOURTEENTH CENTURY. IN THREE
VOLUMES.

> London: Printed at the Minerva-Press for A. K. Newman and Co. Leadenhall-Street,
> 1812.
> I vi, 234p; II 234p; III 251p. 12mo. 15s (ECB, ER, QR).
> ER 20: 252 (July 1812); QR 7: 231 (Mar 1812); WSW I: 17.
> Corvey; CME 3-628-47268-7; ECB 66; NSTC S4207 (BI BL).

*Notes.* Preface states: 'this work was begun in the year 1805, since which time its progress has
been impeded by a variety of obstacles, of consequence only to the author; and in the interim
several publications have appeared on a similar plan' (p. iv). Text proper in vol. 1 ends at
p. 208, and is followed by notes, pp. 209–34; vol. 2 text ends at p. 218, followed by notes
(pp. 219–34); vol. 3 text ends at p. 249 (notes, pp. 250–1).

1812: 59    STUART, Augusta Amelia.
CAVA OF TOLEDO; OR, THE GOTHIC PRINCESS. A ROMANCE. IN
FIVE VOLUMES. BY AUGUSTA AMELIA STUART, AUTHOR OF
LUDOVICO'S TALE; THE ENGLISH BROTHERS; EXILE OF PORTU-
GAL, &C. &C.

> London: Printed at the Minerva-Press, for A. K. Newman and Co. Leadenhall-Street,
> 1812.
> I ii, 259p; II 240p; III 252p; IV 224p; V 286p. 12mo. 25s (ECB, ER, QR).
> ER 20: 502 (Nov 1812); QR 7: 231 (Mar 1812).
> Corvey; CME 3-628-48683-1; ECB 567; xNSTC.

*Notes.* ER, QR, Allibone (and Block and Summers) have 'Cave' rather than 'Cava'.

SURR, Thomas Skinner, MODERN ADVENTURES IN FASHIONABLE
LIFE; OR, THE PRYER FAMILY
See CONSEQUENCES: OR, ADVENTURES AT RRAXALL CASTLE, Vol. 1, 1796: 84;
also present Vol., Appendix E: 6

1812: 60    [SYKES, Henrietta].
SIR WILLIAM DORIEN. A DOMESTIC STORY. IN THREE VOLUMES.
BY THE AUTHOR OF MARGIANA; OR, WIDDRINGTON TOWER.

London: Printed at the Minerva-Press, for A. K. Newman and Co. Leadenhall-Street, 1812.

I 269p; II 252p; III 262p. 12mo. 15s (ECB, QR).

QR 7: 231 (Mar 1812).

Corvey; CME 3-628-48747-1; ECB 539; NSTC S4579 (BI BL).

1812: 61    [THOMAS, Elizabeth].

THE VINDICTIVE SPIRIT. A NOVEL. IN FOUR VOLUMES. BY MRS. BRIDGET BLUEMANTLE, AUTHOR OF HUSBAND AND WIFE; MONTE VIDEO; MORTIMER HALL; THREE OLD MAIDS, &C. &C.

London: Printed at the Minerva-Press, for A. K. Newman and Co. Leadenhall-Street, 1812.

I 233p; II 227p; III 200p; IV 215p. 12mo. 22s (ECB); 21s (ER, QR).

ER 20: 502 (Nov 1812); QR 7: 471 (June 1812).

Corvey; CME 3-628-47156-7; ECB 63; xNSTC.

1812: 62    [VENTUM, Harriet].

*THE DANGERS OF INFIDELITY: A NOVEL.

London: Chapple, 1812.

3 vols. 12mo. 18s (ECB, ER, QR).

ER 21: 258 (Feb 1813); QR 8: 512 (Dec 1812).

No copy located; ECB 612.

*Notes.* ECB lists under Ventum, Harriet; ER and QR give without author.

1812: 63    [?WATSON, Miss].

ROSAMUND, COUNTESS OF CLARENSTEIN. IN THREE VOLUMES.

London: Printed by A. J. Valpy; Tooke's Court, Chancery Lane, 1812.

I viii, 324p; II 344p; III 288p. 12mo.

MH-H *EC8.W3310.812r; xNSTC.

*Notes.* Vol. 1, first leaf, MS ink addition reads: 'From the Authoress Miss Watson, Eldest Daughter of the late Bishop of Llandaff, Richard Watson D.D.'. Text in vol. 1 ends at p. 317; followed by advs., pp. 319–24.

1812: 64    [WEST, Jane].

THE LOYALISTS: AN HISTORICAL NOVEL. BY THE AUTHOR OF "LETTERS TO A YOUNG MAN," "A TALE OF THE TIMES," &C. IN THREE VOLUMES.

London: Printed for Longman, Hurst, Rees, Orme, and Brown, Paternoster-Row, 1812.

I 364p; II 307p; III 352p. 12mo. 21s (ECB, ER, QR).

ER 20: 501 (Nov 1812); QR 7: 471 (June 1812); WSW I: 557.

BRu ENC; ECB 631; NSTC W1348 (BI BL, C, O).

*Notes.* Further edns: 2nd edn. 1812 (Corvey), CME 3-628-48893-1; Boston 1813 (NUC).

1812: 65   WHYTE, Alexander.

**VELINA. A MORAL TALE. IN TWO VOLUMES. BY ALEXANDER WHYTE, ESQ.**

London: Printed for William Miller, Albemarle Street, 1812.
I xix, 216p; II 196p. 8vo. 10s 6d (ECB, QR).
QR 7: 471 (June 1812).
BL N.1476; ECB 636; NSTC W1797.

*Notes.* Preface dated 12 Dec 1811.

1812: 66   [WILSON, Ann].

**SCOTCH LAWSUITS; OR, A TALE OF THE EIGHTEENTH AND NINE-TEENTH CENTURIES. BY THE AUTHOR OF THE "TWO BROTHERS", &C. &C.**

London: Printed for George Robinson, Paternoster-Row; by J. Swan, 76, Fleet Street, 1812.
210p. 12mo.
ER 21: 259 (Feb 1813); WSW I: 565.
E Vts.115.b.3; ECB 641; NSTC S739.

*Notes.* ECB lists as by Miss Ann Wilson, also attributing to her *Lady Geraldine Beaufort* (1802: 61) and *Letters on ancient history* (1809); the latter also appears as by Anne Wilson in Allibone, NSTC and NUC.

# 1813

1813: 1   ANON.

**DEMETRIUS, A RUSSIAN ROMANCE. IN TWO VOLUMES.**

London: Printed for Longman Hurst Rees Orme and Brown, Paternoster-Row, 1813.
I 260p; II 232p. 12mo. 10s 6d (ECB); 10s 6d boards (ER, QR).
ER 21: 481 (July 1813); QR 9: 502 (July 1813); WSW I: 32.
Corvey; CME 3-628-47410-8; ECB 158; xNSTC.

*Notes.* With an Appendix on Demetrius, vol. 2, pp. 214–32, extracted from Coxe's *Travels in Russia.*
Further edn: Baltimore 1818 (NUC).

1813: 2   ANON.

**IT WAS ME, A TALE, BY ME, ONE WHO CARES FOR NOTHING OR NOBODY. IN TWO VOLUMES.**

London: Printed for the Author, and sold by A. K. Newman and Co. Leadenhall-Street, 1813.

I 227p; II 225p, ill. 12mo. 10s (ECB); 10s boards (ER, QR).
ER 21: 481 (July 1813); QR 9: 502 (July 1813).
Corvey; CME 3-628-47875-8; ECB 302; NSTC I539 (BI BL, O).

1813: 3    ANON.
THE ORDEAL; A NOVEL. IN THREE VOLUMES.

> London: Printed for Gale, Curtis, and Fenner; and G. and S. Robinson, Paternoster-Row. Sold also by Macredie and Co., and G. R. Clarke, Edinburgh; Smith and Son, Glasgow; and M. Keene, and J. Cumming, Dublin, 1813.
> I 264p; II 260p; III 208p. 12mo. 18s (ECB, ER, QR).
> ER 22: 490 (Jan 1814); QR 10: 544 (Jan 1814), 12: 524 (Jan 1815); WSW I: 87.
> Corvey; CME 3-628-48311-5; ECB 424; NSTC O419 (BI BL).

1813: 4    ANON.
A PICTURE OF SOCIETY, OR, THE MISANTHROPIST.

> London: Printed for T. Hookham, jun. and E. T. Hookham, No. 15, Old Bond Street; and M. Keene, College Green, Dublin, 1813.
> 202p. 12mo.
> O 249.r.44; NSTC P1671 (BI BL).

*Notes.* Drop-head title reads: 'The Misanthropist; or, a Picture of Society'.

1813: 5    ANON.
THE RUINS OF SELINUNTI; OR, THE VAL DE MAZZARA, SICILIAN, CALABRIAN, AND NEAPOLITAN SCENERIES. IN THREE VOLUMES. BY A LATE RAMBLER IN THESE COUNTRIES.

> London: Printed at the Minerva-Press, for A. K. Newman and Co. Leadenhall-Street, 1813.
> I 221p; II 256p; III 248p. 12mo. 15s (ECB, ER, QR).
> ER 22: 246 (Oct 1813); QR 10: 296 (Oct 1813).
> Corvey; CME 3-628-48559-2; ECB 506; NSTC S1108 (BI BL).

1813: 6    ANON.
SHE THINKS FOR HERSELF. IN THREE VOLUMES.

> London: Printed for Longman, Hurst, Rees, Orme, and Brown, Paternoster-Row, 1813.
> I 263p; II 261p; III 345p. 12mo. 16s 6d (ECB, ER).
> ER 21: 258 (Feb 1813); WSW I: 110–11.
> Corvey; CME 3-628-48650-5; ECB 532; NSTC S1607 (BI BL).

*Notes.* ECB dates Feb 1812.

AGG, John, THE SECRET MEMOIRS OF AN ILLUSTRIOUS PRINCESS
See 1810: 21

1813: 7    [AUSTEN, Jane].
PRIDE AND PREJUDICE: A NOVEL. IN THREE VOLUMES. BY THE AUTHOR OF "SENSE AND SENSIBILITY."

London: Printed for T. Egerton, Military Library, Whitehall, 1813.

I 307p; II 239p; III 323p. 12mo. 18s (ECB, ER).

ER 21: 259 (Feb 1813); WSW I: 136.

BRu ENC; ECB 33; NSTC A2017 (BI BL, C, Dt, E, O).

*Notes.* Colophon 'Printed by C. Roworth, Bell-yard, Temple-bar' in vol. 1; 'G. Sidney, Printer, Northumberland-Street, Strand' in vols. 2 and 3.

Further edns: 2nd edn. 1813 (Corvey), CME 3-628-48078-7; 3rd edn. 1817 (NSTC); 1833 (NSTC); 1839 (NSTC); 1844 (NSTC); 1846 (NSTC); Philadelphia 1832, as *Elizabeth Bennet* (NSTC); French trans., 1822; German trans., 1830.


1813: 8    [BALLANTYNE, John].

**THE WIDOW'S LODGINGS; A NOVEL. IN TWO VOLUMES.**

Edinburgh: Printed by James Ballantyne and Co. and published by John Ballantyne and Co. Hanover-Street; and Longman, Hurst, Rees, Orme, and Brown, London, 1813.

I xxiii, 202p; II x, 218p. 12mo. 9s (ECB).

O Vet.A6e.349; ECB 636; NSTC B342.

*Notes.* ECB dates Apr 1813. 'Advertisement' signed Daniel Dawson, Ramsgate, 1 Aug 1812.

Further edn: 2nd edn. 1813 (Corvey), CME 3-628-48969-5.


1813: 9    BARRETT, Eaton Stannard.

**THE HEROINE, OR ADVENTURES OF A FAIR ROMANCE READER, BY EATON STANNARD BARRETT, ESQ. IN THREE VOLUMES.**

London: Printed for Henry Colburn, Public Library, Conduit-Street, Hanover-Square; and sold by George Goldie, Edinburgh, and John Cumming, Dublin, 1813.

I xx, 224p; II 239p; III 302p. 12mo. 18s (ECB, ER, QR).

ER 22: 245 (Oct 1813); QR 10: 296 (Oct 1813); WSW I: 143.

BL 012635.d.8; ECB 41; NSTC B670 (BI O).

*Notes.* Dedication to George Canning.

Further edns: 2nd edn. 1814 as *The Heroine, or the Adventures of Cherubina* (NSTC, NUC); 3rd edn. 1815 as *The Heroine, or the Adventures of Cherubina* (NSTC, NUC); Philadelphia 1815 (from London, 2nd edn.) (NUC).


1813: 10    BEAUCHAMP, Henry [pseud.?].

**THE INTERESTING ADVENTURES OF A HACKNEY COACH, (AS RELATED BY THE COACHMAN;) WRITTEN BY HENRY BEAU-CHAMP. CONTAINING A GREAT VARIETY OF CURIOUS OCCUR-RENCES, TAKEN CHIEFLY FROM THE PRESENT TIMES.**

London: Published by S. Hood, 39, Tottenham-Court-Road; and sold by all other Booksellers, 1813.

ii, iv, 154p, ill. 12mo.

O 249.s.58; NSTC B1128.

*Notes.* 'To the Reader', pp. [i]–ii, is followed by an unheaded statement concerning the present aim to provide a 'second volume' to 'that ingenious little work, entitled "The Adventures of a Hackney Coach," published in the year 1781'; this is signed 'The Author' and dated London 1813 (pp. [i]–iv, second sequence). Collates in sixes.

Further edn: 1815 (NSTC).

1813: 11   BENGER, [Elizabeth Ogilvy].
THE HEART AND THE FANCY, OR VALSINORE. A TALE. BY MISS BENGER. IN TWO VOLUMES.

London: Printed for Longman, Hurst, Rees, Orme, and Brown, Paternoster-Row, 1813.
I 243p; II 312p. 12mo. 12s (ECB); 12s boards (ER, QR).
ER 21: 481 (July 1813); QR 9: 502 (July 1813); WSW I: 152.
Corvey; CME 3-628-47236-9; ECB 50; NSTC B1551 (BI BL, O).

*Notes.* Further edns: Philadelphia 1815 (NUC); French trans., 1816 [as *Valsinore, ou le coeur et l'imagination* (BN)].

1813: 12   BREWER, J[ames] N[orris].
SIR FERDINAND OF ENGLAND. A ROMANCE. IN FOUR VOLUMES. BY J. N. BREWER, AUTHOR OF A WINTER'S TALE; AN OLD FAMILY LEGEND; SECRETS MADE PUBLIC, &C.

London: Printed at the Minerva-Press, for A. K. Newman and Co. Leadenhall-Street, 1813.
I ii, 216p; II 255p; III 268p; IV 271p. 12mo. 22s (ECB, ER).
ER 21: 258 (Feb 1813).
Corvey; CME 3-628-47203-2; ECB 73; NSTC B4251 (BI BL).

*Notes.* Notes at the end of all vols: vol. 1, 4 pp. (unn.); vol. 2, 2 pp. (unn.); vol. 3, 3 pp. (unn.); vol. 4, 4 pp. (unn.). Summers (p. 506) lists as 4 vols., Minerva Press, 1802, with 2nd edn. Newman 1813. But Blakey, ECB, Hardy, and NSTC all date this work 1813; and the earliest publication by Brewer discovered is 1807.

1813: 13   BREWER, James Norris.
SIR GILBERT EASTERLING, A STORY, SUPPOSED TO HAVE BEEN WRITTEN BY HIMSELF ABOUT THE YEAR 1598. IN FOUR VOLUMES. PREPARED FOR THE PRESS BY JAMES NORRIS BREWER, AUTHOR OF A WINTER'S TALE, SIR FERDINAND OF ENGLAND, &C.

London: Printed at the Minerva-Press, for A. K. Newman and Co. Leadenhall-Street, 1813.
I iii, 264p; II 270p; III 241p; IV 255p. 12mo. 22s (ECB).
Corvey; CME 3-628-47067-6; ECB 73; xNSTC.

*Notes.* 'Introductory Remarks, by the Editor', vol. 1, pp. [i]–iii. Notes at the end of all vols: vol. 1 and 2, 4 pp. (unn.); vol. 3, 5 pp. (unn.); vol. 4, 6 pp. (unn.).

CHARLTON, Mary, ROSAURA DI VIRALVA
See 1805: 19

1813: 14   COXE, Eliza A.
**LIBERALITY AND PREJUDICE, A TALE; BY ELIZA A. COXE. IN THREE VOLUMES.**

> London: Printed by E. & H. Hodson, Cross-Street, Hatton-Garden, for B. & R. Crosby
> & Co. Stationers' Court, Paternoster Row, 1813.
> I 312p; II 292p; III 379p. 12mo. 18s (ECB, ER, QR).
> ER 22: 246 (Oct 1813); QR 10: 544 (Jan 1814); WSW I: 224.
> BL 1153.i.13; ECB 141; NSTC C3996.

*Notes.* 8 pp. unn. list of 'Subscribers' (154 listed) at beginning of vol. 1.


1813: 15   [CUTHBERTSON, Catherine].
**ADELAIDE: OR, THE COUNTERCHARM. A NOVEL. IN FIVE VOL-UMES. BY THE AUTHOR OF "SANTO SEBASTIANO; OR, THE YOUNG PROTECTOR:" "ROMANCE OF THE PYRENEES:" AND "THE FOREST OF MONTALBANO."**

> London: Printed for G. and S. Robinson, and Cradock and Joy, Paternoster-Row, 1813.
> I 429p; II 419p; III 432p; IV 436p; V 424p. 12mo. 35s (ECB).
> ER 22: 245 (Oct 1813); QR 10: 544 (Jan 1814); WSW I: 233.
> Corvey; CME 3-628-47015-3; ECB 5; NSTC C4642 (BI BL, O).

*Notes.* Further edn: German trans., 1833.


1813: 16   DARLING, P[eter] M[iddleton].
**THE FOREST OF VALANCOURT, OR THE HAUNT OF THE BAN-DITTI; A ROMANCE. BY P. M. DARLING, AUTHOR OF "THE ROM-ANCE OF THE HIGHLANDS."**

> Edinburgh: Printed by J. Hay & Co. for the Author; sold by William M'William, Lawn-market, 1813.
> 10, 287p. 12mo.
> O Vet.A6.e.350; NSTC D305.

*Notes.* Prefatory 'Beauty and Virtue, an Ode' addressed to 'Miss Margaret Susannah Ander-son', pp. [5]–10, followed by an address to reader (1 p. unn.) dated Edinburgh, 24 Apr 1813. Collates in sixes.


1813: 17   [DAVENPORT, Selina].
**THE SONS OF THE VISCOUNT, AND THE DAUGHTERS OF THE EARL, A NOVEL. DEPICTING RECENT SCENES IN FASHIONABLE LIFE. BY A LADY. IN FOUR VOLUMES.**

> London: Printed for Henry Colburn, Public Library, Conduit-Street, Hanover-Square;
> and sold by George Goldie, Edinburgh; and John Cumming, Dublin, 1813.
> I 220p; II 235p; III 222p; IV 250p. 12mo. 24s (ECB, ER).
> ER 21: 259 (Feb 1813).
> Corvey; CME 3-628-48711-0; ECB 550; NSTC D391 (BI BL).

*Notes.* Dedication to 'the Right Honourable the Lady Louisa Cadogan'.

1813:18　DE RENZY, S[parow] S.

THE FAITHFUL IRISHWOMAN, OR THE HOUSE OF DUNDER. BY
CAPTAIN S. S. DE RENZY. IN TWO VOLUMES.

> London: Printed by J. Gillet, Crown-Court, Fleet-Street; and sold by Sherwood, Neely,
> and Jones, Paternoster-Row; and to be had of all Booksellers, 1813.
> I xx, 215p; II 232p. 12mo. 10s 6d (ECB, ER).
> ER 22: 245 (Oct 1813); WSW I: 241.
> CLU-S/C PR.4539.DAAAf; ECB 159; xNSTC.

*Notes.* Dedication to 'my Uncle, Sir Solomon Dunder, Bart.' signed 'Your affectionate
Nephew, S. S. Dunder'. 'Subscribers' Names' (67 listed), vol. 1 (3 pp. unn.).

1813:19　{FRERE, B}[enjamin].

THE ADVENTURES OF A DRAMATIST ON A JOURNEY TO THE
LONDON MANAGERS. IN TWO VOLUMES.

> London: Printed for Lackington, Allen and Co. Finsbury Square; and sold by all Book-
> sellers, 1813.
> I vi, 204p; II 204p. 12mo. 12s (ECB, QR).
> QR 8: 512 (Dec 1812); WSW I: 274.
> BL N.2496; ECB 6; NSTC F1763.

*Notes.* Dedication to Samuel Whitbread, Esq. M.P., signed B. Frere and dated Handsworth,
Staffordshire, 1 Nov 1812. Printer's mark on verso of half-titles reads: 'Printed by Swinney
and Ferrall, Birmingham'. ECB dates Nov 1812; and ECB 189 (under Ererf [pseud.]) also lists
Groombridge edn., Dec 1831, 12s.
Further edns: 2nd edn. 1813 (Corvey), CME 3-628-47611-9; 1832 (NUC); 1832 (NUC).

1813:20　GREEN, [Sarah].

DECEPTION. A FASHIONABLE NOVEL, IN THREE VOLUMES,
FOUNDED ON FACTS. BY MRS. GREEN. AUTHORESS OF THE PRI-
VATE HISTORY OF THE COURT OF ENGLAND—GOOD MEN OF
MODERN DATE, &C. &C. &C.

> London: Published by Sheerwood [*sic*], Neely, and Jones, Paternoster-Row. And sold
> by all Booksellers, 1813.
> I 216p; II 204p; III 216p. 12mo.
> ViU PZ2.G74D.1813; xNSTC.

*Notes.* The last pages of vol. 3 are mistakenly numbered 111–116. Colophon 'P. White,
Printer, 25, New Street, Bishopsgate, London' in vol. 1; 'T. Wallis, Printer, Highgate' in
vols. 2 and 3.

1813:21　HAMILTON, [Ann] M[ary].

THE MAIDEN WIFE: OR, THE HEIRESS OF DE COURCEY. A MOST
INTERESTING TALE. IN FOUR VOLUMES. BY MISS M. HAMILTON,
AUTHORESS OF THE FOREST OF ST. BERNARDO, &C. &C.

> London: Published by Sherwood Neely & Jones Paternoster-Row, and Taylor and Co.
> Oxford Street. And sold by all Booksellers, 1813.

I 215p; II 216p; III 214p; IV 185p. 12mo. 20s (ER).

ER 21: 258 (Feb 1813).

Corvey; CME 3-628-47587-2; ECB 252; NSTC H301 (BI O).

*Notes.* Drop-head title reads: 'The Heiress of De Courcy' [*sic*]. Final two pages of vol. 1 wrongly numbered as 114 and 115. Mistakenly attributed in some catalogues to Emma Hamilton. ECB dates 1812.

1813: 22   HAMILTON, [Emma].
**"I CAN'T AFFORD IT." AND OTHER TALES, BY MRS. HAMILTON. IN TWO VOLUMES.**

> London: Printed by W. Oxberry, 11, Clarendon Square Somers Town. Published by
>    C. Chapple, Pall Mall, 1813.
> I 240p; II 191p. 12mo. 10s (ECB, ER); 10s 6d (ER); 15s (ER).
> ER 21: 258 (Feb 1813), 21: 481 (July 1813), 22: 245 (Oct 1813).
> Corvey; CME 3-628-51030-9; ECB 252; NSTC H331 (BI BL).

*Notes.* ER has 10s July 1813, 10s 6d Oct 1813.

1813: 23   HILL, Mary.
**ANSELMO; OR, THE DAY OF TRIAL. A ROMANCE. IN FOUR VOL-UMES. BY MARY HILL, AUTHOR OF THE FOREST OF COMALVA, &C.**

> London: Printed at the Minerva-Press, for A. K. Newman and Co. Leadenhall-Street,
>    1813.
> I 252p; II 231p; III 211p; IV 236p. 12mo. 22s (ECB, ER); 21s (QR).
> ER 22: 245 (Oct 1813); QR 10: 296 (Oct 1813).
> Corvey; CME 3-628-47711-5; ECB 268; NSTC H1687 (BI O).

1813: 24   HITCHENER, William Henry.
**ST. LEONARD'S FOREST; OR, THE CHILD OF CHANCE. A NOVEL. BY WILLIAM HENRY HITCHENER, OF THE SURREY THEATRE. IN TWO VOLUMES.**

> London: Printed for C. Chapple, Pall-Mall, 1813.
> I vi, 223p; II 224p. 12mo. 10s (ECB); 10s boards (ER, QR).
> ER 21: 481 (July 1813); QR 9: 502 (July 1813).
> Corvey; CME 3-628-47673-9; ECB 274; xNSTC.

*Notes.* Dedication 'to Robert William Elliston, Esq.', dated Blackfriars Road, 6 Nov 1812.

1813: 25   HITCHENER, William Henry.
**THE TOWERS OF RAVENSWOLD; OR, DAYS OF IRONSIDE. A ROMANCE. BY WILLIAM HENRY HITCHENER, OF THE SURRY [*sic*] THEATRE: AUTHOR OF ST. LEONARD'S FOREST, &C. IN TWO VOLUMES.**

> London: Printed for C. Chapple. Pall Mall, 1813.
> I 204p; II 202p. 12mo. 10s (ER, QR).
> ER 22: 490 (Jan 1814); QR 10: 544 (Jan 1814), 12: 524 (Jan 1815); WSW I: 314.
> Corvey; CME 3-628-47674-7; NSTC H1927 (BI O).

1813: 26 [HOFLAND, Barbara].
THE DAUGHTER-IN-LAW, HER FATHER, AND FAMILY. IN TWO VOL-
UMES. BY THE AUTHOR OF THE OFFICER'S WIDOW AND FAMILY;
THE CLERGYMAN'S WIDOW AND FAMILY; LITTLE DRAMAS, &C.

> London: Printed at the Minerva-Press, for A. K. Newman and Co. Leadenhall-Street,
> 1813.
> I 232p, ill.; II 240p, ill. 12mo. 10s (ER).
> ER 21: 258 (Feb 1813).
> Corvey; CME 3-628-47424-8; xNSTC.

*Notes.* Further edns: 1825 (NSTC 2H29380); 1829 (NSTC); [1830] (NSTC).

1813: 27 [HOFLAND, Barbara].
IWANOWNA; OR, THE MAID OF MOSCOW. A NOVEL. IN TWO VOL-
UMES. BY THE AUTHOR OF THE CLERGYMAN'S WIDOW, OFFI-
CER'S WIDOW, SON OF A GENIUS, SISTERS, &C.

> London: Printed for G. and S. Robinson, Paternoster Row, 1813.
> I 265p; II 279p. 12mo. 12s (ECB, ER, QR).
> ER 21: 481 (July 1813); QR 9: 502 (July 1813); WSW I: 327.
> BL 12613.f.18; ECB 303; NSTC H2421.

*Notes.* Further edns: 2nd edn. 1816 as *The Maid of Moscow; or Iwanowna* (Corvey—a reissue
by A. K. Newman), CME 3-638-47663-1; Philadelphia 1815 (NUC).

1813: 28 [HOFLAND, Barbara].
PATIENCE AND PERSEVERANCE; OR, THE MODERN GRISELDA. A
DOMESTIC TALE. IN FOUR VOLUMES. BY THE AUTHOR OF SAYS
SHE TO HER NEIGHBOUR, WHAT? &C.

> London: Printed at the Minerva-Press, for A. K. Newman and Co. Leadenhall-Street,
> 1813.
> I iii, 283p; II 282p; III 262p; IV 223p. 12mo. 22s (ER, QR).
> ER 22: 245 (Oct 1813); QR 10: 296 (Oct 1813).
> Corvey; CME 3-628-48404-9; NSTC H2424 (BI BL, O).

*Notes.* Preface 'To the Reader' acknowledges author's debt to 'the admirable little work of
Miss Edgeworth's, entitled *The Modern Griselda*'.
Further edn: Philadelphia 1816 (NUC).

1813: 29 [HOFLAND, Barbara].
THE SISTERS; A DOMESTIC TALE, BY THE AUTHOR OF THE OFFI-
CER'S WIDOW AND FAMILY; CLERGYMAN'S WIDOW AND FAMILY;
LITTLE DRAMAS, &C. &C.

> Ipswich: Printed by J. Raw, and sold by Longman, Hurst, Rees, Orme and Brown, Lon-
> don, 1813.
> 249p. 12mo. 5s (ECB); 5s boards (ER, QR).
> ER 21: 481 (July 1813); QR 9: 502 (July 1813); WSW I: 112.
> Dt OLS.B-3-906; ECB 540; NSTC H2428 (BI BL, C).

*Notes.* Further edns: London 1814 (BRu ENC—A. K. Newman); new edn. 1828 (NSTC); Hartford 1815 (NUC); French trans., 1832.

1813: 30   [HOGG, Thomas Jefferson].
**MEMOIRS OF PRINCE ALEXY HAIMATOFF. TRANSLATED FROM THE ORIGINAL LATIN MSS. UNDER THE IMMEDIATE INSPECTION OF THE PRINCE, BY JOHN BROWN, ESQ.**

> London: Printed for T. Hookham, jun. and E. T. Hookham, 15, Old Bond Street, 1813.
> iv, 236p. 12mo.
> BL C.39.e.63; ECB 380; NSTC H2105 (BI O).

*Notes.* Preface dated 4 Feb 1813, begins: 'From this Translation, which is so very free, as, in many parts, to be rather a paraphrase than a translation, it is impossible to form any just idea of the classic eloquence and pure Latinity of the original'. Vol. ends with advs. (4 pp. unn.), including review extracts.
Further edn: 1825 (NSTC).

1813: 31   HOLCROFT, [Frances].
**THE WIFE AND THE LOVER. A NOVEL, BY MISS HOLCROFT. IN THREE VOLUMES.**

> London: Printed for Henry Colburn, Public Library, Conduit-Street, Hanover-Square;
>     and sold by George Goldie, Edinburgh, and John Cumming, Dublin, 1813/14.
> I (1813) 204p; II (1814) 238p; III (1814) 294p. 12mo. 18s (ECB, ER, QR).
> ER 22: 490 (Jan 1814); QR 10: 544 (Jan 1814); WSW I: 319.
> Corvey; CME 3-628-47731-X; ECB 276; xNSTC.

*Notes.* ECB dates Nov 1813.

1813: 32   HOLSTEIN, Anthony Frederick [pseud.].
**LADY DURNEVOR; OR, MY FATHER'S WIFE. A NOVEL. IN THREE VOLUMES. BY ANTHONY FREDERICK HOLSTEIN, AUTHOR OF SIR OWEN GLENDOWR; THE ASSASSIN OF ST. GLENROY; LOVE, MYSTERY, AND MISERY; MODERN KATE; INHABITANTS OF EARTH; MISERIES OF AN HEIRESS; BOUVERIE, &C. &C.**

> London: Printed at the Minerva-Press, for A. K. Newman and Co. Leadenhall-Street,
>     1813.
> I iv, 247p; II 240p; III 232p. 12mo. 16s 6d (ECB).
> Corvey; CME 3-628-47736-0; ECB 278; xNSTC.

*Notes.* Preface dated Jan 1813.

1813: 33   HOLSTEIN, Anthony Frederick [pseud.].
**L'INTRIGUANTE; OR, THE WOMAN OF THE WORLD. BY ANTHONY FREDERICK HOLSTEIN. AUTHOR OF ISADORA OF MILAN, MISERIES OF AN HEIRESS, BOUVERIE, OR THE PUPIL OF THE WORLD, &C. IN FOUR VOLUMES.**

> London: Printed for Henry Colburn, Public Library, Conduit Street, Hanover Square;
>     and sold by George Goldie, Edinburgh; and John Cumming, Dublin, 1813.

I ix, 216p; II 202p; III 200p; IV 208p. 12mo. 24s (ECB); 22s (ER).
ER 21: 259 (Feb 1813); WSW I: 324.
Corvey; CME 3-628-47737-9; ECB 278; xNSTC.

*Notes.* Preface dated Jan 1813. Vols. 1 and 2 have 'Printed by J. Dennett, Leather Lane, London' on verso of t.p. and colophon of 'Vigurs, Printer, 14, York-Street, Covent Garden'; in vols. 3 and 4 these appear the other way round.

1813: 34 HOUGHTON, [Mary].
**THE BORDER CHIEFTAINS; OR, LOVE AND CHIVALRY. A NOVEL. IN THREE VOLUMES. BY MISS HOUGHTON, AUTHOR OF "THE MYS-TERIES OF THE FOREST."**

London: Printed for G. and S. Robinson, Paternoster Row, 1813.
I vi, 258p; II 273p; III 312p. 12mo. 18s (ECB, QR).
ER 22: 245 (Oct 1813); QR 10: 296 (Oct 1813); WSW I: 329.
Corvey; CME 3-628-47806-5; ECB 284; xNSTC.

*Notes.* 'To the Public', signed 'The Author. Hampstead'.
Further edns: 2nd edn. 1815 (Blakey); German trans., 1817 [as *Die feindlichen Stammhäupter, oder Liebe und Ritterthum* (RS)].

1813: 35 HUTTON, Catherine.
**THE MISER MARRIED. A NOVEL. IN THREE VOLUMES. BY CATHER-INE HUTTON.**

London: Printed for Longman, Hurst, Rees, Orme, and Brown. Paternoster Row, 1813.
I xii, 288p; II 283p; III 268p. 12mo. 15s (ECB, ER).
ER 21: 481 (July 1813); WSW I: 337.
Corvey; CME 3-628-47864-2; ECB 291; NSTC H3424 (BI O).

*Notes.* Dedication 'to my Father, my beloved and respected Father', dated Birmingham, 1 May 1813. Preface states that the author gained the confidence to write fiction as a result of her dissatisfaction with 'a celebrated Novel, written by a celebrated Lady, which appeared to me of that kind called prose run mad' (p. x). See also the same author's *Oakwood Hall* (1819: 43).
Further edn: Philadelphia 1814 (NUC).

1813: 36 ILIFF, [Maria].
**THE PRIOR CLAIM. A TALE. IN TWO VOLUMES. BY MRS. ILIFF.**

London: Published for the Author, by J. Burch, White-Hart-Court, Lombard-Street, 1813.
I xvi, 228p; II 236p. 12mo. 9s (ECB); 9s boards (ER, QR).
ER 21: 481 (July 1813); QR 9: 502 (July 1813).
Corvey; CME 3-628-47879-0; ECB 292; xNSTC.

*Notes.* 'Dedication. To my Friends! And who, it may be asked, are they?', dated London, 4 Mar 1813. 'List of Subscribers' (183 names, headed by the Duke of Kent), vol. 1, pp. [vii]–xvi. ECB gives Newman as publisher, but not discovered in this form.

1813: 37   JOHNSON, Mrs. D.

*THE BROTHERS IN HIGH LIFE; OR, THE NORTH OF IRELAND. A ROMANCE, IN THREE VOLUMES. BY MRS D. JOHNSON.

> London: Printed for G. Kearsley, No. 46, Fleet Street; and sold by J. Jones, 4, St. Michael's
> Alley, Cornhill, and 24, Blackman Street, Southwark, 1820 [first published 1813].
> I 184p; II 179p; III 186p. 12mo.
> WSW I: 346.
> No copy of 1st edn. located.

*Notes.* First published in 1813, but no copy with this date located. Details above follow 1820 edn. (CtY-BR In.J631.813Bb).

Further edn: 1820 (see note above).

1813: 38   KELLY, Isabella.

JANE DE DUNSTANVILLE; OR, CHARACTERS AS THEY ARE. A NOVEL. IN FOUR VOLUMES. BY ISABELLA KELLY, AUTHOR OF MADELINE, ABBEY OF ST. ASAPH, AVONDALE PRIORY, JOSCELINA, EVA, RUTHINGLENNE, MODERN INCIDENT, BARON'S DAUGHTER, SECRET, LITERARY INFORMATION, FRENCH GRAMMAR, POEMS, &C. &C.

> London: Published for the Author, by J. Souter, 1, Paternoster Row; and sold by Mr.
> Mozley, Gainsborough; Messrs. Wilson and Co. York; Messrs. Doig and Sterling,
> Edinburgh; and by all Booksellers, 1813.
> I xi, 232p; II 232p; III 220p; IV 220p. 12mo. 21s (ER, QR).
> ER 22: 246 (Oct 1813); QR 10: 544 (Jan 1814); WSW I: 350.
> IU 823.K296j; xNSTC.

*Notes.* Dedication 'to Her Royal Highness the Princess of Wales', signed Isabella Hedgeland, York Place, Brompton, 1 Sept 1813. 'Subscribers' Names' (57 listed), vol. 1, pp. [ix]–xi.

Further edn: 2nd edn. 1819 (Corvey—a reissue by A. K. Newman), CME 3-628-47979-7.

1813: 39   LAFONTAINE, [August Heinrich Julius].

AGE AND YOUTH; OR, THE FAMILIES OF ABENSTEDT. A NOVEL. IN FOUR VOLUMES. FROM THE GERMAN OF LA FONTAINE, AUTHOR OF THE FAMILY OF HALDEN; THE REPROBATE; HERMANN AND EMILIA; DOLGORUCKI AND MENZIKOFF, &C.

> London: Printed at the Minerva-Press, for A. K. Newman and Co. Leadenhall-Street,
> 1813.
> I 207p; II 247p; III 233p; IV 255p. 12mo. 21s (ECB, ER); 22s (QR).
> ER 22: 245 (Oct 1813); QR 10: 296 (Oct 1813).
> BL 12547.dd.8; ECB 326; NSTC L146.

*Notes.* German original not discovered.

1813: 40   LLEWELLYN, Mrs.

READ, AND GIVE IT A NAME. A NOVEL. IN FOUR VOLUMES. BY MRS. LLEWELLYN.

London: Printed at the Minerva-Press, for A. K. Newman and Co. Leadenhall-Street, 1813.

I iv, 273p; II 281p; III 255p; IV 274p. 12mo. 22s (ECB, ER, QR).

ER 22: 245 (Oct 1813); QR 10: 296 (Oct 1813); WSW I: 375.

Corvey; CME 3-628-48035-3; ECB 350; xNSTC.

1813: 41    MALDEN, Miriam.
### HOPE; OR, JUDGE WITHOUT PREJUDICE. A NOVEL. IN FOUR VOL-UMES. BY MIRIAM MALDEN.

London: Printed at the Minerva-Press, for A. K. Newman and Co. Leadenhall-Street, 1813.

I 254p; II 268p; III 258p; IV 327p. 12mo. 22s (ECB, ER, QR).

ER 22: 246 (Oct 1813); QR 10: 296 (Oct 1813).

Corvey; CME 3-628-48153-8; ECB 364; NSTC M807 (BI BL).

1813: 42    MORIARTY, H[enrietta] M[aria].
### A HERO OF SALAMANCA; OR, THE NOVICE ISABEL. A NOVEL, IN THREE VOLUMES. BY H. M. MORIARTY, AUTHOR OF "BRIGHTON IN AN UPROAR," &C. &C. &C.

London: Printed for the Author; and sold by J. Souter, No. 1, Paternoster-Row; and to be had of all Booksellers, 1813.

I 237p; II 183p; III 159p. 12mo. 18s (ER).

ER 21: 258 (Feb 1813); WSW I: 409.

Corvey; CME 3-628-48331-X; ECB 396; xNSTC.

1813: 43    OPIE, [Amelia Alderson].
### TALES OF REAL LIFE. BY MRS. OPIE. IN THREE VOLUMES.

London: Printed for Longman, Hurst, Rees, Orme, and Brown, Paternoster-Row, 1813.

I 322p; II 294p; III 297p. 12mo. 18s (ECB, ER, QR).

ER 22: 245 (Oct 1813); QR 10: 296 (Oct 1813); WSW I: 422.

BL 12613.aaa.2; ECB 423; NSTC O388.

*Notes.* Further edns: 2nd edn. 1813 (Corvey), CME 3-628-48307-7; 3rd edn. 1816 (NSTC); Boston 1827 (NSTC); French trans., 1814; German trans., 1816 [as *Darstellungen aus dem wirklichen Leben,* published as vols. 3 and 4 of *Bibliothek neuer englischer Romane* (RS)].

1813: 44    PARKER, Emma.
### ARETAS, A NOVEL. IN FOUR VOLUMES. BY EMMA PARKER, AUTHOR OF "ELFRIDA, HEIRESS OF BELGROVE," AND "VIRGINIA, OR THE PEACE OF AMIENS."

London: Printed for B. and R. Crosby and Co. Stationers' Court, Paternoster Row, 1813.

I viii, 344p; II 375p; III 367p; IV 382p. 12mo. 24s (ECB, ER).

ER 21: 259 (Feb 1813); WSW I: 429.

Corvey; CME 3-628-48384-0; ECB 433; xNSTC.

*Notes.* Preface states: '"Elfrida" was ready for the press, a considerable time before it was published; that delay was so far disadvantageous to "Virginia" as making it appear to come out too soon after the former, though still near a year elapsed between the publishing of the two works, though they have been spoken of as if they had actually accompanied each other. It is now a year and a half since I finished the latter'.

1813: 45    PAYNTER, D[avid] W[illiam].
THE HISTORY AND ADVENTURES OF GODFREY RANGER; IN THREE VOLUMES. BY D. W. PAYNTER.
> Manchester: Printed and sold by R. & W. Dean, Market-Street, 1813.
> I xiii, 259p; II v, 272p; III viii, 345p. 12mo.
> O 249.s.101-103; NSTC P787.

*Notes.* 'The Publisher's Preface', vol. 1, pp. [iii]–x, (humorously?) deprecating the work as if to forestall criticism. Collates in sixes.
Further edn: London 1816 as *Godfrey Ranger. A Novel* (Corvey—a reissue by A. K. Newman), CME 3-628-48405-7.

1813: 46    PECK, [Frances].
*VAGA; OR, A VIEW OF NATURE. A NOVEL. IN THREE VOLUMES. BY MRS. PECK.
> London: Robinson, 1813.
> 3 vols. 12mo. 18s (ECB); 18s boards (ER).
> ER 21: 259 (Feb 1813); WSW I: 435.
> No copy of 1st edn. located; ECB 439.

*Notes.* Title details based on 2nd edn. of 1815 (see below).
Further edn: 2nd edn. 1815 (Corvey—a reissue by A. K. Newman), CME 3-628-48410-3.

1813: 47    [?PHIBBS, Mary].
THE LADY OF MARTENDYKE; AN HISTORICAL TALE OF THE FIF-TEENTH CENTURY. BY A LADY. IN FOUR VOLUMES.
> London: Published for the Author, by Henry Colburn, Public Library, Conduit-Street, Hanover-Square, 1813.
> I xv, 222p; II 210p; III 248p; IV 292p. 12mo.
> WSW I: 63.
> Corvey; CME 3-628-47892-8; NSTC P1399.5 (BI BL).

*Notes.* Dedication 'to the Most Noble the Marchioness of Ely', dated Laura House, Bath, Dec 1812. List of 'Subscribers' (320 names), vol. 1, pp. [v]–[x]. Preface dated Laura House, Bath, Dec 1812. In ViU copy (PR.3991.A6L3.1813) t.p. to vols. 1 and 2 has 'A Lady' deleted and 'Mary Phibbs' written alongside; t.p. to vol. 1 also has the inscription 'Margaret Phibbs given by her beloved father W. H. Phibbs' (in all 12 'Phibbs' entries, including 'Wm H. Phibbs Esq', are found in the subscription list). In vol. 1 the following is written in pencil in Michael Sadleir's hand: 'With Autograph of Author (Mary Phibbs) on fly leaf'. Care perhaps needs to be taken before accepting the attribution: the hand of Mary Phibbs seems rather immature, and the appropriation of the work could possibly be part of a childish game.

1813: 48   PLUMPTRE, Anne.

THE HISTORY OF MYSELF AND MY FRIEND, A NOVEL: BY ANNE PLUMPTRE. IN FOUR VOLUMES.

> London: Printed for Henry Colburn, English and Foreign Public Library, Conduit Street, Hanover Square, 1813.
> I vi, 308p; II 322p; III 315p; IV 316p. 12mo. 28s (ECB, ER, QR).
> ER 21: 258 (Feb 1813); QR 8: 512 (Dec 1812); WSW I: 441.
> Corvey; CME 3-628-48476-6; ECB 455; NSTC P2160 (BI BL, C).

1813: 49   POTTER, John.

OLIVIA; OR THE NYMPH OF THE VALLEY: A NOVEL, IN TWO VOLUMES. BY JOHN POTTER, M.D.

> London: Printed for W. Earle, Albemarle-Street, 1813.
> I missing; II 208p. 12mo. 10s 6d (ER, QR).
> ER 22: 490 (Jan 1814); QR 10: 544 (Jan 1814), 12: 524 (Jan 1815).
> BL 1154.c.28; NSTC P2735.

*Notes.* Vol. 1 is missing in BL, and no other copy has been located.

1813: 50   POTTER, Matilda.

MOUNT ERIN; AN IRISH TALE. IN TWO VOLUMES. BY MATILDA POTTER.

> London: Printed for J. Souter, 1, Paternoster-Row, by G. Sidney, Northumberland-Street, Strand, 1813.
> I 211p; II 212p. 12mo. 10s 6d (ER, QR).
> ER 21: 481 (July 1813); QR 10: 296 (Oct 1813); WSW I: 448.
> Corvey; CME 3-628-48366-2; xNSTC.

1813: 51   ROCHE, Regina Maria.

THE MONASTERY OF ST. COLUMB; OR, THE ATONEMENT. A NOVEL. IN FIVE VOLUMES. BY REGINA MARIA ROCHE, AUTHOR OF THE CHILDREN OF THE ABBEY; HOUSES OF OSMA AND ALMERIA; DISCARDED SON, &C.

> London: Printed at the Minerva-Press, for A. K. Newman and Co. Leadenhall-Street, 1813.
> I 273p; II 244p; III 208p; IV 203p; V 215p. 12mo. 27s 6d (ECB); 27s 6d boards (ER).
> ER 21: 258 (Feb 1813); WSW I: 470.
> Corvey; CME 3-628-48460-X; ECB 498; NSTC D149.5 (BI BL).

*Notes.* ECB dates Dec 1812.
Further edns: New York & Philadelphia 1813 (NUC); German trans., 1816 [as *Die Geheimnisse der Abtei von Santa Columba, oder der Ritter mit den rothen Waffen* (RS)]; French trans., 1819 [as *Le Monastère de Saint-Columba, ou le chevalier des armes rouges* (BN)].

1813: 52   [ROSS, Mrs].

THE MARCHIONESS!!! OR, "THE MATURED ENCHANTRESS." IN THREE VOLUMES. BY LADY ――.

London: Printed at the Minerva-Press, for A. K. Newman and Co. Leadenhall-Street,
1813.
I 197p; II 224p; III 214p. 12mo. 16s 6d (ECB); 18s (ER).
ER 21: 481 (July 1813); WSW I: 473.
Corvey; CME 3-628-48083-3; ECB 367; NSTC R1705 (BI BL).

1813: 53   ROSS, Mrs.
THE STRANGERS OF LINDENFELDT; OR, WHO IS MY FATHER? A
NOVEL. IN THREE VOLUMES. BY MRS. ROSS, AUTHOR OF THE
COUSINS, &C.

London: Printed at the Minerva-Press, for A. K. Newman and Co. Leadenhall-Street,
1813.
I 262p; II 267p; III 256p. 12mo. 15s (ECB, ER).
ER 21: 259 (Feb 1813); WSW I: 474.
Corvey; CME 3-628-48555-X; ECB 503; NSTC R1707 (BI BL).

1813: 54   {SCOTT, Honoria} [pseud.?].
STRATHMAY: OR SCENES IN THE NORTH, ILLUSTRATIVE OF
SCOTTISH MANNERS, &C. A TALE. BY THE AUTHOR OF A WINTER
IN EDINBURGH, AMATORY TALES, VALE OF CLYDE, &C. IN TWO
VOLUMES.

Edinburgh: Printed for J. Dick, 142, High Street; and T. Tegg, 111, Cheap Side, London,
1813.
I 197p; II 175p. 12mo. 9s (ECB, ER, QR).
ER 23: 256 (Apr 1814); QR 11: 255 (Apr 1814).
IU 823.Sco82s; ECB 520; xNSTC.

*Notes*. List of 5 novels 'Just Published' by Tegg and Dick, facing t.p. to vol. 1, includes 'A Win-
ter in Edinburgh [. . .] by Honoria Scott', effectively acknowledging author of present title.
For her possible true identity, see 1810: 74. At end of vol. 2 fuller list of 'New and Valuable
Publications', paginated to 7, begins on verso of p. 175. ECB, ER, QR all relate to the 2nd edn.
Further edn: 2nd edn., London 1814, as *The Castle of Strathmay, or Scenes in the North; A Tale*
(BL 12613.cc.7; NSTC S760), with Tegg's name first on the imprint.

1813: 55   [SMITH, Julia].
THE OLD SCHOOL. IN TWO VOLUMES.

London: Printed for J. Booth, Duke Street, Portland Place, 1813.
I viii, 300p; II vi, 272p. 12mo. 12s (ECB, ER).
ER 22: 245 (Oct 1813); WSW I: 86.
BL 12614.g.24; ECB 422; NSTC S2535 (BI C).

1813: 56   SPENCE, Elizabeth Isabella.
THE CURATE AND HIS DAUGHTER; A CORNISH TALE. BY ELIZA-
BETH ISABELLA SPENCE, AUTHOR OF SUMMER EXCURSIONS—A
CALEDONIAN EXCURSION—THE NOBILITY OF THE HEART—THE
WEDDING DAY, &C. &C. IN THREE VOLUMES.

London: Printed for Longman, Hurst, Rees, Orme, & Brown, Paternoster-Row, 1813.
I 239p; II 256p; III 247p. 12mo. 15s (ECB).
WSW I: 518.
Corvey; CME 3-628-48666-1; ECB 554; xNSTC.

*Notes.* ECB dates Apr 1813.


1813: 57   STAËL-HOLSTEIN, [Anne Louise Germaine] de.
ZULMA, AND OTHER TALES: TO WHICH IS PREFIXED AN ESSAY ON
FICTIONS. BY THE BARONESS DE STAEL HOLSTEIN. TRANSLATED
FROM THE FRENCH. IN TWO VOLUMES.

London: Printed for Henry Colburn, Conduit-Street, Hanover-Square, 1813.
I 187p; II 201p. 12mo. 10s 6d (ECB, ER, QR).
ER 22: 246 (Oct 1813); QR 10: 296 (Oct 1813).
BL 12510.e.15; ECB 557; NSTC S3443.

*Notes.* Trans. of *Zulma, et trois nouvelles: précédé d'un essai sur les fictions*, published by Colburn (Londres, 1813). The three novellas are 'Mirza', 'Adelaide and Theodore', and 'History of Pauline'.


1813: 58   [SYKES, Henrietta].
STORIES OF THE FOUR NATIONS, CONTAINING MONTARGIS, A
FRENCH STORY; MY AUNT PATTY, AN ENGLISH STORY; LILLIAS DE
LARA, A SPANISH STORY; THE CALABRIAN, AN ITALIAN STORY. IN
FIVE VOLUMES. BY THE AUTHOR OF MARGIANA; SIR WILLIAM
DORIEN, &C. &C.

London: Printed at the Minerva-Press, for A. K. Newman and Co. Leadenhall-Street,
    1813.
I 270p; II 218p; III 278p; IV 294p; V 296p. 12mo. 27s 6d (ECB, QR).
QR 8: 512 (Dec 1812).
Corvey; CME 3-628-48673-4; ECB 564; NSTC S4582 (BI BL, O).

*Notes.* ECB dates Dec 1812.


1813: 59   [TEMPLE, Edmond].
THE LIFE OF PILL GARLICK; RATHER A WHIMSICAL SORT OF FELLOW.

London: Printed for the Author; and sold by John Miller, 25, Bow Street, Covent Gar-
    den; and N. Mahon, Dublin, 1813.
xlviii, 321p. 12mo. 8s 6d (ER).
ER 22: 245 (Oct 1813).
BL N.2067; NSTC P1785 (BI C, E, O).

*Notes.* See below *Memoirs of Myself* (1816: 56), which describes itself as a second vol. to this item.
Further edn: 2nd edn. 1815 (NSTC).


1813: 60   [UTTERSON, Sarah Elizabeth].
TALES OF THE DEAD. PRINCIPALLY TRANSLATED FROM THE
FRENCH.

London: Printed for White, Cochrane, and Co., Fleet-Street, 1813.

viii, 248p. 8vo. 9s (ECB, ER, QR).

ER 22: 246 (Oct 1813); QR 10: 297 (Oct 1813).

BL 12547.d.8; ECB 576; NSTC U261 (BI O).

*Notes.* Mainly translated and adapted from of *Fantasmagoriana, ou Recueil d'histoires, d'apparitions de spectres, revenants [. . .] traduit de l'allemand, par un Amateur* [by Jean Baptiste Benoit Eyriès] (Paris, 1812). 'Advertisement', pp. [i]–ii, states: 'The first four tales in this collection, and the last, are imitated from a small French work, which professes to be translated from the German [. . .] The last tale has been considerably curtailed [. . .] The fifth tale [. . .] is founded on an incident similar in its features, which was some years since communicated to me, by a female friend of very deserved celebrity'. 'Preface of the French Translator', pp. [iii]–viii. Six tales in all. In the Introduction to the 1831 edn. of her *Frankenstein*, Mary Shelley mentions that a reading of the French version of this work in the company of Byron, Polidori and Percy B. Shelley, in Italy in 1816, prompted their decision to write ghost stories. No German original has been discovered.

1813: 61    [VULPIUS, Christian August]; [?SOANE, George (*trans.*) or ?BOHN, Henry George (*trans.*)].

**FERRANDINO: BY THE AUTHOR OF RINALDO RINALDINI. A CONTINUATION OF THAT CELEBRATED ROMANCE. TRANSLATED FROM THE GERMAN. IN TWO VOLUMES.**

London: Printed and published by W. Oxberry, and sold by all Booksellers, 1813.

I ii, 220p; II 180p. 12mo. 10s 6d boards (ER); 10s (ER, QR).

ER 21: 258 (Feb 1813), 21: 481 (July 1813); QR 9: 260 (May 1813).

ViU PZ2.V84F.1813; xNSTC.

*Notes.* Trans. of *Ferrandino; Fortsetzung der Geschichte Rinaldinis* (Leipzig, 1800). ER and QR both state 'Translated from the German by G. Soane, A.B.'. Block, DNB, and NUC, however, all attribute the translation to Henry George Bohn (1796–1884). ECB 204 lists Colburn edn., Apr 1813, price 10s 6d. Summers (p. 323) gives only a Colburn 1813 edn., 'by Henry G. Bohn', later adv. by Newman. It is possible that this represents a rival version, though no copy with this imprint has been located. ER 10s Feb 1813, 10s 6d boards July 1813; Soane is mentioned in the first instance only.

1813: 62    [WALKER, George].

**THE TRAVELS OF SYLVESTER TRAMPER THROUGH THE INTERIOR OF THE SOUTH OF AFRICA: WITH THE ADVENTURES & ACCIDENTS THAT HE ENCOUNTERED IN A JOURNEY OF MORE THAN TWO THOUSAND MILES THROUGH THESE UNKNOWN WILDERNESSES, CONSTANTLY EXPOSED TO DANGER FROM BEASTS OF PREY, AND THE ATTACKS OF SAVAGES. EMBELLISHED WITH PLATES.**

London: Published and sold by G. Walker, Publisher of Books and Music, 106, Great Portland Street, 1813.

216p, ill. 12mo. 3s 6d (ECB); 3s 6d boards (ER, QR).

ER 21: 481 (July 1813); QR 9: 502 (July 1813).

BL 836.c.9; ECB 596; NSTC W216.

*Notes.* 'W. Wilson, Printer, 4, Greville-Street, Hatton-Garden, London', after t.p. imprint date.
Further edns: 2nd edn. 1813 (NSTC); 3rd edn. 1816 (NUC); 4th edn. 1817 (NSTC).

1813: 63    WARD, Catharine G[eorge].
MY NATIVE LAND; OR, THE TEST OF HEROISM. A NOVEL. BY
CATHARINE G. WARD, AUTHOR OF THE DAUGHTER OF ST. OMER;
A BACHELOR'S HEIRESS, &C. &C.

> London: Printed at the Minerva-Press, for A. K. Newman and Co. Leadenhall-Street,
> 1813.
> 222p. 12mo. 5s (ECB).
> Corvey; CME 3-628-48823-0; ECB 623; xNSTC.

# 1814

1814: 1    ANON.
BACHELORS' MISERIES. A NOVEL. IN FOUR VOLUMES. BY AN OLD
MAID OF DISTINCTION, AUTHOR OF SEVERAL POPULAR WORKS.

> London: Printed at the Minerva-Press, for A. K. Newman and Co. Leadenhall-Street,
> 1814.
> I 269p; II 285p; III 275p; IV 223p. 12mo. 24s (ER, QR).
> ER 24: 268 (Nov 1814); QR 12: 274 (Oct 1814).
> Corvey; CME 3-628-47090-0; xNSTC.

1814: 2    ANON.
THE CABRONAZOS, OR A SPANIARD IN LONDON. A NOVEL IN TWO
VOLUMES. BY A GRADUATE.

> London: Printed by R. Juigné, 17, Margaret Street, Cavendish Square. Sold by Sher-
> wood, Neely and Jones, Paternoster Row, and all other Booksellers, 1814.
> I ii, 240p; II 246p. 12mo. 14s (ER, QR).
> ER 23: 509 (Sept 1814); QR 11: 511 (July 1814).
> BL 12613.d.18; NSTC G1594.

*Notes.* Dedicatory letter, in French, from the author 'A Madame La Marquise De W___',
dated 'A Londres, ce 20 Mars, 1814'.
Further edn: 2nd edn. 1815 as *The Spaniard in London; or, the Cabronazos* (Corvey—a reissue, with replacement t.p., by Thomas Tegg), CME 3-628-48665-3.

1814: 3    ANON.
CŒLEBS MARRIED. BEING INTENDED AS A CONTINUATION OF
CŒLEBS IN SEARCH OF A WIFE.

London: Published and sold by G. Walker, Publisher of Books and Music, No. 106, Great Portland-Street, 1814.

iv, 428p. 12mo. 7s (ER).

ER 22: 490 (Jan 1814); WSW I: 25.

BL 1488.g.24; NSTC C2784 (BI C, O).

*Notes.* 'This volume is neither written by, nor with the knowledge of the admirable writer of the work which this professes to continue' (p. iv).

1814: 4   ANON.
**CONDUCT. A NOVEL. IN THREE VOLUMES.**

London: Printed at the Minerva-Press, for A. K. Newman and Co. Leadenhall-Street, 1814.

I xii, 231p; II 204p; III 239p. 12mo. 21s (ECB); 18s (ER, QR).

ER 22: 490 (Jan 1814); QR 10: 544 (Jan 1814), 12: 524 (Jan 1815); WSW I: 26.

Corvey; CME 3-628-47308-X; ECB 130; NSTC C3332 (BI BL).

*Notes.* 'To the Subscribers and the Public' states that the work 'never would have been published, but for the benefit of her seven, now orphan, children'. Followed by a 'List of Subscribers' (255 names), vol. 1, pp. [iii]–[xiii]. ECB dates 1813.

1814: 5   ANON.
**THE IRISH GIRL. A RELIGIOUS TALE. BY THE AUTHOR OF CŒLEBS MARRIED.**

London: Published by George Walker, 106, Great-Portland-Street. Sold also by Cradock and Joy, Paternoster-Row, 1814.

102p, ill. 12mo.

BL 864.h.1; NSTC I461.

*Notes.* Frontispiece, 'The Irish Girl Found', dated at foot, 12 Aug 1814. Collates in sixes. Further edn: 2nd edn. 1814 (NSTC).

1814: 6   ANON.
**PNEUMANEE; OR, THE FAIRY OF THE NINETEENTH CENTURY. IN TWO VOLUMES.**

London: Printed for J. Hatchard, Bookseller to the Queen, 190, opposite Albany, Piccadilly, 1814.

I viii, 264p; II 254p. 12mo. 10s 6d (ECB, ER, QR).

ER 23: 509 (Sept 1814); QR 12: 274 (Oct 1814); WSW I: 94.

BL N.2367; ECB 456; NSTC P2225.5 (BI O).

*Notes.* Further edn: Philadelphia & New York 1815 (NUC).

1814: 7   ANON.
**POPULARITY: OR THE VOTARY OF WEALTH: IN THREE VOLUMES. BY A MISER.**

London: Published by Sherwood, Neely, and Jones, Paternoster-Row; and C. Chapple, Pall-Mall; and sold by all Booksellers, 1814.

I 188p; II 196p; III 214p. 12mo. 15s (Summers).

Corvey; CME 3-628-48484-7; NSTC P2553.5 (BI BL).

*Notes.* Adv. facing t.ps. for: 'The Marquis & his Wife: or, fashionable Infidelity: a highly finished Novel, in three Volumes [. . .] by an Author of Celebrity'; vol. 2, 'The Carthusian Friar;
or Mysteries of Montanville: A posthumous Romance in four Volumes by an Author of
Celebrity'; vol. 3, 'Just published, The Ballad Singer [. . .] by Mrs. Edgeworth'. T.p. imprint
changes in vols. 2 and 3 to 'London: Printed for J. and M. Taylor, 96, Lucas Street, Brunswick
Square; Sherwood, Neely, and Jones, Paternoster Row; and C. Chapple, Pall-Mall, 1814'.


1814: 8    ANON.

THE SPLENDOUR OF ADVERSITY: A DOMESTIC STORY. IN THREE
VOLUMES. BY THE AUTHOR OF BLACK ROCK HOUSE, WINTER
IN BATH, CORINNA OF ENGLAND, THE DEAD LETTER OFFICE, &C.
&C.

London: Printed by C. Baldwin, New Bridge-Street, for B. and R. Crosby, and Co.,
Stationers'-Court, Ludgate-Street, 1814.

I 299p; II 275p; III 276p. 12mo. 15s (ECB, ER, QR).

ER 22: 490 (Jan 1814); QR 11: 255 (Apr 1814); WSW I: 147.

Corvey; CME 3-628-48728-5; ECB 556; NSTC B1034 (BI BL).

*Notes.* Sometimes attributed to Mrs E. G. Bayfield and also to J. H. James, though both attributions are doubtful. ECB dates Dec 1813.


1814: 9    [AGG, John].

A MONTH IN TOWN. A SATIRICAL NOVEL. BY HUMPHRY
HEDGEHOG, ESQ. AUTHOR OF "THE GENERAL-POST BAG,"
"REJECTED ODES," &C. &C. &C.

London: Printed for J. Johnston, 98, Cheapside, 1814.

I 200p; II 191p; III 184p. 12mo. 16s 6d (ER).

ER 24: 268 (Nov 1814).

BL 1154.k.13; NSTC A591 (BI C).

*Notes.* Further edns: 2nd edn. 1815 (NUC); 3rd edn., corrected, with new preface, 1816 (NSTC).


1814: 10    [AIKIN, Lucy].

LORIMER. A TALE.

London: Printed for Henry Colburn, Conduit-Street, Hanover-Square: and sold by
G. Goldie, Edinburgh; and J. Cumming, Dublin, 1814.

230p. 12mo. 5s (ECB); 6s (ER).

ER 23: 255 (Apr 1814); WSW I: 68.

BL N.2495; ECB 353; NSTC A691.

*Notes.* Further edn: Philadelphia 1816, as *Lorimer; A Modern Novel* (NUC).


1814: 11    [AUSTEN, Jane].

MANSFIELD PARK: A NOVEL. IN THREE VOLUMES. BY THE AUTHOR
OF "SENSE AND SENSIBILITY," AND "PRIDE AND PREJUDICE."

London: Printed for T. Egerton, Military Library, Whitehall, 1814.
I 360p; II 294p; III 354p. 12mo. 18s (ECB; ER; QR, 1st and 2nd edns.).
ER 23: 509 (Sept 1814); QR 11: 511 (July 1814), 14: 554 (Jan 1816, 2nd edn.).
BRu ENC; ECB 33; NSTC A2016 (BI BL, C, O).

*Notes.* Imprint on vol. 2 differs: 'London: Printed for T. Egerton, Whitehall, 1814'. Colophon 'G. Sidney, Printer, Northumberland-street, Strand' vols. 1 and 3; 'Printed by C. Roworth, Bell-yard, Temple-bar' in vol. 2.
Further edns: 2nd edn. 1816 (Corvey), CME 3-628-48078-7; 1833 (NSTC); 1837 (NSTC); Belfast 1846 (NSTC); 1847 (NSTC); Philadelphia 1832 (NUC); French trans., 1816 [as *Le Parc de Mansfield, ou les trois cousines* (BN)].

1814: 12   BATTERSBY, John.
TELL-TALE SOPHAS, AN ECLECTIC FABLE, IN THREE VOLUMES. FOUNDED ON ANECDOTES, FOREIGN AND DOMESTIC. BY JOHN BATTERSBY.

London: Printed by D. N. Shury, and sold by J. Wallis, 77, Berwick-Street, Soho, 1814.
I 259p; II 287p; III 280p. 12mo.
Corvey; CME 3-628-47129-X; ECB 581; NSTC B977 (BI BL).

*Notes.* Further edn: 1826 (NUC).

1814: 13   [BEAUCLERC, Amelia].
MONTREITHE; OR, THE PEER OF SCOTLAND. A NOVEL. IN FOUR VOLUMES.

London: Printed at the Minerva-Press, for A. K. Newman and Co. Leadenhall-Street, 1814.
I 259p; II 308p; III 288p; IV 303p. 12mo. 22s (ER, QR).
ER 24: 269 (Nov 1814); QR 12: 523 (Jan 1815); WSW I: 79.
Corvey; CME 3-628-48275-5; NSTC B1130 (BI BL, C).

1814: 14   [BRUNTON, Mary].
DISCIPLINE: A NOVEL. BY THE AUTHOR OF "SELF-CONTROL."

Edinburgh: Printed by George Ramsay & Co. for Manners and Miller; and Longman, Hurst, Rees, Orme, and Brown, London, 1814.
I ix, 290p; II 306; III 292p. 8vo. 24s (ECB, ER).
ER 24: 544 (Feb 1815); WSW I: 177.
BL N.1942/4; ECB 164; NSTC B5016 (BI C, E, NCu, O).

*Notes.* Preface dated Edinburgh, Nov 1814. ECB dates Jan 1815.
Further edns: 2nd edn. 1815 (Corvey), CME 3-628-47436-1; 3rd edn. 1815 (NSTC); 1832 (NSTC); 1849 (NSTC); Boston 1815 (NUC); German trans., 1823 [as *Ellen Percy, oder Erziehung durch Schicksale* (RS)].

BURNEY, Frances
See D'ARBLAY, Frances

1814: 15   [BYRON, 'Medora Gordon'].
THE ENGLISH EXPOSÉ; OR, MEN AND WOMEN "ABROAD" AND "AT
HOME." IN FOUR VOLUMES. BY A MODERN ANTIQUE, AUTHOR OF
CELIA IN SEARCH OF A HUSBAND, &C.

> London: Printed at the Minerva-Press, for A. K. Newman and Co. Leadenhall-Street,
> 1814.
> I 227p; II 258p; III 238; IV 242p. 12mo. 22s (ER, QR).
> ER 22: 490 (Jan 1814); QR 10: 544 (Jan 1814), 12: 524 (Jan 1815); WSW I: 193.
> Corvey; CME 3-628-47910-X; NSTC B6039 (BI BL).

1814: 16   CULLEN, Margaret.
MORNTON. A NOVEL. IN THREE VOLUMES. BY MARGARET CULLEN,
AUTHOR OF "HOME."

> London: Printed for J. Mawman, No. 39, Ludgate-Street; and for Wilson and Sons,
> York, 1814.
> I viii, 335p; II 342p; III 400p. 12mo. 18s (ECB, ER, QR).
> ER 23: 256 (Apr 1814), 23: 509 (Sept 1814); QR 11: 510 (July 1814); WSW I: 229.
> Corvey; CME 3-628-47359-4; ECB 146; xNSTC.

Notes. Dedication 'to Thomas Clarkson, Esq.', praising him for his efforts against the Slave
Trade, dated Fulford, 11 Apr 1814. Colophon in each vol. reads: 'From the Office of Thomas
Wilson & Sons, High-Ousegate, York'.
Further edns: 3rd edn. 1829 (NSTC 2C45830); 4th edn. 1835 (NUC); Boston 1816 (NUC).

1814: 17   {D'ARBLAY, F}[rances].
THE WANDERER; OR FEMALE DIFFICULTIES. BY THE AUTHOR OF
EVELINA; CECILIA; AND CAMILLA, IN FIVE VOLUMES.

> London: Printed for Longman, Hurst, Rees, Orme, and Brown, Paternoster-Row, 1814.
> I xxvii, 443p; II 458p; III 438p; IV 359p; V 395p. 12mo. 42s (ECB, ER, QR).
> ER 23: 256 (Apr 1814), 24: 320–38 (Feb 1815) full review; QR 11: 123–30 (Apr 1814) full
> review, 11: 510 (July 1814); WSW I: 181.
> BL 248.e.36–40; ECB 622; NSTC B5713 (BI C, O).

Notes. Dedication 'to Doctor Burney, F.R.S. and Correspondent to the Institute of France',
signed F. B. D'Arblay, 14 Mar 1814. Full review in ER (Feb 1815) under the page-top heading 'Standard Novels and Romances'.
Further edns: 2nd edn. 1814 (Corvey), CME 3-628-48878-8; New York 1814 (NUC); French
trans., 1815 [as La Femme errante (BN)].

1814: 18   DAVENPORT, Selina.
THE HYPOCRITE; OR, THE MODERN JANUS. A NOVEL. IN FIVE
VOLUMES. BY SELINA DAVENPORT.

> London: Printed at the Minerva-Press, for A. K. Newman and Co. Leadenhall-Street,
> 1814.
> I 221p; II 222; III 243p; IV 259p; V 261p. 12mo. 25s (ER, QR).
> ER 24: 269 (Nov 1814); QR 12: 523 (Jan 1815); WSW I: 237–8.
> Corvey; CME 3-628-47429-9; ECB 153; NSTC D390 (BI BL, O).

DUNN, Lady, SUSPICION; OR, THE BENEVOLENT RECLUSE
See 1810: 40

1814: 19   EDGEWORTH, Mrs.
THE BALLAD SINGER; OR, MEMOIRS OF THE BRISTOL FAMILY: A
MOST INTERESTING NOVEL. IN FOUR VOLUMES. BY MRS. EDGE-
WORTH, AUTHOR OF THE CHATEAU DE ST. PIERRE, FATHERLESS
FANNY, &C. &C. &C.

> London: Published by Sherwood, Neely, and Jones, Paternoster Row; and sold by all
> Booksellers, 1814.
> I 217p; II 246p; III 191p; IV 192p. 12mo. 20s (ECB).
> Corvey; CME 3-628-47528-7; ECB 178; NSTC E223 (BI BL, E, O).

*Notes.* ECB gives Newman as publisher, but not discovered in this form.

1814: 20   EDGEWORTH, Maria.
PATRONAGE. BY MARIA EDGEWORTH, AUTHOR OF "TALES OF FASH-
IONABLE LIFE," "BELINDA," "LEONORA," &C. IN FOUR VOLUMES.

> London: Printed for J. Johnson and Co. St. Paul's Church-Yard, 1814.
> I 418p; II 431p; III 402p; IV 389p. 12mo. 28s (ECB, QR).
> ER 22: 416–34 (Jan 1814) full review; QR 10: 301–22 (Jan 1814) full review, 11: 255 (Apr
> 1814); WSW I: 256–7.
> BRu ENC; ECB 178; NSTC E241 (BI BL, C, Dt, E, O).

*Notes.* Dedication 'to the Reader' signed Richard Lovell Edgeworth, Edgeworth's Town,
6 Oct 1813. Novel dated at end 26 Mar 1813. Novel proper ends p. 388 followed by errata,
2 pp.
*Further edns:* 2nd edn. 1814 (Corvey), CME 3-628-47574-0; 3rd edn. 1814 (NSTC); 3rd edn.
1815 [*sic*] (NSTC); Philadelphia 1814 (from London, 2nd edn.) (NUC); French trans., 1816
[as *Les Protecteurs et les protégés* (BN)]; German trans., 1828 [as *Die Gönnerschaft* (RS)].

1814: 21   [FOSCOLO, Niccolo Ugo].
*THE LETTERS OF ORTIS TO LORENZO: TAKEN FROM THE ORI-
GINAL MANUSCRIPTS, PUBLISHED AT MILAN IN 1802. TRANS-
LATED FROM THE ITALIAN.

> London: Printed for Henry Colburn, 1814.
> iv, 233p, ill. 12mo. 8s 6d (ECB, ER, QR).
> ER 23: 255 (Apr 1814); QR 11: 255 (Apr 1814).
> No copy of 1st edn. located; ECB 342.

*Notes.* Trans. of *Ultime Lettere di Jacopo Ortis* (Milan, 1802). 'Preface, by the Translator'
signed F. B. and dated London, 1 Jan 1814. Details from NUC (copy cited not found in ICU)
together with microfilm copy (t.p. missing) in ICU. Frontispiece portrait in 2nd edn. bears
legend: 'Published Jan.ʸ 1 1814 by Henry Colburn. Conduit Street'. An Italian language version ('Londra, 1811') was reviewed in QR 8: 438–45 (Dec 1812).
*Further edn:* 2nd edn. 1818 (BL 12410.ccc.29; NSTC 2O5322).

1814: 22    GAMBLE, John.
SARSFIELD: OR WANDERINGS OF YOUTH: AN IRISH TALE. BY
JOHN GAMBLE, ESQ. STRABANE; AUTHOR OF SKETCHES, &C. IN
IRELAND. IN THREE VOLUMES.

> London: Printed for C. Cradock and W. Joy, 32 Paternoster-Row; Doig and Stirling,
> Edinburgh; M. Keene, Dublin; and S. Archer, Belfast, 1814.
> I viii, 204p; II 232p; III 219p. 12mo. 16s 6d (ECB, ER, QR).
> ER 23: 509 (Sept 1814); QR 12: 274 (Oct 1814), 16: 283 (Oct 1816); WSW I: 276.
> Corvey; CME 3-628-47755-7; ECB 222; NSTC G125 (BI BL, Dt).

1814: 23    [GILLIES, Robert Pierce].
THE CONFESSIONS OF SIR HENRY LONGUEVILLE. A NOVEL. IN
TWO VOLUMES.

> Edinburgh: Printed by James Ballantyne and Co. for Longman, Hurst, Rees, Orme, and
> Brown, London, 1814.
> I 220p; II 204p. 12mo. 10s 6d (ECB, QR).
> QR 12: 274 (Oct 1814); WSW I: 279.
> Corvey; CME 3-628-47316-0; ECB 231; NSTC G956 (BI BL, E).

1814: 24    [GREEN, Sarah].
THE CARTHUSIAN FRIAR, OR THE MYSTERIES OF MONTANVILLE;
A POSTHUMOUS ROMANCE. IN FOUR VOLUMES. CORRECTED
AND REVISED BY AN AUTHOR OF CELEBRITY.

> London: Published by Sherwood, Neely, and Jones, Paternoster-Row; C. Chapple,
> Pallmall [sic]; and sold by all Booksellers, 1814.
> I 216p; II 192p; III 179p; IV 212p. 12mo.
> Corvey; CME 3-628-47217-2; xNSTC.

*Notes.* Advs. facing t.ps. as follows: vol. 1: The Ballad Singer; vol. 2: The Maiden Wife; or the
Heiress of De Courcy [...] By Miss M. Hamilton; vol. 3: Fitzherbert; or the Brothers. A Tale.
In three Volumes. By Mrs Yorke; vol. 4: Popularity.

1814: 25    [GREEN, Sarah].
THE FUGITIVE, OR FAMILY INCIDENTS. IN THREE VOLUMES. BY
THE AUTHOR OF PRIVATE HISTORY OF THE COURT OF ENGLAND,
ROMANCE READERS AND ROMANCE WRITERS, &C. &C.

> London: Printed for Black, Parry, & Co. Leadenhall-Street, 1814.
> I 220p; II 233p; III 236p. 12mo. 13s 6d (ECB, ER, QR).
> ER 24: 545 (Feb 1815); QR 13: 281 (Apr 1815); WSW I: 289.
> BL N.1858; ECB 220; NSTC G1945.

*Notes.* Further edn: 1815 (Corvey), CME 3-628-47843-X.

1814: 26    HANWAY, {M}[ary] {A}[nn].
CHRISTABELLE, THE MAID OF ROUEN. A NOVEL, FOUNDED ON
FACTS. BY MRS. HANWAY, AUTHOR OF "ELLINOR," "ANDREW
STUART," AND "FALCONBRIDGE ABBEY." IN FOUR VOLUMES.

London: Printed for Longman, Hurst, Rees, Orme, and Brown, Paternoster-Row, 1814.
I xiii, 335p; II 351p; III 320p; IV 322p. 12mo. 24s (ECB, ER).
ER 24: 545 (Feb 1815); WSW I: 297.
Corvey; CME 3-628-47600-3; ECB 254; NSTC H476 (BI BL).

*Notes.* Dedication 'to His Royal Highness the Duke of Sussex' signed by 'M. A. Hanway',
Blackheath, 1 Sept 1814.

### HARVEY, Jane, AUBERRY STANHOPE
See 1812: 33

### 1814: 27   HARVEY, Jane.
### RECORDS OF A NOBLE FAMILY, BY JANE HARVEY, AUTHOR OF "MEMOIRS OF AN AUTHOR," &C. &C. &C. IN FOUR VOLUMES.

London: Sold by Longman, Hurst, Rees, Orme and Brown, and printed and sold by H.
    Mozley, Gainsborough. September, 1814.
I 253p; II 252p; III 262p, IV 276p. 12mo. 18s (ECB, ER, QR).
ER 24: 544 (Feb 1815); QR 12: 523 (Jan 1815); WSW I: 301.
Corvey; CME 3-628-47647-X; ECB 257; NSTC H765 (BI BL).

*Notes.* Collates in sixes. Colophon of 'H. Mozley, Printer, Gainsborough'. ECB dates Nov
1814.

### 1814: 28   [HATTON, Anne Julia Kemble].
### CONVICTION; OR, SHE IS INNOCENT! A NOVEL. IN FIVE VOLUMES. BY ANN OF SWANSEA, AUTHOR OF CAMBRIAN PICTURES; SICILIAN MYSTERIES, &C. &C.

London: Printed at the Minerva-Press, for A. K. Newman and Co. Leadenhall-Street,
    1814.
I 238p; II 260p; III 239p; IV 246p; V 266p. 12mo. 27s 6d (ECB, ER, QR).
ER 23: 256 (Apr 1814), 23: 509 (Sept 1814); QR 11: 511 (July 1814), 12: 274 (Oct 1814).
Corvey; CME 3-628-48744-7; ECB 133; NSTC A1351 (BI BL).

*Notes.* Dedication 'to an unnamed Friend', subscribed 'Swansea, College Street'.

### 1814: 29   HAWKINS, Lætitia Matilda.
### ROSANNE; OR, A FATHER'S LABOUR LOST. IN THREE VOLUMES. BY LÆTITIA-MATILDA HAWKINS.

London: Printed for F. C. and J. Rivington, No. 62, St. Paul's Church-Yard, 1814.
I xii, 352p; II 366p; III 370p. 8vo. 27s (ECB, ER, QR).
ER 23: 509 (Sept 1814), 24: 544 (Feb 1815); QR 11: 511 (July 1814), 12: 523 (Jan 1815);
    WSW I: 303.
Corvey; CME 3-628-47542-2; ECB 259; NSTC H991 (BI BL, C, E, O).

*Notes.* Dedication 'to the Right Honourable Elizabeth-Laura, Countess of Waldegrave'.

### 1814: 30   HAYNES, D. F.
### PIERRE AND ADELINE; OR THE ROMANCE OF THE CASTLE. IN TWO VOLUMES. BY D. F. HAYNES, ESQ.

London: Printed for B. and R. Crosby and Co. Stationers' Court, 1814.
I 355p; II 356p. 12mo. 12s (ECB, ER, QR).
ER 22: 490 (Jan 1814); QR 10: 544 (Jan 1814), 12: 524 (Jan 1815); WSW I: 305.
NIC PR.4769.H2.P5; ECB 260; xNSTC.

*Notes.* Pagination at the end of vol. 2 incorporates 4 pp. list of 'Books now publishing by B. and R. Crosby and Co.'; the text of the novel ends at p. 352. ECB dates Dec 1813.
Further edn: 1841 as *The Romance of the Castle* (NSTC 2H14188).

1814: 31   HELME, Elizabeth.
MODERN TIMES; OR, THE AGE WE LIVE IN. A POSTHUMOUS NOVEL. IN THREE VOLUMES. DEDICATED, BY PERMISSION, TO THE RIGHT HONORABLE COUNTESS COWPER. BY ELIZABETH HELME, AUTHOR OF THE FARMER OF INGLEWOOD FOREST, THE PILGRIM OF THE CROSS, THE PENITENT OF GODSTOW, &C. &C.

Brentford: Printed by and for P. Norbury; sold by C. Cradock and W. Joy, No. 32, Pater-noster-Row; and by all other Booksellers, 1814.
I 284p; II 280p; III 303p. 12mo. 16s 6d (ER, QR).
ER 24: 545 (Feb 1815); QR 13: 281 (Apr 1815).
Corvey; CME 3-628-47726-3; NSTC H1228 (BI BL, O).

*Notes.* Dedication 'to the Right Honourable Countess Cowper', signed 'William Helme'. Elizabeth Helme died in 1810 (FC).
Further edn: 2nd edn. 1817 (NUC).

1814: 32   HERVEY, {Eliz}[abeth].
AMABEL; OR, MEMOIRS OF A WOMAN OF FASHION. BY MRS. HER-VEY, AUTHOR OF THE MOURTRAY FAMILY, &C. IN FOUR VOL-UMES.

London: Printed for Henry Colburn, Public Library, Conduit-Street, Hanover-Square; and sold by George Goldie, Edinburgh, and John Cumming, Dublin, 1814.
I 326p; II 335p; III 302p; IV 317p. 12mo. 28s (ECB, ER, QR).
ER 22: 490 (Jan 1814); QR 10: 544 (Jan 1814), 11: 255 (Apr 1814), 12: 524 (Jan 1815).
Corvey; CME 3-628-47790-5; ECB 266; NSTC H1457 (BI BL, C).

*Notes.* Dedication to the Queen, signed 'Eliz. Hervey'. ECB dates Dec 1813.
Further edns: 2nd edn. (A. K. Newman remainder issue with new t.p.) 1818 (CG, NUC); French trans., 1819.

1814: 33   [HOFLAND, Barbara].
THE MERCHANT'S WIDOW AND HER FAMILY. BY THE AUTHOR OF THE OFFICER'S WIDOW AND HER FAMILY; CLERGYMAN'S WIDOW AND FAMILY; DAUGHTER-IN-LAW, &C.

London: Printed at the Minerva-Press, for A. K. Newman and Co. Leadenhall-Street, 1814.
iii, 236p. 12mo. 4s (ECB, ER, QR).

ER 22: 490 (Jan 1814); QR 10: 544 (Jan 1814), 12: 524 (Jan 1815).
Corvey; CME 3-628-48066-3; ECB 381; NSTC H2423 (BI BL, O).

*Notes.* 'Advertisement' dated 30 July 1813. ECB dates 1813.
Further edns: 1820? as *The History of a Merchant's Widow* (NUC); 4th edn. 1823 (NSTC);
6th edn. 1826 (NSTC); [1830?] (NSTC); Great Yarmouth, [1840?] (NSTC); [1847] (NSTC);
French trans., 1831.


1814: 34   HOFLAND, {B}[arbara].
A VISIT TO LONDON; OR, EMILY AND HER FRIENDS. A NOVEL. IN
FOUR VOLUMES. BY MRS. HOFLAND, AUTHOR OF THE CLERGY-
MAN'S WIDOW; OFFICER'S WIDOW; MERCHANT'S WIDOW;
DAUGHTER-IN-LAW; SISTERS; SAYS SHE TO HER NEIGHBOUR;
PANORAMA OF EUROPE, &C.

>London: Printed at the Minerva-Press, for A. K. Newman and Co. Leadenhall-Street,
>1814.
>I 251p; II 272p; III 306p; IV 289p. 12mo. 24s (ECB, ER, QR).
>ER 23: 509 (Sept 1814); QR 12: 274 (Oct 1814).
>Corvey; CME 3-628-47678-X; ECB 275; xNSTC.

*Notes.* Dedication to the Queen, signed 'B. Hofland'.


1814: 35   HOLSTEIN, Anthony Frederick [pseud.].
THE SCOTCHWOMAN. A NOVEL. IN THREE VOLUMES. BY
ANTHONY FREDERICK HOLSTEIN, AUTHOR OF SIR OWEN GLEN-
DOWR; LOVE, MYSTERY, AND MISERY; THE ASSASSIN OF ST. GLEN-
ROY; INHABITANTS OF EARTH; BOUVERIE; THE MODERN KATE;
MISERIES OF AN HEIRESS, &C. &C.

>London: Printed at the Minerva-Press, for A. K. Newman and Co. Leadenhall-Street,
>1814.
>I 233p; II 211p; III 226p. 12mo. 15s (ECB, ER, QR).
>ER 23: 256 (Apr 1814); QR 11: 510 (July 1814); WSW I: 324.
>Corvey; CME 3-628-47738-7; ECB 278; xNSTC.


1814: 36   [JOHNSTONE, Christian Isobel].
THE SAXON AND THE GAËL; OR, THE NORTHERN METROPOLIS:
INCLUDING A VIEW OF THE LOWLAND AND HIGHLAND CHARAC-
TER. IN FOUR VOLUMES.

>London: Printed for Thomas Tegg, 111, Cheapside; and T. Dick, 142, High-Street,
>Edinburgh, 1814.
>I 216p; II 198p; III 203p; IV 200p. 12mo. 21s (ER).
>ER 24: 545 (Feb 1815); WSW I: 347.
>Corvey; CME 3-628-48527-4; NSTC J847 (BI BL, C, E).

*Notes.* Printer's mark after imprint date on t.p. reads: 'Printed by J. & A. Aikman, Edinburgh'.

1814: 37    LEADBE[A]TER, Mary and SHAKLETON, Elizabeth.
TALES FOR COTTAGERS, ACCOMODATED [*sic*] TO THE PRESENT
CONDITION OF THE IRISH PEASANTRY. BY MARY LEADBETTER,
AND ELIZABETH SHAKLETON.

> Dublin: Printed by James Cumming & Co. Hibernia Press-Office, for John Cumming,
> Lower Ormond Quay; and Gale, Curtis, and Fenner, Paternoster Row, London,
> 1814.
> 227p, ill. 12mo. 4s (ER, QR).
> ER 24: 544 (Feb 1815); QR 12: 523 (Jan 1815); WSW I: 117, 366.
> PU PR.4879.L85.T14; NSTC L880 (BI BL, Dt).

*Notes.* BL copy (1389.b.51(2)) lacks frontispiece; its imprint also does not include the London publishers.


1814: 38    [LOFTUS, George].
MILFORD HOUSE; OR, FOLLY AS IT FLIES. BY A LATE OFFICER OF
THE THIRD GUARDS. IN THREE VOLUMES.

> London: Printed for William Lindsell, Wimpole Street; by Dove, St. John's Square,
> 1814.
> I 243p; II 203p; III 162p. 12mo. 18s (ER, QR).
> ER 24: 268 (Nov 1814); QR 12: 274 (Oct 1814).
> Corvey; CME 3-628-48131-7; NSTC L2222 (BI BL).

*Notes.* Dedication to the Marchioness of Townshend.


1814: 39    MATHEW, Richard.
COURTLY ANNALS; OR, INDEPENDENCE THE TRUE NOBILITY. A
NOVEL. IN FOUR VOLUMES. BY RICHARD MATHEW, ESQ.

> London: Printed at the Minerva-Press, for A. K. Newman and Co. Leadenhall-Street,
> 1814.
> I 254p, ill.; II 242p; III 260p; IV 251p. 12mo. 22s (ECB, ER, QR).
> ER 22: 490 (Jan 1814); QR 10: 544 (Jan 1814), 12: 524 (Jan 1815).
> Corvey; CME 3-628-48196-1; ECB 373; NSTC M1658 (BI BL).

*Notes.* Dedication 'to Myself'. ECB dates 1813.


1814: 40    MEEKE, [Mary].
CONSCIENCE. A NOVEL. IN FOUR VOLUMES. BY MRS. MEEKE,
AUTHOR OF MATRIMONY, MIDNIGHT WEDDINGS, NINE DAYS'
WONDER, TALE OF MYSTERY, &C. &C.

> London: Printed at the Minerva-Press, for A. K. Newman and Co. Leadenhall-Street,
> 1814.
> I 312p; II 267p; III 264p; IV 247p. 12mo. 24s (ER, QR).
> ER 23: 509 (Sept 1814); QR 12: 274 (Oct 1814).
> Corvey; CME 3-628-48207-0; ECB 378; NSTC M1953 (BI BL).

1814: 41   MORGAN, Lady {Sydney} [née OWENSON, Sydney].
**O'DONNEL. A NATIONAL TALE. BY LADY MORGAN, (LATE MISS OWENSON) AUTHOR OF THE WILD IRISH GIRL; NOVICE OF ST. DOMINICK, &C. IN THREE VOLUMES.**

> London: Printed for Henry Colburn, Public Library, Conduit Street, Hanover-Square, and sold by George Goldie, Edinburgh, and John Cumming, Dublin, 1814.
> I xii, 295p; II 331p; III 339p. 12mo. 21s (ECB, ER, QR).
> ER 23: 256 (Apr 1814); QR 11: 256 (Apr 1814); WSW I: 426.
> Corvey; CME 3-628-48329-8; ECB 396; NSTC O733 (BI BL, E, O).

*Notes.* Dedication 'to His Grace William Spencer Cavendish, Duke of Devonshire', signed Sydney Morgan. Preface also signed Sydney Morgan, and dated 35, Kildare-Street, Dublin, 1 Mar 1814.
Further edns: New edn. 1815 (NUC); 1835 (NSTC); 1836 (NUC); 1848 (NUC); New York 1814 (NUC); French trans., 1815 [as *O'Donnel, ou l'Irlande* (BN)]; German trans., 1823 [as *O'Donnel, oder die Reise nach dem Riesendamm* (RS)].
Facs: IAN (1979).

1814: 42   [MURRAY, Hugh].
**CORASMIN, OR, THE MINISTER; A ROMANCE. IN THREE VOLUMES. BY THE AUTHOR OF THE SWISS EMIGRANTS.**

> London: Printed for Longman, Hurst, Rees, Orme, and Brown, Paternoster Row, 1814.
> I iii, 269p; II 243p; III 275p. 12mo. 15s (ECB, ER, QR).
> ER 23: 256 (Apr 1814); QR 11: 256 (Apr 1814); WSW I: 414.
> Corvey; CME 3-628-47337-3; ECB 135; NSTC M3701 (BI BL, E, O).

*Notes.* Colophon of 'Walker and Greig, Printers, Edinburgh' in all vols. See *The Swiss Emigrants* (1804: 52) for a possible connection with Louisa Theresa Bellenden Ker. But a letter to Hugh Murray in the Longman Letter Books, I, 98, no. 96, dated 24 Nov 1813, indicates that *Corasmin* is almost certainly his: 'We will thank you to give your Novel to Walker & Greig to print to be done similar to "Marian" which they printed for us [...]. Please send us a copy of the Title of the work that we may include it in our list of new publications.' The same letter authorises an impression of 750 copies.

1814: 43   [O'KEEFFE, Adelaide].
**ZENOBIA, QUEEN OF PALMYRA; A NARRATIVE, FOUNDED ON HISTORY. IN TWO VOLUMES. BY THE AUTHOR OF PATRIARCHAL TIMES.**

> London: Printed by J. Dennett, Leather Lane, Holborn; for F. C. and J. Rivington, St. Paul's Church Yard, 1814.
> I viii, 347p; II viii, 310p. 12mo. 12s (ECB, ER, QR).
> ER 23: 256 (Apr 1814); QR 11: 511 (July 1814); WSW I: 132.
> Corvey; CME 3-628-48247-X; ECB 421; NSTC Z39 (BI BL).

*Notes.* Further edns: 1814 (NUC); 1824 (NUC).

OWENSON, Sydney
See MORGAN, Lady Sydney

1814: 44   [PILKINGTON, Mary].
THE NOVICE; OR, THE HEIR OF MONTGOMERY CASTLE. A NOVEL.
IN THREE VOLUMES. BY MATTHEW MORAL, ESQ.

> London: Printed at the Minerva-Press, for A. K. Newman and Co. Leadenhall-Street,
>     1814.
> I 235p; II 240p; III 230p. 12mo. 16s 6d (ECB, ER).
> ER 24: 545 (Feb 1815).
> Corvey; CME 3-628-48280-1; ECB 395; NSTC M3122 (BI BL).

*Notes.* Frank (Item 330) notes the bibliographical confusion over Miss Pilkington and Mary Pilkington, listing this as by the latter. He comments 'The fact that *The Novice* bears the signature, "Matthew Moral, esq.", suggests the soberly didactic direction which Mrs. Pilkington gives to her rewriting of Mrs Radcliffe's *The Italian*' (p. 283). Mrs Mary Pilkington (1766–1839), the prolific author of children's books, was evidently a different figure from the shadowy 'Miss Pilkington' who wrote four novels for the Minerva Press, ending with *The Accusing Spirit* (see 1802: 54).

1814: 45   [PINCHARD, Elizabeth].
MYSTERY AND CONFIDENCE: A TALE. BY A LADY. IN THREE VOL-
UMES.

> London: Printed for Henry Colburn, Public Library, Conduit-Street, Hanover-Square,
>     and sold by George Goldie, Edinburgh, and John Cumming, Dublin, 1814.
> I 230p; II 222p; III 199p. 12mo. 18s (ECB, ER, QR).
> ER 23: 256 (Apr 1814); QR 11: 255 (Apr 1814).
> Corvey; CME 3-628-48183-X; ECB 403; NSTC P1795 (BI BL, O).

1814: 46   PORTER, Anna Maria.
THE RECLUSE OF NORWAY. BY MISS ANNA MARIA PORTER. IN
FOUR VOLUMES.

> London: Printed for Longman, Hurst, Rees, Orme, and Brown, Paternoster-Row, 1814.
> I viii, 247p; II 317p; III 300p; IV 333p. 12mo. 24s (ECB, ER, QR).
> ER 24: 269 (Nov 1814); QR 12: 523 (Jan 1815); WSW I: 447.
> Corvey; CME 3-628-48302-6; ECB 464; NSTC P2592 (BI BL, E, O).

*Notes.* Dedication 'to the Author of "A Fortnight's Ramble to the Lakes"', signed Anna Maria Porter. Preface dated Long-Ditton, 3 Sept 1814.
Further edns: 2nd edn. 1816 (NSTC); New York 1815 (NUC) [also Philadelphia 1815 (NUC)]; French trans., 1815.

1814: 47   ROBERTS, [Margaret].
DUTY, A NOVEL, BY THE LATE MRS. ROBERTS, AUTHOR OF "ROSE
AND EMILY:" INTERSPERSED WITH POETRY AND PRECEDED BY A
CHARACTER OF THE AUTHOR BY MRS. OPIE. IN THREE VOLUMES.

> London: Printed for Longman, Hurst, Rees, Orme, and Brown, Paternoster-Row, 1814.
> I 212p; II 199p; III 180p. 12mo. 12s (ECB, ER, QR).
> ER 24: 268 (Nov 1814); QR 12: 274 (Oct 1814), 13: 531 (July 1815); WSW I: 467.
> Corvey; CME 3-628-48614-9; ECB 496; NSTC R1194 (BI BL, O).

*Notes.* 'Sketch of the Character of the Author', signed Amelia Opie, vol. 1, pp. [3]–22. This gives the name of the author's husband as Revd Richard Roberts, a clergyman in Surrey, making NUC's attribution of 1806: 57 (by Mrs D. Roberts) to Margaret Roberts seem less likely.

Further edns: New York 1815, as *Duty; or, the White Cottage* (NUC); French trans., 1816.


1814: 48   [ROCHE, Mrs].
**LONDON TALES; OR, REFLECTIVE PORTRAITS.**

> London: Printed for John Booth, Duke Street, Portland Place, 1814.
> I iv, 138p; II 159p. 12mo. 7s (ECB, ER, QR).
> ER 23: 509 (Sept 1814); QR 12: 274 (Oct 1814).
> Corvey; CME 3-628-51094-5; ECB 498; NSTC D148 (BI BL).

*Notes.* For the authorship see: Natalie Schroeder, 'Regina Maria Roche, Popular Novelist, 1789–1834: The Rochean Canon', *Papers of the Bibliographical Society of America*, 73 (1979), 462–8. She doubts the work is by Regina Maria Roche. See also 1814: 49 below for evidence of a different author writing under the name of Mrs Roche.


1814: 49   ROCHE, Mrs.
**PLAIN TALES. BY MRS. ROCHE, AUTHOR OF "THE MOOR", &C. IN TWO VOLUMES.**

> London: Published and sold by G. Walker, Publisher of Books and Music, 106, Great
>     Portland-Street. Sold also by Cradock and Joy, Paternoster-Row, 1814.
> I vi, 211p; II 271p. 12mo.
> BRu ENC; xNSTC.

*Notes.* 'Introduction' states 'These Plain Tales were composed for the amusement of a dear sister'. Almost certainly not by Regina Maria Roche. See also *London Tales* and *Anna; or, Edinburgh* (Entries 1814: 48, 1815: 42), which with the present title appear to form a distinct group. Printer information after imprint date reads: 'W. Wilson, Printer, 4, Greville-Street, Hatton-Garden, London'.


1814: 50   ROCHE, Regina Maria.
**TRECOTHICK BOWER; OR, THE LADY OF THE WEST COUNTRY. A TALE. IN THREE VOLUMES. BY REGINA MARIA ROCHE, AUTHOR OF THE CHILDREN OF THE ABBEY; DISCARDED SON; HOUSES OF OSMA AND ALMERIA; MONASTERY OF ST. COLUMB; VICAR OF LANSDOWNE, &C. &C.**

> London: Printed at the Minerva-Press, for A. K. Newman and Co. Leadenhall-Street,
>     1814.
> I 264p; II 258p; III 263p. 12mo. 18s (ECB, ER, QR).
> ER 22: 490 (Jan 1814); QR 10: 544 (Jan 1814), 12: 523 (Jan 1815); WSW I: 470.
> Corvey; CME 3-628-48465-0; ECB 498; NSTC D151 (BI BL, O).

*Notes.* ECB dates 1813.

Further edn: Philadelphia & Boston 1816 (NUC).

1814: 51   ROSS, Mrs.

THE MODERN CALYPSO; OR, WIDOW'S CAPTIVATION. A NOVEL. IN FOUR VOLUMES. BY MRS. ROSS, AUTHOR OF THE COUSINS, STRANGERS OF LINDENFELDT, &C.

London: Printed at the Minerva-Press, for A. K. Newman and Co. Leadenhall-Street, 1814.
I 248p; II 246p; III 244p; IV 236p. 12mo. 22s (ECB, ER, QR).
ER 22: 490 (Jan 1814); QR 10: 544 (Jan 1814), 12: 524 (Jan 1815).
Corvey; CME 3-628-48553-3; ECB 503; xNSTC.

*Notes.* ECB dates 1813.

SCOTT, Honoria, THE CASTLE OF STRATHMAY
See 1813: 54

1814: 52   [SCOTT, Sir Walter].

WAVERLEY; OR, 'TIS SIXTY YEARS SINCE. IN THREE VOLUMES.

Edinburgh: Printed by James Ballantyne and Co. for Archibald Constable and Co.; and Longman, Hurst, Rees, Orme, and Brown, London, 1814.
I 358p; II 370p; III 371p. 12mo. 21s (ECB, ER).
ER 23: 509 (Sept 1814, for 2nd edn.), 24: 208–43 (Nov 1814, for 3rd edn.) full review, 24: 268 (Nov 1814, for 3rd edn.); QR 11: 354–77 (July 1814) full review; WSW I: 484.
BL C.59.g.16; ECB 627; NSTC S893 (BI C, E, O).

*Notes.* 'This day published', 7 July 1814, *Edinburgh Evening Courant.*
Further edns: 2nd edn. 1814 (Corvey), CME 3-628-48598-3; 3rd edn. 1814 (NSTC); 4th edn. 1814 (NSTC); 5th edn. 1815 (NSTC); 6th edn. 1816 (NSTC); 7th edn. 1817 (NSTC); 8th edn. 1821 (NSTC); Boston 1815 (NUC) [also New York 1815 (NUC)]; French trans. (of 4th edn.), 1818; German trans., 1821. Numerous reprintings in collected edns.

1814: 53   STANHOPE, Louisa Sidney.

MADELINA. A TALE FOUNDED ON FACTS. IN FOUR VOLUMES. BY LOUISA SIDNEY STANHOPE, AUTHOR OF MONTBRASIL ABBEY; DI MONTRANZO; THE AGE WE LIVE IN; STRIKING LIKENESSES; CONFESSIONAL OF VALOMBRE, &C. &C.

London: Printed at the Minerva-Press, for A. K. Newman and Co. Leadenhall-Street, 1814.
I 245p; II 263p; III 257p; IV 269p. 12mo. 22s (ECB, ER); 21s (QR).
ER 22: 246 (Oct 1813); QR 10: 544 (Jan 1814).
Corvey; CME 3-628-48777-3; ECB 558; NSTC S3497 (BI C).

*Notes.* ECB dates 1813.

1814: 54   STIVEN, Alexander.

*LOVE AND WAR: AN HISTORICAL ROMANCE. BY ALEXANDER STIVEN.

London: Printed for the Author, 1814.

2 vols. 12mo. 12s (ER, QR).
ER 23: 256 (Apr 1814); QR 11: 510 (July 1814); WSW I: 522.
No copy located.

*Notes.* Imprint details from Block.

1814: 55    [THOMAS, Elizabeth].
THE PRISON-HOUSE; OR, THE WORLD WE LIVE IN. A NOVEL. IN
FOUR VOLUMES. BY MRS. BRIDGET BLUEMANTLE, AUTHOR OF
THE VINDICTIVE SPIRIT, HUSBAND AND WIFE, MONTE VIDEO,
&C. &C.

London: Printed at the Minerva-Press, for A. K. Newman and Co. Leadenhall-Street,
1814.
I 235p; II 226p; III 229p; IV 235p. 12mo. 22s (ECB, ER, QR).
ER 23: 509 (Sept 1814); QR 12: 274 (Oct 1814).
Corvey; CME 3-628-47155-9; ECB 63; NSTC B3417 (BI BL).

1814: 56    TORRENS, Robert.
THE VICTIM OF INTOLERANCE; OR, THE HERMIT OF KILLARNEY.
A CATHOLIC TALE. BY ROBERT TORRENS, MAJOR IN THE ROYAL
MARINES.

London: Printed for Gale, Curtis, and Fenner, Paternoster-Row, 1814.
I 181p; II 238p; III 221p; IV 288p. 12mo. 20s (ECB, ER, QR).
ER 23: 256 (Apr 1814); QR 11: 511 (July 1814); WSW I: 266, 542.
Corvey; CME 3-628-47458-2; ECB 594; NSTC T1337 (BI O).

*Notes.* Dedication 'to the People of Ireland'. Colophon throughout of W. Flint, Printer, Old
Bailey, London. WSW I: 266 (mistakenly) lists under Robert Ferrers.

1814: 57    TUCKETT, T. R.
THE VAULTS OF LEPANTO. A ROMANCE. IN THREE VOLUMES. BY
T. R. TUCKETT, ESQ.

London: Printed at the Minerva-Press, for A. K. Newman and Co. Leadenhall-Street,
1814.
I 220p; II 227p; III 286p. 12mo. 15s (ECB, ER, QR).
ER 23: 256 (Apr 1814); QR 11: 510 (July 1814); WSW I: 545.
Corvey; CME 3-628-48840-0; ECB 602; xNSTC.

*Notes.* Drop-head title reads: 'Urbino; or, the Vaults of Lepanto', the title also given in Blakey
(copy not seen), ECB, Frank, and WSW I: 545.

1814: 58    WARD, Catherine G[eorge].
A BACHELOR'S HEIRESS; OR, A TALE WITHOUT WONDER! A
NOVEL, IN THREE VOLUMES. BY CATHARINE G. WARD, AUTHOR
OF THE DAUGHTER OF ST. OMAR, AND MY NATIVE LAND.

Lynn: Printed by W. G. Whittingham, and published by R. Baldwin, Pater-Noster Row,
London, 1814.

I 219p; II 210p; III 168p. 12mo. 15s (ECB, ER, QR).
ER 22: 490 (Jan 1814); QR 10: 544 (Jan 1814), 11: 255 (Apr 1814), 12: 524 (Jan 1815).
Corvey; CME 3-628-48821-4; ECB 623; xNSTC.

*Notes.* Dedication to the Countess of Craven, signed C. G. Ward, Coventry, 1 Dec 1813. ECB dates Dec 1813.

1814: 59    WARD, Catherine G[eorge].
THE SON AND THE NEPHEW; OR, MORE SECRETS THAN ONE. A NOVEL. IN THREE VOLUMES. BY CATHERINE G. WARD, AUTHOR OF DAUGHTER OF ST. OMER; MY NATIVE LAND; A BACHELOR'S HEIRESS; CORINNA, &C. &C. DEDICATED (BY PERMISSION) TO MRS. BOEHM.

London: Printed for Sherwood, Neely and Jones, Paternoster Row; and may be had of all Booksellers, 1814.
I iv, 248p; II 232p; III 248p. 12mo.
IU 823.M383s; ECB 623; xNSTC.

*Notes.* Dedication to Mrs Boehm. ECB dates 1815.

1814: 60    [WEST, Jane].
ALICIA DE LACY; AN HISTORICAL ROMANCE. BY THE AUTHOR OF "THE LOYALISTS," &C. IN FOUR VOLUMES.

London: Printed for Longman, Hurst, Rees, Orme, and Brown, Paternoster-Row, 1814.
I xv, 348p; II 362p; III 358p; IV 312p. 12mo. 28s (ECB, ER, QR).
ER 23: 509 (Sept 1814); QR 12: 274 (Oct 1814); WSW I: 557.
Corvey; CME 3-628-48889-3; ECB 630; NSTC W1342 (BI C, O).

*Notes.* Introduction dated 7 Mar 1814.
Further edns: French trans., 1820; German trans., 1821 [as *Die Ritter der rothen Rose* (RS)].

1814: 61    WESTON, Anna Maria.
PLEASURE AND PAIN, OR THE FATE OF ELLEN; A NOVEL. IN THREE VOLUMES. BY ANNA MARIA WESTON.

London: Printed for Thomas Tegg, No. 111, Cheapside, 1814.
I 236p; II 236p; III 244p. 12mo. 18s (ECB, ER, QR).
ER 23: 256 (Apr 1814); QR 11: 256 (Apr 1814).
BL 12604.h.12; ECB 631; NSTC W1416.

1815: 1   ANON.
## AMURATH, PRINCE OF PERSIA. AN ARABIAN TALE.

> London: Published and sold by G. Walker, (Publisher of Books and Music), 105 and
> 106, Great Portland-Street: sold also by Baldwin, Cradock, and Joy, Paternoster-
> Row; Sharpe, Juvenile Library, London Museum, Piccadilly: and Sutherland,
> Calton-Street, Edinburgh, 1815.
> iv, 221p, ill. 12mo.
> WSW I: 11.
> BL N.2034; NSTC A1172 (BIE).

1815: 2   ANON.
## THE ANNALS OF ORLINGBURY: A NOVEL. BY THE AUTHOR OF LOVE AND HORROR; A MODERN ROMANCE. A SHORT EXCURSION IN FRANCE, &C. IN TWO VOLUMES.

> London: Printed for J. J. Stockdale, No. 41, Pall-Mall, 1815.
> I 220p; II 128p. 12mo. 10s (ER, QR).
> ER 25: 560 (Oct 1815); QR 13: 531 (July 1815).
> Corvey; CME 3-628-47062-5; xNSTC.

*Notes.* Novel dated 14 June 1815 at end. For an earlier novel evidently by the same author, written under the pseudonym of Ircastrensis, see *Love and Horror* (1812: 41).

1815: 3   ANON.
## THE CAVERN OF ASTOLPHO, A SPANISH ROMANCE. IN TWO VOLUMES.

> London: Printed for W. Simpkin and R. Marshall, Stationers' Court, Ludgate Street, 1815.
> I v, 274p; II 291p. 12mo. 10s 6d (ECB, QR); 10s (ER).
> ER 25: 560 (Oct 1815); QR 14: 279 (Oct 1815); WSW I: 22.
> Corvey; CME 3-628-47241-5; ECB 103; xNSTC.

*Notes.* 'To the Reader' states that 'the following Romance was formed, and the whole nearly written, some years ago'. Collates in sixes.
Further edn: French trans., 1816?.

1815: 4   ANON.
## THE CURSE OF ULRICA; OR THE WHITE CROSS KNIGHTS OF RIDDARHOLMEN. A SWEDISH ROMANCE OF THE SIXTEENTH CENTURY. IN THREE VOLUMES.

> London: Printed for Black, Parry, and Co. Booksellers to the Hon. East India Company,
> Leadenhall Street, 1815.
> I xii, 299p; II 335p; III 327p. 12mo. 18s (ECB, ER, QR).

ER 25: 278 (June 1815); QR 13: 531 (July 1815).
Corvey; CME 3-628-47364-0; ECB 148; NSTC U15 (BI BL).

*Notes.* Preface, dated London, Feb 1815, implies male authorship.

1815: 5 ANON.
DANGEROUS SECRETS. A NOVEL. IN TWO VOLUMES.

London: Printed at the Minerva-Press, for A. K. Newman and Co. Leadenhall-Street, 1815.
I vii, 201p; II 210p. 12mo. 10s 6d (QR).
QR 13: 281 (Apr 1815).
Corvey; CME 3-628-47418-3; NSTC S1040 (BI BL).

*Notes.* Introductory lines (in verse) concerning the work being a novel, at the beginning of vol. 1.

1815: 6 ANON.
LADY JANE'S POCKET. A NOVEL. IN FOUR VOLUMES. BY THE AUTHOR OF SILVANELLA, OR THE GIPSEY.

London: Printed at the Minerva Press for A. K. Newman and Co. Leadenhall-Street, 1815.
I 228p; II 245p; III 268p; IV 235p. 12mo. 22s (ER, QR).
ER 25: 560 (Oct 1815); QR 14: 279 (Oct 1815); WSW I: 63.
Corvey; CME 3-628-47891-X; NSTC L93 (BI BL, C).

1815: 7 ANON.
LIFE, SMOOTH AND ROUGH AS IT RUNS.

London: Printed by Whittingham and Rowland, Goswell-Street, for John Martin, Holles Street Cavendish Square, 1815.
iv, 215p. 12mo. 6s (ECB, ER).
ER 25: 278 (June 1815); WSW I: 66.
ABu SB.82379.Lifes; ECB 346; NSTC L1604 (BI BL).

*Notes.* Preface states that 'this is no novel, nor aught so worthy as a good one [. . .] [but] only a narrative of the every day concerns of Life, smooth and rough as it runs' (pp. [i]–ii).

1815: 8 ANON.
THE MISERIES AND PLEASURES OF MATRIMONY; OR, THE FIRST HUSBAND AND THE SECOND. A NOVEL. IN FOUR VOLUMES.

London: Printed at the Minerva-Press, for A. K. Newman and Co. Leadenhall-Street, 1815.
I 300p; II 297p; III 291p; IV 312p. 12mo. 24s (ECB, ER, QR).
ER 25: 278 (June 1815); QR 13: 281 (Apr 1815).
Corvey; CME 3-628-48212-7; ECB 389; NSTC M2669 (BI BL).

1815: 9 ANON.
THE OBSERVANT PEDESTRIAN MOUNTED; OR A DONKEY TOUR TO BRIGHTON, A COMIC SENTIMENTAL NOVEL. IN THREE VOLUMES. BY THE AUTHOR OF THE MYSTIC COTTAGER—OBSERVANT PEDESTRIAN—MONTROSE—SPLENDID FOLLIES, &C.

London: Printed for W. Simpkin and R. Marshall, No. 4, Stationers' Court, Ludgate Street, 1815.

I iv, 327p; II iv, 282p; III iv, 300p. 12mo. 16s 6d (ECB, ER, QR).

ER 25: 278 (June 1815); QR 13: 281 (Apr 1815), 13: 531 (July 1815); WSW I: 84.

BL 12611.dd.14; ECB 419; NSTC P934.

### THE SPANIARD IN LONDON

See 1814: 2

### 1815: 10   ANON.
### A TALE, FOR GENTLE AND SIMPLE.

London: Printed for Rowland Hunter, Successor to J. Johnson, St. Paul's Church-Yard, 1815.

xi, 456p. 12mo. 7s (ECB, ER).

ER 25: 278 (June 1815).

BL N.1873; ECB 574; NSTC T105 (BI C).

*Notes.* 'Inscribed, without permission, to Miss Edgeworth, by a very sincere Admirer Unknown'. Printer's mark verso of t.p.: 'Printed by J. Belcher & Son, High-Street, Birmingham'. Collates in sixes.

### 1815: 11   ANON.
### THERESA; OR, THE WIZARD'S FATE. A ROMANCE. IN FOUR VOLUMES. BY A MEMBER OF THE INNER TEMPLE.

London: Printed at the Minerva-Press, for A. K. Newman and Co. Leadenhall-Street, 1815.

I 258p; II 262p; III 259p; IV 258p. 12mo. 22s (QR).

QR 13: 531 (July 1815).

Corvey; CME 3-628-48951-2; NSTC T596 (BI BL, C, O).

### 1815: 12   ANON.
### VARIETIES OF LIFE; OR, CONDUCT AND CONSEQUENCES. A NOVEL. IN THREE VOLUMES. BY THE AUTHOR OF "SKETCHES OF CHARACTER."

London: Printed for Longman, Hurst, Rees, Orme, and Brown, Paternoster Row, 1815.

I 346p; II 270p; III 295p. 12mo. 18s (ECB, ER, QR).

ER 25: 278 (June 1815); QR 13: 531 (July 1815), 14: 554 (Jan 1816); WSW I: 125–6.

Corvey; CME 3-628-48860-5; ECB 610; NSTC V132 (BI BL, C).

*Notes.* Further edn: Philadelphia 1816 (NSTC).

### 1815: 13   ANON.
### ZELUCA; OR, EDUCATED AND UNEDUCATED WOMAN. A NOVEL. IN THREE VOLUMES.

Brighton: Printed for the Author, by J. Forbes, No. 8, Market-Street; and published by Baldwin, Craddock, and Joy, Paternoster Row, London; and may be had of all Booksellers, 1815.

I 406p; II 344p; III 343p. 12mo. 21s (ECB, ER, QR).

ER 25: 560 (Oct 1815); QR 14: 279 (Oct 1815); WSW I: 132.

Corvey; CME 3-628-48999-7; ECB 654; NSTC Z34 (BI BL, C).

*Notes.* Collates in sixes.

1815: 14  [AGG, John].

A MONTH AT BRUSSELS, A SATIRICAL NOVEL. IN THREE VOLUMES. BY THE AUTHOR OF "A MONTH IN TOWN," "REJECTED ODES," "GENERAL POST BAG," &C. &C.

London: Printed for M. Iley, Somerset Street, Portman Square, sold by Sherwood, Neely, and Jones, Paternoster Row, and all Booksellers, 1815.

I vii, 184p; II 180p; III 185p. 12mo. 16s 6d (ER, QR).

ER 25: 560 (Oct 1815); QR 14: 279 (Oct 1815); WSW I: 79.

Corvey; CME 3-628-48274-7; NSTC A590 (BI BL, O).

*Notes.* Preface dated London, 22 Aug 1815. Collates in sixes.

1815: 15  ALGERNON [pseud.].

THE ROYAL WANDERER, OR THE EXILE OF ENGLAND. A TALE. BY ALGERNON. IN THREE VOLUMES.

London: Printed for J. Johnston, 98, Cheapside, 1815.

I 248p; II 231p; III 190p. 12mo. 18s (ER, QR).

ER 25: 560 (Oct 1815); QR 14: 279 (Oct 1815); WSW I: 3.

Corvey; CME 3-628-47039-0; NSTC A896 (BI BL).

*Notes.* ECB 505 lists Newman edn., 1815, 16s 6d; but not discovered in this form.

1815: 16  BENSON, Maria.

SYSTEM AND NO SYSTEM; OR, THE CONTRAST. BY MARIA BENSON, AUTHOR OF THOUGHTS ON EDUCATION.

London: Printed for J. Hatchard, Bookseller to the Queen, No. 190, opposite Albany, Piccadilly; and sold by W. A. Justice, Howden, 1815.

xx, 264p. 12mo. 6s (ECB); 6s boards (s.l.).

WSW I: 153.

ABu SB.82379.Bens; ECB 51; NSTC B1619 (BI BL).

*Notes.* T.p. details also appear on outer front board. Dedication 'to the Honourable Viscountess Pollington'. Preface signed Ousefleet Grange. 'List of Subscribers' (97 names), pp. [viii]–xii, headed by an apology for 'a small addition' to the price owing to 'a considerable advance [. . .] in the price of paper'. ECB dates Jan 1815.

1815: 17  BUONAPARTE, Louis.

MARIA; OR, THE HOLLANDERS: BY LOUIS BUONAPARTE. IN THREE VOLUMES.

London: Printed by J. Gillet, Crown-Court, Fleet-Street, for H. Colburn, Conduit-Street; and Longman, Hurst, Rees, Orme, and Brown, Paternoster-Row, 1815.

I xvi, 225p; II 189p; III 251p. 12mo. 16s 6d (ECB, ER); 16s (QR).

ER 25: 278 (June 1815); QR 13: 281 (Apr 1815); WSW I: 180.

BL N.1820; ECB 64; NSTC L2387 (BI C, Dt).

*Notes.* Trans. of *Marie, ou les Hollandoises* (Paris, 1814), which is the second edn. of *Marie, ou les peines de l'amour* (Gratz, 1812). Preface to the Translation, signed E. A. K., 6 Feb 1815, reads: 'The first edition, under the title of *Marie, ou les peines de l'amour*, was printed at Gratz, in the year 1812. Of that edition, a reprint appeared in Paris, but, from whatever cause, not before the beginning of the year 1814. In the interim, the author had made several alterations in his work, changing some of the minor incidents of the story, and consequently suppressing some of his pages, and adding others; and, in the month of June, 1814, he conveyed, by a written paper, dated at Lausanne, in Switzerland, and signed "L. de St. Leu," to a particular bookseller in Paris, authority to print, from the original manuscript, with its alterations, a second edition of his book, under the new title of *Marie, ou les Hollandoises*. From this edition, the following translation has been made' (pp. [v]–vi).

1815: 18    BYRON, ['Medora Gordon'].

**THE BACHELOR'S JOURNAL, INSCRIBED (WITHOUT PERMISSION) TO THE GIRLS OF ENGLAND. IN TWO VOLUMES. EDITED BY MISS BYRON, AUTHOR OF THE ENGLISHWOMAN, THE ENGLISHMAN, HOURS OF AFFLUENCE AND DAYS OF INDIGENCE, ALDERMAN AND PEER, &C. &C.**

> London: Printed at the Minerva-Press, for A. K. Newman and Co. Leadenhall-Street, 1815.
> I 249p; II 237p. 12mo. 10s 6d (ECB, ER).
> ER 24: 545 (Feb 1815); WSW I: 185.
> Corvey; CME 3-628-47178-8; ECB 91; NSTC B6037 (BI BL, O).

1815: 19    [CLAYTON, W.].

**THE INVISIBLE HAND. A TALE.**

> London: Printed for Cadell & Davies, in the Strand, and Hatchard, Piccadilly, 1815.
> 160p. 12mo. 5s (ER, QR).
> ER 25: 560 (Oct 1815); QR 14: 279 (Oct 1815); WSW I: 58.
> Corvey; CME 3-628-47939-8; NSTC I396 (BI O).

*Notes.* ECB 120 lists Cadell edn., 1817, 5s.

Further edns: 2nd edn. 1817 (with 'By W. Clayton' on t.p., and also containing dedication 'to Mrs. Clayton, of Highbury Place [. . .] by her dutiful, indebted, and affectionate son, the author' (MH 18478.7.5)); New York 1815 (Early American imprints. Second series; no. 34363 (microfilm)).

1815: 20    DAVENPORT, Selina.

**DONALD MONTEITH, THE HANDSOMEST MAN OF THE AGE. A NOVEL. IN FIVE VOLUMES. BY SELINA DAVENPORT, AUTHOR OF THE HYPOCRITE, OR THE MODERN JANUS; THE SONS OF THE VISCOUNT AND DAUGHTERS OF THE EARL, &C.**

> London: Printed at the Minerva Press for A. K. Newman and Co. Leadenhall-Street, 1815.

I 212p; II 229p; III 251p; IV 264p; V 268p. 12mo. 22s (ECB); 25s (ER, QR).
ER 25: 560 (Oct 1815); QR 14: 279 (Oct 1815).
Corvey; CME 3-628-47428-0; ECB 153; NSTC D389 (BI BL, C, O).

*Notes.* Further edn: 2nd edn. 1832 (NUC).

1815: 21   {DESPOURRINS, M.}.
THE NEVILLE FAMILY; AN INTERESTING TALE, FOUNDED ON
FACTS. BY A LADY. IN THREE VOLUMES.

London: Printed for T. Hughes, 35, Ludgate Street, 1815.
I v, 250p; II 220p; III 188p. 12mo. 13s 6d (QR).
QR 13: 531 (July 1815).
Corvey; CME 3-628-48190-2; xNSTC.

*Notes.* Dedication 'to the Right Honorable Lady Kinsale', signed 'M. Despourrins'. Collates
in sixes.

1815: 22   [DOHERTY, Ann].
THE KNIGHT OF THE GLEN. AN IRISH ROMANCE. BY THE AUTHOR
OF THE CASTLES OF WOLFNORTH AND MONTEAGLE, RONALD-
SHA, &C. IN TWO VOLUMES.

London: Printed for G. Walker, Publisher of Books and Music, 106, Great Portland
    Street. Sold also by Baldwin, Cradock, and Joy, Paternoster-Row; and J. Sutherland,
    Calton-Street, Edinburgh, 1815.
I 242p; II 210p. 12mo. 8s (ER).
ER 25: 278 (June 1815).
Corvey; CME 3-628-47982-7; NSTC K762 (BI BL).

*Notes.* For the chain leading to author attribution, see Entries 1808: 41 and 1812: 31.

1815: 23   [FENTON, Richard].
MEMOIRS OF AN OLD WIG.

London: Printed for Longman, Hurst, Rees, Orme, and Brown, Paternoster-Row, 1815.
xvi, 164p. 8vo. 7s (ECB, QR).
QR 14: 279 (Oct 1815).
Dt OLS.B-1-978; ECB 379; NSTC F469 (BI BL, C, E, O).

*Notes.* Vignette illustration of a wig (t.p.); Preface signed 'the Editor'.

1815: 24   [GALT, John].
THE MAJOLO: A TALE.

London: Published by H. Colburn, Conduit Street, Hanover Square, 1815.
252p. 12mo. 6s (ECB); 10s 6d (QR).
QR 16: 557 (Jan 1817); WSW I: 275.
Corvey; CME 3-628-48150-3; ECB 222; xNSTC.

*Notes.* 'Introductory Address' dated Apr 1815. ECB dates 1816. QR and WSW evidently refer
to the 1816 edn. (see below).
Further edn: 1816 (BL 12613.g.6; NSTC 2G1384). This 2-volumed edn. contains additional
text, as explained in a Preface, vol. 1, pp. [iii]–iv, dated 'Lindsey Place, Chelsea, November 5,

1816', which begins: 'The original sketch of this little work was so well received by several friends, in whose judgment the author had naturally great confidence, as some of them are persons to whom a large circle of acquaintance have, in matters of taste, been accustomed to pay much deference, that he was induced to suspend the sale of the first volume, and complete the narrative'. The imprint of the BL copy of this edn. reads: 'Printed for T. Faulkner, Bookseller, Paradise Row, Chelsea; and Sherwood, Neely, and Jones, Paternoster Row'. Galt is acknowledged as the author on t.p.

1815: 25   GAMBLE, John.
HOWARD; BY JOHN GAMBLE, ESQ. AUTHOR OF IRISH SKETCHES, SARSFIELD, &C. IN TWO VOLUMES.

> London: Printed for Baldwin, Cradock, and Joy, 47, Paternoster Row, 1815.
> I 228p; II 208p. 12mo. 9s (ECB, QR); 10s (ER).
> ER 25: 278 (June 1815); QR 13: 531 (July 1815); WSW I: 276.
> Corvey; CME 3-628-47908-8; ECB 222; NSTC G124 (BI BL).

*Notes.* Text proper in vol. 1 ends at p. 226, followed by advs., pp. [227]–228.

1815: 26   {GIBSON, A.}.
THE LIFE OF A RECLUSE. IN TWO VOLUMES.

> Newark: Printed and sold by M. Hage, Stodman-Street: and may be had of all Country
>    Booksellers; and of Messrs. Longman, Hurst, and Co. Paternoster Row, 1815.
> I 200p; II 222p. 12mo. 10s 6d (ER).
> ER 27: 537 (Dec 1816).
> MH-H *EC8.G3570.815l; xNSTC.

*Notes.* 'Address to Subscribers', signed A. Gibson, Screveton, near Bingham, 1 Aug 1815; followed by 'List of Subscribers' (10 pp. unn.), with 405 names. The author is listed as Ann Gibson in F. J. G. Robinson and P. J. Wallis, *Book Subscription Lists: A Revised Guide* (Newcastle upon Tyne, 1975), p. 55, where Newark Public Library is given as a source.
Further edn: reissued by A. K. Newman, London 1817 (Corvey; NSTC 2G6538), CME 3-628-47815-4.

1815: 27   GIFFARD, Edward Castleton.
FRANCE & ENGLAND; OR, SCENES IN EACH. COMPILED FROM THE ORIGINAL PAPERS, BY EDWARD CASTLETON GIFFARD, ESQ. IN TWO VOLUMES.

> London: Printed for G. & S. Robinson, 25, Paternoster-Row, by T. Davison, White-
>    Friars, 1815.
> I 204p; II 204p. 12mo. 10s 6d (ECB).
> Corvey; CME 3-628-47816-2; ECB 230; xNSTC.

*Notes.* 'The Editor's Preface' is signed G. C. Giffard [*sic*], London, 5 Mar 1814; the novel itself ends with the initials E. C. G. ECB dates May 1815.

GUNNING, Elizabeth, THE MAN OF FASHION
See THE VICTIMS OF SEDUCTION, below

1815: 28   GUNNING, [Elizabeth] [afterwards PLUNKETT].
THE VICTIMS OF SEDUCTION; OR, MEMOIRS OF A MAN OF FASH-
ION: A TALE OF MODERN TIMES. IN TWO VOLUMES. BY THE LATE
MISS GUNNING.

> London: Printed for M. Jones, 5, Newgate Street, 1815.
> I xi, 179p; II 182p. 12mo. 10s 6d (ECB, ER).
> ER 24: 545 (Feb 1815).
> Corvey; CME 3-628-47549-X; ECB 248; xNSTC.

*Notes.* Dedication 'to Her Royal Highness the Princess Charlotte of Wales [. . .] by the
Daughter of the late Lieut.-General Gunning, and the Niece of the late Duchess of Argyle,
and Countess of Coventry'. Followed by a dedicatory poem, 'The Fable of Trees, inscribed to
Her Royal Highness the Princess Charlotte of Wales'. Drop-head title reads: 'The Man of
Fashion'. Also published in the same year with an alternative t.p., as *The Man of Fashion; A
Tale of Modern Times* (see O 249.s.243; NSTC G2398).

1815: 29   [HATTON, Anne Julia Kemble].
SECRET AVENGERS; OR, THE ROCK OF GLOTZDEN. A ROMANCE.
IN FOUR VOLUMES. BY ANNE OF SWANSEA, AUTHOR OF CAM-
BRIAN PICTURES; SICILIAN MYSTERIES; CONVICTION, &C. &C.

> London: Printed at the Minerva-Press, for A. K. Newman and Co. Leadenhall-Street,
>    1815.
> I 281p; II 278p; III 305p; IV 310p. 12mo. 24s (ECB, ER).
> ER 24: 545 (Feb 1815); WSW I: 351.
> Corvey; CME 3-628-48805-2; ECB 20; NSTC A1353 (BI BL).

*Notes.* Dedication to Miss Smith, of the Theatre Royal, Drury-Lane, dated Swansea, 2 Mar 1814.

1815: 30   HOFLAND, {B}[arbara].
A FATHER AS HE SHOULD BE. A NOVEL. IN FOUR VOLUMES. BY
MRS. HOFLAND, AUTHOR OF SAYS SHE TO HER NEIGHBOUR,
CLERGYMAN'S WIDOW, VISIT TO LONDON, PATIENCE AND PER-
SEVERANCE, &C. &C.

> London: Printed at the Minerva-Press, for A. K. Newman and Co. Leadenhall-Street, 1815.
> I 262p; II 276p; III 274p; IV 291p. 12mo. 24s (ECB, ER).
> ER 24: 545 (Feb 1815); WSW I: 327.
> Corvey; CME 3-628-47677-1; ECB 275; NSTC H2418 (BI BL).

*Notes.* Dedication 'to Her Royal Highness the Princess Elizabeth', signed B. Hofland.
Further edns: 2nd edn. 1824 (NSTC); Philadelphia 1816 (NSTC).

1815: 31   HOLSTEIN, Anthony Frederick [pseud.].
THE DISCONTENTED MAN; OR LOVE AND REASON. A NOVEL. IN
THREE VOLUMES. BY ANTHONY FREDERICK HOLSTEIN, AUTHOR
OF SIR OWEN GLENDOWR; LOVE, MYSTERY, AND MISERY; BOU-
VERIE; THE INHABITANTS OF EARTH; MODERN KATE; MISERIES
OF AN HEIRESS; LADY DURNEVOR; SCOTCHWOMAN, &C. &C.

London: Printed at the Minerva Press for A. K. Newman and Co. Leadenhall-Street, 1815.
I xi, 219p; II 225p; III 244p. 12mo. 16s 6d (ECB, ER, QR).
ER 25: 560 (Oct 1815); QR 13: 531 (July 1815); WSW I: 324.
Corvey; CME 3-628-47734-4; ECB 278; NSTC H2274 (BI BL, C).

*Notes.* Preface dated Jan 1815.

1815: 32    [JOHNSTONE, Christian Isobel].
## CLAN-ALBIN: A NATIONAL TALE. IN FOUR VOLUMES.

London: Printed for Longman, Hurst, Rees, Orme, & Brown; Macredie, Skelly, and Muckersy, Edinburgh; and John Cumming, Dublin, 1815.
I iv, 300p; II 328p; III 354p; IV 348p. 12mo. 28s (ECB, QR).
QR 13: 281 (Apr 1815); WSW I: 347.
Corvey; CME 3-628-47285-7; ECB 117; NSTC J846 (BI BL, C, E, O).

*Notes.* 'Advertisement by the Editor' states (p. iii) 'that the first half of this Tale was not only written but *printed* long before' the appearance of *Waverley.* Colophon in vol. 4 reads: 'Printed by John Moir, Edinburgh, 1815'. Collates in sixes. Copy in National Library of Scotland (Vts.13.f.19) has t.p. with an Edinburgh imprint (Edinburgh: Printed by John Moir, Royal Bank Close, for Macredie, Skelly, and Muckersy; Longman [etc.], London; and John Cumming, Dublin, 1815), though vols. 2 and 3 of this set belong to the 'Second Edition' (also with an Edinburgh imprint). The likelihood is that edns. were published simultaneously in London and Edinburgh with different t.ps.
Futher edns: 2nd edn. 1815 (NSTC); 2nd edn. Edinburgh 1815 (NSTC); Philadelphia 1815 (NUC); German trans., 1821 (ascribed to Walter Scott).

1815: 33    JONES, J[ohn].
## HAWTHORN COTTAGE; OR, THE TWO CUPIDS: A TALE, IN TWO VOLUMES. BY J. JONES.

London: Printed for James Asperne, at the Bible, Crown, and Constitution, 32, Cornhill, 1815.
I xv, 293p; II xxi, 330p. 12mo. 10s 6d (ER).
ER 24: 545 (Feb 1815); WSW I: 347.
Corvey; CME 3-628-47999-1; ECB 312; NSTC J943 (BI BL).

1815: 34    MANT, Alicia Catherine.
## CAROLINE LISMORE: OR, THE ERRORS OF FASHION. A TALE. BY ALICIA CATHERINE MANT, AUTHOR OF ELLEN: OR, THE YOUNG GODMOTHER.

Southampton: Printed by T. Skelton; for Law and Whittaker, Ave-Maria-Lane, London, 1815.
136p, ill. 12mo. 3s 6d (ECB, ER, QR).
ER 25: 560 (Oct 1815); QR 14: 279 (Oct 1815); WSW I: 333, 386–7.
MH-H *EC8.M3184.816c; ECB 366; NSTC M1040 (BI BL, C, O).

*Notes.* Collates in sixes.

1815: 35   MATHERS, John [pseud.].

THE HISTORY OF MR. JOHN DECASTRO AND HIS BROTHER BAT, COMMONLY CALLED OLD CRAB. IN FOUR VOLUMES. THE MERRY MATTER WRITTEN BY JOHN MATHERS; THE GRAVE BY A SOLID GENTLEMAN.

> London: Printed for T. Egerton, Whitehall, 1815.
> I vi, 338p; II 404p; III 366p; IV 406p. 12mo. 24s (ER).
> ER 25: 278 (June 1815); WSW I: 54.
> Corvey; CME 3-628-47715-8; NSTC M1648 (BI BL, C).

*Notes.* Dedication to the Right Honourable Earl of ******, signed John Mathers, and the Solid Gentleman. Announced 'this day published' in *The Times*, 25 Apr 1815, 'price 24s in boards'. Block and Summers attribute to George Colman the Younger. An article devoted to this novel in *Blackwood's Magazine*, 81 (Jan 1857), 99–121 is, however, unable to identify the author. See also the same author's *History of Elsmere and Rosa* (1817: 41).
Further edn: 1834 (NSTC).

1815: 36   MEEKE, [Mary].

THE SPANISH CAMPAIGN; OR, THE JEW. A NOVEL. IN THREE VOL-UMES. BY MRS. MEEKE, AUTHOR OF CONSCIENCE, MATRIMONY, MIDNIGHT WEDDINGS, NINE DAYS' WONDER, TALE OF MYSTERY, &C. &C.

> London: Printed at the Minerva-Press, for A. K. Newman and Co. Leadenhall-Street, 1815.
> I 209p; II 202p; III 244p. 12mo. 18s (ECB, ER).
> ER 24: 545 (Feb 1815).
> Corvey; CME 3-628-48263-1; ECB 378; NSTC M1956 (BI BL).

1815: 37   MORDAUNT, Henry.

CHRONICLES OF THE TON; OR A SPRING AND SUMMER IN LON-DON. BY HENRY MORDAUNT, ESQ. IN THREE VOLUMES.

> London: Printed for the Booksellers, 1815.
> I 260p; II 215p; III 232p. 12mo.
> CtY In.M811.815; xNSTC.

1815: 38   PARKER, Emma.

THE GUERRILLA CHIEF: A NOVEL. IN THREE VOLUMES. BY EMMA PARKER, AUTHOR OF "ELFRIDA, HEIRESS OF BELGROVE;"—"VIR-GINIA, OR THE PEACE OF AMIENS;"—AND "ARESTAS."

> London: Printed for William Lindsell, Wimpole Street; by J. F. Dove, St John's Square, 1815.
> I 366p; II 302p; III 328p. 12mo. 21s (ER, QR).
> ER 24: 544 (Feb 1815); QR 13: 281 (Apr 1815); WSW I: 428.
> CtY In.P224.815G; NSTC P395 (BI O).

*Notes.* Vol. 3, pp. [326] and [327] misprinted as 236 and 237. Vol. 3 of the Bodleian copy (249.s.308-310) has engraving of 'The Druid', drawn by R. Westall, engraved by Heath, dated

1 Apr 1812, positioned as a frontispiece, but this was probably added after publication from another source.
Further edns: 2nd edn. 1817 (Corvey), CME 3-628-48386-7; German trans., 1817.

1815: 39   PILKINGTON, [Mary].
CELEBRITY; OR THE UNFORTUNATE CHOICE. A NOVEL. IN THREE VOLUMES. BY MRS. PILKINGTON, AUTHOR OF CRIMES AND CHARACTERS; SINCLAIR, OR THE MYSTERIOUS ORPHAN; NOVICE, OR THE HEIR OF MONTGOMERY CASTLE, &C. &C.

> London: Printed at the Minerva Press for A. K. Newman and Co. Leadenhall-Street, 1815.
> I 238p; II 249p; III 238p. 12mo. 15s (ECB, ER).
> ER 25: 560 (Oct 1815).
> Corvey; CME 3-628-48441-3; ECB 450; NSTC P1761 (BI BL).

1815: 40   PINCHARD, [Elizabeth].
THE WARD OF DELAMERE, A TALE. IN THREE VOLUMES. BY MRS. PINCHARD, AUTHOR OF "MYSTERY AND CONFIDENCE, THE BLIND CHILD, &C." INSCRIBED, BY PERMISSION, TO MRS. G. A. ROBINSON.

> London: Printed for Black, Parry, & Co. Booksellers to the East India Company, Leadenhall-Street, 1815.
> I 308p; II 324p; III 328p. 12mo. 16s 6d (ECB, ER, QR).
> ER 25: 278 (June 1815); QR 13: 531 (July 1815); WSW I: 440.
> Corvey; CME 3-628-48472-3; ECB 451; NSTC P1796 (BI BL).

*Notes.* Dedication to Mrs George Abercrombie Robinson, dated Taunton, 1815.
Further edn: Philadelphia 1816 (NSTC).

PLUNKETT, Elizabeth
See GUNNING, Elizabeth

1815: 41   PRICKETT, Miss.
WARWICK CASTLE, AN HISTORICAL NOVEL, IN THREE VOLUMES. BY MISS PRICKETT. DEDICATED TO THE RIGHT HONOURABLE THE COUNTESS OF CLONMELL. CONTAINING, AMONGST OTHER DESULTORY INFORMATION, THE DESCENT AND ACHIEVEMENTS OF THE ANCIENT EARLS OF WARWICK, FROM THE EARLIEST PERIOD OF THEIR CREATION TO THE PRESENT TIME. WITH SOME ACCOUNT OF WARWICK, BIRMINGHAM, LEMMINGTON [*sic*], KENILWORTH, STRATFORD-UPON-AVON, &C. &C.; INTERSPERSED WITH PIECES OF LOCAL POETRY, INCIDENTAL BIOGRAPHY, AND AUTHENTIC ANECDOTES OF ENGLISH HISTORY.

> London: Printed for Baldwin, Cradock, and Joy, 47, Paternoster Row, 1815.
> I xi, 299p; II 338p; III 293p. 12mo. 21s (ECB, QR); 15s (ER).

ER 25: 278 (June 1815); QR 13: 281 (Apr 1815), 13: 531 (July 1815); WSW I: 451.
Corvey; CME 3-628-48372-7; ECB 469; NSTC P3026 (BI C, O).

*Notes.* Dedication 'to the Right Honourable the Countess of Clonmell'.

1815: 42    ROCHE, Mrs.

ANNA; OR, EDINBURGH. A NOVEL, IN TWO VOLUMES. BY MRS. ROCHE, AUTHOR OF "LONDON TALES, OR REFLECTIVE POR-TRAITS," "THE MOOR," "PLAIN TALES;" &C.

London: Printed for R. Hill, 71, Borough. Sold also by Cradock and Joy, 32, Paternoster-Row; and all other Booksellers, 1815.
I 15, 215p; II 15, 172p. 12mo. 10s (ECB, ER).
ER 24: 545 (Feb 1815); WSW I: 470.
Corvey; CME 3-628-48427-8; ECB 498; xNSTC.

*Notes.* For the issue of authorship see: Natalie Schroeder, 'Regina Maria Roche, Popular Novelist, 1789–1834: The Rochean Canon', *Papers of the Bibliographical Society of America*, 73 (1979), 462–8. She doubts the work is by Regina Maria Roche. See also 1814: 48, 49. ECB dates Dec 1814.

1815: 43    ROSS, Mrs.

THE FAMILY ESTATE; OR LOST AND WON. A NOVEL. IN THREE VOLUMES. BY MRS. ROSS, AUTHOR OF THE COUSINS, MODERN CALYPSO, STRANGERS OF LINDENFELDT, &C. &C.

London: Printed at the Minerva Press for A. K. Newman and Co. Leadenhall-Street, 1815.
I 225p; II 252p; III 234p. 12mo. 15s (ECB, ER, QR).
ER 25: 560 (Oct 1815); QR 14: 279 (Oct 1815).
Corvey; CME 3-628-48552-5; ECB 503; NSTC R1704 (BI BL, C).

1815: 44    ROSS, Mrs.

PAIRED—NOT MATCHED; OR, MATRIMONY IN THE NINETEENTH CENTURY. A NOVEL. IN FOUR VOLUMES. BY MRS. ROSS, AUTHOR OF THE MODERN CALYPSO, &C. &C.

London: Printed at the Minerva-Press, for A. K. Newman and Co. Leadenhall-Street, 1815.
I 253p; II 252p; III 200p; IV 210p. 12mo. 20s (ECB, ER).
ER 24: 545 (Feb 1815); WSW I: 474.
Corvey; CME 3-628-48554-1; ECB 503; NSTC R1706 (BI BL).

*Notes.* Further edn: Philadelphia 1816 (NUC).

1815: 45    SARRAZIN, Adrien de.

BARDOUC; OR, THE GOAT-HERD OF MOUNT TAURUS: AN EASTERN TALE. TRANSLATED FROM THE FRENCH OF ADRIEN DE SARRAZIN.

London: Printed by B. M'Millan, Bow-Street, Covent-Garden: sold by Sherwood, Neely, and Jones, Paternoster-Row, 1815.

iv, 187p. 12mo.

BL 12655.bb.37; NSTC S475.

*Notes.* Trans. of *Bardouc, ou le pâtre du Mont-Taurus* (Paris, 1814).

Further edns: 1821 (NSTC); Boston 1850 (NSTC).


1815: 46    [SCOTT, Sir Walter].

GUY MANNERING; OR, THE ASTROLOGER. BY THE AUTHOR OF "WAVERLEY." IN THREE VOLUMES.

> Edinburgh: Printed by James Ballantyne and Co. for Longman, Hurst, Rees, Orme, and Brown, London; and Archibald Constable and Co., 1815.
>
> I 341p; II 346p; III 358p. 12mo. 21s (ER).
>
> ER 24: 544 (Feb 1815); QR 12: 501–9 (Jan 1815) full review; WSW I: 485.
>
> BL 636.e.2; ECB 249; NSTC S866 (BI C, E, NCu, O).

*Notes.* Published Mar 1815, according to Corson, but actually released in Edinburgh on 24 Feb 1815 (see Constable Letter Books, National Library of Scotland, MS 789, pp. 227–32). ECB mistakenly dates Dec 1814.

Futher edns: 2nd edn. 1815 (Corvey), CME 3-628-48617-3; 3rd edn. 1815 (NSTC); 4th edn. 1817 (NSTC); 6th edn. 1820 (NSTC); Boston 1815 (NUC); French trans., 1816; German trans., 1816 [as *Der Astrolog; eine caledonische Wundersage* (RS)]. Numerous reprintings in collected edns.


1815: 47    SMITH, [Catherine].

BAROZZI; OR THE VENETIAN SORCERESS. A ROMANCE OF THE SIX-TEENTH CENTURY. IN TWO VOLUMES. BY MRS. SMITH, AUTHOR OF THE CALEDONIAN BANDIT, &C. &C.

> London: Printed at the Minerva Press for A. K. Newman and Co. Leadenhall-Street, 1815.
>
> I 229p; II 241p. 12mo. 10s 6d (ECB, QR); 10s (ER); 12s (ER, QR).
>
> ER 21: 258 (Feb 1813), 25: 560 (Oct 1815); QR 9: 260 (May 1813), 13: 531 (July 1815).
>
> Corvey; CME 3-628-48758-7; ECB 544; NSTC S2362 (BI BL, C).

*Notes.* ECB dates July 1815. No explanation has been found for the earliness of the first review listings. ER Oct 1815 prices 10s, QR July 1815 at 10s 6d.

Further edn: French trans., 1817.

Facs: GNIII (1977).


1815: 48    STANHOPE, Louisa Sidney.

TREACHERY; OR, THE GRAVE OF ANTOINETTE. A ROMANCE, INTERSPERSED WITH POETRY. IN FOUR VOLUMES. BY LOUISA SIDNEY STANHOPE, AUTHOR OF DI MONTRANZO; CONFES-SIONAL OF VALOMBRE; AGE WE LIVE IN; MONTBRASIL ABBEY; THE BANDIT'S BRIDE, &C. &C.

> London: Printed at the Minerva-Press, for A. K. Newman and Co. Leadenhall-Street, 1815.
>
> I 267p; II 258p; III 271p; IV 274p. 12mo. 22s (ECB, ER).

ER 25: 278 (June 1815).
Corvey; CME 3-628-48783-8; ECB 558; NSTC S3499 (BI BL).

1815: 49   SURR, T[homas] S[kinner].
THE MAGIC OF WEALTH. A NOVEL. IN THREE VOLUMES. BY T. S.
SURR, AUTHOR OF A WINTER IN LONDON, &C.

> London: Printed for T. Cadell & W. Davies, Strand; by G. Sidney, Northumberland
> Street, 1815.
> I 276p; II 267p; III 240p. 12mo. 18s (ECB, ER, QR).
> ER 24: 544 (Feb 1815); QR 13: 281 (Apr 1815); WSW I: 527.
> Corvey; CME 3-628-48737-4; ECB 570; NSTC S4390 (BI BL, O).

*Notes.* Dedication 'to Sir William Paxton, of Middleton Hall, Caermarthenshire'. 'Advertisement' dated Islington, Mar 1815. Text in vol. 3 ends on p. 222, followed by 'Notes',
pp. [224]–240.
Further edn: Philadelphia 1815 (NUC).

1815: 50   TAYLOR, Jane.
DISPLAY. A TALE FOR YOUNG PEOPLE. BY JANE TAYLOR, ONE OF THE
AUTHORS OF "ORIGINAL POEMS FOR INFANT MINDS," "HYMNS
FOR INFANT MINDS," &C.

> London: Printed for Taylor and Hessey, 93, Fleet-Street; and J. Coder, St. Paul's
> Church-Yard, 1815.
> 214p. 12mo. 6s (ECB, QR).
> QR 14: 279 (Oct 1815); WSW I: 531.
> BL 838.a.14; ECB 579; NSTC T313 (BI C, Dt, O).

*Notes.* This title is commonly found in contemporary circulating library catalogues, and
clearly enjoyed a wide currency.
Further edns: 2nd edn. 1815 (NSTC); 3rd edn. 1815 (NSTC); 4th edn. 1816 (NUC); 5th edn.
1816 (NSTC); 6th edn. 1817 (NSTC); [at least 8 more edns. to 1850]; Boston 1831 (NUC).

1815: 51   [THOMAS, Elizabeth].
THE BARON OF FALCONBERG; OR, CHILDE HAROLDE IN PROSE. IN
THREE VOLUMES. BY MRS. BRIDGET BLUEMANTLE, AUTHOR OF
THE PRISON HOUSE, VINDICTIVE SPIRIT, MORTIMER HALL,
MONTE VIDEO, HUSBAND AND WIFE, &C. &C.

> London: Printed at the Minerva-Press, for A. K. Newman and Co. Leadenhall-Street,
> 1815.
> I 209p; II 256p; III 234p. 12mo. 15s (ECB, QR).
> QR 13: 281 (Apr 1815).
> Corvey; CME 3-628-47123-0; ECB 63; NSTC T668 (BI BL, C).

1815: 52   WEEKS, Harriett Waller.
MEMOIRS OF THE VILLARS FAMILY; OR, THE PHILANTHROPIST: A
NOVEL, IN THREE VOLUMES. BY HARRIETT WALLER WEEKS.

London: Printed for the Author, and published by C. Chapple, No. 66, Pall-Mall, 1815.
I x, 193p; II 219p; III 262p. 12mo. 18s (ABu s.l.).
Corvey; CME 3-628-48881-8; NSTC W1048 (BI BL, C).

*Notes.* 'List of Subscribers' (*c.*75 names), vol. 1, pp. [vii]–x. Drop-head titles and running-titles read: 'The Philanthropist'.

1815: 53    [WEST, Jane].
## VICISSITUDES OF LIFE; EXEMPLIFIED IN THE INTERESTING MEMOIRS OF A YOUNG LADY, IN A SERIES OF LETTERS. IN TWO VOLUMES.

London: Printed for E. Cox and Son, St. Thomas's Street, Borough, 1815.
I 258p; II 234p. 12mo. 10s 6d (ER).
ER 26: 247 (Feb 1816).
Corvey; CME 3-628-48913-X; NSTC W1354 (BI O).

*Notes.* Half-titles read: 'Memoirs of a Young Lady, &c. &c.'

1815: 54    [WILLIAMS, William].
## THE JOURNAL OF LLEWELLIN PENROSE, A SEAMAN. IN FOUR VOLUMES.

London: Printed for John Murray, Albemarle Street, and William Blackwood, Edinburgh, 1815.
I xvi, 239p; II 217p; III 215p; IV 197p. 8vo. 24s (ECB, ER, QR).
ER 25: 278 (June 1815); QR 13: 531 (July 1815); WSW I: 255.
Corvey; CME 3-628-47922-3; ECB 314; NSTC W2145 (BI BL, C, E, O).

*Notes.* Dedication to Benjamin West, Esq., signed John Eagles. 'Advertisement' signed John Eagles. Text dated New York, 2 May 1783 at end. Colophons read: 'Caledonian Mercury Press, Edinburgh'. Williams (1727–91), who was a painter and the first tutor of Benjamin West, wrote the novel in America between 1774 and 1775, and it has been consequently claimed as the first novel written in America. The published version of 1815 was much altered by Williams's benefactor in Bristol, Thomas Eagles, and was later submitted for publication by his son, the Revd John Eagles. John Murray, the publisher, offered £200, the work apparently having been read and approved by Walter Scott. For an edn. based on Williams's original manuscript and a useful introduction describing its publication history, see David Howard Dickason, *Mr. Penrose: The Journal of Penrose, Seaman* (Bloomington: Indiana University Press, 1969).
Further edns: new edn. [1 vol. abridged] 1825 (NSTC); German trans., 1817 [as *Der neue Robinson, oder Tagebuch Llewellin Penroses, eines Matrosen* (RS)].

1816: 1   ANON.

## THE COTTAGERS OF THE LAKES.

> London: Printed for J. Harris, Successor to E. Newberry, Corner of St. Paul's Church Yard; Wm. Darton, Holborn; and A. K. Newman, Leadenhall Street, by J. Raw, Ipswich, 1816.
>
> ii, 235p, ill. 12mo. 3s 6d (ECB).
>
> WSW I: 28.
>
> Corvey; CME 3-628-47345-4; ECB 138; NSTC 2C39123 (BI O).

*Notes.* ECB gives Longman as publisher, June 1816, but not discovered in this form as a 1st edn.

Further edn: 1820 (NSTC). BL 1608/3511 (on which NSTC is based) has the imprint of: Longman, Hurst, Rees, Orme, and Brown [etc.]; Ipswich, A. K. Cowell.

1816: 2   ANON.

## DIURNAL EVENTS; OR THE ANTIPODES TO ROMANCE. A NOVEL. IN FOUR VOLUMES. BY THE AUTHOR OF THE SAILOR AND SOLDIER BOY.

> London: Printed at the Minerva Press for A. K. Newman and Co. Leadenhall-Street, 1816.
>
> I 232p; II 204p; III 221p; IV 236p. 12mo. 20s (ER, QR).
>
> ER 26: 247 (Feb 1816); QR 14: 554 (Jan 1816).
>
> Corvey; CME 3-628-47440-X; NSTC 2E14291 (BI BL, C).

*Notes.* Evidently by the same author as *The Sailor Boy* (1800: 13), *The Soldier Boy* (1801: 13), and *Nobility Run Mad* (1802: 9).

1816: 3   ANON.

## ELIZABETH DE MOWBRAY; OR THE HEIR OF DOUGLAS. A ROMANCE OF THE THIRTEENTH CENTURY. IN FOUR VOLUMES.

> London: Printed at the Minerva Press for A. K. Newman and Co. Leadenhall-Street, 1816.
>
> I 283p; II 320p; III 355p; IV 284p. 12mo.
>
> Corvey; CME 3-628-47531-7; NSTC 2D8910 (BI BL).

1816: 4   ANON.

## GULZARA, PRINCESS OF PERSIA; OR, THE VIRGIN QUEEN. COLLECTED FROM THE ORIGINAL PERSIAN.

> London: Printed for John Souter, No. 1, Paternoster Row; by J. Adlard, 23, Bartholomew Close, 1816.
>
> xiii, 248p. 8vo. 10s 6d (ECB, ER).

ER 26: 248 (Feb 1816).

BL 1080.i.23(4); ECB 248; NSTC 2G25229 (BI C, Dt, E, O; NA DLC, MH).

*Notes.* Dedication 'to the British Public', dated London, 1 Jan 1816. A satire concerning Charlotte Caroline Augusta, Princess of Wales.

Further edn: Philadelphia 1816 (NSTC).

1816: 5    ANON.

JULIA OF ARDENFIELD; A NOVEL. IN TWO VOLUMES.

London: Printed for Law and Whittaker, Ave-Maria Lane, Ludgate Street, 1816.
I 231p; II 224p. 12mo. 10s 6d (ECB, ER, QR).
ER 26: 498 (June 1816); QR 15: 295 (Apr 1816); WSW I: 61.
Corvey; CME 3-628-48007-8; ECB 315; NSTC 2J13207 (BI BL; NA MH).

1816: 6    ANON.

LAVINIA FITZ-AUBYN, WITH OTHER TALES; SKETCHED FROM LIFE. IN FOUR VOLUMES.

London: Printed for P. Martin, 198, Oxford Street, Corner of Orchard Street; and J.
    Rees, Bristol, 1816.
I 310p; II 348p; III 250p; IV 218p. 12mo. 28s (ER).
ER 27: 271 (Sept 1816); WSW I: 64.
Corvey; CME 3-628-51077-5; NSTC 2F7317 (BI BL).

*Notes.* Introductory preface indicates female authorship. Final page of vol. 4 mistakenly numbered as p. 156.

1816: 7    ANON.

*MALVERN HILLS; OR, HISTORY OF HENRY FREEMANTLE. A NOVEL. IN TWO VOLUMES. SECOND EDITION.

London: Printed for Thomas Mason, Russell-Street; and sold by A. K. Newman & Co.
    Leadenhall-Street; and Simpkin & Marshall, Stationers' Court, 1816.
I 192p; II 249p. 12mo.
MH-H 19463.31.125; NSTC 2F15501 (BI O).

*Notes.* Half-titles read: 'Malvern Hills. A Novel'; running-title reads: 'Henry Freemantle'. Block lists a novel *c*.1810 with the title 'Henry Freemantle' which may represent the 1st edn. of this work, though no copy has been located.

1816: 8    ANON.

MEMOIRS OF OLIVER CROMWELL AND HIS CHILDREN. SUPPOSED TO BE WRITTEN BY HIMSELF. IN THREE VOLUMES.

London: Printed for, and published by, C. Chapple, PallMall [*sic*]. Bookseller to their
    Royal Highnesses the Prince Regent, and the Dukes of York and Cambridge, 1816.
I viii, 264p; II 288p; III 279p. 12mo. 18s (ECB, ER).
ER 26: 498 (June 1816).
Corvey; CME 3-628-48064-7; ECB 380; NSTC 2C43873 (BI BL, C, E, O; NA DLC, MH).

*Notes.* Dedication 'to His Majesty's Ministers', signed R. H. Introduction claims source as papers in possession of a descendant of the Fairfax family in America.

1816: 9   ANON.

THE PRINCE OR THE ROYAL LIBERTINES. IN THREE VOLUMES.

> London: Printed for Sherwood, Neeley and Jones, Paternoster-Row, 1816.
> I 191p; II iii, 189p; III iv, 176p. 12mo.
> WSW I: 98.
> Corvey; CME 3-628-48304-2; xNSTC.

*Notes.* Text proper ends in vol. 1 at p. 186, followed by 'Contents of the First Volume', pp. [187]–191. 'Contents' in other vols. paginated in small roman numerals, though in the 2nd vol. (mis)bound at the end. ECB 470 lists Newman edn. 1818, 15s.
Further edn: 2nd edn. 1818 (NSTC 2P26676). BLC indicates that 2nd edn. was also published by Sherwood.


1816: 10   ANON.

ROMANTIC FACTS; OR WHICH IS HIS WIFE? IN FOUR VOLUMES. BY THE AUTHOR OF VERONICA, OR THE MYSTERIOUS STRANGER.

> London: Printed at the Minerva Press for A. K. Newman and Co. Leadenhall-Street, 1816.
> I xi, 205p; II 201p; III 206p; IV 196p. 12mo. 22s (ECB, ER, QR).
> ER 25: 560 (Oct 1815); QR 14: 279 (Oct 1815).
> Corvey; CME 3-628-48510-X; ECB 501; NSTC 2F668 (BI BL, C).

*Notes.* Dedication 'to E—— L——'. *Veronica; or, the Mysterious Stranger* (1798), cited as a work by the same author in the title, was published as 'by Lister' on its original t.p. No further information about this apparent pseudonym has been discovered. See also, as part of the same chain, 1819: 14 and 1822: 3 below.


1816: 11   ANON.

ST. CLYDE; A NOVEL. IN THREE VOLUMES.

> London: Printed for Gale and Fenner, Paternoster-Row, by S. Hamilton, Weybridge, Surrey, 1816.
> I 272p; II 333p; III 308p. 12mo. 15s (ECB, ER).
> ER 26: 498 (June 1816); WSW I: 107.
> Corvey; CME 3-628-48596-7; ECB 511; NSTC 2S2009 (BI BL, O).

*Notes.* Dedication 'to Thomas Campbell, Esq., Author of "The Pleasures of Hope"', dated 27 Mar 1816.


1816: 12   ANON.

UNCLE TWEAZY AND HIS QUIZZICAL NEIGHBOURS: A COMI-SATIRIC NOVEL. IN THREE VOLUMES. BY THE AUTHOR OF THE "OBSERVANT PEDESTRIAN," &C. &C. &C.

> London: Printed for W. Simpkin and R. Marshall, Stationers'-Court, Ludgate-Street, 1816.
> I 206p; II 307p; III 228p. 12mo. 15s (ECB, ER, QR).
> ER 26: 248 (Feb 1816); QR 14: 554 (Jan 1816), 15: 295 (Apr 1816).
> BL N.1684; ECB 606; NSTC 2T21106 (BI C).

1816: 13　[AGG, John].

EIGHTEEN HUNDRED AND FIFTEEN; A SATIRICAL NOVEL. BY HUMPHREY HEDGEHOG, ESQ. AUTHOR OF "A MONTH IN TOWN"— "THE GENERAL POST BAG," "REJECTED ODES, &C. &C." IN THREE VOLUMES.

> London: Printed for James Johnston, Cheapside, 1816.
> I 215p; II 210p; III 212p. 12mo. 18s (ER, QR).
> ER 26: 248 (Feb 1816); QR 14: 554 (Jan 1816).
> Corvey; CME 3-628-47720-4; NSTC 2A5128 (BI BL; NA MH).

*Notes.* Sometimes erroneously attributed to John Gifford, who also used this pseudonym.


1816: 14　APPLETON, {Elizabeth}.

EDGAR: A NATIONAL TALE. BY MISS APPLETON, AUTHOR OF PRIVATE EDUCATION, &C. IN THREE VOLUMES.

> London: Printed for Henry Colburn, Public Library, Conduit Street, Hanover Square, 1816.
> I viii, 275p; II 274p; III 276p. 12mo. 21s (ECB, ER, QR).
> ER 27: 271 (Sept 1816); QR 15: 295 (Apr 1816), 18: 545 (Jan 1818); WSW I: 133–4.
> Corvey; CME 3-628-47066-8; ECB 23; NSTC 2A14441 (BI BL, C).

*Notes.* Dedication 'to Her Royal Highness the Princess Charlotte of Wales, and of Saxe Cobourg Saalfeld' signed 'Elizabeth Appleton'. 'To the Public', explaining why 'Tale' rather than 'Novel' has been used in the title, as more appropriate for 'moral fiction'; this is dated London, 4 June 1816. Extensive historical notes at the end of each vol.


1816: 15　ASHE, [Thomas].

THE SOLDIER OF FORTUNE: AN HISTORICAL AND POLITICAL ROMANCE. BY CAPT. ASHE, AUTHOR OF THE SPIRIT OF BOOK, LIBERAL CRITIC, &C. &C. IN TWO VOLUMES.

> London: Printed by B. M'Millan, Bow Street, Covent Garden. Sold by Sherwood, Neely, and Jones, Paternoster-Row; and at Galignani's French and English Library, 18, Rue Vivienne, Paris, 1816.
> I viii, 307p; II 319p. 12mo.
> Corvey; CME 3-628-47075-7; ECB 28; NSTC 2A17457 (BI BL, O).

*Notes.* Dedication 'to the Right Honourable the Lord Viscount Castlereagh'. 'Note' stating that 'This Historical and Political Romance is framed upon real incidents recorded in the Annals of Ancient Spain', but that 'the characters are all drawn from existing personages, such as Lord Wellington, Buonaparte, &c.'.


1816: 16　[AUSTEN, Jane].

EMMA: A NOVEL. IN THREE VOLUMES. BY THE AUTHOR OF "PRIDE AND PREJUDICE," &C. &C.

> London: Printed for John Murray, 1816.
> I 322p; II 351p; III 363p. 12mo. 21s (ECB, ER, QR).

ER 26: 247 (Feb 1816); QR 14: 188–201 (Oct 1815) full review, 14: 554 (Jan 1816); WSW I: 136.

Corvey; CME 3-628-47704-2; ECB 186; NSTC 2A19394 (BI BL, C; NA DLC).

*Notes.* Dedication 'to His Royal Highness the Prince Regent'. Colophon 'Printed by C. Roworth, Bell-yard, Temple-bar' in vols. 1 and 2; 'Printed by J. Moyes, Greville Street, Hatton Garden, London' in vol. 3. Adv. ('Lately were published, by the author of *Emma*') on verso of vol. 3, p. 363, for: *Sense and Sensibility*, 2nd edn; *Pride and Prejudice*, 2nd edn.; *Mansfield Park*. Published Dec 1815 (Gilson).

Further edns: 1833 (NSTC); 1836 (NSTC); 1841 (NSTC); 1849 (NSTC); Philadelphia 1816 (NSTC); French trans., 1816 [as *La Nouvelle Emma, ou les caractères anglais du siècle* (BN)].

**BAYLEY, Catharine, THE HAUT-TON**
See 1812: 20

1816: 17   [BEAUCLERC, Amelia].
**HUSBAND HUNTERS!!! A NOVEL. IN FOUR VOLUMES. BY THE AUTHOR OF MONTREITHE, OR THE PEER OF SCOTLAND.**
> London: Printed at the Minerva Press for A. K. Newman and Co. Leadenhall-Street, 1816.
> I 232p; II 229p; III 249p; IV 230p. 12mo. 20s (ER, QR).
> ER 26: 247 (Feb 1816); QR 14: 554 (Jan 1816).
> Corvey; CME 3-628-47919-3; NSTC 2B13635 (BI BL).

1816: 18   [BENKOWITZ, Carl Friedrich]; GEISWEILER, Maria (*trans.*).
**ANGELION, OR THE WIZARD IN ELIS. A ROMANCE. TAKEN FROM THE GERMAN, BY MARIA DE GEISWEILER. IN THREE VOLUMES.**
> London: Published by Sherwood, Neely, and Jones, Paternoster-Row; and Tabart and Co. 85, Piccadilly, 1816.
> I xii, 211p; II 191p; III 208p. 12mo. 18s (ECB, ER).
> ER 27: 271 (Sept 1816).
> BL 12554.bbb.17; ECB 224; NSTC 2G4208.

*Notes.* Trans. of *Angelion, der Zauberer in Elis* (Berlin, 1798–1800). 'List of Subscribers' (174 names), vol. 1, pp. [v]–xii.

1816: 19   BENNETT, Elizabeth.
**FAITH AND FICTION, OR SHINING LIGHTS IN A DARK GENERATION. A NOVEL. IN FIVE VOLUMES. BY ELIZABETH BENNETT.**
> London: Printed at the Minerva Press for A. K. Newman and Co. Leadenhall-Street, 1816.
> I 256p; II 306p; III 336p; IV 328p; V 284p. 12mo. 27s 6d (ECB, ER, QR).
> ER 26: 498 (June 1816); QR 15: 295 (Apr 1816).
> Corvey; CME 3-628-47113-3; ECB 50; NSTC 2B18047 (BI BL, C).

*Notes.* BLC attributes to A. M. Bennett, while Blakey, Block, Summers and ECB all have Elizabeth Bennet(t). Anna Maria Bennett died in 1808, but DNB claims a posthumous publication, citing R. Watt's *Bibliotheca Britannica* (1824).

Further edn: French trans., 1816 [as *L'Orpheline du presbytère, fiction et vérité* (BN under Bennett, Agnes Maria)].

1816: 20   BURNEY, S{arah} H{arriet}.
**TALES OF FANCY: BY S. H. BURNEY, AUTHOR OF 'CLARENTINE,' 'GERALDINE FAUCONBERG,' AND 'TRAITS OF NATURE.'**

> London: Printed for Henry Colburn, Public Library, Conduit Street, Hanover Square, 1816/20.
> I (1816) viii, 400p; II (1820) 432p; III (1820) 470p. 12mo. 24s (ECB); 7s 6d (ER, QR, for vol. 1); 12s (QR, vols. 2–3).
> ER 26: 247 (Feb 1816), 33: 519 (May 1820); QR 14: 554 (Jan 1816), 22: 564 (Mar 1820); WSW I: 181.
> MH-H 18477.42.2; ECB 87; NSTC 2B60607 (BI BL, C).

*Notes.* T.p. to vol. 1 also gives the title of the tale which makes up this volume, 'The Shipwreck'. Those to vols. 2 and 3 similarly announce 'Country Neighbours; or the Secret', while describing Burney as 'author of Clarentine, Traits of Nature &c.'; imprint details remain unchanged, apart from the addition of '& Co.' after Colburn and the changed date. Dedication in vol. 1 to the Right Hon. Lady Crewe, dated Chelsea College, 1 Dec 1815; dedication in vol. 2 'to Her Royal Highness the Princess Elizabeth, Hereditary Princess of Hesse Hombourg', signed Sarah Harriet Burney. Colophon in vol. 1 reads: 'B. Clarke, Printer, Well Street, London'; in vols. 2 and 3: 'Printed by J. Nichols and Son, Red Lion Passage, Fleet Street, London'. ECB dates 1815–20.
Further edns: 2nd edn. 1816/20 (Corvey), CME 3-628-47145-1; Boston 1816 (NSTC); French trans., of 'The Shipwreck' 1815 and of 'Country Neighbours' 1820; German trans., of 'The Shipwreck' 1821.

1816: 21   [BYRON, 'Medora Gordon'].
**THE SPINSTER'S JOURNAL. IN THREE VOLUMES. BY A MODERN ANTIQUE, AUTHOR OF CELIA IN SEARCH OF A HUSBAND, ENGLISH EXPOSÉ, &C.**

> London: Printed at the Minerva Press for A. K. Newman and Co. Leadenhall-Street, 1816.
> I 251p; II 282p; III 267p. 12mo. 16s 6d (ECB, ER).
> ER 26: 498 (June 1816).
> Corvey; CME 3-628-48726-9; ECB 555; NSTC 2B64949 (BI BL, C).

1816: 22   CONSTANT DE [REBECQUE], Benjamin [Henri]; [WALKER, Alexander (*trans.*)].
**ADOLPHE: AN ANECDOTE FOUND AMONG THE PAPERS OF AN UNKNOWN PERSON, AND PUBLISHED BY M. BENJAMIN DE CONSTANT.**

> London: Printed for H. Colburn, Conduit Street, 1816.
> xvi, 222p. 12mo.
> WSW I: 239.
> BL 837.b.30; NSTC 2C34835 (BI C, E; NA MH).

*Notes.* Trans. of *Adolphe: anecdote trouvée dans les papiers d'un inconnu* (Paris, 1816).
Includes 'Preface to the second French edition; or an essay on the character and the moral
result of the work'.
Further edn: Philadelphia 1817 (NSTC).

1816: 23   {CORDOVA, Cordelia}.
**HUMAN NATURE. A NOVEL. IN THREE VOLUMES.**

> London: Printed for Henry Colburn, Public Library, Conduit Street, Hanover Square,
>    1816.
> I xxviii, 188p; II 231p; III 224p. 12mo. 18s (QR).
> QR 14: 279 (Oct 1815); WSW I: 56.
> BL 12655.bb.36; NSTC 2C37861.

*Notes.* 'Dedicatory Preface' 'to Mrs. V——', signed Cordelia Cordova, Dover, 20 Mar 1813.
Running-titles read: 'Human Nature; or the Dangers of Platonism'. Some preliminary pages
are wrongly bound together.

1816: 24   [CUNNINGHAM, John William].
**SANCHO, OR THE PROVERBIALIST.**

> London: Printed by Ellerton and Henderson, Johnson's Court, for T. Cadell and
>    W. Davies, Strand; and J. Hatchard, Piccadilly, 1816.
> 181p. 12mo. 5s (ECB, QR).
> QR 15: 295 (Apr 1816); WSW I: 232.
> C Syn.7.81.101; ECB 147; NSTC 2C46845 (BI BL, O).

*Notes.* Dedication dated May 1816.
Further edns: 2nd edn. 1816 (NSTC); 3rd edn. 1817 (NSTC); Boston 1817 (NSTC) [also New
York 1817 (NSTC)].

1816: 25   DALBERG, Baron [Johann Friedrich Hugo von].
**MEHALED AND SEDLI; OR, THE HISTORY OF A DRUSE FAMILY:
WITH SOME ACCOUNT OF THE DRUSES, AN ANCIENT PEOPLE OF
SYRIA. IN TWO VOLUMES. BY THE BARON DE DALBERG, BROTHER
OF THE GRAND DUKE OF FRANKFORT.**

> London: Printed for Gale and Fenner, Paternoster-Row, 1816.
> I iv, 202p; II 203p. 12mo. 10s (ER).
> ER 26: 248 (Feb 1816).
> Corvey; CME 3-628-47389-6; NSTC 2D703 (BI BL, C).

*Notes.* Trans. of *Geschichte einer Drusenfamilie* (Frankfurt, 1808). 'Advertisement' quotes
from 'an English critic' (presumably a review of the German original).

1816: 26   DAVENPORT, Selina.
**THE ORIGINAL OF THE MINIATURE. A NOVEL. IN FOUR VOLUMES.
BY SELINA DAVENPORT, AUTHOR OF THE HYPOCRITE, OR MOD-
ERN JANUS, THE SONS OF THE VISCOUNT AND DAUGHTERS OF
THE EARL, DONALD MONTEITH, &C. &C.**

London: Printed at the Minerva Press for A. K. Newman and Co. Leadenhall-Street, 1816.
I 227p; II 229p; III 246p; IV 246p. 12mo. 22s (ECB, QR).
QR 15: 578 (July 1816).
Corvey; CME 3-628-47373-X; ECB 153; NSTC 2D3612 (BI BL, C).

1816: 27   [ENGLISH, John].
*CASTLETHORPE LODGE; OR, THE CAPRICIOUS MOTHER. INCLUDING THE CURIOUS ADVENTURES OF ANDREW GLAS- MORE, A NOVEL, IN THREE VOLUMES. BY THE AUTHOR OF "MOD- ERN TIMES, OR ANECDOTES OF AN ENGLISH FAMILY;"—"THE GREY FRIAR, AND THE BLACK SPIRIT OF THE WYE," &C. SECOND EDITION.

London: Printed and published by Allen and Co. No. 15, Paternoster-Row, 1816.
I 237p; II 216p; III 208p. 12mo.
Corvey; CME 3-628-47237-7; xNSTC.

*Notes.* Drop-head title reads: 'The Capricious Mother'. A novel titled *The Capricious Mother; or Accidents and Chances*, 3 vols., 15s, is listed in ER July 1812 and QR Mar 1812; and this pos- sibly represents the 1st edn. of this work, though no copy with this title has been located.

GALT, John, THE MAJOLO: A TALE
See 1815: 24

GEISWEILER, Maria
See BENKOWITZ, Carl Friedrich

1816: 28   GENLIS, [Stephanie-Félicité, Comtesse] de.
JANE OF FRANCE, AN HISTORICAL NOVEL, BY MADAME DE GENLIS. TRANSLATED FROM THE FRENCH. IN TWO VOLUMES.

London: Printed for Henry Colburn, Conduit Street, Hanover Square, 1816.
I iv, 194p; II 175p. 12mo. 12s (ECB).
WSW I: 240.
BL N.2191; ECB 225; NSTC 2B54548 (BI O).

*Notes.* Trans. of *Jeanne de France* (Paris, 1816). ECB dates May 1816.
Further edn: Boston 1817 (NSTC).

1816: 29   GLUMP, Humphrey [pseud.].
A TOUR TO PURGATORY AND BACK. A SATIRICAL NOVEL. BY HUMPHREY GLUMP. ESQ.

London: Printed by A. Redford, London Road, Southwark, n.d. [1816].
xii, 219p. 12mo.
BL 12316.ee.43; NSTC 2G10950.

*Notes.* 'Prefatory Introduction', pp. [v]–xii, signed Tothill Street, Westminster, 1 Nov 1816.

GREEN, Sarah, PERCIVAL ELLINGFORD: OR THE REFORMIST
See 1810: 45

1816: 30   GRIFFITH, Sophia.
SHE WOULD BE A HEROINE. BY SOPHIA GRIFFITH. IN THREE
VOLUMES.

> London: Printed for Baldwin, Cradock, & Joy, Paternoster-Row; and for Doig & Stir-
> ling, Edinburgh, 1816.
> I 323p; II 266p; III 269p. 12mo. 15s (ECB, ER).
> ER 26: 498 (June 1816); WSW I: 290.
> Corvey; CME 3-628-47912-6; ECB 246; NSTC 2G22902 (BI BL, C; NA MH).

1816: 31   GRIFFITHS, Griffiths ap.
THE SONS OF ST. DAVID. A CAMBRO-BRITISH HISTORICAL TALE,
OF THE FOURTEENTH CENTURY. WITH EXPLANATORY NOTES
AND REFERENCES. IN THREE VOLUMES. BY GRIFFITHS AP GRIF-
FITHS, ESQ.

> London: Printed at the Minerva Press for A. K. Newman and Co. Leadenhall-Street,
> 1816.
> I ii, 232p; II 222p; III 236p. 12mo. 15s (ECB, ER, QR).
> ER 27: 271 (Sept 1816), 28: 268 (Mar 1817); QR 15: 578 (July 1816).
> Corvey; CME 3-628-47821-9; ECB 246; NSTC 2G23032 (BI BL, C, E, O).

*Notes.* 'Notes' at end of each vol.

1816: 32   HARVEY, Jane.
BROUGHAM CASTLE. A NOVEL. IN TWO VOLUMES. BY JANE HAR-
VEY, AUTHOR OF AUBERRY STANHOPE, ETHELIA, CASTLE OF
TYNEMOUTH, WARKFIELD CASTLE, &C. &C.

> London: Printed at the Minerva Press for A. K. Newman and Co. Leadenhall-Street,
> 1816.
> I 242p; II 226p. 12mo. 10s 6d (ECB, ER).
> ER 26: 498 (June 1816).
> Corvey; CME 3-628-47640-2; ECB 257; NSTC 2H11035 (BI BL, C, O).

1816: 33   [HATTON, Anne Julia Kemble].
CHRONICLES OF AN ILLUSTRIOUS HOUSE; OR THE PEER, THE
LAWYER, AND THE HUNCHBACK. A NOVEL. IN FIVE VOLUMES.
EMBELLISHED WITH CHARACTERS AND ANECDOTES OF WELL-
KNOWN PERSONS. BY ANNE OF SWANSEA, AUTHOR OF CAM-
BRIAN PICTURES, SICILIAN MYSTERIES, CONVICTION, SECRET
AVENGERS, &C. &C.

> London: Printed at the Minerva Press for A. K. Newman and Co. Leadenhall-Street,
> 1816.
> I 269p; II 267p; III 343p; IV 346p; V 330p. 12mo. 27s 6d (ECB, ER, QR).

ER 26: 248 (Feb 1816), 27: 271 (Sept 1816); QR 14: 554 (Jan 1816); WSW I: 351.
Corvey; CME 3-628-48743-9; ECB 20; NSTC 2A13189 (BI BL, C; NA MH).

## HOFLAND, Barbara, THE MAID OF MOSCOW
See 1813: 27

1816: 34   ISAACS, Mrs.
TALES OF TO-DAY. BY MRS. ISAACS, AUTHOR OF "ARIEL"—"ELLA
ST. LAURENCE"—"WANDERINGS OF FANCY"—&C. &C. &C. IN
THREE VOLUMES.
London: Printed for C. Chapple, Pall-Mall, opposite St. James's Palace, 1816.
I 335p; II 336p; III 375p. 12mo. 24s (ECB).
ER 26: 498 (June 1816); WSW I: 343.
Corvey; CME 3-628-51068-6; ECB 301; NSTC 2I4897 (BI BL, C, O).

*Notes.* I The Heiress of Riversdale; II Continuation of The Heiress of Riversdale. Juliet; III
Continuation of Juliet. The Sisters.
Further edn: French trans., 1817 [as *Les Trois Romans, ou contes d'aujourd'hui* (NUC)].

1816: 35   [JACSON, Frances].
RHODA. A NOVEL. BY THE AUTHOR OF "THINGS BY THEIR RIGHT
NAMES," AND "PLAIN SENSE." IN THREE VOLUMES.
London: Printed for Henry Colburn, Conduit Street; and G. and S. Robinson, Pater-
noster Row, 1816.
I 336p; II 1st pt. 244p, 2nd pt. 252p; III 424p. 12mo. 28s (ECB); 15s (QR).
QR 14: 554 (Jan 1816); WSW I: 103–4.
BL N.1821,1822; ECB 491; NSTC 2R8420 (BI E, O).

*Notes.* Mistakenly attributed in some catalogues to Alethea Lewis. For the present attribution, see note to *Things By Their Right Names* (1812: 42). Part I and II in vol. 2 each have their
own t.p. and separate pagination, making this in effect a four-volumed work. Copy in BRu
ENC is actually bound in 4 vols. ECB dates Nov 1815.
Further edns: 2nd edn. 1816 (Corvey), CME 3-628-48540-1; Boston 1816 (NUC).

1816: 36   JENNER, Mrs. J.
MELMOTH HOUSE: A NOVEL. IN THREE VOLUMES, BY MRS. J.
JENNER.
London: Printed for the Author, and sold by G. Austin, Battle; sold also by Baldwin,
Cradock and Joy, No. 47; Walker and Edwards, No. 44 Paternoster Row, and R.
Nunn, No. 48 Great Queen Street, 1816.
I iv, 250p; II 265p; III 270p. 12mo. 20s (ER).
ER 27: 271 (Sept 1816).
Corvey; CME 3-628-47988-6; NSTC 2J4726 (BI BL, O; NA MH).

*Notes.* 'List of Subscribers' (235 names), vol. 3, pp. [1]–10. Colophon at end of each vol. reads
'Battle: Printed by G. Austin'.

1816: 37   JOHNSTON, Mary.
## THE LAIRDS OF GLENFERN; OR, HIGHLANDERS OF THE NINETEENTH CENTURY. A TALE. IN TWO VOLUMES. BY MARY JOHNSTON.

> London: Printed at the Minerva Press for A. K. Newman and Co. Leadenhall-Street, 1816.
> I vi, 245p; II 236p. 12mo. 10s 6d (ECB, ER).
> ER 27: 271 (Sept 1816).
> Corvey; CME 3-628-47990-8; ECB 310; NSTC 2J9505 (BI BL, C, E).

*Notes.* Preface attempts to forestall claims that the novel is imitative of 'those exquisite delineations of Scottish scenery and manners which have lately appeared, under the titles of *Waverly* [*sic*], *Discipline*, &c.', stating that 'The whole of the first, and great part of the second volume, have been written nearly four years' (pp. v–vi).


1816: 38   JUVENIS [pseud.].
## MARY AND FANNY. A NARRATIVE. BY JUVENIS.

> London: Printed at the Minerva Press for A. K. Newman and Co. Leadenhall-Street, 1816.
> 263p, ill. 12mo. 4s (ECB, QR).
> QR 15: 578 (July 1816).
> Corvey; CME 3-628-48089-2; ECB 371; NSTC 2J13745 (BI BL, C).

*Notes.* Presentationally targeted at youth, but written in an orthodox novel style.


1816: 39   [KELLY, Mrs].
## THE MATRON OF ERIN: A NATIONAL TALE. IN THREE VOLUMES.

> London: Published by Simpkin and Marshall, Stationer's Court; and by Richard Coyne, Parliament Street, Dublin, 1816.
> I 334p; II 306p; III 359p. 12mo. 18s (ECB, ER, QR).
> ER 26: 248 (Feb 1816), 26: 498 (June 1816); QR 15: 554 (Jan 1816).
> Corvey; CME 3-628-47463-9; ECB 373; NSTC 2K2013 (BI BL, C, E, O; NA MH).

*Notes.* Mrs Kelly is to be distinguished from Mrs Isabella Kelly, afterwards Mrs Hedgeland. Collates in sixes.


1816: 40   [LAMB, Lady Caroline].
## GLENARVON. IN THREE VOLUMES.

> London: Printed for Henry Colburn, 1816.
> I 295p; II 390p; III 322p. 12mo. 21s (ECB); 24s (ER).
> ER 26: 498 (June 1816); QR 15: 295 (Apr 1816); WSW I: 358.
> BL N.1834-36; ECB 233; NSTC 2L2306 (BI E, O; NA MH).

*Notes.* Further edns: 2nd edn. 1816 (NSTC); 3rd edn. 1816 (Corvey), CME 3-628-47814-6; 4th edn. 1817 (NSTC); Philadelphia 1816 (NSTC); French trans., 1819. Facs: RR (1993); RWN (1995).


1816: 41   LANCASTER, Agnes.
## THE ABBESS OF VALTIERA; OR, THE SORROWS OF A FALSEHOOD. A ROMANCE. IN FOUR VOLUMES. BY AGNES LANCASTER.

London: Printed at the Minerva Press for A. K. Newman and Co. Leadenhall-Street, 1816.
I 265p; II 252p; III 236p; IV 238p. 12mo. 22s (QR).
QR 15: 554 (Jan 1816); WSW I: 361.
Corvey; CME 3-628-47897-9; NSTC 2L3129 (BI BL, C).

1816: 42   LAYTON, {Jemima}.
SPANISH TALES, TRANSLATED FROM LE SAGE, AND SELECTED FROM OTHER AUTHORS: WHEREIN ARE CONTAINED A DESCRIPTION OF MADRID, GRENADA, SARAGOZA, SEVILLE, MILAN, PARMA, PALERMO, &C. &C. BY MRS. FREDERICK LAYTON. IN THREE VOLUMES.

London: Printed for Hatchard, Piccadilly; Barrett, Bath; and Deighton, Cambridge, 1816.
I xiii, 248p; II 273p; III 275p. 12mo. 21s (ER, QR).
ER 27: 536 (Dec 1816); QR 15: 578 (July 1816).
BL 837.c.34; ECB 335; NSTC 2L7465 (BI C, E).

*Notes.* Half-title to vol. 1 states: 'Published for the Benefit of Distressed Clergymen with a large Family'. Dedication to the Earl of Buchan, signed Jemima Layton. 'List of Subscribers' (78 names) and 'List of Benefactors' (26 listed) at the beginning of vol. 1 (4 pp. unn.). The subscribers include Hannah More and William Roscoe, as well as a number of M.P.s, among them Thomas Johnes and Samuel Whitbread; the benefactors include Walter Scott.

1816: 43   LEFANU, Alicia.
STRATHALLAN. BY ALICIA LEFANU, GRAND-DAUGHTER TO THE LATE THOMAS SHERIDAN, M.A. IN FOUR VOLUMES.

London: Printed for Sherwood, Neely, and Jones, Paternoster-Row, 1816.
I iv, 536p; II 363p; III 344p; IV 305p. 12mo. 24s (ECB, ER, QR).
ER 27: 537 (Dec 1816); QR 15: 578 (July 1816); WSW I: 368.
Corvey; CME 3-628-47978-9; ECB 336; NSTC 2L9899 (BI BL, O; NA MH).

*Notes.* The first of a sequence of novels by Alicia Lefanu (*c.*1795–*c.*1826), grand-daughter to the novelist and dramatist Frances Sheridan, and the daughter of Elizabeth Sheridan Lefanu, the author of *The India Voyage* (1804: 39). Her aunt, Alicia Lefanu (1753–1817), was also a writer.
Further edns: 2nd edn. 1816 (NSTC); 3rd edn. 1817 (NSTC); French trans., 1818.

1816: 44   {M'MULLAN, Mary Anne}.
THE WANDERINGS OF A GOLDFINCH; OR, CHARACTERISTIC SKETCHES IN THE NINETEENTH CENTURY.

London: Printed by W. Clowes, Northumberland-Court, Strand; for Messrs. Longman, Hurst, Rees, and Co.; T. Egerton, Military Library, Whitehall; and E. Lloyd, Harley-Street, 1816.
vii, xii, 355p. 8vo. 12s (ER).
ER 26: 498 (June 1816).
BL 1457.h.8; NSTC 2M7531.

*Notes.* Dedication 'to her Royal Highness the Princess Mary', signed 'Mary Anne M'Mullan', London, 22 Apr 1816. Preface, pp. [v]–vii, followed by Subscription list headed 'Previous to Publication Copies of this Work were ordered by', pp. [i]–xii (new sequence). 314 subscribers, including Dr Burney, John Galt, Sir William Knighton, Mrs Opie, and William Wordsworth.

1816: 45   [?MOSSE, Henrietta Rouviere].
## CRAIGH-MELROSE PRIORY; OR, MEMOIRS OF THE MOUNT LINTON FAMILY. A NOVEL. IN FOUR VOLUMES.

> London: Printed for C. Chapple, Pall-Mall, 1816.
> I vii, 347p; II 307p; III 332p; IV 311p. 12mo. 24s (ER).
> ER 26: 247 (Feb 1816).
> Corvey; CME 3-628-47347-0; NSTC 2C41946 (BI BL, C).

*Notes.* Preface states that this represents a first appearance before the world, and indicates female authorship. The writer adds that 'it was written towards the close of the last year, when she was only three and twenty—and not originally intended for publication' (p. vi). This makes the attribution to Mosse, found in Block and Summers, seem doubtful. It is also noticeable that, unlike Mosse's other titles, this work does not bear the author's name on the t.p. and is not published by the Minerva Press.
*Further edn:* French trans., 1817.

1816: 46   NOOTH, Charlotte.
## EGLANTINE; OR, THE FAMILY OF FORTESCUE. A NOVEL. IN TWO VOLUMES. BY CHARLOTTE NOOTH.

> London: Printed by A. J. Valpy, Tooke's Court, Chancery-Lane. Sold by Sherwood, Neely, and Jones, Paternoster-Row; and all other Booksellers, 1816.
> I xi, 300p; II 321p. 12mo. 12s (ER).
> ER 27: 271 (Sept 1816); WSW I: 418.
> Corvey; CME 3-628-48233-X; NSTC 2N9605 (BI BL).

*Notes.* Dedication 'to Lady Shepherd', dated Kew, 20 July 1816. Adv. for 'Original Poems', 'lately published, by the same Author', on separate page between the Dedication and the Preface.

1816: 47   OPIE, [Amelia Alderson].
## VALENTINE'S EVE. BY MRS. OPIE. IN THREE VOLUMES.

> London: Printed for Longman, Hurst, Rees, Orme, and Brown, Paternoster-Row, 1816.
> I 348p; II 388p; III 240p. 12mo. 21s (ECB, ER).
> ER 26: 248 (Feb 1816); WSW I: 422.
> BL N.1675-77; ECB 423; NSTC 2O4405 (BI Dt, E, O).

*Notes.* Further edns: 2nd edn. 1816 (Corvey), CME 3-628-48309-3; Boston 1827 (NSTC); French trans., 1816 [as *Catherine Shirley, ou la veille de Saint-Valentin* (BN)].

1816: 48   PARKER, Emma.
## SELF-DECEPTION. IN A SERIES OF LETTERS. BY EMMA PARKER, AUTHOR OF "THE GUERRILLA CHIEF," "ARETAS," &C. &C.

London: Printed for T. Egerton, Military Library, Whitehall, 1816.
I iv, 326p; II 324p. 12mo. 12s (ECB, ER).
ER 27: 271 (Sept 1816), 28: 268 (Mar 1817); WSW I: 429.
Corvey; CME 3-628-48387-5; ECB 433; NSTC 2P3702 (BI BL; NA MH).

## PAYNTER, David William, GODFREY RANGER. A NOVEL

See 1813: 45

## 1816: 49    [PEACOCK, Thomas Love].
## HEADLONG HALL.

London: Printed for T. Hookham, jun. and Co. Old Bond Street, 1816.
216p. 12mo. 6s (ECB).
WSW I: 433.
BL N.1687; ECB 260; NSTC 2P8172 (BI C, O; NA MH).

*Notes.* Further edns: 2nd edn. 1816 (NSTC); 3rd edn. 1822 (NSTC); 1837 (NSTC); Philadelphia 1816 (NSTC).

## 1816: 50    PORTER, Rippin.
## LOVE, RASHNESS, AND REVENGE; OR, TALES OF THREE PASSIONS. IN TWO VOLUMES. BY RIPPIN PORTER, ESQ.

London: Printed for W. Simpkin and R. Marshall, Stationers' Court, Paternoster Row.
   By J. Noble, Market-Place, Boston, 1816.
I xi, 264p; II 318p. 12mo. 10s 6d (ECB, ER, QR).
ER 26: 248 (Feb 1816); QR 14: 554 (Jan 1816).
Corvey; CME 3-628-48363-8; ECB 464; NSTC 2P22528 (BI BL, C, O).

*Notes.* The tales are: 'Rashness; or Maurice and Charlotte. An English Tale'; 'Benallen and Kaphira; or, Constancy Rewarded. An Othman Tale'; 'Revenge; or, Feudal Strife. A Spanish Tale'. The last two of these tales have separate t.ps.

## RYLEY, Samuel William, THE ITINERANT

See 1808: 93

## 1816: 51    SCOTT, Caroline.
## HERMIONE; OR, THE DEFAULTER. A NOVEL. IN TWO VOLUMES. BY CAROLINE SCOTT.

London: Printed at the Minerva Press for A. K. Newman and Co. Leadenhall-Street,
   1816.
I 231p; II 223p. 12mo. 10s 6d (ECB, ER, QR).
ER 27: 271 (Sept 1816); QR 15: 578 (July 1816).
Corvey; CME 3-628-48537-1; ECB 520; NSTC 2S8312 (BI BL, C; NA MH).

## 1816: 52    [SCOTT, Sir Walter].
## THE ANTIQUARY. BY THE AUTHOR OF "WAVERLEY" AND "GUY MANNERING." IN THREE VOLUMES.

Edinburgh: Printed by James Ballantyne and Co. for Archibald Constable and Co.; and
   Longman, Hurst, Rees, Orme, and Brown, London, 1816.
I viii, 336p; II 348p; III 372p. 12mo. 24s (ECB, ER).
ER 26: 498 (June 1816); QR 15: 125–39 (Apr 1816) full review; WSW I: 485–6.
Corvey; CME 3-628-48541-X; ECB 21; NSTC 2S9452 (BI BL, C, Dt, E, O; NA MH).

*Notes.* Novel proper ends vol. 3, p. 355, and is followed by 'Glossary', pp. [357]–372. 'This
day published', 4 May 1816, *Edinburgh Evening Courant.*
Further edns: 2nd edn. 1816 (NSTC); 5th edn. 1818 (NSTC); 6th edn. 1821 (NSTC); New
York 1816 (NSTC, NUC); French trans., 1817; German trans., 1821. Numerous reprintings
in collected edns.

1816: 53   [SCOTT, Sir Walter].
**TALES OF MY LANDLORD, COLLECTED AND ARRANGED BY JEDE-
DIAH CLEISHBOTHAM, SCHOOLMASTER AND PARISH-CLERK OF
GANDERCLEUGH. IN FOUR VOLUMES.**

Edinburgh: Printed for William Blackwood, Prince's Street: and John Murray, Albe-
   marle Street, London, 1816.
I 363p; II 340p; III 349p; IV 347p. 12mo. 28s (ECB, ER, QR).
ER 27: 536 (Dec 1816), 28: 193–259 (Mar 1817) full review; QR 16: 283 (Oct 1816), 16:
   430–80 (Jan 1817) full review; WSW I: 486.
E NG.1175.d.5; ECB 575; NSTC 2S10281 (BI BL, O; NA MH).

*Notes.* 'This day published', 2 Dec 1816, *Edinburgh Evening Courant.* Contains 'The Black
Dwarf' (vol. 1) and 'Old Mortality' (vols. 2–4).
Further edns: 2nd edn. 1817 (NSTC); 3rd edn. 1817 (Corvey, NSTC); 4th edn. 1818 (NSTC);
5th edn. 1819 (NSTC); Philadelphia 1817 (NUC); French trans., 1817 [as *Les Puritains
d'Ecosse, et le nain mystérieux, contes de mon hôte* (NSTC)]; German trans., of 'The Black
Dwarf' 1819 and 'Old Mortality' 1820 [as *Die Schwärmer* (RS)]. Numerous reprintings in
collected edns.

1816: 54   SULLIVAN, Mary Ann.
**OWEN CASTLE, OR, WHICH IS THE HEROINE? A NOVEL. IN FOUR
VOLUMES. DEDICATED BY PERMISSION TO THE RIGHT HON-
OURABLE LADY COMBERMERE, BY MARY ANN SULLIVAN, LATE OF
THE THEATRES ROYAL, LIVERPOOL, MANCHESTER, NEWCASTLE,
BIRMINGHAM, AND NORWICH.**

London: Printed for Simpkin and Marshall, Stationer's Court, Ludgate Hill, 1816.
I iv, 292p; II 264p; III 244p; IV 227p. 12mo. 20s (ECB, ER, QR).
ER 26: 498 (June 1816); QR 15: 295 (Apr 1816); WSW I: 526.
Corvey; CME 3-628-48729-3; ECB 568; NSTC 2S46208 (BI BL, C).

*Notes.* Dedication to Lady Combermere.
Further edn: 2nd edn. 1823 (NUC).

1816: 55   TAYLOR, B.
**FORTITUDE; OR, EUPHEMIA: A NOVEL, IN TWO VOLUMES. BY B.
TAYLOR, ESQ.**

London: Printed for W. Simpkin and R. Marshall, Stationers' Court, Ludgate Street, 1816.

I 270p; II 260p. 12mo. 10s 6d (ECB, ER).

ER 26: 498 (June 1816).

Corvey; CME 3-628-48942-3; ECB 578; NSTC 2T3044 (BI BL, C).

1816: 56    [TEMPLE, Edmond].

**MEMOIRS OF MYSELF. BY PILL GARLICK.**

London: Sold by John Miller, 34, Bow-Street, Covent-Garden; and N. Mahon, and M. Keen, Dublin, 1816.

xv, 275p. 12mo. 7s (ER).

ER 26: 248 (Feb 1816).

BL N.2068; NSTC 2P17090/1 (BI C).

*Notes.* 'N.B.' at end of Introduction states: 'This book is in fact the Second Volume of the one alluded to above; the Author has only changed the title from "Life Of Pill Garlick," to "Memoirs of Myself"' (p. iv). See *The Life of Pill Garlick* (1813: 59).

1816: 57    [THOMAS, Elizabeth].

**PURITY OF HEART, OR THE ANCIENT COSTUME, A TALE, IN ONE VOLUME, ADDRESSED TO THE AUTHOR OF GLENARVON. BY AN OLD WIFE OF TWENTY YEARS.**

London: Printed for W. Simpkin and R. Marshall, Stationers'-Court, Ludgate-Street, 1816.

viii, 273p. 12mo. 5s 6d (ECB, QR); 4s (ER).

ER 27: 536 (Dec 1816); QR 16: 283 (Oct 1816); WSW I: 536.

BL N.1945; ECB 475; NSTC 2T8193 (BI O).

*Notes.* Further edn: 2nd edn. 1817 (Corvey), CME 3-628-48420-0.

1816: 58    [WHITFIELD, Henry].

**EARLY FEUDS; OR FORTUNE'S FROLICS. A NOVEL. IN THREE VOLUMES. BY THE AUTHOR OF GERALDWOOD, BUT WHICH? VILLEROY, SIGISMAR, &C.**

London: Printed at the Minerva Press for A. K. Newman and Co. Leadenhall-Street, 1816.

I 226p; II 274p; III 260p. 12mo. 15s (ECB, QR).

QR 14: 279 (Oct 1815).

Corvey; CME 3-628-47507-4; ECB 176; NSTC 2F5051 (BI BL).

*Notes.* Spine labels are provided at end of vol. 1: these state price as 15s.

1816: 59    ZIEGENHIRT, Sophia F.

**THE ORPHAN OF TINTERN ABBEY. A NOVEL. IN THREE VOLUMES. BY SOPHIA F. ZIEGENHIRT, AUTHOR OF SEABROOK VILLAGE, AND SEVERAL HISTORICAL ABRIDGEMENTS.**

London: Printed at the Minerva Press for A. K. Newman and Co. Leadenhall-Street, 1816.

I 220p; II 253p; III 258p. 12mo. 15s (ECB, ER).
ER 26: 248 (Feb 1816), 27: 271 (Sept 1816); WSW I: 577.
Corvey; CME 3-628-49000-6; ECB 655; NSTC 2Z321 (BI BL, C).

# 1817

1817: 1    ANON.
## THE ACTRESS OF THE PRESENT DAY. IN THREE VOLUMES.

London: Printed for James Harper, 46, Fleet-Street, 1817.
I 295p; II 293p; III 318p. 12mo. 18s (ECB, ER).
ER 29: 512 (Feb 1818); WSW I: 7.
Corvey; CME 3-628-47009-9; ECB 4; NSTC 2A2305 (BI BL).

*Notes.* ECB lists Milliken (Dublin), Harper edn., Jan 1818; but not discovered in this form.

1817: 2    ANON.
## CONIRDAN; OR, THE ST. KILDIANS. A MORAL TALE. BY THE AUTHOR OF HARDENBRASS AND HAVERILL.

London: Printed for Sherwood, Neely, and Jones, Paternoster-Row, 1817.
xi, 319p. 12mo. 7s (ER, QR).
ER 29: 255 (Nov 1817); QR 17: 256 (July 1817); WSW I: 27.
Corvey; CME 3-628-47317-9; NSTC 2C34015 (BI C, E).

*Notes.* For the issue of authorship, see *Hardenbrass and Haverill* (1817: 3, below).

1817: 3    ANON.
## HARDENBRASS AND HAVERILL; OR, THE SECRET OF THE CASTLE, A NOVEL, IN FOUR VOLUMES. CONTAINING A MADMAN AND NO MADMAN—WHO WALKS—DEEDS OF DARKNESS, &C.—REMARKABLE CHARACTERS, INCIDENTS, ADVENTURES, &C. &C. INSTRUCTIVE AND ENTERTAINING.

London: Published by Sherwood, Neely, and Jones, Paternoster-Row, 1817.
I xi, 422p; II 606p; III 382p; IV 420p. 12mo. 31s 6d (ECB, ER).
ER 28: 552 (Aug 1817); WSW I: 51.
Corvey; CME 3-628-47626-7; ECB 254; NSTC 2J10655 (BI BL, C, O; NA MH).

*Notes.* Attributed in some catalogues to James Athearn Jones, but perhaps as a mistake arising from his authorship of *Haverill; or, Memoirs of an Officer in the Army of Wolfe* (New York, 1831). The sequence of novels following on from this title, and especially *Reft Rob* (1817: 7), has also been incorrectly associated with David Carey.

1817: 4 ANON.

HOWARD CASTLE; OR A ROMANCE FROM THE MOUNTAINS. IN
FIVE VOLUMES. BY A NORTH BRITON.

> London: Printed at the Minerva Press for A. K. Newman and Co. Leadenhall-Street,
> 1817.
> I vii, 295p; II 292p; III 304p; IV 288p; V 302p. 12mo. 27s 6d (ECB, ER).
> ER 28: 553 (Aug 1817), 29: 255 (Nov 1817).
> Corvey; CME 3-628-47745-X; ECB 285; NSTC 2N10031 (BI BL).

*Notes.* Preface 'to the Public'.

1817: 5 ANON.

MODERN MANNERS; OR, A SEASON AT HARROWGATE. IN TWO
VOLUMES.

> London: Printed for Longman, Hurst, Rees, Orme, & Brown, Paternoster-Row, 1817.
> I 269p; II 352p. 12mo. 12s (ECB, ER); 10s (ER).
> ER 28: 552 (Aug 1817), 29: 255 (Nov 1817); WSW I: 77.
> Corvey; CME 3-628-48217-8; ECB 390; NSTC 2H10124 (BI BL, O).

1817: 6 ANON.

PONSONBY. IN TWO VOLUMES.

> London: Printed for John Richardson, Royal Exchange, 1817.
> I 211p; II 208p. 8vo.
> ER 28: 268 (Mar 1817); WSW I: 98.
> Corvey; CME 3-628-48483-9; NSTC 2P21097 (BI BL, O; NA MH).

1817: 7 ANON.

REFT ROB; OR, THE WITCH OF SCOT-MUIR, COMMONLY CALLED
MADGE THE SNOOVER. A SCOTTISH TALE. BY THE AUTHOR OF
HARDENBRASS AND HAVERILL.

> London: Printed for Sherwood, Neely, and Jones, Paternoster Row, 1817.
> iv, 192p. 12mo. 5s (ECB).
> WSW I: 102.
> Corvey; CME 3-628-48525-8; ECB 484; NSTC 2J10658 (BI, BL E).

*Notes.* For the issue of author attribution, see 1817: 3. ECB dates Aug 1817.
Further edns: 1825 (NSTC); 1834 as *The Nuptial Doom, or the Witch of Scots-muir*
(NSTC).

1817: 8 ANON.

THE REVEALER OF SECRETS; OR THE HOUSE THAT JACK BUILT, A
NEW STORY UPON AN OLD FOUNDATION. IN THREE VOLUMES.
BY THE AUTHOR OF EVERSFIELD ABBEY, BANKS OF THE WYE,
AUNT AND NIECE, SUBSTANCE AND SHADOW, &C. &C.

> London: Printed at the Minerva Press for A. K. Newman and Co. Leadenhall-Street,
> 1817.

I 231p; II 219p; III 218p. 12mo. 15s (ECB, ER, QR).

ER 27: 536 (Dec 1816); QR 15: 578 (July 1816).

Corvey; CME 3-628-48539-8; ECB 489; NSTC 2R7623 (BI BL, C, O; NA MH).

*Notes.* The last in a chain of novels linked variously by title attributions to Mrs E. G. Bayfield, Mrs E. M. Foster, and J. H. James. ECB dates Nov 1816.

1817: 9 ANON.
## THREE WEEKS AT FLADONG'S. A NOVEL. BY A LATE VISITANT. IN THREE VOLUMES.

London: Printed for the Author, and sold by all Booksellers in Town and Country, 1817.
I iii, 220p; II 227p; III 245p. 12mo. 20s (s.l., ECB, ER).
ER 28: 553 (Aug 1817); WSW I: 121.
BL 1153.g.22; ECB 590; NSTC 2F7765 (BI O).

*Notes.* ECB lists Iley as publisher, but not discovered in this form.

1817: 10 [AGG, John].
## THE PAVILION; OR, A MONTH IN BRIGHTON. A SATIRICAL NOVEL. BY HUMPHREY HEDGEHOG, ESQ. AUTHOR OF "A MONTH IN TOWN," "GENERAL POST BAG," "REJECTED ODES," &C.

London: Printed for J. Johnston, 98, Cheapside, and 335, Oxford Street, and sold by all Booksellers, 1817.
I 239p; II 244p; III 224p. 12mo.
BL 12614.bb.14; ECB 437; NSTC 2A5134 (BI O; NA MH).

*Notes.* Last four pages of vol. 2 are mistakenly numbered 155–158.

1817: 11 [BARRETT, Eaton Stannard].
## SIX WEEKS AT LONG'S. BY A LATE RESIDENT. IN THREE VOLUMES.

London: Printed for the Author; and sold by all Booksellers, 1817.
I xii, 235p; II 230p; III 226p. 12mo. 21s (ECB, QR).
ER 28: 268 (Mar 1817); QR 16: 557 (Jan 1817); WSW I: 143.
O 12.Õ.1841-1843; ECB 540; NSTC 2B9426.

*Notes.* Contains portraits of contemporary literary figures: Lord Leander (Byron) is first encountered reading Scott. ECB lists as 'Six weeks at Long's Hotel', and gives Colburn as publisher; but not discovered in either form.
Further edns: 2nd edn. 1817 (Corvey), CME 3-628-48750-1; 3rd edn. 1817 (NSTC).

1817: 12 BEAUCLERC, Amelia.
## THE DESERTER. A NOVEL. IN FOUR VOLUMES. BY AMELIA BEAU-CLERC, AUTHOR OF MONTREITHE, OR THE PEER OF SCOTLAND; HUSBAND HUNTERS, &C. &C.

London: Printed at the Minerva Press for A. K. Newman and Co. Leadenhall-Street, 1817.
I 263p; II 245p; III 217p; IV 245p. 12mo. 22s (ECB, QR).
QR 17: 256 (July 1817).
Corvey; CME 3-628-47131-1; ECB 45; NSTC 2B13633 (BI BL, C, O).

1817: 13    [?BELL, Nugent].
**ALEXENA; OR, THE CASTLE OF SANTA MARCO, A ROMANCE, IN THREE VOLUMES. EMBELLISHED WITH ENGRAVINGS.**

> London: Printed at the Minerva Press, for A. K. Newman and Co. Leadenhall-St., 1817.
> I 287p, ill.; II 300p, ill.; III 219p, ill. 12mo.
> ViU PZ2.A445.1817; xNSTC.

*Notes.* Frontispiece, depicting different scenes in Gothic mode from the novel, at the beginning of each vol. Imprint on t.p. of vols. 2 and 3, instead of that of the Minerva Press, reads: 'Dublin: Printed by Brett Smith, Mary-Street, 1817'. Another copy (IU 823.A1272) has all 3 t.ps. as vol. 1 in this copy (i.e. A. K. Newman).


1817: 14    [BELLIN DE LA LIBORLIÈRE, Louis François Marie; SHEDDEN, Sophia Elizabeth (*trans.*)].
**THE HERO; OR, THE ADVENTURES OF THE NIGHT: A ROMANCE. TRANSLATED FROM THE ARABIC INTO IROQUESE; FROM THE IROQUESE INTO HOTTENTOT; FROM THE HOTTENTOT INTO FRENCH; AND FROM THE FRENCH INTO ENGLISH. IN TWO VOLUMES.**

> London: Printed for T. and J. Allman, Princes Street, Hanover Square; C. Rice, Berkley Square; and Baldwin, Cradock, and Joy, Paternoster Row, 1817.
> I 171p; II 162p. 12mo. 10s (s.l.).
> ER 28: 553 (Aug 1817), 29: 255 (Nov 1817); QR 17: 294 (Apr 1817); WSW I: 52.
> ICU PR.3391.H5.1817; NSTC 2B16703 (NA MH).

*Notes.* Trans. of *La Nuit anglaise* (Paris, 1799). 'Dedicated with all due Humility to the Authors of The Mysteries of Udolpho; The Tomb; Grasville Abbey; The Monk; Hubert de Sevrac; Celestina; and the Heroine'. Mrs Shedden wrote in the following terms to Sir Walter Scott about her publication in a letter dated 24 Jan 1819: 'I thank you for the kind expressions you use concerning my little translation, but you have mistaken me. It was published two years ago, so that all I wished was that you would ask for it at a circulating Library in your *Northern Athens*, as the more copies are disposed of, the sooner Mr. Allman, of Princes Street, Hanover Square, will give £25 which he promised to give me when he had sold the first edition. The title is *The Hero or the Adventures of a Night*. I dare say you are acquainted with the original *La Nuit Anglaise*—a very witty French work' (*Private Letter Books of Sir Walter Scott*, ed. Wilfred Partington (London, 1930), pp. 229–30). Summers (p. 353) lists Colburn edn., 3 vols., 1815, but not discovered in this form.
Further edn: Philadelphia 1817 (NSTC).


1817: 15    BRAMBLE, Robert [pseud.].
**THE ROYAL BRIDES; OR, SKETCHES OF EXALTED CHARACTERS. A NOVEL, IN THREE VOLUMES. BY ROBERT BRAMBLE, ESQ.**

> London: Printed for M. Iley, Somerset Street, Portman Square; sold by Sherwood, Neely, and Jones, Paternoster-Row; and may be had of all other Booksellers, 1817.
> I 278p; II 300p; III 262p. 12mo. 18s (ER).
> ER 27: 537 (Dec 1816).
> BL 12611.d.15; NSTC 2B46008 (BI C).

1817: 16   BRETON, Marianne.
THE WIFE OF FITZALICE, AND THE CALEDONIAN SIREN. A
ROMANCE, WITH HISTORICAL NOTES. IN FIVE VOLUMES. BY
MARIANNE BRETON.

> London: Printed at the Minerva Press for A. K. Newman and Co. Leadenhall-Street,
> 1817.
> I xii, 268p; II 308p; III 282p; IV 260p; V 290p. 12mo. 27s 6d (ECB, ER, QR).
> ER 27: 536 (Dec 1816); QR 16: 283 (Oct 1816).
> Corvey; CME 3-628-47195-8; ECB 73; NSTC 2B47097 (BI BL, C, O).

*Notes.* In all vols. 'Historical Notes' follow text: vol. 1, pp. [264]–268; vol. 2, pp. [306]–308;
vol. 3, p. [283]; vol. 4, pp. [259]–260; vol. 5, p. [291]. ER describes author as 'Marianne
Wilton', but no other source for this surname has been discovered. ECB dates Nov 1816.

1817: 17   CHIARI, [Pietro]; WHITE, Thomas Evanson (*trans.*).
THE PRIZE IN THE LOTTERY; OR, THE ADVENTURES OF A YOUNG
LADY, WRITTEN BY HERSELF. FROM THE ITALIAN OF L'ABBATE
CHIARI. TRANSLATED BY THOMAS EVANSON WHITE, WITH AN
INTRODUCTION AND NOTES.

> London: Printed by B. M'Millan, Bow-Street, Covent-Garden; sold by Sherwood, Neely
> and Jones, Paternoster-Row; and Wilson, Royal Exchange, 1817.
> I x, 182p; II vi, 196p. 12mo. 10s (ECB, QR).
> QR 16: 557 (Jan 1817).
> BL 1153.e.23; ECB 471; NSTC 2C18340.

*Notes.* Trans. of *La giocatrice di lotto* (Parma, 1757).

1817: 18   CLARK, Emily.
TALES AT THE FIRE SIDE; OR, A FATHER AND MOTHER'S STORIES.
IN THREE VOLUMES. DEDICATED BY PERMISSION TO COLONEL
M'MAHON. BY MISS EMILY CLARK, GRAND-DAUGHTER OF THE
UNFORTUNATE COLONEL FREDERICK, AND AUTHOR OF THE
BANKS OF THE DOURO, POEMS, &C. &C.

> Brentford: Printed by and for P. Norbury; and sold by Baldwin, Cradock, and Joy,
> Paternoster-Row; and all Booksellers in Town and Country, 1817.
> I 223p; II 216p; III 204p. 12mo.
> BL N.1711; ECB 118; NSTC 2C23241 (BI C, O).

*Notes.* Dedicatory verses (1 p. unn.). 7 stories, evidently directed towards younger readers,
but in the style and form of conventional fiction.

1817: 19   [CORP, Harriet].
CŒLEBS DECEIVED. BY THE AUTHOR OF "AN ANTIDOTE TO THE
MISERIES OF HUMAN LIFE," "COTTAGE SKETCHES," &C. &C.

> London: Printed for the Author: and sold by Baldwin, Cradock, and Joy, 47, Paternos-
> ter-Row; Nisbet, 15, Castle-Street, Oxford-Street; T. Inkersley, Bradford; Robinson
> & Co. Leeds; and by all other Booksellers, 1817.

I xi, 189p; II 185p. 12mo. 8s (ECB); 18s (ER, for 3 vols.).
ER 29: 255 (Nov 1817); WSW I: 219.
Corvey; CME 3-628-47301-2; ECB 123; NSTC 2C38495 (BI BL, O).

*Notes.* Collates in sixes. ER price apparently calculated mistakenly on 3 vols.
Further edn: Philadelphia 1817 (NUC).

1817: 20   [CUTHBERTSON, Catherine].
**ROSABELLA: OR, A MOTHER'S MARRIAGE. A NOVEL. IN FIVE VOL-
UMES. BY THE AUTHOR OF THE ROMANCE OF THE PYRENEES;
SANTO SEBASTIANO, OR, THE YOUNG PROTECTOR; THE FOREST
OF MONTALBANO; AND ADELAIDE, OR, THE COUNTERCHARM.**

London: Printed for Baldwin, Cradock, and Joy, Paternoster-Row, 1817.
I 352p; II 348p; III 346p; IV 335p; V 396p. 12mo. 30s (ECB, ER, QR).
ER 29: 512 (Feb 1818); QR 18: 256 (Oct 1817), 18: 545 (Jan 1818); WSW I: 233.
Corvey; CME 3-628-48512-6; ECB 502; NSTC 2C48146 (BI BL, C, NCu, O).

*Notes.* Text proper in vol. 1 ends on p. 349, followed by advs. pp. 350–2; in vol. 5 'Errata' fill
pp. 395–6.
Further edn: New York 1818 (NUC).

1817: 21   D'ARCY, Azilé.
**PREJUDICE; OR PHYSIOGNOMY. A NOVEL. IN THREE VOLUMES.
BY AZILÉ D'ARCY.**

London: Printed at the Minerva Press for A. K. Newman and Co. Leadenhall-Street,
   1817.
I 221p; II 233p; III 223p. 12mo. 15s (ECB, ER, QR).
ER 29: 255 (Nov 1817); QR 17: 256 (July 1817).
Corvey; CME 3-628-47419-1; ECB 152; NSTC 2D2851 (BI BL, C).

1817: 22   DAVENPORT, Selina.
**LEAP YEAR; OR WOMAN'S PRIVILEGE. A NOVEL. IN FIVE VOL-
UMES. BY SELINA DAVENPORT, AUTHOR OF THE HYPOCRITE, OR
MODERN JANUS; DONALD MONTEITH; ORIGINAL OF THE MINIA-
TURE, &C. &C.**

London: Printed at the Minerva Press for A. K. Newman and Co. Leadenhall-Street,
   1817.
I 209p; II 214p; III 211p; IV 235p; V 185p. 12mo. 25s (ECB, ER).
ER 28: 553 (Aug 1817).
Corvey; CME 3-628-47372-1; ECB 153; NSTC 2D3611 (BI BL, C).

1817: 23   DUCRAY-DUM[I]NIL, [François-Guillaume]; [ST. CLAIR,
Rosalia [pseud.] (*trans.*)].
**THE BLIND BEGGAR; OR THE FOUNTAIN OF ST. CATHERINE. A
NOVEL. IN FOUR VOLUMES. BY DUCRAY DUMENIL, AUTHOR OF
JULIEN, OR MY FATHER'S HOUSE; LITTLE CHIMER; TALE OF MYS-
TERY; VICTOR, OR CHILD OF THE FOREST, &C. &C.**

London: Printed at the Minerva Press for A. K. Newman and Co. Leadenhall-Street, 1817.

I 263p; II 240p; III 291p; IV 280p. 12mo. 22s (ECB).

Corvey; CME 3-628-47492-2; ECB 61; NSTC 2D21007 (BI BL, C).

*Notes.* Trans. of *La Fontaine Sainte-Catherine* (Paris, 1813). For St. Clair as translator, see attribution in title of *The Son of O'Donnel* (1819: 59).

1817: 24   EDGEWORTH, Maria.
HARRINGTON, A TALE; AND ORMOND, A TALE. IN THREE VOL-UMES. BY MARIA EDGEWORTH, AUTHOR OF COMIC DRAMAS, TALES OF FASHIONABLE LIFE, &C. &C.

London: Printed for R. Hunter, Successor to Mr. Johnson, 72, St. Paul's Church-Yard, and Baldwin, Cradock, and Joy, Paternoster-Row, 1817.

I iv, 521p; II 422p; III 352p. 12mo. 21s (ECB, ER).

ER 28: 390–418 (Aug 1817) full review, 28: 553 (Aug 1817); WSW I: 257.

BRu ENC; ECB 178; NSTC 2E2217 (BI BL, C, Dt, E, O).

*Notes.* 'To the Reader' signed Richard Lovell Edgeworth, Edgeworth's Town, 31 May 1817, followed by 'Note.—He died a few days after he wrote this Preface—the 13th June, 1817'. *Harrington* fills vol. 1, *Ormond* vols. 2 and 3.
Further edns: 2nd edn. 1817 (Corvey), CME 3-628-47570-8; New York 1817 (NSTC) [also Philadelphia 1817 (NUC)]; French trans., of 'Harrington' and of 'Ormond' 1817.
Facs: IAN (1979), of 'Ormond'.

1817: 25   [ENNIS, Alicia Margaret].
MEMOIRS OF THE MONTAGUE FAMILY. IN THREE VOLUMES.

London: Printed for Edmund Lloyd, Harley-Street, by W. Clowes, Northumberland-Court, Strand, 1817.

I vii, 506p; II 509p; III 499p. 12mo. 21s (ER).

ER 30: 542 (Sept 1818).

Corvey; CME 3-628-48065-5; NSTC 2M33576 (BI Dt, O).

*Notes.* For chain leading to author attribution, see 1820: 22.
Further edn: 1820 as *Ireland; or, Memoirs of the Montague Family* (Corvey), CME 3-628-47947-9. This is a reissue with imprint: 'Printed for E. Lloyd, Harley-Street; and sold by A. K. Newman and Co., Leadenhall-Street'. Apart from different t.ps. the texts are identical. For further details, see Appendix E: 7.

1817: 26   FIELDING, James Holroyd.
BEAUCHAMP; OR, THE WHEEL OF FORTUNE. A NOVEL. IN FOUR VOLUMES. BY JAMES HOLROYD FIELDING, EDITOR OF "SOME ACCOUNT OF MYSELF, BY CHARLES EARL OF ERPINGHAM," &C. &C.

London: Printed at the Minerva Press for A. K. Newman and Co. Leadenhall-Street, 1817.

I 237p; II 240p; III 244p; IV 238p. 12mo. 22s (ECB, ER).

ER 29: 255 (Nov 1817), 29: 512 (Feb 1818).

Corvey; CME 3-628-47550-3; ECB 45; NSTC 2F5591 (BI BL, C, O).

*Notes.* Chapter 1, p. 3 states: 'We are a single individual, as the reader may perceive, by simply looking to the titlepage of our book, whose innate diffidence would have led us to remain in obscurity, had not our bookseller urged, that a thing without a name was little better than no thing at all'. Vol. 1, p. 7 reads: '[. . .] we have commenced the writing of this our book, on the seventh day of November, in the year 1816'.

Further edn: French trans., 1819 [as *La roue de fortune, ou l'héritière de Beauchamp. Par Fielding* (NSTC, which, following BL, wrongly gives as a trans. of 1806: 41 falsely ascribed to Henry Fielding)].

1817: 27    [FIELDING, James Holroyd].
**SOME ACCOUNT OF MYSELF. BY CHARLES EARL OF ERPINGHAM, &C. &C. &C. IN FOUR VOLUMES.**

>   London: Printed for W. Simpkin & R. Marshall, Stationers' Court, Ludgate Street, 1817.
>   I iv, 263p; II 252p; III 254p; IV 263p. 12mo. 22s (ECB, ER).
>   ER 28: 553 (Aug 1817), 29: 255 (Nov 1817).
>   BL N.2039; ECB 549; NSTC 2M33124 (BI C, Dt, O; NA DLC, MH).

*Notes.* Authorship attributed on basis of 1817: 26, above. NSTC, NUC, BLC all treat Charles Monkton, Earl of Erpingham as a pseudonym, but without identifying authorship.

1817: 28    GENLIS, [Stéphanie-Félicité, Comtesse] de; JAMIESON, Alexander (*trans.*).
**PLACIDE, A SPANISH TALE. IN TWO VOLS. TRANSLATED FROM LES BATTUÉCAS, OF MADAME DE GENLIS. BY ALEXANDER JAMIESON.**

>   London: Printed for W. Simpkin & R. Marshall, Stationers' Court, Ludgate Street, 1817.
>   I vi, 204p; II 206p. 12mo. 8s (ECB, QR).
>   ER 28: 268 (Mar 1817); QR 16: 557 (Jan 1817).
>   Corvey; CME 3-628-47804-9; ECB 225; NSTC 2G4572 (BI BL, C, Dt, E).

*Notes.* Trans. of *Les Batuécas* (Paris, 1816).
Further edn: New York 1817 (NSTC).

1817: 29    GODWIN, William.
**MANDEVILLE. A TALE OF THE SEVENTEENTH CENTURY IN ENGLAND. BY WILLIAM GODWIN. IN THREE VOLUMES.**

>   Edinburgh: Printed for Archibald Constable and Co. and Longman, Hurst, Rees, Orme, and Brown, London, 1817.
>   I xii, 306p; II 316p; III 367p. 12mo. 21s (ECB, ER); 21s boards (QR).
>   ER 29: 255 (Nov 1817); QR 18: 176–7 (Oct 1817) full review, 18: 257 (Oct 1817); WSW I: 282.
>   Corvey; CME 3-628-47849-9; ECB 234; NSTC 2G11519 (BI BL, C, Dt, E, NCu, O; NA DLC, MH).

*Notes.* Dedication to 'the late John Philpot Curran', dated 25 Oct 1817.
Further edns: 1818 (NSTC); New York 1818 (NSTC) [also Philadelphia 1818 (NSTC)]; French trans., 1818. See also 1818: 11.

1817: 30   [HATTON, Anne Julia Kemble].
GONZALO DE BALDIVIA; OR, A WIDOW'S VOW. A ROMANTIC LEG-
END. IN FOUR VOLUMES. INSCRIBED, BY PERMISSION, TO WILLIAM
WILBERFORCE, ESQ. BY THE AUTHOR OF CAMBRIAN PICTURES,
SICILIAN MYSTERIES, CONVICTION, SECRET AVENGERS, CHRONI-
CLES OF AN ILLUSTRIOUS HOUSE, &C. &C.

> London: Printed at the Minerva Press for A. K. Newman and Co. Leadenhall-Street, 1817.
> I 299p; II 292p; III 300p; IV 292p. 12mo. 22s (ECB, ER).
> ER 27: 537 (Dec 1816).
> Corvey; CME 3-628-48802-8; ECB 20; NSTC 2A13192 (BI BL, C, O).

*Notes.* Dedication 'to W. Wilberforce, Esq.', signed 'Ann of Swansea. Swansea, July 13, 1816,
Carr Street'.


1817: 31   HERBERT, Caroline.
HUMAN LIFE, WITH VARIATIONS; OR THE CHAPTER OF ACCI-
DENTS. BY CAROLINE HERBERT.

> London: Printed for Longman, Hurst, Rees, Orme, and Brown, Paternoster Row; and
> Lake, Uxbridge, 1817.
> 188p. 12mo. '4s 6d bds' (s.l.).
> ABu SB.82379.Her; NSTC 2H18098 (BI BL, C, O; NA MH).

*Notes.* 'Advertisement' states of the author 'she is an orphan, only eighteen, and this is the
first production she has ever submitted to the clemency of the public'.


1817: 32   HOFLAND, [Barbara].
THE GOOD GRANDMOTHER, AND HER OFFSPRING; A TALE. BY
MRS. HOFLAND, AUTHOR OF "THE SON OF A GENIUS," &C. &C.

> London: Printed for R. Hunter, (Successor to Mr. Johnson) St. Paul's Church-Yard, 1817.
> iv, 164p. 12mo. 3s 6d (ER).
> ER 28: 553 (Aug 1817); WSW I: 294.
> ABu SB.82379.Hof.g; ECB 275; NSTC 2H29392 (BI BL, C, O; NA MH).

*Notes.* Dedication 'to Mrs. Haugh of Doncaster'. ECB 275 also lists Newman edn., 1830,
2s 6d; but not discovered in this form.
Further edns: 2nd edn. 1828 (NSTC); Boston 1821 (NUC).


1817: 33   HOLCROFT, Fanny.
FORTITUDE AND FRAILTY; A NOVEL. IN FOUR VOLUMES. INSCRIBED
TO THE REVERED MEMORY OF HER LAMENTED FATHER, BY FANNY
HOLCROFT.

> London: Printed by W. Clowes, Northumberland-Court, Strand, for W. Simpkin and
> R. Marshall, Stationers'-Court, Ludgate-Street, 1817.
> I 230p; II 294p; III 271p; IV 230p. 12mo. 22s (ECB, QR).
> ER 28: 268 (Mar 1817); QR 16: 557 (Jan 1817); WSW I: 319.
> Corvey; CME 3-628-47730-1; ECB 276; NSTC 2H26025 (BI BL, C).

*Notes.* 'Lines to the Memory of the late Thomas Holcroft', recto page following t.p.

1817: 34   HUTTON, Catharine.
THE WELSH MOUNTAINEER: A NOVEL. BY CATHARINE HUTTON,
AUTHOR OF THE MISER MARRIED. IN THREE VOLUMES.

> London: Printed for Longman, Hurst, Rees, Orme, and Brown, Paternoster-Row, 1817.
> I 264p; II 258p; III 294p. 12mo. 16s 6d (ECB); 18s (ER).
> ER 28: 553 (Aug 1817); WSW I: 337.
> Corvey; CME 3-628-47866-9; ECB 291; NSTC 2H39194 (BI BL, C, O; NA MH).

*Notes.* Further edn: Philadelphia 1817 (Gecker).

1817: 35   [JERDAN, William].
SIX WEEKS IN PARIS; OR, A CURE FOR THE GALLOMANIA. BY A
LATE VISITANT. IN THREE VOLUMES.

> London: Printed for J. Johnston, 98, Cheapside; Macredie and Co. Edinburgh; and sold
>    by all Booksellers, 1817.
> I vii, 256p; II 240p; III 241p. 12mo. 18s (ECB, QR).
> ER 29: 255 (Nov 1817); QR 17: 256 (July 1817).
> BL 1152.g.3; ECB 540; NSTC 2J4968.

*Notes.* Further edn: 2nd edn. 1818 (Corvey), CME 3-628-48751-X.

1817: 36   KER, Anne.
EDRIC, THE FORESTER: OR, THE MYSTERIES OF THE HAUNTED
CHAMBER. AN HISTORICAL ROMANCE, IN THREE VOLUMES. BY
MRS. ANNE KER, OF HIS GRACE THE DUKE OF ROXBURGH'S FAM-
ILY, AUTHOR OF THE HEIRESS DI MONTALDE—ADELINE ST.
JULIAN—EMMELINE, OR THE HAPPY DISCOVERY—MYSTERIOUS
COUNT—AND MODERN FAULTS.

> London: Printed for the Author, by D. N. Shury, Berwick Street, Soho; and sold by
>    T. Hughes, Ludgate Street, 1817.
> I 214p; II 216p; III 216p. 12mo.
> WSW I: 354.
> Corvey; CME 3-628-47995-9; xNSTC.

*Notes.* Further edn: 1841 (NSTC 2K4083).

1817: 37   [LESTER, Elizabeth B.].
THE BACHELOR AND THE MARRIED MAN, OR THE EQUILIBRIUM
OF THE "BALANCE OF COMFORT." IN THREE VOLUMES.

> London: Printed for Longman, Hurst, Rees, Orme, and Brown, Paternoster-Row, 1817.
> I 254p; II 207p; III 216p. 12mo. 16s 6d (ECB); 10s 6d (ER); 16s 6d boards (QR).
> ER 29: 512 (Feb 1818); QR 18: 256 (Oct 1817); WSW I: 14.
> Corvey; CME 3-628-47089-7; ECB 34; NSTC 2B1385 (BI BL, C).

*Notes.* Block, NSTC and NUC attribute this novel to Mrs Ross, though no author is given in
ECB and Summers. The present attribution is based on fresh evidence discovered in
the Longman Letter Books at the University of Reading. In a letter dated 1 Apr 1818, the
publishers write to Miss E. B. Lester in the following terms: 'We have looked over the

Physiognomist and will with pleasure put it to press on the same terms as we arranged for the Bachelor & Married Man—your early answer will oblige' (Longman I, 100, no. 239). *The Physiognomist [...] by the Author of "The Bachelor and the Married Man"* (see 1818: 39) represents one of a chain of novels, all published by Longmans, which likewise have been attributed to Mrs Ross. Elizabeth B. Lester is the acknowledged author of *The Quakers: A Tale* (see 1817: 38, below), hitherto the only work of fiction she is known to have written. Further proof of Lester's likely authorship of *The Bachelor and the Married Man*, and its successors, is found in another letter from Longman & Co., addressed to Miss Lester on 20 Nov 1818, concerning her next novel (probably *Hesitation; or to Marry or not to Marry?*: see 1819: 45): 'Agreeably to your request we now send you a copy of the opinion & suggestions of our literary friend and by adopting them we have no doubt you will add greatly to the interest of the Novel. We do not think the Title a happy one—if you could give us several we would point out the one we thought best. Our friend suggests Isadora or the Force of First Love. The Batchelor & Married Man was an excellent title—as soon as we hit upon a good title the work should be announced' (Longman I, 100, no. 248). Isadora Argyle is the heroine of *Hesitation; or to Marry or not to Marry?*. Longman Divide Ledger D2 (p. 73) records an impression of 750 copies of *The Bachelor and the Married Man* in Dec 1817, with 720 sold, and a second edn. of 500 copies in June 1818: figures and dates which are confirmed in Impression Ledger 6, ff. 124v, 169. No other record of this 2nd edn. has been discovered. Thanks are due to Michael Bott and Frances Miller, of the University of Reading Library, for their help in researching these letters and other materials in the Longman archives. ECB dates Jan 1818.

Further edns: New York 1818 (NSTC); German trans., 1818 [as *Der Ehemann und der Hagestolz* (RS)]. For evidence of a 2nd edn., see note above.

1817: 38   LESTER, Elizabeth B.
### THE QUAKERS; A TALE. BY ELIZABETH B. LESTER.

> London: Printed for Baldwin, Cradock, and Joy, Paternoster-Row, 1817.
> 269p. 12mo. 6s (ECB, ER); 6s boards (QR).
> ER 29: 512 (Feb 1818); QR 18: 256 (Oct 1817); WSW I: 370.
> Corvey; CME 3-628-48038-8; ECB 339; NSTC 2L12419 (BI BL, C).

*Notes.* Further edn: New York 1818 (NSTC).

1817: 39   M'GENNIS, Alicia.
### STRATHBOGIE; OR THE RECLUSE OF GLENMORRIS. A ROMANCE. IN FIVE VOLUMES. BY ALICIA M'GENNIS.

> London: Printed at the Minerva Press for A. K. Newman and Co. Leadenhall-Street, 1817.
> I 244p; II 277p; III 270p; IV 237p; V 231p. 12mo. 27s 6d (ECB, ER).
> ER 28: 553 (Aug 1817).
> Corvey; CME 3-628-48093-0; ECB 359; NSTC 2M4103 (BI BL, C, O).

1817: 40   MANT, Alicia Catherine.
### MONTAGUE NEWBURGH; OR, THE MOTHER AND SON. IN TWO VOLUMES. BY ALICIA CATHERINE MANT, AUTHOR OF ELLEN; OR THE YOUNG GODMOTHER, AND CAROLINE LISMORE; OR THE ERRORS OF FASHION.

London: Printed for Law and Whittaker, Ave-Maria-Lane, 1817.
I vi, 347p; II 250p. 12mo. 10s 6d (ECB, ER, QR).
ER 28: 552 (Aug 1817), 29: 255 (Nov 1817); QR 17: 294 (Apr 1817); WSW I: 387.
BL N.1794; ECB 366; NSTC 2M13263 (BI C, Dt, O; NA MH).

*Notes.* Dedication 'to My Mother'. Collates in sixes.
Further edn: 3rd edn. 1826 (NSTC).


1817: 41    MATHERS, John [pseud.].
THE HISTORY OF ELSMERE AND ROSA: AN EPISODE. IN TWO VOL-
UMES. THE MERRY MATTER WRITTEN BY JOHN MATHERS; THE
GRAVE, BY A SOLID GENTLEMAN.
Printed for Baldwin, Cradock, and Joy, Paternoster-Row, 1817.
I xx, 306p; II v, 332p. 12mo. 12s (ECB, QR).
QR 18: 256 (Oct 1817).
BL N.1742; ECB 272; NSTC 2M19792 (BI C).

*Notes.* The 'Advertisement' cites a favourable review of *The History of Mr. John Decastro* (see
1815: 35), also written under this pseudonym, as a strong inducement for the undertaking of
the present work. Block and Summers attribute both works to George Colman, the Younger.


MONKTON, Charles, Earl of Erpingham [pseud.]
See FIELDING, James Holroyd


1817: 42    MOORE, Edward.
THE MYSTERIES OF HUNGARY. A ROMANTIC HISTORY, OF THE
FIFTEENTH CENTURY. IN THREE VOLUMES. BY EDWARD MOORE,
ESQ. AUTHOR OF SIR RALPH DE BIGOD, &C. &C.
London: Printed at the Minerva Press for A. K. Newman and Co. Leadenhall-Street,
    1817.
I 266p; II 288p; III 316p. 12mo.
ER 27: 537 (Dec 1816).
Corvey; CME 3-628-48277-1; NSTC 2M34655 (BI BL, C).

*Notes.* Further edn: French trans., 1817.


1817: 43    [MOORE, Frances].
MANNERS: A NOVEL. IN THREE VOLUMES.
London: Printed for Baldwin, Cradock, and Joy, Paternoster Row, 1817.
I 308p; II 336p; III 364p. 12mo. 18s (ECB, ER, QR).
ER 29: 512 (Feb 1818); QR 18: 256 (Oct 1817), 19: 575 (July 1818); WSW I: 403.
Corvey; CME 3-628-48081-7; ECB 366; NSTC 2M34693 (BI BL, C; NA MH).

*Notes.* Text proper in vol. 1 ends on p. 305, followed by advs. pp. 306–8. Block erroneously
attributes to Frances Brooke [née Moore] (1724–89), rather than to Frances Moore (*c*.1789–
1881), the true author.
Further edn: New York 1818 (NSTC).

1817: 44   MOSSE, Henrietta Rouviere.
A BRIDE AND NO WIFE. A NOVEL. IN FOUR VOLUMES. BY MRS.
MOSSE, (LATE HENRIETTA ROUVIERE,) AUTHOR OF LUSSINGTON
ABBEY, HEIRS OF VILLEROY, PEEP AT OUR ANCESTORS, OLD IRISH
BARONET, ARRIVALS FROM INDIA, &C. &C.

> London: Printed at the Minerva Press for A. K. Newman and Co. Leadenhall-Street,
>     1817.
> I 307p; II 305p; III 302p; IV 246p. 12mo. 22s (ECB, ER).
> ER 29: 512 (Feb 1818); WSW I: 412.
> Corvey; CME 3-628-48340-9; ECB 399; NSTC 2R19127 (BI BL, C).

1817: 45   [MOWER, Arthur].
THE WHITE COTTAGE, A TALE.

> Edinburgh: Printed for William Blackwood, Prince's Street: and T. Cadell and W.
>     Davies, Strand, London, 1817.
> 344p. 12mo. 7s (ECB, ER, QR).
> ER 28: 268 (Mar 1817); QR 16: 557 (Jan 1817); WSW I: 412.
> Corvey; CME 3-628-48902-4; ECB 634; NSTC 2M39573 (BI BL, C, E, O; NA MH).

*Notes.* Further edn: Philadelphia 1817 (NUC).

1817: 46   [PEACOCK, Thomas Love].
MELINCOURT. BY THE AUTHOR OF HEADLONG HALL. IN THREE
VOLUMES.

> London: Printed for T. Hookham, jun. and Co. Old Bond Street; and Baldwin,
>     Cradock, and Joy, Paternoster Row, 1817.
> I 224p; II 216p; III 208p. 12mo. 18s (ECB, QR).
> ER 28: 268 (Mar 1817); QR 16: 557 (Jan 1817); WSW I: 434.
> Corvey; CME 3-628-48053-1; ECB 378; NSTC 2P8178 (BI BL, C, Dt, O; NA MH).

*Notes.* Further edns: Philadelphia 1817 (NSTC); French trans., 1818 [as *Anthélia Mélincourt,
ou les enthousiastes* (NSTC)].

1817: 47   PLASTIC, Sir Peter [pseud.].
THE ABSENT MAN, A NARRATIVE. EDITED BY SIR PETER PLASTIC,
KNIGHT OF THE ORDER OF THE TOWER AND SWORD.

> London: Printed for Baldwin, Cradock, and Joy, Paternoster Row, 1817.
> vii, 232p. 12mo. 4s (ECB, QR); 3s (ER).
> ER 28: 269 (Mar 1817); QR 17: 295 (Apr 1817); WSW I: 441.
> BL N.1989; ECB 2; NSTC 2P18767 (BI C).

*Notes.* 'Prefatory Dedication', pp. [iii]–iv, dated 'Tower of London, Jan. 1817'.

1817: 48   PORTER, Anna Maria.
THE KNIGHT OF ST. JOHN, A ROMANCE, BY MISS ANNA MARIA
PORTER, AUTHOR OF "THE RECLUSE OF NORWAY," &C. &C. &C. IN
THREE VOLUMES.

London: Printed for Longman, Hurst, Rees, Orme, and Brown, Paternoster-Row, 1817.
I 333p; II 302p; III 354p. 12mo. 21s (ECB).
ER 29: 255 (Nov 1817); WSW I: 447.
Corvey; CME 3-628-48301-8; ECB 463; NSTC 2P22253 (BI BL, NCu, O; NA MH).

*Notes.* Further edns: 2nd edn. 1817 (NSTC); 3rd edn. 1818 (NSTC); New York 1817 (NSTC);
French trans., 1818.


1817: 49   PORTER, Jane.
THE PASTOR'S FIRE-SIDE, A NOVEL, IN FOUR VOLUMES. BY MISS
JANE PORTER, AUTHOR OF THADDEUS OF WARSAW, SIDNEY'S
APHORISMS, AND THE SCOTTISH CHIEFS.

London: Printed for Longman, Hurst, Rees, Orme, and Brown, Paternoster-Row, 1817.
I 323p; II 405p; III 403p; IV 500p. 12mo. 31s 6d (ECB, ER).
ER 27: 537 (Dec 1816); WSW I: 448.
E Hall.252.g; ECB 464; NSTC 2P22421 (BI BL, Dt, O; NA MH).

*Notes.* Further edns: 2nd edn. 1817 (Corvey), CME 3-628-48359-X; 3rd edn. 1821 (NSTC);
[1822] (NSTC); 1832 (NSTC); 1849 (NSTC); New York 1818 (NUC); French trans., 1817;
German trans., 1822 [as *Des Pfarrers Heimath. Ein romantisches Gemälde* (RS)].


ROSS, Mrs, THE BACHELOR AND THE MARRIED MAN
See LESTER, Elizabeth B.


1817: 50   ROSS, Mrs.
THE BALANCE OF COMFORT; OR THE OLD MAID AND MARRIED
WOMAN. A NOVEL. IN THREE VOLUMES. BY MRS. ROSS, AUTHOR
OF THE MARCHIONESS, THE COUSINS, FAMILY ESTATE, MODERN
CALYPSO, PAIRED—NOT MATCHED, &C.

London: Printed at the Minerva Press for A. K. Newman and Co. Leadenhall-Street,
    1817.
I 269p; II 279p; III 282p. 12mo. 15s (ECB, ER, QR).
ER 27: 536 (Dec 1816); QR 16: 283 (Oct 1816).
Corvey; CME 3-628-48551-7; ECB 503; NSTC 2R17990 (BI BL, O; NA MH).

*Notes.* ECB dates Nov 1816.
Further edns: 2nd edn. 1817 (NSTC); 3rd edn. 1817 (NSTC); 4th edn. 1818 (NSTC); New
York 1817 (NSTC); French trans., 1818 [as *Le Pour et le contre, ou la vieille fille et la femme
mariée* (BN)].


RYLEY, Samuel William, THE ITINERANT
See 1808: 93


1817: 51   ST. GEORGE, Catherine.
MARIA, A DOMESTIC TALE. DEDICATED BY PERMISSION TO HER
ROYAL HIGHNESS THE PRINCESS CHARLOTTE OF SAXE-COBURG.
BY CATHERINE ST. GEORGE. IN THREE VOLUMES.

London: Published by J. Porter, Bookseller to Her Royal Highness the Princess Charlotte, 81, Pall Mall, 1817.

I xvi, 162p; II 208p; III 216p. 12mo. 18s (ER).

ER 28: 553 (Aug 1817); WSW I: 476–7.

IU 823.Sa22m; xNSTC.

*Notes.* Dedication signed Catherine St George, Douglas, Isle of Man, 4 June 1817. 'List of Subscribers' (195 names), vol. 1, pp. [ix]–xvi.


1817: 52    SELDEN, Catharine.

**VILLASANTELLE; OR THE CURIOUS IMPERTINENT. A ROMANCE. BY CATHARINE SELDEN, AUTHOR OF THE ENGLISH NUN, COUNT DE SANTERRE, SERENA, VILLA NOVA, GERMAN LETTERS, &C. &C.**

London: Printed for A. K. Newman and Co. Leadenhall-Street, 1817.

iv, 338p. 12mo. 6s (ECB, ER).

ER 27: 537 (Dec 1816).

Corvey; CME 3-628-48639-4; ECB 525; NSTC 2S12662 (BI BL, C, O).

*Notes.* Colophon of 'R. Snare, Printer, Reading'. Collates in sixes. ECB dates Nov 1816.


1817: 53    TAYLOR, Eliza.

**EDUCATION; OR, ELIZABETH, HER LOVER AND HUSBAND. A TALE FOR 1817. IN THREE VOLUMES. BY ELIZA TAYLOR.**

London: Printed at the Minerva Press for A. K. Newman and Co. Leadenhall-Street, 1817.

I vii, 211p; II 227p; III 233p. 12mo. 15s (ECB, ER).

ER 28: 268 (Mar 1817).

Corvey; CME 3-628-48943-1; ECB 578; NSTC 2T3185 (BI BL, C).

*Notes.* For the probable distinctness of Eliza Taylor from Miss Taylor, also a Minerva author, see 1803: 69.


1817: 54    [?TAYLOR, Jane].

**RACHEL: A TALE.**

London: Printed for Taylor and Hessey, 93, Fleet Street, 1817.

153p, ill. 12mo. 5s (ECB, ER).

ER 28: 553 (Aug 1817); WSW I: 100.

Corvey; CME 3-628-48486-3; ECB 477; NSTC 2R486 (BI BL, O).

*Notes.* Frontispiece bears the legend: 'Published April 21, 1817'. For the issue of attribution, see *The Authoress* (1819: 67). ECB dates June 1817.

Further edns: 2nd edn. (NUC); 3rd edn. 1821 (NSTC); Philadelphia 1818 (NUC).


1817: 55    [THOMAS, Elizabeth].

**CLAUDINE; OR PERTINACITY. A NOVEL. IN THREE VOLUMES. BY MRS. BRIDGET BLUEMANTLE, AUTHOR OF MORTIMER HALL, THE VINDICTIVE SPIRIT, PRISON HOUSE, BARON OF FALCONBERG, &C. &C.**

London: Printed at the Minerva Press for A. K. Newman and Co. Leadenhall-Street, 1817.

I 253p; II 268p; III 255p. 12mo. 15s (ECB, ER, QR).

ER 27: 537 (Dec 1816); QR 16: 283 (Oct 1816).

Corvey; CME 3-628-47124-9; ECB 63; NSTC 2B38497 (BI BL).

*Notes.* ECB dates Nov 1816.

# 1818

1818: 1　ANON.

## THE BANDIT CHIEF; OR, LORDS OF URVINO. A ROMANCE. IN FOUR VOLUMES.

London: Printed at the Minerva Press for A. K. Newman and Co. Leadenhall-Street, 1818.

I 248p; II 284p; III 294p; IV 331p. 12mo. 22s (ECB).

Corvey; CME 3-628-47095-1; ECB 37; NSTC 2B6560 (BI BL, C).

*Notes.* ECB dates Sept 1818. Summers (p. 241) describes also 2nd edn. published by A. K. Newman with t.p. reading: 'By The Author Of Eustace Fitz-Richard, Latham House, In The Days Of John Of Gaunt, etc., etc.'; but no copy of this edn. has been located. For another work evidently by the same author, see 1826: 2.

Further edn: see note above.

1818: 2　ANON.

## BENIGNITY; OR, THE WAYS OF HAPPINESS. A SERIOUS NOVEL. SELECTED (WITH ADDITIONAL CONVERSATIONS,) FROM THE WORKS OF HENRY BROOKE, ESQ. BY A LADY.

Brentford: Printed by P. Norbury; and sold by Baldwin, Cradock and Joy, Paternoster Row; and all other Booksellers in Town and Country, 1818.

vii, 280p. 12mo. 5s (ECB, ER); 5s boards (QR).

ER 30: 268 (June 1818); QR 18: 544 (Jan 1818).

ABu SB.82369.Bro; ECB 50; NSTC 2B50316 (BI BL, C).

*Notes.* An offshoot from Henry Brooke's *The Fool of Quality* (1766–70).

1818: 3　ANON.

## BRAMBLETON HALL, A NOVEL, BEING A SEQUEL TO THE CELE-BRATED EXPEDITION OF HUMPHREY[sic] CLINKER, BY TOBIAS SMOLLET [sic], M.D.

London: Printed by and for T. H. Green, Kennington Cross; A. K. Newman and Co. Leadenhall Street; and Sherwood, Neely and Jones, Paternoster Row, 1818.

xix, 162p, ill. 12mo. 3s 6d (ER).

ER 31: 267 (Dec 1818).

BL 012635.c.44; NSTC 2B46009 (BI C, E, O; NA MH).

*Notes.* Preface, pp. [v]–xv, 'To those readers who may not have perused the preceding volumes of the Expedition of Humphry Clinker'. Drop-head title and running-titles read 'Sequel to Expedition of Humphry Clinker'. Frontispiece bears the legend: 'Pub^d by T. H. Green Kennington Library Park Place Kennington.'

1818: 4   ANON.

## CASTLES IN THE AIR; OR, THE WHIMS OF MY AUNT. A NOVEL. BY THE AUTHORESS OF "DUNETHVIN; OR, A VISIT TO PARIS." IN THREE VOLUMES.

London: Printed for Baldwin, Cradock, and Joy, Paternoster-Row, 1818.

I 256p; II 235p; III 288p. 12mo. 15s (ECB, QR).

QR 19: 575 (July 1818); WSW I: 22.

Corvey; CME 3-628-47224-5; ECB 252; NSTC 2C11054 (BI BL, C, O).

*Notes.* Text proper in vol. 1 ends on p. 250 followed by advs. (6 pp.). ECB lists as by Halliday (Miss), but no further information supporting this attribution has been discovered: see also 1818: 7.

1818: 5   ANON.

## CIVILIZATION; OR THE INDIAN CHIEF. IN THREE VOLUMES.

London: Printed for T. Egerton, Whitehall, 1818.

I 335p; II 301p; III 259p. 12mo. 18s (QR).

QR 18: 545 (Jan 1818); WSW I: 25.

Corvey; CME 3-628-47284-9; NSTC 2C22665 (BI BL, C; NA DLC, MH).

*Notes.* Text proper in vol. 1 ends on p. 307 followed by 'Notes', pp. [309]–335.

1818: 6   ANON.

## DELUSION. A NOVEL. IN TWO VOLUMES.

London: Printed for Law and Whittaker, Ave Maria Lane, Ludgate Street, 1818.

I vi, 281p; II 286p. 12mo. 10s 6d (ECB, ER).

ER 29: 512 (Feb 1818); WSW I: 32.

Corvey; CME 3-628-47409-4; ECB 158; NSTC 2D8567 (BI BL, C, O).

1818: 7   ANON.

## DUNETHVIN; OR, THE VISIT TO PARIS. A NOVEL. IN FOUR VOLUMES. BY A LADY, SOME TIME RESIDENT IN FRANCE.

London: Printed at the Minerva Press for A. K. Newman and Co. Leadenhall-Street, 1818.

I 288p; II 292p; III 264p; IV 282p. 12mo. 22s (ECB, ER, QR).

ER 30: 268 (June 1818); QR 18: 545 (Jan 1818).

Corvey; CME 3-628-47495-7; ECB 174; NSTC 2D22565 (BI BL, C).

*Notes.* For a possible clue to authorship, see *Castles in the Air* (1818: 4).

1818: 8   ANON.
DUNSANY. AN IRISH STORY.
>   London: Printed for Sherwood, Neely, and Jones, Paternoster-Row, 1818.
>   I x, 279p; II 308p. 12mo. 12s (ER, QR).
>   ER 29: 512 (Feb 1818); QR 18: 256 (Oct 1817).
>   Corvey; CME 3-628-47509-0; NSTC 2D23105 (NA MH).

*Notes.* 'List of Subscribers' (136 names), vol. 1, pp. [iii]–x.

1818: 9   ANON.
THE HISTORY OF JULIUS FITZ-JOHN. BY THE AUTHOR OF HARD-
ENBRASS AND HAVERILL; CONIRDAN, OR THE ST. KILDIANS; AND
REFT ROB, OR THE WITCH OF SCOT-MUIR, COMMONLY CALLED
MADGE THE SNOOVER. IN THREE VOLUMES.
>   London: Printed for Sherwood, Neely, and Jones, Paternoster-Row, 1818.
>   I 2, xv, 372p; II 354p; III 364p. 12mo. 21s (ER).
>   ER 29: 512 (Feb 1818); WSW I: 54.
>   Corvey; CME 3-628-47714-X; xNSTC.

*Notes.* For the issue of author attribution, see *Hardenbrass and Haverill* (1817: 3). Advs. with
reviews, vol. 1, pp. [1]–2, first sequence of arabic numbers.

1818: 10   ANON.
JESSY; OR, THE ROSE OF DONALD'S COTTAGE. A TALE. IN FOUR
VOLUMES. BY THE AUTHOR OF THE BRAVO OF BOHEMIA, &C.
>   London: Printed at the Minerva Press for A. K. Newman and Co. Leadenhall-Street,
>       1818.
>   I xi, 246p; II 239p; III 229p; IV 228p. 12mo. 22s (ECB, ER).
>   ER 29: 255 (Nov 1817).
>   Corvey; CME 3-628-47983-5; ECB 308; NSTC 2J5520 (BI BL, C).

*Notes.* Dedication to Lady Cope Sherbrooke, signed 'St. John's, New Brunswick, North
America'. This states: 'I ventured some few years since to enter the list of candidates for their
[the British public's] favour [. . .] induced to hazard the fate of a second work, under the
favourable auspices of our late worthy president, Lieutenant-General Hunter' (pp. v–vi).
Evidently by same author as *Yamboo* (see 1812: 18). ECB dates 1817.

LIONEL: OR, THE LAST OF THE PEVENSEYS
See PHILLIPS, John

1818: 11   ANON.
MANDEVILLE; OR, THE LAST WORDS OF A MANIAC! A TALE OF
THE SEVENTEENTH CENTURY IN ENGLAND. BY HIMSELF. VOL-
UME IV.
>   London: Printed for Effingham Wilson, 88, Royal Exchange; and sold by all other Book-
>       sellers, 1818.
>   216p. 12mo.

WSW I: 71.

Corvey; CME 3-628-47849-9; NSTC 2G11519 (BI O).

*Notes.* A parodic '4th volume' to Godwin's *Mandeville* (see 1817: 29). Collates in sixes.
Further edn: Philadelphia 1818 (NSTC).

1818: 12   ANON.
## PRODIGIOUS!!! OR, CHILDE PADDIE IN LONDON. IN THREE VOLUMES.

London: Printed for the Author, and sold by Wm. Lindsell, 87, Wimpole-Street, 1818.
I xv, 296p; II 336p; III 296p. 12mo. 24s (ECB).
WSW I: 99.

Corvey; CME 3-628-47481-7; ECB 471; NSTC 2P27481 (BI BL, O; NA DLC, MH).

*Notes.* Printer information after imprint date reads: 'W. Wilson, Printer, 4, Greville-Street, London'.

Further edns: 2nd edn. 1818 (NUC); 3rd edn. 1818 (NSTC).

1818: 13   ANON.
## THE PROVINCIALS, A COUNTRY TALE, DEDICATED TO THE INTEL-LIGENT READER IN TOWN AND COUNTRY. IN TWO VOLUMES. BY THE AUTHOR OF "THE RAMSAY FAMILY."

London: Published by J. Bysh, 52, Paternoster-Row, and sold by the Principal Book-sellers in the Kingdom, n.d. [1818? (BLC)].
I xi, 240p; II 269p. 12mo.
WSW I: 99.

BL 12611.b.12; NSTC 2P28280.

*Notes.* Half-titles include printer's mark of 'Bennett, Printer, Bristol'.

1818: 14   ANON.
## SIR JAMES THE ROSS; OR, THE OLD SCOTTISH BARON. A BORDER STORY IN ONE VOLUME. BY A NORTH BRITON.

London: Printed for Matthew Iley, Somerset Street, Portman Square, 1818.
373p, ill. 12mo.
ER 29: 512 (Feb 1818).

Corvey; CME 3-628-48708-0; NSTC 2R17765 (BI E).

*Notes.* ER lists as 'Sir James the Rose, a Border Story'.

1818: 15   ANON.
## THE SOLDIERS OF VENEZUELA: A TALE. IN TWO VOLUMES.

London: Printed for T. Egerton, Whitehall, 1818.
I 267p; II 315p. 12mo. 12s (ECB, QR).
ER 30: 268 (June 1818); QR 18: 544 (Jan 1818).

Corvey; CME 3-628-48720-X; ECB 549; NSTC 2S30263 (BI BL, C).

1818: 16   ANON.
## SOPHIA: OR, THE DANGEROUS INDISCRETION. A TALE, FOUNDED ON FACTS. IN THREE VOLUMES.

London: Printed for Longman, Hurst, Rees, Orme, and Brown, Paternoster-Row, 1818.
I 264p; II 280p; III 204p. 12mo. 16s 6d (ECB, QR); 10s 6d (ER).
ER 30: 268 (June 1818); QR 19: 286 (Apr 1818); WSW I: 114.
Corvey; CME 3-628-48713-7; ECB 550; NSTC 2S31457 (BI BL).

*Notes.* 'The Author's Farewell Address to Sophia', vol. 3, p. [205].

1818: 17    ANON.
SUBMISSION EXEMPLIFIED: OR, THE AMIABLE STRANGER. A NAR-
RATIVE.

London: Printed by R. Watts, for T. Cadell and W. Davies, Strand; Black, Kingsbury,
   Parbury, & Allen, Leadenhall -Street, and Hatchard, Piccadilly, 1818.
251p. 12mo. 6s (ER).
ER 29: 512 (Feb 1818); WSW I: 116.
ABu SB.82379.Sub; NSTC 2S45680 (BI BL, C, Dt; NA MH).

1818: 18    ATKINSON, Charles.
THE LIFE AND ADVENTURES OF AN ECCENTRIC TRAVELLER.
WITH ENGRAVINGS. BY CHARLES ATKINSON; AUTHOR OF "THE
MIND'S MONITOR,"—"ST. HELENA,"—"THE NEIGHBOURHOOD
OF HESLINGTON," &C.

York: Printed for the Author, by M. W. Carrall, opposite the Nelson Inn, Walmgate,
   1818.
iv, 105, ill. 8vo. 'Price to Subscribers, 4s 6d in Boards. Non-Subscribers 5s' (t.p.); 4s 6d
   (ECB).
BL 1164.h.31; ECB 30; NSTC 2A18350.

*Notes.* Preface refers to 'my worthy Subscribers and Patrons' (p. iv), but no subscription list
found.

1818: 19    {AUSTEN, Jane}.
NORTHANGER ABBEY: AND PERSUASION. BY THE AUTHOR OF
"PRIDE AND PREJUDICE," "MANSFIELD-PARK," &C. WITH A BIO-
GRAPHICAL NOTICE OF THE AUTHOR. IN FOUR VOLUMES.

London: John Murray, Albemarle-Street, 1818.
I xxiv, 300p; II 331p; III 280p; IV 308p. 12mo. 24s (ECB); 24s boards (QR).
QR 18: 256 (Oct 1817), 24: 352–376 (Jan 1821) full review ('New Edition'); WSW I: 136.
Corvey; CME 3-628-48238-0; ECB 33; NSTC 2A19396 (BI BL, C, E, O; NA MH).

*Notes.* 'Biographical Notice of the Author', naming her as Jane Austen, vol. 1, pp. [v]–xvi,
dated London, 13 Dec 1817. 'Postscript', vol. 1, pp. xvii–xix, dated London, 20 Dec 1817.
'Advertisement, by the Authoress, to Northanger Abbey', vol. 1, pp. [xxiii]–xxiv, begins:
'This little work was finished in the year 1803'. Published Dec 1817 (Gilson).
Further edns: 1833 (NSTC); 1837 (NSTC); 1848 (Gilson); 1850 (NSTC); Philadelphia 1832
of 'Persuasion' (Gilson); Philadelphia 1833 of 'Northanger Abbey' (Gilson); French trans.,
of 'Persuasion' [as *La Famille Elliot, ou l'ancienne inclination* (BN)] 1821, and of 'Northanger
Abbey' 1824; German trans., of 'Persuasion' [as *Anna: ein Familiengemählde* (Gilson)] 1822.

1818: 20   BRODERICK, Miss.
THE CUMBERLAND COTTAGER. A STORY, FOUNDED ON FACTS. IN
THREE VOLUMES. BY MISS BRODERICK.

> London: Printed at the Minerva Press for A. K. Newman and Co. Leadenhall-Street,
> 1818.
> I 245p; II 234p; III 260p. 12mo. 16s 6d (ECB, ER, QR).
> ER 31: 267 (Dec 1818); QR 19: 574 (July 1818).
> Corvey; CME 3-628-47161-3; ECB 77; NSTC 2B49826 (BI BL, C, O).

1818: 21   [BRONTË, Patrick].
THE MAID OF KILLARNEY; OR, ALBION AND FLORA: A MODERN
TALE; IN WHICH ARE INTERWOVEN SOME CURSORY REMARKS
ON RELIGION AND POLITICS.

> London: Published by Baldwin, Cradock, and Joy, Paternoster-Row; sold also by
> T. Inkersley, Bradford; Robinson and Co. Leeds; and all other Booksellers, 1818.
> vi, 166p. 12mo. 3s 6d (ER).
> ER 30: 268 (June 1818); WSW I: 173.
> Corvey; CME 3-628-48148-1; NSTC 2B50235 (BI BL, C, O).

*Notes.* Collates in sixes.

1818: 22   BROWN, Thomas (the Elder) [pseud.].
BATH; A SATIRICAL NOVEL, WITH PORTRAITS. BY THOMAS
BROWN, THE ELDER: AUTHOR OF BRIGHTON, OR THE STEYNE, IN
THREE VOLUMES.

> London: Printed for the Author; and sold by Sherwood, Neely, and Jones, Paternoster-
> Row, 1818.
> I 220p; II 228p; III 209p. 12mo.
> ER 30: 268 (June 1818); WSW I: 176.
> MH-H 19463.2.3.10*; NSTC 2B53047 (BI O; NA DLC).

*Notes.* Adv. opp. vol. 2 t.p. for the same author's 'Brighton; or, the Steyne, [. . .] Third Edition'; another adv. for the same work at end of vol. 3 includes a long review extract from
'a "London Literary Journal"'.
Further edns: 2nd edn. 1818 (NSTC); 4th edn. 1818 (Corvey), CME 3-628-47140-0.

1818: 23   [BROWN, Thomas (the Elder)] [pseud.].
BRIGHTON; OR, THE STEYNE. A SATIRICAL NOVEL. IN THREE VOL-
UMES.

> London: Printed for the Author. Sold by Sherwood, Neely, and Jones, Paternoster-Row,
> 1818.
> I xii, 252p; II 225p; III 232p. 12mo. 21s (ECB, ER, QR).
> ER 30: 268 (June 1818); QR 18: 545 (Jan 1818); WSW I: 176.
> BL 12611.aaa.1; ECB 74; NSTC 2B53048 (BI E, O; NA DLC, MH).

*Notes.* Further edn: 2nd edn. 1818 (Corvey), CME 3-628-47158-3.

1818: 24 [BUDDEN, Maria Elizabeth].
**WOMAN; OR, MINOR MAXIMS. A SKETCH. IN TWO VOLUMES.**

> London: Printed at the Minerva Press for A. K. Newman and Co. Leadenhall-Street, 1818.
> I 277p; II 281p. 12mo. 11s (ECB, ER, QR).
> ER 30: 268 (June 1818); QR 18: 545 (Jan 1818); WSW I: 131.
> Corvey; CME 3-628-48976-6; ECB 645; NSTC 2W29094 (BI BL, C, O; NA MH).

*Notes.* Sometimes wrongly attributed to Elizabeth Thomas, as a result of both writers having published works titled *Claudine* (see 1817: 55 and note to 1824: 19). Dedication 'to a Tender and Affectionate Mother'.
Further edn: revised as *Helena Egerton; or, Traits of Female Character* (see 1824: 19).

BYRON, Elizabeth
See STRUTT, Elizabeth

1818: 25 {CLARK, Elizabeth}.
**THE ADVERTISEMENT; OR, TWENTY YEARS AGO. A NOVEL, IN THREE VOLUMES.**

> London: Published by Longman, Hurst, Rees, Orme and Brown, Paternoster-Row; and Barratt and Son, Bond-Street, Bath, 1818.
> I xi, 228p; II 212p; III 186p. 12mo. 15s (ECB); 16s 6d (ER).
> ER 29: 512 (Feb 1818); WSW I: 8.
> Corvey; CME 3-628-47022-6; ECB 118; NSTC 2C23239 (BI BL, C).

*Notes.* Dedication 'to the Rev. Bence Bence, Beccles, Suffolk', signed 'Elizabeth Clark'. For the possible appearance of the same author under another surname, see E. D. Carr, *Fears and Cares* (1821: 27). ECB lists as Newman, 1818; but not discovered in this form.

1818: 26 CROKER, M[argaret] S[arah].
**THE QUESTION, WHO IS ANNA? A TALE. BY MISS M. S. CROKER. IN THREE VOLUMES.**

> London: Printed for the Author, and published by J. Souter, No. 73, St. Paul's Church-Yard, 1818.
> I viii, 280p; II 276p; III 312p. 12mo.
> WSW I: 227–8.
> Corvey; CME 3-628-47349-7; NSTC 2C43628 (BI BL, C, Dt).

*Notes.* 'Dedication. Humbly inscribed to the Right Hon. Lord Erskine'.

1818: 27 DALLAS, Alexander R[obert] C[harles].
**FELIX ALVAREZ; OR, MANNERS IN SPAIN: CONTAINING DESCRIP-TIVE ACCOUNTS OF SOME OF THE PROMINENT EVENTS OF THE LATE PENINSULAR WAR; AND AUTHENTIC ANECDOTES ILLUS-TRATIVE OF THE SPANISH CHARACTER; INTERSPERSED WITH POETRY, ORIGINAL, AND FROM THE SPANISH. BY ALEXANDER R. C. DALLAS, ESQ. IN THREE VOLUMES.**

London: Printed for Baldwin, Cradock, and Joy, Paternoster-Row, 1818.

I xvi, 259p; II iv, 273p; III iv, 304p. 12mo. 18s (ECB, ER, QR).

ER 30: 268 (June 1818); QR 19: 286 (Apr 1818); WSW I: 234.

Corvey; CME 3-628-47391-8; ECB 150; NSTC 2D1015 (BI BL, C, Dt, E, O).

*Notes.* Dedication 'to the Right Honourable General Graham, Lord Lynedoch', signed 'Alexander R. C. Dallas, Morden, 4th May, 1818'. Notes at end of all vols., vol. 1, pp. [231]–259; vol. 2, pp. [249]–273; vol. 3, pp. [274]–304.

Further edn: New York 1818 (NSTC).

1818: 28   DAVENPORT, Selina.

AN ANGEL'S FORM AND A DEVIL'S HEART. A NOVEL. IN FOUR VOL-UMES. BY SELINA DAVENPORT, AUTHOR OF THE HYPOCRITE, OR MODERN JANUS, DONALD MONTEITH, ORIGINAL OF THE MINIA-TURE, LEAP YEAR, &C.

London: Printed at the Minerva Press for A. K. Newman and Co. Leadenhall-Street, 1818.

I 227p; II 248p; III 242p; IV 266p. 12mo. 22s (ECB).

Corvey; CME 3-628-47426-4; ECB 153; NSTC 2D3609 (BI BL, C).

*Notes.* ECB dates Sept 1818.

1818: 29   [FERRIER, Susan Edmonstone].

MARRIAGE, A NOVEL. IN THREE VOLUMES.

Edinburgh: William Blackwood, Prince's-Street: and John Murray, Albemarle-Street, London, 1818.

I 319p; II 314p; III 343p. 12mo. 21s (ECB, ER, QR).

ER 30: 268 (June 1818); QR 19: 286 (Apr 1818); WSW I: 267.

Corvey; CME 3-628-48159-7; ECB 368; NSTC 2F4879 (BI BL, C, E, O; NA MH).

*Notes.* Further edns: 2nd edn. 1819 (NSTC); 3rd edn. 1826 (NSTC); 1841 (NSTC); 1842 (NSTC); 1847 (NSTC); New York 1818 (NUC); French trans., 1825; German trans., 1827.

1818: 30   [FOUQUÉ, Friedrich Heinrich Karl, Baron de la Motte]; SOANE, George (*trans.*).

UNDINE, A ROMANCE. TRANSLATED FROM THE GERMAN. BY GEORGE SOANE, A.B.

London: Printed for W. Simpkin, and R. Marshall, Stationer's Court, Ludgate Street, 1818.

205p. 12mo. 5s 6d (ECB, QR).

ER 30: 268 (June 1818); QR 19: 574 (July 1818).

BL 12548.dd.4; ECB 213; NSTC 2L2885 (BI O; NA MH).

*Notes.* Trans. of *Undine* (Berlin, 1811). Dedication to 'Edward Knight, Esq. of the Theatre Royal, Drury Lane'. 'Advertisement' begins: 'It may be right to observe, that in translating this work, I have taken neither few nor trifling liberties with the original'. ECB gives co-publisher as Bell & B[radfute], Edinburgh, but no copy discovered with this imprint.

Further edns: 1830 (NSTC); 1843 (NSTC); 1844 (NSTC); Philadelphia 1824 (NSTC); French trans., 1819. Numerous later American and British translations.

1818: 31   [GAMBLE, John].
NORTHERN IRISH TALES. IN TWO VOLUMES.

> London: Printed for Longman, Hurst, Rees, Orme, and Brown, Paternoster-Row, 1818.
> I 258p; II 276p. 12mo. 12s (ECB).
> ER 29: 512 (Feb 1818); WSW I: 84.
> Corvey; CME 3-628-51019-8; ECB 417; NSTC 2I4039 (BI BL, Dt, O).

*Notes.* 3 tales: 'Stanley', 'Nelson', and 'Lesley'.


1818: 32   GENLIS, [Stéphanie-Félicité, Comtesse] de.
ZUMA, OR THE TREE OF HEALTH. TO WHICH ARE ADDED, THE
FAIR PAULINE,—ZENEIDA,—THE REEDS OF THE TIBER,—AND
THE WIDOW OF LUZI. BY MADAME DE GENLIS.

> London: Printed for Henry Colburn, Conduit Street, Hanover Square, 1818.
> iv, 277p. 12mo. 6s (QR).
> QR 18: 545 (Jan 1818).
> BL 837.b.24; NSTC 2B54580 (BI E).

*Notes.* Trans. of *Zuma, ou la découverte de quinquina* (Paris 1817). Dedication 'to Countess
de Choiseul' signed 'La Comtess de Genlis'. As well as 'Zuma' (to p. 53), the other tales are
'Fair Pauline' (54–104), 'Zeneida' (105–92), 'Reeds of the Tiber' (193–251), 'Widow of Luzi'
(252–77).
Further edn: New York 1818 (NSTC).


GOLLAND, Mrs. C. D.
See HAYNES, Miss C. D.


1818: 33   [HARDING, Anne Raikes].
CORRECTION. A NOVEL. IN THREE VOLUMES.

> London: Printed for Longman, Hurst, Rees, Orme, and Brown, Paternoster-Row, 1818.
> I 338p; II 336p; III 384p. 12mo. 21s (ECB, QR); 15s (ER).
> ER 29: 512 (Feb 1818); QR 18: 545 (Jan 1818); WSW I: 297.
> Corvey; CME 3-628-47340-3; ECB 137; NSTC 2H7485 (BI BL, C; NA MH).

*Notes.* Further edns: 2nd edn. 1819 (NUC); Philadelphia 1818 (Early American imprints.
Second series; no. 43741 (microfilm)).


1818: 34   [HATTON, Anne Julia Kemble].
SECRETS IN EVERY MANSION; OR THE SURGEON'S MEMORAN-
DUM-BOOK. A SCOTTISH RECORD. IN FIVE VOLUMES. BY ANNE
OF SWANSEA, AUTHOR OF CAMBRIAN PICTURES, SICILIAN MYS-
TERIES, CONVICTION, SECRET AVENGERS, CHRONICLES OF AN
ILLUSTRIOUS HOUSE, GONZALO DE BALDIVIA, &C.

> London: Printed at the Minerva Press for A. K. Newman and Co. Leadenhall-Street,
>     1818.
> I xv, 310p; II 356p; III 370p; IV 390p; V 344p. 12mo. 27s 6d (ECB, ER); 27s 6d boards
>     (QR).

ER 29: 512 (Feb 1818); QR 18: 545 (Jan 1818).

Corvey; CME 3-628-48806-0; ECB 20; NSTC 2A13195 (BI BL, C).

*Notes.* Introduction in form of a poem 'to Louis St. Clair', vol. 1, pp. [v]–xv.

1818: 35   HAYNES, Miss C. D. [afterwards GOLLAND, Mrs. C. D.].
THE FOUNDLING OF DEVONSHIRE; OR, "WHO IS SHE?" A NOVEL.
IN FIVE VOLUMES. BY MISS C. D. HAYNES, AUTHOR OF CASTLE LE
BLANC, &C. &C.

> London: Printed at the Minerva Press for A. K. Newman and Co. Leadenhall-Street,
> 1818.
> I viii, 240p; II 266p; III 259p; IV 260p; V 270p. 12mo. 27s 6d (ECB, ER).
> ER 29: 512 (Feb 1818).
> Corvey; CME 3-628-47717-4; ECB 260; NSTC 2H14181 (BI BL, C).

*Notes.* 'The Castle of Le Blanc', as apparently mentioned in the title above, was serialized in
the *Lady's Magazine* (21 parts, 1816–19), but apparently not published separately (see Robert
B. Mayo, 'Gothic Romance in the Magazines', PMLA 65 (1950), 783–4). ECB dates the present work 1817.

1818: 36   [HILLARY, Joseph].
THE PARISH PRIEST IN IRELAND. IN TWO VOLUMES.

> London: Printed for T. Hughes, Ludgate-Street, and W. Mathews, Cork, 1818.
> I 236p; II 228p. 12mo. 10s (ER).
> ER 30: 268 (June 1818).
> Corvey; CME 3-628-48360-3; xNSTC.

*Notes.* Collates in sixes.

1818: 37   HOGG, James.
THE BROWNIE OF BODSBECK; AND OTHER TALES. BY JAMES HOGG,
AUTHOR OF "THE QUEEN'S WAKE," &C. &C. IN TWO VOLUMES.

> Edinburgh: Printed for William Blackwood, Prince's-Street: and John Murray, Albe-
> marle-Street, London, 1818.
> I xii, 295p; II 346p. 12mo. 14s (ECB, ER, QR).
> ER 30: 268 (June 1818); QR 19: 286 (Apr 1818); WSW I: 318.
> Corvey; CME 3-628-51047-3; ECB 276; NSTC 2H25690 (BI BL, C, E, O).

*Notes.* Dedication in verse 'to the Right Honourable Lady Anne Scott, of Buccleuch', dated
Eltrive Lake, 1 Apr 1818. The other tales are: 'The Wool-Gatherer', vol. 2, pp. [89]–228; 'The
Hunt of Eildon', vol. 2, pp. [231]–346.
Further edn: Philadelphia 1833 (NUC).

1818: 38   LEFANU, Alicia.
HELEN MONTEAGLE. BY ALICIA LEFANU, AUTHOR OF STRATHAL-
LAN. IN THREE VOLUMES.

> London: Printed for Sherwood, Neely, & Jones, Paternoster-Row, 1818.
> I 342p; II 483p; III 400p. 12mo. 21s (ER, QR).

ER 29: 512 (Feb 1818); QR 18: 256 (Oct 1817).
Corvey; CME 3-628-47975-4; NSTC 2L9894 (NA MH).

1818: 39    [LESTER, Elizabeth B.].
THE PHYSIOGNOMIST. A NOVEL. BY THE AUTHOR OF "THE BACH-
ELOR AND THE MARRIED MAN." IN THREE VOLUMES.
London: Printed for Longman, Hurst, Rees, Orme, and Brown, Paternoster-Row, 1818.
I ix, 266p; II 231p; III 183p. 12mo. 16s 6d (ECB, ER); 16s 6d boards (QR).
ER 30: 268 (June 1818); QR 19: 286 (Apr 1818); WSW I: 92.
Corvey; CME 3-628-48435-9; ECB 448; NSTC 2P15649 (BI BL, C).

*Notes.* For attribution to Lester, rather than to Mrs Ross, see note to *The Bachelor and the Married Man* (1817: 37).
Further edn: New York 1820 (NSTC).

1818: 40    LOURDOUEIX, [Henri] de.
CHARENTON; OR, THE FOLLIES OF THE AGE: A PHILOSOPHICAL
ROMANCE. BY M. DE LOURDOUEIX. TRANSLATED FROM THE
FRENCH.
London: Printed for Baldwin, Cradock, and Joy, Paternoster-Row, 1818.
iv, 252, ill. 8vo. 7s 6d (ECB, QR).
QR 19: 574 (July 1818).
BRu ENC; ECB 354; NSTC 2L11030 (BI BL, C, D, E, O).

*Notes.* Trans. of *Les Folies du siècle, roman philosophique* (Paris, 1817). 'Translator's Preface',
pp. [iii]–iv.

1818: 41    [MATURIN, Charles Robert].
WOMEN; OR, POUR ET CONTRE. A TALE. BY THE AUTHOR OF
"BERTRAM," &C. IN THREE VOLUMES.
Edinburgh: Printed by James Ballantyne and Co. for Archibald Constable and Co.; and
Longman, Hurst, Rees, Orme, and Brown, London, 1818.
I v, 275p; II 276p; III 408p. 12mo. 21s (ECB, ER, QR).
ER 29: 512 (Feb 1818), 30: 234–57 (June 1818) full review; QR 19: 286 (Apr 1818),
19: 321–8 (July 1818) full review, 19: 574 (July 1818); WSW I: 390.
Corvey; CME 3-628-48977-6; ECB 645; NSTC 2M20504 (BI BL, C, Dt, E, O; NA MH).

*Notes.* Dedication 'to the Right Honourable the Countess of Essex'. Preface, vol. 1, pp. [iii]–v,
discusses the unpopularity of Maturin's earlier fiction.
Further edns: New York 1818 (NSTC) [also Philadelphia 1818 (NSTC)]; French trans., 1818
[as *Éva, ou amour et religion* (BN)].
Facs: IAN (1979).

1818: 42    MONTENGON, Pedro; SMITH, Charles Hervey (*trans.*).
EUDOXIA: DAUGHTER OF BELISARIUS. A NOVEL. TRANSLATED
FROM THE SPANISH OF DON PEDRO MONTENGON, BY CHARLES
HERVEY SMITH. IN TWO VOLS.

London: Printed for J. J. Stockdale, 41, Pall-Mall, 1818.
I 187p; II 224p. 12mo.
Corvey; CME 3-628-48761-7; xNSTC.

*Notes.* Trans. of *Eudoxia, hija de Belisario*, (Madrid, 1793). Dedication 'to my Country-women', by the Translator. Collates in sixes.

1818: 43    [MOORE, Frances].
A YEAR AND A DAY. A NOVEL. IN TWO VOLUMES. BY MADAME
PANACHE, AUTHOR OF MANNERS.

London: Printed for Baldwin, Cradock, and Joy, Paternoster-Row, 1818.
I 276p; II 340p. 12mo. 12s (ECB, QR).
QR 19: 575 (July 1818); WSW I: 403.
Corvey; CME 3-628-48380-8; ECB 431; NSTC 2M34692 (BI BL, C, Dt, O; NA MH).

*Notes.* Block erroneously attributes to Frances Brooke [née Moore] (1724–89), rather than to
Frances Moore (*c.*1789–1881), the true author.
Further edns: 1819 (NSTC); New York 1819 (NUC); French trans., 1820.

1818: 44    MORGAN, Lady [Sydney] [née OWENSON, Sydney].
FLORENCE MACARTHY: AN IRISH TALE. BY LADY MORGAN, AUTHOR
OF "FRANCE," "O'DONNEL," &C. IN FOUR VOLUMES.

London: Printed for Henry Colburn, Public Library, Conduit Street, Hanover Square,
    1818.
I vi, 331p; II 283p; III 295p; IV 283p. 12mo. 28s (ER).
ER 31: 267 (Dec 1818); WSW I: 426.
BL N.1827,28; NSTC 2M36478 (BI O).

*Notes.* Further edns: 2nd edn. 1819 (NSTC); 3rd edn. 1819 (NSTC); 4th edn. 1819 (Corvey),
CME 3-628-48327-1; 5th edn. 1819 (NSTC); 1839 (NSTC); Baltimore 1819 (NUC) [also New
York 1819 (NUC) and Philadelphia 1819 (NUC)]; French trans., 1819; German trans., 1821.
Facs: IAN (1979).

1818: 45    [OLLIER, Charles].
ALTHAM AND HIS WIFE. A DOMESTIC TALE.

London: Printed for C. & J. Ollier, Vere Street, Bond Street, 1818.
198p. 12mo.
WSW I: 421.
Corvey; CME 3-628-47047-1; NSTC 2O3539 (BI BL).

*Notes.* Collates in sixes.

1818: 46    OPIE, [Amelia Alderson].
NEW TALES. BY MRS. OPIE. IN FOUR VOLUMES.

London: Printed for Longman, Hurst, Rees, Orme, and Brown, Paternoster-Row, 1818.
I 356p; II 408p; III 312p; IV 363p. 12mo. 28s (ECB, ER); 28s boards (QR); 24s (QR).
ER 30: 542 (Sept 1818); QR 19: 286 (Apr 1818), 19: 574 (July 1818); WSW I: 422–3.
Corvey; CME 3-628-51115-1; ECB 423; NSTC 2O4393 (BI BL, C, Dt, E, O).

*Notes.* Further edns: 3rd edn. 1819 (NUC); New York 1818 (NUC) [also Philadelphia 1818 (NUC)]; French trans., 1818.

OWENSON, Sydney
See MORGAN, Lady Sydney

1818: 47    [PASCOE, Charlotte Champion, and WILLYAMS, Jane Louisa].
**COQUETRY. IN THREE VOLUMES.**

> Edinburgh: Printed by James Ballantyne and Co. (for the Author;) sold by Archibald
> Constable and Co. Edinburgh; and Longman, Hurst, Rees, Orme, and Brown, Lon-
> don, 1818.
> I 294p; II 343p; III 328p. 12mo. 21s (ECB, ER).
> ER 31: 267 (Dec 1818).
> Corvey; CME 3-628-47333-0; ECB 135; NSTC 2P5866 (BI BL, C, E; NA MH).

*Notes.* The authors were sisters (née Willyams), Charlotte having married Revd Thomas Pascoe by the time of the publication (see Corson). National Library of Scotland MS 322, f. 285v
(19 Jan 1818) shows Walter Scott recommending the work to Robert Cadell (Constable's
partner), having read it in MS, and suggesting 'Trevanion' would be a better title. ECB dates
Mar 1819.

1818: 48    [PEACOCK, Thomas Love].
**NIGHTMARE ABBEY: BY THE AUTHOR OF HEADLONG HALL.**

> London: Printed for T. Hookham, jun. Old Bond-Street; and Baldwin, Cradock, and
> Joy, Paternoster-Row, 1818.
> 218p. 12mo. 6s 6d (ECB, ER, QR).
> ER 31: 267 (Dec 1818); QR 19: 574 (July 1818); WSW I: 434.
> Corvey; CME 3-628-48228-3; ECB 414; NSTC 2P8180 (BI BL, C, O; NA MH).

*Notes.* Further edns: 1837 (NSTC); Philadelphia 1819 (NUC); German trans., 1819 [as *Die
Burg Alphausen, oder Zyprians Frauenwahl* (RS)].
Facs: RR (1992).

1818: 49    PECK, {Frances}.
**THE BARD OF THE WEST; COMMONLY CALLED EMAN AC KNUCK,
OR NED OF THE HILLS. AN IRISH HISTORICAL ROMANCE,
FOUNDED ON FACTS OF THE SEVENTH CENTURY. IN THREE VOL-
UMES. BY MRS. PECK, AUTHOR OF THE "MAID OF AVON," "WELCH
PEASANT BOY," "YOUNG ROSINIÈRE," "VAGA," &C.**

> London: Published by Baldwin, Cradock, and Joy, Paternoster-Row, and John Cum-
> ming, Dublin, 1818.
> I 5, 244p; II 224p; III 194p. 12mo. 15s (ECB, QR).
> QR 19: 574 (July 1818).
> Corvey; CME 3-628-48408-1; ECB 439; NSTC 2P8908 (BI BL, C, O; NA MH).

*Notes.* Dedication 'to His Royal Highness Prince Edward', signed Frances Peck. 'Argument',
vol. 1, pp. [3]–5, dated Dublin, 28 Nov 1818. ECB dates Dec 1818.

1818:50    [?PHILLIPS, John].
## LIONEL: OR, THE LAST OF THE PEVENSEYS. A NOVEL. IN THREE VOLUMES.

> London: Printed for Longman, Hurst, Rees, Orme, and Brown, Paternoster-Row, 1818.
> I 309p; II 315p; III 383p. 12mo. 21s (ECB, ER, QR).
> ER 30: 268 (June 1818), 31: 267 (Dec 1818); QR 19: 286 (Apr 1818), 19: 574 (July 1818); WSW I: 67.
> Corvey; CME 3-628-48032-9; ECB 347; NSTC 2L16997 (BI BL, C; NA MH).

*Notes.* Copies of two letters from the publishers to J. Phillips, Ferrybridge, Yorkshire, survive in the Longman Letter Books (I, 100, nos. 234, 236): the first, dated 12 Mar 1818, recommending terms 'on the same plan as we do those of Mrs. Opie &c. &c. namely that of Dividing Profits'; the second (24 Mar 1818) concerning the choice of title. A Longman ledger refers to the addressee more fully as John Phillips.


1818:51    PLUMPTRE, Anne and Annabella.
## TALES OF WONDER, OF HUMOUR, AND OF SENTIMENT; ORIGINAL AND TRANSLATED. BY ANNE AND ANNABELLA PLUMPTRE. IN THREE VOLUMES.

> London: Printed for Henry Colburn, Public Library, Conduit Street, Hanover Square, 1818.
> I 340p; II 354p; III 355p. 12mo. 21s (ECB, ER).
> ER 29: 512 (Feb 1818); WSW I: 441.
> Corvey; CME 3-628-51119-4; ECB 455; NSTC 2P19456 (BI BL, C; NA DLC, MH).

*Notes.* I Containing Zelis, or the Way to be Happy; The Weathercock; and the Magic Dollar; II Containing the Spectre of Presburg; The Fair of Beaucaire; and Tsching-Quang; III Containing the Family of Valencia; Fanny; Omar and Zemida; and Philosophy and Love. Drop-head titles for the first story in each volume read: 'Zelis: an Indian Tale'; 'The Spectre of Presburg. A Hungarian Tale'; 'The Family of Valencia. A Spanish Tale'. Individual t.ps. for separate stories contained within volumes read: 'The Weathercock. A Burgundian Tale'; 'The Magic Dollar. A Tale of Alsace'; 'The Fair of Beaucaire. A Provençal Tale'; 'Tsching-Quang. A Chinese Tale'; 'Fanny. A Tale of Lorraine'; 'Omar and Zemida: or the Principle of True Love. A Peruvian Tale'; 'Philosophy and Love. A Milesian Tale'. Adv. for Colburn's British and Foreign Public Library facing t.ps. of vols. 1 and 3.


1818:52    PORTER, Anna Maria.
## THE FAST OF ST. MAGDALEN, A ROMANCE. BY ANNA MARIA PORTER. IN THREE VOLUMES.

> London: Printed for Longman, Hurst, Rees, Orme, and Brown, Paternoster-Row, 1818.
> I 347p; II 317p; III 346p. 12mo. 21s (ECB, ER); 21s boards (QR).
> ER 31: 267 (Dec 1818); QR 19: 574 (July 1818); WSW I: 447.
> BL 12612.ee.15; ECB 463; NSTC 2P22246 (BI Dt, E, O; NA MH).

*Notes.* Further edns: 2nd edn. 1819 (Corvey), CME 3-628-48298-4; 3rd edn. 1819 (NUC); Boston 1819 (NSTC) [also New York 1819 (NSTC, NUC)]; French trans., 1819 [as *Le Jeûne de Sainte Madeleine, ou les illustres proscrits* (BLC)].

1818: 53   PUZZLEBRAIN, Peregrine [pseud.].
**TALES OF MY LANDLADY. EDITED BY PEREGRINE PUZZLEBRAIN. ASSISTANT TO THE SCHOOLMASTER OF GANDERCLEUGH. IN THREE VOLUMES.**

> London: Printed for M. Iley, Somerset Street, Portman Square, and may be had of all Booksellers, 1818.
> I 339p; II 261p; III 343p. 12mo.
> ER 29: 512 (Feb 1818), 30: 268 (June 1818); WSW I: 118.
> Corvey; CME 3-628-48869-9; NSTC 2P29951 (BI BL; NA MH).

1818: 54   RYLEY, Ann.
**FANNY FITZ-YORK, HEIRESS OF TREMORNE. IN THREE VOLUMES. BY ANN RYLEY.**

> London: Printed for Sherwood, Neely, and Jones, Paternoster-Row, 1818.
> I viii, 407p; II 410p; III 467p. 12mo. 21s (QR).
> QR 18: 256 (Oct 1817).
> Corvey; CME 3-628-48589-4; NSTC 2R22758 (BI BL).

*Notes.* Dedication 'to Mrs. Buckley, Manchester', dated 'Cottage of Comfort, Park-gate, September 1, 1817'. Preface dated Parkgate, 7 Nov 1817.

1818: 55   [SCOTT, Sir Walter].
**ROB ROY. BY THE AUTHOR OF "WAVERLEY," "GUY MANNERING," AND "THE ANTIQUARY." IN THREE VOLUMES.**

> Edinburgh: Printed by James Ballantyne and Co. for Archibald Constable and Co.; and Longman, Hurst, Rees, Orme, and Brown, London, 1818.
> I viii, 321p; II 324p; III 348p. 12mo. 24s (ECB); 24s boards (ER).
> ER 29: 403–32 (Feb 1818) full review, 29: 512 (Feb 1818); WSW I: 487.
> BL Cup.400.b.40; ECB 495; NSTC 2S10179 (BI C, Dt, E, NCu, O; NA MH).

*Notes.* 'This day published', 1 Jan 1818, *Edinburgh Evening Courant.*
Further edns: 2nd edn. 1818 (NSTC); 3rd edn. 1818 (Corvey), CME 3-628-48584-3; 4th edn. 1818 (NSTC); 1821 (NSTC); New York 1818 (NSTC) [also Philadelphia 1818 (NSTC)]; French trans., 1818 [as *Robert le Rouge Mac-Gregor, ou les montagnards écossais* (NSTC)]; German trans., 1819 [as *Robin, der Rothe* (NSTC)]. Numerous reprintings in collected edns.

1818: 56   [SCOTT, Sir Walter].
**TALES OF MY LANDLORD. SECOND SERIES, COLLECTED AND ARRANGED BY JEDEDIAH CLEISHBOTHAM, SCHOOLMASTER AND PARISH-CLERK OF GANDERCLEUGH. IN FOUR VOLUMES.**

> Edinburgh: Printed for Archibald Constable and Company, 1818.
> I 333p; II 322p; III 328p; IV 375p. 12mo. 32s (ECB, ER, QR).
> ER 30: 268 (June 1818); QR 19: 574 (July 1818); WSW I: 487–8.
> Corvey; ECB 575; NSTC 2S10293 (BI BL, Dt, E, O; NA DLC).

*Notes.* 'This day published', 25 July 1818, *Edinburgh Evening Courant.* Comprises 'The Heart of Mid-Lothian'.

Further edns: 2nd edn. 1818 (NSTC); 3rd edn. 1818 (NSTC); Philadelphia 1818 (NSTC); French trans., 1818; German trans. 1821 [as *Der Kerker von Edinburgh* (RS)]. Numerous reprintings in collected edns.

1818: 57    [SHELLEY, Mary Wollstonecraft].
**FRANKENSTEIN; OR, THE MODERN PROMETHEUS. IN THREE VOLUMES.**

> London: Printed for Lackington, Hughes, Harding, Mavor, & Jones, Finsbury Square, 1818.
> I xii, 181p; II 156p; III 192p. 12mo. 16s 6d (ECB, ER).
> ER 29: 512 (Feb 1818); QR 18: 379–85 (Jan 1818) full review; WSW I: 496–7.
> Corvey; CME 3-628-47833-2; ECB 216; NSTC 2S18445 (BI BL, C, Dt; NA DLC, MH).

*Notes.* Dedication to William Godwin.
Further edns: 1823 (NSTC); 1831 (NSTC); 1832 (NUC); 1836 (BRu ENC); 1839 (NSTC); 1849 (NSTC); Philadelphia 1833 (NSTC, NUC); French trans., 1821.
Facs: RR (of 1823 New edn.; 1993).

1818: 58    STANHOPE, Louisa Sidney.
**THE NUN OF SANTA MARIA DI TINDARO. A TALE. IN THREE VOLUMES. BY LOUISA SIDNEY STANHOPE, AUTHOR OF MONTBRAZIL ABBEY, DI MONTRANZO, BANDIT'S BRIDE, TREACHERY, &C. &C.**

> London: Printed at the Minerva Press for A. K. Newman and Co. Leadenhall-Street, 1818.
> I xxiv, 254p; II 249p; III 250p. 12mo. 16s 6d (ECB, ER).
> ER 30: 542 (Sept 1818).
> Corvey; CME 3-628-48778-1; ECB 558; NSTC 2S36110 (BI BL, C).

1818: 59    [STEVENS, Grace Buchanan].
**LLEWELLEN, OR, THE VALE OF PHLINLIMMON: A NOVEL. IN THREE VOLUMES.**

> Edinburgh: Printed by John Moir, Royal Bank Close, for Macredie, Skelly, & Co. 52, Prince Street; and T. & G. Underwood, 32, Fleet Street, London, 1818.
> I 300p; II 270p; III 285p. 12mo. 21s (ECB, ER, QR).
> ER 30: 268 (June 1818); QR 19: 286 (Apr 1818); WSW I: 520.
> Corvey; CME 3-628-48034-5; ECB 350; NSTC 2S39227 (BI BL, C; NA MH).

1818: 60    STRUTT, [Elizabeth] [formerly BYRON].
**GENEVIEVE; OR, THE ORPHAN'S VISIT. A NOVEL. IN THREE VOLUMES. BY MRS. STRUTT, AUTHOR OF THE BORDERERS, ANTI-DELPHINE, &C.**

> London: Printed at the Minerva Press for A. K. Newman and Co. Leadenhall-Street, 1818.
> I viii, 274p; II 292p; III 311p. 12mo. 15s 6d (ECB); 16s 6d (ER).
> ER 30: 268 (June 1818).
> Corvey; CME 3-628-48682-3; ECB 566; NSTC 2S44850 (BI BL, C).

1818: 61	WARD, Catherine G[eorge].
ROBERTINA; OR, THE SACRED DEPOSIT. A NOVEL. IN TWO VOL-
UMES. BY CATHERINE G. WARD, AUTHOR OF THE DAUGHTER OF
ST. OMER, THE BACHELOR'S HEIRESS, MY NATIVE LAND, THE SON
AND THE NEPHEW, &C. &C.

> London: Printed at the Minerva Press for A. K. Newman and Co. Leadenhall-Street, 1818.
> I ii, 215p; II 226p. 12mo. 10s (ECB).
> Corvey; CME 3-628-47695-X; ECB 623; NSTC 2W4968 (BI BL, C, O).

*Notes.* Dedication 'to the unknown ———', dated 6 Aug 1817. ECB dates 1817.

1818: 62	YOSSY, {A}[nn].
CONSTANCY AND LEOPOLD. BY MADAME YOSSY, AUTHOR OF
SWITZERLAND. IN FOUR VOLUMES.

> London: Printed for Matthew Iley, Somerset Street, Portman Square; and sold by M.
> Galignani, Paris; and M. Le Double, Geneva; and all other Booksellers, 1818.
> I xv, 263p; II 253p; III 237p; IV 233p. 12mo. 24s (ER).
> ER 30: 268 (June 1818).
> BRu ENC; xNSTC.

*Notes.* Dedication to Lady Mary Ross, signed A. Yossy. Introduction dated Apr 1818.
Further edn: French trans., 1823 [as *Glorianna et Léopold, ou l'empire du préjugé* (BN)].

# 1819

1819: 1	ANON.
ALBANY. A NOVEL. IN THREE VOLUMES. BY THE AUTHOR OF BEAU
MONDE, &C. &C. &C.

> London: Printed at the Minerva Press for A. K. Newman and Co. Leadenhall-Street,
> 1819.
> I 260p; II 255p; III 237p. 12mo. 16s 6d (ECB, QR).
> QR 21: 268 (Jan 1819).
> Corvey; CME 3-628-47035-8; ECB 10; NSTC 2A6422 (BI BL, C).

1819: 2	ANON.
THE BLACK CONVENT; OR, A TALE OF FEUDAL TIMES. IN TWO
VOLUMES.

> London: Printed at the Minerva Press for A. K. Newman and Co. Leadenhall-Street,
> 1819.
> I 244p; II 249p. 12mo. 11s (ECB, ER, QR).
> ER 32: 514 (Oct 1819); QR 22: 270 (July 1819).
> Corvey; CME 3-628-47200-8; ECB 59; NSTC 2C34982 (BI BL, C, O).

1819: 3   ANON.

THE CASTLE OF VILLA-FLORA. A PORTUGUESE TALE, FROM A MANUSCRIPT LATELY FOUND BY A BRITISH OFFICER OF RANK IN AN OLD MANSION IN PORTUGAL. IN THREE VOLUMES.

London: Printed at the Minerva Press for A. K. Newman and Co. Leadenhall-Street, 1819.
I 219p; II 257p; III 266p. 12mo. 16s 6d (ECB, ER, QR).
ER 32: 514 (Oct 1819); QR 22: 270 (July 1819).
Corvey; CME 3-628-47221-0; ECB 100; NSTC 2C10991 (BI BL, C, O).

1819: 4   ANON.

CORALY. A NOVEL. IN THREE VOLUMES.

London: Printed for Longman, Hurst, Rees, Orme, and Brown, Paternoster-Row, 1819.
I 260p; II 210p; III 167p. 12mo. 10s 6d (ECB).
WSW I: 27.
Corvey; CME 3-628-47336-5; ECB 135; NSTC 2C37654 (BI BL, C, O).

*Notes.* Item in Longman Letter Books (I, 101, no. 111C), dated 9 Apr 1821 and concerning the remaindering of unsold copies, indicates male authorship. ECB dates Jan 1819.

1819: 5   ANON.

EDWARD WORTLEY, AND THE EXILE OF SCOTLAND. IN THREE VOLUMES.

London: Printed for J. W. Whiteley, 103, Newgate Street, 1819.
I xi, 343p; II 316p; III 229p. 12mo.
WSW I: 35.
Corvey; CME 3-628-47512-0; xNSTC.

*Notes.* I Edward Wortley; II Edward Wortley; III Exile of Scotland.

1819: 6   ANON.

THE ENGLISHMAN IN PARIS; A SATIRICAL NOVEL. WITH SKETCHES OF THE MOST REMARKABLE CHARACTERS THAT HAVE RECENTLY VISITED THAT CELEBRATED CAPITAL. IN THREE VOLUMES.

London: Printed for Sherwood, Neely, and Jones, Paternoster-Row, 1819.
I 248p; II 220p; III 240p. 12mo. 21s (ER).
ER 31: 267 (Dec 1818).
Corvey; CME 3-628-47653-4; NSTC 2E10528 (BI BL, E, O; NA MH).

1819: 7   ANON.

ERRORS AND THEIR CONSEQUENCES; OR, MEMOIRS OF AN ENGLISH FAMILY. IN TWO VOLUMES.

London: Printed for Longman, Hurst, Rees, Orme, and Brown, Pater-Noster-Row, 1819.
I xx, 389p; II 318p. 12mo. 13s (ECB, ER, QR).
ER 32: 257 (July 1819); QR 21: 563 (Apr 1819); WSW I: 39.
Corvey; CME 3-628-47620-8; ECB 190; NSTC 2E10072 (BI BL, C, O).

*Notes.* Preface, vol. 1, pp. [i]–xx. Continuous roman and arabic pagination, with novel proper beginning at p. [21].

1819: 8   ANON.
**THE FAMILIES OF OWEN AND DE MONTFORT. A TALE OF ANCIENT DAYS. IN THREE VOLUMES.**

> London: Printed at the Minerva Press for A. K. Newman and Co. Leadenhall-Street, 1819.
> I iii, 228p; II 222p; III 202p. 12mo. 15s (ABu s.l.).
> Corvey; CME 3-628-47607-0; NSTC 2O6929 (BI BL, O).

*Notes.* 'Preface. To the Reader', signed 'The Author'.

1819: 9   ANON.
**GOGMAGOG-HALL; OR, THE PHILOSOPHICAL LORD AND THE GOVERNESS. BY THE AUTHOR OF "PRODIGIOUS!!! OR, CHILDE PADDIE IN LONDON." IN THREE VOLUMES.**

> London: Printed for G. and W. B. Whittaker, Ave-Maria Lane, Ludgate-Street, 1819.
> I 355p; II 311p; III 334p. 12mo. 21s (ER).
> ER 32: 256 (July 1819); QR 21: 563 (Apr 1819); WSW I: 49.
> Corvey; CME 3-628-47911-8; NSTC 2G11875 (BI BL).

1819: 10   ANON.
**THE INTRIGUING BEAUTY, AND THE BEAUTY WITHOUT INTRIGUE. IN THREE VOLUMES.**

> London: Printed for T. and J. Allman, Princes-Street, Hanover-Square; and sold by Baldwin, Cradock, and Joy, Paternoster-Row; and Bell and Bradfute, Edinburgh, 1819.
> I 216p; II 254p; III 224p. 12mo.
> WSW I: 58.
> Corvey; CME 3-628-47920-7; NSTC 2B13911 (BI BL).

1819: 11   ANON.
**LONDON: OR, A MONTH AT STEVENS'S, BY A LATE RESIDENT. A SATIRICAL NOVEL. IN THREE VOLUMES.**

> London: Printed for Sherwood, Neely, and Jones, Paternoster-Row, 1819.
> I iv, 236p; II 210p; III 214p. 12mo.
> BL 12611.aa.13; NSTC 2LON6986 (BI E, O; NA MH).

*Notes.* Further edn: 2nd edn. 1819 (Corvey), CME 3-628-48111-2.

1819: 12   ANON.
**MELCOMBE LODGE; OR, TRAITS OF FAMILY PRIDE! A NOVEL, IN FOUR VOLUMES. BY A LADY.**

> Lynn: Printed by and for W. Whittingham, and published by Baldwin, Cradock, and Joy, London, 1819.

I 254p; II 218p; III 224p; IV 289p. 12mo.
BL N.1767,68; NSTC 2M23644 (BI C, O).

1819: 13 ANON.
*THE METROPOLIS. A NOVEL, BY THE AUTHOR OF LITTLE
HYDROGEN, OR THE DEVIL ON TWO STICKS IN LONDON. IN
THREE VOLUMES.
London: Printed for J. J. Stockdale, 41, Pall Mall, 1819.
I iv, 267p; II 273p; III 260p. 12mo.
No copy of 1st edn. located.

*Notes.* Details above follow Bodleian copy of 2nd edn. (249.s.263). Introduction presents the
(female) narrator's account. A different work from Eaton Stannard Barrett's *The Metropolis*
(1811: 18). ECB 383 lists 8th edn., 1819, 24s.
Further edns: 2nd edn. (NSTC 2M26045); 8th edn. 1819 (NSTC).

1819: 14 ANON.
MY OLD COUSIN; OR, A PEEP INTO COCHIN-CHINA. A NOVEL. IN
THREE VOLUMES. BY THE AUTHOR OF ROMANTIC FACTS, OR WHICH
IS HIS WIFE? VERONICA, OR THE MYSTERIOUS STRANGER, &C.
London: Printed at the Minerva Press for A. K. Newman and Co. Leadenhall-Street,
1819.
I vi, 226p; II 218p; III 209p. 12mo. 16s 6d (ER).
ER 31: 267 (Dec 1818).
Corvey; CME 3-628-48174-0; NSTC 2C40017 (BI BL, C, O).

*Notes.* 'Preface. To the Reader' states that 'the character of Mr. St. Paul is faithfully delineated
from an oral tradition of the author's maternal grandfather respecting an "*old cousin*," from
whom he derived considerable estates in Yorkshire', and that it offers a record of 'nearly a
hundred years ago'. Nafferton Abbey in the novel 'may be yet seen at Watton, near Beverley'.
For a possible connection with the pseudonym 'Lister', see 1816: 10.

1819: 15 ANON.
NORMANBURN; OR, THE HISTORY OF A YORKSHIRE FAMILY. A
NOVEL. BY THE AUTHOR OF HARDENBRASS AND HAVERILL; OR,
THE SECRET OF THE CASTLE; REFT ROB, OR THE WITCH OF SCOT-
MUIR, COMMONLY CALLED MADGE THE SNOOVER;—CONIRDAN,
OR THE ST. KILDIANS; AND THE HISTORY OF JULIUS FITZ-JOHN.
IN FOUR VOLUMES.
London: Printed for Sherwood, Neely, and Jones, Paternoster Row; and sold by every
Bookseller in the United Kingdom, 1819.
I iv, 316p; II 247p; III 251p; IV 296p. 12mo. 21s (ER, QR).
ER 31: 557 (Mar 1819); QR 21: 268 (Jan 1819).
Corvey; CME 3-628-48225-9; xNSTC.

*Notes.* 'To the Reader' signed 'The Editor'. For the issue of author attribution see *Hardenbrass and Haverill* (1817: 3).

1819: 16   ANON.

THE PLEASURES OF WANT; OR, IN LOVE AND NOT IN LOVE. A NOVEL, BY A POPULAR AUTHOR. IN THREE VOLUMES.

> London: William Fearman, Library, 170, New Bond Street, 1819.
> I 282p; II 294p; III 201p. 12mo. 21s (ECB).
> Corvey; CME 3-628-48475-8; ECB 455; NSTC 2P19213 (BI BL).

*Notes.* ECB gives publisher as 'Fearson' (evidently a mistake).

1819: 17   ANON.

PRINCIPLE AND PASSION. A NOVEL. IN TWO VOLUMES.

> Derby: Printed by and for Henry Mozley; and sold by Longman, Hurst, Rees, Orme, and Brown, 1819.
> I 308p; II 280p. 12mo. 10s (ECB).
> WSW I: 98.
> Corvey; CME 3-628-48354-9; ECB 470; NSTC 2P26866 (BI BL).

*Notes.* ECB dates Dec 1818. Collates in sixes.

1819: 18   ANON.

ROBIN HOOD; A TALE OF THE OLDEN TIME. IN TWO VOLUMES.

> Edinburgh: Oliver & Boyd, High Street; G. & W. B. Whittaker, Ave-Maria-Lane, London; and W. Turnbull, Glasgow, 1819.
> I 246p; II 221p. 12mo. 12s (ER).
> ER 32: 257 (July 1819).
> Corvey; CME 3-628-48615-7; NSTC 2H28683 (BI BL).

*Notes.* 8 pp. of separately-paged advs. at the end of vol. 2.
Further edns: 2nd edn. 1819 (NSTC).

1819: 19   ANON.

A SENTIMENTAL JOURNEY THROUGH MARGATE AND HASTINGS. BY DR. COMPARATIVE, JUN.

> London: Printed for A. K. Newman and Co. Leadenhall-Street, 1819.
> viii, 214p, ill. 12mo.
> Corvey; CME 3-628-48644-0; NSTC 2S38997 (BI BL, C, O).

*Notes.* According to NSTC, sometimes attributed to John Graham.

1819: 20   ANON.

THE UNITED IRISHMAN, OR THE FATAL EFFECTS OF CREDULITY; A TALE FOUNDED ON FACTS. IN TWO VOLUMES.

> Dublin: Printed for the Author, 1819.
> I 295p; II 286p. 12mo. 13s (QR).
> QR 21: 563 (Apr 1819).
> Dt OLS.186.o.20; NSTC 2U749 (BI O).

*Notes.* Collates in sixes.
Further edn: 1821 as *The Cavern in the Wicklow Mountains, or Fate of the O'Brien Family*

(BL 12808.ff.10). This is a reissue (replacement t.p.), with the Dublin imprint: 'Printed for the Author, by James Charles, No. 57, Mary-Street'; the original drop-head titles in both vols. in the BL copy have also been crudely pasted over with the new title. For further details, see Appendix E: 8.

1819: 21   ANON.
**VARIETIES IN WOMAN. A NOVEL, IN THREE VOLUMES.**
> London: Printed for Baldwin, Cradock, and Joy Paternoster-Row, 1819.
> I 261p; II 240p; III 249p. 12mo. 16s 6d (ECB).
> WSW I: 125.
> Corvey; CME 3-628-48859-1; ECB 610; NSTC 2V1178 (BI BL, C, O).

*Notes.* ECB dates Nov 1819.

1819: 22   ASHE, [Thomas].
**THE CHARMS OF DANDYISM; OR LIVING IN STYLE. IN THREE VOL-UMES. BY OLIVIA MORELAND, CHIEF OF THE FEMALE DANDIES; AND EDITED BY CAPTAIN ASHE, AUTHOR OF THE SPIRIT OF THE BOOK, &C.**
> London: Printed at the Minerva Press for A. K. Newman and Co. Leadenhall-Street, 1819.
> I 221p; II 218p; III 209p. 12mo. 21s (ECB).
> Corvey; CME 3-628-48290-9; ECB 396; NSTC 2A17456 (BI BL, C, O; NA MH).

*Notes.* ECB dates Jan 1819.

1819: 23   [BALFOUR, Alexander].
**CAMPBELL; OR, THE SCOTTISH PROBATIONER. A NOVEL. IN THREE VOLUMES.**
> Edinburgh: Published by Oliver and Boyd, High-Street; G. and W. B. Whittaker, London; W. Turnbull, Glasgow; and Johnston and Deas, Dublin, 1819.
> I 335p; II 325p; III 270p. 12mo. 21s (ECB, ER).
> ER 31: 267 (Dec 1818); WSW I: 139.
> Corvey; CME 3-628-47206-7; ECB 94; NSTC 2B4165 (BI BL, C, E, O).

*Notes.* 5 pp. of separately-paged advs. at the end of vol. 3.
Futher edn: New York 1819 (NSTC).

1819: 24   BALL, Edward.
**THE BLACK ROBBER; A ROMANCE. IN THREE VOLUMES. BY EDWARD BALL.**
> London: Printed for A. K. Newman and Co. Leadenhall-Street, 1819.
> I iv, 241p; II [241]–472p; III 203p. 12mo. 16s 6d (ECB, ER, QR).
> ER 32: 256 (July 1819), 32: 514 (Oct 1819); QR 21: 268 (Jan 1819), 22: 270 (July 1819).
> Corvey; CME 3-628-47093-5; ECB 36; NSTC 2B4418 (BI BL, O).

*Notes.* 'Dedication. To Mrs. ——.', signed 'E. B.'.
Further edn: 2nd edn. 1832 (NUC).

1819: 25 BENNET[T], Elizabeth.
EMILY, OR, THE WIFE'S FIRST ERROR; AND BEAUTY & UGLINESS,
OR, THE FATHER'S PRAYER AND THE MOTHER'S PROPHECY. TWO
TALES. IN FOUR VOLUMES. BY ELIZABETH BENNET, AUTHOR OF
FAITH AND FICTION, &C. &C.

> London: Printed at the Minerva Press for A. K. Newman and Co. Leadenhall-Street, 1819.
> I xvi, 224p; II 212p; III 245p; IV 234p. 12mo. 20s (ECB, ER, QR).
> ER 31: 556 (Mar 1819); QR 21: 268 (Jan 1819).
> Corvey; CME 3-628-47109-5; ECB 50; NSTC 2B18046 (BI BL, C).

*Notes.* For the issue of attribution, see note to the same author's *Faith and Fiction* (1816: 19).
Further edn: French trans., 1820 [as *Beauté et laideur* (BN under Bennett, Agnes Maria)].

1819: 26 BENSON, Maria.
THE CARRIAGE: BY MARIA BENSON, AUTHOR OF "THOUGHTS ON
EDUCATION." "SYSTEM AND NO SYSTEM." "IMITATION." &C.

> London: Published by E. Wallis, 42, Skinner Street, 1819.
> 168p. 12mo.
> BL N.2070(2); ECB 51; NSTC 2B18702 (BI C).

*Notes.* Dedication 'to Arnold Knight, M.D. Sheffield', dated Sheffield, 10 Feb 1819. Collates in sixes.

1819: 27 BROWN, Elizabeth Cullen.
THE SISTERS OF ST GOTHARD. A TALE. IN TWO VOLUMES. BY
ELIZABETH CULLEN BROWN.

> London: Printed at the Minerva Press for A. K. Newman and Co. Leadenhall-Street,
> 1819.
> I vii, 228p; II 240p. 12mo. 10s 6d (ECB, ER).
> ER 32: 256 (July 1819).
> Corvey; CME 3-628-47358-6; ECB 78; NSTC 2B51981 (BI BL, C, O).

*Notes.* 'List of Subscribers' (63 names), vol. 1, pp. v–vii.

BRYDGES, Sir Samuel Egerton, CONINGSBY and LORD BROCKENHURST
See 1820: 18

1819: 28 BRUNTON, Mary.
EMMELINE. WITH SOME OTHER PIECES. BY MARY BRUNTON,
AUTHOR OF SELF-CONTROL, AND DISCIPLINE. TO WHICH IS PRE-
FIXED A MEMOIR OF HER LIFE, INCLUDING SOME EXTRACTS
FROM HER CORRESPONDENCE.

> Edinburgh: Printed for Manners and Miller, and Archibald Constable and Co., Edin-
> burgh; and John Murray, Albemarle Street, London, 1819.
> cxxi, 195p, ill. 8vo. 10s 6d (ECB, QR); 10s 6d boards (ER).
> ER 31: 556 (Mar 1819); QR 21: 563 (Apr 1819); WSW I: 177–8.
> Corvey; CME 3-628-52301-X; ECB 81; NSTC 2B54747 (BI BL, C, E, O; NA MH).

*Notes.* Portrait of Mrs Brunton (opp. t.p.). Dedication 'to Captain William Balfour, R.N.'. 'Memoir', pp. [v]–cxxi, signed 'Alex. Brunton', Edinburgh, 2 Mar 1819.
Further edns: 2nd edn. 1820 (NSTC); New York 1819 (NSTC).
Facs: BWN (1992).

1819: 29    [BUSK, Mrs. M. M.].
## ZEAL AND EXPERIENCE: A TALE. IN TWO VOLUMES.

> London: Printed for T. Hookham, jun., Old Bond Street, and Baldwin, Cradock, and Joy, Paternoster-Row; by Jas.-W. and Chas. Adlard, 23, Bartholomew Close, 1819.
> I 254p; II 245p. 12mo. 10s 6d (ECB, ER).
> ER 31: 556 (Mar 1819), 32: 256 (July 1819); WSW I: 132.
> Corvey; CME 3-628-48998-9; ECB 654; xNSTC.

*Notes.* Block, ECB, and NSTC all attribute *Tales of Fault and Feeling* 'by the author of *Zeal and Experience*' (see 1825: 17) to Busk, who is given as Mrs Busk in Block and ECB. The intials 'M. M.' are found in BLC. The catalogue of Trinity College, Dublin, describes this author as Mrs William Busk.

CHATEAUBRIAND, François René, Vicomte de, THE TWO MARTYRS
See 1812: 28

1819: 30    CLARK, Emily.
## THE ESQUIMAUX; OR, FIDELITY. A TALE. IN THREE VOLUMES. BY MISS EMILY CLARK, GRAND-DAUGHTER OF THE LATE COLONEL FREDERICK, AND AUTHOR OF TALES AT THE FIRESIDE, BANKS OF THE DOURO, POEMS DEDICATED TO LADY LONSDALE, &C. &C.

> London: Printed at the Minerva Press for A. K. Newman and Co. Leadenhall-Street, 1819.
> I 268p; II 268p; III 267p. 12mo. 16s 6d (ECB, ER, QR).
> ER 32: 256 (July 1819); QR 21: 268 (Jan 1819).
> Corvey; CME 3-628-47291-1; ECB 118; NSTC 2C23240 (BI BL, C, O).

1819: 31    D'AUBIGNE, Frances.
## THE EXPRESS. A NOVEL. IN THREE VOLUMES. BY FRANCES D'AUBIGNE.

> London: Printed at the Minerva Press for A. K. Newman and Co. Leadenhall-Street, 1819.
> I 218p; II 210p; III 208p. 12mo. 15s (ABu s.l.)
> Corvey; CME 3-628-47423-X; NSTC 2D3378 (BI BL, C, O).

*Notes.* 'Advertisement', dated Jan 1819. 'Notes', vol. 3, pp. [185]–208.

1819: 32    DUTTON, T[homas] (*trans.?*).
## THE NECROMANCER. COMPRISING A SERIES OF WONDERFUL EVENTS, FOUNDED ON FACT. TRANSLATED FROM A NEW GERMAN WORK, BY T. DUTTON, ESQ.

> Battle: Printed and published by T. Garland, 1819.
> 119p. 12mo.
> BL 1077.d.52; NSTC 2D23815.

*Notes.* No German original discovered. Colophon reads: 'T. Garland, Printer, Battle, Sussex'. 'The first book printed at Battle?' (BLC); but compare 1816: 36. Collates in sixes.

1819: 33   GENLIS, [Stephanie-Félicité, Comtesse] de.
THE NEW ÆRA; OR, ADVENTURES OF JULIEN DELMOUR: RELATED
BY HIMSELF. IN FOUR VOLUMES. BY MADAME DE GENLIS.

> London: Printed for Henry Colburn, Public Library, Conduit Street, Hanover Square,
> 1819.
> I viii, 304p; II 240p; III 276p; IV 232p. 12mo. 24s (ER, QR).
> ER 32: 257 (July 1819); QR 21: 563 (Apr 1819), 22: 270 (July 1819); WSW I: 240.
> BL N.1150; NSTC 2G4574 (BI Dt, O; NA MH).

*Notes.* Trans. of *Les Parvenus, ou les aventures de Julien Delmours* (Paris, 1819). QR July 1819 gives as *Adventures of Julien Delmour.*

GOLLAND, Mrs. C. D.
See HAYNES, Miss C. D.

1819: 34   GROSETT, Emilia.
THE FREEBOOTER'S WIFE; OR, THE HAG OF GLENBURNE; A SCOT-
TISH ROMANCE. BY EMILIA GROSETT, AUTHOR OF "THE MATER-
NAL SPECTRE," &C. &C. &C.

> London: Printed and published by W. Mason, 21, Clerkenwell Green: sold also by
> Simpkin & Marshall, Stationers' Court, 1819.
> iv, 183p. 12mo. 'Price Four Shillings' (t.p.).
> E Hall.277.e; NSTC 2G23913.

*Notes.* Dedication 'to the Ladies of Great Britain; the Constant Admirers of Romance and Fiction, [. . .] by the Author'. Collates in sixes.

1819: 35   H., E. H.
THE HIGHLANDER; OR, A TALE OF MY LANDLADY. IN TWO VOL-
UMES. BY E. H. H.

> London: Printed at the Minerva Press for A. K. Newman and Co. Leadenhall-Street,
> 1819.
> I xxvi, 230p; II 263p. 12mo. 11s (QR).
> QR 22: 270 (July 1819).
> Corvey; CME 3-628-47709-3; NSTC 2H21027 (BI BL, C, E).

*Notes.* Preface in vol. 1, pp. [i]–xiv, satirising the contemporary novel, particularly its stock phrases. 'To the Reader' in vol. 1, pp. [xv]–xxvi, avows indebtedness to Scott. Continuous roman and arabic pagination, with novel proper beginning at p. [27].

1819: 36   HAMILTON, Terrick.
ANTAR, A BEDOUEEN ROMANCE. TRANSLATED FROM THE ARA-
BIC. BY TERRICK HAMILTON, ESQ. ORIENTAL SECRETARY TO THE
BRITISH EMBASSY AT CONSTANTINOPLE.

London: John Murray, Albemarle-Street, 1819/20.
I (1819) viii, 356p; II (1820) xlii, 350p; III (1820) 375p; IV (1820) 406p. 8vo. 36s 6d (ECB).
Corvey; CME 3-628-49015-4; ECB 253; NSTC 2H5426 (BI BL, C, Dt, E, O).

*Notes.* A part trans. of *The Romance of Antar* ('Sirat Antar ibn Shaddad'), an extensive poem, long handed down by oral tradition only, centred on the Arabian poet and warrior, Antara ibn Shaddad. Introduction, vol. 1, pp. [i]–viii, in which the 'Editor' states the translator to be presently 'out of England'. Drop-head title reads: 'Life and Adventures of Antar'. T.ps. of vols. 2, 3, and 4 carry 'Part The First' at the end of the title. Statement on page following 'The Translator's Preface', vol. 2, pp. [i]–xlii, reads: 'The Binder is requested to prefix this preface to the first volume when bound'. ECB enters as 'Life and Adventures of Antar', and dates Mar 1820.

1819: 37    [HARDING, Anne Raikes].
DECISION. A TALE. BY THE AUTHOR OF CORRECTION, &C. IN THREE VOLUMES.

London: Printed for Longman, Hurst, Rees, Orme, and Brown, Paternoster-Row, 1819.
I vii, 348p; II 356p; III 363p. 12mo. 21s (ECB, QR).
QR 21: 563 (Apr 1819); WSW I: 297.
Corvey; CME 3-628-51013-9; ECB 156; NSTC 2H7486 (BI BL, C, O; NA MH).

*Notes.* Preface dated Bath, June 1819. A different work from the anonymous *The Decision; A Novel* (see 1811: 6), and from Barbara Hofland's *Decision: A Tale* (1824: 48).
Further edn: New York 1819 (NSTC).

1819: 38    [HARLEY, Edward].
THE VETERAN; OR, MATRIMONIAL FELICITIES. IN THREE VOLUMES.

London: Printed for Longman, Hurst, Rees, Orme, and Brown, Paternoster-Row, 1819.
I xii, 310p; II viii, 323p; III viii, 348p. 12mo. 21s (ECB, QR).
ER 32: 256 (July 1819); QR 21: 563 (Apr 1819); WSW I: 298.
Corvey; CME 3-628-48911-3; ECB 612; NSTC 2H8476 (BI BL, C).

1819: 39    HARVEY, Jane.
ANY THING BUT WHAT YOU EXPECT. BY JANE HARVEY, AUTHOR OF MONTEITH—ETHELIA—MEMOIRS OF AN AUTHOR—RECORDS OF A NOBLE FAMILY, ETC. ETC. ETC. IN THREE VOLUMES.

Derby: Printed by and for Henry Mozley, 1819.
I 334p; II 315p; III 311p. 12mo. 15s (ECB).
Corvey; CME 3-628-47632-1; ECB 257; xNSTC.

*Notes.* ECB lists as Mozley and Longman, and dates Oct 1819. Collates in sixes.

1819: 40    [HATTON, Anne Julia Kemble].
CESARIO ROSALBA; OR, THE OATH OF VENGEANCE. A ROMANCE. IN FIVE VOLUMES. BY ANN OF SWANSEA, AUTHOR OF SICILIAN MYSTERIES, CONVICTION, GONZALO DE BALDIVIA, SECRET AVENGERS, SECRETS IN EVERY MANSION, CAMBRIAN PICTURES, CHRONICLES OF AN ILLUSTRIOUS HOUSE, &C.

London: Printed at the Minerva Press for A. K. Newman and Co. Leadenhall-Street, 1819.

I 299p; II 291p; III 296p; IV 274p; V 295p. 12mo. 27s 6d (ECB, ER, QR).

ER 32: 514 (Oct 1819); QR 22: 270 (July 1819).

Corvey; CME 3-628-48742-0; ECB 20; NSTC 2A13188 (BI BL, C).

*Notes.* 'Inscription' to Mrs Coutts, dated Swansea, St John's, 5 Mar 1819.


1819: 41   HAYNES, Miss C. D. [afterwards GOLLAND, Mrs. C. D.]
**AUGUSTUS & ADELINA; OR, THE MONK OF ST. BARNARDINE. A ROMANCE. IN FOUR VOLUMES. BY MISS C. D. HAYNES, AUTHOR OF THE FOUNDLING OF DEVONSHIRE, CASTLE OF LE BLANC, &C.**

London: Printed at the Minerva Press for A. K. Newman and Co. Leadenhall-Street, 1819.

I 220p; II 247p; III 240p; IV 217p. 12mo. 20s (ECB, ER).

ER 32: 256 (July 1819).

Corvey; CME 3-628-47641-0; ECB 260; NSTC 2H14179 (BI BL, C; NA MH).


1819: 42   [HOPE, Thomas].
**ANASTASIUS: OR, MEMOIRS OF A GREEK; WRITTEN AT THE CLOSE OF THE EIGHTEENTH CENTURY. IN THREE VOLUMES.**

London: John Murray, Albemarle-Street, 1819.

I iii, 376p; II 429p; III 457p. 8vo. 31s 6d (ECB).

ER 35: 92–102 (Mar 1821) full review; QR 24: 511–29 (Jan 1821) full review (3rd edn.); WSW I: 328 and II: 119.

BL 12612.g.13; ECB 16; NSTC 2H29859 (BI C, E, O; NA MH).

*Notes.* 'Preface of the Editor', vol. 1, pp. [i]–iii. 'Notes' at end of each vol: vol. 1, pp. [357]–376; vol. 2, pp. [419]–429; vol., 3 pp. [453]–457. 'Works Recently Published' (8 pp. unn.), dated Nov 1819, at end of vol. 1. The first 3-decker novel at a guinea-and-a-half. Thomas Cadell wrote to his partner Archibald Constable on 5 Dec 1819 (apropos Walter Scott's forthcoming *Ivanhoe*): 'Murray yesterday subscribed a book in three volumes crown 8vo at £1 11s 6d!!! [. . .] it is a novel, and why may we not do the same thing?' (National Library of Scotland, MS 323, f. 84). On its first appearance this book was credited to Lord Byron, who, however, told Lady Blessington that he wept bitterly on reading "Anastasius" for two reasons—one that he had not written it, and the other that Hope had (CG). ECB dates Jan 1820. The 3rd edn. (see below) contains a dedication signed 'Thos. Hope. Duchess-Street, April 1825'.
Further edns: 2nd edn. 1820 (NSTC); 3rd edn. 1820 (Corvey), CME 3-628-47057-9; 4th edn. 1827 (NSTC); 1836 (NSTC); New York 1820 (NSTC); French trans., 1820; German trans., 1821.


1819: 43   HUTTON, Catherine.
**OAKWOOD HALL, A NOVEL; INCLUDING A DESCRIPTION OF THE LAKES OF CUMBERLAND AND WESTMORELAND, AND A PART OF SOUTH WALES. BY CATHERINE HUTTON, AUTHOR OF "THE MISER MARRIED," AND "THE WELSH MOUNTAINEER." IN THREE VOLUMES.**

London: Printed by Strahan and Spottiswoode, Printers-Street; for Longman, Hurst,
    Rees, Orme, and Brown, Paternoster-Row, 1819.

I vii, 271p; II 253p; III 244p. 12mo. 16s 6d (ECB, QR).

QR 21: 268 (Jan 1819); WSW I: 337.

Corvey; CME 3-628-47865-0; ECB 291; NSTC 2H39192 (BI BL, C, O).

*Notes.* Preface, signed Catherine Hutton, dated 'Bennett's Hill, near Birmingham, Feb.
1819'. This opens: 'Oakwood Hall, though last published as an entire work, was my first
attempt at writing for the press, and is the one alluded to in the preface of the Miser Married,
as having been undertaken upon reading a celebrated novel of great exuberance. The novel,
which occasioned it will be found in Mrs. Oakwood's library in the present work. // Oakwood
Hall was cut into shreds, and published some years since, under the title of Oakwood House,
in the periodical publication called La Belle Assemblée: the work, as it is now offered to the
Public, has received great additions, and, I hope, many improvements'.
Further edn: Philadelphia 1819 (NUC).

1819: 44   LEFANU, Alicia.
**LEOLIN ABBEY. A NOVEL. BY ALICIA LEFANU, AUTHOR OF STRAT-
HALLAN AND HELEN MONTEAGLE. IN THREE VOLUMES.**

London: Printed by Strahan and Spottiswoode, Printers-Street; for Longman, Hurst,
    Rees, Orme, and Brown, Paternoster-Row, 1819.

I 395p; II 286p; III 276p. 12mo. 21s (ECB, ER, QR).

ER 32: 257 (July 1819); QR 21: 563 (Apr 1819); WSW I: 368.

Corvey; CME 3-628-47977-0; ECB 336; NSTC 2L9896 (BI BL, C).

*Notes.* Further edn: French trans., 1824 [as *L'Abbaye de Léolin. Traduit de l'anglais de Regina
Maria Roche* (BN)].

**LE NOIR, Elizabeth Anne, THE MAID OF LA VENDEE**
See 1808: 71

1819: 45   [LESTER, Elizabeth B.].
**HESITATION; OR, TO MARRY, OR, NOT TO MARRY? IN THREE VOLUMES.**

London: Printed by Strahan and Spottiswoode, Printers-Street; for Longman, Hurst,
    Rees, Orme, and Brown, Paternoster-Row, 1819.

I 287p; II 243p; III 269p. 12mo. 18s (ECB).

WSW I: 53.

Corvey; CME 3-628-47682-8; ECB 267; NSTC 2R17993 (BI BL, C; NA MH).

*Notes.* For attribution to Lester, rather than to Mrs Ross, see note to *The Bachelor and the
Married Man* (1817: 37). ECB dates Mar 1819.
Further edn: New York 1819 (NUC).

1819: 46   [MACDONOGH, Felix].
**THE HERMIT IN LONDON; OR, SKETCHES OF ENGLISH MANNERS.**

London: Printed for Henry Colburn, Public Library, Conduit Street, 1819/20.

I (1819) iii, 237p; II (1819) iii, 251p; III (1819) iii, 264p; IV (1820) ii, 245p; V (1820) ii,
    243p. 12mo. 30s (ECB); 18s (ER, QR for 3 vols.).

ER 32: 514 (Oct 1819); QR 22: 270 (July 1819).

Corvey; CME 3-628-51058-9; ECB 265; NSTC 2M3276 (Bl BL, C, Dt, E, O).

*Notes.* Further edns: 1821 (NSTC); 1822 (NSTC); [1850?] (NSTC); New York 1820 (NSTC); French trans., 1820/1.

1819: 47   {M}[ASKELL], {M. W.}.
## OLD TAPESTRY; A TALE OF REAL LIFE. IN TWO VOLUMES.

Edinburgh: Printed by James Ballantyne and Co. for W. and C. Tait, Prince's Street; and
   G. and W. B. Whittaker, Ave-Maria-Lane, London, 1819.
I xiii, 325p; II 319p. 12mo. 12s (ECB, ER, QR).
ER 31: 556 (Mar 1819); QR 21: 268 (Jan 1819).
Corvey; CME 3-628-48253-4; ECB 422; NSTC 2M18581 (Bl BL, C, E, O).

*Notes.* Dedication 'to Flint Popham, Esq.', signed 'M. W. M. Brasen-Nose College', Oxford,
Mar 1819.

1819: 48   MEEKE, [Mary].
## THE VEILED PROTECTRESS; OR, THE MYSTERIOUS MOTHER. A NOVEL. IN FIVE VOLUMES. BY MRS. MEEKE, AUTHOR OF MATRIMONY, NINE DAYS' WONDER, OLD WIFE AND YOUNG HUSBAND, SPANISH CAMPAIGN, CONSCIENCE, THERE IS A SECRET! ELLESMERE, &C. &C.

London: Printed at the Minerva Press for A. K. Newman and Co. Leadenhall-Street,
   1819.
I 257p; II 280p; III 263p; IV 240p; V 240p. 12mo. 27s 6d (ECB, ER).
ER 31: 267 (Dec 1818).
Corvey; CME 3-628-47960-6; ECB 378; NSTC 2M23137 (Bl BL, C).

1819: 49   MOORE, Mrs. Robert.
## EVELEEN MOUNTJOY; OR, VIEWS OF LIFE. A NOVEL. BY MRS. ROBERT MOORE. IN FOUR VOLUMES.

London: Printed for Longman, Hurst, Rees, Orme, and Brown, Paternoster-Row, 1819.
I vii, 372p; II 256p; III 296p; IV 256p. 12mo. 24s (ECB, ER, QR).
ER 32: 514 (Oct 1819); QR 22: 270 (July 1819); WSW I: 405.
Corvey; CME 3-628-48286-0; ECB 394; NSTC 2M35055 (Bl BL, C).

*Notes.* Preface dated Weymouth, July 1819.

## MORELAND, Olivia, THE CHARMS OF DANDYISM
See ASHE, Thomas

1819: 50   [MOYSEY, Abel].
## FORMAN. A TALE. IN THREE VOLUMES.

London: Printed for Ogle, Duncan, and Co. 37, Paternoster Row, and 295, Holborn;
   and Ogle, Allardice, and Thomson, Edinburgh, 1819.
I viii, 309p; II 328p; III 317p. 12mo. 18s (ECB, ER).

ER 32: 257 (July 1819); WSW I: 173.
Corvey; CME 3-628-47822-7; ECB 211; NSTC 2M39621 (BI BL, C).

*Notes.* Dedication 'to Walter Scott, Esq.'. Preface opens: 'The original hint for the following story may be found in the proceedings upon the Widow Turner's case, for the murder of Sir Thomas Overbury, 1 State Trials, 3d Edition, p. 339'. H&L attributes to Brougham, Lord Henry.

1819: 51   NATHAN, [Eliza].
**ELVINGTON. A NOVEL. IN THREE VOLUMES. BY MRS. NATHAN.**

London: Printed for J. J. Stockdale, 41, Pall-Mall, 1819.
I xii, 287p; II 288p; III 280p. 12mo. 21s (ER).
ER 32: 256 (July 1819); WSW I: 415.
Corvey; CME 3-628-48186-4; NSTC 2N1558 (BI BL).

*Notes.* Dedication 'to my husband'. 'Prospectus of an Academy for Vocal Music, on Mr. Nathan's System of Teaching Singing', vol. 1, pp. [x]–xi. ECB 406 lists Newman edn., June 1822, 16s 6d; but not discovered in this form.

1819: 52   O'KEEFFE, {Adelaide}.
**DUDLEY. BY MISS O'KEEFFE, AUTHOR OF PATRIARCHAL TIMES, OR THE LAND OF CANAAN; ZENOBIA, QUEEN OF PALMYRA; &C. IN THREE VOLUMES.**

London: Printed by Strahan and Spottiswoode, Printers-Street; for Longman, Hurst, Rees, Orme, and Brown, Paternoster-Row, 1819.
I viii, 369p; II iv, 452p; III iv, 453p. 12mo. 21s (ECB, ER, QR).
ER 32: 257 (July 1819); QR 21: 563 (Apr 1819); WSW I: 420.
Corvey; CME 3-628-48245-3; ECB 421; NSTC 2O2585 (BI BL, C; NA MH).

*Notes.* 'To the Public', signed 'Adelaide O'Keeffe. Chichester, Sussex. May 1819'. Epistolary novel with list of 'Correspondents' at beginning of vol. 1 after 'the good old-fashioned custom of Richardson and others'.
Further edn: French trans., 1824 [as *Dudley et Claudy, ou l'isle de Teneriffe* (DBI)].

1819: 53   [PARNELL, William].
**MAURICE AND BERGHETTA; OR, THE PRIEST OF RAHERY. A TALE.**

London: Printed for Rowland Hunter, Successor to Mr. Johnson, 72, St. Paul's Church-Yard; and C. P. Archer, Dublin, 1819.
xliii, 356p. 12mo. 7s (ECB, ER).
ER 32: 514 (Oct 1819); WSW I: 429–30.
Corvey; CME 3-628-48198-8; ECB 434; NSTC 2P4919 (BI BL, C, O; NA MH).

*Notes.* Dedication 'to the Catholic Priesthood of Ireland'. Drop-head title reads: 'The Priest of Rahery's Tale'.
Further edns: 2nd edn. Dublin 1820 (NSTC); 1825 as *The Priest of Rahery* (NSTC); Boston 1820 (NSTC).

1819: 54   POLIDORI, John William.
**ERNESTUS BERCHTOLD; OR, THE MODERN OEDIPUS. A TALE. BY JOHN WILLIAM POLIDORI, M.D.**

London: Printed for Longman, Hurst, Rees, Orme, and Brown, Paternoster-Row, 1819.
viii, 275p. 12mo. 6s (ECB, ER).
ER 32: 514 (Oct 1819); WSW I: 443.
Corvey; CME 3-628-48480-4; ECB 460; NSTC 2P20555 (BI BL, C, O; NA MH).

1819: 55   [POLIDORI, John William].
THE VAMPYRE; A TALE.
London: Printed for Sherwood, Neely, and Jones, Paternoster-Row, 1819.
xxv, 84p. 8vo. 4s 6d (ER).
ER 32: 256 (July 1819); WSW I: 442–3.
Corvey; CME 3-628-51148-8; ECB 90; NSTC 2P20559 (BI BL, C, Dt, E, O; NA DLC, MH).

Notes. '[Entered at Stationers' Hall, March 27, 1819.]' after imprint date. 'Extract from a Letter to Geneva', with t.p. 'Extract of a Letter to the Editor', pp. [vii]–xvi. Introduction, pp. [xix]–xxv. Continuous roman and arabic pagination in vol. 1, with tale beginning at p. [27]. 'Extract of a Letter, containing an Account of Lord Byron's Residence in the Island of Mitylene', introduced by separate t.p., pp. [75]–84: this has been ascribed to John Mitford, R.N. The story was also published in the New Monthly Magazine, Apr 1819, and attributed by the publisher to Byron; subsequently repudiated by him, and claimed by Polidori. ECB lists as by Byron.
Further edns: [1830?] (NSTC); Albany, NY, 1819 (Early American imprints. Second series; no. 47487 (microfilm)) [also Philadelphia 1819 (Early American imprints. Second series; No. 47488 (microfilm))]; French trans., 1819; German trans., 1819.
Facs: RR (1990).

1819: 56   [REED, Andrew].
NO FICTION: A NARRATIVE, FOUNDED ON RECENT AND INTER-
ESTING FACTS. IN TWO VOLUMES.
London: Printed by H. Teape, Tower-Hill. Sold by Cadell & Davies, Strand; Hatchard, Piccadilly; Hamilton, Paternoster-Row; Conder, St. Paul's Church-Yard; Westley, Stationers' Court; Nisbet, Castle-Street; Wilson, Royal Exchange; Blanshard, City-Road; and W. Wilson & Co. George Street, Edinburgh, 1819.
I xi, 327p; II 340p. 8vo. 12s (ECB, ER); 10s 6d (QR).
ER 32: 257 (July 1819); QR 21: 563 (Apr 1819); WSW I: 83.
ABu SB.82379.Ree; ECB 415; NSTC 2R4715 (BI BL, C; NA MH).

Notes. Dedication 'to Youth'.
Further edns: 2nd edn. 1819 (NSTC); 2nd edn. 1820 (Corvey), CME 3-628-48926-8; 3rd edn. 1820 (NSTC); 4th edn. 1820 (NUC); 6th edn. 1822 (NSTC); 7th edn. 1823 (NSTC); Baltimore 1821 (NSTC) [also Boston 1821 (NUC), Hartford 1821 (NUC), and Philadelphia 1821 (NUC)]; German trans., 1834.

1819: 57   [RENNIE, James].
SAINT PATRICK: A NATIONAL TALE OF THE FIFTH CENTURY. BY
AN ANTIQUARY. IN THREE VOLUMES.
Edinburgh: Printed for Archibald Constable and Co. Edinburgh; Longman, Hurst, Rees, Orme, and Brown, and Hurst, Robinson, and Company, London, 1819.

I xlviii, 264p; II 359p; III 320p. 12mo. 21s (ECB, ER).
ER 31: 267 (Dec 1818).
Corvey; CME 3-628-48576-2; ECB 512; NSTC 2R7037 (BI BL, Dt, E, O).

*Notes.* 'The Author's Personal Narrative. To be read either before or after the Tale, or not at all, as the Reader may incline', vol. 1, pp. [i]–xlviii, dated 'Stephen's Green, Dublin, Nov. 2, 1818'. Colophons read: 'Printed by George Ramsay and Co, Edinburgh, 1818'.

1819: 58    RICHARDSON, [Sarah] (*trans.?*).
THE EXILE OF POLAND; OR, THE VOW OF CELIBACY; A NOVEL, TRANSLATED FROM THE FRENCH, BY MRS. RICHARDSON, AUTHOR OF THE TRAGEDIES OF "ETHELRED," "GERTRUDE," "ORIGINAL POEMS FOR YOUTH," &C. IN THREE VOLUMES.

> London: Published by W. Simpkin and R. Marshall, Stationers' Court, Ludgate Street,
>     and C. Chapple, 66, Pall-Mall, 1819.
> I 213p; II 230p; III 240p. 12mo. 16s 6d (ECB, QR).
> QR 22: 564 (Mar 1822).
> BL N.2734; ECB 196; NSTC 2R9843.

*Notes.* No French original discovered. ECB dates Dec 1819.
Further edn: 1824 (Corvey—a reissue by A. K. Newman), CME 3-628-48572-X.

1819: 59    ST. CLAIR, Rosalia [pseud.].
THE SON OF O'DONNEL. A NOVEL. IN THREE VOLUMES. BY ROSALIA ST. CLAIR, AUTHOR OF THE BLIND BEGGAR, &C. &C.

> London: Printed at the Minerva Press for A. K. Newman and Co. Leadenhall-Street,
>     1819.
> I 220p; II 215p; III 244p. 12mo. 16s 6d (ECB).
> Corvey; CME 3-628-48501-0; ECB 511; NSTC 2S2000 (BI BL).

1819: 60    [SANDHAM, Elizabeth].
LUCILLA; OR, THE RECONCILIATION. BY THE AUTHOR OF THE TWIN SISTERS, ADOPTED DAUGHTER, WILLIAM SELWYN, &C. &C. &C.

> London: Printed for Sherwood, Neely, and Jones, No. 20, Paternoster-Row, 1819.
> I xi, 247p; II 250p. 12mo. 7s (ECB).
> WSW I: 477–8.
> Corvey; CME 3-628-48120-1; ECB 355; NSTC 2S4110 (BI BL).

*Notes.* ECB lists publisher as Harris, but not discovered in this form.

1819: 61    [SCOTT, Sir Walter].
TALES OF MY LANDLORD, THIRD SERIES, COLLECTED AND ARRANGED BY JEDEDIAH CLEISHBOTHAM, SCHOOLMASTER AND PARISH-CLERK OF GANDERCLEUGH. IN FOUR VOLUMES.

> Edinburgh: Printed for Archibald Constable and Co.; Longman, Hurst, Rees, Orme, and
>     Brown, Paternoster-Row; and Hurst, Robinson, and Co. 90, Cheapside, London, 1819.

> I 333p; II 324p; III 333p; IV 330p. 12mo. 32s (ECB, ER).
>
> ER 32: 257 (July 1819); QR 21: 563 (Apr 1819); WSW I: 488.
>
> BL 636.e.8,9; ECB 575; NSTC 2S10296 (BI E, O; NA DLC).

*Notes.* 'This day published', 21 June 1819, *Edinburgh Evening Courant.* Contains 'The Bride of Lammermoor' (ends vol. 3, p. 131) and 'A Legend of Montrose' (begins vol. 3, p. [135]). Further edns: 2nd edn. 1819 (NSTC); 3rd edn. 1819 (Corvey); Philadelphia 1819 (NSTC); French trans., of 'The Bride of Lammermoor' 1819 and 'A Legend of Montrose' [as *L'Officier de fortune* (NSTC)] 1819; German trans., of 'The Bride of Lammermoor' [as *Die Braut* (RS)] 1820, and of 'A Legend of Montrose' [as *Allan Mac-Aulay, der Seher des Hochlandes* (RS)] 1821.


1819: 62    S[?MITH], M.

**FRANCES; OR, THE TWO MOTHERS. A TALE. IN THREE VOLUMES. BY M. S.**

> London: Printed at the Minerva Press for A. K. Newman and Co. Leadenhall-Street, 1819.
>
> I 242p; II 237p; III 210p. 12mo. 15s (ECB, QR).
>
> QR 21: 268 (Jan 1819).
>
> Corvey; CME 3-628-47827-8; ECB 215; NSTC 2F13731 (BI BL, C, Dt, O).

*Notes.* Dt copy completes 'M. Smith' as author's name on t.p., written in pencil (NSTC).


1819: 63    SPENCE, Elizabeth Isabella.

**A TRAVELLER'S TALE OF THE LAST CENTURY: BY ELIZABETH ISABELLA SPENCE, AUTHOR OF LETTERS FROM THE NORTH HIGHLANDS; AND THE CURATE AND HIS DAUGHTER. IN THREE VOLUMES.**

> London: Printed by Strahan and Spottiswoode, Printers-Street; for Longman, Hurst, Rees, Orme, and Brown, Paternoster-Row, 1819.
>
> I xv, 243p; II 213p; III 262p. 12mo. 16s 6d (ECB, QR).
>
> QR 21: 268 (Jan 1819); WSW I: 518.
>
> Corvey; CME 3-628-48723-4; ECB 554; NSTC 2S33539 (BI BL, C).

*Notes.* Dedication to Lady Hamlyn Williams, signed 'Northumberland-Street, Nottingham-Place'. ECB dates Mar 1817, probably in error.


1819: 64    SPENSER, Arthur.

**ISKANDER; OR, THE HERO OF EPIRUS. A ROMANCE. IN THREE VOLUMES. BY ARTHUR SPENSER.**

> London: Printed at the Minerva Press for A. K. Newman and Co. Leadenhall-Street, 1819.
>
> I iv, 218p; II 227p; III 218p. 12mo. 15s (ECB, ER).
>
> ER 32: 514 (Oct 1819).
>
> Corvey; CME 3-628-48725-0; ECB 554; NSTC 2S33983 (BI BL, C, O).


1819: 65    [SUTHERLAND, Alexander].

**REDMOND THE REBEL; OR, THEY MET AT WATERLOO. A NOVEL. IN THREE VOLUMES.**

London: Printed at the Minerva Press for A. K. Newman and Co. Leadenhall-Street, 1819.
I 252p; II 260p; III 265p. 12mo. 16s 6d (ECB).
WSW I: 101.
Corvey; CME 3-628-48519-3; ECB 482; NSTC 2S47482 (BI BL, C, E, O).

*Notes.* ECB dates Apr 1819.

1819: 66   TAYLOR, [Ann].
THE FAMILY MANSION. A TALE. BY MRS. TAYLOR, OF ONGAR,
AUTHOR OF 'MATERNAL SOLICITUDE, PRACTICAL HINTS,' &C.
&C. &C.

London: Printed for Taylor and Hessey, Fleet Street, 1819.
206p, ill. 12mo. 5s 6d (ECB).
WSW I: 530.
BL 1507/891; ECB 578; NSTC 2T3021 (BI O; NA MH).

*Notes.* ECB dates Nov 1819.
Further edns: 2nd edn. 1820 (NSTC); 4th edn. 1820 (NUC); 5th edn. 1827 (NSTC); 5th [*sic*]
edn. 1830 (NSTC); Philadelphia 1820 (NUC).

1819: 67   [?TAYLOR, Jane].
THE AUTHORESS. A TALE. BY THE AUTHOR OF "RACHEL."

London: Printed for Taylor and Hessey, Fleet Street, 1819.
vii, 168p, ill. 12mo. 5s (ECB, ER); 5s boards (QR).
ER 32: 514 (Oct 1819); QR 21: 563 (Apr 1819), 22: 270 (July 1819); WSW I: 13.
Corvey; CME 3-628-47082-X; ECB 33; NSTC 2A19807 (BI BL, C, NCu, O; NA MH).

*Notes.* Frontispiece carries the legend: 'Published Mar 1, 1819'. 2nd edn. is attributed to Jane
Taylor (1783–1824) in NUC. For further arguments in favour of Jane Taylor's authorship of
this and two allied titles, see Rainer Schöwerling's Introduction to the Edition Corvey Fac-
simile of *The Authoress* (Stuttgart, 1988), pp. 23–5, 34–5.
Further edn: 2nd edn. 1822 (NUC).
Facs: EC (1988).

1819: 68   WARD, Catherine G[eorge].
*THE THORN, OR DOUBTFUL PROPERTY. BY CATHERINE G.
WARD, AUTHOR OF 'THE ORPHAN BOY,' 'COTTAGE ON THE
CLIFF,' 'FISHER'S DAUGHTER,' 'MYSTERIOUS MARRIAGE,' 'FAM-
ILY PORTRAITS,' &C.

London: Published by J. Robins and Co. Ivy Lane, Paternoster Row; G. Virtue, Ivy Lane,
and Bath Street, Bristol; and J. Robins jun. and Co. Lower Ormond Quay, Dublin,
1825 [first published 1819?].
726p, ill. 8vo.
No copy of 1st edn. of 1819 located.

*Notes.* Details above replicate edn. of 1825 (O Pettingell.635), which collates in fours. Sum-
mers (p. 209) dates 'The Thorn; or Doubtful Property' as 1819 in his listing of Ward's works.
It also appears as one of the works by the author in the titles of 1823: 83 and 84.
Further edns: 1825 (see note above); 1830 (BL RB.23.a.12505).

1819: 69   WENTWORTH, Zara.
## THE RECLUSE OF ALBYN HALL. A NOVEL. IN THREE VOLUMES. BY ZARA WENTWORTH.

> London: Printed at the Minerva Press for A. K. Newman and Co. Leadenhall-Street, 1819.
> I 242p; II 258p; III 264p. 12mo. 16s 6d (ECB, ER).
> ER 30: 542 (Sept 1818).
> Corvey; CME 3-628-48891-5; ECB 630; NSTC 2W12930 (BI BL, C).

*Notes.* ECB also dates Sept 1818.

1819: 70   WICKENDEN, W[illiam] S.
## COUNT GLARUS OF SWITZERLAND. INTERSPERSED WITH SOME PIECES OF POETRY. BY W. S. WICKENDEN, THE BARD OF THE FOREST. DEDICATED, BY PERMISSION, TO EDWARD JENNER, ESQ. M.D.F.R.S.

> Gloucester: Printed by J. Roberts, Herald Office; sold by Longman, Hurst, Rees, Orme, and Brown, Paternoster Row, London; Barry and Son, Bristol; and all other Booksellers, n.d. [1819].
> 109p. 12mo.
> WSW I: 562.
> ABu SB.82379.Wic; ECB 636; NSTC 2W19034 (BI BL, O).

*Notes.* Dedication to Edward Jenner, dated Dean-Forest, Apr 1819. 6 pp. (unn.) 'List of Subscribers' (132 names).

1819: 71   WILKINSON, [Sarah Scudgell].
## NEW TALES BY MRS. WILKINSON, IN THREE VOLUMES.

> London: Printed for Matthew Iley, 1, Somerset Street, Portman Square, 1819.
> I 300p; II 286p; III 231p. 12mo. 18s (ECB, ER).
> ER 32: 257 (July 1819).
> Corvey; CME 3-628-48925-3; ECB 637; xNSTC.

*Notes.* I The Bandit of Florence; and the Fugitive Nun; II The Bandit of Florence; and the Fugitive Nun, continued; III Imbecility of Mind; addressed to the Author of "Purity of Heart". Dedication to the Earl of Pomfret. ECB dates *c.* 1825, and places this title apart from those listed as by Sarah Wilkinson.

1819: 72   [WOODROOFFE, Anne].
## THE HISTORY OF MICHAEL KEMP, THE HAPPY FARMER'S LAD.

> Bath: Printed by Wood and Co. at the Bath and Cheltenham Gazette Office, Union-Street, 1819.
> I 149p; II [161]p. 12mo.
> O 1489.f.2966; NSTC 2W30517 (BI BL, C).

*Notes.* Vol. 2 t.p. imprint differs by also including 'and sold by Hatchard, London; Binns and Robinson, Bath; Richardson, Bristol; and all other Booksellers'; it also states 'Part II' rather than 'Vol. II'. The last page in Bodleian copy is written in hand, presumably as a result of the original printed page having been damaged; the same occurs with pp. 5/6 of vol. 1. Collates in sixes.

Further edns: 3rd edn. London 1823 (C S727.d.82.81); 4th edn. London 1830 (NSTC); New York 1841 (from 6th London edn.) (NSTC, NUC).

1819: 73    {?W}[YNDHAM], {Alicia}.
**HAROLD THE EXILE. IN THREE VOLUMES.**

>   London: * * * * * * *, 1819.
>   I 284p; II 312p; III 322p. 12mo.
>   WSW I: 51.
>   Corvey; CME 3-628-47627-5; NSTC 2H8648 (BI BL, C, Dt, O; NA MH).

*Notes.* First of a sequence of 'Introductory Letters' from Geneva to the correpondent's sister, vol. 1, pp. [1]–83, signed 'Alicia W.'; and further letters in this sequence, similiarly written to a sister, signed 'A. W.'. It seems unclear from the context whether these are entirely fictitious or not. List of 'Popular Novels' (2 pp. unn.) published by Henry Colburn at end of vol. 3. Sadleir (Item 87) states 'This curious novel is a satire on Byron, Caroline Lamb and other contemporaries. The asterisked imprint is unique in my experience in nineteenth-century publishing'. A note on the catalogue card at Dt records: 'Possibly by Alicia Wyndham, a member of the noted Welsh family who intermarried with the Wyndham-Quinn family of Adare from whence this copy comes.'

# 1820

1820: 1    ANON.
**AUGUSTUS; OR, THE AMBITIOUS STUDENT.**

>   London: Printed for Baldwin, Cradock, and Joy, Paternoster-Row, 1820.
>   viii, 356p. 8vo. 9s (ECB); 7s (QR).
>   QR 24: 276 (Oct 1820); WSW II: 4.
>   Corvey; CME 3-628-47032-3; ECB 32; NSTC 2A19261 (BI BL, C, O; NA DLC).

1820: 2    ANON.
**DE CLIFFORD; OR, PASSION MORE POWERFUL THAN REASON. A NOVEL. IN FOUR VOLUMES.**

>   London: Printed at the Minerva Press for A. K. Newman and Co. Leadenhall-Street, 1820.
>   I 263p; II 239p; III 240p; IV 306p. 12mo. 22s (ECB, ER).
>   ER 34: 263 (Aug 1820).
>   Corvey; CME 3-628-47294-6; ECB 157; NSTC 2D7144 (BI BL, C, O).

1820: 3   ANON.

**EDINBURGH: A SATIRICAL NOVEL. BY THE AUTHOR OF LONDON; OR, A MONTH AT STEVENS'S. IN THREE VOLUMES.**

> London: Printed for Sherwood, Neely, and Jones, Paternoster-Row, 1820.
> I viii, 251p; II 309p; III 235p. 12mo. 21s (ECB, ER, QR).
> ER 35: 266 (Mar 1821); QR 24: 571 (Jan 1821).
> Corvey; CME 3-628-47517-1; ECB 178; NSTC 2E4172 (BI BL, E, O; NA MH).

1820: 4   ANON.

**EDWARD, OR THE PURSUIT OF HAPPINESS.**

> London: Printed for T. Cadell and W. Davies, Strand; by J. M'Creery, Black-Horse-Court, 1820.
> 180p. 8vo. 6s 6d (ECB); 6s 6d boards (ER).
> ER 33: 519 (May 1820).
> Corvey; CME 3-628-47513-9; ECB 180; NSTC 2E4809 (BI BL, C, O).

1820: 5   ANON.

**THE EXILE: OR, MATILDA OF THE CASTLE, AND ROUSINA OF THE ALPS; AN HISTORICAL MEMOIR.**

> London: William Sams, Bookseller, by Appointment, to H.R.H. the Duke of York, No. 1, St. James's Street, 1820.
> xi, 118p. 12mo.
> ABu SB.82379.Exi; NSTC 2M20195 (BI BL, O).

*Notes.* Prefatory dedication signed 'Horatio'. Drop-head title reads: 'Matilda the Exile, and the Maid of the Alps'. 1 p. adv. at end for 'Sams's Circulating Library, Corner of Pall Mall, opposite St. James's Palace'.

1820: 6   ANON.

**GOOD-HUMOUR; OR MY UNCLE, THE GENERAL. BY A THIRD COUSIN. IN TWO VOLUMES.**

> London: Printed for T. Egerton, Whitehall, 1820.
> I xi, 310p; II 367p. 12mo. 12s (ECB, ER, QR).
> ER 33: 519 (May 1820); QR 23: 283 (May 1820); WSW I: 49.
> Corvey; CME 3-628-47842-1; ECB 236; NSTC 2G13170 (BI BL, C, O).

1820: 7   ANON.

**NICE DISTINCTIONS: A TALE.**

> Dublin: Printed at the Hibernia Press Office, 1, Temple-Lane for J. Cumming 16, Lower Ormond-Quay; and Longman, Hurst, Rees, Orme, and Brown, London, 1820.
> vii, 330p. 8vo. 10s 6d (ECB, ER).
> ER 33: 518 (May 1820), 34: 263 (Aug 1820).
> Corvey; CME 3-628-48223-2; ECB 413; NSTC 2N7355 (BI BL, C, Dt, O).

*Notes.* Preface to 'Jedediah Cleishbotham', dated Dublin, 30 Sept 1819.

1820: 8   ANON.
**OLIVIA, OR THE ORPHAN. A TALE. IN TWO VOLUMES. BY A LADY OF DISTINCTION.**

London: Printed for Matthew Iley, Somerset-Street, Portman-Square, 1820.
I 240p; II 207p. 12mo. 12s 6d (ECB, ER).
ER 33: 519 (May 1820).
Corvey; CME 3-628-48256-9; ECB 423; NSTC 2O3379 (BI BL).

1820: 9   ANON.
**THE SMUGGLERS, A TALE, DESCRIPTIVE OF THE SEA-COAST MANNERS OF SCOTLAND. IN THREE VOLUMES.**

Edinburgh: Printed for J. Dick, High-Street, 1820.
I 243p; II 243p; III 267p. 12mo. 18s (QR).
QR 21: 563 (Apr 1819).
Corvey; CME 3-628-48716-1; NSTC 2S29249 (BI BL).

*Notes.* ECB 547 lists Newman edn., Mar 1820, 16s 6d; but not discovered in this form.

1820: 10   ANON.
**TALES OF MY LANDLORD, NEW SERIES, CONTAINING PONTEFRACT CASTLE. IN THREE VOLUMES.**

London: Printed for William Fearman, New Bond-Street, 1820.
I xlvi, 226p; II 290p; III 319p. 12mo.
Corvey; CME 3-628-48870-2; ECB 575; NSTC 2T1406 (BI BL, E; NA MH).

*Notes.* Vol. 1 includes a long 'Publisher's Preface' containing details of a dispute with John Ballantyne, Walter Scott's literary agent, concerning the copyright of the *Tales of My Landlord* series.
Further edns: French trans., 1821 [as *Le Château de Pontefract* (Pigoreau)]; German trans., 1824 [as *Das Schloss von Pontefract* (RS)].

1820: 11   ANON.
**THE WEST-INDIAN, OR THE BROTHERS; A NOVEL, IN THREE VOLUMES.**

Dublin: Printed at the Hibernia Press Office, 1, Temple Lane, for John Cumming, 16,
    Lower Ormond Quay, and A. K. Newman and Co. Leadenhall-Street. London, 1820.
I vii, 189p; II 233p; III 181p. 12mo. 15s (ECB, QR); 15s boards (ER).
ER 34: 509 (Nov 1820); QR 24: 276 (Oct 1820).
Corvey; CME 3-628-48896-6; ECB 630; xNSTC.

1820: 12   ANON.
**ZELICA, THE CREOLE; A NOVEL, BY AN AMERICAN. IN THREE VOLUMES.**

London: Printed for William Fearman, Library, 170, New Bond-Street, 1820.
I 243p; II 254p; III 309p. 12mo. 21s (ECB).
ER 35: 266 (Mar 1821); WSW II: 41.
Corvey; CME 3-628-47473-6; ECB 654; NSTC 2A10534 (BI BL).

*Notes.* ER gives 'Madame de Sansée' as the author. Adv. opp. t.p. of vol. 1 for 'American Novels', announcing two titles 'In the Press, by the same Author', viz. 'The Scarlet Hand-kerchief, 3 vols.', and 'The Stranger in Mexico, 3 vols.', which with the present work 'form a Series of Novels that have been transmitted to the Publisher from America'. For the first of these titles, though from another publisher, see 1823: 12.

1820: 13    [BARHAM, Richard Harris].
BALDWIN; OR, A MISER'S HEIR. A SERIO-COMIC TALE. IN TWO VOLUMES. BY AN OLD BACHELOR.

> London: Printed at the Minerva Press for A. K. Newman and Co. Leadenhall-Street, 1820.
> I vi, 245p; II 270p. 12mo. 11s (ECB, ER, QR).
> ER 34: 509 (Nov 1820); QR 24: 276 (Oct 1820).
> Corvey; CME 3-628-47091-9; ECB 36; NSTC 2B7767 (BI BL, C, O; NA MH).

*Notes.* Dedication 'To Anybody', signed 'G. H. E.'. NSTC gives the author's pseudonym as George Hector Epaminondas. Copy at Harvard (*EC8.B2395.8206) includes author's MS revisions, evidently in preparation for a 2nd edn.

1820: 14    BARRON, Edward.
THE ROYAL WANDERER, OR SECRET MEMOIRS OF CAROLINE: THE WHOLE FOUNDED ON RECENT FACTS, AND CONTAINING AMONG OTHER THINGS, AN AUTHENTIC AND HITHERTO UNPUBLISHED ACCOUNT OF COURT-CABALS, AND ROYAL TRAVELS. BY EDWARD BARRON, ESQ. EMBELLISHED WITH ENGRAVINGS.

> London: Printed and published by H. Rowe, 11, Warwick-Square, Paternoster-Row, 1820.
> 860p, ill. 8vo.
> NN CK.Barron; NSTC 2B9759 (NA DLC).

*Notes.* Preface dated 'January 1st'. A 'secret history' of Princess Caroline, distinct from *The Royal Wanderer*, 'by Algernon', 3 vols. (see 1815: 15). The copy seen is bound with the same author's *The Wrongs of Royalty; being a continuation of the Royal Wanderer* (1820: 15). Collates in fours.
Further edn: 1823 (NSTC).

1820: 15    BARRON, Edward.
THE WRONGS OF ROYALTY; BEING, A CONTINUATION OF THE ROYAL WANDERER, OR, MEMOIRS OF HER PRESENT MAJESTY QUEEN CAROLINE. [. . .] BY EDWARD BARRON, ESQ.

> London: Printed and published by H. Rowe, 11, Warwick-Square, Paternoster-Row, 1820.
> iv, 288p, ill. 8vo.
> NN CK.Barron; xNSTC.

*Notes.* Preface dated London, June 1820. T.p. description above omits more than 100 words of additional text outlining contents. Collates in fours.

1820: 16    BEAUCLERC, Amelia.
**DISORDER AND ORDER. A NOVEL. IN THREE VOLUMES. BY AMELIA BEAUCLERC, AUTHOR OF MONTREITHE, OR THE PEER OF SCOTLAND; ALINDA, OR CHILD OF MYSTERY; THE DESERTER; HUSBAND HUNTERS, &C.**

> London: Printed at the Minerva Press for A. K. Newman and Co. Leadenhall-Street, 1820.
> I 258p; II 264p; III 275p. 12mo. 16s 6d (ECB, QR).
> QR 22: 564 (Mar 1820).
> Corvey; CME 3-628-47133-8; ECB 45; NSTC 2B13634 (BI BL, C, O).

1820: 17    [?BROWN, James].
**CARNWATH MUIR, A TALE, FOUNDED ON FACTS.**

> Edinburgh: Printed for the Author. Sold by Oliver and Boyd, Edinburgh; William Turnbull, Glasgow; and William Robertson, Lanark, 1820.
> xii, 409p. 12mo. 7s 6d (ER).
> ER 34: 264 (Aug 1820).
> E Hall.197.f; NSTC 2C8118.

*Notes.* With MS note (on recto of blank leaf before t.p.), identifying author as 'James Brown, Farmer, [. . .] Carluke'. Dedication 'to Sir Charles M'Donald Lockhart of Lee and Carnwath, Baronet'.

1820: 18    BRYDGES, Sir [Samuel] Egerton.
**TRAGIC TALES. CONINGSBY, AND LORD BROKENHURST. BY SIR EGERTON BRYDGES, BART.**

> London: Printed for Robert Triphook, 23, Old Bond-Street, 1820.
> I 186p; II 198p. 8vo. 10s boards (ER); 10s (QR).
> ER 34: 264 (Aug 1820); QR 24: 276 (Oct 1820); WSW I: 178.
> Corvey; CME 3-628-47143-5; NSTC 2B55206 (BI BL, C; NA MH).

*Notes.* Preface dated Geneva, 23 Aug 1819. *Coningsby, a Tragic Tale* was printed separately, with Paris, Geneva and London publishers on the t.p., in 1819. *Lord Brokenhurst, or Fragments of Winter Leaves, a Tragic Tale* was also published separately, with a Geneva imprint, 1819. In addition to these titles, Brydges published *Sir Ralph Willoughby: An Historical Tale of the Sixteenth Century* under a Florence imprint of 1820, but no London issue of this has been discovered (copies at BL, C, E, O, and MH, all have Florence only imprint).

**BURNEY, Sarah Harriet, COUNTRY NEIGHBOURS**
See 1816: 20

1820: 19    [CAREY, David].
**LOCHIEL; OR, THE FIELD OF CULLODEN. IN THREE VOLUMES.**

> London: Printed for G. and W. B. Whittaker, Ave-Maria-Lane, 1820.
> I xxiii, 358p; II 347p; III 396p. 12mo. 21s (ECB); 21s boards (ER).
> ER 34: 264 (Aug 1820); WSW I: 198 and II: 70.
> Corvey; CME 3-628-48109-0; ECB 350; NSTC 2C7017 (BI BL, C, E; NA MH).

*Notes.* Dedication to John Crichton Stuart, Marquis of Bute.

Further edns: French trans., 1822 [as *Édouard en Écosse, ou la bataille de Culloden* (BN)]. NSTC 1826 edn. at MH is in fact 1820, as above.


1820: 20   CORDELIA [pseud.].

**DACRESFIELD; OR, VICISSITUDES ON EARTH. A NOVEL. IN FOUR VOLUMES. BY CORDELIA, CHIEF LADY AT THE COURT OF QUEEN MAB!**

> London: Printed at the Minerva Press for A. K. Newman and Co. Leadenhall-Street, 1820.
>
> I xiv, 220p; II 230p; III 221p; IV 236p. 12mo. 20s (ECB, ER).
>
> ER 33: 254 (Jan 1820).
>
> Corvey; CME 3-628-47384-5; ECB 149; NSTC 2C37797 (BI BL, C, O).

*Notes.* Introduction 'by her Elfin Majesty'.


1820: 21   DALLAS, R[obert] C[harles].

**SIR FRANCIS DARRELL; OR THE VORTEX: A NOVEL. BY R. C. DALLAS, ESQ. AUTHOR OF PERCIVAL, AUBREY, MORLAND, &C. &C. IN FOUR VOLUMES.**

> London: Printed for Longman, Hurst, Rees, Orme, and Brown, Paternoster-Row, 1820.
>
> I vii, 300p; II 290p; III 306p; IV 336p. 12mo. 28s (ECB, ER, QR).
>
> ER 34: 509 (Nov 1820); QR 24: 276 (Oct 1820); WSW I: 235 and II: 84.
>
> Corvey; CME 3-628-47416-7; ECB 150; NSTC 2D1116 (BI BL, C, E, O; NA MH).

*Notes.* Preface signed St Adresse, 6 Apr 1820.


1820: 22   ENNIS, A{licia} M{argaret}.

**THE CONTESTED ELECTION; OR A COURTIER'S PROMISES. IN THREE VOLUMES. DEDICATED BY PERMISSION, TO HIS GRACE THE DUKE OF LEINSTER, &C. &C. BY A. M. ENNIS, AUTHOR OF IRELAND, OR THE MONTAGUE FAMILY.**

> London: Printed at the Minerva Press for A. K. Newman and Co. Leadenhall-Street, 1820.
>
> I viii, 302p; II 305p; III 316p. 12mo. 18s (ECB, ER).
>
> ER 34: 509 (Nov 1820); WSW I: 261.
>
> Corvey; CME 3-628-47461-2; ECB 188; NSTC 2E10671 (BI BL, C, O).

*Notes.* Dedication to the Duke of Leinster, signed Alicia Margaret Ennis, Grenville-Street, Mountjoy-Square, Dublin, Aug 1820.


**ENNIS, Alicia Margaret, IRELAND; OR, MEMOIRS OF THE MONTAGUE FAMILY**

See 1817: 25 and Appendix E: 7

1820: 23    FOUQUÉ, Friedrich [Heinrich Karl], Baron de la Motte; [HARE, Julius Charles (*trans.*)].

SINTRAM AND HIS COMPANIONS: A ROMANCE. FROM THE GER-MAN OF FREDERIC BARON DE LA MOTTE FOUQUÉ, AUTHOR OF UNDINE, &C.

> London: C. and J. Ollier, Vere Street, Bond Street; and William Blackwood, Edinburgh, 1820.
> xiv, 267p. 12mo.
> ER 34: 264 (Aug 1820).
> BL 12547.c.11; NSTC 2L2874 (BI C, O).

*Notes.* Trans. of *Sintram und seine Gefährten* (Vienna, 1815).
Further edns: NSTC includes 4 edns. between 1841 and 1848, at least two of which are another trans.

1820: 24    FURBO, [Francisco] and VALLADERRAS, Leandra [de].

ANDREW OF PADUA, THE IMPROVISATORE; A TALE FROM THE ITALIAN OF THE ABBATE FURBO. AND THE VINDICTIVE FATHER, FROM THE SPANISH OF LEANDRA OF VALLADERRAS.

> London: Printed for Sir Richard Phillips and Co. Bride Court, Bridge Street; sold by W. Sams, opposite St. James's Palace, and to be had of all Booksellers, 1820.
> xiv, 294p. 12mo. 'Price 6s. half-bound and lettered' (t.p.).
> BL 1458.d.12; NSTC 2F18650 (NA MH).

*Notes.* Foreign originals not discovered. Half-title missing, but the following is readable by being faintly mirrored on the preceding blank page: 'The Periodical Novelist, or Circulating Library. Vol III. Andrew of Padua and the Vindictive Father'. Cf. 1820: 26 and 28(a), below. Preface by the Translator to the first tale, plus 'Biographical Sketch of the Abbate Furbo', pp. [v]–vii. 'The Vindictive Father, or Lorenzo and Claudia' is without preliminaries, and begins on p. [195].

1820: 25    [GALT, John].

THE EARTHQUAKE; A TALE. BY THE AUTHOR OF "THE AYRSHIRE LEGATEES." IN THREE VOLUMES.

> Edinburgh: Printed for William Blackwood: and T. Cadell and W. Davies, Strand, Lon-don, 1820.
> I 310p; II 297p; III 276p. 12mo. 21s boards (QR).
> QR 24: 571 (Jan 1821); WSW I: 275 and II: 96.
> Corvey; CME 3-628-47525-2; NSTC 2G1364 (BI BL, C, Dt, E).

*Notes.* Dedication to 'the Right Honourable Earl of Guilford'.
Further edns: 2nd edn. 1821 (NSTC); New York 1821 (NUC).

1820: 26    [GALT, John].

GLENFELL; OR, MACDONALDS AND CAMPBELLS. AN EDINBURGH TALE OF THE NINETEENTH CENTURY.

> London: Printed for Sir Richard Phillips and Co. Bride Court, Bridge Street; sold by W. Sams, opposite St. James's Palace, and to be had of all Booksellers, 1820.

viii, 328p. 12mo. 'Price 6s half-bound and lettered, or 5s. 3d. in quires' (t.p.); 6s 'half-bound and lettered' (ER).

ER 33: 254 (Jan 1820); WSW I: 48.

E RB.S.39; NSTC 2G10462 (NA MH).

*Notes.* Preface is dated 'Covenanters' Close, High-Street, Edinburgh, December 31, 1819'. 4 pp. (unn.) 'Advertisement to the Series' placed before preliminaries: half-title reads 'The Circulating Library. Vol. I. Glenfell'. First vol. in 'The Circulating Library' (for the second and third, see 1820: 28(a) and 24). The last page is mistakenly numbered 238.
Further edn: French trans., 1823.

1820: 27    [GASPEY, Thomas].
**THE MYSTERY; OR, FORTY YEARS AGO. A NOVEL. IN THREE VOL-UMES.**

> London: Printed for Longman, Hurst, Rees, Orme, and Brown, Paternoster-Row, 1820.
> I 340p; II 323p; III 324p. 12mo. 21s (ECB, ER).
> ER 33: 519 (May 1820); WSW I: 276 and II: 100.
> Corvey; CME 3-628-48184-8; ECB 403; NSTC 2G3297 (BI BL, C, E; NA DLC, MH).

*Notes.* Further edns: New York 1820 (NSTC); French trans., 1821.

1820: 28(a)    GENLIS, [Stéphanie-Félicité, Comtesse] de.
**PETRARCH AND LAURA, BY MADAME DE GENLIS. TRANSLATED FROM THE FRENCH.**

> London: Printed for Sir Richard Phillips and Co. Bride Court, Bridge Street; sold by W. Sams, opposite St. James's Palace, and to be had of all Booksellers, 1820.
> 374p. 12mo. 'Price 6s half-bound and lettered, or 5s. 3d. in quires' (t.p.).
> BL 1152.k.6; NSTC 2B54566.

*Notes.* Trans. of *Pétrarque et Laure* (Paris, 1819). Half-title reads 'The Circulating Library. Vol II. Petrarch and Laura'. Main text followed by 24 pp. (unn.) of Notes.

1820: 28(b)    GENLIS, [Stéphanie-Félicité, Comtesse] de.
**PETRARCH AND LAURA. BY MADAME DE GENLIS. TRANSLATED FROM THE FRENCH.**

> London: Printed for Henry Colburn & Co. Public Library, Conduit Street, Hanover Square, 1820.
> I xii, 195p; II 213p. 12mo. 10s 6d (ECB).
> BL 837.b.27; ECB 225; NSTC 2B54567 (BI Dt, O).

*Notes.* Trans. of *Pétrarque et Laure* (Paris, 1819).

GORDON, Percival
See NODIER, Jean Emmanuel Charles

1820: 29    GRANT, M[ary] A[nne].
**TALES. FOUNDED ON FACTS. BY M. A. GRANT, AUTHOR OF SKETCHES OF LIFE AND MANNERS, WITH DELINEATIONS OF SCENERY, &C. &C.**

London: Boosey and Sons, Broad Street, Royal Exchange, 1820.
268p. 12mo.
ER 34: 509 (Nov 1820); WSW I: 287 and II: 103.
Corvey; CME 3-628-51051-1; NSTC 2G17839 (BI O).

*Notes*. Dedication to 'the Right Hon. Sir William Grant, late Master of the Rolls'. 3 pp. adv. for 'Park House, Croydon. Mrs Grant's Establishment for the Education of Young Ladies' at the end of the novel, numbered pp. [1]–3.

1820: 30   HALES, J. M. H.
THE ASTROLOGER; OR, THE EVE OF SAN SEBASTIAN; A ROMANCE, BY J. M. H. HALES, ESQ. IN THREE VOLUMES.

London: Printed for William Fearman, Library, 170, New Bond-Street, 1820.
I xii, 298p; II 294p; III 352p. 12mo.
ER 33: 519 (May 1820); WSW I: 13.
Corvey; CME 3-628-47598-8; xNSTC.

*Notes*. Further edn: 2nd edn. 1820 (NSTC 2H2237).

HAMILTON, Terrick, ANTAR
See 1819: 36

1820: 31   {H}[EDGE], {M}[ary] {A}[nn].
THE RETREAT; OR, SKETCHES FROM NATURE. A DESCRIPTIVE TALE. BY THE AUTHOR OF AFFECTION'S GIFT, TREASURES OF THOUGHT, LETTERS ON HISTORY, &C. IN TWO VOLUMES.

London: Published by Baldwin, Cradock, and Joy, Paternoster-Row; and Swinborne and Walter, Colchester, 1820.
I ix, 227p; II 247p. 12mo. 12s (ECB).
ER 34: 263 (Aug 1820); WSW I: 308.
Corvey; CME 3-628-48567-3; ECB 489; NSTC 2H15925 (BI BL, C).

*Notes*. Introduction signed 'M. A. H.'. Colophon reads: 'Printed by Swinborne and Walter, Colchester'.
Further edns: 2nd edn. 1822 (NUC); New York 1821 (NSTC).

1820: 32   HEFFORD, John.
CRESTYPHON, A THEBAN TALE: AND THE VANDAL ROBBERY, A CATHARGINIAN TALE. BY JOHN HEFFORD, ESQ. FORMERLY PRO-FESSOR IN THE COMMERCIAL COLLEGE, WOODFORD.

London: Printed for Matthew Iley, 1, Somerset-Street, Portman-Square; and sold by all Booksellers in Town and Country, 1820.
vi, 301p. 12mo. 6s (ECB, QR).
QR 24: 276 (Oct 1820).
Corvey; CME 3-628-51045-7; ECB 583; NSTC 2H16012 (BI BL).

*Notes*. Preface dated Kentish Town, 24 Apr 1820. QR lists as 'Theban and Carthaginian Tales. By John Hifford'.

1820: 33   HOFLAND, [Barbara].
**TALES OF THE PRIORY. BY MRS. HOFLAND. IN FOUR VOLUMES.**

> London: Printed for Longman, Hurst, Rees, Orme, and Brown, Paternoster-Row, 1820.
> I 298p; II 317p; III 361p; IV 309p. 12mo. 28s (ECB); 28s boards (ER); 24s (QR).
> ER 34: 263 (Aug 1820); QR 24: 276 (Oct 1820); WSW I: 327.
> Corvey; CME 3-628-51040-6; ECB 275; NSTC 2H29421 (BI BL, C, E, O; NA MH).

*Notes.* Further edn: New York 1820 (NUC).


1820: 34   HOGG, James.
**WINTER EVENING TALES, COLLECTED AMONG THE COTTAGERS IN THE SOUTH OF SCOTLAND. BY JAMES HOGG, AUTHOR OF "THE QUEEN'S WAKE," &C. &C. IN TWO VOLUMES.**

> Edinburgh: Printed for Oliver & Boyd, High-Street; and G. & W. B. Whittaker, Ave-
>     Maria-Lane, London, 1820.
> I 340p; II 335p. 12mo. 14s (ECB, ER).
> ER 33: 519 (May 1820); WSW I: 319 and II: 115.
> Corvey; CME 3-628-51027-9; ECB 276; NSTC 2H25732 (BI BL, C, E, NCu, O; NA
>     MH).

*Notes.* Further edns: 2nd edn. 1821 (NSTC); New York 1820 (NUC); German trans., 1821 [as *Die Wanderer im Hochlande* (RS)].


1820: 35   HOLFORD, {Margaret} [afterwards HODSON].
**WARBECK OF WOLFSTEIN. BY MISS HOLFORD, AUTHOR OF WAL-LACE, &C. IN THREE VOLUMES.**

> London: Printed for Rodwell and Martin, New Bond-Street, 1820.
> I iv, 342p; II 399p; III 372p. 12mo. 24s (ER, QR).
> ER 34: 264 (Aug 1820), 35: 266 (Mar 1821); QR 24: 571 (Jan 1821); WSW II: 117.
> Corvey; CME 3-628-47698-4; NSTC 2H26271 (BI BL, C, O; NA MH).

*Notes.* Dedication to Joanna Baillie, signed 'Margaret Holford, Hendon Place, May 18th'.
Further edns: 1847 (NUC); French trans., 1821 [as *Warbeck de Wolfstein, ou les dangers du fatalisme* (BN)]; German trans., 1822.


1820: 36   HUISH, Robert.
**THE BROTHERS; OR THE CASTLE OF NIOLO. A ROMANCE. BY ROBERT HUISH ESQ. AUTHOR OF "KELLY'S CELEBRATED MEMOIRS OF HER LATE ROYAL HIGHNESS PRINCESS CHARLOTTE;"—"THE PERUVIANS, A POEM;"—"A TREATISE ON THE MANAGEMENT OF BEES;"—"FERNEY CASTLE;" &C. &C.**

> London: Published by William Emans, Nos. 1 and 2, Peacock Street, Newington, 1820.
> I iv, 393p, ill.; II 413p, ill. 8vo.
> BL 012611.l.20; NSTC 2H35867 (NA MH).

*Notes.* Adv. at end of *Fatherless Rosa*, below, describes this title as 'completed in Thirty-four numbers, price sixpence each'. Collates in fours.

1820: 37   HUISH, Robert.
FATHERLESS ROSA; OR, THE DANGERS OF THE FEMALE LIFE.
EXPRESSLY WRITTEN AS A COMPANION TO FATHERLESS
FANNY[.] BY ROBERT HUISH, ESQ. AUTHOR OF "KELLY'S CELE-
BRATED MEMOIRS OF HER LATE ROYAL HIGHNESS THE PRINCESS
CHARLOTTE;"—"THE BROTHERS; OR, THE CASTLE OF NIOLO;"—
"LIFE OF OUR LAMENTED SOVEREIGN GEORGE THE THIRD." &C.
&C.

> London: Printed by T. Kaygill, 20, Wych Street, Strand; for William Emans, No. 7, Lon-
> don Road, 1820.
> iv, 522p, ill. 8vo.
> BL 1509/3479; NSTC 2F1800 (BI C).

*Notes.* Additional engraved t.p., bearing the imprint of Thomas Kelly, London, also dated
1820. Frontispiece portrait of the author, with legend 'Published by Tho$^s$. Kelly, 17 Paternoster-Row, Sep 1 1820'; this is amongst 8 engraved illustrations. Collates in fours.

1820: 38   HUMDRUM, Lady [pseud.].
DOMESTIC SCENES. A NOVEL. IN THREE VOLUMES. BY LADY
HUMDRUM, AUTHOR OF MORE WORKS THAN BEAR HER NAME.

> London: Printed for Longman, Hurst, Rees, Orme, and Brown, Paternoster-Row, 1820.
> I 368p; II 359p; III 386p. 12mo. 21s (ECB, ER).
> ER 33: 518 (May 1820); WSW I: 333.
> Corvey; CME 3-628-47801-4; ECB 168; NSTC 2H36417 (BI BL, C, O).

*Notes.* Distinct from *Domestic Scenes* by Mrs Showes (1806: 61).

1820: 39   ISAACS, Mrs
EARL OSRIC; OR, THE LEGEND OF ROSAMOND. A ROMANCE. BY
MRS. ISAACS, AUTHOR OF "TALES OF TO-DAY,"—"WANDERINGS
OF FANCY," &C. &C. &C. IN THREE VOLUMES.

> London: Published by C. Chapple, Royal Subscription Circulating Library, 66, Pall-
> Mall, and Simpkin and Marshall, Stationers' Court, Ludgate Street, 1820.
> I 263p; II 315p; III 436p. 12mo. 24s (ECB, ER).
> ER 33: 254 (Jan 1820), 33: 519 (May 1820).
> Corvey; CME 3-628-47948-7; ECB 301; xNSTC.

*Notes.* Vol. 3 is divided into two parts, paginated to p. 236, and pp. 238–436.

1820: 40   [JONES, George].
SUPREME BON TON: AND BON TON BY PROFESSION. A NOVEL. BY
THE AUTHOR OF "PARGA." &C. &C. IN THREE VOLUMES.

> London: John C. Spence, King-Street, Bloomsbury, 1820.
> I viii, 345p; II 342p; III 305p. 12mo. 18s (ER).
> ER 34: 509 (Nov 1820); WSW I: 116 and II: 74.
> Corvey; CME 3-628-48736-6; NSTC 2J10360 (BI BL; NA MH).

*Notes.* 'Preliminary Epistle from the Author' states 'Given at our residence, in Euston Square, this 12th Day of August, 1820, being the first day of publication'. ECB 569 lists Newman edn., Nov 1820, 18s, but not discovered in this form.

1820: 41    [KING, Frances Elizabeth].
**THE RECTOR'S MEMORANDUM BOOK, BEING THE MEMOIRS OF A FAMILY IN THE NORTH.**
> London: Printed for the Editor, and sold by Messrs. Rivington, St. Paul's Church Yard, and J. Hatchard, Piccadilly, n.d. [1820].
> 272p. 18mo. 7s (ECB); 6s boards (ER).
> ER 34: 264 (Aug 1820).
> Corvey; CME 3-628-48602-5; ECB 482; NSTC 2K5502 (BI BL, C, O).

*Notes.* 'Introductory Letter', pp. [3]–11, dated 'Harrowgate, Oct. 16th, 1780', states the fictional 'Mr. Wilson is our author', but clearly indicates actual female authorship. 'Notice by the Editor' draws attention both to the date of the Introductory Letter and to the fact that the MS 'has been in the Editor's possession ever since that period, which is now over forty years'. Dated in some catalogues as 1819, but ECB lists as July 1820. On ABu copy (SB.82379.Kin.f) 'date 1820' has been added in hand at foot of t.p.

1820: 42    LATHOM, Francis.
**ITALIAN MYSTERIES; OR, MORE SECRETS THAN ONE. A ROMANCE. IN THREE VOLUMES. BY FRANCIS LATHOM, AUTHOR OF THE MYSTERIOUS FREEBOOTER; LONDON; THE UNKNOWN; MEN AND MANNERS; ROMANCE OF THE HEBRIDES; HUMAN BEINGS; FATAL VOW; MIDNIGHT BELL; IMPENETRABLE SECRET; MYSTERY; &C. &C.**
> London: Printed at the Minerva Press for A. K. Newman and Co. Leadenhall-Street, 1820.
> I vi, 246p; II 246p; III 274p. 12mo. 16s 6d (ECB, ER).
> ER 33: 159 (May 1820); WSW I: 59.
> Corvey; CME 3-628-47904-5; ECB 330; NSTC 2L5031 (BI BL, C, E).

*Notes.* Prefatory letter 'to Mr. A. K. Newman', dated New York, 24 Oct 1819.
Further edn: French trans., 1823 [as *Les Mystères italiens, ou le Château della Torrida* (BN)].

1820: 43    LATHOM, Francis.
**THE ONE-POUND NOTE, AND OTHER TALES. IN TWO VOLUMES. BY FRANCIS LATHOM, AUTHOR OF ITALIAN MYSTERIES; MYSTERIOUS FREEBOOTER; LONDON; ROMANCE OF THE HEBRIDES; THE UNKNOWN; MEN AND MANNERS; MYSTERY; FATAL VOW; VERY STRANGE BUT VERY TRUE; ASTONISHMENT, &C. &C.**
> London: Printed for A. K. Newman and Co. Leadenhall-Street, 1820.
> I 271p; II 245p. 12mo. 11s (ECB, QR).
> QR 24: 276 (Oct 1820); WSW I: 87.
> Corvey; CME 3-628-51075-9; ECB 330; NSTC 2L5037 (BI BL, C, E, O).

1820: 44 LAYTON, Jemima.
HULNE ABBEY, A NOVEL, IN THREE VOLUMES. BY MRS. FREDER-
ICK LAYTON, FORMERLY MISS JEMIMA PLUMPTRE. DEDICATED
BY PERMISSION TO THE DUKE OF NORTHUMBERLAND.
> London: Printed for William Fearman, Library, 170, New Bond-Street, 1820.
> I xvi, 305p; II 312p; III 290p. 12mo.
> ER 34: 509 (Nov 1820).
> Corvey; CME 3-628-47972-X; NSTC 2L7466 (NA MH).

1820: 45 [LESTER, Elizabeth B.].
TALES OF THE IMAGINATION. BY THE AUTHOR OF THE BACHE-
LOR AND THE MARRIED MAN, THE PHYSIOGNOMIST, AND HESI-
TATION. IN THREE VOLUMES.
> London: Printed for Longman, Hurst, Rees, Orme, and Brown, Paternoster-Row, 1820.
> I 227p; II 261p; III 252p. 12mo. 18s (ECB, ER); 21s (QR).
> ER 34: 264 (Aug 1820); QR 24: 276 (Oct 1820); WSW I: 118.
> Corvey; CME 3-628-48863-X; ECB 576; NSTC 2R17994 (BI BL, C; NA MH).

*Notes.* For attribution to Lester, rather than to Mrs Ross, see note to *The Bachelor and the Married Man* (1817: 37).

LLOYD, Charles, ISABEL, A TALE
See 1810: 60

1820: 46 [LUCAS, Charles].
GWELYGORDD; OR, THE CHILD OF SIN. A TALE OF WELSH ORIGIN. IN
THREE VOLUMES. BY THE AUTHOR OF THE INFERNAL QUIXOTE,
ABYSSINIAN REFORMER, CASTLE OF ST. DONATS, &C. &C.
> London: Printed at the Minerva Press for A. K. Newman & Co. Leadenhall-Street, 1820.
> I 275p; II 322p; III 280p. 12mo. 16s 6d (ECB); 16s boards (ER).
> ER 34: 264 (Aug 1820); WSW I: 378 and II: 137.
> Corvey; CME 3-628-47590-2; ECB 355; NSTC 2L24395 (BI BL).

1820: 47 MAC DONNELL, Eneas.
THE HERMIT OF GLENCONELLA; A TALE. BY ENEAS MAC DON-
NELL.
> London: Printed for G. Cowie and Co., in the Poultry, 1820.
> vi, 293p. 12mo. 7s (ECB, ER).
> ER 33: 519 (May 1820), 34: 263 (Aug 1820).
> Corvey; CME 3-628-48076-0; ECB 359; NSTC 2M3200 (BI BL, C, Dt, O).

*Notes.* Preface dated Rossbeg, near Westport, 26 Oct 1819.

1820: 48 [MACDONOGH, Felix].
THE HERMIT IN THE COUNTRY; OR, SKETCHES OF ENGLISH MAN-
NERS.

London: Printed for Henry Colburn & Co. Public Library, Conduit Street, 1820/22.

I (1820) xi, 279p; II (1820) vii, 237p; III (1820) vii, 231p; IV (1822) vii, 264p. 12mo. 25s (ECB); 18s vols. 1–3, 7s vol. 4 (ER); 7s vol. 4 (QR).

ER 34: 509 (Nov 1820) vols. 1–3, 37: 536 (Nov 1822) vol. 4; QR 27: 558 (July 1822) vol. 4.

Corvey; CME 3-628-51035-X; ECB 265; NSTC 2M3280 (BI BL, C, Dt, E; NA DLC, MH).

*Notes.* Further edns: New edn. 1823 (NSTC); New York 1820 (NUC).

## MACDONOGH, Felix, THE HERMIT IN LONDON

See 1819: 46

1820: 49   [MACKENZIE, Mary Jane].

## GERALDINE; OR, MODES OF FAITH AND PRACTICE. A TALE, IN THREE VOLUMES. BY A LADY.

London: Printed for T. Cadell and W. Davies, in the Strand; and W. Blackwood, Edinburgh, 1820.

I vii, 293p; II 285p; III 296p. 12mo. 21s (ECB, ER, QR).

ER 33: 518 (May 1820), 35: 525 (July 1821); QR 25: 276 (Apr 1821); WSW I: 382 and II: 140.

Corvey; CME 3-628-47784-0; ECB 228; NSTC 2M5897 (BI BL, C, E, O).

*Notes.* Preface dated 13 Jan 1820.

Further edns: 2nd edn. 1821 (NSTC); Boston 1821 (NSTC).

1820: 50   MAC NALLY, {Louisa}.

## ECCENTRICITY: A NOVEL. IN THREE VOLUMES. BY MRS. MAC NALLY.

Dublin: Printed at the Hibernia Press Office, 1, Temple Lane, for J. Cumming, 16, Lower Ormond Quay; and Longman, Hurst, Rees, Orme, and Brown, London, 1820.

I iv, 346p; II 340p; III 318p. 12mo. 31s (ER).

ER 34: 509 (Nov 1820).

Corvey; CME 3-628-48138-4; NSTC 2M7643 (BI BL, C, Dt; NA MH).

*Notes.* 'Advertisement' signed Louisa Mac Nally. Otherwise identical copy at Urbana (IU 823.M.2322e) has London imprint, with Longmans the main publisher, and John Cumming the Dublin subsidiary. ECB 361 lists Newman edn., June 1822, 18s, but not discovered in this form.

1820: 51   [MATURIN, Charles Robert].

## MELMOTH THE WANDERER: A TALE. BY THE AUTHOR OF "BERTRAM," &C. IN FOUR VOLUMES.

Edinburgh: Printed for Archibald Constable and Company, and Hurst, Robinson, and Co. Cheapside, London, 1820.

I xii, 341p; II 321p; III 368p; IV 453p. 12mo. 28s (ECB); 28s boards (ER).

ER 34: 509 (Nov 1820), 35: 353–62 (July 1821) full review; QR 24: 303–11 (Jan 1821) full review; WSW I: 391 and II: 142–3.

Corvey; CME 3-628-48054-X; ECB 378; NSTC 2M20497 (BI BL, C, Dt, E, O; NA DLC, MH).

*Notes*. Dedication to the Marchioness of Abercorn. Preface dated Dublin, 31 Aug 1820.
Further edns: 2nd edn. 1821 (NUC); Boston 1821 (NSTC); French trans., 1821 [as *L'Homme du mystère, ou histoire de Melmoth le voyageur* (MLC); also as *Melmoth, ou l'homme errant* (MLC)]; German trans., 1821.

1820: 52   MILNER, H[enry] M. (*trans.?*).
THE ITALIAN DON JUAN; OR, MEMOIRS OF THE DEVIL SACRIPANTI, THE BRIGAND OF THE APENNINES. TRANSLATED FREELY FROM THE ITALIAN. BY M. H. MILNER. AUTHOR OF BARMECIDE: JEW OF LUBECK; &C.

London: Printed and published for C. Chapple, Royal Library, 66, Pall-Mall, 1820.
iii, 160p. 12mo. 5s (ECB, ER).
ER 34: 263 (Aug 1820).
Corvey, CME 3-628-48166-X; ECB 302; xNSTC.

*Notes*. No Italian original discovered.

1820: 53   [MORE, Olivia].
THE WELSH COTTAGE.

Wellington, Salop: Printed by and for F. Houlston and Son. And sold by Scatcherd and Letterman, Ave-Maria-Lane, London, 1820.
ix, 223p, ill. 12mo. 4s (ECB); 4s boards (ER).
ER 33: 519 (May 1820); WSW II: 62.
Corvey; CME 3-628-48883-4; ECB 629; NSTC 2M35930 (BI BL, O).

*Notes*. 'Entered at Stationer's Hall', on t.p. after imprint date. Sometimes attributed erroneously to Mary M. Sherwood.
Further edns: 2nd edn. 1822 (CFu); 3rd edn. 1828 (AWn).

1820: 54   [MOYSEY, Abel].
THE WHARBROKE LEGEND: A TALE OF THE DEAD. BY ALBERT MARMACOPT, LATE OF COPT HALL, ESQ., F.S.A. IN TWO VOLUMES.

London: Printed for Ogle, Duncan, and Co. 37, Paternoster-Row, and 295, Holborn; and Ogle, Allardice, and Thomson, Edinburgh, 1820.
I vii, 351p; II 359p. 12mo. 14s (ECB, ER, QR).
ER 33: 519 (May 1820), 34: 509 (Nov 1820); QR 23: 283 (May 1820), 24: 276 (Oct 1820); WSW II: 154.
Corvey; CME 3-628-48158-9; ECB 632; NSTC 2M14772 (BI BL, C, O; NA MH).

*Notes*. 'To the Editor of a Former Publication, entitled "Tales of the Dead!" ', signed Albert Marmacopt.

1820: 55   [MUDIE, Robert].
GLENFERGUS. IN THREE VOLUMES.

Edinburgh: Oliver & Boyd, High-Street. G. & W. B. Whittaker, Ave-Maria-Lane, London, 1820.
I 348p; II 342p; III 339p. 12mo. 21s (ECB, ER, QR).
ER 33: 254 (Jan 1820); QR 22: 564 (Mar 1820); WSW I: 413.
Corvey; CME 3-628-47818-9; ECB 233; NSTC 2M39903 (BI BL, E, O; NA DLC, MH).

1820: 56    [NODIER, Jean Emmanuel Charles]; GORDON, Percival (*trans.*).
GIOVANNI SBOGARRO, A VENETIAN TALE. TAKEN FROM THE
FRENCH. BY PERCIVAL GORDON.

London: Printed for Baldwin, Cradock, and Joy, Paternoster-Row, 1820.
I iv, 270p; II 360p. 12mo. 12s (ECB, QR); 12s boards (ER).
ER 34: 264 (Aug 1820); QR 24: 276 (Oct 1820).
Corvey; CME 3-628-47796-4; ECB 231; xNSTC.

*Notes*. Trans. of *Jean Sbogar* (Paris, 1818). Preface, dated Jan 1820, states the 'present account' to be 'taken from an anonymous French work, but with considerable alterations'. ECB lists as 'Transl. from French by Percival Gordon'.
Further edn: New York 1820 (NUC).

1820: 57    OPIE, [Amelia Alderson].
TALES OF THE HEART. BY MRS. OPIE. IN FOUR VOLUMES.

London: Printed for Longman, Hurst, Rees, Orme, and Brown, Paternoster-Row, 1820.
I 350p; II 419p; III 396p; IV 353p. 12mo. 28s (ECB); 28s boards (ER).
ER 34: 264 (Aug 1820); WSW I: 423 and II: 156.
Corvey; CME 3-628-48306-9; ECB 423; NSTC 2O4402 (BI BL, C, E, O).

*Notes*. Further edns: 2nd edn. 1820 (BRu ENC); New York 1820 (NSTC); German trans., 1820 [as *Geschichten fürs Herz* (RS)]; French trans., 1831.

1820: 58    PRINCEPS, Elizabeth Louisa Slater.
VARIETY. A NOVEL. BY ELIZABETH LOUISA SLATER PRINCEPS.
WITH POETRY. IN THREE VOLUMES.

London: Printed for W. Fearman, Library, 170, New Bond-Street, 1820.
I 264p; II 259p; III 224p. 12mo. 21s (ER, QR).
ER 34: 509 (Nov 1820); QR 24: 276 (Oct 1820); WSW I: 126.
Corvey; CME 3-628-54706-7; NSTC 2P26813 (BI BL).

1820: 59    [PURCELL, Mrs].
THE ORIENTALIST, OR ELECTIONEERING IN IRELAND; A TALE, BY
MYSELF. IN TWO VOLUMES.

London: Printed for Baldwin, Cradock, and Joy, 47, Paternoster-Row; J. Thomson & Co., Edinburgh; William Gribbin, Dublin; and Samuel Archer, Belfast, 1820.
I viii, 345p; II 419p. 12mo. 15s (ECB, ER).
ER 33: 519 (May 1820), 34: 263 (Aug 1820); WSW I: 454.
Corvey; CME 3-628-48312-3; ECB 424; NSTC 2P29125 (BI BL, C, O; NA DLC, MH).

1820: 60   ROCHE, Regina Maria.
THE MUNSTER COTTAGE BOY. A TALE. IN FOUR VOLUMES. BY
REGINA MARIA ROCHE, AUTHOR OF THE CHILDREN OF THE ABBEY,
TRECOTHICK BOWER, MONASTERY OF ST. COLUMB, &C. &C.

> London: Printed at the Minerva Press for A. K. Newman and Co. Leadenhall-Street, 1820.
> I 283p; II 327p; III 303p; IV 282p. 12mo. 28s (ECB).
> ER 33: 254 (Jan 1820); WSW I: 470.
> Corvey; CME 3-628-48461-8; ECB 498; NSTC 2D1379 (BI BL, O).

*Notes.* ECB dates Nov 1819.
Further edns: New York 1820 (NSTC); French trans., 1821.


1820: 61   ST. CLAIR, Rosalia [pseud.].
THE HIGHLAND CASTLE, AND THE LOWLAND COTTAGE. A
NOVEL. IN FOUR VOLUMES. BY ROSALIA ST. CLAIR, AUTHOR OF
THE SON OF O'DONNEL, BLIND BEGGAR, &C. &C.

> London: Printed at the Minerva Press for A. K. Newman and Co. Leadenhall-Street,
> 1820.
> I 248p; II 248p; III 235p; IV 234p. 12mo. 22s (ECB, ER).
> ER 33: 518 (May 1820).
> Corvey; CME 3-628-48497-9; ECB 511; NSTC 2S1996 (BI BL, O).


1820: 62   [SCOTT, Sir Walter].
THE ABBOT. BY THE AUTHOR OF "WAVERLEY." IN THREE VOL-
UMES.

> Edinburgh: Printed for Longman, Hurst, Rees, Orme, and Brown, London; and for
> Archibald Constable and Company, and John Ballantyne, 1820.
> I iv, 348p; II 351p; III 367p. 12mo. 24s (ECB, ER).
> ER 34: 263 (Aug 1820); QR 24: 276 (Oct 1820), 26: 109–48 (Oct 1821) full review; WSW
> I: 489–90 and II: 173.
> Corvey, CME 3-628-48545-2; ECB 1; NSTC 2S9409 (BI BL, C, Dt, E, NCu, O; NA MH).

*Notes.* 'This day published', 2 Sept 1820, *Edinburgh Evening Courant.* This is one of eight
novels by Scott which are together given full reviews in QR (Oct 1821).
Further edns: Philadelphia 1820 (NSTC); French trans., 1820; German trans., 1821 [as *Der
Abt, ein romantisches Gemählde* (RS)]. Numerous reprintings in collected edns.


1820: 63   [SCOTT, Sir Walter].
IVANHOE; A ROMANCE. BY THE AUTHOR OF "WAVERLEY," &C. IN
THREE VOLUMES.

> Edinburgh: Printed for Archibald Constable and Co; and Hurst, Robinson, and Co. 90,
> Cheapside, London, 1820.
> I xxxiii, 298p; II 327p; III 371p. 8vo. 30s (ECB, ER, QR).
> ER 33: [1]–54 (Jan 1820) full review, 33: 254 (Jan 1820); QR (2nd edn.) 22: 564
> (Mar 1820), 26: 109–48 (Oct 1821) full review; WSW I: 488–9 and II: 173.
> BL 247.e.25–27; ECB 303; NSTC 2S9692 (BI C, O; NA DLC, MH).

*Notes.* 'This day published', 20 Dec 1819, *Edinburgh Evening Courant*. This is one of eight novels by Scott which are together given full reviews in QR (Oct 1821).
Further edns: 2nd edn. 1820 (Corvey); 3rd edn. 1821 (NCBEL); Philadelphia 1820 (NSTC); French trans., 1820 [as *Ivanhoé, ou le retour du croisé* (BN)]; German trans., 1820. Numerous reprintings in collected edns.

1820: 64   [SCOTT, Sir Walter].
THE MONASTERY. A ROMANCE. BY THE AUTHOR OF "WAVER-LEY." IN THREE VOLUMES.

> Edinburgh: Printed for Longman, Hurst, Rees, Orme, and Brown, London; and for
>   Archibald Constable and Co., and John Ballantyne, Bookseller to the King, 1820.
> I 331p; II 330p; III 351p. 12mo. 24s (ECB, ER, QR).
> ER 33: 518 (May 1820); QR 23: 283 (May 1820), 26: 109–48 (Oct 1821) full review;
>   WSW I: 489.
> Corvey; CME 3-628-48578-9; ECB 391; NSTC 2S10043 (BI BL, C, Dt, E, NCu, O; NA
>   DLC, MH).

*Notes.* 'This day published', 23 Mar 1820, *Edinburgh Evening Courant*. This is one of eight novels by Scott which are together given full reviews in QR (Oct 1821).
Further edns: 2nd edn. 1820 (NSTC); Philadelphia 1820 (NSTC); French trans., 1820; German trans., 1821. Numerous reprintings in collected edns.

1820: 65   SEBRIGHT, Paul.
COINCIDENCE; OR, THE SOOTHSAYER. A NOVEL. IN THREE VOL-UMES. BY PAUL SEBRIGHT.

> London: Printed at the Minerva Press for A. K. Newman and Co. Leadenhall-Street,
>   1820.
> I 243p; II 247p; III 284p. 12mo. 16s 6d (ECB, ER).
> ER 33: 519 (May 1820); WSW I: 490.
> Corvey; CME 3-628-48629-7; ECB 524; NSTC 2S12005 (BI BL, C, O).

1820: 66   STANHOPE, Louisa Sidney.
THE CRUSADERS. AN HISTORICAL ROMANCE, OF THE TWELFTH CENTURY. IN FIVE VOLUMES. BY LOUISA SIDNEY STANHOPE, AUTHOR OF MONTBRAZIL ABBEY, THE BANDIT'S BRIDE, DI MON-TRANZO, CONFESSIONAL OF VALOMBRE, &C. &C.

> London: Printed at the Minerva Press for A. K. Newman and Co. Leadenhall-Street,
>   1820.
> I 262p; II 252p; III 258p; IV 275p; V 301p. 12mo. 27s 6d (ECB, ER).
> ER 34: 264 (Aug 1820); WSW I: 519.
> Corvey; CME 3-628-48774-9; ECB 558; NSTC 2S36108 (BI BL, C, E).

1820: 67   [SUTHERLAND, Alexander].
ST. KATHLEEN; OR, THE ROCK OF DUNNISMOYLE. A NOVEL. IN FOUR VOLUMES. BY THE AUTHOR OF REDMOND THE REBEL.

London: Printed at the Minerva Press for A. K. Newman and Co. Leadenhall-Street, 1820.

I 294p; II 262p; III 242p; IV 241p. 12mo. 22s (ECB); 22s boards (ER).

ER 34: 509 (Nov 1820); WSW I: 107.

Corvey; CME 3-628-48490-1; ECB 511; NSTC 2S47483 (BI BL, C, E, O).

VALLADERRAS, Leandra de
See FURBO, Francisco

1820: 68   WARD, Catherine G[eorge].
**THE MYSTERIOUS MARRIAGE, OR THE WILL OF MY FATHER, BY CATHERINE G. WARD, AUTHORESS OF "THE DAUGHTER OF ST OMER", "MY NATIVE LAND", "BACHELORS HEIRESS", "THE PRIMROSE GIRL" &C. &C.**

London: Published by J. Tallis, 7, Warwick Squ^e. Newgate Street, n.d. [1820].
646p, ill. 8vo.
WSW II: 199.
BL 012634.ppp.11; NSTC 2W4966 (BI E).

*Notes.* No date, but frontispiece facing t.p. bears the legend 'Published by T. Kinnersley Feb. 7 1820'. Engraved t.p. only (from which title, headed by the words 'Founded on Facts', is taken above). Collates in fours. ECB 623 lists 4 vols., 1824 edn., 21s.
Further edns: 1822 (ScU); 1824 (NSTC); 4 vols. 1824 (Corvey), CME 3-628-48824-9; New York 1834 (NSTC). The 4 vol. edn. at Corvey was published by George Virtue, with an 'Advertisement' dated London, July 1824, stating that 'the Publisher, in offering the present edition, is actuated by a wish to introduce it [*The Mysterious Marriage*] to the notice of the numerous supporters of Public Libraries'.

1820: 69   WARD, Catherine G[eorge].
**THE ROSE OF CLAREMONT, OR DAUGHTER, WIFE & MOTHER, BY CATHERINE G. WARD, AUTHORESS OF THE "MYSTERIOUS MARRIAGE," "THE DAUGHTER OF ST. OMER," "MY NATIVE LAND," &C. &C.**

London: Published by J. Tallis, 7 Warwick Square, Newgate Street; and G. Virtue, 6, Cannon Row, Parliament Street, n.d. [1820].
I 600p, ill.; II 602p, ill. 8vo.
BL 12654.p.23; ECB 623; NSTC 2W4969 (BI C).

*Notes.* Dedication to Queen Caroline, signed Catherine G. Ward, London, 1820. Collates in fours. ECB dates 1820.
Further edns: [1821] (NUC); 1823 (CG, Summers).

1820: 70   WILKINSON, Sarah [Scudgell].
**THE SPECTRE OF LANMERE ABBEY, OR THE MYSTERY OF THE BLUE AND SILVER BAG; A ROMANCE. BY SARAH WILKINSON: AUTHORESS OF THE BANDIT OF FLORENCE, FUGITIVE COUNTESS, WHEEL OF FORTUNE, &C. IN TWO VOLUMES.**

London: Printed and published by W. Mason, Clerkenwell Green, 1820.
I 212p; II 213p. 12mo. 'Eight Shillings' (t.p.).
BL 12612.bb.28; ECB 638; NSTC 2W21064.

*Notes.* Preface (1 p. unn.) acknowledges 'profit' as a main motive: 'Knowing how eager the fair sex are for something *new* and *romantic*, I determined on an attempt to *please* my fair sisterhood, hoping to *profit* myself thereby'.

# 1821

### 1821: 1    ANON.
### ANECDOTES OF A CROAT.

London: Published by Sherwood, Neely, and Jones, Paternoster-Row, 1821.
iv, 425p. 12mo. 5s (ECB).
C Rom.6.31; ECB 19; NSTC 2A12592 (BI BL, O).

*Notes.* ECB dates Dec 1821.
Further edn: reissued in an extended form as *Anecdotes of a Croat; or, the Castle of Serai, comprehending hints for the improvement of public works, agriculture, and domestic life*, 2 vols, Simpkin and Marshall (compare 1823: 2).

### 1821: 2    ANON.
### BANNOCKBURN; A NOVEL. IN THREE VOLUMES.

Edinburgh: Printed for John Warren, Old Bond Street, London; and William Blackwood, Prince's-Street, 1821.
I 238p; II 228p; III 288p. 12mo. 18s (ECB); 18s boards (ER).
ER 35: 526 (July 1821); WSW II: 5.
Corvey; CME 3-628-47099-4; ECB 38; NSTC 2B7054 (BI BL, C, E, O).

*Notes.* Further edn: Philadelphia 1822 (NSTC).

### 1821: 3    ANON.
### BIGOTRY; OR, THE WARNING VOICE. A NOVEL. IN FOUR VOLUMES.

London: Printed for A. K. Newman and Co. Leadenhall-Street, 1821.
I 305p; II 342p; III 312p; IV 316p. 12mo. 24s (ECB, ER).
ER 36: 280 (Oct 1821).
Corvey; CME 3-628-47202-4; ECB 56; NSTC 2B33448 (BI BL, C).

### THE CAVERN IN THE WICKLOW MOUNTAINS
See 1819: 20 and Appendix E: 8

1821:4 ANON.

CONCEALMENT. A NOVEL. IN THREE VOLUMES.

> London: John Warren, Old Bond Street, 1821.
> I viii, 438p; II 475p; III 456p. 12mo. 21s (ECB); 21s boards (ER).
> ER 35: 526 (July 1821); WSW II: 7.
> Corvey; CME 3-628-47278-4; ECB 129; NSTC 2C33484 (BI BL, C).

1821:5 ANON.

THE FEUDS OF LUNA AND PEROLLO; OR, THE FORTUNES OF THE
HOUSE OF PANDOLFINA. AN HISTORIC TALE OF THE SIXTEENTH
CENTURY. IN FOUR VOLUMES.

> London: Printed for A. K. Newman and Co. Leadenhall-Street, 1821.
> I iv, 275p; II 271p; III 274p; IV 322p. 12mo. 22s (ECB).
> Corvey; CME 3-628-47505-8; ECB 204; NSTC 2F5052 (BI C).

*Notes.* ECB dates June 1821.

1821:6 ANON.

HAPPINESS; A TALE, FOR THE GRAVE AND THE GAY. IN TWO VOL-
UMES.

> London: Printed for Francis Westley, 10, Stationer's-Court; and sold by Longman,
>    Hurst, Rees, Orme, & Brown, Paternoster-Row, 1821.
> I 301p; II 312p. 8vo. 12s (ECB, ER).
> ER 36: 571 (Feb 1822); WSW II: 14.
> BL 12612.f.9; ECB 254; NSTC 2H7230 (BI C; NA MH).

*Notes.* Further edns: 3rd edn. 1821 (Corvey), CME 3-628-47543-0; Boston 1822 (NSTC).

1821:7 ANON.

MAURICE POWELL: AN HISTORICAL WELSH TALE OF ENGLAND'S
TROUBLES. IN THREE VOLUMES.

> London: Printed for Baldwin, Cradock, and Joy, Paternoster-Row, 1821.
> I 263p; II 272p; III 352p. 12mo. 18s (ECB, ER, QR).
> ER 36: 571 (Feb 1822); QR 26: 544 (Jan 1822); WSW II: 22.
> Corvey; CME 3-628-48199-6; ECB 374; NSTC 2P23803 (BI BL, O; NA MH).

1821:8 ANON.

MEMOIRS OF A MAN OF FASHION. WRITTEN BY HIMSELF.
INCLUDING ANECDOTES OF MANY CELEBRATED PERSONS, WITH
WHOM HE HAD INTERCOURSE AND CONNEXION. IN THREE VOL-
UMES.

> London: Printed for Sherwood, Neely, and Jones, Paternoster-Row, 1821.
> I xvi, 240p; II viii, 208p; III viii, 214p. 12mo. 21s (ECB, ER).
> ER 36: 280 (Oct 1821); WSW II: 22.
> Corvey; CME 3-628-48062-0; ECB 379; NSTC 2M24179 (NA DLC).

*Notes.* Dedication to 'Lord ****'.

1821:9   ANON.

NATIONAL FEELING; OR, THE HISTORY OF FITZSIMON; A NOVEL.
WITH HISTORICAL AND POLITICAL REMARKS. IN TWO VOLUMES.
BY AN IRISHMAN.

> Dublin: Printed for the Author, by A. O'Neil, at the Minerva Printing-Office, 17,
> Chancery-Lane, 1821.
> I viii, 238p; II 252p. 12mo.
> WSW II: 24.
> Dt OLS.181.q.106; NSTC 2N1651 (NA MH)

*Notes.* 'To you, my Countrymen', dated 16 Mar 1821.


1821:10   ANON.
OLD WIVES' TALES.

> London: Printed for F. C. & J. Rivington, No. 62, St. Paul's Church-Yard, and No. 3,
> Waterloo-Place, Pall-Mall, 1821.
> 195p. 12mo. 3s (ECB).
> Corvey; CME 3-628-51109-7; ECB 422; NSTC 2W28639 (BI BL, O).

*Notes.* ECB dates July 1821.


THE ONLY CHILD
See OPIE, Amelia Alderson


1821:11   ANON.
THE PRIEST: IN THREE VOLUMES.

> London: Printed for Baldwin, Cradock, and Joy, Paternoster-Row, 1821.
> I 268p; II 261p; III 270p. 12mo. 18s (ECB, ER).
> ER 36: 571 (Feb 1822); WSW II: 29.
> Corvey; CME 3-628-48294-1; ECB 469; NSTC 2P26389 (BI BL, C, O).


1821:12   ANON.
THE PRIVATEER; A TALE, IN TWO VOLUMES.

> London: Printed for John Andrews, 167, New Bond-Street, 1821.
> I 212p; II 219p. 8vo.
> ER 36: 279 (Oct 1821); WSW II: 29.
> Corvey; CME 3-628-48365-4; NSTC 2P27264 (BI BL, C, O).

*Notes.* 4 pp. (unn.) addition at the end of vol. 2 announces opening of J. Andrews's Library,
167 New Bond-Street, near Grafton-Street, and gives subscription terms and regulations.
Further edn: Philadelphia 1821 (NSTC).


1821:13   ANON.
ST. AUBIN; OR, THE INFIDEL. IN TWO VOLUMES.

> Edinburgh: Oliver & Boyd, High-Street; sold also by G. & W. B. Whittaker, Ave-Maria-
> Lane, London; and W. Turnbull, Glasgow, 1821.
> I 316p; II 348p. 12mo. 12s (ECB); 14s boards (ER); 12s boards (ER, QR).

ER 35: 266 (Mar 1821), 35: 525 (July 1821); QR 25: 276 (Apr 1821); WSW II: 32.
Corvey; CME 3-628-48593-2; ECB 511; NSTC 2S1527 (BI BL, NCu).

*Notes.* ER gives price as 14s boards in Mar 1821, and as 12s boards in July 1821.
Further edn: 2nd edn. 1824 (NUC).

1821: 14 ANON.
SCHEMING; A NOVEL, IN THREE VOLUMES.

London: Henry Colburn and Co. Public Library, Conduit Street, 1821.
I 235p; II 228p; III 245p. 12mo. 21s (ECB, ER).
ER 35: 266 (Mar 1821); WSW II: 32.
Corvey; CME 3-628-48533-9; ECB 517; NSTC 2S6401 (BI BL, C, O; NA MH).

1821: 15 ANON.
SUCH IS THE WORLD. IN THREE VOLUMES.

London: Printed for G. and W. B. Whittaker, Ave-Maria-Lane, 1821.
I xix, 323p; II 312p; III 311p. 12mo. 21s (ECB, ER).
ER 35: 266 (Mar 1821); WSW II: 35–6.
Corvey; CME 3-628-48790-0; ECB 568; NSTC 2S45711 (BI BL; NA MH).

*Notes.* Preface states the manuscript was completed on 15 Aug 1820. Apparently by the same
author as that of *The Village Coquette* (1822: 13).

1821: 16 ANON.
A TALE OF THE OLDEN TIME. BY A HARROW BOY.

London: Printed for John Andrews, 167, New Bond-Street, 1821.
174p. 12mo. 6s 6d (ECB).
ER 35: 526 (July 1821); WSW II: 107.
Corvey; CME 3-628-48794-3; ECB 575; NSTC 2T1218 (BI BL, C, O).

*Notes.* Dedication to 'his school-fellows' by 'the author'. Statement (1 p. unn.) at the end of
vol. that the work was begun when the author was 14, and completed two years later; this is
dated 12 Mar 1821.

1821: 17 ANON.
TALES OF MY LANDLORD, NEW SERIES, CONTAINING THE FAIR
WITCH OF GLAS LLYN. IN THREE VOLUMES.

London: Printed for William Fearman, New Bond-Street, 1821.
I xcvi, 256p; II 360p; III 368p. 12mo. 24s (ER, QR).
ER 35: 525 (July 1821); QR 24: 571 (Jan 1821).
Corvey; ECB 575; NSTC 2T1407 (BI BL, E).

*Notes.* Further edns: French trans., 1821 [as *La Belle Sorcière de Glas-Llyn* (Pigoreau)];
German trans., 1822 [as *Die Circe von Glas-Llyn* (RS)].

1821: 18 ANON.
TRAITS AND TRIALS: A NOVEL. IN TWO VOLUMES.

London: Printed for James Cawthorn, Cockspur-Street, 1821.

I iv, 297p; II 314p. 12mo. 14s (ECB); 21s (ER).
ER 35: 525 (July 1821); WSW II: 38.
Corvey; CME 3-628-48767-6; ECB 596; NSTC 2T16298 (BI BL).

*Notes*. ER gives as 'by an American'. ECB dates Jan 1821 and lists 2 vols. ER lists 3 vols., which explains the price difference between the two sources.

1821: 19   ANON.
THE VICAR OF IVER: A TALE. BY THE AUTHOR OF "THE ITALIAN CONVERT."

London: Printed for Francis Westley, 10, Stationers' Court, and Ave-Maria-Lane, 1821.
130p, ill. 12mo. 3s 6d (ECB, ER, QR).
ER 35: 526 (July 1821); QR 25: 276 (Apr 1821); WSW II: 39–40.
Corvey; CME 3-628-48912-1; ECB 613; NSTC 2V3242 (NA MH).

1821: 20   ARGUS, Arabella [pseud.].
OSTENTATION AND LIBERALITY. A TALE. IN TWO VOLUMES. BY ARABELLA ARGUS, AUTHOR OF "THE JUVENILE SPECTATOR;" "THE ADVENTURES OF A DONKEY," &C.

London: William Darton, 58, Holborn Hill, 1821.
I 216p, ill.; II 216p, ill. 18mo. 5s (ECB).
WSW II: 42.
Corvey; CME 3-628-47397-7; ECB 24; NSTC 2A15250 (BI BL, C, O; NA MH).

*Notes*. ECB dates Apr 1821.
Further edn: [1825?] (NSTC).

1821: 21   ARLINCOURT, [Charles] Vicomte d'.
THE RECLUSE; A TRANSLATION OF "LE SOLITAIRE," BY M. LE VICOMTE D'ARLINCOURT. IN TWO VOLUMES.

London: Henry Colburn and Co. Public Library, Conduit Street, Hanover Square, 1821.
I v, 218p; II 218p. 12mo. 12s (ECB, ER).
ER 36: 570 (Feb 1822).
Corvey; CME 3-628-47456-6; ECB 152; NSTC 2A15600 (BI BL, C, E, O).

*Notes*. Trans. of *Le Solitaire* (Paris, 1821). Preface likens aspects of the work to 'the historical character and dramatic style of the novels of the author of Waverley' (p. [iii]), while pointing also to its own extensive fame in France. 'Preface to the Fifth Edition of the Original' also in vol. 1, pp. [1]–3.
Further edn: New York 1822 (NUC).

1821: 22   [BENNET, William].
THE CAVALIER. A ROMANCE. BY LEE GIBBONS, STUDENT OF LAW. IN THREE VOLUMES.

London: Printed for Longman, Hurst, Rees, Orme, and Brown, Paternoster-Row, 1821.
I xxxi, 437p; II 370p; III 359p. 12mo. 21s (ECB); 21s boards (ER, QR).

ER 35: 525 (July 1821); QR 25: 275 (Apr 1821); WSW II: 101.

Corvey; CME 3-628-47813-8; ECB 229; NSTC 2B18425 (BI BL, C).

*Notes.* Dedication to 'my very dear friend, C—— G——, Esq.', signed Lee Gibbons [pseud.], Chapel-en-le-Frith, Aug 1820.

Further edns: Philadelphia 1822 (NSTC); German trans., 1822 [as *Der Cavalier, ein historischer Roman* (RS)].

BRAYER DE SAINT-LÉON, Louise Marguerite
See CAMPBELL, Margaret

1821: 23   BRYDGES, Sir S[amuel] E[gerton].
**THE HALL OF HELLINGSLEY; A TALE. BY SIR S. E. BRYDGES, BART. &C. &C. &C. IN THREE VOLUMES.**

London: Printed for Longman, Hurst, Rees, Orme, and Brown, Paternoster-Row, 1821.
I vii, 209p; II viii, 245p; III viii, 293p. 12mo. 18s (ECB); 18s boards (ER).
ER 36: 570 (Feb 1822); WSW II: 59.
Corvey; CME 3-628-47142-7; ECB 81; NSTC 2B55163 (BI BL, C, E, O; NA DLC, MH).

1821: 24   CAMPBELL, D[orothea] P[rimrose].
**HARLEY RADINGTON. A TALE. IN TWO VOLUMES. BY MISS D. P. CAMPBELL.**

London: Printed for A. K. Newman and Co. Leadenhall-Street, 1821.
I 278p, II 234p. 12mo. 10s 6d (ECB); 10s 6d boards (ER).
ER 36: 279 (Oct 1821).
Corvey; CME 3-628-47208-3; ECB 94; NSTC 2C4397 (BI BL, C, O; NA MH).

1821: 25   CAMPBELL, Margaret.
**THE MIDNIGHT WANDERER; OR A LEGEND OF THE HOUSES OF ALTENBERG AND LINDENDORF. A ROMANCE. IN FOUR VOLUMES. BY MARGARET CAMPBELL.**

London: Printed for A. K. Newman and Co. Leadenhall-Street, 1821.
I 227p; II 224p; III 222p; IV 257p. 12mo. 22s (ECB, ER, QR).
ER 35: 266 (Mar 1821), 36: 280 (Oct 1821); QR 24: 571 (Jan 1821).
Corvey; CME 3-628-47209-1; ECB 95; NSTC 2C4895 (BI BL, C).

*Notes.* A free trans. of *Alexina, ou la vieille tour du château de Holdheim* (Paris 1813), by Mme. Louise Marguerite Brayer de Saint-Léon (Summers). NUC (but not NSTC) catalogues *The Midnight Wanderer* under Brayer de Saint-Léon's authorship.

Further edn: According to a note in BN, this work was re-translated into French as a work by Ann Radcliffe under the title of *Rose d'Altenberg, ou le spectre dans les ruines* (Paris, 1830).

1821: 26   [CAREY, David].
**A LEGEND OF ARGYLE; OR 'TIS A HUNDRED YEARS SINCE. IN THREE VOLUMES.**

London: Printed for G. & W. B. Whittaker, Ave-Maria-Lane, 1821.
I 324p; II 331p; III 312p. 12mo. 21s (ECB).

WSW II: 70.
Corvey; CME 3-628-48048-5; ECB 337; NSTC 2C7015 (BI BL, C, E, O; NA MH).
*Notes.* ECB dates Apr 1821.

1821: 27    CARR, E. D.
FEARS AND CARES. A NOVEL. IN THREE VOLUMES. BY E. D. CARR,
AUTHOR OF THE ADVERTISEMENT, OR TWENTY YEARS AGO, &C.
>London: Printed for A. K. Newman and Co. Leadenhall-Street, 1821.
>I 235p; II 231p; III 267p. 12mo. 16s 6d (ECB); 16s 6d boards (ER).
>ER 35: 525 (July 1821).
>Corvey; CME 3-628-47216-4; ECB 99; NSTC 2C9359 (BI BL, C, O).

*Notes.* ECB gives the title as 'Fears and cares; or, an uncle and his nephew'. For the possible appearance of the same author under another surname, see Elizabeth Clark, *The Advertisement* (1818: 25).

1821: 28    [COOPER, James Fenimore].
PRECAUTION, A NOVEL. IN THREE VOLUMES.
>London: Henry Colburn and Co. Public Library, Conduit Street, Hanover Square,
>1821.
>I 307p; II 301p; III 315p. 12mo. 21s (ECB, ER, QR).
>ER 35: 525 (July 1821); QR 25: 276 (Apr 1821); WSW II: 77.
>Corvey; CME 3-628-47332-2; ECB 467; NSTC 2C36867 (BI BL, C; NA MH).

*Notes.* Originally published New York 1820 (Blanck).
Further edns: 1839 (NSTC); French trans., 1825; German trans., 1825 [as *Mosely-Hall, oder die Wahl des Gatten* (RS)].

1821: 29    [CRADOCK, Joseph].
FIDELIA; OR THE PREVALENCE OF FASHION.
>London: Printed by John Nichols and Son, 25, Parliament Street; and sold by C. Chapple, Royal Library, Pall Mall, 1821.
>v, 173p. 12mo. 5s 6d boards (ER).
>ER 36: 279 (Oct 1821); WSW II: 80–1.
>BL 12620.c.9; NSTC 2C41724 (BI O; NA MH).

*Notes.* 'Advertisement' from 'the Editor' states the novel 'was written some time since, and is evidently of the Old School'. This leaf has been mis-bound in the BL copy at the very end of the book.

1821: 30    EDMESTON, James.
ANSTON PARK, A TALE. BY JAMES EDMESTON, AUTHOR OF SACRED
LYRICS.
>London: Printed for B. J. Holdsworth, 18, (South Side,) St. Paul's Church Yard, 1821.
>243p. 12mo. 5s 6d (ECB); 6s (ER, QR).
>ER 35: 266 (Mar 1821); QR 24: 572 (Jan 1821); WSW II: 92.
>Corvey; CME 3-628-47519-8; ECB 179; NSTC 2E4488 (BI BL, C).

*Notes.* Dedication to Captain John Pudner, 'late Commissary of Ordnance at Allahabad'.

1821: 31    EGAN, Pierce.
LIFE IN LONDON; OR, THE DAY AND NIGHT SCENES OF JERRY
HAWTHORN, ESQ. AND HIS ELEGANT FRIEND CORINTHIAN TOM,
ACCOMPANIED BY BOB LOGIC, THE OXONIAN, IN THEIR RAM-
BLES AND SPREES THROUGH THE METROPOLIS. BY PIERCE EGAN,
AUTHOR OF WALKS THROUGH BATH, SPORTING ANECDOTES,
PICTURE OF THE FANCY, BOXIANA, &C. DEDICATED TO HIS MOST
GRACIOUS MAJESTY KING GEORGE THE FOURTH. EMBELLISHED
WITH THIRTY-SIX SCENES FROM REAL LIFE, DESIGNED AND
ETCHED BY I. R. & G. CRUIKSHANK; AND ENRICHED ALSO WITH
NUMEROUS ORIGINAL DESIGNS ON WOOD, BY THE SAME
ARTISTS.

> London: Printed for Sherwood, Neely, and Jones, Paternoster-Row, 1821.
> xvi, 376p, ill., music. 8vo. 36s (ECB).
> Corvey; CME 3-628-51309-X; ECB 181; NSTC 2E5884 (BI BL, E; NA DLC, MH).

Notes. Dedication to 'his Most Excellent Majesty King George the Fourth', dated 19 July
1821. ECB dates July 1821. Previously issued in monthly numbers from 1820.
Further edns: 2nd edn. 1821 (NSTC); 1822 (NSTC); 1823 (NSTC); New Orleans 1837
(NSTC).


1821: 32    [?EGAN, Pierce].
REAL LIFE IN IRELAND; OR, THE DAY AND NIGHT SCENES, ROV-
INGS, RAMBLES, AND SPREES, BULLS, BLUNDERS, BODDERATION
AND BLARNEY, OF BRIAN BORU, ESQ. AND HIS ELEGANT FRIEND
SIR SHAWN O'DOGHERTY. EXHIBITING A REAL PICTURE OF
CHARACTERS, MANNERS, &C. IN HIGH AND LOW LIFE, IN DUBLIN
AND VARIOUS PARTS OF IRELAND. EMBELLISHED WITH HUMOR-
OUS COLOURED ENGRAVINGS, FROM ORIGINAL DESIGNS BY THE
MOST EMINENT ARTISTS. BY A REAL PADDY.

> London: Printed by B. Bensley, Bolt Court, Fleet Street. Published by Jones and Co. 3,
> Warwick Square; and J. L. Marks, Piccadilly; and sold by all Booksellers and News-
> men in Town and Country, 1821.
> vii, 296p, ill. 8vo.
> MH-H 21473.51.2.50*; NSTC 2E5909 (BI BL, C, O).

Notes. Before main t.p. there is a t.p. of number 12 of the 'about Twenty-four Weekly Numbers' of Real Life in Ireland, priced at 6d. At top of this t.p. is printed: 'A Sequel to Life in London.' Opp. t.p. (proper), frontispiece with legend at foot: 'Published by Jones & Cº. Janʸ. 28,
1822'. The illustrations throughout have various dates in 1821 and 1822. Collates in fours.
Further edns: 4th edn. 1829 (NSTC); [1850?] (NSTC).


1821: 33    [EGAN, Pierce].
REAL LIFE IN LONDON; OR, THE RAMBLES AND ADVENTURES OF
BOB TALLYHO, ESQ. AND HIS COUSIN, THE HON. TOM DASHALL,
THROUGH THE METROPOLIS; EXHIBITING A LIVING PICTURE OF

FASHIONABLE CHARACTERS, MANNERS, AND AMUSEMENTS IN HIGH AND LOW LIFE. BY AN AMATEUR. EMBELLISHED AND ILLUS-TRATED WITH A SERIES OF COLOURED PRINTS, DESIGNED AND ENGRAVED BY MESSRS. ALKEN, DIGHTON, BROOK, ROWLAND-SON, &C.

London: Printed for Jones & Co. 3, Warwick Square, 1821/22.

I (1821) x, 656p, ill.; II (1822) ix, 668p, ill. 8vo. '28s; l.p., 42s' (ECB).

BL C.70.e.1; ECB 481; NSTC 2E5885 (BI C, O; NA DLC, MH).

*Notes.* T.p. to vol. 2 differs by reading 'Further Adventures' rather than 'Adventures'; addition-ally, 'Heath' is listed as one of the engravers (appearing first). ECB dates *c.* 1825. Collates in fours. Further edns: 1822 (NSTC); 1823 (NSTC); 1824 (NSTC); 1831 (NSTC).

1821: 34    [FOUQUÉ, Friedrich Heinrich Karl, Baron de la Motte]; SOANE, George (*trans.*).
MINSTREL-LOVE; FROM THE GERMAN OF THE AUTHOR OF UNDINE. BY GEORGE SOANE, A.B. IN TWO VOLUMES.

London: Printed for W. Simpkin & R. Marshall, Stationers' Court, 1821.

I lx, 256p; II 380p. 12mo. 12s (ECB); 12s boards (QR).

QR 26: 275 (Oct 1821).

BL 12553.e.17; ECB 213; NSTC 2L2870 (BI O).

*Notes.* Trans. of *Sängerliebe* (Stuttgart, 1816). Dedication by the Translator to Robert G. Pen-nington, Esq. QR lists under 'Poetry'.
Further edns: 1823 (NUC); another trans., 1845 (NSTC).

1821: 35    FRERE, {B}[enjamin].
RANK AND FASHION! OR THE MAZES OF LIFE; A NOVEL, IN THREE VOLUMES. BY MR. FRERE.

London: Printed for William Fearman, Library, 170, New Bond-Street, 1821.

I vi, 288p; II 256p; III 266p. 12mo. 21s (ECB).

ER 36: 279 (Oct 1821).

Corvey; CME 3-628-47840-5; ECB 219; NSTC 2F16467 (BI BL, O; NA MH).

*Notes.* Dedication to 'the Author of Waverly [*sic*]', signed B. Frere.
Further edn: French trans., 1821 [as *L'Aventurier grand seigneur, ou les embarras de la vie* (BLC)].

1821: 36    [GALT, John].
ANNALS OF THE PARISH; OR THE CHRONICLE OF DALMAILING; DURING THE MINISTRY OF THE REV. MICAH BALWHIDDER. WRITTEN BY HIMSELF. ARRANGED AND EDITED BY THE AUTHOR OF "THE AYRSHIRE LEGATEES," &C.

Edinburgh: Printed for William Blackwood; and T. Cadell, Strand, London, 1821.

400p. 12mo. 8s (ECB, ER); 8s boards (QR).

ER 35: 526 (July 1821), 39: 158–96 (Oct 1823) full review; QR 25: 147–53 (Apr 1821) full review, 25: 578 (July 1821); WSW II: 96.

Corvey; CME 3-628-47063-3; ECB 222; NSTC 2G1353 (BI BL, C, E, O; NA DLC, MH).

*Notes.* This is one of twelve novels which are together given full reviews in ER (Oct 1823) under the title 'Secondary Scottish Novels'.
Further edns: 2nd edn. 1822 (NSTC); 1841 (NSTC); 1844 (NSTC); 1845 (NSTC); 1850 (NSTC); Philadelphia 1821 (NSTC); French trans., 1824.

1821: 37   [GALT, John].
THE AYRSHIRE LEGATEES; OR, THE PRINGLE FAMILY. BY THE AUTHOR OF "ANNALS OF THE PARISH," &C.

> Edinburgh: Printed for William Blackwood, and T. Cadell, Strand, London, 1821.
> 303p. 12mo. 7s (ER).
> ER 36: 279, 280 (Oct 1821), 39: 158–96 (Oct 1823) full review; WSW II: 96.
> Corvey; CME 3-628-47088-9; NSTC 2G1357 (BI BL, C, E, O; NA MH).

*Notes.* Page facing t.p. bears the legend 'Originally published in Blackwood's Edinburgh Magazine'. This is one of twelve novels which are together given full reviews in ER (Oct 1823) under the title 'Secondary Scottish Novels'.
Further edns: 2nd edn. (with *The Gathering of the West*) 1823 (NSTC); 1841 (with *Annals of the Parish*) (NSTC); 1850 (NSTC); New York 1823 (NSTC); German trans., 1823 [as *Die Erben, ein Familiengemälde* (RS)].

1821: 38   GASCOIGNE, Henry Barnet.
SYMPATHY IN SEARCH OF PEACE AT HOME: A NOVEL OF A NOVEL KIND—A TALE OF THE TIMES, FROM CARLTON HOUSE TO THE POORHOUSE—AN EVENING'S AMUSEMENT FOR YOURSELF AND FRIENDS, AT WHICH EVERY ONE IS INVITED TO LAUGH, BUT NO ONE OBLIGED TO CRY. BY HENRY BARNET GASCOIGNE.

> London: Published by John Robinson, Paternoster-Row; and to be had of all Book-sellers, 1821.
> xi, 276p. 12mo. 5s boards (ECB, ER).
> ER 36: 280 (Oct 1821); WSW II: 100.
> BL 12611.cc.12; ECB 224; NSTC 2G3149 (BI C).

*Notes.* Dedication to 'William Wilberforce, Esq. M.P.', dated Rugby, Warwickshire, 10 Apr 1821.

1821: 39   [GASPEY, Thomas].
CALTHORPE; OR, FALLEN FORTUNES: A NOVEL. BY THE AUTHOR OF THE MYSTERY; OR, FORTY YEARS AGO. IN THREE VOLUMES.

> London: Printed for Longman, Hurst, Rees, Orme, and Brown, Paternoster-Row, 1821.
> I vi, 324p; II 295p; III 345p. 12mo. 21s (ECB); 21s boards (ER, QR).
> ER 35: 265 (Mar 1821); QR 24: 571 (Jan 1821); WSW II: 100.
> Corvey; CME 3-628-47183-4; ECB 93; NSTC 2G3281 (BI BL, C, E; NA MH).

*Notes.* Further edns: Philadelphia 1821 (NSTC); French trans., 1821; German trans., 1823.

GOLLAND, Mrs. C. D.
See HAYNES, Miss C. D.

1821: 40   GORDON, Alexander.
MACGRIGOR AND CLARENDON, OR THE RECLUSE LOVERS. A
NOVEL. BY ALEXANDER GORDON.

> Aberdeen: Printed by D. Chalmers and Co. Adelphi Court, Union Street, 1821.
> 192p. 12mo.
> MH-H 18488.7.10*; NSTC 2G14328 (BI E).

1821: 41   GRIFFIN, James.
THE FREEBOOTER OF THE ALPS. A ROMANCE. IN TWO VOLUMES.
BY JAMES GRIFFIN.

> London: Printed for A. K. Newman and Co. Leadenhall-Street, 1821.
> I 254p; II 248p. 12mo. 11s (ECB, ER).
> ER 36: 280 (Oct 1821).
> Corvey; CME 3-628-47914-2; ECB 246; NSTC 2G22671 (BI BL, C).

1821: 42   HALES, [J]. M. H.
DE WILLENBERG; OR, THE TALISMAN. A TALE OF MYSTERY. IN
FOUR VOLUMES. BY I. M. H. HALES, ESQ. AUTHOR OF THE
ASTROLOGER.

> London: Printed for A. K. Newman and Co. Leadenhall-Street, 1821.
> I iv, 249p; II 271p; III 243p; IV 236p. 12mo. 22s (ECB, ER, QR).
> ER 36: 280 (Oct 1821); QR 26: 275 (Oct 1821).
> Corvey; CME 3-628-47591-0; ECB 250; NSTC 2H2238 (BI BL, C).

*Notes.* Further edn: French trans., 1827.

1821: 43   [HATTON, Anne Julia Kemble].
LOVERS AND FRIENDS; OR, MODERN ATTACHMENTS. A NOVEL.
IN FIVE VOLUMES. BY ANNE OF SWANSEA, AUTHOR OF CONVIC-
TION, GONZOLA DE BALDIVIA, CHRONICLES OF AN ILLUSTRIOUS
HOUSE, SECRET AVENGERS, SECRETS IN EVERY MANSION, CAM-
BRIAN PICTURES, CESARIO ROSALBA, &C. &C.

> London: Printed at the Minerva Press for A. K. Newman and Co. Leadenhall-Street,
> 1821.
> I viii, 257p; II 286p; III 321p; IV 319p; V 315p. 12mo. 27s 6d (ECB).
> WSW II: 108.
> Corvey; CME 3-628-48804-4; ECB 20; NSTC 2A13194 (BI BL, C).

*Notes.* Dedication to John Edmin, Esq., signed College-Street, Swansea, 10 July 1820. ECB
dates Nov 1820.

1821: 44   HAWKINS, Lætitia Matilda.
HERALINE; OR, OPPOSITE PROCEEDINGS. BY LÆTITIA-MATILDA
HAWKINS. IN FOUR VOLUMES.

> London: Printed for F. C. and J. Rivington, Waterloo Place, Pall-Mall, and St. Paul's
> Churchyard; and T. Hookham, Old Bond Street, 1821.

I iv, 362p; II 362p; III 349p; IV 408p. 12mo. 32s (ECB, ER, QR).
ER 36: 279 (Oct 1821); QR 25: 578 (July 1821); WSW II: 108.
BL 12613.bbb.21; ECB 259; NSTC 2H13208 (BI C, O).

*Notes.* Dedication 'to Her Royal Highness the Duchess of Gloucester'.
Further edn: 2nd edn. 1821 (Corvey), CME 3-628-47541-4.

1821: 45   HAYNES, Miss C. D. [afterwards GOLLAND, Mrs. C. D.].
ELEANOR; OR, THE SPECTRE OF ST. MICHAEL'S. A ROMANTIC
TALE. IN FIVE VOLUMES. BY MISS C. D. HAYNES, AUTHOR OF CAS-
TLE LE BLANC; FOUNDLING OF DEVONSHIRE; AUGUSTUS AND
ADELINA, &C. &C.

London: Printed at the Minerva Press for A. K. Newman and Co. Leadenhall-Street,
1821.
I 276p; II 257p; III 259p; IV 246p; V 278p. 12mo. 27s 6d (ECB, ER).
ER 34: 509 (Nov 1820).
Corvey; CME 3-628-47716-6; ECB 260; NSTC 2H14180 (BI BL, C).

*Notes.* ECB also dates Nov 1820.
Further edn: French trans., 1824 [as *Le Spectre de Saint-Michel, ou les deux Éléonore* (BN)].

1821: 46   HENRY, Alexander.
ROLANDO: A ROMANCE. BY ALEXANDER HENRY, ESQ. IN TWO
VOLUMES.

London: Printed by A. J. Valpy, Tooke's-Court, Chancery-Lane, for A. K. Newman and
Co. Leadenhall-Street, 1821.
I 215p; II 207p. 12mo. 10s (ECB, ER).
ER 36: 280 (Oct 1821).
Corvey; CME 3-628-47778-6; ECB 264; NSTC 2H17522 (BI BL).

*Notes.* Collates in sixes.

1821: 47   HERON, Mrs.
CONVERSATION; OR, SHADES OF DIFFERENCE. A NOVEL. IN
THREE VOLUMES. BY MRS. HERON.

London: Printed for A. K. Newman and Co. Leadenhall-Street, 1821.
I 236p; II 238p; III 219p. 12mo. 16s 6d (ECB, ER).
ER 36: 570 (Feb 1822).
Corvey; CME 3-628-47886-3; ECB 266; NSTC 2H18810 (BI BL, C, O).

1821: 48   HOOLE, Innes.
SCENES AT BRIGHTON; OR, "HOW MUCH?" A SATIRICAL NOVEL.
IN THREE VOLUMES. BY INNES HOOLE, ESQ. AUTHOR OF SOCIETY
AND SOLITUDE, &C.

London: Printed for A. K. Newman and Co. Leadenhall-Street, 1821.
I 222p; II 203p; III 197p. 12mo. 15s (ECB); 15s boards (ER).
ER 36: 279 (Oct 1821).
Corvey; CME 3-628-47693-3; ECB 280; NSTC 2H29445 (BI BL, C, O; NA MH).

1821: 49   HOOLE, Innes.
SOCIETY AND SOLITUDE. A NOVEL. IN THREE VOLUMES. BY
INNES HOOLE, ESQ.

> London: Printed for A. K. Newman and Co. Leadenhall-Street, 1821.
> I 206p; II 194p; III 203p. 12mo. 15s (ECB, ER, QR).
> ER 35: 266 (Mar 1821); QR 24: 571 (Jan 1821).
> Corvey; CME 3-628-47694-1; ECB 280; NSTC 2H29446 (BI BL, C, E, O).

1821: 50   [JOHNSON, Arthur].
DINAN. A ROMANCE.

> London: Printed for G. and W. B. Whittaker, Ave Maria Lane, 1821.
> 114p. 12mo. 3s 6d (ER, QR).
> ER 36: 570 (Feb 1822); QR 26: 544 (Jan 1822).
> Corvey; CME 3-628-47435-3; NSTC 2J8096 (BI BL, C, O; NA MH).

*Notes.* Collates in sixes.

1821: 51   [JONES, Hannah Maria].
GRETNA GREEN; OR, THE ELOPEMENT OF MISS D—— WITH A
GALLANT SON OF MARS. FOUNDED ON RECENT FACTS.

> London: Published by George Virtue, 6, Panyer Alley, Paternoster Row. Printed by
>    C. Baynes, Cook's Court, Carey Street, 1821.
> 694p, ill. 8vo.
> BL 012638.r.28; NSTC 2J10429 (BI E).

*Notes.* Additional engraved t.p. [n.d.], with variant London imprint: 'Published by J. Tallis,
16, Warwick Squᵉ. Newgate Street'. Collates in fours.
Further edns: 1823 (NSTC); 1836 (NSTC).

1821: 52   KELLY, Mrs.
THE FATALISTS; OR, RECORDS OF 1814 AND 1815. A NOVEL. IN FIVE
VOLUMES. BY MRS. KELLY, AUTHOR OF THE MATRON OF ERIN, &C.

> London: Printed for A. K. Newman and Co. Leadenhall-Street, 1821.
> I ii, 275p; II 265p; III 291p; IV 294p; V 301p. 12mo. 27s 6d (ECB, ER).
> ER 35: 525 (July 1821).
> Corvey; CME 3-628-48008-6; ECB 317; NSTC 2K2012 (BI BL, C, O).

1821: 53   {KELLY, Richard N.}.
DE RENZEY; OR, THE MAN OF SORROW. WRITTEN BY HIMSELF,
EDITED BY HIS NEPHEW. IN THREE VOLUMES.

> London: Printed for W. Simpkin and R. Marshall, Stationer's Court, Ludgate-Street,
>    1821.
> I 202p; II 245p; III 286p. 12mo. 15s (ECB, ER); 15s boards (ER, QR).
> ER 35: 526 (July 1821), 36: 571 (Feb 1822); QR 25: 276 (Apr 1821); WSW II: 127.
> Corvey; CME 3-628-48565-7; ECB 317; xNSTC.

*Notes.* Dedication to Lady Morgan, signed Richard N. Kelly, Dublin, 18 Jan 1821.

1821:54    [KELTY, Mary Ann].
**THE FAVOURITE OF NATURE. A TALE. IN THREE VOLUMES.**

> London: Printed for G. and W. B. Whittaker, Ave-Maria-Lane, 1821.
>
> I iv, 366p; II 414p; III 383p. 12mo. 21s (ECB); 21s boards (ER).
>
> ER 35: 525 (July 1821); WSW II: 128.
>
> Corvey; CME 3-628-47503-1; ECB 201; NSTC 2K2397 (BI BL, C, Dt, E, O; NA MH).

*Notes.* Dedication to Joanna Baillie.

Further edns: 2nd edn. 1821 (NSTC); 3rd edn. 1822 (NSTC); 4th edn. 1840 (NUC); French trans., 1823 [as *Éliza Rivers, ou la favorite de la nature* (BN)].


1821:55    [LESTER, Elizabeth B.].
**THE WOMAN OF GENIUS. IN THREE VOLUMES.**

> London: Printed for Longman, Hurst, Rees, Orme, and Brown, Paternoster-Row, 1821/22.
>
> I (1821) 227p; II (1821) 230p; III (1822) 207p. 12mo. 16s 6d (ECB); 16s (ER, QR).
>
> ER 36: 570 (Feb 1822); QR 26: 544 (Jan 1822); WSW II: 41.
>
> Corvey; CME 3-628-48975-X; ECB 645; NSTC 2W29105 (BI BL, C, O; NA MH).

*Notes.* List of 'Popular Novels' by Longmans at end of vol. 2 in the Corvey copy of *Fire-side Scenes* (1825: 52) has this title as 'By the Author of the "Bachelor and Married Man"'. For attribution of this chain of novels to Elizabeth Lester, rather than to Mrs Ross, see note to *The Bachelor and the Married Man* (1817: 37).

Further edn: German trans., 1823 [as *Die genialischen Frauen, oder Geheimnisse liebender Herzen.* (RS)].


1821:56    [LOCKHART, John Gibson].
**VALERIUS; A ROMAN STORY. IN THREE VOLUMES.**

> Edinburgh: Printed for William Blackwood, and T. Cadell, Strand, London, 1821.
>
> I 311p; II 347p; III 312p. 12mo. 24s (ECB, ER, QR).
>
> ER 35: 266 (Mar 1821), 35: 525 (July 1821), 39: 158–96 (Oct 1823) full review; QR 25: 276 (Apr 1821); WSW II: 136.
>
> Corvey; CME 3-628-48852-4; ECB 609; NSTC 2L19491 (BI BL, C, E, O; NA MH).

*Notes.* This is one of twelve novels which are together given full reviews in ER (Oct 1823) under the title 'Secondary Scottish Novels'.

Further edns: New edn. 1842 (NSTC); Boston 1821 (NSTC).


1821:57    M'LEOD, Miss [E. H.].
**TALES OF TON; THE FIRST SERIES; CONTAINING FASHIONABLE CHARACTERS. A NOVEL. IN FOUR VOLUMES. BY MISS M'LEOD.**

> London: Printed for A. K. Newman and Co. Leadenhall-Street, 1821.
>
> I iii, 250p; II 327p; III 344p; IV 380p. 12mo. 24s (ER, QR).
>
> ER 35: 266 (Mar 1821); QR 24: 571 (Jan 1821); WSW II: 140.
>
> Corvey; CME 3-628-48087-6; ECB 361; NSTC 2M7092 (BI BL, C, E, O).

*Notes.* ECB lists three series, price 72s.

1821: 58   M'LEOD, Miss [E. H.].
### TALES OF TON; THE SECOND SERIES. BY MISS M'LEOD. IN FOUR VOLUMES.

London: Printed for A. K. Newman and Co. Leadenhall-Street, 1821.
I 307p; II 274p; III 320p; IV 314p. 12mo. 24s boards (ER).
ER 35: 526 (July 1821).
Corvey; CME 3-628-48087-6; ECB 361; NSTC 2M7092 (BI BL, C, E, O).

*Notes.* ECB lists three series, price 72s.

1821: 59   MARSHAL, Thomas Henry.
### THE IRISH NECROMANCER; OR, DEER PARK. A NOVEL. IN THREE VOLUMES. BY THOMAS HENRY MARSHAL.

London: Printed for A. K. Newman and Co. Leadenhall-Street, 1821.
I 250p; II 243p; III 225p. 12mo. 16s 6d (ECB, QR); 16s 6d boards (ER).
ER 35: 526 (July 1821); QR 25: 276 (Apr 1821).
Corvey; CME 3-628-48092-2; ECB 300; NSTC 2M16082 (BI BL, C, E, O).

*Notes.* Further edns: French trans., 1824; German trans., 1824 [as *Der irländische Schwarzkünstler und die Giftmischerin* (RS)].

1821: 60   [MOORE, Alicia].
### THE SISTERS: A NOVEL, IN FOUR VOLUMES.

London: Printed for Baldwin, Cradock, and Joy, Paternoster-Row, 1821.
I 284p; II 236p; III 244p; IV 248p. 8vo. 28s (ECB, ER).
ER 36: 279 (Oct 1821); WSW II: 150.
Corvey; CME 3-628-48748-X; ECB 540; NSTC 2M34520 (BI BL, C).

*Notes.* Later printed in 1854 as *Rosalind and Felicia; or, The Sisters* (NSTC 2S23167).

1821: 61   [?OPIE, Amelia Alderson].
### THE ONLY CHILD; OR, PORTIA BELLENDEN. A TALE.

London: J. Ebers, 27, Old Bond Street, 1821.
326p. 12mo. 7s 6d boards (ER, QR).
ER 35: 266 (Mar 1821); QR 24: 572 (Jan 1821); WSW II: 26.
Corvey; CME 3-628-48257-7; NSTC 2B16619 (BI BL).

*Notes.* Dedication to the Marquis of Lansdowne. In an unpublished letter of 21 June 1839 to Sir John Gurney, Amelia Opie apparently acknowledges this work: 'I got 100 L for ye novel— *the only child*'. This letter, which also refers to a dedication to Lord Lansdowne, is in the possession of Paula R. Feldman of the University of South Carolina.

1821: 62   PORTER, Anna Maria.
### THE VILLAGE OF MARIENDORPT. A TALE. BY MISS ANNA MARIA PORTER, AUTHOR OF THE FAST OF ST. MAGDALEN, KNIGHT OF ST. JOHN, &C. &C. &C. IN FOUR VOLUMES.

London: Printed for Longman, Hurst, Rees, Orme, and Brown, Paternoster-Row, 1821.
I vi, 303p; II 336p; III 313p; IV 455p. 12mo. 28s (ECB, ER, QR).

ER 35: 266 (Mar 1821); QR 24: 571 (Jan 1821); WSW II: 163.

Corvey; CME 3-628-48305-0; ECB 464; NSTC 2P22260 (BI BL, NCu, O; NA DLC, MH).

*Notes.* Dedication to 'the principal Inhabitants of Long-Ditton and Thames-Ditton', dated Long-Ditton, Dec 1820.

Further edns: Boston 1821 (NSTC); French trans., 1821.

1821: 63    RICHARDSON, Charlotte Caroline.
THE SOLDIER'S CHILD: OR, VIRTUE TRIUMPHANT. A NOVEL. BY
CHARLOTTE CAROLINE RICHARDSON, AUTHOR OF "HARVEST, A
POEM:" ALSO OF "ISAAC AND REBECCA; AND OTHER POEMS." IN
TWO VOLUMES.

London: Printed for J. Robinson, Paternoster Row, 1821.
I 303p; II 300p. 12mo. 12s (ECB); 12s boards (ER).
ER 36: 280 (Oct 1821); WSW II: 168.
Corvey; CME 3-628-48575-4; ECB 492; NSTC 2R9457 (BI BL, C).

1821: 64    [SCOTT, Sir Walter].
KENILWORTH; A ROMANCE. BY THE AUTHOR OF "WAVERLEY,"
"IVANHOE," &C. IN THREE VOLUMES.

Edinburgh: Printed for Archibald Constable and Co.; and John Ballantyne; and Hurst,
Robinson, and Co., London, 1821.
I 320p; II 339p; III 348p. 8vo. 31s 6d (ECB, QR); 31s 6d boards (ER).
ER 35: 265 (Mar 1821); QR 24: 571 (Jan 1821), 26: 109–48 (Oct 1821) full review; WSW
II: 173–4.
Corvey; CME 3-628-48582-7; ECB 318; NSTC 2S9760 (BI BL, C, DE, E, NCu, O; NA
DLC, MH).

*Notes.* 'This day published', 8 Jan 1821, *Edinburgh Evening Courant.* This is one of eight
novels by Scott which are together given full reviews in QR (Oct 1821).

Further edns: 2nd edn. 1821 (NSTC); Philadelphia 1821 (NSTC); French trans., 1821 [as *Le
Château de Kenilworth* (BN)]; German trans., 1821. Numerous reprintings in collected edns.

1821: 65    SIDNEY, Philip Francis.
THE RULING PASSION. A COMIC STORY, OF THE SIXTEENTH CEN-
TURY. REVIVED, REVISED, AND EDITED, BY PHILIP FRANCIS SID-
NEY, AUTHOR OF "THE HERMIT IN YORK," AND VARIOUS OTHER
POPULAR WORKS. IN THREE VOLUMES.

York: Printed for the Proprietors of the Hull Packet, Hull, 1821.
I xii, 252p; II viii, 269p; III vii, 252p. 12mo.
BL N.2749; NSTC 2S21036.

*Notes.* Introduction, dated Jan 1821, mentions 'an old Work, entitled "The Force of Blood"',
in a Cervantesque style, which is 're-edited' here.

1821: 66    SMITH, Charlotte.
THE REPUBLICAN'S MISTRESS; A NOVEL FOUNDED UPON FACTS.
BY CHARLOTTE SMITH. IN THREE VOLUMES.

London: Printed for W. Wright, Fleet-Street, 1821.
I 286p; II 287p; III 345p. 12mo. 18s (ECB, ER, QR).
ER 35: 525 (July 1821); QR 25: 276 (Apr 1821).
Corvey; CME 3-628-48661-0; ECB 544; NSTC 2S25620 (BI BL).

*Notes.* Sometimes ascribed to Charlotte (Turner) Smith, 1749–1806, but more probably the work of another author.

1821: 67 SOUZA[-BOTELHO], [Adélaide-Marie-Émilie Filleul, Marquise de Flahaut].
**HELEN DE TOURNON: A NOVEL. BY MADAME DE SOUZA. TRANS-LATED FROM THE FRENCH. IN TWO VOLUMES.**

London: Printed for Longman, Hurst, Rees, Orme, and Brown, Paternoster-Row, 1821.
I 269p; II 263p. 12mo. 10s 6d (ECB); 10s 6d boards (ER, QR).
ER 35: 266 (Mar 1821); QR 24: 571 (Jan 1821).
BL N.368; ECB 552; NSTC 2F7815 (BI C).

*Notes.* Trans. of *Mademoiselle de Tournon* (vol. 6 of *Oeuvres Complètes*, Paris, 1821–2). Further edn: Boston 1822 (NUC).

1821: 68 STANHOPE, Louisa Sidney.
**THE FESTIVAL OF MORA. AN HISTORICAL ROMANCE. BY LOUISA SIDNEY STANHOPE, AUTHOR OF MONTBRAZIL ABBEY, THE BAN-DIT'S BRIDE, THE CRUSADERS, &C. &C. &C. IN FOUR VOLUMES.**

London: Printed for John Richardson, Royal Exchange, 1821.
I 291p; II 284p; III 277p; IV 258p. 12mo. 24s (ECB); 24s boards (ER).
ER 36: 570 (Feb 1822).
Corvey; CME 3-628-48776-5; ECB 558; NSTC 2S36109 (BI BL, C; NA MH).

*Notes.* Further edn: 2nd edn. 1824 (NUC).

1821: 69 {STERNDALE, Mary}.
**THE LIFE OF A BOY. BY THE AUTHOR OF THE PANORAMA OF YOUTH. IN TWO VOLUMES.**

London: Printed for G. and W. B. Whittaker, Ave-Maria-Lane, 1821.
I vii, 432p; II 453p. 12mo. 14s (ECB, ER).
ER 36: 279 (Oct 1821).
Corvey; CME 3-628-48050-7; ECB 563; NSTC 2S41197 (BI BL, C, O; NA MH).

*Notes.* Dedication to the Countess of Besborough, signed Mary Sterndale, Sheffield, May 1821. ECB mistakenly lists as by Mary Stockdale.

1821: 70 TAYLOR, [Ann].
**RETROSPECTION: A TALE. BY MRS. TAYLOR, OF ONGAR, AUTHOR OF "MATERNAL SOLICITUDE," &C. &C.**

London: Printed for Taylor and Hessey, Fleet Street, 1821.
230p, ill. 12mo.
WSW II: 192–3.
Corvey; CME 3-628-48944-X; NSTC 2T3029 (BI BL; NA MH).

*Notes.* Further edns: 2nd edn. 1822 (NSTC); 3rd edn. 1823 (NSTC); 4th edn. 1823 (NSTC); 1830 (NSTC); Philadelphia 1822 (NSTC).

1821: 71   [?TAYLOR, Jane].
**PRUDENCE AND PRINCIPLE: A TALE. BY THE AUTHOR OF "RACHEL," AND "THE AUTHORESS."**

> London: Printed for Taylor and Hessey, Fleet Street, 1821.
> vii, 213p, ill. 12mo.
> WSW II: 29.
> BL 1152.e.8; NSTC 2P28313 (BI C, O).

*Notes.* For arguments in favour of Jane Taylor's authorship of *Rachel* and *The Authoress*, see 1819: 67. This title, though not usually associated with her, apparently forms part of the same group.
Further edn: Wellington [Salop] [1823?] (NSTC).

1821: 72   THORNTON, Alfred.
**DON JUAN. VOLUME THE FIRST. BY ALFRED THORNTON, ESQ. WITH FIFTEEN COLOURED ENGRAVINGS.**

> London: Printed for Thomas Kelly, 17 Paternoster-Row, 1821/22.
> I (1821) xii, 619p, ill.; II (1822) xi, 660p, ill. 8vo.
> DLC PR.5670.T65D7; ECB 588; NSTC 2T10996 (NA MH).

*Notes.* T.p. of vol. 2 differs as follows: 'Don Juan; Volume the Second: containing his Life in London, or, a true Picture of the British Metropolis. By Alfred Thornton, Esq. with coloured Engravings. London: Printed for Thomas Kelly, 17, Paternoster-Row, 1822'. Collates in fours. ECB dates 1825–36.
Further edn: 1825–36 (NSTC).

1821: 73   WARD, Catherine G[eorge].
**THE ORPHAN BOY, OR TEST OF INNOCENCE. BY MRS CATHERINE G. WARD, AUTHORESS OF "THE ROSE OF CLAREMONT;" "MYSTERIOUS MARRIAGE;" "MY NATIVE LAND;" "DAUGHTER OF ST. OMER;" "SACRED DEPOSIT;" "BACHELOR'S HEIRESS;" "ROBERTINA;" "POEMS;" &C. &C. &C. &C.**

> London: Published by G. Virtue, 6, Canon Row, Westminster; W. S. Couchman, 10, Throg-
>    morton Street; and J. S. Wellington, 1, Dufour's Place, Broad Street, Golden Square, 1821.
> 768p, ill. 8vo.
> BL N.2008; NSTC 2W4967 (BI C, Dt, O).

*Notes.* 'Founded on Fact' printed at head of t.p., and 'Entered at Stationer's Hall' above publisher's imprint. Collates in fours.
Further edns: 1822 (NUC); 1825 (NSTC); 1846 (NUC); New York 1835 (NSTC).

1821: 74   WENTWORTH, Zara.
**THE HERMIT'S CAVE; OR, THE FUGITIVE'S RETREAT. A ROMANCE. IN FOUR VOLUMES: BY ZARA WENTWORTH, AUTHOR OF THE RECLUSE OF ALBYN HALL, &C.**

London: Printed for A. K. Newman and Co. Leadenhall-Street, 1821.
I 225p; II 239p; III 221p; IV 247p. 12mo. 20s (ECB, ER).
ER 36: 279 (Oct 1821).
Corvey; CME 3-628-48885-0; ECB 629; NSTC 2W12929 (BI BL, C).

1821: 75(a)    WICKENDEN, W[illiam] S.
**BLEDDYN; A WELCH NATIONAL TALE. BY W. S. WICKENDEN, THE BARD OF THE FOREST, AUTHOR OF "COUNT GLARUS OF SWITZERLAND."**

London: Printed for Baldwin, Cradock, and Joy, Paternoster-Row, 1821.
I viii, 120p; II 115p. 12mo.
WSW II: 202.
AWn 620.g.I.25.B64; xNSTC.

*Notes.* 'Names of Subscribers' (95 listed), vol. 1, pp. [v]–viii. Adv. on verso of vol. 2, p. 115, for *Count Glarus of Switzerland*, 'By the same Author'. Colophon in both vols: 'Printed by J. Nichols and Son, 25, Parliament Street, Westminster'.

1821: 75(b)    WICKENDEN, W[illiam] S.
**BLEDDYN; A WELCH NATIONAL TALE, BEING THE FIRST OF A SERIES. BY W. S. WICKENDEN, THE BARD OF THE FOREST, AUTHOR OF "COUNT GLARUS OF SWITZERLAND."**

London: Published for the author, by C. Chapple, Royal Library, Pall-Mall, 1821.
235p. 12mo. 7s (ER).
ER 35: 526 (July 1821); WSW II: 202.
Corvey; CME 3-628-48968-7; ECB 636; NSTC 2W19033 (BI BL).

*Notes.* Lacks the subscription list found in copy above. Colophon reads: 'Printed by J. Nichols and Son, 25, Parliament Street, Westminster'. These appear to be identical sheets to those used for the 2 volumed-version above, apart from the continuous pagination.

# 1822

1822: 1    ANON.
**AGNES; OR, THE TRIUMPH OF PRINCIPLE.**

London: Printed by J. S. Hughes, 66, Paternoster Row; published by B. J. Holdsworth, 18, (South Side,) St. Paul's Church Yard; and sold by Waugh and Innes, Edinburgh; and Chalmers and Collins, Glasgow, 1822.
iv, 272p. 12mo. 6s (ECB).
WSW II: 3.
Corvey; CME 3-628-47027-7; ECB 8; NSTC 2A5159 (BI C).

*Notes.* ECB dates Feb 1822.

1822: 2   ANON.

BLIGHTED AMBITION; OR, THE RISE AND FALL OF THE EARL OF SOMERSET. A ROMANCE, IN THREE VOLUMES.

London: Printed for G. and W. B. Whittaker, 13, Ave-Maria-Lane, 1822.
I x, 334p; II 368p; III 407p. 12mo. 21s (ECB, ER).
ER 37: 280 (June 1822); WSW II: 5.
Corvey; CME 3-628-47230-X; ECB 61; NSTC 2B37807 (BI BL, C; NA MH).

1822: 3   ANON.

THE BLUE MOUNTAINS. A WEST-INDIAN TALE. IN THREE VOL-UMES. BY THE AUTHOR OF ROMANTIC FACTS, OR WHICH IS HIS WIFE? VERONICA, OR THE MYSTERIOUS STRANGER; MY OLD COUSIN, &C.

London: Printed for A. K. Newman and Co. Leadenhall-Street, 1822.
I vi, 267p; II 243p; III 232p. 12mo. 16s 6d (ECB).
WSW II: 5.
Corvey; CME 3-628-47232-6; ECB 63; NSTC 2B38463 (BI BL, C, O).

*Notes.* Dedication to S. Jenyns Soame, Esq., dated 2 Nov 1821. For a possible connection with the pseudonym 'Lister', see 1816: 10. ECB dates June 1822.

1822: 4   ANON.

THE COURT OF HOLYROOD; FRAGMENTS OF AN OLD STORY.

Edinburgh: Macredie, Skelly, & Co. 34 Princes Street; and T. & G. Underwood, Fleet Street, London, 1822.
v, 194p. 12mo. 5s (ECB).
WSW II: 8.
MH-H 19463.12.10*; ECB 139; NSTC 2H27596.

*Notes.* Preface, suggesting that the imminent publication of Scott's *The Abbot* motivated the return to a tale 'sketched some years ago', is signed 'the Authors'. ECB dates Aug 1822. Collates in sixes.
Further edns: 2nd edn. 1822 (Corvey), CME 3-628-47343-8; 3rd edn. 1825 (NSTC).

DANGEROUS ERRORS

See BARBER, Elizabeth

1822: 5   ANON.

THE DAYS OF QUEEN MARY; OR, A TALE OF THE FIFTEENTH CEN-TURY.

London: Printed for the Author; and published by Longman, Hurst, Rees, Orme, & Brown. Paternoster-Row, 1822.
iv, 239p. 12mo. 5s boards (ER); 5s (QR).
ER 39: 512 (Jan 1824); QR 28: 269 (Oct 1822); WSW II: 8.
Corvey; CME 3-628-47379-9; xNSTC.

1822: 6　ANON.

**THE FRENCH PROTESTANT; A TALE. BY THE AUTHOR OF THE "ITALIAN CONVERT," "VICAR OF IVER," &C. &C.**

> London: Printed for Francis Westley, 10 Stationers'-Court, and Ave-Maria-Lane, 1822.
> 144p. 12mo.
> WSW II: 12.
> IU 823.F.888; NSTC 2F16234 (BI BL).

*Notes.* The same author's *The Italian Convert, a Narrative, Founded on Fact* (1821), a shorter piece (70 pp.) also published by Westley, is not entered separately.

1822: 7　ANON.

**LEMIRA OF LORRAINE. A ROMANCE. IN THREE VOLUMES.**

> London: Printed for G. and W. B. Whittaker, Ave Maria Lane, 1822.
> I 272p; II 255p; III 260p. 12mo. 28s (ECB); 18s (ER).
> ER 36: 570 (Feb 1822); WSW II: 19.
> Corvey; CME 3-628-47952-5; ECB 338; NSTC 2L11106 (BI BL, C).

1822: 8　ANON.

**MARIA; A TALE OF A SOUTHERN VALLEY: FOUNDED ON REAL EVENTS IN HIGH LIFE.**

> London: Printed for W. Wright, 46, Fleet-Street, 1822.
> vii, 166p. 12mo.
> WSW II: 22.
> Corvey; CME 3-628-48154-6; NSTC 2M14251 (BI C).

*Notes.* Under title t.p. reads in smaller letters: 'The hero of the tale is an officer of high rank in the army, and Maria, a lady of noble birth'. Frontispiece illustration, with legend 'Published by W. Wright, 49, Fleet Steet, July 1822'.

1822: 9　ANON.

**NO ENTHUSIASM; A TALE OF THE PRESENT TIMES. IN TWO VOLUMES.**

> London: Printed for Francis Westley, 10, Stationers' Court, 1822.
> I 317p; II 298p. 8vo.
> WSW II: 25.
> Corvey; CME 3-628-48295-X; NSTC 2E10856 (BI BL).

1822: 10　ANON.

**REFORMATION: A NOVEL. IN THREE VOLUMES.**

> London: Printed for Longman, Hurst, Rees, Orme, and Brown, Paternoster-Row, 1822.
> I 362p; II 303p; III 333p. 12mo. 18s (ECB, ER).
> ER 38: 522 (May 1823); WSW II: 30.
> Corvey; CME 3-628-48523-1; ECB 484; NSTC 2R5611 (BI BL, C).

1822: 11　ANON.

**TALES, BY AN UNWILLING AUTHOR.**

> Dublin: Richard Milliken, Grafton-Street, Bookseller to his Majesty, his Royal Highness

the Duke of Clarence, his Excellency the Lord Lieutenant, and the University of
Dublin, 1822.

I iv, 263p; II 224p. 12mo. 10s 6d (ECB, ER, QR).

ER 42: 513 (Aug 1825); QR 32: 549 (Oct 1825); WSW II: 36.

MH-H 19464.29.5*; ECB 575; NSTC 2T1324 (BI BL, C, E).

*Notes.* 'To the Reader' dated Feb 1818. 'Subscribers' Names' (*c.*65 listed), 4 pp. unn., at end
of vol. 2.

Further edn: reissued with Longmans as main publishers, London 1825 (Corvey), CME 3-
628-48866-4.

1822: 12    ANON.
**TALES FROM SWITZERLAND.**

London: Printed for Francis Westley, 10, Stationers' Court, and Ave-Maria Lane; and
L. B. Seeley, 169 Fleet Street, 1822/23.

I (1822) viii, 177p; II (1823) 196p, ill.; III (1823) 221p, ill. 12mo. 10s (ECB).

Corvey; CME 3-628-51161-5; ECB 575; NSTC 2Y1229 (BI BL, C, E, O; NA MH).

*Notes.* Attributed in some catalogues to A. Yosy, possibly as a result of Ann Yosy's authorship
of *Switzerland* [. . .] *interspersed with historical anecdotes* (2 vols., 1815); see also 'Tales from
Afar' (1824: 13). Vol. 3 has 'Third Series' on t.p.

1822: 13    ANON.
**THE VILLAGE COQUETTE; A NOVEL, IN THREE VOLUMES. BY THE
AUTHOR OF "SUCH IS THE WORLD."**

London: Printed for G. and W. B. Whittaker, Ave-Maria-Lane, 1822.

I vii, 278p; II 247p; III 236p. 12mo. 18s (ECB, ER, QR).

ER 36: 571 (Feb 1822); QR 26: 544 (Jan 1822); WSW II: 40.

Corvey; CME 3-628-48918-0; ECB 613; NSTC 2V4200 (BI BL, C).

*Notes.* Preface signed F. J., Kensington, Dec 1821.

1822: 14    ANON.
**WHICH IS THE HEROINE? IN TWO VOLUMES.**

London: J. Robins and Co. Ivy Lane, Paternoster Row, 1822.

I 255p; II 219p. 12mo. 12s (ECB).

WSW II: 41.

Corvey; CME 3-628-48900-8; ECB 633; xNSTC.

*Notes.* ECB dates Nov 1822.

1822: 15    AIMWELL, Miss [pseud.].
**GOOD-NATURE: OR, SENSIBILITY: AND OTHER TALES. BY MISS
AIMWELL. IN THREE VOLUMES.**

London: Printed for A. K. Newman and Co. Leadenhall-Street, 1822.

I 271p; II 277p; III 258p. 12mo. 16s 6d (ECB, ER, QR).

ER 36: 570 (Feb 1822); QR 26: 275 (Oct 1821).

Corvey; CME 3-628-47029-3; ECB 9; NSTC 2A5708 (BI BL, C, Dt, O).

*Notes.* ECB dates Dec 1821.

1822: 16    ARLINCOURT, [Charles] Vicomte d'.
**THE RENEGADE, TRANSLATED FROM THE FRENCH OF M. LE VICOMTE D'ARLINCOURT.**

>London: J. Robins and Co. Ivy Lane, Paternoster Row, 1822.
>I viii, 256p; II 272p. 8vo. 12s (ECB).
>BL 1152.i.17; ECB 152; NSTC 2A15599.

*Notes.* Trans. of *Le Renégat* (Paris, 1822). Preface begins: 'The interesting nature of this novel, and the eloquence of its descriptions, no less than its great popularity at this moment, are the reasons which have caused it to be presented to the public in an English dress. The avidity with which the first copies were bought up in Paris is almost unexampled. Four editions were published in immediate succession, and it still continues in the highest esteem' (vol. 1, p. [v]). ECB dates Mar 1822.
Further edns: 1826 (NSTC); New York 1822 (NSTC) [also Philadelphia & New York 1822 (NSTC)].

1822: 17    [BALFOUR, Alexander].
**THE FARMERS' THREE DAUGHTERS. A NOVEL. IN FOUR VOLUMES.**

>London: Printed for A. K. Newman and Co. Leadenhall-Street, 1822.
>I 272p; II 256p; III 246p; IV 284p. 12mo. 24s (ECB, ER).
>ER 36: 570 (Feb 1822).
>Corvey; CME 3-628-47615-1; ECB 200; NSTC 2B4168 (BI BL, C, O).

*Notes.* ECB and ER mistakenly give the title as 'The Farmer's Three Daughters'. ECB dates Oct 1821.

1822: 18    BALL, Edward.
**THE SIBYL'S WARNING. A NOVEL. IN TWO VOLUMES. BY EDWARD BALL.**

>London: Printed for C. Chapple, Royal Subscription Circulating Library, Pall-Mall, 1822.
>I vi, 372p; II 215p. 12mo. 12s (ECB, ER).
>ER 36: 570 (Feb 1822); WSW II: 44.
>Corvey; CME 3-628-47094-3; ECB 536; NSTC 2B4496 (BI BL).

*Notes.* 'Advertisement' signed 'Norwich: Palace House'.

1822: 19    [BARBER, Elizabeth].
**DANGEROUS ERRORS: A TALE.**

>London: Printed for Lupton Relfe, 13, Cornhill, 1822.
>vii, 254p, ill. 12mo. 6s (ECB, QR).
>QR 27: 270 (Apr 1822); WSW II: 8.
>Corvey; CME 3-628-47395-0; ECB 151; NSTC 2B7216 (BI BL, C, O; NA MH).

*Notes.* Author attribution from 1823: 22 and 1824: 17.

1822: 20    [BENNET, William].
**MALPAS; OR, LE POURSUIVANT D'AMOUR. A ROMANCE. BY THE AUTHOR OF "THE CAVALIER." IN THREE VOLUMES.**

London: Printed for Longman, Hurst, Rees, Orme, and Brown, Paternoster-Row, 1822.
I xvi, 372p; II 374p; III 329p. 12mo. 21s (ECB).
WSW II: 50.
Corvey; CME 3-628-48144-9; ECB 364; NSTC 2G6332 (BI BL, C).

*Notes.* Dedication to the Duke of Devonshire, signed Lee Gibbons [pseud.], 23 Nov 1821.
ECB dates June 1822.
Further edn: German trans., 1824 [as *Malpas. Ein historischer Roman aus dem Anfange des 14. Jahrhunderts* (RS)].


1822: 21    BROWN, Charles Brockden.
CARWIN, THE BILOQUIST, AND OTHER AMERICAN TALES AND
PIECES. BY CHARLES BROCKDEN BROWN, AUTHOR OF WIELAND,
ORMOND, ARTHUR MERVYN, &C. &C. IN THREE VOLUMES.

London: Printed for Henry Colburn and Co. Public Library, Conduit Street, 1822.
I iv, 256p; II 287p; III 259p. 12mo. 18s (ECB, ER, QR).
ER 37: 281 (June 1822); QR 27: 270 (Apr 1822); WSW II: 58.
Corvey; CME 3-628-47135-4; ECB 78; NSTC 2B51807 (BI BL, C, E, O; NA DLC, MH).

*Notes.* Editor's Preface mentions 'The incomplete state, in which some of the following posthumous pieces have been left . . .'. For the original composition of 'Carwin' in 1798 and its American publication in instalments 1803–5, see S. W. Reid, 'Brockden Brown in England: Notes on Henry Colburn's 1822 Editions of his Novels', *Early American Literature*, 9 (1974), 188–95.


1822: 22    [BURY, Lady Charlotte Susan Maria].
CONDUCT IS FATE. IN THREE VOLUMES.

Edinburgh: William Blackwood, and T. Cadell, London, 1822.
I 312p; II 301p; III 352p. 12mo. 21s (ECB, ER).
ER 36: 571 (Feb 1822); WSW II: 61.
Corvey; CME 3-628-47309-8; ECB 130; NSTC 2C33699 (BI BL, C, E, O; NA MH).


1822: 23    CAREY, David.
LIFE IN PARIS; COMPRISING THE RAMBLES, SPREES, AND
AMOURS, OF DICK WILDFIRE, OF CORINTHIAN CELEBRITY, AND
HIS BANG-UP COMPANIONS, SQUIRE JENKINS AND CAPTAIN
O'SHUFTLETON; WITH THE WHIMSICAL ADVENTURES OF THE
HALIBUT FAMILY; INCLUDING SKETCHES OF A VARIETY OF
OTHER ECCENTRIC CHARACTERS IN THE FRENCH METROPOLIS.
BY DAVID CAREY. EMBELLISHED WITH TWENTY-ONE COLOURED
PLATES, REPRESENTING SCENES FROM REAL LIFE, DESIGNED AND
ENGRAVED BY MR. GEORGE CRUIKSHANK. ENRICHED ALSO WITH
TWENTY-TWO ENGRAVINGS ON WOOD, DRAWN BY THE SAME
ARTIST, AND EXECUTED BY MR. WHITE.

London: Printed for John Fairburn, Broadway, Ludgate-Hill; sold by Sherwood, Neely,
and Jones; Longman, Hurst, Rees, Orme, and Brown; and Baldwin, Craddock, and

Joy; Paternoster-Row; Simpkin and Marshall, Stationers' Court; Whittakers, Ave-Maria-Lane; Humphrey, St. James's Street, and Wilson, Royal Exchange, 1822.
xxiv, 489p, ill. 8vo. '21s; l.p., 31s 6d' (ECB).
Corvey; ECB 97; NSTC 2C7016 (BI BL, C, E, O; NA DLC, MH).

*Notes.* ECB dates Dec 1822. Collates in fours.
Further edn: 1837 (NSTC).

1822: 24    [COOPER, James Fenimore].
THE SPY; A TALE OF THE NEUTRAL GROUND; REFERRING TO SOME PARTICULAR OCCURRENCES DURING THE AMERICAN WAR: ALSO POURTRAYING AMERICAN SCENERY AND MANNERS. IN THREE VOLUMES.

London: G. and W. B. Whittaker, Ave-Maria-Lane, 1822.
I x, 318p; II 314p; III 312p. 12mo. 21s (ECB, ER); 18s (ER).
ER 37: 280 (June 1822), 38: 522 (May 1823); WSW II: 77.
Corvey; ECB 135; NSTC 2C36880 (BI BL, C).

*Notes.* ER gives price as 21s in June 1822, and as 18s in May 1823. Originally published New York 1821 (Blanck).
Further edns: 1823 (Blanck); 1831 (Blanck); 1849 (Blanck); French trans., 1822; German trans., 1824.

1822: 25    CUNNINGHAM, Allan.
TRADITIONAL TALES OF THE ENGLISH AND SCOTTISH PEAS-ANTRY. BY ALLAN CUNNINGHAM, AUTHOR OF SIR MARMADUKE MAXWELL, A DRAMATIC POEM; &C. IN TWO VOLUMES.

London: Printed for Taylor and Hessey, Fleet-Street, 1822.
I x, 322p; II 357p. 12mo. 12s (ECB, ER, QR).
ER 37: 536 (Nov 1822); QR 27: 558 (July 1822); WSW II: 82–3.
Corvey; CME 3-628-51010-4; ECB 147; NSTC 2C46750 (BI BL, C, Dt, E, O; NA DLC, MH).

*Notes.* Preface notes that 'all these stories, with the exception of the first, appeared at different periods in the London Magazine'.
Further edn: German trans., 1823 [as *Schottische Erzählungen* (RS)].

1822: 26    D., A.
THE ACCOMPLISHED HYPOCRITE; OR BRASS GLITTERS MORE THAN GOLD. A MORAL TALE, FOUNDED ON FACTS. IN TWO VOL-UMES. BY A. D.

London: Printed for A. K. Newman and Co. Leadenhall-Street, 1822.
I 240p; II 301p. 12mo. 12s (ECB).
Corvey; CME 3-628-47003-X; ECB 2; NSTC 2D26 (BI BL).

*Notes.* ECB dates Dec 1821.

1822: 27    DE LUCE, Joan.
CURIOSITY. A NOVEL. IN THREE VOLUMES. BY JOAN DE LUCE.

London: Printed for A. K. Newman and Co. Leadenhall-Street, 1822.
I 240p; II 229p; III 237p. 12mo. 16s 6d (ECB, QR).
QR 27: 558 (July 1822).
Corvey; CME 3-628-48122-8; ECB 158; NSTC 2D8559 (BI BL, C, O).

1822: 28   DERENZY, S. S[parow].
MARIAN DE BRITTOON, OR THE RECTOR'S ORPHAN GRANDAUGHTER.
A NOVEL. IN THREE VOLUMES. BY CAPTAIN S. S. DERENZY, FORMERLY
CAPTAIN IN THE ROYAL SOUTH GLOUCESTER REGIMENT; AND SINCE
CAPTAIN AND ADJUTANT OF H.R.H. THE DUKE OF YORK'S NEW FOREST
RANGERS.

London: Printed for W. Wright, Fleet Street, 1822.
I 309p; II 305p; III 303p. 12mo.
WSW II: 86.
Corvey; CME 3-628-47432-9; ECB 159; NSTC 2D9986 (BI BL).

1822: 29   [DILLON, Henry Augustus Dillon-Lee, Viscount].
THE LIFE AND OPINIONS OF SIR RICHARD MALTRAVERS, AN ENG-
LISH GENTLEMAN OF THE SEVENTEENTH CENTURY. IN TWO VOL-
UMES.

London: Printed for G. and W. B. Whittaker, Ave-Maria-Lane, 1822.
I 274p; II 287p. 8vo. 16s (ECB).
Corvey; CME 3-628-48097-3; ECB 345; NSTC 2D13576 (BI BL, C, E, O; NA DLC).
*Notes.* ECB dates May 1822.

EGAN, Pierce, REAL LIFE IN LONDON
See 1821: 33

1822: 30   EDRIDGE, Rebecca.
THE SCRINIUM, IN TWO VOLUMES. BY REBECCA EDRIDGE.

London: Printed for G. & W. B. Whittaker, Ave-Maria-Lane, 1822.
I viii, 355p; II iv, 380p. 12mo. 15s (ECB, QR).
QR 27: 558 (July 1822); WSW II: 92–3.
Corvey; CME 3-628-47514-7; ECB 179; NSTC 2E4721 (BI BL, C, Dt, E, O; NA DLC).

1822: 31   [FLETCHER, Grenville].
RHODOMALDI; OR, THE CASTLE OF ROVEGGIANO! A ROMANCE.
IN THREE VOLUMES.

London: J. C. Spence, 32, Euston Street, Euston Square, and 218, High Holborn, 1822.
I 254p; II 233p; III 220p. 12mo. 16s 6d (ECB).
WSW II: 30.
Corvey; CME 3-628-48569-X; ECB 491; xNSTC.
*Notes.* ECB dates Apr 1822.

1822: 32    [GALT, John].
## THE PROVOST. BY THE AUTHOR OF ANNALS OF THE PARISH; AYR-SHIRE LEGATEES; AND SIR ANDREW WYLIE.

> Edinburgh: William Blackwood, and T. Cadell, London, 1822.
> 360p. 12mo. 7s (ECB); 7s boards (ER).
> ER 37: 281 (June 1822), 39: 158–96 (Oct 1823) full review; QR 27: 270 (Apr 1822); WSW II: 96.
> E Hall.197.e; ECB 222; NSTC 2G1392 (BI BL, O; NA MH).

*Notes.* Dedication 'to Robert Downie, of Appin, Esquire, M.P. from his friend, the Author'. This is one of twelve novels which are together given full reviews in ER (Oct 1823) under the title 'Secondary Scottish Novels'.
Further edns: 2nd edn. 1822 (Corvey, NSTC); New York 1822 (NSTC); French trans., 1824.

1822: 33    [GALT, John].
## SIR ANDREW WYLIE, OF THAT ILK. BY THE AUTHOR OF "ANNALS OF THE PARISH," &C. IN THREE VOLUMES.

> Edinburgh: Printed for William Blackwood, and T. Cadell, Strand, London, 1822.
> I 336p; II 336p; III 310p. 12mo. 21s (ECB, ER, QR).
> ER 36: 570 (Feb 1822), 39: 158–96 (Oct 1823) full review; QR 26: 544 (Jan 1822); WSW II: 96–7.
> Corvey; CME 3-628-48706-4; ECB 222; NSTC 2G1398 (BI BL, C, Dt, E, O; NA MH).

*Notes.* This is one of twelve novels which are together given full reviews in ER (Oct 1823) under the title 'Secondary Scottish Novels'. ECB dates Mar 1822; *The Provost* as May 1822; and *The Steam-Boat* as Aug 1822.
Further edns: 2nd edn. 1822 (NSTC); London 1841 (NSTC); 1845 (NSTC); New York 1822 (NSTC); French trans., 1823.

1822: 34    [GALT, John].
## THE STEAM-BOAT. BY THE AUTHOR OF ANNALS OF THE PARISH; AYRSHIRE LEGATEES; SIR ANDREW WYLIE; AND THE PROVOST.

> Edinburgh: William Blackwood, and T. Cadell, London, 1822.
> v, 359p. 12mo. 7s (ECB, QR).
> ER 39: 158–96 (Oct 1823) full review; QR 27: 558 (July 1822); WSW II: 96.
> Corvey; CME 3-628-48785-4; ECB 222; NSTC 2G1402 (BI BL, C, Dt, E, O; NA MH).

*Notes.* Dedication to Lord Gwydir signed 'Thomas Duffle' and dated Boyle's Land, Salt Market, Glasgow, 1 July 1822. Page facing t.p. states 'Originally printed in Blackwood's Edinburgh Magazine and now reprinted with corrections and additions'. This is one of twelve novels which are together given full reviews in ER (Oct 1823) under the title 'Secondary Scottish Novels'.
Further edns: 1842, with *The Provost* (NSTC); New York 1823 (NSTC); German trans., 1826.

1822: 35    [GASPEY, Thomas].
## THE LOLLARDS: A TALE, FOUNDED ON THE PERSECUTIONS WHICH MARKED THE EARLY PART OF THE FIFTEENTH CENTURY. BY THE AUTHOR OF THE MYSTERY, OR FORTY YEARS AGO; AND OF CALTHORPE, OR FALLEN FORTUNES. IN THREE VOLUMES.

London: Printed for Longman, Hurst, Rees, Orme, and Brown, Paternoster-Row, 1822.
I xvi, 347p; II 353p; III 334p. 12mo. 21s (ECB, ER, QR).
ER 37: 281 (June 1822), 38: 277 (Feb 1823); QR 28: 268 (Oct 1822); WSW II: 100.
Corvey; CME 3-628-48110-4; ECB 351; NSTC 2G3295 (BI BL, C, E, O; NA DLC, MH).

*Notes.* Further edns: 1843 (NSTC); German trans., 1822.

1822: 36    GREEN, [Sarah].
WHO IS THE BRIDEGROOM? OR, NUPTIAL DISCOVERIES. A NOVEL. IN THREE VOLUMES. BY MRS. GREEN, AUTHOR OF GOOD MEN OF MODERN DATE, THE FUGITIVE, ROMANCE-READERS AND ROMANCE-WRITERS, REFORMIST, FESTIVAL OF ST. JAGO, CARTHUSIAN FRIAR, ROYAL EXILES, &C. &C.

London: Printed for A. K. Newman and Co. Leadenhall-Street, 1822.
I 267p; II 229p; III 262p. 12mo. 16s 6d (ECB, ER, QR).
ER 37: 536 (Nov 1822); QR 27: 558 (July 1822), 28: 269 (Oct 1822); WSW II: 104.
Corvey; CME 3-628-47852-9; ECB 243; NSTC 2G20160 (BI BL).

1822: 37    [HARDING, Anne Raikes].
THE REFUGEES, AN IRISH TALE. BY THE AUTHOR OF CORRECTION, DECISION, &C. &C. IN THREE VOLUMES.

London: Printed for Longman, Hurst, Rees, Orme, and Brown, Paternoster-Row, 1822.
I 287p; II 301p; III 354p. 12mo. 21s (ECB, ER).
ER 37: 281 (June 1822); WSW II: 106.
Corvey; CME 3-628-47459-0; ECB 484; NSTC 2H7491 (BI BL, Dt; NA MH).

*Notes.* Further edn: French trans., 1830 [as *Les Réfugies, histoire irlandaise, par Mrs Sinclair* (BN, under Sinclair)].

1822: 38    HARVEY, Jane.
SINGULARITY. A NOVEL. IN THREE VOLUMES. BY JANE HARVEY, AUTHOR OF BROUGHAM CASTLE, WARKFIELD CASTLE, &C.

London: Printed for A. K. Newman and Co. Leadenhall-Street, 1822.
I 297p; II 296p; III 349p. 12mo. 18s (ECB).
WSW II: 107–8.
Corvey; CME 3-628-47634-8; ECB 257; NSTC 2H11043 (BI BL, C).

*Notes.* ECB dates June 1822.

1822: 39    [HATTON, Anne Julia Kemble].
GUILTY OR NOT GUILTY; OR, A LESSON FOR HUSBANDS. A TALE. IN FIVE VOLUMES. BY ANN OF SWANSEA, AUTHOR OF CONVICTION, CESARIO ROSALBA, SECRETS IN EVERY MANSION, CHRONICLES OF AN ILLUSTRIOUS HOUSE, LOVERS AND FRIENDS, GONZALO DI BALDIVIA, SECRET AVENGERS, CAMBRIAN PICTURES, &C. &C.

London: Printed for A. K. Newman and Co. Leadenhall-Street, 1822.

I ii, 294p; II 296p; III 328p; IV 326p; V 290p. 12mo. 30s (ECB, ER).
ER 36: 571 (Feb 1822); WSW II: 108.
Corvey; CME 3-628-48803-6; ECB 20; NSTC 2A13193 (BI BL, C; NA MH).

*Notes*. Dedication to 'Mrs. Sheppard, of Fox-Hole', dated Orchard-Street, Swansea, 17 Dec 1821.


1822: 40    HEDGE, Mary Anne.
THE FLATTERER; OR, FALSE FRIENDSHIP. A TALE. BY MARY ANNE HEDGE, AUTHOR OF AFFECTION'S GIFT, &C.

London: Printed for Baldwin, Cradock, and Joy; and Swinborne and Walter, 1822.
160p, ill. 12mo. 4s (ECB, ER).
ER 36: 570 (Feb 1822).
Corvey; CME 3-628-51034-1; ECB 208; NSTC 2H15917 (BI BL).

*Notes*. Colophon reads: 'Printed by Swinborne and Walter, Colchester'. Collates in sixes.


1822: 41    HEDGE, Mary Anne.
LIFE; OR, FASHION AND FEELING. A NOVEL. IN THREE VOLUMES. BY MARY ANNE HEDGE, AUTHOR OF AFFECTION'S GIFT; THE RETREAT; LETTERS ON HISTORY, SACRED AND PROFANE; YOUNG INFIDEL; MEMOIRS OF JAMES II; TWILIGHT HOURS IMPROVED; TREASURES OF THOUGHT, &C.

London: Printed for A. K. Newman and Co. Leadenhall-Street, 1822.
I 249p; II 243p; III 240p. 12mo. 16s 6d (ECB, ER, QR).
ER 36: 571 (Feb 1822); QR 26: 544 (Jan 1822); WSW II: 111.
Corvey; CME 3-628-47719-0; ECB 262; NSTC 2H15921 (BI BL, C, O; NA MH).

*Notes*. Dedication to 'Miss Harris'.


1822: 42    HILL, Isabel.
CONSTANCE, A TALE. BY ISABEL HILL, AUTHOR OF 'THE POET'S CHILD,' A TRAGEDY.

London: John Warren, Old Bond Street, 1822.
vii, 279p. 12mo. 7s (ECB, ER).
ER 36: 570 (Feb 1822); WSW II: 114.
Corvey; CME 3-628-47689-5; ECB 269; xNSTC.

*Notes*. Introduction dated London, Dec 1821.


1822: 43    HOFLAND, [Barbara].
TALES OF THE MANOR. BY MRS. HOFLAND. IN FOUR VOLUMES.

London: Printed for Longman, Hurst, Rees, Orme, and Brown, Paternoster-Row, 1822.
I 344p; II 309p; III 342p; IV 309p. 12mo. 24s (ECB, ER, QR).
ER 37: 281 (June 1822); QR 27: 270 (Apr 1822); WSW II: 114.
Corvey; CME 3-628-51039-2; ECB 275; NSTC 2H29420 (BI BL, C, E, O).

*Notes*. Further edns: 2nd edn. 1822 (NSTC); New York 1822 (NSTC).

1822: 44   HOGG, James.
THE THREE PERILS OF MAN; OR, WAR, WOMEN, AND WITCHCRAFT.
A BORDER ROMANCE. BY JAMES HOGG, AUTHOR OF "WINTER-
EVENING TALES," "BROWNIE OF BODSBECK," "QUEEN'S WAKE,"
&C. &C. IN THREE VOLUMES.

>London: Longman, Hurst, Rees, Orme, and Brown, Paternoster-Row, 1822.
>I 341p; II 353p; III 449p. 12mo. 24s (ECB, ER).
>ER 37: 281 (June 1822); QR 27: 270 (Apr 1822); WSW II: 116.
>Corvey; CME 3-628-47697-6; ECB 276; NSTC 2H25728 (BI BL, C, Dt, E, NCu, O; NA
>DLC, MH).

*Notes.* 'John Moir, Printer, Edinburgh, 1822' on verso of t.ps. Dedication 'to William Stewart Rose, Esq. as a small memorial of Yarrow, and the Shepherd's humble sheil'.


1822: 45   [HOOK, James].
PEN OWEN. IN THREE VOLUMES.

>Edinburgh: William Blackwood, and T. Cadell, London, 1822.
>I 331p; II 364p; III 419p. 8vo. 31s 6d (ECB, QR); 31s 6d boards (ER).
>ER 37: 281 (June 1822); QR 27: 270 (Apr 1822); WSW II: 118.
>Corvey; CME 3-628-48412-X; ECB 440; NSTC 2H28909 (BI BL, C, Dt, E, O; NA DLC,
>MH).

*Notes.* Further edns: 1842 (NSTC); New York 1822 (NSTC); French trans., 1823.


1822: 46   [IRVING, Washington].
BRACEBRIDGE HALL; OR, THE HUMORISTS. BY GEOFFREY
CRAYON, GENT. IN TWO VOLUMES.

>London: John Murray, Albemarle-Street, 1822.
>I iv, 393p; II iv, 404p. 12mo. 24s (ECB, ER).
>ER 37: 281 (June 1822), 37: 337-50 (Nov 1822) full review; QR 31: 473–87 (Mar 1825)
>    full review; WSW II: 123.
>Corvey; ECB 301; NSTC 2C42718 (BI BL, C, E, O; NA DLC, MH).

*Notes.* Also published New York 1822, simultaneously with the London edn. (Blanck).
Reviewed in QR (Mar 1825) with three other of Irving's works.
Further edns: New edn. 1823 (NUC); 1824 (NSTC); 1845 (NSTC); 1848 (NSTC); 1850
(NSTC); New York 1822 (NSTC); French trans., 1822; German trans., 1822–3.


1822: 47   JAMIESON, [Frances].
THE HOUSE OF RAVENSPUR, A ROMANCE. BY MRS. JAMIESON. IN
FOUR VOLUMES.

>London: Printed for G. and W. B. Whittaker, Ave-Maria Lane, 1822.
>I 312p; II 306p; III 300p; IV 329p. 12mo. 24s (ECB, QR).
>QR 27: 270 (Apr 1822); WSW II: 124.
>Corvey; CME 3-628-47930-4; ECB 306; NSTC 2T12204 (BI BL; NA MH).

1822: 48    JOHNSTON, Mary.
**DOMESTIC TALES; CONTAINING THE MERCHANT'S WIFE AND HER SISTER. BY MARY JOHNSTON, AUTHOR OF "THE LAIRDS OF GLENFERN; OR, HIGHLANDERS OF THE NINETEENTH CENTURY."**

> London: G. and W. B. Whittaker, Ave-Maria Lane, 1822.
> 220p. 12mo. 5s (ECB).
> WSW II: 125.
> Corvey; CME 3-628-51080-5; ECB 310; NSTC 2J9504 (BI BL, C, O).

*Notes.* Dedication to 'Lieut. Colonel Gordon, of Cluny'. ECB dates May 1822.

1822: 49    [JONES, George].
**THE KNIGHTS OF RITZBERG. A ROMANCE. BY THE AUTHOR OF "SUPREME BON TON," "PARGA," &C. IN THREE VOLUMES.**

> London: J. C. Spence, 32, Euston Street, Euston Square, and 218, High Holborn, 1822.
> I viii, 276p; II 250p; III 236p. 12mo. 16s 6d (ECB).
> WSW II: 74.
> Corvey; CME 3-628-47980-0; ECB 324; NSTC 2K8102 (BI C).

*Notes.* Dedication 'to His Grace, the Duke of Devonshire'. Preface dated Fitzroy Square, July 1822. ECB dates July 1822.

1822: 50    KELLY, R[ichard] N.
**FREDERICK DORNTON; OR, THE BROTHERS. A NOVEL. IN FOUR VOLUMES. BY R. N. KELLY, ESQ. AUTHOR OF DE RENZEY.**

> London: Printed for A. K. Newman and Co. Leadenhall-Street, 1822.
> I 238p; II 268p; III 290p; IV 319p. 12mo. 22s (ECB).
> WSW II: 127.
> Corvey; CME 3-628-47926-6; ECB 317; NSTC 2K2223 (BI BL, C; NA MH).

1822: 51    [KELTY, Mary Ann].
**OSMOND, A TALE. BY THE AUTHOR OF "THE FAVOURITE OF NATURE:" IN THREE VOLUMES.**

> London: Printed for G. and W. B. Whittaker, Ave-Maria Lane, 1822.
> I iv, 312p; II 327p; III 396p. 12mo. 21s (ECB, ER, QR).
> ER 37: 536 (Nov 1822); QR 27: 558 (July 1822), 28: 268 (Oct 1822); WSW II: 128.
> BL N.118; ECB 318; NSTC 2K2406 (BI C, E; NA MH).

*Notes.* Dedication to 'Lady Dacre'.
Further edns: 2nd edn. 1823 (Corvey), CME 3-628-48317-4; German trans., 1822 [as *Osmond, oder der Sturm der Leidenschaft* (RS)]; French trans., 1824.

1822: 52    [LAMB, Lady Caroline].
**GRAHAM HAMILTON.**

> London: Printed for Henry Colburn and Co. Conduit-Street, Hanover-Square, 1822.
> I 221p; II 186p. 12mo. 16s (ECB, ER).
> ER 37: 281 (June 1822); WSW II: 130.
> Corvey; CME 3-628-47791-3; ECB 238; NSTC 2L2307 (BI BL, C, E, O; NA MH).

*Notes.* Notice, dated 2 Apr 1822, stating that 'The Manuscript of these Volumes was placed in Mr. Colburn's hands two years ago, with an earnest injunction neither to name the author, nor to publish it at that time: having fully obeyed the writer's wishes, he has now the pleasure of laying the work before the public'.
Further edns: 2nd edn. 1823 (NSTC); Philadelphia 1822 (NSTC).

1822: 53   LATHOM, Francis.
PUZZLED AND PLEASED; OR, THE TWO OLD SOLDIERS: AND OTHER TALES. IN THREE VOLUMES. BY FRANCIS LATHOM, AUTHOR OF THE MYSTERIOUS FREEBOOTER, UNKNOWN, VERY STRANGE BUT VERY TRUE, MEN AND MANNERS, ROMANCE OF THE HEBRIDES, LONDON, MYSTERY, ONE POUND NOTE, IMPENE-TRABLE SECRET, HUMAN BEINGS, ITALIAN MYSTERIES, ASTON-ISHMENT, FATAL VOW, MIDNIGHT BELL, &C. &C.

> London: Printed for A. K. Newman and Co. Leadenhall-Street, 1822.
> I 274p; II 270p; III 225p. 12mo. 18s (ECB, ER, QR).
> ER 36: 570 (Feb 1822); QR 26: 275 (Oct 1821).
> Corvey; CME 3-628-47902-9; ECB 331; NSTC 2L5039 (BI BL, C, E).

*Notes.* ECB dates Dec 1821.

1822: 54   [LOCKHART, John Gibson].
SOME PASSAGES IN THE LIFE OF MR ADAM BLAIR MINISTER OF THE GOSPEL AT CROSS-MEIKLE.

> Edinburgh: William Blackwood, and T. Cadell, London, 1822.
> 337p. 8vo. 10s 6d (ECB, ER).
> ER 36: 570 (Feb 1822), 39: 158–96 (Oct 1823) full review; WSW II: 136.
> Corvey; CME 3-628-48671-8; ECB 549; NSTC 2L19485 (BI BL, C, Dt, E, O; NA MH).

*Notes.* This is one of twelve novels which are together given full reviews in ER (Oct 1823) under the title 'Secondary Scottish Novels'.
Further edns: 2nd edn. 1824 (NSTC); 1843 (NSTC); Boston 1822 (NUC).

1822: 55   M'CHRONICLE, Ronald [pseud.].
LEGENDS OF SCOTLAND. FIRST SERIES. IN THREE VOLUMES. CON-TAINING FAIR HELEN OF KIRKONNEL, AND ROSLIN CASTLE. BY RONALD M'CHRONICLE, ESQ.

> London: Printed for A. K. Newman and Co. Leadenhall-Street, 1822.
> I 224p; II 240p; III 255p. 12mo. 16s 6d (ER, QR).
> ER 37: 280 (June 1822); QR 27: 270 (Apr 1822); WSW II: 138.
> Corvey; CME 3-628-48070-1; ECB 358; NSTC 2M1928 (BI BL, C, Dt, E, O).

*Notes.* ECB lists three series, price 49s 6d.

MACDONOUGH, Felix, THE HERMIT IN THE COUNTRY
See 1820: 48

1822: 56   M'LEOD, Miss [E. H.].
**TALES OF TON. THIRD SERIES. BY MISS M'LEOD. IN FOUR VOL-UMES.**

> London: Printed for A. K. Newman and Co. Leadenhall-Street, 1822.
> I 294p; II 286p; III 262p; IV 290p. 12mo. 24s boards (ER, QR).
> ER 36: 571 (Feb 1822); QR 26: 544 (Jan 1822).
> Corvey; CME 3-628-48087-6; ECB 361; NSTC 2M7092 (BI BL, C, E).

*Notes.* ECB lists three series, price 72s.

1822: 57   [MAINWARING, Mrs. M.].
**MOSCOW; OR, THE GRANDSIRE. AN HISTORICAL TALE. IN THREE VOLUMES.**

> London: Printed for A. K. Newman and Co. Leadenhall-Street, 1822.
> I 286p; II 264p; III 286p. 12mo. 18s (ECB, ER, QR).
> ER 37: 536 (Nov 1822); QR 27: 558 (July 1822).
> Corvey; CME 3-628-48338-7; ECB 398; NSTC 2M10325 (BI BL, C, O).

1822: 58   MERRYWHISTLE, Marmaduke [pseud.].
**ISN'T IT ODD? BY MARMADUKE MERRYWHISTLE. IN THREE VOL-UMES.**

> London: Printed for G. and W. B. Whittaker, Ave-Maria Lane, 1822.
> I viii, 290p, ill.; II 246p, ill.; III 311p, ill. 12mo. 21s (ECB).
> WSW II: 145.
> Corvey; CME 3-628-48127-9; ECB 382; NSTC 2M25604 (BI BL, C, O; NA DLC, MH).

*Notes.* ECB dates July 1822.

1822: 59   NATHAN, {Eliza}.
**LANGREATH, A TALE. BY MRS. NATHAN, AUTHORESS OF ELVING-TON. IN THREE VOLUMES.**

> London: Printed for G. and W. B. Whittaker, Ave-Maria Lane, 1822.
> I 350p; II 348p; III 468p. 12mo. 21s (ECB, ER).
> ER 36: 570 (Feb 1822); WSW II: 155.
> Corvey; CME 3-628-48250-X; ECB 406; NSTC 2N1559 (BI BL, C).

*Notes.* Preface (1 p. unn.) signed Eliza Nathan. Adv. by G. and W. B. Whittaker, verso of Preface, for 'The following new Compositions of Mr. [*sic*] Nathan': all four items listed are based on poetry (and priced between 1s 6d and 2s 6d).

1822: 60   OPIE, [Amelia Alderson].
**MADELINE, A TALE. BY MRS. OPIE.**

> London: Printed for Longman, Hurst, Rees, Orme, and Brown, Paternoster Row, 1822.
> I 345p; II 333p. 12mo. 14s (ECB, ER).
> ER 36: 571 (Feb 1822); QR 26: 544 (Jan 1822); WSW II: 156.
> Corvey; CME 3-628-48262-3; ECB 423; NSTC 2O4389 (BI BL, C, Dt, E, O; NA MH).

*Notes.* Further edns: Boston 1827 (NSTC); French trans., 1822.

1822: 61   [PEACOCK, Thomas Love].
**MAID MARIAN. BY THE AUTHOR OF HEADLONG HALL.**

> London: Printed for T. Hookham, 15, Old Bond Street; and Longman, Hurst, Rees,
> Orme, and Brown, Paternoster Row, 1822.
> 262p. 12mo. 7s (ECB, QR).
> QR 27: 270 (Apr 1822); WSW II: 159–60.
> Corvey; CME 3-628-48146-5; ECB 438; NSTC 2P8173 (BI BL, C, O; NA MH).

*Notes.* Preliminary Notice, dated 15 Mar 1822, reads: 'This little work, with the exception of
the three last chapters, was written in the autumn of 1818'.
Further edns: 1837 (NSTC); German trans., 1823 [as *Der Forstgraf, oder Robin Hood und
Mariane* (RS)]; French trans., 1826 [as *Robin Hood, ou la forêt de Sherwood* (BN)].

1822: 62   PORTER, Anna Maria.
**ROCHE-BLANCHE; OR, THE HUNTERS OF THE PYRENEES. A
ROMANCE. BY MISS ANNA MARIA PORTER, AUTHOR OF "THE
VILLAGE OF MARIENDORPT," &C. IN THREE VOLUMES.**

> London: Printed for Longman, Hurst, Rees, Orme, and Brown, Paternoster-Row, 1822.
> I xi, 374p; II 419p; III 568p. 12mo. 24s (ECB, QR).
> QR 27: 558 (July 1822); WSW II: 163.
> Corvey; CME 3-628-48303-4; ECB 463; NSTC 2P22258 (BI BL, E, NCu, O; NA DLC, MH).

*Notes.* Dedication 'to his Excellency Doctor Leighton, actual State Counsellor of His Imperial Majesty the Emperor of all the Russias', signed Anna Maria Porter, Long-Ditton, June
1812. 'Address to the Reader' dated Long-Ditton, 12 June 1822. Notice on page facing beginning of novel states 'The Reader is requested to substitute the name of Roche-Blanche, for
Roche Blanc, throughout this work'.
Further edns: Boston 1822 (NSTC); French trans., 1822; German trans., 1823 [as *Ritter Ade-
mar von Bourbon* (RS)].

1822: 63   POYNET, Quintin.
**THE WIZARD PRIEST AND THE WITCH. A ROMANCE. IN THREE
VOLUMES. BY QUINTIN POYNET, ESQ.**

> London: Printed for A. K. Newman and Co. Leadenhall-Street, 1822.
> I vi, 240p; II 225p; III 247p. 12mo. 16s 6d (ECB, ER, QR).
> ER 36: 571 (Feb 1822); QR 26: 544 (Jan 1822).
> Corvey; CME 3-628-48367-0; ECB 466; NSTC 2P24194 (BI BL, C, O).

1822: 64   [RUSSELL, Lord John].
**THE NUN OF ARROUCA, A TALE.**

> London: John Murray, Albemarle-Street, 1822.
> 87p. 8vo. 3s 6d (ECB, QR).
> QR 27: 271 (Apr 1822); WSW II: 171.
> Corvey; CME 3-628-51106-2; ECB 418; NSTC 2R21271 (BI BL, C, Dt, E, O; NA DLC,
> MH).

*Notes.* Collates in fours.
Further edn: French trans., 1826.

1822:65   ST. CLAIR, Rosalia [pseud.].
CLAVERING TOWER. A NOVEL. IN FOUR VOLUMES. BY ROSALIA ST. CLAIR, AUTHOR OF THE BLIND BEGGAR, SON OF O'DONNEL, HIGHLAND CASTLE AND LOWLAND COTTAGE, &C.

> London: Printed for A. K. Newman and Co. Leadenhall-Street, 1822.
> I 241p; II 206p; III 268p; IV 219p. 12mo. 22s (ECB, QR).
> QR 27: 270 (Apr 1822); WSW II: 172.
> Corvey; CME 3-628-48492-8; ECB 511; NSTC 2S1991 (BI BL, O).

1822:66   [SCOTT, Sir Walter].
THE FORTUNES OF NIGEL. BY THE AUTHOR OF "WAVERLEY, KENILWORTH," &C. IN THREE VOLUMES.

> Edinburgh: Printed for Archibald Constable and Co.; and Hurst, Robinson, and Co., London, 1822.
> I xlviii, 313p; II 334p; III 349p. 8vo. 31s 6d (ECB, ER).
> ER 37: 204–25 (June 1822) full review, 37: 280 (June 1822); QR 27: 337–64 (July 1822) full review; WSW II: 175–6.
> Corvey; CME 3-628-48577-0; ECB 212; NSTC 2S9583 (BI BL, C, Dt, E, NCu, O; NA DLC, MH).

*Notes.* 'Introductory Epistle' signed 'Cuthbert Clutterbuck', Kennaquhair, 1 Apr 1822. 'This day published', 30 May 1822, *Edinburgh Evening Courant.*
Further edns: 2nd edn. 1822 (NSTC); 3rd edn. 1822 (NSTC); New York 1822 (NSTC) [also Philadelphia 1822 (NCBEL)]; French trans., 1822; German trans., 1822. Numerous reprintings in collected edns.

1822:67   [SCOTT, Sir Walter].
PEVERIL OF THE PEAK. BY THE AUTHOR OF "WAVERLEY, KENIL-WORTH," &C. IN FOUR VOLUMES.

> Edinburgh: Printed for Archibald Constable and Co.; and Hurst, Robinson, and Co. London, 1822.
> I xxxii, 302p; II 319p; III 315p; IV 320p. 8vo. 42s (ECB); 42s boards (ER).
> ER 38: 277 (Feb 1823); QR 28: 268 (Oct 1822), 35: 518–66 (Mar 1827) full review; WSW II: 175.
> Corvey; CME 3-628-48579-7; ECB 444; NSTC 2S10093 (BI BL, C, Dt, E, NCu, O; NA DLC, MH).

*Notes.* 'Prefatory Letter' signed 'Jonas Driasdust', Michaelmas-day, 1822, York. Published Jan 1823 (Corson). This is one of nine novels which are together given full reviews in QR (Mar 1827) under the page-top heading 'Historical Romance'.
Further edns: 2nd edn. 1823 (NSTC); Philadelphia 1823 (NSTC); German trans., 1822 [as *Ritter Gottfried Peveril; eine romantische Darstellung* (RS)]; French trans., 1823–4. Numerous reprintings in collected edns.

1822:68   [SCOTT, Sir Walter].
THE PIRATE. BY THE AUTHOR OF "WAVERLEY, KENILWORTH," &C. IN THREE VOLUMES.

Edinburgh: Printed for Archibald Constable and Co.; and Hurst, Robinson, and Co. London, 1822.

I vii, 322p; II 332p; III 346p. 8vo. 31s 6d (ECB, ER, QR).

ER 36: 570 (Feb 1822); QR 26: 454–74 (Jan 1822) full review, 26: 544 (Jan 1822); WSW II: 174.

Corvey; CME 3-628-48580-0; ECB 452; NSTC 2S10118 (BI BL, C, Dt, E, NCu, O; NA DLC, MH).

*Notes.* 'Advertisement', signed 'The Author of Waverley', dated 1 Nov 1821. 'This day published', 22 Dec 1821, *Edinburgh Evening Courant.*
Further edns: 2nd edn. 1822 (NSTC); 3rd edn. 1822 (NSTC); Boston 1822 (NSTC) [also Philadelphia 1822 (NSTC)]; French trans., 1822; German trans., 1822. Numerous reprintings in collected edns.

1822: 69   [SEDGWICK, Catharine Maria].
A NEW-ENGLAND TALE. FROM THE SECOND AMERICAN EDITION, REVISED AND CORRECTED BY THE AUTHOR.

London: John Miller, 69, Fleet Street, 1822.
xi, 297p. 12mo. 6s (QR).
QR 28: 269 (Oct 1822); WSW II: 180.
O Douce.T.158; CME 3-628-48191-0; NSTC 2S12235 (BI C).

*Notes.* Dedication to Maria Edgeworth. 'Preface to the First Edition' stating an aim to augment 'the scanty stock of American literature', dated 30 Mar 1822; followed by 'Preface to the Second Edition', dated 18 July 1822. 2nd Preface gives original title as 'A New England Tale, or Sketches of New England Characters and Manners'. Originally published New York 1822 (Blanck, NSTC).

1822: 70   SIMONDE DE SISMONDI, J[ean] C[harles] L[éonard].
JULIA SEVERA; OR THE YEAR FOUR HUNDRED AND NINETY-TWO; TRANSLATED FROM THE FRENCH OF J. C. L. SIMONDE DE SIS-MONDI, AUTHOR OF NEW PRINCIPLES OF POLITICAL ECONOMY; THE HISTORY OF FRANCE; THE ITALIAN REPUBLICS OF THE MIDDLE AGE; THE LITERATURE OF THE SOUTH OF EUROPE, &C. IN TWO VOLUMES.

London: Printed for G. and W. B. Whittaker, Ave-Maria-Lane; and Munday and Slatter, High-Street, Oxford, 1822.
I xii, 245p; II 256p. 12mo.
BL 12510.cc.20; NSTC 2S21933 (BI Dt, E, O).

*Notes.* Trans. of *Julia Sévéra, ou l'an quatre cent quatre-vingt-douze* (Paris, 1822). 'Advertisement' by Translator, dated Oxford, 16 Apr 1822. Collates in sixes.
Further edn: 1824 (NSTC).

1822: 71   SPENCE, [Elizabeth Isabella].
OLD STORIES. BY MISS SPENCE, AUTHOR OF "A TRAVELLER'S TALE," &C. &C. IN TWO VOLUMES.

London: Printed for Longman, Hurst, Rees, Orme, and Brown, Paternoster-Row, 1822.

I vii, 184p; II 208p. 12mo. 10s 6d (ECB, ER).
ER 36: 571 (Feb 1822); QR 26: 544 (Jan 1822); WSW II: 189.
Corvey; CME 3-628-51135-6; ECB 554; NSTC 2S33538 (BI BL, C, E, O; NA MH).

*Notes.* Dedication 'to Mrs. Myddelton Biddulph, the present possessor of Chirk Castle'.

1822: 72    [STODDART, Lady Isabella Wellwood].
TALES OF MY AUNT MARTHA; CONTAINING I. THE LAIRD, A SCOT-
TISH TALE; II. THE SISTERS, AN ENGLISH TALE; III. THE CHATEAU
IN LA VENDEE, A FRENCH TALE.

London: William Fearman, Library, 170, New Bond-Street, 1822.
I xxiv, 344p; II 372p; III 341p. 12mo. 24s (ECB).
WSW II: 190.
Corvey; CME 3-628-48868-0; ECB 60; NSTC 2B36121 (BI BL, C).

*Notes.* ECB dates July 1823, and gives the author as Mrs Martha Blackford, which is the pseudonym of Isabella Stoddart. For further evidence on authorship, see works attributed to the
author in title of 1823: 79.
Further edn: French trans., 1830.

1822: 73    [SUTHERLAND, Alexander].
COSPATRICK OF RAYMONDSHOLM. A WESTLAND TALE. IN TWO
VOLUMES. BY THE AUTHOR OF REDMOND THE REBEL, OR THEY
MET AT WATERLOO; ST. KATHLEEN, &C.

London: Printed for A. K. Newman and Co. Leadenhall-Street, 1822.
I ii, 252p; II 269p. 12mo. 12s (ECB, ER).
ER 36: 570 (Feb 1822).
Corvey; CME 3-628-47369-1; ECB 137; NSTC 2C38878 (BI BL, C).

*Notes.* 'To the Reader', dated July 1821. ECB dates Oct 1821.

1822: 74    [TAYLER, Charles Benjamin].
MAY YOU LIKE IT. BY A COUNTRY CURATE.

London: Printed for T. Boys, Ludgate-Hill, 1822/23.
I (1822) xii, 272p, ill.; II (1823) ix, 386p, ill., music. 12mo. 14s (ECB); 6s vol. 1, 8s vol. 2
(ER).
ER 36: 571 (Feb 1822) for vol. 1, 39: 271 (Oct 1823) for vol. 2; WSW II: 192.
BL 012640.m.38 (vol. 1), Corvey (vol. 2); CME 3-628-54783-0 (2 vols., 1823); ECB 375;
NSTC 2T2793.

*Notes.* The Corvey set has 1823 on the t.p. of both vols; vol. 1 in this set also includes a 'Second Edition' t.p., dated 1822, as well as an additional 'Preface to the Second Edition' (a similar pattern is found in BL N.1505). The 2nd vol. includes a Dedication to Ralph Winstanley
Wood, Esq. ECB dates Jan 1822, May 1823.
Further edns: 3rd edn. 1823–4 (NSTC); 5th edn. 1832 (NSTC); Philadelphia 1822 (NSTC).

THORNTON, Alfred, DON JUAN
See 1821: 72

1822: 75   T[IGHE], H[ugh Usher].

**PASSION. A TALE. BY H. T. WRITTEN DURING HIS RESIDENCE AT ETON.**

> Oxford: Printed by W. Baxter, for J. Vincent, near Brasenose College. Sold also by G. and W. B. Whittaker, London, 1822.
>
> vii, 122p. 12mo.
>
> BL 12614.dd.7(1); NSTC 2T12560 (BI O).

*Notes.* Dedication 'to the Hon. William Ashley'. Collates in sixes.

1822: 76   TROTTER, Robert.

**LOWRAN CASTLE, OR THE WILD BOAR OF CURRIDOO: WITH OTHER TALES, ILLUSTRATIVE OF THE SUPERSTITIONS, MANNERS, AND CUSTOMS OF GALLOWAY. BY ROBERT TROTTER, STUDENT OF MEDICINE.**

> Dumfries: Printed by J. Swan, 77, English Street, 1822.
>
> 157p. 12mo.
>
> E NG.1177.f.4; NSTC 2T18510.

*Notes.* Dedication 'to the Honourable John Gordon of Kenmore'. Preface, dated New Galloway, 26 May 1822, introduces 'the following [10] tales' as 'the first production of a young Author, and undertaken with the view of assisting him to complete his education at College'; this also mentions 'his list of highly respectable Subscribers', though no actual list is present in the volume seen. Collates in sixes.

1822: 77   WARD, Catherine G[eorge].

**FAMILY PORTRAITS; OR, DESCENDANTS OF TRELAWNEY. BY CATHERINE G. WARD, AUTHORESS OF—THE MYSTERIOUS MARRIAGE,—THE ROSE OF CLAREMONT,—POEMS,—THE ORPHAN BOY,—BACHELOR'S HEIRESS,—MY NATIVE LAND,—&C. &C.**

> London: Printed by C. Baynes, 13, Duke Street, Lincoln's-Inn-Fields. Published by G. Virtue, 6, Panyer Alley, Paternoster Row; and 28, Temple Street, Bristol. Sold also by John Tallis, 16, Warwick Square, Newgate Street, and 47, Digbeth, Birmingham; and W. Baynes, Leeds, 1822.
>
> 694p, ill. 8vo.
>
> C 8450.c.21; NSTC 2W4959.

*Notes.* Originally published in 29 numbers. Sequel to *The Mysterious Marriage*. Additional engraved t.p. [n.d.]. Collates in fours. A copy in the Cooper Library, University of South Carolina is titled *The Mysterious Marriage; or Family Portraits [. . .] Vol. II*; it is dated 1822 and the main publisher is G. Virtue.
Further edns: 1824 (NSTC); New York 1843 (NUC).

1822: 78   [WELLS, Charles Jeremiah].

**STORIES AFTER NATURE.**

> London: T. and J. Allman, Princes Street, Hanover Square; and C. and J. Ollier, Vere Street, Oxford Street, 1822.

iv, 251p. 12mo. 6s (ECB).

WSW II: 201.

Corvey; CME 3-628-51136-4; ECB 564; NSTC 2W12392 (BI BL, C, Dt, O; NA MH).

*Notes.* ECB dates Feb 1822.

1822: 79  WENTWORTH, Zara.

THE UNCLES; OR, SELFISHNESS AND LIBERALITY. A NOVEL. IN
THREE VOLUMES. BY ZARA WENTWORTH, AUTHOR OF THE HER-
MIT'S CAVE, RECLUSE OF ALBYN HALL, &C. &C.

London: Printed for A. K. Newman and Co. Leadenhall-Street, 1822.

I 235p; II 281p; III 266p. 12mo. 16s 6d (ECB, ER, QR).

ER 37: 536 (Nov 1822); QR 27: 558 (July 1822).

Corvey; CME 3-628-48887-7; ECB 630; NSTC 2W12931 (BI BL, C, O).

1822: 80  [WHITE, Joseph Blanco].

VARGAS: A TALE OF SPAIN. IN THREE VOLUMES.

London: Printed for Baldwin, Cradock, and Joy, 1822.

I xii, 308p; II 339p; III 327p. 12mo. 18s (ECB).

WSW II: 51–2.

Corvey; CME 3-628-48858-3; ECB 610; NSTC 2B37342 (BI BL, C, O; NA MH).

*Notes.* Attributed in the Preface to the editor's friend, 'the late Cornelius Villiers'. ECB dates
Apr 1822.

Further edn: German trans., 1825 [as *Vargas. Ein spanisches Volksgemälde* (RS)].

1822: 81  [WILKINS, George, and others?].

BODY AND SOUL.

London: Printed for Longman, Hurst, Rees, Orme, and Brown, Paternoster-Row,
1822/23.

I (1822) xi, 391p; II (1823) x, 380p. 8vo. 21s (ECB); 9s vol. 2 (ER); 12s (QR).

ER 38: 523 (May 1823); QR 27: 558 (July 1822); WSW II: 203.

BL 865.h.4; ECB 64; NSTC 2B39202 (BI E, O).

*Notes.* For a possible co-author, the Revd Shepherd, see note to *The Village Pastor* (1825: 88).
Further edns: 2nd edn. 1823 (Corvey), CME 3-628-49007-3; 3rd edn. 1823 (NSTC); 4th edn.
1824, 'with additions and corrections' (NSTC, p.c.); Philadelphia 1824 (NSTC).

1822: 82  [WILSON, John].

LIGHTS AND SHADOWS OF SCOTTISH LIFE, A SELECTION FROM
THE PAPERS OF THE LATE ARTHUR AUSTIN.

Edinburgh: William Blackwood, and T. Cadell, London, 1822.

viii, 430p. 8vo. 10s 6d boards (ER).

ER 37: 281 (June 1822), 39: 158–96 (Oct 1823) full review; WSW II: 204–5.

E Bi.5/3; ECB 346; NSTC 2W25742 (BI BL, C, O; NA DLC).

*Notes.* Dedication to Sir Walter Scott, by 'the Editor'. This is one of twelve novels which are
together given full reviews in ER (Oct 1823) under the title 'Secondary Scottish Novels'.

Further edns: 2nd edn. 1822 (Corvey), CME 3-628-51088-0; 3rd edn. 1823 (NSTC); London 1824 (NSTC); Boston 1822 (NSTC); German trans., 1824 [as *Erzählungen aus dem Leben in Schottland* (RS)]; French trans., 1825 [as *Nouvelles écossaises, tirées des manuscrits d'Arthur Austin* (BN)].

# 1823

1823: 1   ANON.

AN ALPINE TALE: SUGGESTED BY CIRCUMSTANCES WHICH OCCURRED TOWARDS THE COMMENCEMENT OF THE PRESENT CENTURY. BY THE AUTHOR OF "TALES FROM SWITZERLAND."

> London: Printed for Francis Westley, 10, Stationers'-Court, and Ave-Maria-Lane; and L. B. Seely [*sic*], 169, Fleet-Street, 1823.
> I vi, 280p; II 282p. 12mo. 10s (ECB).
> WSW II: 207–8.
> Corvey; CME 3-628-47046-3; ECB 14; NSTC 2Y1228 (BI BL, C, O).

*Notes.* ECB dates Apr 1823. Attributed in some catalogues to A. Yosy, but see *Tales from Afar* (1824: 13).

1823: 2   ANON.

ANECDOTES OF A CROAT; OR, THE CASTLE OF SERAI, COMPREHENDING HINTS FOR THE IMPROVEMENT OF PUBLIC WORKS, AGRICULTURE, AND DOMESTIC LIFE. IN TWO VOLUMES.

> London: Published by W. Simpkin and R. Marshall, Stationers' Hall Court, 1823.
> I iv, 425p; II 396p. 12mo. 12s (ECB).
> Corvey; CME 3-628-47058-7; ECB 19; NSTC 2C43423 (BI BL).

*Notes.* An extended version of 1821: 1; vol. 1 is identical to the earlier publication, apart from a new t.p. ECB dates this version May 1823.

1823: 3   ANON.

EDWARD NEVILLE; OR, THE MEMOIRS OF AN ORPHAN. IN FOUR VOLUMES.

> London: Printed for Longman, Hurst, Rees, Orme, and Brown, Paternoster-Row, 1823.
> I 514p; II 424p; III 442p; IV 418p. 12mo. 28s (ECB, QR); 28s boards (ER).
> ER 39: 272 (Oct 1823); QR 29: 280 (Apr 1823); WSW II: 9.
> Corvey; CME 3-628-47511-2; ECB 180; NSTC 2N3642 (BI BL, O).

1823: 4   ANON.

FIRST AFFECTIONS. AN OXFORDSHIRE STORY. IN TWO VOLUMES.

London: Printed for T. Boys, Ludgate-Hill, 1823.
I xix, 244p; II 305p. 12mo. 12s (ECB, ER).
ER 39: 271 (Oct 1823); WSW II: 12.
Corvey; CME 3-628-47553-8; ECB 206; NSTC 2F6370 (BI O).

*Notes.* Introduced by 'Brief Prefatory Remarks on Novel-Writing', vol. 1, pp. [iii]–xix.


## INFLUENCE AND EXAMPLE
See BARBER, Elizabeth


1823: 5   ANON.
## ISABEL DE BARSAS; A TRADITION OF THE TWELFTH CENTURY. IN THREE VOLUMES.

London: Published by Baldwin, Cradock, and Joy, 1823.
I 339p; II 327p; III 329p. 12mo. 24s (ECB).
WSW II: 17.
Corvey; CME 3-628-47871-5; ECB 301; NSTC 2B10109 (BI BL).

*Notes.* ECB dates Apr 1823.


1823: 6   ANON.
## JUSTINA; OR, RELIGION PURE AND UNDEFILED. A MORAL TALE. IN TWO VOLUMES.

London: Printed for A. K. Newman and Co. Leadenhall-Street, 1823.
I 272p; II 277p. 12mo. 12s (ECB, ER).
ER 39: 272 (Oct 1823).
Corvey; CME 3-628-48011-6; ECB 315; NSTC 2J13580 (BI BL, C, O).

*Notes.* Dated 24 Mar 1823 on final page of text.


1823: 7   ANON.
## THE KOROMANTYN SLAVES; OR, WEST-INDIAN SKETCHES. BY THE AUTHOR OF "THE SOLACE OF AN INVALID," &C. &C. &C.

London: Printed for J. Hatchard and Son, Piccadilly, 1823.
viii, 278p. 12mo. 5s 6d (ECB).
Corvey; CME 3-628-47888-X; ECB 325; NSTC 2K8887 (BI BL, O).

*Notes.* ECB dates Dec 1823.


1823: 8   ANON.
## MAMMON IN LONDON; OR, THE SPY OF THE DAY. IN TWO VOLUMES.

London: Printed for W. Sams, 1, St. James's Street. Bookseller to H.R.H. The Duke of
    York, 1823.
I xii, 355p; II 288p. 12mo. 12s (ECB); 12s boards (ER).
ER 39: 513 (Jan 1824); WSW II: 21.
Corvey; CME 3-628-48077-9; ECB 365; NSTC 2M11431 (BI BL, C, O; NA MH).

1823: 9 ANON.

MARIA; OR, A SHANDEAN JOURNEY OF A YOUNG LADY, THROUGH FLANDERS AND FRANCE, DURING THE SUMMER OF 1822. BY MY UNCLE ODDY.

London: Printed for John Hatchard and Son, 187, Piccadilly, 1823.
xii, 156p. 12mo. 4s (ECB).
Corvey; CME 3-628-48243-7; ECB 368; NSTC 2M14252 (BI BL, C, O).

*Notes.* Dedication 'to Miss Emma Bayley, of Britwell, Buckinghamshire'. ECB dates May 1823.

1823: 10 ANON.

MODES OF LIFE; OR, TOWN AND COUNTRY. A NOVEL. IN THREE VOLUMES.

London: Printed for A. K. Newman and Co. Leadenhall-Street, 1823.
I 284p; II 280p; III 238p. 12mo. 18s (ECB).
Corvey; CME 3-628-48220-8; ECB 390; NSTC 2M31882 (BI BL, C).

*Notes.* ECB dates Mar 1823.

1823: 11 ANON.

THE PLEASURES OF FRIENDSHIP. A TALE.

London: Printed for G. and W. B. Whittaker, Ave Maria Lane, 1823.
ii, 306p. 12mo. 5s (ECB).
WSW II: 28.
BL N.139; ECB 455; NSTC 2P19206 (BI C).

*Notes.* Preface refers to 'the first attempt of a young and inexperienced female'. ECB dates Mar 1823.

1823: 12 ANON.

THE SCARLET HANDKERCHIEF. A NOVEL. IN THREE VOLUMES. BY AN AMERICAN, AUTHOR OF ZELICA THE CREOLE, &C. &C.

London: Printed for A. K. Newman and Co. Leadenhall-Street, 1823.
I 272p; II 264p; III 302p. 12mo. 18s (ECB).
Corvey; CME 3-628-48531-2; ECB 516; NSTC 2A10524 (BI BL).

*Notes.* ECB dates Feb 1823.

1823: 13 ANON.

THE SCHOOL FOR MOTHERS; WITH THE POLITICS OF A VILLAGE. IN THREE VOLUMES.

London: Printed for G. and W. B. Whittaker, Ave-Maria-Lane, 1823.
I xi, 312p; II 303p; III 332p. 12mo. 21s (ECB).
QR 27: 558 (July 1822); WSW II: 32.
Corvey; CME 3-628-48534-7; ECB 518; NSTC 2S7369 (BI BL, C).

*Notes.* 'Prefatory Remarks by a Friend of the Authoress', vol. 1, pp. [i]–xi. Further edn: 1827 (NSTC).

1823: 14   ANON.
## SELF-DELUSION; OR, ADELAIDE D'HAUTEROCHE: A TALE. BY THE AUTHOR OF "DOMESTIC SCENES." IN TWO VOLUMES.

London: Printed for Longman, Hurst, Rees, Orme, and Brown, Paternoster-Row, 1823.
I 365p; II 353p. 12mo. 14s (ECB, QR); 14s boards (ER).
ER 39: 272 (Oct 1823); QR 29: 280 (Apr 1823); WSW II: 33.
Corvey; CME 3-628-48641-6; ECB 526; NSTC 2S12804 (BI BL, C).

*Notes. Domestic Scenes* was written under the pseudonym of Lady Humdrum (see 1820: 38).

## TALES FROM SWITZERLAND
See 1822: 12

1823: 15   ANON.
## TALES OF MY FATHER, AND MY FRIENDS.

London: Printed for T. and G. Underwood, Fleet Street; and Macredie, Skelly, and Co., Edinburgh, 1823.
172p. 8vo. 5s (ECB).
WSW II: 36.
Corvey; CME 3-628-51153-4; ECB 575; NSTC 2T1402 (BI BL; NA MH).

*Notes.* 4 tales. ECB dates Jan 1823. BL copy (N.187(1)) has different imprint: 'London: Printed for the Author. Sold by Thomas and George Underwood, Fleet Street, 1823'.

1823: 16   ANON.
## TRACEY THE POET. A SKETCH FROM THE LIFE. IN THREE VOLUMES.

London: Printed for A. K. Newman and Co. Leadenhall-Street, 1823.
I 264p; II 239p; III 238p. 12mo. 16s 6d (ECB).
Corvey; CME 3-628-48766-8; ECB 595; NSTC 2T15791 (BI BL, C).

*Notes.* ECB dates Feb 1823.

1823: 17   ANON.
## WILLOUGHBY; OR REFORMATION. THE INFLUENCE OF RELIGIOUS PRINCIPLES. BY THE AUTHOR OF "THE DECISION," "CAROLINE ORMSBY," "VILLAGE COUNSEL," &C. &C. IN TWO VOLUMES.

London: C. and J. Rivington, St. Paul's Church-Yard, and Waterloo-Place, Pall-Mall, 1823.
I 372p; II 323p. 12mo. 15s (ECB).
WSW II: 128–9.
Corvey; CME 3-628-48934-2; ECB 641; NSTC 2W24300 (BI BL, C, O).

*Notes.* Wrongly attributed in some catalogues to Grace Kennedy: see note to *The Decision* (1811: 6). ECB dates May 1823.

1823: 18   [AINSWORTH, William Harrison].
## DECEMBER TALES.

London: Printed for G. and W. B. Whittaker, Ave-Maria Lane, 1823.

231p. 12mo. 5s 6d (ECB).

WSW II: 2.

Corvey; CME 3-628-51012-0; ECB 156; NSTC 2A5871 (BI BL, O).

*Notes.* Dedication to Reverend George Croly. ECB dates Jan 1823.

1823: 19    ARLINCOURT, [Charles] Vicomte d'.

**IPSIBOÉ. TRANSLATED FROM THE FRENCH OF M. LE VICOMTE D'ARLINCOURT.**

London: J. Robins and Co. Ivy Lane, Paternoster-Row, 1823.

I viii, 284p; II 270p. 8vo. 12s (ECB).

O 8°.W.304.B5; ECB 26; NSTC 2A15598 (BI C).

*Notes.* Trans. of *Ipsiboé* (Paris, 1823). ECB dates June 1823.

1823: 20    [ASHWORTH, John Harvey].

**HURSTWOOD: A TALE OF THE YEAR 1715. IN THREE VOLUMES.**

London: Printed for Longman, Hurst, Rees, Orme, Brown, and Green, Paternoster-Row, 1823.

I v, 241p; II 250p; III 218p. 12mo. 16s 6d (ECB, ER).

ER 39: 512 (Jan 1824); WSW II: 42.

Corvey; CME 3-628-47753-0; ECB 290; NSTC 2A17728 (BI BL, C, O; NA DLC, MH).

*Notes.* Dedication to Archer Clunn, Esq. of Griffynhavel, dated Hallcar, Radnor, June 1823.

Further edn: 1827 (NSTC: a reissue).

1823: 21    [BALFOUR, Alexander].

**THE FOUNDLING OF GLENTHORN; OR, THE SMUGGLERS' CAVE. A NOVEL. IN FOUR VOLUMES. BY THE AUTHOR OF THE FARMER'S THREE DAUGHTERS.**

London: Printed for A. K. Newman and Co. Leadenhall-Street, 1823.

I 274p; II 307p; III 286p; IV 314p. 12mo. 24s (ECB, ER, QR).

ER 39: 271 (Oct 1823); QR 29: 280 (Apr 1823); WSW II: 44.

Corvey; CME 3-628-47826-X; ECB 213; NSTC 2G10560 (BI BL, C).

1823: 22    [BARBER, Elizabeth].

**INFLUENCE AND EXAMPLE; OR, THE RECLUSE. A TALE. BY THE AUTHOR OF "DANGEROUS ERRORS."**

London: Printed for Lupton Relfe, 13, Cornhill, 1823.

iv, 236p, ill. 12mo. 6s (ECB, ER, QR).

ER 39: 272 (Oct 1823); QR 29: 280 (Apr 1823); WSW II: 16.

Corvey; CME 3-628-47883-9; ECB 295; NSTC 2I2147 (BI BL, O).

*Notes.* For author attribution, see 1822: 19 and 1824: 17.

Further edn: 1832 (NSTC).

1823: 23    [BENNET, William].

**THE KING OF THE PEAK. A ROMANCE. BY THE AUTHOR OF "THE CAVALIER," &C. IN THREE VOLUMES.**

London: Printed for Longman, Hurst, Rees, Orme, and Brown, Paternoster-Row, 1823.
I xvi, 333p; II 412p; III 376p. 12mo. 21s (ECB, ER).
ER 38: 523 (May 1823); WSW II: 50.
Corvey; CME 3-628-47998-3; ECB 321; NSTC 2K5303 (BI BL, E; NA MH).

*Notes.* Dedication to the Mayor of Liverpool, signed Lee Gibbons [pseud.].
Further edn: German trans., 1824 [as *Der Empörer* (RS)].

1823: 24    [BEVERLEY, Robert Mackenzie].
**THE DEVOTEE. A TALE.**

Cambridge: Printed by J. Hodson, Trinity-Street; sold by J. Shipp, Bookseller, Blandford, 1823.
xi, 150p. 12mo.
C Cam.d.823.9; NSTC 2B21121.

*Notes.* Dedication to Lady W. Smith.

1823: 25    BREBNER, Henry.
**HAUBERK HALL, A SERIES OF FACTS. BY HENRY BREBNER. IN TWO
VOLUMES.**

London: Printed for Sherwood, Jones, and Co. Paternoster-Row, 1823.
I 295p; II 276p. 12mo. 10s 6d (ECB).
WSW II: 57.
Corvey; CME 3-628-47194-X; ECB 72; NSTC 2B46650 (BI C).

*Notes.* Dedication to Sir Humphrey Davy, Bart. ECB dates June 1823.

1823: 26    [CHAMISSO, Adelbert von]; [BOWRING, Sir John (*trans.*)].
**PETER SCHLEMIHL: FROM THE GERMAN OF LAMOTTE FOUQUÉ.
WITH PLATES BY GEORGE CRUICKSHANK.**

London: G. and W. B. Whittaker, Ave-Maria Lane, 1823.
xii, 165p, ill. 12mo. 6s 6d (ECB).
MH HEW.3.9.6; ECB 213; NSTC 2C14268 (BI O).

*Notes.* Trans. of *Peter Schlemihls wundersame Geschichte* (Nürnberg, 1814), ed. Friedrich de
la Motte Fouqué. ECB dates Jan 1824.
Further edns: 1st edn. 2nd issue 1824 (NSTC); 1st edn. 3rd issue 1824 (NSTC); 2nd edn. 1824
(NSTC); Boston 1824 (NSTC).

1823: 27    [CLARKE, Hewson].
**HERWALD DE WAKE; OR, THE TWO APOSTATES. A ROMANCE. IN
THREE VOLUMES.**

London: Printed for G. and W. B. Whittaker, Ave-Maria-Lane, 1823.
I 259p; II 270p; III 273p. 12mo. 18s (ECB).
WSW II: 73–4.
Corvey; CME 3-628-47758-1; ECB 266; NSTC 2C24213 (BI BL, C, O).

*Notes.* ECB dates Dec 1823.

1823: 28   [COOPER, James Fenimore].
THE PIONEERS, OR THE SOURCES OF THE SUSQUEHANNA; A DESCRIPTIVE TALE. BY THE AUTHOR OF "THE SPY." IN THREE VOLUMES.

> London: John Murray, Albemarle-Street, 1823.
> I viii, 268p; II 274p; III 364p. 12mo. 18s (ER).
> ER 38: 522 (May 1823); WSW II: 77.
> BL N.175; ECB 452; NSTC 2C36864 (BI C, O).

*Notes.* Preface 'to Mr. Charles Wiley, Bookseller', signed 'the Author, New-York, January 1st, 1823'. Originally published New York 1823 (Blanck).
Further edns: 1827 (NSTC); 1832 (NSTC); 1844 (NSTC); French trans., 1823; German trans., 1824 [as *Die Ansiedler* (RS)].

1823: 29   [CORBETT, Marion and Margaret].
PETTICOAT TALES.

> Edinburgh: Printed for W. and C. Tait; and Longman, Hurst, Rees, Orme, and Brown, London, 1823.
> I 339p; II 342p. 12mo. 14s (ECB, ER).
> ER 39: 271–2 (Oct 1823); WSW II: 27.
> Corvey; CME 3-628-51118-6; ECB 444; NSTC 2C37724 (BI BL, E).

*Notes.* NSTC lists under both 'Margaret Corbett' and 'Marion and Margaret Corbett' (NSTC 2C37725).

1823: 30   CRUMPE, Miss [M. G. T.].
ISABEL ST ALBE: OR VICE AND VIRTUE. A NOVEL. IN THREE VOLUMES. BY MISS CRUMPE.

> Edinburgh: Printed for Archibald Constable and Company; and Hurst, Robinson, and Co. London; and John Cumming, Dublin, 1823.
> I vi, 293p; II 260p; III 230p. 12mo. 18s (ECB, ER).
> ER 38: 522 (May 1823).
> Corvey; CME 3-628-47354-3; ECB 146; NSTC 2C45429 (BI BL, C, E, O; NA MH).

*Notes.* Dedication to Sir Walter Scott, dated Limerick, 24 Feb 1823.

1823: 31   [CUTHBERTSON, Catherine].
THE HUT AND THE CASTLE; A ROMANCE. BY THE AUTHOR OF "THE ROMANCE OF THE PYRENEES;" "SANTO SEBASTIANO; OR, THE YOUNG PROTECTOR," &C. IN FOUR VOLUMES.

> London: Printed for Hurst, Robinson and Co. 90, Cheapside, and 8, Pall-Mall; and Archibald Constable & Co. Edinburgh, 1823.
> I 347p; II 305p; III 310p; IV 389p. 12mo. 28s (ECB, ER).
> ER 38: 522 (May 1823); WSW II: 83.
> Corvey; CME 3-628-47862-6; ECB 290; NSTC 2C48144 (BI BL, C, O).

DE QUINCEY, Thomas, THE STRANGER'S GRAVE
See GLEIG, George Robert

1823: 32   [GALT, John].

THE ENTAIL: OR THE LAIRDS OF GRIPPY. BY THE AUTHOR OF
ANNALS OF THE PARISH, SIR ANDREW WYLIE, &C. IN THREE VOL-
UMES.

> Edinburgh: William Blackwood, and T. Cadell, London, 1823.
> I 321p; II 333p; III 304p. 12mo. 21s (ECB, QR); 21s boards (ER).
> ER 38: 277 (Feb 1823), 39: 158–96 (Oct 1823) full review; QR 28: 269 (Oct 1822); WSW
> II: 97.
> Corvey; CME 3-628-47610-0; ECB 222; NSTC 2G1368 (BI BL, C, Dt, E, O; NA MH).

*Notes.* Dedication to the King, dated Edinburgh, 3 Dec 1822. Colophon in all 3 vols. reads
'Printed by George Ramsay & Co. Edinburgh 1822'. This is one of twelve novels which are
together given full reviews in ER (Oct 1823) under the title 'Secondary Scottish Novels'. ECB
dates Dec 1822.

Further edns: 1842 (NSTC); 1850 (NSTC); New York 1823 (NSTC) [also Philadelphia 1823
(NSTC)]; French trans., 1824 [as *Les Lairds de Grippy, ou le domaine substitué* (BN)]; German
trans., 1824 [as *Das Gewissen, oder die Heimkehr ins Vaterhaus. Ein Familiengemälde* (RS)].

1823: 33   [GALT, John].

THE GATHERING OF THE WEST: (ORIGINALLY PUBLISHED IN
BLACKWOOD'S EDINBURGH MAGAZINE.) BY THE AUTHOR OF THE
AYRSHIRE LEGATEES, THE ENTAIL, ANNALS OF THE PARISH, ETC.

> Edinburgh: William Blackwood, and T. Cadell, London, 1823.
> 131p. 12mo.
> BL N.119(1); NSTC 2W13387 (BI C, E, O).

*Notes.* Lacks a t.p.; the title appears on the front cover.
Further edn: 2nd edn. (with *The Ayrshire Legatees*) 1823 (NSTC).

1823: 34   [GALT, John].

RINGAN GILHAIZE; OR THE COVENANTERS. BY THE AUTHOR OF
"ANNALS OF THE PARISH," "SIR ANDREW WYLIE," "THE ENTAIL,"
&C. IN THREE VOLUMES.

> Edinburgh: Printed for Oliver & Boyd, High Street; and G. & W. B. Whittaker, London,
> 1823.
> I 308p; II 324p; III 323p. 12mo. 21s (ECB); 21s boards (ER).
> ER 38: 522–3 (May 1823), 39: 158–96 (Oct 1823) full review.
> Corvey; CME 3-628-48608-4; ECB 494; NSTC 2G1396 (BI BL, C, Dt, E, NCu, O; NA
> MH).

*Notes.* This is one of twelve novels which are together given full reviews in ER (Oct 1823)
under the title 'Secondary Scottish Novels'.
Further edn: New York 1823 (NSTC).

1823: 35   [GALT, John].

THE SPAEWIFE; A TALE OF THE SCOTTISH CHRONICLES. BY THE
AUTHOR OF "ANNALS OF THE PARISH," "RINGAN GILHAIZE," &C.
IN THREE VOLUMES.

Edinburgh: Published by Oliver & Boyd, Tweeddale-Court; and G. & W. B. Whittaker, Ave-Maria-Lane, London, 1823.

I 312p; II 318p; III 315p. 12mo. 21s (ECB, QR); 21s boards (ER).

ER 39: 512 (Jan 1824); QR 30: 295 (Oct 1823); WSW II: 97.

Corvey; CME 3-628-48664-5; ECB 552; NSTC 2G1400 (BI BL, C, Dt, E, O).

*Notes.* Further edns: Philadelphia 1824 (NSTC); German trans., 1825.

1823: 36    GAMBLE, John.
## CHARLTON, OR SCENES IN THE NORTH OF IRELAND; A TALE. IN THREE VOLUMES. BY JOHN GAMBLE, ESQ. AUTHOR OF "IRISH SKETCHES," "SARSFIELD," "HOWARD," &C. &C. &C.

London: Printed for Baldwin, Cradock, and Joy, 1823.

I xi, 275p; II 276p; III 244p. 12mo. 18s (ECB).

ER 40: 276 (Mar 1824); WSW II: 99.

Corvey; CME 3-628-47860-X; ECB 222; NSTC 2G1526 (BI BL, C, E, O).

*Notes.* ECB dates Dec 1823.

Further edn: 1827 as *Charlton, or Scenes in Ireland* (NSTC).

1823: 37    [GASPEY, Thomas].
## OTHER TIMES; OR, THE MONKS OF LEADENHALL. BY THE AUTHOR OF THE LOLLARDS;—THE MYSTERY; CALTHORPE, OR FALLEN FORTUNES; &C. &C. IN THREE VOLUMES.

London: Printed for Longman, Hurst, Rees, Orme, and Brown, Paternoster-Row, 1823.

I viii, 294p; II 282p; III 320p. 12mo. 18s (ECB, ER).

ER 38: 522 (May 1823); WSW II: 100–1.

Corvey; CME 3-628-48318-2; ECB 426; NSTC 2G3299 (BI BL, C, E; NA DLC, MH).

*Notes.* Pagination in vol. 3 continues through a 3 pp. list of 'Other Works by the same Author' (text proper ends at p. 317).

Further edn: German trans., 1823.

1823: 38    [GLEIG, George Robert].
## THE STRANGER'S GRAVE.

London: Printed for Longman, Hurst, Rees, Orme, Brown, and Green, Paternoster-Row, 1823.

vii, 306p. 12mo. 6s (ECB, ER).

ER 39: 512 (Jan 1824); WSW II: 35.

Corvey; CME 3-628-48678-5; ECB 565; NSTC 2S43885 (BI BL, C, O).

*Notes.* 'Advertisement' dated London, Oct 1823. Until recently, considered by modern scholars to be most probably by Thomas De Quincey: see, e.g., Grevel Lindop, 'Innocence and Revenge: The Problems of De Quincey's Fiction', in Robert Lance Snyder, *Thomas De Quincey: Bicentenary Studies* (Norman and London, 1985), pp. 213–38. Gleig's authorship however is established convincingly through evidence from the Longman archives by Barry Symonds, 'The Stranger's Grave: Laying a De Quinceyan Ghost', *The Charles Lamb Bulletin*, n.s. 83 (July 1993), 105–7.

Further edns: Exeter 1828 (NSTC); 1845 (NSTC); Boston 1824 (NUC).

1823: 39   [GRATTAN, Thomas Colley].
**HIGH-WAYS AND BY-WAYS; OR TALES OF THE ROADSIDE, PICKED UP IN THE FRENCH PROVINCES. BY A WALKING GENTLEMAN.**

> London: Printed for G. and W. B. Whittaker, Ave-Maria-Lane, 1823.
> xxiii, 432p. 8vo. 13s (ECB).
> ER 38: 454–67 (May 1823) full review; QR 28: 269 (Oct 1822); WSW II: 103.
> Corvey; CME 3-628-51028-7; ECB 268; NSTC 2G18165 (BI BL, C, Dt, E).

*Notes.* Dedication to Washington Irving. [1st series].
Further edns: 2nd edn. 1823 (NSTC); 1833 (NSTC); Boston 1824 (NSTC); German trans., 1824 [as *Heer- und Querstraßen, oder Erzählungen gesammelt auf einer Wanderung durch Frankreich, von einem fußreisenden Gentleman*, vols. 1–2 (RS)]; French trans., 1825 [as *Contes sur les grandes et petites routes* (BN)].

1823: 40   GREEN, [Sarah].
**GRETNA GREEN MARRIAGES; OR, THE NIECES. A NOVEL. IN THREE VOLUMES. BY MRS. GREEN, AUTHOR OF WHO IS THE BRIDEGROOM? THE CARTHUSIAN FRIAR; DECEPTION; THE FUGITIVE; GOOD MEN OF MODERN DATE; FESTIVAL OF ST. JAGO, ROYAL EXILE, &C.**

> London: Printed for A. K. Newman and Co. Leadenhall-Street, 1823.
> I 236p; II 238p; III 240p. 12mo. 16s 6d (ECB, ER).
> ER 39: 272 (Oct 1823).
> Corvey; CME 3-628-47907-X; ECB 243; NSTC 2G20157 (BI BL, E).

1823: 41   HARVEY, Jane.
**MOUNTALYTH, A TALE. IN THREE VOLUMES. BY JANE HARVEY, AUTHOR OF "SINGULARITY," &C.**

> London: Printed for Baldwin, Cradock, and Joy, 1823.
> I 234p; II 243p; III 240p. 12mo. 16s 6d (ECB); 15s (ER).
> ER 39: 512 (Jan 1824); WSW II: 108.
> Corvey; CME 3-628-47633-X; ECB 257; NSTC 2H11039 (BI BL, C).

1823: 42   HOFLAND, [Barbara].
**INTEGRITY. A TALE. BY MRS. HOFLAND, AUTHOR OF TALES OF THE PRIORY, TALES OF THE MANOR, AND A SON OF A GENIUS, &C. &C.**

> London: Printed for Longman, Hurst, Rees, Orme, and Brown, Paternoster-Row, 1823.
> 264p, ill. 12mo. 6s (ECB, ER).
> ER 38: 523 (May 1823); WSW II: 114.
> Corvey; CME 3-628-47664-X; ECB 275; NSTC 2H29399 (BI BL, C, Dt).

*Notes.* Further edns: 2nd edn. 1824 (NSTC); 1834 (NUC); Philadelphia 1823 (NUC).

1823: 43   HOGG, James.
**THE THREE PERILS OF WOMAN; OR, LOVE, LEASING, AND JEAL-OUSY. A SERIES OF DOMESTIC SCOTTISH TALES. BY JAMES HOGG, AUTHOR OF "THE THREE PERILS OF MAN," "QUEEN'S WAKE," &C. &C. IN THREE VOLUMES.**

London: Longman, Hurst, Rees, Orme, Brown, and Green, Paternoster-Row, 1823.
I 335p; II 333p; III 372p. 12mo. 21s boards (ER).
ER 39: 272 (Oct 1823); WSW II: 116.
Corvey; CME 3-628-47732-8; ECB 276; NSTC 2H25729 (BI BL, C, Dt, E, O).

*Notes.* Dedication to John Gibson Lockhart.
Further edns: New York 1823 (NUC); French trans., 1825.


1823: 44   HOLFORD, [Margaret] [afterwards HODSON] (*trans.*).
ITALIAN STORIES. TRANSLATED BY MISS HOLFORD, AUTHOR OF
"WALLACE," "WARBECK OF WOLFSTEIN," ETC.

London: Printed for J. Andrews, 167, New Bond Street, 1823.
vi, 188p. 12mo. 5s (ECB, ER, QR).
ER 39: 272 (Oct 1823); QR 29: 280 (Apr 1823); WSW II: 117.
BL 636.d.35; ECB 277; NSTC 2H26268 (BI C, O).

*Notes.* Dedication to Lady Wilmot dated 'London, June 19th'. Printer's mark of C. Whittingham, College House, Chiswick verso of t.p. and on last page. Collates in sixes.


1823: 45   HOOLE, Innes.
HEARTS VERSUS HEADS; OR, DIAMOND CUT DIAMOND. A NOVEL.
IN THREE VOLUMES. BY INNES HOOLE, ESQ. AUTHOR OF SCENES
AT BRIGHTON, SOCIETY AND SOLITUDE, &C.

London: Printed for A. K. Newman and Co. Leadenhall-Street, 1823.
I 235p; II 217p; III 228p. 12mo. 16s 6d (ECB).
Corvey; CME 3-628-47692-5; ECB 280; NSTC 2H29444 (BI BL, C, E, O; NA MH).

*Notes.* ECB dates Apr 1823.


1823: 46   HUME, Grace Stuart.
ALICE, OR INFIDELITY; THE TRIFLER; AND MY AUNT ANNE.
THREE TALES. BY GRACE STUART HUME. IN FIVE VOLUMES.

London: Printed for A. K. Newman and Co. Leadenhall-Street, 1823.
I iv, 319p; II 287p; III 310p; IV 289p; V 324p. 12mo. 30s (ECB).
Corvey; CME 3-628-51052-X; ECB 288; NSTC 2H36600 (BI BL).

*Notes.* ECB dates Dec 1822.


1823: 47   [JACSON, Frances].
ISABELLA. A NOVEL. BY THE AUTHOR OF "RHODA," &C. IN THREE
VOLUMES.

London: Printed for Henry Colburn and Co., 1823.
I 392p; II 348p; III 366p. 12mo. 24s (ECB, ER, QR).
ER 38: 277 (Feb 1823); QR 28: 269 (Oct 1822); WSW II: 17.
Corvey; CME 3-628-47872-3; ECB 301; NSTC 2L13755 (BI BL; NA MH).

*Notes.* Mistakenly ascribed in some catalogues to Alethea Lewis: see note to 1812: 42.
Further edn: Boston 1823 (NSTC).

1823: 48   JEFFERSON, Mr. [pseud.].

TALES OF OLD MR. JEFFERSON, OF GRAY'S INN. COLLECTED BY
YOUNG MR. JEFFERSON, OF LYON'S INN. THE FIRST SERIES. IN
TWO VOLUMES.

> London: G. and W. B. Whittaker, 13, Ave-Maria-Lane, 1823/25.
> I (1823) xii, 340p; II (1823) 334p; III (1825) 432p. 12mo. 22s 6d (ECB); 15s boards
> ([vols. 1 and 2] ER); 7s 6d (vol. 3, ER, QR).
> ER 38: 523 (May 1823) [vols. 1 and 2], 42: 513 (Aug 1825) vol. 3; QR 28: 269 (Oct 1822)
> Series I, 32: 267 (June 1825) vol. 3; WSW II: 125.
> Corvey; CME 3-628-51072-4; ECB 575; NSTC 2J3902 (3 vols. 1823/25 BI O; 2 vols. 1823
> BI BL, C; NA DLC, MH).

*Notes.* Vol. 3 t.p. reads: 'Tales of Old Mr. Jefferson, of Gray's Inn. Collected by Young Mr. Jefferson, of Lyon's Inn. In Three Volumes'. This volume has the imprint 'London: G. B. Whittaker, Ave-Maria-Lane, 1825'. ECB dates 1823–5.


1823: 49   [JONES, George].

TEMPTATION. A NOVEL. BY LEIGH CLIFFE, AUTHOR OF "THE
KNIGHTS OF RITZBERG,"—"PARGA," "SUPREME BON TON," &C.
IN THREE VOLUMES.

> London: J. C. Spence, Euston-Street, Euston Square, 1823.
> I 265p; II 263p; III 266p. 12mo.
> WSW II: 74.
> Corvey; CME 3-628-47293-8; NSTC 2C26368 (BI BL, C, O; NA MH).

*Notes.* Dedication to 'Sir Geo. R. Colier, Bart. K.C.B. &c.'. Preface signed 'L. C.', Fitzroy
Square, 30 Nov 1822.


1823: 50   JOUY, [Victor Joseph] É[tienne de] and JAY, A[ntoine].

THE HERMIT IN PRISON; TRANSLATED FROM THE FRENCH OF E.
JOUY, MEMBER OF THE INSTITUTE, AND AUTHOR OF THE HER-
MIT OF THE CHAUSSÉE D'ANTIN, SYLLA, &C.; AND A. JAY. IN TWO
VOLUMES.

> London: G. and W. B. Whittaker, Ave-Maria Lane, 1823.
> I viii, 263p; II 252p. 12mo. 14s (ECB); 14s boards (ER).
> ER 39: 272 (Oct 1823).
> BL N.153; ECB 314; NSTC 2J12621 (BI Dt, E, O).

*Notes.* Trans. of *Les Hermites en prison* (Paris, 1823).


1823: 51   [KENNEDY, Grace].

FATHER CLEMENT; A ROMAN CATHOLIC STORY. BY THE AUTHOR
OF "THE DECISION," &C.

> Edinburgh: Published by William Oliphant, 22, South Bridge Street; and sold by M.
> Ogle, and Chalmers & Collins, Glasgow; J. Finlay, Newcastle; Beilby & Knotts, Birm-
> ingham; J. Hatchard & Son, T. Hamilton, J. Nisbet, Ogle, Duncan & Co., B. J.
> Holdsworth, F. Westley, and Knight & Lacey, London, 1823.

370p. 18mo.
WSW II: 128.
BL 1509/3275; NSTC 2K3086 (BI E).

*Notes.* Further edns: 2nd edn. 1824 (NSTC); 3rd edn. 1825 (NSTC); 4th edn. 1825 (NSTC); 5th edn. 1826 (NSTC); 6th edn. 1828 (NSTC); [at least 4 more edns. to 1850]; New York 1827 (NSTC); French trans., 1825 [as *Le Père Clément, ou le jésuite confesseur* (BN)]; German trans., 1826 [as *Der Pater Clemens, oder der Jesuit als Beichtvater* (RS)].

1823: 52   [LAMB, Lady Caroline].
**ADA REIS, A TALE. IN THREE VOLUMES.**

> London: John Murray, Albemarle-Street, 1823.
> I xxiv, 243p; II 217p, music; III 149p. 8vo. 15s (ECB, ER).
> ER 38: 522 (May 1823); WSW II: 130.
> Corvey; CME 3-628-47010-2; ECB 4; NSTC 2L2304 (BI BL, C, E, O; NA MH).

*Notes.* Dedication to Lydia White.
Further edn: German trans., 1834.

1823: 53   LATHOM, Francis.
**LIVE AND LEARN; OR, THE FIRST JOHN BROWN, HIS FRIENDS, ENEMIES, AND ACQUAINTANCE, IN TOWN AND COUNTRY. A NOVEL. IN FOUR VOLUMES. BY FRANCIS LATHOM, AUTHOR OF PUZZLED AND PLEASED, THE MYSTERIOUS FREEBOOTER, THE UNKNOWN, VERY STRANGE BUT VERY TRUE, MEN AND MANNERS, ROMANCE OF THE HEBRIDES, ONE POUND NOTE, ITALIAN MYSTERIES, ASTONISHMENT, &C. &C.**

> London: Printed for A. K. Newman and Co. Leadenhall-Street, 1823.
> I xi, 260p; II 290p; III 317p; IV 292p. 12mo. 24s (ECB).
> Corvey; CME 3-628-47903-7; ECB 330; NSTC 2L5033 (BI BL, C, E, O).

*Notes.* Introductory 'A Few Words to Begin With', dated 1 Oct 1822. ECB dates Jan 1823.

1823: 54   LEFANU, [Alicia].
**DON JUAN DE LAS SIERRAS, OR, EL EMPECINADO. A ROMANCE. IN THREE VOLUMES. BY MISS LEFANU, AUTHOR OF HELEN MONTEAGLE, LEOLIN ABBEY, STRATHALLAN, TALES OF A TOURIST, &C.**

> London: Printed for A. K. Newman and Co. Leadenhall-Street, 1823.
> I iv, 210p; II 212p; III 298p. 12mo. 16s 6d (ECB, ER).
> ER 39: 512 (Jan 1824).
> Corvey; CME 3-628-47974-6; ECB 336; NSTC 2L9893 (BI BL, C, Dt, O).

*Notes.* Preface dated 10 Apr 1823.

1823: 55   LEFANU, [Alicia].
**TALES OF A TOURIST. CONTAINING THE OUTLAW, AND FASHIONABLE CONNEXIONS. IN FOUR VOLUMES. BY MISS LEFANU, AUTHOR OF STRATHALLAN, LEOLIN ABBEY, HELEN MONTEAGLE, &C.**

London: Printed for A. K. Newman and Co. Leadenhall-Street, 1823.
I 257p; II 268p; III 267p; IV 250p. 12mo. 22s (ECB).
QR 27: 271 (Apr 1822).
Corvey; CME 3-628-48046-9; ECB 336: NSTC 2L9900 (BI BL, C, O).
*Notes.* ECB dates Dec 1822.

1823: 56    LEWIS, Miss M. G.
GWENLLEAN. A TALE. BY MISS M. G. LEWIS. IN THREE VOLUMES.

London: J. C. Spence, Euston-Street, Euston Square, 1823.
I 250p; II 269p; III 251p. 12mo. 16s 6d (ECB).
WSW II: 134.
Corvey; CME 3-628-48041-8; ECB 249; NSTC 2L14111 (BI C).
*Notes.* ECB dates Feb 1823.

1823: 57    [LOCKHART, John Gibson].
REGINALD DALTON. BY THE AUTHOR OF VALERIUS, AND ADAM
BLAIR. IN THREE VOLUMES.

Edinburgh: William Blackwood, and T. Cadell. London, 1823.
I 346p; II 343p; III 337p. 8vo. 31s 6d (ECB, ER).
ER 38: 523 (May 1823), 39: 158-96 (Oct 1823) full review; WSW II: 136.
Corvey; CME 3-628-48561-4; ECB 484: NSTC 2L19483 (BI BL, C, E, O; NA DLC, MH).
*Notes.* Dedication to Henry Mackenzie. This is one of twelve novels which are together given
full reviews in ER (Oct 1823) under the title 'Secondary Scottish Novels'.
Further edns: 1842 (NSTC); 1849 (NSTC); New York 1823 (NSTC); German trans., 1824?

1823: 58    [LOGAN, Eliza].
ST JOHNSTOUN; OR, JOHN, EARL OF GOWRIE. IN THREE VOL-
UMES.

Edinburgh: Printed for MacLachlan and Stewart; and Baldwin, Cradock, and Joy, Lon-
    don, 1823.
I iv, 306p; II 300p; III 292p. 12mo. 21s (ECB); 21s boards (ER).
ER 39: 512 (Jan 1824); WSW II: 137.
Corvey; CME 3-628-48787-0; ECB 511; NSTC 2L19800 (BI BL, C, Dt, E, O; NA MH).
*Notes.* Dedication to 'the inhabitants of Perth'. 'Prefatory Notice to the Reader', alluding to
Scott as 'the Prince of Novelists', signed 'Peregrine Rover', 3 Sept 1823. 'Concluding Letter'
at end of vol. 3, pp. [207]–292, signed 'Peregrine Rover' and dated Edinburgh, 30 Sept 1823.
Further edns: 2nd edn. 1839 (NUC); German trans., 1824 [as *Der letzte Graf von Gowrie. His-
torischer Roman* (RS)].

1823: 59    M'CHRONICLE, Ronald [pseud.].
LEGENDS OF SCOTLAND. SECOND SERIES. IN THREE VOLUMES.
CONTAINING DAFT MARGET. BY RONALD M'CHRONICLE, ESQ.

London: Printed for A. K. Newman and Co. Leadenhall-Street, 1823.
I xx, 260p; II 253p; III 259p. 12mo. 16s 6d (QR).

QR 29: 280 (Apr 1823).

Corvey; CME 3-628-48070-1; ECB 358; NSTC 2M1928 (BI BL, C, Dt, E, O).

*Notes.* ECB lists three series, price 49s 6d.

1823: 60    [MACDONOGH, Felix].

**THE HERMIT ABROAD. BY THE AUTHOR OF THE HERMIT IN LONDON, AND HERMIT IN THE COUNTRY.**

> London: Printed for Henry Colburn and Co. Conduit-Street, Hanover-Square, 1823.
> I viii, 269p; II iv, 266p; III iv, 311p; IV iv, 316p. 12mo. 28s (ECB, ER).
> ER 40: 276 (Mar 1824); WSW II: 139.
> BL N.158; CME 3-628-47657-7 (vols. 1–3 only); ECB 265; NSTC 2M3272 (BI C, Dt, E, O; NA DLC, MH).

*Notes.* Further edn: French trans., 1824 [as *L'Hermite rôdeur* (NSTC)].

1823: 61    [MACHENRY, James].

**THE WILDERNESS; OR THE YOUTHFUL DAYS OF WASHINGTON. A TALE OF THE WEST. IN THREE VOLUMES. BY SOLOMON SECONDSIGHT.**

> London: Printed for A. K. Newman and Co. Leadenhall-Street, 1823.
> I iv, 291p; II 286p; III 299p. 12mo. 18s (ECB, ER, QR).
> ER 39: 272 (Oct 1823); QR 29: 280 (Apr 1823).
> Corvey; CME 3-628-47501-5; ECB 637; NSTC 2M4789 (BI BL, C).

*Notes.* Further edns: New York 1823 (NUC); German trans., 1827.

1823: 62    MAXWELL, Caroline.

**THE ACTRESS, OR COUNTESS AND NO COUNTESS. A NOVEL. BY CAROLINE MAXWELL, AUTHOR OF "MALCOLM DOUGLAS," "ALFRED OF NORMANDY," "EARL OF DESMOND," "FEUDAL TALES," &C. &C. IN FOUR VOLUMES.**

> London: Printed for Sherwood, Jones, and Co. Paternoster-Row, 1823.
> I xiv, 207p; II 200p; III 226p; IV 204p. 12mo. 16s (ECB).
> WSW II: 144.
> Corvey; CME 3-628-48201-1; ECB 375; NSTC 2M21270 (BI C).

*Notes.* ECB dates Mar 1823.

1823: 63    MEEKE, [Mary].

**WHAT SHALL BE, SHALL BE. A NOVEL. IN FOUR VOLUMES. BY MRS. MEEKE, AUTHOR OF THE VEILED PROTECTRESS; OLD WIFE AND YOUNG HUSBAND; THERE IS A SECRET! FIND IT OUT; WHICH IS THE MAN? THE SPANISH CAMPAIGN, &C.**

> London: Printed for A. K. Newman and Co. Leadenhall-Street, 1823.
> I 270p; II 315p; III 295p; IV 316p. 12mo. 24s (ECB, ER, QR).
> ER 39: 272 (Oct 1823); QR 29: 280 (Apr 1823).
> Corvey; CME 3-628-48051-5; ECB 378; NSTC 2M23138 (BI BL, C, O).

1823: 64    [MEMES, Mrs. John Smythe].
**PRECIPITANCE: A HIGHLAND TALE. BY A LADY. IN TWO VOLUMES.**

> Edinburgh: Printed for the Author; sold by Bell & Bradfute; Reid & Henderson, Glasgow; D. Weir, Greenock; Longman, Hurst, Rees, Orme, & Brown, London; and by J. Cumming, Dublin, 1823.
>
> I v, 275p; II 233p. 12mo. 12s (ECB); 12s boards (ER, QR).
>
> ER 39: 272 (Oct 1823); QR 29: 280 (Apr 1823); WSW II: 28.
>
> Corvey; CME 3-628-48368-9; ECB 468; NSTC 2M24105 (BI BL, C, E, O; NA MH).

*Notes.* Dedication 'to the Right Honourable Sir William Arbuthnot, Bart. Lord Provost of Edinburgh'.

1823: 65    [MOYSEY, Abel].
**THE CONFEDERATES: A STORY, IN THREE VOLUMES.**

> London: Printed for T. Hookham, Old Bond Street, 1823.
>
> I 359p; II 350p; III 342p. 12mo. 21s (ECB).
>
> WSW II: 154.
>
> Corvey; CME 3-628-47310-1; ECB 130; NSTC 2M39620 (BI BL, C, E, O; NA MH).

*Notes.* ECB dates Dec 1822.

1823: 66    [NEAL, John].
**LOGAN, A FAMILY HISTORY. IN FOUR VOLUMES.**

> London: Printed for A. K. Newman and Co. Leadenhall-Street, 1823.
>
> I ii, 300p; II 286p; III 302p; IV 321p. 12mo. 24s (ECB, ER).
>
> ER 38: 522 (May 1823); WSW II: 155.
>
> Corvey; CME 3-628-48049-3; ECB 351; NSTC 2N1997 (BI BL, C).

*Notes.* Originally published Philadelphia 1822 (Blanck).

1823: 67    [NEAL, John].
**SEVENTY-SIX. BY THE AUTHOR OF LOGAN. IN THREE VOLUMES.**

> Baltimore: Printed. London: Reprinted for G. and W. B. Whittaker, Ave-Maria-Lane, 1823.
>
> I 358p; II 327p; III 352p. 12mo. 18s (ECB); 18s boards (ER).
>
> ER 38: 523 (May 1823); WSW II: 155.
>
> Corvey; CME 3-628-48648-3; ECB 528; NSTC 2N2006 (BI BL, C).

*Notes.* Printer's mark and colophon in vol. 1 'Printed by Cox and Baylis, Great Queen Street'; in vol. 2 'Printed by William Clowes, Northumberland-Court'; in vol. 3 'Printed by Law and Gilbert, St. John's Square'. Originally published Baltimore 1823 (Blanck).

1823: 68    [PAULDING, James Kirke].
**KONINGSMARKE, THE LONG FINNE, A STORY OF THE NEW WORLD. IN THREE VOLUMES.**

> New York: Printed. London: Re-printed for G. and W. B. Whittaker, 1823.
>
> I 274p; II 257p; III 264p. 12mo. 18s (ECB, ER).
>
> ER 39: 512 (Jan 1824); WSW II: 159.
>
> Corvey; CME 3-628-47887-1; ECB 324; NSTC 2K8851 (BI BL, C; NA MH).

*Notes.* Printer's mark and colophon in vols. 1 and 2 'Printed by Cox and Baylis, Great Queen Street'; in vol. 3 colophon 'Printed by W. Clowes, Northumberland-Court', but printer's mark of 'Cox and Baylis, Great Queen Street'. Originally published New York 1823 (Blanck). Further edn: German trans., 1824.

1823: 69    [PROCTOR, George].
THE LUCUBRATIONS OF HUMPHREY RAVELIN, ESQ. LATE MAJOR IN THE ** REGIMENT OF INFANTRY.

> London: Printed for G. and W. B. Whittaker, Ave-Maria-Lane, 1823.
> 414p. 8vo. 12s (QR).
> QR 28: 269 (Oct 1822).
> Corvey; CME 3-628-51085-6; ECB 355; NSTC 2P27438 (BI BL, C, E, O; NA DLC).

*Notes.* Further edns: 2nd edn. 1824 (NSTC); German trans., 1824 [as *Humoristische Nachtwachen des ehemaligen brittischen Majors Humphrey Ravelin* (RS)].

1823: 70    [PYNE, William Henry].
WINE AND WALNUTS; OR, AFTER DINNER CHIT-CHAT. BY EPHRAIM HARDCASTLE, CITIZEN AND DRY-SALTER. IN TWO VOLUMES.

> London: Printed for Longman, Hurst, Rees, Orme, and Brown, Paternoster-Row, 1823.
> I viii, 324p; II viii, 340p. 8vo. 15s (ECB); 10s (ER).
> ER 38: 522 (May 1823).
> Corvey; CME 3-628-52903-4; ECB 254; NSTC 2H7390 (BI BL, C, Dt, E, O; NA DLC).

*Notes.* Further edn: 2nd edn. 1824 (NSTC).

1823: 71    REED, Andrew.
MARTHA: A MEMORIAL OF AN ONLY AND BELOVED SISTER. BY ANDREW REED, AUTHOR OF "NO FICTION; A NARRATIVE FOUNDED ON FACT." IN TWO VOLUMES.

> London: Printed for Francis Westley, 10, Stationers' Court, Ludgate Hill, and Longman, Hurst, Rees, Orme, and Brown, Paternoster-Row, 1823.
> I xii, 308p; II 334p. 8vo. 12s (ECB, ER).
> ER 38: 523 (May 1823); WSW II: 167.
> Corvey; CME 3-628-48521-5; ECB 482; NSTC 2R4712 (BI BL, C, O; NA MH).

*Notes.* Further edn: New York 1836 (NSTC).

1823: 72    ROCHE, Regina Maria.
BRIDAL OF DUNAMORE; AND LOST AND WON. TWO TALES. BY REGINA MARIA ROCHE, AUTHOR OF THE CHILDREN OF THE ABBEY, TRECOTHICK BOWER, MAID OF THE HAMLET, MUNSTER COTTAGE BOY, VICAR OF LANSDOWN, HOUSES OF OSMA AND ALMERIA, &C. IN THREE VOLUMES.

> London: Printed for A. K. Newman and Co. Leadenhall-Street, 1823.
> I 306p; II 282p; III 300p. 12mo. 21s (ECB, QR).
> QR 28: 269 (Oct 1822).
> Corvey; CME 3-628-48428-6; ECB 498; NSTC 2R14777 (BI BL, C, O).

*Notes.* ECB dates Dec 1822.
Further edn: French trans., 1824.

1823: 73   RUSSELL, Miss.
**SKETCH OF HER OWN CIRCLE: BY MISS RUSSELL. IN FOUR VOL-
UMES.**

> London: Printed for A. K. Newman and Co. Leadenhall-Street, 1823.
> I 286p; II 269p; III 268p; IV 284p. 12mo. 24s (ECB).
> Corvey; CME 3-628-48560-6; ECB 507; NSTC 2R20923 (BI BL, C, O).

*Notes.* ECB dates Mar 1823.

1823: 74   [SCOTT, Sir Walter].
**QUENTIN DURWARD. BY THE AUTHOR OF "WAVERLEY, PEVERIL
OF THE PEAK," &C. IN THREE VOLUMES.**

> Edinburgh: Printed for Archibald Constable and Co.; and Hurst, Robinson, and Co.
> London, 1823.
> I lxiii, 273p; II 331p; III 360p. 8vo. 31s 6d (ECB, ER).
> ER 38: 522 (May 1823); QR 35; 518–66 (Mar 1827) full review; WSW II:177.
> Corvey; CME 3-628-48583-5; ECB 476; NSTC 2S10140 (BI BL, C, Dt, E, NCu, O;
> NA MH).

*Notes.* 'This day published', 22 May 1823, *Edinburgh Evening Courant.* This is one of nine
novels which are together given full reviews in QR (Mar 1827) under the page-top heading
'Historical Romance'.
Further edns: 2nd edn. 1823 (NSTC); Philadelphia 1823 (NSTC); French trans., 1823; German trans., 1823. Numerous reprintings in collected edns.

1823: 75   [SHELLEY, Mary Wollstonecraft].
**VALPERGA: OR, THE LIFE AND ADVENTURES OF CASTRUCCIO,
PRINCE OF LUCCA. BY THE AUTHOR OF "FRANKENSTEIN." IN
THREE VOLUMES.**

> London: Printed for G. and W. B. Whittaker, Ave-Maria-Lane, 1823.
> I iv, 293p; II 287p; III 269p. 12mo. 21s (ECB).
> WSW II: 181–2.
> Corvey; CME 3-628-48856-7; ECB 532; NSTC 2S18457 (BI BL, C, Dt, O; NA DLC,
> MH).

*Notes.* ECB dates Feb 1823.
Further edn: German trans., 1824.
Facs: RR (1995).

1823: 76   SIMPSON, John.
**RICARDO THE OUTLAW: A ROMANCE. IN TWO VOLUMES. BY CAP-
TAIN JOHN SIMPSON, OF THE ROYAL MARINES.**

> London: Printed by W. Myers, Bedford Place, Commercial Road. For J. J. Jones,
> 28 Leadenhall Street, 1823.

I 294p; II 286p. 12mo. 14s (ECB).

Corvey; CME 3-628-48701-3; ECB 538; NSTC 2S22245 (BI BL; NA DLC).

*Notes.* ECB dates Mar 1823.

Further edn: 2nd edn. 1823 (NUC).

1823: 77    SPENCE, Elizabeth Isabella.

**HOW TO BE RID OF A WIFE, AND THE LILY OF ANNANDALE: TALES, BY ELIZABETH ISABELLA SPENCE, AUTHOR OF "LETTERS FROM THE NORTH HIGHLANDS," "OLD STORIES," &C. &C. IN TWO VOLUMES.**

London: Printed for Longman, Hurst, Rees, Orme, Brown, and Green, Paternoster-Row, 1823.

I 327p; II 256p. 12mo. 12s (ECB, ER).

ER 41: 266 (Oct 1824); WSW II: 189.

Corvey; CME 3-628-48721-8; ECB 554; NSTC 2S33536 (BI BL, C, E, O; NA MH).

*Notes.* ECB dates Jan 1834 [*sic*].

1823: 78    STEPHENS, Nella.

**DE MOWBRAY; OR, THE STRANGER KNIGHT. A ROMANCE. IN FOUR VOLUMES. BY NELLA STEPHENS.**

London: Printed for A. K. Newman and Co. Leadenhall-Street, 1823.

I 235p; II 236p; III 240p; IV 247p. 12mo. 24s (ECB); 22s (ER).

ER 39: 271 (Oct 1823).

Corvey; CME 3-628-48621-1; ECB 561; NSTC 2S38610 (BI BL, C).

1823: 79    [STODDART, Lady Isabella Wellwood].

**ANNALS OF THE FAMILY OF M'ROY. IN THREE VOLUMES. BY MRS. BLACKFORD, AUTHOR OF "TALES OF MY AUNT MARTHA," "SCOTTISH ORPHANS," &C.**

London: W. Wetton, 65, Paternoster-Row. To be had at all Circulating Libraries in Town or Country, 1823.

I viii, 260p; II 260p; III 234p. 12mo. 24s (ECB).

WSW II: 190–1.

Corvey; CME 3-628-47226-1; ECB 59; NSTC 2B36116 (BI BL, C, E, O).

*Notes.* Preface signed Martha Blackford. ECB dates July 1823.

Further edn: German trans., 1826 [as *Die Schwestern, oder die Gefahren der Verheimlichung, ein Spiegel für junge Töchter; aus den Denkwürdigkeiten der Familie Mac Roy* (RS)].

1823: 80    [SUTHERLAND, Alexander].

**MACRIMMON. A HIGHLAND TALE. IN FOUR VOLUMES. BY THE AUTHOR OF REDMOND THE REBEL, COSPATRICK OF RAYMONDSHOLM, ST. KATHLEEN, &C.**

London: Printed for A. K. Newman and Co. Leadenhall-Street, 1823.

I 305p; II 316p; III 307p; IV 281p. 12mo. 24s (ECB, ER, QR).

ER 37: 536 (Nov 1822); QR 28: 268 (Oct 1822); WSW II: 192.
Corvey; CME 3-628-48140-6; ECB 361; NSTC 2S474781 (BI BL, C, E).

*Notes.* ECB dates Dec 1822.

**TAYLER, Charles Benjamin, MAY YOU LIKE IT**
See 1822: 74

1823: 81　[WALKER, . . .].
**RICH AND POOR.**
　　　Edinburgh: William Blackwood, and T. Cadell, London, 1823.
　　　401p. 8vo. 10s 6d (ECB, ER, QR).
　　　ER 39: 272 (Oct 1823); QR 29: 280 (Apr 1823); WSW II: 198.
　　　Corvey; CME 3-628-48570-3; ECB 492; NSTC 2R8959 (BI BL, C, O; NA MH).

*Notes.* CG gives author as Walker, Mrs, but no further evidence for this prefix has been found.

1823: 82　WARD, Catherine G[eorge].
**THE COTTAGE ON THE CLIFF. A SEA-SIDE STORY. BY CATHERINE
G. WARD, AUTHORESS OF—THE ROSE OF CLAREMONT,—THE
MYSTERIOUS MARRIAGE,—FAMILY PORTRAITS, &C. &C. &C.**
　　　London: Printed by C. Baynes, 13, Duke Street, Lincoln's-Inn-Fields. Published by
　　　　　George Virtue, No. 26, Ivy Lane, Paternoster-Row, and Bath Street, Bristol, 1823.
　　　750p, ill. 8vo. 16s (ECB).
　　　Corvey; CME 3-628-48825-7; ECB 623; NSTC 2W4955 (BI BL, C, Dt, E; NA MH).

*Notes.* Collates in fours.
Further edns: 1825 (Corvey); New York 1834 (NSTC).

1823: 83　WARD, Catherine G[eorge].
**THE MYSTERIES OF ST. CLAIR; OR, MARIETTE MOULINE. BY MRS.
CATHERINE G. WARD, AUTHORESS OF THE FOLLOWING POPULAR
NOVELS, VIZ. THE MYSTERIOUS MARRIAGE—THE ROSE OF CLARE-
MONT—ORPHAN　BOY—THE　THORN—FAMILY　PORTRAITS—
COTTAGE ON THE CLIFF—WIDOW'S CHOICE, &C.**
　　　London: Printed and published by Jaques and Wright, Eagle Office, Cross Street, New-
　　　　　ington Butts. Sold also by D. Jaques, Chelsea; and all other Booksellers, 1823.
　　　624p, ill. 8vo.
　　　NjP 3850.64.366; xNSTC.

*Notes.* Collates in fours.
Further edn: 1824 (NSTC 2W4965).

1823: 84　WARD, Catherine G[eorge].
**THE WIDOW'S CHOICE; OR, ONE, TWO, THREE. BY CATHERINE G.
WARD, AUTHORESS OF THE ROSE OF CLAREMONT; MYSTERIOUS
MARRIAGE; ORPHAN BOY; THORN, OR DOUBTFUL PROPERTY;
FAMILY PORTRAITS; AND THE COTTAGE ON THE CLIFF.**

London: Published by J. Saunders, 24, Ivy Lane, Paternoster-Row; Bartlett and Hinton, Oxford; J. Bennett, 5, Cornwall Street, Plymouth; and may be had at every respectable Bookseller throughout the United Kingdom, 1823.

621p, ill. 8vo.

BL P.P.241(13); NSTC 2W4971 (BI C, Dt, O).

*Notes.* Title details from BL copy, consisting of first number (24 pp.) only. Original wrapper announces: 'This truly interesting Work will be printed from Stereotype Plates on a superfine paper, embellished with beautiful Copperplate Engravings, and completed in about 25 numbers, price 6d each, or in Parts, at 2s each.' Pagination from the Harvard copy (MH 18495.3.3.15), which includes an engraved t.p. with the imprint 'London: Published Nov. 7 1823 by J. Saunders 1. Little Bartholomew Close. West Smithfield'. Opposite this is an illustration with imprint: 'Published by J. Saunders, 24 Ivy Lane, Paternoster Row. London, March 29, 1823'. Another t.p. in this Harvard copy bears the date 1824.

Further edn: 1824 (NSTC).


1823: 85

WIELAND, Christoph M[artin]; COKE, Charles Richard (*trans.*).

**CRATES AND HIPPARCHIA. A TALE, IN A SERIES OF LETTERS; TRANSLATED FROM THE GERMAN OF CHRISTOPHER M. WIELAND: BY CHARLES RICHARD COKE.**

Norwich: Printed by and for John Stacy, and sold in London, by Longman, Hurst, Rees, Orme, and Brown; Baldwin, Cradock, and Joy; G. and W. B. Whittaker; Harvey and Darton; W. Wright; C. H. Baldwyn; and Henry Mozley, Derby, 1823.

xii, 132p. 8vo.

BL 12611.d.9; NSTC 2W19328 (BI O).

*Notes.* Trans. of *Krates und Hipparchia* (Stuttgart, 1805). 'Subscribers' (*c.*260 listed), pp. [v]–ix, including Mrs Opie.


**WILKINS, George, BODY AND SOUL**

See 1822: 81


1823: 86   [WILSON, James].

**THE FIRE-EATER.**

Edinburgh: John Anderson, jun., 55, North Bridge Street; and Simpkin & Marshall, London, 1823.

xi, 368p. 12mo. 8s (ECB, ER).

ER 39: 272 (Oct 1823); WSW II: 204.

Corvey; CME 3-628-47606-2; ECB 206; NSTC 2W25420 (BI BL, C, E; NA MH).

*Notes.* Introductory Address 'to the Courteous Reader' signed 'the Editor', Edinburgh, 10 July 1823. Dedication to John Wilson.


1823: 87   [WILSON, John].

**THE TRIALS OF MARGARET LYNDSAY. BY THE AUTHOR OF LIGHTS AND SHADOWS OF SCOTTISH LIFE.**

Edinburgh: William Blackwood, and T. Cadell, London, 1823.
403p. 8vo. 10s 6d (ECB).
ER 39: 158–96 (Oct 1823) full review; WSW II: 205.
Corvey; CME 3-628-48830-3; ECB 599; NSTC 2W25754 (BI BL, E, O; NA DLC, MH).

*Notes.* This is one of twelve novels which are together given full reviews in ER (Oct 1823) under the title 'Secondary Scottish Novels'.
Further edns: 2nd edn. 1823 (NSTC); 3rd edn. 1827 (NSTC); New York 1823 (NSTC); French trans., 1823; German trans., 1827 [as *Margarethens Prüfungen. Ein Familiengemälde* (RS)].

# 1824

**1824: 1 ANON.**
**ARTHUR SEYMOUR. IN TWO VOLUMES.**

London: Printed for Longman, Hurst, Rees, Orme, Brown, and Green, Paternoster-Row, 1824.
I 214p; II 259p. 12mo. 12s (ECB).
WSW II: 4.
Corvey; CME 3-628-47073-0; ECB 28; NSTC 2S14512 (BI BL; NA MH).

*Notes.* Dedication 'to myself'. ECB dates Dec 1823.

**1824: 2 ANON.**
**CAPRICE: OR ANECDOTES OF THE LISTOWEL FAMILY. AN IRISH NOVEL, IN THREE VOLUMES, BY AN UNKNOWN.**

London: Sherwood, Jones and Co. Paternoster-Row, and C. P. Archer, Dublin, 1824.
I 286p; II 346p; III 376p. 12mo. 21s (ECB, QR); 21s boards (ER).
ER 41: 267 (Oct 1824), 41: 519 (Jan 1825); QR 31: 260 (Dec 1824); WSW II: 6.
Corvey; CME 3-628-47211-3; ECB 96; NSTC 2U872 (BI BL).

**THE CONFESSIONS OF A GAMESTER**

See PEERS, J. W.

**1824: 3 ANON.**
**EMILY; OR, TRAITS OF PRINCIPLE. A TALE. BY A LADY.**

London: Otridge and Rackham, in the Strand; and W. Sams, St. James's Street, n.d. [1824].
iv, 302p. 8vo. 6s (ECB).
WSW II: 10.
BL 12651.g.60; ECB 186; NSTC 2E9258 (NA MH).

*Notes.* ECB dates June 1824.

1824: 4   ANON.

THE FAMILY PICTURE GALLERY; OR, EVERY-DAY SCENES. DEPICTED BY MANY CLOSE OBSERVERS, AND BY THEM SELECTED. IN FOUR VOLUMES.

> London: Printed for John Booth, Duke Street, Portland Place, 1824.
> I 368p; II 404p; III 400p; IV 374p. 8vo. 42s (ECB, QR).
> QR 30: 590 (Jan 1824).
> Corvey; CME 3-628-47546-5; ECB 199; NSTC 2F1611 (BI BL, C, O).

1824: 5   ANON.

THE FATHER AND SON, A TALE, BY A FRIEND TO YOUTH.

> London: Printed by the Philanthropic Society, St. George's Fields, 1824.
> iv, 209p. 12mo. 5s (QR).
> QR 32: 267 (June 1825).
> Corvey; CME 3-628-47499-X; NSTC 2F2774 (BI BL, C, O).

*Notes.* ECB 201 lists Simpkin edn., Feb 1825, but not discovered in this form.

1824: 6   ANON.

FIRST LOVE; A TALE OF MY MOTHER'S TIMES. IN TWO VOLUMES.

> London: L. Relfe, Cornhill, 1824.
> I 244p; II 244p. 12mo. 10s 6d (ECB).
> WSW II: 12.
> Corvey; CME 3-628-47555-4; ECB 206; xNSTC.

*Notes.* Prefatory statement (1 p. unn.) claims: 'The author of the following pages is totally unknown to the publisher', the manuscript having been placed in his hands 'by a literary friend, to whom it had been confided'. Distinct from the epistolary *First Love* (1801: 6). ECB dates Dec 1823.

1824: 7   ANON.

GILMOUR; OR, THE LAST LOCKINGE. IN THREE VOLUMES.

> London: Printed for Geo. B. Whittaker, Ave-Maria-Lane, 1824.
> I 348p; II 319p; III 387p. 12mo. 21s (ECB, ER, QR).
> ER 41: 520 (Jan 1825); QR 31: 532 (Mar 1825); WSW II: 13.
> Corvey; CME 3-628-47817-0; ECB 231; NSTC 2G8574 (BI BL, C, O; NA MH).

*Notes.* 'Advertisement' dated Birkrigge, 28 May 1824.
Further edn: French trans., 1829.

1824: 8   ANON.

THE HUMAN HEART.

> London: Printed for Taylor and Hessey, 93, Fleet Street, and 13, Waterloo Place, Pall Mall, 1824.
> xii, 370p. 8vo. 10s 6d (ECB, ER).
> ER 41: 267 (Oct 1824); WSW II: 15.
> Corvey; CME 3-628-51041-4; ECB 288; NSTC 2H36299 (BI BL, E, O; NA DLC).

1824: 9   ANON.
**JAMES FORBES; A TALE, FOUNDED ON FACTS.**

> London: Printed for J. Hatchard and Son, 187, Piccadilly, 1824.
> 275p. 8vo. 7s (ECB, ER).
> ER 41: 520 (Jan 1825); WSW II: 18.
> Corvey; CME 3-628-47942-8; ECB 305; NSTC 2F10215 (BI BL, C, O).

*Notes.* Dedication 'to Mrs. Mackinnon'.

**MUCH TO BLAME**
See OPIE, Amelia Alderson

1824: 10   ANON.
**PROCRASTINATION; OR, THE VICAR'S DAUGHTER. A TALE.**

> London: Printed for Burton and Smith, Leadenhall-Street; and sold by W. Simpkin and
>     R. Marshall, Stationers' Court, 1824.
> 236p, ill. 12mo. 5s (ECB).
> Corvey; CME 3-628-48416-2; ECB 471; NSTC 2P27362 (BI BL, C).

*Notes.* ECB dates Jan 1824.

1824: 11   ANON.
**THE RELAPSE; OR, TRUE AND FALSE MORALITY.**

> London: Printed for J. Hatchard and Son, 187, Piccadilly, 1824.
> 209p. 12mo. 4s 6d (ECB).
> O 24.430; ECB 485; NSTC 2R6372.

*Notes.* ECB dates June 1824.

**SINCERITY: A TALE**
See TAYLOR, Jane

1824: 12   ANON.
**SIR ANDREW SAGITTARIUS; OR, THE PERILS OF ASTROLOGY. A NOVEL, IN THREE VOLUMES.**

> London: James Haldane, Tottenham Court Road, 1824.
> I vii, 235p; II 232p; III 240p. 12mo. 18s (ECB).
> WSW II: 33.
> Corvey; CME 3-628-48705-6; ECB 539; NSTC 2S1358 (BI BL, O).

*Notes.* ECB dates Feb 1824.

1824: 13   ANON.
**TALES FROM AFAR. BY A CLERGYMAN. LATELY RESIDENT ABROAD; AUTHOR OF 'AN ALPINE TALE,' 'TALES FROM SWITZER-LAND', &C. &C.**

> London: Printed for Francis Westley, 10, Stationers' Court, and Ave-Maria-Lane, 1824.
> 241p, ill. 12mo. 4s 6d (ECB); 4s 6d boards (ER).

ER 41: 266 (Oct 1824); WSW II: 36.

Corvey; CME 3-628-51145-3; ECB 575; xNSTC.

*Notes.* The works given to the author in the title are attributed in some catalogues to [Madame] A. Yosy, though mention also here of 'a Clergyman' points to male authorship— see also 1822: 12 and 1823: 1. One of the 6 items in this collection, 'The Drooping Lily', is a poem; another ('The Village Pastor') is 'concluded from vol. 1 of *Tales from Switzerland*' (see 1822: 12).

1824: 14   ANDERSON, Major.

**LEAVE OF ABSENCE, BY THE LATE MAJOR ANDERSON, AUTHOR OF "THE WANDERER IN CEYLON," &C. &C.**

> Cardiff: Printed by R. Lloyd, and sold by W. Bird, Bookseller; and by Longman, Hurst, Rees, Orme, Brown, and Green, London, 1824.
>
> 168p. 8vo.
>
> IU 823.An.235c; xNSTC.

*Notes.* List of Subscribers (76 names), pp. [165]–168. Collates in fours.

1824: 15   [BANIM, John].

**REVELATIONS OF THE DEAD-ALIVE.**

> London: Printed for W. Simpkin and R. Marshall, Stationers'-Hall Court, Ludgate Street, 1824.
>
> 376p. 12mo. 10s 6d (ECB).
>
> BL N.242; ECB 490; NSTC 2B6674 (BI C, Dt, E, O).

*Notes.* Fold-out 'Prophetical Chart' between pp. 96 and 97, 'to face Page xix'; but this is probably misbound in BL copy and relates to another text. ECB dates Nov 1824.

Further edn: 1845 as *London and its Eccentricities in the year 2023* (NSTC).

1824: 16   BARBER, Agnes Anne.

**COUNTRY BELLES; OR, GOSSIPS OUTWITTED. BY AGNES ANNE BARBER. IN THREE VOLUMES.**

> London: Printed for Longman, Hurst, Rees, Orme, Brown, and Green, Paternoster-Row, 1824.
>
> I xi, 245p; II 255p; III 279p. 12mo.
>
> WSW II: 46.
>
> Corvey; CME 3-628-47101-X; ECB 139; NSTC 2B7196 (BI BL, C).

*Notes.* Dedication 'to Mrs. Northmore, Cleve House, Devonshire', signed Agnes A. Barber, —— Priory, 12 July 1823.

1824: 17   BARBER, Elizabeth.

**TALES OF MODERN DAYS. BY ELIZABETH BARBER, AUTHOR OF "DANGEROUS ERRORS"—"INFLUENCE AND EXAMPLE."**

> London: Published by Sherwood, Jones, and Co., Paternoster-Row, 1824.
>
> ix, 340p. 12mo. 6s (ECB, ER).
>
> ER 41: 267 (Oct 1824), 41: 520 (Jan 1825); WSW II: 46.

Corvey; CME 3-628-47102-8; ECB 39; xNSTC.

*Notes.* Further edn: 1840 (NSTC 2B7218).

1824: 18    [BRISTOW, Amelia].
THE FAITHFUL SERVANT; OR, THE HISTORY OF ELIZABETH
ALLEN. A NARRATIVE OF FACTS.

London: Printed for Francis Westley, 10, Stationers' Court; and Ave-Maria Lane, 1824.
xii, 216p. 12mo.
O 24.1; NSTC 2B48810.

*Notes.* Dedication 'to her Subscribers' by the Author. List of Subscribers (152 names),
pp. [v]–vii.
Further edns: 2nd edn. 1824 (NSTC); 4th edn. 1832 as *Elizabeth Allen; or, the Faithful Servant*
(NSTC).

1824: 19    {B}[UDDEN], {M}[aria] {E}[lizabeth].
HELENA EGERTON; OR, TRAITS OF FEMALE CHARACTER. IN TWO
VOLUMES. BY THE AUTHOR OF ALWAYS HAPPY, CLAUDINE, &C.
NEW EDITION, REVISED AND CORRECTED BY THE AUTHOR.

London: Printed for A. K. Newman and Co. Leadenhall-Street, 1824.
I 246p; II 248p. 12mo. 10s (ER).
ER 41: 267 (Oct 1824); WSW II: 194.
BL 12614.k.2; ECB 263; NSTC 2B56480 (BI C, O).

*Notes.* Dedication 'to an Affectionate Mother', signed 'M. E. B. London, 1824'. Note in vol. 1,
p. [3], reads: 'The following Work has already appeared before the Public, under another title
(Woman, or Minor Maxims). The present edition, it is hoped, is free from the faults of the
former one.' A reissue, with authorial revisions, of 1818: 24. Both this title and the previous
version have been mistakenly attributed to Elizabeth Thomas, as the result of each writer
having written a work titled *Claudine*. For Thomas's *Claudine; or Pertinacity*, see 1817: 55.
Budden's *Claudine, or Humility the basis of all virtues* (1822), a didactic work directed at children, is not included as an entry in this Bibliography. ECB lists price as 2s, apparently in
error.

1824: 20    BUTT, George.
THE SPANISH DAUGHTER. BY THE REV. GEORGE BUTT, LATE
CHAPLAIN IN ORDINARY TO HIS MAJESTY; REVISED AND COR-
RECTED BY HIS DAUGHTER, MRS. SHERWOOD, AUTHOR OF "STO-
RIES ON THE CHURCH CATECHISM," "THE FAIRCHILD FAMILY,"
&C. &C. IN TWO VOLUMES.

London: Published by Knight and Lacey, 24, Paternoster-Row; and M. A. Nattali, Tavi-
stock-Street, Covent-Garden, 1824.
I xxiv, 217p; II 222p. 8vo. 16s (ECB, ER, QR).
ER 40: 547 (July 1824); QR 30: 590 (Jan 1824); WSW II: 61–2.
Corvey; CME 3-628-48667-X; ECB 89; NSTC 2B63194 (BI BL, C, O).

*Notes.* Further edns: Boston 1824 (NSTC) [also New York 1824 (NSTC)].

1824: 21    [CAREY, David].
**FREDERICK MORLAND; BY THE AUTHOR OF "LOCHIEL; OR, THE FIELD OF CULLODEN," &C. &C. IN TWO VOLUMES.**

> London: Printed for G. and W. B. Whittaker, Ave-Maria-Lane, 1824.
> I vii, 280p; II 251p. 12mo. 14s (ECB).
> WSW II: 70.
> Corvey; CME 3-628-47836-7; ECB 216; NSTC 2C7014 (BI BL, C; NA MH).

*Notes.* ECB dates Feb 1824.

1824: 22    CAREY, Joanna.
**LASTING IMPRESSIONS: A NOVEL, IN THREE VOLUMES. BY MRS. JOANNA CAREY.**

> London: Printed for Longman, Hurst, Rees, Orme, Brown, and Green, Paternoster-
>     Row, 1824.
> I v, 367p; II 382p; III 370p. 12mo. 21s (ECB).
> WSW II: 70.
> Corvey; CME 3-628-47214-8; ECB 97; NSTC 2C7139 (BI BL, C, E, O).

*Notes.* 'Advertisement' dated West Square, Nov 1824. ECB dates Nov 1824.

1824: 23    CHARLTON, Mary.
**GRANDEUR AND MEANNESS; OR, DOMESTIC PERSECUTION. A NOVEL. IN THREE VOLUMES. BY MARY CHARLTON, AUTHOR OF THE WIFE AND MISTRESS, ROSELLA, &C. &C.**

> London: Printed for A. K. Newman and Co. Leadenhall-Street, 1824.
> I 331p; II 318p; III 342p. 12mo. 21s (ECB, ER).
> ER 41: 266 (Oct 1824).
> Corvey; CME 3-628-47254-7; ECB 107; NSTC 2C16520 (BI BL, C, O).

1824: 24    [CHARLTON, Mary].
**PAST EVENTS; AN HISTORICAL NOVEL, OF THE EIGHTEENTH CEN-TURY, BY THE AUTHOR OF "THE WIFE AND THE MISTRESS," "THE PIRATE OF NAPLES," "ROSELLA," "ANDRONICA," &C., &C. IN THREE VOLUMES.**

> London: Printed for R. P. Moore, Store Street, Bedford Square, 1824.
> I xi, 318p; II 308p; III 315p. 12mo. 21s (ECB).
> WSW II: 72.
> Corvey; CME 3-628-48403-0; ECB 436; NSTC 2C16521 (BI BL, C, O; NA MH).

*Notes.* ECB dates May 1824.
Further edn: 1830 as *Past Events; or the Treacherous Guide, a Romance* (NjP, NUC).

1824: 25    [COLQUHOUN, John Campbell].
**ZOE: AN ATHENIAN TALE.**

> Edinburgh: Printed for Archibald Constable & Co.; and Hurst, Robinson & Co. Lon-
>     don, 1824.

ix, 115p. 12mo. 3s 6d (ECB); 3s 6d boards (ER).
ER 40: 276 (Mar 1824); WSW II: 76.
Corvey; CME 3-628-49003-0; ECB 655; NSTC 2C32174 (BI BL, C, E, O).

*Notes.* Dedication dated Edinburgh, Mar 1824.

1824: 26    [COOPER, James Fenimore].
**THE PILOT; A TALE OF THE SEA. BY THE AUTHOR OF "THE SPY," "PIONEERS," &C. &C. &C. IN THREE VOLUMES.**

London: John Miller, 5, New Bridge Street, Blackfriars, 1824.
I viii, 268p; II 342p; III 303p. 12mo. 21s (ECB).
WSW II: 77–8.
Corvey; ECB 134; NSTC 2C36860 (BI BL, C, Dt, O).

*Notes.* ECB dates Jan 1824. Originally published New York 1823 (Blanck, NSTC).
Further edns: 3rd edn. 1831 (NSTC); London & Liverpool 1831 (Blanck); 1835 (NSTC);
1836 (NSTC); 1839 (NSTC); French trans., 1824; German trans., 1824 [as *Der Lootse, oder Abentheuer an Englands Küste. Ein Seegemälde* (RS)].

1824: 27    [CRAWFORD, Archibald.]
**THE TALES OF MY GRANDMOTHER.**

Ayr: Printed for the Author, and sold by John Dick, Bookseller, Sandgate, 1824.
viii, 300p. 12mo.
E Bl.9/3; NSTC 2C42498.

*Notes.* Introduction in the facetious manner of Walter Scott. Collates in sixes. Republished in 2 vols., with additional tales, by Archibald Constable (compare 1825: 22).

1824: 28    DAVENPORT, Selina.
**PREFERENCE. A NOVEL. IN TWO VOLUMES. BY SELINA DAVENPORT, AUTHOR OF THE HYPOCRITE, OR MODERN JANUS; DONALD MONTEITH; AN ANGEL'S FORM AND DEVIL'S HEART; ORIGINAL OF THE MINIATURE; LEAP YEAR, &C. &C.**

London: Printed for A. K. Newman and Co. Leadenhall-Street, 1824.
I 283p; II 224p. 12mo. 12s (ECB).
WSW II: 29.
Corvey; CME 3-628-47375-6; ECB 153; NSTC 2D3614 (BI BL, C, O).

*Notes.* ECB dates July 1824.

1824: 29    [DILLON, Henry Augustus Dillon-Lee, Viscount].
**ROSALINE DE VERE. IN TWO VOLUMES.**

London: Treuttel and Würtz, Treuttel, jun. and Richter, 30 Soho Square, 1824.
I v, 281p; II 277p. 8vo. 16s (ECB).
WSW II: 87.
Corvey; CME 3-628-48547-9; ECB 502; NSTC 2D13577 (BI BL, C, O; NA MH).

*Notes.* ECB dates May 1824.

1824: 30   DUBOIS, Henr[i] L[eopold].

ADOLPHE AND SELANIE, OR, THE POWER OF ATTACHMENT. A MORAL TALE. FOUNDED ON FACTS. BY HENRY L. DUBOIS, TEACHER OF FRENCH LANGUAGE, EDINBURGH.

> Edinburgh: John Carfrae & Son; and Longman & Co., 1824.
> xvi, 382p. 12mo.
> WSW II: 90.
> BL 12510.dd.24; NSTC 2D20842.

*Notes.* 'Subscribers' Names' (*c.*350 listed, mainly Scottish, including Sir Walter Scott, Francis Jeffrey, J. G. Lockhart, and John Galt), pp. [ix]–xvi.

1824: 31(a)   DURAS, [Claire Louise Rose Bonne, Duchesse de].

OURIKA, A TALE. BY THE DUCHESS DE DURAS.

> London: Printed for James Cawthorn, Cockspur-Street, 1824.
> 107p. 8vo.
> C Rom.1.44¹; NSTC 2D23442 (BI BL, O; NA MH).

*Notes.* Trans. of *Ourika* (Paris, 1824). Extract quoted from the *Literary Gazette*, No. 383, between t.p. and half-titles (1 p. unn.): 'About a month ago a very pretty story under this title was published in Paris. It soon not only attracted attention, but became "quite the rage", and every thing in fashion, and drama, and picture, has since been Ourika. There are Ourika dresses, Ourika vaudevilles, Ourika prints.'

1824: 31(b)   [DURAS, Claire Louise Rose Bonne, Duchesse de].

OURIKA.

> London: Printed for Longman, Hurst, Rees, Orme, Brown, and Green, Paternoster-
>    Row, 1824.
> 136p. 12mo. 3s (ECB).
> C Rom.1.44²; ECB 175; NSTC 23441 (BI BL, Dt).

*Notes.* Another trans. of *Ourika* (Paris, 1824). ECB dates May 1824.

1824: 32   E., T.

ORIENTAL WANDERINGS; OR, THE FORTUNES OF FELIX. A ROMANCE. IN THREE VOLUMES. BY T. E.

> London: Printed for A. K. Newman and Co. Leadenhall-Street, 1824.
> I 251p; II 282p; III 301p. 12mo. 18s (ECB); 12s (ER).
> ER 41: 267 (Oct 1824); WSW II: 26.
> Corvey; CME 3-628-48313-1; ECB 424; NSTC 2E278 (BI BL, C, O; NA DLC).

*Notes.* ECB gives as 'By R. C.'.

1824: 33   [FERRIER, Susan Edmonstone].

THE INHERITANCE. BY THE AUTHOR OF MARRIAGE. IN THREE VOLUMES.

> Edinburgh: William Blackwood, and T. Cadell, London, 1824.
> I 387p; II 415p; III 359p. 8vo. 31s 6d (ECB, QR); 31s 6d boards (ER).

ER 40: 547 (July 1824); QR 30: 590 (Jan 1824); WSW II: 94.

Corvey; CME 3-628-47877-4; ECB 296; NSTC 2F4876 (BI BL, C, Dt, E, O; NA MH).

*Notes.* Further edns: 2nd edn. 1825 (NSTC); 1841 (NSTC); 1847 (NSTC); Philadelphia 1824 (NSTC); French trans., 1824; German trans., 1826.

1824: 34  FLETCHER, Grenville.
**ROSALVIVA, OR THE DEMON DWARF! A ROMANCE. BY GRENVILLE FLETCHER, ESQ. AUTHOR OF "RHODOMALDI," &C. IN THREE VOLUMES.**

London: Matthew Iley, Somerset Street, Portman Square, 1824.
I 206p; II 261p; III 248p. 12mo. 18s (ECB).
QR 31: 532 (Mar 1825).
Corvey; CME 3-628-47605-4; ECB 208; NSTC 2F8398 (BI BL, O).

*Notes.* Dedication to Lady Caroline Lamb. 'Prefatory Address' dated London, May 1824.

1824: 35  [FORRESTER, Charles Robert].
**CASTLE BAYNARD; OR, THE DAYS OF JOHN. BY HAL WILLIS, STU-DENT AT LAW.**

London: Printed for G. and W. B. Whittaker, Ave-Maria-Lane, 1824.
286p. 8vo. 8s (ECB, QR).
QR 30: 590 (Jan 1824); WSW II: 6.
Corvey; CME 3-628-48932-6; ECB 640; NSTC 2W23990 (BI BL, C, E, O).

1824: 36  [FOUQUÉ, Caroline] {de la Motte}; SOANE, George (*trans.*).
**THE OUTCASTS. A ROMANCE. TRANSLATED FROM THE GERMAN. BY GEORGE SOANE. IN TWO VOLUMES.**

London: Printed for G. and W. B. Whittaker, Ave-Maria-Lane, 1824.
I xv, 258p; II 287p. 8vo. 16s (ECB).
BL N.250; ECB 213; NSTC 2L2850 (BI C, O; NA DLC).

*Notes.* Trans. of *Die Vertriebenen* (Leipzig, 1823). Preface identifies 'the Baroness de la Motte' as the author, and classifies her work 'as decidedly a copy of the Scotch romances' (p. iv). ECB dates Jan 1824.

1824: 37  GALT, John.
**THE BACHELOR'S WIFE; A SELECTION OF CURIOUS AND INTER-ESTING EXTRACTS, WITH CURSORY OBSERVATIONS. BY JOHN GALT, ESQ.**

Edinburgh: Published by Oliver & Boyd, Tweeddale-Court, and G. & W. B. Whittaker, London, 1824.
vii, 444p. 8vo. 10s 6d (ECB).
WSW II: 98.
Corvey; CME 3-628-54796-2; ECB 222; NSTC 2G1358 (BI BL, C, E, O; NA DLC, MH).

*Notes.* Preface dated 20 Feb 1824. ECB dates Mar 1824.

1824: 38   [GALT, John].

ROTHELAN; A ROMANCE OF THE ENGLISH HISTORIES. BY THE AUTHOR OF ANNALS OF THE PARISH, RINGAN GILHAIZE, THE SPAEWIFE, &C. IN THREE VOLUMES.

> Edinburgh: Published by Oliver & Boyd, Tweeddale-Court; and Geo. B. Whittaker, London, 1824.
>
> I 299p; II 309p; III 314p. 12mo. 21s (ECB); 21s boards (ER).
>
> ER 41: 519 (Jan 1825); WSW II: 98.
>
> Corvey; CME 3-628-51123-2; ECB 503; NSTC 2G1397 (BI BL, C, E, O; NA MH).

*Notes.* Dedication 'to the Right Honourable Lady Sarah Robinson'. Also containing: *The Quarantine, or Tales of Lazaretto*, vol. 3, pp. [115]–314, incorporating 3 tales. 'Advertisement' (vol. 1, 1 p. unn.) states 'The Manuscript of *Rothelan* not proving sufficient to fill three volumes, three additional Tales have been added, forming part of a design which the Author had some intention of hereafter completing'. ECB dates Nov 1824.

Further edns: New York 1825 (NUC); French trans., 1825; German trans., 1826.


1824: 39   [GASPEY, Thomas].

THE WITCH-FINDER; OR, THE WISDOM OF OUR ANCESTORS. A ROMANCE. BY THE AUTHOR OF "THE LOLLARDS," "OTHER TIMES," "CALTHORPE," &C. IN THREE VOLUMES.

> London: Printed for Longman, Hurst, Rees, Orme, Brown, and Green, Paternoster-Row, 1824.
>
> I xi, 392p; II 350p; III 366p. 12mo. 21s (ECB, ER).
>
> ER 40: 547 (July 1824); WSW II: 101.
>
> Corvey; CME 3-628-48972-5; ECB 644; NSTC 2G3304 (BI BL, C, E, O; NA MH).


1824: 40   GOETHE, [Johann Wolfgang von]; [CARLYLE, Thomas (*trans.*)].

WILHELM MEISTER'S APPRENTICESHIP. A NOVEL. FROM THE GERMAN OF GOETHE. IN THREE VOLUMES.

> Edinburgh: Published by Oliver & Boyd, Tweeddale-Court; and G. & W. B. Whittaker, London, 1824.
>
> I xviii, 324p; II 351p; III 294p. 8vo. 31s 6d (ECB, ER, QR).
>
> ER 40: 547 (July 1824), 42: 409–49 (Aug 1825) full review; QR 30: 590 (Jan 1824).
>
> BL 12550.g.23; ECB 235; NSTC 2G11798 (BI C, Dt, E, O; NA MH).

*Notes.* Trans. of *Wilhelm Meisters Lehrjahre* (Berlin, 1794). ECB dates June 1824.

Further edns: 1828 (NSTC); London 1839 (NSTC); London 1842 (NSTC).


1824: 41   GORE, [Catherine Grace Frances].

THERESA MARCHMONT; OR, THE MAID OF HONOUR. A TALE. BY MRS. CHARLES GORE.

> London: Printed for J. Andrews, 167, New Bond Street, 1824.
>
> 120p. 12mo. 3s 6d (ECB, ER).
>
> ER 41: 267 (Oct 1824); WSW II: 103.
>
> BL N.121(2); ECB 584; NSTC 2G14894 (BI C, O).

*Notes.* ECB dates July 1824. Collates in sixes.
Further edn: 1845 (NSTC).

1824: 42    [GREEN, Sarah].
SCOTCH NOVEL READING; OR, MODERN QUACKERY. A NOVEL
REALLY FOUNDED ON FACTS. IN THREE VOLUMES. BY A COCKNEY.

> London: Printed for A. K. Newman and Co. Leadenhall-Street, 1824.
> I 242p; II 238p; III 245p. 12mo. 16s 6d (ECB).
> WSW II: 104.
> Corvey; CME 3-628-47300-4; ECB 519; NSTC 2G20159 (BI BL, E, O).

*Notes.* ECB dates Feb 1824.

1824: 43    GREEN, W{illiam}C{hild}.
THE PROPHECY OF DUNCANNON; OR, THE DWARF AND THE
SEER: A CALEDONIAN LEGEND. BY W. C. GREEN, ESQ. AUTHOR OF
THE WOODLAND FAMILY; FAYS OF LOCHLOMOND, &C.

> London: Printed by J. M'Gowan, Great Windmill Street; published by Joseph Emans,
>     Ivy Lane, Paternoster-Row; and sold by Jones & Co., 3, Acton Place, Kingsland Road,
>     1824.
> ii, 553p, ill. 8vo.
> O 256.d.397; NSTC 2G20224 (BI E).

*Notes.* 'Prefatory' (pp. i–ii), signed W. C. G., and dated Walworth, 18 Jan 1825. Frontispiece
portrait of Will^m. Child Green, Esq. Collates in fours.

1824: 44    GREEN, William Child.
*THE WOODLAND FAMILY; OR, THE SONS OF ERROR, AND
DAUGHTERS OF SIMPLICITY. A DOMESTIC TALE, BY WILLIAM
CHILD GREEN, ESQ.

> London: Joseph Emans, No. 91 Waterloo Road, 1824.
> 1 vol. 8vo.
> No copy located.

*Notes.* Details chiefly from Summers (p. 563); his dating tallies with the appearance of this
title as a work by the author in *The Prophecy of Duncannon* (see 1824: 43).
Further edn: 1826 (MH 18488.8.10; NSTC 2G20225). This Harvard copy has the author's
name on t.p., and the imprint of 'J. M'Gowan and Son Great Windmill Street, Haymarket'.

1824: 45    [HATTON, Anne Julia Kemble].
WOMAN'S A RIDDLE. A ROMANTIC TALE. IN FOUR VOLUMES. BY
ANN OF SWANSEA, AUTHOR OF CONVICTION, CESARIO ROSALBA,
SECRETS IN EVERY MANSION, CHRONICLES OF AN ILLUSTRIOUS
HOUSE, LOVERS AND FRIENDS, GONZALO DI BALDIVIA, GUILTY
OR NOT GUILTY, &C. &C.

> London: Printed for A. K. Newman and Co. Leadenhall-Street, 1824.
> I 312p; II 319p; III 228p; IV 328p. 12mo. 28s (ECB, ER).

ER 39: 512 (Jan 1824).

Corvey; CME 3-628-48789-7; ECB 20; NSTC 2A13197 (BI BL, C, O).

*Notes.* Dedication to Mrs Faugeres, New York, dated Swansea, Orchard-Street, 1 Nov 1823.

1824: 46   [HAWKINS, Lætitia Matilda].
**ANNALINE; OR, MOTIVE-HUNTING.**

London: Printed for James Carpenter and Son, Old Bond Street, 1824.

I 346p; II 307p; III 310p. 8vo. 30s (ECB, QR).

QR 30: 590 (Jan 1824); WSW II: 108.

Corvey; CME 3-628-47061-7; ECB 20; NSTC 2H13207 (BI BL, C, O; NA MH).

1824: 47   HOFFMANN, E[rnst] T[heodor] A[madeus]; [GILLIES, Robert Pierce (*trans.*)].
**THE DEVIL'S ELIXIR. FROM THE GERMAN OF E. T. A. HOFFMANN.**

Edinburgh: William Blackwood, and T. Cadell, London, 1824.

I vii, 379p; II 339p. 12mo. 14s (ECB).

BL N.230; ECB 275; NSTC 2H25417 (BI C, E, O; NA DLC, MH).

*Notes.* Trans. of *Die Elixiere des Teufels* (Berlin, 1815–16). Translator's Preface dated Edinburgh, 5 June 1824. ECB dates June 1824.

1824: 48   HOFLAND, [Barbara].
**DECISION. A TALE. BY MRS. HOFLAND, AUTHOR OF INTEGRITY A TALE, PATIENCE A TALE, THE SON OF A GENIUS; TALES OF THE PRIORY; TALES OF THE MANOR, &C. &C.**

London: Printed for Longman, Hurst, Rees, Orme, Brown, and Green, Paternoster-Row, 1824.

272p, ill. 12mo. 6s (ECB).

WSW II: 114–15.

Corvey; CME 3-628-47665-8; ECB 275; NSTC 2H29382 (BI BL, C, E, O; NA MH).

*Notes.* A different work from the anonymous *The Decision; A Novel* (1811: 6), and from Anne Raikes Harding's *Decision: A Tale* (1819: 37). ECB dates Nov 1824.

Further edns: 1835 (NUC); 1836 (NUC); 1840 (NSTC); New York 1825 (NSTC).

1824: 49   HOFLAND, [Barbara].
**PATIENCE. A TALE BY MRS. HOFLAND, AUTHOR OF INTEGRITY, A TALE; THE SON OF A GENIUS, TALES OF THE PRIORY, TALES OF THE MANOR, &C. &C.**

London: Printed for Longman, Hurst, Rees, Orme, Brown, and Green, Paternoster-Row, 1824.

298p, ill. 12mo. 6s (ECB).

WSW II: 115.

BL N.219; ECB 275; NSTC 2H29409 (BI C, E, O).

*Notes.* ECB dates Jan 1824.

Further edns: 1836 (NSTC); 1838 (NSTC); New York 1825 (NUC).

1824: 50   [HOGG, James].

THE PRIVATE MEMOIRS AND CONFESSIONS OF A JUSTIFIED SIN-
NER: WRITTEN BY HIMSELF: WITH A DETAIL OF CURIOUS TRAD-
ITIONARY FACTS, AND OTHER EVIDENCE, BY THE EDITOR.

> London: Printed for Longman, Hurst, Rees, Orme, Brown, and Green, Paternoster
> Row, 1824.
> 390p. 8vo. 10s 6d (ECB).
> WSW II: 116.
> Corvey; CME 3-628-47313-6; ECB 471; NSTC 2M24211 (BI BL, C, Dt, E, O; NA MH).

*Notes.* Dedication 'to the Hon. William Smith, Lord Provost of Glasgow'. Printer's mark,
verso of t.p., reads: 'Edinburgh: Printed by James Clarke and Co. 1824'. 'Fac Simile' between
pp. 366 and 367; though in other copies seen (e.g. E Hall.201.e) this appears as a frontispiece.
ECB dates June 1824.

Further edn: reissued (replacement t.p.) as *The Suicide's Grave; or, Memoirs and Confessions
of a Sinner,* 'edited by J. Hogg', Edinburgh 1828 (SEK).

1824: 51   [HOOK, James].

PERCY MALLORY. BY THE AUTHOR OF PEN OWEN. IN THREE VOL-
UMES.

> Edinburgh: William Blackwood, and T. Cadell, London, 1824.
> I 349p; II 344p; III 350p. 8vo. 30s (ECB); 30s boards (ER).
> ER 39: 512 (Jan 1824); WSW II: 118–19.
> Corvey; CME 3-628-48415-4; ECB 442; NSTC 2H28910 (BI BL, C, Dt, E, O).

*Notes.* ECB dates Dec 1823.
Further edns: Philadelphia 1824 (NSTC); French trans., 1824.

1824: 52   [HOOK, Theodore Edward].

SAYINGS AND DOINGS. A SERIES OF SKETCHES FROM LIFE. IN
THREE VOLUMES.

> London: Printed for Henry Colburn, New Burlington-Street, 1824.
> I v, 336p; II 350p; III 358p. 12mo. 30s (ECB, ER).
> ER 40: 276 (Mar 1824); WSW II: 119.
> BL N.1297; ECB 516; NSTC 2H28950 (BI Dt, C, O; NA DLC, MH).

*Notes.* 'Advertisement' dated London, 26 Jan 1824. [1st series].
Further edns: 2nd edn. 1824 (Corvey), CME 3-628-48529-0; 1836 (NSTC); Philadelphia
1824 (NSTC).

1824: 53   HUGHES, Robert.

COBERLEY HALL. A GLOUCESTERSHIRE TALE OF THE FOUR-
TEENTH CENTURY. BY ROBERT HUGHES, CHELTENHAM.

> Cheltenham: Printed by S. Y. Griffith and Co. Chronicle Office, 1824.
> viii, 91p, ill. 8vo.
> BL 012611.i.32; ECB 287; NSTC 2H35368 (BI C, O; NA DLC).

*Notes.* Dedication to Lady Anna-Eliza, Duchess of Buckingham and Chandos, dated Cheltenham, Mar 1824.

1824: 54    [IRVING, Washington].
## TALES OF A TRAVELLER. BY GEOFFREY CRAYON, GENT. IN TWO VOLUMES.

> London: John Murray, Albemarle-Street, 1824.
> I xvi, 364p; II vi, 394p. 8vo. 24s (ECB, ER, QR).
> ER 41: 267 (Oct 1824); QR 31: 260 (Dec 1824), 31: 473–87 (Mar 1825) full review; WSW II: 123–4.
> BL 838.f.7; ECB 301; NSTC 2C42720 (BI C, E, O; NA DLC, MH).

*Notes.* Reviewed in QR (Mar 1825) with three other of Irving's works.
Further edns: New edn. 1825 (Corvey, NSTC); 1848 (NSTC); 1850 (Blanck); Philadelphia 1824 (Blanck); French trans. 1825; German trans., 1825.


1824: 55    JONES, H[annah] M[aria].
## THE FORGED NOTE: OR, JULIAN AND MARIANNE. A MORAL TALE, FOUNDED ON RECENT FACTS. BY MRS. H. M. JONES, AUTHORESS OF GRETNA GREEN,—WEDDING RING,—BRITISH OFFICER, &C.

> London: Printed and published by J. Jaques & W. Wright, Eagle Office, Cross Street, Newington Butts. Sold also by D. Jaques, Chelsea; and all other Booksellers, 1824.
> 661p, ill. 8vo.
> BL 1570/1499; NSTC 2J10424.

*Notes.* Collates in fours.


1824: 56    [JONES, Hannah Maria].
## THE GAMBLERS; OR, THE TREACHEROUS FRIEND: A MORAL TALE, FOUNDED ON RECENT FACTS. BY THE AUTHOR OF SEVERAL POPULAR WORKS.

> London: Printed and Published by E. Livermore, Albion Press, 50, Fetter Lane; and sold by George Virtue, 26, Ivy Lane, Paternoster Row, and Bath Street, Bristol, 1824.
> 672p, ill. 8vo.
> BL 012646.bbb.2; NSTC 2J10425 (BI O).

*Notes.* Originally issued in 28 parts including 4 double numbers, all at 6d (see Mihai H. Handrea, 'Books in Parts and the Number Trade', in *Bookselling and Book Buying: Aspects of the Nineteenth-Century British and North American Book Trade*, ed. Richard G. Landon (Chicago: American Library Association, 1978), p. 42. Collates in fours.
Further edns: 1825 as *The Victim of Fashion, or the Gamblers, Founded on Recent Facts* (NUC); 1836 also as *The Victim of Fashion* (NUC).


1824: 57(a)    JONES, Hannah Maria.
## THE WEDDING RING; OR, MARRIED AND SINGLE: A DOMESTIC TALE. BY HANNAH MARIA JONES, AUTHORESS OF GRETNA GREEN, THE BRITISH OFFICER, &C. &C. IN FOUR VOLUMES.

> London: George Virtue, 26, Ivy Lane, Paternoster Row; Bath Street, Bristol; and Queen Square, Liverpool, 1824.
> I vii, 292p; II 280p; III 284p; IV 310p. 12mo. 21s (ECB).

WSW II: 125.

Corvey; CME 3-628-48000-0; ECB 311; xNSTC.

*Notes.* 'To the Reader' dated London, Oct 1824. ECB dates Sept 1824.

1824: 57(b)    JONES, H[annah] M[aria].
THE WEDDING RING; OR MARRIED AND SINGLE. A DOMESTIC
TALE. BY H. M. JONES, AUTHORESS OF GRETNA GREEN, THE
BRITISH OFFICER, &C. &C.

> London: Printed by C. Baynes, 13, Duke Street, Lincoln's Inn Fields. Published by
>    George Virtue, 26, Ivy Lane, Paternoster Row, and Bath Street, Bristol, 1824.
> 718p, ill. 8vo.
> BL 1560/1181; NSTC 2J10445.

*Notes.* Additional engraved t.p. with imprint: 'London, printed for G. Virtue 26 Ivy Lane, &
Bath Street, Bristol'. Originally issued in 28 numbers, 6d each (Summers). Collates in fours.

KEELIVINE, Christopher [pseud.]
See PICKEN, Andrew

1824: 58    [KELTY, Mary Ann].
TRIALS; A TALE. BY THE AUTHOR OF "THE FAVOURITE OF
NATURE," &C. &C. IN THREE VOLUMES.

> London: Printed for G. and W. B. Whittaker, Ave-Maria Lane, 1824.
> I 328p; II 315p; III 314p. 12mo. 21s (ECB, ER, QR).
> ER 40: 547 (July 1824); QR 30: 590 (Jan 1824); WSW II: 128.
> Corvey; CME 3-628-48828-1; ECB 599; NSTC 2K2417 (BI BL, C, Dt, O; NA MH).

*Notes.* Further edns: Philadelphia 1824 (NUC); French trans., 1824 [as *Les Épreuves de la vie*
(BN)].

1824: 59    LATHOM, Francis.
THE POLISH BANDIT; OR, WHO IS MY BRIDE? AND OTHER TALES.
IN THREE VOLUMES. BY FRANCIS LATHOM, AUTHOR OF PUZZLED
AND PLEASED, THE MYSTERIOUS FREEBOOTER, THE UNKNOWN,
VERY STRANGE BUT VERY TRUE, MEN AND MANNERS, ROMANCE
OF THE HEBRIDES, ONE POUND NOTE, ITALIAN MYSTERIES, LIVE
AND LEARN, ASTONISHMENT, &C.

> London: Printed for A. K. Newman and Co. Leadenhall-Street, 1824.
> I 241p; II 257p; III 276p. 12mo. 18s (ECB).
> Corvey; CME 3-628-51076-7; ECB 331; NSTC 2L5038 (BI BL, C).

*Notes.* ECB dates Feb 1824.

1824: 60    [LOCKHART, John Gibson].
THE HISTORY OF MATTHEW WALD.

> Edinburgh: William Blackwood, and T. Cadell, London, 1824.

382p. 8vo. 10s 6d (ECB, QR); 10s 6d boards (ER).

ER 40: 276 (Mar 1824); QR 30: 590 (Jan 1824); WSW II: 136–7.

Corvey; CME 3-628-47707-7; ECB 273; NSTC 2L19450 (BI BL, C, E, O; NA MH).

*Notes.* Further edns: 1840 (NSTC); 1843 (NSTC); German trans., 1825.


1824: 61    [MACDONOGH, Felix].

**THE HERMIT IN EDINBURGH; OR, SKETCHES OF MANNERS AND REAL CHARACTERS AND SCENES IN THE DRAMA OF LIFE.**

London: Printed for Sherwood, Jones and Co. Paternoster-Row, 1824.

I x, 257p; II vi, 294p; III vi, 247p. 12mo. 18s (ECB, ER).

ER 41: 267 (Oct 1824).

Corvey; CME 3-628-51036-8; ECB 265; NSTC 2M3273 (BI BL, C, E, O; NA DLC, MH).


1824: 62    [MACDONOGH, Felix].

**THE HIGHLANDERS: A TALE. BY THE AUTHOR OF THE HERMIT IN LONDON, HERMIT ABROAD, &C. IN THREE VOLUMES.**

London: Printed for Henry Colburn, New Burlington Street, 1824.

I iv, 310p; II 312p; III 320p. 12mo. 21s (ECB, ER).

ER 40: 547 (July 1824); WSW II: 139–40.

Corvey; CME 3-628-47658-5; ECB 268; NSTC 2M3283 (BI BL, C, Dt, E, O; NA MH).

*Notes.* Preface signed 'The Hermit in London'.

Further edn: New York 1824 (NSTC).


1824: 63    [MACHENRY, James].

**THE INSURGENT CHIEF; OR, O'HALLORAN. AN IRISH HISTORICAL TALE OF 1798. IN THREE VOLUMES. BY SOLOMON SECONDSIGHT, AUTHOR OF THE WILDERNESS, THE SPECTRE OF THE FOREST, &C.**

Philadelphia: Printed for H. C. Carey and I. Lea. London: Re-printed for A. K. Newman & Co. Leadenhall-Street, 1824.

I xxiii, 290p; II 285p; III 287p. 12mo. 18s (ECB, ER, QR).

ER 41: 267 (Oct 1824), 41: 519 (Jan 1825); QR 31: 260 (Dec 1824); WSW II: 140.

Corvey; CME 3-628-48630-0; ECB 359; NSTC 2M4780 (BI BL, C, O).

*Notes.* Colophon reads: 'Printed by J. Darling, Leadenhall-Street, London'. Originally published Philadelphia 1824 as *O'Halloran; or, the Insurgent Chief; an Irish Historical Tale of 1798* (Blanck).

Further edns: London 1842 as *O'Halloran; or, the Insurgent Chief* (NSTC); Belfast 1847, also as *O'Halloran* (NSTC).


1824: 64    [MACHENRY, James].

**THE SPECTRE OF THE FOREST; OR, ANNALS OF THE HOUSATONIC. A NEW-ENGLAND ROMANCE. IN THREE VOLUMES. BY SOLOMON SECONDSIGHT, AUTHOR OF THE WILDERNESS, &C.**

London: Printed for A. K. Newman and Co. Leadenhall-Street, 1824.

I xxiv, 244p; II 236p; III 250p. 12mo. 16s 6d (ECB).

WSW II: 140.

Corvey; CME 3-628-48631-9; ECB 553; NSTC 2M4786 (BI BL, C).

*Notes.* ECB dates Dec 1823. Originally published New York 1823 (NSTC).


1824: 65    M'LEOD, Miss [E. H.].

PRINCIPLE! A FASHIONABLE TALE. IN FOUR VOLUMES. BY MISS
M'LEOD: AUTHOR OF TALES OF TON, FIRST, SECOND, AND THIRD
SERIES.

London: Printed for A. K. Newman and Co. Leadenhall-Street, 1824.
I 263p; II 266p; III 261p; IV 268p. 12mo. 22s (ECB).
WSW II: 140.
Corvey; CME 3-628-48139-2; ECB 361; NSTC 2M7091 (BI BL, C, E, O).

*Notes.* Dedication to Sir Walter Scott, dated Norwich, 1824. ECB dates May 1824.


1824: 66    [MATURIN, Charles Robert].

THE ALBIGENSES, A ROMANCE. BY THE AUTHOR OF "BERTRAM,"
A TRAGEDY: "WOMAN; OR, POUR ET CONTRE," &C. IN FOUR VOL-
UMES.

London: Printed for Hurst, Robinson, and Co. 90, Cheapside, and 8, Pall-Mall; and A.
    Constable and Co. Edinburgh, 1824.
I viii, 439p; II 366p; III 335p; IV 277p. 12mo. 32s (ECB); 32s boards (ER).
ER 40: 276 (Mar 1824); WSW II: 143.
Corvey; CME 3-628-47036-6; ECB 10; NSTC 2M20487 (BI BL, C, E, O).

*Notes.* Dedication to Mrs Smith, Fitzwilliam Street, Dublin.
Further edns: Philadelphia 1824 (NSTC); French trans., 1825.
Facs: GNII (1974).


1824: 67    MITFORD, Mary Russell.

OUR VILLAGE: SKETCHES OF RURAL CHARACTER AND SCENERY.
BY MARY RUSSELL MITFORD, AUTHOR OF JULIAN, A TRAGEDY.

London: G. and W. B. Whittaker, Ave-Maria-Lane, 1824/32.
I (1824) viii, 292p; II (1826) vii, 311p; III (1828) viii, 315p; IV (1830) viii, 345p; V (1832)
    iv, 362p. 8vo. 7s 6d (vol. 1, ECB); 7s 6d boards (vol. 1, ER); 8s 6d (vol. 2, ECB, QR); 9s
    (vol. 3, ECB, QR); 10s 6d (vol. 4, ECB); 10s 6d (vol. 5, ECB).
ER 40: 547 (July 1824); QR 31: 166–74 (Dec 1824) full review, 35: 319 (Jan 1827) vol. 2,
    38: 303 (July 1828) vol. 3; WSW II: 148.
Corvey; CME 3-628-48216-X; ECB 389; NSTC 2M31679 (BI BL, C, E, O).

*Notes.* T.p. imprint publisher description differs as follows: vols. 2 and 3, 'Geo B. Whittaker,
Ave-Maria-Lane'; vols. 4 and 5, 'Whittaker, Treacher, & Co. Ave-Maria-Lane'. ECB dates
vol. 1, May 1824; vol. 2, Oct 1826; vol. 3, May 1828; vol. 4, May 1830; vol. 5, Sept 1832.
Further edns: 2nd edn. 1824 (see below); 3rd edn. 1825 (BLC); '2nd edn.' 1835 (NUC: 3 vols.);
new edn. 1848 (NUC); New York 1830 (NUC: 4th ser.).
Facs: RR (of 2nd edn. 1824; 1996).

1824: 68   MOORE, Hannah W.
**ELLEN RAMSAY. IN THREE VOLUMES. BY MISS HANNAH W. MOORE.**

> London: Printed for Longman, Hurst, Rees, Orme, Brown, and Green, Paternoster-Row, 1824.
> I 311p; II 390p; III 349p. 12mo. 21s (ECB).
> WSW II: 150.
> Corvey; CME 3-628-48282-8; ECB 394; NSTC 2M34776 (BI BL, C, Dt, O).

*Notes.* ECB dates Mar 1824.

1824: 69   [MOORE, Thomas].
**MEMOIRS OF CAPTAIN ROCK, THE CELEBRATED IRISH CHIEFTAIN, WITH SOME ACCOUNT OF HIS ANCESTORS. WRITTEN BY HIMSELF.**

> London: Printed for Longman, Hurst, Rees, Orme, Brown, and Green, 1824.
> xiv, 376p. 12mo. 9s (ECB).
> ER 41: 143–53 (Oct 1824) 4th edn., full review; WSW II: 152–3.
> BL 8145.aa.2; ECB 379; NSTC 2M35448 (BI C, Dt, E, O).

*Notes.* Preface by the Editor, signed 'S. E.', dated 31 Mar 1824.
Further edns: 2nd edn. 1824 (BL G.4356); 3rd edn. 1824 (Corvey, NSTC); 4th edn. 1824 (NSTC); 5th edn. 1824 (NSTC); New York 1824 (NSTC); German trans., 1825.

1824: 70   [MORIER, James Justinian].
**THE ADVENTURES OF HAJJI BABA, OF ISPAHAN. IN THREE VOLUMES.**

> London: John Murray, Albemarle-Street, 1824.
> I lxxv, 272p; II 403p; III 387p. 8vo. 21s (ECB, ER, QR).
> ER 40: 276 (Mar 1824); QR 30: 199–216 (Oct 1823) full review, 30: 295 (Oct 1823); WSW II: 153.
> Corvey; CME 3-628-47016-1; ECB 396; NSTC 2M36628 (BI BL, C, Dt, E, O; NA MH).

*Notes.* Introductory Epistle to Rev. Dr. Fundgruben, signed 'Peregrine Persic', London, 1 Dec 1823. ECB dates Dec 1823. The last page of vol. 3 is mistakenly numbered 388.
Further edns: 2nd edn. 1824 (NSTC); 1835 (NSTC); 1849 (NUC); Philadelphia 1824 (NUC); French trans., 1824; German trans., 1824.

1824: 71   {OAKLEY, Peregrine}.
**AUREUS; OR THE LIFE AND OPINIONS OF A SOVEREIGN. WRITTEN BY HIMSELF.**

> London: Printed for George Wightman, 46, Fleet-Street, 1824.
> viii, 438p. 12mo. 7s 6d (ECB).
> Corvey; CME 3-628-47080-3; ECB 32; NSTC 2O265 (BI BL, C, Dt, O; NA MH).

*Notes.* Preface signed 'Peregrine Oakley, North Street, Brighton', dated 1 Jan 1821. ECB dates Feb 1824.

1824: 72   OLLIER, Charles.
**INESILLA, OR THE TEMPTER, A ROMANCE; WITH OTHER TALES. BY CHARLES OLLIER, AUTHOR OF "ALTHAM AND HIS WIFE."**

London: Printed for E. Lloyd and Son, Harley-Street; and William Blackwood, Edinburgh, 1824.
viii, 287p. 12mo. 7s (ECB).
WSW II: 156.
Corvey; CME 3-628-51110-0; ECB 295; NSTC 2O3543 (BI BL, C, O).

*Notes.* Dedication to Chandos Leigh, Esq. 'Advertisement' signed 'C. O.', Dec 1823. ECB dates Feb 1824.

1824: 73    [?OPIE, Amelia Alderson].
MUCH TO BLAME, A TALE. BY A CELEBRATED AUTHOR. IN THREE VOLUMES.

London: John Templeman, 39, Tottenham Court Road, 1824.
I 294p; II 295p; III 336p. 12mo. 21s (ECB, ER, QR).
ER 40: 547 (July 1824); QR 30: 590 (Jan 1824); WSW II: 24.
Corvey; CME 3-628-48390-5; ECB 400; NSTC 2M39786 (BI O).

*Notes.* Amelia Opie talks in her letter of 21 June 1839 to Sir John Gurney (see note to 1821: 61 for details) of a 3 vol. novel of hers, which she intended to publish anonymously but then decided to withdraw on joining the Society of Friends; the publisher however was far advanced in printing, and the work unknown to her was issued as a 'tale by a *celebrated authoress*'. This is the only novel of this period found with such a title, and the date of publication corresponds with Opie's official conversion to the Society of Friends. The novel is written in a proficient style, not unlike Opie's own.
Further edn: NSTC lists 1830 edn. at MH, but copy seen there is 1824.

1824: 74    [?PEERS, John].
THE CONFESSIONS OF A GAMESTER.

London: Printed for J. Hatchard and Son, 187, Piccadilly, 1824.
244p. 8vo. 7s (ECB, QR); 7s boards (ER).
ER 41: 519 (Jan 1825); QR 31: 260 (Dec 1824).
Corvey; CME 3-628-47311-X; ECB 130; NSTC 2G1602 (BI BL, C, E, O; NA MH).

*Notes.* NSTC gives as 'ed. J. Peers'; John Peers is the attributed author of *Typical Instruction* (1828), also published by Hatchard.

1824: 75    [PENNIE, John Fitzgerald].
CORFE CASTLE; OR KENESWITHA.

London: Hurst, Robinson & Co. 90, Cheapside, and 8, Pall-Mall, 1824.
vii, 434p, ill. 8vo. 12s (ECB); 12s boards (ER).
ER 39: 512 (Jan 1824); WSW II: 7.
Corvey; CME 3-628-47439-6; ECB 136; NSTC 2P10392 (BI BL, C, O; NA DLC, MH).

*Notes.* Preface to 'Henry Bankes, Esq. M.P.', dated London, Nov 1823. ECB dates Dec 1823.

1824: 76    [PICKEN, Andrew].
TALES AND SKETCHES OF THE WEST OF SCOTLAND. BY CHRISTOPHER KEELIVINE.

Glasgow: Printed for Robertson and Atkinson; and sold by Archibald Constable and Co. Edinburgh, and Hurst, Robinson, and Co. London, 1824.

366p. 12mo. 6s boards (ER).

ER 40: 276 (Mar 1824); WSW II: 127.

Corvey; CME 3-628-51084-8; xNSTC.

*Notes.* Collates in sixes. A recently-acquired copy in the Cambridge University Library has t.p. with same year imprint reading 'Edinburgh, Oliver and Boyd; G. & W. B. Whittaker, London; and Robertson & Atkinson, Glasgow'.

Further edn: German trans., 1824 [as *Erzählungen, aus dem Leben in Schottland* (RS)].

1824: 77    PORTER, Jane.
DUKE CHRISTIAN OF LUNEBURG; OR, TRADITION FROM THE HARTZ. BY MISS JANE PORTER, AUTHOR OF "THADDEUS OF WAR-SAW," &C. &C. &C. IN THREE VOLUMES.

London: Printed for Longman, Hurst, Rees, Orme, Brown, and Green, Paternoster-Row, 1824.

I viii, 357p; II 416p; III 402p, 6p. 12mo. 24s (ECB); 24s boards (ER).

ER 40: 276 (Mar 1824); WSW II: 163.

Corvey; CME 3-628-48358-1; ECB 464; NSTC 2P22418 (BI BL, C, E, O; NA DLC, MH).

*Notes.* Dedication to George the Fourth, dated Long Ditton, 24 Jan 1824.

Further edns: 2nd edn. 1824 (NSTC); Boston 1824 (NSTC); French trans., 1824; German trans., 1825 [as *Herzog Christian von Braunschweig-Lüneburg. Eine Sage vom Harz* (RS)].

1824: 78    REEVE, Sophia.
STANMORE; OR, THE MONK, AND THE MERCHANT'S WIDOW. BY SOPHIA REEVE. IN THREE VOLUMES.

London: Printed for G. and W. B. Whittaker, 1824.

I 278p; II 258p; III 271p. 12mo. 18s (ECB, ER, QR).

ER 41: 519 (Jan 1825); QR 31: 260 (Dec 1824); WSW II: 167.

Corvey; CME 3-628-48522-3; ECB 483; NSTC 2R5346 (BI BL, C, E, O; NA MH).

*Notes.* Further edn: German trans., 1825.

1824: 79    RENOU, Sarah.
THE IONIAN; OR, WOMAN IN THE NINETEENTH CENTURY. BY SARAH RENOU, AUTHOR OF 'VILLAGE CONVERSATIONS, OR THE VICAR'S FIRE-SIDE;' AND 'THE TEMPLE OF TRUTH, AN ALLEGORI-CAL POEM.' IN THREE VOLUMES.

London: Printed for Sherwood, Jones, and Co. Paternoster Row, 1824.

I xii, 264p; II 257p; III 252p. 12mo. 21s (ECB).

WSW II: 167.

Corvey; CME 3-628-48563-0; ECB 487; NSTC 2R7148 (BI BL, C).

*Notes.* ECB dates Dec 1823.

1824: 80    ROCHE, Regina Maria.
THE TRADITION OF THE CASTLE; OR, SCENES IN THE EMERALD

ISLE. IN FOUR VOLUMES. BY REGINA MARIA ROCHE, AUTHOR OF
THE CHILDREN OF THE ABBEY, VICAR OF LANSDOWN, MAID OF
THE HAMLET, &C.

London: Printed for A. K. Newman and Co. Leadenhall-Street, 1824.
I 386p; II 364p; III 342p; IV 322p. 12mo. 28s (ECB, ER).
ER 39: 512 (Jan 1824).
Corvey; CME 3-628-48464-2; ECB 498; NSTC 2D1381 (BI BL, O).

*Notes.* ECB dates Oct 1823.
Further edn: French trans., 1824.

1824: 81   ST. CLAIR, Rosalia [pseud.].
THE BANKER'S DAUGHTERS OF BRISTOL; OR, COMPLIANCE AND
DECISION. A NOVEL. IN THREE VOLUMES. BY ROSALIA ST. CLAIR,
AUTHOR OF THE BLIND BEGGAR, HIGHLAND CASTLE, &C.

London: Printed for A. K. Newman and Co. Leadenhall-Street, 1824.
I 255p; II 308p; III 294p. 12mo. 18s (ECB, ER).
ER 39: 512 (Jan 1824); WSW II: 73.
Corvey; CME 3-628-48595-9; ECB 511; NSTC 2S1990 (BI BL).

*Notes.* 'Advertisement' dated Sept 1823. ECB dates Oct 1823.

1824: 82   [SAINT LEGER, Francis Barry Boyle].
SOME ACCOUNT OF THE LIFE OF THE LATE GILBERT EARLE, ESQ.
WRITTEN BY HIMSELF.

London: Printed for Charles Knight, Pall-Mall, East, 1824.
vii, 250p. 8vo. 8s (ECB).
Corvey; CME 3-628-48670-X; ECB 549; NSTC 2S2245 (BI BL, C, Dt, O; NA DLC).

*Notes.* 'Preface by the Editor' dated May 1824.
Further edn: 2nd edn. 1826 (NSTC).

1824: 83   [SCOTT, Sir Walter].
REDGAUNTLET. A TALE OF THE EIGHTEENTH CENTURY. BY THE
AUTHOR OF "WAVERLEY." IN THREE VOLUMES.

Edinburgh: Printed for Archibald Constable and Co.; and Hurst, Robinson, and Co.
London, 1824.
I 319p; II 328p; III 331p. 8vo. 31s 6d (ECB, ER, QR).
ER 40: 547 (July 1824); QR 30: 590 (Jan 1824), 35: 518–66 (Mar 1827) full review; WSW
II: 178–9.
Corvey; CME 3-628-48581-9; ECB 482; NSTC 2S10163 (BI BL, C, Dt, E, NCu, O; NA
DLC, MH).

*Notes.* 'This day published', 17 June 1824, *Edinburgh Evening Courant.* This is one of nine
novels which are together given full reviews in QR (Mar 1827) under the page-top heading
'Historical Romance'.
Further edns: Boston 1824 (NSTC) [also Philadelphia 1824 (CG, NCBEL)]; French trans.,
1824; German trans., 1824. Numerous reprintings in collected edns.

1824: 84   [SCOTT, Sir Walter].
ST RONAN'S WELL. BY THE AUTHOR OF "WAVERLEY, QUENTIN DURWARD," &C. IN THREE VOLUMES.

> Edinburgh: Printed for Archibald Constable and Co.; and Hurst, Robinson, and Co. London, 1824.
>
> I 310p; II 325p; III 323p. 8vo. 31s 6d (ECB, QR); 31s 6d boards (ER).
>
> ER 39: 512 (Jan 1824); QR 30: 295 (Oct 1823), 35: 518–66 (Mar 1827) full review; WSW II: 177–8.
>
> Corvey; CME 3-628-48585-1; ECB 512; NSTC 2S10227 (BI BL, C, Dt, E, NCu, O; NA MH).

*Notes.* 'This day published', 27 Dec 1823, *Edinburgh Evening Courant.* This is one of nine novels which are together given full reviews in QR (Mar 1827) under the page-top heading 'Historical Romance'.
Further edns: 1824 (NCBEL); Boston 1824 (NCBEL) [also New York 1824 (NSTC), also Philadelphia 1824 (NSTC)]; French trans., 1824; German trans., 1824. Numerous reprintings in collected edns.

1824: 85   SCRIBLERUS SECUNDUS [pseud.].
TORRENWALD. A ROMANCE. IN FOUR VOLUMES. BY SCRIBLERUS SECUNDUS, SOMETIME INSTRUCTOR OF YOUTH, VULGO GRINDER.

> London: Printed for A. K. Newman and Co. Leadenhall-Street, 1824.
>
> I 315p; II 291p; III 304p; IV 317p. 12mo. 26s (ECB).
>
> WSW II: 38.
>
> Corvey; CME 3-628-48762-5; ECB 594; NSTC 2S11201 (BI BL, C, O).

*Notes.* ECB dates May 1824.

1824: 86   SEBRIGHT, Paul.
ADÉLE; OR, THE TOMB OF MY MOTHER. A NOVEL. IN FOUR VOLUMES. BY PAUL SEBRIGHT, AUTHOR OF COINCIDENCE, OR THE SOOTHSAYER, &C. &C.

> London: Printed for A. K. Newman and Co. Leadenhall-Street, 1824.
>
> I vi, 246p; II 289p; III 299p; IV 274p. 12mo. 24s (ECB).
>
> Corvey; CME 3-628-48628-9; ÉCB 524; NSTC 2S12004 (BI BL, C, O).

*Notes.* Preface dated 1 Dec 1823. ECB dates Feb 1824.

1824: 87   [SEDGWICK, Catharine Maria].
REDWOOD; A TALE. BY THE AUTHOR OF "A NEW ENGLAND TALE." IN THREE VOLUMES.

> London: John Miller, 5, New Bridge Street, and William Blackwood, Edinburgh, 1824.
>
> I xv, 295p; II 282p; III 297p. 12mo. 21s (ECB); 21s boards (ER).
>
> ER 40: 547 (July 1824), 41: 267 (Oct 1824); WSW II: 180.
>
> Corvey; CME 3-628-48520-7; ECB 482; NSTC 2S12240 (BI BL, C, E, O; NA MH).

*Notes.* Preface dated New York, June 1824. Originally published New York 1824 (Blanck).
Further edn: German trans., 1825 [as *Redwood, ein amerikanischer Roman von Cooper* (RS)].

1824: 88    SMITH, Anna White.

CAROLINE, AND ZELITE; OR, TRANSATLANTIC TALES, TAKEN FROM REAL LIFE. BY ANNA WHITE SMITH.

London: Charles Frederick Cock, 64, Paternoster Row, 1824.
139p. 12mo. 4s (ECB).
WSW II: 184.
BL N.270(1); ECB 544; NSTC 2S25296 (BI O).

*Notes.* Dedication 'to Colonel David Stewart, of Garth'. Two tales: 'Caroline', pp. [5]–88; 'Zelite', pp. [89]–139. ECB dates July 1824.

1824: 89    [SMITH, Margaret].

A WINTER IN WASHINGTON; OR, MEMOIRS OF THE SEYMOUR FAMILY. IN THREE VOLUMES.

New-York: Printed for E. Bliss and E. White. London: Reprinted for A. K. Newman and Co. Leadenhall-Street, 1824.
I xii, 272p; II 293p; III 287p. 12mo.
WSW II: 41.
Corvey; CME 3-628-48937-7; NSTC 2W27490 (BI C, O).

*Notes.* Originally published New York 1824 (NUC).

1824: 90    STANHOPE, Louisa Sidney.

THE SIEGE OF KENILWORTH. AN HISTORICAL ROMANCE. IN FOUR VOLUMES. BY LOUISA SIDNEY STANHOPE, AUTHOR OF THE BANDIT'S BRIDE, THE CRUSADERS, THE FESTIVAL OF MORA, AGE WE LIVE IN, DI MONTRANZO, TREACHERY, &C.

London: Printed for A. K. Newman and Co. Leadenhall-Street, 1824.
I vi, 275p; II 278p; III 293p; IV 306p. 12mo. 24s (ECB, ER).
ER 39: 512 (Jan 1824).
Corvey; CME 3-628-48781-1; ECB 558; NSTC 2S36114 (BI BL, C; NA MH).

*Notes.* Preface dated Upper Edmonton, 4 Oct 1823. ECB dates Nov 1823.

1824: 91    [?TAYLOR, Jane].

SINCERITY: A TALE. BY THE AUTHOR OF "RACHEL," &C.

London: Published by Knight and Lacey, 24, Pater-Noster-Row, 1824.
iv, 176p, ill. 12mo. 5s (ECB).
WSW II: 193.
Corvey; CME 3-628-48702-1; ECB 539; NSTC 2S22570 (BI BL, C, O).

*Notes.* The claimed authorship of *Rachel* appears to place this tale as one of the fictions attributable to Jane Taylor (see also 1819: 67, 1821: 71); though a number of other elements, including different publishers, make this the least firm attribution in the group. ECB dates Dec 1823.

1824: 92    [UPHAM, Edward].

RAMESES; AN EGYPTIAN TALE: WITH HISTORICAL NOTES, OF THE ERA OF THE PHARAOHS. IN THREE VOLUMES.

London: Printed for G. B. Whittaker, Ave-Maria-Lane; John Upham, Bath; and Charles
Upham, Exeter, 1824.

I viii, 341p; II 321p; III 328p. 8vo. 30s (ECB); 30s boards (ER, QR).

ER 41: 519 (Jan 1825); QR 31: 260 (Dec 1824); WSW II: 197.

Corvey; CME 3-628-48449-9; ECB 479; NSTC 2U1035 (BI BL, C, Dt, E, O; NA MH).

*Notes.* 'Advertisement' dated June 1824.

1824: 93    WARD, Catherine G[eorge].
THE FIRST CHILD; OR, THE HEIRESS OF MONTEITH. BY MRS.
CATHERINE G. WARD, AUTHORESS OF THE FOLLOWING POPULAR
WORKS: MYSTERIOUS MARRIAGE—ROSE OF CLAREMONT—
ORPHAN BOY—FAMILY PORTRAITS—THE COTTAGE ON THE
CLIFF—THE WIDOW'S CHOICE—AND MARRIETTE MOULINE. &C.
&C. &C.

London: Printed by J. M'Gowan, Great Windmill Street, published by Joseph Emans, 5,
Ivy Lane, Paternoster-Row, 1824.

627p, ill. 8vo.

IU 823.M.383fir; xNSTC.

*Notes.* Portrait of the authoress, opp. additional engraved t.p., with legend 'Mrs. Catherine
Ward. Published Jany. 1. 1824 by J. Emans, Ivy Lane'. Collates in fours.

1824: 94    WARD, Catherine G[eorge].
THE FISHER'S DAUGHTER, OR THE WANDERINGS OF WOLF, AND
THE FORTUNES OF ALFRED. BEING THE SEQUEL TO THAT SO
GREATLY ADMIRED AND POPULAR WORK, ENTITLED, THE COT-
TAGE ON THE CLIFF, OR A SEA-SIDE STORY. BY MRS. CATHERINE
G. WARD, AUTHORESS OF—MYSTERIOUS MARRIAGE—FAMILY
PORTRAITS—ORPHAN BOY—WIDOW'S CHOICE—THE THORN,
&C. &C.

London: Published by G. Virtue, 26, Ivy-Lane, Paternoster-Row; Bath-Street, Bristol;
and Queen-Square, Liverpool, 1824.

911p, ill. 8vo. 19s 6d (ECB).

IU 823.M383fi.1824; ECB 623; NSTC 2W4960 (BI O).

*Notes.* Printer's mark opp. first page of full text: 'Oxford: Printed by Bartlett and Hinton'.
Adv. at end of Hannah Maria Jones's, *The Wedding Ring* (1824: 57(b)) describes *The Fisher's
Daughter* as 'This day published [. . .] to be completed in about twenty-four nos at Sixpence,
or Six Parts, at Two Shillings Each'. ECB dates 1825. Collates in fours.

Further edns: 1825 (Corvey, NSTC); 1827 (NSTC); 1835 (NSTC); 1836 (NSTC); New York
1835 (NUC).

1824: 95    WHITE, Mary.
BEATRICE; OR, THE WYCHERLY FAMILY. A NOVEL. IN FOUR VOL-
UMES. BY MARY WHITE.

London: Printed for A. K. Newman and Co. Leadenhall-Street, 1824.

I ii, 347p; II 311p; III 354p; IV 313p. 12mo. 26s (ECB).

WSW II: 5.

Corvey; CME 3-628-48903-2; ECB 634; NSTC 2W17293 (BI BL, C, E, O).

*Notes.* ECB dates Apr 1824.

1824: 96    [WHITTY, Michael James].

**TALES OF IRISH LIFE, ILLUSTRATIVE OF THE MANNERS, CUS-TOMS, AND CONDITION OF THE PEOPLE. WITH DESIGNS BY GEORGE CRUIKSHANK.**

London: Published by J. Robins and Co. Ivy Lane, Paternoster Row, 1824.

I iv, 242p, ill.; II 249p, ill. 8vo. 12s (ECB, ER, QR).

ER 41: 520 (Jan 1825); QR 31: 532 (Mar 1825); WSW II: 202.

Corvey; CME 3-628-51018-X; ECB 575; NSTC 2W18777 (BI BL, C, Dt, O; NA DLC, MH).

*Notes.* Further edn: German trans., 1825.

1824: 97    [WILKINS, George].

**THE TWO RECTORS.**

London: Printed for Longman, Hurst, Rees, Orme, Brown, and Green, Paternoster-Row, 1824.

xvi, 458p. 12mo. 10s 6d (ECB).

WSW II: 203.

Corvey; CME 3-628-48849-4; ECB 605; NSTC 2W20716 (BI BL, Dt, E, O).

*Notes.* Dedication 'to the Right Honourable the Earl of E****'. 10 interlinking stories. ECB dates May 1824. According to NSTC and Wolff (Item 7228) 2nd edn. t.p. includes the wording 'by one of the authors of *Body and Soul*. It has been wholly reset'.

Further edn: 2nd edn. 1825 (NSTC).

1824: 98    [WILSON, James].

**TOURNAY; OR ALASTER OF KEMPENCAIRN. BY THE AUTHOR OF THE FIRE-EATER.**

Edinburgh: John Anderson, jun., 55, North Bridge Street; and Simpkin & Marshall, London, 1824.

471p. 12mo. 8s 6d (ECB); 8s 6d boards (ER).

ER 40: 547 (July 1824); WSW II: 204.

Corvey; CME 3-628-48763-3; ECB 594; NSTC 2W25418 (BI BL, E; NA MH).

*Notes.* Dedication to Sir Walter Scott, dated Edinburgh 18 May 1824.

1824: 99    [WOODROOFFE, Anne].

**SHADES OF CHARACTER; OR, THE INFANT PILGRIM. BY THE AUTHOR OF "THE HISTORY OF MICHAEL KEMP."**

Bath: Printed for the Author; and sold by Relfe, Cornhill, and Hatchard, and Seeley, London; and by all other Booksellers, 1824.

I 474p; II 621p; III 390p. 8vo. 23s (ECB); 7s (vol. 3, QR).

QR 32: 267 (June 1825).

Corvey; CME 3-628-48649-1; ECB 529; NSTC 2S14760 (BI BL, C, E).

*Notes*. Dedication 'To the friend of my youth' signed 'the author'. Note, dated 16 Feb 1824, at the end of vol. 2: 'As the Public have been kept so long in waiting for this little work, it has been thought advisable to print the Two Volumes for the present, and to publish the Third in the Summer'. Collates in fours. ECB 647 lists 2 vols., Hatchard 1832 edn., 20s.

Further edns: '4th edn.', London 1841 as *Shades of Character: or, Mental and Moral Delineations* (BL 4413.ccc.48); London 1844 (NUC).

# 1825

1825:1   ANON.

## THE ABDUCTION; OR, THE ADVENTURES OF MAJOR SARNEY. A STORY OF THE TIMES OF CHARLES THE SECOND. IN THREE VOLUMES.

London: Printed for Charles Knight, Pall-Mall East, 1825.

I 286p; II 267p; III 237p. 12mo. 21s (ECB, QR).

QR 32: 267 (June 1825); WSW II: 3.

Corvey; CME 3-628-47011-0; ECB 1; NSTC 2A1007 (BI BL, C, E, O; NA MH).

1825:2   ANON.

## THE ADVENTURERS; OR, SCENES IN IRELAND, IN THE REIGN OF ELIZABETH. IN THREE VOLUMES.

London: Printed for Longman, Hurst, Rees, Orme, Brown, and Green, Paternoster Row, 1825.

I iv, 341p; II 321p; III 322p. 12mo. 21s (ER, QR).

ER 42: 514 (Aug 1825), 43: 356-72 (Feb 1826) full review; QR 32: 549 (Oct 1825).

Corvey; CME 3-628-47021-8; NSTC 2A4376 (BI C, E, O).

*Notes*. This is one of four novels which are together given full reviews in ER (Feb 1826) under the page-top heading 'Irish Novels'.

1825:3   ANON.

## COLONEL BERKLEY AND HIS FRIENDS; CONTAINING SKETCHES OF LIFE SOUTH OF THE POTOMAC. A TALE. IN THREE VOLUMES.

New-York: Printed for W. B. Gilley, 92, Broadway; London: Reprinted for A. K. Newman & Co. Leadenhall-Street, 1825.

I 289p; II 284p; III 243p. 12mo. 18s (ECB, QR).

QR 32: 267 (June 1825).

Corvey; CME 3-628-47305-5; ECB 127; NSTC 2B19708 (BI C; NA DLC).

*Notes.* Colophon reads: 'Printed by J. Darling, Leadenhall-Street, London'. No original New York edn. discovered.

Further edn: 1826 (NSTC).


1825: 4   ANON.
**ENGLISH LIFE; OR, MANNERS AT HOME. IN FOUR PICTURES. IN TWO VOLUMES.**

> London: Printed for G. Wightman, Fleet Street, 1825.
> I 279p; II 286p. 8vo. 14s (ECB).
> WSW II: 10.
> Corvey; CME 3-628-47608-9; ECB 188; NSTC 2E10222 (BI BL, O).

*Notes.* ECB dates Nov 1824.

Further edns: 1829 (Sadleir 84a); New York 1825 (NUC).


1825: 5   ANON.
**EVERY DAY OCCURRENCES. IN TWO VOLUMES.**

> London: Printed for Charles Knight, Pall Mall East, 1825.
> I 227p; II 262p. 12mo. 14s (ECB, ER, QR).
> ER 42: 513 (Aug 1825); QR 32: 267 (June 1825).
> Corvey; CME 3-628-47652-6; ECB 194; NSTC 2E14745 (BI BL, C, E, O; NA MH).

*Notes.* Colophon of Charles Knight, Printer, Windsor.


1825: 6   ANON.
**GOING TOO FAR: A TALE FOR ALL AGES. IN TWO VOLUMES.**

> London: Printed for Baldwin, Cradock, and Joy, 1825.
> I viii, 316p; II 327p. 12mo. 12s (ECB, QR).
> QR 32: 267 (June 1825); WSW II: 13.
> Corvey; CME 3-628-47909-6; ECB 235; NSTC 2G11890 (BI BL, C, Dt, E, O).

*Notes.* Preface indicates female authorship.


1825: 7   ANON.
**HUSBAND HUNTING; OR, THE MOTHER AND DAUGHTERS. A TALE OF FASHIONABLE LIFE. IN THREE VOLUMES.**

> London: Printed for Geo B. Whittaker, Ave Maria Lane, 1825.
> I iv, 288p; II 298p; III 326p. 12mo. 21s (ECB, ER, QR).
> ER 42: 514 (Aug 1825); QR 32: 549 (Oct 1825); WSW II: 16.
> Corvey; CME 3-628-47861-8; ECB 290; NSTC 2H38645 (BI BL, O; NA DLC).

*Notes.* 'Preface by S——L J——N, Esq.' signed 'S. J., Bolt-court, London'. This is written in an inflated Johnsonian style, and is presumably fictitous (Johnson's last residence was at 8, Bolt Court, off Fleet Street).

Further edn: Boston 1825 (NSTC).


1825: 8   ANON.
**THE MISSIONARY.**

Edinburgh: Printed for the Author, and sold by Archibald Constable & Co., 1825.
7, 339p. 8vo.

E T.145.f; NSTC 2M30795.

*Notes.* 'Printed for Private Circulation' appears at the foot of t.p. below imprint date.

1825: 9   ANON.

## NEW LANDLORD'S TALES; OR, JEDEDIAH IN THE SOUTH. IN TWO VOLUMES.

London: Printed for T. Hookham, Old Bond Street, 1825.
I 347p; II 351p. 12mo. 14s (ECB).
Corvey; CME 3-628-51102-X; ECB 410; NSTC 2C25545 (BI BL, E, O).

*Notes.* 'Introductory, by Jedediah Cleishbotham', vol. 1, pp. [1]–16. ECB dates Jan 1825.

1825: 10   ANON.

## ST. HUBERT; OR, THE TRIALS OF ANGELINA. A NOVEL. IN THREE VOLUMES.

London: Printed [*sic*] and sold by G. B. Whittaker, Ave-Maria Lane, 1825.
I 239p; II 226p; III 256p. 12mo. 21s (ECB, ER); 18s (QR).
ER 42: 513 (Aug 1825); QR 32: 267 (June 1825).
Corvey; CME 3-628-48488-X; ECB 511; NSTC 2H34551 (BI BL, O).

*Notes.* Printer's mark of 'R. Snare, Minster-Street, Reading', verso of t.ps., also colophon of R. Snare, Printer, Reading in last vol.

1825: 11   ANON.

## THE WRITER'S CLERK; OR, THE HUMOURS OF THE SCOTTISH METROPOLIS. IN THREE VOLUMES.

London: Printed for G. B. Whittaker, Ave-Maria-Lane, 1825.
I 302p; II 392p; III 426p. 12mo. 21s (ECB).
Corvey; CME 3-628-48983-0; ECB 650; NSTC 2W34332 (BI BL, C, O; NA MH).

*Notes.* ECB dates Dec 1824.

1825: 12   ARCHER, E. A.

## SARAGOSSA; OR, THE HOUSES OF CASTELLO AND DE ARNO. A ROMANCE. IN FOUR VOLUMES. BY E. A. ARCHER.

London: Printed for A. K. Newman and Co. Leadenhall-Street, 1825.
I vi, 245p; II 272p; III vi, 295p; IV 300p. 12mo. 24s (ECB); 26s (ER, QR).
ER 41: 520 (Jan 1825); QR 31: 260 (Dec 1824); WSW II: 42.
Corvey; CME 3-628-47396-9; ECB 23; NSTC 2A14896 (BI BL, C, O).

*Notes.* ECB dates Oct 1824.

1825: 13   [BANIM, John and Michael].

## TALES, BY THE O'HARA FAMILY: CONTAINING CROHOORE OF THE BILL-HOOK. THE FETCHES, AND JOHN DOE. IN THREE VOLUMES.

London: Printed for W. Simpkin and R. Marshall, Stationers'-Hall Court, Ludgate-
Street, 1825.
I 367p; II 392p; III 404p. 12mo. 30s (ECB); 24s (ER, QR).
ER 42: 267 (Apr 1825), 43: 356–72 (Feb 1826) full review; QR 32: 267 (June 1825); WSW
II: 45.
Corvey; CME 3-628-47950-9; ECB 575; NSTC 2O2238 (BI BL, C, E, O; NA DLC, MH).

*Notes.* This is one of four novels which are together given full reviews in ER (Feb 1826) under
the page-top heading 'Irish Novels'. [1st series].
Further edns: 2nd edn. 1826 (NSTC); 3rd edn. 1831 (NUC); Philadelphia 1827 (NSTC); German trans., of 'John Doe' [as *Hauptmann Reh* (RS)] 1828 and 'Crohoore' [as *Der Zwerg, ein
Irländisches Sittengemälde* (RS)] 1828; French trans., of 'Crohoore' [as *Croohore na bilhoge,
ou les White boys* (BN)] and 'John Doe' [as *John Doe, ou le chef des rebelles* (BN)] 1829.
Facs: IAN (1979).

1825: 14    BEDFORD, John Harman.
**WANDERINGS OF CHILDE HAROLDE. A ROMANCE OF REAL LIFE.
INTERSPERSED WITH MEMOIRS OF THE ENGLISH WIFE, THE FOR-
EIGN MISTRESS, AND VARIOUS OTHER CELEBRATED CHARACTERS.
BY JOHN HARMAN BEDFORD, LIEUT. R.N. AUTHOR OF VIEWS
ON THE SHORES OF THE BLACK SEA, &C. IN THREE VOLUMES.**

London: Printed for Sherwood, Jones & Co. Paternoster-Row, 1825.
I xv, 241p; II xi, 208p; III xi, 235p. 12mo. 21s (ECB).
WSW II: 49.
Corvey; CME 3-628-47187-7; ECB 47; NSTC 2B14545 (BI BL, C, Dt, O; NA MH).

*Notes.* Introductory 'A Few Words to the Reader' dated White Cottage, Camberwell, 8 Nov
1824. ECB dates Dec 1824.

1825: 15    [?BORROW, George or ?DODS, Mary Diana].
**TALES OF THE WILD AND THE WONDERFUL.**

London: Printed for Hurst, Robinson, and Co. 5 Waterloo-Place, Pall Mall; and A. Constable and Co. Edinburgh, 1825.
x, 356p. 8vo. 10s 6d (ECB).
WSW II: 53–4.
Corvey; CME 3-628-51167-4; ECB 576; NSTC 2B41787 (BI BL, C, O; NA DLC, MH).

*Notes.* For a summary of evidence concerning the authorship of this title, see Wolff, Item 601
(vol. I, p. 111); Wolff proposes Miss Dods, a friend of Mary Shelley and a contributor to
*Blackwood's Magazine*, as an alternative solution to the contested issue of Borrow's authorship. Dedication to Joanna Baillie. ECB dates Oct 1825.
Further edn: Philadelphia 1826 (NSTC).

1825: 16    [BOSWELL, Thomas Alexander].
**THE JOURNAL OF AN EXILE. IN TWO VOLUMES.**

London: Printed for Saunders and Otley, British and Foreign Public Library, Conduit-
Street, Hanover-Square, 1825.

I 330p; II 328p. 12mo. 18s (ECB).

Corvey; CME 3-628-48009-4; ECB 314; NSTC 2J12551 (BI BL, C, E).

*Notes.* ECB dates Mar 1825.

Further edn: 2nd edn. 1825 (NSTC).


1825: 17    [BUSK, Mrs. M. M.].

TALES OF FAULT AND FEELING. BY THE AUTHOR OF "ZEAL AND EXPERIENCE."

London: T. Hookham, Old Bond-Street, 1825.

I 314p; II 333p; III 303p. 12mo. 21s (ECB, QR).

QR 32: 267 (June 1825); WSW II: 61.

Corvey; CME 3-628-51147-X; ECB 575; NSTC 2B62413 (BI BL, C, E, O).

*Notes.* 9 tales, the last 2 in verse. The author is styled as Mrs Busk in ECB; see also *Zeal and Experience* (1819: 29).


1825: 18    [CADELL, Cecilia Mary].

MASSENBURG. A TALE. IN THREE VOLUMES.

London: Printed for T. Cadell, Strand; and W. Blackwood, Edinburgh, 1825.

I iv, 328p; II 359p; III 308p. 12mo. 21s (ECB, ER, QR).

ER 42: 514 (Aug 1825); QR 32: 549 (Oct 1825); WSW II: 69.

Corvey; CME 3-628-48135-X; ECB 372; NSTC 2C939 (BI BL, C, E, O).

*Notes.* Preface dated 23 May 1825.


1825: 19    [CHENEY, Harriet Vaughan Foster].

A PEEP AT THE PILGRIMS IN SIXTEEN HUNDRED THIRTY-SIX. A TALE OF OLDEN TIMES. BY THE AUTHOR OF DIVERS UNFINISHED MANUSCRIPTS, &C. &C. IN THREE VOLUMES.

London: Printed for Geo. B. Whittaker, Ave-Maria Lane, 1825.

I 299p; II 326p; III 352p. 12mo. 18s (ECB, QR).

QR 32: 267 (June 1825); WSW II: 72.

Corvey; CME 3-628-48411-1; ECB 440; NSTC 2C17675 (BI C; NA DLC).

*Notes.* Originally published Boston 1824.


1825: 20    [COOPER, James Fenimore].

LIONEL LINCOLN; OR, THE LEAGUER OF BOSTON. BY THE AUTHOR OF THE "SPY," "PIONEERS," "PILOT," &C. &C. &C. IN THREE VOLUMES.

London: John Miller, 5, New Bridge Street, Blackfriars, 1825.

I 319p; II 300p; III 275p. 12mo. 21s (ECB, ER, QR).

ER 42: 266 (Apr 1825); QR 32: 267 (June 1825); WSW II: 78.

Corvey; ECB 134; NSTC 2C36836 (BI BL, C, Dt, O; NA MH).

*Notes.* Originally published New York 1824.

Further edns: 1832 (NSTC); 1839 (Blanck); French trans., 1825; German trans., 1825.

1825: 21    [COX, Frances Clarinda Adeline].
**THE CAMISARD; OR, THE PROTESTANTS OF LANGUEDOC: A TALE IN THREE VOLUMES.**

> London: Printed for Geo B. Whittaker, Ave-Maria Lane, 1825.
> I 360; II 405p; III 444p. 12mo. 21s (ECB, QR).
> QR 33: 279 (Dec 1825); WSW II: 80.
> BL N.334; ECB 94; NSTC 2C40920 (BI C, E, O).

*Notes.* Dedication to Thomas Denman, Esq., M.P.


1825: 22    [CRAWFORD, Archibald].
**TALES OF MY GRANDMOTHER.**

> Edinburgh: Printed for Archibald Constable and Co.; and Hurst, Robinson, & Co. London, 1825.
> I vi, 374p; II 312p. 12mo. 14s (ECB, ER).
> ER 42: 267 (Apr 1825); WSW II: 81.
> BL N.331; ECB 575; NSTC 2C42498 (BI C, E, O).

*Notes.* An extended version of 1824: 27. It omits 3 tales from the earlier 1 vol. version, while adding 4 new tales through its second vol. The original Introduction is replaced by a shorter Preface.


1825: 23    [?CROWE, Eyre Evans or ?PHIPPS, Constantine Henry, Marquis of Normanby].
**THE ENGLISH IN ITALY. IN THREE VOLUMES.**

> London: Printed for Saunders and Otley, British and Foreign Public Library, Conduit Street, Hanover Square, 1825.
> I ii, 305p; II 323p; III 318p. 12mo. 30s (ECB); 31s 6d (QR).
> QR 32: 549 (Oct 1825); WSW II: 161.
> Corvey; CME 3-628-47830-8; ECB 187; NSTC 2P15297 (BI BL, C, E, O; NA MH).

*Notes.* Preface, dated Aug 4 1825, mentions the author's 'residence of several years in the Peninsula', and apologizes for the mangling of Italian phrases in the text, first apparent to him when 'the sheets of the first and second volumes' reached him in 'his foreign abode'. Wolff (I, 323) ascribes to Crowe, in preference to the more conventional attribution to Constantine Henry Phipps, Marquis of Normanby. The grounds for this include its listing as one of his works in DNB, from information acquired from Crowe's son, and Crowe's much longer residence on the Continent compared with Phipps. It is worth adding that Crowe made a number of contributions to *Blackwood's Edinburgh Magazine* on French and Italian subjects during the early 1820s, including a series of 'Letters from Italy'. ECB lists as 'By Marquis of Normanby'. QR adds 'By a Distinguished Resident'. Wolff also uses similar arguments to reclaim the following two titles, usually attributed to Phipps, for Crowe: *Historiettes* (1827: 28), and *The English in France* (1828: 34).


1825: 24    [CROWE, Eyre Evans].
**TO-DAY IN IRELAND. IN THREE VOLUMES.**

> London: Printed for Charles Knight, Pall Mall East, 1825.

I 291p; II 319p; III 305p. 12mo. 24s (ECB, ER, QR).

ER 42: 514 (Aug 1825), 43: 356–72 (Feb 1826) full review; QR 32: 268 (June 1825); WSW II: 82.

Corvey; CME 3-628-48962-8; ECB 592; NSTC 2C44612 (BI BL, C, Dt, E, O; NA MH).

*Notes.* I The Carders; II The Carders; Connemara; III Old and New Light; The Toole's Warning. This is one of four works of fiction which are together given full reviews in ER (Feb 1826) under the page-top heading 'Irish Novels'. ECB dates May 1825, and gives Colburn (who brought out the 2nd edn.) as publisher.

Further edns: 2nd edn. 1826 (NSTC). French trans., of 'The Carders' and 'Connemara' 1830, and of 'The Toole's Warning' [as *La Fée de la famille O'Toole, ou le signal du départ* (MGD)] 1833.

Facs: IAN (1979).


1825: 25   DENNISTON, James.

**LEGENDS OF GALLOWAY; BEING A SERIES OF TRADITIONS, ILLUS- TRATIVE OF ITS ANCIENT HISTORY, CUSTOMS, MANNERS, AND SUPERSTITIONS BY JAMES DENNISTON, ESQ.**

> Edinburgh: Printed for Archibald Constable and Co. and Hurst, Robinson and Co. London, 1825.

> xiv, 294p. 8vo. 7s (ECB, QR); 7s boards (ER).

> ER 42: 266 (Apr 1825); QR 32: 267 (June 1825).

> Corvey; CME 3-628-47412-4; ECB 159; NSTC 2D9574 (BI BL, C, Dt, E, O; NA DLC, MH).

*Notes.* Dedication to the Right Honourable the Earl of Galloway. Preface dated Creetown, 20 Jan 1825.


**DE QUINCEY, Thomas, WALLADMOR**

See HÄRING, Georg Wilhelm Heinrich


1825: 26   DE RENZY, {S.} Sparow.

**LIFE, LOVE, AND POLITICS; OR THE ADVENTURES OF A NOVICE. A TALE. BY CAPTAIN SPAROW DE RENZY, AUTHOR OF "MARIAN DE BRITTOON," &C. &C. IN TWO VOLUMES.**

> London: Published by Knight and Lacey, Paternoster Row, 1825.

> I vii, 353p; II 336p. 12mo. 12s (ECB, QR).

> QR 32: 267 (June 1825).

> Corvey; CME 3-628-48566-5; ECB 345; NSTC 2D9985 (BI BL, C, O).

*Notes.* Preface signed S. Sparow De Renzy. Collates in sixes.


DODS, Mary Diana

See BORROW, George


1825: 27   {DOUGLAS, Mrs}.

**SUNGROVE ABBEY. AN INTERESTING DOMESTIC TALE.**

London: Published by G. Virtue, 26, Ivy-Lane, Paternoster-Row; and Bath-Street, Bristol; and sold by W. Black, Queen-Square, Liverpool, 1825.
592p, ill. 8vo.
BL RB.23.a.12456; xNSTC.

*Notes.* Additional engraved t.p. preceding t.p. proper reads: 'Sungrove Abbey, A Domestic Tale by Mrs. Douglas, author of several popular works'. This also carries the London imprint of G. Virtue, and is dated 1825. Collates in fours.
Further edn: 1844 (NSTC 2D17437).

1825: 28    EDRIDGE, Rebecca.
THE HIGHEST CASTLE AND THE LOWEST CAVE; OR, EVENTS OF
THE DAYS WHICH ARE GONE. BY REBECCA EDRIDGE, AUTHOR OF
THE SCRINIUM. IN THREE VOLUMES.

London: Printed for Geo. B. Whittaker, Ave-Maria Lane, 1825.
I 312p; II 300p; III 271p. 12mo. 18s (ECB).
WSW II: 93.
Corvey; CME 3-628-47515-5; ECB 179; NSTC 2E4720 (BI BL, C, O; NA MH).

*Notes.* Dedication 'to Every Body'.

1825: 29    EGAN, Pierce.
THE LIFE OF AN ACTOR. BY PIERCE EGAN, AUTHOR OF "LIFE IN
LONDON," "TOM AND JERRY," "A MUSICAL DRAMA," ETC. DEDI-
CATED TO EDMUND KEAN, ESQ. THE POETICAL DESCRIPTIONS BY
T. GREENWOOD. EMBELLISHED WITH TWENTY-SEVEN CHARAC-
TERISTIC SCENES, ETCHED BY THEODORE LANE; ENRICHED ALSO
WITH SEVERAL ORIGINAL DESIGNS ON WOOD, EXECUTED BY MR.
THOMPSON.

London: Printed for C. S. Arnold, Tavistock Street, Covent Garden, 1825.
xvi, 272p, ill. 8vo. 27s (ECB).
Corvey; CME 3-628-51310-3; ECB 181; NSTC 2E5902 (BI BL, C, O; NA DLC, MH).

*Notes.* Dedication dated 113, Strand, London, 18 Dec 1824. ECB dates Jan 1825. Collates in fours.

1825: 30    FOUQUÉ, [Friedrich Heinrich Karl], Baron de la Motte.
THE MAGIC RING; A ROMANCE, FROM THE GERMAN OF FREDER-
ICK, BARON DE LA MOTTE FOUQUÉ. IN THREE VOLUMES.

Edinburgh: Published by Oliver & Boyd, Tweeddale-Court; and Geo. B. Whittaker, London, 1825.
I xv, 319p; II 344p; III 332p. 12mo. 21s (ECB).
BL N.278; ECB 213; NSTC 2L2906 (BI C, Dt, E, O).

*Notes.* Trans. of *Der Zauberring* (Nürnberg, 1813). Dedication 'to Conrad Charles, Freyherr von Ämselnburg, in Berlin, translator of "The Lady of the Lake", "The Bridal of Triermain" and "The Antiquary" '. ECB dates Nov 1825.
Further edn: another trans. 1846 (NSTC).

1825: 31    [GALT, John].

## THE OMEN.

Edinburgh: William Blackwood, and T. Cadell, London, 1825.
160p. 8vo. 4s 6d (ECB).
WSW II: 98–9.
BL N.354(1); ECB 423; NSTC 2G1387 (BI C, E, O; NA MH).

*Notes.* 'Postscript' signed 'B. A. M., Castle-Bromage, 10th Jan. 1826'. ECB dates Feb 1826.
Further edns: 1842 with *The Provost* (NSTC); 1844 (NSTC).

1825: 32    [GLASSE, Francis].

## NED CLINTON; OR, THE COMMISSARY: COMPRISING ADVENTURES, AND EVENTS DURING THE PENINSULAR WAR: WITH CURIOUS AND ORIGINAL ANECDOTES OF MILITARY, AND OTHER REMARKABLE CHARACTERS. IN THREE VOLUMES.

London: Printed for William Marsh, 145, Oxford Street, 1825.
I viii, 287p; II ix, 271p; III viii, 270p. 12mo. 21s (ECB, ER, QR).
ER 42: 266 (Apr 1825); QR 32: 267 (June 1825).
Corvey; CME 3-628-48188-0; ECB 409; NSTC 2G10123 (BI BL, C, O).

*Notes.* Further edns: 2nd edn. 1832 (NSTC); 1839 (NSTC).

1825: 33    [GLEIG, George Robert].

## THE SUBALTERN.

Edinburgh: William Blackwood, and T. Cadell, London, 1825.
373p. 12mo. 7s (ECB, QR).
QR 33: 597 (Mar 1826), 34: 406–21 (Sept 1826) full review.
BRu ENC; ECB 568; NSTC 2G10330 (BI BL, Dt, C, E, O; NA DLC, MH).

*Notes.* 'Originally published in *Blackwood's Edinburgh Magazine*' on verso of half-title. This is one of three novels which are together given full reviews in QR (Sept 1826) under the page-top heading 'Military Memoirs'.
Further edns: 2nd edn. 1826 (NSTC); 3rd edn. 1828 (NSTC); 1845 (NSTC); German trans., 1830 [as *Soldatenleben. Kriegsabentheuer in den Pyrenäen und Süd-Frankreich* (RS)].

1825: 34    [GODWIN, Catherine Grace].

## REINE CANZIANI: A TALE OF MODERN GREECE. IN TWO VOLUMES.

London: Printed for Hurst, Robinson and Co., 90 Cheapside, and 8 Pall-Mall; and A.
   Constable and Co., Edinburgh, 1825.
I viii, 309p; II 292p. 12mo. 14s (ECB, ER, QR).
ER 42: 514 (Aug 1825); QR 32: 268 (June 1825); WSW II: 30.
Corvey; CME 3-628-48562-2; ECB 485; NSTC 2C6383 (BI BL, C, E, O).

1825: 35    [GRATTAN, Thomas Colley].

## HIGH-WAYS AND BY-WAYS; OR, TALES OF THE ROADSIDE, PICKED UP IN THE FRENCH PROVINCES. BY A WALKING GENTLEMAN. SECOND SERIES. IN THREE VOLUMES.

London: Printed for Henry Colburn, New Burlington Street, 1825.
I 293p; II 324p; III 348p. 12mo. 30s (ECB).
WSW II: 104.
Corvey; CME 3-628-51059-7; ECB 268; NSTC 2G18165 (BI BL, Dt, E, O; NA DLC).
*Notes.* ECB dates Dec 1824.
Further edns: 1827 (NSTC); 1833 (NSTC); Philadelphia 1827 (NSTC); French trans., 1825
[as *Grandes routes et chemins de traverse, ou contes recueillis dans les provinces françaises*
(BN)]; German trans., 1825–8 [as *Heer- und Querstraßen, oder Erzählungen gesammelt auf
einer Wanderung durch Frankreich, von einem fußreisenden Gentleman,* vols. 3–5 (RS)].

1825: 36   GREEN, [Sarah].
PARENTS AND WIVES; OR, INCONSISTENCY AND MISTAKES. A
NOVEL. IN THREE VOLUMES. BY MRS. GREEN, AUTHOR OF WHO IS
THE BRIDEGROOM? GRETNA GREEN MARRIAGES; GOOD MEN OF
MODERN DATE; FESTIVAL OF ST. JAGO; FUGITIVE; &C.

London: Printed for A. K. Newman and Co. Leadenhall-Street, 1825.
I 248p; II 230p; III 227p. 12mo. 16s 6d (ECB, QR).
QR 32: 549 (Oct 1825); WSW II: 104.
Corvey; CME 3-628-47927-4; ECB 243; NSTC 2G20158 (BI BL, E, O).

1825: 37   GRIMSTONE, M[ary] L{eman}.
THE BEAUTY OF THE BRITISH ALPS; OR, LOVE AT FIRST SIGHT. BY
M. L. GRIMSTONE.

Plymouth: Printed for and published by J. Bennett, 5, Cornwall-Street, 1825.
iv, 549p, ill. 8vo.
BRu ENC; NSTC 2G23371 (NA MH).
*Notes.* Frontispiece portrait of 'M. Leman Grimstone' facing t.p. Harvard copy (MH-H
21483 46.8.5*) has a different t.p., with the following imprint: 'Published by G. Virtue, 26,
Ivy-Lane, Paternoster-Row; Bath-Street, Bristol; and Queen-Square, Liverpool, 1825.' Col-
lates in fours.
Further edn: [1840] (NSTC).

1825: 38   [HÄRING, Georg Wilhelm Heinrich]; [DE QUINCEY, Thomas
(*trans.*)].
WALLADMOR: "FREELY TRANSLATED INTO GERMAN FROM THE
ENGLISH OF SIR WALTER SCOTT." AND NOW FREELY TRANS-
LATED FROM THE GERMAN INTO ENGLISH. IN TWO VOLUMES.

London: Printed for Taylor and Hessey, 93 Fleet Street, and 13 Waterloo Place, Pall
Mall, 1825.
I xxx, 247p; II 311p. 8vo. 16s (ECB, QR); 21s (QR).
QR 31: 260 (Dec 1824), 31: 532 (Mar 1825); WSW II: 86.
BL N.327; ECB 521; NSTC 2H1245 (BI C, Dt, E, O; NA MH).
*Notes.* Trans. of *Walladmor. Frei nach dem Englischen des Walter Scott. Von W\*\*\*\*s* (Berlin,
1824). Advertisement to the Reader (about the German provenance (ironic)); Dedication to
W\*\*\*\*s, the German 'Translator' of *Walladmor;* German 'Translator's' Dedication to Sir

Walter Scott, Bart. In spite of its alleged provenance, the German 'translation' is a German original, masquerading as a novel by Scott. For an account of the differences between Häring's and De Quincey's narratives, see Frederick Burwick, 'How to Translate a Waverley Novel: Sir Walter Scott, Willibald Alexis, and Thomas De Quincey', *Wordsworth Circle*, 25: 2 (1994), 93–100. Willibald Alexis was Häring's pseudonym. ECB dates Oct 1824, which is the date of De Quincey's *London Magazine* review of the *German* novel, though the English counterpart almost certainly appeared early in 1825. QR lists as 21s in Dec 1824, and 16s in Mar 1825.

1825: 39   [HARDING, Anne Raikes].
**REALITIES, NOT A NOVEL. A TALE FROM REAL LIFE. IN FOUR VOL-UMES. BY THE AUTHOR OF CORRECTION, DECISION, REFUGEES, &C.**

> London: Printed for A. K. Newman and Co. Leadenhall-Street, 1825.
> I viii, viii, 284p; II 254p; III 263p; IV 243p. 12mo. 24s (ECB).
> WSW II: 106.
> Corvey; CME 3-628-48456-1; ECB 481; NSTC 2H7490 (BI BL, O).

*Notes*. Preface dated Bath, Aug 1825. ECB dates Aug 1825.

1825: 40   HARTSTONGE, Matthew Weld.
**THE EVE OF ALL-HALLOWS; OR, ADELAIDE OF TYRCONNEL; A ROMANCE. IN THREE VOLUMES. BY MATTHEW WELD HART-STONGE, ESQ. M.R.I.A.**

> London: Printed for G. B. Whittaker, Ave Maria Lane, 1825.
> I 330p; II 298p; III 199p. 12mo. 18s (ECB).
> ER 42: 513 (Aug 1825); QR 32: 268 (June 1825); WSW II: 107.
> Corvey; CME 3-628-47630-5; ECB 257; NSTC 2H10836 (BI E).

*Notes*. Dedication to Sir Walter Scott, of Abbotsford, Bart., dated Molesworth-Street, Dublin, Feb 1825.

1825: 41   HIGGINSON, Francis S.
**MANDERVILLE; OR, THE HIBERNIAN CHILIARCH: A TALE. BY FRANCIS S. HIGGINSON, R.N. LATE COMMANDER OF HIS MAJESTY'S CUTTER LYNX. IN TWO VOLUMES.**

> London: Printed and published by Thomas Dolby, Catherine Street, Strand, 1825.
> I vii, 287p; II 277p. 12mo.
> WSW II: 113.
> Corvey; CME 3-628-47685-2; ECB 268; NSTC 2H20893 (BI BL, C, O; NA MH).

*Notes*. ECB dates Apr 1825.

1825: 42   HOFLAND, [Barbara].
**MODERATION. A TALE. BY MRS. HOFLAND, AUTHOR OF INTEGRITY A TALE, PATIENCE A TALE, DECISION A TALE, THE SON OF A GENIUS; TALES OF THE PRIORY; TALES OF THE MANOR, &C.**

London: Printed for Longman, Hurst, Rees, Orme, Brown, and Green, Paternoster-
Row, 1825.
253p, ill. 12mo. 6s (ECB, QR).
QR 32: 549 (Oct 1825); WSW II: 115.
Corvey; CME 3-628-47662-3; ECB 275; NSTC 2H29407 (BI BL, C, E, O).

*Notes.* Colophon reads 'Bungay: Stereotyped and Printed by J. and R. Childs'.
Further edns: 2nd edn. 1826 (NSTC); 1836 (NSTC); 1838 (NSTC).


1825: 43    [HOOK, Theodore Edward].
**SAYINGS AND DOINGS, OR SKETCHES FROM LIFE. SECOND
SERIES. IN THREE VOLUMES.**

London: Printed for Henry Colburn, New Burlington-Street, 1825.
I viii, 326p; II 344p; III 412p. 12mo. 31s 6d (ECB).
WSW II: 119.
O 256.e.15896; ECB 516; NSTC 2H28950 (BI BL, C, Dt).

*Notes.* Preface dated London, 19 Jan 1825. ECB dates Feb 1825.
Further edns: New edn. 1825 (Corvey), CME 3-628-48529-0; 1838 (NSTC); Philadelphia
1825 (NSTC).


1825: 44    [HUGO, Victor].
**HANS OF ICELAND.**

London: J. Robins and Co. Ivy Lane, Paternoster Row, 1825.
225p, ill. 12mo. 7s 6d (ECB, QR).
QR 32: 267 (June 1825).
Corvey; CME 3-628-47659-3; ECB 254; NSTC 2H35719 (BI BL, C, Dt, O; NA MH).

*Notes.* Trans. of *Han d'Islande* (Paris, 1823).
Further edns: [1841] (NSTC); [1845] (NSTC); 1847 as *The Demon Dwarf; or, Hans of Iceland*
(NSTC).


1825: 45    [INGLIS, Henry David].
**TALES OF ARDENNES. BY DERWENT CONWAY.**

London: Printed for G. B. Whittaker, Ave Maria Lane, 1825.
xiv, 242p. 8vo. 8s (ECB, QR).
QR 32: 267 (June 1825); WSW II: 76–7.
Corvey; CME 3-628-51017-1; ECB 296: NSTC 2I2443 (BI BL, C, E, O).

*Notes.* Introduction dated Liege, Mar 1824. Contains 8 tales plus a short verse drama.


**JEFFERSON, Mr. [pseud.], TALES OF OLD MR. JEFFERSON**
See 1823: 48


**JONES, Hannah Maria, THE VICTIM OF FASHION**
See 1824: 56

1825:46   [JONES, James Athearn].

THE REFUGEE. A ROMANCE. IN THREE VOLUMES. BY CAPTAIN MATTHEW MURGATROYD, OF THE NINTH CONTINENTALS IN THE REVOLUTIONARY WAR.

> New York: Printed for Wilder & Campbell. London: Reprinted for A. K. Newman & Co. Leadenhall-Street, 1825.
>
> I 285p; II 270p; III 280p. 12mo. 18s (ECB, ER, QR).
>
> ER 42: 513 (Aug 1825); QR 32: 268 (June 1825).
>
> Corvey; CME 3-628-48394-8; ECB 401; NSTC 2J10659 (BI BL, C, O).

*Notes.* Originally published New York 1825 (NSTC).


1825:47   KENDRICK, Tertius T. C.

THE TRAVELLERS. A TALE, ILLUSTRATIVE OF THE MANNERS, CUSTOMS, AND SUPERSTITIONS OF MODERN GREECE. BY TERTIUS T. C. KENDRICK, AUTHOR OF THE "IONIAN ISLANDS," THE "KAKO-DÆMON," ETC. ETC. IN THREE VOLUMES.

> London: Published by C. S. Arnold, 21, Tavistock Street, Covent Garden; sold also by Oliver and Boyd, Edinburgh; and Westley and Tyrrell, Dublin, 1825.
>
> I 248p; II 216p; III 258p. 12mo. 18s (ECB, ER, QR); 18s boards (ER, QR).
>
> ER 42: 513, 514 (Aug 1825); QR 32: 268 (June 1825), 32: 549 (Oct 1825).
>
> Corvey; CME 3-628-47993-2; ECB 318; NSTC 2K2832 (BI BL, C, O).

*Notes.* 'Address to the Reader' (1 p. unn.) at end of vol. 3, subscribed Malta. Colophon of 'C. and C. Whittingham, College House, Chiswick'. ER 42: 513 and QR 32: 549 (Oct 1825) list as 18s boards.


1825:48   [KENNEDY, Grace].

DUNALLAN; OR, KNOW WHAT YOU JUDGE; A STORY. IN THREE VOLUMES. BY THE AUTHOR OF "THE DECISION," "FATHER CLEMENT," &C. &C.

> Edinburgh: Published by W. Oliphant, 22, South Bridge; and Hamilton, Adams & Co. 33, Paternoster Row, London, 1825.
>
> I 270p; II 272p; III 220p. 12mo. 18s (ER).
>
> ER 41: 520 (Jan 1825); WSW II: 129.
>
> BL 012642.n.244; NSTC 2K3058 (BI C, E, O).

*Notes.* Further edns: 2nd edn. 1825 (Corvey), CME 3-628-47494-9; 3rd edn. 1826 (Jarndyce XCIV, Item 614); 4th edn. 1829 (NSTC); 5th edn. 1836 (BL RB.23.a.12244); 6th edn. 1841 (NSTC); New York 1828 (NSTC); French trans., 1828; German trans., 1835 [as vols. 3–4 of *Der Miss Grace Kennedy sämmtliche Werke* (RS)].


1825:49   [KENNEDY, Grace].

PHILIP COLVILLE; OR, A COVENANTER'S STORY. UNFINISHED. BY THE AUTHOR OF "THE DECISION," "FATHER CLEMENT," &C. &C.

> Edinburgh: Published by W. Oliphant, 22, South Bridge; and sold by M. Ogle, and Chalmers & Collins, Glasgow; J. Finlay, Newcastle; Beilby & Knotts, Birmingham;

J. Hatchard and Son, Hamilton, Adams & Co., J. Nisbet, J. Duncan, B. J. Holdsworth, and F. Westley, London: and R. M. Tims, and W. Curry, jun. & Co. Dublin, 1825.
272p. 12mo. 6s (ECB).
WSW II: 129.
Corvey; CME 3-628-48434-0; ECB 445; NSTC 2K3092 (BI C, E, O; NA MH).

*Notes.* ECB dates Oct 1825.
Further edn: German trans., 1836 [as vol. 6 of *Der Miss Grace Kennedy sämmtliche Werke* (RS)].

1825: 50    [LAUDER, Sir Thomas Dick].
LOCHANDHU A TALE OF THE EIGHTEENTH CENTURY. IN THREE VOLUMES.

Edinburgh: Printed for Archibald Constable and Co.; and Hurst, Robinson and Co. London, 1825.
I xii, 300p, ill.; II 312p, ill.; III 287p, ill. 12mo. 21s (ECB); 21s boards (ER); 35s (QR).
ER 42: 266 (Apr 1825), 42: 513 (Aug 1825); QR 32: 549 (Oct 1825); WSW II: 133.
Corvey; CME 3-628-48037-X; ECB 350; NSTC 2L5420 (BI BL, C, E, O; NA DLC, MH).

*Notes.* Introductory Address signed Charles Montague Montgomery, Gladstanes' Lodgings, James' Court, 10 Nov 1824.
Further edn: French trans., 1828.

1825: 51    [LAURENCE, Miss H.].
LONDON IN THE OLDEN TIME; OR, TALES INTENDED TO ILLUS-TRATE THE MANNERS AND SUPERSTITIONS OF ITS INHABITANTS, FROM THE TWELFTH TO THE SIXTEENTH CENTURY.

London: Longman, Hurst, Rees, Orme, Brown, and Green; Paternoster-Row, 1825.
viii, 324p. 8vo. 10s (ECB, ER, QR).
ER 42: 514 (Aug 1825); QR 32: 268 (June 1825), 32: 549 (Oct 1825); WSW II: 133.
Corvey; CME 3-628-51089-9; ECB 352; NSTC 2L5526 (BI BL, Dt, E, O; NA DLC).

*Notes.* 8 tales, plus a prefatory poem.
Further edn: 2nd edn. 1827 (NSTC).

1825: 52    [LESTER, Elizabeth B.].
FIRE-SIDE SCENES. BY THE AUTHOR OF THE BACHELOR AND MARRIED MAN, &C. &C. &C. IN THREE VOLUMES.

London: Printed for Longman, Hurst, Rees, Orme, Brown, and Green, 1825.
I 312p; II 283p; III 300p. 12mo. 21s (ECB).
Corvey; CME 3-628-47551-1; ECB 206; NSTC 2F6346 (BI BL, E, O; NA MH).

*Notes.* For attribution to Lester, rather than to Mrs Ross, see note to *The Bachelor and the Married Man* (1817: 37). ECB dates Dec 1824.

1825: 53    [LEWIS, Miss M. G.].
AMBITION. IN THREE VOLUMES.

London: Printed for T. Cadell, Strand, and W. Blackwood, Edinburgh, 1825.

I 299p; II 365p; III 413p. 12mo. 24s (ECB, ER, QR).
ER 42: 514 (Aug 1825); QR 32: 549 (Oct 1825); WSW II: 135.
Corvey; CME 3-628-47053-6; ECB 15; NSTC 2L14110 (BI BL, C, E, O).

1825: 54    LITT, W[illiam].
HENRY AND MARY, A LOCAL TALE; ILLUSTRATIVE OF THE PECU-
LIAR HABITS, CUSTOMS, AND DIVERSIONS OF THE INHABITANTS
OF THE WEST OF CUMBERLAND, DURING THE GREATER PART OF
THE EIGHTEENTH AND PRECEDING CENTURY. BY W. LITT,
AUTHOR OF WRESTLIANA.

> Whitehaven: Printed by Robert Gibson, King-Street: sold by John Richardson, Royal
> Exchange, London, 1825.
> ii, 382p. 8vo.
> BL RB.23.a.12379; xNSTC.

*Notes.* 'Preliminary Observations' states 'As for the Tale itself, there is in reality more *truth*
than *fiction*' (p. ii). Collates in fours.

1825: 55    [LLANOS GUTIERREZ, Valentin].
DON ESTEBAN; OR, MEMOIRS OF A SPANIARD. WRITTEN BY HIM-
SELF. IN THREE VOLUMES.

> London: Henry Colburn, New Burlington Street, 1825.
> I x, 303p; II iv, 267p; III v, 292p. 12mo. 27s (ECB); 24s (ER, QR); 21s (QR).
> ER 42: 267 (Apr 1825); QR 32: 267 (June 1825), 33: 205–17 (Dec 1825) full review, 33:
> 597 (Mar 1826); WSW II: 105.
> Corvey; CME 3-628-47444-2; ECB 168; NSTC 2L18566 (BI BL, C, E, O; NA MH).

*Notes.* QR lists as 24s in June 1825, and 21s in Mar 1826.
Further edns: 2nd edn. 1826 (NSTC); German trans., 1827 [as *Der Pflegesohn. Historischer
Roman, aus den Papieren eines Spaniers* (RS)].

1825: 56    M'CHRONICLE, Ronald [pseud.].
BURTON. A NOVEL. IN THREE VOLUMES. BY RONALD M'CHRON-
ICLE, ESQ. AUTHOR OF LEGENDS OF SCOTLAND, (FIRST AND SEC-
OND SERIES,) &C.

> London: Printed for A. K. Newman and Co. Leadenhall-Street, 1825.
> I 268p; II 254p; III 230p. 12mo. 18s (ECB).
> WSW II: 138.
> Corvey; CME 3-628-48072-8; ECB 358; NSTC 2M1927 (BI BL, C, O).

*Notes.* ECB dates Nov 1824.

1825: 57    M'DERMOT, [Martin].
THE MYSTERY DEVELOPED. A NOVEL. IN THREE VOLUMES. BY MR.
M'DERMOT, AUTHOR OF A CRITICAL DISSERTATION ON THE
NATURE AND PRINCIPLES OF TASTE; PHILOSOPHICAL INQUIRY INTO
THE SOURCES OF THE PLEASURES DERIVED FROM TRAGIC REPRE-
SENTATIONS; THE BEAUTIES OF MODERN LITERATURE, &C. &C.

London: Printed for A. K. Newman and Co. Leadenhall-Street, 1825.
I 262p; II 282p; III 246p. 12mo. 16s 6d (ECB, ER, QR).
ER 42: 266 (Apr 1825); QR 31: 532 (Mar 1825).
Corvey; CME 3-628-48068-X; ECB 358; NSTC 2M2797 (BI BL, C, O).

1825: 58    [MACHENRY, James].
THE HEARTS OF STEEL, AN IRISH HISTORICAL TALE OF THE LAST
CENTURY. BY THE AUTHOR OF "THE WILDERNESS," "O'HALLO-
RAN," &C. IN THREE VOLUMES.

London: Printed for Wightman and Cramp, Paternoster-Row, 1825.
I xii, 315p; II 321p; III 346p. 12mo. 24s (ECB).
WSW II: 140.
Corvey; CME 3-628-47718-2; ECB 261; NSTC 2M4778 (BI BL, C).

*Notes.* Preface dated London, 15 July 1825. ECB dates Nov 1825.
Further edns: Philadelphia 1825 (Blanck, NSTC); French trans., 1830.

1825: 59    [MAXWELL, William Hamilton].
O'HARA; OR, 1798. IN TWO VOLUMES.

London: Printed for J. Andrews, 167, New Bond-Street; and Miliken, Dublin, 1825.
I xl, 264p; II 294p. 8vo. 16s (ECB, ER, QR).
ER 42: 514 (Aug 1825), 43: 356–72 (Feb 1826) full review; QR 32: 549 (Oct 1825); WSW
II: 144.
Corvey; CME 3-628-48244-5; ECB 421; NSTC 2M21428 (BI BL, C, Dt, O; NA MH).

*Notes.* In IinFII, Item 46, authorship is given to Robert Ashworth, apparently correcting the
attribution to Maxwell in IinFI, Item 1118; but no other evidence concerning this claim has
been discovered. Dedication to the most noble the Marquess of Sligo, K.P., dated 1 June
1825. This is one of four novels which are together given full reviews in ER (Feb 1826) under
the page-top heading 'Irish Novels'.
Facs: IAN (1979).

1825: 60    MOSSE, Henrietta Rouviere.
A FATHER'S LOVE AND A WOMAN'S FRIENDSHIP; OR, THE WIDOW
AND HER DAUGHTERS. A NOVEL. IN FIVE VOLUMES. BY HENRI-
ETTA ROUVIERE MOSSE, AUTHOR OF LUSSINGTON ABBEY, HEIRS
OF VILLEROY, OLD IRISH BARONET, PEEP AT OUR ANCESTORS,
ARRIVALS FROM INDIA, BRIDE AND NO WIFE, &C.

London: Printed for A. K. Newman and Co. Leadenhall-Street, 1825.
I 319p; II 326p; III 336p; IV 355p; V 306p. 12mo. 30s (ECB, ER, QR).
ER 42: 513 (Aug 1825); QR 32: 549 (Oct 1825); WSW II: 154.
Corvey; CME 3-628-48343-3; ECB 399; NSTC 2R19128 (BI BL, C, E, O).

1825: 61    [NEAL, John].
BROTHER JONATHAN: OR, THE NEW ENGLANDERS. IN THREE
VOLUMES.

Edinburgh: William Blackwood, and T. Cadell, Strand, London, 1825.

I 421p; II 451p; III 452p. 8vo. 31s 6d (ECB, QR); 20s boards (ER).
ER 42: 514 (Aug 1825); QR 32: 549 (Oct 1825); WSW II: 155.
Corvey; CME 3-628-47164-8; ECB 78; NSTC 2N1990 (BI BL, C, E, O; NA DLC, MH).

1825: 62   [NOVELLO, Mary Sabilla].
## A DAY IN STOWE GARDENS.
London: Printed for J. & H. L. Hunt, Tavistock Street, Covent Garden, 1825.
x, 315p. 8vo. 9s (ECB, QR).
QR 31: 532 (Mar 1825); WSW II: 156.
Corvey; CME 3-628-47378-0; ECB 155; NSTC 2N11615 (BI BL, C, E, O).

*Notes.* Dedication to Leigh Hunt. QR sub-titles 'A Collection of Tales on the Plan of the Decameron'. NSTC classes under 635, 'Garden crops, Vegetables', but clearly fiction.

1825: 63   [OGLE, Nathaniel].
## MARIAMNE: AN HISTORICAL NOVEL OF PALESTINE.
London: Geo. B. Whittaker, Ave-Maria Lane, 1825.
I viii, 269p; II 246p; III 232p. 12mo. 18s (ECB, ER, QR).
ER 42: 266 (Apr 1825); QR 32: 267 (June 1825); WSW II: 23.
Corvey; CME 3-628-48155-4; ECB 368; NSTC 2M1470 (BI BL, E).

*Notes.* Dedication 'to Sir Walter Scott, Baronet, &c. &c.', dated 10 Mar 1825. Preface to later edn. of 1839 (see below) notes how the work was originally published 'during the crash and panic of 1824' and 'lost amid the confusion'.
Further edns: 1839 as *Mariamne, the last of the Asmonean Princesses* (BL N.1622); 1843 (NUC); German trans., 1828.

1825: 64   O'TARA, Mac-Erin [pseud.].
## THOMAS FITZ-GERALD THE LORD OF OFFALEY. A ROMANCE OF THE SIXTEENTH CENTURY. IN THREE VOLUMES. BY MAC-ERIN O'TARA, THE LAST OF THE SEANACHIES. BEING THE FIRST OF A PROJECTED SERIES ILLUSTRATIVE OF THE HISTORY OF IRELAND.
London: Printed for A. K. Newman and Co. Leadenhall-Street; and sold by John Cumming, Dublin, 1825.
I xxx, 372p; II 306p; III 258p. 12mo. 27s (ECB).
WSW II: 157.
Corvey; CME 3-628-48071-X; ECB 585; NSTC 2O6047 (BI BL, C, E, O).

*Notes.* Introduction, vol. 1, pp. [i]–xxx. Continuous roman and arabic pagination, with novel proper beginning at p. [31]. ECB dates Mar 1825.

**PARNELL, William, THE PRIEST OF RAHERY**
See 1819: 53

1825: 65   [PAULDING, James Kirke].
## JOHN BULL IN AMERICA; OR, THE NEW MUNCHAUSEN.
London: John Miller, New Bridge Street, Blackfriars, 1825.

xix, 327p. 12mo. 7s (ECB).
WSW II: 159.
BL 837.d.26; CME 3-628-47991-6; ECB 309; NSTC 2P7326 (BI C, O; NA DLC).

*Notes.* 'Preface of the Editor', pp. [iii]–xix, dated Washington, 10 Oct 1824. ECB dates Apr 1825. Originally published New York 1825 (Blanck, NSTC).

**PHIPPS, Constantine Henry, Marquis of Normanby, THE ENGLISH IN ITALY**
See CROWE, Eyre Evans

1825: 66    [PHIPPS, Constantine Henry, Marquis of Normanby].
**MATILDA; A TALE OF THE DAY.**

> London: Henry Colburn, New Burlington Street, 1825.
> v, 379p. 12mo. 10s 6d (ECB, ER, QR).
> ER 42: 513 (Aug 1825); QR 32: 549 (Oct 1825), 33: 474–90 (Mar 1826) full review; WSW II: 161.
> Corvey; CME 3-628-48137-6; ECB 373; NSTC 2P15312 (BI BL, Dt, NCu).

*Notes.* This is one of three novels which are together given full reviews in QR (Mar 1826) under the page-top heading 'Novels of Fashionable Life'.
Further edns: 2nd edn. 1825 (NSTC); 3rd edn. 1825 (NSTC); 4th edn. 1826 (NSTC); New York 1825 (NUC) [also Philadelphia 1825 (NUC)]; French trans., 1826 [as *Mathilde; ou les Anglais en Italie* (BLC)]; German trans., 1827.

1825: 67    PICARD, L[ouis] B[enoit].
**THE GIL BLAS OF THE REVOLUTION. BY L. B. PICARD. IN THREE VOLUMES.**

> London: Printed for Saunders and Otley, British and Foreign Public Library, Conduit Street, Hanover Square; and Geo. B. Whittaker, Ave-Maria-Lane, 1825.
> I 341p; II 358p; III 385p. 12mo. 21s (ECB).
> BL N.283; ECB 373; NSTC 2P15708 (BI C, E, O; NA MH).

*Notes.* Trans. of *Le Gilblas de la révolution* (Paris, 1824). Half-titles read 'The Gil Blas of the Revolution, or the Confessions of Lawrence Giffard'. ECB dates Jan 1825.

1825: 68    PICARD, L[ouis] B[enoit].
**THE NOVICE; OR, THE MAN OF INTEGRITY. FROM THE FRENCH OF L. B. PICARD, AUTHOR OF THE GIL BLAS OF THE REVOLUTION, &C. &C. IN THREE VOLUMES.**

> London: Printed for Baldwin, Cradock and Joy, 1825.
> I 264p; II 280p; III 246p. 12mo. 16s 6d (ECB); 21s (QR).
> QR 32: 267 (June 1825); WSW II: 161.
> BL N.303; ECB 449; NSTC 2P15709 (BI C, O).

*Notes.* Trans. of *L'Honnête Homme, ou le niais* (Paris, 1825).

1825: 69    [PYNE, William Henry].
**THE TWENTY-NINTH OF MAY: RARE DOINGS AT THE RESTORA-TION. BY EPHRAIM HARDCASTLE, AUTHOR OF "WINE AND WAL-NUTS." IN TWO VOLUMES.**

London: Printed for Knight and Lacey, Paternoster Row; and Westley and Tyrrell, Dublin, 1825.

I xii, 354p; II iv, 366p. 12mo. 18s (ECB, ER, QR).

ER 42: 514 (Aug 1825); QR 32: 268 (June 1825); WSW II: 165.

Corvey; CME 3-628-47625-9; ECB 254; NSTC 2H7389 (BI BL).

*Notes.* Dedication 'to his most excellent Majesty King George the Fourth'. QR gives as the title 'The Twenty-ninth of May; or, Joyous Doings at the Restoration'.

Further edn: 2nd edn. 1825 (NSTC).

1825: 70   R——N., F.

**TRUTH AND FASHION, A SKETCH. BY F. R——N. IN TWO VOLUMES.**

London: Printed for Geo. B. Whittaker, Ave-Maria Lane, 1825.

I 292p; II 261p. 12mo. 14s (ECB, ER, QR).

ER 42: 514 (Aug 1825); QR 32: 549 (Oct 1825); WSW II: 165.

Corvey; CME 3-628-48838-9; ECB 601; xNSTC.

1825: 71   ROCHE, Regina Maria.

**THE CASTLE CHAPEL. A ROMANTIC TALE. IN THREE VOLUMES. BY REGINA MARIA ROCHE, AUTHOR OF THE CHILDREN OF THE ABBEY; BRIDAL OF DUNAMORE; CLERMONT; DISCARDED SON; HOUSES OF OSMA AND ALMERIA; MUNSTER COTTAGE BOY; TRADITION OF THE CASTLE; TRECOTHICK BOWER; MAID OF THE HAMLET; VICAR OF LANSDOWNE, &C.**

London: Printed for A. K. Newman and Co. Leadenhall-Street, 1825.

I 292p; II 307p; III 284p. 12mo. 21s (ECB, QR).

QR 32: 267 (June 1825).

Corvey; CME 3-628-48429-4; ECB 498; NSTC 2D1372 (BI BL, O).

*Notes.* Further edns: French trans., 1825 [as *La Chapelle du vieux château de Saint-Doulagh, ou les bandits de Newgate* (BN)]; German trans. (based on the French trans.), 1827 [as *Die Kapelle des alten Schlosses von Saint-Doulagh, oder die Banditen von Newgate* (RS)].

1825: 72   ROLFE, Ann.

**CHOICE AND NO CHOICE; OR, THE FIRST OF MAY. BY MRS. ANN ROLFE, AUTHOR OF "MISCELLANEOUS POEMS FOR A WINTER'S EVENING." IN TWO VOLUMES.**

London: Charles Frederick Cock, 64, Paternoster-Row, 1825.

I xi, 161p; II 179p. 12mo. 10s (ECB, ER, QR).

ER 42: 513 (Aug 1825); QR 32: 268 (June 1825).

Corvey; CME 3-628-48467-7; ECB 500; NSTC 2R16110 (BI BL, C, O).

*Notes.* Preface describes the author's internal debate before embarking on a novel, a new form for her, rather than poetry; this is signed 'A. R.'.

1825: 73   [SCOTT, Sir Walter].

**TALES OF THE CRUSADERS. BY THE AUTHOR OF "WAVERLEY, QUENTIN DURWARD," &C. IN FOUR VOLUMES.**

Edinburgh: Printed for Archibald Constable and Co.; and Hurst, Robinson, and Co. London, 1825.

I xxviii, 327p; II 355p; III 325p; IV 364p. 8vo. 42s (ECB); 42s boards (ER).

ER 42: 513 (Aug 1825); QR 35: 518–66 (Mar 1827) full review; WSW II: 179.

Corvey; CME 3-628-48597-5; ECB 576; NSTC 2S10307 (BI BL, C, E, NCu, O; NA DLC, MH).

*Notes.* I The Betrothed; II The Betrothed; III The Talisman; IV The Talisman. 'This day published', 23 June 1825, *Edinburgh Evening Courant.* This is one of nine titles which are together given full reviews in QR (Mar 1827) under the page-top heading 'Historical Romance'.

Further edns: New York 1825 (NSTC) [also Philadelphia 1825 (NSTC)]; French trans., 1825 [as *Histoires du temps des croisades*: 'The Betrothed' as 'Le Connètable de Chester; ou les Fiancés' and 'The Talisman' as 'Le Talisman; ou, Richard en Palestine' (BN)]; German trans., 1825 [as *Erzählungen von den Kreuzfahrern*: 'The Betrothed' as 'Die Verlobten' and 'The Talisman' as 'Richard Löwenherz in Palästina' (RS)]. Numerous reprintings in collected edns.

SHEPHERD, Revd
See WILKINS, George

1825: 74   [SHERER, Joseph Moyle].
THE STORY OF A LIFE. BY THE AUTHOR OF SCENES AND IMPRESSIONS IN EGYPT AND ITALY, RECOLLECTIONS OF THE PENINSULA, &C. IN TWO VOLUMES.

London: Printed for Longman, Hurst, Rees, Orme, Brown, and Green, Paternoster-Row, 1825.

I xii, 316p; II 364p. 8vo. 18s (ECB, ER).

ER 42: 514 (Aug 1825); WSW II: 183.

CtY-BR In.Sh52.825S; ECB 564; NSTC 2S19131 (BI BL, C, E, O; NA DLC, MH).

*Notes.* NSTC misleadingly indicates that BL and E copies are 1st edn., instead of 2nd.
Further edns: 2nd edn. 1825 (Corvey), CME 3-628-48674-2; 3rd edn. 1825 (NUC); German trans., 1826 [as *Buntes Leben* (RS)].

1825: 75   SLINGSBY, Henry.
MY GRANDMOTHER'S GUESTS AND THEIR TALES. BY HENRY SLINGSBY. IN TWO VOLUMES.

London: James Robins and Co. Ivy Lane, Paternoster Row, and Joseph Robins, jun. and Co. Lower Ormond Quay, Dublin, 1825.

I xl, 273p; II 303p. 8vo. 16s (ECB, ER, QR).

ER 42: 514 (Aug 1825); QR 32: 268 (June 1825); WSW II: 184.

Corvey; CME 3-628-51139-9; ECB 543; NSTC 2S24428 (BI BL, C, Dt, O).

1825: 76   STANHOPE, Louisa Sidney.
RUNNEMEDE. AN ANCIENT LEGEND. IN THREE VOLUMES. BY LOUISA SIDNEY STANHOPE, AUTHOR OF THE BANDIT'S BRIDE; THE CRUSADERS; THE SIEGE OF KENILWORTH; FESTIVAL OF MORA; AGE WE LIVE IN, &C. &C.

London: Printed for A. K. Newman and Co., Leadenhall-Street, 1825.
I vi, 282p; II 292p; III 274p. 12mo. 18s (ECB).
WSW II: 189.
Corvey; CME 3-628-48779-X; ECB 558; NSTC 2S36112 (BI BL, C, O).

*Notes.* Preface dated Upper Edmonton, 1 Dec 1824. ECB dates Nov 1824, and gives the title as 'Runnemede; or, the Days of King John'. 'Note' fills vol. 3, pp. [271]–274.

1825: 77   STEPHENS, Nella.
THE ROBBER CHIEFTAIN; OR, DINAS LINN. A ROMANCE. IN FOUR VOLUMES. BY NELLA STEPHENS, AUTHOR OF DE MOWBRAY, OR THE STRANGER KNIGHT, &C.

London: Printed for A. K. Newman and Co. Leadenhall-Street, 1825.
I 244p; II 227p; III 237p; IV 232p. 12mo. 22s (ECB).
WSW II: 190.
Corvey; CME 3-628-48622-X; ECB 561; NSTC 2S38611 (BI BL, C, O).

*Notes.* ECB dates Oct 1824.

1825: 78   TIECK, [Johann Ludwig]; [THIRWALL, Connop (*trans.*)].
THE PICTURES; THE BETROTHING. NOVELS, TRANSLATED FROM THE GERMAN OF LEWIS TIECK.

London: Printed for Geo. B. Whittaker, Ave-Maria-Lane, 1825.
xxxix, 255p. 8vo. 9s (ECB, QR).
QR 32: 267 (June 1825).
BL 12611.d.7; ECB 591; NSTC 2T7685 (BI NCu, O; NA MH).

*Notes.* Trans. of *Die Gemälde* (Dresden, 1823) and *Die Verlobung* (Dresden, 1823). 'The Pictures', [1]–151p; 'The Betrothing', [153]–255p.

1825: 79   TROTTER, Robert.
DERWENTWATER; OR THE ADHERENTS OF KING JAMES. A TALE OF THE FIRST REBELLION. WITH AN APPENDIX, CONTAINING GENEALOGICAL NOTICES AND ANECDOTES OF SEVERAL ANCI-ENT AND HONOURABLE FAMILIES. BY ROBERT TROTTER, GENT. CHIEF OF THE NAME IN SCOTLAND.

Edinburgh: John Anderson, jun. North Bridge Street; Sherwood, Jones, and Co. London; Edward Baines, Leeds; and J. Johnstone, Dumfries, 1825.
viii, 272p. 12mo.
BL 12654.m.16; NSTC 2T18509 (BI E; NA MH).

*Notes.* Tale proper ends at p. 103; Appendix runs from pp. [107]–272, thus outweighing the tale!

1825: 80   [TUCKER, George].
THE VALLEY OF SHENANDOAH; OR, MEMOIRS OF THE GRAYSONS. IN THREE VOLUMES.

New-York: Printed for C. Wiley, Wall-Street. London: Reprinted for A. K. Newman & Co. Leadenhall-Street, 1825.

I 295p; II 318p; III 293p. 12mo.
Corvey; CME 3-628-48854-0; NSTC 2G19188 (BI BL).

*Notes.* Originally published New York 1824 (NSTC).

1825: 81 VIEUSSEUX, A[ndré].
ANSELMO: A TALE OF ITALY. BY A. VIEUSSEUX, AUTHOR OF
"ITALY AND THE ITALIANS," &C. &C. &C. IN TWO VOLUMES.

London: Printed for Charles Knight, Pall-Mall East, 1825.
I viii, 282p; II 271p. 8vo. 16s (ECB).
WSW II: 198.
Corvey; CME 3-628-48915-6; ECB 613; NSTC 2V3932 (BI BL, C, E, O; NA DLC).

*Notes.* ECB dates Nov 1825.
Further edn: German trans., 1826 [as *Anselmo, ein Gemälde nach dem Leben in Rom und Neapel* (RS)].

1825: 82 [VILLEMAREST, Charles Maxime Catherinet, de].
THE HERMIT IN ITALY, OR OBSERVATIONS ON THE MANNERS
AND CUSTOMS OF ITALY; BEING A CONTINUATION OF THE
SKETCHES OF FRENCH MANNERS, BY M. DE JOUY, AUTHOR OF
"L'HERMITE EN PRISON," "L'HERMITE DE LA CHAUSSÉE
D'ANTIN," &C. IN THREE VOLS.

London: Printed for Geo. B. Whittaker, Ave-Maria Lane, 1825.
I vii, 267p; II 281p; III 295p. 12mo. 18s (ECB, ER, QR).
ER 41: 520 (Jan 1825); QR 31: 532 (Mar 1825).
BL 12613.bbb.23; ECB 265; NSTC 2I5351 (BI Dt, E, O; NAMH).

*Notes.* Trans. of *L'Hermite en Italie* (Paris, 1824–5). ECB dates Dec 1824.

1825: 83 [WALKER, . . . ].
COMMON EVENTS: A CONTINUATION OF RICH AND POOR.

Edinburgh: William Blackwood, and T. Cadell, London, 1825.
382p. 8vo. 10s 6d (ECB, QR); 10s 6d boards (ER).
ER 42: 266 (Apr 1825); QR 32: 267 (June 1825).
Corvey; CME 3-628-47276-8; ECB 128; NSTC 2W1903 (BI BL, C, E, O; NA DLC).

*Notes.* For author, see note to *Rich and Poor* (1823: 81).

1825: 84 [WALLACE, Robert Grenville].
FORTY YEARS IN THE WORLD; OR, SKETCHES AND TALES OF A
SOLDIER'S LIFE. BY THE AUTHOR OF "FIFTEEN YEARS IN INDIA,"
"MEMOIRS OF INDIA," &C. &C. &C. IN THREE VOLUMES.

London: Printed for Geo. B. Whittaker, Ave-Maria Lane, 1825.
I x, 318p; II 326p; III 319p. 12mo. 30s (ECB, ER, QR).
ER 42: 514 (Aug 1825); QR 32: 549 (Oct 1825); WSW II: 199.
IU 823.W1552f; ECB 212; xNSTC.

*Notes.* Dedication to Ross Thompson, Esq., of Greenwood Park, near Newry.
Further edns: 2nd edn. 1825 (NSTC 2W3221); 3rd edn. 1825 (NUC).

1825: 85    [WARD, Robert Plumer].
**TREMAINE, OR THE MAN OF REFINEMENT. IN THREE VOLUMES.**

> London: Printed for Henry Colburn, New Burlington Street, 1825.
> I xii, 356p, ill.; II 402p; III 357p. 12mo. 31s 6d (ECB, ER, QR).
> ER 42: 266 (Apr 1825); QR 32: 267 (June 1825), 33: 474-90 (Mar 1826) full review;
>     WSW II: 199.
> BL N.1949,1950; ECB 598; NSTC 2W5229 (BI Dt, E, O; NA MH).

*Notes.* Preface addressed to the Right Honourable William Sturges Bourne, M.P., of Test-wood Park, Hampshire. This is one of three novels which are together given full reviews in QR (Mar 1826) under the page-top heading 'Novels of Fashionable Life'.
Further edns: 2nd edn. 1825 (Corvey), CME 3-628-48826-5; 3rd edn. 1825 (NSTC); 1839 (NSTC); Philadelphia 1825 (NSTC); French trans., 1830; German trans., 1838.


1825: 86    WENTWORTH, Zara.
**DE SANTILLANA; OR, THE FORCE OF BIGOTRY. A ROMANTIC TALE. IN FOUR VOLUMES. BY ZARA WENTWORTH, AUTHOR OF THE HERMIT'S CAVE, RECLUSE OF ALBYN HALL, UNCLES, &C. &C.**

> London: Printed for A. K. Newman and Co. Leadenhall-Street, 1825.
> I 276p; II 262p; III 290p; IV 247p. 12mo. 24s (ECB, QR).
> QR 32: 267 (June 1825).
> Corvey; CME 3-628-48884-2; ECB 629; NSTC 2W12928 (BI BL, C, O).

*Notes.* Dedication to Lady William Bentinck, signed Zara Wentworth.


1825: 87    [WESTMACOTT, Charles Molloy].
**FITZALLEYNE OF BERKELEY. A ROMANCE OF THE PRESENT TIMES. BY BERNARD BLACKMANTLE, AUTHOR OF THE ENGLISH SPY. IN TWO VOLUMES.**

> London: Published by Sherwood and Co. Paternoster-Row, 1825.
> I xx, 219p, ill.; II x, 201p. 8vo. 13s (ECB, QR).
> QR 32: 267 (June 1825); WSW II: 202.
> Corvey; CME 3-628-47228-8; ECB 207; NSTC 2W14202 (BI BL, C; NA MH).


1825: 88    [?WILKINS, George or ?SHEPHERD, Revd].
**THE VILLAGE PASTOR. BY ONE OF THE AUTHORS OF BODY AND SOUL.**

> London: Printed for Longman, Hurst, Rees, Orme, Brown, and Green, Paternoster
>     Row, 1825.
> x, 335p. 12mo. 8s (ECB, ER, QR).
> ER 42: 513 (Aug 1825); QR 32: 268 (June 1825); WSW II: 203.
> BL 865.h.7; ECB 614; NSTC 2W20695 (BI C, E, O).

*Notes.* The Longman Letter Books contain a letter of 17 Feb 1825 addressed to the 'Rev. Mr. Shepherd', which begins: 'We have received a letter from Dr Wilkins, in which he consents to the insertion of "by one of the authors of Body & Soul" in the title of the "Village Pastor"' (Longman I, 101, no. 495A). The same letter then goes on to state terms for an edition of

1,250, with payment of £50 immediately, and a further £20 'should the edition be sold off within twelve months'. For an associated work, *The Two Rectors* (1824: 97), Longmans wrote directly to Wilkins, offering noticeably stronger terms. This might open up the possibility that Shepherd was in fact the author of the present title, as well as being a co-author of *Body and Soul* (1822: 81).

1825: 89   WILSON, Alexander.
### ALICE ALLAN. THE COUNTRY TOWN. ET CET. BY ALEXANDER WIL-SON.

> London: Geo. B. Whittaker, Ave-Maria-Lane, 1825.
> 295p. 8vo. 8s 6d (ECB, ER, QR).
> ER 41: 520 (Jan 1825); QR 31: 532 (Mar 1825); WSW II: 204.
> Corvey; CME 3-628-51165-8; ECB 641; NSTC 2W24729 (BI BL, C, E, O; NA MH).

*Notes.* 6 stories. ECB dates Nov 1824.

1825: 90   [WILSON, John].
### THE FORESTERS. BY THE AUTHOR OF LIGHTS AND SHADOWS OF SCOTTISH LIFE; AND THE TRIALS OF MARGARET LYNDSAY.

> Edinburgh: William Blackwood, and T. Cadell, Strand, London, 1825.
> 413p. 8vo. 10s 6d (ECB, ER, QR).
> ER 42: 266 (Apr 1825); QR 32: 268 (June 1825); WSW II: 205.
> Corvey; CME 3-628-47536-8; ECB 211; NSTC 2W25716 (BI BL, C, E, O; NA MH).

*Notes.* Further edns: New edn. 1840 (NUC); 1846 (NSTC); New York 1825 (NUC) [also Philadelphia 1825 (NUC)].

1825: 91   WINTER, L. F.
### CASTLE HARCOURT; OR, THE DAYS OF KING RICHARD THE THIRD. A TALE OF 1483. IN THREE VOLUMES. BY L. F. WINTER, ESQ.

> London: Printed for A. K. Newman and Co. Leadenhall-Street, 1825.
> I 243p; II 280p; III 241p. 12mo. 16s 6d (ECB, QR).
> QR 31: 532 (Mar 1825).
> Corvey; CME 3-628-48938-5; ECB 644; NSTC 2W27556 (BI BL, C, E, O).

# 1826

1826: 1 ANON.

**THE ECCENTRIC TRAVELLER. IN FOUR VOLUMES. WITH FORTY-FOUR ENGRAVINGS.**

> London: Printed for Longman, Rees, Orme, Brown, and Green, Paternoster-Row, 1826.
>
> I ix, 323p, ill.; II ix, 311p, ill.; III x, 311p, ill.; IV x, 324p, ill. 12mo. 36s (ECB).
>
> Corvey; CME 3-628-47527-9; ECB 177; NSTC 2T16476 (BI BL, E, O; NA DLC, MH).

*Notes.* ECB dates Apr 1826.

1826: 2 ANON.

**EUSTACE FITZ-RICHARD. A TALE OF THE BARONS' WARS. IN FOUR VOLUMES. BY THE AUTHOR OF THE BANDIT CHIEF, OR LORDS OF URVINO.**

> London: Printed for A. K. Newman and Co. Leadenhall-Street, 1826.
>
> I xi, 300p; II 315p; III 266p; IV 348p. 12mo. 24s (ECB, QR).
>
> QR 33: 597 (Mar 1826); WSW II: 10.
>
> Corvey; CME 3-628-47614-3; ECB 193; NSTC 2F7629 (BI BL, E, O).

1826: 3 ANON.

**MONTVILLE; OR, THE DARK HEIR OF THE CASTLE. A NOVEL. IN THREE VOLUMES.**

> London: Printed for A. K. Newman and Co. Leadenhall-Street, 1826.
>
> I 263p; II 254p; III 254p. 12mo. 16s 6d (ECB, QR).
>
> QR 33: 597 (Mar 1826); WSW II: 24.
>
> Corvey; CME 3-628-48276-3; ECB 393; NSTC 2M34286 (BI BL, O).

*Notes.* ECB dates Dec 1825.

1826: 4 ANON.

**THE MOSS-TROOPERS. A BORDER TALE. IN THREE VOLUMES. BY THE AUTHOR OF BANNOCKBURN, &C.**

> London: Printed for A. K. Newman and Co. Leadenhall-Street, 1826.
>
> I v, 248p; II 223p; III 255p. 12mo. 16s 6d (QR).
>
> QR 34: 611 (Sept 1826).
>
> Corvey; CME 3-628-48267-4; NSTC 2M38796 (BI BL, C, E, O).

1826: 5 ANON.

**PAYWICKE; OR, THE BEGINNING OF HOPE.**

> Edinburgh: Printed for Waugh and Innes; M. Ogle, Glasgow; R. M. Tims, Dublin; James Duncan, J. Nisbet, and F. Westley, London, 1826.

206p, ill. 18mo. 2s 6d (ECB).

E Hall.248.h; ECB 437; NSTC 2P7761.

*Notes.* ECB dates Apr 1826, listing as if 'Paywicke' were the author and with the title as 'Essay on the beginning of hope'.


### 1826: 6    ANON.
### THE REBEL: A TALE. IN TWO VOLUMES.

London: Printed for Longman, Rees, Orme, Brown, and Green, Paternoster-Row, 1826.

I xi, 368p; II 355p. 12mo. 14s (ECB, QR).

QR 33: 597 (Mar 1826); WSW II: 29.

Corvey; CME 3-628-48518-5; ECB 481; NSTC 2R4078 (BI BL, C, E, O).

*Notes.* Introduction by 'the Editor', dated 27 Oct 1825. He states the novel was by his great-uncle, 'the late Horace Stanhope', and that the MS 'is dated October the 28th, 1787'.


### 1826: 7    ANON.
### STORIES FOR THE CHRISTMAS WEEK. IN TWO VOLUMES.

London: Printed for Howell and Stewart, 295, Holborn, 1826.

I vi, 330p; II 325p. 12mo. 14s (ECB, QR).

QR 33: 597 (Mar 1826).

Corvey; CME 3-628-48624-6; ECB 564; xNSTC.

*Notes.* ECB dates Dec 1825.


### 1826: 8    ANON.
### STRANGER OF THE VALLEY; OR, LOUISA AND ADELAIDE. AN AMERICAN TALE. IN THREE VOLUMES. BY A LADY.

New-York: Printed for Collins and Hannay. London: Reprinted for A. K. Newman and Co. Leadenhall-Street, 1826.

I 273p; II 271p; III 262p. 12mo. 16s 6d (ECB).

Corvey; CME 3-628-47472-8; ECB 565; NSTC 2L1432 (BI BL, C).

*Notes.* ECB dates Aug 1825. Colophon in each vol. reads: 'J. Darling, Leadenhall-Street, London'. Originally published New York 1825 (NSTC).


### 1826: 9    [AINSWORTH, William Harrison (and ASTON, John Partington?)].
### SIR JOHN CHIVERTON. A ROMANCE.

London: John Ebers, Old Bond Street, 1826.

vii, 317p. 8vo. 10s 6d (ECB).

QR 34: 611 (Sept 1826); WSW II: 2.

Corvey; CME 3-628-48709-9; ECB 539; NSTC 2C19503 (BI BL, C).

*Notes.* NSTC gives authorship as William Harrison Ainsworth and J. P. Aston. Sadleir (Items 27, 27a) also notes that this work was written in collaboration with a school friend J. P. Aston. Further edn: 2nd edn. 1827 (Sadleir 27a).

1826: 10   {A}[NLEY], {C}[harlotte].
MIRIAM; OR, THE POWER OF TRUTH. A JEWISH TALE. BY THE
AUTHOR OF "INFLUENCE."

> London: John Hatchard and Son, Piccadilly, 1826.
> vii, 384p. 8vo. 10s 6d (ECB, QR).
> QR 34: 302 (June 1826); WSW II: 2.
> BL N.1243; ECB 388; NSTC 2A13077 (BI C, E, O).

*Notes.* Preface signed C. A., Newport, Isle of Wight, Feb 1826. Dedication to Miss Curry (of Clanville).
Further edns: 2nd edn. 1829 (p.c.); 3rd edn. 1832 (NSTC); 9th edn. 1849 (NUC); Boston 1833 (NSTC).

1826: 11   APPENZELLER, [Johann Konrad].
GERTRUDE DE WART; OR, FIDELITY UNTIL DEATH. TRANSLATED
FROM THE ORIGINAL GERMAN OF APPENZELLER.

> London: Published by Longman, Rees, Orme, Brown, & Green Paternoster Row, 1826.
> xi, 167p. 12mo. 6s (ECB)
> Dt 196.u.9.no.1; ECB 22; NSTC 2A14380 (BI BL, C, E, O)

*Notes.* Trans. of *Gertrud von Wart, oder Treue bis in den Tod* (Zurich, 1813). ECB dates Feb 1826.

ASTON, John Partington
See AINSWORTH, William Harrison

1826: 12   [BALFOUR, Alexander].
HIGHLAND MARY. A NOVEL. IN FOUR VOLUMES. BY THE AUTHOR
OF THE FOUNDLING OF GLENTHORN, FARMER'S THREE DAUGH-
TERS, &C. &C.

> London: Printed for A. K. Newman and Co. Leadenhall-Street, 1826.
> I 306p; II 250p; III 243p; IV 290p. 12mo. 22s (ECB).
> WSW II: 44.
> Corvey; CME 3-628-47710-7; ECB 268; NSTC 2B4170 (BI BL, C, E, O).

*Notes.* ECB dates May 1826.

1826: 13   [BANIM, John and Michael].
THE BOYNE WATER, A TALE, BY THE O'HARA FAMILY. AUTHORS
OF TALES, COMPRISING CROHOORE OF THE BILL-HOOK, THE
FETCHES, AND JOHN DOE. IN THREE VOLUMES.

> London: Printed for W. Simpkin and R. Marshall, Stationer's-Hall Court, Ludgate-Street, 1826.
> I xxix, 375p; II 421p; III 436p. 12mo. 31s 6d (ECB, QR).
> QR 34: 302 (June 1826); WSW II: 45.
> Corvey; CME 3-628-47272-5; ECB 70; NSTC 2O2242 (NA DLC).

*Notes.* Introductory letter dated Inismore, 2 Feb 1826 and signed 'A. O'H.'.

Further edns: 2nd edn. 1826 (NSTC); French trans., 1829.
Facs: IAN (1979).

1826: 14    [BANIM, John and Michael].
TALES BY THE O'HARA FAMILY. SECOND SERIES. COMPRISING
THE NOWLANS, AND PETER OF THE CASTLE. IN THREE VOLUMES.
> London: Henry Colburn, New Burlington Street, 1826.
> I 318p; II 360p; III 381p. 12mo. 31s 6d (ECB); 31s 6d boards (ER).
> ER 45: 257 (Dec 1826); QR 35: 319 (Jan 1827); WSW II: 45.
> Corvey; CME 3-628-47940-1; ECB 575; NSTC 2O2239 (BI BL).

*Notes.* Further edns: New edn. 1827 (NUC); French trans., 1829 [separately as *L'Apostat, ou
la famille Nowlan* (BN), and *Padhré na moulh, ou le mendiant des ruines* (BN)]; German
trans., of 'Peter of the Castle' 1834; German trans., of 'The Nowlans' [as *Das Haus Nowlan,
oder Hang und Geschick. Ein irländisches Familiengemälde* (RS)] 1835.
Facs: IAN (1979).

1826: 15    [BARBAROUX, Charles Ogé and LARDIER, Joseph Alexandre].
ADVENTURES OF A FRENCH SERJEANT, DURING HIS CAMPAIGNS
IN ITALY, SPAIN, GERMANY, RUSSIA, ETC. FROM 1805 TO 1823.
WRITTEN BY HIMSELF.
> London: Henry Colburn, New Burlington-Street, 1826.
> xvi, 345p. 12mo. 9s 6d (ECB).
> QR 34: 406–21 (Sept 1826) full review.
> BL 612.i.12; ECB 6; NSTC 2B7181 (BI C, O).

*Notes.* Trans. of *Mémoires de Robert Guillemard, sergent en retraite* (Paris, 1826). Dedication
'To the Non-Commissioned Officers of the French Army', signed 'Your Fellow Soldier,
Robert Guillemard'. This is one of three novels which are together given full reviews in QR
(Sept 1826) under the page-top heading 'Military Memoirs'.
Further edn: Philadelphia 1826 (NSTC).

1826: 16    [BLESSINGTON, Charles John Gardiner, Earl of].
DE VAVASOUR: A TALE OF THE FOURTEENTH CENTURY. IN THREE
VOLUMES.
> London: Henry Colburn, New Burlington Street, 1826.
> I viii, 342p; II 383p; III 479p. 8vo. 31s 6d (ECB, QR).
> QR 34: 302 (June 1826); WSW II: 99.
> Corvey; CME 3-628-48861-3; ECB 160; NSTC 2D10538 (BI BL, C, E, O; NA MH).

1826: 17    BOLEN, C. A.
THE MYSTERIOUS MONK; OR, THE WIZARD'S TOWER. AN HISTOR-
ICAL ROMANCE. IN THREE VOLUMES. BY C. A. BOLEN.
> London: Printed for A. K. Newman and Co. Leadenhall-Street, 1826.
> I 242p; II 234p; III 239p. 12mo. 16s 6d (ECB); 16s 6d boards (QR).
> QR 34: 611 (Sept 1826).
> Corvey; CME 3-628-47265-2; ECB 64; NSTC 2B39615 (BI BL, C, O).

1826: 18   [BOSWELL, Thomas Alexander].
RECOLLECTIONS OF A PEDESTRIAN. BY THE AUTHOR OF "THE JOURNAL OF AN EXILE." IN THREE VOLUMES.

> London: Saunders and Otley, British and Foreign Public Library, Conduit Street, Hanover Square, 1826.
> I 290p; II 307p; III 353p. 12mo. 27s (ECB).
> Corvey; CME 3-628-51308-1; ECB 481; NSTC 2B42245 (BI BL, C, E, O; NA DLC, MH).

*Notes.* ECB dates Mar 1826.


1826: 19   BRAY, Anna Eliza.
DE FOIX; OR, SKETCHES OF THE MANNERS AND CUSTOMS OF THE FOURTEENTH CENTURY. AN HISTORICAL ROMANCE. BY ANNA ELIZA BRAY, LATE MRS. CHARLES STOTHARD, AUTHOR OF LET-TERS WRITTEN DURING A TOUR THROUGH NORMANDY, BRI-TANNY, AND OTHER PARTS OF FRANCE, IN 1818; MEMOIRS OF THE LIFE OF THE LATE CHARLES ALFRED STOTHARD, F.S.A. &C. &C. &C. IN THREE VOLUMES.

> London: Printed for Longman, Rees, Orme, Brown, and Green, Paternoster-Row, 1826.
> I v, 286p; II 283p; III 288p. 8vo. 27s (ECB, QR).
> QR 34: 302 (June 1826); WSW II: 57.
> Corvey; CME 3-628-47275-X; ECB 72; NSTC 2S42908 (BI BL, C, E, O; NA MH).

*Notes.* 'Advertisement' dated Vicarage, Tavistock, Devon, 1 Nov 1825.
Further edns: 1833 (NSTC); German trans., 1834 [as *De Foix, oder Französisches Leben im 14. Jahrhundert*, published as vols. 1–3 of Bray's *Historische Romane* (RS)] .


1826: 20   [BRISTOW, Amelia].
SOPHIA DE LISSAU; OR, A PORTRAITURE OF THE JEWS OF THE NINETEENTH CENTURY: BEING AN OUTLINE OF THE RELIGIOUS AND DOMESTIC HABITS OF THIS MOST INTERESTING NATION, WITH EXPLANATORY NOTES, BY THE AUTHOR OF "ELIZABETH ALLEN; OR, THE FAITHFUL SERVANT."

> London: Published for the Author, by Gardiner & Son, Princes Street, Cavendish Square and Simpkin & Marshall, Stationers' Court, 1826.
> 4, 269p. 18mo. 5s (ECB).
> BL 696.c.9(1); ECB 550; NSTC 2B48814.

*Notes.* Preface (pp. [3]–4, first sequence) ends with the following statement: 'The Author intended to prefix a List of the Subscribers, but as it was found difficult to procure the Names correctly, and many of her immediate Friends requested that their Names might not appear, it is omitted; though she would have been proud to record the distinguished names that have been obtained.' Text proper ends on p. 257, followed by 'Explanatory Notes' (pp. 259–69). ECB dates Mar 1828.
Further edns: 2nd edn. 1828 (Corvey), CME 3-628-48712-9; 3rd edn. 1829 (NSTC); 1833 (NSTC); 5th edn. 1840 (NSTC); German trans., 1829 [as *Die Familie de Lissa* (RS)].

1826: 21    [BRODIE, Alexander].
THE PROPHETESS: A TALE OF THE LAST CENTURY, IN ITALY. IN
THREE VOLUMES.

> Edinburgh: Printed for Thomas Clark, 32, George Street; and Longman, Rees, Orme,
> Brown, and Green, London, 1826.
> I viii, 372p; II 346p; III 331p. 12mo. 24s (ECB, QR).
> QR 35: 319 (Jan 1827); WSW II: 58.
> Corvey; CME 3-628-48417-0; ECB 472; NSTC 2B49894 (BI BL, C, O; NA MH).

1826: 22    [BUNBURY, Selina].
THE PASTOR'S TALES. BY THE AUTHOR OF "EARLY RECOLLEC-
TIONS".

> Edinburgh: Published by William Oliphant, 22, South Bridge Street; and sold by M.
> Ogle, and Chalmers & Collins, Glasgow—J. Finlay, Newcastle—Beilby & Knotts,
> Birmingham—Hamilton, Adams & Co., J. Nisbet, J. Duncan, J. Hatchard & Son, and
> B. J. Holdsworth, London—and R. M. Tims, and W. Curry jun. & Co. Dublin, 1826.
> 116p, ill. 12mo.
> E Hall.250.h; NSTC 2B57690.

*Notes.* Collates in sixes.

1826: 23    [BURY, Lady Charlotte Susan Maria].
"ALLA GIORNATA;" OR, TO THE DAY. IN THREE VOLUMES.

> London: Saunders and Otley, Conduit Street, 1826.
> I 348p; II 300p; III 310p. 12mo. 30s (ECB).
> QR 34: 612 (Sept 1826); WSW II: 61.
> Corvey; CME 3-628-47043-9; ECB 13; NSTC 2C4338 (BI BL, E, O; NA DLC, MH).

1826: 24    CHATEAUBRIAND, [François René], Vicomte de.
ABEN-HAMET, THE LAST OF THE ABENCERAGES; A ROMANCE, BY
THE VISCOUNT DE CHATEAUBRIAND. TRANSLATED FROM THE
FRENCH.

> London: Treuttel and Würtz, Treuttel jun., and Richter, 30, Soho Square, 1826.
> xxviii, 207p, ill., music. 12mo. 7s (ECB, QR).
> QR 34: 612 (Sept 1826).
> BL N.424(1); ECB 107; NSTC 2C16958 (BI C, Dt, O; NA DLC).

*Notes.* Trans. of *Les Aventures du dernier Abencérage* (Londres, 1826).

1826: 25    [COOPER, James Fenimore].
THE LAST OF THE MOHICANS; A NARRATIVE OF 1757. BY THE
AUTHOR OF "THE SPY," "THE PILOT," "THE PIONEERS," &C. &C. IN
THREE VOLUMES.

> London: John Miller, New Bridge Street, 1826.
> I xi, 287p; II 276p; III 295p. 12mo. 21s (ECB, QR).
> QR 34: 302 (June 1826); WSW II: 78.
> Corvey; ECB 134; NSTC 2C36830 (BI BL, C, Dt, E; NA MH).

*Notes.* Originally published Philadelphia 1826 (Blanck, NSTC).
Further edns: 1831 (NSTC); 1836 (NSTC); 1838 (NSTC); 1849 (Blanck, NSTC); 1850 (NSTC); German trans., 1826; French trans., 1830.

1826: 26    [CORBETT, Marion and Margaret].
## THE ODD VOLUME.
> Edinburgh: Printed for Daniel Lizars; Thomas Ogilvie, Glasgow; and G. B. Whittaker, London, 1826.
> 375p, music. 8vo. 21s (1st and 2nd series, ECB).
> E NF.605.h.13; ECB 420; NSTC 2C37700 (BI BL, C, O; NA MH).

*Notes.* [1st series]. ECB dates Aug 1826.
Further edns: 2nd edn. 1826 (Corvey), CME 3-628-51108-9; Boston 1827 (NSTC).

1826: 27    CUNNINGHAM, Allan.
## PAUL JONES; A ROMANCE. BY ALLAN CUNNINGHAM, AUTHOR OF "SIR MARMADUKE MAXWELL," "TRADITIONAL TALES," &C. IN THREE VOLUMES.
> Edinburgh: Published by Oliver & Boyd ; Longman, Rees, Orme, Brown & Green, London, 1826.
> I 380p; II 372p; III 371p. 8vo. 31s 6d (ECB); 31s 6d boards (ER).
> ER 45: 257 (Dec 1826); WSW II: 83.
> Corvey; CME 3-628-47362-4; ECB 147; NSTC 2C46742 (BI BL, C, Dt, E, O; NA MH).

*Notes.* Further edns: Philadelphia 1827 (NSTC); German trans., 1826.

1826: 28    [DEACON, William Frederick].
## NOVEMBER NIGHTS; OR, TALES FOR WINTER EVENINGS. BY THE AUTHOR OF "WARRENIANA."
> London: Thomas Maclean, 26, Haymarket, 1826.
> vi, 468p. 12mo. 12s (ECB); 10s 6d (QR).
> QR 33: 597 (Mar 1826); WSW II: 85.
> Corvey; CME 3-628-51105-4; ECB 418; NSTC 2D6423 (BI BL, C, Dt).

*Notes.* Preface dated 30 Nov 1825. ECB dates Dec 1825.

1826: 29    DES STRAELLA, Leonora.
## THE ENGLISH BARONET. A NOVEL. IN THREE VOLUMES. BY LEONORA DES STRAELLA.
> London: Printed for A. K. Newman and Co. Leadenhall-Street, 1826.
> I 230p; II 219p; III 195p. 12mo. 16s 6d (ECB, QR).
> QR 33: 597 (Mar 1826).
> Corvey; CME 3-628-47431-0; ECB 565; NSTC 2S43765 (BI BL, C, O).

1826: 30    [DISRAELI, Benjamin, Earl of Beaconsfield].
## VIVIAN GREY.
> London: Henry Colburn, New Burlington Street, 1826/27.

I (1826) 266p; II (1826) 236p; III (1827) 333p; IV (1827) 362p; V (1827) 324p, 25p.
12mo. 18s (ECB vols. 1–2); 31s 6d (ECB vols. 3–5); 31s 6d boards (ER).
ER 45: 544 (Mar 1827), vols. 3–5; WSW II: 87–8.
Corvey; CME 3-628-48807-9; ECB 165; NSTC 2D14247 (BI BL, C, E, O; NA MH).

*Notes.* Last 25 pp. of vol. 5 contain 'Key to Vivian Grey', with the imprint 'London: Printed for William Marsh, 137, Oxford Street, 1827'. ECB dates first 2 vols. as Apr 1826, and final 3 vols. Feb 1827.
Further edns: 3rd edn. 1827 (NSTC); 1834 (NSTC); New York 1826 (NUC); German trans., 1827.

1826: 31    [DUNCAN, Henry].
**WILLIAM DOUGLAS; OR, THE SCOTTISH EXILES. A HISTORICAL NOVEL. IN THREE VOLUMES.**

Edinburgh: Published by Oliver & Boyd; and Longman, Rees, Orme, Brown, & Green, London, 1826.
I 326p; II 308p; III 324p. 12mo. 21s (ECB, QR).
QR 34: 302 (June 1826), 34: 612 (Sept 1826); WSW II: 90.
Corvey; CME 3-628-48927-X; ECB 638; NSTC 2D22189 (BI BL, C, E, O).

1826: 32    {DURAS}, [Claire Louise Rose Bonne], {Duchesse de}.
**EDWARD. TRANSLATED FROM THE FRENCH OF THE AUTHOR OF OURIKA.**

London: Printed for Longman, Rees, Orme, Brown, and Green, Paternoster Row, 1826.
186p. 12mo. 7s (ECB, QR).
QR 34: 611 (Sept 1826).
C Rom.1.44³; ECB 180; NSTC 2D23440 (BI BL, O).

*Notes.* Trans. of *Édouard* (Paris, 1825). Opening statement (1 p. unn.) identifying 'the Duchess of Duras' as the author of this novel and of *Ourika*; this is dated July 1826. Collates in sixes.

1826: 33    [DYER, Robert].
**THE STORY OF A WANDERER; FOUNDED UPON HIS RECOLLEC-TIONS OF INCIDENTS IN RUSSIAN AND COSSACK SCENES.**

London: Printed for Charles Knight, Pall Mall East, 1826.
294p. 8vo. 9s 6d (ECB); 9s boards (QR).
QR 35: 319 (Jan 1827); WSW II: 91.
Corvey; CME 3-628-48675-0; ECB 564; NSTC 2D24305 (BI BL, C, Dt, E, O).

1826: 34    [EATON, Charlotte Anne].
**CONTINENTAL ADVENTURES. A NOVEL. IN THREE VOLUMES.**

London: Printed for Hurst, Robinson & Co. 5, Waterloo-Place, Pall-Mall, 1826.
I xi, 384p; II 321p; III 400p. 8vo. 31s 6d (ECB, QR).
QR 34: 612 (Sept 1826); WSW II: 91.
Corvey; CME 3-628-47324-1; ECB 132; NSTC 2E1358 (BI BL, E, O; NA MH).

*Notes.* Further edns: 2nd edn. 1827 (NSTC); Boston 1826 (NSTC).

1826: 35   ENGEL, J[ohann] J[akob]; GANS, J. (*trans.*).
LORENZ STARK, A CHARACTERISTIC PICTURE OF A GERMAN
FAMILY. BY J. J. ENGEL. TRANSLATED FROM THE GERMAN, BY J.
GANS. IN TWO VOLUMES.

> London: Treuttel & Würtz, Treuttel jun. & Richter, Soho Square, 1826.
> I 207p; II 204p. 12mo. 12s (ECB).
> BL N.362; ECB 186; NSTC 2E9745 (BI C, E, O; NA MH).

*Notes.* Trans. of *Herr Lorenz Stark* (2nd edn., Berlin, 1801); ECB dates June 1826.


1826: 36   [GALT, John].
THE LAST OF THE LAIRDS: OR, THE LIFE AND OPINIONS OF
MALACHI MAILINGS, ESQ. OF AULDBIGGINGS. BY THE AUTHOR
OF ANNALS OF THE PARISH, THE ENTAIL, ETC.

> Edinburgh: William Blackwood, and T. Cadell, Strand, London, 1826.
> 364p. 8vo. 10s 6d (ECB); 10s 6d boards (ER).
> ER 45: 257 (Dec 1826); QR 35: 319 (Jan 1827); WSW II: 98.
> Corvey; CME 3-628-47905-3; ECB 330; NSTC 2G1375 (BI BL, C, Dt, E, O; NA MH).

*Notes.* Further edn: New York 1827 (NSTC).


1826: 37   GILLIES, R[obert] P[ierce] (*trans.*).
GERMAN STORIES: SELECTED FROM THE WORKS OF HOFFMANN,
DE LA MOTTE FOUQÉ, PICHLER, KRUSE, AND OTHERS. BY R. P.
GILLIES, ESQ. IN THREE VOLUMES.

> Edinburgh: William Blackwood, and T. Cadell, Strand, London, 1826.
> I xiv, 333p; II 358p; III 363p. 12mo. 21s (ECB).
> BL N.426; ECB 231; NSTC 2G5621 (BI C, Dt, E, O; NA DLC, MH).

*Notes.* 11 stories in all. ECB dates Nov 1826.


1826: 38   [GILLIES, Robert Pierce].
TALES OF A VOYAGER TO THE ARCTIC OCEAN. IN THREE VOL-
UMES.

> London: Henry Colburn, New Burlington Street, 1826.
> I 347p; II 336p; III 350p. 12mo. 28s 6d (ECB).
> WSW II: 101.
> Corvey; CME 3-628-48875-3; ECB 575; NSTC 2G8248 (BI BL, C, E, O; NA DLC, MH).

*Notes.* [1st series]. ECB dates Dec 1826
Further edns: 1834 (NSTC); Philadelphia 1827 (NSTC); German trans., 1827.


1826: 39   [GLASCOCK, William Nugent].
NAVAL SKETCH-BOOK; OR, THE SERVICE AFLOAT AND ASHORE;
WITH CHARACTERISTIC REMINISCENCES, FRAGMENTS, AND
OPINIONS ON PROFESSIONAL, COLONIAL, AND POLITICAL SUB-
JECTS; INTERSPERSED WITH COPIOUS NOTES, BIOGRAPHICAL,

HISTORICAL, CRITICAL, AND ILLUSTRATIVE. BY AN OFFICER OF RANK. IN TWO VOLUMES.

> London: Printed for the Author; and sold by H. Colburn; Geo. B. Whittaker; Simpkin & Marshall; and all Booksellers, 1826.
>
> I xxiv, 251p; II vi, 286p. 8vo. 18s (ECB).
>
> BL 838.d.3; ECB 408; NSTC 2G9532 (BI E; NA DLC, MH).

*Notes.* [1st series]. ECB dates 1st series Jan 1826 and 2nd series Apr 1834.
Further edns: 2nd edn. 1826 (Corvey, NSTC); 1831 (NSTC).

1826: 40    [?GORE, Catherine Grace Frances].
RICHELIEU; OR, THE BROKEN HEART. AN HISTORICAL TALE.

> London: Printed for W. Sams, Royal Library, 1, St. James's-Street, 1826.
>
> v, 158p. 8vo. 5s 6d (ECB).
>
> QR 33: 597 (Mar 1826).
>
> Corvey; CME 3-628-48604-1; ECB 493; NSTC 2G14803 (BI BL).

*Notes.* NSTC (matching DNB and NCBEL) states 'attributed to Mrs. Gore'. Preface, however, implies male authorship. Tale proper ends p. 150, followed by Appendix (Notes consisting of translations of passages from the Duke of Richelieu's *Vie Privée*, which are given in French in the main narrative).
Further edn: 1833 (NSTC).

1826: 41    GREEN, William Child.
ABBOT OF MONTSERRAT; OR, THE POOL OF BLOOD. A ROMANCE. IN TWO VOLUMES. BY WILLIAM CHILD GREEN, AUTHOR OF THE FAYS OF LOCH LOMOND, SICILIAN BOY, THE PROPHECY OF DUN-CANNON, &C. &C.

> London: Printed for A. K. Newman and Co. Leadenhall-Street, 1826.
>
> I ii, 229p; II 256p. 12mo. 10s 6d (ECB, QR).
>
> QR 33: 597 (Mar 1826).
>
> Corvey; CME 3-628-47853-7; ECB 244; NSTC 2G20221 (BI BL, C, E, O).

*Notes.* Facs: GNIII (1977).

GREEN, William Child, THE WOODLAND FAMILY
See 1824: 44

1826: 42    HALL, Mrs. A. C.
OBSTINACY. A TALE. BY MRS. A. C. HALL.

> London: Printed for Longman, Rees, Orme, Brown, and Green, Paternoster-Row, 1826.
>
> 338p, ill. 12mo. 6s (ECB, QR).
>
> QR 33: 597 (Mar 1826), 34: 302 (June 1826); WSW II: 105.
>
> Corvey; CME 3-628-47622-4; ECB 250; NSTC 2H2466 (BI BL, C, O).

1826: 43    [HATTON, Anne Julia Kemble].
DEEDS OF THE OLDEN TIME. A ROMANCE. IN FIVE VOLUMES. BY ANN OF SWANSEA, AUTHOR OF WOMAN'S A RIDDLE, GUILTY OR

NOT GUILTY, GONZALO DI BALDIVIA, LOVERS AND FRIENDS, CHRONICLES OF AN ILLUSTRIOUS HOUSE, SECRETS IN EVERY MANSION, CONVICTION, CESARIO ROSALBA, &C. &C.

> London: Printed for A. K. Newman and Co., Leadenhall-Street, 1826.
>
> I ii, 296p; II 326p; III 343p; IV 331p; V 319p. 12mo. 30s (ECB).
>
> Corvey; CME 3-628-48797-8; ECB 20; NSTC 2A13190 (BI BL, C, O).

*Notes.* ECB dates Apr 1826. Dedication to Mrs Carsgill, dated 'Swansea, February 3, 1826, (22, Orchard-Street.)'.

1826: 44   [HEUN, Carl Gottlieb Samuel]; HAAS, J[ames] D. (*trans.*).
LIESLI, A SWISS TALE BY H. CLAUREN. TRANSLATED FROM THE GERMAN BY J. D. HAAS.

> London: Printed for G. B. Whittaker Ave Maria Lane, and J. Rees, Bristol, 1826.
>
> 144p, ill. 8vo. 6s (ECB); 6s boards (ER, QR).
>
> ER 45: 257 (Dec 1826); QR 35: 319 (Jan 1827).
>
> BL 12554.b.25; ECB 120; NSTC 2C24985.

*Notes.* Trans. of *Liesli und Elsi, zwei Schweizergeschichten* (Dresden, 1821). H[einrich] Clauren is a pseudonym. ECB dates Nov 1826.
Further edns: 1839 (NSTC); 1845 (NSTC).

1826: 45   [HOCKLEY, William Browne].
PANDURANG HARI, OR MEMOIRS OF A HINDOO. IN THREE VOLUMES.

> London: Printed for Geo. B. Whittaker, Ave-Maria Lane, 1826.
>
> I xv, 345p; II 354p; III 398p. 12mo. 24s (ECB).
>
> WSW II: 114.
>
> Corvey; CME 3-628-48381-6; ECB 344; NSTC 2H24562 (BI BL, C, E, O; NA MH).

*Notes.* Sadleir (Item 1196) says 'This novel was actually written by Cyrus Redding, from rough notes sent from India by Hockley'. ECB dates Oct 1835 [*sic*].
Further edn: German trans., 1826.

1826: 46   HOFLAND, [Barbara].
REFLECTION. A TALE. BY MRS. HOFLAND, AUTHOR OF INTEGRITY, A TALE; PATIENCE, A TALE; DECISION, A TALE; MODERATION, A TALE; THE SON OF A GENIUS; TALES OF THE PRIORY; TALES OF THE MANOR; &C, &C.

> London: Printed for Longman, Rees, Orme, Brown, and Green, Paternoster-Row, 1826.
>
> 267p, ill. 12mo. 6s (ECB, QR).
>
> QR 34: 612 (Sept 1826); WSW II: 115.
>
> Corvey; CME 3-628-47661-5; ECB 275; NSTC 2H29410 (BI BL, E, O).

*Notes.* Further edns: 1835 (NSTC); 1838 (NSTC).

1826: 47   [HUDSON, Marianne Spencer].
ALMACK'S[.] A NOVEL. IN THREE VOLUMES.

> London: Saunders and Otley, Public Library, Conduit Street, 1826.

I xi, 390p; II 346p; III 413p. 12mo. 31s 6d (ECB); 31s 6d boards (ER).
ER 45: 257 (Dec 1826); WSW II: 190.
BL N.383,384; ECB 14; NSTC 2H34816 (BI E, O; NA MH).

*Notes.* ECB 320 gives also 'Key to "Almacks"', 8vo, Literary Gazette Office, 1827. Sadleir (Item 3136) states *Key to Almacks* was reprinted from the *Literary Gazette* of 9 Nov 1826. Further edns: 2nd edn. 1827 (Corvey), CME 3-628-47048-X; 3rd edn. 1827 (NSTC); New York 1827 (NSTC).

1826: 48   [KELTY, Mary Ann].
THE STORY OF ISABEL; BY THE AUTHOR OF "THE FAVOURITE OF NATURE," &C. &C. &C. IN THREE VOLUMES.

London: Printed for Longman, Rees, Orme, Brown, and Green, Paternoster-Row, 1826.
I xii, 367p; II 325p; III 332p. 12mo. 24s (ECB); 24s boards (QR).
QR 33: 597 (Mar 1826); WSW II: 128.
Corvey; CME 3-628-48676-9; ECB 564; NSTC 2K2414 (BI BL, O).

*Notes.* Dedication to Mrs Murray.
Further edn: German trans., 1826.

LARDIER, Joseph Alexandre
See BARBAROUX, Charles Ogé

1826: 49   LEFANU, Alicia.
HENRY THE FOURTH OF FRANCE. A ROMANCE. IN FOUR VOL-UMES. BY ALICIA LEFANU, AUTHOR OF MEMOIRS OF THE LIFE AND WRITINGS OF MRS. FRANCES SHERIDAN; DON JUAN DE LAS SIERRAS; HELEN MONTEAGLE; LEOLIN ABBEY; TALES OF A TOURIST; &C.

London: Printed for A. K. Newman and Co. Leadenhall-Street, 1826.
I 231p; II 229p; III 240p; IV 226p. 12mo. 22s (ECB).
WSW II: 134.
Corvey; CME 3-628-47976-2; ECB 336; NSTC 2L9895 (BI BL, C, E, O).

*Notes.* ECB dates Apr 1826.

1826: 50   [LEFROY, Christopher Edward].
OUTALISSI; A TALE OF DUTCH GUIANA.

London: J. Hatchard and Son, Piccadilly, 1826.
viii, 324p. 8vo. 9s 6d (ECB).
Corvey; CME 3-628-48322-0; ECB 427; NSTC 2L10009 (BI BL, C, E, O; NA DLC, MH).

*Notes.* Dedication to William Wilberforce, Esq. dated Dutch Guiana, 1 Jan 1826. 'Editorial Epilogue' dated Dutch Guiana, 18 Jan 1826. ECB dates Dec 1826.

1826: 51   [LISTER, Thomas Henry].
GRANBY. A NOVEL. IN THREE VOLUMES.

London: Henry Colburn, New Burlington Street, 1826.

I 324p; II 342p; III 330p. 12mo. 27s (ECB, QR).

ER 43: 395-406 (Feb 1826) full review; QR 33: 474–90 (Mar 1826) full review, 33: 597 (Mar 1826); WSW II: 135.

Corvey; CME 3-628-51024-4; ECB 240; NSTC 2L17194 (BI BL, C, Dt, E; NA MH).

*Notes.* ECB dates Dec 1825. This is one of three novels together given full reviews in QR (Mar 1826) under the page-top heading 'Novels of Fashionable Life'.

Further edns: 2nd edn. 1826 (NSTC); 3rd edn. 1826 (NSTC); 1833 (NSTC); 1836 (NSTC); New York 1826 (NSTC); French trans., 1829.

1826: 52   {LITTLE, Thomas}.
**CONFESSIONS OF AN OXONIAN. IN THREE VOLUMES. EMBELL-
ISHED WITH THIRTY-SIX COLOURED PLATES.**

London: J. J. Stockdale, Printer, No. 24, Opera Colonnade, 1826.
I viii, xii, 212p, ill.; II 243p, ill.; III 284p, ill. 12mo.
C Lib.7.82.22; NSTC 2L17488 (BI BL, O).

*Notes.* 'Advertisement' signed by Thomas Little, alleging that the true author died of typhus, leaving a manuscript concerning his life and adventures at College. Collates in sixes.

1826: 53   [LLANOS GUTIERREZ, Valentin].
**SANDOVAL; OR, THE FREEMASON. A SPANISH TALE. BY THE
AUTHOR OF "DON ESTEBAN." IN THREE VOLUMES.**

London: Henry Colburn, New Burlington Street, 1826.
I viii, 345p; II 422p; III 450p. 12mo. 28s 6d (ECB).
QR 34: 488–506 (Sept 1826) full review; WSW II: 105.
Corvey; CME 3-628-48507-X; ECB 514; NSTC 2L18570 (BI BL, C, E, O).

*Notes.* Further edns: New York & Philadelphia 1826 (NSTC); German trans., 1827.

1826: 54   [MACDONOGH, Felix].
**THE HEROINE OF THE PENINSULA; OR, CLARA MATILDA OF
SEVILLE. BY THE AUTHOR OF THE "HERMIT IN LONDON," AND
OTHER POPULAR WORKS. IN TWO VOLUMES.**

London: Sherwood, Gilbert and Piper, Paternoster Row, C. Chapple, Royal Library,
    Pall Mall; A. K. Newman and Co., 1826.
I 244p; II 244p. 12mo. 12s (ECB, QR).
QR 34: 302 (June 1826).
Corvey; CME 3-628-47781-6; ECB 266; NSTC 2M3282 (BI BL, E, O).

1826: 55   M'LEOD, Miss E. H.
**GERALDINE MURRAY. A TALE OF FASHIONABLE LIFE. IN FOUR
VOLUMES. BY E. H. P. LATE MISS M'LEOD, AUTHOR OF TALES OF
TON, FIRST, SECOND, AND THIRD SERIES, PRINCIPLE, &C. &C.**

London: Printed for A. K. Newman and Co., Leadenhall-Street, 1826.
I 264p; II 241p; III 259p; IV 264p. 12mo. 22s (ECB, QR).

QR 35: 319 (Jan 1827); WSW II: 140.
Corvey; CME 3-628-47744-1; ECB 361; NSTC 2M7090 (BI BL, C, E, O).

*Notes.* Preface dated Fingringhoe Hall, Essex, Sept 1826.

1826: 56   [MÄMPEL, Johann C.].
ADVENTURES OF A YOUNG RIFLEMAN, IN THE FRENCH AND ENG-
LISH ARMIES, DURING THE WAR IN SPAIN AND PORTUGAL, FROM
1806 TO 1816. WRITTEN BY HIMSELF.

London: Henry Colburn, New Burlington Street, 1826.
iv, 414p. 12mo. 9s 6d (ECB).
QR 34: 406–21 (Sept 1826) full review.
MH-H 19463.01.5*; ECB 6; NSTC 2A4411.

*Notes.* Trans. of vols. 1 and 2 of *Der junge Feldjäger* (1826–7). This is one of three novels
together given full reviews in QR (Sept 1826) under the page-top heading 'Military Memoirs'.
Further edns: 2nd edn. 1826 (NSTC); Philadelphia 1826 (NSTC).

1826: 57   [MÄMPEL, Johann C.].
THE YOUNG RIFLEMAN'S COMRADE. A NARRATIVE ON HIS MILI-
TARY ADVENTURES, CAPTIVITY, AND SHIPWRECK.

London: Henry Colburn, New Burlington Street, 1826.
xxiv, 310p. 12mo. 9s 6d (ECB).
WSW II: 141.
BL 1201.d.18; ECB 653; NSTC 2M9241 (BI C; NA DLC).

*Notes.* Trans. of *Des jungen Feldjägers Kriegskamerad* (vol. 3 of *Der junge Feldjäger*). 'Editor's
Preface' of the original title is signed Goethe, Weimar, 14 Jan 1826. Dedication by the trans-
lator to 'His Excellency Freiherrn von Göthe Minister of State to His Royal Highness the
Grand Duke of Saxe Weimar' dated London, 12 Oct 1826. ECB dates Oct 1826.

1826: 58   MARTEN, Ambrose.
THE STANLEY TALES, ORIGINAL AND SELECT. CHIEFLY COL-
LECTED BY THE LATE AMBROSE MARTEN, OF STANLEY PRIORY,
TEESDALE.

London: Published by W. Morgan, 45, Dean-Street, Soho, 1826/27.
I (1826) xxii, 334p, ill.; II (1826) 356p, ill.; III (1826) 356p, ill.; IV (1827) 356p, ill.;
    V (1827) 356p, ill.; VI (1827) 359p, ill. 18mo. 2s 6d (QR, 'Part I'); 33s (ECB, 6 vols.).
QR 34: 612 (Sept 1826).
Corvey; CME 3-628-51099-6; ECB 558; NSTC 2M16350 (BI BL, C, O).

*Notes.* T.p. imprint in vols. 4 and 5 changes to 'Published by W. Morgan, 33, Old Bond Street;
and W. Tait, Princes Street, Edinburgh'; and in vol. 6 reads 'Published by Thomas Hurst and
Co., 65, St. Paul's Church Yard. W. Morgan, 33, Old Bond-Street; and W. Tait, Princes
Street, Edinburgh'.
Further edn: 1827 (NSTC).

MITFORD, Mary Russell, OUR VILLAGE
See 1824: 67

1826: 59   MOSSE, Henrietta Rouviere.
**GRATITUDE; AND OTHER TALES. IN THREE VOLUMES. BY HENRI-
ETTA ROUVIERE MOSSE, AUTHOR OF LUSSINGTON ABBEY, HEIRS
OF VILLEROY, OLD IRISH BARONET, PEEP AT OUR ANCESTORS,
ARRIVALS FROM INDIA, BRIDE AND NO WIFE, A FATHER'S LOVE
AND A WOMAN'S FRIENDSHIP, &C.**

> London: Printed for A. K. Newman and Co. Leadenhall-Street, 1826.
> I xv, 304p; II 278p; III 315p. 12mo. 18s (ECB).
> WSW II: 154.
> Corvey; CME 3-628-48346-8; ECB 399; NSTC 2R19129 (BI BL, C, O).

*Notes.* ECB dates Oct 1825.


1826: 60   [OLIVER, Mrs. N. W.].
**SEPHORA; A HEBREW TALE, DESCRIPTIVE OF THE COUNTRY OF
PALESTINE, AND OF THE MANNERS AND CUSTOMS OF THE
ANCIENT ISRAELITES. TWO VOLUMES.**

> London: J. Hatchard and Son, 187, Piccadilly, 1826.
> I viii, 280p; II 280p. 8vo. 14s (ECB).
> QR 33: 597 (Mar 1826); WSW II: 34.
> Corvey; CME 3-628-48647-5; ECB 527; NSTC 2O3311 (BI BL, E, O).

*Notes.* Further edn: Worcester, Mass., 1835 (NSTC).


1826: 61   PECK, [Frances].
**NAPOLEON; OR, THE MYSTERIES OF THE HUNDRED DAYS, AN HIS-
TORICAL NOVEL, BY MRS. PECK, AUTHOR OF THE "BARD OF THE
WEST."**

> London: Published by Simpkin and Marshall, Stationer's-Court, and Westley and
>    Tyrrell, Sackville-Street, Dublin, 1826.
> I xxix, 265p; II 245p. 8vo. 16s (ECB, QR).
> QR 34: 612 (Sept 1826); WSW II: 160.
> Corvey; CME 3-628-48409-X; ECB 439; NSTC 2P8910 (BI C; NA MH).

*Notes.* 'Advertisement' states how the author was pre-empted in using the originally
intended title of 'The Hundred Days'. Introduction dated Dublin, 1 June 1826.


1826: 62   [PICKERING, Ellen].
**THE MARRIAGE OF THE FAVOURITE; OR, SHE BRED HIM A SOL-
DIER. A NOVEL. BY THE AUTHOR OF "THE HEIRESS." IN THREE
VOLUMES.**

> London: G. B. Whittaker, Ave-Maria-Lane, 1826.
> I 280p; II 307p; III 300p. 12mo. 18s (ECB, QR); 18s boards (ER).
> ER 45: 257 (Dec 1826); QR 35: 319 (Jan 1827).
> Corvey; CME 3-628-48161-9; ECB 369; NSTC 2P15851 (BI BL, C, O).

1826: 63   PORTER, A[nna] M[aria].

**HONOR O'HARA. A NOVEL, IN THREE VOLUMES. BY MISS A. M. PORTER, AUTHOR OF "THE HUNGARIAN BROTHERS," "THE RECLUSE OF NORWAY," &C. &C. &C.**

> London: Printed for Longman, Rees, Orme, Brown, and Green, Paternoster-Row, 1826.
> I vii, 400p; II 453p; III 536p. 12mo. 21s (ECB); 24s boards (ER); 24s (QR).
> ER 45: 257 (Dec 1826); QR 35: 319 (Jan 1827), 39: 525 (Apr 1829); WSW II: 163.
> Corvey; CME 3-628-48299-2; ECB 463; NSTC 2P22249 (BI BL, C, E, O; NA DLC, MH).

*Notes.* Prefatory notice dated Esher, Aug 1826.
Further edns: New York 1827 (NSTC); French trans., 1827.

1826: 64   PORTER, Jane and Anna Maria.

**TALES ROUND A WINTER HEARTH. BY JANE AND ANNA MARIA PORTER. IN TWO VOLUMES.**

> London: Printed for Longman, Rees, Orme, Brown, and Green, Paternoster-Row, 1826.
> I vi, 343p; II 458p. 12mo. 16s (ECB).
> QR 33: 597 (Mar 1826), 34: 302 (June 1826); WSW II: 163.
> Corvey; CME 3-628-54704-0; ECB 464; NSTC 2P22429 (BI BL, C, Dt, E, O; NA DLC, MH).

*Notes.* 'To the Reader' dated Esher, Surry [*sic*], Feb 1826. Anna Maria contributed 'Glenrowan', 'Lord Howth', 'Jeannie Halliday'; Jane Porter wrote the remainder.
Further edn: German trans., 1827 [as *Erzählungen beim Kaminfeuer* (RS)].

1826: 65   PUTNEY, Charlotte.

**THE BRAZEN MASK. A ROMANCE. IN FOUR VOLUMES. BY MRS. CHARLOTTE PUTNEY, AUTHOR OF CORA, &C.**

> London: Printed for A. K. Newman and Co. Leadenhall-Street, 1826.
> I 269p; II 261p; III 254p; IV 252p. 12mo. 22s (ECB).
> Corvey; CME 3-628-48421-9; ECB 475; NSTC 2P29894 (BI BL, C, O).

*Notes.* ECB dates Oct 1825.

1826: 66   RADCLIFFE, Ann.

**GASTON DE BLONDEVILLE, OR THE COURT OF HENRY III. KEEPING FESTIVAL IN ARDENNE, A ROMANCE. ST. ALBAN'S ABBEY, A METRICAL TALE; WITH SOME POETICAL PIECES. BY ANNE RADCLIFFE, AUTHOR OF "THE MYSTERIES OF UDOLPHO," "ROMANCE OF THE FOREST," &C. TO WHICH IS PREFIXED A MEMOIR OF THE AUTHOR, WITH EXTRACTS FROM HER JOURNALS. IN FOUR VOLUMES.**

> London: Henry Colburn, New Burlington Street, 1826.
> I 132, 186p; II 399p; III 375p; IV 331p. 12mo. 38s (ECB, QR).
> QR 34: 611 (Sept 1826); WSW II: 165–6.
> Corvey; CME 3-628-48445-6; ECB 477; NSTC 2R573 (BI BL, C, Dt, E, O; NA MH).

*Notes.* 'Memoir of the Life and Writings of Mrs. Radcliffe' in vol. 1, pp. [3]–132. Vols. 3 and 4 have the half-titles 'The Posthumous Works of Mrs. Radcliffe'.

Further edns: 1833 (NSTC); 1839 (NUC); New York 1826 (NSTC) [also Philadelphia 1826 (NSTC)]; French trans., 1826; German trans., 1826.

1826: 67    [SAINT LEGER, Francis Barry Boyle].
**MR. BLOUNT'S MSS. BEING SELECTIONS FROM THE PAPERS OF A MAN OF THE WORLD. BY THE AUTHOR OF GILBERT EARLE. IN TWO VOLUMES.**

> London: Printed for Charles Knight, Pall-Mall East, 1826.
> I 255p; II 279p. 8vo. 14s (ECB, QR).
> QR 34: 302 (June 1826).
> Corvey; CME 3-628-47231-8; ECB 62; NSTC 2S2243 (BI BL, C, O; NA DLC, MH).

1826: 68    [?SCARGILL, William Pitt].
**TRUTH. A NOVEL BY THE AUTHOR OF NOTHING. IN THREE VOLUMES.**

> London: Printed for Hunt and Clarke, Tavistock Street, Covent Garden, 1826.
> I 356p; II 354p; III 314p. 12mo. 24s (ECB, QR).
> QR 34: 612 (Sept 1826); WSW II: 172.
> Corvey; CME 3-628-48837-0; ECB 601; NSTC 2S6013 (BI BL, C).

*Notes.* NCBEL states that this novel was not by Scargill. Certainly its publisher, and that of two successors (1827: 61 and 1828: 70), sets it apart from the chain of titles Scargill published with Colburn.

1826: 69    [SCHULZE, Friedrich August].
**\*THE GIPSY, A ROMANTIC TALE, FROM THE GERMAN OF FREDERICK LAUN.**

> London: C. Chapple, 1826.
> 12mo. 8s (ECB); 8s boards (ER, QR).
> ER 45: 257 (Dec 1826); QR 35: 319 (Jan 1827).
> No copy located; ECB 231.

*Notes.* Trans. of *Die Zigeunerin* (Leipzig, 1825). Friedrich Laun was the pseudonym of Friedrich August Schulze. Title above has been mainly reconstituted from a list of 'Novels, Romances, and Tales, Published by C. Chapple, Royal Subscription Library, Pall Mall', in *Life in the West* (1828: 38).

1826: 70    [SCOTT, Sir Walter].
**WOODSTOCK; OR, THE CAVALIER. A TALE OF THE YEAR SIXTEEN HUNDRED AND FIFTY-ONE. BY THE AUTHOR OF "WAVERLEY, TALES OF THE CRUSADERS," &C. IN THREE VOLUMES.**

> Edinburgh: Printed for Archibald Constable and Co.; and Longman, Rees, Orme, Brown, and Green, London, 1826.
> I xvi, 315p; II 332p; III 370p. 8vo. 31s 6d (ECB, QR).

QR 34: 302 (June 1826), 35: 518-66 (Mar 1827) full review; WSW II: 179-80.

Corvey; CME 3-628-48599-1; ECB 647; NSTC 2S10385 (BI BL, C, Dt, E, NCu, O; NA MH).

*Notes.* Published 28 Apr 1826 (Corson). This is one of nine novels together given full reviews in QR (Mar 1827) under the page-top heading 'Historical Romance'.

Further edns: Boston 1826 (NSTC) [also New York 1826 (NSTC) and Philadelphia 1826 (NSTC)]; French trans., 1826; German trans., 1826. Numerous reprintings in collected edns.


1826: 71    [SHELLEY, Mary Wollstonecraft].

**THE LAST MAN. BY THE AUTHOR OF FRANKENSTEIN. IN THREE VOLUMES.**

London: Henry Colburn, New Burlington Street, 1826.

I xi, 358p; II 328p; III 352p. 12mo. 27s (ECB, QR).

QR 33: 597 (Mar 1826); WSW II: 182.

Corvey; CME 3-628-47901-0; ECB 532; NSTC 2S18448 (BI BL, C, Dt, O; NA MH).

*Notes.* Further edns: 2nd edn. 1826 (NSTC); Philadelphia 1833 (NSTC).


1826: 72    [SMITH, Horatio].

**BRAMBLETYE HOUSE; OR, CAVALIERS AND ROUNDHEADS. A NOVEL. BY ONE OF THE AUTHORS OF THE "REJECTED ADDRESSES." IN THREE VOLUMES.**

London: Henry Colburn, New Burlington Street, 1826.

I 378p; II 399p; III 413p. 12mo. 31s 6d (ECB).

QR 33: 597 (Mar 1826), 35: 518–66 (Mar 1827) full review; WSW II: 185.

Corvey; CME 3-628-47273-3; ECB 71; NSTC 2S26638 (BI E, O; NA MH).

*Notes.* This is one of nine novels which are together given full reviews in QR (Mar 1827) under the page-top heading 'Historical Romance'.

Further edns: 2nd edn. 1826 (NSTC); 3rd edn. 1826 (NSTC); 1833 (NSTC); [1835] (NSTC); 1839 (NSTC); French trans., 1826; German trans., 1827 [as *Brambletye-house und der schwarze Geist. Romantische Darstellung aus den Zeiten Cromwells* (RS)].


1826: 73    [SMITH, Horatio].

**THE TOR HILL. BY THE AUTHOR OF "BRAMBLETYE HOUSE," "GAI-ETIES AND GRAVITIES," &C. &C. IN THREE VOLUMES.**

London: Henry Colburn, New Burlington Street, 1826.

I 310p; II 350p; III 326p. 12mo. 31s 6d (ECB, QR); 31s 6d boards (ER).

ER 45: 257 (Dec 1826); QR 35: 319 (Jan 1827), 35: 518–66 (Mar 1827) full review; WSW II: 185.

BL N.389; ECB 594; NSTC 2S26653 (BI C, Dt, E, O; NA MH).

*Notes.* This is one of nine novels which are together given full reviews in QR (Mar 1827) under the page-top heading 'Historical Romance'.

Further edns: New edn. 1827 (Corvey), CME 3-628-48964-4; 1835 (NSTC); Philadelphia 1826 (NSTC); French trans., 1827; German trans., 1827.

1826: 74   WARD, Catherine G[eorge].

THE FOREST GIRL; OR, THE MOUNTAIN HUT: AN ORIGINAL AND INTERESTING DOMESTIC TALE. BY CATHERINE G. WARD, AUTHORESS OF THE MYSTERIOUS MARRIAGE, COTTAGE ON THE CLIFF, THE FISHER'S DAUGHTER, &C. &C.

> London: Published by George Virtue, Ivy-Lane, Paternoster-Row; and Bath Street, Bristol, 1826.
> 838p, ill. 8vo.
> MH 18495.3.3.30; NSTC 2W4961 (BI O).

*Notes.* Collates in fours.


1826: 75   [WILKINS, George].

THE CONVERT. BY THE AUTHOR OF "THE TWO RECTORS."

> London: Published by Longman, Rees, Orme, Brown, and Green, Paternoster-Row, 1826.
> viii, 444p. 12mo. 10s 6d (ECB).
> WSW II: 203.
> BL N.415; ECB 133; NSTC 2W20700 (BI C, Dt, E, O).

*Notes.* Dedication to the Duke of Newcastle. ECB dates Jan 1826.


1826: 76   [?WILLIAMS, Mitchell].

FEUDAL DAYS; OR, THE FREEBOOTER'S CASTLE. A ROMANCE. IN THREE VOLUMES.

> London: Printed for Mitchell Williams, 42, St. Andrew's Hill, Doctors Commons, 1826.
> I xii, 201p; II 204p; III 214p. 12mo.
> BL N.1713; NSTC 2W22898 (BI C, O).

*Notes.* Statement opp. t.p. reads: 'This Work is the first of an intended series, illustrative of the less noticed phenomena of history,—Subject, *The People, Democracy, Revival of Civilization.*'


1826: 77   [WOOD, George].

THE RAMBLES OF REDBURY ROOK; OR, A CAUTION TO HIS OWN SPECIES HOW THEY EMBRACE THE PROFESSION OF ARMS. BY THE AUTHOR OF THE SUBALTERN OFFICER.

> London: Printed and published by G. Wood, 27, Leman Street, Goodman's Fields; and sold by all Booksellers, 1826.
> viii, 231p, ill. 12mo. 5s (ECB).
> Corvey; CME 3-628-48448-0; ECB 479; NSTC 2W29455 (BI BL, E, O; NA MH).

*Notes.* ECB dates Aug 1826 and gives the author as 'Geo. Wood'. See Wolff (Item 7255) for documentation of an attempt by the author to blackmail Lord Palmerston into paying for the suppression of this work. *The Subaltern Officer* (1825), mentioned in the title, is not a novel.

1827: 1   ANON.

THE BRIDE OF OBEYDA; AND OTHER TALES. IN THREE VOLUMES. BY THE AUTHOR OF MONTVILLE, OR THE DARK HEIR OF THE CASTLE.

> London: Printed for A. K. Newman and Co., 1827.
> I 300p; II 295p; III 285p. 12mo. 18s (ECB).
> Corvey; CME 3-628-47122-2; ECB 74; NSTC 2B47664 (BI BL, C, E, O).

*Notes.* ECB dates Aug 1827.

1827: 2   ANON.

CHATEAU OF LEASPACH; OR, THE STRANGER IN SWITZERLAND. A TALE: IN THREE VOLUMES.

> London: Printed for A. K. Newman and Co., 1827.
> I 278p; II 251p; III 233p. 12mo. 16s 6d (ECB).
> Corvey; CME 3-628-47259-8; ECB 107; NSTC 2C16942 (BI BL, C, E, O).

*Notes.* ECB dates July 1827.

1827: 3   ANON.

ELLMER CASTLE; A ROMAN CATHOLIC STORY OF THE NINE-TEENTH CENTURY.

> Dublin: William Curry, jun. and Co. 9, Upper Sackville-Street. Hamilton, Adams, and
> Co. J. Nisbet, and J. Hatchard and Son, London; William Oliphant, Waugh and
> Innes, and William Whyte and Co. Edinburgh, 1827.
> 320p, ill. 12mo. 3s 6d (ECB).
> BL 4413.f.37(1); ECB 185; NSTC 2E8242 (BI Dt).

*Notes.* ECB dates June 1827, and gives Hurst as publisher (but not discovered in this form). Further edns: 2nd edn. 1827 (BRu ENC); 3rd edn. 1828 (Corvey), CME 3-628-47488-4; Boston 1833 (NSTC).

1827: 4   ANON.

THE GUARDS. A NOVEL. IN THREE VOLUMES.

> London: T. Clerc Smith, St. James's Street, 1827.
> I 261p; II 259p; III 266p. 12mo. 28s 6d (ECB); 28s 6d boards (ER).
> ER 46: 534 (Oct 1827).
> Corvey; CME 3-628-47772-7; ECB 247; NSTC 2G24480 (BI BL, C, E, O).

*Notes.* Further edn: New York 1827 (NSTC).

1827: 5   ANON.

HAMEL, THE OBEAH MAN. IN TWO VOLUMES.

London: Printed for Hunt and Clarke, York Street, Covent Garden, 1827.
I 336p; II 327p. 8vo. 16s (ECB); 18s (QR).
QR 36: 603 (Oct 1827).
Corvey; CME 3-628-47544-9; ECB 252; NSTC 2H4629 (BI BL, C, E, O; NA DLC).

1827: 6   ANON.
**HIGH LIFE, A NOVEL. IN THREE VOLUMES.**

London: Saunders and Otley, Conduit Street, 1827.
I 303p; II 372p; III 376p. 12mo. 31s 6d (ECB); 31s 6d boards (ER).
ER 46: 534 (Oct 1827).
Corvey; CME 3-628-47687-9; ECB 268; NSTC 2L15127 (BI BL, C, E, O; NA DLC).

*Notes.* Wolff (V, 14; Item 7486) mentions a tentative attribution to Mrs C. D. Burdett.
Further edn: New York 1827 (NSTC).

1827: 7   ANON.
**HYDE NUGENT. A TALE OF FASHIONABLE LIFE. IN THREE VOL-
UMES.**

London: Henry Colburn, New Burlington Street, 1827.
I iv, 328p; II 298p; III 296p. 12mo. 28s 6d (ECB); 28s 6d boards (ER).
ER 46: 534 (Oct 1827).
Corvey; CME 3-628-47868-5; ECB 291; NSTC 2N11826 (BI BL, E, O).

1827: 8   ANON.
**THE ROMAN CATHOLIC PRIEST.**

Dublin: William Curry, jun. and Co. Hamilton, Adams and Co. London; and
    W. Oliphant, Edinburgh, 1827.
298p, ill. 18mo. 3s 6d (ECB).
BL 4413.f.39(2); ECB 500; NSTC 2R16326.

*Notes.* ECB lists publisher as Hurst, May 1828, but not discovered in this form.

1827: 9   ANON.
**ROMANCES AND TALES FOR THE WINTER FIRE-SIDE. IN TWO
VOLUMES.**

London: Printed for Howell and Stewart, 1827.
I 330p; II 325p. 12mo.
BL 12611.aaa.22; NSTC 2R16444.

*Notes.* 'Azanaga the Moor' (ends at vol. 1, p. 223); 'The News at Nadiska' (from vol. 1 p. [225]
to end of vol. 2).

1827: 10   ANON.
**STORIES OF CHIVALRY AND ROMANCE.**

London: Published by Longman, Rees, Orme, Brown, and Green, 1827.
275p. 12mo. 6s (ECB).
Corvey; CME 3-628-51129-1; ECB 564; NSTC 2S42437 (BI BL, C, O; NA MH).

*Notes.* 6 stories. ECB dates Mar 1827.

1827: 11   ANON.
VERITAS VINCIT: OR, INCIDENTS OF REAL LIFE.

> Dublin: Carson & Knox, Grafton-Street; William Curry, jun. & Co. Sackville-Street.
> Hamilton, Adams, & Co. Paternoster-Row, London. M. Jellett, Belfast, 1827.
> iv, 248p. 12mo.
> BL 12611.f.15; NSTC 2V2542.

*Notes.* 'To the Public' at end offers thanks 'to the Ladies and Gentlemen of Larne and its vicinity, for their kind support'. Collates in sixes.


1827: 12   ANN OF KENT [pseud.].
THE CASTLE OF VILLEROY; OR, THE BANDIT CHIEF. BY ANN OF KENT. AUTHOR OF FACTS ELUCIDATED AND THE ROSE OF CLERMONT.

> London: Published by W. Simpkin and R. Marshall, Stationers' Court, Ludgate Street, 1827.
> 346p. 12mo. 8s (ECB).
> Corvey; CME 3-628-47951-7; ECB 20; NSTC 2A13106 (BI O).

*Notes.* Distinct from *Castle of Villeroy* (1801: 52), by Frances Mary Mills. *The Rose of Claremont*, as possibly mentioned in the present title, was written by Catherine George Ward (see 1820: 69). 'Advertisement' dated Mar 27, 1287 [*sic*]. ECB dates Apr 1827. Further edn: 1829 edn. at MH, listed in NSTC, is in fact 1827 as present entry.


1827: 13   [ANWYL, Edward Trevor].
TALES OF WELSH SOCIETY AND SCENERY. IN TWO VOLUMES.

> London: Printed for Longman, Rees, Orme, Brown, and Green, Paternoster-Row, 1827.
> I vi, 431p; II 393p. 12mo. 18s (ECB).
> Corvey; CME 3-628-48876-1; ECB 576; NSTC 2T1461 (BI BL, C, E, O).

*Notes.* Dedication 'to my Dear Mother'. 'Advertisement' dated London, Feb 1827. Vol. 1 contains: 'The Youth of Edward Ellis' (pp. [3]–270), 'The Cousins' (pp. 273–431); vol. 2 contains: 'Frederic Anwyl' (pp. [3]–199), 'The Prediction' (pp. 203–393). For author attribution, see 1829: 14, effectively a reissue of this work. ECB dates Mar 1827.


1827: 14   {B}[ARROW], {J}[ohn Henry].
EMIR MALEK, PRINCE OF THE ASSASSINS. AN HISTORICAL NOVEL OF THE THIRTEENTH CENTURY. IN THREE VOLUMES.

> London: Printed for Longman, Rees, Orme, Brown, and Green, Paternoster-Row, 1827.
> I xx, 248p; II 244p; III 298p. 12mo. 18s (ECB); 18s boards (ER).
> ER 46: 534 (Oct 1827), 47: 524 (May 1828); QR 37: 302 (Jan 1828).
> Corvey; CME 3-628-47564-3; ECB 186; NSTC 2B9876 (BI BL, C, E, O).

*Notes.* 'Advertisement' at the beginning of 1st vol. signed J. B.
Further edn: German trans., 1828.

1827: 15    [BAYLY, Nathaniel Thomas Haynes].
**THE AYLMERS. A NOVEL. IN THREE VOLUMES.**

> London: Saunders and Otley, Conduit Street, 1827.
> I iv, 247p; II 247p; III 193p. 12mo. 27s (ECB); 27s boards (ER).
> ER 46: 534 (Oct 1827).
> Corvey; CME 3-628-47087-0; ECB 33; NSTC 2B12682 (BI BL, C, E, O).

*Notes.* Further edn: 2nd edn. 1827 (NSTC).


1827: 16    [BENNET, William].
**OWAIN GOCH[.] A TALE OF THE REVOLUTION. BY THE AUTHOR OF "THE CAVALIER," "KING OF THE PEAK," &C. &C. IN THREE VOLUMES.**

> London: Printed for Longman, Rees, Orme, Brown, and Green, Paternoster-Row, 1827.
> I xxiv, 368p; II 408p; III 464p. 12mo. 24s (ECB); 24s boards (ER).
> ER 46: 534 (Oct 1827).
> Corvey; CME 3-628-48323-9; ECB 428; NSTC 2G6333 (BI BL, C).

*Notes.* Prefatory Letter from Lee Gibbons [pseud.] to Norman Courtdelois, Esq., dated May 1827.


1827: 17    BOLEN, C. A.
**WALTER THE MURDERER; OR, THE MYSTERIES OF EL DORADO. AN HISTORICAL ROMANCE. IN THREE VOLUMES. BY C. A. BOLEN, AUTHOR OF THE MYSTERIOUS MONK, &C.**

> London: Printed for A. K. Newman and Co., 1827.
> I 233p; II 243p; III 236p. 12mo. 16s 6d (ECB).
> Corvey; CME 3-628-47266-0; ECB 64; NSTC 2B39616 (BI BL, C, O).

*Notes.* ECB dates May 1827.


1827: 18    [BULWER LYTTON, Edward George].
**FALKLAND.**

> London: Henry Colburn, New Burlington Street, 1827.
> ix, 264p. 12mo. 9s 6d (ECB, QR); 9s 6d boards (ER).
> ER 45: 544 (Mar 1827); QR 36: 301 (June 1827).
> Corvey; CME 3-628-47168-0; ECB 198; NSTC 2B57409 (BI BL, C, Dt, E, O; NA DLC, MH).

*Notes.* Preface dated London, 7 Mar 1827.
Further edns: 1834 (NSTC); New York 1830 (NSTC); German trans., 1827; French trans., 1833.


1827: 19    [BUNBURY, Selina].
**CABIN CONVERSATIONS AND CASTLE SCENES. AN IRISH STORY. BY THE AUTHOR OF "EARLY RECOLLECTIONS," "A VISIT TO MY BIRTH-PLACE," &C. &C.**

London: James Nisbet, Berners Street, 1827.
173p, ill. 18mo. 2s 6d (ECB).
BL N.271(3); ECB 91; NSTC 2B57666 (BI C, O).

*Notes.* ECB dates Aug 1827.


1827: 20    [BURDETT, Mrs. C. D.].
**ENGLISH FASHIONABLES ABROAD. A NOVEL. IN THREE VOLUMES.**

London: Henry Colburn, New Burlington Street, 1827.
I 322p; II 348p; III 346p. 12mo. 31s 6d (ECB, QR); 31s 6d boards (ER).
ER 46: 534 (Oct 1827); QR 36: 301 (June 1827).
Corvey; CME 3-628-47764-6; ECB 187; NSTC 2E10074 (BI C, E, O; NA DLC, MH).

*Notes.* ECB dates Apr 1825 [*sic*].
Further edns: 1837 (NSTC); Boston 1828 (MH, NSTC).


1827: 21    [BURY, Lady Charlotte Susan Maria].
**FLIRTATION. A NOVEL. IN THREE VOLUMES.**

London: Henry Colburn, New Burlington Street, 1827.
I 304p; II 316p; III 380p. 12mo. 31s 6d (ECB); 31s 6d boards (ER, QR).
ER 47: 525 (May 1828); QR 37: 302 (Jan 1828).
E NF.658.g.24; ECB 209; NSTC 2C4347 (BI NCu; NA DLC).

*Notes.* Further edns: 2nd edn. 1828 (Corvey), CME 3-628-47593-7; 3rd edn. 1828 (NSTC); 1834 (NSTC); New York 1828 (NSTC).


1827: 22    [CARRINGTON, Edmund Frederick John].
**CONFESSIONS OF AN OLD BACHELOR.**

London: Henry Colburn, New Burlington Street, 1827.
371p. 12mo. 10s 6d (ECB).
Corvey; CME 3-628-47312-8; ECB 130; NSTC 2C9601 (BI BL, E, O; NA MH).

*Notes.* ECB dates Jan 1827.


1827: 23    CHATEAUBRIAND, [François René], Vicomte de.
**THE NATCHEZ; AN INDIAN TALE. BY THE VISCOUNT DE CHATEAUBRIAND, AUTHOR OF ATALA, THE BEAUTIES OF CHRIS-TIANITY, TRAVELS IN THE HOLY LAND, &C. IN THREE VOLUMES.**

London: Henry Colburn, New Burlington Street, 1827.
I xl, 299p; II 335p; III 412p. 8vo. 21s (ECB).
BL N.463; ECB 108; NSTC 2C16979 (BI C, Dt, E, O; NA DLC).

*Notes.* Trans. of *Les Natchez*, first published in 1826 as vols. 19 and 20 of *Oeuvres complètes*. ECB dates Jan 1827.
Further edn: 2nd edn. 1832, as *Celuta, or, The Natchez* (NSTC).


1827: 24    [COOPER, James Fenimore].
**THE PRAIRIE, A TALE, BY THE AUTHOR OF THE SPY, THE PILOT, &C. &C. IN THREE VOLUMES.**

London: Henry Colburn, New Burlington Street, 1827.

I viii, 339p; II 370p; III 366p. 12mo. 24s (ECB); 24s boards (ER).

ER 46: 534 (Oct 1827).

Corvey; CME 3-628-47331-4; ECB 135; NSTC 2C36866 (BI BL, C, Dt, E, O; NA DLC, MH).

*Notes.* This was set from advance sheets of the Paris (1827) edn., and preceded the first American edn. (Blanck).

Further edns: 1832 (NSTC); 1834 (NSTC); 1836 (NSTC); Liverpool 1839 (NSTC); 1850 (NSTC); Philadelphia 1827 (NSTC); French trans., 1827; German trans., 1827.


1827: 25   [COOPER, James Fenimore].

**THE RED ROVER, A TALE. BY THE AUTHOR OF "THE SPY," "THE PILOT," "THE PRAIRIE," &C. IN THREE VOLUMES.**

London: Henry Colburn, New Burlington Street, 1827.

I ix, 336p; II 309p; III 341p. 12mo. 28s 6d (ECB); 28s 6d boards (ER); 49s (QR).

ER 47: 525 (May 1828); QR 37: 302 (Jan 1828).

BL 1608/4013; ECB 135; NSTC 2C36871 (BI C, O; NA MH).

*Notes.* Dedication to W. B. Shubrick, Esquire, U.S. Navy. First published in Paris (Hector Bossange) and in London (see Blanck, vol. 2 (1957), pp. 279-80, who indicates that Paris edn. was marginally earlier). Corvey copy is identical to the BL copy listed above, apart from its 1828 imprint.

Further edns: 1828 (Corvey, NSTC); 1834 (NSTC); 1836 (NSTC); Liverpool 1839 (NSTC); 1840 (NSTC); [at least 2 more edns. to 1850]; Philadelphia 1828 (NSTC); German trans., 1828; French trans., 1830.


1827: 26   [CORBETT, Marion and Margaret].

**THE BUSY-BODIES; A NOVEL. BY THE AUTHORS OF "THE ODD VOLUME." IN THREE VOLUMES.**

London: Printed for Longman, Rees, Orme, Brown, and Green, and Adam Black, Edinburgh, 1827.

I 355p; II 336p; III 359p. 12mo. 24s (ECB); 24s boards (ER).

ER 46: 534 (Oct 1827).

Corvey; CME 3-628-47147-8; ECB 88; NSTC 2C37717 (BI BL, C, E, O; NA MH).


1827: 27   [CORBETT, Marion and Margaret].

**THE ODD VOLUME. SECOND SERIES.**

London: Printed for Longman, Rees, Orme, Brown, and Green, Paternoster-Row, 1827.

381p, music. 8vo. 21s (1st and 2nd series, ECB).

Corvey; CME 3-628-51108-9; ECB 420; NSTC 2C37701 (BI BL, C, Dt, O; NA DLC, MH).

*Notes.* ECB dates Apr 1827; it also gives publishers as Lizars (Edinburgh), Whittaker, for both series, but 2nd series not discovered in this form. Colophon reads: 'Edinburgh: Printed by James Ballantyne and Co.'.

Further edn: 3rd edn. 1827 (NSTC).

1827: 28   [?CROWE, Eyre Evans or ?PHIPPS, Constantine Henry, Marquis of Normanby].
HISTORIETTES, OR TALES OF CONTINENTAL LIFE. BY THE AUTHOR OF "THE ENGLISH IN ITALY." IN THREE VOLUMES.

> London: Saunders and Otley, Conduit Street, 1827.
> I xii, 333p; II 352p; III 316p. 12mo. 31s 6d (ECB, QR); 31s 6d boards (ER).
> ER 46: 534 (Oct 1827); QR 36: 301 (June 1827).
> Corvey; CME 3-628-51060-9; ECB 271; NSTC 2P15300 (BI C, E, O; NA DLC, MH).

*Notes.* For the issue of author attribution, see *The English in Italy* (1825: 23).

1827: 29   [?CROWE, Eyre Evans or ?EATON, Charlotte Anne].
VITTORIA COLONNA: A TALE OF ROME, IN THE NINETEENTH CENTURY. IN THREE VOLUMES.

> Edinburgh: William Blackwood, and T. Cadell, London, 1827.
> I 278p; II 247p; III 252p. 12mo. 18s (ECB, QR); 18s boards (ER).
> ER 46: 534 (Oct 1827); QR 36: 603 (Oct 1827).
> Corvey; CME 3-628-48919-9; ECB 616; NSTC 2E1362 (BI BL, C, O; NA DLC, MH).

*Notes.* See Wolff (I, 323) for arguments for attributing this title to Crowe, as opposed to Charlotte Anne Eaton.
Further edn: German trans., 1828.

DISRAELI, Benjamin, VIVIAN GREY
See 1826: 30

EATON, Charlotte Anne, VITTORIA COLONNA
See CROWE, Eyre Evans

1827: 30   [FORRESTER, Charles Robert].
SIR ROLAND. A ROMANCE OF THE TWELFTH CENTURY. IN FOUR VOLUMES. BY HAL WILLIS, STUDENT AT LAW, AUTHOR OF "CASTLE BAYNARD."

> London: Printed for A. K. Newman and Co., 1827.
> I xii, 266p; II 254p; III 239p; IV 232p. 12mo. 22s (ECB, QR); 22s boards (ER).
> ER 45: 544 (Mar 1827); QR 36: 301 (June 1827).
> Corvey; CME 3-628-48933-4; ECB 640; NSTC 2W23991 (BI BL, C, E, O).

*Notes.* Dedication to 'my right worthy and excellent friend, J. J. McCracken'. ECB dates Mar 1822 [*sic*].

GAMBLE, John, CHARLTON, OR SCENES IN IRELAND
See 1823: 36

1827: 31   GOLLAND, Mrs. [C. D.] [née HAYNES, Miss C. D.].
THE RUINS OF RUTHVALE ABBEY. A NOVEL. IN FOUR VOLUMES. BY MRS. GOLLAND, (LATE MISS HAYNES,) AUTHOR OF THE

FOUNDLING OF DEVONSHIRE, ELEANOR, OR THE SPECTRE OF ST. MICHAEL'S, AUGUSTUS AND ADELINE, &C. &C.

London: Printed for A. K. Newman and Co. Leadenhall-Street, 1827.
I 285p; II 249p; III 250p; IV 259p. 12mo. 22s (ECB, QR).
QR 35: 319 (Jan 1827).
Corvey; CME 3-628-47841-3; ECB 260; NSTC 2H14183 (BI BL, C, E, O).

*Notes.* ECB dates Nov 1826.

1827: 32    [GORE, Catherine Grace Frances].
THE LETTRE DE CACHET; A TALE. THE REIGN OF TERROR; A TALE.

London: J. Andrews, 167, New Bond-Street.
v, 406p. 8vo. 10s 6d (ECB).
Corvey; CME 3-628-48030-2; ECB 342; NSTC 2G14846 (BI BL, C, E, O; NA DLC, MH).

*Notes.* Preface (pp. [iii]–v) argues in favour of the single-volume form. 'The Lettre de Cachet' pp. [1]–188; 'The Reign of Terror' pp. [191]–406. ECB dates June 1827.

1827: 33    [GRATTAN, Thomas Colley].
HIGH-WAYS AND BY-WAYS; OR, TALES OF THE ROADSIDE, PICKED UP IN THE FRENCH PROVINCES. BY A WALKING GENTLE-MAN. THIRD SERIES. IN THREE VOLUMES.

London: Henry Colburn, New Burlington Street, 1827.
I 333p; II 319p; III 367p. 12mo. 31s 6d (ECB, QR).
QR 37: 302 (Jan 1828).
Corvey; CME 3-628-51042-2; ECB 268; NSTC 2G18165 (BI BL, C, Dt, E, O).

*Notes.* Further edns: 1833 (NSTC); Philadelphia 1833 (NSTC).

1827: 34    [GRIFFIN, Gerald Joseph].
"HOLLAND-TIDE;" OR, MUNSTER POPULAR TALES.

London: Printed for W. Simpkin and R. Marshall, Stationers' Hall Court, Ludgate-Street, 1827.
378p. 12mo. 8s 6d (ECB).
Corvey; CME 3-628-51038-4; ECB 277; NSTC 2G22647 (BI BL, Dt, O).

*Notes.* ECB dates Feb 1827.
Further edn: 2nd edn. 1827 (NSTC).
Facs: IAN (1979).

1827: 35    [GRIFFIN, Gerald Joseph].
TALES OF THE MUNSTER FESTIVALS CONTAINING, CARD DRAW-ING; THE HALF SIR; AND SUIL DHUV, THE COINER. BY THE AUTHOR OF "HOLLAND-TIDE, OR IRISH POPULAR TALES." IN THREE VOLUMES.

London: Saunders and Otley, Conduit Street, 1827.
I xxiii, 355p; II 326p; III 316p. 12mo. 31s 6d (ECB, QR).
QR 37: 302 (Jan 1828), 38: 601 (Oct 1828).
Corvey; CME 3-628-48867-2; ECB 576; NSTC 2G22655 (BI BL, C, Dt, E, O).

*Notes.* Further edns: 2nd edn. 1829 (NSTC); 1848 (NSTC); German trans., 1829 [as *Suil Dhuv, der Falschmünzer und die Kartenschlägerin* (RS)].
Facs: IAN (1979).

1827: 36    HALE, S[arah] J[osepha Buell].
SIDNEY ROMELEE. A TALE OF NEW ENGLAND. IN THREE VOL-
UMES. BY MRS. S. J. HALE.

> Boston: Printed for Bowles and Dearborn. London: Re-printed for A. K. Newman and
>     Co., 1827.
> I 274p; II 260p; III 274p. 12mo. 16s 6d (ECB).
> Corvey; CME 3-628-47466-3; ECB 250; NSTC 2H2147 (BI BL, C, O).

*Notes.* Colophon reads: 'Printed by J. Darling, Leadenhall-Street, London'. ECB dates Aug 1827.
Originally published as *Northwood; A Tale of New England*, in 2 vols., Boston 1827 (Blanck).

1827: 37    [HAMILTON, Thomas].
THE YOUTH AND MANHOOD OF CYRIL THORNTON. IN THREE
VOLUMES.

> Edinburgh: William Blackwood, and T. Cadell, London, 1827.
> I 365p; II 384p; III 380p. 8vo. 31s 6d (ECB, QR); 31s boards (ER); 8s (QR).
> ER 46: 534 (Oct 1827); QR 36: 301 (June 1827), 37: 581 (Mar 1828).
> Corvey; CME 3-628-48996-2; ECB 654; NSTC 2H5434 (BI BL, Dt, E, O; NA DLC).

*Notes.* QR lists as 8s in June 1827 and as 31s 6d in Mar 1828.
Further edns: 2nd edn. 1829 (NSTC); 1842 (NSTC); 1848 (NSTC); Boston 1827 (NSTC).

1827: 38    [HARDING, Anne Raikes].
DISSIPATION. A TALE OF SIMPLE LIFE. IN FOUR VOLUMES. BY THE
AUTHOR OF "REALITIES," "CORRECTION," &C.

> London: Printed for A. K. Newman and Co., 1827.
> I x, 290p; II 264p; III 252p; IV 292p. 12mo; 24s (ECB).
> Corvey; CME 3-628-47438-8; ECB 166; NSTC 2H7487 (BI BL, C, O).

*Notes.* ECB dates Apr 1827.

1827: 39    [HAWORTH, Euphrasia Fanny].
THE PINE TREE DELL, AND OTHER TALES. IN TWO VOLUMES.

> London: J. Andrews, 167, New Bond-Street, 1827.
> I 324p; II 299p. 8vo. 18s (ECB, QR).
> QR 36: 603 (Oct 1827).
> Corvey; CME 3-628-54707-5; ECB 451; NSTC 2H13402 (BI BL, C, E, O; NA MH).

*Notes.* NSTC states 'By E. F. Haworth, edited by A. Dyce'. 'Advertisement' (1 p. unn.) states
'The Pine Tree Dell', the first story, 'is neither translated nor borrowed from a foreign ori-
ginal'; half-title gives 'A German Tale' as sub-title for this tale. ECB and QR sub-title *The Pine
Tree Dell* as 'A German Legend'.

HAYNES, Miss C. D.
See GOLLAND, Mrs. C. D.

1827: 40    [HOCKLEY, William Browne].

**THE ZENANA; OR A NUWAB'S LEISURE HOURS; BY THE AUTHOR OF "PANDURANG HARI; OR MEMOIRS OF A HINDOO." IN THREE VOLUMES.**

> London: Saunders and Otley, Conduit Street, 1827.
> I viii, 423p; II 438p; III 435p. 12mo. 24s (ECB); 24s boards (ER).
> ER 45: 544 (Mar 1827).
> Corvey; CME 3-628-49006-5; ECB 654; NSTC 2H24564 (BI BL, C, Dt, O).

*Notes.* Further edn: German trans., 1827 [as *Das indische Serail, oder Mussestunden eines Nuwabs* (RS)].

1827: 41    HOFLAND, [Barbara].

**SELF-DENIAL. A TALE. BY MRS. HOFLAND, AUTHOR OF INTEGRITY, A TALE; PATIENCE, A TALE; DECISION, A TALE; MODERATION, A TALE; REFLECTION, A TALE; THE SON OF A GENIUS; TALES OF THE PRIORY; TALES OF THE MANOR, &C. &C.**

> London: Printed for Longman, Rees, Orme, Brown, and Green, Paternoster-Row, 1827.
> 254p, ill. 12mo. 6s (ECB, QR).
> QR 39: 253 (Jan 1829).
> Corvey; CME 3-628-47660-7; ECB 275; NSTC 2H29415 (BI BL, E, O; NA MH).

*Notes.* Colophon reads 'Bungay: Printed by J. and R. Childs'. ECB dates Oct 1827.
Further edns: New edn. 1831 (NUC); New edn. 1834 (NUC); New edn. 1835 (NUC); Harrogate 1837 (NSTC); Harrogate 1838 (NSTC); New York 1828 (NUC).

1827: 42    HOOD, Thomas.

**NATIONAL TALES. BY THOMAS HOOD, AUTHOR OF "WHIMS AND ODDITIES." IN TWO VOLUMES.**

> London: William H. Ainsworth, Old Bond Street, 1827.
> I viii, 244p, ill.; II 238p, ill. 12mo. 21s (ECB).
> Corvey; CME 3-628-51050-3; ECB 279; NSTC 2H28777 (BI BL, C, E, O; NA DLC, MH).

*Notes.* Advs. (1 p. unn.) at end of vol. 2 headed 27, Old Bond-Street, Feb 1827. ECB dates Mar 1827.
Further edns: Philadelphia 1839 (NUC); German trans., 1828 [as *Ausgewählte Erzählungen* (RS)].

1827: 43    [HORNE, Moffat James].

**THE ADVENTURES OF NAUFRAGUS. WRITTEN BY HIMSELF.**

> London: Published by Smith, Elder, and Co. 65, Cornhill, 1827.
> xii, 225p. 8vo. 8s (ECB, QR).
> QR 36: 603 (Oct 1827).
> Corvey; CME 3-628-47031-5; ECB 6; NSTC 2H30993 (BI BL, C, Dt, E, O; NA MH).

*Notes.* Further edn: 2nd edn. 1828 (NSTC).

1827: 44   [JOHNSTONE, Christian Isobel].
ELIZABETH DE BRUCE. BY THE AUTHOR OF CLAN-ALBIN. IN
THREE VOLUMES.

>Edinburgh: William Blackwood, and T. Cadell, London, 1827.
>I 387p; II 404p; III 400p. 8vo. 31s 6d (ECB); 31s 6d boards (ER).
>ER 45: 544 (Mar 1827); QR 35: 617 (Mar 1827).
>Corvey; CME 3-628-47522-8; ECB 183; NSTC 2J9645 (BI BL, C, E, O; NA MH).

*Notes.* Further edns: New York 1827 (NUC); German trans., 1827.

1827: 45   JONES, E. H. de St. Pierre [pseud.?].
ROCKAVON: A TALE OF THE THIRTEENTH CENTURY. BY E. H. DE
ST. PIERRE JONES. IN THREE VOLUMES.

>London: Printed at the Caxton Press, by H. Fisher, Son, and Co. Published at 38, New-
>gate-Street; and sold by all Booksellers, 1827.
>I 326p; II 346p; III 310p. 12mo. 15s (ECB).
>Corvey; CME 3-628-48002-7; ECB 311; NSTC 2J10180 (BI BL, C, O).

*Notes.* The author's name, combining elements of Hannah Maria Jones and J. H. Bernardin
de Saint Pierre, may possibly be a pseudonym. Collates in sixes.
Further edn: 1834 (Jarndyce CXXV, Item 113).

1827: 46(a)   [JONES, Hannah Maria].
ROSALINE WOODBRIDGE. IN THREE VOLUMES.

>London: Matthew Iley, Somerset Street, Portman Square, 1827.
>I 304p; II 323p; III 316p. 12mo. 25s (ECB); 25s boards (ER).
>ER 45: 257 (Dec 1826).
>Corvey; CME 3-628-48548-7; ECB 502; NSTC 2J10435 (BI BL, C, O).

*Notes.* Colophon reads: 'C. Baynes, Printer, Duke-Street, Lincoln's-inn-fields.' ECB dates
Dec 1826.

1827: 46(b)   JONES, Hannah Maria.
ROSALINE WOODBRIDGE; OR, THE MIDNIGHT VISIT. A ROMAN-
TIC TALE. BY HANNAH MARIA JONES, AUTHORESS OF THE WED-
DING RING, THE VICTIM OF FASHION, THE FORGED NOTE, THE
BRITISH OFFICER, &C. &C.

>London: Printed by C. Baynes, Duke Street, Lincoln's Inn Fields; for George Virtue,
>Ivy Lane, Paternoster Row, Bath-Street Bristol; and St. Vincent Street, Liverpool,
>1827.
>712p, ill. 8vo.
>Dt OLS.L-2-27; NSTC 21J10436 (BI BL).

*Notes.* Additional vignette t.p. plus 8 engraved illustrations. Collates in fours.

1827: 47   JONES, Hannah Maria.
THE STRANGERS OF THE GLEN; OR, THE TRAVELLERS
BENIGHTED. A TALE OF MYSTERY. BY HANNAH MARIA JONES,

# AUTHORESS OF THE WEDDING RING, GRETNA GREEN, THE VICTIM OF FASHION, &C. &C.

> London: Printed by C. Baynes, Duke-Street, Lincoln's-Inn-Fields; published by G. Virtue, Ivy-Lane, Paternoster-Row; Bath Street, Bristol; and St. Vincent Street, Liverpool: and sold by all Booksellers, 1827.
> 715p, ill. 8vo.
> BRu ENC; NSTC 2J10440 (BI BL).

*Notes.* Additional engraved t.p. with imprint 'London: Published by G. Virtue, 26 Ivy Lane, & Bath St., Bristol' [n.d.]. BL 1509/997 has Preface, pp. [iii]–iv, signed William Leman Rede, which evidently relates to another work. Collates in fours.

## 1827: 48    [LAUDER, Sir Thomas Dick].
# THE WOLFE OF BADENOCH; A HISTORICAL ROMANCE OF THE FOURTEENTH CENTURY. BY THE AUTHOR OF "LOCHANDHU."

> Edinburgh: Printed for Cadell & Co.; and Simpkin & Marshall, London, 1827.
> I 399p; II 424p; III 474p. 12mo. 24s boards (ER).
> ER 45: 544 (Mar 1827); QR 35: 617 (Mar 1827).
> Corvey; CME 3-628-48973-3; NSTC 2L5427 (BI BL, C, E; NA MH).

*Notes.* ECB 645 lists 2nd edn., Feb 1827, price 24s.
Further edns: 2nd edn. 1827 (NUC); German trans., 1827; French trans., 1828.

## 1827: 49    [LAURENCE, Miss H.].
# LONDON IN THE OLDEN TIME; OR, TALES INTENDED TO ILLUSTRATE THE MANNERS AND SUPERSTITIONS OF ITS INHABITANTS FROM THE TWELFTH TO THE SIXTEENTH CENTURY. SECOND SERIES.

> London: Longman, Rees, Orme, Brown, and Green; Paternoster Row, 1827.
> vi, 329p. 8vo. 10s (ECB).
> Corvey; CME 3-628-51089-9; ECB 352; NSTC 2L5527 (BI BL; NA DLC).

*Notes.* ECB dates May 1827.

## 1827: 50    [LOUDON, Jane C.].
# THE MUMMY! A TALE OF THE TWENTY-SECOND CENTURY. IN THREE VOLUMES.

> London: Henry Colburn, New Burlington Street, 1827.
> I viii, 300p; II 348p; III 303p. 12mo. 28s 6d (ECB, QR); 28s 6d boards (ER).
> ER 46: 534 (Oct 1827); QR 37: 302 (Jan 1828).
> BL N.458,459; ECB 400; NSTC 2W10092 (BI C, Dt, E, O; NA DLC).

*Notes.* Begins: 'In the year 2126 England enjoyed peace and tranquility under the absolute dominion of a female sovereign'.
Further edn: 2nd edn. 1828 (Corvey), CME 3-628-48392-1.

## 1827: 51    [?MAGINN, William].
# THE MILITARY SKETCH-BOOK. REMINISCENCES OF SEVENTEEN YEARS IN THE SERVICE ABROAD AND AT HOME. BY AN OFFICER OF THE LINE. IN TWO VOLUMES.

London: Henry Colburn, New Burlington Street, 1827.
I 347p; II 347p. 12mo. 21s (ECB).
IU 823.M.5991; ECB 384; NSTC 2S3536 (BI BL, C, E, O).

*Notes.* Attributed in Block and in some library catalogues to William Maginn, but perhaps erroneously: see also the same author's *Tales of Military Life* (1829: 58). ECB dates Apr 1827. Further edns: 2nd edn. 1831 (NSTC); New York 1827 (NUC).

1827: 52   [MAGINN, William].
**WHITEHALL; OR, THE DAYS OF GEORGE IV.**

London: William Marsh, 137, Oxford-Street, n.d. [1827].
vi, 330p. 8vo. 10s 6d (ECB).
QR 37: 84–100 (Jan 1828) full review, 37: 302 (Jan 1828).
Corvey; CME 3-628-48905-9; ECB 635; NSTC 2M9550 (BI BL, C, Dt, E, O; NA DLC, MH).

*Notes.* Dedication to Sir Edmund Nagle, K.C.B., dated Green Arbour Court, 21 Oct 1827. Reviewed together in QR (Jan 1828) with *May Fair: A Poem* (1827) and a collection of contemporary annuals. ECB dates Nov 1827.

**MARTEN, Ambrose, THE STANLEY TALES**
See 1826: 58

1827: 53   MOORE, Thomas.
**THE EPICUREAN, A TALE. BY THOMAS MOORE.**

London: Printed for Longman, Rees, Orme, Brown, and Green, Paternoster-Row, 1827.
vii, 332p. 12mo. 9s (ECB).
QR 36: 603 (Oct 1827).
BL 634.e.1; ECB 394; NSTC 2M35206 (BI Dt; NA DLC, MH).

*Notes.* Dedication to Lord John Russell.
Further edns: 2nd edn. 1827 (Corvey), CME 3-628-48287-9; 3rd edn. 1827 (NSTC); 4th edn. 1827 (NSTC); 5th edn. 1828 (NSTC); 6th edn. 1831 (NSTC); [at least 2 more edns. to 1850]; Philadelphia 1827 (NSTC); French trans., 1827 [as *L'Épicurien, ou la vierge de Memphis* (BN)]; German trans., 1828.

1827: 54   MORGAN, Lady {Sydney} [née OWENSON, Sydney].
**THE O'BRIENS AND THE O'FLAHERTYS; A NATIONAL TALE. BY LADY MORGAN. IN FOUR VOLUMES.**

London: Henry Colburn, New Burlington-Street, 1827.
I xi, 295p; II 340p; III 332p; IV 362p. 12mo. 42s (ECB); 36s boards (ER).
ER 47: 525 (May 1828).
Corvey; CME 3-628-48328-X; ECB 396; NSTC 2O7617 (BI BL, Dt, E, O; NA DLC, MH).

*Notes.* Preface signed Sydney Morgan, Kildare-Street, Dublin, 1 Oct 1827. ECB dates Nov 1827. Further edns: 2nd edn. 1828 (NSTC); 1838 (NSTC); Philadelphia 1828 (NSTC); French trans., 1828; German trans., 1828.
Facs: IAN (1979).

1827: 55   MOSSE, Henrietta Rouviere.
**WOMAN'S WIT & MAN'S WISDOM; OR, INTRIGUE. A NOVEL. IN
FOUR VOLUMES. BY HENRIETTA ROUVIERE MOSSE, AUTHOR OF A
FATHER'S LOVE AND A WOMAN'S FRIENDSHIP, BRIDE AND NO
WIFE, GRATITUDE, &C. &C.**

> London: Printed for A. K. Newman and Co., 1827.
> I iv, 308p; II 299p; III 290p; IV 296p. 12mo.
> Corvey; CME 3-628-48351-4; ECB 399; NSTC 2R19130 (BI BL, C, O).

*Notes.* 'A Short Preface' dated Queen-Street, Camden-Town, 26 Apr 1827.

OWENSON, Sydney
See MORGAN, Lady Sydney

1827: 56   [PENNIE, John Fitzgerald].
**THE TALE OF A MODERN GENIUS; OR, THE MISERIES OF PARNAS-
SUS. IN A SERIES OF LETTERS. IN THREE VOLUMES.**

> London: J. Andrews, 167, New Bond Street, 1827.
> I xviii, 348p; II ix, 358p; III xii, 331p. 12mo. 24s (ECB, QR).
> QR 37: 302 (Jan 1828).
> BL 615.c.34; ECB 441; NSTC 2P10399 (BI C; NA MH).

*Notes.* Dedication to Sir Richard Colt Hoare, Bart., signed 'Sylvaticus' [the pseudonymous author of the letters], pp. [v]–vii; poetry at the end of all vols. Preface concludes: 'The letters have been revised and corrected, and all the notes added at the time of preparing them for the press; and this appears to the author all that is necessary at present to state respecting them, save and mereover [*sic*] that three or four of the letters, as well as several of the poetical pieces, have appeared in different respectable periodicals' (p. xi). ECB dates Oct 1827.

**PHIPPS, Constantine Henry, HISTORIETTES**
See CROWE, Eyre Evans

1827: 57   REDE, William Leman.
**THE WEDDED WANDERER; OR, THE SOLDIER'S FATE. A NOVEL, BY
WILLIAM LEMAN REDE.**

> London: Published by G. Virtue, Ivy Lane, Paternoster Row; Bath-Street, Bristol; and
>     Vincent-Street, Liverpool: and sold by all Booksellers, 1827.
> 787p, ill. 8vo.
> BL 1609/5661; NSTC 2R4414 (BI C, E; NA MH).

*Notes.* Additional engraved t.p., also dated 1827. Collates in fours.

**RYLEY, Samuel William, THE ITINERANT IN SCOTLAND**
See 1808: 93

1827: 58   ST. CLAIR, Rosalia [pseud.].
**FASHIONABLES AND UNFASHIONABLES. A NOVEL. IN THREE VOL-
UMES. BY ROSALIA ST. CLAIR, AUTHOR OF THE HIGHLAND**

CASTLE AND LOWLAND COTTAGE, THE BANKER'S DAUGHTERS
OF BRISTOL, SON OF O'DONNELL, FIRST AND LAST YEARS OF
WEDDED LIFE, &C.

> London: Printed for A. K. Newman and Co., 1827.
> I 279p; II 265p; III 271p. 12mo. 16s 6d (ECB); 16s 6d boards (ER).
> ER 46: 534 (Oct 1827).
> Corvey; CME 3-628-48495-2; ECB 511; NSTC 2S1994 (BI BL, E, O).

1827: 59    ST. CLAIR, Rosalia [pseud.].
THE FIRST AND LAST YEARS OF WEDDED LIFE. A NOVEL. IN FOUR
VOLUMES. BY ROSALIA ST. CLAIR, AUTHOR OF THE HIGHLAND
CASTLE AND LOWLAND COTTAGE, &C.

> London: Printed for A. K. Newman and Co. Leadenhall-Street, 1827.
> I 270p; II 264p; III 271p; IV 243p. 12mo. 22s (ECB, QR); 22s boards (ER).
> ER 45: 257 (Dec 1826); QR 35: 319 (Jan 1827).
> Corvey; CME 3-628-48496-0; ECB 511; NSTC 2S1995 (BI BL, E, O; NA MH).

*Notes.* ECB dates Oct 1826.

1827: 60    [SCARGILL, William Pitt].
BLUE-STOCKING HALL. IN THREE VOLUMES.

> London: Henry Colburn, New Burlington Street, 1827.
> I iv, 320p; II 328p; III 258p. 12mo. 27s (ECB); 27s boards (ER).
> ER 46: 534 (Oct 1827).
> Corvey; CME 3-628-47264-4; ECB 63; NSTC 2S6000 (BI BL, C, Dt, O).

*Notes.* Further edns: 2nd edn. 1829 (NSTC); New York 1828 (NSTC).

1827: 61    [?SCARGILL, William Pitt].
ELIZABETH EVANSHAW. THE SEQUEL OF "TRUTH," A NOVEL. IN
THREE VOLUMES.

> London: Published by Hunt and Clarke, York Street, Covent Garden, 1827.
> I vii, 386p; II 347p; III 342p. 12mo. 24s (ECB).
> Corvey; CME 3-628-47523-6; ECB 183; NSTC 2S6001 (BI BL, C, E, O; NA MH).

*Notes.* For the issue of author attribution, see *Truth: A Novel by the Author of Nothing* (1826: 68).

1827: 62    [SCARGILL, William Pitt].
TRUCKLEBOROUGH HALL; A NOVEL. IN THREE VOLUMES.

> London: Henry Colburn, New Burlington-Street, 1827.
> I 368p; II 359p; III 313p. 12mo. 28s 6d (ECB).
> Corvey; CME 3-628-48832-X; ECB 601; NSTC 2S6012 (BI BL, C, O; NA MH).

*Notes.* ECB dates Jan 1827.
Further edn: German trans., 1827.

1827: 63    {SCOTT}, [Sir] {Walter}.
CHRONICLES OF THE CANONGATE; BY THE AUTHOR OF "WAVER-
LEY," &C. IN TWO VOLUMES.

Edinburgh: Printed for Cadell and Co.; and Simpkin and Marshall, London, 1827.
I xxviii, 351p; II 374p. 8vo. 21s (ECB).
QR 37: 302 (Jan 1828).
Corvey; CME 3-628-48542-8; ECB 521; NSTC 2S9527 (BI BL, C, Dt, E, NCu, O; NA DLC, MH).

*Notes.* Introduction signed Walter Scott, Abbotsford, 1 Oct 1827. [1st series]. 'This day published', 8 Nov 1827, *Edinburgh Evening Courant.*
Further edns: New York 1827 (NSTC) [also Philadelphia 1827 (NSTC)]; French trans., 1827; German trans., 1828. Numerous reprintings of its tales ('The Highland Widow', 'The Two Drovers', and 'The Surgeon's Daughter') in collected edns.

1827: 64    [SMITH, Horatio].
**REUBEN APSLEY. BY THE AUTHOR OF BRAMBLETYE HOUSE, THE TOR HILL, &C. IN THREE VOLUMES.**

London: Henry Colburn, New Burlington Street, 1827.
I viii, 340p; II 369p; III 392p. 12mo. 31s 6d (ECB); 31s 6d boards (ER).
ER 46: 534 (Oct 1827).
Corvey; CME 3-628-48568-1; ECB 489; NSTC 2S26650 (BI BL, C, E, O; NA MH).

*Notes.* Dedication 'to Sir Walter Scott, Bart. &c.', dated Brighton, June 1827.
Further edns: New edn. 1827 (BRu ENC); Philadelphia 1827 (NUC); French trans., 1827; German trans., 1827.

1827: 65    [SPENCE, Elizabeth Isabella].
**DAME REBECCA BERRY, OR, COURT SCENES IN THE REIGN OF CHARLES THE SECOND. IN THREE VOLUMES.**

London: Printed for Longman, Rees, Orme, Brown, and Green, Paternoster-Row, 1827.
I vii, 323p; II 312p; III 260p. 12mo. 18s (ECB); 18s boards (ER).
ER 45: 544 (Mar 1827).
Corvey; CME 3-628-47417-5; ECB 151; NSTC 2S33535 (BI BL, C, E, O; NA MH).

*Notes.* Further edn: German trans., 1827 [as *Rebekka Berry, oder Scenen und Charaktere am Hofe Carls des Zweiten* (RS)].

1827: 66    SPIE[SS], [Christian Heinrich].
**THE DWARF OF WESTERBOURG. FROM THE GERMAN OF J. C. SPIETZ.**

London: Printed for the Author; and published by W. Morgan, 33, Old Bond Street, 1827.
I v, 249p, ill.; II 248p, ill. 12mo. 16s (s.l.).
BL 12611.i.17; NSTC 2S34175 (NA MH).

*Notes.* Trans. of *Das Petermännchen* (Prague 1791–2). Coloured frontispiece. ECB 175 has a title entry which reads: 'Dwarf of Westerbony. 2 vols. Sm. 8vo, 18s, Chapple, [18]27'.

1827: 67    STANHOPE, Louisa Sidney.
**THE SEER OF TIVIOTDALE. A ROMANCE. IN FOUR VOLUMES. BY LOUISA SIDNEY STANHOPE, AUTHOR OF THE BANDIT'S BRIDE,**

THE CRUSADERS, THE FESTIVAL OF MORA, RUNNEMEDE, AGE WE
LIVE IN, DI MONTRANZO, SIEGE OF KENILWORTH, CONFES-
SIONAL OF VALOMBRE, &C.

> London: Printed for A. K. Newman and Co., 1827.
> I iii, 312p; II 300p; III 295p; IV 270p. 12mo. 24s (ECB); 24s boards (ER).
> ER 45: 544 (Mar 1827).
> Corvey; CME 3-628-48780-3; ECB 558; NSTC 2S36113 (BI BL, C, E, O).


1827: 68    [?SURR, Thomas Skinner].
RICHMOND; OR, SCENES IN THE LIFE OF A BOW STREET OFFICER,
DRAWN UP FROM HIS PRIVATE MEMORANDA. IN THREE VOL-
UMES.

> London: Henry Colburn, New Burlington Street, 1827.
> I viii, 312p; II viii, 322p; III vii, 310p. 12mo. 31s 6d (ECB); 38s 6d boards (ER); 38s 6d
> (QR).
> ER 45: 544 (Mar 1827); QR 36: 302 (June 1827).
> Corvey; CME 3-628-48605-X; ECB 493; NSTC 2S47158 (BI BL, C, Dt, O; NA DLC,
> MH).

*Notes.* Also attributed to Thomas Gaspey, though most modern sources give Surr. 'Notice'
dated London, 16 Mar 1827.
Further edn: New York 1827 (NUC).


1827: 69    [SUTHERLAND, Alexander].
TALES OF A PILGRIM. BY THE AUTHOR OF "A SUMMER RAMBLE IN
THE NORTH HIGHLANDS."

> Edinburgh: William Hunter, 23, Hanover Street; and James Duncan, London, 1827.
> 394p. 8vo. 10s 6d (ECB, QR).
> QR 35: 617 (Mar 1827).
> Corvey; CME 3-628-51158-5; ECB 575; NSTC 2S47479 (BI BL, C, O).

*Notes.* Dedication to Sir Walter Scott, of Abbotsford, Baronet. List of of recently published
works (4 pp. unn.) at end of vol. headed Jan 1827.
Further edn: 2nd edn. 1827 (NSTC).


1827: 70    {?TEMPEST, Basil}.
THE VALLIES; OR, SCENES AND THOUGHTS FROM SECLUDED
LIFE. IN TWO VOLUMES.

> London: Printed for Longman, Rees, Orme, Brown, & Green, Paternoster-Row, 1827.
> I viii, 213p; II 223p. 12mo. 10s (ECB, QR).
> QR 35: 617 (Mar 1827).
> Corvey; CME 3-628-47434-5; ECB 609; NSTC 2T5149 (BI BL, C, O).

*Notes.* Prefatory dedication 'to the Lady Susan Tempest', stating how the present work at her
request has been prepared from the papers of Mr Basil Tempest. 4 pp. adv. list for 'Popular
Novels' published by Longmans, at end of vol. 2, is dated Feb. 1827.

1827: 71    [TONNA], Charlotte Elizabeth.
THE SYSTEM; A TALE OF THE WEST INDIES. BY CHARLOTTE ELIZA-
BETH, AUTHOR OF CONSISTENCY, PERSEVERANCE, OSRIC, ALLAN
M'LEOD, &C.

> London: Frederick Westley, and A. H. Davis, 10, Stationers' Court and Ave Maria Lane.
>     Sold by Westley and Tyrrell, Dublin, and Waugh and Innes, Edinburgh, 1827.
> 233p. 12mo. 5s (ECB).
> Corvey; CME 3-628-47521-X; ECB 183; NSTC 2C16478 (BI BL, C, Dt, E, O; NA MH).

*Notes.* ECB dates Mar 1827.
Further edn: 1832 (NSTC).


1827: 72    [UPHAM, Edward].
KARMATH. AN ARABIAN TALE. BY THE AUTHOR OF "RAMESES,"
AN EGYPTIAN TALE. ETC. ETC.

> London: Printed for Charles Frederick Cock, 21, Fleet Street. Sold by G. B. Whittaker,
>     Ave-Maria Lane; and John Upham, Bath, 1827.
> ix, 341p. 12mo. 8s (ECB, QR).
> QR 36: 603 (Oct 1827).
> Corvey; CME 3-628-48022-1; ECB 316; NSTC U1034 (BI BL, C, Dt, E, O).

*Notes.* Preface dated London, Apr 1827.


1827: 73    [VAN DYK, Harry Stoe].
THE GONDOLA.

> London: Lupton Relfe, 13, Cornhill, 1827.
> vi, 246p. 12mo. 8s 6d (ECB, QR).
> QR 36: 301 (June 1827); WSW II: 198.
> Corvey; CME 3-628-47595-3; ECB 236; NSTC 2V838 (BI BL, C, E, O; NA MH).

*Notes.* Dedication to James Wadmore, jun. Esq., dated Dec 1826. ECB dates Dec 1826, and
(incorrectly) sub-titles as 'A Poem'; QR as 'A Series of Tales related at Sea'.


1827: 74    VELDE, C[arl] F[ranz] van der.
ARWED GYLLENSTERNA, A TALE OF THE EARLY PART OF THE
EIGHTEENTH CENTURY; FROM THE GERMAN OF C. F. VANDER
VELDE. IN TWO VOLUMES.

> London: Printed for E. Lloyd and Son, Harley-Street, 1827.
> I iv, 247p; II 251p. 8vo. 16s (ECB, QR).
> QR 35: 617 (Mar 1827).
> BL N.501; ECB 609; NSTC 2V1964 (BI E, O; NA MH).

*Notes.* Trans. of *Arwed Gyllenstierna* (Dresden, 1823).
Further edn: 1846 (NSTC).


1827: 75    WARD, Catherine G[eorge].
THE KNIGHT OF THE WHITE BANNER; OR, THE SECRETS OF THE
CASTLE. BY MRS. MASON, LATE CATHERINE G. WARD. AUTHORESS

OF THE MYSTERIOUS MARRIAGE, THE COTTAGE ON THE CLIFF, THE FISHER'S DAUGHTER, THE FOREST GIRL &C. &C.

> London: Printed by C. Baynes, Duke Street, Lincoln's Inn Fields; for George Virtue, 26, Ivy-Lane, Paternoster-Row; Bath Street, Bristol; and St. Vincent Street, Liverpool. 1827.
> 768p, ill. 8vo.
> BL 1456.g.11; ECB 623; NSTC 2W4962 (BI C; NA MH).

*Notes.* Collates in fours.

1827: 76    [WARD, Robert Plumer].
DE VERE; OR, THE MAN OF INDEPENDENCE. BY THE AUTHOR OF TREMAINE. IN FOUR VOLUMES.

> London: Henry Colburn, New Burlington Street, 1827.
> I vii, xix, 343p; II 388p; III 338p; IV 325p. 12mo. 42s (ECB, QR); 42s boards (ER).
> ER 46: 534 (Oct 1827); QR 36: 301 (June 1827), 36: 269–85 (June 1827) full review.
> Corvey; CME 3-628-47185-0; ECB 160; NSTC 2W5292 (BI BL, C, Dt, O).

*Notes.* Dedication to Henry, Earl of Mulgrave, dated London, 6 Mar 1827.
Further edns: 2nd edn. 1827 (NUC); 3rd edn. 1827 (NSTC); 1833 (NSTC); Philadelphia 1827 (NSTC); German trans., 1827.
Facs: EC (1988).

1827: 77    WELLS, {Sarah} Wilmot.
TALES; MOURNFUL, MIRTHFUL, AND MARVELLOUS. BY MRS. WILMOT WELLS, OF MARGATE. IN THREE VOLUMES.

> London: Longman, Rees, Orme, Brown, and Green, Paternoster Row; and J. Denne, Margate, 1827.
> I xii, 216p; II 248p; III 211p. 8vo. 21s (ECB).
> Corvey; CME 3-628-51164-X; ECB 629; NSTC 2W12566 (BI BL, C, O).

*Notes.* Additional t.p. for the first story, 'The Rose-bud of Deal', states 'Written in the Spring of 1823.' 'Apologetical Preface' signed Sarah Wilmot Wells. Paradise Place, Dane Hill, Margate, Sept 1827. 'Subscribers' (*c.*115 listed), vol. 1, pp. [ix]–xii. ECB dates Oct 1827.

1827: 78    [WEST, Jane].
RINGROVE; OR, OLD FASHIONED NOTIONS. BY THE AUTHOR OF "LETTERS TO A YOUNG MAN," "A TALE OF THE TIMES," &C. &C. IN TWO VOLUMES.

> London: Printed for Longman, Rees, Orme, Brown, and Green, Paternoster-Row, 1827.
> I 413p; II 427p. 12mo. 16s (ECB); 16s boards (ER, QR).
> ER 46: 534 (Oct 1827); QR 37: 302 (Jan 1828).
> Corvey; CME 3-628-48609-2; ECB 494; NSTC 2W13752 (BI BL, C, E, O).

1827: 79    [WOODROOFFE, Anne].
MICHAEL, THE MARRIED MAN; OR, THE SEQUEL TO THE HISTORY OF MICHAEL KEMP. BY THE AUTHOR OF "SHADES OF CHARACTER," "HISTORY OF MICHAEL KEMP," &C. &C.

London: John Hatchard and Son, Piccadilly, 1827.
I 285p, ill.; II [291]–579p. 12mo. 8s (ECB).
Corvey; CME 3-628-48067-1; ECB 383; NSTC 2W30518 (BI BL, C, Dt, E, O).

*Notes.* ECB dates May 1827.

# 1828

1828: 1   ANON.

## DE BEAUVOIR; OR, SECOND LOVE. IN THREE VOLUMES.

London: Printed for Longman, Rees, Orme, Brown, and Green, Paternoster-Row, 1828.
I 399p; II 431p; III 447p. 12mo. 24s (ECB, QR); 24s boards (ER).
ER 47: 524 (May 1828); QR 37: 581 (Mar 1828).
Corvey; CME 3-628-47186-9; ECB 156; NSTC 2D6907 (BI BL, C, E, NCu, O; NA DLC, MH).

1828: 2   ANON.

## DE LACY; OR, PASSION'S SLAVE. A NOVEL. IN THREE VOLUMES. BY THE AUTHOR OF MODES OF LIFE, OR TOWN AND COUNTRY.

London: Printed for A. K. Newman and Co., 1828.
I 298p; II 295p; III 316p. 12mo. 18s (ECB, QR).
QR 37: 302 (Jan 1828).
Corvey; CME 3-628-47889-8; ECB 157; NSTC 2D7970 (BI BL, C, E, O; NA DLC).

*Notes.* ECB dates Oct 1827.

1828: 3   ANON.

## EDMUND O'HARA, AN IRISH TALE; BY THE AUTHOR OF "ELLMER CASTLE."

Dublin: William Curry, jun. and Co. 9, Upper Sackville-Street, 1828.
358p, ill. 12mo. 3s 6d (ECB).
Corvey; CME 3-628-47487-6; ECB 179; NSTC 2O2257 (BI BL, O).

*Notes.* ECB dates Jan 1829, and gives Hurst as second publisher (but not discovered in this form).

1828: 4   ANON.

## THE HEBREW, A SKETCH IN THE NINETEENTH CENTURY: WITH THE DREAM OF SAINT KENYA.

Edinburgh: Printed for W. Blackwood, and T. Cadell, Strand, London, 1828.
viii, 232p. 12mo. 5s 6d (ECB).
Corvey; CME 3-628-51037-6; ECB 262; NSTC 2H15773 (BI BL, E, O).

*Notes.* Pp. [221]–232 contain 'The Dream of Saint Kenya' (poem). ECB dates Mar 1828.

1828: 5   ANON.

**A HUNDRED YEARS HENCE; OR THE MEMOIRS OF CHARLES, LORD MORESBY, WRITTEN BY HIMSELF.**

> London: Published by Longman, Rees, Orme, Brown, and Green, Paternoster-Row, 1828.
> iv, 210p. 12mo. 6s (ECB).
> Corvey; CME 3-628-47785-9; ECB 288; NSTC 2M36097 (BI BL, C, O).

*Notes.* ECB dates Apr 1828. Collates in sixes.

1828: 6   ANON.

**THE LAIRDS OF FIFE. IN THREE VOLUMES.**

> Edinburgh: Printed for Constable & Co. and Hurst, Chance & Co. London, 1828.
> I 309p; II 302p; III 309p. 8vo. 24s (ECB, QR).
> QR 38: 601 (Oct 1828).
> Corvey; CME 3-628-47893-6; ECB 326; NSTC 2F5653 (BI BL, C, E; NA MH).

1828: 7   ANON.

**MARCELLA: OR, THE MISSIONARY ABROAD AND AT HOME. CONTAINING SKETCHES AND INCIDENTS FROM LIFE. IN TWO VOLUMES.**

> London: J. Hatchard and Son, 187, Piccadilly, 1828.
> I 343p; II 287p. 12mo. 15s (ECB, QR).
> QR 38: 601 (Oct 1828).
> Corvey; CME 3-628-48084-1; ECB 367; NSTC 2M13848 (BI BL, C, E, O).

*Notes.* Notice (1 p. unn.) after t.p. lists donations (totalling £25) to be made to four Charities, 'If this Work should pass through a Second Edition'.

1828: 8   ANON.

**MARLY; OR, A PLANTER'S LIFE IN JAMAICA.**

> Glasgow: Published by Richard Griffin & Co. and Hunt and Clarke, London, 1828.
> 363p. 8vo. 9s (ECB).
> Corvey; CME 3-628-48292-5; ECB 368; NSTC 2M14771 (BI BL, C; NA DLC).

*Notes.* ECB dates Mar 1828. Collates in fours.
Further edns: 1828 (NSTC); 1831 (NSTC).

1828: 9   ANON.

**MARY HARLAND; OR, THE JOURNEY TO LONDON. A TALE OF HUMBLE LIFE.**

> Edinburgh: Published by Oliver & Boyd, Tweeddale Court; and Geo. B. Whittaker, London, 1828.
> 320p. 18mo. 4s (ECB).
> BL 1210.c.18(2); ECB 371; NSTC 2H8444.

*Notes.* ECB dates Mar 1828.

1828: 10   ANON.

### THE MORTIMERS, OR THE VALE OF MACHYNLLAETH.

> London: Printed for R. P. Moore, Store Street, Bedford Square, 1828.
> I vi, 316p; II 356p; III 317p. 12mo. 21s (ECB); 21s boards (ER).
> ER 47: 524 (May 1828).
> Corvey; CME 3-628-48336-0; ECB 398; NSTC 2M38166 (BI BL, C).

1828: 11   ANON.

### THE NIGHT WATCH; OR, TALES OF THE SEA. IN TWO VOLUMES.

> London: Henry Colburn, New Burlington Street, 1828.
> I vii, xi, 328p; II viii, 340p. 12mo. 18s (ECB).
> Corvey; CME 3-628-48227-5; ECB 414; NSTC 2N8498 (BI BL, C, E, O; NA DLC, MH).

*Notes.* ECB dates Mar 1828.

1828: 12   ANON.

### THE RECTOR OF OVERTON, A NOVEL. IN THREE VOLUMES.

> London: Fisher, Son, and Co. 38, Newgate Street, 1828.
> I iv, 310p; II 279p; III 306p. 12mo. 21s (ECB).
> QR 38: 303 (July 1828).
> Corvey; CME 3-628-48601-7; ECB 482; NSTC 2O6742 (BI BL, C, E).

*Notes.* Dedication to Mrs Watts Russel. Collates in sixes.
Further edn: 2nd edn. 1828 (NSTC).

1828: 13   ANON.

### THE SUBALTERN'S LOG BOOK: INCLUDING ANECDOTES OF WELL KNOWN MILITARY CHARACTERS. IN TWO VOLUMES.

> London: James Ridgway, 169, Piccadilly, 1828.
> I xiv, 304p; II 311p. 8vo. 21s (ECB).
> Corvey; CME 3-628-48686-6; ECB 568; NSTC 2S45665 (BI BL, C, E).

*Notes.* Sometimes attributed, but erroneously, to George Robert Gleig. Dedication to Conrad Vetter, Esq. ECB dates 1827.
Further edn: New York 1829 (NSTC).

1828: 14   ANON.

### THE TOWER OF CLANMALLOCH. A ROMANCE.

> Dublin: Saunders and Kempston, 36, Nassau-Street, 1828.
> viii, 317p. 8vo. 7s (ECB).
> Corvey; CME 3-628-48765-X; ECB 595; NSTC 2T15124 (BI BL).

*Notes.* ECB cites Newman edn., 1828, but not discovered in this form.

1828: 15   ANON.

### VICTORIA, OR THE MALE COQUETTE AND THE DUPE. IN THREE VOLUMES.

> London: J. Robins and Co. Ivy Lane, Paternoster-Row, and Upper Ormond Quay, Dublin, 1828.

I 269p; II 253p; III 284p. 12mo. 18s (ECB); 18s boards (ER).
ER 48: 538 (Dec 1828).
Corvey; CME 3-628-48914-8; ECB 613; NSTC 2V3385 (BI BL, C, E, O).

1828: 16    [BANIM, John].
THE ANGLO-IRISH OF THE NINETEENTH CENTURY. A NOVEL. IN
THREE VOLUMES.

London: Henry Colburn, New Burlington Street, 1828.
I 308p; II 305p; III 303p. 12mo. 31s 6d (ECB, QR); 31s 6d boards (ER).
ER 48: 538 (Dec 1828); QR 38: 601 (Oct 1828), 39: 253 (Jan 1829).
Corvey; CME 3-628-47060-9; ECB 19; NSTC 2B6659 (BI BL, C, Dt, E, O; NA MH).

*Notes.* Further edns: 1838 (NUC); French trans., 1829.

1828: 17    [BANIM, John and Michael].
THE CROPPY; A TALE OF 1798. BY THE AUTHORS OF "THE O'HARA
TALES," "THE NOWLANS," AND "THE BOYNE WATER." IN THREE
VOLUMES.

London: Henry Colburn, New Burlington Street, 1828.
I 314p; II 299p; III 318p. 12mo. 31s 6d (ECB); 31s 6d boards (ER).
ER 47: 524 (May 1828).
Corvey; CME 3-628-47353-5; ECB 145; NSTC 2B6685 (BI BL, C, Dt, E, O; NA MH).

*Notes.* Dedication 'to Sheffield Grace, Esq, F.S.A. &c.', signed 'The O'Hara Family'.
Further edns: 1834 (NUC); Philadelphia 1839 (NUC); French trans., 1833.
Facs: IAN (1979).

1828: 18    [BEAZLEY, Samuel].
THE ROUÉ. IN THREE VOLUMES.

London: Henry Colburn, New Burlington Street, 1828.
I 350p; II 362p; III 408p. 12mo. 31s 6d (ECB); 31s 6d boards (ER).
ER 47: 524 (May 1828).
Corvey; CME 3-628-48556-8; ECB 504; NSTC 2B13992 (BI BL, C, E, O; NA DLC, MH).

*Notes.* Further edn: New York 1828 (NSTC).

1828: 19    [BECKE, Richard].
THE PRIMA DONNA. A TALE OF TO-DAY.

London: Edward Bull, Holles Street, 1828.
vi, 320p. 12mo. 10s 6d (ECB).
Corvey; CME 3-628-54705-9; ECB 469; NSTC 2B14142 (BI BL, C, E, O).

*Notes.* ECB dates May 1828.

1828: 20    [BOADEN, James].
THE MAN OF TWO LIVES. A NARRATIVE WRITTEN BY HIMSELF. IN
TWO VOLUMES.

London: Henry Colburn, New Burlington Street, 1828.

I 273p; II 303p. 12mo. 18s (ECB).

Corvey; CME 3-628-48082-5; ECB 365; NSTC 2B38843 (BI BL, C, E, O; NA DLC, MH).

*Notes.* Signed at end Edward Sydenham (fictional). ECB dates Nov 1828.

Further edn: Boston 1829 (NSTC).

1828: 21   [BRAY, Anna Eliza].

THE PROTESTANT; A TALE OF THE REIGN OF QUEEN MARY. BY THE AUTHOR OF 'DE FOIX', 'THE WHITE HOODS,' &C. IN THREE VOLUMES.

London: Henry Colburn, New Burlington Street, 1828.

I 344p; II 326p; III 281p. 12mo. 31s 6d (ECB); 31s 6d boards (ER).

ER 48: 538 (Dec 1828); QR 39: 253 (Jan 1829).

Corvey; CME 3-628-48418-9; ECB 72; NSTC 2P27826 (BI BL, C, E, O; NA DLC, MH).

*Notes.* Wolff (I, 160; Item 792), citing the author's *Autobiography*, notes how this (her third) novel was inspired by Foxe's *Book of Martyrs*; it was begun 18 Sept, finished 19 Nov 1827, and ready for the press on 31 Jan 1828. Colburn made better terms than Longman, offering £200 'in advance of half profits' and taking the risk. The book appeared in Nov 1828, and Colburn took advantage of the anti-Catholic feeling prevalent on the eve of the Catholic Emancipation Act to puff the book as political propaganda, which distressed Mrs Bray.

Further edns: 1833 (NUC); New York 1829 (NUC).

1828: 22   BRAY, Anna Eliza.

THE WHITE HOODS; AN HISTORICAL ROMANCE. BY ANNA ELIZA BRAY, LATE MRS. CHARLES STOTHARD, AUTHOR OF "DE FOIX;" "LETTERS WRITTEN DURING A TOUR THROUGH NORMANDY AND BRITANNY;" "MEMOIRS OF THE LATE CHARLES A. STOTHARD, F.S.A." &C. &C. IN THREE VOLUMES.

London: Printed for Longman, Rees, Orme, Brown, and Green, Paternoster-Row, 1828.

I 309p; II 299p; III 371p. 8vo. 31s 6d (ECB); 31s 6d boards (ER).

ER 47: 525 (May 1828); QR 37: 581 (Mar 1828).

Corvey; CME 3-628-47193-1; ECB 72; NSTC 2S42928 (BI BL, C, O; NA MH).

*Notes.* 'Advertisement' dated Vicarage, Tavistock, Devon, 30 Nov 1826. Finished in July 1826, according to the author's *Autobiography*, and published 11 Feb 1828 (see Wolff, Item 798).

Further edns: 1833 (NUC); 1845 (NUC); French trans., 1828; German trans., 1834 [as *Die Weißkappen, oder Anna von Gent*, published as vols. 4–6 of Bray's *Historische Romane* (RS)].

1828: 23   [BRISTOW, Amelia].

EMMA DE LISSAU; A NARRATIVE OF STRIKING VICISSITUDES, AND PECULIAR TRIALS; WITH EXPLANATORY NOTES, ILLUSTRATIVE OF THE MANNERS AND CUSTOMS OF THE JEWS. BY THE AUTHOR OF "SOPHIA DE LISSAU," "ELIZABETH ALLEN," &C. &C. IN TWO VOLUMES.

London: Published by T. Gardiner and Son, Princes Street, Cavendish Square. Sold by

Hatchard and Son, Piccadilly; Simpkin and Marshall, Stationers' Hall Court, and all other Booksellers, 1828.

I viii, 269p; II viii, 258p. 12mo. 12s (ECB).

Corvey; CME 3-628-47560-0; ECB 186; NSTC 2L17104 (BI BL, C, O).

*Notes.* Preface dated Pimlico, 30 May 1828. 'List of Subscribers' (*c.* 210 listed), 8 pp. unn., at end of vol. 2. ECB dates June 1828. Collates in sixes.

Further edns: 2nd edn. 1829 (NSTC); 3rd edn. 1830 (NSTC); 1837 (NUC); 6th edn. 1847 (NUC).

1828: 24    [BULWER LYTTON, Edward George].
**PELHAM; OR, THE ADVENTURES OF A GENTLEMAN. IN THREE VOLUMES.**

London: Henry Colburn, New Burlington Street, 1828.

I 339p; II 316p; III 366p. 12mo. 31s 6d (ECB, QR).

QR 38: 303 (July 1828).

Corvey; CME 3-628-47171-0; ECB 440; NSTC 2B57442 (BI BL, C, Dt, E, O; NA DLC, MH).

*Notes.* Further edns: 2nd edn. 1828 (NSTC); 1833 (NSTC); 1839 (NSTC); 1849 (NSTC); New York 1829 (NSTC); French trans., 1828; German trans., 1829.

1828: 25    [BUNBURY, Selina].
**THE ABBEY OF INNISMOYLE: A STORY OF ANOTHER CENTURY. BY THE AUTHOR OF "EARLY RECOLLECTIONS," "A VISIT TO MY BIRTH-PLACE," &C.**

Dublin: William Curry, jun. and Co. 9, Upper Sackville-Street, 1828.

333p, ill. 12mo. 3s 6d (ECB).

Corvey; CME 3-628-47001-3; ECB 1; NSTC 2A408 (BI C, Dt).

*Notes.* ECB gives publisher as Orr, and dates July 1828.

Further edn: 2nd edn. 1829 (Jarndyce XCIV, Item 268).

1828: 26    [BURDETT, Mrs. C. D.].
**AT HOME. A NOVEL. BY THE AUTHOR OF ENGLISH FASHIONABLES ABROAD. IN THREE VOLUMES.**

London: Henry Colburn, New Burlington Street, 1828.

I 300p; II 300p; III 359p. 12mo. 31s 6d (ECB); 31s 6d boards (ER).

ER 48: 538 (Dec 1828).

Corvey; CME 3-628-47077-3; ECB 30; NSTC 2A18110 (BI BL, C, E; NA MH).

*Notes.* Drop-head titles and running-titles read: 'English Fashionables At Home'.

1828: 27    CADDICK, Mrs. [H. C.].
**TALES OF THE AFFECTIONS: BEING SKETCHES FROM REAL LIFE. BY MRS. CADDICK.**

London: Longman, Rees, Orme, Brown, and Green; and T. Sowler, Manchester, n.d. [1828].

v, 199p. 8vo. 7s (ECB, QR).

QR 38: 601 (Oct 1828).

BL N.680(2); CME 3-628-47182-6; ECB 92; NSTC 2C945 (BI C, O).

*Notes.* ECB dates July 1828.

1828: 28    [CARNE, John].
## TALES OF THE WEST. BY THE AUTHOR OF LETTERS FROM THE EAST. IN TWO VOLUMES.

London: Henry Colburn, New Burlington Street, 1828.

I 315p; II 319p. 12mo. 21s (ECB); 18s (QR).

QR 37: 581 (Mar 1828).

Corvey; CME 3-628-51166-6; ECB 98; NSTC 2C8059 (BI BL, C, O; NA DLC, MH).

*Notes.* Pagination in vol. 1 runs incorrectly from 314 to 317 (i.e. no pp. 315 and 316).

Further edn: New York 1828 (NUC).

1828: 29    [CARRINGTON, Edmund Frederick John].
## CONFESSIONS OF AN OLD MAID. IN THREE VOLUMES.

London: Henry Colburn, New Burlington Street, 1828.

I 295p; II 294p; III 291p. 12mo. 28s 6d (ECB).

Corvey; CME 3-628-47314-4; ECB 130; NSTC 2C9602 (BI BL, C, E, O; NA MH).

*Notes.* ECB dates Jan 1828.

1828: 30    [CLARKE, Hewson].
## FELICIAN ALPHERY; OR, THE FORTUNES OF THE RALEIGH FAMILY. BY THE AUTHOR OF "HERWALD DE WAKE." IN THREE VOLUMES.

London: Printed for A. K. Newman and Co., 1828.

I 268p; II 248p; III 254p. 12mo. 16s 6d (ECB); 16s 6d boards (ER).

ER 48: 538 (Dec 1828).

Corvey; CME 3-628-47484-1; ECB 202; NSTC 2C24212 (BI BL, C, E, O).

1828: 31    [CORBETT, Marion and Margaret].
## TALES AND LEGENDS. BY THE AUTHORS OF "THE ODD VOLUME," &C. IN THREE VOLUMES.

Edinburgh: Printed for Cadell and Co.; and Simpkin and Marshall, London, 1828.

I 352p; II 358p; III 404p. 8vo. 31s 6d (ECB, ER).

ER 47: 524 (May 1828).

Corvey; CME 3-628-51146-1; ECB 575; NSTC 2C37699 (BI BL, C, Dt, E; NA MH).

1828: 32    [CROLY, George].
## SALATHIEL. A STORY OF THE PAST, THE PRESENT, AND THE FUTURE. IN THREE VOLUMES.

London: Henry Colburn, New Burlington Street, 1828.

I viii, 338p; II 324p; III 417p. 12mo. 31s 6d (ECB).

Corvey; CME 3-628-48505-3; ECB 512; NSTC 2C43772 (BI BL, Dt, NCu, O; NA MH).

*Notes.* Dedication to the Duke of Newcastle. ECB dates Mar 1828.

Further edns: 2nd edn. 1828 (NSTC); 1829 (NSTC); 1842 (NSTC); New York 1828 (NUC); French trans., 1828 [as *Salathiel, ou le juif-errant* (BN)]; German trans., 1829 [as *Salathiel, oder Memoiren des ewigen Juden*; also as *Der ewige Jude, eine historische Novelle der Vorzeit* (RS)].

1828: 33    [CROLY, George].
## TALES OF THE GREAT ST. BERNARD. IN THREE VOLUMES.

> London: Henry Colburn, New Burlington Street, 1828.
> I 336p; II 336p; III 321p. 12mo. 31s 6d (ECB).
> BL Cup.402.d.3; ECB 576; NSTC 2C43779 (BI Dt, O).

*Notes.* S.l. of BL copy reads 'Second Edition', but no suggestion of this in the text itself. ECB dates Nov 1828.

Further edns: 2nd edn. 1829 (Corvey), CME 3-628-51149-6; New York 1829 (NSTC).

1828: 34    [?CROWE, Eyre Evans or ?PHIPPS, Constantine Henry, Marquis of Normanby].
## THE ENGLISH IN FRANCE. BY THE AUTHOR OF "THE ENGLISH IN ITALY." IN THREE VOLUMES.

> London: Saunders and Otley, Conduit Street, 1828.
> I 327p; II 357p; III 338p. 12mo. 31s 6d (ECB); 31s 6d boards (ER).
> ER 47: 524 (May 1828).
> Corvey; CME 3-628-47828-6; ECB 187; NSTC 2P15296 (BI BL, C, Dt, E; NA MH).

*Notes.* Additional unn. page bound at end of vol. 3, stating: 'Should any errors be discovered in the following pages, the reader is requested to consider them as arising from the author's absence from England, and the consequent impossibility of his personal correction of the press.' The case for attribution to Crowe, rather than to Phipps, is made by Wolff (I, 323): for further details, see *The English in Italy* (1825: 23).

Further edns: 2nd edn. 1828 (NSTC); Philadelphia 1829 (NUC).

1828: 35    CUNNINGHAM, Allan.
## SIR MICHAEL SCOTT, A ROMANCE, BY ALLAN CUNNINGHAM. IN THREE VOLUMES.

> London: Henry Colburn, New Burlington-Street, 1828.
> I viii, 296p; II 307p; III 307p. 12mo. 28s 6d (ECB); 28s 6d boards (ER).
> ER 47: 525 (May 1828).
> Corvey; CME 3-628-47363-2; ECB 147; NSTC 2C46747 (BI BL, C, Dt, E, O; NA MH).

*Notes.* ECB dates Nov 1827.

Further edn: German trans., 1829.

1828: 36    DAGLEY, Elizabeth Frances.
## THE BIRTHDAY: WITH OTHER TALES. BY ELIZABETH FRANCES DAGLEY, AUTHORESS OF "FAIRY FAVOURS."

> London: James Bulcock, 163, Strand, 1828.

vi, 270p, ill. 8vo. 6s (ECB).
Corvey; CME 3-628-51014-7; ECB 149; NSTC 2D569 (BI BL, C, O).

*Notes.* Additional engraved t.p., where the title appears as 'The Birth-day and other Tales, by Eliz[th] Frances Dagley, author of "Fairy Favors [*sic*]" &c.'. Dedication to Mrs Hemans. 13 children-orientated tales. ECB dates Feb 1828.

1828: 37  DAVENPORT, Selina.
ITALIAN VENGEANCE AND ENGLISH FORBEARANCE. A ROMANCE. BY SELINA DAVENPORT, AUTHOR OF THE HYPOCRITE, OR MODERN JANUS; LEAP YEAR; ANGEL'S FORM AND DEVIL'S HEART: ORIGINAL OF THE MINIATURE; DONALD MONTEITH, &C. &C.

London: A. K. Newman & Co. Leadenhall-Street, 1828.
I 274p; II 274p; III 270p. 12mo. 16s 6d (ECB).
Corvey; CME 3-628-47427-2; ECB 153; NSTC 2D3610 (BI BL, C, E, O).

*Notes.* ECB dates Mar 1828.

1828: 38  [?DEALE, . . . or ?LUTTRELL, Henry].
LIFE IN THE WEST; OR, THE CURTAIN DRAWN. A NOVEL. DEDICATED, BY PERMISSION, TO THE RIGHT HON. ROBERT PEEL, M.P. CONTAINING SKETCHES, SCENES, CONVERSATIONS, AND ANECDOTES OF THE LAST IMPORTANCE TO FAMILIES, AND MEN OF RANK, FASHION, AND FORTUNE. FOUNDED ON FACTS. BY A FLAT ENLIGHTENED. IN TWO VOLUMES.

London: C. Chapple, Royal Library, 59, Pall-Mall, 1828.
I x, 309p; II 318p. 12mo. 21s (ECB); 21s boards (ER).
ER 47: 525 (May 1828).
Corvey; CME 3-628-48103-1; ECB 345; NSTC 2D6460 (BI BL, C, O; NA MH).

*Notes.* Wolff (see Item 7637; V, 35–6) doubts the attribution to Deale found in Block, NSTC, and NUC. As he notes, *Craven Derby, or the Lordship by Tenure* (1832/33), which carries on its t.p. 'by the author of Crockford's: or Life in the West', is ascribed to Henry Luttrell (as as an alternative to '—— Deale') in H & L. Dedication to the Right Hon. Robert Peel, M.P., dated London, 1 Dec 1827. ECB dates Nov 1827.
Further edns: 2nd edn. 1828, as *Crockford's; or, Life in the West* (NSTC); 3rd edn. 1828 (NSTC); New York 1828 (NSTC).

1828: 39  [DERENZY, Margaret G.].
THE OLD IRISH KNIGHT: A MILESIAN TALE OF THE FIFTH CENTURY. BY THE AUTHOR OF "A WHISPER TO A NEWLY-MARRIED PAIR," "PARNASSIAN GEOGRAPHY," &C.

London: Printed for Poole and Edwards, (Successors to Scatcherd and Letterman,) 12, Ave-Maria Lane, 1828.
186p. 12mo. 4s (ECB).
Corvey; CME 3-628-48291-7; ECB 422; NSTC 2D9981 (BI BL, C, E).

*Notes.* ECB dates Feb 1828.

1828: 40    [DISRAELI, Benjamin, Earl of Beaconsfield].
THE VOYAGE OF CAPTAIN POPANILLA. BY THE AUTHOR OF
"VIVIAN GREY."

> London: Henry Colburn, New Burlington Street, 1828.
> viii, 243p. 12mo. 9s 6d (ECB); 7s (QR).
> QR 38: 303 (July 1828).
> Corvey; CME 3-628-48810-9; ECB 617; NSTC 2D14249 (BI BL, C, E, O; NA MH).

*Notes.* Dedication 'to Robert Ward, Esq., &c. &c. &c. of Chesham Woburn Hall, in the
County of Bucks'.
Further edns: 1829 (NSTC); Philadelphia 1828 (Jarndyce CX, Item 313).


1828: 41    DUBOIS, Henr[i] L[eopold] (*trans.?*).
THE HISTORY OF A FRENCH DAGGER; AN ANECDOTE OF THE REVO-
LUTION. TRANSLATED FROM THE FRENCH, BY HENRY L. DUBOIS,
LATE SURGEON OF CAVALRY IN THE IMPERIAL ARMY.

> London: Printed for the Author, by G. Duckworth, 76, Fleet-Street, 1828.
> I iv, xvi, 200p; II 199p. 12mo.
> BL 1208.k.2; NSTC 2D20843.

*Notes.* No French original discovered. Dedication 'To my Subscribers', vol. 1, pp. iii–iv. 'List
of Subscribers' (*c.*330 names), vol. 1, pp. [i]–xvi (2nd sequence).


1828: 42    FITZ-GEORGE, George [pseud.?].
MONTAUBAN AND THE MONK HILARIO. A LEGEND OF THE THIR-
TEENTH CENTURY. BY GEORGE FITZ-GEORGE, ESQ. IN THREE
VOLUMES.

> London: Printed for A. K. Newman and Co., 1828.
> I xxii, 327p; II 310p; III 326p. 12mo. 18s (ECB).
> Corvey; CME 3-628-47603-8; ECB 207; NSTC 2F7359 (BI BL, E).

*Notes.* 'Preface, by the Editor', vol. 1, pp. [i]–xxii, signed George Fitz-George, 10 Oct 1827.
Continuous roman and arabic pagination in vol. 1, with novel proper beginning at p. [23].
ECB dates Oct 1827.


1828: 43    [FRASER, James Baillie].
THE KUZZILBASH. A TALE OF KHORASAN. IN THREE VOLUMES.

> London: Henry Colburn, New Burlington Street, 1828.
> I 348p; II 359p; III 332p. 12mo. 31s 6d (ECB); 31s 6d boards (ER).
> ER 47: 524 (May 1828); QR 39: 73–99 (Jan 1829) full review.
> Corvey; CME 3-628-49016-2; ECB 325; NSTC 2F14798 (BI BL, C, E, O; NA DLC, MH).

*Notes.* ECB dates 1826, but no copy with this imprint date discovered. Reviewed in QR
(Jan 1829) together with Morier's *The Adventures of Hajji Baba, of Ispahan, in England* (1828: 60).


1828: 44    [GASPEY, Thomas].
HISTORY OF GEORGE GODFREY. WRITTEN BY HIMSELF. IN THREE
VOLUMES.

London: Henry Colburn, New Burlington Street, 1828.
I vii, 351p; II viii, 287p; III viii, 306p. 12mo. 28s 6d (ECB).
Corvey; CME 3-628-47699-2; ECB 273; NSTC 2G3291 (BI BL, C, E, O; NA MH).

*Notes.* ECB dates Mar 1828.

1828: 45    [GREY, Elizabeth Caroline].
**DE LISLE; OR, THE SENSITIVE MAN. IN THREE VOLUMES.**

London: Edward Bull, Holles Street, 1828.
I 325p; II 416p; III 425p. 12mo. 31s 6d (ECB); 31s 6d boards (ER); 28s (QR).
ER 47: 525 (May 1828); QR 37: 581 (Mar 1828).
Corvey; CME 3-628-48031-0; ECB 158; NSTC 2G22142 (BI O).

*Notes.* Also issued with the same year imprint as *De Lisle; or, the Distrustful Man.* ER and QR both list title as in the present entry. ECB gives variant title and dates Dec 1827. BL N.572-73, which has the variant title, is similar in all other respects: for other libraries holding this version see NSTC 2G22141.
Further edn: New York 1828 (NUC).

1828: 46    [HARDING, Anne Raikes].
**EXPERIENCE. A TALE FOR ALL AGES. BY THE AUTHOR OF CORREC-TION, REALITIES, DISSIPATION, &C. IN FOUR VOLUMES.**

London: Printed for A. K. Newman and Co., 1828.
I 260p; II 241p; III 256p; IV 233p. 12mo. 22s (ECB); 22s boards (ER).
ER 48: 538 (Dec 1828); QR 38: 601 (Oct 1828).
Corvey; CME 3-628-47617-8; ECB 196; NSTC 2H7488 (BI BL, C, E, O).

1828: 47    HARVEY, Jane.
**THE AMBASSADOR'S SECRETARY. A TALE. IN FOUR VOLUMES. BY JANE HARVEY, AUTHOR OF BROUGHAM CASTLE; ETHELIA; MOUNTALYTH; RECORDS OF A NOBLE FAMILY; SINGULARITY; WARKFIELD CASTLE, &C.**

London: Printed for A. K. Newman and Co., 1828.
I 262p; II 249p; III 241p; IV 250p. 12mo. 22s (ECB); 22s boards (ER).
ER 47: 525 (May 1828).
Corvey; CME 3-628-47631-3; ECB 15; NSTC 2H11034 (BI BL, C, E, O).

*Notes.* ECB dates Nov 1827.

1828: 48    [HATTON, Anne Julia Kemble].
**UNCLE PEREGRINE'S HEIRESS. A NOVEL. BY ANN OF SWANSEA, AUTHOR OF GUILTY OR NOT GUILTY; WOMAN'S A RIDDLE; DEEDS OF THE OLDEN TIME; GONZALO DE BALDIVIA; CONVICTION, &C. IN FIVE VOLUMES.**

London: Printed for A. K. Newman and Co., 1828.
I 324p; II 351p; III 346p; IV 337p; V 364p. 12mo. 30s (ECB); 30s boards (ER).
ER 47: 525 (May 1828).
Corvey; CME 3-628-48788-9; ECB 20; NSTC 2A13196 (BI BL, C, E, O).

*Notes.* Dedication 'to W. M'Cready, Esq., Manager of the Theatre Royal, Bristol; Cardiff and Swansea theatres', signed 'Ann of Swansea, Swansea, January 22, 1828, 22, Orchard-Street'.

1828: 49   [HAY, William].
**TALES AND SKETCHES, BY JACOB RUDDIMAN, A.M. OF MARIS-CHAL COLLEGE, ABERDEEN.**

> Edinburgh: John Anderson, jun. 55, North Bridge Street, and Simpkin & Marshall, London, 1828.
> 300p. 8vo. 10s 6d (ECB).
> Corvey; CME 3-628-51124-0; ECB 505; NSTC 2R20055 (BI BL, C, Dt, E, O; NA MH).

*Notes.* 18 tales. ECB dates May 1828.

1828: 50   [HOCKLEY, William Browne].
**THE ENGLISH IN INDIA. BY THE AUTHOR OF "PANDURANG HARI," AND "THE ZENANA." IN THREE VOLUMES.**

> London: Printed for W. Simpkin and R. Marshall, Stationers'-Hall Court, 1828.
> I vii, 328p; II 382p; III 353p. 12mo. 24s (ECB, QR); 24s boards (ER).
> ER 47: 525 (May 1828); QR 37: 581 (Mar 1828).
> Corvey; CME 3-628-47829-4; ECB 187; NSTC 2H24560 (BI BL, C, O).

*Notes.* Further edn: 1835 (NUC).

1828: 51   [HOFLAND, Barbara].
**KATHERINE. A TALE. IN FOUR VOLUMES.**

> London: A. K. Newman & Co. Leadenhall-Street, 1828.
> I 247p; II 231p; III 234p; IV 240p. 12mo. 22s (ECB).
> Corvey; CME 3-628-48004-3; ECB 275; NSTC 2H29400 (BI BL, C, E, O).

*Notes.* ECB dates July 1828.

**HOGG, James, THE SUICIDE'S GRAVE**
See 1824: 50

1828: 52   [HOOK, Theodore Edward].
**SAYINGS AND DOINGS; OR SKETCHES FROM LIFE. THIRD SERIES. IN THREE VOLUMES.**

> London: Henry Colburn, New Burlington Street, 1828.
> I 378p; II 326p; III 333p. 12mo. 31s 6d (ECB, QR); 31s 6d boards (ER).
> ER 47: 525 (May 1828); QR 37: 581 (Mar 1828).
> Corvey; CME 3-628-48529-0; ECB 516; NSTC 2H28950 (BI BL, C, E, O).

*Notes.* 'Advertisement' dated London, 24 Jan 1828.
Further edns: 1834 (NUC); 1839 (NSTC); Philadelphia 1828 (NUC).

1828: 53   [?HUISH, Robert or ?MAGINN, William].
**THE RED BARN, A TALE, FOUNDED ON FACT.**

> London: Printed for Knight and Lacey, 55, Paternoster-Row, and sold by all Book-sellers, 1828.

vi, 716p, ill. 8vo.

BL 1509/24; NSTC 2H35895 (BI O; NA MH).

*Notes.* BLC attributes this copy to Robert Huish, and another (C.140.c.25) to William Maginn. Sadleir (Item 1521), notes that 'Halkett & Laing attribute the work to William Maginn on the strength of a paragraph by Charles Welch, published in *The Library Journal*, vol. v, p. 88, March 1880', adding that Welch's identification cannot be disregarded, even though DNB and several other bibliographers make no mention of it. Folding facsimile letter between pages 612 and 613; pp. [617]–716 contain 'Trial of William Corder, for the Murder of Maria Marten' plus other supplementary material. Collates in fours.

Further edn: 1831 (NSTC).

1828: 54   LATHOM, Francis.

**YOUNG JOHN BULL; OR, BORN ABROAD AND BRED AT HOME. A NOVEL. BY FRANCIS LATHOM, AUTHOR OF THE MYSTERIOUS FREEBOOTER; PUZZLED AND PLEASED; LONDON; HUMAN BEINGS; VERY STRANGE BUT VERY TRUE; ASTONISHMENT; POLISH BANDIT; UNKNOWN; FATAL VOW; MIDNIGHT BELL; LIVE AND LEARN; MEN AND MANNERS; &C. &C. IN THREE VOLUMES.**

London: A. K. Newman & Co. Leadenhall-Street, 1828.

I viii, 327p; II 286p; III 283p. 12mo. 18s (ECB).

Corvey; CME 3-628-47966-5; ECB 331; NSTC 2L5041 (BI BL, C, E, O).

*Notes.* 'The Author's Address to the Reader', dated Philadelphia, 1 Mar 1828. ECB dates Apr 1828.

1828: 55   [LISTER, Thomas Henry].

**HERBERT LACY. BY THE AUTHOR OF GRANBY. IN THREE VOLUMES.**

London: Henry Colburn, New Burlington Street, 1828.

I vi, 305p; II 289p; III 285p. 12mo. 31s 6d (ECB, QR); 31s 6d boards (ER).

ER 47: 525 (May 1828); QR 37: 581 (Mar 1828).

Corvey; CME 3-628-47706-9; ECB 265; NSTC 2L17196 (BI BL, C, E, O).

*Notes.* Dedication 'to Thomas Lister, Esq. of Armitage Park, Staffordshire', signed 'Your very affectionate son, the author'. ECB dates Dec 1827.

Further edn: Philadelphia 1828 (NSTC).

LUTTRELL, Henry

See DEALE

1828: 56   M'CHRONICLE, Ronald [pseud.].

**LEGENDS OF SCOTLAND. THIRD SERIES. IN THREE VOLUMES. CONTAINING EDWARD FALCONER. BY RONALD M'CHRONICLE, ESQ.**

London: A. K. Newman & Co. Leadenhall-Street, 1828.

I 241p; II 233p; III 226p. 12mo.

Corvey; CME 3-628-48070-1; ECB 358; NSTC 2M1928 (BI BL, C, Dt, E, O).

*Notes.* ABu copy s.l. gives price as 16s 6d. ECB lists three series, 49s 6d.

MAGINN, William
See HUISH, Robert

1828: 57    MANZONI, Alessandro; [SWAN, Charles (*trans.*)].
THE BETROTHED LOVERS; A MILANESE TALE OF THE XVIIth. CEN-
TURY: TRANSLATED FROM THE ITALIAN OF ALESSANDRO MAN-
ZONI. IN THREE VOLUMES.
> Pisa: Nicolo Capurro, Lung Arno, 1828.
> I xvii, 390p; II 397p; III 347p. 12mo. 21s (ECB); 21s boards (ER).
> ER 48: 538 (Dec 1828); QR 38: 303 (July 1828).
> BL 635.f.28; ECB 367; NSTC 2M13705 (BI O).

*Notes.* Trans. of *I promessi sposi* (Milan 1825–6, but not published until 1827). ECB lists Riv-
ington as publisher, and dates June 1828; along with the review listings, this indicates that
Swan's translation had a full circulation in Britain.
Further edns: 1834 (NSTC, another trans.); 1845 (NSTC, another trans.).

**MITFORD, Mary Russell, OUR VILLAGE**
See 1824: 67

1828: 58    [MOIR, David Macbeth].
THE LIFE OF MANSIE WAUCH, TAILOR IN DALKEITH. WRITTEN BY
HIMSELF.
> Edinburgh: William Blackwood, and T. Cadell, London, 1828.
> viii, 374p. 12mo. 7s (ECB).
> Corvey; ECB 627; NSTC 2M32196 (BI BL, C, E, O).

*Notes.* Dedication 'to John Galt, Esq. of Guelph, Upper Canada'. 'Part of this Autobiography
originally appeared in Blackwood's Magazine' appears on verso of half-title. ECB dates Apr
1828.
Further edns: 1839 (NSTC); 1845 (NSTC); New York & Philadelphia 1828 (NSTC).

1828: 59    [MONKLAND, Anne Catherine].
LIFE IN INDIA; OR, THE ENGLISH AT CALCUTTA. IN THREE VOL-
UMES.
> London: Henry Colburn, New Burlington Street, 1828.
> I 259p; II 268p; III 296p. 12mo. 28s 6d (ECB, QR); 28s 6d boards (ER).
> ER 48: 538 (Dec 1828); QR 39: 253 (Jan 1829).
> Corvey; CME 3-628-48098-1; ECB 345; NSTC 2M33113 (BI BL, C, Dt, E, O; NA DLC,
>     MH).

1828: 60    [MORIER, James Justinian].
THE ADVENTURES OF HAJJI BABA, OF ISPAHAN, IN ENGLAND. IN
TWO VOLUMES.
> London: John Murray, Albemarle-Street, 1828.
> I xxxii, 306p; II 352p. 12mo. 15s (ECB).

QR 38: 303 (July 1828), 39: 73–99 (Jan 1829) full review.
BL N.564; ECB 396; NSTC 2M36629 (BI C, E, NCu, O; NA MH).

*Notes.* Introduction dated London, 19 Apr 1828. Reviewed in QR (Jan 1829) together with Fraser's *The Kuzzilbash* (1828: 43).
Further edns: 1835 (NSTC); 1850 (NSTC); New York 1828 (NSTC) [also Philadelphia 1828 (NUC)]; German trans., 1829.

1828: 61   NEELE, Henry.
THE ROMANCE OF HISTORY. ENGLAND. BY HENRY NEELE. IN THREE VOLUMES.

> London: Printed for Edward Bull, 26, Holles Street, Cavendish Square, 1828.
> I ix, vi, 355p; II vi, 364p; III vi, 352p. 12mo. 31s 6d (ECB, QR); 31s 6d boards (ER).
> ER 47: 331–67 (May 1828) full review, 47: 525 (May 1828); QR 37: 302 (Jan 1828).
> Corvey; CME 3-628-51101-1; ECB 409; NSTC 2R16432 (BI BL).

*Notes.* Dedication 'to the King's Most Excellent Majesty'. ECB dates Oct 1827.
Further edns: 2nd edn. 1828 (NUC); 3rd edn. 1828 (NUC); 4th edn. 1831 (NSTC); 1833 (NSTC); Philadelphia 1828 (NSTC); German trans., 1828 [as *Romantische Erzählungen aus der Geschichte Englands* (RS)].

1828: 62   [PHIPPS, Constantine Henry, Marquis of Normanby].
YES AND NO: A TALE OF THE DAY. BY THE AUTHOR OF "MATILDA." IN TWO VOLUMES.

> London: Henry Colburn, New Burlington Street, 1828.
> I vii, 335p; II 270p. 12mo. 21s (ECB); 21s boards (ER).
> ER 47: 525 (May 1828).
> Corvey; CME 3-628-48985-7; ECB 652; NSTC 2P15316 (BI BL, C, Dt, E, O; NA DLC, MH).

*Notes.* ECB dates Dec 1827.
Further edns: Philadelphia 1828 (NUC); French trans., 1830.

PHIPPS, Constantine Henry
See also CROWE, Eyre Evans

1828: 63   PICHLER, [Karoline]; ROSENTHAL, J. D. (*trans.*).
WALDSTEIN; OR, THE SWEDES IN PRAGUE. FROM THE GERMAN OF MADAME C. PICHLER, BY J. D. ROSENTHAL. IN TWO VOLUMES.

> London: T. Rodwell, New Bond-Street, 1828.
> I viii, 280p; II 293p. 12mo. 15s (ECB, QR).
> QR 38: 303 (July 1828).
> BL N.546; ECB 449; NSTC 2P15726 (BI C, E, O).

*Notes.* Trans. of *Die Schweden in Prag* (Leipzig, 1827). Dedication to 'Her Serene Highness The Princess Paul Esterhazy' signed J. D. Rosenthal. BLC states that J. D. Rosenthal is the same as James D. Haas, and that the latter surname was used afterwards. This chronology, however, does not accord with the appearance of Haas as translator on the t.p. of C. G. S. Heun's *Liesli* (see 1826: 44). ECB dates May 1828.

Further edns: 1839 as *The Swedes in Prague*, trans. J. D. Haas (NSTC); 1845 as *The Swedes in Prague*, trans. J. D. Haas (NSTC).

1828: 64	PORTER, Anna Maria and Jane.
**COMING OUT; AND THE FIELD OF THE FORTY FOOTSTEPS. BY JANE AND ANNA MARIA PORTER. IN THREE VOLUMES.**
> London: Printed for Longman, Rees, Orme, Brown, and Green, Paternoster-Row, 1828.
> I ix, 508p; II 575p; III 680p. 12mo. 30s (ECB); 30s boards (ER).
> ER 47: 525 (May 1828); QR 37: 581 (Mar 1828).
> Corvey; CME 3-628-48357-3; ECB 464; NSTC 2P22243 (BI BL, C, Dt, E, O; NA MH).

*Notes.* 'Prefatory Address to the Reader of "Coming Out"', signed Anna Maria Porter, Esher, Nov 1827. 'Preface to "The Field of the Forty Footsteps"', signed Jane Porter, Esher, Dec 1827. Vols. 1 and 2 include 'Coming Out: A Tale of the Nineteenth Century' [by A. M. Porter]; Jane Porter's 'The Field of the Forty Footsteps; A Romance of the Seventeenth Century' fills vol. 3.
Further edns: New York 1828 (NSTC); French trans., 1828 [separately as *Le Champ des quarante pas* (BN), and *Entrée dans le monde* (BN)]; German trans., 1828/29 [*Das Feld der vierzig Fußstapfen. Romantische Erzählung* (RS)].

1828: 65	PRICHARD, T[homas] J[effery] Llewelyn.
**THE ADVENTURES AND VAGARIES OF TWM SHON CATTI, DESCRIPTIVE OF LIFE IN WALES: INTERSPERSED WITH POEMS. BY T. J. LLEWELYN PRICHARD.**
> Aberystwyth: Printed for the Author, by John Cox, 1828.
> 252p. 12mo.
> BL 12614.dd.11; NSTC 2P26274 (BI C, E; NA MH).

*Notes.* Collates in sixes. Claimed as the first indigenous Welsh novel (see Gerald Morgan, 'The First Anglo-Welsh Novel', *The Anglo-Welsh Review*, 17 (1968), 114–22).
Further edn: Cowbridge [1839] (NSTC).

1828: 66	[REEVE, Sophia].
**CUTHBERT. A NOVEL. IN THREE VOLUMES.**
> London: Sustenance and Stretch, Percy Street, 1828.
> I 264p; II 254p; III 286p. 12mo. 28s 6d (ECB); 28s 6d boards (ER).
> ER 47: 525 (May 1828).
> Corvey; CME 3-628-47365-9; ECB 149; NSTC 2R5344 (BI BL, C, E, O).

*Notes.* ECB dates Dec 1827.

1828: 67	ROCHE, Regina Maria.
**CONTRAST. IN THREE VOLUMES. BY REGINA MARIA ROCHE, AUTHOR OF THE CHILDREN OF THE ABBEY; DISCARDED SON; VICAR OF LANSDOWN; BRIDAL OF DUNAMORE; TRADITION OF THE CASTLE; CASTLE CHAPEL, &C. &C.**
> London: A. K. Newman & Co. Leadenhall-Street, 1828.

I xxiv, 372p; II 358p; III 326p. 12mo. 21s (ECB, QR); 21s boards (ER).
ER 47: 524 (May 1828); QR 38: 303 (July 1828).
Corvey; CME 3-628-48457-X; ECB 498; NSTC 2D1378 (BI BL, E, O).

*Notes.* Dedication to her Royal Highness the Princess Augusta, dated London, 10 Apr 1828.
'List of Subscribers' (*c.*205 names), vol. 1, pp. [xvii]–xxiv.
Further edn: New York 1828 (NUC).

1828: 68   ROLFE, Ann.
THE WILL; OR, TWENTY-ONE YEARS. IN ONE VOLUME. BY MRS.
ANN ROLFE, AUTHOR OF "MISCELLANEOUS POEMS FOR A WIN-
TER'S EVENING;" "CHOICE AND NO CHOICE."

Saxmundham: Printed and sold by L. Brightly, 1828.
xii, 402p, vi. 12mo. 6s 6d (QR).
QR 41: 557 (Nov 1829).
O 249.s.457; NSTC 2R16113.

*Notes.* Prefatory 'Author, Reviewer, and Reader', in the form of a dialogue. The text is in
small print, and in word length matches a contemporary three-volumed novel. 'List of Subscribers', at end (separately paginated [i]–vi); this contains 187 names (all with place of residence, the majority from East Anglia). ECB 500 lists Newman edn., Mar 1830, price 6s 6d,
but not discovered in this form.

1828: 69   ST. CLAIR, Rosalia [pseud.].
ULRICA OF SAXONY. A ROMANTIC TALE OF THE FIFTEENTH CEN-
TURY. BY ROSALIA ST. CLAIR, AUTHOR OF THE BANKER'S DAUGH-
TERS OF BRISTOL; FIRST AND LAST YEARS OF WEDDED LIFE;
CLAVERING TOWER; SON OF O'DONNEL; FASHIONABLES AND
UNFASHIONABLES; &C. &C. IN THREE VOLUMES.

London: A. K. Newman & Co. Leadenhall-Street, 1828.
I 252p; II 286p; III 241p. 12mo. 16s 6d (ECB).
Corvey; CME 3-628-48502-9; ECB 511; NSTC 2S2001 (BI BL, E, O).

*Notes.* ECB dates June 1828.

1828: 70   [?SCARGILL, William Pitt].
PENELOPE: OR, LOVE'S LABOUR LOST. A NOVEL. IN THREE VOL-
UMES.

London: Printed for Hunt and Clarke, York Street, Covent Garden, 1828.
I 358p; II 331p; III 296p. 8vo. 31s 6d (ECB, QR); 31s 6d boards (ER).
ER 47: 524 (May 1828); QR 38: 303 (July 1828).
Corvey; CME 3-628-48413-8; ECB 440; NSTC 2S6005 (BI BL, C, E, O; NA MH).

*Notes.* For the issue of author attribution, see *Truth: A Novel by the Author of Nothing*
(1826: 68).

1828: 71   [SCOTT, Lady Caroline Lucy].
A MARRIAGE IN HIGH LIFE. EDITED BY THE AUTHORESS OF 'FLIR-
TATION.' IN TWO VOLUMES.

London: Henry Colburn, New Burlington Street, 1828.
I iv, 300p; II 308p. 12mo. 21s (ECB); 21s boards (ER).
ER 48: 538 (Dec 1828); QR 38: 303 (July 1828).
Corvey; CME 3-628-48160-0; ECB 369; NSTC 2S8316 (BI BL, C, O; NA DLC, MH).

*Notes.* Wolff (IV, 192; Item 6217) of the author notes: 'This novel, her first, was edited by her relative, Lady Charlotte Susan Maria Bury.'
Further edns: Philadelphia 1833 (NUC); French trans., 1830; German trans., 1837.

1828: 72    [SCOTT, Sir Walter].
CHRONICLES OF THE CANONGATE. SECOND SERIES. BY THE AUTHOR OF "WAVERLEY," &C. IN THREE VOLUMES.

Edinburgh: Printed for Cadell and Co.; and Simpkin and Marshall, London, 1828.
I 336p; II 336p; III 348p. 8vo. 31s 6d (ECB, QR); 31s 6d boards (ER).
ER 47: 524 (May 1828); QR 38: 303 (July 1828).
Corvey; CME 3-628-48542-8; ECB 521; NSTC 2S9531 (BI BL, C, Dt, E, NCu, O; NA MH).

*Notes.* 'Saint Valentine's Day; or, the Fair Maid of Perth' (drop-head title) begins at vol. 1, p. 23. 'This day published', 15 May 1828, *Edinburgh Evening Courant.*
Further edns: 2nd edn. 1828 as *St Valentine's Day; or, The Fair Maid of Perth* (Victoria and Albert Museum, Dyce 8769); New York 1828 (NSTC) [also Philadelphia 1828 (NSTC)]; French trans., 1828 [as *La Jollie Fille de Perth* (see note below)]; German trans., 1828 [as *Das schöne Mädchen von Perth* (RS)]. Numerous reprintings in collected edns. Robert Cadell on 15 Aug 1828 wrote to Scott saying he was sending 'a Copy of an old friend in a new dress "La Jolie Fille de Perth"' (see *The Letters of Sir Walter Scott*, ed. H. J. C Grierson, 12 vols. (London, 1932–37), X, 485). This would suggest a French translation in circulation before the 1829 imprint found in BN.

1828: 73    [SEDGWICK, Catharine Maria].
HOPE LESLIE; OR, EARLY TIMES IN THE MASSACHUSETTS. BY THE AUTHOR OF REDWOOD. IN THREE VOLUMES.

London: John Miller, 40, Pall-Mall, 1828.
I 286p; II 292p; III 302p. 12mo. 21s (ECB); 21s boards (ER, QR).
ER 47: 525 (May 1828); QR 37: 302 (Jan 1828).
Corvey; CME 3-628-47690-9; ECB 281; NSTC 2L12052 (BI BL, C, E, O).

*Notes.* ECB dates Nov 1827, and lists Colburn (actually the publisher with Bentley of the 1830 edn.) as publisher. Originally published New York 1827, with the Miller (London) edn. appearing slightly later (Blanck).
Further edns: 1830 (NUC); 1850 (NUC); French trans., 1828 [as *La Jeune sauvage, ou les premières années de la province de Massachusetts* (BN)].

1828: 74    [?SHOBERL, Frederick].
TALES OF WOMAN. IN TWO VOLUMES.

London: Henry Colburn, New Burlington Street, 1828.
I vi, 331p; II 271p. 12mo. 18s (ECB); 18s boards (ER).
ER 49: 528 (June 1829).
Corvey; CME 3-628-51168-2; ECB 576; NSTC 2S20069 (BI BL, C, E, O).

*Notes.* I The Wife; Helen [Lindorf]; II Helen, concluded; The Russian Daughter; The Mother. In the Preface the 'Editor' states that the tales, by different hands, are 'designed to illustrate the character of that sex, on which lordly Man, in some of his lofty moods, is apt to look down with a degree of contempt; and to show him that if there are qualities of mind in which he surpasses Woman, yet it would be difficult for him to exhibit such sublime examples of the heroism of affection as she has to produce' (p. [iii]). Block and NSTC list as 'edited by' Shoberl; Wolff (IV, 114–15; Item 6296) questions the attribution.

1828: 75    [SMITH, Horatio].
**ZILLAH; A TALE OF THE HOLY CITY. BY THE AUTHOR OF "BRAM-BLETYE HOUSE," "THE TOR HILL," "REUBEN APSLEY," &C. IN FOUR VOLUMES.**

> London: Henry Colburn, New Burlington Street, 1828.
> I xxiii, 300p; II 309p; III 307p; IV 316p. 12mo. 22s (ECB); 42s boards (ER).
> ER 48: 538 (Dec 1828); QR 39: 253 (Jan 1829).
> Corvey; CME 3-628-49001-4; ECB 655; NSTC 2S26656 (BI BL, E, O; NA MH).

*Notes.* Dedication 'to Barron Field, Esq. late Judge of the Supreme Court, New South Wales'. 'Advertisement' states that the work was 'placed in the Publisher's hands early in March last', but publication deferred owing to its similarity in setting to *Salathiel* (see 1828: 32). QR gives the title as 'Zilla [*sic*]; A Tale of Jerusalem'.
*Further edns:* 2nd edn. 1828 (NSTC); 1839 (NSTC); New York 1829 (NSTC); French trans., 1829; German trans., 1829 [as *Zilla, romantisches Gemälde aus der Geschichte Jerusalems* (RS)].

1828: 76    [SMYTH, Amelia Gillespie].
**TALES OF THE MOORS: OR, RAINY DAYS IN ROSS-SHIRE. BY THE AUTHOR OF SELWYN IN SEARCH OF A DAUGHTER.**

> Edinburgh: William Blackwood, and T. Cadell, Strand, London, 1828.
> xix, 437p. 8vo. 10s 6d (ECB, QR).
> QR 37: 581 (Mar 1828).
> Corvey; CME 3-628-48865-6; ECB 576; NSTC 2S29276 (BI BL, C, Dt, E, O).

*Notes.* Dedication to Sir Walter Scott, Baronet. ECB gives the author as 'Car. Bowles', an erroneous attribution to Caroline Anne Bowles (afterwards Southey). 'Selwyn in Search of a Daughter' (as mentioned in the title) was first serialized in *Blackwood's Edinburgh Magazine*, during 1827, and only appeared in book form in 1835.

1828: 77    [TAYLER, Charles Benjamin].
**A FIRESIDE BOOK, OR THE ACCOUNT OF A CHRISTMAS SPENT AT OLD COURT. BY THE AUTHOR OF MAY YOU LIKE IT.**

> London: Printed for J. A. Hessey, 93, Fleet-Street, 1828.
> 229p, ill. 8vo. 6s (ECB).
> BL N.192(2); CME 3-628-47619-4; ECB 206; NSTC 2T2779 (BI C, E, O; NA MH).

*Notes.* Legend of the frontispiece illustration reads: 'London. Published, Decr. 20, 1827, by J. A. Hessey, Fleet Street'. Dedication 'To My Sisters, Fancy and Charlotte'. ECB dates Dec 1827.
*Further edns:* 2nd edn. 1830 (NSTC); Boston 1832 (NUC).

1828: 78   TAYLOR, Sarah.
**GLENALPIN, OR THE BANDIT'S CAVE. BY MISS SARAH TAYLOR. IN TWO VOLUMES.**

> London: Longman, Rees, Orme, Brown, and Green, and S. Wilkin, Norwich, 1828.
> I iii, 304p; II 305p. 12mo. 10s 6d (ECB); 10s 6d boards (ER).
> ER 47: 524 (May 1828).
> Corvey; CME 3-628-48945-8; ECB 580; xNSTC.

*Notes.* 'Preface addressed to the Subscribers', signed Sarah Taylor, 7 Apr 1828. Colophon of 'S. Wilkin, Printer, Norwich, March 21st. 1828' at end of vol. 1. Jarndyce XCV, Item 1099, notes vi–pp. subscribers' list in vol. 2, but none found in the Corvey copy.
Further edn: 1832 (NSTC 2T4263).

1828: 79   [THOMSON, Richard].
**TALES OF AN ANTIQUARY: CHIEFLY ILLUSTRATIVE OF THE MAN-NERS, TRADITIONS, AND REMARKABLE LOCALITIES OF ANCIENT LONDON. IN THREE VOLUMES.**

> London: Henry Colburn, New Burlington Street, 1828.
> I vi, 360p; II 393p; III 353p. 12mo. 31s 6d (ECB, QR).
> QR 38: 303 (July 1828).
> Corvey; CME 3-628-52306-0; ECB 575; NSTC 2T10488 (BI BL, Dt, E, O).

*Notes.* Dedication to the Author of *Waverley*.
Further edns: 1832 as *Legends of London* (NSTC); German trans., 1829.

1828: 80   TRUEBA Y COSIO, [Joaquin] Telesforo de.
**GOMEZ ARIAS; OR, THE MOORS OF THE ALPUJARRAS. A SPANISH HISTORICAL ROMANCE. BY DON TELESFORO DE TRUEBA Y COSIO. IN THREE VOLUMES.**

> London: Hurst, Chance, and Co. 65, St. Paul's Church Yard, 1828.
> I xi, 262p; II 260p; III 235p. 12mo. 27s (ECB, QR).
> QR 38: 303 (July 1828).
> Corvey; CME 3-628-48834-6; ECB 601; NSTC 2T18797 (BI BL, C, E, O; NA MH).

*Notes.* Preface mentions 'the work being written in English by a Spaniard' (p. xi). Dedication to the Right Honourable Lord Holland, dated London, Mar 1828.
Further edns: German trans., 1828; French trans., 1829.

1828: 81   [WHITE, Charles].
**ALMACK'S REVISITED. IN THREE VOLUMES.**

> London: Saunders and Otley, Conduit Street, 1828.
> I 384p; II 336p; III 368p. 12mo. 31s 6d (ECB, ER).
> ER 47: 525 (May 1828).
> Corvey; CME 3-628-47049-8; ECB 14; NSTC 2W16615 (BI BL, C, Dt, E, O; NA DLC, MH).

*Notes.* The same book as *Herbert Milton* (see 1828: 82) with another t.p. and a different type setting. Colophon in all vols: 'Printed by J. F. Dove, St. John's Square'. ECB dates Dec 1827.
Further edns: 2nd edn. 1828 (NSTC); New York 1828 (NUC).

1828: 82   [WHITE, Charles].
**HERBERT MILTON. IN THREE VOLUMES.**

> London: Saunders and Otley, Conduit Street, 1828.
> I 381p; II 327p; III 366p. 12mo. 31s 6d (ECB).
> Corvey; CME 3-628-47779-4; ECB 265; NSTC 2W16625 (NA MH).

*Notes.* A notice at the beginning of vol. 1 (after t.p., and before beginning of main text) claims that 'the following work was originally written under the title of "Almack's", and before the Publication of that popular Novel'—see entry above for the same text under a different title, and 1826: 47 for the original *Almack's.* Colophon in all vols: 'Printed by S. and R. Bentley, Dorset Street'. ECB dates Dec 1827.
Further edn: German trans., 1828 [as *Herbert Milton, oder Leben der höheren Stände in London* (RS)].

1828: 83   [WIGHTWICK, George].
**THE LIFE AND REMAINS OF WILMOT WARWICK. EDITED BY HIS FRIEND HENRY VERNON.**

> London: James Ridgway, Piccadilly, 1828/29.
> I (1828) 326p; II (1829) 314p. 8vo. 18s (ECB, QR).
> QR 41: 557 (Nov 1829).
> Corvey; ECB 345; NSTC 2W7023 (BI BL, C, Dt, E, O; NA DLC).

*Notes.* Dedication to 'Geoffrey Crayon, Esq.', signed 'Henry Vernon'. ECB dates Sept 1828, Sept 1829.

# 1829

1829: 1   ANON.
**THE DAVENELS; OR, A CAMPAIGN OF FASHION IN DUBLIN. IN TWO VOLUMES.**

> London: Henry Colburn, New Burlington Street, 1829.
> I vii, 320p; II 271p. 12mo. 18s (ECB, QR).
> QR 41: 557 (Nov 1829).
> Corvey; CME 3-628-47425-6; ECB 153; NSTC 2D3470 (BI Dt, E; NA DLC, MH).

*Notes.* Dedication to His Grace the Duke of Wellington.

1829: 2   ANON.
**D'ERBINE; OR, THE CYNIC. IN THREE VOLUMES.**

> London: Printed for W. Simpkin and R. Marshall, Stationers'-Hall Court, 1829.
> I 334p; II 278p; III 310p. 12mo. 24s (ECB); 24s boards (ER).
> ER 49: 529 (June 1829).
> Corvey; CME 3-628-47413-2; ECB 159; NSTC 2D9893 (BI BL, C, E, O).

1829: 3   ANON.
## THE FATE OF GRAYSDALE. A LEGEND. IN TWO VOLUMES.

> London: James Duncan, 37, Paternoster Row, 1829.
> I 312p; II 285p. 12mo. 14s (ECB); 14s boards (ER).
> ER 49: 529 (June 1829).
> Corvey; CME 3-628-47485-X; ECB 201; NSTC 2F2748 (BI BL, C; NA MH).

## THE INDIAN CHIEF
See POSTL, Karl Magnus

1829: 4   ANON.
## JESUITISM AND METHODISM. A NOVEL. IN TWO VOLUMES.

> London: Printed for the Author, and published by Saunders and Otley, Conduit Street,
>     1829.
> I 256p; II 218p. 12mo. 18s (ECB).
> QR 41: 287 (July 1829).
> Corvey; CME 3-628-47989-4; ECB 308; NSTC 2J5575 (BI BL, C, O).

*Notes.* ECB lists Simpkin as publisher, May 1829; but not discovered in this form.

1829: 5   ANON.
## THE LIFE OF A MIDSHIPMAN, A TALE FOUNDED ON FACTS: AND INTENDED TO CORRECT AN INJUDICIOUS PREDILECTION IN BOYS FOR THE LIFE OF A SAILOR.

> London: Henry Colburn, New Burlington Street, 1829.
> xii, 264p, ill. 12mo. 9s 6d (ECB, QR).
> QR 42: 279 (Jan 1830).
> Corvey; CME 3-628-48108-2; ECB 345; NSTC 2N38 (BI BL, C, E, O).

*Notes.* Introduction signed 'E. N.'.

1829: 6   ANON.
## MY GRANDFATHER'S FARM; OR, PICTURES OF RURAL LIFE.

> Edinburgh: Published by Oliver & Boyd, Tweeddale-Court; and Geo. B. Whittaker,
>     London, 1829.
> 335p. 12mo. 7s (ECB, QR).
> QR 39: 525 (Apr 1829).
> Corvey; CME 3-628-51100-3; ECB 403; NSTC 2G17267 (BI BL, C, Dt, E).

*Notes.* ECB dates Nov 1828.

1829: 7   ANON.
## PACOCOCO. A ROMANCE.

> London: Printed and published by I. Pesman, 63, Cromer Street, Gray's Inn Road, 1829.
> 131p. 12mo.
> C. Rom.52.47[3]; NSTC 2P691 (BI BL, E, O).

*Notes.* Collates in sixes.

1829: 8 ANON.

## REAY MORDEN: A NOVEL. IN THREE VOLUMES.

Edinburgh: George A. Douglas; Simpkin & Marshall, London; and J. Cumming, Dublin, 1829.
I iii, 315p, II 289p; III 367p. 8vo. 24s (ECB); 24s boards (ER).
ER 49: 529 (June 1829).
Corvey; CME 3-628-48517-7; ECB 481; xNSTC.

*Notes.* 'The Author's Advertisement', dated Edinburgh, 1829. NSTC attributes to 'Nibbs, Missionary in Jamaica', but no further evidence concerning this has been discovered.
Further edn: 2nd edn. 1829 (NSTC 2N7307).

1829: 9 ANON.

## THE SCHOOL OF FASHION, A NOVEL. IN THREE VOLUMES.

London: Henry Colburn, New Burlington Street, 1829.
I viii, 288p; II 300p; III 312p. 12mo. 27s (ECB); 27s boards (ER).
ER 49: 529 (June 1829); QR 41: 287 (July 1829), 41: 557 (Nov 1829).
Corvey; CME 3-628-48535-5; ECB 518; NSTC 2S7378 (BI BL, C, O).

*Notes.* Further edn: New York 1829 (NSTC).

1829: 10 ANON.

## TALES OF FOUR NATIONS. IN THREE VOLUMES.

London: Whitaker[*sic*], Treacher, and Arnot. Ave-Maria Lane, 1829.
I ix, 312p; II 311p; III 310p. 12mo. 27s (ECB, QR).
QR 41: 557 (Nov 1829).
Corvey; CME 3-628-48799-4; ECB 575; NSTC 2T1384 (BI BL, C, Dt, O).

*Notes.* Further edn: 1831 (NSTC).

1829: 11 ANON.

## TALES OF PERPLEXITY. THE RENDEZVOUS. THE DISINHERITED. CROSS PURPOSES.

London: Published by Sampson Low, 42, Lamb's Conduit Street, 1829.
223p. 12mo. 7s 6d (ECB).
Corvey; CME 3-628-51157-7; ECB 576; NSTC 2T1413 (BI BL, C, O).

*Notes.* ECB dates June 1829.

1829: 12 ANON.

## WALDEGRAVE, A NOVEL. IN THREE VOLUMES.

London: Henry Colburn, New Burlington Street, 1829.
I 305p; II 287p; III 318p. 12mo. 27s (ECB); 27s boards (ER).
ER 49: 529 (June 1829).
Corvey; CME 3-628-48812-5; ECB 618; NSTC 2W1638 (BI BL, C, E, O; NA MH).

1829: 13 ANWYL, Edward Trevor.

## REGINALD TREVOR; OR, THE WELSH LOYALISTS. A TALE OF THE SEVENTEENTH CENTURY. BY EDWARD TREVOR ANWYL. IN THREE VOLUMES.

London: Printed for A. K. Newman and Co., 1829.
I xi, 270p; II 247p; III 281p. 12mo. 18s 6d (ECB); 18s boards (ER).
ER 49: 529 (June 1829).
Corvey; CME 3-628-47065-X; ECB 21; NSTC 2A13965 (BI BL, C, E, O).

*Notes.* Dedication 'to Sir Watkin Williams Wynn (of Wynnstay, in the County of Denbigh) Bart, M.P., Lord Lieutenant of the Counties of Denbigh and Merioneth'. Prefatory address 'to Philip Sydney Arundel Esq., of Gray's Inn, London' dated 'G——, near Dolgelley, N.W. December 1828'.

1829: 14   [ANWYL, Edward Trevor].
**YOUTH AND MANHOOD OF EDWARD ELLIS, AND THE COUSINS; ROMANTIC TALES OF WELCH SOCIETY AND SCENERY. IN TWO VOLUMES.**

London: Printed for W. Reeves, Bridge Court, Near Westminster Bridge, 1829.
I vi, 431p; II 393p. 12mo.
DLC PR.3991.A1Y59; NSTC 2E7776.

*Notes.* Dedication to the author's mother. 'Advertisement' dated London, Feb 1827. Author attribution from a later collection, *Tales of Welshland and Welsherie* (1831), an A. K. Newman publication which states on its t.p. 'by the author of Reginald Trevor, Youth of Edward Ellis, &c.'. (For *Reginald Trevor*, see 1829: 13 above.) Vol. 1 contains: 'The Youth of Edward Ellis' (up to p. 270), 'The Cousins' (pp. 273–431); vol. 2 contains: 'Frederic Anwyl' (up to p. 199), 'The Prediction' (pp. 203–393). For an earlier issue of the same stories, see 1827: 13. ECB 654 lists Newman, 1830 edn., price 12s 6d (an edn. also given in Summers); but not discovered in this form.

1829: 15   BARNUM, H. L.
**THE SPY UNMASKED; OR, MEMOIRS OF ENOCH CROSBY, ALIAS HARVEY BIRCH, THE HERO OF THE "SPY, A TALE OF THE NEUTRAL GROUND," BY MR. COOPER, AUTHOR OF "THE PILOT," "THE RED ROVER," &C. &C. BY H. L. BARNUM. IN TWO VOLUMES.**

London: A. K. Newman and Co. New York: J. & J. Harper, Cliff-Street, 1829.
I xxi, 234p; II 222p. 12mo. 10s (ECB); 10s boards (ER).
ER 48: 538 (Dec 1828).
Corvey; CME 3-628-47104-4; ECB 41; NSTC 2B9202 (BI BL, C, Dt, E, O; NA DLC, MH).

*Notes.* Dedication 'to James F. Cooper, Esq., author of "The Spy", "Red Rover", &c.', vol. 1, pp. [vii]–viii. Introduction, pp. [ix]–xxi. Continuous roman and arabic pagination in vol. 1, with novel proper beginning at p. [23]. Originally published New York 1828 (NUC). ECB dates Oct 1828.

1829: 16   [BEAMISH, North Ludlow].
**PEACE CAMPAIGNS OF A CORNET. IN THREE VOLUMES.**

London: John Ebers and Co., Old Bond Street, 1829.
I vii, 307p; II 299p; III 258p. 12mo. 27s (ECB).
QR 39: 525 (Apr 1829).
Corvey; CME 3-628-48406-5; ECB 438; NSTC 2B13220 (BI BL, C, E, O; NA DLC).

*Notes.* 'Advertisement' dated Regent's Park, Apr 1829.
Further edn: New York 1829 (NSTC).

1829: 17   BEDINGFIELD, Mrs. [Mary] Bryan.
**LONGHOLLOW: A COUNTRY TALE. BY MRS. BRYAN BEDINGFIELD.
IN THREE VOLUMES.**

> London: Whittaker, Treacher, and Arnot, Ave Maria Lane, 1829.
> I xv, 334p; II 291p; III 261p. 8vo. 24s (ECB); 24s boards (ER).
> ER 49: 529 (June 1829).
> Corvey; CME 3-628-47188-5; ECB 47; NSTC 2B14569 (BI O).

*Notes.* ECB gives the title as 'Longfellow: a tale of the West'.

1829: 18   [BERNARD, William Bayle].
**THE FREEBOOTER'S BRIDE; OR, THE BLACK PIRATE OF THE
MEDITERRANEAN: INCLUDING THE MYSTERY OF THE MORESCOES.
A ROMANCE, INTERSPERSED WITH HISTORICAL ALLUSIONS TO
THE REIGN OF CHARLES V. IN FIVE VOLUMES.**

> London: Printed for A. K. Newman and Co., 1829.
> I viii, 278p; II 276p; III 258p; IV 262p; V 257p. 12mo. 27s 6d (ECB).
> Corvey; CME 3-628-47809-X; ECB 216; NSTC 2F15201 (BI BL, E, O).

*Notes.* ECB dates Sept 1829.

1829: 19   [BOWLES, Caroline Anne].
**CHAPTERS ON CHURCHYARDS. BY THE AUTHORESS OF ELLEN
FITZARTHUR, WIDOW'S TALE, SOLITARY HOURS, ETC. IN TWO
VOLUMES.**

> Edinburgh: William Blackwood, and T. Cadell, London, 1829.
> I 303p; II 316p. 8vo. 12s (ECB).
> BL 837.d.28; ECB 106; NSTC 2B43724 (BI BL, C, Dt, E, O; NA MH).

*Notes.* Versos of half-titles to vol. 1 and vol. 2 carry the legend: 'Originally published in Black-
wood's Edinburgh Magazine.' Vol. 1 contains 'Churchyards', 'Broad Summerford', and 'The
Haunted Churchyard'; vol. 2 contains 'Andrew Cleaves' and 'The Grave of the Broken
Heart'. ECB dates May 1829.
Further edns: 1841 (NSTC); New York 1842 (NSTC).

1829: 20   [BREWER, James Norris].
**THE FITZWALTERS, BARONS OF CHESTERTON; OR, ANCIENT TIMES
IN ENGLAND. BY THE AUTHOR OF A WINTER'S TALE, SECRETS
MADE PUBLIC, SIR FERDINAND OF ENGLAND, SIR GILBERT EASTER-
LING, OLD FAMILY LEGEND, &C. &C. IN FOUR VOLUMES.**

> London: Printed for A. K. Newman and Co., 1829.
> I ii, 296p; II 266p; III 257p; IV 256p. 12mo. 24s (ECB).
> Corvey; CME 3-628-47604-6; ECB 207; NSTC 2F7679 (BI BL, C, E, O).

*Notes.* ECB dates Oct 1829.

1829: 21 [BULWER LYTTON, Edward George].
## DEVEREUX. A TALE. BY THE AUTHOR OF "PELHAM." IN THREE VOLUMES.

> London: Henry Colburn, New Burlington Street, 1829.
> I vii, 299p; II 310p; III 344p. 12mo. 31s 6d (ECB); 31s 6d boards (ER).
> ER 49: 528 (June 1829); QR 41: 287 (July 1829).
> Corvey; CME 3-628-47150-8; ECB 160; NSTC 2B57397 (BI BL, C, Dt, E, O; NA DLC, MH).

*Notes.* Further edns: 1831 (NSTC); 1836 (NSTC); New York 1829 (NSTC); French trans., 1829; German trans., 1830.

1829: 22 [BULWER LYTTON, Edward George].
## THE DISOWNED. BY THE AUTHOR OF "PELHAM." IN FOUR VOLUMES.

> London: Henry Colburn, New Burlington Street, 1829.
> I xlix, 384p; II 341p; III 273p; IV 354p. 12mo. 31s boards (ER).
> ER 49: 528 (June 1829); QR 39: 253 (Jan 1829).
> Corvey; CME 3-628-47166-4; ECB 84; NSTC 2B57399 (NA DLC, MH).

*Notes.* Dedication to William Lytton Bulwer, Esq., dated 8 Nov 1828. ECB dates Nov 1828. ER price relates to 3 vols., the form in which the 2nd edn. appeared.
Further edns: 2nd edn. 1829 (NSTC); 3rd edn. 1829 (NSTC); 1835 (NSTC); New York 1829 (NSTC); French trans., 1829 [as *L'Enfant désavoué* (BN)]; German trans., 1829 [as *Der Verstoßene* (RS)].

1829: 23 [BUNBURY, Selina].
## MY FOSTER BROTHER.

> Dublin: R. M. Tims, 85, Grafton-Street; Houlston and Son, and Hamilton and Adams, Paternoster-Row; J. Nesbitt, Berner's-St.; Hatchard and Son, Piccadilly, London; W. Oliphant; Waugh and Innes, Edinburgh; and Chalmers and Collins, Glasgow, 1829.
> 134p, ill. 12mo.
> D Ir.3991.m.26; NSTC 2M42679 (BI Dt).

*Notes.* Further edn: 2nd edn. 1833 (NSTC).

1829: 24 [BUNBURY, Selina].
## RETROSPECTIONS; A SOLDIER'S STORY. BY THE AUTHOR OF "A VISIT TO MY BIRTH-PLACE," "ABBEY OF INNISMOYLE," "STORIES FROM CHURCH HISTORY," &C. &C.

> Dublin: William Curry, jun. and Co. 9, Upper Sackville Street, 1829.
> 294p, ill. 12mo. 3s (ECB).
> BL 4413.f.41(3); ECB 489; NSTC 2B57692.

*Notes.* ECB lists as Hurst (Dublin) 1829, but not discovered with this imprint.

1829: 25 [CARLETON, William].
## FATHER BUTLER. THE LOUGH DEARG PILGRIM. BEING SKETCHES OF IRISH MANNERS.

Dublin: William Curry, jun. and Co., 9, Upper Sackville-Street, 1829.

iv, 302p, ill. 12mo. 3s 6d (ECB).

BL 4413.f.40(3); ECB 201; NSTC 2C7486 (BI Dt).

*Notes.* 'Notice to the Reader', dated 20 Feb 1829, stating that the original was published in a magazine. The second story begins on p. 201. ECB dates Apr 1829.

Further edns: 2nd edn. 1839 (NSTC); Philadelphia 1839 (NSTC).

Facs: IAN (1979).

1829: 26   [CARNE, John].

STRATTON HILL, A TALE OF THE CIVIL WARS. BY THE AUTHOR OF "LETTERS FROM THE EAST," "TALES OF THE WEST OF ENGLAND," &C. &C. IN THREE VOLUMES.

London: Henry Colburn, New Burlington Street, 1829.

I iv, 304p; II 308p; III 309p. 12mo. 31s 6d (ECB); 31s 6d boards (ER).

ER 49: 529 (June 1829); QR 41: 287 (July 1829).

Corvey; CME 3-628-48679-3; ECB 566; NSTC 2C8056 (BI BL, C, E, O; NA DLC).

*Notes.* Further edn: New York 1829 (NSTC).

1829: 27   [COOPER, James Fenimore].

THE BORDERERS: A TALE. BY THE AUTHOR OF "THE SPY," "THE RED ROVER," "THE PRAIRIE," &C. &C. &C.

London: Henry Colburn and Richard Bentley, New Burlington-Street, 1829.

I xiv, 299p; II 311p; III 316p. 12mo. 31s 6d (ECB); 31s 6d boards (ER).

ER 50: 284 (Oct 1829); QR 41: 557 (Nov 1829).

Corvey; CME 3-628-47328-4; ECB 134; NSTC 2C36778 (BI BL, C, Dt, E, O; NA MH).

*Notes.* This edn. narrowly preceded the first American issue (Blanck).

Further edns: 1833 (NSTC); 1849 (NSTC); Philadelphia 1829 as *The Wept of Wish Ton-Wish* (Blanck, NSTC); German trans., 1829 [as *Conanchet und die Puritaner in Connecticut* (RS) and as *Die Grenzbewohner, oder die Beweinte von Wish-Ton-Wish* (RS)].

1829: 28   [CORP, Harriet].

TALES CHARACTERISTIC, DESCRIPTIVE, AND ALLEGORICAL. BY THE AUTHOR OF "AN ANTIDOTE TO THE MISERIES OF HUMAN LIFE," &C. &C. WITH A FRONTISPIECE.

London: Printed for Baldwin and Cradock, 1829.

vi, 222p, ill. 12mo. 6s (ECB).

Corvey; CME 3-628-51144-5; ECB 575; NSTC 2C38500 (BI BL, C, O).

*Notes.* ECB dates Jan 1829.

1829: 29   CROKER, T[homas] Crofton.

LEGENDS OF THE LAKES; OR, SAYINGS AND DOINGS AT KILLAR-NEY. COLLECTED CHIEFLY FROM THE MANUSCRIPTS OF R. ADOL-PHUS LYNCH, ESQ. H. P. KING'S GERMAN LEGION. BY T. CROFTON CROKER.

London: John Ebers and Co. Old Bond Street, 1829.
I viii, 245p, ill., map, music; II vi, 247p, ill., music. 8vo. 18s (ECB, QR).
QR 39: 253 (Jan 1829).
Corvey; CME 3-628-51008-2; ECB 144; NSTC 2C43658 (BI BL, C, Dt, E, O; NA MH).

*Notes.* Dedication 'to Miss Edgeworth, of Edgeworth's Town, Ireland'. Vol. 2, pp. [245]–247 contains 'Topographical Index'. ECB dates Dec 1828.

1829: 30    [CROWE, Eyre Evans].
**YESTERDAY IN IRELAND. BY THE AUTHOR OF "TO DAY IN IRE-LAND." IN THREE VOLS.**

London: Henry Colburn, New Burlington Street, 1829.
I 313p; II 327p; III 332p. 12mo. 31s 6d (ECB); 31s 6d boards (ER).
ER 49: 529 (June 1829).
Corvey; CME 3-628-48986-5; ECB 652; NSTC 2C44613 (BI BL, C, Dt, E, O; NA MH).

*Notes.* I Corramahon; II Corramahon. The Northerns of 1798; III Corramahon. The Northerns of 1798. 'Corramahon' ends at vol. 2, p. 287, and 'The Northerns of Ninety-Eight' begins vol. 2, p. [291]; t.p. to vol. 3 wrongly indicates that 'Corramahon' is in that volume. Dedication to the Marquis of Lansdowne.
Further edn: New York 1829 (NSTC).
Facs: IAN (1979).

1829: 31    [CRUMPE, Miss M. G. T.].
**GERALDINE OF DESMOND, OR IRELAND IN THE REIGN OF ELIZA-BETH. AN HISTORICAL ROMANCE. IN THREE VOLUMES.**

London: Henry Colburn, New Burlington Street, 1829.
I xxiii, 352p; II 323p; III 287p. 12mo. 31s 6d (ECB); 31s 6d boards (ER).
ER 49: 529 (June 1829); QR 41: 557 (Nov 1829).
Corvey; CME 3-628-47749-2; ECB 228; NSTC 2C45428 (BI BL, C, Dt, E, O; NA MH).

*Notes.* Dedication to Thomas Moore, Esq., dated Welbeck Street, Cavendish Square, 1 May 1829.
Further edn: 2nd edn. 1830 (NSTC).

1829: 32    [EAST, Timothy].
**THE MODERN MARTYR. BY THE AUTHOR OF "THE EVANGELICAL RAMBLER."**

London: Frederick Westley and A. H. Davis, 10, Stationers'-Hall-Court, and Ave-Maria-Lane; John Boyd, Edinburgh; R. Wrightson, Birmingham; and G. Tyrrell, Dublin, 1829.
I vi, 311p; II 318p. 12mo. 10s (ECB).
Corvey; CME 3-628-48218-6; ECB 390; NSTC 2M17638 (BI BL, C, Dt, E, O).

*Notes.* Preface dated 1 Jan 1829. ECB dates Jan 1829.

1829: 33    [GILLIES, Robert Pierce].
**TALES OF A VOYAGER TO THE ARCTIC OCEAN. SECOND SERIES. IN THREE VOLUMES.**

London: Henry Colburn, New Burlington Street, 1829.

I 342p; II 352p; III 337p. 12mo. 31s 6d (ECB).

Corvey; CME 3-628-48875-3; ECB 575; NSTC 2G8248 (BI BL, C, E, O; NA DLC, MH).

*Notes.* ECB dates Feb 1829.

Further edn: 1834 (NSTC).

1829: 34    [GLASCOCK, William Nugent].

**SAILORS AND SAINTS; OR, MATRIMONIAL MANŒUVRES. BY THE AUTHORS OF THE "NAVAL SKETCH BOOK." IN THREE VOLUMES.**

London: Henry Colburn, New Burlington Street, 1829.

I vii, 315p; II 327p; III 316p. 12mo. 31s 6d (ECB); 31s 6d boards (ER).

ER 49: 529 (June 1829); QR 39: 525 (Apr 1829).

Corvey; CME 3-628-51125-9; ECB 511; NSTC 2G9531 (BI BL, C, Dt, E, O).

*Notes.* Further edns: 2nd edn. 1829 (NSTC); New York 1829 (NSTC).

1829: 35    [GLEIG, George Robert].

**THE CHELSEA PENSIONERS. BY THE AUTHOR OF "THE SUBAL-TERN." IN THREE VOLUMES.**

London: Henry Colburn, New Burlington Street, 1829.

I 318p; II 307p; III 328p. 12mo. 31s 6d (ECB); 31s 6d boards (ER).

ER 49: 529 (June 1829).

Corvey; CME 3-628-47262-8; ECB 108; NSTC 2G10267 (BI BL, C, Dt, E, O; NA DLC, MH).

*Notes.* Further edns: 1833 (NSTC); 1841 (NSTC); German trans., 1830 [as *Der Invaliden-Klub, Kriegsabentheuer aus dem Leben gedienter Officiere* (RS)].

1829: 36    [GORE, Catherine Grace Frances].

**HUNGARIAN TALES. BY THE AUTHOR OF "THE LETTRE DE CACHET." IN THREE VOLUMES.**

London: Saunders and Otley, Conduit Street, 1829.

I x, 328p; II [329]–427p, 250p; III 339p. 12mo. 31s 6d (ECB); 31s 6d boards (ER).

ER 49: 529 (June 1829); QR 39: 253 (Jan 1829).

Corvey; CME 3-628-48862-1; ECB 288; NSTC 2G14842 (BI BL, C, Dt, E, O; NA DLC, MH).

*Notes.* ECB dates Dec 1828. QR lists as 'written during a Residence in that Country'.

1829: 37    [GORE, Catherine Grace Frances].

**ROMANCES OF REAL LIFE. BY THE AUTHOR OF "HUNGARIAN TALES." IN THREE VOLUMES.**

London: Henry Colburn, New Burlington Street, 1829.

I vi, 329p; II 323p; III 354p. 12mo. 31s 6d (ECB); 31s 6d boards (ER).

ER 49: 529 (June 1829).

Corvey; CME 3-628-51120-8; ECB 501; NSTC 2G14881 (BI BL, C, E, O; NA DLC, MH).

*Notes.* Further edn: New York 1829 (NSTC).

1829: 38    [GRATTAN, Thomas Colley].
## TRAITS OF TRAVEL; OR, TALES OF MEN AND CITIES. BY THE AUTHOR OF "HIGH-WAYS AND BY-WAYS." IN THREE VOLUMES.

> London: Henry Colburn, New Burlington Street, 1829.
> I viii, 336p; II 366p; III 335p. 12mo. 31s 6d (ECB); 31s 6d bound (ER).
> ER 49: 529 (June 1829); QR 39: 525 (Apr 1829).
> Corvey; CME 3-628-51143-7; ECB 241; NSTC 2G18175 (BI BL, C, Dt, E, O; NA DLC, MH).

*Notes.* 'Advertisement' dated Brussels, 1829.
Further edns: New York 1829 (NSTC); German trans., 1829.

1829: 39    GRESLEY, Roger.
## SIR PHILIP GASTENEYS: A MINOR. BY SIR ROGER GRESLEY, BART.

> London: Henry Colburn, New Burlington Street, 1829.
> vii, 209p. 12mo. 8s 6d (ECB, QR).
> QR 41: 287 (July 1829).
> Corvey; CME 3-628-51062-7; ECB 539; NSTC 2G21774 (BI BL, C, E, O; NA DLC, MH).

*Notes.* Preface dated Paris, 25 Mar 1829.

1829: 40    [GREY, Elizabeth Caroline].
## THE TRIALS OF LIFE. BY THE AUTHOR OF "DE LISLE." IN THREE VOLUMES.

> London: Edward Bull, Holles Street, 1829.
> I 319p; II 285p; III 279p. 12mo. 31s 6d (ECB, QR); 31s 6d boards (ER).
> ER 48: 538 (Dec 1828); QR 39: 252 (Jan 1829).
> Corvey; CME 3-628-48829-X; ECB 599; NSTC 2G22168 (BI BL, C, E, NCu, O; NA DLC, MH).

*Notes.* ECB dates Nov 1828.
Further edn: New York & Philadelphia 1829 (NSTC).

1829: 41    [GRIFFIN, Gerald Joseph].
## THE COLLEGIANS. IN THREE VOLUMES.

> London: Saunders and Otley, Conduit Street, 1829.
> I 330p; II 349p; III 322p. 12mo. 31s 6d (ECB); 31s 6d boards (ER).
> ER 49: 529 (June 1829); QR 39: 525 (Apr 1829).
> Corvey; CME 3-628-47304-7; ECB 125; NSTC 2G22641 (BI BL, C, Dt, E, O; NA DLC, MH).

*Notes.* Half-titles read: 'A Second Series of Tales of the Munster Festivals.'
Further edns: 2nd edn. 1829 (NSTC); 1847 (NSTC); New York 1829 (NSTC); German trans., 1848.
Facs: IAN (1979).

1829: 42    [GRIFFIN, Gerald Joseph].
## THE RIVALS. TRACY'S AMBITION. BY THE AUTHOR OF "THE COL-LEGIANS." IN THREE VOLUMES.

London: Saunders and Otley, Conduit Street, 1829.
I xxx, 306p; II 321p; III 302p. 12mo. 31s 6d (ECB, ER, QR).
ER 51: 294 (Apr 1830); QR 42: 280 (Jan 1830).
Corvey; CME 3-628-48613-0; ECB 246; NSTC 2G22651 (BI O).

*Notes.* Half-titles read: 'Third Series of Tales of the Munster Festivals.'
Further edns: 1830 (NSTC); 1842 (NSTC); New York 1830 (NSTC). Sadleir (Item 1071) notes of the unavowed 2nd edn., 1830, that internally the only difference from the 1st edn. is the date on the titles.
Facs: IAN (1979).

1829: 43   HALL, [Anna Maria].
**SKETCHES OF IRISH CHARACTER. BY MRS. S. C. HALL.**

London: Frederick Westley, and A. H. Davis, Stationers'-Hall Court, 1829.
I ix, 224p; II 220p. 8vo. 12s (ECB).
Corvey; CME 3-628-51029-5; ECB 250; NSTC 2H2562 (BI BL, C, Dt, O; NA DLC).

*Notes.* 'Introduction' addressed to 'my dear Miss Mitford'. ECB dates Apr 1829. 2nd series (1 vol.) published in 1831.
Further edn: New York 1829 (NSTC).
Facs: IAN (1979).

1829: 44   HARRISON, W[illiam] H.
**TALES OF A PHYSICIAN. BY W. H. HARRISON.**

London: Robert Jennings, Poultry, 1829.
vi, 248p. 8vo. 7s 6d (ECB, QR).
QR 41: 287 (July 1829).
Corvey; CME 3-628-51031-7; ECB 256; NSTC 2H9972 (BI BL, C, E, O; NA MH).

*Notes.* 2nd series (1 vol.) published in 1831, with the imprint of Jennings and Chaplin.
Further edns: Philadelphia 1835 (NSTC); French trans., 1833 [as *Les Mémoires d'un médicin* (MGD)].

1829: 45   [HEAD, Catharine].
**RYBRENT DE CRUCE. IN THREE VOLUMES.**

London: Henry Colburn, New Burlington Street, 1829.
I 318p; II 309p; III 332p. 12mo. 28s 6d (ECB); 28s 6d boards (ER).
ER 49: 529 (June 1829); QR 42: 279 (Jan 1830).
Corvey; CME 3-628-48588-6; ECB 509; NSTC 2H14825 (BI BL, C, E, O; NA MH).

*Notes.* Further edn: New York 1829 (NSTC).

1829: 46   [HESELTINE, William].
**THE LAST OF THE PLANTAGENETS: AN HISTORICAL ROMANCE. ILLUSTRATING SOME OF THE PUBLIC EVENTS, AND DOMESTIC AND ECCLESIASTICAL MANNERS, OF THE FIFTEENTH AND SIX- TEENTH CENTURIES.**

London: Smith, Elder, and Co., Cornhill, 1829.

xxiv, 464p. 8vo. 12s (ECB).

Corvey; CME 3-628-47906-1; ECB 330; NSTC 2H19331 (BI BL, C, Dt, O).

*Notes.* ECB dates Jan 1829.

Further edns: 2nd edn. 1829 (NSTC); New York 1829 (NSTC).


1829: 47    HOFLAND, [Barbara].

**BEATRICE, A TALE FOUNDED ON FACTS. BY MRS. HOFLAND. IN THREE VOLUMES.**

London: Printed for Longman, Rees, Orme, Brown, and Green, Paternoster-Row, 1829.

I 324p; II 354p; III 312p. 12mo. 21s (ECB, QR); 21s boards (ER).

ER 50: 284 (Oct 1829); QR 41: 557 (Nov 1829).

Corvey; CME 3-628-47675-5; ECB 275; NSTC 2H29375 (BI C, E, O; NA DLC, MH).

*Notes.* Further edn: New York 1830 (NSTC).


1829: 48    [JAMES, George Payne Rainsford].

**RICHELIEU, A TALE OF FRANCE. IN THREE VOLUMES.**

London: Henry Colburn, New Burlington Street, 1829.

I xix, 290p; II 315p; III 348p. 12mo. 31s 6d (ECB); 31s 6d boards (ER).

ER 49: 529 (June 1829).

Corvey; CME 3-628-47936-3; ECB 493; NSTC 2J2162 (BI BL, C, E, O; NA MH).

*Notes.* Further edns: 2nd edn. 1831 (NSTC); 1839 (NSTC); New York 1829 (NUC); French trans., 1830; German trans., 1830 [as *Kardinal Richelieu. Eine historisch-romantische Schilderung Frankreichs im Jahr 1642* (RS)].


1829: 49    [JONES, George].

**MARGARET CORYTON. BY LEIGH CLIFFE, ESQ. AUTHOR OF "PARGA," &C. IN THREE VOLUMES.**

London: R. & S. A. Bielefeld, Rathbone-Place, and Galignani, Paris, 1829.

I 267p; II 282p; III 251p. 12mo. 27s (ECB); 27s bound (ER).

ER 49: 529 (June 1829).

Corvey; CME 3-628-47292-X; ECB 121; NSTC 2C26363 (BI BL, C, E, O).

*Notes.* Dedication to Lady Charlotte Bury. Preface dated London, May 1829.


1829: 50(a)    {J}[ONES], {H}[annah] {M}[aria].

**EMILY MORELAND; OR, THE MAID OF THE VALLEY: BY THE AUTHOR OF "ROSALINE WOODBRIDGE." IN THREE VOLUMES.**

London: Printed for the Proprietor, by C. Baynes, Duke Street, Lincoln's Inn Fields. Published by Sherwood, Gilbert, & Piper, Paternoster Row, 1829.

I vii, 360p; II 383p; III 353p. 12mo. 21s (ECB).

Corvey; CME 3-628-47559-7; ECB 186; xNSTC.

*Notes.* Preface signed H. M. J. ECB dates 1830.

1829: 50(b)   JONES, Hannah Maria.
EMILY MORELAND; OR, THE MAID OF THE VALLEY. BY HANNAH
MARIA JONES, AUTHORESS OF ROSALINE WOODBRIDGE,
STRANGERS OF THE GLEN, THE WEDDING RING, GRETNA GREEN,
THE VICTIM OF FASHION, &C. &C. &C.

> London: Printed by C. Baynes, Duke Street, Lincoln's Inn Fields, for George Virtue, Ivy
> Lane, Paternoster Row, Bath-Street Bristol; and St. Vincent Street, Liverpool, 1829.
> 760p, ill. 8vo.
> BL 12646.i.21; NSTC 2J10423 (BI C, E).

Notes. Additional engraved t.p., with imprint 'London, published by G. Virtue, 26, Ivy Lane,
1829'. Frontispiece plus 8 other engraved ills. Collates in fours.
Further edn: 1836 (NSTC).

1829: 51   [JONES, James Athearn].
TALES OF AN INDIAN CAMP. IN THREE VOLUMES.

> London: Henry Colburn and Richard Bentley, New Burlington Street, 1829.
> I xxxiii, 312p; II iv, 336p; III iv, 341p. 12mo. 31s 6d (ECB).
> Corvey; CME 3-628-51151-8; ECB 575; NSTC 2J10660 (BI BL, C, E, O).

Notes. 29 items. ECB dates Nov 1829.
Further edn: 2nd edn. 1830 as Traditions of the North American Indians (NSTC).

1829: 52   [KENNEDY, Grace].
FLORENCE: OR THE ASPIRANT. A NOVEL, IN THREE VOLUMES.

> London: Whittaker, Treacher, and Co. Ave Maria Lane, 1829.
> I 296p; II 293p; III 311p. 8vo. 24s (ECB, QR); 24s boards (ER).
> ER 49: 529 (June 1829); QR 41: 287 (July 1829).
> Corvey; CME 3-628-47797-2; ECB 209; NSTC 2K3090 (BI BL, C, E, O; NA DLC, MH).

Notes. Dedication to the King.

1829: 53   LATHOM, Francis.
FASHIONABLE MYSTERIES; OR, THE RIVAL DUCHESSES, AND OTHER
TALES. BY FRANCIS LATHOM, AUTHOR OF THE MYSTERIOUS FREE-
BOOTER; PUZZLED AND PLEASED; LONDON; YOUNG JOHN BULL;
VERY STRANGE BUT VERY TRUE; ASTONISHMENT; POLISH BANDIT;
UNKNOWN; FATAL VOW; MIDNIGHT BELL; LIVE AND LEARN;
HUMAN BEINGS; MEN AND MANNERS; &C. &C. IN THREE VOLUMES.

> London: Printed for A. K. Newman and Co., 1829.
> I 297p; II 274p; III 281p. 12mo. 18s (ECB).
> Corvey; CME 3-628-47957-6; ECB 330; NSTC 2L5029 (BI BL, C, E, O).

Notes. ECB dates Dec 1828.

1829: 54   LÉVIS, [Pierre Marc Gaston] de.
THE CARBONARO. A PIEDMONTESE TALE. BY THE DUKE DE LEVIS.
IN TWO VOLUMES.

London: Henry Colburn, New Burlington Street, 1829.
I xi, 314p; II 404p. 12mo. 18s (ECB); 18s boards (ER).
ER 49: 529 (June 1829); QR 39: 525 (Apr 1829).
BL N.659; ECB 343; NSTC 2L13574 (BI C, O; NA DLC).

*Notes.* Trans. of *La Conspiration de mil huit cent vingt et un, ou les jumeaux de Chevreuse* (Paris, 1829).

1829: 55 [LOGAN, Eliza].
**RESTALRIG; OR, THE FORFEITURE. BY THE AUTHOR OF ST JOHN-STOUN, OR JOHN EARL OF GOWRIE. IN TWO VOLUMES.**
Edinburgh: MacLachlan & Stewart; and Simpkin & Marshall, London, 1829.
I viii, 308p; II 346p. 8vo. 21s (ECB).
Corvey; CME 3-628-48564-9; ECB 489; NSTC 2L19798 (BI BL, C, E; NA MH).

*Notes.* Dedication to the Right Honourable James, Baron Ruthven, dated Edinburgh, 1 Dec 1828. ECB dates Feb 1829.
Further edn: French trans., 1829 [as *Logan de Restalrig* (BLC)].

1829: 56 [LOUDON, Jane C.].
**STORIES OF A BRIDE; BY THE AUTHOR OF THE MUMMY. IN THREE VOLUMES.**
London: Henry Colburn and Richard Bentley, New Burlington Street, 1829.
I 307p; II 323p; III 296p. 12mo. 28s 6d (ECB); 28s 6d boards (ER).
ER 50: 284 (Oct 1829).
Corvey; CME 3-628-48625-4; ECB 564; NSTC 2S42434 (BI BL, C, E, O).

1829: 57 [MACKENZIE, Mary Jane].
**PRIVATE LIFE; OR, VARIETIES OF CHARACTER AND OPINION. IN TWO VOLUMES. BY THE AUTHOR OF "GERALDINE," &C. &C.**
London: Printed for T. Cadell, Strand; and W. Blackwood, Edinburgh, 1829.
I 361p; II 391p. 8vo.
Corvey; CME 3-628-48356-5; NSTC 2M5900 (BI BL, Dt, C, E).

*Notes.* ECB 360 lists 3rd edn., Cadell, 1835.
Further edns: 2nd edn. 1830 (NUC); 3rd edn. 1835 (NSTC); New York 1829 (NUC).

1829: 58 [?MAGINN, William].
**TALES OF MILITARY LIFE. BY THE AUTHOR OF "THE MILITARY SKETCH BOOK." IN THREE VOLUMES.**
London: Henry Colburn, New Burlington Street, 1829.
I vii, 335p; II 322p; III 331p. 12mo. 31s 6d (ECB); 31s 6d bound (ER); 28s 6d (QR).
ER 49: 529 (June 1829); QR 41: 287 (July 1829).
Corvey; CME 3-628-48864-8; ECB 575; NSTC 2M9549 (BI BL, C, Dt, E, O; NA DLC, MH).

*Notes.* I Vandeleur; II Vandeleur; III Vandeleur concluded; Gentleman Gray. Dedication 'to the Colonel of the 42nd (Royal Highlanders,) Lieutenant-General the Right Hon. Sir George Murray, G.C.B. and G.C.H.'. Preface mentions the author having spent the 'greatest part' of his life in the army. Wolff (Item 7574) suggests that the attribution of this title to William Maginn by Block is likely to be wrong—see also *The Military Sketch-book* (1827: 51). Further edns: 1834 (NUC); 1849/51 (Wolff, Item 7575).

1829: 59    [MARRYAT, Frederick].
THE NAVAL OFFICER; OR, SCENES AND ADVENTURES IN THE LIFE OF FRANK MILDMAY. IN THREE VOLUMES.

> London: Henry Colburn, New Burlington Street, 1829.
> I 297p; II 310p; III 270p. 12mo. 31s 6d (ECB); 28s 6d boards (ER).
> ER 49: 529 (June 1829).
> Corvey; CME 3-628-48259-3; ECB 408; NSTC 2M15125 (BI BL, C, E, O).

*Notes.* Further edns: 1834 (NSTC); 1836 (NSTC); 1839 (NSTC); Philadelphia 1833 (NUC); French trans., 1833; German trans., 1835.

1829: 60    [MAXWELL, William Hamilton].
STORIES OF WATERLOO; AND OTHER TALES. IN THREE VOLUMES.

> London: Henry Colburn and Richard Bentley, New Burlington Street, 1829.
> I 336p; II 279p; III 296p. 12mo. 28s 6d (ECB).
> Corvey; CME 3-628-51133-X; ECB 564; NSTC 2M21432 (BI BL, C, Dt, E, O).

*Notes.* 32 tales. ECB dates Oct 1829.
Further edns: 1833 (NSTC); 1834 (NSTC).

1829: 61    MOSSE, Henrietta Rouviere.
THE BLANDFORDS; OR, FATE AND FORTUNE. A NOVEL. BY HENRI-ETTA ROUVIERE MOSSE, AUTHOR OF A FATHER'S LOVE AND A WOMAN'S FRIENDSHIP, BRIDE AND NO WIFE, GRATITUDE, WOMAN'S WIT AND MAN'S WISDOM &C. &C. IN FOUR VOLUMES.

> London: Printed for A. K. Newman and Co., 1829.
> I 298p; II 295p; III 267p; IV 298p. 12mo. 24s (ECB); 24s boards (ER).
> ER 49: 529 (June 1829).
> Corvey; CME 3-628-48342-5; ECB 399; NSTC 2R19126 (BI BL, C, E, O).

*Notes.* Dedication to the Marchioness Cornwallis, dated London, 24 June 1829.

1829: 62    [MUDFORD, William].
THE FIVE NIGHTS OF ST. ALBANS. IN THREE VOLUMES.

> Edinburgh: William Blackwood, and T. Cadell, Strand, London, 1829.
> I viii, 312p; II 285p; III 286p. 12mo. 29s 6d (ECB); 28s 6d boards (ER).
> ER 49: 529 (June 1829); QR 41: 287 (July 1829).
> Corvey; CME 3-628-47616-X; ECB 207; NSTC 2M39802 (BI BL, C, E, O; NA DLC).

*Notes.* Preface dated London, 22 May 1829.
Further edns: 2nd edn. London 1835 (NUC); Philadelphia 1833 (NSTC); German trans., 1830.

1829: 63    [PARDOE, Julia S. H.].

## LORD MORCAR OF HEREWARD. A ROMANCE OF THE TIMES OF WILLIAM THE CONQUEROR. IN FOUR VOLUMES.

London: Printed for A. K. Newman and Co., 1829.
I 293p; II 272p; III 278p; IV 288p. 12mo. 22s (ECB); 22s boards (ER).
ER 49: 529 (June 1829).
Corvey; CME 3-628-48114-7; ECB 353; NSTC 2P3006 (BI BL, C, E, O; NA DLC, MH).

1829: 64    [PEACOCK, Thomas Love].

## THE MISFORTUNES OF ELPHIN. BY THE AUTHOR OF HEADLONG HALL.

London: Published by Thomas Hookham, Old Bond Street, 1829.
240p. 12mo. 7s (ECB, QR).
QR 39: 525 (Apr 1829).
Corvey; CME 3-628-48214-3; ECB 438; NSTC 2P8179 (BI BL, C, Dt, E, O; NA DLC, MH).

1829: 65    [PICKEN, Andrew].

## THE SECTARIAN; OR, THE CHURCH AND THE MEETING-HOUSE. IN THREE VOLUMES.

London: Henry Colburn, New Burlington Street, 1829.
I 282p; II 306p; III 324p. 12mo. 27s (ECB); 27s boards (ER).
ER 49: 529 (June 1829).
Corvey; CME 3-628-48672-6; ECB 525; NSTC 2P15789 (BI BL, C, E, O).

1829: 66    [POSTL, Karl Magnus].

## THE INDIAN CHIEF; OR, TOKEAH AND THE WHITE ROSE. A TALE OF THE INDIANS AND THE WHITES. IN THREE VOLUMES.

London: A. K. Newman and Co. Philadelphia: Carey, Lea, and Carey, 1829.
I viii, 261p; II 234p; III 244p. 12mo. 16s 6d (ECB); 16s 6d boards (ER).
ER 49: 529 (June 1829).
Corvey; CME 3-628-47471-X; ECB 295; NSTC 2I1784 (BI BL, C, E, O).

*Notes.* ECB gives the title as 'The Indian chief: an American novel'. Originally published Philadelphia 1829, as *Tokeah; or, the White Rose* (NUC). Postl wrote pseudonymously as Charles Sealsfield and also as C. Sidon, and *Tokeah* is catalogued by NUC under the first of these names. Further edn: this novel served as the basis for a larger work, in German, *Der Legitime und die Republikaner* (Zurich, 1833).

1829: 67    [RICHARDSON, John].

## ÉCARTÉ; OR, THE SALONS OF PARIS. IN THREE VOLUMES.

London: Henry Colburn, New Burlington Street, 1829.
I 327p; II 329p; III 343p. 12mo. 28s 6d (ECB).
Corvey; CME 3-628-47526-0; ECB 177; NSTC 2R9646 (BI BL, C, Dt, E, O; NA DLC, MH).

*Notes.* ECB dates Mar 1829.

1829: 68   RITCHIE, Leitch.
**TALES AND CONFESSIONS. BY LEITCH RITCHIE.**

> London: Smith, Elder, & Co. 65, Cornhill, 1829.
> xii, 364p. 12mo. 10s 6d (ECB, QR).
> QR 39: 253 (Jan 1829).
> Corvey; CME 3-628-51128-3; ECB 495; NSTC 2R11602 (BI BL, C, O).

*Notes*. Dedication to James Augustus St John, Esq., dated London, 18 Nov 1828. ECB dates Dec 1828.
Further edn: 1833 (NSTC).

1829: 69   ST. CLAIR, Rosalia [pseud.].
**ELEANOR OGILVIE THE MAID OF THE TWEED. A ROMANTIC LEG-END. BY ROSALIA ST. CLAIR, AUTHOR OF THE HIGHLAND CASTLE; BANKER'S DAUGHTERS; SON OF O'DONNEL; &C. &C. IN THREE VOLUMES.**

> London: Printed for A. K. Newman and Co., 1829.
> I 268p; II 240p; III 251p. 12mo. 16s 6d (ECB).
> Corvey; CME 3-628-48494-4; ECB 511; NSTC 2S1993 (BI BL, E, O).

*Notes*. ECB dates Mar 1829.

1829: 70   [SAINT LEGER, Francis Barry Boyle].
**TALES OF PASSION: LORD LOVEL'S DAUGHTER. THE BOHEMIAN.—SECOND LOVE. BY THE AUTHOR OF "GILBERT EARLE." IN THREE VOLUMES.**

> London: Henry Colburn, New Burlington-Street, 1829.
> I 315p; II 319p; III 356p. 12mo. 31s 6d (ECB); 31s 6d boards (ER).
> ER 49: 529 (June 1829); QR 39: 253 (Jan 1829).
> Corvey; CME 3-628-48872-9; ECB 576; NSTC 2S2248 (BI BL, C, Dt, O; NA DLC, MH).

*Notes*. 'Notice' by the Author, dated 17 Jan 1829.
Further edn: New York 1829 (NSTC).

1829: 71   [SALUCES, Mme. de].
**FOSCARINI OR THE PATRICIAN OF VENICE. IN TWO VOLUMES.**

> London: Printed for Rowland Hunter, St. Paul's Churchyard, 1829.
> I 365p; II 395p. 12mo. 21s (ECB); 20s boards (ER).
> ER 49: 529 (June 1829).
> Corvey; CME 3-628-47768-9; ECB 212; NSTC 2F11603 (BI BL, C, E, O).

*Notes*. Trans. of *Foscarini, ou le patricien de Venise* (Paris, 1826). Alternate running-titles read: 'Tales of our Neighbours'; this is explained in a 'Notice to the Reader' as the result of an original intention to include an additional tale relating to France.

1829: 72   [SCARGILL, William Pitt].
**RANK AND TALENT; A NOVEL. BY THE AUTHOR OF "TRUCKLEBOROUGH-HALL." IN THREE VOLUMES.**

London: Henry Colburn, New Burlington Street, 1829.
I 328p; II 323p; III 293p. 12mo. 28s 6d (ECB); 28s 6d boards (ER).
ER 49: 529 (June 1829).
Corvey; CME 3-628-48450-2; ECB 479; NSTC 2S6008 (BI BL, C, O; NA MH).

1829: 73    [SCARGILL, William Pitt].
TALES OF A BRIEFLESS BARRISTER. IN THREE VOLUMES.

London: Henry Colburn and Richard Bentley, New Burlington Street, 1829.
I vi, 306p; II 309p; III 300p. 12mo. 28s 6d (ECB).
Corvey; CME 3-628-48795-1; ECB 575; NSTC 2S6010 (BI BL, C, Dt, E, O; NA DLC).

*Notes.* ECB dates Nov 1829.
Further edn: [1831?] (NSTC).

1829: 74    [SCARGILL, William Pitt].
TALES OF MY TIME. BY THE AUTHOR OF BLUE-STOCKING HALL.
IN THREE VOLUMES.

London: Henry Colburn and Richard Bentley, New Burlington Street, 1829.
I 297p; II 311p; III 351p. 12mo. 28s 6d (ECB); 28s 6d boards (ER).
ER 50: 284 (Oct 1829); QR 41: 557 (Nov 1829).
Corvey; CME 3-628-48871-0; ECB 575; NSTC 2S6011 (BI BL, C, Dt, E, O; NA DLC).

*Notes.* I Who Is She?; II Who Is She?; The Young Reformers; III The Young Reformers.

1829: 75    [SCOTT, Sir Walter].
ANNE OF GEIERSTEIN; OR, THE MAIDEN OF THE MIST. BY THE
AUTHOR OF "WAVERLEY," &C. IN THREE VOLUMES.

Edinburgh: Printed for Cadell and Co.; and Simpkin and Marshall, London, 1829.
I 336p; II 346p; III 381p. 8vo. 31s 6d (ECB); 31s 6d boards (ER).
ER 49: 528 (June 1829); QR 41: 287 (July 1829).
Corvey; CME 3-628-48546-0; ECB 521; NSTC 2S9436 (BI BL, C, Dt, E, NCu, O; NA
MH).

*Notes.* Published May 1829 (Corson).
Further edns: New York 1829 (NSTC) [also Philadelphia 1829 (NSTC)]; French trans., 1829;
German trans., 1829. Numerous reprintings in collected edns.

SEALSFIELD, Charles
See POSTL, Karl Magnus

1829: 76    [SHEE, Martin Archer].
OLDCOURT; A NOVEL, IN THREE VOLUMES.

London: Henry Colburn, New Burlington Street, 1829.
I iv, 366p; II 392p; III 396p. 12mo. 31s 6d (ECB, QR).
ER 49: 529 (June 1829); QR 41: 557 (Nov 1829).
Corvey; CME 3-628-48248-8; ECB 422; NSTC 2O2792 (BI BL, C, E, O; NA DLC, MH).

1829: 77    [SHERER, Joseph Moyle].
TALES OF THE WARS OF OUR TIMES. BY THE AUTHOR OF "RECOL-
LECTIONS OF THE PENINSULA," &C. &C. &C. IN TWO VOLUMES.

> London: Printed for Longman, Rees, Orme, Brown, and Green, Paternoster-Row,
> 1829.
> I vii, 364p; II 369p. 8vo. 21s (ECB).
> QR 41: 287 (July 1829).
> Corvey; CME 3-628-51162-3; ECB 576; NSTC 2S19132 (BI BL, C, E, O).

*Notes.* Further edn: German trans., 1832 [as *Bilder aus dem Kriegsleben* (RS)].


1829: 78    [SMITH, Horatio].
THE NEW FOREST. A NOVEL. BY THE AUTHOR OF "BRAMBLETYE
HOUSE," &C. IN THREE VOLUMES.

> London: Henry Colburn, New Burlington Street, 1829.
> I 305p; II 311p; III 327p. 12mo. 31s 6d boards (ER).
> ER 49: 529 (June 1829); QR 41: 287 (July 1829).
> Corvey; CME 3-628-48192-9; ECB 545; NSTC 2S26649 (BI BL, C, E, O; NA MH).

*Notes.* Further edns: 1830 (NSTC); New York 1829 (NSTC); German trans., 1830 [as *Der
Wald von Hampshire, oder des Sonderlings Glück* (RS)]; French trans., 1831.


1829: 79    [TONNA], Charlotte Elizabeth.
THE ROCKITE, AN IRISH STORY. BY CHARLOTTE ELIZABETH,
AUTHOR OF OSRIC, THE SYSTEM, CONSISTENCY, &C. &C.

> London: James Nisbet, Berners Street, 1829.
> 286p. 12mo. 5s (ECB).
> Corvey; CME 3-628-47577-5; ECB 183; NSTC 2C16472 (BI BL, C, Dt, E, O; NA MH).

*Notes.* Dedication 'to Lord Mount Sandford'. ECB dates June 1829.
Further edns: 2nd edn. 1830 (NUC); 3rd edn. 1836 (NUC); 4th edn. 1846 (NSTC); New York
1844 (NUC).


1829: 80    TRUEBA Y COSIO, Joaquin Telesforo de.
THE CASTILIAN. BY DON TELESFORO DE TRUEBA Y COSIO, AUTHOR
OF "GOMEZ ARIAS." IN THREE VOLUMES.

> London: Henry Colburn, New Burlington Street, 1829.
> I viii, 310p; II 369p; III 371p. 12mo. 31s 6d (ECB); 31s 6d boards (ER).
> ER 49: 529 (June 1829); QR 39: 253 (Jan 1829).
> Corvey; CME 3-628-48833-8; ECB 601; NSTC 2T18796 (BI BL, C, E, O; NA MH).

*Notes.* Preface dated Richmond, 30 Sept 1828. ECB dates Dec 1828.
Further edns: French trans., 1829 [as *Le Castillan, ou le prince noir en Espagne* (BN)]; German
trans., 1829.


1829: 81    [WHITE, Charles].
THE ADVENTURES OF A KING'S PAGE. BY THE AUTHOR OF
"ALMACK'S REVISITED." IN THREE VOLUMES.

London: Henry Colburn, New Burlington Street, 1829.
I 308p; II 312p; III 394p. 12mo. 31s 6d (ECB); 31s 6d boards (ER).
ER 49: 529 (June 1829); QR 39: 525 (Apr 1829).
Corvey; CME 3-628-47017-X; ECB 6; NSTC 2W16614 (BI BL, C, E; NA DLC, MH).

*Notes.* Further edns: New York 1829 (NUC); German trans., 1829 [as *Arthur Beverley, des König's Page* (RS)].

## WIGHTWICK, George, THE LIFE AND REMAINS OF WILMOT WAR-WICK

See 1828: 83

# APPENDIX

This Appendix is not intended as an overflow for works of fiction that should have been included in the main listings, nor is it meant in any way to be all-inclusive. Rather the different sections include representative examples of those kinds of work which have been excluded as not matching the requirements for entry in this volume. Sections A-D provide illustrations of types of fiction in the period which are considered not to represent novels in the sense required for entry in the main listings. Section E offers a selection of titles that have been omitted on the basis that they are reissues of earlier publications or translations later than the first English translation. Section F includes representative examples of titles which, apparently not having survived, leave an element of doubt about their existence or suitability for entry.

## A: Children's Tales / Tales for Youth

A: 1   [ZIEGENHIRT, Sophia F.].
**SEABROOK VILLAGE AND ITS INHABITANTS. OR THE HISTORY OF MRS. WORTHY AND HER FAMILY; FOUNDED ON FACTS. WRITTEN FOR THE INSTRUCTION AND AMUSEMENT OF YOUNG PEOPLE.**
> London: Printed by T. Harper, jun. Crane Court, Fleet Street, for Henry Colburn, English and Foreign Public Library, Conduit Street, New Bond Street, 1811.
> 228p. 12mo. 4s 6d (ECB); 7s (ER).
> ER 18: 265 (May 1811); WSW I: 577.
> Corvey; CME 3-628-48611-4; ECB 524; NSTC S1002 (BI BL, C).

*Notes.* Adv. facing t.p. for 'New Books. To be had at Colburn's Library, Conduit Street, New Bond Street'. 5 titles listed (all educational in emphasis).

A: 2   ?P[ORTER], A[nna] M[aria].
**TALES OF PITY ON FISHING, SHOOTING, AND HUNTING. INTENDED TO INCULCATE IN THE MIND OF YOUTH, SENTIMENTS OF HUMANITY, TOWARD THE BRUTE CREATION. BY A. M. P.**
> London: Printed for J. Harris, Corner of St. Paul's Church Yard, 1814.
> 154p, ill. 18mo.
> O 25325.f.34; NSTC P4.

*Notes.* Attributed to Porter by FC, NCBEL and NUC. Frontispiece illustration of 'Fishing'. 3 stories. Very small pages, and written in a simplistic moral style.

A: 3   {HOFLAND}, [Barbara].
**MATILDA; OR THE BARBADOES GIRL. A TALE FOR YOUNG PEOPLE.**

BY THE AUTHOR OF THE CLERGYMAN'S WIDOW AND FAMILY,
MERCHANT'S WIDOW AND FAMILY, AFFECTIONATE BROTHERS,
PANORAMA OF EUROPE, THE SISTERS, &C.

London: Printed at the Minerva Press for A. K. Newman and Co. Leadenhall-Street,
1816.
250p, ill. 12mo. 4s (s.l., ECB, ER).
ER 27: 271 (Sept 1816).
Corvey; CME 3-628-48195-3; ECB 373; NSTC 2H29402 (BI BL, C).

*Notes.* Includes dialogues under speaker headings. Unused spine label at end of book reading: 'The Barbadoes Girl. A Tale. By Mrs. Hofland. Price 4s. 1816'. ER also gives author's
name. One of several fictions by this author aimed directly at children and 'young people'
and not included among the main entries of this Bibliography.
Further edns: 2nd edn. 1818, as *The Barbadoes Girl* (NSTC); 3rd edn. 1819 (NSTC); 5th edn.
1825 (NSTC); Philadelphia 1817 (NUC).

A: 4    SULLIVAN, W[illiam] F[rancis].
THE RECLUSE, OR THE HERMIT OF WINDERMERE: A NARRATIVE
FOUNDED UPON FACTS; BEING AN IMPORTANT LESSON FOR
YOUTH. BY W. F. SULLIVAN, A.M. TEACHER OF ELOCUTION AND
BELLES LETTRES.

London: Printed for C. Chapple, No. 66, Pall-Mall, opposite St. James's Palace, 1818.
viii, 182p, ill. 12mo.
WSW I: 526.
Corvey; 3-628-48730-7; NSTC 2S46266 (BI BL, O).

*Notes.* List (2 pp. unn.) at end of 'Books of Instruction and Amusement, for the use of
Schools, Children, & Young Persons, recently published by C. Chapple, Pall-Mall'. BLC
records as '1818 [1819]'.

A: 5    ELLIOTT, Mary.
CONFIDENTIAL MEMOIRS; OR, ADVENTURES OF A PARROT, A
GREYHOUND, A CAT, AND A MONKEY. BY MARY ELLIOTT, LATE
BELSON.

London: William Darton, 58, Holborn Hill, 1821.
254p, ill. 8vo. 6s (ECB).
Corvey; CME 3-628-52303-6; ECB 49; NSTC 2E7562 (BI BL, C).

*Notes.* Concludes with poem 'Little Frank's Dream', pp. 251–4. Adv. at end (2 pp. unn.),
headed 'A List of Juvenile Books, published by William Darton [. . .]'. ECB dates Feb 1822.
By a prolific author of children's books in this period.

A: 6    [STODDART, Lady Isabella Wellwood].
THE SCOTTISH ORPHANS: A MORAL TALE. FOUNDED ON AN HIS-
TORICAL FACT; AND CALCULATED TO IMPROVE THE MINDS OF
YOUNG PEOPLE. BY MRS. BLACKFORD, AUTHOR OF THE ESKDALE
HERD-BOY, 'A VERY SUPERIOR WORK; AND WE HAVE READ IT
OURSELVES WITH MUCH INTEREST.'—LONDON MAGAZINE.

London: Printed for Wetton and Jarvis, 65, Paternoster Row, Cheapside; by J. J. Cowing, Barnet, 1822.

213p, ill. 12mo. 3s 6d (ECB, ER).

ER 36: 571 (Feb 1822); WSW II: 190.

Corvey; CME 3-628-47227-X; ECB 59; NSTC 2B36120 (BI BL).

*Notes.* Preface (2 pp. unn.) states that the narrative is based 'on an event which actually took place in Scotland'. One of a series of tales by the author aimed at 'young people'. These include *Arthur Monteith: a Moral Tale* (1822), a continuation; *The Eskdale Herd-boy, a Scottish Tale* (1819); and *William Montgomery; or, the Young Artist* (1829).

Further edns: 2nd edn. 1823 (NSTC); 1850 (NSTC); New York 1824 (NUC); French trans., 1825 [as *Arthur Monteith, ou les Orphelins écossais* (BN)].

A: 7   ANON.
**EMILY, A TALE FOR YOUNG PERSONS.**

London: John Harris, Corner of St. Paul's Church-Yard, 1825.

195p, ill. 12mo. 5s (ECB, QR).

QR 31: 531 (Mar 1825).

Corvey; 3-628-47562-7; ECB 186; NSTC 2E9255 (BI BL).

*Notes.* Collates in sixes. Adv. at end (4 pp. unn.) for 'New and Useful Books for Young People, published by J. Harris'.

# B:  Shorter Tales and Miscellanies

B: 1   M[ARGRAVINE] OF [BRANDENBURG-] A[NSPACH], [Elizabeth] [formerly CRAVEN, Elizabeth].
**THE SOLDIER OF DIERENSTEIN; OR, LOVE AND MERCY. AN AUSTRIAN STORY, BY H.S.H. THE M. OF A——.**

Newbury: Printed by T. Mayo, and published by J. White, Fleet-Street, London, 1802.

40p, ill. 8vo. 3s 6d (CR).

CR 2nd ser. 36: 479 (Dec 1802); WSW I: 226.

Corvey; CME 3-628-51134-8; NSTC C4136 (BI BL, C, O).

*Notes.* 'To the Austrian Eagle' (1 p. unn.). Text divided into 'Stanza[s]', [1st]–26th. Frontispiece states 'Published [. . .] Feby. 20 1802'. Collates in fours.

B: 2   MATHEWS, [Eliza Kirkham].
**ANECDOTES OF THE CLAIRVILLE FAMILY; TO WHICH IS ADDED, THE HISTORY OF EMILY WILMONT. BY MRS. C. MATHEWS.**

York: Printed by and for T. Wilson and R. Spence, High-Ousegate, 1802.

107p, ill. 18mo. 'Price one shilling' (t.p.).

BL 12614.ccc.8; NSTC M1661.

*Notes.* Extremely small pages (only 13cm high); includes two woodcuts.

Further edn: 1809 (NSTC).

B: 3   ANON.
**ODD MOMENTS; OR TIME BEGUILED.**

> London: For Thomas Boys, Ludgate Hill, 1825.
> 290p, ill. 12mo. 6s (ECB, QR).
> QR 32: 267 (June 1825); WSW II: 26.
> Corvey; CME 3-628-51107-0; ECB 420; NSTC 2M32555 (BI BL, O).

*Notes.* Dedication 'To Caroline Frances Boys, the friend of my earlier days'. 'Advertisement' (1 p. unn.) states intention to follow in path of 'those beautifully written Tales under the title of "May you like it" ': see 1822: 74. Later followed by *More Odd Moments* (1826). Further edn: 1834 (NSTC).


# C:  Didactic Fiction

C: 1   RICE, Mrs.
**THE NABOB: A MORAL TALE. BY MRS. RICE, AUTHOR OF THE DESERTED WIFE, MONTEITH, ETC.**

> London: Printed for J. Harris, St. Paul's Church Yard; and Longman, Hurst, Rees, and
>     Orme, Paternoster Row; and M. Hage, Newark, 1807.
> 144p, ill. 12mo.
> BL 1210.h.51; ECB 492; NSTC R822.

*Notes.* Frontispiece illustration of Pagoda Lodge carries the legend: 'Published by M. Hage, Newark, Sep$^r$. 1806'. A didactic tale, aimed primarily at youthful readership.


C: 2   [SHERWOOD, Mary Martha].
**THE HISTORY OF GEORGE DESMOND; FOUNDED ON FACTS WHICH OCCURRED IN THE EAST INDIES, AND NOW PUBLISHED AS A USEFUL CAUTION TO YOUNG MEN GOING OUT TO THAT COUNTRY.**

> Wellington, Salop: Printed by and for F. Houlston and Son. And sold by Scatcherd and
>     Letterman, Ave-Maria Lane, London, 1821.
> 290p. 8vo. 7s (ECB).
> WSW II: 15.
> Corvey; CME 3-628-47703-4; ECB 273; NSTC 2D10339 (BI BL).

*Notes.* Imprint date followed by 'Entered at Stationers' Hall'. Collates in fours. ECB dates Oct 1821. One of the more 'adult' of numerous children's books written by this author in the period.


C: 3   ANON.
**THE WIDOW'S NARRATIVE; COMPRISING REMARKS ON THE CONDUCT OF HUMBLE LIFE.**

> London: Printed for Francis Westley, 10, Stationers' Court, and Ave Maria-Lane, 1822.

v, 130p. 8vo.
Corvey; CME 3-628-48970-9; NSTC 2N3040 (BI BL, C).

*Notes.* Introduction contains a fictitious letter of a poor widow, Mary Nelson, whose memorandum provides the main narrative: this addresses the author/editor as 'Honored sir,' and is dated 4 Jan 1815. Concluding editorial frame signed 'E. M—'.

C: 4   ANON.
**TALES OF HUMBLE LIFE.**

London: Printed for Charles Knight, Pall-Mall East, 1824.
103p. 12mo.
WSW II: 36.
Corvey; CME 3-628-51150-X; ECB 575; NSTC 2T1390 (BI BL).

*Notes.* Colophon reads: C. Knight, Printer, Windsor. 'Advertisement' (1 p. unn.) states: 'The following Tales were published in a Periodical Work, which was the first to perceive the necessity for a wholesome Popular Literature [. . .] The original object of the writer may, perhaps, be advanced by their republication.' 7 tales in all ECB dates Mar 1825.

# D:  Historical Memoirs

D: 1   DILLON, John Talbot.
**ALPHONSO AND ELEONORA; OR, THE TRIUMPHS OF VALOUR AND VIRTUE. ILLUSTRATED BY HISTORICAL FACTS. BY JOHN TALBOT DILLON, ESQ. M.R.I.A. LATE CAPTAIN IN THE 2D SURREY REGIMENT OF MILITIA. &C. &C. &C. AUTHOR OF TRAVELS THROUGH SPAIN, &C. &c. IN TWO VOLUMES.**

London: Printed by J. Barker, No. 19, Great Russell-Street, Covent-Garden. Sold by him, and W. Taylor, Brompton-Terrace, Knightsbridge, 1800.
I viii, 216p; II 176p. 12mo.
BL 12613.cc.11; EM 201: 4; ESTC t070071 (NA CLU-S/C, MH-H).

*Notes.* 'To The Right Honourable Patrick Dillon, Earl of Roscommon; Baron of Kilkenny-West; In The Kingdom of Ireland' signed John Talbot Dillon and dated Michael Place, Brompton, 19 May 1800. An account of Alphonso VIII, King of Castile, and his consort, Eleanor, daughter of Henry II, King of England.

D: 2   HAMILTON, Elizabeth.
**MEMOIRS OF THE LIFE OF AGRIPPINA, THE WIFE OF GERMANICUS. BY ELIZABETH HAMILTON, AUTHOR OF "LETTERS ON THE ELEMENTARY PRINCIPLES OF EDUCATION;" &C. &C.**

Bath: Printed by R. Cruttwell; for G. and J. Robinson, Pater-Noster-Row, London, 1804.
I xxxviii, 319p; II v, 340p; III viii, 352p. 8vo. 18s (ECB).
WSW I: 295.
BL 609.e.12; ECB 252; NSTC H322 (BI C, Dt, E, O).

*Notes.* 'Additional Notes' in vol. 1, pp. [291]–319; vol. 2, pp. [323]–340; vol. 3, pp. [343]–352. ECB (erroneously?) gives publisher as Johnson, Oct 1804. Historical narrative, but in novel form, with fictional dialogue.
Further edn: 2nd edn. London 1811 (NSTC).

D: 3    [IRELAND, Samuel William Henry].
EFFUSIONS OF LOVE FROM CHATELOR TO MARY QUEEN OF SCOT-LAND. TRANSLATED FROM A GALLIC MANUSCRIPT, IN THE SCOTCH COLLEGE, AT PARIS. INTERSPERSED WITH SONGS, SONNETS, AND NOTES EXPLANATORY, BY THE TRANSLATOR.
> London: Printed for C. Chapple, Pall-Mall, and Southampton-Row, Bloomsbury, 1805.
> vi, 151p. 8vo. 5s (ECB).
> WSW I: 340.
> BL 1568/571; ECB 181; NSTC I430 (BI E).

*Notes.* Frontispiece states 'pub. Aug. 7. 1805, by C. Chapple, Pall-Mall'. ECB gives Crosby as publisher, Aug 1805.
Further edn: 2nd edn. 1808 (NSTC).

# E:  Reissues/reprints and later translations

E: 1    ANON.
THE LIBERTINES; OR, MONKISH MYSTERIES! A ROMANCE.
> Cork: Printed by John Connor, Chatterton's-Buildings, Grand-Parade, 1800.
> 291p. 12mo.
> ViU PZ.2.L5451800; EM 1007: 23; ESTC n002907 (BI BL, D; NA MH-H).

*Notes.* Collates in sixes. A reprint of *The Libertines: a novel* (London, 2 vols., 1798): see Vol. 1, 1798: 11.

E: 2    {KNIGGE}, [Adolf Franz Friedrich Ludwig von)].
FAMILY MISFORTUNES; OR THE HISTORY OF FREDERICK GUT-MAN, AMTSRATH OF MEHLBACH, WITH ANECDOTES OF THE FUERSTENRUFS. FROM THE GERMAN.
> London: Printed for A. Cleugh, Ratcliff-Highway, 1802.
> xi, 312p, ill. 12mo. 'Three Shillings and Six-Pence' (t.p.).
> OBgU PT2281.G98.F313; xNSTC.

*Notes.* Trans. of *Geschichte des Amtsraths Gutmann* (Hanover, 1794). Frontispiece facing t.p. 'Preface of the Translator', pp. [v]–xi, implies male translator; also attributes authorship to Baron Knigge. Drop-head title reads 'The History of the Amtsrath Gutman'. A reissue with cancel t.p. of *The History of the Amtsrath Gutman, written by himself. Published by Adolphus Baron Knigge. Translated from the German* (London 1799): see Vol. 1, 1799: 57.

E: 3   FLORIAN, [Jean Pierre Claris de]; HIGHLEY, {Harriet} (*trans.*).
**GALATEA: A PASTORAL ROMANCE. FROM THE FRENCH OF MON-
SIEUR FLORIAN. BY MISS HIGHLEY. DEDICATED BY PERMISSION
TO THE MARCHIONESS OF SALISBURY.**

> London: Printed for S. Highley (Successor to the late Mr. John Murray) No. 24, Fleet
> Street; and A. Constable and Co. Edinburgh, 1804.
> 16, 157p, ill. 8vo. 7s boards (CR); 7s (ECB).
> CR 3rd ser. 3: 238 (Oct 1804).
> BL 12490.aa.19; ECB 209; NSTC F942 (BI E, O).

*Notes.* Trans. of *Galatée, roman pastoral* (Paris, 1783). Dedication to the 'Most Honourable The
Marchioness of Salisbury', signed 'Harriet Highley' and dated London, 20 Apr 1804 (pp. 1–4);
preface (pp. 5–8); 'M. Florian's Introduction' (pp. 9–16), concluding first arabic sequence. An
earlier trans. 'by an officer', appeared with a Dublin imprint in 1791: see Vol. 1, 1791: 35.
Further edn: another trans. 1813 (BLC).


E: 4   CAZOTTE, [Jacques].
**BIONDETTA, OR THE ENAMOURED SPIRIT: A ROMANCE. TRANSLATED
FROM LE DIABLE AMOUREUX OF M. CAZOTTE; AND DEDICATED
(WITHOUT PERMISSION) TO M. G. LEWIS, ESQ. AUTHOR OF THE MONK.**

> London: Printed for John Miller, 72, Chancery Lane, 1810.
> xiii, 220p. 12mo. 5s (ER).
> ER 16: 259 (Apr 1810).
> BL 1458.d.16; NSTC C1157 (BI O).

*Notes.* Trans of *Le Diable amoureux* (Paris, 1772). Dedication to 'M. G. Lewis, Esq.' signed
'The Translator'. Preceded by earlier translations under different titles: see Vol. 1, 1791: 32.


E: 5   LONEY, T. C.
**SEBASTIAN AND ISABEL; OR, THE INVISIBLE SWORD. A ROMANCE.
BY T. C. LONEY.**

> London: Printed for Henry Colburn, English and Foreign Library, Conduit-Street, New
> Bond-Street, 1811.
> 186p. 12mo.
> ViU PZ2.L65S.1811; xNSTC.

*Notes.* Printer's mark on verso of t.p. reads: 'B. Clarke, printer'; colophon at foot of p. 186
reads 'J. Wilson, printer, Macclesfield'. Collates in sixes. A reissue, with new t.p. but lacking
the preliminaries, of *The Man in Armour, or The Invisible Sword* (see 1807: 39).


E: 6   SURR, Thomas Skinner.
**MODERN ADVENTURES IN FASHIONABLE LIFE; OR, THE PRYER
FAMILY[.] A NOVEL, BY THOMAS SKINNER SURR, ESQ. AUTHOR OF
"THE WINTER IN LONDON," "SPLENDID MISERY," &C.**

> Dublin: Printed for H. Colbert, Wholesale Bookseller, 148, Capel-Street, 1812.
> 250p. 12mo.
> CtY-BR In.SU78.812; xNSTC.

*Notes.* 'Introduction' (pp. 1–11). 23 letters. Apparently a reprinting of Surr's *Consequences: or, Adventures at Rraxall Castle*: see Vol. 1, 1796: 84.

E: 7   [ENNIS, Alicia Margaret].
**IRELAND; OR, MEMOIRS OF THE MONTAGUE FAMILY. IN THREE VOLUMES.**

> London: Printed for E. Lloyd, Harley-Street; and sold by A. K. Newman and Co. Leadenhall-Street, 1820.
> I vii, 506p; II 509p; III 499p. 12mo. 18s (ECB).
> Corvey; CME 3-628-47947-9; ECB 188; xNSTC.

*Notes.* A reissue (replacement t.p.), of *Memoirs of the Montague Family* (1817: 25). ECB dates Nov 1820.


E: 8   ANON.
**THE CAVERN IN THE WICKLOW MOUNTAINS, OR FATE OF THE O'BRIEN FAMILY; A TALE FOUNDED ON FACTS. IN TWO VOLUMES.**

> Dublin: Printed for the Author, by James Charles, No. 57, Mary-Street, 1821.
> I 295p; II 286p. 12mo.
> BL 12808.ff.10; NSTC 2O433.

*Notes.* A reissue (replacement t.p.) of *The United Irishman, or The Fatal Effects of Credulity* (1819: 20). The original drop-head titles in both vols. of the BL copy have been crudely pasted over with this new title.


# F:  Uncertain reconstituted/unseen titles

F: 1   [?ISDELL, Sarah or ?PILKINGTON, Mary].
*****FITZHERBERT. A NOVEL.**

> London: J. F. Hughes, 1810?
> 3 vols?
> No copy located.

*Notes.* Adv. facing t.p. of vol. 2 of *The Spanish Lady, and the Norman Knight* (1810: 25), lists three items that 'Speedily will be published' by J. F. Hughes, the second of which is '*Fitzherbert*, a Novel, in 3 vols. By Sarah Isdell, author of the 'Irish Recluse', &c. &c.'. The catalogue (1824) of Horne's circulating library, Cheapside, itemises (as 8741) a novel with the same title by Sarah Isdell in 3 vols. It is possible that such a work was remaindered as a result of Hughes's bankruptcy in 1810. '*Fitzherbert*, a Novel, 4 vols. By Mrs. Pilkington' is adv. as 'In the Press' at the end of vol. 3 of an earlier Hughes publication, *The Child of Mystery* (1808: 110); Summers also lists a *Fitzherbert*, 4 vols., 1808, by Mrs Pilkington (enlarged to Mrs Mary Pilkington in his Index of Authors). This earlier announcement appears to be the less reliable of the two as a source for an actual authored work.

F: 2   SINCLAIR, Mrs.
\*JULIA FITZCLARENCE AND OTHER TALES. BY MRS. SINCLAIR.

>London: Allen, 1810.
>3 vols. 15s.
>No copy located.

*Notes.* Title and date from Block; publisher and price from Bent22; listed in several circulating catalogues as by 'Mrs. Sinclair' and in some with the extended title 'and other tales'. Adv. list (1 p. unn.) of works 'Just Published by J. F. Hughes' at end of vol. 1 of *Yorkshire Characters* (1810: 28) includes '*Julia Fitzclarence*; 3 vols. 15s'.

F: 3   [COOPER, Maria Susanna].
\*THE WIFE; OR, CAROLINE HERBERT. BY THE LATE AUTHOR OF THE "EXEMPLARY MOTHER".

>London: Printed for Becket and Porter, 1813.
>2 vols. 8vo. 10s (ECB).
>WSW I: 218.
>No copy located; ECB 98.

*Notes.* Main details from Hardy (Item 326). This title is not evident as a novel in contemporary circulating library catalogues. The same author's *Moral Tales* (1811), also posthumously published, is a work directed at children.

F: 4   DARLING, P[eter] M[iddleton].
\*PATERNAL LOVE; OR, THE REWARD OF FRIENDSHIP. BY P. M. DARLING.

>London: Gale and Co., 1814.
>1 vol.
>No copy located.

*Notes.* Imprint details from Summers. The title and author are also given in Part II of A. K. Newman's Minerva Library catalogue [1814–19], and in the Appendix [1814] to the catalogue of Robert Kinnear's library in Edinburgh; but no other information about its existence has been discovered. Possibly a short tale.

F: 5   MATHEWS, Mrs.
\*THE PHANTOM; OR MYSTERIES OF THE CASTLE. A TALE OF OTHER TIMES. BY THE LATE MRS. MATHEWS, OF THE THEATRES ROYAL, YORK AND HULL.

>London: Baldwin, Craddock, and Joy; and I. Wilson, Hull, 1825.
>1 vol.
>No copy located.

*Notes.* Main details from Summers, supported by Block. The title with author is also found as Item 6767 in Eneas Mackenzie's *Catalogue of the Newcastle General Circulating Library* (1832), held in Newcastle Public Library. Under his Index of Authors, Summers attributes *Perplexities; or, the Fortunate Elopement* (1794) to the same Mrs Mathews, and gives the date of her death as 1823. Possibly a short tale.

# Index of Authors and Translators

The index lists both real author names and pseudonyms. Where a pseudonym has been identified, the true author name provides the entry, with cross-reference from the pseudonym. Where pseudonyms are unidentified these provide the entry. In cases of authors appearing under more than one name during the period, the name most commonly found (e.g., Owenson, Sydney as opposed to Morgan, Lady Sydney) provides the entry, with cross-reference from the other name or names used. Cross-references are also provided generally from other names (e.g. a married name) or forms of name by which an author might be known. Normally, *see* refers to information in the '*Notes*' field of entries.

# Index of Titles

The index generally offers the shortest form of title by which a work can be recognized. Initial definite and indefinite articles are normally omitted, as too are sub-titles (unless required to distinguish between otherwise similar titles). Normally, *see* refers to information in the '*Notes*' field of entries.

# Index of Publishers, Booksellers, and Printers

All indexed names are alphabetically ordered under the town of publication. Names follow the form found on the imprint, unless egregiously in error, and the fullest form found normally provides the entry, with cross-reference from the shortened form or forms where required. The index lists concerns as found on imprints (e.g. Longman, Hurst, Rees, and Orme) and also provides separate entries where partnerships were expanded or changed in other ways.

Names without symbols are normally booksellers or publishers alone (as found in imprints under 'published by', 'printed for', and 'sold by'). Symbols are used to indicate the following exceptions:

†     Both printer and bookseller (as under 'Printed and sold by')
(†)    Printer only (as under 'Printed by')

Additionally asterisks (*) are used to denote cases where a work was printed or sold 'for the Author'.

Where symbols precede the entry number they relate only to that particular item. Where symbols are placed after the indexed name they relate to all the following entries; further symbols against entry numbers indicate further exceptions.

Normally, *see* refers to information in the '*Notes*' field of entries. This index, however, generally does not include information relating to Further editions.

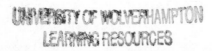